2023
安徽统计年鉴
ANHUI STATISTICAL YEARBOOK

(总第35期　NO.35)

安徽省统计局
Anhui Provincial Bureau of Statistics
国家统计局安徽调查总队
Survey Office of the National Bureau of Statistics in Anhui
编
COMPILED

中国统计出版社
China Statistics Press

《安徽统计年鉴2023》

ANHUI STATISTICAL YEARBOOK 2023

图书在版编目（CIP）数据

安徽统计年鉴. 2023 = Anhui Statistical Yearbook 2022 : 汉英对照 / 安徽省统计局, 国家统计局安徽调查总队编. -- 北京 : 中国统计出版社, 2023.11
ISBN 978-7-5230-0298-8

Ⅰ. ①安… Ⅱ. ①安… ②国… Ⅲ. ①统计资料－安徽－2023－年鉴－汉、英 Ⅳ. ①C832.54-54

中国国家版本馆CIP数据核字(2023)第202334号

安徽统计年鉴2023

作　　者/ 安徽省统计局 · 国家统计局安徽调查总队
责任编辑/ 周小睿
执行编辑/ 刘　琛
装帧设计/ 朴书堂文化 · 陈　强
出版发行/ 中国统计出版社有限公司
通信地址/ 北京市丰台区西三环南路甲6号　邮政编码/100073
发行电话/ 邮购（010）63376909　书店（010）68783171
网　　址/ http://www.zgtjcbs.com/
印　　刷/ 安徽新华印刷股份有限公司
经　　销/ 新华书店
开　　本/ 890mm×1240mm　1/16
字　　数/ 1500 千字
印　　张/ 43.25　彩页0.75
版　　别/ 2023 年 11 月第 1 版
版　　次/ 2023 年 11 月第 1 次印刷
定　　价/ 450.00元　Price:450.00 yuan (RMB)

《安徽统计年鉴2023》编辑委员会

AnHui Statistical Yearbook 2023 Editorial Board

《安徽统计年鉴2023》编辑部

AnHui Statistical Yearbook 2023 Editorial Department

Editor-in-Chief: Guo Jinsong

Associate Editor-in-Chief: Xu Jingwen Wu Jiang

Coordinators: Zhou Xiaorui

Execute Editing: Liu Chen

Editorial Staff: (in order of strokes of Chinese surname)

Ding Yuan	Wang Fang	Wang Qian	Wang Xuesong
Wei Wei	Shi Dongling	Fu Shuyun	Ji Xiaojun
L ü Xuefeng	Zhu Guangyu	Wu Manqi	Ren Hu
Liu Qiang	Liu Yanli	Liu Chenyu	Jiang Lijing
An Jian	Li Xian	Li Zhongwei	Li Jiaxin
Wu Han	Wu Jiajia	Zou Shanshan	Wang Xin
Wang Zhong	Zhang Wei	Zhang Wei	Zhang Weiwei
Zhang Junfeng	Zhang Zhiyong	Chen Lingxin	Chen Chunsong
Yue Linfeng	Zhou Wenwen	Zheng Quanyu	Zhao Dejun
Hao Li	Hu Longxiang	Hu Yongming	Bo Lin
Shi Wenyue	Xu Qun	Xu Guowei	Xu Chengzhou
Gao Wei	Guo Changhu	Huang Shaolin	Peng Yin

English Translator: Sun Naijing

CD-ROM Designer: Xu GuoWei Ren Hu

编辑说明

一、《安徽统计年鉴2023》全面、系统地收录了2022年全省及各市、县经济和社会各方面统计数据，重点展示统计部门服务新阶段现代化美好安徽建设的成果，是一部全面反映安徽省国民经济和社会发展情况的资料性年刊。

二、全书内容共分23个篇章和附录，即：综合；国民经济核算；人口；就业人员和工资；固定资产投资；能源生产和消费；财政与金融；物价指数；城乡人民生活；城市概况；自然资源和环境保护；农业；工业；建筑业；运输和邮电；国内贸易；对外经济贸易；旅游；教育和科技；卫生和社会服务；文化和体育；公共管理及其他；省级和县级主要经济指标及位次。附录部分主要有：安徽农民工非农就业基本情况。为帮助读者理解和使用有关数据，各篇章附有简要说明和主要指标解释，介绍了统计范围和统计方法。

三、本年鉴使用国民经济行业分类(GB/T4754-2017)。

四、本年鉴中使用的度量衡单位均采用国际统一标准计量单位。

五、本年鉴符号使用说明,年鉴各表中的“空格”表示该项统计指标数据不足本表最小单位数、数据不详或无该项数据，“#”表示其中的主要项。

六、本年鉴中部分合计数或相对数由于单位取舍不同产生的计算误差，均未作机械调整。全书中英文对照，配套出版磁质光盘。

Preface

Ⅰ. *Anhui Statistical Yearbook 2023* comprehensively and systematically includes the economic and social statistical data of the whole province and all cities and counties in 2022, and focuses on displaying the achievements of statistical departments in serving the construction of modern and beautiful Anhui in the new stage. It is an annual reference magazine that comprehensively reflects the national economic and social development of Anhui province.

Ⅱ. The contents of the book are divided into 23 chapters and appendices, namely: General survey; National accounts; Population; Employment and wages; Investment in fixed assets; Production and consumption of energy; Government finance and finance; Price indices; Livelihood of urban and rural people; General survey of cities; Natural resources and environmental protection; Agriculture; Industry; Construction; Transport, post and telecommunication services; Domestic trade; Foreign trade and economic cooperation; Tourism; Education and science; Public health and social services; Culture and sports; Public management and others; Main economic indicators and their orders of precedence of province and county. The appendix mainly includes: the basic situation of non–agricultural employment of migrant workers in Anhui. In order to help readers understand and use the relevant data, each chapter is accompanied by a brief description and explanation of the main indicators, and introduces the statistical scope and statistical methods.

Ⅲ. In this yearbook , We use the classification of national economic industries (GB / T4754–2017).

Ⅳ. The units of measurement used in this book are internationally standardized measurement units.

Ⅴ. Notations used in this book: （blank space） indicates that the figure is not large enough to be measured with the smallest unit in the table, or data are unknown, or are not available. “#” indicates a major items of the total.

Ⅵ. Statistical discrepancies due to rounding are not adjusted in this book. Anhui Statistical Yearbook is compiled bilingually in Chinese and English and a magnetic CD–ROM has been published to form a complete set.

目　　录
CONTENTS

一、　综　合
General Survey

1—1　全省行政区划（2022年末）…… 3
Administrative Divisions in Anhui (End of 2022)

1—2　全省县以上行政区划（2022年末）…… 4
Administrative Divisions of Counties and Above in Anhui (End of 2022)

1—3　各行业机构单位数（2022年）…… 5
Number of Grass Root Units in Various Sectors （2022）

1—4　各市按三次产业和机构类型分法人单位数（2022年）…… 8
Number of Legal Entities by Three Strata of Industry and Type of Institutions and Region （2022）

1—5　各市按控股情况分企业法人单位数（2022年）…… 9
Numbers of Corporate Enterprises the Status of Holdings by Region （2022）

1—6　国民经济和社会发展总量与速度指标…… 10
Principal Aggregate Indicators On National Economic and Social Development and Their Related Indices and Growth Rates

1—7　国民经济和社会发展结构指标…… 22
Structural Indicators on National Economic and Social Development

1—8　国民经济和社会发展比例和效益指标…… 25
Indicators on Proportions and Efficiency in National Economic and Social Development

1—9　社会经济主要指标人均水平…… 28
Major Per Capita Indicators of Social and Economy

1—10　人民物质文化生活提高情况…… 29
Improvement of People's Material and Cultural Life

1—11　平均每天主要社会经济活动…… 30
Selected Indicators on Average Daily Social and Economic Activities

1—12　长三角国民经济和社会发展主要指标（2022年）…… 31
Main Indicators of National Economic and Social Development in Yangtze River Delta （2022）

1—13　中部6省国民经济和社会发展主要指标（2022年）…… 32
Main Indicators of National Economic and Social Development of 6 Middle Provinces （2022）

1—14　黄山旅游区域主要经济指标（2022年）…… 33
Main Economic Indicators of Tourist Region of Mount Huang （2022）

1—15　九华山旅游区域主要经济指标（2022年）…… 34
Main Economic Indicators of Tourist Region of Mount Jiu Hua （2022）

主要统计指标解释…… 35
Explanatory Notes for Major Statistical Indicators

二、　国民经济核算
National Accounts

2—1　安徽生产总值…… 43
Gross Domestic Product

2—2　安徽生产总值构成…… 44
Composition of Gross Domestic Product

2—3　安徽生产总值指数（上年为100）…… 45
Indices of Gross Domestic Product （preceding year=100）

2—4　安徽生产总值指数（1978=100）…… 46
Indices of Gross Domestic Product （1978=100）

2—5　三次产业贡献率…… 47
Contribution Rate of the Three Industries

2—6　三次产业拉动率…… 48
Pulling Rate of the Three Industries

2—7　按行业、产业构成分的安徽生产总值（2021年）…… 49
According to the Industry and the Industry Method of GDP in Anhui （2021）

2—8 按行业、产业构成分的安徽生产总值（2022年）…… 50
According to the Industry and the Industry Method of GDP in Anhui（2022）
2—9 各市生产总值…… 51
Gross Domestic Product by Region
2—10 各市生产总值指数…… 52
Gross Domestic Product Index by Region
2—11 各市第一产业增加值…… 53
Added Value of the Primary Industry by Region
2—12 各市第一产业增加值指数…… 54
Value Added Index of Primary Industry by Region
2—13 各市第二产业增加值…… 55
Added Value of the Secondary Industry by Region
2—14 各市第二产业增加值指数…… 56
Value-added Index of Secondary Industry by Region
2—15 各市第三产业增加值…… 57
Value-added of Tertiary Industry by Region
2—16 各市第三产业增加值指数…… 58
Value-added Index of Tertiary Industry by Region
2—17 各市分产业分行业增加值（2022年）…… 59
Value-added by Industry and Sector by Region (2022)
2—18 各市、县生产总值及指数…… 61
Gross Domestic Product and Indices by County or City
主要统计指标解释…… 64
Explanatory Notes for Major Statistical Indicators

三、 人 口
Population

3—1 主要年份人口指标…… 69
Major Population Indicators in Main Year
3—2 主要年份人口系数…… 69
Ratio of Population in Main Year
3—3 七次全省人口普查基本情况…… 70
Basic Statistics on National Population Census in 1953, 1964, 1982, 1990, 2000, 2010 and 2020
3—4 各市主要年份人口城镇化率…… 72
Main Year Rate of Urbanization by Region
3—5 各市常住人口出生率、死亡率（2022年）…… 73
Resident Population Birth Rate, Mortality by Region （2022）
3—6 各市主要人口指标（2022年）…… 74
Main Population Indicators by Region （2022）
3—7 各市主要年份总人口文盲率…… 75
Illiteracy Ratio by Region in the Primary Years
3—8 各市人均受教育年限…… 76
Average Number of Years of Education by Region
3—9 按年龄和性别分人口数（2022年）…… 77
Population by Age and Sex （2022）
3—10 各市家庭户规模和常住人口性别比（2022）…… 78
Household Size and Sex Ratio of Permanent Residents by Region (2022)
3—11 各市人口年龄结构（2022年）…… 79
Age Composition of Population by Region （2022）
3—12 各市按性别分的15岁及以上文盲人口（2022年）…… 80
Illiterate Population Aged 15 and Over by Sex and Region （2022）
3—13 各市每十万人口拥有受教育程度人口（2022年）…… 81
Population by Educational Level and Region Per 100 Thousand Persons （2022）
3—14 各市婚姻人口构成（2022年）…… 82
Composition of Marriage Status by Region （2022）
3—15 全省育龄妇女分年龄孩次的生育率（2022年）…… 83
Fertility Rate of Women At Childbearing Age by Age and Children's Order （2022）
3—16 各市外出半年以上人口比重、性别比及流向（2022年）…… 84
Proportion, Sexual Distinction and Floating Direction of Persons Going Out for More Than Half a Year

by Region （2022）
3—17 各市流向省外半年以上的流动人口构成（2022年）…… 85
Composition of Persons Floating Out of the Province for More Than Half a Year by Region （2022）
3—18 全省外出半年以上人口分年龄构成（2022年）…… 86
Composition of Population Going out More Than Half a Year in the Whole Province （2022）
3—19 各市按外出时间分的外出人口比例（2022年）…… 87
Proportion of Persons Going Out by Time and Region （2022）
主要统计指标解释…… 88
Explanatory Notes for Major Statistical Indicators

四、 就业人员和工资
Employment and Wages

4—1 就业基本情况…… 93
Basic Conditions of Employment
4—2 主要年份按城乡分的就业人员数…… 94
Number of Employed Persons by Residence in Urban and Rural Areas and Region in Main Year
4—3 各市分行业城镇非私营单位就业人员数（2022年）…… 95
Number of Employed Persons by Sector and Region （2022）
4—4 主要年份私营企业年末户数…… 97
Number of Households of Private Enterprises at the end of Main Years
4—5 各市私营企业年末户数（2022年）…… 97
Number of Private Enterprises at the End of the Year by Region (2022)
4—6 主要年份个体年末户数…… 98
Number of Households at the end of Main Years
4—7 各市个体年末户数（2022年）…… 98
Number of Individual Households at the end of Each by Region (2022)
4—8 城镇非私营单位就业人员数…… 99
Number of Employed Persons of Urban Non-private Owned Units
4—9 城镇非私营单位分行业就业人员数（2022年）…… 100
Number of Employed Persons of Urban Non-private Owned Units by Status （2022）
4—10 城镇非私营单位分行业女性就业人员占全部就业人员比重（2022年）…… 103
Proportion of Female Employed to Total of Urban Non-private Owned Units by Status by Sector （2022）
4—11 城镇非私营单位主要年份就业人员工资总额和指数…… 106
Total Wages of Employed Persons and Related Index of Urban Non-private Owned Units in Major Years
4—12 城镇非私营单位主要年份就业人员平均工资及指数…… 107
Average Wage of Employed Persons and Related Index of Urban Non-private Owned Units in Major Years
4—13 城镇非私营单位分行业就业人员工资总额（2022年）…… 108
Total Wages of Employed Persons of Urban Non-private Owned Units by Sector （2022）
4—14 各市城镇非私营单位分行业就业人员工资总额（2022年）…… 111
Total Wages of Employed Persons of Urban Non-private Owned Units by Sector and Region （2022）
4—15 城镇非私营单位分行业就业人员年平均工资…… 113
Average Wage of Employed Persons of Urban Non-private Owned Units by Sector
4—16 各市城镇非私营单位分行业就业人员年平均工资（2022年）…… 114
Average Wage of Employed Persons of Urban Non-private Owned Units by Sector By Region （2022）
4—17 城镇非私营单位就业人员年平均工资（2022年）…… 116
Average Wage of Employed Persons of Urban Non-private Owned Units at Their Posts （2022）
4—18 各市城镇非私营单位就业人员年平均工资（2022年）…… 117
Average Wage of Employed Persons of Urban Non-private Owned Units at Their Posts by Region (2022)
4—19 城镇私营单位就业人员和工资情况（2022年）…… 118
Wages of Employed Persons in Private Enterprises of Urban Areas （2022）
4—20 城镇非私营单位分行业就业人员年平均工资（2022年）…… 119
Average Wage of Employed Persons of Urban Non-private Owned Units by Sector （2022）
主要统计指标解释…… 122
Explanatory Notes for Major Statistical Indicators

五、 固定资产投资
Investment in Fixed Assets

5—1 固定资产投资主要指标增长情况…… 127

Growth of Main Indicators of Fixed Asset Investment
5—2 各行业按登记注册类型分固定资产投资增长情况（2022年）…… 128
Growth of Investment in Fixed Assets by Industry by Type of Registration (2022)
5—3 各行业按隶属构成控股分固定资产投资增长情况（2022年）…… 134
Growth of Investment in Fixed Assets in Various Industries According to Their Membership (2022)
5—4 各行业固定资产投资资金来源增长情况（2022年）…… 140
Growth of Sources of Funds for Fixed Assets Investment in Various Industries (2022)
5—5 各行业按建设性质项目分固定资产投资增长情况（2022年）…… 146
Growth of Investment in Fixed Assets by Construction Projects in Various Industries (2022)
5—6 各市固定资产投资增长情况（2022年）…… 149
Growth of Investment in Fixed Assets by Region (2022)
5—7 各市按登记注册类型分固定资产投资增长情况（2022年）…… 150
Growth of Fixed Asset Investment by Registration Type by Region (2022)
5—8 各市按隶属构成控股分固定资产投资增长情况（2022年）…… 151
Growth of Fixed Asset Investment by Controlling Shares According to Membership Composition by Region (2022)
5—9 各市按行业新增固定资产投资增长情况（2022年）…… 152
Growth of Investment in Newly Added Fixed Assets by Industry by Region (2022)
5—10 各市按行业分固定资产投资增长情况（2022年）…… 153
Growth of Fixed Asset Investment by Industry by Region (2022)
5—11 各市固定资产投资资金来源增长情况（2022年）…… 154
Growth of Capital Sources for Fixed Asset Investment by Region (2022)
5—12 各市按建设性质项目分固定资产投资增长情况（2022年）…… 155
Growth of Investment in Fixed Assets by Construction Projects by Region (2022)
5—13 各市民间投资和技改投资增长情况（2022年）…… 156
Growth of Private Investment and Technological Innovation Investment by Region (2022)
5—14 房地产开发主要指标…… 157
Main Indicators of Real Estate Development
5—15 房地产开发投资（2022年）…… 158
Investment in Real Estate Development （2022）
5—16 房地产开发企业财务状况（2022年）…… 160
Enterprise's Financial Situation in Real Estate Development （2022）
5—17 各市房地产开发企业财务状况（2022年）…… 160
Enterprise's Financial Situation in Real Estate Development by Region （2022）
5—18 房地产开发企业（单位）财务状况…… 162
Enterprise's Financial Situation in Real Estate Development
5—19 房地产开发企业（单位）投资、资金和土地情况…… 163
Investment, Funds and Land Condition of Real Estate Developer
5—20 房地产开发企业（单位）施工、销售和待售情况（2022年）…… 164
Construction, Sale and for Sale in Real Estate Development Units （2022）
5—21 各市房地产开发企业（单位）个数（2022年）…… 165
Number of Enterprises for Real Estate Development by Region （2022）
5—22 各市按控股情况分的房地产企业（单位）个数（2022年）…… 165
Number of Real Estate Enterprises (units) by Controlled Holdings by Region （2022）
5—23 各市房地产开发建设投资总规模及完成投资（2022年）…… 166
General Scale and Actually Completed Investment in Real Estate Development by Region （2022）
5—24 各市按用途分的房地产开发企业（单位）完成投资额（2022年）…… 167
Actually Completed Investment of Enterprises for Real Estate Development by Region and by Use （2022）
5—25 各市房地产开发企业（单位）资金来源（2022年）…… 168
Sources of Funds of Enterprises for Real Estate Development by Region （2022）
5—26 各市房地产开发建设房屋建筑面积和造价（2022年）…… 169
Floor Space of Buildings and their Cost in Real Estate Development by Region （2022）
5—27 各市按用途分的房地产开发企业（单位）新开工房屋面积（2022年）…… 170
Floor Space Started in Real Estate Development by Region and by Use （2022）
5—28 各市商品房屋销售情况（2022年）…… 171
Selling of Commercial Houses by Region （2022）
5—29 各市按用途分的商品房屋实际销售面积（2022年）…… 172
Floor Space of Commercial Houses Actually Sold by Use and by Region （2022）
5—30 各市按用途分的商品房待售情况（2022年）…… 173
Commercial House for Sale by Used by Region （2022）
主要统计指标解释…… 174

Explanatory Notes for Major Statistical Indicators

六、 能源生产和消费 Production and Consumption of Energy

6—1 能源生产和消费总量及电力生产和消费量 …… 181
Total Production and Consumption of Energy and Electricity
6—2 综合能源平衡表 …… 181
Overall Energy Balance
6—3 能源生产弹性系数 …… 182
Elasticity Ratio of Energy Production
6—4 能源消费弹性系数 …… 182
Elasticity Ratio of Energy Consumption
6—5 能源加工转换效率 …… 182
Efficiency of Energy Conversion
6—6 主要年份电力平衡表 …… 183
Electricity Balance Sheet in Main Year
6—7 主要年份平均每天各种能源消费量 …… 183
Average Daily Energy Consumption by Variety in Main Year
6—8 主要年份生活能源消费量 …… 184
Average Annual Energy Consumption for Households in Main Year
6—9 主要年份人均生活能源消费量 …… 184
Annual per Capita Energy Consumption of Households in Main Year
6—10 主要年份能源消耗指标 …… 185
Energy Consumption Indices in Main Year
6—11 各市能源消耗指标（2022年） …… 185
Energy Consumption Indices by Region （2022）
6—12 全社会用电情况 …… 186
Electricity Used in Whole Society
6—13 电力建设情况 …… 187
Electric Power Construction Situation
6—14 经销企业能源购进、销售与库存情况（2022年） …… 187
Energy Distribution Enterprise Purchase, Sales and Inventory （2022）
6—15 主要年份全社会工业分行业用电量 …… 188
Electricity Consumption of the Whole Society, Industry and Sub-industry in Major Years
6—16 规模以上工业企业分行业取水情况（2022年） …… 189
Water Intake by Industries of Industrial Enterprises Above Designated Size （2022）
6—17 规模以上工业企业分行业主要能源品种消费量（2022年） …… 190
Industrial Enterprises Above Designated Size Consume Major Energy Resources in Different Industries （2022）
6—18 规模以上工业企业能源购进、消费及库存（2022年） …… 192
Buys, Consumes and Stock of the Energy of Above Designated Size Industrial Enterprises （2022）
6—19 地区能源消费 …… 193
Regional Energy Consumption
6—20 各市全社会用电情况（2022年） …… 193
Electricity Used in Whole Society by Region （2022）
6—21 各市主要年份工业用电量 …… 194
Industrial Electricity Used in Main Year by Region
6—22 各市规模以上工业企业取水情况（2022年） …… 194
Water Intake by Industrial Enterprises Above Designated Size by Region （2022）
主要统计指标解释 …… 195
Explanatory Notes for Major Statistical Indicators

七、 财政与金融 Government Finance and Finance

7—1 一般公共预算收支及增长速度 …… 199
General Public Budget Revenue and Expenditure and Growth Rate
7—2 一般公共预算收入相当于生产总值的比例 …… 199
General Public Budget Revenue As a Percentage of Gross Domestic Product
7—3 税收收入和非税收入及比重 …… 200

Total Revenue and Proportion of Tax and Non-tax
7—4 各项税收收入 200
Government Tax Revenue
7—5 一般公共预算收支情况 201
General Public Budget Revenue and Expenditure
7—6 各市一般公共预算收入（2022年） 202
General Public Budget Revenue by Region (2022)
7—7 各市一般公共预算支出（2022年） 204
Expenditures in General Public Budgets by Region (2022)
7—8 各县（市）一般公共预算收入（2022年） 206
General Public Budget Revenue by County (City) (2022)
7—9 各县（市）一般公共预算支出（2022年） 212
Expenditures in General Public Budgets by County (City) (2022)
7—10 金融机构（含外资）人民币信贷资金平衡表（资金来源） 218
Financial Institutions (including foreign) RMB Credit Balance Sheet (funding)
7—11 金融机构（含外资）人民币信贷资金平衡表（资金运用） 219
Financial Institutions (including foreign) RMB Credit Balance Sheet (fund use)
7—12 金融机构（含外资）本外币合并信贷收支 220
Local and Foreign Financial Institutions (including foreign) Merging the Credit Balance of Payments
7—13 各市金融机构（含外资）本外币合并信贷收支（2022年） 221
Local and Foreign Financial Institutions (including foreign) Merging the Credit Balance of Payments by Region （2022）
7—14 人民币信贷收支情况（2022年） 222
Credit Receipts and Payments （2022）
7—15 上市公司数量 223
Number of Listed Companies
7—16 股票发行及筹资情况 223
Issuing Summary for Stocks
7—17 各市股票发行情况及筹资情况（截至2022年） 224
Issuing Summary for Stocks by Region (As of 2022)
7—18 保险公司业务经济技术指标（2022年） 225
Main Professional Technical Indicators of Insurance Companies （2022）
主要统计指标解释 226
Explanatory Notes for Major Statistical Indicators

八、 物价指数
Price Indices

8—1 各种价格总指数 233
Price Indices
8—2 各种价格定基指数 233
Fixed-base Price Indices
8—3 居民消费价格分类指数（2022年） 234
Consumer Price Indices by Category （2022）
8—4 调查市、县居民消费价格分类指数（2022年） 236
Consumer Price Indices by Category and by Surveyed City and County （2022）
8—5 农产品生产者价格指数 237
Producer Price Indices of Agricultural Products
8—6 工业生产者出厂价格主要分组指数（按生产生活资料分） 238
Producer Price Indices for Industrial Products by Category
8—7 工业生产者出厂价格主要分组指数（按轻重工业分） 239
Sub-index of Light and Heavy industry of Ex-factory Industrial Producer Price Index
8—8 工业生产者购进价格主要分组指数 240
Industrial Products Purchased from the Price Indices by Category
主要统计指标解释 241
Explanatory Notes for Major Statistical Indicators

九、 城乡人民生活
Livelihood of Urban and Rural People

9—1 人民物质文化生活情况…… 245
People's Material and Cultural Life
9—2 全体居民家庭基本情况…… 246
Basic Information About The Households of all The Residents
9—3 全体居民可支配收入及构成…… 247
Household Disposable Income and Composition
9—4 全体居民按收入五等份分组的人均可支配收入…… 247
Per Capita Disposable Income of All Residents Divided Into Five Equal Groups
9—5 全体居民消费支出…… 248
Consumption Expenditure of Total Residents
9—6 全体居民消费支出构成…… 249
Composition of Household Consumption Expenditure
9—7 全体居民年末主要耐用消费品拥有量…… 250
Ownership of Major Durable Consumer Goods by the End of The Year
9—8 各市全体居民人均可支配收入…… 250
Per Capita Disposable Income of All Residents by Region
9—9 城镇居民家庭基本情况…… 251
Basic Conditions of Urban Households
9—10 城镇居民现金可支配收入及构成…… 252
Urban Residents Cash Disposable Income and Composition
9—11 城镇居民年末主要耐用消费品拥有量…… 252
Ownership of Major Durable Consumer Goods by Urban Residents at The Year-end
9—12 各市城镇居民人均可支配收入…… 253
Per Capita Disposable Income of Urban Residents by Region
9—13 农村居民家庭基本情况…… 254
Basic Conditions of Rural Households
9—14 农村居民可支配收入及构成…… 255
Disposable Income and Composition of Rural Residents
9—15 农村居民现金可支配收入及构成…… 256
Rural Residents Cash Disposable Income and Composition
9—16 农村居民消费支出…… 257
Consumption Expenditure of Rural Residents
9—17 农村居民消费支出构成…… 258
Composition of Rural Residents' Consumption Expenditure
9—18 农村居民主要食品消费量…… 259
Main Food Consumption of Rural Residents
9—19 农村居民年末主要耐用消费品拥有量…… 260
Ownership of Major Durable Consumer Goods by Rural Residents at The End of The Year
9—20 各市农村居民人均可支配收入…… 261
Per Capita Disposable Income of Rural Residents by Region
9—21 分市、县（市、区）居民人均可支配收入…… 262
Per Capita Disposable Income of Residents in Cities and Counties (cities and districts)
主要统计指标解释…… 265
Explanatory Notes for Major Statistical Indicators

十、 城市概况 General Survey of Cities

10—1 地级城市基本情况（2022年）…… 269
Basic Statement of Cities at Prefectural Level （2022）
10—2 地级城市市区基本情况（2022年）…… 272
Basic Statement of Cities at Prefectural Level by Region （2022）
10—3 城市市政公用基础设施基本情况…… 278
Basic Statistics on Urban Public Utilities
10—4 各市城市建设情况（2022年）…… 279
Statistics on City Construction by Region （2022）
10—5 各市城市市政设施情况（2022年）…… 280
Basic Statistics on Municipal Infrastructure in Cities by Region （2022）
10—6 各市城市设施水平（2022年）…… 281
Level of Public Facilities in Cities by Region （2022）

10—7 各市城市公共交通情况（2022年）………… 282
Basic Statistics on Public Transportation in Cities by Region （2022）
10—8 各市城市绿地和园林（2022年）………… 283
Basic Statistics on Parks and Green Areas in Cities by Region （2022）
10—9 各市城市燃气情况（2022年）………… 284
Basic Statistics on Supply of Gas in Cities by Region （2022）
10—10 城市供水用水情况………… 285
Water Supply and Water Use of Cities
10—11 各市城市供水用水情况（2022年）………… 286
Water Supply and Water Use of Cities by Region （2022）
10—12 各市城市污水排放和处理情况（2022年）………… 287
City Sewage Emission and Processing by Region （2022）
10—13 各市城市市容环境卫生情况（2022年）………… 288
Basic Statistics on Urban Sanitation in Cities by Region （2022）
主要统计指标解释………… 289
Explanatory Notes for Major Statistical Indicators

十一、 自然资源和环境保护
Natural Resources and Environment Protection

11—1 自然状况………… 293
Natural Conditions
11—2 自然资源………… 294
Natural Resources
11—3 主要城市平均气温（2022年）………… 295
Monthly Average Temperature in Major Cities （2022）
11—4 主要城市降水量（2022年）………… 295
Monthly Precipitation in Major Cities （2022）
11—5 各市全年降水量（2022年）………… 296
Total Precipitation by Region （2022）
11—6 流域分区全年降水量（2022年）………… 296
Total Precipitation by Area of Rivers （2022）
11—7 各市水资源总量（2022年）………… 297
Water Resources by Region （2022）
11—8 流域分区水资源总量（2022年）………… 298
Water Resources by Area of Rivers （2022）
11—9 主要年份供水和用水情况………… 299
Water Supply and Water Use in Rural Area
11—10 各市供水和用水情况（2022年）………… 299
Water Supply and Water Use by Region （2022）
11—11 环境综合整治………… 300
Environmental Improvement
11—12 环保系统机构、人员数………… 302
Environmental Protection Agencies and Persons Engaged
11—13 生活污染物排放………… 302
Discharge of Pollutants from Daily Life
11—14 工业企业“三废”排放及治理………… 303
Discharge and Treatment of Waste Water, Waste Gas and Solid Wastes by Industry Enterprises
11—15 各市工业废水排放及处理（2021年）………… 304
Discharge and Treatment of Industrial Waste Water by Region （2021）
11—16 各市工业废气排放及处理（2021年）………… 305
Emission and Treatment of Industrial Waste Gas by Region （2021）
11—17 各市工业固体废物产生及处理利用（2022年）………… 306
Discharge, Treatment and Utilization of Industrial Solid Wastes by Region （2022）
11—18 各市城市空气质量指标（2022年）………… 307
Ambient Air Quality in Main Cities by Region （2022）
11—19 各市城市道路交通噪声监测情况（2022年）………… 307
Monitoring of Urban Road Traffic Noise in Key Cities by Region （2022）
11—20 水资源情况………… 308
Water Resources

11—21 各市水资源情况（2022年）…… 308
Water Resources by Region （2022）
11—22 农村环境状况…… 309
The Environment of Rural Areas
11—23 各市农村环境状况（2022年）…… 309
The Environment of Rural Areas by Region （2022）
11—24 突发环境事件情况…… 310
Environmental Accidents
11—25 各市突发环境事件情况（2022年）…… 310
Environmental Accidents by Region （2022）
11—26 地质灾害及防治情况…… 311
Geological Disasters and Prevention and Cure
11—27 各市地质灾害及防治情况（2022年）…… 311
Geological Disasters and Prevention and Cure by Region （2022）
11—28 自然保护基本情况…… 312
Basic Situation of Natural Protection
11—29 造林面积…… 313
Area of Afforestation
11—30 各市造林面积（2022年）…… 313
Area of Afforestation by Region （2022）
主要统计指标解释…… 314
Explanatory Notes for Major Statistical Indicators

十二、 农 业
Agriculture

12—1 乡（镇）、村数及主要农业机械年末拥有量…… 323
Number of Townships (towns), Villages and Year-end Ownership of Main Agricultural Machinery
12—2 主要年份农林牧渔业生产情况…… 324
Output of Farming, Forestry, Animal Husbandry and Fishery
12—3 主要年份农作物播种面积…… 325
Sown Area of Crops in Major Years
12—4 农林牧渔业总产值及指数…… 326
Gross Output Value of Farming, Forestry, Animal Husbandry and Fishery and Related Indices
12—5 主要年份林业生产情况…… 327
Basic Data of Forest Production in Major Years
12—6 主要年份茶叶、水果生产情况…… 327
Tea, Fruits Production in Major Years
12—7 主要年份牲畜饲养情况…… 328
Number of Livestock in Major Years
12—8 主要年份畜产品产量…… 328
Output of Livestock Products in Major Years
12—9 农林牧渔业总产值（2022年）…… 329
Gross Output Value of Farming, Forestry, Animal Husbandry and Fishery （2022）
12—10 农作物主要产品生产情况（2022年）…… 330
Production of Main Crops (2022)
12—11 各市乡（镇）、村数（2022年）…… 331
Number of Townships (towns) and Villages by Region (2022)
12—12 各市农、林、牧、渔业总产值及指数（2022年）…… 332
Gross Output Value of Farming, Forestry, Animal Husbandry and Fishery and Related Indices by Region （2022）
12—13 各市主要农业机械年末拥有量（2022年）…… 334
Agricultural Machinery at the Year-end by Region （2022）
12—14 各市主要粮食作物播种面积（2022年）…… 335
Area Sown With Main Grain Crops in Each by Region (2022)
12—15 各市主要经济作物播种面积（2022年）…… 336
Area Sown to Main Cash Crops in Each by Region (2022)
12—16 各市主要农产品单位面积产量（2022年）…… 338
Yield of Major Farm Crops per Hectare by Region （2022）
12—17 各市主要粮食作物产量（2022年）…… 339
Output of Major Food Crops in Each by Region (2022)

12—18 各市主要经济作物产量（2022年） ······ 340
Output of Main Cash Crops in Each by Region (2022)
12—19 各市茶叶、水果生产情况（2022年） ······ 341
Tea, Fruits Production by Region （2022）
12—20 各市牲畜饲养情况（2022年） ······ 342
Number of Livestock by Region （2022）
12—21 各市畜产品产量（2022年） ······ 343
Output of Livestock Products by Region （2022）
12—22 各市水产品产量（2022年） ······ 344
Output of Aquatic Products by Region （2022）
12—23 国有农场基本情况 ······ 345
Basic Statistics on State Farms
12—24 各县（市）乡（镇）、村数（2022年） ······ 346
Number of Townships (towns) and Villages by County or City (2022)
12—25 各县（市）农林牧渔业总产值（2022年） ······ 348
Gross Output Value of Agriculture, Forestry, Animal Husbandry and Fishery by County or City （2022）
12—26 各县（市）主要粮食作物产量（2022年） ······ 350
Area Sown With Main Grain Crops in Each by County or City (2022)
12—27 各县（市）主要经济作物产量（2022年） ······ 352
Yield of Farm Crops and Area of Cultivated Land by County or City （2022）
12—28 各县（市）茶叶、水果生产情况（2022年） ······ 354
Tea, Fruits Production by County or City （2022）
12—29 各县（市）畜牧业、渔业生产情况（2022年） ······ 356
Production of Animal Husbandry, Fishery by County or City （2022）
主要统计指标解释 ······ 358
Explanatory Notes for Major Statistical Indicators

十三、 工 业
Industry

13—1 工业分行业职工人数 ······ 363
Number of Staff and Workers in Industry by Industrial Branch
13—2 规模以上工业企业主要经济指标（2022年） ······ 364
Main Indicators Above Designated Size Industrial Enterprises （2022）
13—3 规模以上工业企业主要经济效益指标（2022年） ······ 372
Main Indicators on Economic Benefit Above Designated Size Industrial Enterprises by Industrial Branch （2022）
13—4 国有控股工业企业主要经济指标（2022年） ······ 376
Main Indicators of State-owned and State-holding Industrial Enterprises （2022）
13—5 国有控股工业企业主要经济效益指标（2022年） ······ 380
Main Indicators on Economic Benefit of State-owned and State-holding Industrial Enterprises （2022）
13—6 外商投资和港澳台商投资工业企业主要经济指标（2022年） ······ 382
Main Indicators of Industrial Enterprises with Hong Kong, Macao, Taiwan and Foreign Funds （2022）
13—7 外商投资和港澳台商投资工业企业主要经济效益指标（2022年） ······ 386
Main Indicators on Economic Benefit of Industrial Enterprises with Hong Kong, Macao, Taiwan and Foreign Funds （2022）
13—8 私营工业企业主要经济指标（2022年） ······ 388
Main Indicators of Private Enterprises （2022）
13—9 私营工业企业主要经济效益指标（2022年） ······ 392
Main Indicators on Economic Benefit of Private Industrial Enterprises （2022）
13—10 大中型工业企业主要经济指标（2022年） ······ 394
Main Indicators of Large and Medium-sized Industrial Enterprises （2022）
13—11 大中型工业企业主要经济效益指标（2022年） ······ 398
Main Indicators on Economic Benefit of Large and Medium-sized Industrial Enterprises （2022）
13—12 各市全部规模以上工业企业主要经济指标（2022年） ······ 400
Main Indicators Above Designated Size Industrial Enterprises by Region （2022）
13—13 各市国有控股工业企业主要经济指标（2022年） ······ 401
Main Indicators of State-owned and State Holding Majority Shares Industrial Enterprises by Region （2022）
13—14 各市外商投资和港澳台商投资工业企业主要经济指标（2022年） ······ 402
Main Indicators on Economic Benefit of Industrial Enterprises with Hong Kong, Macao, Taiwan and Foreign Funds by Region （2022）

13—15 各市私营工业企业主要经济指标（2022年）…… 403
Main Indicators of Private Enterprises by Region （2022）
13—16 各市大中型工业企业主要经济指标（2022年）…… 404
Main Indicators of Large and Medium-sized Industrial Enterprises by Region （2022）
13—17 工业主要产品生产能力…… 405
Production Capacity of Major Industrial Products
13—18 主要工业产品产量…… 406
Output of Major Industrial Products
13—19 各市主要工业产品产量（2022年）…… 408
Output of Major Industrial Products by Region （2022）
主要统计指标解释…… 410
Explanatory Notes for Major Statistical Indicators

十四、 **建 筑 业**
Construction

14—1 建筑业企业概况…… 417
Main Indicators on Construction Enterprises
14—2 主要年份建筑业企业主要经济指标…… 418
Main Economic Indicators on Construction Enterprises
14—3 建筑业企业房屋建筑完成情况（2022年）…… 419
Floor Space of Buildings Completed by Construction Enterprises （2022）
14—4 建筑业企业主要生产指标（2022年）…… 420
Main Indicators on Construction Enterprises （2022）
14—5 建筑业企业主要财务指标（2022年）…… 422
Main Financial Indicators on Construction Enterprises （2022）
14—6 按登记注册类型分建筑业企业主要经济指标（2022）…… 426
According to the Construction Enterprise Registration Type Points Leading Economic Indicators （2022）
14—7 各市建筑业企业房屋建筑完成情况（2022年）…… 428
Floor Space of Buildings Completed by Construction Enterprises by Region （2022）
14—8 各市按登记注册类型和行业分的建筑业企业单位数（2022年）…… 429
Number of Construction Enterprises by Registration Status, Section and Region （2022）
14—9 各市按经济类型和行业分的建筑业总产值（2022年）…… 430
Overall Output Value of Enterprises in Charge of Construction by Ownership and Region （2022）
14—10 各市建筑业企业生产情况（2022年）…… 431
Production Indicators on Construction Enterprises by Region （2022）
14—11 各市建筑业企业主要财务指标（2022年）…… 432
Main Financial Indicators on Construction Enterprises by Region （2022）
主要统计指标解释…… 433
Explanatory Notes for Major Statistical Indicators

十五、 **运输和邮电**
Transport, Post and Telecommunication Services

15—1 交通运输业基本情况…… 437
Basic Conditions of Transportation
15—2 运输路线长度…… 438
Length of Transportation Routes
15—3 运输线路质量…… 439
Quality of Transportation Routes
15—4 内河港口码头吞吐量…… 439
Volume of Passenger and Freight Handled in Ports of Inland Rivers
15—5 主要港口分货类吞吐量…… 440
Volume of Throughput in Major Ports by Type of Freight
15—6 各市公路客货运输量（2022年）…… 440
Highway Passenger and Freight Traffic Volume By Region （2022）
15—7 主要年份公路线路年底到达数（按技术等级分）…… 441
Length of Highway Routes at the Year-end (classified by technical level)
15—8 公路线路年底到达数（按技术等级分）（2022年）…… 441
Length of Highway Routes at the Year-end (classified by technical level) （2022）

15—9 各市公路线路年底到达数（按技术等级分）（2022年）…… 442
Length of Highway Routes at the Year-end by Region (classified by technical level) (2022)
15—10 公路密度及通达情况…… 442
Density and Reaching Status of Highways
15—11 主要年份民用车辆拥有量…… 443
Possession of Civil Vehicles
15—12 主要年份私人车辆拥有量…… 443
Possession of Private Vehicles
15—13 民用车辆拥有量营运情况（2022年）…… 444
Civilian Vehicles Capacity of Transportation Situation (2022)
15—14 各市民用车辆拥有量（2022年）…… 445
Possession of Civil Vehicles by Region (2022)
15—15 各市私人车辆拥有量（2022年）…… 445
Possession of Private Vehicles by Region (2022)
15—16 公路营运汽车拥有量…… 446
Possession of Vehicles for Highway Business Transportation
15—17 各市公路营运汽车拥有量（2022年）…… 446
Possession of Vehicles for Highway Business Transportation by Region (2022)
15—18 各市民用运输船舶拥有量（2022年）…… 447
Number of Civil Transport Vessels Owned by Region (2022)
15—19 各市私人运输船舶拥有量（2022年）…… 447
Number of Private-owned Transport Vessels Owned by Region (2022)
15—20 全省机场运输业务量（2022年）…… 448
Traffic Capacity of Airports (2022)
15—21 民航机场吞吐量（2022年）…… 448
Volume of Passenger and Freight Handled in Civil Airports (2022)
15—22 东航安徽分公司基本情况…… 449
Basic Information of Anhui Branch of China Eastern Airlines
15—23 邮电业务基本情况…… 449
Basic Statistics of Postal and Telecommunications Services
15—24 各市邮电业务量（2022年）…… 450
Post and Telecommunication Services by Region (2022)
15—25 邮电局所数及邮递线路（年底数）…… 451
Postal and Telecommunication Services Facilities (year-end)
15—26 各市邮电局所数及邮递线路（2022年）…… 451
Postal and Telecommunication Services Facilities by Region (2022)
主要统计指标解释…… 452
Explanatory Notes for Major Statistical Indicators

十六、 国内贸易 Domestic Trade

16—1 国内贸易基本情况…… 459
Basic Conditions of Domestic Trade
16—2 限额以上批发零售、住宿餐饮业基本情况（2022年，按登记注册类型分）…… 460
Basic Conditions of Enterprises Above Designated Size in Wholesale and Retail Sale and Catering Trade by Registration (2022)
16—3 限额以上批发零售业商品购进、销售和库存情况（2022年，按注册类型分）…… 462
Total Purchases, Sales and Inventory of Enterprises Above Designated Size in Wholesale and Retail Trade by Registration (2022)
16—4 限额以上批发零售业商品购进、销售和库存情况（2022年，按行业分）…… 463
Total Purchases, Sales and Inventory of Enterprises Above Designated Size in Wholesale and Retail Trade by Sector (2022)
16—5 限额以上批发零售业主要商品分类销售额（2022年）…… 467
Total Sales of Enterprises Above Designated Size in Wholesale and Retail Sale by Category of Main Commodities (2022)
16—6 限额以上批发零售企业主要财务指标情况（2022年，按登记注册类型分）…… 468
Main Financial Indicators of Enterprises Above Designated Size in Wholesale and Retail Sale by Registration (2022)
16—7 限额以上批发零售企业主要财务指标情况（2022年，按行业分）…… 472

Main Financial Inventory of Enterprises Above Designated Size in Wholesale and Retail by Sector （2022）
16—8 限额以上住宿餐饮业经营情况（2022年）…… 476
Above Designated Accommodation Catering Business （2022）
16—9 限额以上住宿业和餐饮企业主要财务指标情况（2022年）…… 478
Main Financial Indicators of Enterprises Above Designated Size in Catering Trades by Status of Registration and by Sector （2022）
16—10 限额以上批发和零售业连锁经营情况（2022年）…… 482
Basic Conditions of Chain-Enterprise Above Quota Wholesale and Retail （2022）
16—11 限额以上住宿和餐饮业连锁经营情况（2022年）…… 482
Basic Conditions of Chain-Enterprise Above Quota Lodging and food and Beverage Industry （2022）
16—12 各市限额以上批发和零售业连锁经营情况（2022年）…… 483
Basic Conditions of Chain-Enterprise Above Quota Wholesale and Retail by Region （2022）
16—13 各市限额以上住宿和餐饮业连锁经营情况（2022年）…… 483
Basic Conditions of Chain-Enterprise Above Quota Lodging and Food and Beverage Industry by Region （2022）
16—14 各市限额以上批发零售企业主要财务指标情况（2022年）…… 484
Main Financial Indicators of Enterprises Above Designated Size in Wholesale and Retail by Region （2022）
16—15 各市限额以上住宿和餐饮企业主要财务指标情况（2022年）…… 484
Main Financial Indicators of Enterprises Above Designated Size in Catering Trades by Status of Registration by Region （2022）
16—16 各市限额以上批发零售业商品购进、销售和库存情况（2022年）…… 488
Total Purchases, Sales and Inventory of Enterprises Above Designated Size in Wholesale and Retail and Inventory by Region （2022）
16—17 各市限额以上住宿餐饮业经营情况（2022年）…… 488
Above Designated Accommodation Catering Business by Region （2022）
16—18 亿元以上商品交易市场情况（2022年）…… 489
Market Situation of Commodity Trading Above 100 million Yuan （2022）
16—19 各市亿元以上商品交易市场情况（2022年）…… 489
Market Situation of Commodity Trading Above 100 million Yuan by Region （2022）
16—20 亿元以上商品交易市场摊位分类情况（2022年）…… 490
Classification of Commodity Exchange Markets of Transaction Value over 100 Million Yuan （2022）
16—21 各市社会消费品零售总额（2022年）…… 491
Total Retail Sale of Consumer Goods in Major Years by Region （2022）
16—22 各县（市）社会消费品零售总额（2022年）…… 492
Total Retail Sale of Consumer Goods in Major Years by County or City （2022）
主要统计指标解释…… 494
Explanatory Notes for Major Statistical Indicators

十七、 对外经济贸易 Foreign Trade and Economic Cooperation

17—1 对外经济贸易基本情况…… 499
Foreign Trade and Economic Cooperation
17—2 海关出口商品分类金额…… 500
Value of Exports by Category of Commodities (Customs Statistics)
17—3 海关进口商品分类金额…… 500
Value of Imports by Category of Commodities (Customs Statistics)
17—4 海关进出口商品分类金额…… 501
Value of Imports and Exports by Category of Commodities (Customs Statistics)
17—5 安徽省同各国（地区）进出口总额…… 503
Anhui's Foreign Trade With Related Countries and Territories
17—6 进出口商品贸易方式总值（2022年）…… 508
Total Value of Import and Export Trade Way （2022）
17—7 外国和港澳台地区直接投资（按行业）（2022年）…… 509
Foreign and Hong Kong, Macao and Taiwan Direct Investment (by Industry) （2022）
17—8 外国和港澳台地区直接投资（按国别和地区）（2022年）…… 510
Direct Investment of Foreign Countries and Hong Kong, Macao and Taiwan by Countries and Regions （2022）
17—9 按国别（地区）对外投资…… 512
According to the Country (region) of Foreign Investment
17—10 按国别（地区）对外承包工程和劳务合作…… 514
According to the Country (region) of Foreign Contracted Projects and Labor Service Cooperation

17—11 外商投资企业年末企业数、投资总额及注册资本（2022年）…… 516
Number, Investment and Registered Capital of Foreign-funded Enterprises （2022）
17—12 各市外商投资企业年末企业数、投资总额及注册资本（2022年）…… 517
Number, Investment and Registered Capital of Foreign-funded Enterprises by Region （2022）
17—13 各市商品进出口总额…… 518
Import and Export Commodities by Region
17—14 各市外商直接投资…… 518
Foreign Direct Investment by Region
17—15 各市外国和港澳台地区直接投资（2022年）…… 519
Direct Investment of Foreign Countries, Hong Kong, Macao and Taiwan by Sector by Region （2022）
主要统计指标解释…… 520
Explanatory Notes for Major Statistical Indicators

十八、 旅　游
Tourism

18—1 旅游事业发展…… 525
Development of Tourism
18—2 各市旅行社数…… 526
Number of Travel Agencies by Region
18—3 主要年份旅游景点基本情况…… 527
Basic Information of Tourist Attractions in Main Years
18—4 各市旅游景点基本情况（2022年）…… 527
Basic Information of Tourist Attractions by Region (2022)
18—5 各市旅游星级饭店（宾馆）住宿设施情况（2022年）…… 528
Accommodation Facilities of Hotels Concerning Foreign Affairs by Region （2022）
18—6 国际旅游外汇收入及构成…… 529
Foreign Exchange Earnings and It's Composition
18—7 接待外国人旅游人数（按国别分）…… 530
Number of Foreign Tourists by Country
18—8 国内旅游情况人数结构（按年龄、身份和职业分）（2022年）…… 530
Number of Domestic Tourists by Age, Identity and Occupation （2022）
18—9 国内旅游主要经济指标…… 531
Main Economic Indicators of Domestic Tourism
18—10 各市国内旅游主要经济指标（2022年）…… 531
Main Economic Indicators of Domestic Tourism by Region （2022）
18—11 国内旅游人均花费（2022年）…… 532
Per Capita Costs of Domestic Tourism （2022）
18—12 各市国内旅游人均花费（2022年）…… 532
Per Capita Costs of Domestic Tourism by Region （2022）
18—13 国家级黄山风景区旅游事业发展情况…… 533
Development of Tourism of Huang Shan Scenic at National Level
18—14 国家级九华山风景区旅游事业发展情况…… 534
Development of Tourism of Jiu Hua Shan Scenic at National Level
主要统计指标解释…… 535
Explanatory Notes for Major Statistical Indicators

十九、 教育和科技
Education and Science

19—1 教育事业基本情况…… 539
Basic Statistics on Education
19—2 研究生数…… 540
Number of Postgraduates
19—3 普通高等学校本科分科学生数…… 540
Number of Students of the Ordinary College Undergraduate Course Branch
19—4 普通高职高专（专科）分科学生数…… 541
Number of Students in Ordinary Vocational Colleges by Subject
19—5 普通本科高等学校分科专任教师数（2022年）…… 541
Number of Full-time Teachers in Regular Undergraduate Institutions of Higher Learning by Subject （2022）

19—6 普通高职高专（专科）专任教师数（2022年） …… 542
Number of Full-time Teachers in Ordinary Vocational Colleges (2022)
19—7 普通中等职业学校分科学生数（2022年） …… 543
Number of Students in General Secondary Vocational Schools by Subject (2022)
19—8 中等职业学校分科专任教师数（2022年） …… 544
Number of Full-time Teachers in Secondary Vocational Schools by Subject (2022)
19—9 技工学校数和学生数 …… 544
Number of Technical Schools, Students, Staff and Teachers
19—10 平均每万人口各级教育在校学生及构成情况 …… 545
All Levels of Education Students per 10000 Population and Composition
19—11 各级各类学校生师比 …… 545
At Various Levels and School Teacher Ratio
19—12 各级学校女学生和女教师数 …… 546
Number of Female Students and Teachers by Level of School
19—13 各级各类成人教育基本情况（2022年） …… 547
Basic Situation of Adult Education of All Types and at All Levels （2022）
19—14 民办教育基本情况（2022年） …… 547
Basic Information on Private Education （2022）
19—15 各市普通高等学校和中职学校情况（2022年） …… 548
General Institutions of Higher Learning and Secondary Vocational Schools by Region (2022)
19—16 各市特殊教育情况（2022年） …… 548
Basic Statistics on Special Education by Region （2022）
19—17 各市普通中学分城乡学校数和在校学生数（2022年） …… 549
Number of Regular Secondary Schools and Student Enrollment by Urban and Rural Areas and by Region （2022）
19—18 各市普通中学分城乡招生数和毕业生数（2022年） …… 550
Number of New Student Enrollment and Graduates of Regular Secondary Schools by Urban and Rural Areas and by Region （2022）
19—19 各市普通高中、初中和小学分城乡专任老师数（2022年） …… 551
Regular Senior High School, Junior High School and Primary School by Urban and Rural Full-time Teachers by Region (2022)
19—20 各市小学分城乡情况（2022年） …… 552
Primary Schools by Urban and Rural Conditions by Region (2022)
19—21 各市幼儿园基本情况（2022年） …… 553
Basic Statistics on Kindergartens by Region （2022）
19—22 各级各类学校教育经费收入情况（2022年） …… 554
Basic Statistics on Educational Funds in Various Schools （2022）
19—23 全省科技活动基本情况 …… 555
Basic Statistics on Scientific and Technological Activities
19—24 县级以上政府部门属研究与开发机构及科技信息与文献机构数、人员数 …… 556
State-owned Research and Development Institutions and Information and Literature Institutions at and Above County Level and Persons Engaged
19—25 县级以上政府部门属研究与开发机构及科技信息与文献机构科技经费筹集和支出总额 …… 556
Total Funds and Total Expenditures of State-owned Research and Development Institutions and Information and Literature Institutions at and Above County Level
19—26 科协系统科技活动情况（2022年） …… 557
Basic Statistics on Scientific and Technological Activities of Associations for Science and Technology （2022）
19—27 各市规上企业分行业创新情况（2022年） …… 558
Innovation of Enterprises by Industry by Region (2022)
19—28 规上企业创新情况（2022年） …… 559
Enterprise Innovation on Regulation (2022)
19—29 规上企业产品和工艺创新情况（2022年） …… 560
Product and Process Innovation of Enterprises on The Regulation (2022)
19—30 规上企业组织和营销创新情况（2022年） …… 561
Enterprise Organization and Marketing Innovation on Regulation (2022)
19—31 规上企业创新合作情况（2022年） …… 562
Innovation Cooperation of Enterprises in Accordance With Regulations (2022)
19—32 规上工业企业创新情况（2022年） …… 563
Innovation of Industrial Enterprises on Regulation (2022)
19—33 规上工业企业产品和工艺创新情况（2022年） …… 564
Product and Process Innovation of Industrial Enterprises (2022)

19—34 规上工业企业组织和营销创新情况（2022年）…… 565
Organizational and Marketing Innovation of Industrial Enterprises on Regulation (2022)
19—35 规上工业企业创新合作情况（2022年）…… 566
Innovation Cooperation Among Industrial Enterprises (2022)
19—36 研究与试验发展人员（2022年）…… 567
Research and Experimental Development Personnel (2022)
19—37 研究与试验发展经费支出情况（2022年）…… 568
Research and Development Funds and Internal Expenditure （2022）
19—38 高等学校科技活动情况…… 568
Basic Statistics on Higher Education for Scientific and Technological Activities
19—39 各市研究与试验发展人员（2022年）…… 569
Research and Experimental Development Personnel by Region (2022)
19—40 各市研究与试验发展经费支出情况（2022年）…… 571
Research and Development Funds and Internal Expenditure by Region （2022）
19—41 各市工业企业享受相关政策情况（2022年）…… 572
Industrial Enterprises Enjoy Relevant Policies by Region (2022)
19—42 工业企业科技活动基本情况…… 573
Basic Statistics on Science and Technology Activities of Industrial Enterprises
19—43 各市工业企业研究与试验发展基本情况（2022年）…… 574
Research and Development Basic Situation of Industrial Enterprise by Region （2022）
19—44 各市工业企业研究与试验发展经费情况（2022年）…… 575
Research and Development Funds Basic Situation of Industrial Enterprise by Region （2022）
19—45 各市工业企业自主知识产权和技术情况（2022年）…… 576
Self-owned Intellectual Property Rights and Technology Situation Industrial Enterprise by Region （2022）
19—46 省级以上开发区主要经济指标…… 577
Main Economic Indicators of Development Areas above the Provincial Level
19—47 部分国家级开发区主要经济指标（2022年）…… 578
Main Economic Indicators of Some National Development Zones (2022)
19—48 各市省级以上开发区主要经济指标（2022年）…… 580
Main Economic Indicators of Development Areas above the Provincial Level by Region （2022）
19—49 合肥国家高新技术产业开发区企业经营状况（2022年）…… 581
Enterprises Business of Hefei National Development Zone for New and High-level Technology Industries （2022）
19—50 合肥国家高新技术产业开发区产品概况（2022年）…… 581
Products of Hefei National Development Zone for New and High-level Technology Industries （2022）
19—51 全省监督抽查产品质量情况…… 582
Results of Sampling Check on Product Quality Under Provincial Supervision
19—52 技术市场成交情况（2022年）…… 582
Situation of Technological Markets （2022）
19—53 三种专利申请授权量…… 583
Three Kinds of Patent Applications Granted
19—54 各市三种专利申请授权量（2022年）…… 583
Three Kinds of Patent Applications Granted by Region （2022）
主要统计指标解释…… 584
Explanatory Notes for Major Statistical Indicators

二十、 卫生和社会服务
Public Health and Social Services

20—1 医疗卫生机构数…… 589
Number of Health Institutions
20—2 医疗卫生机构人员数…… 589
Number of Engaged Persons in Health Institutions
20—3 医疗卫生机构、床位、人员数（2022年）…… 590
Number of Health Units, Beds and Staff （2022）
20—4 医疗卫生机构各类人员数（2022年）…… 591
Persons Engaged in Health Care Institutions by Type of Occupation （2022）
20—5 各市医疗卫生机构人员数（2022年）…… 592
Number of Persons Engaged in Health Institutions by Region （2022）
20—6 各市医疗卫生机构数（2022年）…… 593
Number of Medical Health Institutions by Region （2022）

20—7 各市医疗卫生机构床位数（2022年）…… 594
Number of Beds of Medical Health Institutions by Region （2022）
20—8 医疗机构门诊、住院服务情况（2022年）…… 595
The Situation of Outpatient Service and Hospitalization Service in Medical Institution(2022)
20—9 重大传染病救治及救助情况…… 596
Significant Infectious Diseases Treatment and Rescue Situation
20—10 医疗机构病床使用情况（2022年）…… 596
Utilization of Hospital Beds（2022）
20—11 主要年份医院病床使用情况…… 597
Utilization of Hospital Beds in Main Years
20—12 各市医院病床使用情况（2022年）…… 597
Utilization of Hospital Beds by Region （2022）
20—13 主要年份乡镇卫生院病床使用情况…… 598
Utilization of Hospital Beds of Township Hospitals in Main Years
20—14 各市乡镇卫生院病床使用情况（2022年）…… 598
Utilization of Hospital Beds of Township Hospitals by Region （2022）
20—15 主要年份村卫生室基本情况…… 599
The Basic Situation of Health Room in Main Years
20—16 各市村卫生室基本情况（2022年）…… 599
The Basic Situation of Health Room by Region （2022）
20—17 民政行业单位基本情况（2022年）…… 600
Basic Conditions of Civil Affairs Agencies（2022）
20—18 全省民政服务事业费支出情况…… 600
Expenditure on Civil Affairs Service in the Province
20—19 社会福利事业单位基本情况（2022年）…… 601
Basic Statistics on Social Welfare Institutions （2022）
20—20 享受补助、救济人员情况…… 601
Persons Receiving Subsidies or Relief Funds
20—21 婚姻服务情况…… 602
Number of Marriage and Divorces
20—22 各市婚姻服务情况（2022年）…… 602
Number of Marriage and Divorces by Region （2022）
20—23 城乡居民最低生活保障情况…… 603
Basic Living Allowances for Urban and Rural Residents
20—24 各市城乡居民最低生活保障情况（2022年）…… 603
Basic Living Allowances for Urban and Rural Residents by Region（2022）
20—25 工伤保险情况…… 604
Situation of Employment Injury Insurance
20—26 各市职工基本医疗保险情况（2022年）…… 604
Basic Medical Insurance for Employees by Region (2022)
20—27 城镇职工基本养老保险情况…… 605
Basic Endowment Insurance for Urban Employees
20—28 各市城镇职工基本养老保险情况（2022年）…… 605
Basic Endowment Insurance for Urban Employees by Region (2022)
20—29 主要年份城乡居民参加基本医疗保险情况…… 606
Participation of Urban and Rural Residents in Basic Medical Insurance in Major Years
20—30 各市城乡居民参加基本医疗保险情况（2022年）…… 607
Participation of Urban and Rural Residents in Basic Medical Insurance by Region (2022)
20—31 各市失业保险基本情况（2022年）…… 608
Basic Information About Unemployment Insurance by Region （2022）
20—32 城乡居民基本养老保险情况…… 609
Situation of Rural and Rural Residents Endowment Insurance
20—33 各市生育保险情况（2022年）…… 609
Birth Insurance Situation by Region （2022）
20—34 人力资源服务机构综合情况（2022年）…… 610
Human Resources Service Organization Comprehensive Situation （2022）
20—35 人力资源服务业务基本情况（2022年）…… 611
Human Resources Service Basic Situation （2022）
20—36 各市职业技能鉴定综合情况（2022年）…… 612
Comprehensive Situation of Vocational Skill Evaluation and Appraisal by Region (2022)

主要统计指标解释…… 613
Explanatory Notes for Major Statistical Indicators

二十一、文化和体育
Culture and Sports

21—1 文化艺术和文物事业机构、人员情况（2022年）…… 621
Number of Institutions and Personnel in Culture, Art and Cultural Relies （2022）
21—2 艺术表演团体演出情况（2022年）…… 622
Basic Statistics on Performance of Art Troupes （2022）
21—3 群众艺术馆、文化馆站业务活动及经费情况（2022年）…… 622
Basic Statistics on Activities and Expenditures of Mass Art Centers and Cultural Centers （2022）
21—4 公共图书馆业务活动及经费情况（2022年）…… 623
Facilities, Services and Expenditures of Public Libraries （2022）
21—5 博物馆、文物机构业务活动及经费情况（2022年）…… 623
Facilities, Services and Expenditures of Museums and Cultural Relic Agencies （2022）
21—6 全省档案事业基本情况（2022年）…… 624
Provincial Archives Cause Basic Situation (2022)
21—7 广播、电视事业发展情况…… 625
Basic Statistics on Broadcasting and Television Stations
21—8 广播、电视覆盖率…… 625
Listeners and Viewers Rate
21—9 广播、电视节目制作时间…… 625
Produces Length of Broadcasting and Television
21—10 广播、电视宣传基本情况（2022年）…… 626
Basic Statistics on Broadcasting and Television （2022）
21—11 图书、杂志和报纸出版数量…… 626
Number of Books, Magazines and Newspaper Published
21—12 主要年份少年儿童读物和课本出版情况…… 627
Number of Books Published for Children and Textbooks in Major Years
21—13 主要年份出版印刷生产情况…… 627
Conditions of Printing in Main Year
21—14 主要年份出版物发行机构数和网点数…… 627
Issuing Institutions and Spots of Publication in Main Year
21—15 规模以上文化及相关产业法人单位基本情况（2022年）…… 628
Basic Information of Cultural and Related Industry Legal Entities above Designated Size(2022)
21—16 分地区规模以上文化及相关产业法人单位基本情况（2022年）…… 629
Basic Information of Cultural and Related Industry Legal Entities above Designated Size by Region(2022)
21—17 全省体育场地数（2020年）…… 630
Number of Stadiums and Gymnasiums（2020）
21—18 体育系统职工人数（2022年）…… 630
Number of Staff and Workers in Sports System （2022）
21—19 等级运动员、等级裁判员发展人数（2022年）…… 631
Number of Athletes and Referees in Grades by Type of Sports （2022）
21—20 体育活动基本情况…… 632
Basic Statement of Sports
主要统计指标解释…… 633
Explanatory Notes for Major Statistical Indicators

二十二、公共管理及其他
Public Management and Others

22—1 历届安徽省人民代表大会代表人数…… 637
Number of Anhui Province the National People's Congress Represents
22—2 历届政协安徽省委员会委员人数…… 637
Number of Anhui Province Political Consultative Conference Committee Member
22—3 妇联组织及工作情况…… 638
Basic Statistics of Women's Associations
22—4 工会组织情况…… 638
Basic Statistics on Trade Unions

22—5 妇女参政议政状况…… 639
Basic Conditions on Women's Participating in the Administration and Discussion of State Affairs
22—6 妇女卫生保健状况…… 640
Basic Conditions on Women Hygiene
22—7 儿童卫生保健状况…… 640
Basic Conditions on Children Hygiene
22—8 残疾人事业基本情况…… 641
Basic Information of People with Disabilities
22—9 律师、公证、调解、司法鉴定、法律援助工作基本情况…… 643
Basic Statistics on Lawyers, Notarization and Mediation
22—10 劳动人事争议仲裁委员会受理及处理案件情况（2022年）…… 644
Accepted and Settled Cases by Labor Dispute Arbitration Committee （2022）
22—11 公安机关立案的刑事案件情况…… 645
Criminal Cases Registered in Public Security Organs
22—12 公安机关受理、查处治安案件情况…… 645
Offense Cases Against Public Order Handled by Public Security Organs
22—13 各市公安机关立案的刑事案件情况（2022年）…… 646
Criminal Cases Registered in Public Security Organs By Region （2022）
22—14 各市公安机关查处治安案件情况（2022年）…… 647
Investigation of Public Security Cases by Public Security Organs By Region （2022）
22—15 检察机关处理申诉案件情况（2022年）…… 648
Appeals Handled by Procurator's Offices （2022）
22—16 人民法院行政一审案件受理结案情况（2022年）…… 648
People's Courts Have Accepted and Concluded Cases of First Instance (2022)
22—17 人民法院刑事一审案件受理结案情况（2022年）…… 648
People's Courts Have Accepted and Concluded Criminal Cases of First Instance (2022)
22—18 人民法院合同纠纷一审案件受理结案情况（2022年）…… 649
Settlement of Cases of First Instance Concerning Contract Disputes in People's Courts (2022)
22—19 人民法院婚姻家庭、继承、权属、侵权纠纷及其他民事一审案件受理结案情况（2022年）…… 650
Settlement of Marriage and Family, Inheritance, Ownership, Infringement Disputes and Other Civil Cases of First Instance in People's Courts (2022)
22—20 主要年份交通事故发生情况…… 651
Traffic Accidents in Main Years
22—21 交通事故情况（2022年）…… 651
Basic Statistics on Traffic Accidents （2022）
22—22 各市交通事故情况（2022年）…… 652
Basic Statistics on Traffic Accidents by Region （2022）
22—23 灾害情况（2022年）…… 653
Statistics on Disasters （2022）
22—24 救灾情况…… 653
Statistics on Disaster Relief
22—25 福利彩票…… 653
Welfare Lottery
22—26 体育彩票…… 653
Sport Lottery
主要统计指标解释…… 654
Explanatory Notes for Major Statistical Indicators

二十三、省级和县级主要经济指标及位次
Main Economic Indicators and Their Orders of Precedence of Province and County

23—1 全国分省（市）主要年份生产总值及位次（2022年）…… 659
Gross Domestic Product and Their Orders of Precedence in Major Years by Province or City（2022）
23—2 全国分省（市）主要年份固定资产投资及位次…… 660
Urban Investment in Fixed Assets and Their Orders of Precedence in Main Years by Province or City
23—3 全国分省（市）主要年份房地产开发企业本年完成投资及位次…… 661
Major Years Real Estate Development Enterprises Completed Investment in Current Year and Ranking by Province or City
23—4 全国分省（市）主要年份农林牧渔业总产值及位次…… 662
Gross Output Value of Farming, Forestry, Animal Husbandry, and Fishery and Their Orders of Precedence

in Main Years by Province or City
23—5　全国分省（市）主要年份工业增速位次…… 663
Growth Rank of Industry in Main Years by Province or City
23—6　全国分省（市）主要年份社会消费品零售总额及位次…… 664
Total Retail Sales of Consumer Goods and Their Orders of Precedence in Main Years by Province or City
23—7　全省分县（市）主要经济指标及位次（2022年）…… 665
Main Economic Indicators and Their Orders of Precedence of All Counties （2022）

附　录
Appendix

附录1　安徽农民工非农就业基本情况…… 671
Basic Situation of Non-agricultural Employment of Migrant Workers in Anhui Province

第一篇

Chapter 1

综合

GENERAL SURVEY

简要说明

一、本篇包括我省行政区划、国民经济综合资料等内容。

二、国民经济综合资料中的“各部门单位数”为第四次全国经济普查后部分行业企业资料更新维护数据。

三、国民经济总量、速度、结构、比例和效益指标均取自本年鉴各篇；国民经济综合资料由省统计局综合处整理。

四、我省境内国家级旅游景点黄山、九华山风景区旅游基本情况，由所在地统计部门提供。

Brief Introduction

I. This chapter covers the summary data on national economy.

II. "Number of departments and units" in the comprehensive data of national economy is the updated and maintained data of enterprises in some industries after the fourth national economic census.

III. Data on the total value, speed, structure, ratio and effects on the national economy are extracted from the concerned data in other chapters in this yearbook. The summary data on national economy are prepared by the Division of Integrated Statistics of Anhui Statistical Bureau.

IV. Data on the basic conditions of national scenic spot-Mount Huang and Mount Jiuhua are provided by the statistical department where they are.

1—1　全省行政区划（2022年末）
Administrative Divisions in Anhui (End of 2022)

单位：个（unit）

市名称 Name of City		市级区划数 Number of Regions at Cities Level	县级区划数 Number of Regions at County Level	县级市 Cities at County Level	县 Counties	市辖区 Districts under the Jurisdiction of Cities	街道办事处 Street Office	乡镇级区划数 Number of Regions at Townships Level	镇 Towns	乡 Townships
总　计	**Total**	**16**	**104**	**9**	**50**	**45**	**287**	**1235**	**1011**	**224**
合肥市	Hefei	1	9	1	4	4	50	81	70	11
淮北市	Huaibei	1	4		1	3	15	18	18	
亳州市	Bozhou	1	4		3	1	9	79	72	7
宿州市	Suzhou	1	5		4	1	18	94	93	1
蚌埠市	Bengbu	1	7		3	4	22	55	47	8
阜阳市	Fuyang	1	8	1	4	3	18	149	125	24
淮南市	Huainan	1	7		2	5	19	71	59	12
滁州市	Chuzhou	1	8	2	4	2	22	94	85	9
六安市	Luan	1	7		4	3	10	130	95	35
马鞍山市	Maanshan	1	6		3	3	13	35	33	2
芜湖市	Wuhu	1	7	1	1	5	27	44	44	
宣城市	Xuancheng	1	7	2	4	1	21	78	62	16
铜陵市	Tongling	1	4		1	3	5	31	27	4
池州市	Chizhou	1	4		3	1	11	45	37	8
安庆市	Anqing	1	10	2	5	3	23	130	85	45
黄山市	Huangshan	1	7		4	3	4	101	59	42

1—2 全省县以上行政区划（2022年末）

Administrative Divisions of Counties and Above in Anhui (End of 2022)

省辖市 City Under Province Administration	县（市、区） Name of County (City), District Under Administative
合肥市 Hefei	蜀山区、庐阳区、瑶海区、包河区、巢湖市、长丰县、肥东县、肥西县、庐江县 Shushan District，Luyang District, Yaohai District，Baohe District，Chaohu，Changfeng，Feidong，Feixi，Lujiang
淮北市 Huaibei	相山区、杜集区、烈山区、濉溪县 Xiangshan District，Duji District，Lieshan District，Suixi
亳州市 Bozhou	谯城区、涡阳县、蒙城县、利辛县 Qiaocheng District，Guoyang，Mengcheng，Lixin
宿州市 Suzhou	埇桥区、砀山县、萧　县、灵璧县、泗　县 Yongqiao District，Dangshan，Xiaoxian，Lingbi，Sixian
蚌埠市 Bengbu	蚌山区、龙子湖区、禹会区、淮上区、怀远县、五河县、固镇县 Bengshan District，Longzihu District，Yuhui District，Huaishang District，Huaiyuan，Wuhe，Guzhen
阜阳市 Fuyang	颍州区、颍东区、颍泉区、界首市、临泉县、太和县、阜南县、颍上县 Yingzhou District，Yingdong District，Yingquan District，Jieshou，Linquan，Taihe，Funan，Yingshang
淮南市 Huainan	田家庵区、大通区、谢家集区、八公山区、潘集区、凤台县、寿　县 Tianjiaan District，Datong District，Xiejiaji District，Bagongshan District，Panji District，Fengtai，Shouxian
滁州市 Chuzhou	琅琊区、南谯区、明光市、天长市、来安县、全椒县、定远县、凤阳县 Langya District，Nanqiao District，Mingguang，Tianchang，Laian，Quanjiao，Dingyuan，Fengyang
六安市 Luan	金安区、裕安区、叶集区、霍邱县、舒城县、金寨县、霍山县 Jinan District，Yuan District，Yeji District, Huoqiu，Shucheng，Jinzhai，Huoshan
马鞍山市 Maanshan	雨山区、花山区、博望区、当涂县、含山县、和　县 Yushan District，Huashan District，Bowang District，Dangtu，Hanshan，Hexian
芜湖市 Wuhu	镜湖区、鸠江区、弋江区、湾沚区、繁昌区、无为市、南陵县 Jinghu District，Jiujiang District，Yijiang District，Wanzhi District，Fanchang District，Wuwei，Nanling
宣城市 Xuancheng	宣州区、宁国市、广德市、郎溪县、泾　县、旌德县、绩溪县 Xuanzhou District，Ningguo，Guangde，Langxi，Jingxian，Jingde，Jixi
铜陵市 Tongling	铜官区、郊　区、义安区、枞阳县 Tongguan District，Suburban District，Yian District，Zongyang
池州市 Chizhou	贵池区、东至县、石台县、青阳县 Guichi District，Dongzhi，Shitai，Qingyang
安庆市 Anqing	大观区、迎江区、宜秀区、桐城市、潜山市、怀宁县、太湖县、宿松县、望江县、岳西县 Daguan District，Yingjiang District，Yixiu District，Tongcheng，Qianshan，Huaining，Taihu，Susong，Wangjiang，Yuexi
黄山市 Huangshan	屯溪区、黄山区、徽州区、歙　县、休宁县、黟　县、祁门县 Tunxi District，Huangshan District，Huizhou District，Shexian，Xiuning，Yixian，Qimen

1—3　各行业机构单位数（2022年）
Number of Grass Root Units in Various Sectors (2022)

单位：个（unit）

行业类别	Industrial Category	单位数 Number of Units	#法人单位 Legal Entities	#“四上”单位 Legal Entities with Certain Scale, Qualification or Quota
合　计	**Total**	**1596080**	**1454978**	**53144**
农、林、牧、渔业	**Agriculture, Forestry, Animal Husbandry and Fishery**	**125565**	**124583**	
农　业	Farming	65275	65030	
林　业	Forestry	6969	6861	
畜牧业	Animal Husbandry	22311	22189	
渔　业	Fishery	9081	9049	
农、林、牧、渔专业及辅助性活动	Agriculture, Forestry, Animal Husbandry and Fishery Major and Supporting Activities	21929	21454	
采矿业	**Mining**	**1843**	**1632**	**345**
煤炭开采和洗选业	Mining and Washing of Coal	142	84	19
石油和天然气开采业	Extraction of Petroleum and Natural Gas	5	2	1
黑色金属矿采选业	Mining and Processing of Ferrous Metal Ores	272	254	56
有色金属矿采选业	Mining and Processing of Non-Ferrous Metal Ores	207	168	28
非金属矿采选业	Mining and Processing of Non-metal Ores	1108	1031	238
开采专业及辅助性活动	Mining Profession and Auxiliary Activities	54	47	3
其他采矿业	Mining of Other Ores	55	46	
制造业	**Manufacturing**	**176351**	**171586**	**20448**
农副食品加工业	Processing of Food from Agricultural Products	8922	8541	1411
食品制造业	Manufacture of Foods	5021	4854	432
酒、饮料和精制茶制造业	Manufacture of Liquor, Beverages and Refined Tea	4895	4748	268
烟草制品业	Manufacture of Tobacco	16	7	5
纺织业	Manufacture of Textile	6097	6018	768
纺织服装、服饰业	Manufacture of Textile, Wearing Apparel and Accessories	13397	13161	656
皮革、毛皮、羽毛及其制品和制鞋业	Manufacture of Leather, Fur, Feather and Related Products and Footwear	2478	2441	338
木材加工和木、竹、藤、棕、草制品业	Processing of Timber, Manufacture of Wood, Bamboo, Rattan, Palm and Straw Products	10013	9867	535
家具制造业	Manufacture of Furniture	5486	5412	249
造纸和纸制品业	Manufacture of Paper and Paper Products	3131	3092	245
印刷和记录媒介复制业	Printing and Reproduction of Recording Media	3792	3702	395
文教、工美、体育和娱乐用品制造业	Manufacture of Articles for Culture, Education, Arts and Crafts, Sport and Entertainment Activities	4911	4834	566
石油、煤炭及其他燃料加工业	Petroleum, Coal and Other Fuel Processing Industries	594	570	47
化学原料和化学制品制造业	Manufacture of Raw Chemical Materials and Chemical Products	5845	5648	1200
医药制造业	Manufacture of Medicines	3055	2945	561
化学纤维制造业	Manufacture of Chemical Fibres	312	304	70
橡胶和塑料制品业	Manufacture of Rubber and Plastics Products	10149	9987	1253
非金属矿物制品业	Manufacture of Non-metallic Mineral Products	16375	15707	2518
黑色金属冶炼和压延加工业	Smelting and Pressing of Ferrous Metals	696	665	137
有色金属冶炼和压延加工业	Smelting and Pressing of Non-ferrous Metals	1201	1153	326
金属制品业	Manufacture of Metal Products	15118	14811	1371
通用设备制造业	Manufacture of General Purpose Machinery	13202	12890	1505

1—3 续表1 continued

单位：个（unit）

行业类别	Industrial Category	单位数 Number of Units	#法人单位 Legal Entities	#"四上"单位 Legal Entities with Certain Scale, Qualification or Quota
专用设备制造业	Manufacture of Special Purpose Machinery	11254	10880	1103
汽车制造业	Manufacture of Automobiles	5028	4805	1156
铁路、船舶、航空航天和其他运输设备制造业	Manufacture of Railway, Ship, Aerospace and Other Transport Equipments	1129	1086	202
电气机械和器材制造业	Manufacture of Electrical Machinery and Apparatus	8238	7920	1502
计算机、通信和其他电子设备制造业	Manufacture of Computers, Communication and Other Electronic Equipment	5855	5669	1073
仪器仪表制造业	Manufacture of Measuring Instruments and Machinery	3022	2963	183
其他制造业	Other Manufacture	2719	2672	105
废弃资源综合利用业	Comprehensive Utilization of Waste Resources	2279	2235	253
金属制品、机械和设备修理业	Repair Service of Metal Products, Machinery and Equipment	2121	1999	15
电力、热力、燃气及水生产和供应业	**Production and Supply of Electricity, Heat, Gas and Water**	**7843**	**6685**	**648**
电力、热力的生产和供应业	Production and Supply of Electric Power and Heat Power	5196	4494	375
燃气生产和供应业	Production and Supply of Gas	569	358	139
水的生产和供应业	Production and Supply of Water	2078	1833	134
建筑业	**Construction**	**173676**	**156893**	**8899**
房屋建筑业	Construction of Buildings	44957	38446	4413
土木工程建筑业	Civil Engineering	36530	31032	2967
建筑安装业	Building Installation	16800	15137	541
建筑装饰、装修和其他建筑业	Architectural Decoration, Decoration and Other Construction Industries	75389	72278	978
批发和零售业	**Wholesale and Retail Trades**	**417008**	**382064**	**10159**
批发业	Wholesale Trade	197457	189770	4698
零售业	Retail Trade	219551	192294	5461
交通运输、仓储和邮政业	**Transport, Storage and Post**	**46646**	**39777**	**1408**
铁路运输业	Railway Transport	131	99	6
道路运输业	Road Transport	30809	28411	916
水上运输业	Water Transport	1629	1458	210
航空运输业	Air Transport	116	90	6
管道运输业	Transport Via Pipelines	15	12	1
多式联运和运输代理业	Multimodal Transport and Transportation Agency	5186	4744	80
装卸搬运和仓储业	Handling and warehousing industry	4318	3660	113
邮政业	Post	4442	1303	76
住宿和餐饮业	**Hotels and Catering Services**	**32710**	**27441**	**2613**
住宿业	Hotels	6963	6296	850
餐饮业	Catering Services	25747	21145	1763
信息传输、软件和信息技术服务业	**Information Transmission, Software and Information Technology**	**68812**	**63669**	**769**
电信、广播电视和卫星传输服务	Telecommunication, Radio and Television and Satellite Transmission Service	3583	1305	86
互联网和相关服务	Internet and Related Service	11818	11321	176
软件和信息技术服务业	Software and Information Technology	53411	51043	507

1—3 续表2 continued

单位：个（unit）

行业类别	Industrial Category	单位数 Number of Units	#法人单位 Legal Entities	#"四上"单位 Legal Entities with Certain Scale, Qualification or Quota
金融业	**Financial Intermediation**	**13912**	**3913**	
货币金融服务	Monetary and Financial Service	7696	1363	
资本市场服务	Capital Market Service	1552	1023	
保险业	Insurance	3903	904	
其他金融业	Other Financial Activities	761	623	
房地产业	**Real Estate**	**49502**	**41233**	**4350**
租赁和商务服务业	**Leasing and Business Services**	**197857**	**186060**	**1605**
租赁业	Leasing	26843	25916	140
商务服务业	Business Services	171014	160144	1465
科学研究和技术服务业	**Scientific Research and Technical Services**	**91498**	**83221**	**738**
研究和试验发展	Research and Experimental Development	9692	9344	57
专业技术服务业	Professional Technical Services	43852	37530	573
科技推广和应用服务业	Science and Technology Popularization and Application Services	37954	36347	108
水利、环境和公共设施管理业	**Management of Water Conservancy, Environment and Public Facilities**	**15266**	**13526**	**178**
水利管理业	Management of Water Conservancy	1578	1011	1
生态保护和环境治理业	Ecological Protection and Environmental Treatment	1416	1294	30
公共设施管理业	Management of Public Facilities	8876	8050	138
土地管理业	Land Management	3396	3171	9
居民服务、修理和其他服务业	**Service to Households, Repair and Other Services**	**31276**	**29293**	**259**
居民服务业	Service to Households	12546	11674	98
机动车、电子产品和日用产品修理业	Repair of Motor Vehicle, Electronics and Household Products	13123	12441	85
其他服务业	Other Services	5607	5178	76
教　育	**Education**	**36377**	**29132**	**147**
卫生和社会工作	**Health and Social Service**	**15294**	**12769**	**205**
卫　生	Health	10857	8609	175
社会工作	Social Service	4437	4160	30
文化、体育和娱乐业	**Culture, Sports and Entertainment**	**29278**	**27812**	**373**
新闻和出版业	Journalism and Publishing Activities	406	372	29
广播、电视、电影和录音制作业	Radio, Television, Film and Recording Production	4498	4232	119
文化艺术业	Cultural and Art Activities	8834	8316	68
体　育	Sports Activities	3462	3256	16
娱乐业	Entertainment	12078	11636	141
公共管理、社会保障和社会组织	**Public Management, Social Security and Social Organization**	**65366**	**53689**	
中国共产党机关	Organs of Communist Party of China	1463	1230	
国家机构	Government Agencies	24017	13333	
人民政协、民主党派	People's Political Consultative Conference and Democratic Parties	262	259	
社会保障	Social Security	548	365	
群众团体、社会团体和其他成员组织	Non-Governmental Organizations, Social Organizations and Other Organizations	20543	20213	
基层群众自治组织及其他组织	Land Management Industry of Grassroots Mass Self-Governing Organizations and Other Organizations	18533	18289	

注："四上"单位是指规模以上工业、限额以上批零住宿餐饮业、规模以上服务业、具有资质的建筑法人单位和有开发经营活动的房地产开发经营业法人单位。

a) Legal entities with certain scale, qualification or quota units refer to industrial entities above designated size, accommodation and catering industries above designated size, service industries above designated size, qualified construction legal entities and real estate development and business legal entities with development and operation activities.

1—4 各市按三次产业和机构类型分法人单位数（2022年）

Number of Legal Entities by Three Strata of Industry and Type of Institutions and Region (2022)

单位：个（unit）

地区 Region		法人单位数 Number of Legal Entities	按三次产业分 Grouped by Three Strata of Industry			按机构类型分 By Type of Institutions				
			第一产业 Primary Industry	第二产业 Secondary Industry	第三产业 Tertiary Industry	企业法人 Business Entity	事业法人 Institution Entity	机关法人 Government Entity	社会团体 Social Organization	其他 Others
总计	**Total**	**1454978**	**103129**	**334750**	**1017099**	**1289473**	**20326**	**8276**	**16708**	**120195**
合肥市	Hefei	442315	10177	79547	352591	425808	2423	813	2816	10455
淮北市	Huaibei	30331	1551	7417	21363	26630	581	288	492	2340
亳州市	Bozhou	95346	20171	18587	56588	75333	937	343	688	18045
宿州市	Suzhou	78958	11870	18468	48620	62052	1492	415	697	14302
蚌埠市	Bengbu	67729	3418	14347	49964	58770	1064	460	1005	6430
阜阳市	Fuyang	126737	12746	32144	81847	109301	1747	704	1058	13927
淮南市	Huainan	49093	3087	10807	35199	39987	1317	673	862	6254
滁州市	Chuzhou	86249	5918	25172	55159	74299	1339	528	1269	8814
六安市	Luan	91263	12624	23619	55020	76132	1699	556	1723	11153
马鞍山市	Maanshan	52539	2239	14494	35806	48091	757	410	580	2701
芜湖市	Wuhu	96045	4213	21974	69858	87914	1230	550	1187	5164
宣城市	Xuancheng	50489	2137	16715	31637	44260	960	510	921	3838
铜陵市	Tongling	29495	2509	7030	19956	26149	650	278	550	1868
池州市	Chizhou	31223	1995	8389	20839	25625	895	397	936	3370
安庆市	Anqing	92249	7016	27496	57737	80091	2075	821	1144	8118
黄山市	Huangshan	34917	1458	8544	24915	29031	1160	530	780	3416

1—5　各市按控股情况分企业法人单位数（2022年）
Numbers of Corporate Enterprises the Status of Holdings by Region (2022)

单位：个（unit）

地　区	Region	企业单位数 Number of Enterprises	国有控股 State-holding	集体控股 Collective-holding	私人控股 Private-holding	港澳台商控股 Hong Kong, Macao and Taiwan-holding	外商控股 Foreign-holding	其他 Others
总　计	**Total**	**1347478**	**14805**	**10978**	**1274561**	**1232**	**1175**	**44727**
合肥市	Hefei	430979	3805	1884	417435	374	386	7095
淮北市	Huaibei	27676	469	152	26181	23	17	834
亳州市	Bozhou	86919	662	588	77157	30	13	8469
宿州市	Suzhou	70753	991	574	64540	52	32	4564
蚌埠市	Bengbu	61581	721	525	58343	68	54	1870
阜阳市	Fuyang	113514	859	644	109980	53	21	1957
淮南市	Huainan	41651	656	471	39311	38	19	1156
滁州市	Chuzhou	77367	800	402	73141	80	134	2810
六安市	Luan	82620	714	1271	77631	49	44	2911
马鞍山市	Maanshan	49426	525	402	47287	92	86	1034
芜湖市	Wuhu	90707	1068	731	86037	133	150	2588
宣城市	Xuancheng	45764	868	384	42027	61	55	2369
铜陵市	Tongling	26996	460	331	25619	36	17	533
池州市	Chizhou	27507	447	670	24896	23	52	1419
安庆市	Anqing	83520	1216	1143	77119	73	64	3905
黄山市	Huangshan	30498	544	806	27857	47	31	1213

1—6 国民经济和社会发展总量与速度指标

指　　标		Item		总量指标 2010
人口与就业		**Population and Employment**		
人　　口		**Population**		
常住人口	（万人）	Permanent Populations	(10000 persons)	5957
#城镇人口		Urban		2573
乡村人口		Rural		3384
#男性人口		Male		3028
女性人口		Female		2929
出生人口	（万人）	Births	(10000 persons)	75.7
死亡人口	（万人）	Deaths	(10000 persons)	35.4
就　　业	**（万人）**	**Employment**	**(10000 persons)**	
从业人员		Practitioners		4050.0
城镇就业人员		Urban Employed Persons		973.5
#国有经济		State-owned Units		206.0
城镇集体经济		Urban of Other Types of Ownership		17.9
港澳台投资经济		Economic Units Funded by Entrepreneurs from Hong Kong Macao and Taiwan		7.0
外商投资经济		Foreign Funded Units		14.7
城镇私营经济		Urban Private Enterprises		133.3
城镇个体		Urban Self-employed Individuals		264.1
城镇非私营单位就业人员数		The Non-private Institutions in Cities and Towns of Employment		372.9
国有经济		State-owned Units		206.0
城镇集体经济		Urban of Other Types of Ownership		17.9
其他经济		Units of Other Types of Ownership		149.1
城镇登记失业人数		Registered Unemployed in Urban Areas		28.5
宏观经济		**Macroeconomic Indicator**		
国民经济核算	**（亿元）**	**National Accounting**	**(100 million yuan)**	
生产总值		Gross Domestic Product		13249.78
第一产业		Primary Industry		1600.57
第二产业		Secondary Industry		6395.99
#工　　业		Industry		4949.15
第三产业		Tertiary Industry		5253.23

注：2020年起就业人数为常住口径就业人员数，往年均为户籍口径（下同）。

Principal Aggregate Indicators On National Economic and Social Development and Their Related Indices and Growth Rates

Aggregate Indicator				速度指标　(%)　Indices and Growth Rates						
				指　数　(2022年为以下各年) Index (2022 as Percentage of the Following Years)				平均增长速度 Average Annual Growth Rate		
2015	2020	2021	2022	2010	2015	2020	2021	2011—2015	2016—2020	2021—2022
6011	6105	6113	6127	102.9	101.9	100.4	100.2	0.2	0.3	0.2
3064	3561	3631	3685	143.2	120.3	103.5	101.5	3.5	3.1	1.7
2947	2544	2482	2442	72.2	82.8	96.0	98.4	-2.7	-2.9	-2.0
3048	3112	3121	3127	103.3	102.6	100.5	100.2	0.1	0.4	0.2
2963	2993	2992	3000	102.4	101.2	100.2	100.3	0.2	0.2	0.1
77.6	57.6	49.2	43.8	57.9	56.5	76.1	89.1	0.5	-5.8	-12.8
35.7	48.5	48.9	49.5	139.9	138.7	102.1	101.2	0.2	6.3	1.0
4342.1	3243.0	3215.0	3176.0	78.4	73.1	97.9	98.8	1.4	-5.7	-1.0
1292.1	1791.0	1816.0	1790.0	183.9	138.5	99.9	98.6	5.8	6.7	0.0
189.1	175.9	179.3	178.4	86.6	94.4	101.4	99.5	-1.7	-1.4	0.7
14.7	7.7	7.1	6.5	36.4	44.1	84.4	91.4	-3.8	-12.2	-8.1
15.9	13.4	15.0	15.6	223.2	98.4	116.4	104.0	17.8	-3.3	7.9
19.8	19.0	19.6	18.9	128.7	95.1	99.3	96.1	6.2	-0.8	-0.4
325.0	420.9	482.4	464.2	348.2	142.8	110.3	96.2	19.5	5.3	5.0
423.1										
513.8	565.6	563.2	576.8	154.7	112.3	102.0	102.4	6.6	1.9	1.0
189.1	175.9	179.3	178.4	86.6	94.4	101.4	99.5	-1.7	-1.4	0.7
14.7	7.7	7.1	6.5	36.4	44.1	84.4	91.5	-3.8	-12.2	-8.1
310.0	382.0	376.8	392.0	262.9	126.5	102.6	104.0	15.8	4.3	1.3
30.9	30.0	25.5						1.6	-0.6	
23831.18	38061.51	42565.17	45045.02	262.4	159.0	112.0	103.5	10.5	7.3	5.8
2376.05	3184.95	3363.88	3513.70	160.3	129.9	111.7	104.0	4.3	3.1	5.7
10838.34	15216.46	17240.14	18588.03	282.5	161.0	113.3	105.1	11.9	7.3	6.4
8360.56	11235.53	12790.84	13791.97	295.1	162.5	114.0	104.8	12.7	7.3	6.8
10616.78	19660.10	21961.14	22943.30	271.2	163.9	111.1	102.2	10.6	8.1	5.4

a) Number of people employed since 2020 is the number of people employed by permanent residence caliber, and in previous years is the household registration caliber (the same below).

1—6 续表1 continued

指 标	Item	总量指标 2010
财 政 （亿元）	**Public Finance (100 million yuan)**	
一般公共预算收入	General Public Budget Revenue	1149.4
#增值税	Value-added Tax	129.5
契 税	Contract Tax	95.9
企业所得税	Enterprises' Income Tax	106.6
一般公共预算支出	Expenditures in General Public Budget Revenue	2587.6
#一般公共服务	General Public Service	273.7
教 育	Education	386.3
社会保障和就业	Social Security and Employment	334.2
物价总指数 （上年=100）	**Price Indices (preceding year=100)**	
居民消费价格指数	Consumer Price Index	103.1
农产品生产价格指数	Production Price Indices of Agricultural Products	110.8
工业生产者出厂价格指数	Ex-factory Industrial Producer Price Index	109.0
工业生产者购进价格指数	Industrial Producer Purchasing Price Index	111.8
利用外资 （万美元）	**Utilization of Foreign Capital (USD 10000)**	
外商直接投资合同金额	The Contract Amount of Foreign Investment	216462
实际利用外商直接投资额	The Actual Use of Foreign Direct Investment	501446
能源生产与消费 （万吨标准煤）	**Production and Consumption of Energy (10000 tons of SCE)**	
能源生产总量	Total Energy Production	9673.8
能源消费总量	Total Energy Consumption	9414.0
产 业	**Industry**	
农 业	**Agriculture**	
粮食播种面积 （千公顷）	Sown Area of Grain Crops (1000 hectares)	6947.7
经济作物播种面积 （千公顷）	Area Sown to Cash Crops (1000 hectares)	1631.6
农林牧渔业总产值 （亿元）	Gross Output Value of Farming, Forestry, Animal Husbandry and Fishery (100 million yuan)	2815.0
主要农产品产量	Output of Major Farm Products	
粮 食 （万吨）	Grain (10000 tons)	3207.7
棉 花 （万吨）	Cotton (10000 tons)	25.8
油 料 （万吨）	Oil-bearing Crops (10000 tons)	176.1
生黄红麻 （万吨）	Raw Huang Hongma (10000 tons)	0.25
烟 叶 （万吨）	Tobacco (10000 tons)	1.77
茶 叶 （万吨）	Tea (10000 tons)	8.0
猪 肉 （万吨）	Pork (10000 tons)	234.9
牛 肉 （万吨）	Beef (10000 tons)	13.6
羊 肉 （万吨）	Mutton (10000 tons)	11.4
肉猪出栏 （万头）	Number of Slaughtered Fattened Hogs (10000 heads)	2737.2
奶 类 （万吨）	Milk (10000 tons)	19.1
水产品 （万吨）	Aquatic Products (10000 tons)	193.3
农业机械总动力 （万千瓦）	Total Agricultural Machinery Power (10000 kW)	5409.8
机耕面积 （千公顷）	Machine-cultivated Area (1000 hectares)	4056.4
机播面积 （千公顷）	Mechanical Sowing Area (1000 hectares)	3606.6
机收面积 （千公顷）	Receive a Area (1000 hectares)	5264.3

注：2022年实际利用外商直接投资额统计口径是商务部口径，往年为省口径，数据不可比。

Aggregate Indicator				速度指标 (%) Indices and Growth Rates						
2015	2020	2021	2022	指　数 (2022年为以下各年) Index (2022 as Percentage of the Following Years)				平均增长速度 Average Annual Growth Rate		
				2010	2015	2020	2021	2011—2015	2016—2020	2021—2022
2454.3	3216.0	3498.2	3589.1					16.4	5.6	
273.1	943.2	1007.6	845.1					16.1	28.1	
172.5	226.2	262.1	231.6					12.5	5.6	
235.6	362.5	392.4	392.5					17.2	9.0	
5239.0	7473.6	7591.1	8379.8	323.8	159.9	112.1	110.4	15.2	7.4	5.9
400.1	515.1	522.6	585.3	213.9	146.3	113.6	112.0	7.9	5.2	6.6
856.7	1261.9	1315.7	1420.9	367.8	165.8	112.6	108.0	17.3	8.1	6.1
691.5	1173.1	1229.6	1427.1	427.0	206.4	121.7	116.1	15.7	11.1	10.3
101.3	102.7	100.9	102.0	129.9	114.1	102.9	102.0	2.6	2.1	1.4
99.8	115.6	101.3	102.8	155.9	129.4	104.1	102.8	3.8	4.5	2.0
93.9	99.1	107.7	103.2	115.9	121.2	111.2	103.2	-0.9	1.7	5.4
93.5	98.5	111.5	104.0	123.6	129.0	116.0	104.0	-0.9	2.2	7.7
393800	517192	688168	429034							
1361945	1830542	1929728	215507							
9972.6	8602.0	9317.5	9401.1	97.2	94.3	109.3	100.9	0.6	-2.9	4.5
12301.2	14697.9	15342.6	15882.7	168.7	129.1	108.1	103.5	5.5	3.6	4.0
7280.7	7289.5	7309.6	7314.2	105.3	100.5	100.3	100.1	0.9	0.02	0.2
1500.1	1528.5	1577.2	1619.3	99.3	108.0	105.9	102.7	-1.7	0.4	2.9
4183.1	5680.9	6004.3	6278.0	163.9	132.5	114.2	104.5	4.3	3.0	6.9
4077.2	4019.2	4087.6	4100.1	127.8	100.6	102.0	100.3	4.9	-0.3	1.0
14.8	4.1	2.9	2.6	9.9	17.3	62.4	87.8	-10.6	-22.6	-21.0
171.4	162.5	167.1	173.4	98.5	101.1	106.7	103.8	-0.5	-1.1	3.3
0.18	0.26	0.22	0.24	97.7	132.6	94.0	109.0	-5.9	7.1	-3.1
2.63	2.04	2.01	2.18	122.9	82.7	106.7	108.0	8.2	-5.0	3.3
11.0	12.9	13.7	14.2	176.8	128.4	110.1	103.2	6.6	3.1	4.9
249.8	183.4	238.7	248.3	105.7	99.4	135.4	104.0	1.2	-6.0	16.4
8.3	9.9	11.2	11.7	85.8	140.5	117.9	104.9	-9.4	3.6	8.6
10.3	20.7	21.9	22.5	197.8	217.6	108.9	102.8	-1.9	14.8	4.4
2872.2	2150.5	2797.8	2920.9	106.7	101.7	135.8	104.4	1.0	-5.6	16.5
28.6	37.6	47.6	50.7	264.9	177.2	134.7	106.6	8.4	5.6	16.1
209.3	232.4	236.5	245.5	127.0	117.3	105.6	103.8	1.6	2.1	2.8
6581.0	6799.5	6924.3	7070.1	130.7	107.4	104.0	102.1	4.0	0.7	2.0
4287.9	7668.4	7646.2	7642.0	188.4	178.2	99.7	99.9	1.1	12.3	-0.2
5003.9	6124.6	6281.8	6551.4	181.7	130.9	107.0	104.3	6.8	4.1	3.4
6440.6	7420.1	7314.1	7520.8	142.9	116.8	101.4	102.8	4.1	2.9	0.7

1—6 续表2 continued

指 标		Item		总量指标 2010
工 业（规模以上）		**Industry**		
主要工业产品产量		Output of Major Industrial Products		
布	（亿米）	Cloth	(100 million m)	10.9
家用电冰箱	（万台）	Household Refrigerators	(10000 units)	2078.9
房间空气调节器	（万台）	Air Conditioners	(10000 units)	1666.1
家用洗衣机	（万台）	Household Washing Machines	(10000 units)	1267.0
彩色电视机	（万部）	Colour Television Sets	(10000 units)	395.3
原 煤	（亿吨）	Coal	(100 million tons)	1.30
发电量	（亿千瓦时）	Electricity	(100 million kwh)	1443.9
钢 材	（万吨）	Rolled Steel	(10000 tons)	2446.4
水 泥	（万吨）	Cement	(10000 tons)	7874
汽 车	（辆）	Motor Vehicles	(unit)	1244735
蓄电池	（千伏安时）	Storage Battery	(KVA.h)	6610665
微型电子计算机	（万部）	Micro-computers	(10000 unit)	1.8
企业单位数	（个）	Number of Industrial Enterprises	(unit)	16277
#大型企业		Large		100
资产总计	（亿元）	Total Assets	(100 million yuan)	15930.3
负债合计	（亿元）	Total Liabilities	(100 million yuan)	9565.9
营业收入	（亿元）	Business Revenue	(100 million yuan)	
利润总额	（亿元）	Total Profits	(100 million yuan)	1445.6
建 筑 业		**Construction**		
企业单位数	（个）	Number of Enterprises	(unit)	2469
企业从业人员	（万人）	Number of Persons Engaged	(10000 persons)	158.0
建筑业总产值	（亿元）	Gross Output Value	(100 million yuan)	2865.0
房屋建筑施工面积	（万平方米）	Floor Space of Buildings Under Construction	(10000 sq.m)	23295.7
房屋建筑竣工面积	（万平方米）	Floor Space of Buildings Completed	(10000 sq.m)	10512.4
#住宅面积		Residential Buildings		6461.5
交通运输		**Transportation**		
货 运 量	（万吨）	Freight Traffic	(10000 tons)	228106
铁 路		Railways		12091
公 路		Highways		183658
水 运		Waterways		32355
民 航		Total Civil Aviation Routes		2.2
客 运 量	（万人）	Passenger Traffic	(10000 persons)	159597
铁 路		Railways		5552
公 路		Highways		153697
水 运		Waterways		139
民 航		Total Civil Aviation Routes		208
内河港口货物吞吐量	（万吨）	Volume of Freight Handled in Major Ports	(10000 tons)	32502
公路里程	（公里）	Total Length of Highways	(km)	149382
等级公路里程	（公里）	Length of Expressway and Class Ⅰ to Ⅳ Highway	(km)	142340
邮电通信业		**Postal and Telecommunication Services**		
邮电业务总量	（亿元）	Total Business Revenue	(100 million yuan)	300.3
函 件	（亿件）	Number of Letters Delivered	(100 million pieces)	2.1
报刊期发数	（万份）	Number of Newspapers and Magazines Distributed	(10000 copies)	602.2
移动电话年末用户	（万户）	Year-end Mobile Phone Users	(10000 subscribers)	2798.7
#4G移动电话用户		4G Mobile Phone Subscribers		
5G移动电话用户		5G Mobile Phone Subscribers		
固定电话年末用户	（万户）	Year-end Fixed-line Subscribers	(10000 subscribers)	1231.0

注：1. 自2011年起，规模以上工业企业统计范围为年主营业务收入2000万元及以上工业企业。自2019年起，主营业务收入指标调整为营业收入指标。

2. 2021年邮电业务总量按上年不变单价计算（下同）。

Aggregate Indicator				速度指标 (%) Indices and Growth Rates						
				指　数 (2022年为以下各年) Index (2022 as Percentage of the Following Years)				平均增长速度 Average Annual Growth Rate		
2015	2020	2021	2022	2010	2015	2020	2021	2011—2015	2016—2020	2021—2022
14.1	8.0	7.7	4.9	45.1	34.7	61.3	64.1	5.4	-10.8	-21.7
2888.2	2437.9	2381.4	2633.5	126.7	91.2	108.0	110.6	6.8	-3.3	3.9
3176.1	3009.7	3385.5	2691.1	161.5	84.7	89.4	79.5	13.8	-1.1	-5.4
1725.2	2380.4	2627.4	2545.2	200.9	147.5	106.9	96.9	6.4	6.7	3.4
1176.9	1611.8	1224.8	1026.3	259.6	87.2	63.7	83.8	24.4	6.5	-20.2
1.34	1.11	1.13	1.12	85.8	83.4	100.8	99.1	0.6	-3.7	0.4
2034.2	2682.0	2911.8	3135.0	217.1	154.1	116.9	107.7	7.1	5.7	8.1
3334.7	3607.5	3820.3	3963.0	162.0	118.8	109.9	103.7	6.4	1.6	4.8
13085	14176	14992	14211	180.5	108.6	100.2	94.8	10.7	1.6	0.1
1257681	1160724	1452112	1746876	140.3	138.9	150.5	120.3	0.2	-1.6	22.7
19170259	20208640	20828210	23094438	349.4	120.5	114.3	110.9	23.7	1.1	6.9
1801.5	3097.1	3694.8	2950.2	162835.2	163.8	95.3	79.8	297.7	11.4	-2.4
19077	18447	19880	21484	132.0	112.6	116.5	108.1	3.2	-0.7	7.9
278	254	277	279	279.0	100.4	109.8	100.7	22.7	-1.8	4.8
31360.0	43846.6	50052.3	56457.8	354.4	180.0	128.8	112.8	14.5	6.9	13.5
18028.2	24376.5	28059.4	31899.8	333.5	176.9	130.9	113.7	13.5	6.2	14.4
39554.5	38549.3	45519.5	46889.5		118.5	121.6	103.0		-0.5	10.3
2000.1	2439.6	2871.0	2386.6	165.1	119.3	97.8	83.1	6.7	4.1	-1.1
2867	5878	7274	8362	338.7	291.7	142.3	115.0	3.0	15.4	19.3
168.8	203.7	196.2	211.6	134.0	125.3	103.9	107.9	1.3	3.8	1.9
5695.9	9365.1	10584.0	11702.6	408.5	205.5	125.0	110.6	14.7	10.5	11.8
41479.7	49377.0	53887.4	49670.7	213.2	119.7	100.6	92.2	12.2	3.5	0.3
15553.6	14516.0	14006.5	14856.9	141.3	95.5	102.3	106.1	8.1	-1.4	1.2
10501.8	9772.8	8647.2	8459.9	130.9	80.6	86.6	97.8	10.2	-1.4	-7.0
345756	374318	401242	393920	172.7	113.9	105.2	98.2	8.7	1.6	2.6
10158	7549	7617	7769	64.3	76.5	102.9	102.0	-3.4	-5.8	1.5
230649	243529	259044	245982	133.9	106.6	101.0	95.0	4.7	1.1	0.5
104947	123239	134580	140167	433.2	133.6	113.7	104.2	26.5	3.3	6.6
2.3	1.6	1.7	1.0	44.3	42.2	59.0	57.7	1.0	-6.5	-23.2
87107	32570	27673	14695	9.2	16.9	45.1	53.1	-11.4	-17.9	-32.8
8553	9455	10996	7201	129.7	84.2	76.2	65.5	9.0	2.0	-12.7
78072	22776	16284	7284	4.7	9.3	32.0	44.7	-12.7	-21.8	-43.4
185	111	161	87	62.8	47.2	78.9	54.2	5.9	-9.8	-11.2
297	229	231	123	59.2	41.5	53.8	53.2	7.4	-5.1	-26.7
48044	54095	58326	60793	187.0	126.5	112.4	104.2	8.1	2.4	6.0
186940	236483	237411	237967	159.3	127.3	100.6	100.2	4.6	4.8	0.3
182877	236424	237388	237944	167.2	130.1	100.6	100.2	5.1	5.3	0.3
740.0	5663.2	987.7	1044.7	347.9	141.2	18.4	105.8	19.8	50.2	-57.1
0.8	0.2	0.4	0.5	22.2	55.9	192.6	108.6	-16.9	-21.9	38.8
597.0	466.6	429.7	424.6	70.5	71.1	91.0	98.8	-0.2	-4.8	-4.6
4232.6	6025.6	6192.6	6379.4	227.9	150.7	105.9	103.0	8.6	7.3	2.9
1253.7	4752.2	3978.5	3510.2		280.0	73.9	88.2		30.5	-14.1
		1263.9	2082.2				164.7			
739.4	559.5	541.0	521.4	42.4	70.5	93.2	96.4	-9.7	-5.4	-3.5

a) Since 2011, the statistical scope of the industrial enterprises were industrial companies with revenue from principal business over 20 million yuan. Since 2019, the main business income index has been adjusted to the operating income index.

b) Total amount of post and telecommunications business in 2021 is calculated at the constant unit price of the previous year (the same below).

1—6 续表3 continued

指 标	Item	总量指标 2010
国内商业	**Domestic Trade**	
社会消费品零售总额 (亿元)	Total Retail Sales of Consumer Goods (100 million yuan)	5139.0
批发零售业购进总额 (亿元)	Total Goods Purchases of Enterprises in Wholesale and Retail Sale Trade (100 million yuan)	4653.0
批发零售业销售总额 (亿元)	Total Sales of Enterprises in Wholesale and Retail Sale Trade (100 million yuan)	5144.1
批发零售业库存总额 (亿元)	Total Inventory of Enterprises in Wholesale and Retail Sale Trade (100 million yuan)	397.5
对外经济贸易	**Foreign Trade**	
进出口总额 (万美元)	Total Exports and Tourists (USD 10000)	2427677
进口额	Imports	1186388
出口额	Exports	1241288
国际旅游	**International Tourism**	
入境旅游人数 (万人次)	Total Number of Tourists (10000 persons)	198.4
#外国人	Foreigners	117.4
旅游外汇收入 (万美元)	Foreign Exchange Earnings from Tourism (USD 10000)	82025
旅游星级宾馆个数 (个)	Number of Tourist Hotel of Star Class (unit)	453
金融保险	**Finance and Insurance**	
金融机构人民币存款余额 (亿元)	Financial Institutions Renminbi Deposit Balance (100 million yuan)	16366.1
金融机构人民币贷款余额 (亿元)	Financial Institutions RMB Loan Balance (100 million yuan)	11452.3
保险公司保费收入 (亿元)	Income From Premium of Insurance Companies (100 million yuan)	438.2
保险公司赔款及给付 (亿元)	Amount Reparations of Insurance Companies (100 million yuan)	104.6
教育、科技、文化	**Education, Science and Technology and Culture**	
教 育	**Education**	
幼儿园数 (个)	Number of Kindergartens (unit)	4018
入园儿童数 (万人)	Student Enrollment in Kindergartens (10000 persons)	100.82
学龄儿童入学率 (%)	Percentage of School-age Children Enrolled (%)	
专任教师数 (万人)	Full-time Teachers (10000 persons)	
普通高等学校	Regular Institutions of Higher Education	4.93
中等职业学校	Secondary Vocational School	2.17
普通中学	Regular Secondary Schools	23.01
#高 中	Senior Secondary Schools	6.69
小 学	Primary Schools	24.57
在校学生数 (万人)	Student Enrollment (10000 persons)	
普通高等学校	Regular Institutions of Higher Education	93.90
中等职业学校	Secondary Vocational School	77.61
普通中学	Regular Secondary Schools	406.58
#高 中	Senior Secondary Schools	127.60
小 学	Primary Schools	460.44

注：2021年起中等职业学校各项指标含成人中专，口径略大（下同）。

Aggregate Indicator				速度指标 (%) Indices and Growth Rates						
				指 数 (2022年为以下各年) Index (2022 as Percentage of the Following Years)				平均增长速度 Average Annual Growth Rate		
2015	2020	2021	2022	2010	2015	2020	2021	2011—2015	2016—2020	2021—2022
11184.9	18333.7	21471.2	21518.4	418.7	192.4	117.4	100.2	16.8	10.4	8.3
8389.5	13676.3	17665.1	19715.9	423.7	235.0	144.2	111.6	12.5	10.3	20.1
9454.9	15693.4	19727.8	21963.5	427.0	232.3	140.0	111.3	12.9	10.7	18.3
757.1	1054.0	973.7	1095.4	275.6	144.7	103.9	112.5	13.8	6.8	1.9
4880808	7859430	10700787	11315512	466.1	231.8	144.0	105.7	15.0	10.0	20.0
1569384	3301562	4363312	4174306	351.8	266.0	126.4	95.7	5.8	16.0	12.4
3311424	4557868	6337476	7141206	575.3	215.7	156.7	112.7	21.7	6.6	25.2
444.6	69.3	11.5	4.8	2.4	1.1	6.9	41.7	17.5	-31.1	-73.7
259.2	44.0	6.1	2.7	2.3	1.0	6.1	44.3	17.2	-29.9	-75.2
226287	27466	4532	2248	2.7	1.0	8.2	49.6	22.5	-34.4	-71.4
441	262	242	217	47.9	49.2	82.8	89.7	-0.5	-9.9	-9.0
34482.9	59897.8	66271.9	74492.7	455.2	216.0	124.4	112.4	16.1	11.7	11.5
25489.1	51520.5	58151.0	67048.4	585.5	263.0	130.1	115.3	17.4	15.1	14.1
698.9	1403.5	1379.7	1418.2	323.6	202.9	101.0	102.8	9.8	15.0	0.5
276.9	477.4	519.3	562.5	537.7	203.2	117.8	108.3	21.5	11.5	8.6
6988	10876	11478	11577	288.1	165.7	106.4	100.9	11.7	9.3	3.2
185.65	216.81	214.06	204.30	202.6	110.0	94.2	95.4	13.0	3.2	-2.9
99.96	99.99	99.99	100.00							
5.81	6.56	7.02	7.50	152.1	129.1	114.3	106.8	3.3	2.5	6.9
2.72	2.76	3.12	3.23	148.8	118.8	117.0	103.5	4.6	0.3	8.2
22.72	24.76	25.65	26.13	113.6	115.0	105.5	101.9	-0.2	1.7	2.7
7.63	8.21	8.63	9.02	134.9	118.2	109.9	104.5	2.7	1.5	4.8
23.83	26.04	26.90	26.97	109.8	113.2	103.6	100.3	-0.6	1.8	1.8
113.07	136.85	150.50	155.35	165.5	137.4	113.5	103.2	3.8	3.9	6.5
58.43	56.36	75.21	72.80	93.8	124.6	129.2	96.8	-5.5	-0.7	13.7
303.63	337.31	346.21	348.86	85.8	114.9	103.4	100.8	-5.7	2.1	1.7
113.55	113.36	116.34	120.10	94.1	105.8	105.9	103.2	-2.3		2.9
422.50	468.24	468.73	470.25	102.1	111.3	100.4	100.3	-1.7	2.1	0.2

a) Indicators of secondary vocational schools since 2021 include adult technical secondary schools, with a slightly larger caliber (the same below).

1—6 续表4 continued

指 标		Item		总量指标 2010
在校学生毕业生数	(万人)	Graduates of Student Enrollment	(10000 persons)	
普通高等学校		Regular Institutions of Higher Education		23.22
中等职业学校		Secondary Vocational School		27.37
普通中学		Regular Secondary Schools		136.57
#高 中		Senior Secondary Schools		44.38
小 学		Primary Schools		87.41
预算内教育经费支出	(亿元)	Government Expenditures on Education	(100 million yuan)	436.06
科 技		**Science and Technology**		
研究与试验发展人员	(万人)	Research and Experimental Developers	(10000 persons)	
研究与试验发展经费支出	(亿元)	Expenditures on Research and Development	(100 million yuan)	163.72
输出技术合同成交额	(亿元)	Export Technology Contract Turnover	(100 million yuan)	46.15
文 化		**Culture**		
出版数量		Number of Published		
图 书	(万册)	Number of Books Published	(10000 copies)	23891
杂 志	(万册)	Number of Magazines Issued	(10000 copies)	5842
报 纸	(万份)	Number of Newspapers Issued	(10000 copies)	116988
公共图书馆	(个)	Number of Public Libraries	(unit)	88
公共图书馆藏书量	(万册)	Total Collections of Public Libraries	(10000 volumes)	1235.8
电视节目制作时间	(小时)	Production Hours of TV Programs	(hours)	82427
广播覆盖率	(%)	Broadcast Covering Rate	(%)	97.31
电视覆盖率	(%)	TV Covering Rate	(%)	97.50
家庭、生活、环境		**Family, People's Livelihood and Environment**		
婚 姻	**(万对)**	**Marriages and Divorces**	**(10000 couple)**	
结婚数		Number of Marriages		65.09
离婚数		Number of Divorces		10.96
居 住	**(平方米)**	**Housing**	**(sq.m)**	
城镇居民人均居住面积		Per Capita Gross Floor Space of Urban Residents		31.6
农村居民人均居住面积		Per Capita Net Floor Space of Rural Residents		32.1
生 活		**People's Livelihood**		
城镇居民人均可支配收入	(元)	Per Capita Annual Disposable Income of Urban Households	(yuan)	
城镇居民人均消费性支出	(元)	Per Capita Annual Living Expenditures of Urban Residents	(yuan)	
#食品支出		Food		
农村居民人均可支配收入	(元)	Rural Residents per Capita Disposable Income	(yuan)	
农村居民人均消费支出	(元)	Per Capita Annual Living Expenditures of Rural Residents	(yuan)	
#食品支出		Food		
工资、居民生活和保障		**Wages, Residents' Livelihood and Security**		
城镇非私营单位就业人员工资总额	(亿元)	Total Wages of Employed Persons of Urban Non-private Owned Units	(100 million yuan)	1225.12
国有单位		State-owned Units		691.48
城镇集体单位		Urban Collective Unit		42.56
其他单位		Units of Other Types of Ownership		491.07
城镇非私营单位就业人员平均工资	(元)	Average Wage of Employed Persons of Urban Non-private Owned Units	(yuan)	33341
城镇居民最低生活保障人数	(人)	Number of Subsistence Allowances for Urban Residents	(person)	883944
农村居民最低生活保障人数	(人)	Number of Subsistence Allowances for Rural Residents	(person)	2146238

Aggregate Indicator				速度指标 (%) Indices and Growth Rates						
				指　数 (2022年为以下各年) Index (2022 as Percentage of the Following Years)				平均增长速度 Average Annual Growth Rate		
2015	2020	2021	2022	2010	2015	2020	2021	2011—2015	2016—2020	2021—2022
29.25	32.68	32.70	41.89	180.4	143.2	128.2	128.1	4.7	2.2	13.2
22.03	16.47	26.31	23.88	87.2	108.4	145.0	90.8	-4.2	-5.7	20.4
107.39	105.88	106.09	114.98	84.2	107.1	108.6	108.4	-4.7	-0.3	4.2
43.30	35.13	35.99	38.07	85.8	87.9	108.4	105.8	-0.5	-4.1	4.1
64.32	74.01	75.72	74.95	85.7	116.5	101.3	99.0	-6.0	2.8	0.6
951.43	1257.11	1315.42	1420.07	325.7	149.3	113.0	108.0	16.9	5.7	6.3
20.48	27.88	35.02	37.50		183.1	134.5	107.1		6.4	16.0
431.75	883.18	1006.12	1152.51	704.0	266.9	130.5	114.5	21.4	15.4	14.2
190.53	742.44	1754.55	2216.72	4803.6	1163.4	298.6	126.3	32.8	31.3	72.8
27329	31793	32294	32772	137.2	119.9	103.1	101.5	2.7	3.1	1.5
5251	3485	3443	3429	58.7	65.3	98.4	99.6	-2.1	-7.9	-0.8
104830	56092	54808	50871	43.5	48.5	90.7	92.8	-2.2	-11.8	-4.8
122	131	133	133	151.1	109.0	101.5	100.0	6.8	1.4	0.8
1942.4	3545.8	3770.0	4203	340.1	216.4	118.5	111.5	9.5	12.8	8.9
77470	76041	78637	77187	93.6	99.6	101.5	98.2	-1.2	-0.4	0.8
98.77	99.93	99.94	99.95							
98.93	99.90	99.92	99.94							
73.80	47.13	42.02	33.89	52.1	45.9	71.9	80.6	2.5	-8.6	-15.2
18.12	23.77	15.00	14.32	130.6	79.0	60.2	95.4	10.6	5.6	-22.4
34.7	42.1	42.3	42.4	134.4	122.2	100.7	100.2	1.9	3.9	0.4
46.8	54.6	54.7	54.7	170.7	117.0	100.3	100.0	7.8	3.1	0.1
26936	39442	43009	45133		167.6	114.4	104.9		7.9	7.0
17234	22683	26495	26832		155.7	118.3	101.3		5.6	8.8
5802	7401	8469	8925		153.8	120.6	105.4		5.0	9.8
10821	16620	18372	19575		180.9	117.8	106.5		9.0	8.5
8975	15024	17163	17980		200.3	119.7	104.8		10.9	9.4
3212	5146	5769	6354		197.8	123.5	110.1		9.9	11.1
2823.84	4740.34	5224.58	5646.16	460.9	199.9	119.1	108.1	18.2	10.9	9.1
1135.30	1884.51	2077.06	2191.17	316.9	193.0	116.3	105.5	10.4	10.7	7.8
69.69	57.76	59.50	57.45	135.0	82.4	99.5	96.5	10.4	-3.7	-0.3
1618.86	2798.07	3088.02	3397.54	691.9	209.9	121.4	110.0	26.9	11.6	10.2
55139	85854	93861	98649	295.9	178.9	114.9	105.1	10.6	9.3	7.2
646672	344316	316695	276271	31.3	42.7	80.2	87.2	-6.1	-11.8	-10.4
1963293	1836832	1769270	1698699	79.1	86.5	92.5	96.0	-1.8	-1.3	-3.8

1—6 续表5 continued

指 标		Item		总量指标 2010
卫 生		**Health Care**		
卫生机构数	(个)	Number of Health Institutions	(unit)	23019
医院、卫生院		Hospitals		2167
疾病防治中心		Disease Prevention and Controlling		124
妇幼保健站		Maternity and Child Care Centers		119
卫生机构床位数	(张)	Number of Beds in Health Institutions	(unit)	186116
#医院、卫生院		Hospitals		171389
卫生机构人员数	(人)	Number of Persons Engaged in Health Institutions	(person)	247493
专业卫生技术人员	(人)	Number of Technical Personnel in Hospitals	(person)	205403
#执业（助理）医师		Licensed (Assistant) Doctors		81097
注册护士		Registered Nurse		76550
市政建设		**City Construction**		
供水管道长度	(公里)	Length of Water Supply Pipelines	(km)	14730
供水总量	(万立方米)	Total Annual Volume of Water Supply	(10000 cu.m)	160816
#居民家庭用水		Household Water		50889
天然气供气量	(万立方米)	Supply of Natural Gas	(10000 cu.m)	112190
#家庭用量		Consumption of Coal Gas for Residential Use		25154
液化石油气供气量	(吨)	Liquefied Petroleum Gas	(ton)	615770
#家庭用量		Consumption of Liquefied Gas for Residential Use		166335
污水排放量	(万立方米)	Volume of Sewage Discharged	(10000 cu.m)	124449
污水处理厂处理量	(万立方米)	Sewage Treatment Plant Capacity	(10000 cu.m)	89086
排水管长度	(公里)	Length of Drainage	(km)	13136
生活垃圾清运量	(万吨)	Volume of Garbage Swept Away	(10000 tons)	435.3
生活垃圾无公害处理量	(万吨)	Volume of Garbage Treated	(10000 tons)	281.0
公共汽（电）车总数	(辆)	Total Number of Public Buses and Trolley Buses	(unit)	11875
出租汽车数	(辆)	Number of Taxis	(unit)	50068
铺装道路长度	(公里)	Length of Paved Roads	(km)	10157
公园面积	(公顷)	Area of Parks	(hectare)	8685
园林绿地面积	(公顷)	Area of Urban Green Areas	(hectare)	71463
建成区绿化覆盖率	(%)	Afforestation Covering Rate in the Constructed Area	(%)	37.5
环境、灾害		**Environment and Disaster**		
化学需氧量排放量	(万吨)	Amount of CoD Discharged	(10000 tons)	41.1
二氧化硫排放量	(万吨)	Volume of Sulphur Dioxide Emission	(10000 tons)	53.3
突发环境事件次数	(次)	Number of Environmental Accidents	(time)	30
环境污染直接经济损失	(万元)	Losses Converted Into Cash	(10000 yuan)	231.6
交通事故发生数	(起)	Number of Traffic Accidents	(cases)	7714
交通受伤人数	(人)	Number of Injured in Traffic Accidents	(person)	9364
交通死亡人数	(人)	Number of Death in Traffic Accidents	(person)	2808
交通事故损失金额	(万元)	Loss of Traffic Accidents	(10000 yuan)	2349.6

注：生态环境部根据二污普数据对2016—2019年环境指标进行了动态更新，前期数据未做调整。

a) Ministry of Ecology and Environment dynamically updated the environmental indicators from 2016 to 2019 based on the general pollution data, and did not adjust the previous data.

Aggregate Indicator				速度指标 (%) Indices and Growth Rates						
2015	2020	2021	2022	指数 (2022年为以下各年) Index (2022 as Percentage of the Following Years)				平均增长速度 Average Annual Growth Rate		
				2010	2015	2020	2021	2011—2015	2016—2020	2021—2022
24853	29391	29554	30176	131.1	121.4	102.7	102.1	1.5	3.4	1.3
2400	2744	2685	2677	123.5	111.5	97.6	99.7	2.1	2.7	-1.2
121	121	122	124	100.0	102.5	102.5	101.6	-0.5		1.2
121	123	126	127	106.7	105.0	103.3	100.8	0.3	0.3	1.6
267405	407679	411023	443917	238.5	166.0	108.9	108.0	7.5	8.8	4.3
253716	387743	389444	419512	244.8	165.3	108.2	107.7	8.2	8.9	4.0
377387	503226	519677	553360	223.6	146.6	110.0	106.5	8.8	5.9	4.9
280768	412247	435334	471176	229.4	167.8	114.3	108.2	6.5	8.0	6.9
107792	164325	172670	185983	229.3	172.5	113.2	107.7	5.9	8.8	6.4
119303	188253	200980	221426	289.3	185.6	117.6	110.2	9.3	9.6	8.5
23842	36257	34120	35916	243.8	150.6	99.1	105.3	10.1	8.7	-0.5
174263	238126	255083	261031	162.3	149.8	109.6	102.3	1.6	6.4	4.7
68319	99121	101662	102099	200.6	149.4	103.0	100.4	6.1	7.7	1.5
234585	414417	451842	501514	447.0	213.8	121.0	111.0	15.9	12.1	10.0
71773	128570	134921	151169	601.0	210.6	117.6	112.0	23.3	12.4	8.4
736312	157719	160115	159206	25.9	21.6	100.9	99.4	3.6	-26.5	0.5
104259	87248	82192	85158	51.2	81.7	97.6	103.6	-8.9	-3.5	-1.2
150642	208669	228288	227265	182.6	150.9	108.9	99.6	3.9	6.7	4.4
138293	199819	219407	218797	245.6	158.2	109.5	99.7	9.2	7.6	4.6
24399	35393	36505	37867	288.3	155.2	107.0	103.7	13.2	7.7	3.4
491.9	660.7	714.9	745.4	171.3	151.5	112.8	104.3	2.5	6.1	6.2
489.7	660.7	714.9	745.4	265.3	152.2	112.8	104.3	11.8	6.2	6.2
18622	28331	28301	27785	234.0	149.2	98.1	98.2	9.4	8.8	-1.0
55217	54136	55298	55205	110.3	100.0	102.0	99.8	2.0	-0.4	1.0
13375	17750	19433	20372	200.6	152.3	114.8	104.8	5.7	5.8	7.1
12043	18795	20547	22931	264.0	190.4	122.0	111.6	6.8	9.3	10.5
93786	119533	127602	132363	185.2	141.1	110.7	103.7	5.6	5.0	5.2
41.2	42.0	44.1	45.3	120.8	110.1	107.9	102.8	1.9	0.4	3.9
87.1	118.6	120.0						16.2	6.4	
48.0	10.9	8.6						-2.1	-25.7	
8	10	2	3	10.0	37.5	30.0	150.0	-23.2	4.6	-45.2
75.3	695.7	512.6	101.4	43.8	134.7	14.6	19.8	-20.1	56.0	-61.8
13736	10706	10284	8668	112.4	63.1	81.0	84.3	12.2	-4.9	-10.0
15342	12252	11278	9198	98.2	60.0	75.1	81.6	10.4	-4.4	-13.4
2595	2373	2231	2215	78.9	85.4	93.3	99.3	-1.6	-1.8	-3.4
6122.5	5526.8	5168.8	4259.1	181.3	69.6	77.1	82.4	21.1	-2.0	-12.2

1—7 国民经济和社会发展结构指标

Structural Indicators on National Economic and Social Development

单位：%

指　　标	Item	2010	2015	2020	2021	2022
人口与就业	**Population and Employment**					
人　　口	**Population**					
城乡结构	Urban and Rural Structure					
城　镇	Urban	43.2	51.0	58.3	59.4	60.2
乡　村	Rural	56.8	49.0	41.7	40.6	39.8
性别结构	Sexual Structure					
男	Male	50.83	50.66	50.97	51.06	51.04
女	Female	49.17	49.34	49.03	48.94	48.96
就　　业	**Employment**					
产业结构	Industrial Structure					
第一产业	Primary Industry	39.1	32.1	25.1	24.2	24.9
第二产业	Secondary Industry	25.1	28.4	31.5	31.9	32.1
第三产业	Tertiary Industry	35.8	39.5	43.4	43.9	43.0
宏观经济	**Macro Economy**					
国民核算	**National Accounting**					
生产总值产业结构	Structure of Total Investment in Fixed Assets					
第一产业	Primary Industry	12.1	10.0	8.4	7.9	7.8
第二产业	Secondary Industry	48.3	45.5	40.0	40.5	41.3
第三产业	Tertiary Industry	39.6	44.5	51.6	51.6	50.9
投　　资	**Investment**					
固定资产投资产业结构	Structure of Total Investment in Fixed Assets					
第一产业	Primary Industry	1.9	3.2	1.5	1.9	2.1
第二产业	Secondary Industry	47.4	44.6	30.1	31.3	33.8
第三产业	Tertiary Industry	50.7	52.2	68.3	66.8	64.1
资金来源结构	Structure of Funded Sources					
国家预算内资金	State Budgetary Appropriation	7.3	5.1	5.4	6.4	9.2
国内贷款	Domestic Loans	9.4	5.2	9.0	7.1	7.6
利用外资	Foreign Investment	0.9	0.3	0.2	0.2	0.1
自筹和其他投资	Fundraising	82.4	89.5	85.4	86.3	83.1
财　　政	**Government Finance**					
一般公共预算收入结构	Revenue Structure of the General Public Budget					
税收收入	Tax Revenue	75.4	73.3	68.4	68.3	62.6
非税收入	Non-tax Revenue	24.6	26.7	31.6	31.7	37.4
能源生产与消费	**Energy Production and Consumption**					
能源生产总量结构	Composition of Total Energy Production					
原　煤	Coal	98.4	96.0	85.8	83.3	81.6
一次电力	Primary Power	1.2	2.2	8.7	10.8	12.3
能源消费总量结构	Composition of Total Energy Consumption					
煤　品	Coal	86.2	77.1	69.8	67.7	67.6
油　品	Petroleum	10.3	16.0	15.4	15.7	13.9
天 然 气	Natural Gas	1.8	3.8	5.1	4.8	6.0
非化石能源	Non-fossil Energy	1.7	3.2	9.7	11.8	12.5

注：2020年起就业结构为常住口径，往年均为户籍口径（下同）。

a) Since 2020, the employment structure is of permanent residence caliber, and in previous years, it is of household registration caliber (the same below).

1—7 续表1 continued

单位：%

指　标	Item	2010	2015	2020	2021	2022
产　业	**Industrial**					
农　业	**Agriculture**					
农林牧渔业产值结构	Structure of Gross Output Value					
农　业	Farming	52.5	49.7	44.5	46.7	46.8
林　业	Forestry	4.8	6.9	6.8	6.9	7.5
牧　业	Animal Husbandry	29.5	28.9	33.4	30.2	28.9
渔　业	Fishery	9.5	10.3	9.6	10.4	10.5
工　业	**Industry**					
工业总产值规模结构	Structure of Gross Output Value of Industry					
大型企业	Large Enterprises	34.3	31.6	34.4	38.3	39.3
中型企业	Medium-sized Enterprises	25.9	19.7	18.9	19.1	19.3
小微型企业	Small and Mini Enterprises	39.9	48.8	46.7	42.6	41.4
建筑业	**Construction**					
建筑业总产值结构	Structure of Gross Output Value of Construction Enterprises					
建筑工程	Construction Projects	87.5	85.7	85.0	84.8	85.9
安装工程	Installation Projects	8.6	7.6	7.2	7.4	7.2
其　他	Others	3.9	6.6	7.7	7.7	6.9
运输业	**Transportation**					
货运量结构	Structure of Freight Traffic					
铁　路	Railways	5.3	2.9	2.0	1.9	2.0
公　路	Highways	80.5	66.7	65.1	64.6	62.4
水　运	Waterways	14.2	30.4	32.9	33.5	35.6
民　航	Total Civil Aviation Routes	0.001	0.0007	0.0004	0.0004	0.0002
国内商业	**Domestic Trade**					
社会消费品零售总额构成	Composition of Retail Sales of Consumer Goods					
城　镇	Urban			82.4	82.5	84.1
乡　村	Rural			17.6	17.5	15.9
对外经济贸易	**Foreign Trade**					
出口商品结构	Structure of Exports					
初级产品	Primary Goods	6.3	5.5	3.2	2.8	2.7
工业制成品	Manufactured Goods	93.7	94.5	96.8	97.2	97.3
进口商品结构	Structure of Imports					
初级产品	Primary Goods	53.1	50.8	46.9	48.5	46.3
工业制成品	Manufactured Goods	46.9	49.2	53.1	51.5	53.7
国际旅游	**International Tourism**					
来华旅游人数结构	Structure of Tourists					
外国人	Foreigners	59.2	58.3	63.5	52.9	56.2
港澳台同胞	Compatriots form Hong Kong, Macao and Taiwan	40.8	41.7	36.5	47.1	43.8
金融保险业	**Finance and Insurance**					
金融机构资金来源结构	Structure of Sources of Funds in State Banks					
#各项存款	Deposits	103.4	98.0	92.4	92.8	92.4
应付及暂收款	Account Payable and Temporary Credit	1.9	2.7	2.5	2.5	2.5
各项准备	Every Capital Reserve	1.2	1.8	2.1	2.3	2.2
所有者权益	Owners' Equity	3.7	4.6	5.1	4.9	4.7
金融机构资金运用结构	Structure of Fund Uses in State Banks					
#各项贷款	Loans	72.4	72.5	79.5	81.5	83.2
债券投资	Bond Investment		6.6	8.3	8.3	9.0
股权及其他投资	Equity and Other Investment		5.1	5.6	5.3	4.4
教育、科技、文化	**Education, Science and Culture**					
教　育	**Education**					
在校学生结构	Structure of Student Enrollment					
大学生	College and University Students	8.2	10.4	11.2	12.0	12.4
中学生	Secondary School Students	42.4	33.4	32.3	33.5	33.6
小学生	Primary School Students	40.4	38.9	38.4	37.2	37.4

1—7 续表2 continued

单位：%

指 标	Item	2010	2015	2020	2021	2022
专任教师结构	Full-time Teachers by Type					
大 学	College and University Students	8.5	9.4	9.2	9.2	9.7
中 学	Secondary School Students	43.6	41.1	38.4	37.9	37.9
小 学	Primary School Students	42.5	38.5	36.4	35.4	34.8
科 技	**Science and Technology**					
研究与试验发展经费	Research and Experimental Development Funding					
筹集款结构	Structure					
#政府资金	Government Fund	22.0	20.0	15.3	14.6	16.2
企业资金	Enterprise Fund	72.6	76.7	81.5	82.9	81.1
研究与试验发展经费支出	Research and Development Expenses					
#基础研究	Basic Research	7.5	5.6	6.9	7.4	9.0
应用研究	Applied research	9.6	7.8	8.9	8.4	8.4
试验发展	Experimental development	83.0	86.6	84.2	84.3	82.6
生活、环境	**People's Livelihood and Environment**					
生 活	**People's Livelihood**					
城镇居民消费结构	Consumption Structure of Urban Residents					
食品类	Food	38.0	33.7	32.6	32.0	33.3
衣着类	Clothing	10.6	8.1	6.8	6.8	6.6
居 住	Residence	10.7	20.1	23.6	22.0	22.7
生活用品及服务	Household Facilities, Articles and Services	5.9	5.4	6.0	6.3	6.1
医疗保健	Health Care and medical Services	6.4	6.2	7.2	7.1	7.2
交通通信	Transport and Communications	11.8	13.1	11.8	11.5	10.8
教育文化娱乐服务	Education, Cultural and Recreation Services	12.9	11.1	10.1	12.0	10.7
其他商品及服务	Other Goods and Services	3.8	2.3	1.9	2.4	2.7
农村居民消费结构	Consumption Structure of Rural Residents					
食品类	Food	40.7	35.8	34.3	33.6	35.3
衣着类	Clothing	5.8	5.6	5.8	6.1	5.8
居 住	Residence	21.6	21.2	22.6	20.2	20.6
生活用品及服务	Household Facilities, Articles and Services	5.8	5.6	5.7	5.8	5.9
交通通信	Transport and Communications	8.5	11.8	11.1	11.1	11.3
教育文化娱乐服务	Education, Cultural and Recreation Services	9.1	9.3	9.5	11.5	10.7
医疗保健	Health Care and medical Services	6.6	9.0	9.7	9.7	8.6
其他商品及服务	Other Goods and Services	2.0	1.8	1.5	1.9	1.7
卫 生	**Health Care**					
卫生技术人员结构	Composition of medical Technical personnel					
#执业（助理）医师	Licensed (Assistant) Doctors	39.5	38.4	39.9	39.7	39.5
注册护士	Registered Nurses	37.3	42.5	45.7	46.2	47.0
医院床位结构	Hospital Beds by Area					
综合医院	Comprehensive Hospitals		71.2	66.8	65.5	64.7
中医医院	Hospitals of Traditional Chinese Medicine		13.5	14.5	14.5	15.1
专科医院	Specialized Hospitals		14.3	15.9	17.1	17.1
环境、灾害	**Environment and Disasters**					
自然灾害直接经济损失	Direct Economic Losses From Natural Disasters					
洪涝灾	Floods	74.8	61.9	99.6	46.4	5.4

1—8　国民经济和社会发展比例和效益指标
Indicators on Proportions and Efficiency in National Economic and Social Development

指　标	Item	2010	2015	2020	2021	2022
人　口	**Population**					
出生率 (‰)	Birth Rate (‰)	12.70	12.92	9.45	8.05	7.16
死亡率 (‰)	Death Rate (‰)	5.95	5.94	7.96	8.00	8.09
自然增长率 (‰)	Natural Growth Rate (‰)	6.75	6.98	1.49	0.05	-0.93
就　业	**Employment**					
三次产业从业者比例（以第一产业为100）	Employment Ratio by Type of Industry (Employment in primary industry=100)					
第一产业	Primary Industry	100.0	100.0	100.0	100.0	100.0
第二产业	Secondary Industry	64.2	88.2	125.2	131.7	129.1
第三产业	Tertiary Industry	91.6	122.7	172.8	181.0	172.9
城镇登记失业率 (%)	Registered Unemployment Rate in Urban Areas	3.66	3.14	2.80	2.50	
国民核算	**National Accounting**					
全社会劳动生产率 （元/人）	Overall Labor Productivity (yuan/person)	32968	55081	117004	131822	140964
第一产业	Primary Industry	10163	16902		42207	44789
第二产业	Secondary Industry	63563	1127		168525	181701
第三产业	Tertiary Industry	36534	62481		155863	165298
人均生产总值 (元)	Per Capita GDP (yuan)	21923	39692	62411	69676	73603
固定资产投资	**Investment in Fixed Assets**					
房地产开发企业房屋建筑面积竣工率 (%)	Real Estate Development Enterprise Housing Construction Area Completion Rate (%)	17.2	16.2	11.3	15.0	14.6
财　政	**Finance**					
一般公共预算收入相当于生产总值比例 (%)	Proportion of General Public Budget Revenue to GDP (%)	8.67	10.30	8.40	8.20	8.00
一般公共预算支出相当于生产总值比例 (%)	Proportion of General Public Budget Expenditure to GDP (%)	19.53	21.98	19.64	17.83	18.6
利用外资	**Utilization of Foreign Capital**					
实际利用外资额相当于签订利用外资额比例 (%)	Proportion of Foreign Capital Actually Used to Total Amount of Foreign Capital for Utilization by Signed Contracts or Agreements (%)	231.66	345.85	353.94	280.42	50.23
能源生产与消费	**Production and Consumption of Energy**					
电力生产弹性系数	Elasticity Ratio of Electricity Production	0.69	0.16		1.18	2.00
能源消费弹性系数	Elasticity Ratio of Energy Consumption	0.62	0.31	1.55	0.53	1.00
电力消费弹性系数	Elasticity Ratio of Electricity Consumption	0.90	0.40	1.43	1.43	2.91
每万元生产总值消耗的能源 （吨标准煤）	Energy Consumption per 10000 yuan GDP (ton of SCE)	0.97	0.56	0.43	0.37	0.37

注1：2020年起就业比例、全社会劳动生产率为常住口径，往年均为户籍口径。

a) Since 2020, the employment ratio and labor productivity of the whole society have been registered as permanent residents. In previous years, they have been registered as permanent residents.

注2：2022年实际利用外商直接投资额统计口径是商务部口径，往年为省口径，数据不可比。

1—8 续表1 continued

指　　标	Item	2010	2015	2020	2021	2022
农　业	**Agriculture**					
每公顷播种面积农产品产量（公斤）	Output of Farm Crops per Hectare of Sown Area (kg)					
粮　食	Grain	4617	5600	5514	5592	5606
棉　花	Cotton	918	881	801	846	844
油　料	Oil-bearing Crops	2546	2982	3116	3083	3086
工　业	**Industry**					
总资产贡献率 （%）	Ratio of Total Assets to Industrial Output Value (%)	16.22	12.25	9.63	9.86	7.78
资产负债率 （%）	Assets-liability Ratio (%)	60.05	57.49	55.59	56.06	56.50
成本费用利润率 （%）	Ratio of Profits to Industrial Cost (%)	8.63	5.41	6.79	6.78	5.40
流动资产周转次数 （次/年）	Number of Times of Annual of Turnover Circulating Funds (times/year)	2.63	2.83	1.69	1.70	1.58
产品销售率 （%）	Proportion of products Sold (%)	97.57	97.3	97.7	97.90	97.20
建筑业	**Construction**					
产值利润率 （%）	Ratio of Profit to Gross Output Value (%)	3.43	3.29	2.66	2.53	2.37
劳动生产率 （元/人）	Overall Labor Productivity (yuan/person)	177486	340696	457314	533025	507177
交通运输业	**Transportation**					
铁路网密度 （公里/万平方公里）	Railway Density (km/10000 sq.km)	203	298	368	376	376
公路网密度 （公里/万平方公里）	Highway Density (km/10000 sq.km)	10716	13410	16680	16946	16986
铁路货运密度 （吨/公里）	Railway Freight Traffic Density (ton/km)	42424	24367	14631	14472	14758
公路货运密度 （吨/公里）	Highway Freight Traffic Density (ton/km)	12295	12338	10298	10911	10337
邮电通信业	**Postal and Telecommunications Services**					
全省电话普及率（按年末常住人口计算） （部/百人）	Access to Telephones, National (set/100 persons)	67.65	82.72	107.86	110.15	112.63
#移动电话普及率	Access to Mobile Phones	46.98	70.41	98.70	101.30	104.12
对外经济贸易	**Foreign Trade**					
进出口总额相当于生产总值比例 （%）	Proportion of Total Imports & Exports to GDP (%)	13.3	13.8	14.2	16.3	16.7
国际旅游	**International Tourism**					
每一来华游客花费 （美元）	Expenditure per International Tourist in China(USD)	413	509	397	394	468
国内旅游人均花费 （元）	Expenditure per Domestic Tourist (yuan)	838	896	897	961	935

1—8　续表2　continued

指　　标	Item	2010	2015	2020	2021	2022
金融保险	**Finance and Insurance**					
金融机构存款相当于生产总值比例 (%)	Bank Deposits as Percentage of GDP (%)	123.52	144.70	157.37	155.70	165.37
金融机构贷款相当于生产总值比例 (%)	Bank Loans as Percentage of GDP (%)	86.43	106.96	135.36	136.62	148.85
教　育	**Education**					
学校教师负担系数 (%)	Student-teacher Ratio (in percentage) (%)					
高等学校	Colleges and Universities	19.05	19.46	20.86	21.44	20.71
中等学校	Secondary Schools	19.23	14.23	14.30	14.65	14.36
小学学校	Primary Schools	18.74	17.73	17.98	17.42	17.44
科　技	**Science and Technology**					
研究与发展经费支出相当于生产总值比例 (%)	Expenditure on Research and Development is Equivalent to the Proportion of GDP (%)	1.32	1.96	2.28	2.34	2.56
卫　生	**Health Care**					
每万人执业(助理)医师数 (人)	Number of Doctors per 10000 Persons (person)	11.91	15.51	23.06	24.22	26.11
每万人医院床位数 (张)	Number of Hospital Beds per 10000 Persons (unit)	17.90	29.17	44.68	44.66	47.62
医院病床使用率 (%)	Utilization Rate of Hospital Beds (%)	85.9	85.0	72.2	71.2	68.4
文　化	**Culture**					
每百万人有艺术表演团体 (个)	Number of Troupes per Million Persons (unit)	0.81	23.24	32.75	40.26	53.43
每百万人有公共图书馆 (个)	Number of Public Libraries per Million Persons (unit)	1.29	1.76	1.84	1.87	1.87
每百万人有博物馆 (个)	Number of Museums per Million Persons (unit)	1.76	2.46	3.23	3.13	3.16
家　庭	**Family**					
负担少儿系数 (%)	Dependency Ratio of Children (%)	24.68	25.99	29.27	28.30	27.23
负担老年系数 (%)	Dependency Ratio of the Aged (%)	14.21	16.74	22.83	23.43	23.87
婚　姻	**Marriages and Divorces**					
离 婚 率 (‰)	Divorce Rate (‰)	3.22	5.22	6.67	4.21	4.02
生　活	**People's Livelihood**					
城镇与农村居民收入增长率比例（实际扣除价格因素）	Proportion of Growth Rate of Annual Income of Urban Residents to the Growth Rate of Annual Net Income of Rural Residents		0.91	0.98	0.98	0.60
市政建设	**City Construction**					
城市用水普及率 (%)	Urban Water Penetration Rate (%)	96.06	98.79	99.60	99.81	99.76
城市燃气普及率 (%)	Urban Gas Penetration Rate (%)	90.52	97.55	99.24	99.48	99.42
人均公园绿地面积 (平方米)	Public Green Areas per Person (sq.m)	10.95	13.37	14.88	14.49	16.98

1—9 社会经济主要指标人均水平
Major Per Capita Indicators of Social and Economy

项　目		Item		2020	2021	2022
地区生产总值	**（元）**	**Gross Domestic Product**	**(yuan)**	**62411**	**69676**	**73603**
农林牧渔业总产值	**（元）**	**Gross Output Value of Farming, Forestry, Animal Husbandry and Fishery**	**(yuan)**	**7972**	**8422**	**8814**
主要产品产量		**Output of Major Products**				
原　煤	（吨）	Coal	(ton)	1.56	1.58	1.57
焦　炭	（吨）	Coke	(ton)	0.17	0.18	0.18
发电量	（千瓦小时）	Electricity	(kWh)	3763.7	4084.4	4401.3
钢　材	（公斤）	Steel Products	(kg)	506.2	535.9	556.4
水　泥	（公斤）	Cement	(kg)	1989.4	2103.0	1995.1
布	（米）	Cloth	(m)	11.2	10.7	6.9
粮　食	（公斤）	Grain	(kg)	564.0	573.4	575.6
棉　花	（公斤）	Cotton	(kg)	0.58	0.41	0.36
油　料	（公斤）	Oil-bearing Crops	(kg)	22.8	23.4	24.3
肉　类	（公斤）	Meat	(kg)	55.4	64.0	66.7
社会消费品零售额	**（元）**	**Total Retail Sales of Consumer Goods**	**(yuan)**	**25727.9**	**30118.1**	**30210.2**
人民生活	**（元）**	**People's Livelihood**	**(yuan)**			
城镇非私营单位就业人员平均工资		Average Wage of Employed Persons and Related Index of Urban Non-private Owned Units		85854	93861	98649
国　有		State-owned Units		107953	116898	123493
集　体		Urban Collective-owned Units		76836	85045	89738
城镇常住居民可支配收入		Annual Disposable Income of Urban Residents		39442	43009	45133
城镇居民消费性支出		Living Expenditure of Urban Residents		22683	26495	26832
农村常住居民可支配收入		Farmers Disposable Income		16620	18372	19575
农民家庭生活消费支出		Living Expenditure of Rural Residents		15024	17163	17980

1—10 人民物质文化生活提高情况
Improvement of People's Material and Cultural Life

项　目	Item	2020	2021	2022
城乡居民收入　（元）	**Income of Rural and Urban Residents (yuan)**			
城镇常住居民人均可支配收入	Annual Per Capita Disposable Income of Urban Residents	39442	43009	45133
农村常住居民人均可支配收入	Per Capita Disposable Income of Farmers	16620	18372	19575
城镇非私营单位就业人员平均工资	Average Wage of Employed Persons and Related Index of Urban Non-private Owned Units	85854	93861	98649
平均每人住房面积　（平方米）	**Per Capita Floor Space of Residential Buildings (sq.m)**			
城镇居民建筑面积	Urban Residents	42.09	42.31	42.40
农村居民建筑面积	Rural Residents	54.55	54.68	54.70
生活、文化、教育、卫生	**Livelihood, Culture, Education and Public Health**			
每百户拥有（抽样）	Number of Durable Consumer Goods Owned Per 100 Households by Sample			
彩色电视机　（台）	TV (Color) (unit)			
城镇居民	Urban Residents	138.60	132.73	133.32
农　民	Rural Residents	134.78	133.82	133.14
洗衣机　（台）	Washing Machine (unit)			
城镇居民	Urban Residents	100.80	99.17	99.29
农　民	Rural Residents	90.70	93.47	94.17
移动电话　（部）	Mobile Telephone (unit)			
城镇居民	Urban Residents	252.70	256.99	256.76
农　民	Rural Residents	272.72	278.86	277.71
每百人每天拥有报纸　（份）	Newspapers per 100 Persons per Day (copy)	2.16	2.11	1.96
每人每年拥有期刊　（册）	Number of Magazines per Person per Year (copy)	0.49	0.48	0.48
每万人口中在校大学生　（人）	Number of Enrollment Students of Regular Institutions of Higher Education per 10000 Persons (person)	191.9	211.2	218.2
每千人口中医院床位数　（张）	Number of Hospital Bed per 1000 persons (unit)	4.5	4.5	4.8
每千人口中卫生技术人员（人）	Number of Medical Technical Personnel Per 1000 Persons (person)	6.8	7.1	7.7

1—11 平均每天主要社会经济活动
Selected Indicators on Average Daily Social and Economic Activities

指　　标	Item	2010	2015	2020	2021	2022
每天创造的财富	**Daily Production**					
安徽生产总值　（万元）	Gross Domestic Product　(10000 yuan)	363008	652909	1039932	1166169	1234110
第一产业	Primary Industry	43851	65097	87020	92161	96266
第二产业	Secondary Industry	175233	296941	415750	472333	509261
工　业	Industry	135593	229056	306982	350434	377862
建筑业	Construction	39639	68363	109351	122582	132039
第三产业	Tertiary Industry	143924	290871	537161	601675	628584
一般公共预算收入（万元）	General Public Budget Revenue　(10000 yuan)	31490	67241	87869	95841	98333
粮　食　（吨）	Grain　(ton)	87882	111705	109815	111988	112332
棉　花　（吨）	Cotton　(ton)	706	404	112	80	70
油　料　（吨）	Oil-bearing Crops　(ton)	4825	4697	4439	4579	4751
布　（万米）	Cloth　(10000 m)	298	387	217	210	134
原　煤　（万吨）	Coal　(10000 tons)	35.70	36.7	30.3	30.9	30.6
发电量　（亿千瓦时）	Electricity　(100 million kWh)	3.96	5.57	7.33	7.98	8.59
钢　材　（万吨）	Rolls Steel　(10000 tons)	6.70	9.14	9.88	10.47	10.86
水　泥　（万吨）	Cement　(10000 tons)	21.57	35.85	38.73	41.07	38.93
家用电冰箱　（台）	Household Refrigerator　(unit)	56956	79129	66792	65244	72151
家用洗衣机　（台）	Household Washing Machines　(unit)	34712	47266	65216	71984	69732
每天消费量	**Daily National Consumption**					
能源消费量（万吨标准煤）	Energy Consumption　(10000 tons of SCE)	25.8	33.7	40.2	42.0	43.5
每天其他经济活动	**Other Daily Economic Activities**					
货物运输量　（万吨）	Volume of Freight Traffic　(10000 tons)	624.9	947.3	1022.7	1099.3	1079.2
旅客运输量　（万人）	Volume of Passenger Traffic　(10000 persons)	437.3	238.6	89.0	75.8	40.3
邮电业务总量　（万元）	Business Volume of Postal and Telecommunications Services　(10000 yuan)	8228	20275	154733	27060	28621
出版图书　（万册）	Books Published　(10000 copies)	65.5	74.9	87.1	88.2	89.8
出版杂志　（万册）	Publishing Magazines　(10000 copies)	16.0	14.4	9.5	9.4	9.4
出版报纸　（万份）	Newspaper Published　(10000 copies)	320.5	287.2	153.7	149.7	139.4
社会消费品零售总额（万元）	Total Retail Sales of Consumer Goods (10000 yuan)	140795	306436	500921	588252	589545
进出口总额　（万美元）	Total Value of Imports and exports　(USD 10000)	6651	13372	21474	29317	31001
出口额	Exports	3401	9072	12453	17363	19565
进口额	Imports	3250	4300	9021	11954	11436
实际利用外资额　（万美元）	Foreign Capital Actually Used　(USD 10000)	1373.8	3731.4	5001.5	5286.9	590.4
国际旅游外汇收入（万美元）	Foreign Exchange Earnings from International Tourism　(USD 10000)	224.7	620.0	75.0	12.4	6.2
每天人口变动和婚姻	**Daily Population Changes and Marriages**					
出　生　（人）	Births　(person)	2074	2126	1574	1348	1201
死　亡　（人）	Deaths　(person)	970	978	1325	1340	1356
结　婚　（对）	Marriages　(couple)	1783	2022	1288	1151	928
离　婚　（对）	Divorces　(couple)	300	496	649	411	392

1—12 长三角国民经济和社会发展主要指标（2022年）
Main Indicators of National Economic and Social Development in Yangtze River Delta （2022）

指　　标	Item	全国总计 National Total	上海市 Shanghai	江苏省 Jiangsu	浙江省 Zhejiang	安徽省 Anhui
总人口（年末）　(万人)	Population at Year-end　(10000 persons)	141175	2475	8515	6577	6127
国内(地区)生产总值　(亿元)	Gross Domestic Product　(100 million yuan)	1210207	44653	122876	77715	45045
第一产业	Primary Industry	88345	97	4959	2325	3514
第二产业	Secondary Industry	483165	11458	55889	33205	18588
第三产业	Tertiary Industry	638698	33097	62028	42185	22943
地方一般公共预算收入(亿元)	General Public Budget Revenue　(100 million yuan)	108819	7608	9259	8039	3589
地方一般公共预算支出(亿元)	General Public Budget Expenditure　(100 million yuan)	225039	9393	14903	12018	8379
社会消费品零售总额　(亿元)	Total Retail Sales of Consumer Goods　(100 million yuan)	439733	16442	42752	30467	21518
货物进出口总额　(亿元)	Total Value of Imports and Exports　(100 million yuan)	420678	41903	54455	46837	7531
出　口	Exports	239654	17134	34816	34325	4764
进　口	Imports	181024	24769	19639	12511	2767
主要农产品产量	Output of Major Farm Products					
粮　食　(万吨)	Grain　(10000 tons)	68652.8	95.6	3769.1	621.0	4100.1
棉　花　(万吨)	Cotton　(10000 tons)	598.0		0.6	0.5	2.6
油　料　(万吨)	Oil-bearing Crops　(10000 tons)	3654.2	0.3	96.3	33.0	173.4
主要工业产品产量	Output of Major Industrial Products					
原　煤　(亿吨)	Coal　(100 million tons)	45.6		0.1		1.1
天然气　(亿立方米)	Natural Gas　(100 million cu.m)	2201.1	19.5	0.8		2.5
水　泥　(万吨)	Cement　(10000 tons)	212951.3	369.6	14235.7	12953.7	14218.7
钢　材　(万吨)	Rolled Steel　(10000 tons)	134033.5	1920.9	14882.2	2934.8	3963.0
汽　车　(万辆)	Motor Vehicles　(10000 sets)	2718.0	302.5	94.4	124.9	174.7
发电量　(亿千瓦小时)	Electricity　(100 million kWh)	88487.1	955.0	6077.3	4349.9	3298.8
铁路营业里程　(公里)	Length of Railways in Operation　(km)	154907		4276.9		5265
公路里程　(万公里)	Length of Highways　(10000 km)	535	1.3	15.8	12.3	23.8
#高速公路　(公里)	Expressway　(km)	177252	851	5087	5290	5477
客运量　(万人)	Passenger Traffic　(10000 persons)	558738	8630	46350	33761	14695
货运量　(万吨)	Freight Traffic　(10000 tons)	5152571	141374	292305	320785	393920
邮政行业业务总量　(亿元)	Total Postal Business　(100 million yuan)	14316.7	1849.9	1022.1	2187.0	436.0
电信业务总量　(亿元)	Total Telecom Service　(100 million yuan)	17497.5	575.4	1375.7	1122.0	608.7
普通高等学校数　(个)	Number of Regular Institutions of Higher Education (unit)	2760	64	168	109	121
本专科在校学生数　(万人)	Graduates of Undergraduates and College Students　(10000 persons)	3659.4	55.5	221.9		155.4
医院数　(个)	Number of Hospitals　(unit)	37000	455	2087	1520	1338
执业(助理)医师　(万人)	Licensed (Assistant) Doctors　(10000 persons)	443.5	8.5	27.9	24.8	18.6
医院床位数　(万张)	Number of Beds of Medical Institutions　(10000 beds)	766.3		44.4	33.9	33.9

1—13 中部6省国民经济和社会发展主要指标（2022年）
Main Indicators of National Economic and Social Development of 6 Middle Provinces (2022)

指 标	Item	山西省 Shanxi	江西省 Jiangxi	河南省 Henan	湖北省 Hubei	湖南省 Hunan	安徽省 Anhui
总人口（年末） (万人)	Population at Year-end (10000 persons)	3481	4528	9872	5844	6604	6127
国内(地区)生产总值 (亿元)	Gross Domestic Product (100 million yuan)	25643	32075	61345	53735	48670	45045
第一产业	Primary Industry	1340	2452	5818	4987	4603	3514
第二产业	Secondary Industry	13841	14360	25465	21241	19183	18588
第三产业	Tertiary Industry	10461	15264	30062	27508	24885	22943
地方一般公共预算收入(亿元)	General Public Budget Revenue (100 million yuan)	3454	2948	4262	3281	3102	3589
地方一般公共预算支出(亿元)	General Public Budget Expenditure (100 million yuan)	5873	7288	10645	8626	9005	8379
社会消费品零售总额 (亿元)	Total Retail Sales of Consumer Goods (100 million yuan)	7563	12853	24407	22165	19051	21518
货物进出口总额 (亿元)	Total Value of Imports and Exports (100 million yuan)	1846	6713	8524	6171	7058	7531
出 口	Exports	1211	5088	5247	4209	5155	4764
进 口	Imports	634	1625	3277	1962	1904	2767
主要农产品产量	Output of Major Farm Products						
粮 食 (万吨)	Grain (10000 tons)	1464.3	2151.9	6789.4	2741.1	3018.0	4100.1
棉 花 (万吨)	Cotton (10000 tons)		2.2	1.4	10.3	8.2	2.6
油 料 (万吨)	Oil-bearing Crops (10000 tons)	15.0	137.5	684.0	374.2	277.0	173.4
主要工业产品产量	Output of Major Industrial Products						
原 煤 (亿吨)	Coal (100 million tons)	13.2		1.0	0.007	0.1	1.1
天然气 (亿立方米)	Natural Gas (100 million cu.m)	132.1		3.9	1.4		2.5
水 泥 (万吨)	Cement (10000 tons)	4844.6	8997.2	11488.4	11056.2	9998.4	14218.7
钢 材 (万吨)	Rolled Steel (10000 tons)	6354.6	3457.0	4158.0	3911.1	3038.3	3963.0
汽 车 (万辆)	Motor Vehicles (10000 sets)	16.5	41.4	55.3	189.6	26.3	174.7
发电量 (亿千瓦小时)	Electricity (100 million kWh)	4298.8	1725.0	3429.8	3108.7	1768.1	3298.8
铁路营业里程 (公里)	Length of Railways in Operation (km)		4822	6332		6078	5265
公路里程 (万公里)	Length of Highways (10000 km)	14.5	21.1	27.7	30.2	24.2	23.8
#高速公路 (公里)	Expressway (km)	5859	6728	8009	7598	7331	5477
客运量 (万人)	Passenger Traffic (10000 persons)	6274	16891	26900	26607	38915	14695
货运量 (万吨)	Freight Traffic (10000 tons)	211540	196932	258700	209480	214266	393920
邮政行业业务总量 (亿元)	Total Postal Business (100 million yuan)	124.9	243.6	567.2	427.6	328.2	436.0
电信业务总量 (亿元)	Total Telecom Service (100 million yuan)	359.8	437.7	1007.7	567.8	666.9	608.7
普通高等学校数 (个)	Number of Regular Institutions of Higher Education (unit)		106			116	121
本专科在校学生数 (万人)	Graduates of Undergraduates and College Students (10000 persons)	94.6	146.4	282.3	177.3	168.5	155.4
医院数 (个)	Number of Hospitals (unit)			2467	1182	1733	1338
执业(助理)医师 (万人)	Licensed (Assistant) Doctors (10000 persons)		11.3	31.2	17.7	19.7	18.6
医院床位数 (万张)	Number of Beds of Medical Institutions (10000 beds)			56.1	32.4	39.9	33.9

1—14 黄山旅游区域主要经济指标（2022年）
Main Economic Indicators of Tourist Region of Mount Huang (2022)

指　标	Item	黄山市市区 Huangshan Region Of City	歙　县 Shexian	休宁县 Xiuning	黟　县 Yixian	祁门县 Qimen
土地面积（平方公里）	Total Land Area (sq.km)	2357	2122	2126	857	2215
年末总人口（万人）	Population at the Year-end (10000 persons)	54.30	35.50	20.70	7.50	14.30
生产总值（万元）	Gross Domestic Product (10000 yuan)	4819985	2373830	1376939	543696	908857
第一产业	Primary Industry	234683	223954	179604	53212	90328
第二产业	Secondary Industry	1644517	886468	555777	182250	283418
第三产业	Tertiary Industry	2940785	1263407	641557	308234	535111
农业总产值（可比价）（万元）	Gross Agricultural Output Value (Constant Price) (10000 yuan)	415148	357416	301229	91032	137298
农业增加值（万元）	Value-added of Agriculture (10000 yuan)	238665	227048	185084	54842	91770
工业增加值（万元）	e-added of Industry (10000 yuan)	1098034	625074	360576	96783	164545
公路通车里程（公里）	Length of Highways (km)	2079	2091	1620	620	1349
邮电业务总量（万元）	Business Volume of Post and Telecommunications (10000 yuan)	79227	30246	18691	8720	13787
全社会固定资产投资增速（%）	Growth Rate of Fixed Assets Investment in the Whole Society %	-5.7	1.7	13.4	13.5	6.6
#500万元以上项目投资增速	Investment Growth Rate of Projects with More than 5 Million Yuan	12.8	6.6	41.0	18.0	11.3
房地产投资额（万元）	Investment in Real Estate Development (10000 yuan)	975374	183603	86773	114606	72016
社会消费品零售总额（万元）	Total Retail Sales of Consumer Goods (10000 yuan)	2702159	1046528	688160	238580	419530
年末职工人数（在岗）（万人）	Number of Staff and Workers at the Year-end (Fully Employed) (10000 persons)	74732.32	18380.31	9270.21	5288.04	7246.02
职工工资总额（在岗）（万元）	Total Wages of Staff and Workers (Fully Employed) (10000 yuan)	704335	183921	96716	49295	71512
一般公共预算收入（不含基金）（万元）	General Public Budget Revenue (Excluding Funds) (10000 yuan)	546813	149180	105178	43969	61959
一般公共预算支出（不含基金）（万元）	General Public Budget Expenditure (Excluding Funds) (10000 yuan)	115282	20010	27403	15911	19328
住户存款（万元）	Household Deposits (10000 yuan)	5308727	3242581	1795503	791661	1401518
农村居民人均可支配收入（元）	Per Capita Disposable Income of Rural Residents (yuan)	21712	21532	21426	21910	21365
接待旅游人数（万人）	Tourists Received (10000 persons)	2887.4	875.9	519.0	1201.1	239.7
#国际游客	International Tourists	0.9	0.2	0.1	0.3	0.02
国内游客	Domestic Tourists	2886.5	875.7	518.9	1200.8	239.7
旅游外汇收入（万美元）	Foreign Exchange Earnings from Tourism (USD 10000)	260.1	44.2	27.5	68.0	0.6

注：1. 农村居民人均可支配收入国家队不汇总市区数据，以全市数据替代。
2. 邮电业务总量按上年不变单价计算。

a) Per capita disposable income of rural residents the national team does not aggregate urban data, instead using citywide data.

b) Total amount of post and telecommunications business is calculated at the constant unit price of the previous year.

1—15 九华山旅游区域主要经济指标（2022年）
Main Economic Indicators of Tourist Region of Mount Jiu Hua (2022)

指 标	Item	池州市市区 Chizhou Region Of City	青阳县 Qingyang	石台县 Shitai	东至县 Dongzhi
年末总人口 （万人）	Population at the Year-end (10000 persons)	66.6	29.0	10.6	53.9
生产总值 （万元）	Gross Domestic Product (10000 yuan)	5935050	1749437	342122	2594592
第一产业	Primary Industry	406269	149047	57059	365878
第二产业	Secondary Industry	3032521	742957	82219	1161457
第三产业	Tertiary Industry	2496260	857433	202844	1067256
农业总产值（现行价） （万元）	Gross Agricultural Output Value (Current Price) (10000 yuan)	695165	251596	100779	676163
农业增加值 （万元）	Value-added of Agriculture (10000 yuan)	419944	154165	58019	395363
工业增加值 （万元）	Value-added of Industry (10000 yuan)	2587220	634251	63109	947301
公路通车里程 （公里）	Length of Highways (km)	3444	1706	1090	3319
全社会固定资产投资增速（%）	Growth Rate of Fixed Assets Investment in the Whole Society	14.3	16.0	22.3	15.4
#500万元以上项目投资增速	Investment Growth Rate of Projects with More than 5 Million Yuan	18.1	16.8	25.7	19.5
社会消费品零售总额 （万元）	Total Retail Sales of Consumer Goods (10000 yuan)	2616815	801692	153672	1019024
一般公共预算收入（不含基金） （万元）	General Public Budget Revenue (Excluding Funds) (10000 yuan)	516932	119093	28987	131913
一般公共预算支出（不含基金） （万元）	General Public Budget Expenditure (Excluding Funds) (10000 yuan)	1105764	283375	155287	425651
城乡居民储蓄存款年末余额 （万元）	Outstanding Amount of Saving Deposits in Urban and Rural Areas at the Year-end (10000 yuan)	5406980	2231468	715801	3193080
农村居民可支配收入 （元）	Rural Residents' Disposable Income (yuan)	21418	21640	14951	20596
接待旅游人数 （人）	Tourists Received (person)	15870111	13210057	8808833	10248668
#国际游客	International Tourists	445	380	220	273
国内游客	Domestic Tourists	15869666	13209677	8808613	10248395
旅游营业收入 （万元）	Income of Tourism (10000 yuan)	1983705	1667883	682945	919019
旅游外汇收入 （万美元）	Foreign Exchange Earnings from Tourism (USD 10000)	11	9	4	6

注：年末总人口为户籍人口。
a) Total population at the end of the year is registered population.

主要统计指标解释

可比价格

指计算各种总量指标所采用的扣除了价格变动因素的价格，可进行不同时期总量指标的对比。按可比价格计算总量指标有两种方法：一种是直接用产品产量乘某一年的不变价格计算；另一种是用价格指数进行缩减。

平均增长速度

我国计算平均增长速度有两种方法：一种是习惯上经常使用的“水平法”，又称几何平均法，是以间隔期最后一年的水平同基期水平对比来计算平均每年增长（或下降）速度；另一种是“累计法”，又称代数平均法或方程法，是以间隔期内各年水平的总和同基期水平对比来计算平均每年增长（或下降）速度。在一般正常情况下，两种方法计算的平均每年增长速度比较接近；但在经济发展不平衡、出现大起大落时，两种方法计算的结果差别较大。

本《年鉴》内所列的平均增长速度，均用“水平法”计算。从某年到某年平均增长速度的年份，均不包括基期年在内。如建国四十三年的平均增长速度是以1949年为基期计算的，则写为1950-1992年平均增长速度，其余类推。

企业（单位）登记注册类型

以市场监管部门登记注册的各类企业为划分对象，以市场监管部门对企业登记注册的类型为依据，将企业登记注册类型分为内资企业、港澳台商投资企业和外商投资企业三大类。内资企业包括国有企业、集体企业、股份合作企业、联营企业、有限责任公司、股份有限公司、私营公司和其他企业；港澳台商投资企业和外商投资企业分别包括合资经营企业、合作经营企业、独资经营企业和股份有限公司。

对不在市场监管部门进行登记注册的行政机关、事业单位和社会团体，主要按其经费来源和管理方式进行划分。

法人单位

指具备以下条件的单位：（一）依法成立，有自己的名称、组织机构和场所，能够独立承担民事责任；（二）独立拥有和使用（或授权使用）资产，承担负债，有权与其他单位签订合同；（三）会计上独立核算，能够编制资产负债表。法人单位包括企业法人、事业单位法人、机关法人、社会团体法人和其他法人。按照下属是否有产业活动单位，又分为单产业法人和多产业法人。

产业活动单位

法人单位所属的产业活动单位，指具备以下条件的单位：（一）在一个场所从事一种或主要从事一种社会经济活动；（二）相对独立组织生产经营或业务活动；（三）能够掌握收入和支出等业务核算资料。

单位数

表中的单位数为单产业法人数和多产业法人所属的产业活动单位数之和。

国有企业

指企业全部资产归国家所有，并按《中华人民共和国企业法人登记管理条例》规定登记注册的非公司制的经济组织。不包括有限责任公司中的国有独资公司。

集体企业

指企业资产归集体所有，并按《中华人民共和国企业法人登记管理条例》规定登记注册的经济组织。

股份合作企业

指以合作制为基础，由企业职工共同出资入股，吸收一定比例的社会资产投资组建，实行自主经营，自负盈亏，共同劳动，民主管理，按劳分配与按股分红相结合的一种集体经济组织。

联营企业

指两个及两个以上相同或不同所有制性质的企业法人或事业单位法人，按自愿、平等、互利的原则，共同投资组成的经济组织。联营企业包括国有联营企业、集体联营企业、国有与集体联营企业和其他联营企业。

有限责任公司

指根据《中华人民共和国公司登记管理条例》规定登记注册，由两个以上、五十个以下的股东共同出资，每个股东以其所认缴的出资额对公司承担有限责任，公司以其全部资产对其债务承担责任的经济组织。有限责任公司包括国有独资公司以及其他有限责任公司。

股份有限公司

指根据《中华人民共和国公司登记管理条例》规定登记注册，其全部注册资本由等额股份构成并通过发行股票筹集资本，股东以其认购的股份对公司承担有限责任，公司以其全部资产对其债务承担责任的经济组织。

私营企业

指由自然人投资设立或由自然人控股，以雇佣劳动为基础的营利性经济组织。包括按照《公司法》《合伙企业法》《私营企业暂行条例》规定登记注册的私营有限责任公司、私营股份有限公司、私营合伙企业和私营独资企业。

其他内资企业

指上述企业之外的其他内资经济组织。

与港澳台商合资经营企业

指港澳台地区投资者与内地企业依照《中华人民共和国外商投资法》及有关法律的规定，按合同规定的比例投资设立、分享利润和分担风险的企业。

与港澳台商合作经营企业

指港澳台地区投资者与内地企业依照《中华人民共和国外商投资法》及有关法律的规定，依照合作合同的约定进行投资或提供条件设立、分配利润和分担风险的企业。

港澳台商独资经营企业

指依照《中华人民共和国外商投资法》及有关法律的规定，在内地由港澳台地区投资者全额投资设立的企业。

港澳台商投资股份有限公司

指根据国家有关规定，经外经贸部依法批准设立，其中港、澳、台商的股本占公司注册资本的比例达 25% 以上的股份有限公司。凡其中港、澳、台商的股本占公司注册资本的比例小于 25%的，属于内资企业中的股份有限公司。

中外合资经营企业

指外国企业或外国人与中国内地企业依照《中华人民共和国外商投资法》及有关法律的规定，按合同规定的比例投资设立、分享利润和分担风险的企业。

中外合作经营企业

指外国企业或外国人与中国内地企业依照《中华人民共和国外商投资法》及有关法律的规定，依照合作合同的约定进行投资或提供条件设立、分配利润和分担风险的企业。

外资企业

指依照《中华人民共和国外商投资法》及有关法律的规定，在中国内地由外国投资者全额投资设立的企业。

外商投资股份有限公司

指根据国家有关规定，经外经贸部依法批准设立，其中外资的股本占公司注册资本的比例达 25% 以上的股份有限公司。凡其中外资股本占公司注册资本的比例小于 25%的，属于内资企业中的股份有限公司。

行政机关、事业单位和社会团体

参照企业登记注册类型，主要按其经费来源和管理方式划分。具体规定如下：

⑴行政机关：包括国家机关和政党机关，原则上均列为“国有”。但有特殊规定的，如供销社等，则列为“集体”。

⑵事业单位：包括经国家机构编制部门和有关业务主管部门批准成立的各类事业单位，不包括实行企业化管理的事业单位。事业单位的划分办法如下：

①由国家财政预算拨款或列入财政预算外资金管理以及经费主要来源于国有主管部门或国有上级单位的事业单位，列为“国有”。

②经费主要来源于集体单位的事业单位，列为“集体”。

③公民个人（或个人合伙）开办的事业单位，列为“私营”。

④上述以外的其他事业单位，如果其经费来源不明确，按管理方式进行归类。

⑶社会团体：包括经民政部门批准成立以及未纳入社会团体管理条例范围的工会、妇联等各类社会团体。社会团体的划分办法如下：

①未纳入民政部社会团体管理条例范围的工会、妇联、共青团、青联、工商联、科协、侨联等社会团体，国家拨款设立的基金会或基金管理组织以及经费主要来源于国有业务主管部门或国有上级单位的社会团体，列为“国有”。

②经费主要来源于集体单位的社会团体，列为“集体”。

③公民个人（或个人合伙）开办的社会团体，划为“私营”。

④上述以外的其他社会团体，如果其经费来源不明确，改按管理方式进行归类。

Explanatory Notes for Major Statistical Indicators

Comparable Prices

Refer to prices that are used to remove the factors of price change in calculating economic aggregates, so as to facilitate comparison of aggregates over time. Two methods are used for calculating economic aggregates at comparable prices: 1.Multiplying the output of products by their constant prices of certain year; 2.Deflation of data at current prices by relevant price index.

Average Annual Growth Rate

Two methods for calculating average annual growth rate are applied in China, one is often called "level approach" or the method of calculating geometric average, which is derived by comparing the level of the last year of the interval with that of the beginning year; the other is called "accumulative approach" or algebraic average or equation method, which is derived by the summation of the actual figure of each year in the interval divided by the figure in the base year.

Usually the results calculated by the two methods are fairly close, but they differed sharply when uneven economic development occurred with striking fluctuations in growth.

The average annual growth rates listed in this statistical yearbook are calculated by level approach except for the growth rate of investment in fixed assets. The base years are not listed when the years are listed for average annual growth rates. For instance, the average annual growth rate of 43 years since 1949 is listed as average annual growth rate of 1950-1992 without listing the base year 1949. And the analogy of this is also the same for the rest of the years.

Registration Status of Enterprises

According to the types of enterprises registered by market supervision departments, the types of enterprises registered by market supervision departments are divided into three categories: domestic enterprises, enterprises invested by Hong Kong, Macao and Taiwan enterprises and enterprises invested by foreign investors. Domestic enterprises include state-owned enterprises, collective enterprises, joint-stock cooperative enterprises, joint ventures, limited liability companies, joint stock limited companies, private companies and other enterprises; Hong Kong, Macao and Taiwan invested enterprises and foreign invested enterprises respectively include joint venture enterprises, cooperative enterprises, sole proprietorship enterprises and joint stock limited companies.

Administrative organs, institutions and social organizations that are not registered with market supervision departments shall be classified mainly according to their sources of funds and modes of management.

State-owned Enterprises

Refer to non-corporation economic units where the entire assets are owned by the state and which have registered in accordance with the Regulation of the People's Republic of China on the Management of Registration of Corporate Enterprises. Excluded from this category are sole state-funded corporations in the limited liability corporations.

Collective-owned Enterprises

Refer to economic units where the assets are owned collectively and which have registered in accordance with the Regulation of the People's Republic of China on the Management of Registration of Corporate Enterprises.

Cooperative Enterprises

refer to a form of collective economic units (enterprises) where capitals come mainly from employees as their shares, with certain proportion of capital from the outside, where production is organized on the basis of independent operation, independent accounting for profits and losses, joint work, democratic management, and a distribution system that integrates remuneration according to work with dividend according to capital share.

Joint Ownership Enterprises

Refer to economic units established by two or more corporate enterprises or corporate institutions of the same or different ownership, through joint investment on the basis of equality, voluntary participation and mutual benefits. They include state joint ownership enterprises, collective joint ownership enterprises, joint state-collective enterprises, other joint ownership enterprises.

Limited Liability Corporations

Refer to economic units established with investment from 2-50 investors and registered in accordance with the Regulation of the People's Republic of China on the Management of Registration of Corporations, each investor bearing limited liability to the corporation depending on its share of investment, and the corporation bearing liability to its debt to the maximum of its total assets. Limited liability corporations include exclusive state-funded limited liability corporations and other limited liability corporations.

Share-holding Corporations Ltd

Refer to economic units registered in accordance with the Regulation of the People's Republic of China on the Management of Registration of Corporations, with total registered capitals divided into equal shares and raised through issuing stocks. Each investor bears limited liability to the corporation depending on the holding of shares, and the corporation bears liability to its debt to the maximum of its total assets.

Private Enterprises

Refer to profit-making economic units invested and established by natural persons, or controlled by natural persons using employed labour. Included in this category are private limited liability corporations, private share-holding corporations Ltd., private partnership enterprises and private-funded enterprises registered in accordance with the Corporation Law, Partnership Enterprises Law and Interim Regulations on Private Enterprises.

Other Domestic-funded Enterprises

Refer to domestic-funded economic units other than those mentioned above.

Joint-venture Enterprises with Funds from Hong Kong, Macao and Taiwan

Refer to enterprises jointly established by investors from Hong Kong, Macao and Taiwan with enterprises in the mainland of China in accordance with the Foreign Investment Law of the People's Republic of China and other relevant laws, where the share of investment, profits and risks is stipulated in the contract.

Cooperative Enterprises with Funds from Hong Kong Macao and Taiwan

Established by investors from Hong Kong, Macao and Taiwan with enterprises in the mainland of China in accordance with the Foreign Investment Law of the People's Republic of China and other relevant laws, where the investment or provision of facilities, and the share of profits and risks is stipulated in the cooperative contract.

Enterprises with Sole (exclusive) Investment from Hong Kong, Macao and Taiwan

Refer to enterprises established in the mainland of China with exclusive investment from investors from Hong Kong, Macao and Taiwan in accordance with the Foreign Investment Law of the People's Republic of China and other relevant laws.

Share-holding Corporations Ltd. with Investment from Hong Kong, Macao and Taiwan

refer to share-holding corporations Ltd. established with the approval from the Ministry of Foreign Trade and Economic Relations in line with relevant state regulations, where the share of investment from Hong Kong, Macao or Taiwan businessmen exceeds 25% of the total registered capital of the corporation. In case the share of investment from Hong Kong, Macao or Taiwan is less than 25% of the total registered capital, the enterprise is to be classified as domestic-funded share-holding corporation Ltd.

Joint-venture Enterprises with Foreign Investment

Refer to enterprises jointly established by foreign enterprises or foreigners with enterprises in the mainland of China in accordance with the Foreign Investment Law of the People's Republic of China and other relevant laws, where the share of investment, profits and risks is stipulated in the contract.

Cooperation Enterprises with Foreign Investment

Refer to enterprises jointly established by foreign enterprises or foreigners with enterprises in the mainland of China in accordance with the Foreign Investment Law of the People's Republic of China and other relevant laws, where the investment or provision of facilities, and the share of profits and risks is stipulated in the cooperative contract.

Enterprises with Sole (exclusive) Foreign Investment

Refer to enterprises established in the mainland of China with exclusive investment from foreign investors in accordance with the Foreign Investment Law of the People's Republic of China and other relevant laws.

Share-holding Corporations Ltd. with Foreign Investment

refer to share-holding corporations Ltd. established with the approval from the Ministry of Foreign Trade and Economic Relations in line with relevant state regulations, where the share of investment from foreign investors exceeds 25% of the total registered capital of the corporation. In case the share of foreign investment is less than 25% of the total registered capital, the enterprise is to be classified as domestic-funded share-holding corporation Ltd.

Government Agencies, Institutions and Social Organizations

are classified into following categories by source of funds and way of management taking reference of the registration status of enterprises:

(1) Government agencies: include state and party agencies, classified in principle as “state-owned”. There are exceptions, such as supply and marketing cooperatives which are classified as “collective”.

(2) Institutions: include institutions of various types established with the approval by organization and staffing departments of the government, but exclude institutions where enterprise management system is introduced. Institutions are further classified as follows:

a) Institutions whose main budget is listed in the government budget appropriations or extra-budget funds, or allocated from the budget of their competent government agencies. Such institutions are classified as “state-owned”.

b) Institutions whose budget mainly comes from collective units. Such institutions are classified as “collective”.

c) Institutions other than those mentioned above whose source of budget are not clear. Such institutions are classified by way of management.

(3) Social organizations: include social organizations established with the approval from the Ministry of Civil Affairs, and organizations that are not covered by social organization management regulations such as trade unions, women's federations etc. Social organizations are further classified as follows:

a) Social organizations that are not covered by social organization management regulations of the Ministry of Civil Affairs such as trade unions, women's federations, communist youth leagues, youth associations, industrial and commerce associations, scientists associations, overseas Chinese associations, etc., foundations and fund management organizations established with funds from the state, and social organizations whose funds mainly come from the budget of their competent government agencies. Such institutions are classified as “state-owned”.

b) Social organizations whose budget mainly comes from collective units. Such institutions are classified as “collective”.

c) Social organizations established by individual or a group of citizens, which are classified as “private”.

d) Social organizations other than those mentioned above whose source of budget are not clear. Such organizations are classified by way of management.

第二篇

Chapter 2

国民经济核算

NATIONAL ACCOUNTS

简要说明

一、本年鉴公布的地区生产总值以及与之有关的指标数据，最后一年数据不是最终数，还会在获得更多的财务和行政记录等资料后发生变动。如果遇到普查或者重大核算方法改革，在能够获得更详细的基础资料的情况下，地区生产总值的历史数据还会发生变动。2018 年，根据全国第四次经济普查结果和国家统计局地区生产总值统一核算要求，对历史年份全省生产总值进行了修订。

二、有关“指数”部分包括“以上年为 100 的指数”和“以 1978 年为 100 的指数”两个方面，“以上年为 100 的指数”表中 2000 年的数据按 1990 年价格计算，2001—2005 年的数据按 2000 年价格计算，2006—2010 年的数据按 2005 年价格计算，2011—2015 年的数据按 2010 年价格计算，2016-2020 年的数据按 2015 年价格计算，2021 年以后的数据按 2020 年价格计算；“以 1978 年为 100 的指数”是以 1978 年为基数，每年指数相乘得到的。

三、人均 GDP 按年平均常住人口测算，2011-2019 年人均 GDP 有关数据为根据第七次人口普查数据修订。

四、本篇资料由省统计局国民经济核算处整理编制。

Brief Introduction

I. Gross regional product and related indicators published in this yearbook are not final and subject to change as additional financial and administrative records become available. Historical GDP figures may change in the event of censuses or major accounting reforms, when more detailed basic information is available. In 2018, the province's Historical GDP was revised in accordance with the results of the fourth National Economic census and the unified calculation requirements of the National Bureau of Statistics on regional GDP.

II. The "index" includes two aspects: "Index 100 in previous year" and "Index 100 in 1978". The data in the table of "Index 100 in previous year" are calculated at 1990 prices, while the data from 2001 to 2005 are calculated at 2000 prices. Data from 2006 to 2010 are calculated at 2005 prices, data from 2011 to 2015 are calculated at 2010 prices, data from 2016 to 2020 are calculated at 2015 prices, and data after 2021 are calculated at 2020 prices. "Index of 100 in 1978" is derived by multiplying the index each year based on 1978.

III. Per capita GDP is calculated based on the annual average resident population. Data on per capita GDP from 2011 to 2019 are revised based on the seventh census data.

Ⅳ. This data is compiled by national economic accounting Department of provincial Bureau of Statistics.

2—1 安徽生产总值
Gross Domestic Product

本表按当年价格计算。 Data in value terms in this table are calculated at current price.

年份 Year	生产总值（亿元）Gross Domestic Product (100 million yuan)	第一产业 Primary Industry	第二产业 Secondary Industry	第三产业 Tertiary Industry	工业 Industry	建筑业 Construction	人均生产总值（元/人）Per Capita GDP (yuan/person)
2000	3125.33	741.77	1062.23	1321.33	841.48	220.75	5147
2005	5675.85	966.50	2197.40	2511.95	1664.58	532.82	9193
2006	6500.31	1011.03	2653.16	2836.11	2031.20	621.96	10630
2007	7941.61	1116.32	3371.80	3453.49	2604.93	766.88	12989
2008	9517.68	1313.08	4194.45	4010.14	3238.44	956.02	15535
2009	10864.68	1382.68	4918.65	4563.35	3743.65	1175.00	17715
2010	13249.78	1600.57	6395.99	5253.23	4949.15	1446.83	21923
2011	16284.92	1867.99	8189.09	6227.83	6424.71	1764.38	27303
2012	18341.67	2018.57	9247.89	7075.22	7279.71	1968.17	30697
2013	20584.04	2173.16	10233.43	8177.44	8045.39	2203.75	34404
2014	22519.65	2294.95	10982.59	9242.11	8595.16	2405.06	37580
2015	23831.18	2376.05	10838.34	10616.78	8360.56	2495.26	39692
2016	26307.70	2489.76	11517.48	12300.46	8909.39	2626.72	43686
2017	29676.22	2582.27	12681.24	14412.71	9739.86	2961.74	49092
2018	34010.91	2638.00	14094.44	17278.47	10639.84	3476.85	56063
2019	36845.49	2915.97	14970.00	18959.52	11181.67	3811.57	60561
2020	38061.51	3184.95	15216.46	19660.10	11235.53	4002.25	62411
2021	42565.17	3363.88	17240.14	21961.14	12790.84	4474.26	69676
2022	45045.02	3513.70	18588.03	22943.30	13791.97	4819.43	73603

注：2022年数据为初步核算数（下同）。

a) The data in 2022 are preliminary accounting data (the same below).

2—2 安徽生产总值构成
Composition of Gross Domestic Product

本表按当年价格计算。（单位：%） Data in value terms in this table are calculated at current price. (%)

年 份 Year	生产总值 Gross Domestic Product	第一产业 Primary Industry	第二产业 Secondary Industry	第三产业 Tertiary Industry	工 业 Industry	建筑业 Construction
2000	100.0	23.7	34.0	42.3	26.9	7.1
2005	100.0	17.0	38.7	44.3	29.3	9.4
2006	100.0	15.6	40.8	43.6	31.2	9.6
2007	100.0	14.0	42.5	43.5	32.8	9.7
2008	100.0	13.8	44.1	42.1	34.0	10.0
2009	100.0	12.7	45.3	42.0	34.5	10.8
2010	100.0	12.1	48.3	39.6	37.4	10.9
2011	100.0	11.5	50.3	38.2	39.5	10.8
2012	100.0	11.0	50.4	38.6	39.7	10.7
2013	100.0	10.6	49.7	39.7	39.1	10.7
2014	100.0	10.2	48.8	41.0	38.2	10.7
2015	100.0	10.0	45.5	44.5	35.1	10.5
2016	100.0	9.5	43.8	46.7	33.9	10.0
2017	100.0	8.7	42.7	48.6	32.8	10.0
2018	100.0	7.8	41.4	50.8	31.3	10.2
2019	100.0	7.9	40.6	51.5	30.3	10.3
2020	100.0	8.4	40.0	51.6	29.5	10.5
2021	100.0	7.9	40.5	51.6	30.1	10.5
2022	100.0	7.8	41.3	50.9	30.6	10.7

2—3 安徽生产总值指数
Indices of Gross Domestic Product

本表按不变价格计算。 （上年为100） The indices in this table are calculated at constant price. (preceding year=100)

年 份 Year	生产总值 Gross Domestic Product	第一产业 Primary Industry	第二产业 Secondary Industry	第三产业 Tertiary Industry	工 业 Industry	建 筑 业 Construction	人 均 生产总值 Per Capita GDP
2000	108.6	101.2	109.5	111.9	108.6	114.2	107.9
2005	111.0	101.7	116.4	110.3	118.9	108.4	111.4
2006	112.6	104.5	118.6	110.5	119.6	115.5	113.7
2007	114.1	103.6	119.2	113.1	121.4	112.1	114.1
2008	112.6	106.2	115.8	111.6	117.4	110.1	112.4
2009	113.1	105.0	116.8	111.9	117.1	115.5	113.0
2010	114.3	104.6	120.1	111.0	121.5	114.9	116.0
2011	113.4	104.0	117.0	111.9	118.8	110.6	114.9
2012	111.2	105.4	112.8	110.9	114.6	106.1	111.0
2013	110.3	103.3	111.9	110.2	112.2	111.4	110.2
2014	109.2	104.6	109.7	109.7	110.1	108.2	109.0
2015	108.7	104.2	108.3	110.3	108.0	109.3	108.5
2016	108.8	102.7	107.9	111.1	108.3	106.3	108.5
2017	108.6	104.1	108.2	110.0	108.2	108.0	108.2
2018	108.0	103.1	108.2	108.8	108.9	105.6	107.6
2019	107.3	103.2	107.5	107.8	107.0	108.9	106.9
2020	103.7	102.2	104.6	103.0	104.3	105.7	103.4
2021	108.2	107.4	107.8	108.7	108.8	105.2	108.1
2022	103.5	104.0	105.1	102.2	104.8	105.6	103.3

2—4 安徽生产总值指数
Indices of Gross Domestic Product

本表按不变价格计算。 (1978=100) The indices in this table are calculated at constant price. (1978=100)

年份 Year	生产总值 Gross Domestic Product	第一产业 Primary Industry	第二产业 Secondary Industry	第三产业 Tertiary Industry	工业 Industry	建筑业 Construction	人均生产总值 Per Capita GDP
2000	885.3	297.4	1257.3	2137.7	1197.7	1724.6	678.9
2005	1450.1	319.5	2287.6	3861.4	2136.3	3359.2	1092.9
2006	1632.8	333.9	2713.1	4266.8	2555.0	3879.9	1242.6
2007	1863.0	345.9	3234.0	4825.8	3101.8	4349.4	1417.8
2008	2097.7	367.3	3745.0	5385.6	3641.5	4788.7	1593.6
2009	2372.5	385.7	4374.2	6026.5	4264.2	5530.9	1800.8
2010	2711.8	403.4	5253.4	6689.4	5181.0	6355.0	2088.9
2011	3075.2	419.5	6146.5	7485.4	6155.0	7028.6	2400.1
2012	3419.6	442.2	6933.3	8301.3	7053.6	7457.3	2664.1
2013	3771.8	456.8	7758.4	9148.0	7914.1	8307.4	2935.8
2014	4118.8	477.8	8511.0	10035.4	8713.4	8988.6	3200.0
2015	4477.1	497.9	9217.4	11069.0	9410.5	9824.5	3472.0
2016	4871.1	511.3	9945.6	12297.7	10191.6	10443.4	3767.1
2017	5290.0	532.3	10761.1	13527.5	11027.3	11278.9	4076.0
2018	5713.2	548.8	11643.5	14717.9	12008.7	11910.5	4385.8
2019	6130.3	566.4	12516.8	15865.9	12849.3	12970.5	4688.4
2020	6357.1	578.9	13092.6	16341.9	13401.8	13709.8	4847.8
2021	6878.4	621.7	14113.8	17763.6	14581.2	14422.7	5240.5
2022	7119.1	646.6	14833.6	18154.4	15281.1	15230.4	5413.4

2—5 三次产业贡献率
Contribution Rate of the Three Industries

本表按不变价格计算。（单位：%） The indices in this table are calculated at constant price. (%)

年　份 Year	生产总值 Gross Domestic Product	第一产业 Primary Industry	第二产业 Secondary Industry	第三产业 Tertiary Industry
2000	100.0	3.0	47.9	49.1
2005	100.0	2.6	53.4	44.0
2006	100.0	6.1	57.1	36.8
2007	100.0	4.0	55.6	40.4
2008	100.0	7.1	53.4	39.5
2009	100.0	5.2	56.1	38.7
2010	100.0	4.1	63.6	32.3
2011	100.0	3.6	61.1	35.3
2012	100.0	5.4	56.7	37.9
2013	100.0	3.4	58.1	38.5
2014	100.0	4.9	54.1	41.0
2015	100.0	4.6	49.1	46.3
2016	100.0	3.1	40.6	56.3
2017	100.0	4.5	42.7	52.8
2018	100.0	3.4	45.8	50.8
2019	100.0	3.8	46.5	49.7
2020	100.0	5.0	57.2	37.8
2021	100.0	8.3	39.8	51.9
2022	100.0	9.6	57.4	33.0

注：产业贡献率指各产业增加值增量与GDP增量之比。

a) Industrial Contributing refers to the proportion of increment of every industrial value-added to increment of GDP.

2—6 三次产业拉动率
Pulling Rate of the Three Industries

本表按不变价格计算。 （单位：百分点） The indices in this table are calculated at constant price. (percentage points)

年 份 Year	生产总值 Gross Domestic Product	第一产业 Primary Industry	第二产业 Secondary Industry	第三产业 Tertiary Industry
2000	8.6	0.3	4.1	4.2
2005	11.0	0.3	5.9	4.8
2006	12.6	0.8	7.2	4.6
2007	14.1	0.6	7.8	5.7
2008	12.6	0.9	6.7	5.0
2009	13.1	0.7	7.3	5.1
2010	14.3	0.6	9.1	4.6
2011	13.4	0.5	8.2	4.7
2012	11.2	0.6	6.4	4.2
2013	10.3	0.3	6.0	4.0
2014	9.2	0.4	5.0	3.8
2015	8.7	0.4	4.3	4.0
2016	8.8	0.3	3.6	4.9
2017	8.6	0.4	3.7	4.5
2018	8.0	0.3	3.6	4.1
2019	7.3	0.3	3.4	3.6
2020	3.7	0.2	2.1	1.4
2021	8.2	0.7	3.3	4.2
2022	3.5	0.3	2.0	1.2

注：产业拉动率指GDP增长速度与各产业贡献率之乘积。

a) The industrial pulling rate to GDP growth refers to the growth rate of GDP multiplying the industrial contributing rate.

2—7　按行业、产业构成分的安徽生产总值（2021年）

According to the Industry and the Industry Method of GDP in Anhui（2021）

本表按当年价格计算。　　Data in this table are calculated at current price.

指　　标	Item	总　量（亿元）Total (100 million yuan)	构　成（%）Composition (%)
安徽生产总值	**Gross Domestic Product**	**42565.17**	**100.0**
按行业分	**Grouped by Sector**		
农、林、牧、渔业	Agriculture, Forestry, Animal Husbandry and Fishery	3548.66	8.3
工　业	Industry	12790.84	30.1
建筑业	Construction	4474.26	10.5
批发和零售业	Wholesale and Retail Trades	4067.76	9.6
交通运输、仓储和邮政业	Transport, Storage and Post	2099.67	4.9
住宿和餐饮业	Hotels and Catering Services	815.61	1.9
信息传输、软件和信息技术服务业	Information Transmission, Software and Information Technology	1009.99	2.4
金融业	Financial Intermediation	2701.92	6.3
房地产业	Real Estate	3144.58	7.4
租赁和商务服务业	Leasing and Business Services	1300.63	3.1
科学研究和技术服务业	Scientific Research and Technical Services	901.57	2.1
水利、环境和公共设施管理业	Management of Water Conservancy, Environment and Public Facilities	252.52	0.6
居民服务、修理和其他服务业	Service to Households, Repair and Other Services	1049.39	2.5
教　育	Education	1731.12	4.1
卫生和社会工作	Health and Social Service	948.11	2.2
文化、体育和娱乐业	Culture, Sports and Entertainment	348.56	0.8
公共管理、社会保障和社会组织	Public Management, Social Security and Social Organization	1379.98	3.2
按产业分	**Grouped by Industry**		
第一产业	Primary Industry	3363.88	7.9
第二产业	Secondary Industry	17240.14	40.5
第三产业	Tertiary Industry	21961.15	51.6

2—8 按行业、产业构成分的安徽生产总值（2022年）
According to the Industry and the Industry Method of GDP in Anhui（2022）

本表按当年价格计算。

Data in value terms in this table are calculated at current price.

指　标	Item	总量（亿元）Total (100 million yuan)	构成（%）Composition (%)
安徽生产总值	**Gross Domestic Product**	**45045.02**	**100.0**
按行业分	**Grouped by Sector**		
农林牧渔业	Agriculture, Forestry, Animal Husbandry and Fishery	3722.28	8.3
工　业	Industry	13791.97	30.6
建筑业	Construction	4819.43	10.7
批发和零售业	Wholesale and Retail Trades	4240.79	9.4
交通运输、仓储和邮政业	Transport, Storage and Post	2171.72	4.8
住宿和餐饮业	Hotels and Catering Services	825.91	1.8
金融业	Financial Intermediation	2935.07	6.5
房地产业	Real Estate	2937.07	6.5
其他服务业	Other Services	9600.78	21.3
按产业分	**Grouped by Industry**		
第一产业	Primary Industry	3513.70	7.8
第二产业	Secondary Industry	18588.03	41.3
第三产业	Tertiary Industry	22943.30	50.9

注：本表为初步核算数。

a) This table is the preliminary accounting data.

2—9 各市生产总值
Gross Domestic Product by Region

本表按当年价格计算。
Data in this table are calculated at current price.

(单位：亿元)
(100 million yuan)

地 区	Region	2010	2012	2013	2014	2015	2016
合 肥 市	Hefei	2976.08	4167.98	4696.01	5250.09	5830.95	6544.26
淮 北 市	Huaibei	492.27	636.15	720.43	770.28	774.64	823.09
亳 州 市	Bozhou	582.63	811.12	931.80	1017.85	1066.93	1200.86
宿 州 市	Suzhou	650.57	914.95	1025.20	1151.32	1235.77	1404.84
蚌 埠 市	Bengbu	672.74	925.72	1099.72	1227.20	1337.70	1501.98
阜 阳 市	Fuyang	924.09	1248.05	1436.67	1584.57	1687.45	1887.35
淮 南 市	Huainan	707.02	893.26	941.57	928.91	917.36	979.46
滁 州 市	Chuzhou	837.80	1212.45	1418.89	1596.45	1812.28	2035.94
六 安 市	Luan	614.12	860.38	944.50	1019.48	1053.43	1190.73
马鞍山市	Maanshan	932.22	1210.54	1273.06	1330.80	1366.11	1448.90
芜 湖 市	Wuhu	1329.42	1844.76	2075.66	2298.79	2366.24	2620.22
宣 城 市	Xuancheng	552.04	795.43	894.39	982.51	1009.66	1101.08
铜 陵 市	Tongling	455.88	629.41	675.38	706.15	720.94	852.26
池 州 市	Chizhou	312.57	433.03	480.07	528.44	569.94	618.17
安 庆 市	Anqing	937.65	1307.67	1379.09	1517.87	1557.40	1684.74
黄 山 市	Huangshan	310.13	425.68	473.77	513.85	540.15	594.39

地 区	Region	2017	2018	2019	2020	2021	2022
合 肥 市	Hefei	7366.64	8605.13	9370.21	10005.56	11392.75	12013.08
淮 北 市	Huaibei	942.91	1009.54	1077.94	1119.07	1223.04	1302.79
亳 州 市	Bozhou	1351.51	1551.33	1740.26	1805.96	1962.68	2101.50
宿 州 市	Suzhou	1573.08	1757.82	1953.03	1969.24	2127.72	2224.59
蚌 埠 市	Bengbu	1690.26	1906.50	2016.02	2018.35	1948.99	2012.28
阜 阳 市	Fuyang	2128.51	2407.34	2686.05	2724.45	3021.50	3233.32
淮 南 市	Huainan	1086.04	1197.10	1283.21	1305.69	1437.05	1541.07
滁 州 市	Chuzhou	2282.01	2594.07	2888.70	2946.84	3342.11	3609.98
六 安 市	Luan	1296.84	1448.48	1616.89	1669.45	1913.49	2004.64
马鞍山市	Maanshan	1671.58	1923.74	2085.64	2102.70	2389.27	2520.96
芜 湖 市	Wuhu	2880.49	3282.96	3586.46	3714.14	4267.64	4502.13
宣 城 市	Xuancheng	1233.84	1418.86	1557.44	1591.36	1798.89	1914.40
铜 陵 市	Tongling	921.36	954.65	950.56	1003.69	1165.59	1209.95
池 州 市	Chizhou	681.33	753.93	830.07	853.10	1004.16	1078.55
安 庆 市	Anqing	1902.12	2196.75	2356.72	2381.45	2611.91	2767.46
黄 山 市	Huangshan	662.71	738.88	816.33	850.37	957.40	1002.33

2—10 各市生产总值指数

Gross Domestic Product Index by Region

本表按不变价格计算。（上年为100） The indices in this table are calculated at constant price. (preceding year=100)

地 区	Region	2010	2012	2013	2014	2015	2016
合肥市	Hefei	116.4	112.4	111.3	109.8	110.3	109.9
淮北市	Huaibei	113.6	112.1	109.1	109.5	104.6	105.0
亳州市	Bozhou	113.4	111.0	109.9	108.0	109.2	108.9
宿州市	Suzhou	112.9	112.5	111.6	109.7	108.9	109.1
蚌埠市	Bengbu	114.1	112.0	111.1	110.1	110.2	109.4
阜阳市	Fuyang	113.6	111.0	110.0	108.9	109.6	109.0
淮南市	Huainan	112.3	111.6	109.4	100.6	103.8	106.6
滁州市	Chuzhou	115.2	112.3	111.2	109.6	110.1	109.3
六安市	Luan	111.5	110.5	108.2	108.0	106.9	107.2
马鞍山市	Maanshan	113.9	111.5	110.6	109.5	108.8	108.8
芜湖市	Wuhu	117.0	112.5	111.7	110.4	110.0	109.7
宣城市	Xuancheng	115.0	112.5	110.7	109.0	108.2	108.7
铜陵市	Tongling	116.1	110.5	111.3	109.7	109.4	109.1
池州市	Chizhou	115.7	111.8	110.2	109.2	108.5	108.1
安庆市	Anqing	112.9	110.9	110.2	109.1	107.3	107.9
黄山市	Huangshan	112.5	110.9	109.5	107.6	106.2	107.8

地 区	Region	2017	2018	2019	2020	2021	2022
合肥市	Hefei	108.5	108.5	107.5	104.3	109.1	103.5
淮北市	Huaibei	107.6	103.6	103.0	103.3	103.4	100.2
亳州市	Bozhou	109.2	110.1	109.3	104.1	108.4	104.2
宿州市	Suzhou	109.1	108.5	108.4	103.6	108.1	103.9
蚌埠市	Bengbu	109.1	108.5	104.7	102.3	97.5	102.0
阜阳市	Fuyang	109.0	109.5	108.8	103.3	108.6	103.9
淮南市	Huainan	106.9	104.3	105.0	102.9	105.4	102.0
滁州市	Chuzhou	109.0	109.1	109.5	103.9	109.8	105.5
六安市	Luan	107.9	107.6	108.3	104.1	110.9	104.2
马鞍山市	Maanshan	108.7	108.2	107.7	103.6	108.7	104.6
芜湖市	Wuhu	108.9	108.4	108.0	103.5	111.4	104.1
宣城市	Xuancheng	108.5	108.3	107.7	103.9	109.7	104.2
铜陵市	Tongling	108.2	103.9	98.1	103.2	107.2	102.9
池州市	Chizhou	105.5	105.7	107.8	103.7	110.2	105.4
安庆市	Anqing	108.2	107.8	106.8	103.5	106.2	102.9
黄山市	Huangshan	107.8	107.7	107.6	102.8	109.1	100.6

2—11 各市第一产业增加值
Added Value of the Primary Industry by Region

本表按当年价格计算。
Data in this table are calculated at current price.

（单位：亿元）
(100 million yuan)

地 区	Region	2010	2012	2013	2014	2015	2016
合肥市	Hefei	172.54	220.71	237.39	246.47	256.53	262.32
淮北市	Huaibei	48.02	49.00	54.21	56.70	57.85	59.85
亳州市	Bozhou	132.70	172.73	184.30	193.61	194.02	204.98
宿州市	Suzhou	173.08	222.18	232.64	245.37	251.69	242.39
蚌埠市	Bengbu	118.84	154.88	167.68	177.07	187.03	198.22
阜阳市	Fuyang	187.24	233.25	251.22	265.05	272.37	286.05
淮南市	Huainan	83.90	94.73	101.58	105.62	108.36	114.69
滁州市	Chuzhou	141.42	181.11	194.08	202.05	207.53	209.75
六安市	Luan	115.92	154.52	162.33	170.82	176.82	185.13
马鞍山市	Maanshan	54.48	68.12	72.66	75.90	78.14	82.24
芜湖市	Wuhu	80.31	102.55	111.41	117.89	119.85	122.86
宣城市	Xuancheng	82.92	104.39	111.44	117.74	121.09	127.33
铜陵市	Tongling	31.97	37.87	40.60	43.26	44.62	45.94
池州市	Chizhou	43.54	59.38	64.27	68.20	70.16	70.68
安庆市	Anqing	124.76	158.10	171.55	179.31	185.75	191.96
黄山市	Huangshan	38.09	46.51	50.55	51.92	53.43	54.50

地 区	Region	2017	2018	2019	2020	2021	2022
合肥市	Hefei	270.07	277.59	291.86	335.21	358.26	379.23
淮北市	Huaibei	65.29	65.29	72.83	81.02	86.32	89.21
亳州市	Bozhou	209.41	210.41	238.19	258.53	271.34	286.55
宿州市	Suzhou	258.45	253.62	287.51	314.94	332.26	338.19
蚌埠市	Bengbu	203.48	207.89	234.32	257.20	275.56	289.46
阜阳市	Fuyang	310.67	310.68	350.43	396.75	417.32	434.21
淮南市	Huainan	119.55	123.46	130.09	143.55	151.08	158.09
滁州市	Chuzhou	217.69	220.73	249.39	274.72	287.99	301.54
六安市	Luan	190.61	196.68	217.08	240.64	255.85	267.84
马鞍山市	Maanshan	85.16	86.85	94.10	100.24	104.50	109.68
芜湖市	Wuhu	126.82	133.03	146.57	162.95	170.13	179.25
宣城市	Xuancheng	130.29	135.40	149.69	163.19	172.05	179.59
铜陵市	Tongling	48.54	50.00	52.73	56.92	59.23	61.86
池州市	Chizhou	72.73	74.95	83.89	89.13	94.25	98.09
安庆市	Anqing	193.29	200.01	216.08	242.20	253.16	262.73
黄山市	Huangshan	56.30	56.90	61.76	67.76	74.60	78.18

2—12 各市第一产业增加值指数
Value Added Index of Primary Industry by Region

本表按不变价格计算。（上年为100） The indices in this table are calculated at constant price. (preceding year=100)

地 区	Region	2010	2012	2013	2014	2015	2016
合肥市	Hefei	103.7	105.0	103.4	104.7	104.4	101.3
淮北市	Huaibei	104.4	104.8	103.5	104.5	104.5	107.9
亳州市	Bozhou	104.6	101.1	102.9	104.1	104.5	96.9
宿州市	Suzhou	106.7	105.2	106.0	106.4	105.9	94.9
蚌埠市	Bengbu	105.1	106.0	103.8	104.9	104.4	104.5
阜阳市	Fuyang	103.3	105.7	103.1	105.0	104.7	107.7
淮南市	Huainan	104.1	104.6	102.9	106.3	105.1	102.0
滁州市	Chuzhou	101.8	103.1	102.0	103.0	102.4	103.1
六安市	Luan	105.5	105.6	101.2	104.6	104.1	104.9
马鞍山市	Maanshan	104.2	105.2	103.5	104.5	104.4	104.9
芜湖市	Wuhu	103.9	105.4	100.7	104.7	102.2	101.5
宣城市	Xuancheng	104.6	105.8	102.7	104.4	104.2	102.6
铜陵市	Tongling	104.8	106.0	103.4	104.6	104.5	106.6
池州市	Chizhou	104.2	106.0	103.4	104.6	104.2	102.7
安庆市	Anqing	104.5	105.4	103.0	104.6	104.0	102.8
黄山市	Huangshan	104.7	105.2	102.9	104.1	103.9	103.5

地 区	Region	2017	2018	2019	2020	2021	2022
合肥市	Hefei	103.7	102.2	101.7	101.2	105.1	103.9
淮北市	Huaibei	103.8	102.0	103.2	100.8	109.6	103.7
亳州市	Bozhou	104.5	103.8	105.6	103.1	109.1	103.8
宿州市	Suzhou	101.0	103.2	103.7	103.1	108.0	104.6
蚌埠市	Bengbu	104.2	103.5	103.6	102.0	106.8	104.3
阜阳市	Fuyang	104.0	103.5	103.7	103.3	108.4	104.0
淮南市	Huainan	104.9	104.7	101.1	101.0	106.9	103.3
滁州市	Chuzhou	102.1	102.4	103.8	101.8	106.7	103.7
六安市	Luan	103.9	102.9	103.4	102.0	108.9	104.5
马鞍山市	Maanshan	103.8	102.8	103.4	101.7	106.7	103.9
芜湖市	Wuhu	104.0	103.1	103.2	102.1	106.4	104.3
宣城市	Xuancheng	104.0	103.1	103.2	102.2	107.0	104.4
铜陵市	Tongling	103.3	103.0	101.9	101.2	106.7	103.8
池州市	Chizhou	103.4	103.3	104.0	101.3	107.6	103.9
安庆市	Anqing	103.7	104.0	102.8	102.1	106.7	103.6
黄山市	Huangshan	103.9	103.6	103.1	102.8	108.2	104.9

2—13 各市第二产业增加值
Added Value of the Secondary Industry by Region

本表按当年价格计算。
Data in this table are calculated at current price.

(单位：亿元)
(100 million yuan)

地 区	Region	2010	2012	2013	2014	2015	2016
合肥市	Hefei	1382.65	1958.06	2156.10	2390.31	2480.46	2719.86
淮北市	Huaibei	239.88	330.80	383.57	404.58	389.56	409.88
亳州市	Bozhou	206.11	307.19	350.18	390.95	413.50	435.10
宿州市	Suzhou	243.55	347.79	399.92	450.74	470.18	515.67
蚌埠市	Bengbu	302.10	444.80	540.15	606.96	601.23	657.17
阜阳市	Fuyang	339.26	480.89	570.33	619.44	640.44	697.24
淮南市	Huainan	406.56	512.79	512.48	458.03	410.64	410.44
滁州市	Chuzhou	388.55	552.16	658.82	744.60	878.64	947.62
六安市	Luan	257.30	350.01	393.51	417.01	410.95	451.73
马鞍山市	Maanshan	588.48	760.11	771.07	767.37	716.66	735.74
芜湖市	Wuhu	801.32	1153.73	1253.88	1334.94	1248.73	1360.96
宣城市	Xuancheng	253.67	404.92	463.63	488.80	498.76	528.58
铜陵市	Tongling	270.47	350.37	367.90	380.17	384.92	419.75
池州市	Chizhou	145.73	209.41	229.51	250.03	262.89	280.38
安庆市	Anqing	424.61	629.10	654.91	737.71	745.09	793.05
黄山市	Huangshan	130.46	185.06	191.18	205.35	202.77	213.33

地 区	Region	2017	2018	2019	2020	2021	2022
合肥市	Hefei	2909.34	3169.98	3341.51	3535.79	4103.56	4394.44
淮北市	Huaibei	460.51	462.27	460.64	463.31	509.93	570.33
亳州市	Bozhou	478.66	554.54	607.84	613.57	664.39	732.65
宿州市	Suzhou	557.77	625.66	683.96	676.59	733.01	771.56
蚌埠市	Bengbu	729.52	810.55	808.61	778.84	647.38	661.76
阜阳市	Fuyang	802.72	923.79	1008.20	990.17	1105.11	1221.26
淮南市	Huainan	450.91	482.51	510.27	505.66	575.43	648.93
滁州市	Chuzhou	1097.78	1268.79	1398.53	1416.45	1633.00	1807.98
六安市	Luan	490.86	524.04	578.30	615.77	736.83	784.88
马鞍山市	Maanshan	855.73	934.73	1002.85	984.39	1159.63	1239.36
芜湖市	Wuhu	1454.69	1581.37	1712.66	1743.67	2012.74	2135.58
宣城市	Xuancheng	583.12	666.47	730.18	745.50	860.49	937.27
铜陵市	Tongling	455.16	477.44	433.40	462.86	579.55	602.80
池州市	Chizhou	304.39	333.11	364.42	371.17	456.68	502.75
安庆市	Anqing	910.03	991.67	1038.19	1019.27	1127.77	1215.23
黄山市	Huangshan	227.54	251.82	279.70	293.42	341.28	355.24

2—14 各市第二产业增加值指数

Value-added Index of Secondary Industry by Region

本表按不变价格计算。 (上年为100) The indices in this table are calculated at constant price. (preceding year=100)

地 区	Region	2010	2012	2013	2014	2015	2016
合 肥 市	Hefei	119.8	112.4	110.6	109.9	109.2	108.2
淮 北 市	Huaibei	118.8	114.4	108.8	111.1	102.1	102.9
亳 州 市	Bozhou	123.2	113.9	111.2	108.5	110.0	109.1
宿 州 市	Suzhou	116.4	113.8	110.7	109.0	108.3	109.3
蚌 埠 市	Bengbu	121.3	115.0	114.6	111.9	110.1	109.4
阜 阳 市	Fuyang	121.2	115.1	113.0	110.8	110.1	111.0
淮 南 市	Huainan	113.7	113.1	108.9	95.5	100.5	107.1
滁 州 市	Chuzhou	123.4	115.4	114.3	110.8	110.3	111.7
六 安 市	Luan	118.0	110.9	111.3	108.4	106.3	106.6
马鞍山市	Maanshan	115.3	111.2	111.4	110.1	108.6	107.9
芜 湖 市	Wuhu	121.4	112.9	110.5	110.4	106.1	109.4
宣 城 市	Xuancheng	121.5	114.6	113.8	110.5	107.8	108.7
铜 陵 市	Tongling	120.8	112.0	112.9	110.7	104.5	109.3
池 州 市	Chizhou	123.1	112.8	112.4	110.3	110.2	108.2
安 庆 市	Anqing	118.4	113.6	110.2	111.4	106.0	108.4
黄 山 市	Huangshan	118.4	112.5	105.5	106.8	104.0	106.8

地 区	Region	2017	2018	2019	2020	2021	2022
合 肥 市	Hefei	107.7	107.7	107.3	106.3	110.4	105.3
淮 北 市	Huaibei	108.6	100.6	97.1	103.4	97.5	99.0
亳 州 市	Bozhou	108.5	111.0	110.2	104.3	107.5	105.8
宿 州 市	Suzhou	109.9	109.1	110.0	104.6	108.5	104.5
蚌 埠 市	Bengbu	109.6	109.1	102.7	102.2	85.9	101.2
阜 阳 市	Fuyang	112.5	112.4	109.9	103.1	107.7	105.0
淮 南 市	Huainan	106.0	103.7	106.3	103.9	103.8	102.3
滁 州 市	Chuzhou	111.6	112.8	111.2	105.2	109.5	107.7
六 安 市	Luan	108.2	108.1	109.0	106.2	112.3	107.2
马鞍山市	Maanshan	108.5	108.6	109.0	104.3	109.7	106.6
芜 湖 市	Wuhu	108.6	108.6	109.0	103.4	111.6	105.3
宣 城 市	Xuancheng	108.7	110.2	109.9	105.3	110.5	106.3
铜 陵 市	Tongling	108.5	105.0	92.3	104.2	108.1	103.8
池 州 市	Chizhou	105.8	107.4	109.5	105.6	111.1	107.5
安 庆 市	Anqing	109.2	107.8	107.4	104.5	104.0	102.5
黄 山 市	Huangshan	107.3	109.5	109.8	104.6	110.1	100.0

2—15 各市第三产业增加值
Value-added of Tertiary Industry by Region

本表按当年价格计算。

Data in this table are calculated at current price.

(单位：亿元)
(100 million yuan)

地 区	Region	2010	2012	2013	2014	2015	2016
合 肥 市	Hefei	1420.89	1989.21	2302.52	2613.31	3093.96	3562.08
淮 北 市	Huaibei	204.36	256.35	282.65	309.01	327.23	353.36
亳 州 市	Bozhou	243.82	331.20	397.32	433.29	459.41	560.78
宿 州 市	Suzhou	233.93	344.98	392.65	455.22	513.90	646.79
蚌 埠 市	Bengbu	251.80	326.04	391.89	443.17	549.44	646.59
阜 阳 市	Fuyang	397.59	533.91	615.12	700.08	774.64	904.06
淮 南 市	Huainan	216.56	285.74	327.51	365.26	398.37	454.34
滁 州 市	Chuzhou	307.83	479.18	565.99	649.80	726.11	878.57
六 安 市	Luan	240.90	355.84	388.65	431.65	465.67	553.88
马鞍山市	Maanshan	289.26	382.31	429.33	487.53	571.31	630.92
芜 湖 市	Wuhu	447.79	588.48	710.37	845.96	997.66	1136.40
宣 城 市	Xuancheng	215.45	286.12	319.32	375.96	389.81	445.17
铜 陵 市	Tongling	153.44	241.16	266.89	282.72	291.39	386.57
池 州 市	Chizhou	123.30	164.24	186.28	210.20	236.88	267.11
安 庆 市	Anqing	388.28	520.48	552.63	600.86	626.56	699.73
黄 山 市	Huangshan	141.58	194.11	232.05	256.58	283.94	326.56

地 区	Region	2017	2018	2019	2020	2021	2022
合 肥 市	Hefei	4187.23	5157.56	5736.84	6134.56	6930.94	7239.40
淮 北 市	Huaibei	417.12	481.97	544.48	574.73	626.80	643.26
亳 州 市	Bozhou	663.44	786.38	894.23	933.85	1026.96	1082.30
宿 州 市	Suzhou	756.86	878.54	981.56	977.72	1062.45	1114.84
蚌 埠 市	Bengbu	757.25	888.06	973.10	982.30	1026.06	1061.07
阜 阳 市	Fuyang	1015.12	1172.88	1327.42	1337.54	1499.08	1577.84
淮 南 市	Huainan	515.59	591.13	642.85	656.48	710.54	734.05
滁 州 市	Chuzhou	966.54	1104.55	1240.78	1255.67	1421.11	1500.46
六 安 市	Luan	615.37	727.75	821.51	813.04	920.82	951.92
马鞍山市	Maanshan	730.69	902.16	988.69	1018.07	1125.14	1171.92
芜 湖 市	Wuhu	1298.98	1568.56	1727.23	1807.51	2084.77	2187.30
宣 城 市	Xuancheng	520.43	616.99	677.57	682.67	766.34	797.53
铜 陵 市	Tongling	417.65	427.21	464.43	483.92	526.80	545.29
池 州 市	Chizhou	304.21	345.86	381.76	392.80	453.24	477.71
安 庆 市	Anqing	798.80	1005.07	1102.45	1119.98	1230.98	1289.50
黄 山 市	Huangshan	378.87	430.16	474.86	489.20	541.52	568.91

2—16 各市第三产业增加值指数
Value-added Index of Tertiary Industry by Region

本表按不变价格计算。（上年为100） The indices in this table are calculated at constant price. (preceding year=100)

地 区	Region	2010	2012	2013	2014	2015	2016
合 肥 市	Hefei	114.5	113.2	112.8	110.2	111.8	112.0
淮 北 市	Huaibei	110.2	111.0	110.8	108.6	107.9	107.2
亳 州 市	Bozhou	110.5	113.6	112.1	109.2	110.5	113.9
宿 州 市	Suzhou	114.4	116.1	115.9	112.2	111.1	115.8
蚌 埠 市	Bengbu	110.0	110.7	109.5	109.7	112.5	111.1
阜 阳 市	Fuyang	112.2	109.6	110.1	108.7	111.0	107.8
淮 南 市	Huainan	112.4	111.4	112.6	108.4	108.9	107.3
滁 州 市	Chuzhou	111.2	111.9	110.2	110.2	112.6	108.3
六 安 市	Luan	107.5	112.1	107.9	108.9	108.5	108.6
马鞍山市	Maanshan	113.0	113.3	110.1	109.0	109.8	110.4
芜 湖 市	Wuhu	113.5	112.8	115.7	111.2	118.1	111.0
宣 城 市	Xuancheng	112.5	112.3	109.5	108.5	109.9	110.8
铜 陵 市	Tongling	109.8	108.7	109.9	108.7	119.9	109.4
池 州 市	Chizhou	112.1	112.5	109.6	109.2	107.5	109.6
安 庆 市	Anqing	110.5	109.4	112.3	107.6	109.7	108.9
黄 山 市	Huangshan	109.8	110.8	115.1	109.1	108.6	109.2

地 区	Region	2017	2018	2019	2020	2021	2022
合 肥 市	Hefei	109.5	109.5	107.9	103.0	108.5	102.4
淮 北 市	Huaibei	107.0	107.5	109.3	103.5	107.3	100.5
亳 州 市	Bozhou	111.5	111.4	109.7	104.2	108.8	103.4
宿 州 市	Suzhou	111.7	109.9	108.6	102.8	108.0	103.3
蚌 埠 市	Bengbu	110.1	109.3	107.1	102.5	104.2	101.8
阜 阳 市	Fuyang	107.7	108.9	109.4	103.6	109.4	103.1
淮 南 市	Huainan	108.2	104.8	104.6	102.3	106.3	101.4
滁 州 市	Chuzhou	107.6	106.1	108.5	102.5	110.7	103.5
六 安 市	Luan	109.1	108.9	109.3	102.8	110.3	101.9
马鞍山市	Maanshan	109.6	108.5	106.6	102.9	107.9	102.7
芜 湖 市	Wuhu	109.7	108.6	107.3	103.7	111.5	103.0
宣 城 市	Xuancheng	109.6	107.4	106.3	102.4	109.5	101.9
铜 陵 市	Tongling	108.6	102.8	105.3	102.2	106.4	102.0
池 州 市	Chizhou	105.8	104.4	106.8	102.1	109.9	103.8
安 庆 市	Anqing	108.3	108.8	107.0	102.6	108.1	103.2
黄 山 市	Huangshan	108.7	107.1	106.8	101.4	108.5	100.3

2—17 各市分产业分行业增加值（2022年）
Value-added by Industry and Sector by Region (2022)

本表绝对数按当年价格计算，指数按不变价格计算。 (单位：亿元)
Absolute numbers in this table are calculated at current prices and indices at constant prices. (100 million yuan)

地区	Region	第一产业 Primary Industry	第二产业 Secondary Industry	第三产业 Tertiary Industry	农林牧渔业 Agriculture, Forestry, Animal Husbandry and Fishery	工业 Industry	建筑业 Construction	批发和零售业 Wholesale, Retail Trade	交通运输、仓储和邮政业 Transport, Storage and Postal Services	住宿和餐饮业 Accommodation and Catering Trade
合肥市	Hefei	379.23	4394.44	7239.40	388.22	2606.50	1791.50	1177.62	558.59	206.90
淮北市	Huaibei	89.21	570.33	643.26	91.81	518.90	51.81	103.71	94.24	19.64
亳州市	Bozhou	286.55	732.65	1082.30	295.94	529.38	203.50	186.58	94.75	43.50
宿州市	Suzhou	338.19	771.56	1114.84	396.04	527.93	243.82	192.93	109.95	47.01
蚌埠市	Bengbu	289.46	661.76	1061.07	299.28	527.57	134.56	159.33	134.87	38.60
阜阳市	Fuyang	434.21	1221.26	1577.84	481.76	978.53	243.05	320.14	175.43	62.76
淮南市	Huainan	158.09	648.93	734.05	162.02	569.06	81.13	148.87	82.10	38.84
滁州市	Chuzhou	301.54	1807.98	1500.46	328.96	1447.04	361.48	269.83	146.86	63.10
六安市	Luan	267.84	784.88	951.92	274.87	552.98	232.11	193.45	102.01	37.16
马鞍山市	Maanshan	109.68	1239.35	1171.92	117.66	989.70	251.05	284.10	76.22	40.46
芜湖市	Wuhu	179.25	2135.58	2187.30	184.01	1677.42	471.13	499.90	208.64	73.53
宣城市	Xuancheng	179.59	937.27	797.53	187.75	724.56	212.90	180.36	97.08	29.88
铜陵市	Tongling	61.86	602.80	545.29	63.64	514.88	88.22	99.22	70.10	24.04
池州市	Chizhou	98.09	502.75	477.71	103.03	423.48	79.51	108.41	48.45	25.13
安庆市	Anqing	262.73	1215.23	1289.50	267.57	963.54	252.78	215.21	124.41	52.04
黄山市	Huangshan	78.18	355.24	568.91	79.74	234.50	120.87	101.12	48.02	23.33

2-17 续表1 continued

地 区 Region		金融业 Banking	房地产业 Real Estate Trade	其他服务业 Other Services	构成(%) Composition 第一产业 Primary Industry	第二产业 Secondary Industry	第三产业 Tertiary Industry	指数 Preceding year=100 生产总值 Gross Domestic Product	第一产业 Primary Industry	第二产业 Secondary Industry	第三产业 Tertiary Industry
合肥市	Hefei	1166.68	1011.71	3105.37	3.2	36.6	60.2	103.5	103.9	105.3	102.4
淮北市	Huaibei	68.06	85.62	269.00	6.8	43.8	49.4	100.2	103.7	99.0	100.5
亳州市	Bozhou	145.78	162.40	439.67	13.6	34.9	51.5	104.2	103.8	105.8	103.4
宿州市	Suzhou	123.56	151.50	431.86	15.2	34.7	50.1	103.9	104.6	104.5	103.3
蚌埠市	Bengbu	123.38	126.21	468.47	14.4	32.9	52.7	102.0	104.3	101.2	101.8
阜阳市	Fuyang	203.88	171.52	596.25	13.4	37.8	48.8	103.9	104.0	105.0	103.1
淮南市	Huainan	105.18	87.46	266.42	10.3	42.1	47.6	102.0	103.3	102.3	101.4
滁州市	Chuzhou	160.98	193.63	638.11	8.3	50.1	41.6	105.5	103.7	107.7	103.5
六安市	Luan	122.59	140.67	348.79	13.4	39.1	47.5	104.2	104.5	107.2	101.9
马鞍山市	Maanshan	100.83	131.61	529.33	4.3	49.2	46.5	104.6	103.9	106.6	102.7
芜湖市	Wuhu	206.02	234.81	946.67	4.0	47.4	48.6	104.1	104.3	105.3	103.0
宣城市	Xuancheng	103.22	77.47	301.18	9.4	48.9	41.7	104.2	104.4	106.3	101.9
铜陵市	Tongling	56.96	59.88	233.01	5.1	49.8	45.1	102.9	103.8	103.8	102.0
池州市	Chizhou	46.11	50.47	193.94	9.1	46.6	44.3	105.4	103.9	107.5	103.8
安庆市	Anqing	141.38	173.88	576.65	9.5	43.9	46.6	102.9	103.6	102.5	103.2
黄山市	Huangshan	60.46	78.22	256.07	7.8	35.4	56.8	100.6	104.9	100.0	100.3

2—18 各市、县生产总值及指数
Gross Domestic Product and Indices by County or City

市、县 County、City		2021年 生产总值（亿元） Gross Domestic Product in 2021 (100 million yuan)	2022年 生产总值（亿元） Gross Domestic Product in 2022 (100 million yuan)	第一产业 Primary Industry	第二产业 Secondary Industry	第三产业 Tertiary Industry	2022年 生产总值指数(%) Indices of Gross Domestic Product in 2022 (2021=100)	第一产业 Primary Industry	第二产业 Secondary Industry	第三产业 Tertiary Industry	2022年 人均生产总值（元/人） Per Capita GDP in 2022 (yuan/person)
合肥市	**Hefei**	**11392.75**	**12013.08**	**379.23**	**4394.44**	**7239.40**	**103.5**	**103.9**	**105.3**	**102.4**	**125798**
巢湖市	Chaohu	571.89	608.01	53.06	237.83	317.12	104.3	104.4	106.1	102.9	83402
长丰县	Changfeng	778.35	823.83	87.26	393.55	343.02	103.7	103.8	113.0	95.4	103496
肥东县	Feidong	814.77	859.39	86.53	294.50	478.37	103.1	103.8	106.9	100.9	95754
肥西县	Feixi	1003.14	1068.36	75.75	449.72	542.89	104.1	104.4	105.5	102.9	108684
庐江县	Lujiang	549.46	601.45	66.32	233.63	301.50	107.8	103.7	119.1	101.6	67579
淮北市	**Huaibei**	**1223.04**	**1302.79**	**89.21**	**570.33**	**643.26**	**100.2**	**103.7**	**99.0**	**100.5**	**66401**
濉溪县	Suixi	540.64	571.18	60.62	291.45	219.11	100.1	103.9	98.1	101.1	61783
亳州市	**Bozhou**	**1962.68**	**2101.50**	**286.55**	**732.65**	**1082.30**	**104.2**	**103.8**	**105.8**	**103.4**	**42258**
涡阳县	Guoyang	412.60	451.69	67.81	166.29	217.59	105.1	103.8	106.8	104.3	38689
蒙城县	Mengcheng	427.72	458.83	70.54	119.27	269.01	104.4	103.9	103.3	105.0	41730
利辛县	Lixin	365.07	386.77	60.70	114.42	211.65	103.5	103.9	104.7	102.8	32791
宿州市	**Suzhou**	**2127.72**	**2224.59**	**338.19**	**771.56**	**1114.84**	**103.9**	**104.6**	**104.5**	**103.3**	**41875**
砀山县	Dangshan	249.40	262.03	45.78	73.75	142.50	104.2	104.3	104.0	104.3	34252
萧　县	Xiaoxian	408.34	431.61	75.66	178.87	177.08	105.1	104.6	106.1	104.4	41421
灵璧县	Lingbi	308.79	324.43	67.52	75.58	181.33	104.8	104.3	104.1	105.3	33292
泗　县	Sixian	282.96	293.24	67.41	81.04	144.78	103.0	104.8	102.1	102.5	38865
蚌埠市	**Bengbu**	**1948.99**	**2012.28**	**289.46**	**661.76**	**1061.07**	**102.0**	**104.3**	**101.2**	**101.8**	**60739**
怀远县	Huaiyuan	345.30	357.25	86.99	70.74	199.51	101.7	104.9	93.3	104.0	38046
五河县	Wuhe	258.33	272.87	76.31	50.01	146.56	104.0	105.1	104.5	103.3	51534
固镇县	Guzhen	291.27	301.73	89.98	92.06	119.69	101.6	103.5	98.3	103.1	60166

注：本表绝对数按当年价格计算，指数按不变价格计算。

a) Absolute numbers in this table are calculated at current prices and indices at constant prices.

2—18 续表1 continued

市、县 County、City		2021年生产总值(亿元) Gross Domestic Product in 2021 (100 million yuan)	2022年生产总值(亿元) Gross Domestic Product in 2022 (100 million yuan)	第一产业 Primary Industry	第二产业 Secondary Industry	第三产业 Tertiary Industry	2022年生产总值指数(%) Indices of Gross Domestic Product in 2022 (2021=100)	第一产业 Primary Industry	第二产业 Secondary Industry	第三产业 Tertiary Industry	2022年人均生产总值(元/人) Per Capita GDP in 2022 (yuan/person)
阜阳市	**Fuyang**	**3021.50**	**3233.32**	**434.21**	**1221.26**	**1577.84**	**103.9**	**104.0**	**105.0**	**103.1**	**39643**
界首市	Jieshou	376.72	411.49	36.20	235.73	139.55	105.6	104.3	106.2	105.0	63896
临泉县	Linquan	428.63	460.27	101.78	113.22	245.27	105.3	104.8	107.2	104.6	27963
太和县	Taihe	499.76	533.63	65.51	218.49	249.62	103.8	103.5	103.3	104.4	38937
阜南县	Funan	308.78	327.05	68.57	95.74	162.74	104.0	103.6	106.1	103.0	27905
颍上县	Yingshang	460.47	505.03	71.96	216.73	216.34	103.5	103.5	103.4	103.5	42227
淮南市	**Huainan**	**1437.05**	**1541.07**	**158.09**	**648.93**	**734.05**	**102.0**	**103.3**	**102.3**	**101.4**	**50802**
凤台县	Fengtai	328.60	348.50	42.60	180.40	125.50	99.1	103.3	96.2	101.3	64892
寿　县	Shouxian	243.35	259.90	61.80	73.50	124.60	105.8	103.4	115.1	102.3	31143
滁州市	**Chuzhou**	**3342.11**	**3609.98**	**301.54**	**1807.98**	**1500.46**	**105.5**	**103.7**	**107.7**	**103.5**	**89800**
天长市	Tianchang	621.96	686.11	44.02	419.03	223.06	107.3	104.4	108.0	106.5	112847
明光市	Mingguang	269.81	288.33	45.60	82.03	160.70	104.8	103.2	106.4	104.5	59145
来安县	Laian	358.01	392.21	29.23	195.56	167.42	106.6	104.5	111.4	101.8	93383
全椒县	Quanjiao	315.88	336.61	31.17	152.65	152.79	104.3	102.7	108.1	101.3	84363
定远县	Dingyuan	357.63	380.09	77.51	122.62	179.95	104.1	104.2	103.6	104.3	56393
凤阳县	Fengyang	457.78	495.38	49.02	222.20	224.16	105.6	103.2	107.0	104.8	77951
六安市	**Luan**	**1913.49**	**2004.64**	**267.84**	**784.88**	**951.92**	**104.2**	**104.5**	**107.2**	**101.9**	**45643**
霍邱县	Huoqiu	274.99	282.38	66.84	88.05	127.49	104.4	104.5	105.8	103.5	29945
舒城县	Shucheng	353.75	375.73	40.78	179.85	155.11	105.2	104.7	107.8	102.6	54101
金寨县	Jinzhai	221.91	236.44	28.52	105.25	102.67	105.7	105.1	108.5	103.1	47814
霍山县	Huoshan	192.72	205.72	23.99	92.01	89.72	106.0	104.9	108.2	104.2	72182
马鞍山市	**Maanshan**	**2389.27**	**2520.96**	**109.68**	**1239.35**	**1171.92**	**104.6**	**103.9**	**106.6**	**102.7**	**116093**
当涂县	Dangtu	513.79	558.65	38.14	286.36	234.14	106.2	103.8	108.6	104.0	134777
含山县	Hanshan	232.82	250.69	25.38	107.52	117.78	107.0	103.8	111.3	104.4	74279
和　县	Hexian	329.74	353.47	31.29	153.97	168.21	106.4	104.1	109.0	104.8	85898
芜湖市	**Wuhu**	**4267.64**	**4502.13**	**179.25**	**2135.58**	**2187.30**	**104.1**	**104.3**	**105.3**	**103.0**	**121630**
无为市	Wuwei	573.26	609.91	63.44	296.65	249.81	105.2	104.5	106.0	104.5	73750

2—18 续表2 continued

市、县 County、City		2021年生产总值(亿元) Gross Domestic Product in 2021 (100 million yuan)	2022年生产总值(亿元) Gross Domestic Product in 2022 (100 million yuan)	第一产业 Primary Industry	第二产业 Secondary Industry	第三产业 Tertiary Industry	2022年生产总值指数(%) Indices of Gross Domestic Product in 2022 (2021=100)	第一产业 Primary Industry	第二产业 Secondary Industry	第三产业 Tertiary Industry	2022年人均生产总值(元/人) Per Capita GDP in 2022 (yuan/person)
南陵县	Nanling	317.22	341.78	40.71	140.69	160.38	106.2	104.5	107.5	105.5	78480
宣城市	**Xuancheng**	**1798.89**	**1914.40**	**179.59**	**937.27**	**797.53**	**104.2**	**104.4**	**106.3**	**101.9**	**76853**
宁国市	Ningguo	419.32	454.28	28.54	269.05	156.69	106.0	104.6	108.4	102.2	116932
广德市	Guangde	375.03	404.29	29.73	202.88	171.69	105.8	104.2	108.2	103.3	80616
郎溪县	Langxi	203.35	214.77	20.97	116.92	76.88	103.8	104.2	105.5	101.1	69058
泾 县	Jingxian	146.45	155.16	22.07	64.92	68.17	104.0	104.8	105.6	102.2	57149
绩溪县	Jixi	99.50	101.57	15.46	45.29	40.83	100.4	104.1	98.5	100.9	74139
旌德县	Jingde	61.33	65.17	9.24	27.42	28.50	104.0	103.9	105.6	102.5	59245
铜陵市	**Tongling**	**1165.59**	**1209.95**	**61.86**	**602.80**	**545.29**	**102.9**	**103.8**	**103.8**	**102.0**	**92823**
枞阳县	Zongyang	188.31	196.66	33.81	55.20	107.65	103.3	103.7	101.3	104.0	42338
池州市	**Chizhou**	**1004.16**	**1078.55**	**98.09**	**502.75**	**477.71**	**105.4**	**103.9**	**107.5**	**103.8**	**81124**
东至县	Dongzhi	240.91	259.46	36.59	116.15	106.73	105.6	103.8	108.9	103.1	65936
石台县	Shitai	31.98	34.21	5.71	8.22	20.28	105.5	104.0	108.3	104.8	43580
青阳县	Qingyang	178.68	191.38	15.17	75.13	101.08	105.4	104.2	107.9	103.9	77955
安庆市	**Anqing**	**2611.91**	**2767.46**	**262.73**	**1215.23**	**1289.50**	**102.9**	**103.6**	**102.5**	**103.2**	**66470**
桐城市	Tongcheng	412.02	452.04	38.32	233.93	179.79	104.5	103.7	104.9	104.2	76294
潜山市	Qianshan	226.21	237.19	32.33	100.70	104.16	103.0	103.9	102.3	103.3	53846
怀宁县	Huaining	325.29	344.93	27.23	179.99	137.71	103.9	103.7	104.7	102.8	69542
太湖县	Taihu	200.81	210.85	34.41	74.99	101.45	103.8	103.7	105.3	102.7	48978
宿松县	Susong	250.03	262.52	55.04	99.47	108.01	103.1	103.2	103.1	103.1	42966
望江县	Wangjiang	198.84	202.49	36.03	79.52	86.95	100.6	103.8	96.6	102.7	43972
岳西县	Yuexi	127.63	132.35	19.17	43.74	69.43	102.1	103.8	99.7	103.1	40975
黄山市	**Huangshan**	**957.40**	**1002.33**	**78.18**	**355.24**	**568.91**	**100.6**	**104.9**	**100.0**	**100.3**	**75505**
歙 县	Shexian	224.84	237.38	22.40	88.65	126.34	102.3	105.0	101.7	102.3	66493
休宁县	Xiuning	130.88	137.69	17.96	55.58	64.16	100.9	105.1	102.8	98.2	66038
黟 县	Yixian	51.06	54.37	5.32	18.23	30.82	102.4	104.0	103.8	101.3	72013
祁门县	Qimen	87.77	90.89	9.03	28.34	53.51	99.7	105.1	97.1	100.1	63118

主要统计指标解释

国内（地区）生产总值（GDP）

指按市场价格计算的一个国家（或地区）所有常住单位在一定时期内生产活动的最终成果。国内（地区）生产总值有三种表现形态，即价值形态、收入形态和产品形态。从价值形态看，它是所有常住单位在一定时期内生产的全部货物和服务价值超过同期投入的全部非固定资产货物和服务价值的差额，即所有常住单位的增加值之和；从收入形态看，它是所有常住单位在一定时期内创造并分配给常住单位和非常住单位的初次收入之和；从产品形态看，它是所有常住单位在一定时期内最终使用的货物和服务价值减去货物和服务进口价值。在实际核算中，国内（地区）生产总值有三种计算方法，即生产法、收入法和支出法。三种方法分别从不同的方面反映国内（地区）生产总值及其构成。

三次产业

三次产业的划分是世界上较为常用的产业结构分类，但各国的划分不尽一致。根据国家统计局2012年制定的三次产业划分规定及相关修订通知：

第一产业是指农、林、牧、渔业（不含农、林、牧、渔专业及辅助性活动）；

第二产业是指采矿业（不含开采专业及辅助性活动），制造业（不含金属制品、机械和设备修理业），电力、热力、燃气及水的生产和供应业，建筑业；

第三产业是指除第一、二产业以外的其他行业。

劳动者报酬

指劳动者因从事生产活动所获得的全部报酬。包括劳动者获得的各种形式的工资、奖金和津贴，既包括货币形式的，也包括实物形式的，还包括劳动者所享受的公费医疗和医药卫生费、上下班交通补贴、单位支付的社会保险费、住房公积金等。

生产税净额

指生产税减生产补贴后的余额。生产税指政府对生产单位从事生产、销售和经营活动以及因从事生产活动使用某些生产要素（如固定资产、土地、劳动力）所征收的各种税、附加费和规费。生产补贴与生产税相反，指政府对生产单位的单方面转移支出，因此视为负生产税，包括政策亏损补贴、价格补贴等。

固定资产折旧

指一定时期内为弥补固定资产损耗按照规定的固定资产折旧率提取的固定资产折旧，或按国民经济核算统一规定的折旧率虚拟计算的固定资产折旧。它反映了固定资产在当期生产中的转移价值。各类企业和企业化管理的事业单位的固定资产折旧是指实际计提的折旧费；不计提折旧的政府机关、非企业化管理的事业单位和居民住房的固定资产折旧是按照统一规定的折旧率和固定资产原值计算的虚拟折旧。原则上，固定资产折旧应按固定资产当期的重置价值计算，但是目前我国尚不具备对全社会固定资产进行重估价的基础，所以暂时只能采用上述办法。

营业盈余

指常住单位创造的增加值扣除劳动者报酬、生产税净额和固定资产折旧后的余额。它相当于企业的营业利润加上生产补贴，但要扣除从利润中开支的工资和福利等。

文化及相关产业

指为社会公众提供文化产品和文化相关产品的生产活动的集合。

文化及相关产业增加值

衡量的是一个地区所有常住单位一定时期内进行文化及相关产业生产活动而创造的增加值。

Explanatory Notes for Major Statistical Indicators

Gross Domestic Product (GDP)

refers to the final products at market prices produced by all resident units in a country (or a region) during a certain period of time. Gross domestic product is expressed in three different perspectives, namely value, income, and products respectively. GDP in its value perspective refers to the total value of all goods and services produced by all resident units during a certain period of time, minus the total value of input of goods and services of the nature of non-fixed assets; in other words, it is the sum of the value-added of all resident units. GDP from the perspective of income includes the primary income created by all resident units and distributed to resident and non-resident units. GDP from the perspective of products refers to the value of all goods and services for final consumption by all resident units minus the net exports of goods and services during a given period of time. In the practice of national accounting, gross domestic product is calculated from three approaches, namely production approach, income approach and expenditure approach, which reflect gross domestic product and its composition from different angles.

Three Strata of Industry

Classification of economic activities into three strata of industry is a common practice in the world, although the grouping varies to some extent form country to country. In China economic activities are categorized into the following three strata of industry:

Primary industry refers to agriculture, forestry, animal husbandry and fishery (excluding professional and auxiliary activities of agriculture, forestry, animal husbandry and fishery);

Secondary industry refers to mining (excluding mining specialized and auxiliary activities), manufacturing (excluding metal products, machinery and equipment repair), production and supply of electricity, heat, gas and water, and construction;

Tertiary industry refers to all other economic activities not included in the primary or secondary industries.

Labourers Remuneration

refers to all remuneration received by workers for engaging in production activities. Including various forms of wages, bonuses and allowances for workers, including both monetary and physical forms, as well as public medical care and medical and health expenses enjoyed by workers, commuting subsidies, social insurance premiums paid by units, housing accumulation funds, etc.

Net Taxes on Production

refers to taxes on production less subsidies on production. The taxes on production refers to the various taxes, extra charges and fees levied on the production units on their production, sale and business activities as well as on the use of some factors of production, such as fixed assets, land and labour in the production activities they are engaged in. In contrast to taxes on production, subsidies on production refer to the unilateral government transfer to the production units and are therefore regarded as negative taxes on production. They include subsidies on the loss due to implementation of government policies, price subsidies, etc.

Depreciation of Fixed Assets

refers to the depreciation of fixed assets in a given period, drawn in accordance with the stipulated depreciation rate for the purpose of compensating the wear-and-tear loss of the fixed assets or the depreciation of fixed assets imputed in accordance with the stipulated unified depreciation rate in the national economic accounting system. It reflects the value of transfer of the fixed assets in the production of the current period. The depreciation of fixed assets in various enterprises and institutions managed as enterprises refers to the depreciation expenses actually drawn. In government agencies and institutions not managed as enterprises which do not draw the depreciation expenses, as well as for the houses of residents, the depreciation of fixed assets is the imputed depreciation, which is calculated in accordance with the stipulated unified depreciation rate.

In principle, the depreciation of fixed assets should be calculated on the basis of the re-purchased value of the fixed assets. However, currently the conditions in China do not facilitate the revaluation of all the fixed assets. Therefore, only the above-mentioned methods can be adopted at present.

Operating Surplus

refers to the balance of the value added created by the resident units after deducting the labourers remuneration, net taxes on production and the depreciation of fixed assets. It is equivalent to the business profit of the enterprises plus subsidies to production, but the wages and welfare expenses paid from the profits should be deducted.

Culture and related industries

refers to the collection of production activities that provide cultural products and cultural related products for the public.

Added value of culture and related industries

it is a measure of the added value created by the cultural and related industrial activities of all resident units in an area during a certain period of time.

第三篇

Chapter 3

人口

POPULATION

简要说明

一、本篇资料反映我省 2022 年及主要年份人口方面的基本情况，包括全省主要人口统计数据，主要指标有：总户数、总人口、家庭户规模、性别比、少年儿童系数、老年系数、老少比、文化程度状况、少年儿童抚养系数、老年抚养系数、总抚养系数、婚姻构成、就业者身份等。

二、本篇资料来源主要有以下两个方面：

1. 家庭户数据、人口性别比、人口受教育程度、抚养系数等资料，根据历年人口抽查调查和人口普查数据整理计算。

2. 历史上七次人口普查资料，根据历次人口普查资料整理。

三、本篇资料均由省统计局人口处整理编制。

Brief Introduction

I. Data in this chapter show the basic conditions of Anhui's population in 2022, including the main data of population statistics of the whole province, such as family size, sex ratio, children ratio, the aged ratio, ratio of the aged to children, educational level, children dependency ratio, the aged dependency ratio, and total dependency ratio.

II. There are two main sources for Data published in this chapter.

1. Materials on Households, sex ratio, educational level and dependency ratio are tabulated according to the data of the population sample survey and census of the past years.

2. Data from seven censuses in history, compiled according to previous censuses.

III. Data in this chapter are prepared by the Population Division, Anhui Statistical Bureau.

3—1 主要年份人口指标
Major Population Indicators in Main Year

年份 Year	户籍人口 Residence Populations 总数（万人）Total (10000 persons)	城镇人口比重（%）Proportion of Urban Populations (%)	常住人口 Permanent Populations 总数（万人）Total (10000 persons)	城镇人口比重（%）Proportion of Urban Populations (%)	出生率（‰）Birth Rate (‰)	死亡率（‰）Death Rate (‰)	自然增长率（‰）Natural Growth Rate (‰)	流向省外半年以上的人数（万人）Floating Out of This Province for More Than Half a Year (10000 persons)
2010	6827	22.71	5957	43.20	12.70	5.95	6.75	1038
2012	6902	22.89	5978	46.30	13.00	6.14	6.86	1157
2013	6929	22.92	5988	47.87	12.88	6.06	6.82	1130
2014	6936	22.69	5997	49.31	12.86	5.89	6.97	1053
2015	6949	27.58	6011	50.97	12.92	5.94	6.98	1045
2016	7027	29.52	6033	52.62	13.02	5.96	7.06	1052
2017	7059	31.07	6057	54.29	14.07	5.90	8.17	1058
2018	7083	32.65	6076	55.65	12.41	5.96	6.45	1048
2019	7119	34.65	6092	57.02	12.03	6.04	5.99	1061
2020			6105	58.33	9.45	7.96	1.49	1152
2021			6113	59.39	8.05	8.00	0.05	1145
2022			6127	60.15	7.16	8.09	-0.93	1126

注：1. 户籍人口为公安户籍统计数，常住人口为人口普查或人口抽样调查年底推算数；
2. 常住人口是指常住本地的人，不包括户籍人口中到省外半年以上的人口，包括外省来我省常住半年以上的人口；
3. 以下各表除加以注明的外，均为常住人口数。

a) Registered population is the number of the public security census, and the resident population is the estimated number at the end of the population census or population sampling survey.

b) Permanent population refers to people inhabit local place, excluding those residence population that going out of this province for more than one year and including the population moving to this province from other province for more than one year.

c) Data in the following tables refer to permanent populations excluding those with notes.

3—2 主要年份人口系数
Ratio of Population in Main Year

单位：%

年份 Year	少年儿童系数 Ratio of Children	老年系数 Aging Coefficient	老少比 Ratio of the Aged to Children	少年儿童抚养系数 Child Support Coefficient	老年抚养系数 The Aged Dependency Ratio	总抚养系数 Dependency Ratio	年龄中位数（岁）Median of Age (year)
2010	17.77	10.23	57.57	24.68	14.21	38.89	36.36
2012	18.35	12.08	65.83	26.37	17.36	43.73	39.79
2013	18.51	12.24	66.15	26.72	17.68	44.40	40.12
2014	18.68	11.71	62.72	26.83	16.83	43.66	39.42
2015	18.21	11.73	64.41	25.99	16.74	42.73	39.68
2016	18.31	12.00	65.54	26.27	17.22	43.49	38.63
2017	18.60	12.38	66.56	26.95	17.94	44.89	39.62
2018	18.85	12.97	68.81	27.65	19.02	46.67	40.08
2019	18.91	13.93	73.66	28.16	20.74	48.90	41.91
2020	19.24	15.01	78.00	29.27	22.83	52.09	40.04
2021	18.65	15.44	82.79	28.30	23.43	51.72	40.24
2022	18.02	15.80	87.68	27.23	23.87	51.10	40.32

注：2010、2020年为普查数据，其余年份为人口变动抽样推算数或调查数（下同）。

a) 2010 and 2020 are census data, and the rest of the years are estimated sampling data or survey data of population change (the same below).

3—3 七次全省人口普查基本情况

Basic Statistics on National Population Census in 1953, 1964, 1982, 1990, 2000, 2010 and 2020

指 标		Item	
总 人 口	**(万人)**	**Total Population**	**(10000 persons)**
男		Male	
女		Female	
育龄妇女 (15—49岁)		Women at Childbearing Age (Age 15-49)	
总 户 数	**(万户)**	**Total Number of Households**	**(10000 household)**
家 庭 户		Family Households	
集 体 户		Non-family Households	
家庭户规模	**(人/户)**	**Average Family Size**	**(person/household)**
各年龄组人口	**(万人)**	**Population by Age**	**(10000 persons)**
0—6岁		Age 0-6	
7—14岁		Age 7-14	
15—64岁		Age 15-64	
65岁以上		Age 65 and Over	
劳动年龄人口		Population Within Working Age	
男60岁、女55岁以上人口		Males Aged 60 and Females Aged 55 and Over	
民族人口	**(万人)**	**Nationality Population**	**(10000 persons)**
汉 族		Han Nationality	
少数民族		Minority Nationalities	
15岁及以上人口	**(万人)**	**Marital Status of Population Aged 15 and Over**	**(10000 persons)**
未 婚		Unmarried	
有 配 偶		Married	
丧 偶		Widowed	
离 婚		Divorced	
每十万人拥有受教育程度人口	**(人)**	**Population with Education Attainment Per 10000 from Population Census**	**(person)**
大专以上		Colleges and Over	
高 中		Senior Secondary School	
初 中		Junior Secondary School	
小 学		Primary School	
文盲人口及文盲率		**Illiterate Population and Illiterate Rate**	
文盲人口	(万人)	Illiterate Population	(10000 persons)
文 盲 率	(%)	Illiterate Rate	(%)
市镇乡人口	**(万人)**	**Population of Cities, Towns and Townships**	**(10000 persons)**
市		City	
镇		Town	
乡		Townships	
人口平均预期寿命	**(岁)**	**Population Life Expectancy**	**(age)**

1953	1964	1982	1990	2000	2010	2020
3066.3	**3124.1**	**4966.6**	**5618.1**	**5900.0**	**5950.0**	**6102.7**
1610.7	1618.2	2576.4	2902.6	3043.8	3024.6	3110.3
1455.7	1506.0	2390.2	2715.5	2856.2	2925.5	2992.4
705.4	741.2	1150.8	1498.8	1576.9	1702.8	1340.2
713.2	**765.2**	**1052.2**	**1337.7**	**1650.5**	**1932.2**	**2288.8**
		1047.1	1332.0	1631.4	1886.2	2191.0
		5.1	5.6	19.2	46.0	97.8
4.3	**4.1**	**4.6**	**4.1**	**3.5**	**3.0**	**2.6**
624.7	542.7	679.9	781.5	515.4	511.7	524.6
481.0	657.6	1115.4	813.4	988.7	545.9	649.6
	1849.6	2968.5	3719.5	3948.0	4284.0	4012.5
	74.2	202.8	303.7	448.0	608.5	915.9
1649.3	1657.6	2615.9	3336.7	3535.1	3725.1	3708.7
		425.7	577.1	761.6	1072.7	1378.8
3052.7	3108.6	4940.4	5585.7	5860.2	5910.5	6059.5
13.6	15.5	26.2	32.4	39.8	39.6	43.3
		3171.3	**4023.2**	**4396.0**	**4892.4**	**4928.4**
		954.6	1112.5	964.2	951.2	842.0
		1959.3	2641.9	3199.9	3582.5	3676.0
		237.2	247.7	177.1	310.3	304.0
		20.2	21.1	54.8	48.4	106.0
	258	408	883	2312	6733	13280
	1010	3977	5037	7653	10840	13294
	3861	14236	19970	32826	38604	33724
	19307	29716	34701	37362	27763	26875
		1900.7	1381.8	602.2	484.4	274.0
		31.8	24.6	10.1	8.1	4.5
112.5	214.7	488.5	692.1	843.5	1218.3	1633.0
153.8	146.7	219.7	310.3	733.2	1339.5	1927.0
2800.1	2762.7	4258.4	4615.7	4323.4	3392.3	2543.0
			70.22	**72.62**	**75.10**	**77.96**

3—4 各市主要年份人口城镇化率
Main Year Rate of Urbanization by Region

单位：%

地 区	Region	2010	2015	2020	2021	2022
总 计	**Total**	**43.20**	**50.97**	**58.33**	**59.39**	**60.15**
合肥市	Hefei	63.00	72.25	82.28	84.04	84.64
淮北市	Huaibei	54.50	59.28	64.16	64.78	64.92
亳州市	Bozhou	29.10	35.94	42.50	43.19	44.05
宿州市	Suzhou	31.40	37.58	43.76	45.03	46.38
蚌埠市	Bengbu	45.00	49.33	55.08	56.90	57.92
阜阳市	Fuyang	31.90	36.48	41.97	42.74	43.47
淮南市	Huainan	54.81	56.86	61.08	61.91	62.05
滁州市	Chuzhou	41.60	51.88	61.84	62.92	63.12
六安市	Luan	35.66	42.65	48.49	49.46	50.50
马鞍山市	Maanshan	58.00	65.77	71.69	72.39	72.90
芜湖市	Wuhu	54.60	64.16	72.31	72.99	73.55
宣城市	Xuancheng	43.30	52.02	60.82	61.75	62.60
铜陵市	Tongling	46.64	58.01	66.17	66.33	66.45
池州市	Chizhou	44.50	53.10	59.68	60.09	60.23
安庆市	Anqing	36.06	48.69	55.52	56.17	56.29
黄山市	Huangshan	41.10	50.61	58.29	59.25	59.38

3—5　各市常住人口出生率、死亡率（2022年）
Resident Population Birth Rate, Mortality by Region (2022)

地　区	Region	出 生 率（‰）Birth Rate（‰）	死 亡 率（‰）Mortality（‰）	自然增长率（‰）Natural Growth Rate（‰）
总　　计	**Total**	**7.16**	**8.09**	**-0.93**
合 肥 市	Hefei	8.97	5.39	3.58
淮 北 市	Huaibei	7.40	7.90	-0.50
亳 州 市	Bozhou	7.30	8.86	-1.56
宿 州 市	Suzhou	8.02	8.94	-0.91
蚌 埠 市	Bengbu	6.55	6.66	-0.11
阜 阳 市	Fuyang	7.95	9.48	-1.52
淮 南 市	Huainan	5.65	8.20	-2.54
滁 州 市	Chuzhou	6.64	8.02	-1.38
六 安 市	Luan	6.14	9.01	-2.87
马鞍山市	Maanshan	6.84	6.90	-0.06
芜 湖 市	Wuhu	6.46	6.88	-0.42
宣 城 市	Xuancheng	6.26	9.47	-3.21
铜 陵 市	Tongling	5.29	9.91	-4.61
池 州 市	Chizhou	6.38	8.60	-2.22
安 庆 市	Anqing	6.07	9.66	-3.59
黄 山 市	Huangshan	5.87	8.75	-2.88

3—6 各市主要人口指标（2022年）
Main Population Indicators by Region (2022)

地 区	Region	常住人口 Permanent Populations 总数（万人）Total (10000 persons)	城镇人口比重（%）Proportion of Urban Populations (%)
总 计	**Total**	**6127.0**	**60.15**
合肥市	Hefei	963.4	84.64
淮北市	Huaibei	195.0	64.92
亳州市	Bozhou	496.0	44.05
宿州市	Suzhou	530.0	46.38
蚌埠市	Bengbu	330.9	57.92
阜阳市	Fuyang	814.1	43.47
淮南市	Huainan	302.7	62.05
滁州市	Chuzhou	405.0	63.12
六安市	Luan	437.9	50.50
马鞍山市	Maanshan	218.6	72.90
芜湖市	Wuhu	373.1	73.55
宣城市	Xuancheng	249.5	62.60
铜陵市	Tongling	130.1	66.45
池州市	Chizhou	132.8	60.23
安庆市	Anqing	415.6	56.29
黄山市	Huangshan	132.3	59.38

3—7 各市主要年份总人口文盲率
Illiteracy Ratio by Region in the Primary Years

单位：%

地区	Region	2000	2005	2010	2015	2020	2021	2022
总计	**Total**	**10.06**	**11.74**	**8.14**	**5.79**	**4.49**	**4.30**	**4.15**
合肥市	Hefei	7.69	8.67	5.28	4.69	3.72	3.59	3.50
淮北市	Huaibei	8.42	7.59	6.54	4.96	5.56	5.11	5.06
亳州市	Bozhou	10.70	14.59	10.76	6.87	6.95	6.85	6.73
宿州市	Suzhou	10.28	11.32	8.64	6.34	2.61	2.36	2.25
蚌埠市	Bengbu	10.60	12.17	6.90	5.38	5.31	5.23	5.16
阜阳市	Fuyang	11.25	13.18	9.25	6.85	5.72	5.50	5.48
淮南市	Huainan	8.32	10.47	6.67	4.95	3.79	3.78	3.77
滁州市	Chuzhou	10.77	13.14	9.07	5.98	2.65	2.35	2.10
六安市	Luan	9.75	12.67	7.92	5.82	2.83	2.60	2.46
马鞍山市	Maanshan	8.87	7.94	5.24	5.02	5.43	5.11	4.91
芜湖市	Wuhu	10.81	10.45	5.87	5.23	4.92	4.79	4.54
宣城市	Xuancheng	8.88	14.47	9.46	5.85	5.20	4.89	4.60
铜陵市	Tongling	10.76	7.20	6.88	7.14	8.24	7.88	7.58
池州市	Chizhou	11.29	11.21	8.53	5.84	7.43	7.36	7.18
安庆市	Anqing	11.84	11.80	8.80	4.97	2.71	2.67	2.60
黄山市	Huangshan	8.35	8.26	6.25	3.92	4.42	4.14	3.95

3—8 各市人均受教育年限
Average Number of Years of Education by Region

单位：年（year）

地 区	Region	2021年人均受教育年限 The average number of years of Education in 2021			2022年人均受教育年限 The average number of years of Education in 2022		
		合 计 Total	男 Male	女 Female	合 计 Total	男 Male	女 Female
总 计	**Total**	**9.51**	**10.06**	**8.95**	**9.63**	**10.16**	**9.09**
合肥市	Hefei	11.02	11.51	10.52	11.02	11.53	10.50
淮北市	Huaibei	9.58	10.14	9.03	9.76	10.42	9.07
亳州市	Bozhou	8.52	9.21	7.82	8.70	9.28	8.14
宿州市	Suzhou	9.71	10.15	9.28	9.82	10.18	9.49
蚌埠市	Bengbu	9.36	9.83	8.90	9.46	9.92	9.01
阜阳市	Fuyang	8.66	9.21	8.12	8.86	9.38	8.37
淮南市	Huainan	9.23	9.68	8.79	9.24	9.75	8.73
滁州市	Chuzhou	10.01	10.52	9.47	10.25	10.68	9.80
六安市	Luan	9.16	9.71	8.61	9.21	9.75	8.64
马鞍山市	Maanshan	9.36	9.94	8.76	9.59	10.24	8.89
芜湖市	Wuhu	9.70	10.27	9.10	9.90	10.46	9.29
宣城市	Xuancheng	8.98	9.47	8.47	9.18	9.55	8.79
铜陵市	Tongling	9.02	9.84	8.22	9.29	10.02	8.57
池州市	Chizhou	8.75	9.54	7.97	8.97	9.63	8.32
安庆市	Anqing	9.30	9.93	8.68	9.38	10.06	8.70
黄山市	Huangshan	9.32	9.80	8.82	9.33	9.87	8.77

3—9　按年龄和性别分人口数（2022年）
Population by Age and Sex (2022)

年　龄 Age	人口数（人） Population (person)			占总人口比重（%） Percentage to Total Population (%)			性别比（女=100） Sex Ratio (female=100)
	合计 Total	男 Male	女 Female	合计 Total	男 Male	女 Female	
总　计 Total	**694637**	**354512**	**340125**	**100.00**	**51.04**	**48.96**	**104.23**
0—4	32030	17432	14598	4.61	54.42	45.58	119.41
5—9	47614	25768	21846	6.85	54.12	45.88	117.95
10—14	45530	24737	20793	6.55	54.33	45.67	118.97
15—19	43429	23346	20083	6.25	53.76	46.24	116.25
20—24	30073	15473	14600	4.33	51.45	48.55	105.98
25—29	39144	20039	19105	5.64	51.19	48.81	104.89
30—34	53133	26406	26728	7.65	49.70	50.30	98.79
35—39	40580	19990	20590	5.84	49.26	50.74	97.09
40—44	41883	21016	20867	6.03	50.18	49.82	100.72
45—49	52481	26361	26120	7.56	50.23	49.77	100.92
50—54	69074	34019	35055	9.94	49.25	50.75	97.04
55—59	61798	31146	30652	8.90	50.40	49.60	101.61
60—64	28133	15154	12979	4.05	53.86	46.14	116.76
65+	109753	53663	56089	15.80	48.89	51.11	95.68

注：本表常住人口数为2022年人口变动抽样调查实际调查数。

a) Data is from the annual national sample survey of population in 2022 。

3—10 各市家庭户规模和常住人口性别比（2022年）
Household Size and Sex Ratio of Permanent Residents by Region (2022)

地 区	Region	家庭户规模（人/户）Size of Family Household (person/household)	人口性别比（女=100）Sex Ratio (female=100)
总 计	**Total**	**2.72**	**104.23**
合肥市	Hefei	2.65	105.87
淮北市	Huaibei	2.76	100.64
亳州市	Bozhou	2.77	105.16
宿州市	Suzhou	2.83	102.94
蚌埠市	Bengbu	2.80	103.07
阜阳市	Fuyang	2.94	103.31
淮南市	Huainan	2.60	104.38
滁州市	Chuzhou	2.77	105.71
六安市	Luan	2.69	106.38
马鞍山市	Maanshan	2.62	105.21
芜湖市	Wuhu	2.71	106.08
宣城市	Xuancheng	2.46	105.21
铜陵市	Tongling	2.59	99.44
池州市	Chizhou	2.53	100.25
安庆市	Anqing	2.77	102.30
黄山市	Huangshan	2.66	102.67

3—11　各市人口年龄结构（2022年）
Age Composition of Population by Region (2022)

单位：%

地　区	Region	总人口（万人）Total Population (10000 persons)	年龄构成 Proportion to Total Populations 0—14岁 Age 0-14	15—64岁 Age 15-64	15—59岁 Age 15-59	65岁及以上 Age 65 and Over	抚养比 Dependency Ratio 总抚养比 Gross Dependency Ratio	少儿抚养比 Children Dependency Ratio	老年抚养比 The Aged Dependency Ratio
总　计	**Total**	**6127.0**	**18.02**	**66.18**	**62.13**	**15.80**	**51.10**	**27.23**	**23.87**
合肥市	Hefei	963.4	16.34	70.92	67.92	12.74	41.00	23.04	17.96
淮北市	Huaibei	195.0	19.63	66.42	62.70	13.95	50.56	29.55	21.01
亳州市	Bozhou	496.0	23.69	61.90	57.78	14.42	61.55	38.26	23.29
宿州市	Suzhou	530.0	22.21	62.29	58.36	15.50	60.54	35.66	24.88
蚌埠市	Bengbu	330.9	20.32	64.51	60.49	15.17	55.03	31.51	23.52
阜阳市	Fuyang	814.1	22.56	63.11	59.19	14.32	58.44	35.74	22.70
淮南市	Huainan	302.7	17.88	64.50	59.57	17.62	55.04	27.72	27.32
滁州市	Chuzhou	405.0	15.48	67.70	63.75	16.82	47.71	22.87	24.84
六安市	Luan	437.9	16.50	65.77	61.18	17.74	52.05	25.09	26.97
马鞍山市	Maanshan	218.6	13.62	67.96	64.14	18.42	47.14	20.04	27.10
芜湖市	Wuhu	373.1	13.75	69.36	65.60	16.89	44.17	19.82	24.34
宣城市	Xuancheng	249.5	12.97	67.88	63.53	19.15	47.33	19.11	28.21
铜陵市	Tongling	130.1	13.62	67.72	62.47	18.66	47.66	20.11	27.55
池州市	Chizhou	132.8	14.43	67.35	61.48	18.22	48.47	21.42	27.05
安庆市	Anqing	415.6	15.59	66.74	62.10	17.67	49.83	23.36	26.47
黄山市	Huangshan	132.3	13.64	67.01	61.47	19.35	49.22	20.35	28.88

3—12 各市按性别分的15岁及以上文盲人口（2022年）
Illiterate Population Aged 15 and Over by Sex and Region (2022)

地 区	Region	15岁及以上人口（人）Population Aged 15 and Over (person)	男 Male	女 Female	文盲人口（人）Illiterate Population (person)	男 Male	女 Female	文盲人口占15岁及以上人口的比重 Percentage of Illiterate Population to Total Aged 15 and Over (%)	男 Male	女 Female
总 计	**Total**	**574042**	**283922**	**290120**	**33587**	**8343**	**25244**	**5.85**	**2.94**	**8.70**
合肥市	Hefei	56401	28213	28188	2996	745	2250	5.31	2.64	7.98
淮北市	Huaibei	19908	10030	9878	1579	399	1180	7.93	3.98	11.94
亳州市	Bozhou	28658	13894	14765	3001	744	2257	10.47	5.36	15.29
宿州市	Suzhou	37374	17539	19835	1396	324	1072	3.74	1.85	5.40
蚌埠市	Bengbu	35436	17438	17998	2927	859	2068	8.26	4.93	11.49
阜阳市	Fuyang	55789	26507	29282	5411	1311	4101	9.70	4.95	14.00
淮南市	Huainan	32079	15872	16207	2183	683	1500	6.81	4.31	9.25
滁州市	Chuzhou	43448	21755	21694	727	165	562	1.67	0.76	2.59
六安市	Luan	39678	19994	19684	1399	370	1029	3.53	1.85	5.23
马鞍山市	Maanshan	28388	14444	13944	1628	361	1266	5.73	2.50	9.08
芜湖市	Wuhu	42843	21973	20870	2045	536	1509	4.77	2.44	7.23
宣城市	Xuancheng	32640	16464	16175	1427	380	1047	4.37	2.31	6.47
铜陵市	Tongling	19925	9504	10421	1562	374	1188	7.84	3.94	11.40
池州市	Chizhou	16618	8175	8443	1489	403	1086	8.96	4.93	12.86
安庆市	Anqing	56162	27762	28400	2480	453	2027	4.42	1.63	7.14
黄山市	Huangshan	28696	14360	14336	1338	235	1103	4.66	1.63	7.70

3—13 各市每十万人口拥有受教育程度人口（2022年）

Population by Educational Level and Region Per 100 Thousand Persons (2022)

单位：人（person）

地区 Region	大专及以上 College and Higher Level	高中和中专 Senior Secondary School	初中 Junior Secondary School	小学 Primary School
总计 Total	**14220**	**13911**	**32957**	**27151**
合肥市 Hefei	27439	15175	26042	19940
淮北市 Huaibei	13283	12844	37237	22733
亳州市 Bozhou	7414	10363	37047	30290
宿州市 Suzhou	9784	17248	36054	26082
蚌埠市 Bengbu	12171	12524	34668	27195
阜阳市 Fuyang	7729	10294	38432	29281
淮南市 Huainan	11980	12138	36435	27729
滁州市 Chuzhou	14158	19509	33063	23912
六安市 Luan	10408	13660	33110	32549
马鞍山市 Maanshan	15955	13369	31756	27017
芜湖市 Wuhu	18507	14032	29043	26895
宣城市 Xuancheng	12075	12707	33934	29976
铜陵市 Tongling	16422	14046	28012	26326
池州市 Chizhou	14191	11464	29422	30358
安庆市 Anqing	13550	13472	30797	31559
黄山市 Huangshan	13445	12343	35663	27988

3—14 各市婚姻人口构成（2022年）
Composition of Marriage Status by Region (2022)

单位：%

地 区	Region	未 婚 Never Married	有配偶 With Spouses	离 婚 Divorced	丧 偶 Widowed
总 计	**Total**	**16.83**	**74.66**	**2.22**	**6.29**
合肥市	Hefei	20.53	73.47	1.79	4.21
淮北市	Huaibei	18.05	74.36	2.33	5.26
亳州市	Bozhou	16.82	74.94	1.89	6.35
宿州市	Suzhou	15.93	75.86	1.76	6.45
蚌埠市	Bengbu	17.18	74.36	2.55	5.91
阜阳市	Fuyang	20.08	72.07	1.67	6.17
淮南市	Huainan	14.76	75.53	2.89	6.82
滁州市	Chuzhou	14.57	77.44	2.22	5.78
六安市	Luan	15.71	75.80	1.58	6.91
马鞍山市	Maanshan	15.32	75.84	2.84	6.00
芜湖市	Wuhu	19.23	71.91	2.91	5.95
宣城市	Xuancheng	12.47	76.83	3.58	7.11
铜陵市	Tongling	14.99	75.49	2.15	7.37
池州市	Chizhou	12.78	77.32	2.10	7.81
安庆市	Anqing	16.11	75.00	1.65	7.24
黄山市	Huangshan	14.07	75.74	2.80	7.40

3—15　全省育龄妇女分年龄孩次的生育率（2022年）
Fertility Rate of Women At Childbearing Age by Age and Children's Order (2022)

单位：‰

年　龄 Age	生育率 Fertility-rate	第一孩生育率 The First Child	第二孩生育率 The Second Child	第三孩及以上生育率 The Third Child and Over
总　计 Total	**29.48**	**13.42**	**12.94**	**2.97**
15-19	**2.49**	**2.32**	**0.21**	
20-24	**38.06**	**27.81**	**9.09**	**1.12**
20	14.47	11.46	3.10	
21	26.49	20.67	5.56	0.33
22	36.01	26.36	8.06	1.67
23	47.98	33.13	12.78	1.94
24	72.46	52.83	17.27	2.18
25-29	**87.31**	**49.27**	**32.06**	**5.75**
25	71.08	44.93	21.96	4.31
26	92.35	58.11	29.78	4.53
27	93.62	52.69	35.44	5.37
28	96.84	52.91	35.41	7.95
29	81.17	39.97	34.86	6.03
30-34	**58.90**	**19.90**	**31.45**	**7.19**
30	76.50	32.85	34.90	8.33
31	64.15	24.15	32.65	7.28
32	59.26	19.00	33.12	6.97
33	53.36	13.99	30.58	8.27
34	41.15	10.03	25.57	5.03
35-39	**23.26**	**4.68**	**13.80**	**4.40**
40-44	**5.57**	**0.89**	**2.93**	**1.54**
45-49	**0.26**	**0.10**	**0.11**	**0.07**

3—16 各市外出半年以上人口比重、性别比及流向（2022年）

Proportion, Sexual Distinction and Floating Direction of Persons Going Out for More Than Half a Year by Region (2022)

地 区 Region	外出人口性别比(女=100) Sexual Distinction of Persons Going Out (Female=100)	外出流向构成(%) Composition of Floating Directions(%)			
		本县其他乡镇街道 Other Township Streets in This County	本市其他县 区 Other Counties or Districts in This City	本省其他市 Other Cities in This Province	外 省 Other Provinces
总 计 Total	**125.10**	**22.31**	**6.62**	**14.10**	**56.97**
合肥市 Hefei	114.47	39.66	24.27	8.38	27.69
淮北市 Huaibei	131.49	18.97	4.68	13.13	63.22
亳州市 Bozhou	126.43	19.67	2.29	15.82	62.22
宿州市 Suzhou	122.89	28.43	3.25	11.75	56.58
蚌埠市 Bengbu	133.42	18.43	4.97	11.78	64.82
阜阳市 Fuyang	121.13	18.47	6.94	10.73	63.86
淮南市 Huainan	135.16	18.48	5.27	18.76	57.49
滁州市 Chuzhou	119.94	26.07	8.33	14.62	50.98
六安市 Luan	123.01	18.14	5.34	20.54	56.00
马鞍山市 Maanshan	126.46	25.41	7.92	12.17	54.50
芜湖市 Wuhu	114.30	25.74	9.15	15.40	49.71
宣城市 Xuancheng	112.29	36.91	8.08	10.02	44.99
铜陵市 Tongling	120.43	19.44	6.05	21.95	52.56
池州市 Chizhou	123.69	21.38	4.77	17.75	56.09
安庆市 Anqing	119.68	23.47	7.15	15.92	53.46
黄山市 Huangshan	126.07	24.73	7.99	13.83	53.45

3—17 各市流向省外半年以上的流动人口构成（2022年）

Composition of Persons Floating Out of the Province for More Than Half a Year by Region (2022)

单位：%

地 区	Region	合计(人) Total (person)	江苏 Jiangsu	浙江 Zhejiang	上海 Shanghai	广东 Guangdong	北京 Beijing	福建 Fujian	山东 Shandong
总 计	**Total**	**104974**	**29.48**	**30.08**	**16.60**	**5.07**	**2.58**	**2.34**	**2.09**
合肥市	Hefei	2571	33.96	17.97	22.60	3.70	4.32	1.91	1.59
淮北市	Huaibei	2379	33.00	27.15	15.22	3.83	1.98	2.40	2.61
亳州市	Bozhou	10807	29.44	36.38	13.32	5.65	1.12	2.74	1.69
宿州市	Suzhou	10433	41.92	30.57	11.03	2.91	1.68	1.26	2.14
蚌埠市	Bengbu	6111	32.89	33.78	18.10	3.91	1.05	2.62	1.52
阜阳市	Fuyang	17867	17.94	38.74	13.24	8.18	3.08	2.56	2.75
淮南市	Huainan	4530	29.80	16.67	36.75	3.66	1.48	2.78	0.93
滁州市	Chuzhou	5278	51.21	19.69	17.45	2.52	1.02	0.81	1.10
六安市	Luan	7212	44.43	19.88	22.19	3.23	1.18	0.71	1.12
马鞍山市	Maanshan	3917	47.54	12.00	10.54	4.29	7.28	1.12	3.24
芜湖市	Wuhu	3078	25.50	10.53	25.89	3.87	11.60	1.53	3.41
宣城市	Xuancheng	4987	22.90	33.37	28.33	2.33	1.08	1.02	0.82
铜陵市	Tongling	4015	49.99	15.44	14.62	2.37	2.19	1.12	0.87
池州市	Chizhou	3888	22.63	33.87	16.18	6.25	5.45	1.67	2.70
安庆市	Anqing	12712	14.72	29.74	13.16	8.36	3.00	5.95	3.33
黄山市	Huangshan	5190	13.72	57.03	13.85	3.60	1.08	1.52	1.68

地 区	Region	天津 Tianjin	河南 Henan	河北 Hebei	新疆 Xinjiang	辽宁 Liaoning	湖北 Hubei	陕西 Shaanxi	流向其他省市 Floating to Other Provinces or Cities
总 计	**Total**	**1.03**	**1.26**	**0.92**	**0.51**	**0.76**	**1.17**	**0.73**	**5.37**
合肥市	Hefei	0.75	1.44	1.56	0.78	1.01	1.79	0.86	5.79
淮北市	Huaibei	0.87	2.98	1.01	0.55	0.34	1.05	0.80	6.23
亳州市	Bozhou	1.44	0.86	0.79	0.65	0.63	0.68	0.33	4.26
宿州市	Suzhou	0.48	1.32	0.75	0.70	0.16	0.85	1.19	3.05
蚌埠市	Bengbu	0.48	0.62	0.31	0.31	0.16	0.61	0.49	3.15
阜阳市	Fuyang	2.34	1.65	1.49	1.15	0.47	0.98	0.73	4.71
淮南市	Huainan	0.49	1.06	0.82	0.44	0.18	0.88	0.38	3.68
滁州市	Chuzhou	0.18	0.51	0.23	0.30	0.42	0.74	0.51	3.31
六安市	Luan	0.55	1.21	0.62	0.15	0.18	1.26	0.35	2.94
马鞍山市	Maanshan	0.34	1.25	1.79	0.28	0.38	1.23	0.59	8.13
芜湖市	Wuhu	1.83	1.33	1.95	0.42	1.01	1.75	1.17	8.21
宣城市	Xuancheng	0.51	0.34	0.54	0.16	0.42	1.20	0.72	6.25
铜陵市	Tongling	0.32	0.77	0.47	0.15	0.85	1.37	0.40	9.07
池州市	Chizhou	0.55	0.44	0.64	0.13	0.67	1.31	1.03	6.47
安庆市	Anqing	1.44	2.38	1.16	0.26	3.19	2.20	1.35	9.76
黄山市	Huangshan	0.19	0.62	0.31	0.19	0.25	1.21	0.29	4.46

3—18 全省外出半年以上人口分年龄构成（2022年）
Composition of Population Going out More Than Half a Year in the Whole Province (2022)

单位：%

年龄 Age	合计 Total	男 Male	女 Female	性别比 (女=100) Sex Ratio (Female=100)
总计 Total	**100.00**	**55.86**	**44.14**	**126.54**
0-4	**3.10**	**1.65**	**1.46**	**113.17**
5-9	**4.77**	**2.66**	**2.10**	**126.59**
10-14	**4.46**	**2.50**	**1.96**	**127.36**
15-19	**7.32**	**4.12**	**3.20**	**128.62**
15	1.06	0.58	0.48	121.03
16	1.38	0.78	0.59	131.95
17	1.48	0.83	0.65	127.72
18	1.64	0.93	0.71	130.49
19	1.76	0.99	0.76	129.80
20-24	**9.00**	**5.02**	**3.98**	**125.93**
20	1.80	1.01	0.80	126.70
21	1.75	0.98	0.78	125.89
22	1.85	1.05	0.80	131.56
23	1.67	0.93	0.74	126.23
24	1.93	1.05	0.88	119.87
25-29	**11.48**	**6.34**	**5.14**	**123.33**
25	1.97	1.09	0.88	124.23
26	2.08	1.15	0.92	125.00
27	2.45	1.32	1.12	117.66
28	2.41	1.31	1.09	120.05
29	2.59	1.46	1.12	130.17
30-34	**14.72**	**8.18**	**6.55**	**124.97**
30	2.64	1.47	1.18	124.38
31	2.90	1.62	1.28	126.74
32	3.46	1.94	1.52	127.36
33	3.07	1.70	1.37	124.33
34	2.65	1.45	1.20	121.39
35-39	**9.98**	**5.65**	**4.33**	**130.71**
35	2.54	1.45	1.09	132.72
36	2.11	1.19	0.92	129.53
37	1.86	1.04	0.81	128.22
38	1.79	1.00	0.79	127.86
39	1.69	0.97	0.72	135.18
40-44	**8.46**	**4.88**	**3.58**	**136.37**
40	1.74	0.99	0.74	133.67
41	1.63	0.92	0.71	129.29
42	1.67	1.00	0.66	151.74
43	1.73	0.98	0.76	129.13
44	1.69	0.99	0.71	139.80
45-49	**8.07**	**4.70**	**3.36**	**139.89**
45	1.53	0.91	0.62	146.05
46	1.54	0.90	0.64	139.87
47	1.54	0.90	0.64	139.86
48	1.67	0.96	0.71	135.74
49	1.79	1.04	0.75	138.77
50-54	**8.74**	**4.89**	**3.84**	**127.44**
50	1.92	1.09	0.83	131.39
51	1.84	1.01	0.83	122.17
52	1.75	0.99	0.77	128.70
53	1.61	0.89	0.72	123.98
54	1.62	0.92	0.70	131.17
55-59	**5.69**	**3.11**	**2.58**	**120.56**
60-64	**1.74**	**0.96**	**0.78**	**123.72**
65+	**2.47**	**1.19**	**1.28**	**92.56**

3—19　各市按外出时间分的外出人口比例（2022年）

Proportion of Persons Going Out by Time and Region (2022)

单位：%

地　区	Region	合　计（人）Total (person)	半年至一年 Six Months To One Year	一年至二年 One to Two Years	二年至五年 Two to Five Years	五年以上 More Than Five Years
总　计	**Total**	**173430**	**49.26**	**11.94**	**16.46**	**22.34**
合 肥 市	Hefei	8513	44.41	14.21	15.56	25.81
淮 北 市	Huaibei	4453	42.38	11.92	20.88	24.81
亳 州 市	Bozhou	13703	62.19	10.25	12.75	14.81
宿 州 市	Suzhou	13793	54.63	15.72	16.97	12.69
蚌 埠 市	Bengbu	10422	33.69	15.78	25.63	24.90
阜 阳 市	Fuyang	21866	67.13	10.58	11.17	11.12
淮 南 市	Huainan	9478	33.76	14.32	19.17	32.75
滁 州 市	Chuzhou	10932	30.54	15.22	24.08	30.16
六 安 市	Luan	12653	57.99	11.50	13.21	17.31
马鞍山市	Maanshan	6648	47.40	11.54	18.65	22.41
芜 湖 市	Wuhu	5656	43.83	11.69	19.78	24.70
宣 城 市	Xuancheng	11489	20.79	12.89	21.67	44.64
铜 陵 市	Tongling	6693	57.54	10.55	12.85	19.06
池 州 市	Chizhou	6972	42.96	10.66	16.28	30.11
安 庆 市	Anqing	19969	67.17	7.87	10.13	14.82
黄 山 市	Huangshan	10190	33.05	10.06	20.70	36.19

主要统计指标解释

人口数

指一定时点、一定地区范围内的有生命的个人的总和。

常住人口

是指具有中华人民共和国国籍并在中华人民共和国境内常住的人。

（1）居住本乡、镇、街道，户口在本乡、镇、街道的人；

（2）居住本乡、镇、街道半年以上，户口在外乡、镇、街道的人；

（3）在本乡、镇、街道居住不满半年，离开户口登记地半年以上的人；

（4）居住本乡、镇、街道，户口待定的人；

（5）原住本乡、镇、街道，现在国外工作学习，暂无户口的人；

常住户口在本乡、镇、街道，但已离开本乡、镇、街道半年以上的人，在户口所在地只登记人数，不计入户口所在地的常住人口数内。

总人口文盲率

15岁及以上不识字人数与总人口数的比例。

出生率（又称粗出生率）

指在一定时期内（通常为一年）平均每千人所出生的人数的比率，一般用千分率表示。

计算公式为：

出生率＝年出生人数/年平均人数×1000‰

式中：出生人数指活产婴儿，即胎儿脱离母体时（不含怀孕月数），有过呼吸或其他生命现象。年平均人数指年初、年底人口数的平均数，也可用年中人口数代替。

死亡率（又称粗死亡率）

指在一定时期内（通常为一年）一定地区的死亡人数与同期平均人数（或期中人数）之比，一般用千分率表示。

计算公式为：

死亡率＝年死亡人数/年平均人数×1000‰

人口自然增长率

指在一定时期内（通常为一年）人口自然增加数（出生人数减死亡人数）与该时期内平均人数（或期中人数）之比，一般用千分率表示。

计算公式为：

人口自然增长率＝（年出生人数－年死亡人数）/年平均人数×1000‰

＝人口出生率－人口死亡率

在业人口（又称就业人口）

指十六周岁及十六周岁以上人口中从事一定的社会劳动并取得劳动报酬或经营收入的人口。

未工作人口

指十六周岁及十六周岁以上人口中未从事社会劳动的人口，包括在校学生、料理家务、待升学、失去工作、离退休、退职、丧失劳动能力等非在业人口。

抚养系数

指被抚养人口（0-14岁和65岁以上人口）与15-64岁人口的比例。

计算公式为：

抚养系数＝被抚养人口/15-64岁人口×100％

老年抚养系数

指老年人口（65岁以上人口）与15-64岁人口的比例。

计算公式为：

老年抚养系数＝老年人口/15-64岁人口×100％

少年儿童抚养系数

指0-14岁少年儿童与15-64岁人口的比例。

计算公式为：

少年儿童抚养系数＝少年儿童人口/15-64岁人口×100％

Explanatory Notes for Major Statistical Indicators

Total Population

refers to the total number of people alive at a certain point of time within a given area.

Permanent Population

refers to the persons who hold the nationality of, and have permanent residing place in the People's Republic of China.

a) Those who reside in the townships, towns and street communities and have their permanent household registration there.

b) Those who have resided in the townships, towns and street communities for more than 6 months but the places of their permanent household registration are elsewhere.

c) Those who have resided in the townships, towns and street communities for less than 6 months but have been away from the place of their permanent household registration for more than 6 months.

d) Those who live in the townships, towns and street communities while the places of their household registration have not yet settled.

e) Those who used to live in the townships, towns and street communities but are working or studying abroad and have no permanent household registration for the time being.

Those who have their permanent household registration in the townships, towns and street communities but have been away from these places for more than 6 months are only registered as total population not counted as permanent population of the places of their household registration.

Total Population Illiterate Ratio

refers to the ratio of the number of illiterate people aged 15 and over to total population.

Birth Rate or (Crude Birth Rate)

refers to the ratio of the number of births to the average population during a certain period of time (usually a year) which is often expressed in‰. The following formula is used:

Birth Rate=Number of Births/Average Number of Population×1000‰

Number of births refers to live births i.e. the births when babies had showed any vital phenomena regardless of the length of pregnancy.

Annual Average Number of Population is the average of the number of population at the beginning of the year and that at the end of the year. Sometimes it is substituted for with the mid year population.

Death Rate (or Crude Death Rate)

refers to the ratio of the number of deaths to the average population (or mid year population) during a certain period of time (usually a year) which is often expressed in ‰. The following formula is used:

Death Rate umber of Deaths=Number of Deaths/Annual Average Number of Population×1000‰

Natural Growth Rate of Population

refers to the ratio of natural increase in population (number of births minus number of deaths) in a certain period of time (usually a year) to the average population (or mid year population) of the same period which is often expressed in‰. The following formulas are applied:

Natural Growth of Population=(Number of Births-Number of Deaths)/Average Number of Population×1000‰

Natural Growth Rate of Population=Birth Rate-Death Rate

Employed Population

refers to population aged 16 or over engaging in social labour which generates income.

Not Working Population

refers to population aged 16 or over not engaging in any social labour which generates income, including students enrolled in schools, house wives, students waiting for entering schools with higher level, persons losing their jobs, retirees, job quitters, disabled, etc.

Total Dependency Ratio

refers to the ratio of number of dependents to the total

population aged 15-64, the number of dependents being population aged 0-14 and population aged 65 and over. The total dependency ratio is calculated as follows:

Total Dependency Ratio=Number of dependents/Population aged 15-64×100%

The Aged Dependency Ratio

refers to the ratio of the number of the aged population to the total population aged 15-64, the aged being population aged 65 and over. The aged dependency ratio is calculated as follows:

The Aged Dependency Ratio=Number of the aged population/Population aged 15-64×100%

The Juvenile and Children Dependency Ratio

refers to the ratio of the number of the juvenile and children to the total population aged 15-64, the juvenile and children being population aged 0-14. The juvenile and children dependency ratio is calculated as follows:

The Juvenile and Children Dependency Ratio=Number of juvenile and children/Population aged 15-64×100%

第四篇

Chapter 4

就业人员和工资

EMPLOYMENT AND WAGES

简要说明

一、本篇资料反映我省 2022 年及主要年份劳动经济方面的基本情况，包括全省和 16 个市主要劳动统计数据。主要指标有：就业人员、私营和个体就业人员、城镇登记失业人员及失业率、单位就业人员、工资总额和平均工资等。

二、本篇资料来源主要有三个方面：

1. 就业人员数、工资总额、平均工资，根据 2022 年度全省劳动工资统计年报汇总整理提供。

2. 私营企业和个体就业人员，根据省市场监督管理局提供的资料整理。

3. 城镇登记失业人数、新增就业人数、城镇登记失业率，根据省人力资源和社会保障厅提供的资料整理。

三、1998 年及以后城镇单位就业人员、职工工资、工资总额、平均工资等指标中不再包括离开本单位仍保留劳动关系的职工及其生活费。

四、表 4—3、14、16、18 中“铁路（国家反馈）”2022 年铁路系统相关数据由国家统计局单独反馈，无法分解到各市，故单独列出。

五、本篇资料均由省统计局人口处整理编制。

Brief Introduction

I. Data in this chapter show the basic conditions of Anhui’s labor economy in 2022 and the mainly previous years, including the main data of labor statistics of the whole province and 16 prefectures such as number of the employed persons, number of persons employed in the urban private enterprises and self-employment, registered urban unemployed persons and unemployment rate, number of employment in units, total wages and average wages.

II. There are three main sources for Data published in this chapter.

1. Number of employed persons, total wages and average wages are summarized and provided according to the 2022 provincial labor and wage statistics annual report.

2. Private enterprise and individual obtain employment personnel, according to the province market supervises the data that administration provides collate.

3. Urban registered unemployment, new employment, urban registered unemployment rate, according to the provincial Human resources and social security department.

III. The scope of statistics on employed person in urban areas, total number of staff and workers, total wage bills, average wages do not include the persons who had left their working units and while keeping their labour contract/employment relation unchanged since 1998.

IV. Tables 4-3, 14, 16, and 18 "Railway (National Feedback)", the relevant data of railway system in 2022 are fed back by the National Bureau of Statistics alone, and cannot be decomposed into cities, so they are listed separately.

Ⅴ. Data in this chapter are prepared by the Population Division, Anhui Statistical Bureau.

4—1 就业基本情况
Basic Conditions of Employment

单位：万人（10000 persons）

项　目	Item	2010	2015	2020	2021	2022
就业人员合计	**Total Number of Employed Persons**	**4050.0**	**4342.1**	**3243.0**	**3215.0**	**3176.0**
第一产业	Primary Industry	1583.6	1396.2	815.0	779.0	790.0
第二产业	Secondary Industry	1016.5	1232.1	1020.0	1026.0	1020.0
第三产业	Tertiary Industry	1449.9	1713.8	1408.0	1410.0	1366.0
就业人员构成（合计=100）	**Composition of Employed Persons (total=100)**					
第一产业	Primary Industry	39.1	32.1	25.1	24.2	24.9
第二产业	Secondary Industry	25.1	28.4	31.5	31.9	32.1
第三产业	Tertiary Industry	35.8	39.5	43.4	43.9	43.0
按城乡分就业人员	**Number of Employed Persons by Urban and Rural Areas**					
城镇就业人员	Urban Employed Persons	973.5	1292.1	1791.0	1816.0	1790.0
#国有单位	State-owned Units	206.0	189.1	175.9	179.3	178.4
城镇集体单位	Urban Collective Owned Units	17.9	14.7	7.7	7.1	6.5
股份合作单位	Share Holding Units	4.7	3.3	2.0	2.0	1.9
联营单位	Joint Owned Units	0.8	0.3	0.8	0.8	0.7
有限责任公司	Limited Liability Corporations	80.0	203.7	266.0	263.8	281.6
股份有限公司	Share-holding Corporations Ltd.	37.7	60.8	72.6	65.4	63.2
港澳台商投资单位	Units Funded by Entrepreneurs from Hong Kong, Macao & Taiwan	7.0	15.9	13.4	15.0	15.6
外商投资单位	Foreign Funded Units	14.7	19.8	19.0	19.6	18.9
乡村就业人员	Rural Employed Persons	3076.5	3050.0	1452.0	1399.0	1386.0
城镇非私营单位就业人数	**The Private Institutions in Cities and Towns of Employment**	**372.9**	**513.8**	**565.6**	**563.2**	**576.8**
国有单位	State-owned Units	206.0	189.1	175.9	179.3	178.4
城镇集体单位	Urban Collective Owned Units	17.9	14.7	7.7	7.1	6.5
其他单位	Units of Other Types of Ownership	149.1	310.0	382.0	376.8	392.0
城镇单位女性就业人员	**Number of Female Employment in Urban Units**	**121.3**	**170.2**	**204.7**	**207.1**	**214.2**

注：2020年起就业人数为常住口径就业人员数，往年均为户籍口径（下同）。

a) Number of employed persons since 2020 is the number of employed persons with permanent residence in previous years (the same below).

4—2 主要年份按城乡分的就业人员数

Number of Employed Persons by Residence in Urban and Rural Areas and Region in Main Year

单位：万人（10000 persons）

年 份 Year	合 计 Total	城镇 Urban Area 小 计 Sub-total	国有单位 State-owned Units	集体单位 Collective-owned Units	股份合作单位 Share Holding Units	联营单位 Joint-owned Units
2005	3669.7	730.5	208.7	30.8	3.9	0.8
2010	4050.0	973.5	206.0	17.9	4.7	0.8
2011	4120.9	1038.3	219.0	18.3	5.2	1.1
2012	4206.8	1141.0	225.7	17.2	4.9	0.8
2013	4275.9	1226.2	196.4	16.2	3.4	0.4
2014	4311.0	1277.4	198.8	15.6	3.3	0.4
2015	4342.1	1292.1	189.1	14.7	3.3	0.3
2016	4361.6	1327.5	191.1	14.2	3.6	0.3
2017	4377.9	1378.5	184.0	13.1	2.9	0.2
2018	4385.3	1385.3	181.2	12.5	2.5	0.3
2019	4384.0	1415.5	170.1	8.0	1.8	0.5
2020	3243.0	1791.0	175.9	7.7	2.0	0.8
2021	3215.0	1816.0	179.3	7.1	2.0	0.8
2022	3176.0	1790.0	178.4	6.5	1.9	0.7

年 份 Year	城镇 Urban Area 有限责任公司 Limited Liability Corporations	股份有限公司 Share Holding Corporations Ltd.	港澳台商投资单位 Economic Units Funded by Entrepreneurs from Hong Kong, Macao and Taiwan	外商投资单位 Foreign Funded Economic Units	乡村小计 Rural Area Sub-total
2005	52.3	24.8	3.7	6.7	2939.2
2010	80.0	37.7	7.0	14.7	3076.5
2011	94.0	43.6	8.3	16.7	3082.6
2012	112.6	45.0	8.0	15.9	3065.8
2013	201.5	59.4	15.9	20.3	3049.7
2014	200.4	58.9	16.7	20.9	3033.6
2015	203.7	60.8	15.9	19.8	3050.0
2016	204.4	62.0	15.4	19.6	3034.1
2017	213.8	61.5	15.7	18.4	2999.4
2018	291.0	69.7	12.4	15.9	3000.0
2019	285.8	68.7	12.0	16.4	2968.5
2020	266.0	72.6	13.4	19.0	1452.0
2021	263.8	65.4	15.0	19.6	1399.0
2022	281.6	63.2	15.6	18.9	1386.0

4—3 各市分行业城镇非私营单位就业人员数（2022年）
Number of Employed Persons by Sector and Region (2022)

单位：人（person）

地区 Region	合计 Total	农林牧渔业 Agriculture, Forestry, Animal Husbandry and Fishery	采矿业 Mining	制造业 Manufacturing	电力、热力、燃气及水的生产和供应业 Production and Supply of Electricity, Heat, Gas and Water	建筑业 Construction	批发和零售业 Wholesale and Retail Trade	交通运输、仓储和邮政业 Transport, Storage, Post & Telecommunications	住宿和餐饮业 Accommodation and Catering Trade	信息传输、计算机服务和软件业 Information, Circulation Computer Services and Software
总计 Total	**5768444**	**23234**	**119001**	**1414370**	**97216**	**938636**	**239289**	**261225**	**62213**	**116904**
合肥市 Hefei	1686058	1842	1167	379043	43377	459078	99453	63210	25253	66772
淮北市 Huaibei	169018	243	39565	30706	4207	9804	4172	2967	1173	2400
亳州市 Bozhou	250653	579	4075	49378	2612	24362	14052	8083	2887	2486
宿州市 Suzhou	288069	573	191	34549	2598	58274	9305	5655	1548	4769
蚌埠市 Bengbu	247485	255		56800	2843	32374	9976	8429	1776	2679
阜阳市 Fuyang	379089	1053	7168	63475	3152	39586	16605	10351	2840	2829
淮南市 Huainan	225527	976	50368	21975	11891	11413	7262	4693	978	1566
滁州市 Chuzhou	330045	1505	931	126205	3387	46808	11433	6553	1343	2072
六安市 Luan	257399	597	5125	61596	3762	17357	5848	5723	2504	2371
马鞍山市 Maanshan	247976	513	5270	83964	4560	42199	5379	6534	1146	3796
芜湖市 Wuhu	681417	1039	15	234638	4583	90423	28826	78440	5088	13889
宣城市 Xuancheng	251958	886	91	89689	2259	26204	6044	2745	1648	2139
铜陵市 Tongling	146644	387	2789	46430	2259	22322	3228	4737	6682	1276
池州市 Chizhou	114715	187	1565	28973	1567	7029	3145	1888	641	1441
安庆市 Anqing	331820	12243	623	84921	3254	37462	11328	9261	3148	4579
黄山市 Huangshan	121013	357	61	22025	906	13940	3233	2401	3556	1839
铁路（国家反馈） Railways (State Feedback)	39555							39555		

注：2020年起非一套表单位采取抽样调查，部分数据因四舍五入的原因，存在总计与分项合计不等的情况（下同）。

a) Starting from 2020, sampling survey will be carried out for non-one set of forms. Due to rounding, some data may vary in total and sub-total (the same below).

4—3 续表 continued

单位：人（person）

地区 Region	金融业 Banking	房地产业 Real Estate	租赁和商务服务业 Leasing and Commercial Services	科学研究和技术服务业 Scientific Research and Technical Services	水利、环境和公共设施管理业 Water Conservancy, Environmental and Public Facilities Management	居民服务、修理和其他服务业 Residents Service, Repair and Other Services	教育 Education	卫生和社会工作 Health and Social Work	文化、体育和娱乐业 Culture, Sports and Entertain-ment	公共管理、社会保障和社会组织 Public Management, Social Security and Social Organization
总计 Total	**190831**	**152830**	**219274**	**117133**	**89232**	**27371**	**688551**	**373527**	**35788**	**601818**
合肥市 Hefei	61798	52847	50934	64757	7547	3087	124360	70611	13071	97851
淮北市 Huaibei	5341	3129	5500	1665	2239	298	24790	10843	727	19247
亳州市 Bozhou	8007	8254	7137	1284	8568	1490	48880	21830	1209	35480
宿州市 Suzhou	9560	9804	2206	4356	7399	459	56420	30604	1332	48466
蚌埠市 Bengbu	6606	8043	8066	5387	4537	3916	43087	22852	1471	28388
阜阳市 Fuyang	12962	10020	6168	3602	11513	585	82426	47956	2160	54640
淮南市 Huainan	9526	6342	10709	2375	4578	266	33057	18930	1248	27373
滁州市 Chuzhou	11295	7687	4613	3138	7309	1626	38429	17504	841	37367
六安市 Luan	12946	4732	5442	2800	9852	651	45834	28562	1308	40391
马鞍山市 Maanshan	10469	4051	5951	4710	1978	690	26233	13962	1133	25440
芜湖市 Wuhu	9828	14152	69722	9252	2331	4397	44760	20837	2365	46835
宣城市 Xuancheng	8532	3992	17921	2147	3680	1125	27530	16964	1053	37309
铜陵市 Tongling	4075	5570	3358	2288	1864	398	16821	8583	978	12598
池州市 Chizhou	6085	2475	13001	2959	2630	1284	13838	7413	738	17853
安庆市 Anqing	8617	8333	5508	4220	8932	6836	46766	27265	2591	45934
黄山市 Huangshan	5184	3399	3038	2195	4274	264	15323	8811	3563	26646
铁路(国家反馈) Railways (State Feedback)										

4—4 主要年份私营企业年末户数
Number of Households of Private Enterprises at the end of Main Years

单位：户（household）

年 份 Year	合 计 Total	城 镇 Urban Areas	乡 村 Rural Areas
2005	105998	63586	42412
2010	228670	128891	99779
2013	353841	268220	85621
2014	452338	367081	85257
2015	570835	482899	87936
2016	733289	630108	103181
2017	915621	733832	181789
2018	1128262	768022	360240
2019	1345811	696771	649040
2020	1515981	615513	900468
2021	1756051	563968	1192083
2022	1947190	508245	1438945

4—5 各市私营企业年末户数（2022年）
Number of Private Enterprises at the End of the Year by Region (2022)

单位：户（household）

地 区	Region	合 计 Total	城 镇 Urban Areas	乡 村 Rural Areas
总 计	**Total**	**1947190**	**508245**	**1438945**
合肥市	Hefei	580971	137898	443073
淮北市	Huaibei	41502	9679	31823
亳州市	Bozhou	168812	18297	150515
宿州市	Suzhou	114464	28541	85923
蚌埠市	Bengbu	78918	22785	56133
阜阳市	Fuyang	191622	42917	148705
淮南市	Huainan	61909	20450	41459
滁州市	Chuzhou	115385	37427	77958
六安市	Luan	117248	34400	82848
马鞍山市	Maanshan	66353	25810	40543
芜湖市	Wuhu	121631	30919	90712
宣城市	Xuancheng	60650	23810	36840
铜陵市	Tongling	37328	13265	24063
池州市	Chizhou	32422	10621	21801
安庆市	Anqing	121488	39053	82435
黄山市	Huangshan	36450	12348	24102
其 他	Others	37	25	12

4—6 主要年份个体年末户数
Number of Households at the end of Main Years

单位：户（household）

年份 Year	合计 Total	城镇 Urban Areas	乡村 Rural Areas
2005	1110417	522609	587808
2010	1341472	999110	342362
2013	1678333	1399830	278503
2014	1878153	1597745	280408
2015	2018755	1739521	279234
2016	2357198	2036420	320778
2017	2715364	2338868	376496
2018	3115351	2641590	473761
2019	3580407	2862226	718181
2020	4015048	2976310	1038738
2021	4486102	3036536	1449566
2022	4910424	3023944	1886480

4—7 各市个体年末户数（2022年）
Number of Individual Households at the end of Each by Region (2022)

单位：户（household）

地区	Region	合计 Total	城镇 Urban Areas	乡村 Rural Areas
总计	**Total**	**4910424**	**3023944**	**1886480**
合肥市	Hefei	848751	452414	396337
淮北市	Huaibei	153668	94119	59549
亳州市	Bozhou	446133	199692	246441
宿州市	Suzhou	434136	249743	184393
蚌埠市	Bengbu	256851	149991	106860
阜阳市	Fuyang	534022	334483	199539
淮南市	Huainan	212675	146664	66011
滁州市	Chuzhou	321540	219251	102289
六安市	Luan	290705	204638	86067
马鞍山市	Maanshan	169196	125680	43516
芜湖市	Wuhu	362195	182544	179651
宣城市	Xuancheng	229909	176143	53766
铜陵市	Tongling	93298	85624	7674
池州市	Chizhou	118338	71073	47265
安庆市	Anqing	330644	262611	68033
黄山市	Huangshan	108363	69274	39089

4—8 城镇非私营单位就业人员数
Number of Employed Persons of Urban Non-private Owned Units

单位：万人（10000 persons）

行　业	Sector	2021	2022
总　计	**Total**	**563.17**	**576.84**
农、林、牧、渔业	Agriculture, Forestry, Animal Husbandry and Fishery	2.67	2.32
采矿业	Mining	13.01	11.90
制造业	Manufacturing	131.00	141.44
电力、热力、燃气及水的生产和供应业	Production and Supply of Electricity, Heat, Gas and Water	10.30	9.72
建筑业	Construction	98.40	93.86
批发和零售业	Wholesale and Retail Trades	23.85	23.93
交通运输、仓储和邮政业	Transport, Storage and Post	20.86	26.12
住宿和餐饮业	Hotels and Catering Services	5.45	6.22
信息传输、软件和信息技术服务业	Information Transmission, Software and Information Technology	10.03	11.69
金融业	Financial Intermediation	22.21	19.08
房地产业	Real Estate	15.13	15.28
租赁和商务服务业	Leasing and Business Services	21.35	21.93
科学研究和技术服务业	Scientific Research and Technical Services	10.66	11.71
水利、环境和公共设施管理业	Management of Water Conservancy, Environment	7.05	8.92
居民服务、修理和其他服务业	Services to Households, Repair and Other Services	2.41	2.74
教　育	Education	68.19	68.86
卫生和社会工作	Health and Social Service	36.92	37.35
文化、体育和娱乐业	Culture, Sports and Entertainment	3.52	3.58
公共管理、社会保障和社会组织	Public Management, Social Security and Social Organization	60.18	60.18

4—9 城镇非私营单位分行业就业人员数（2022年）
Number of Employed Persons of Urban Non-private Owned Units by Status (2022)

单位：人（person）

行　业	Sector	合　计 Total	国有单位 State-owned Units	城镇集体单位 Urban Collective-owned Units	其他单位 Units of Other Types of Ownership
总　　计	**Total**	**5768444**	**1783755**	**64670**	**3920019**
按执行会计标准类别分组	**Grouped by Executive Accounting System Type**				
企　业	Enterprises	4126470	237047	32522	3856900
政　府	Government	1574211	1531734	28019	14457
民间非营利组织	Non-profit Organizations	64843	13712	4112	47019
其　他	Others	2921	1262	16	1643
按国民经济行业分组	**Grouped by Economic Sector**				
农、林、牧、渔业	**Agriculture, Forestry, Animal Husbandry and Fishery**	**23234**	**19305**	**486**	**3443**
农　业	Farming	6892	5537	194	1161
林　业	Forestry	2751	2390	49	312
畜牧业	Animal Husbandry	786	25		761
渔　业	Fishery	351	75	3	273
农林牧渔专业及辅助性活动	Agriculture, Forestry, Animal Husbandry and Fishery Major and Supporting Activities	12455	11278	240	937
采矿业	**Mining**	**119001**	**4460**	**53**	**114488**
煤炭开采和洗选业	Mining and Washing of Coal	100221	1049		99172
石油和天然气开采业	Extraction of Petroleum and Natural Gas	321			321
黑色金属矿采选业	Mining and Processing of Ferrous Metal Ores	9605	2684	16	6905
有色金属矿采选业	Mining and Processing of Non-Ferrous Metal Ores	3048	61		2987
非金属矿采选业	Mining and Processing of Non-metal Ores	5281	331	37	4913
开采专业及辅助性活动	Mining Profession and Auxiliary Activities	516	335		181
制造业	**Manufacturing**	**1414370**	**27319**	**3314**	**1383737**
农副食品加工业	Processing of Food from Agricultural Products	47293	608	103	46582
食品制造业	Manufacture of Foods	26368	8	11	26349
酒、饮料和精制茶制造业	Manufacture of Liquor, Beverages and Refined Tea	28534	80	720	27734
烟草制品业	Manufacture of Tobacco	6760	5579		1181
纺织业	Manufacture of Textile	33812	562	19	33231
纺织服装、服饰业	Manufacture of Textile, Wearing Apparel and Accessories	55095		10	55085
皮革、毛皮、羽毛及其制品和制鞋业	Manufacture of Leather, Fur, Feather and Related Products and Footwear	17434		1	17433
木材加工和木、竹、藤、棕、草制品业	Processing of Timber, Manufacture of Wood, Bamboo, Rattan, Palm and Straw Products	6843			6843
家具制造业	Manufacture of Furniture	13380			13380
造纸和纸制品业	Manufacture of Paper and Paper Products	10494	376	271	9847
印刷和记录媒介复制业	Printing and Reproduction of Recording Media	16337	142	235	15960
文教、工美、体育和娱乐用品制造业	Manufacture of Articles for Culture, Education, Arts and Crafts, Sport and Entertainment Activities	14419	38	84	14298
石油、煤炭及其他燃料加工业	Petroleum, Coal and Other Fuel Processing Industries	7591			7591
化学原料和化学制品制造业	Manufacture of Raw Chemical Materials and Chemical Products	73795	269	61	73465
医药制造业	Manufacture of Medicines	50512		13	50499
化学纤维制造业	Manufacture of Chemical Fibres	3883			3883
橡胶和塑料制品业	Manufacture of Rubber and Plastics Products	75749	513	349	74887
非金属矿物制品业	Manufacture of Non-metallic Mineral Products	79727	4075	202	75450
黑色金属冶炼和压延加工业	Smelting and Pressing of Ferrous Metals	36473	572	25	35876

4—9 续表1 continued

单位：人（person）

行业	Sector	合计 Total	国有单位 State-owned Units	城镇集体单位 Urban Collective-owned Units	其他单位 Units of Other Types of Ownership
有色金属冶炼和压延加工业	Smelting and Pressing of Non-ferrous Metals	27607	144	1	27462
金属制品业	Manufacture of Metal Products	56280	760	432	55088
通用设备制造业	Manufacture of General Purpose Machinery	93955	1870	119	91966
专用设备制造业	Manufacture of Special Purpose Machinery	62933	859	530	61544
汽车制造业	Manufacture of Automobiles	151268	2969	14	148285
铁路、船舶、航空航天和其他运输设备制造业	Manufacture of Railway, Ship, Aerospace and Other Transport Equipments	13012	1082	80	11850
电气机械和器材制造业	Manufacture of Electrical Machinery and Apparatus	194739		15	194724
计算机、通信和其他电子设备制造业	Manufacture of Computers, Communication and Other Electronic Equipment	179166	2582		176584
仪器仪表制造业	Manufacture of Measuring Instruments and Machinery	11083		7	11076
其他制造业	Other Manufacture	4460	58	12	4390
废弃资源综合利用业	Utilization of Waste Resources	8635	405		8230
金属制品、机械和设备修理业	Repair Service of Metal Products, Machinery and Equipment	6735	3768		2967
电力、热力、燃气及水生产和供应业	**Production and Supply of Electricity, Heat, Gas and Water**	**97216**	**12421**	**325**	**84470**
电力、热力的生产和供应业	Production and Supply of Electric Power and Heat Power	63788	8431	23	55334
燃气生产和供应业	Production and Supply of Gas	12793	101		12692
水的生产和供应业	Production and Supply of Water	20636	3889	302	16444
建筑业	**Construction**	**938636**	**50948**	**19991**	**867697**
房屋建筑业	Construction of Buildings	575008	38388	9338	527282
土木工程建筑业	Civil Engineering	243772	9044	1874	232854
建筑安装业	Building Installation	53513	2175	3656	47682
建筑装饰、装修和其他建筑业	Architectural Decoration, Decoration and Other Construction Industries	66344	1342	5123	59879
批发和零售业	**Wholesale and Retail Trades**	**239289**	**15876**	**897**	**222515**
批发业	Wholesale Trade	97351	13394	346	83611
零售业	Retail Trade	141937	2482	551	138904
交通运输、仓储和邮政业	**Transport, Storage and Post**	**261225**	**18686**	**1173**	**241366**
铁路运输业	Railway Transport	42382	30		42352
道路运输业	Road Transport	127144	11854	855	114435
水上运输业	Water Transport	6010	344	106	5560
航空运输业	Air Transport	3280	633		2647
管道运输业	Transport Via Pipelines	15			15
多式联运和运输代理业	Multimodal Transport and Transportation Agency	5375	313	21	5041
装卸搬运和仓储业	Handling and Storage Industry	11291	3807	191	7293
邮政业	Post	65728	1705		64023
住宿和餐饮业	**Hotels and Catering Services**	**62213**	**1338**	**117**	**60757**
住宿业	Hotels	27435	743	12	26679
餐饮业	Catering Services	34778	595	105	34078
信息传输、软件和信息技术服务业	**Information Transmission, Software and Information Technology**	**116904**	**6397**	**99**	**110408**
电信、广播电视和卫星传输服务	Telecommunication, Radio and Television and Satellite Transmission Service	48785	5578	73	43134
互联网和相关服务	Internet and Related Service	10050	80		9970
软件和信息技术服务业	Software and Information Technology	58070	739	26	57304

4—9 续表2 continued

单位：人（person）

行业	Sector	合计 Total	国有单位 State-owned Units	城镇集体单位 Urban Collective-owned Units	其他单位 Units of Other Types of Ownership
金融业	**Financial Intermediation**	**190831**	**22823**	**191**	**167817**
货币金融服务	Monetary and Financial Service	99618	19837	191	79590
资本市场服务	Capital Market Service	4794	105		4689
保险业	Insurance	84103	2284		81819
其他金融业	Other Financial Activities	2316	597		1720
房地产业	**Real Estate**	**152830**	**3368**	**351**	**149111**
租赁和商务服务业	**Leasing and Business Services**	**219274**	**16987**	**1622**	**200665**
租赁业	Leasing	4782	207	2	4573
商务服务业	Business Services	214491	16780	1620	196092
科学研究和技术服务业	**Scientific Research and Technical Services**	**117133**	**40800**	**952**	**75382**
研究和试验发展	Research and Experimental Development	17176	8202	45	8929
专业技术服务业	Professional Technical Services	83781	27221	748	55813
科技推广和应用服务业	Science and Technology Popularization and Application Services	16175	5377	159	10640
水利、环境和公共设施管理业	**Management of Water Conservancy, Environment and Public Facilities**	**89232**	**25097**	**306**	**63830**
水利管理业	Management of Water Conservancy	9093	8753	16	325
生态保护和环境治理业	Ecological Protection and Environmental Treatment	3250	1417		1833
公共设施管理业	Management of Public Facilities	75418	14231	290	60896
土地管理业	Land Management	1471	695		775
居民服务、修理和其他服务业	**Service to Households, Repair and Other Services**	**27371**	**3630**	**474**	**23267**
居民服务业	Service to Households	12026	2442	303	9280
机动车、电子产品和日用产品修理业	Repair of Motor Vehicle, Electronics and Household Products	3293	247	99	2947
其他服务业	Other Services	12053	940	72	11040
教　育	**Education**	**688551**	**600174**	**12769**	**75608**
卫生和社会工作	**Health and Social Service**	**373527**	**295413**	**19873**	**58241**
卫　生	Health	362558	290110	19187	53261
社会工作	Social Service	10970	5304	685	4981
文化、体育和娱乐业	**Culture, Sports and Entertainment**	**35788**	**19632**	**253**	**15903**
新闻和出版业	Journalism and Publishing Activities	6756	3889		2867
广播、电视、电影和录音制作业	Radio, Television, Film and Recording Production	9872	7091	69	2712
文化艺术业	Cultural and Art Activities	13075	7428	133	5514
体　育	Sports Activities	1806	713	26	1068
娱乐业	Entertainment	4278	511	25	3742
公共管理、社会保障和社会组织	**Public Management, Social Security and Social Organization**	**601818**	**599080**	**1424**	**1315**
中国共产党机关	Organs of Communist Party of China	28994	28985		9
国家机构	Government Agencies	561111	558984	1242	885
人民政协、民主党派	People's Political Consultative Conference and Democratic Parties	4043	4043		
社会保障	Social Security	3690	3647	31	12
群众团体、社会团体和其他成员组织	Non-Governmental Organizations, Social Organizations and Other Organizations	3919	3421	151	347

4—10 城镇非私营单位分行业女性就业人员占全部就业人员比重（2022年）

Proportion of Female Employed to Total of Urban Non-private Owned Units by Status by Sector (2022)

以本类型从业人员为100 (Total number of this item employed=100)　　单位：%

行　业	Sector	合　计 Total	国有单位 State-owned Units	城镇集体单　位 Urban Collective-owned Units	其他单位 Units of Other Types of Ownership
总　　计	**Total**	**37.1**	**44.3**	**44.5**	**33.8**
按执行会计标准类别分组	**Grouped by Executive Accounting System Type**				
企　业	Enterprises	33.1	31.8	27.4	33.2
政　府	Government	46.4	46.0	61.4	61.2
民间非营利组织	Non-profit Organizations	70.0	65.3	64.6	71.9
其　他	Others	42.7	50.2	56.3	36.8
按国民经济行业分组	**Grouped by Economic Sector**				
农、林、牧、渔业	**Agriculture, Forestry, Animal Husbandry and Fishery**	**32.2**	**31.5**	**31.4**	**36.3**
农　业	Farming	28.3	25.0	36.3	42.5
林　业	Forestry	35.1	35.6	22.4	33.5
畜牧业	Animal Husbandry	41.6	36.0		41.8
渔　业	Fishery	23.9	21.3	66.7	24.2
农林牧渔专业及辅助性活动	Agriculture, Forestry, Animal Husbandry and Fishery Major and Supporting Activities	33.3	33.8	28.8	28.7
采矿业	**Mining**	**9.4**	**16.1**	**35.8**	**9.1**
煤炭开采和洗选业	Mining and Washing of Coal	7.7	11.8		7.6
石油和天然气开采业	Extraction of Petroleum and Natural Gas	21.2			21.2
黑色金属矿采选业	Mining and Processing of Ferrous Metal Ores	16.6	17.5	18.8	16.3
有色金属矿采选业	Mining and Processing of Non-Ferrous Metal Ores	19.9	31.1		19.7
非金属矿采选业	Mining and Processing of Non-metal Ores	20.7	16.9	43.2	20.8
开采专业及辅助性活动	Mining Profession and Auxiliary Activities	25.6	14.9		45.3
制造业	**Manufacturing**	**35.9**	**24.7**	**40.9**	**36.1**
农副食品加工业	Processing of Food from Agricultural Products	46.5	24.4	36.0	46.8
食品制造业	Manufacture of Foods	55.6	25.0	72.7	55.6
酒、饮料和精制茶制造业	Manufacture of Liquor, Beverages and Refined Tea	36.8	42.5	55.4	36.3
烟草制品业	Manufacture of Tobacco	27.9	29.3		21.8
纺织业	Manufacture of Textile	62.0	68.0	42.1	61.9
纺织服装、服饰业	Manufacture of Textile, Wearing Apparel and Accessories	75.0		70.0	75.0
皮革、毛皮、羽毛及其制品和制鞋业	Manufacture of Leather, Fur, Feather and Related Products and Footwear	68.2			68.2
木材加工和木、竹、藤、棕、草制品业	Processing of Timber, Manufacture of Wood, Bamboo, Rattan, Palm and Straw Products	41.1			41.1
家具制造业	Manufacture of Furniture	34.1			34.1
造纸和纸制品业	Manufacture of Paper and Paper Products	35.4	16.2	25.8	36.4
印刷和记录媒介复制业	Printing and Reproduction of Recording Media	41.9	33.8	56.2	41.7
文教、工美、体育和娱乐用品制造业	Manufacture of Articles for Culture, Education, Arts and Crafts, Sport and Entertainment Activities	65.8	47.4	52.4	65.9
石油、煤炭及其他燃料加工业	Petroleum, Coal and Other Fuel Processing Industries	15.5			15.5
化学原料和化学制品制造业	Manufacture of Raw Chemical Materials and Chemical Products	26.4	12.3	24.6	26.5
医药制造业	Manufacture of Medicines	52.0		38.5	52.0
化学纤维制造业	Manufacture of Chemical Fibres	36.0			36.0
橡胶和塑料制品业	Manufacture of Rubber and Plastics Products	38.2	29.6	51.0	38.2
非金属矿物制品业	Manufacture of Non-metallic Mineral Products	25.1	14.1	28.0	25.7
黑色金属冶炼和压延加工业	Smelting and Pressing of Ferrous Metals	13.2	10.7	20.0	13.2

4—10 续表1 continued

单位：%

行业	Sector	合计 Total	国有单位 State-owned Units	城镇集体单位 Urban Collective-owned Units	其他单位 Units of Other Types of Ownership
有色金属冶炼和压延加工业	Smelting and Pressing of Non-ferrous Metals	23.5	33.3		23.5
金属制品业	Manufacture of Metal Products	26.7	30.3	24.8	26.7
通用设备制造业	Manufacture of General Purpose Machinery	25.1	22.1	37.0	25.1
专用设备制造业	Manufacture of Special Purpose Machinery	27.2	21.7	35.7	27.2
汽车制造业	Manufacture of Automobiles	27.7	15.0	42.9	28.0
铁路、船舶、航空航天和其他运输设备制造业	Manufacture of Railway, Ship, Aerospace and Other Transport Equipments	23.4	10.0	36.3	24.5
电气机械和器材制造业	Manufacture of Electrical Machinery and Apparatus	37.2		26.7	37.2
计算机、通信和其他电子设备制造业	Manufacture of Computers, Communication and Other Electronic Equipment	37.0	44.5		36.9
仪器仪表制造业	Manufacture of Measuring Instruments and Machinery	31.0		57.1	30.9
其他制造业	Other Manufacture	36.2	22.4	75.0	36.3
废弃资源综合利用业	Utilization of Waste Resources	27.0	23.5		27.1
金属制品、机械和设备修理业	Repair Service of Metal Products, Machinery and Equipment	21.1	24.5		16.7
电力、热力、燃气及水生产和供应业	**Production and Supply of Electricity, Heat, Gas and Water**	**24.1**	**24.2**	**31.8**	**24.1**
电力、热力的生产和供应业	Production and Supply of Electric Power and Heat Power	19.8	19.4	26.1	19.8
燃气生产和供应业	Production and Supply of Gas	31.1	23.8		31.2
水的生产和供应业	Production and Supply of Water	33.2	34.5	32.3	32.9
建筑业	**Construction**	**13.3**	**8.9**	**15.6**	**13.6**
房屋建筑业	Construction of Buildings	13.7	6.8	23.9	14.0
土木工程建筑业	Civil Engineering	13.0	14.8	27.1	12.8
建筑安装业	Building Installation	14.8	15.4	3.4	15.7
建筑装饰、装修和其他建筑业	Architectural Decoration, Decoration and Other Construction Industries	10.3	16.4	4.8	10.7
批发和零售业	**Wholesale and Retail Trades**	**53.5**	**29.4**	**48.4**	**55.2**
批发业	Wholesale Trade	36.5	23.5	33.8	38.6
零售业	Retail Trade	65.2	61.6	57.6	65.3
交通运输、仓储和邮政业	**Transport, Storage and Post**	**28.5**	**30.6**	**25.9**	**28.3**
铁路运输业	Railway Transport	11.4	43.3		11.4
道路运输业	Road Transport	31.7	30.8	23.2	31.9
水上运输业	Water Transport	18.3	24.1	25.6	17.8
航空运输业	Air Transport	35.4	23.5		38.2
管道运输业	Transport Via Pipelines	0.0			0.0
多式联运和运输代理业	Multimodal Transport and Transportation Agency	34.3	34.5	33.3	34.2
装卸搬运和仓储业	Handling and Storage Industry	26.0	22.4	37.7	27.6
邮政业	Post	33.7	50.0		33.2
住宿和餐饮业	**Hotels and Catering Services**	**62.2**	**62.0**	**51.3**	**62.2**
住宿业	Hotels	61.0	60.7	50.0	61.0
餐饮业	Catering Services	63.1	63.7	51.4	63.2
信息传输、软件和信息技术服务业	**Information Transmission, Software and Information Technology**	**40.0**	**32.9**	**42.4**	**40.4**
电信、广播电视和卫星传输服务	Telecommunication, Radio and Television and Satellite Transmission Service	39.5	34.2	46.6	40.1
互联网和相关服务	Internet and Related Service	45.8	43.8		45.8
软件和信息技术服务业	Software and Information Technology	39.4	21.6	30.8	39.6

4—10 续表2 continued

单位：%

行 业	Sector	合 计 Total	国有单位 State-owned Units	城镇集体单位 Urban Collective-owned Units	其他单位 Units of Other Types of Ownership
金融业	**Financial Intermediation**	**54.1**	**44.6**	**56.5**	**55.4**
货币金融服务	Monetary and Financial Service	46.1	43.9	56.5	46.6
资本市场服务	Capital Market Service	40.5	47.6		40.4
保险业	Insurance	64.8	53.0		65.1
其他金融业	Other Financial Activities	39.2	33.5		41.2
房地产业	**Real Estate**	**42.6**	**37.9**	**36.5**	**42.8**
租赁和商务服务业	**Leasing and Business Services**	**40.7**	**34.8**	**44.8**	**41.1**
租赁业	Leasing	21.7	12.6	0.0	22.2
商务服务业	Business Services	41.1	35.0	44.9	41.6
科学研究和技术服务业	**Scientific Research and Technical Services**	**29.1**	**28.9**	**38.5**	**29.1**
研究和试验发展	Research and Experimental Development	33.3	31.6	82.2	34.5
专业技术服务业	Professional Technical Services	27.3	27.8	32.8	26.9
科技推广和应用服务业	Science and Technology Popularization and Application Services	33.9	29.7	52.5	35.8
水利、环境和公共设施管理业	**Management of Water Conservancy, Environment and Public Facilities**	**41.0**	**34.3**	**16.6**	**43.8**
水利管理业	Management of Water Conservancy	24.5	24.7	14.0	18.4
生态保护和环境治理业	Ecological Protection and Environmental Treatment	26.1	26.0		26.3
公共设施管理业	Management of Public Facilities	43.6	40.8	16.8	44.4
土地管理业	Land Management	44.0	38.3		49.0
居民服务、修理和其他服务业	**Service to Households, Repair and Other Services**	**43.9**	**39.7**	**47.3**	**44.5**
居民服务业	Service to Households	43.8	30.0	49.2	47.3
机动车、电子产品和日用产品修理业	Repair of Motor Vehicle, Electronics and Household Products	27.3	25.5	23.2	27.5
其他服务业	Other Services	48.5	68.5	72.2	46.6
教 育	**Education**	**56.8**	**55.0**	**63.6**	**69.8**
卫生和社会工作	**Health and Social Service**	**65.7**	**65.0**	**65.0**	**69.5**
卫 生	Health	65.8	65.2	65.4	69.4
社会工作	Social Service	63.6	58.4	53.6	70.6
文化、体育和娱乐业	**Culture, Sports and Entertainment**	**46.7**	**44.9**	**49.4**	**48.8**
新闻和出版业	Journalism and Publishing Activities	45.7	42.9		49.5
广播、电视、电影和录音制作业	Radio, Television, Film and Recording Production	42.5	39.3	44.9	50.8
文化艺术业	Cultural and Art Activities	50.1	51.8	58.6	47.6
体 育	Sports Activities	41.4	36.8	26.9	44.8
娱乐业	Entertainment	49.5	50.0	36.0	49.5
公共管理、社会保障和社会组织	**Public Management, Social Security and Social Organization**	**30.9**	**30.9**	**28.4**	**37.0**
中国共产党机关	Organs of Communist Party of China	29.3	29.3		55.6
国家机构	Government Agencies	30.8	30.8	25.4	33.9
人民政协、民主党派	People's Political Consultative Conference and Democratic Parties	25.1	25.1		0.0
社会保障	Social Security	52.9	52.9	51.6	50.0
群众团体、社会团体和其他成员组织	Non-Governmental Organizations, Social Organizations and Other Organizations	52.4	54.1	48.3	37.3

4—11 城镇非私营单位主要年份就业人员工资总额和指数
Total Wages of Employed Persons and Related Index of Urban Non-private Owned Units in Major Years

年 份 Year	工 资 总 额 （万元） Total Wages (10000 yuan)				指 数 （上年=100） Index (Preceding year=100)			
	合 计 Total	国有单位 State-owned Units	城镇集体单 位 Urban Collective-owned Units	其他单位 Units of Other Types of Ownership	合 计 Total	国有单位 State-owned Units	城镇集体单 位 Urban Collective-owned Units	其他单位 Units of Other Types of Ownership
2005	4841315	3071572	276909	1492834	114.9	109.5	107.0	129.7
2010	12251179	6914813	425619	4910747	119.3	117.1	117.8	122.8
2013	24637193	9517563	607624	14512006	127.9	94.4	104.7	168.8
2014	26315988	10271162	643610	15401216	106.8	107.9	105.9	106.1
2015	28238432	11353008	696857	16188567	107.3	110.5	108.3	105.1
2016	30128307	12550426	721317	16856565	106.7	110.5	103.5	104.1
2017	33237088	13838446	738939	18659703	110.3	110.3	102.4	110.7
2018	43548900	16776530	797838	25974533	131.0	121.2	108.0	139.2
2019	45211215	16848336	527941	27834938	103.8	100.4	66.2	107.2
2020	47403429	18845081	577630	27980719	104.8	111.9	109.4	100.5
2021	52245849	20770570	595008	30880271	110.2	110.2	103.0	100.4
2022	56461561	21911676	574459	33975425	108.1	105.5	96.5	110.0

4—12 城镇非私营单位主要年份就业人员平均工资及指数

Average Wage of Employed Persons and Related Index of Urban Non-private Owned Units in Major Years

年份 Year	平均货币工资（元） Average Wage in Monetary Terms (yuan)				指数（上年=100） Index (Preceding year=100)			
	合计 Total	国有单位 State-owned Units	城镇集体单位 Urban Collective-owned Units	其他单位 Units of Other Types of Ownership	合计 Total	国有单位 State-owned Units	城镇集体单位 Urban Collective-owned Units	其他单位 Units of Other Types of Ownership
2005	15334	15450	9894	16788	118.6	114.3	126.2	124.8
2010	33341	33793	23869	33867	115.8	115.9	119.1	115.2
2013	47806	48683	37927	47765	107.2	108.6	109.2	105.7
2014	50894	51974	41741	50657	106.5	106.8	110.1	106.1
2015	55139	60433	47261	52302	108.3	116.3	113.2	103.2
2016	59102	66210	50976	55076	107.2	109.6	107.9	105.3
2017	65150	75733	56758	59346	110.2	114.4	111.3	107.8
2018	74378	93210	63843	66089	114.2	123.1	112.5	111.4
2019	79037	99851	66059	70415	106.3	107.1	103.5	106.5
2020	85854	107953	76836	75613	108.6	108.1	116.3	107.4
2021	93861	116898	85045	83022	109.3	108.3	110.7	109.8
2022	98649	123493	89738	87450	105.1	105.6	105.5	105.3

注：本表所涉及指标，2010年以前为在岗职工相关指标，2010年及以后为就业人员相关指标。

a) Before 2010,the indicators involved in this table were related as employment workers, and after 2010 as the staff and workers indicators.

4—13 城镇非私营单位分行业就业人员工资总额（2022年）
Total Wages of Employed Persons of Urban Non-private Owned Units by Sector (2022)

单位：万元（10000 yuan）

行业	Sector	合计 Total	国有单位 State-owned Units	城镇集体单位 Urban Collective-owned Units	其他单位 Units of Other Types of Ownership
总计	**Total**	**56461561**	**21911676**	**574459**	**33975425**
按执行会计标准类别分组	**Grouped by Executive Accounting System Type**				
企业	Enterprises	36254404	2512287	212468	33529648
政府	Government	19782910	19289310	331573	162028
民间非营利组织	Non-profit Organizations	400209	94185	30349	275676
其他	Others	24038	15895	69	8074
按国民经济行业分组	**Grouped by Economic Sector**				
农、林、牧、渔业	**Agriculture, Forestry, Animal Husbandry and Fishery**	**142879**	**120647**	**2641**	**19592**
农业	Farming	44424	38505	804	5115
林业	Forestry	21810	18738	445	2628
畜牧业	Animal Husbandry	4856	35		4821
渔业	Fishery	1460	221	7	1233
农林牧渔专业及辅助性活动	Agriculture, Forestry, Animal Husbandry and Fishery Major and Supporting Activities	70329	63148	1386	5795
采矿业	**Mining**	**1698724**	**62019**	**221**	**1636485**
煤炭开采和洗选业	Mining and Washing of Coal	1483860	10356		1473504
石油和天然气开采业	Extraction of Petroleum and Natural Gas	4397			4397
黑色金属矿采选业	Mining and Processing of Ferrous Metal Ores	119096	43572	66	75458
有色金属矿采选业	Mining and Processing of Non-Ferrous Metal Ores	25735	663		25073
非金属矿采选业	Mining and Processing of Non-metal Ores	60373	3128	154	57090
开采专业及辅助性活动	Mining Profession and Auxiliary Activities	5214	4299		915
制造业	**Manufacturing**	**12396249**	**399449**	**22447**	**11974354**
农副食品加工业	Processing of Food from Agricultural Products	309581	3787	437	305358
食品制造业	Manufacture of Foods	174843	51	45	174747
酒、饮料和精制茶制造业	Manufacture of Liquor, Beverages and Refined Tea	198582	243	3160	195179
烟草制品业	Manufacture of Tobacco	177021	157087		19934
纺织业	Manufacture of Textile	208755	3625	167	204963
纺织服装、服饰业	Manufacture of Textile, Wearing Apparel and Accessories	333554		37	333517
皮革、毛皮、羽毛及其制品和制鞋业	Manufacture of Leather, Fur, Feather and Related Products and Footwear	101305		3	101302
木材加工和木、竹、藤、棕、草制品业	Processing of Timber, Manufacture of Wood, Bamboo, Rattan, Palm and Straw Products	42398			42398
家具制造业	Manufacture of Furniture	105832			105832
造纸和纸制品业	Manufacture of Paper and Paper Products	78645	5040	3146	70460
印刷和记录媒介复制业	Printing and Reproduction of Recording Media	125539	857	1576	123107
文教、工美、体育和娱乐用品制造业	Manufacture of Articles for Culture, Education, Arts and Crafts, Sport and Entertainment Activities	76164	214	358	75592
石油、煤炭及其他燃料加工业	Petroleum, Coal and Other Fuel Processing Industries	113436			113436
化学原料和化学制品制造业	Manufacture of Raw Chemical Materials and Chemical Products	704474	3936	377	700160
医药制造业	Manufacture of Medicines	364743		43	364700
化学纤维制造业	Manufacture of Chemical Fibres	30704			30704
橡胶和塑料制品业	Manufacture of Rubber and Plastics Products	626505	5699	1514	619291
非金属矿物制品业	Manufacture of Non-metallic Mineral Products	646711	44673	987	601052
黑色金属冶炼和压延加工业	Smelting and Pressing of Ferrous Metals	417402	7296	137	409968

4—13 续表1 continued

单位：万元（10000 yuan）

行 业	Sector	合 计 Total	国有单位 State-owned Units	城镇集体单位 Urban Collective-owned Units	其他单位 Units of Other Types of Ownership
有色金属冶炼和压延加工业	Smelting and Pressing of Non-ferrous Metals	231293	1138	3	230152
金属制品业	Manufacture of Metal Products	444264	4296	3507	436461
通用设备制造业	Manufacture of General Purpose Machinery	872427	18673	910	852845
专用设备制造业	Manufacture of Special Purpose Machinery	577256	8942	5468	562845
汽车制造业	Manufacture of Automobiles	1443638	28584	93	1414961
铁路、船舶、航空航天和其他运输设备制造业	Manufacture of Railway, Ship, Aerospace and Other Transport Equipments	142530	17676	384	124470
电气机械和器材制造业	Manufacture of Electrical Machinery and Apparatus	1651469		37	1651431
计算机、通信和其他电子设备制造业	Manufacture of Computers, Communication and Other Electronic Equipment	1854970	16949		1838021
仪器仪表制造业	Manufacture of Measuring Instruments and Machinery	137596		25	137571
其他制造业	Other Manufacture	44614	603	32	43979
废弃资源综合利用业	Utilization of Waste Resources	65223	9309		55914
金属制品、机械和设备修理业	Repair Service of Metal Products, Machinery and Equipment	94777	60772		34005
电力、热力、燃气及水生产和供应业	**Production and Supply of Electricity, Heat, Gas and Water**	**1326398**	**147618**	**2232**	**1176549**
电力、热力的生产和供应业	Production and Supply of Electric Power and Heat Power	1031873	114559	260	917054
燃气生产和供应业	Production and Supply of Gas	113021	940		112081
水的生产和供应业	Production and Supply of Water	181504	32119	1972	147413
建筑业	**Construction**	**6718775**	**355143**	**137811**	**6225820**
房屋建筑业	Construction of Buildings	3680490	261766	45885	3372840
土木工程建筑业	Civil Engineering	2123407	59629	16506	2047272
建筑安装业	Building Installation	419131	21834	28392	368906
建筑装饰、装修和其他建筑业	Architectural Decoration, Decoration and Other Construction Industries	495746	11914	47029	436803
批发和零售业	**Wholesale and Retail Trades**	**1998537**	**215522**	**3764**	**1779251**
批发业	Wholesale Trade	1123185	193532	1492	928161
零售业	Retail Trade	875352	21990	2272	851090
交通运输、仓储和邮政业	**Transport, Storage and Post**	**2491494**	**141365**	**4998**	**2345131**
铁路运输业	Railway Transport	680181	181		680000
道路运输业	Road Transport	944794	88534	3677	852583
水上运输业	Water Transport	56406	4203	467	51736
航空运输业	Air Transport	41292	7689		33603
管道运输业	Transport Via Pipelines	216			216
多式联运和运输代理业	Multimodal Transport and Transportation Agency	47016	1642	47	45327
装卸搬运和仓储业	Handling and Storage Industry	81290	20538	807	59945
邮政业	Post	640300	18579		621721
住宿和餐饮业	**Hotels and Catering Services**	**321319**	**6730**	**442**	**314147**
住宿业	Hotels	145078	3543	34	141501
餐饮业	Catering Services	176242	3188	408	172646
信息传输、软件和信息技术服务业	**Information Transmission, Software and Information Technology**	**1443693**	**84590**	**432**	**1358671**
电信、广播电视和卫星传输服务	Telecommunication, Radio and Television and Satellite Transmission Service	588532	72647	182	515702
互联网和相关服务	Internet and Related Service	113784	1308		112476
软件和信息技术服务业	Software and Information Technology	741377	10635	249	730493

4—13 续表2 continued

单位：万元（10000 yuan）

行 业	Sector	合 计 Total	国有单位 State-owned Units	城镇集体单 位 Urban Collective-owned Units	其他单位 Units of Other Types of Ownership
金融业	**Financial Intermediation**	**2636768**	**343684**	**1453**	**2291632**
货币金融服务	Monetary and Financial Service	1792217	288955	1453	1501809
资本市场服务	Capital Market Service	104642	1924		102718
保险业	Insurance	661886	16368		645517
其他金融业	Other Financial Activities	78023	36437		41586
房地产业	**Real Estate**	**1272599**	**27699**	**1623**	**1243276**
租赁和商务服务业	**Leasing and Business Services**	**1299719**	**131378**	**12641**	**1155701**
租赁业	Leasing	35825	2695	10	33120
商务服务业	Business Services	1263894	128682	12631	1122581
科学研究和技术服务业	**Scientific Research and Technical Services**	**1486852**	**508578**	**7077**	**971198**
研究和试验发展	Research and Experimental Development	257417	105656	160	151601
专业技术服务业	Professional Technical Services	1090574	349936	5747	734891
科技推广和应用服务业	Science and Technology Popularization and Application Services	138860	52986	1170	84705
水利、环境和公共设施管理业	**Management of Water Conservancy, Environment and Public Facilities**	**451810**	**251898**	**2537**	**197375**
水利管理业	Management of Water Conservancy	115006	112110	217	2680
生态保护和环境治理业	Ecological Protection and Environmental Treatment	32440	14091		18349
公共设施管理业	Management of Public Facilities	289133	118797	2320	168016
土地管理业	Land Management	15230	6900		8330
居民服务、修理和其他服务业	**Service to Households, Repair and Other Services**	**169248**	**31113**	**2573**	**135562**
居民服务业	Service to Households	80009	22334	1750	55926
机动车、电子产品和日用产品修理业	Repair of Motor Vehicle, Electronics and Household Products	22754	2005	474	20275
其他服务业	Other Services	66485	6775	349	59361
教 育	**Education**	**8188295**	**7555186**	**121826**	**511282**
卫生和社会工作	**Health and Social Service**	**4911184**	**4177926**	**233704**	**499554**
卫 生	Health	4853463	4147146	230665	475652
社会工作	Social Service	57721	30779	3040	23902
文化、体育和娱乐业	**Culture, Sports and Entertainment**	**348346**	**219298**	**2125**	**126923**
新闻和出版业	Journalism and Publishing Activities	85414	50378		35036
广播、电视、电影和录音制作业	Radio, Television, Film and Recording Production	103008	83713	531	18765
文化艺术业	Cultural and Art Activities	113774	71977	1188	40609
体 育	Sports Activities	14066	7994	235	5837
娱乐业	Entertainment	32084	5236	171	26677
公共管理、社会保障和社会组织	**Public Management, Social Security and Social Organization**	**7158673**	**7131835**	**13913**	**12925**
中国共产党机关	Organs of Communist Party of China	362905	362792		113
国家机构	Government Agencies	6657365	6636030	11643	9693
人民政协、民主党派	People's Political Consultative Conference and Democratic Parties	59229	59229		
社会保障	Social Security	36482	36221	217	44
群众团体、社会团体和其他成员组织	Non-Governmental Organizations, Social Organizations and Other Organizations	42364	37563	2053	2748

4—14 各市城镇非私营单位分行业就业人员工资总额（2022年）
Total Wages of Employed Persons of Urban Non-private Owned Units by Sector and Region (2022)

单位：万元（10000 yuan）

地　区　Region	合　计 Total	农　林牧渔业 Agriculture, Forestry, Animal Husbandry and Fishery	采矿业 Mining	制造业 Manufac-turing	电力、热力、燃气及水的生产和供应业 Production and Supply of Electricity, Heat, Gas and Water	建筑业 Construction	批发和零售业 Wholesale and Retail Trade	交　通运输、仓储和邮政业 Transport, Storage, Post & Telecomm-unications	住宿和餐饮业 Accommo-dation and Catering Trade	信息传输、计算机服务和软件业 Information, Circulation Computer Services and Software
总　计 Total	**56461561**	**142879**	**1698724**	**12396249**	**1326398**	**6718775**	**1998537**	**2491494**	**321319**	**1443693**
合肥市 Hefei	18702288	15758	13435	4246289	701335	3551321	938971	637207	129264	876603
淮北市 Huaibei	1609893	981	490712	217611	48668	68197	30710	23957	4452	21562
亳州市 Bozhou	2028892	2099	48027	285617	23822	146790	113250	48847	13389	30554
宿州市 Suzhou	2382421	2073	2240	193459	25513	398200	55379	46960	7923	38467
蚌埠市 Bengbu	2157146	1277		401766	20656	246976	57726	58724	6225	23591
阜阳市 Fuyang	3198521	4858	104012	356967	31274	234395	103345	55418	12075	25670
淮南市 Huainan	2521354	6570	850949	166998	187783	65516	48745	31567	3966	21414
滁州市 Chuzhou	3023680	11811	5828	1007563	34063	314751	110604	46806	7235	26920
六安市 Luan	2494070	4160	49272	468886	40481	105673	53431	47585	11273	32962
马鞍山市 Maanshan	2646651	4566	84637	808847	62435	351216	43917	58364	5642	44094
芜湖市 Wuhu	6225954	10333	71	2090988	52903	628553	242034	610601	28452	173025
宣城市 Xuancheng	2225479	6381	584	677234	23638	159519	41411	27215	8234	25420
铜陵市 Tongling	1433260	3000	30829	414022	23532	139029	30063	41767	50680	16720
池州市 Chizhou	1085837	1372	12752	221279	15550	38887	24572	16113	2927	17222
安庆市 Anqing	2948729	65424	4907	665843	25319	198827	78301	79335	13499	44667
黄山市 Huangshan	1139000	2218	469	172879	9424	70924	26079	22642	16083	24802
铁路（国家反馈） Railways (State Feedback)	638388							638388		

4—14 续表 continued

单位：万元（10000 yuan）

地 区 Region	金融业 Banking	房地产业 Real Estate	租赁和商务服务业 Leasing and Commercial Services	科学研究和技术服务业 Scientific Research and Technical Services	水利、环境和公共设施管理业 Water Conservancy, Environmental and Public Facilities Management	居民服务、修理和其他服务业 Residents Service, Repair and Other Services	教育 Education	卫生和社会工作 Health and Social Work	文化、体育和娱乐业 Culture, Sports and Entertainment	公共管理、社会保障和社会组织 Public Management, Social Security and Social Organization
总 计 Total	**2636768**	**1272599**	**1299719**	**1486852**	**451810**	**169248**	**8188295**	**4911184**	**348346**	**7158673**
合肥市 Hefei	1057319	466122	381240	959375	76446	22688	1774874	1238025	157858	1458159
淮北市 Huaibei	62416	23219	22627	18825	6344	2356	279360	99161	3820	184914
亳州市 Bozhou	130995	66012	43247	11006	18862	7853	469330	252504	10575	306113
宿州市 Suzhou	100724	69156	18140	41622	17867	2362	595873	342325	9314	414824
蚌埠市 Bengbu	78167	58657	46466	58854	30737	12002	441937	247814	13223	352349
阜阳市 Fuyang	167412	97582	27986	38746	33253	3078	824397	561432	15439	501181
淮南市 Huainan	113839	58040	47686	22241	25841	1987	388780	190822	10951	277658
滁州市 Chuzhou	118794	73895	25565	30314	43786	6824	434834	206260	8365	509465
六安市 Luan	141909	43503	33027	21293	50725	3409	536041	360079	10031	480329
马鞍山市 Maanshan	142731	35707	37184	61629	24306	4686	346379	169248	9595	351470
芜湖市 Wuhu	117800	103797	379768	95862	28424	30208	648825	380095	24351	579864
宣城市 Xuancheng	132193	36638	74600	18200	19211	5627	323706	191621	8391	445655
铜陵市 Tongling	52050	32423	20324	28686	13895	3169	231367	115849	8480	177376
池州市 Chizhou	56334	21427	85502	21602	7180	9696	178057	102367	7048	245950
安庆市 Anqing	103324	57552	26890	38996	40711	50884	518585	350347	20887	564432
黄山市 Huangshan	60761	28870	29468	19601	14222	2419	195948	103236	30018	308935
铁路(国家反馈) Railways (State Feedback)										

4—15 城镇非私营单位分行业就业人员年平均工资
Average Wage of Employed Persons of Urban Non-private Owned Units by Sector

单位：元（yuan）

行　业	Sector	2021	2022
总　计	**Total**	**93861**	**98649**
农、林、牧、渔业	Agriculture, Forestry, Animal Husbandry and Fishery	55304	61363
采矿业	Mining	123744	139477
制造业	Manufacturing	84197	88420
电力、热力、燃气及水的生产和供应业	Production and Supply of Electricity, Heat, Gas and Water	130890	135961
建筑业	Construction	72577	73907
批发和零售业	Wholesale and Retail Trades	75833	83443
交通运输、仓储和邮政业	Transport, Storage and Post	94979	91595
住宿和餐饮业	Hotels and Catering Services	52830	51885
信息传输、软件和信息技术服务业	Information Transmission, Software and Information Technology	111935	123902
金融业	Financial Intermediation	110117	134790
房地产业	Real Estate	82975	80948
租赁和商务服务业	Leasing and Business Services	61432	61210
科学研究和技术服务业	Scientific Research and Technical Services	118465	132305
水利、环境和公共设施管理业	Management of Water Conservancy, Environment	55651	51067
居民服务、修理和其他服务业	Services to Households, Repair and Other Services	62885	63420
教　育	Education	112889	120136
卫生和社会工作	Health and Social Service	125732	133119
文化、体育和娱乐业	Culture, Sports and Entertainment	84665	95935
公共管理、社会保障和社会组织	Public Management, Social Security and Social Organization	113849	119260

4—16 各市城镇非私营单位分行业就业人员年平均工资（2022年）
Average Wage of Employed Persons of Urban Non-private Owned Units by Sector By Region (2022)

单位：元（yuan）

地区 Region	合计 Total	农林牧渔业 Agriculture, Forestry, Animal Husbandry and Fishery	采矿业 Mining	制造业 Manufacturing	电力、热力、燃气及水的生产和供应业 Production and Supply of Electricity, Heat, Gas and Water	建筑业 Construction	批发和零售业 Wholesale and Retail Trade	交通运输、仓储和邮政业 Transport, Storage, Post & Telecommunications	住宿和餐饮业 Accommodation and Catering Trade	信息传输、计算机服务和软件业 Information, Circulation Computer Services and Software
总　计 Total	**98649**	**61363**	**139477**	**88420**	**135961**	**73907**	**83443**	**91595**	**51885**	**123902**
合肥市 Hefei	112019	84677	116768	112936	161255	79532	95046	100945	52527	131564
淮北市 Huaibei	95154	40657	120179	71543	114767	71574	68145	80637	39236	90910
亳州市 Bozhou	81498	39790	123633	57658	91006	64439	80891	59629	46689	124506
宿州市 Suzhou	82542	37858	118486	54649	97157	67559	57056	84653	50114	82047
蚌埠市 Bengbu	87572	49251		70582	72811	79180	57156	66958	34415	89717
阜阳市 Fuyang	85142	45769	144406	57129	97510	59791	62537	52690	44268	90913
淮南市 Huainan	111495	66936	164836	75046	157293	60254	65870	65998	40927	136279
滁州市 Chuzhou	93649	78508	60473	81080	99668	73529	91095	70587	53773	128794
六安市 Luan	97256	70137	95013	76535	109110	65864	90629	81939	42681	137023
马鞍山市 Maanshan	107254	91976	150592	95778	136507	85040	87338	95598	47905	117258
芜湖市 Wuhu	95107	102189	48697	91785	111915	70950	85980	69048	55837	127119
宣城市 Xuancheng	88968	67495	64330	76353	105722	65769	68382	95669	48827	112598
铜陵市 Tongling	98719	77865	110019	89412	106291	66088	91112	86664	72717	130998
池州市 Chizhou	95852	72734	83398	77688	100881	59598	76985	84724	44693	118563
安庆市 Anqing	89207	53109	76296	78246	77523	54019	68661	85085	43294	96491
黄山市 Huangshan	94611	61364	77239	76501	103282	55911	78697	92782	45401	132774
铁路（国家反馈） Railways (State Feedback)	160391							160391		

4—16 续表 continued

单位：元（yuan）

地区 Region	金融业 Banking	房地产业 Real Estate	租赁和商务服务业 Leasing and Commercial Services	科学研究和技术服务业 Scientific Research and Technical Services	水利、环境和公共设施管理业 Water Conservancy, Environmental and Public Facilities Management	居民服务、修理和其他服务业 Residents Service, Repair and Other Services	教育 Education	卫生和社会工作 Health and Social Work	文化、体育和娱乐业 Culture, Sports and Entertainment	公共管理、社会保障和社会组织 Public Management, Social Security and Social Organization
总计 Total	**134790**	**80948**	**61210**	**132305**	**51067**	**63420**	**120136**	**133119**	**95935**	**119260**
合肥市 Hefei	165734	84009	74689	152911	99805	74628	144452	177035	118333	149584
淮北市 Huaibei	114232	72475	47120	112344	28573	77261	115684	91890	51706	94362
亳州市 Bozhou	162334	79493	57049	84871	21942	53541	96850	116600	81135	86579
宿州市 Suzhou	98337	69374	75887	95375	28492	51467	106471	112731	70117	86336
蚌埠市 Bengbu	114377	68431	62871	114515	67006	30945	103723	109540	88158	122866
阜阳市 Fuyang	121673	95383	50286	111119	29072	52432	101390	120498	72284	91436
淮南市 Huainan	118443	91153	47404	94624	55804	73741	117748	100355	87585	102176
滁州市 Chuzhou	108560	95060	54798	99867	59849	55497	114249	119672	98299	139216
六安市 Luan	106179	90312	62659	74502	51158	52246	116098	127304	76365	119340
马鞍山市 Maanshan	133803	85082	62579	134143	123278	72659	133246	122452	84358	139018
芜湖市 Wuhu	120252	72669	59069	132974	114707	70054	146177	185856	98429	124835
宣城市 Xuancheng	151214	91040	39287	88053	52078	48490	119125	113751	84026	119210
铜陵市 Tongling	126523	58693	59800	125732	74427	79151	139657	137485	86567	137242
池州市 Chizhou	88653	84235	68763	73837	27320	72733	129626	139533	96494	138236
安庆市 Anqing	120577	67976	48192	92375	45461	76123	112775	130511	81347	122511
黄山市 Huangshan	114806	83629	100444	91837	33458	91813	129478	118493	81977	115401
铁路（国家反馈）Railways (State Feedback)										

4—17 城镇非私营单位就业人员年平均工资（2022年）

Average Wage of Employed Persons of Urban Non-private Owned Units at Their Posts (2022)

单位：元（yuan）

行业	Sector	合计 Total	在岗职工 On-the-job Worker	国有单位 State-owned Units	城镇集体单位 Urban Collective-owned Units	其他单位 Units of Other Types of Ownership
总计	**Total**	**98649**	**101999**	**123493**	**89738**	**87450**
按执行会计标准类别分组	**Grouped by Executive Accounting System Type**					
企业	Enterprises	88563	91413	105465	65818	87702
政府	Government	126589	129998	126834	120000	113313
民间非营利组织	Non-profit Organizations	62327	63338	67230	74256	59780
其他	Others	83434	84031	125452	43188	50523
按国民经济行业分组	**Grouped by Economic Sector**					
农、林、牧、渔业	Agriculture, Forestry, Animal Husbandry and Fishery	61363	70765	62038	55116	58351
采矿业	Mining	139477	140458	131534	41604	139841
制造业	Manufacturing	88420	88678	144968	67801	87333
电力、热力、燃气及水的生产和供应业	Production and Supply of Electricity, Heat, Gas and Water	135961	136580	117492	69488	138953
建筑业	Construction	73907	76005	67205	69980	74422
批发和零售业	Wholesale and Retail Trade	83443	84053	135243	41853	79904
交通运输、仓储和邮政业	Transport, Storage and Postal Services	91595	96835	74999	43096	93059
住宿和餐饮业	Accommodation and Catering Trade	51885	52159	49326	37458	51971
信息传输、计算机服务和软件业	Information Circulation, Computer Service and Software	123902	128829	132638	42304	123471
金融业	Banking	134790	170547	150393	76463	132788
房地产业	Real Estate	80948	83969	85356	45948	80935
租赁和商务服务业	Leasing and Commercial Services	61210	62736	79134	69736	59596
科学研究和技术服务业	Scientific Research and Technical Services	132305	133833	125136	76183	137156
水利、环境和公共设施管理业	Water Conservancy, Environmental and Public Facilities Management	51067	54957	99846	82639	31360
居民服务、修理和其他服务业	Residents Service, Repair and Other Services	63420	63092	86167	55874	59942
教育	Education	120136	122905	127169	97647	68168
卫生和社会工作	Health and Social Work	133119	134493	143512	118756	85933
文化、体育和娱乐业	Culture, Sports and Entertainment	95935	98179	111236	84333	77657
公共管理、社会保障和社会组织	Public Management, Social Security and Social Organization	119260	123444	119352	98027	99857

4—18 各市城镇非私营单位就业人员年平均工资（2022年）
Average Wage of Employed Persons of Urban Non-private Owned Units at Their Posts by Region (2022)

单位：元（yuan）

地　区	Region	合　计 Total	在岗职工 On-the-job Worker
总　计	**Total**	**98649**	**101999**
合 肥 市	Hefei	112019	117760
淮 北 市	Huaibei	95154	97564
亳 州 市	Bozhou	81498	83187
宿 州 市	Suzhou	82542	85159
蚌 埠 市	Bengbu	87572	89218
阜 阳 市	Fuyang	85142	87591
淮 南 市	Huainan	111495	115829
滁 州 市	Chuzhou	93649	95083
六 安 市	Luan	97256	99416
马鞍山市	Maanshan	107254	109561
芜 湖 市	Wuhu	95107	96390
宣 城 市	Xuancheng	88968	90205
铜 陵 市	Tongling	98719	100968
池 州 市	Chizhou	95852	98596
安 庆 市	Anqing	89207	93278
黄 山 市	Huangshan	94611	96695
铁　路(国家反馈)	Railways (State Feedback)	160391	162865

4—19 城镇私营单位就业人员和工资情况（2022年）
Wages of Employed Persons in Private Enterprises of Urban Areas (2022)

行　业	Sector	单位就业人员年末人数（人）Number of Employed Persons per Unit at the End of the Year (person)	工资总额（千元）Total Wage (1000 yuan)	平均工资（元）Average Wage (yuan)
总　计	**Total**	**4641626**	**256474593**	**57095**
按国民经济行业分组	**Grouped by Economic Sector**			
农、林、牧、渔业	Agriculture, Forestry, Animal Husbandry and Fishery	27660	1296512	45936
采矿业	Mining	6409	485659	76107
制造业	Manufacturing	1366254	81791540	61150
电力、热力、燃气及水的生产和供应业	Production and Supply of Electricity, Heat, Gas and Water	8632	459515	54236
建筑业	Construction	1195355	66988701	59091
批发和零售业	Wholesale and Retail Trade	463004	23593303	51511
交通运输、仓储和邮政业	Transport, Storage and Postal Services	119531	6489911	55425
住宿和餐饮业	Accommodation and Catering Trade	136132	6096104	45391
信息传输、计算机服务和软件业	Information Circulation, Computer Service	97893	7012074	73751
金融业	Banking	12927	1079079	84014
房地产业	Real Estate	161215	8138778	50078
租赁和商务服务业	Leasing and Commercial Services	579164	29299806	54222
科学研究和技术服务业	Scientific Research and Technical Services	126463	7397027	59454
水利、环境和公共设施管理业	Water Conservancy, Environmental and Public Facilities Management	47811	1717338	37477
居民服务、修理和其他服务业	Residents Service, Repair and Other Services	66584	2743871	42548
教　育	Education	141887	6922768	49644
卫生和社会工作	Health and Social Work	56026	3565222	64809
文化、体育和娱乐业	Culture, Sports and Entertainment	28681	1397383	49291
公共管理、社会保障和社会组织	Public Management, Social Security and Social Organization			

4—20 城镇非私营单位分行业就业人员年平均工资（2022年）

Average Wage of Employed Persons of Urban Non-private Owned Units by Sector (2022)

单位：元（yuan）

行　业	Sector	合　计 Total	国有单位 State-owned Units	城镇集体单位 Urban Collective-owned Units	其他单位 Units of Other Types of Ownership
总　计	**Total**	**98649**	**123493**	**89738**	**87450**
按国民经济行业分组	**Grouped by Economic Sector**				
农、林、牧、渔业	**Agriculture, Forestry, Animal Husbandry and Fishery**	**61363**	**62038**	**55116**	**58351**
农　业	Farming	62935	67630	42508	43492
林　业	Forestry	79369	79084	90714	79727
畜牧业	Animal Husbandry	65649	29417		66246
渔　业	Fishery	43290	33938	22000	45784
农林牧渔专业及辅助性活动	Agriculture, Forestry, Animal Husbandry and Fishery Major and Supporting Activities	56715	55846	58221	67786
采矿业	**Mining**	**139477**	**131534**	**41604**	**139841**
煤炭开采和洗选业	Mining and Washing of Coal	144679	97789		145169
石油和天然气开采业	Extraction of Petroleum and Natural Gas	131659			131659
黑色金属矿采选业	Mining and Processing of Ferrous Metal Ores	119972	149579	41313	107827
有色金属矿采选业	Mining and Processing of Non-Ferrous Metal Ores	82942	105222		82480
非金属矿采选业	Mining and Processing of Non-metal Ores	113461	96243	41730	115125
开采专业及辅助性活动	Mining Profession and Auxiliary Activities	97274	121110		50525
制造业	**Manufacturing**	**88420**	**144968**	**67801**	**87333**
农副食品加工业	Processing of Food from Agricultural Products	65750	62551	49312	65823
食品制造业	Manufacture of Foods	67203	64000	40727	67215
酒、饮料和精制茶制造业	Manufacture of Liquor, Beverages and Refined Tea	69977	30375	44015	70768
烟草制品业	Manufacture of Tobacco	258878	279614		163391
纺织业	Manufacture of Textile	61106	62493	66960	61078
纺织服装、服饰业	Manufacture of Textile, Wearing Apparel and Accessories	60495		36600	60500
皮革、毛皮、羽毛及其制品和制鞋业	Manufacture of Leather, Fur, Feather and Related Products and Footwear	57119		30000	57120
木材加工和木、竹、藤、棕、草制品业	Processing of Timber, Manufacture of Wood, Bamboo, Rattan, Palm and Straw Products	61963			61963
家具制造业	Manufacture of Furniture	79605			79605
造纸及纸制品业	Manufacture of Paper and Paper Products	74761	130562	114799	71463
印刷和记录媒介复制业	Printing and Reproduction of Recording Media	76226	58306	67575	76515
文教、工美、体育和娱乐用品制造业	Manufacture of Articles for Culture, Education, Arts and Crafts, Sport and Entertainment Activities	52392	56289	42683	52438
石油、煤炭及其他燃料加工业	Petroleum, Coal and Other Fuel Processing Industries	146553			146553
化学原料和化学制品制造业	Manufacture of Raw Chemical Materials and Chemical Products	96812	146873	62867	96655
医药制造业	Manufacture of Medicines	72439		33231	72449
化学纤维制造业	Manufacture of Chemical Fibres	76575			76575
橡胶和塑料制品业	Manufacture of Rubber and Plastics Products	82665	93895	43390	82757
非金属矿物制品业	Manufacture of Non-metallic Mineral Products	82461	109680	49080	81057
黑色金属冶炼和压延加工业	Smelting and Pressing of Ferrous Metals	111806	121603	54960	111685

4—20 续表1 continued

单位：元（yuan）

行 业	Sector	合 计 Total	国有单位 State-owned Units	城镇集体单位 Urban Collective-owned Units	其他单位 Units of Other Types of Ownership
有色金属冶炼和压延加工业	Smelting and Pressing of Non-ferrous Metals	85149	73426	25000	85218
金属制品业	Manufacture of Metal Products	80668	75630	80445	80723
通用设备制造业	Manufacture of General Purpose Machinery	91998	100771	77089	91842
专用设备制造业	Manufacture of Special Purpose Machinery	92215	100930	102213	92002
汽车制造业	Manufacture of Automobiles	99005	93442	66714	99127
铁路、船舶、航空航天和其他运输设备制造业	Manufacture of Railway, Ship, Aerospace and Other Transport Equipments	107456	149792	47988	103691
电气机械和器材制造业	Manufacture of Electrical Machinery and Apparatus	88288		24933	88293
计算机、通信和其他电子设备制造业	Manufacture of Computers, Communication and Other Electronic Equipment	101864	64345		102414
仪器仪表制造业	Manufacture of Measuring Instruments and Machinery	122984		35857	123039
其他制造业	Other Manufacture	100733	103914	26667	100895
废弃资源综合利用业	Utilization of Waste Resources	79273	221645		71614
金属制品、机械和设备修理业	Repair Service of Metal Products, Machinery and Equipment	139406	162884		110851
电力、热力、燃气及水生产和供应业	**Production and Supply of Electricity, Heat, Gas and Water**	**135961**	**117492**	**69488**	**138953**
电力、热力的生产和供应业	Production and Supply of Electric Power and Heat Power	160481	133177	112913	164719
燃气生产和供应业	Production and Supply of Gas	88416	94939		88366
水的生产和供应业	Production and Supply of Water	88642	83143	66139	90356
建筑业	**Construction**	**73907**	**67205**	**69980**	**74422**
房屋建筑业	Construction of Buildings	67379	64315	47931	68006
土木工程建筑业	Civil Engineering	88185	69083	90868	88880
建筑安装业	Building Installation	76477	100573	82992	74961
建筑装饰、装修和其他建筑业	Architectural Decoration, Decoration and Other Construction Industries	73703	88779	96322	71562
批发和零售业	**Wholesale and Retail Trades**	**83443**	**135243**	**41853**	**79904**
批发业	Wholesale Trade	114488	143743	44528	110094
零售业	Retail Trade	61904	88951	40265	61509
交通运输、仓储和邮政业	**Transport, Storage and Post**	**91595**	**74999**	**43096**	**93059**
铁路运输业	Railway Transport	159471	60333		159541
道路运输业	Road Transport	74024	73953	43525	74256
水上运输业	Water Transport	93816	123991	45349	92876
航空运输业	Air Transport	128516	124413		129493
管道运输业	Transport Via Pipelines	143667			143667
多式联运和运输代理业	Multimodal Transport and Transportation Agency	87750	50830	22286	90402
装卸搬运和仓储业	Handling and Storage Industry	71467	53148	42272	81901
邮政业	Post	84523	109093		83958
住宿和餐饮业	**Hotels and Catering Services**	**51885**	**49326**	**37458**	**51971**
住宿业	Hotels	52208	45981	28000	52396
餐饮业	Catering Services	51622	53665	38528	51627
信息传输、软件和信息技术服务业	**Information Transmission, Software and Information Technology**	**123902**	**132638**	**42304**	**123471**
电信、广播电视和卫星传输服务	Telecommunication, Radio and Television and Satellite Transmission Service	120449	130219	24945	119349
互联网和相关服务	Internet and Related Service	111034	167705		110599
软件和信息技术服务业	Software and Information Technology	129138	147572	86000	128926

4—20 续表2 continued

单位：元（yuan）

行业	Sector	合计 Total	国有单位 State-owned Units	城镇集体单位 Urban Collective-owned Units	其他单位 Units of Other Types of Ownership
金融业	**Financial Intermediation**	**134790**	**150393**	**76463**	**132788**
货币金融服务	Monetary and Financial Service	180625	145349	76463	189735
资本市场服务	Capital Market Service	223401	190465		224127
保险业	Insurance	74035	71859		74092
其他金融业	Other Financial Activities	337542	613929		242062
房地产业	**Real Estate**	**80948**	**85356**	**45948**	**80935**
租赁和商务服务业	**Leasing and Business Services**	**61210**	**79134**	**69736**	**59596**
租赁业	Leasing	77448	121964	50000	75226
商务服务业	Business Services	60848	78557	69758	59233
科学研究和技术服务业	**Scientific Research and Technical Services**	**132305**	**125136**	**76183**	**137156**
研究和试验发展	Research and Experimental Development	157522	130662	35556	184644
专业技术服务业	Professional Technical Services	135304	128819	78664	139432
科技推广和应用服务业	Science and Technology Popularization and Application Services	89950	98285	76288	85620
水利、环境和公共设施管理业	**Management of Water Conservancy, Environment and Public Facilities**	**51067**	**99846**	**82639**	**31360**
水利管理业	Management of Water Conservancy	126335	127897	130048	83483
生态保护和环境治理业	Ecological Protection and Environmental Treatment	100550	100411		100656
公共设施管理业	Management of Public Facilities	38706	82662	79916	27985
土地管理业	Land Management	105375	100271		110014
居民服务、修理和其他服务业	**Service to Households, Repair and Other Services**	**63420**	**86167**	**55874**	**59942**
居民服务业	Service to Households	68725	91685	58915	62774
机动车、电子产品和日用产品修理业	Repair of Motor Vehicle, Electronics and Household Products	67922	78468	51792	67516
其他服务业	Other Services	56850	73689	48514	55460
教　育	**Education**	**120136**	**127169**	**97647**	**68168**
卫生和社会工作	**Health and Social Service**	**133119**	**143512**	**118756**	**85933**
卫　生	Health	135551	145076	121450	89407
社会工作	Social Service	53055	58511	44261	48461
文化、体育和娱乐业	**Culture, Sports and Entertainment**	**95935**	**111236**	**84333**	**77657**
新闻和出版业	Journalism and Publishing Activities	127366	129972		123796
广播、电视、电影和录音制作业	Radio, Television, Film and Recording Production	104160	117477	76928	69640
文化艺术业	Cultural and Art Activities	86278	96387	90695	72665
体　育	Sports Activities	77302	109760	87148	54840
娱乐业	Entertainment	68140	101290	68400	64025
公共管理、社会保障和社会组织	**Public Management, Social Security and Social Organization**	**119260**	**119352**	**98027**	**99857**
中国共产党机关	Organs of Communist Party of China	126151	126152		125000
国家机构	Government Agencies	118916	118982	94330	111282
人民政协、民主党派	People's Political Consultative Conference and Democratic Parties	148075	148075		
社会保障	Social Security	98962	99413	69935	37000
群众团体、社会团体和其他成员组织	Non-Governmental Organizations, Social Organizations and Other Organizations	108462	110127	133312	80583

主要统计指标解释

就业人员

指从事一定社会劳动并取得劳动报酬或经营收入的全部劳动力。包括：1. 全部职工；2. 城镇私营企业从业人员；3. 城镇个体劳动者；4. 农村社会劳动者；5. 其他社会劳动者。这一指标反映了一定时期内全部劳动力资源的实际利用情况，是研究基本国情国力的重要指标。

单位就业人员

指在各级国家机关、政党机关、社会团体及企业、事业单位中工作，取得工资或其他形式的劳动报酬的全部人员。包括在岗职工、再就业的离退休人员、民办教师以及在各单位中工作的外方人员和港澳台方人员、兼职人员、借用的外单位人员和第二职业者。不包括离开本单位仍保留劳动关系的职工。各单位的从业人员反映了各单位实际参加生产或工作的全部劳动力。

城镇私营和个体就业人员

城镇私营就业人员指在工商管理部门注册登记，其经营地址设在县城关镇（含城关镇）以上的私营企业从业人员；包括私营企业投资者和雇工。城镇个体从业人员指在工商管理部门注册登记，并持有城镇户口或在城镇长期居住，经批准从事个体工商经营的从业人员；包括个体经营者和在个体工商户劳动的家庭帮工和雇工。

城镇登记失业人员

指有非农业户口，在一定的劳动年龄内，有劳动能力，无业而要求就业，并在当地就业服务机构进行求职登记的人员。

城镇登记失业率

指城镇登记失业人数同城镇从业人数与城镇登记失业人数之和的比。计算公式为：

城镇登记失业率=城镇登记失业人数/（城镇从业人数+城镇登记失业人数）×100%

在岗职工

指在本单位工作并由单位支付工资的人员，以及有工作岗位，但由于学习、病伤产假等原因暂未工作，仍由单位支付工资的人员。

专业技术人员

指从事专业技术工作的人员以及从事专业技术管理工作且已在1983年以前评定了专业技术职称或在1984年以后聘任了专业技术职务的人员。

专业技术人员具体指工程技术人员、农业技术人员、科研人员（含自然科学研究、社会科学研究及实验技术人员）、卫生技术人员、教学人员（含高等院校、中等专业学校、技工学校、中学、小学）、民用航空飞行技术人员、船舶技术人员、经济人员、会计人员、统计人员、翻译人员、图书资料、档案、文博人员、新闻、出版人员、律师、公证人员、广播电视播音人员、工艺美术人员、体育人员、艺术人员及政工人员。

专业技术管理人员具体指企业、事业单位的领导；企业、事业单位下设的职能机构、企业的生产车间和辅助车间（或附属辅助生产单位）中从事生产、技术、经济管理和政治工作的人员。

按照公务员管理或参照公务员管理的人员不统计为专业技术人员。

就业人员工资总额

指根据《关于工资总额组成的规定》（1990年1月1日国家统计局发布的一号令）进行修订，本单位在报告期内（季度或年度）直接支付给本单位全部就业人员的劳动报酬总额。包括计时工资、计件工资、奖金、津贴和补贴、加班加点工资、特殊情况下支付的工资，是在岗职工工资总额、劳务派遣人员工资总额和其他从业人员工资总额之和。

在岗职工工资总额

指本单位在报告期内直接支付给本单位全部在岗职工的劳动报酬总额。在岗职工工资总额由基本工资、绩效工资、工资性津贴和补贴、其他工资四部分组成。工资总额不包括病假、事假等情况的扣款。

就业人员平均工资

指本单位就业人员在报告期内平均每人所得的工资额。

在岗职工平均工资

指本单位在岗职工在报告期内平均每人所得的工资额。

Explanatory Notes for Major Statistical Indicators

Employed Persons

refers to the persons who are engaged in social labor and receive remuneration payment or earn business income, including: (1)Total staff and workers; (2)Employed persons in private enterprises in urban areas; (3)Self-employed individuals in urban areas; (4)Social laborers in rural areas; (5)Other social laborers. It reflects the utilization of total labor force during a given period of time.

Persons Employed in Various Units

refer to all the persons working in government agencies of various levels, political and party organizations, social organizations, enterprises and institutions, and receiving wages or other forms of payment. They include fully-employed staff and workers, re-employed retirees, teachers in schools run by the local people, foreigners and Chinese compatriots from Hong Kong, Macao, and Taiwan working in various units, part-time employees, employees of other units working temporarily at current posts, and employees holding the second job, but exclude staff and workers who have left their working units while keeping their labour contract (employment relation) unchanged. This indicator reflects the total number of laborers actually engaged in production or other operations in various units.

Persons Employed in Private Enterprises and Self-Employed Individuals in Urban Areas

Persons employed in private enterprises refer to the persons employed in the private enterprises which have been registered at the departments of industrial and commercial administration and are situated at a county town (i.e. a town where the county government is located) for business operation or at urban areas with the level higher than a county town. The self-employed individuals in urban areas refer to persons who hold the certificates of residence in urban areas or have resided in the urban areas for a long time and have been registered at the departments of industrial and commercial administration and approved to be engaged in individual industrial or commercial business, including self-employed persons as well as helpers and hired labourers who work in the individual households engaged in industrial or commercial business.

Registered Urban Unemployed Persons

The registered unemployed persons in urban areas refer to the persons who are registered as permanent residents in the urban areas engaged in non-agricultural activities, aged within the range of working age, capable to labour, unemployed but desirous to be employed and have been registered at the local employment service agencies to apply for a job.

Registered Urban Unemployment Rate

Registered unemployment rate in urban areas refers to the ratio of the number of the registered unemployed persons to the sum of the number of employed persons and the registered unemployed persons. The formula is as follows:

Registered urban unemployment rate =number of registered urban unemployed persons/(urban employed person number + registered urban unemployed person number)×100%

Fully Employed Staff and Workers

refer to persons who work in, and receive wages from their working units, as well as persons who have their work posts, but are temporarily absent from work for reasons of study or on sick, injury or maternal leave and still receive wages from their working units.

Professional and Technical Personnel

refers to professional, technical and managerial staff members in institutions who were rated professional and technical titles before 1983 or appointed professional and technical posts after 1984.

Professional and technical personnel includes the following: Engineering, Agriculture, Scientific Research (including natural science, social science and laboratory technique), Health care, Teaching, civil aviation, shipping, economics, accounting, statistics, translating, archives, publishing, lawyer, broadcasting, craft, physical culture, art and political workers.

Managerial staff refers to the leadership of enterprises and institutions and persons engaged in production, technology, economic management and political work in functioning organizations under enterprises or institutions and workshop of enterprises.

Public servants or the personnel in light of public service

are not included.

Total wages of employed persons

According to the "Regulations of total wages" (No.1 decree issued in January 11990 by the National Bureau of Statistics), it is revised, the unit during the report period (quarterly or annual) paid directly to the total remuneration of the units of all employees. Including hourly wages, piece-rate wages, bonuses, allowances and subsidies, overtime wages, wages under special circumstances, It is on the total wages of staff and workers, labor dispatch staff wages and other employees wages .

Total wages of employed staff and workers

Refers to the total amount of labor remuneration paid by the unit directly to all on-duty employees of the unit during the reporting period. The total salary of staff and workers is composed of basic salary, performance salary, salary allowance and subsidy, and other wages. Gross wages do not include deductions for sick leave, personal leave, etc.

The average wage of employed persons

Refers to the average wages of staff in the report period

Average wages of employed staff and workers

Refers to the average wages of employed staff in the report period

第 五 篇

Chapter 5

固定资产投资

INVESTMENT IN FIXED ASSETS

简要说明

一、按照国家统计局现行统计制度规定，固定资产投资统计的范围包括：⑴城镇投资500万元以上项目；⑵房地产开发投资。按登记注册类型分，包括内资、港澳台商及外商投资。

二、固定资产投资统计资料来源为：项目建设单位填报的报表和“一套表”平台房地产开发企业填的报表，由省统计局投资处加工整理提供。

三、固定资产投资统计的调查方法，均为全面统计报表。

Brief Introduction

I. According to the current statistical system stipulated by State Statistical Bureau, the fixed assets investment includes: (1) items in town with investment of five million yean and above; (2) the real estate investment, they include domestic investment, investment from Hong Kong, Macao and Taiwan and investment from foreign countries.

II. Data sources for the statistics of investment in fixed assets are as follows: These tables filled by the project construction units and real estate development enterprises of a set of tables platform are provided and processed by investment department of Anhui Provincial Bureau of Statistics

III. Survey methods of fixed assets investment statistics are all comprehensive statistical reports.

5—1 固定资产投资主要指标增长情况
Growth of Main Indicators of Fixed Asset Investment

单位：%

指　标	Item	2021	2022
固定资产投资	**Investment in Fixed Assets**	**9.4**	**9.0**
按构成分	According to Composition		
建筑安装工程	Construction and Installation	15.7	7.3
设备工器具购置	Purchase of Instruments	2.9	11.7
其他费用	Other Expenses	-11.0	15.2
按三次产业分	According to the Three Industry		
第一产业	Primary Industry	39.1	22.5
第二产业	Secondary Industry	13.5	21.8
第三产业	Tertiary Industry	6.9	2.5
按投资资金来源分	According to the Source of Investment Funds	17.0	5.6
国家预算资金	State Budget Funds	38.9	50.9
国内贷款	Domestic Loans	-6.8	11.8
债　券	Bonds	-78.2	-66.7
利用外资	Foreign Investment	14.4	-18.6
自筹资金	Self-raising Funds	21.5	16.7
其他资金来源	Other Sources of Funding	13.6	-20.5
房屋建筑面积	Building Area		
本年施工房屋面积	Area of Houses Under Construction This Year	4.1	-12.8
#住　宅	Residential	4.3	-12.9
本年竣工房屋面积	Housing Area Completed This Year	37.5	-15.2
#住　宅	Residential	38.1	-19.3

注：由于投资统计方法变化，增速为可比口径。

a) Due to changes in investment statistics methods, the growth rate is comparable.

5—2 各行业按登记注册类型分固定资产投资增长情况（2022年）

Growth of Investment in Fixed Assets by Industry by Type of Registration (2022)

行业	Sector	固定资产投资 Investment in Fixed Assets	内资企业 Domestic Funded Enterprise	国有企业 State-owned Enterprise
总计	**Total**	**9.0**	**9.2**	**15.4**
农、林、牧、渔业	**Agriculture, Forestry, Animal Husbandry and Fishery**	**20.3**	**19.9**	**38.1**
农业	Farming	49.6	49.0	49.8
林业	Forestry	101.4	100.7	172.2
畜牧业	Animal Husbandry	-27.6	-28.3	-18.7
渔业	Fishery	9.3	9.3	9.4
农林牧渔业及辅助性活动	Agriculture, Forestry, Animal Husbandry and Fishery Major and Supporting Activities	-5.4	-5.7	-36.4
采矿业	**Mining**	**30.1**	**29.7**	**162.0**
煤炭开采和洗选业	Mining and Washing of Coal	2.9	2.9	94.0
石油和天然气开采业	Extraction of Petroleum and Natural Gas	994.5	994.5	
黑色金属矿采选业	Mining and Processing of Ferrous Metal Ores	18.3	16.8	-79.1
有色金属矿采选业	Mining and Processing of Non-Ferrous Metal Ores	-40.9	-40.9	
非金属矿采选业	Mining and Processing of Non-metal Ores	110.0	108.6	362.7
开采专业及辅助性活动	Mining Profession and Auxiliary Activities	60.7	60.7	
其他采矿业	Mining of Other Ores	-58.7	-58.7	
制造业	**Manufacturing**	**21.5**	**22.9**	**2.2**
农副食品加工业	Processing of Food from Agricultural Products	-1.3	-1.1	-17.7
食品制造业	Manufacture of Foods	-13.3	-9.9	60.1
酒、饮料和精制茶制造业	Manufacture of Liquor, Beverages and Refined Tea	25.0	21.4	83.8
烟草制品业	Manufacture of Tobacco	-6.4	-7.0	-3.0
纺织业	Manufacture of Textile	7.5	8.2	
纺织服装、服饰业	Manufacture of Textile, Wearing Apparel and Accessories	9.2	10.3	76.1
皮革、毛皮、羽毛及其制品和制鞋业	Manufacture of Leather, Fur, Feather and Related Products and Footwear	47.9	53.5	
木材加工和木、竹、藤、棕、草制品业	Processing of Timber, Manufacture of Wood, Bamboo, Rattan, Palm and Straw Products	22.7	21.7	-23.3
家具制造业	Manufacture of Furniture	-23.0	-23.1	
造纸和纸制品业	Manufacture of Paper and Paper Products	39.5	44.0	122.0
印刷和记录媒介复制业	Printing and Reproduction of Recording Media	-8.2	-11.2	
文教、工美、体育和娱乐用品制造业	Manufacture of Articles for Culture, Education, Arts and Crafts, Sport and Entertainment Activities	81.5	87.0	300.0
石油、煤炭及其他燃料加工业	Petroleum, Coal and Other Fuel Processing Industries	40.1	66.3	
化学原料和化学制品制造业	Manufacture of Raw Chemical Materials and Chemical Products	4.2	7.2	
医药制造业	Manufacture of Medicines	8.5	9.2	-6.8
化学纤维制造业	Manufacture of Chemical Fibres	35.2	41.1	
橡胶和塑料制品业	Manufacture of Rubber and Plastics Products	5.8	7.3	
非金属矿物制品业	Manufacture of Non-metallic Mineral Products	4.8	3.7	384.0
黑色金属冶炼和压延加工业	Smelting and Pressing of Ferrous Metals	37.9	38.6	
有色金属冶炼和压延加工业	Smelting and Pressing of Non-ferrous Metals	26.7	32.4	-33.6

单位：%

集体企业 Collective-owned Enterprise	股份合作企业 Share Holding Cooperative Enterprises	联营企业 Joint Owned Enterprises	有限责任公司 Limited Liability Corporations	股份有限公司 Share-holding Corporations Ltd.	私营企业 Private Enterprises	其他企业 Other Enterprises	港、澳、台商投资企业 Enterprises Funded by Entrepreneurs from Hong Kong, Macao and Taiwan	外商投资企业 Foreign Funded Enterprises	个体经营 Individual Management
45.0	**13.0**	**17.9**	**7.3**	**8.7**	**7.5**	**18.4**	**7.8**	**-11.3**	**92.0**
232.5	**298.9**	**1086.4**	**48.4**	**8.7**	**-10.7**	**36.3**	**26.6**		**125.6**
114.3	368.6	1086.4	173.4	138.4	7.2	28.5	31.6		1372.3
			92.3		-0.7	469.8			
306.8	-72.9		-48.1	-10.8	-25.7	2.7			32.4
			-38.7		-6.7	115.7			
475.5			179.4	-0.7	-12.8	-25.0			30.8
			24.9	**96.0**	**3.5**	**-92.1**		**63.3**	
			-8.7	166.8	-84.4	-91.9			
			994.5						
			20.0		78.8			43.4	
			-68.5	94.3	12.5				
			157.9		-4.8				
			112.0	-90.5	-59.2				
					-58.7				
-26.9	**204.5**	**1101.6**	**37.5**	**11.0**	**18.7**	**9.9**	**15.2**	**-13.1**	**38.2**
1977.3			29.3	266.1	-14.0	121.2	840.0	-57.5	-54.7
			4.6	-77.9	-11.1	279.7	11.0	-47.2	
35.1			-0.2	53.3	-0.8	-28.9	96.5	39.7	20.0
			18.6	-3.5	6.2	-51.2	180.8	-67.9	
			111.2	-48.8	1.4	-38.6	6.4		
			81.3	370.5	40.7			292.7	
			-34.8		50.6	-36.7	10.9		
			-26.1	-74.2	-21.7	-94.7		-39.9	
-70.4			-17.3		70.9	220.3		-27.4	
			23.5	-54.7	-15.5		367.5	-20.8	
			151.7	499.4	72.4	-78.4			
			85.9	96.1	4.5	4980.8	-97.4	-21.5	
			9.5	7.3	5.0		-58.0	-29.9	
			42.6	9.2	-0.4	108.1	34.0	-41.7	
			-19.1	-14.0	144.6				
	-52.3	695.7	29.0	-25.8	3.8	-65.7	0.5	-44.2	
			0.9	10.4	-2.1	-15.2	529.1	-48.5	701.8
			0.1	81.2	9.4	-79.0		-10.5	
			58.8	20.5	33.1		-11.0	-48.2	

5—2 续表1 continued

行业	Sector	固定资产投资 Investment in Fixed Assets	内资企业 Domestic Funded Enterprise	国有企业 State-owned Enterprise
金属制品业	Manufacture of Metal Products	31.6	33.0	78.0
通用设备制造业	Manufacture of General Purpose Machinery	11.3	15.2	307.6
专用设备制造业	Manufacture of Special Purpose Machinery	3.7	3.3	-5.5
汽车制造业	Manufacture of Automobiles	34.1	33.2	-41.4
铁路、船舶、航空航天和其他运输设备制造业	Manufacture of Railway, Ship, Aerospace and Other Transport Equipments	-20.2	-19.1	-72.6
电气机械和器材制造业	Manufacture of Electrical Machinery and Apparatus	80.5	85.7	431.6
计算机、通信和其他电子设备制造业	Manufacture of Computers, Communication and Other Electronic Equipment	31.9	33.5	-55.7
仪器仪表制造业	Manufacture of Measuring Instruments and Machinery	91.4	89.5	1359.8
其他制造业	Other Manufacture	9.4	8.5	-16.5
废弃资源综合利用业	Comprehensive Utilization of Waste Resources	-3.3	-1.1	-12.9
金属制品、机械和设备修理业	Repair Service of Metal Products, Machinery and Equipment	-32.5	-32.5	1397.6
电力、热力、燃气及水生产和供应业	**Production and Supply of Electricity, Heat, Gas and Water**	**22.7**	**22.9**	**35.3**
电力、热力生产和供应业	Production and Supply of Electric Power and Heat Power	21.6	21.7	40.2
燃气生产和供应业	Production and Supply of Gas	5.4	0.4	490.3
水的生产和供应业	Production and Supply of Water	28.4	28.7	30.3
建筑业	**Construction**	**-31.6**	**-31.6**	
房屋建筑业	Construction of Buildings	-10.8	-10.8	
土木工程建筑业	Civil Engineering	-68.5	-68.5	
建筑安装业	Building Installation			
建筑装饰、装修和其他建筑业	Architectural Decoration, Decoration and Other Construction Industries	7.1	7.1	
批发和零售业	**Wholesale and Retail Trades**	**-22.6**	**-21.9**	**-17.3**
批发业	Wholesale Trade	-27.9	-28.5	-76.2
零售业	Retail Trade	-19.3	-17.1	72.9
交通运输、仓储和邮政业	**Transport, Storage and Post**	**22.5**	**22.9**	**20.5**
铁路运输业	Railway Transport	39.8	39.8	27.9
道路运输业	Road Transport	18.3	18.3	19.2
水上运输业	Water Transport	96.9	97.2	143.3
航空运输业	Air Transport	220.2	220.2	51.5
管道运输业	Transport Via Pipelines	0.0	-4.0	1.1
多式联运和运输代理业	Multimodal Transport and Transportation Agency	22.3	11.8	-81.5
装卸搬运和仓储业	Handling and warehousing industry	12.3	18.5	46.0
邮政业	Post	16.7	16.7	313.2
住宿和餐饮业	**Hotels and Catering Services**	**8.2**	**7.5**	**100.8**
住宿业	Hotels	11.2	10.6	121.4
餐饮业	Catering Services	-6.7	-7.2	24.9
信息传输、软件和信息技术服务业	**Information Transmission, Software and Information Technology**	**2.4**	**-0.2**	**68.1**
电信、广播电视和卫星传输服务	Telecommunication, Radio and Television and Satellite Transmission Service	4.7	0.5	33.6
互联网和相关服务	Internet and Related Service	-11.3	-11.3	50.1
软件和信息技术服务业	Software and Information Technology	8.0	7.0	192.4

单位：%

集体企业 Collective-owned Enterprise	股份合作企业 Share Holding Cooperative Enterprises	联营企业 Joint Owned Enterprises	有限责任公司 Limited Liability Corporations	股份有限公司 Share-holding Corporations Ltd.	私营企业 Private Enterprises	其他企业 Other Enterprises	港、澳、台商投资企业 Enterprises Funded by Entrepreneurs from Hong Kong, Macao and Taiwan	外商投资企业 Foreign Funded Enterprises	个体经营 Individual Management
			77.1	-9.3	23.5	-21.7	24.2	-41.2	
			10.3	-12.8	16.2	-30.7	-66.0	-25.5	
		401.5	42.5	-20.5	-7.7	557.1	-2.4	84.4	
			42.5	-10.3	52.8	-35.4	12.4	46.0	
			-24.2	-21.6	-10.1	-38.6	-9.8	-71.9	
	496.6		104.1	-49.7	85.1	665.3	33.2	-29.8	
			46.1	4.3	31.2	-5.5	28.5	-13.6	
			53.9	449.9	87.6		-72.4	1090.0	
			51.8	-69.9	8.0	434.6		616.1	
			6.8	-85.0	6.0	146.3	-64.4		
			-18.3		-75.3				
950.0		**-85.0**	**33.9**	**-9.7**	**-23.4**	**-8.9**	**16.9**	**33.7**	
			42.7	-30.4	-29.4	-26.5	15.5	96.6	
			9.4	809.1	-22.8		47.5	13.9	
			21.1	140.7	31.6	19.3	-11.9		
			-43.7		**32.4**				
			-40.2		4824.0				
			-56.6						
			-51.4		48.4				
	247.1		**-41.6**	**-6.1**	**-8.1**	**37.6**	**-11.6**	**-38.1**	**305.5**
			-40.4	-66.1	-0.8	680.0			
	247.1		-42.6	16.0	-12.7	-6.0	-11.6	-38.1	75.3
80.0		**563.5**	**28.7**	**33.4**	**6.7**	**-8.4**	**-28.8**	**-41.8**	**-80.7**
			52.4	34.9					
-51.9			15.6	73.6	48.2	-12.4			
			150.5	65.1	1.4				
			452.4		-56.8				
								571.7	
			-2.6		50.8				
544.9			27.4	-65.9	-6.8	75.5	-28.2	-73.1	-80.7
			719.6		-50.8				
462.1			**-7.4**	**82.6**	**2.9**	**160.3**	**-66.9**		**119.7**
462.1			-5.2	84.4	5.7	121.6	-66.9		141.3
			-20.4	71.7	-9.3	673.3			32.5
			-2.3	**-5.2**	**-10.7**	**-70.9**	**25.7**	**52.2**	
			-6.9	9.6		-32.5		52.2	
			-24.5	-65.2	47.7	138.8	-10.6		
			48.6	-25.5	-33.8	-85.2			

5—2 续表2 continued

行业	Sector	固定资产投资 Investment in Fixed Assets	内资企业 Domestic Funded Enterprise	国有企业 State-owned Enterprise
金融业	**Financial Intermediation**	**-21.4**	**-14.9**	**-8.6**
货币金融服务	Monetary and Financial Service	-13.0	-13.0	-8.6
资本市场服务	Capital Market Service	57.7	57.7	
保险业	Insurance	-63.5	-63.5	
其他金融业	Other Financial Activities	-22.4	89.6	
房地产业	**Real Estate**	**-7.3**	**-7.2**	**-9.4**
租赁和商务服务业	**Leasing and Business Services**	**21.4**	**20.7**	**55.9**
租赁业	Leasing	34.6	34.6	
商务服务业	Business Services	21.3	20.6	53.5
科学研究和技术服务业	**Scientific Research and Technical Services**	**24.1**	**24.1**	**107.4**
研究和试验发展	Research and Experimental Development	-37.8	-37.8	25.0
专业技术服务业	Professional Technical Services	-13.8	-11.6	83.7
科技推广和应用服务业	Science and Technology Popularization and Application Services	88.6	88.0	272.2
水利、环境和公共设施管理业	**Management of Water Conservancy, Environment and Public Facilities**	**18.7**	**18.8**	**16.6**
水利管理业	Management of Water Conservancy	4.2	4.2	15.2
生态保护和环境治理业	Ecological Protection and Environmental Treatment	17.8	18.9	11.9
公共设施管理业	Management of Public Facilities	23.4	23.4	17.8
土地管理业	Land Management	-59.0	-59.0	-56.7
居民服务、修理和其他服务业	**Service to Households, Repair and Other Services**	**7.0**	**4.5**	**18.6**
居民服务业	Service to Households	9.9	6.9	21.8
机动车、电子产品和日用产品修理业	Repair of Motor Vehicle, Electronics and Household Products	102.4	102.4	
其他服务业	Other Services	-45.2	-45.2	-40.0
教　育	**Education**	**1.9**	**1.8**	**3.3**
卫生和社会工作	**Health and Social Service**	**39.5**	**39.5**	**41.3**
卫　生	Health	43.1	43.1	42.6
社会工作	Social Service	15.4	15.4	21.4
文化、体育和娱乐业	**Culture, Sports and Entertainment**	**2.8**	**2.6**	**17.8**
新闻和出版业	Journalism and Publishing Activities	-24.0	-24.0	-32.0
广播、电视、电影和录音制作业	Radio, Television, Film and Recording Production	-68.6	-68.6	-46.4
文化艺术业	Cultural and Art Activities	12.2	12.6	3.7
体　育	Sports Activities	22.8	19.8	22.8
娱乐业	Entertainment	-4.5	-4.5	151.3
公共管理、社会保障和社会组织	**Public Management, Social Security and Social Organization**	**-5.1**	**-5.1**	**-11.8**
中国共产党机关	Organs of Communist Party of China	-66.8	-66.8	-78.7
国家机构	Government Agencies	-0.7	-0.7	-7.9
社会保障	Social Security	-73.4	-73.4	-73.4
群众团体、社会团体和其他成员组织	Non-Governmental Organizations, Social Organizations and Membership Organizations	87.3	87.3	1054.0
基层群众自治组织及其他组织	Land Management Industry of Grassroots Mass Self-Governing Organizations and Other Organizations	-18.7	-18.7	-5.8

单位：%

集体企业 Collective-owned Enterprise	股份合作企业 Share Holding Cooperative Enterprises	联营企业 Joint Owned Enterprises	有限责任公司 Limited Liability Corporations	股份有限公司 Share-holding Corporations Ltd.	私营企业 Private Enterprises	其他企业 Other Enterprises	港、澳、台商投资企业 Enterprises Funded by Entrepreneurs from Hong Kong, Macao and Taiwan	外商投资企业 Foreign Funded Enterprises	个体经营 Individual Management
-40.4			**93.1**	**-40.5**	**-21.6**	**391.9**	**-51.6**		
-40.4			2679.7	-46.7	2664.8	391.9			
				-9.3					
					-52.7				
			45.7		193.8		-51.6		
-12.5	**13.6**	**-56.4**	**-10.2**	**-4.6**	**-2.4**	**41.9**	**-14.6**	**-38.9**	
-88.1		**28.3**	**14.2**	**-42.0**	**18.3**	**3.8**	**67.4**		
			-50.8		4.0				
-88.1		28.3	14.3	-42.0	19.4	1.8	67.4		
			13.2	**-21.1**	**4.9**	**272.5**	**88.5**		
			-58.0		-23.8				
			-18.0	-32.5	-30.6	-51.8	-73.3		
			89.8	-13.9	29.0	387.2	144.6		
38.7	**-30.5**	**-30.3**	**22.2**	**39.3**	**17.1**	**40.7**	**-76.3**	**29.8**	
	-41.5		-21.5		1830.5	-14.9			
1326.9			22.4	48.0	46.0	87.2	-96.0	-40.5	
10.5	297.2	-30.3	38.2	35.9	-13.0	49.2	-28.7	31.1	
			-63.0						
			56.5		**-42.7**	**-68.9**			**515.6**
			53.9		-62.4	-68.9			515.6
			85.7		109.9				
			81.8		-59.9				
-13.9		**-21.9**	**12.7**	**-51.5**	**-22.1**	**25.6**		**20.4**	
126.3	**-16.5**		**41.2**	**86.2**	**29.7**	**-23.3**			
160.6	-16.5		41.3	31.5	59.6	-33.5			
			40.6		-21.7	-1.8			
-93.0			**21.2**	**-42.6**	**-15.9**	**-49.5**		**1397.0**	**-66.1**
				11.3					
			-59.6		-90.7	-58.3			
-85.7			52.6	-14.7	24.7	-73.7			-60.4
			19.2		10.2	-34.6		1397.0	
			13.4		-20.2	-35.7			
			32.4			**97.1**			
			45.2			91.7			
						-30.5			
			-93.9			167.9			

5—3 各行业按隶属构成控股分固定资产投资增长情况（2022年）

Growth of Investment in Fixed Assets in Various Industries According to Their Membership (2022)

行业	Sector	固定资产投资 Investment in Fixed Assets	按隶属关系分 By Affiliation	
			中央 Central Investment	地方 Local Investment
总计	**Total**	**9.0**	**23.6**	**8.4**
农、林、牧、渔业	**Agriculture, Forestry, Animal Husbandry and Fishery**	**20.3**	**-24.0**	**21.7**
农业	Farming	49.6	10.9	51.1
林业	Forestry	101.4		99.7
畜牧业	Animal Husbandry	-27.6		-26.5
渔业	Fishery	9.3		9.3
农林牧渔业及辅助性活动	Agriculture, Forestry, Animal Husbandry and Fishery Major and Supporting Activities	-5.4	-84.5	1.5
采矿业	**Mining**	**30.1**	**52.1**	**28.3**
煤炭开采和洗选业	Mining and Washing of Coal	2.9	68.5	-1.6
石油和天然气开采业	Extraction of Petroleum and Natural Gas	994.5		994.5
黑色金属矿采选业	Mining and Processing of Ferrous Metal Ores	18.3	7.6	24.5
有色金属矿采选业	Mining and Processing of Non-Ferrous Metal Ores	-40.9		-41.1
非金属矿采选业	Mining and Processing of Non-metal Ores	110.0	597.1	106.8
开采专业及辅助性活动	Mining Profession and Auxiliary Activities	60.7		33.8
其他采矿业	Mining of Other Ores	-58.7		-58.7
制造业	**Manufacturing**	**21.5**	**101.5**	**19.5**
农副食品加工业	Processing of Food from Agricultural Products	-1.3	206.3	-2.2
食品制造业	Manufacture of Foods	-13.3		-13.3
酒、饮料和精制茶制造业	Manufacture of Liquor, Beverages and Refined Tea	25.0	101.9	21.1
烟草制品业	Manufacture of Tobacco	-6.4		-6.4
纺织业	Manufacture of Textile	7.5		5.7
纺织服装、服饰业	Manufacture of Textile, Wearing Apparel and Accessories	9.2		9.2
皮革、毛皮、羽毛及其制品和制鞋业	Manufacture of Leather, Fur, Feather and Related Products and Footwear	47.9		47.9
木材加工和木、竹、藤、棕、草制品业	Processing of Timber, Manufacture of Wood, Bamboo, Rattan, Palm and Straw Products	22.7		22.7
家具制造业	Manufacture of Furniture	-23.0		-23.0
造纸和纸制品业	Manufacture of Paper and Paper Products	39.5		39.5
印刷和记录媒介复制业	Printing and Reproduction of Recording Media	-8.2		-8.2
文教、工美、体育和娱乐用品制造业	Manufacture of Articles for Culture, Education, Arts and Crafts, Sport and Entertainment Activities	81.5		81.5
石油、煤炭及其他燃料加工业	Petroleum, Coal and Other Fuel Processing Industries	40.1	115.0	-7.3
化学原料及化学制品制造业	Manufacture of Raw Chemical Materials and Chemical Products	4.2	-7.7	4.2
医药制造业	Manufacture of Medicines	8.5	7.5	8.5
化学纤维制造业	Manufacture of Chemical Fibres	35.2		35.2
橡胶和塑料制品业	Manufacture of Rubber and Plastics Products	5.8		5.4
非金属矿物制品业	Manufacture of Non-metallic Mineral Products	4.8	42.8	2.9
黑色金属冶炼和压延加工业	Smelting and Pressing of Ferrous Metals	37.9	77.7	3.5
有色金属冶炼和压延加工业	Smelting and Pressing of Non-ferrous Metals	26.7		25.8

单位：%

按构成分 According to Composition				按控股情况分 According to the Holding Situation					
建筑工程 Construction Engineering	安装工程 Installation Engineering	设备工器具购置 Purchase of Equipment, Tools and Appliances	其他费用 Other Expenses	国有控股 State Holding	集体控股 Collective Holding	私人控股 Private Holding	港澳台商控股 Hong Kong, Macao and Taiwan Holding Company	外商控股 Foreign Holding	其他 Other
7.8	**-0.4**	**11.7**	**15.2**	**18.9**	**-23.7**	**1.9**	**-4.2**	**-18.1**	**14.3**
18.8	**7.8**	**0.0**	**129.8**	**53.3**	**148.6**	**-9.9**	**26.6**		**39.0**
45.1	42.9	67.3	221.1	63.4	412.6	7.9	31.6		156.1
133.0	476.1	-98.1	94.4	323.1		-19.9			210.7
-31.7	-25.8	-17.0	53.6	0.6	9.5	-29.5			-41.9
8.5	25.3	54.1	-51.8	-26.0		8.9			21.7
-3.0	-26.0	-21.3	-25.8	-15.7	146.6	22.5			-24.4
-16.8	**-34.9**	**49.5**	**147.2**	**41.3**		**-14.6**			**136.0**
-26.7	-52.9	57.4	-52.7	4.8		-46.1			
1267.4			-68.3	994.5					
1.2	96.7	113.5	-19.8	-6.5		55.1			
-39.9	-80.3	-48.9	-38.1	-89.6		-11.5			182.1
-5.0	-24.9	-10.6	336.9	253.6		-28.2			227.9
-54.0	1354.9	77.3		201.0		-88.0			
-3.1	-100.0	-100.0	-100.0			-85.4			
26.1	**3.6**	**14.0**	**58.4**	**42.0**	**-21.9**	**15.4**	**-6.8**	**-18.0**	**64.6**
4.9	-21.0	-16.7	-0.3	30.8	549.2	-12.2	837.5	-47.6	114.0
-12.8	-23.3	-16.2	39.8	-4.1	101.3	-16.7	33.4	-47.2	83.7
20.6		43.5	18.2	48.2	14.4	9.8	96.5	37.8	32.5
-11.8	-15.4	-13.7	997.2	-3.0		-84.3			
31.2	-45.8	-20.4	0.6	1831.2		5.1		-85.5	0.7
20.8		-13.7	-16.4	62.9	-42.7	8.1	-19.1		41.4
61.2	-15.8	37.8	22.3	-90.0		52.4			276.2
39.1	0.7	-15.9	10.5	-1.1		22.5			73.6
-15.1	-30.8	-39.1	-45.2			-28.5			66.6
54.3	11.7	7.6	220.3	122.0	-53.2	47.9	-9.7	-88.0	45.2
-14.0	-16.2	3.7	-22.9	540.5	-48.3	-14.9		41.9	0.9
98.9	10.9	40.4	109.1	353.6		84.6			37.6
3.4	84.1	100.9	-23.7	93.5	2275.8	-5.7	-97.4		104.6
-8.1	-15.5	25.0	30.1	81.2	-57.2	5.7	-54.4	-27.2	18.0
22.0	-12.1	-20.0	53.6	59.2	1073.7	-9.2	54.5	-64.1	79.2
133.7	82.8	-23.7	33.7	-32.0		85.7			994.9
18.4	-22.4	-7.6	22.6	-7.1	-62.1	3.3	9.5	-40.4	86.9
1.4	12.1	-12.2	166.4	41.3	47.0	-6.0	17.8	-46.7	38.1
78.7	-53.4	0.9	169.0	78.7		5.3		66.7	-1.4
38.8	-9.5	2.3	202.7	1.4	65.6	18.9	10.3	-41.4	331.0

5—3 续表1 continued

行业	Sector	固定资产投资 Investment in Fixed Assets	按隶属关系分 By Affiliation 中央 Central Investment	地方 Local Investment
金属制品业	Manufacture of Metal Products	31.6	167.6	29.7
通用设备制造业	Manufacture of General Purpose Machinery	11.3	-19.7	11.8
专用设备制造业	Manufacture of Special Purpose Machinery	3.7	2317.9	1.8
汽车制造业	Manufacture of Automobiles	34.1	903.7	28.6
铁路、船舶、航空航天和其他运输设备制造业	Manufacture of Railway, Ship, Aerospace and Other Transport Equipments	-20.2	-53.2	-18.7
电气机械和器材制造业	Manufacture of Electrical Machinery and Apparatus	80.5	67.5	80.7
计算机、通信和其他电子设备制造业	Manufacture of Computers, Communication and Other Electronic Equipment	31.9	167.7	30.2
仪器仪表制造业	Manufacture of Measuring Instruments and Machinery	91.4	1215.7	88.8
其他制造业	Other Manufacture	9.4	-17.9	9.9
废弃资源综合利用业	Comprehensive Utilization of Waste Resources	-3.3	1.8	-3.3
金属制品、机械和设备修理业	Repair Service of Metal Products, Machinery and Equipment	-32.5	116.1	-54.8
电力、热力、燃气及水生产和供应业	**Production and Supply of Electricity, Heat, Gas and Water**	**22.7**	**50.6**	**18.2**
电力、热力生产和供应业	Production and Supply of Electric Power and Heat Power	21.6	45.7	15.2
燃气生产和供应业	Production and Supply of Gas	5.4	847.7	2.7
水的生产和供应业	Production and Supply of Water	28.4	104.3	26.3
建筑业	**Construction**	**-31.6**		**-23.2**
房屋建筑业	Construction of Buildings	-10.8		-10.8
土木工程建筑业	Civil Engineering	-68.5		-39.8
建筑安装业	Building Installation			
建筑装饰、装修和其他建筑业	Architectural Decoration, Decoration and Other Construction Industries	7.1		7.1
批发和零售业	**Wholesale and Retail Trades**	**-22.6**	**-5.9**	**-23.8**
批发业	Wholesale Trade	-27.9	22.9	-30.2
零售业	Retail Trade	-19.3	-16.4	-19.6
交通运输、仓储和邮政业	**Transport, Storage and Post**	**22.5**	**29.0**	**22.4**
铁路运输业	Railway Transport	39.8		32.0
道路运输业	Road Transport	18.3	-18.2	19.3
水上运输业	Water Transport	96.9	65.1	97.0
航空运输业	Air Transport	220.2		218.5
管道运输业	Transport Via Pipelines	0.0	68.0	-2.2
多式联运和运输代理业	Multimodal Transport and Transportation Agency	22.3		22.3
装卸搬运和仓储业	Handling and warehousing industry	12.3	2507.0	9.6
邮政业	Post	16.7	1940.2	-6.1
住宿和餐饮业	**Hotels and Catering Services**	**8.2**	**-73.7**	**9.5**
住宿业	Hotels	11.2	-73.7	13.0
餐饮业	Catering Services	-6.7		-6.7
信息传输、软件和信息技术服务业	**Information Transmission, Software and Information Technology**	**2.4**	**6.5**	**-2.9**
电信、广播电视和卫星传输服务	Telecommunication, Radio and Television and Satellite Transmission Service	4.7	9.6	-26.4
互联网和相关服务	Internet and Related Service	-11.3	-78.5	-2.0
软件和信息技术服务业	Software and Information Technology	8.0	23.7	6.6

单位：%

按构成分 According to Composition				按控股情况分 According to the Holding Situation					
建筑工程 Construction Engineering	安装工程 Installation Engineering	设备工器具购置 Purchase of Equipment, Tools and Appliances	其他费用 Other Expenses	国有控股 State Holding	集体控股 Collective Holding	私人控股 Private Holding	港澳台商控股 Hong Kong, Macao and Taiwan Holding Company	外商控股 Foreign Holding	其他 Other
32.3	7.0	25.0	130.3	177.5		29.0	-39.4	-4.3	4.5
24.0	-12.5	-8.1	14.8	37.3	41.2	16.1	-77.8	-24.9	-11.2
5.2	2.4	-4.8	60.3	32.3	-41.2	0.7	-22.2	105.5	15.1
46.8	-27.8	27.3	-2.5	16.6	31.8	41.5	-23.9	47.4	21.7
-23.4	-47.8	3.7	-46.8	-55.8		-8.1	5.6		-43.8
95.4	105.0	54.2	179.7	61.9	123.9	78.4	33.2	-37.2	116.9
41.4	22.0	25.6	57.9	46.4	35.1	16.6	1.2	-58.3	100.2
85.7	-5.3	120.2	159.6	677.4		73.8	153.1	1090.0	779.7
24.6	29.6	-31.5	-57.7	-0.3		7.4		616.1	28.8
-5.6	-27.3	-0.6	63.8	-59.1		-0.4	55.6	-39.4	260.5
-41.3	-100.0	78.4	-100.0	116.1	-41.7	-76.2			
27.7	**21.5**	**18.8**	**-4.6**	**40.8**	**591.3**	**-9.5**	**-23.4**	**-22.6**	**-17.1**
23.3	29.8	23	-17.1	47.4	395.0	-10.0	-33.9	-99.0	-28.3
16.5	-3.4	-16.5	34.8	51.6	76.4	-16.7	62.8	-4.6	-9.3
33.9	14.3	-4.0	21.9	31.7		5.8	-11.9		-0.8
-41.7		**-13.9**	**-32.0**	**-43.5**	**172.7**	**-41.2**			**250.6**
-16.8		169.1	-44.5	10.0	8.7	-36.9			2566.0
-91.4		-43.3		-83.1					130.5
-68.7		139.2				-13.0			
-21.2	**-27.7**	**-46.2**	**-20.6**	**-26.7**	**-28.7**	**-16.8**	**-11.6**	**-37.3**	**-29.9**
-31.4	-31.7	-64.6	32.0	-57.2		-3.4			-70.8
-12.2	-25.5	-40.7	-29.4	4.9	-67.8	-25.2	-11.6	-37.3	-4.3
12.0	**-37.6**	**-24.0**	**131.6**	**23.8**	**50.2**	**5.7**	**-4.8**	**-53.5**	**30.2**
37.7	402.3		28.0	44.8		-78.3			-50.7
6.4	-52.1	-26.3	137.3	17.7	-36.4	27.0			40.7
124.2	-49.1	161.3	55.8	143.9		22.0			111.9
42.0	215.7	-16.9	1957.0	274.2		-25.1			
65.1	34.9	-85.6	971.1	1.1				571.7	
43.5	-22.7	-38.2	6.1	41.6		0.7			
9.4	-6.5	9.5	75.2	36.8	75.6	-0.6	-20.6	-67.7	28.6
-3.6	214.6	21.8	871.6	366.5		2.9			
11.5	**-17.0**	**-46.2**	**69.9**	**40.0**	**103.3**	**0.5**	**-66.9**		**15.2**
14.9	-19.8	-50.2	95.8	71.2	98.1	0.5	-66.9		14.3
-6.0	0.2	-33.7	4.6	-35.5		0.4			34.3
4.5	**54.8**	**-6.3**	**48.2**	**7.5**		**-16.6**		**54.7**	**-38.4**
39.1	70.4	-10.8	47.1	1.4				54.7	-44.6
-19.5	-58.8	7.2	64.1	-7.5		-48.0			631.6
-8.2	317.5	20.5	28.3	99.7		13.6			-70.3

5—3 续表2 continued

行 业	Sector	固定资产投资 Investment in Fixed Assets	按隶属关系分 By Affiliation 中央 Central Investment	地方 Local Investment
金融业	**Financial Intermediation**	**-21.4**	**-58.8**	**-11.4**
货币金融服务	Monetary and Financial Service	-13.0	-68.1	25.7
资本市场服务	Capital Market Service	57.7		57.7
保险业	Insurance	-63.5		-63.5
其他金融业	Other Financial Activities	-22.4		-31.2
房地产业	**Real Estate**	**-7.3**	**-14.5**	**-7.1**
租赁和商务服务业	**Leasing and Business Services**	**21.4**	**537.3**	**20.0**
租赁业	Leasing	34.6		34.6
商务服务业	Business Services	21.3	537.3	19.8
科学研究和技术服务业	**Scientific Research and Technical Services**	**24.1**	**13.0**	**25.0**
研究和试验发展	Research and Experimental Development	-37.8	4.5	-46.1
专业技术服务业	Professional Technical Services	-13.8	5.6	-15.1
科技推广和应用服务业	Science and Technology Popularization and Application Services	88.6	132.9	88.1
水利、环境和公共设施管理业	**Management of Water Conservancy, Environment and Public Facilities**	**18.7**	**-12.6**	**20.0**
水利管理业	Management of Water Conservancy	4.2	74.1	3.0
生态保护和环境治理业	Ecological Protection and Environmental Treatment	17.8	-39.5	23.9
公共设施管理业	Management of Public Facilities	23.4	-16.4	25.0
土地管理业	Land Management	-59.0		-59.0
居民服务、修理和其他服务业	**Service to Households, Repair and Other Services**	**7.0**		**5.2**
居民服务业	Service to Households	9.9		7.8
机动车、电子产品和日用产品修理业	Repair of Motor Vehicle, Electronics and Household Products	102.4		102.4
其他服务业	Other Services	-45.2		-45.2
教 育	**Education**	**1.9**	**-26.2**	**2.8**
卫生和社会工作	**Health and Social Service**	**39.5**	**66.4**	**38.8**
卫 生	Health	43.1	71.2	42.2
社会工作	Social Service	15.4	-78.9	16.0
文化、体育和娱乐业	**Culture, Sports and Entertainment**	**2.8**	**-35.6**	**4.4**
新闻和出版业	Journalism and Publishing Activities	-24.0		-24.0
广播、电视、电影和录音制作业	Radio, Television, Film and Recording Production	-68.6		-66.8
文化艺术业	Cultural and Art Activities	12.2	-35.7	17.2
体 育	Sports Activities	22.8	-33.0	25.5
娱乐业	Entertainment	-4.5		-4.7
公共管理、社会保障和社会组织	**Public Management, Social Security and Social Organization**	**-5.1**	**73.9**	**-9.7**
中国共产党机关	Organs of Communist Party of China	-66.8		-66.8
国家机构	Government Agencies	-0.7	73.9	-5.6
社会保障	Social Security	-73.4		-73.4
群众团体、社会团体和其他成员组织	Non-Governmental Organizations, Social Organizations and Membership Organizations	87.3		87.3
基层群众自治组织及其他组织	Land Management Industry of Grassroots Mass Self-Governing Organizations and Other Organizations	-18.7		-18.7

单位：%

按构成分 According to Composition				按控股情况分 According to the Holding Situation					
建筑工程 Construction Engineering	安装工程 Installation Engineering	设备工器具购置 Purchase of Equipment, Tools and Appliances	其他费用 Other Expenses	国有控股 State Holding	集体控股 Collective Holding	私人控股 Private Holding	港澳台商控股 Hong Kong, Macao and Taiwan Holding Company	外商控股 Foreign Holding	其他 Other
-5.6	**-78.8**	**-12.9**	**-15.8**	**-28.8**	**0.7**	**-11.9**			**8.1**
-18.9	-50.6	67.5	120.2	-25.3	0.7	670.4			76.9
1489.5		-61.1	-98.7	-9.3					
-22.8	-97.9	331.8				-52.7			
-7.7	218.4	-89.8	-46.2	-42.1		46.5			132.0
-9.4	**-13.5**	**-23.5**	**-0.6**	**-3.2**	**-53.5**	**-6.3**	**2.9**	**-38.7**	**-19.7**
20.2	**100.5**	**-22.2**	**36.4**	**30.5**	**-22.4**	**-1.6**	**56.9**		**45.3**
362.7		-15.6				-20.7			
19.7	96.6	-24.9	35.9	29.8	-22.4	-0.8	56.9		40.6
33.9	**-20.7**	**-12.8**	**30.7**	**32.1**	**1096.9**	**4.1**	**144.6**	**-83.0**	**29.7**
-42.8	-45.2	11.7	-70.8	-46.0		-8.0			2569.3
-19.1	11.0	-37.8	1253.3	-15.8		-4.9		-83.0	40.1
104.5	56.4	-24.0	49.3	153.6	1070.9	11.5	144.6		3.1
17.3	**17.8**	**32.0**	**34.0**	**20.1**	**19.0**	**-5.8**	**-90.6**		**19.4**
6.9	136.5	79.0	-29.5	2.2	-60.3	15.6			125.5
16.8	29.7	49.1	17.3	18.5	312.2	28.5	-96.0		-18.0
20.5	1.9	20.3	85.7	26.2	0.2	-11.3	-80.5		10.7
-51.4	-66.2	-48.6	-83.6	-56.7					
5.9	**-5.2**	**-7.5**	**44.7**	**22.3**		**-17.2**			**-15.3**
4.6	39.1	44.0	56.8	24.8		-17.4			-34.9
74.7	372.3	536.8	225.1			105.7			82.9
-28.3	-79.7	-49.6	-56.0	-40.0		-61.6			
-1.7	**47.0**	**7.5**	**10.8**	**4.9**	**-65.5**	**-18.0**		**20.4**	**37.8**
44.4	**19.1**	**24.1**	**21.6**	**50.8**	**71.2**	**-24.0**			**187.5**
50.9	26.5	21.9	-2.2	51.7	108.2	-23.2			289.1
3.3	-23.6	166.6	151.9	42.1	-70.7	-26.4			43.0
6.6	**-25.6**	**-45.0**	**29.1**	**29.8**	**-64.8**	**-22.6**			**8.6**
-28.5	4.4	-12.3		-24.0					
-84.6	-42.1	-30.5	-39.1	-54.1		-90.1			-76.0
13.0	-4.8	-8.1	35.1	10.5	-85.7	36.0			1.1
17.6	25.8	-28.0	123.0	36.2		-10.7			40.5
3.7	-51.2	-67.0	-1.2	158.9	-60.8	-27.0			2.6
-3.6	**-3.0**	**1.0**	**-35.7**	**-7.9**		**292.3**			**173.9**
-65.9	-77.7		-100.0	-68.4					
1.2	-2.3	4.6	-32.4	-3.3					198.6
-70.7	-28.6	-100.0	-100.0	-73.4					
284.1	66.7	-100.0	-87.1	126.3					-30.5
-27.3	204.7	478.0	-17.1	-32.4		36.6			188.1

5—4 各行业固定资产投资资金来源增长情况（2022年）
Growth of Sources of Funds for Fixed Assets Investment in Various Industries (2022)

行　业	Sector	本年资金来源合计 Total Sources of Funds for the Year
总　计	**Total**	**5.6**
农、林、牧、渔业	**Agriculture, Forestry, Animal Husbandry and Fishery**	**27.5**
农　业	Farming	57.1
林　业	Forestry	110.5
畜牧业	Animal Husbandry	-21.9
渔　业	Fishery	10.3
农林牧渔业及辅助性活动	Agriculture, Forestry, Animal Husbandry and Fishery Major and Supporting Activities	10.5
采矿业	**Mining**	**31.0**
煤炭开采和洗选业	Mining and Washing of Coal	7.6
石油和天然气开采业	Extraction of Petroleum and Natural Gas	995.1
黑色金属矿采选业	Mining and Processing of Ferrous Metal Ores	65.4
有色金属矿采选业	Mining and Processing of Non-Ferrous Metal Ores	-29.2
非金属矿采选业	Mining and Processing of Non-metal Ores	83.1
开采专业及辅助性活动	Mining Profession and Auxiliary Activities	121.6
其他采矿业	Mining of Other Ores	-28.1
制造业	**Manufacturing**	**32.4**
农副食品加工业	Processing of Food from Agricultural Products	5.9
食品制造业	Manufacture of Foods	-7.6
酒、饮料和精制茶制造业	Manufacture of Liquor, Beverages and Refined Tea	35.5
烟草制品业	Manufacture of Tobacco	-4.2
纺织业	Manufacture of Textile	15.2
纺织服装、服饰业	Manufacture of Textile, Wearing Apparel and Accessories	15.3
皮革、毛皮、羽毛及其制品和制鞋业	Manufacture of Leather, Fur, Feather and Related Products and Footwear	52.0
木材加工和木、竹、藤、棕、草制品业	Processing of Timber, Manufacture of Wood, Bamboo, Rattan, Palm and Straw Products	42.2
家具制造业	Manufacture of Furniture	-22.2
造纸和纸制品业	Manufacture of Paper and Paper Products	48.3
印刷和记录媒介复制业	Printing and Reproduction of Recording Media	-2.5
文教、工美、体育和娱乐用品制造业	Manufacture of Articles for Culture, Education, Arts and Crafts, Sport and Entertainment Activities	114.2
石油、煤炭及其他燃料加工业	Petroleum, Coal and Other Fuel Processing Industries	53.5
化学原料和化学制品制造业	Manufacture of Raw Chemical Materials and Chemical Products	11.0
医药制造业	Manufacture of Medicines	12.3
化学纤维制造业	Manufacture of Chemical Fibres	32.9
橡胶和塑料制品业	Manufacture of Rubber and Plastics Products	14.7
非金属矿物制品业	Manufacture of Non-metallic Mineral Products	13.2
黑色金属冶炼和压延加工业	Smelting and Pressing of Ferrous Metals	39.4
有色金属冶炼和压延加工业	Smelting and Pressing of Non-ferrous Metals	60.6

单位：%

国家预算资金 State Budget Funds	国内贷款 Domestic Loans	债券 Bonds	利用外资 Foreign Investment	自筹资金 Self-raising Funds	其他资金来源 Other Sources of Funding
50.9	**11.8**	**-66.7**	**-18.6**	**16.7**	**-20.5**
55.6	**-71.3**		**8.6**	**20.5**	**24.0**
52.7	-17.9		2.6	61.8	53.0
508.3	-100.0			69.1	235.1
96.6	-77.7		-100.0	-22.3	-46.2
236.3				3.2	165.4
-10.5	-100.0			33.8	-27.7
-79.8	**96.4**		**-100.0**	**31.6**	**-92.6**
-55.4	-62.4			16.1	-100.0
				920.1	
			-100.0	73.1	-100.0
				-29.3	-80.9
-95.2	508.1			65.7	-73.0
-100.0				127.4	-100.0
				-28.1	
51.5	**96.6**	**-100.0**	**-5.8**	**29.2**	**43.4**
14.5	64.7			2.3	70.5
-23.4	-22.0			-9.0	84.4
-20.6	11.5		-100.0	37.0	39.5
				-5.5	
-10.0	70.2			14.7	6.5
-30.5	-81.8		-92.3	19.7	9.0
	-80.4			52.4	41.0
46.0	35.7			48.4	-36.8
132.4	122.2		-100.0	-23.0	-51.9
	-42.1			49.1	62.7
	22.8		38.7	-2.5	-19.6
	-2.0			117.1	-9.1
-91.7	433.7			-18.9	339.4
1115.3	1.8		-42.6	13.8	-36.2
4689.8	-38.1		58.6	9.2	-26.1
	3851.2		-100.0	4.3	-100.0
12.5	127.7		-69.0	16.2	-33.6
-1.0	42.9			14.7	-45.7
-100.0	-8.0			37.5	452.1
-4.7	235.6			56.6	19.5

5—4 续表1 continued

行 业	Sector	本年资金来源合计 Total Sources of Funds for the Year
金属制品业	Manufacture of Metal Products	44.6
通用设备制造业	Manufacture of General Purpose Machinery	19.7
专用设备制造业	Manufacture of Special Purpose Machinery	13.0
汽车制造业	Manufacture of Automobiles	41.8
铁路、船舶、航空航天和其他运输设备制造业	Manufacture of Railway, Ship, Aerospace and Other Transport Equipments	-15.8
电气机械和器材制造业	Manufacture of Electrical Machinery and Apparatus	82.0
计算机、通信和其他电子设备制造业	Manufacture of Computers, Communication and Other Electronic Equipment	56.7
仪器仪表制造业	Manufacture of Measuring Instruments and Machinery	109.0
其他制造业	Other Manufacture	26.8
废弃资源综合利用业	Comprehensive Utilization of Waste Resources	5.9
金属制品、机械和设备修理业	Repair Service of Metal Products, Machinery and Equipment	-21.6
电力、热力、燃气及水生产和供应业	**Production and Supply of Electricity, Heat, Gas and Water**	**35.5**
电力、热力生产和供应业	Production and Supply of Electric Power and Heat Power	26.8
燃气生产和供应业	Production and Supply of Gas	26.0
水的生产和供应业	Production and Supply of Water	58.7
建筑业	**Construction**	**-38.6**
房屋建筑业	Construction of Buildings	-24.0
土木工程建筑业	Civil Engineering	-67.3
建筑安装业	Building Installation	
建筑装饰、装修和其他建筑业	Architectural Decoration, Decoration and Other Construction Industries	46.1
批发和零售业	**Wholesale and Retail Trades**	**-12.3**
批发业	Wholesale Trade	-20.6
零售业	Retail Trade	-7.1
交通运输、仓储和邮政业	**Transport, Storage and Post**	**52.1**
铁路运输业	Railway Transport	71.6
道路运输业	Road Transport	50.4
水上运输业	Water Transport	137.7
航空运输业	Air Transport	179.1
管道运输业	Transport Via Pipelines	16.4
多式联运和运输代理业	Multimodal Transport and Transportation Agency	27.1
装卸搬运和仓储业	Handling and warehousing industry	24.5
邮政业	Post	27.0
住宿和餐饮业	**Hotels and Catering Services**	**29.6**
住宿业	Hotels	35.4
餐饮业	Catering Services	3.3
信息传输、软件和信息技术服务业	**Information Transmission, Software and Information Technology**	**-12.8**
电信、广播电视和卫星传输服务	Telecommunication, Radio and Television and Satellite Transmission Service	-23.1
互联网和相关服务	Internet and Related Service	13.4
软件和信息技术服务业	Software and Information Technology	10.3

单位：%

国家预算资金 State Budget Funds	国内贷款 Domestic Loans	债券 Bonds	利用外资 Foreign Investment	自筹资金 Self-raising Funds	其他资金来源 Other Sources of Funding
1099.5	153.7		-100.0	44.7	-14.3
94.2	23.3		-100.0	21.8	-24.5
1211.5	150.7		-98.4	9.8	58.4
-100.0	271.0		116.2	39.9	528.7
	284.6			-20.2	547.4
425.8	176.8		191.6	75.2	194.0
556.9	87.5	-100.0	-8.7	47.2	265.2
-100.0	934.7			103.4	404.7
	-48.5			24.5	101.3
384.4	17.2		-100.0	18.5	-74.7
	-100.0			-11.7	
103.2	**-4.9**		**44.1**	**33.2**	**53.2**
24.0	2.9			33.0	42.4
167.1	-39.5			50.8	-92.6
145.6	-25.3		-100.0	27.4	76.6
-29.7	**131.7**			**-6.2**	**-100.0**
				167.7	-100.0
-100.0				-58.2	
				-17.8	
197.0	**15.5**		**-49.3**	**-13.2**	**-27.6**
204.3	9.3			-24.4	-23.9
192.3	35.2		-49.3	-5.4	-27.8
67.1	**60.0**		**137.8**	**50.4**	**39.2**
4.1	4.6			159.1	140.0
65.9	91.0		14.9	45.2	33.1
60.9	88.8			166.3	587.6
176.1	-100.0			157.2	
188.9				-0.8	
	-67.9			24.4	-100.0
85.7	-33.9		466.1	15.7	89.5
				25.9	
130.0	**28.3**			**19.2**	**375.9**
111.7	43.8			23.4	425.4
	-50.8			0.7	86.1
177.3	**-69.3**			**-16.9**	**24.0**
-44.6	307.1			-22.4	-32.7
562.1	-72.3			-9.5	370.5
624.9	-100.0			1.5	-5.5

5—4 续表2 continued

行 业	Sector	本年资金来源合计 Total Sources of Funds for the Year
金融业	**Financial Intermediation**	**-1.2**
货币金融服务	Monetary and Financial Service	13.8
资本市场服务	Capital Market Service	805.2
保险业	Insurance	-53.4
其他金融业	Other Financial Activities	-27.2
房地产业	**Real Estate**	**-23.4**
租赁和商务服务业	**Leasing and Business Services**	**37.5**
租赁业	Leasing	52.8
商务服务业	Business Services	37.3
科学研究和技术服务业	**Scientific Research and Technical Services**	**40.2**
研究和试验发展	Research and Experimental Development	-21.9
专业技术服务业	Professional Technical Services	-10.3
科技推广和应用服务业	Science and Technology Popularization and Application Services	101.5
水利、环境和公共设施管理业	**Management of Water Conservancy, Environment and Public Facilities**	**38.3**
水利管理业	Management of Water Conservancy	13.5
生态保护和环境治理业	Ecological Protection and Environmental Treatment	41.6
公共设施管理业	Management of Public Facilities	46.5
土地管理业	Land Management	-58.8
居民服务、修理和其他服务业	**Service to Households, Repair and Other Services**	**14.6**
居民服务业	Service to Households	16.7
机动车、电子产品和日用产品修理业	Repair of Motor Vehicle, Electronics and Household Products	212.4
其他服务业	Other Services	-43.8
教 育	**Education**	**13.9**
卫生和社会工作	**Health and Social Service**	**46.4**
卫 生	Health	49.5
社会工作	Social Service	25.5
文化、体育和娱乐业	**Culture, Sports and Entertainment**	**22.4**
新闻和出版业	Journalism and Publishing Activities	-23.8
广播、电视、电影和录音制作业	Radio, Television, Film and Recording Production	-75.3
文化艺术业	Cultural and Art Activities	51.3
体 育	Sports Activities	29.2
娱乐业	Entertainment	10.8
公共管理、社会保障和社会组织	**Public Management, Social Security and Social Organization**	**16.7**
中国共产党机关	Organs of Communist Party of China	-67.8
国家机构	Government Agencies	25.2
社会保障	Social Security	-73.4
群众团体、社会团体和其他成员组织	Non-Governmental Organizations, Social Organizations and Membership Organizations	81.1
基层群众自治组织及其他组织	Land Management Industry of Grassroots Mass Self-Governing Organizations and Other Organizations	1.3

单位：%

国家预算资金 State Budget Funds	国内贷款 Domestic Loans	债券 Bonds	利用外资 Foreign Investment	自筹资金 Self-raising Funds	其他资金来源 Other Sources of Funding
				-5.9	**13.8**
				-1.2	
				805.2	
				-100.0	114.4
				114.5	-83.4
28.5	**-15.6**		**-54.6**	**-9.5**	**-32.2**
113.4	**266.0**			**20.0**	**10.0**
				32.3	
113.4	266.0			19.8	8.2
-8.3	**719.1**		**30.2**	**34.8**	**220.0**
-60.2	-73.7		-100.0	-9.1	383.8
748.9	167.0		46.8	-29.8	274.4
110.6				84.1	184.2
42.5	**-4.0**		**-86.0**	**23.3**	**102.6**
16.7	4.6			-14.1	78.1
7.5	-14.1		-51.2	73.6	108.6
64.9	-0.2		-86.1	27.0	108.3
-69.6	-38.1			-78.2	
32.5	**39.5**			**-2.5**	**84.4**
32.5	39.5			-3.5	77.2
				203.4	
				-46.6	
36.2	**-36.3**			**-8.0**	**88.8**
66.1	**-3.3**		**44.6**	**35.3**	**46.1**
58.7	-23.0			48.8	42.2
232.6	71.7		-100.0	-17.6	104.2
127.3	**40.9**			**-4.0**	**215.6**
-100.0				-26.9	
-61.8				-78.8	-57.3
52.7	13.1			31.1	283.2
169.3	-87.7			-6.4	135.7
451.0	1311.8			-12.3	232.7
2.9				**28.7**	**24.3**
52.5				-69.2	-100.0
1.7				65.1	20.1
-53.4				-100.0	-100.0
				41.8	-100.0
65.9				-69.6	977.2

5—5 各行业按建设性质项目分固定资产投资增长情况（2022年）

Growth of Investment in Fixed Assets by Construction Projects in Various Industries (2022)

单位：%

行　业	Sector	新　建 New Construction	扩　建 Expansion Construction	改建和技术改造 Reconstruction and Technical Transformation
总　计	**Total**	**16.0**	**30.4**	**20.6**
农、林、牧、渔业	**Agriculture, Forestry, Animal Husbandry and Fishery**	**18.4**	**33.8**	**170.4**
农　业	Farming	47.5	60.8	269.8
林　业	Forestry	130.1	-73.4	
畜牧业	Animal Husbandry	-29.0	-23.9	185.4
渔　业	Fishery	-2.8	512.9	904.2
农林牧渔业及辅助性活动	Agriculture, Forestry, Animal Husbandry and Fishery Major and Supporting Activities	-8.1		-8.6
采矿业	**Mining**	**129.8**	**-11.2**	**21.8**
煤炭开采和洗选业	Mining and Washing of Coal	-82.8	-99.4	23.9
石油和天然气开采业	Extraction of Petroleum and Natural Gas			994.5
黑色金属矿采选业	Mining and Processing of Ferrous Metal Ores	-46.4	-11.0	88.4
有色金属矿采选业	Mining and Processing of Non-Ferrous Metal Ores	-90.8	-93.7	8.9
非金属矿采选业	Mining and Processing of Non-metal Ores	647.1	176.3	-5.9
开采专业及辅助性活动	Mining Profession and Auxiliary Activities	-89.1	-58.3	277.2
其他采矿业	Mining of Other Ores			-80.3
制造业	**Manufacturing**	**22.5**	**34.1**	**18.5**
农副食品加工业	Processing of Food from Agricultural Products	-6.8	26.0	2.7
食品制造业	Manufacture of Foods	2.2	22.6	-33.3
酒、饮料和精制茶制造业	Manufacture of Liquor, Beverages and Refined Tea	-2.0	49.6	36.2
烟草制品业	Manufacture of Tobacco		836.4	-44.5
纺织业	Manufacture of Textile	-6.5	10.7	27.7
纺织服装、服饰业	Manufacture of Textile, Wearing Apparel and Accessories	23.7	90.2	-15.7
皮革、毛皮、羽毛及其制品和制鞋业	Manufacture of Leather, Fur, Feather and Related Products and Footwear	44.4	331.6	29.2
木材加工和木、竹、藤、棕、草制品业	Processing of Timber, Manufacture of Wood, Bamboo, Rattan, Palm and Straw Products	16.1	5.8	33.2
家具制造业	Manufacture of Furniture	-31.6	35.6	-29.3
造纸和纸制品业	Manufacture of Paper and Paper Products	78.6	34.3	14.4
印刷和记录媒介复制业	Printing and Reproduction of Recording Media	7.8	-47.9	-7.2
文教、工美、体育和娱乐用品制造业	Manufacture of Articles for Culture, Education, Arts and Crafts, Sport and Entertainment Activities	99.1	17.3	102.2
石油、煤炭及其他燃料加工业	Petroleum, Coal and Other Fuel Processing Industries	-1.5	44.5	51.3
化学原料和化学制品制造业	Manufacture of Raw Chemical Materials and Chemical Products	11.5	17.8	6.9
医药制造业	Manufacture of Medicines	9.3	1.2	14.4
化学纤维制造业	Manufacture of Chemical Fibres	125.6	11.7	123.8
橡胶和塑料制品业	Manufacture of Rubber and Plastics Products	7.1	0.4	7.6
非金属矿物制品业	Manufacture of Non-metallic Mineral Products	10.9	1.6	0.8
黑色金属冶炼和压延加工业	Smelting and Pressing of Ferrous Metals	-21.9	142.1	45.2
有色金属冶炼和压延加工业	Smelting and Pressing of Non-ferrous Metals	59.9	-1.1	13.6

5—5 续表1 continued

单位：%

行 业	Sector	新 建 New Construction	扩 建 Expansion Construction	改建和技术改造 Reconstruction and Technical Transformation
金属制品业	Manufacture of Metal Products	31.1	24.6	40.8
通用设备制造业	Manufacture of General Purpose Machinery	6.7	31.8	10.3
专用设备制造业	Manufacture of Special Purpose Machinery	-3.5	-15.3	31.9
汽车制造业	Manufacture of Automobiles	47.9	43.5	22.6
铁路、船舶、航空航天和其他运输设备制造业	Manufacture of Railway, Ship, Aerospace and Other Transport Equipments	-46.5	22.6	-6.2
电气机械和器材制造业	Manufacture of Electrical Machinery and Apparatus	122.9	37.5	54.4
计算机、通信和其他电子设备制造业	Manufacture of Computers, Communication and Other Electronic Equipment	10.4	77.9	32.7
仪器仪表制造业	Manufacture of Measuring Instruments and Machinery	295.8	-29.7	41.9
其他制造业	Other Manufacture	-11.1	29.2	-4.1
废弃资源综合利用业	Comprehensive Utilization of Waste Resources	-3.5	-29.3	3.2
金属制品、机械和设备修理业	Repair Service of Metal Products, Machinery and Equipment	-61.3		105.8
电力、热力、燃气及水生产和供应业	**Production and Supply of Electricity, Heat, Gas and Water**	**13.6**	**25.1**	**39.9**
电力、热力生产和供应业	Production and Supply of Electric Power and Heat Power	26.7	-6.6	18.1
燃气生产和供应业	Production and Supply of Gas	-7.9	-30.1	100.6
水的生产和供应业	Production and Supply of Water	-4.9	69.3	87.0
建筑业	**Construction**	**-37.7**	**15.0**	**4.4**
房屋建筑业	Construction of Buildings	-23.1		
土木工程建筑业	Civil Engineering			
建筑安装业	Building Installation			
建筑装饰、装修和其他建筑业	Architectural Decoration, Decoration and Other Construction Industries	-41.0		60.0
批发和零售业	**Wholesale and Retail Trades**	**-26.7**	**63.3**	**-20.3**
批发业	Wholesale Trade	-39.6	401.4	-13.8
零售业	Retail Trade	-18.6	-62.0	-23.6
交通运输、仓储和邮政业	**Transport, Storage and Post**	**20.4**	**55.1**	**30.4**
铁路运输业	Railway Transport	35.5		122.2
道路运输业	Road Transport	15.8	52.7	28.6
水上运输业	Water Transport	115.6	191.8	23.2
航空运输业	Air Transport	417.5	131.2	-64.1
管道运输业	Transport Via Pipelines	-4.8		64.0
多式联运和运输代理业	Multimodal Transport and Transportation Agency	13.7		
装卸搬运和仓储业	Handling and warehousing industry	14.5	-0.1	-12.1
邮政业	Post	11.7	-87.4	-28.3
住宿和餐饮业	**Hotels and Catering Services**	**11.2**	**-53.3**	**25.1**
住宿业	Hotels	22.0	-54.0	-28.4
餐饮业	Catering Services	-35.5	-37.1	490.9
信息传输、软件和信息技术服务业	**Information Transmission, Software and Information Technology**	**11.6**	**-57.8**	**-44.1**
电信、广播电视和卫星传输服务	Telecommunication, Radio and Television and Satellite Transmission Service	14.0	-93.1	-15.3
互联网和相关服务	Internet and Related Service	10.7		-56.8
软件和信息技术服务业	Software and Information Technology	4.8	1546.3	-36.0

5—5 续表2 continued

单位：%

行 业	Sector	新 建 New Construction	扩 建 Expansion Construction	改建和技术改造 Reconstruction and Technical Transformation
金融业	**Financial Intermediation**	**-27.4**	**-43.2**	**135.9**
货币金融服务	Monetary and Financial Service	-13.6	-43.2	-64.6
资本市场服务	Capital Market Service	-18.9		338.8
保险业	Insurance	-63.1		
其他金融业	Other Financial Activities	-25.4		
房地产业	**Real Estate**	**-14.0**	**66.9**	**20.9**
租赁和商务服务业	**Leasing and Business Services**	**18.5**	**42.7**	**110.0**
租赁业	Leasing	343.3		
商务服务业	Business Services	17.9	42.7	110.0
科学研究和技术服务业	**Scientific Research and Technical Services**	**21.7**	**276.6**	**90.3**
研究和试验发展	Research and Experimental Development	-41.2		308.9
专业技术服务业	Professional Technical Services	-6.7	-73.7	4.3
科技推广和应用服务业	Science and Technology Popularization and Application Services	80.3	1146.7	937.4
水利、环境和公共设施管理业	**Management of Water Conservancy, Environment and Public Facilities**	**20.7**	**1.7**	**9.9**
水利管理业	Management of Water Conservancy	0.8	44.8	47.1
生态保护和环境治理业	Ecological Protection and Environmental Treatment	23.2	81.9	-32.9
公共设施管理业	Management of Public Facilities	27.0	-13.0	10.3
土地管理业	Land Management	-66.4		-31.4
居民服务、修理和其他服务业	**Service to Households, Repair and Other Services**	**7.6**	**-38.2**	**-12.6**
居民服务业	Service to Households	11.7	-58.0	-9.4
机动车、电子产品和日用产品修理业	Repair of Motor Vehicle, Electronics and Household Products	102.4		
其他服务业	Other Services	-51.8		-35.2
教 育	**Education**	**4.0**	**-14.3**	**0.3**
卫生和社会工作	**Health and Social Service**	**39.5**	**37.8**	**60.3**
卫 生	Health	44.1	38.1	52.5
社会工作	Social Service	9.9	34.7	110.8
文化、体育和娱乐业	**Culture, Sports and Entertainment**	**-0.1**	**246.7**	**38.5**
新闻和出版业	Journalism and Publishing Activities	89.2		-15.0
广播、电视、电影和录音制作业	Radio, Television, Film and Recording Production	-71.6		-71.8
文化艺术业	Cultural and Art Activities	6.4	188.2	164.0
体 育	Sports Activities	21.1		17.2
娱乐业	Entertainment	-6.5		22.1
公共管理、社会保障和社会组织	**Public Management, Social Security and Social Organization**	**-8.9**	**-24.7**	**126.7**
中国共产党机关	Organs of Communist Party of China	-69.7		209.5
国家机构	Government Agencies	-3.3	-24.7	95.1
社会保障	Social Security	-73.4		
群众团体、社会团体和其他成员组织	Non-Governmental Organizations, Social Organizations and Membership Organizations	-35.8		
基层群众自治组织及其他组织	Land Management Industry of Grassroots Mass Self-Governing Organizations and Other Organizations	-17.9		

5—6 各市固定资产投资增长情况（2022年）
Growth of Investment in Fixed Assets by Region (2022)

单位：%

地 区	Region	固定资产投 资 Investment in Fixed Assets	项目投资 Project Investment	工业投资 Industrial Investment	基础设施投 资 Infrastructure Investment	其他投资 Other Investments
总 计	**Total**	**9.0**	**17.4**	**21.8**	**19.6**	**5.9**
合肥市	Hefei	9.1	14.4	25.8	13.5	0.1
淮北市	Huaibei	2.9	13.5	11.5	21.5	12.3
亳州市	Bozhou	8.8	19.5	18.8	42.0	1.3
宿州市	Suzhou	9.6	27.7	16.5	45.8	31.0
蚌埠市	Bengbu	0.5	4.2	-3.7	23.4	4.7
阜阳市	Fuyang	6.5	19.3	47.9	16.4	-11.1
淮南市	Huainan	3.6	12.7	19.2	10.8	6.6
滁州市	Chuzhou	16.5	25.5	34.8	22.0	0.7
六安市	Luan	16.2	29.9	47.6	38.9	1.9
马鞍山市	Maanshan	13.2	21.5	23.3	27.4	8.4
芜湖市	Wuhu	5.4	7.7	7.0	13.7	2.9
宣城市	Xuancheng	10.0	25.2	20.3	26.9	41.5
铜陵市	Tongling	8.8	24.4	22.5	27.4	27.1
池州市	Chizhou	15.0	18.5	35.5	-10.7	21.6
安庆市	Anqing	12.3	15.3	18.7	8.1	17.0
黄山市	Huangshan	0.5	15.1	3.5	28.3	7.0

5—7 各市按登记注册类型分固定资产投资增长情况（2022年）
Growth of Fixed Asset Investment by Registration Type by Region (2022)

单位：%

地 区	Region	内资企业 Domestic Funded Enterprise	国有企业 State-owned Enterprise	集体企业 Collective-owned Enterprise	股份合作企业 Share Holding Cooperative Enterprises	联营企业 Joint Owned Enterprises	有限责任公司 Limited Liability Corporations
总 计	**Total**	**9.2**	**15.4**	**45.0**	**13.0**	**17.9**	**7.3**
合肥市	Hefei	9.3	5.2	17.5		16.3	3.1
淮北市	Huaibei	2.3	35.1		192.9	-62.8	-11.2
亳州市	Bozhou	8.4	35.1		-0.3		9.3
宿州市	Suzhou	9.7	28.0	-66.3			5.5
蚌埠市	Bengbu	0.8	11.9	-81.8			0.2
阜阳市	Fuyang	6.2	9.8	174.6	4.0	381.1	9.5
淮南市	Huainan	1.9	-2.8	-20.1	-34.3	482.5	-4.9
滁州市	Chuzhou	17.1	17.9	1779.3	-41.5	-57.1	34.9
六安市	Luan	15.7	19.6	0.6		-29.0	12.7
马鞍山市	Maanshan	15.6	46.1	525.1	20.1		-7.4
芜湖市	Wuhu	6.0	30.9	147.3	496.6		13.1
宣城市	Xuancheng	10.2	24.8	-47.6	-60.7		-1.0
铜陵市	Tongling	10.5	19.8	83.4	8.8		14.8
池州市	Chizhou	15.1	-15.0			529.8	53.4
安庆市	Anqing	12.7	12.5	170.5	129.5	2567.2	16.0
黄山市	Huangshan	1.0	27.6	117.3	338.6		-8.6

地 区	Region	股份有限公司 Share-holding Corporations Ltd.	私营企业 Private Enterprises	其他企业 Other Enterprises	港、澳、台商投资企业 Enterprises Funded by Entrepreneurs from Hong Kong, Macao and Taiwan	外商投资企业 Foreign Funded Enterprises	个体经营 Individual Management
总 计	**Total**	**8.7**	**7.5**	**18.4**	**7.8**	**-11.3**	**92.0**
合肥市	Hefei	-11.2	30.0	36.2	-10.9	11.8	35.1
淮北市	Huaibei	56.3	-6.3	-41.0	42.3	28.5	
亳州市	Bozhou	51.0	-12.0	-74.4			512.0
宿州市	Suzhou	23.3	8.1	31.8	-7.7	-34.7	99.7
蚌埠市	Bengbu	-4.3	-2.9	-32.6	97.2	-48.2	
阜阳市	Fuyang	10.5	-0.2	-12.9	43.0	-17.0	848.2
淮南市	Huainan	67.5	14.7	-9.3	445.8	-23.1	-16.8
滁州市	Chuzhou	-5.0	8.0	11.0	16.0	-18.7	
六安市	Luan	34.2	14.8	65.5	42.5	487.8	221.0
马鞍山市	Maanshan	53.7	15.6	26.3	0.4	-47.7	
芜湖市	Wuhu	-32.1	-5.3	-11.7	-8.3	-4.3	322.8
宣城市	Xuancheng	-23.1	15.5	23.4	36.1	-16.5	
铜陵市	Tongling	-13.6	1.7	80.7	-71.5	121.7	
池州市	Chizhou	6.7	0.9	42.6	19.9	-10.7	163.5
安庆市	Anqing	3.6	8.5	54.0	-7.2	-24.7	111.6
黄山市	Huangshan	-12.9	-12.7	114.4	36.0	-62.0	60.8

5—8 各市按隶属构成控股分固定资产投资增长情况（2022年）
Growth of Fixed Asset Investment by Controlling Shares According to Membership Composition by Region (2022)

单位：%

地 区	Region	按隶属关系分 By Affiliation		按构成分 According to Composition			
		中 央 Central Investment	地 方 Local Investment	建筑工程 Construction Engineering	安装工程 Installation Engineering	设备工器具购置 Purchase of Equipment,Tools and Appliances	其他费用 Other Expenses
总 计	**Total**	**23.6**	**8.4**	**7.8**	**-0.4**	**11.7**	**15.2**
合 肥 市	Hefei	4.2	9.3	8.9	-20.7	18.3	8.3
淮 北 市	Huaibei	125.4	1.7	-3.4	-20.0	21.9	28.5
亳 州 市	Bozhou	-17.0	10.4	1.1	42.0	8.5	32.4
宿 州 市	Suzhou	217.8	8.7	8.3	4.9	10.7	22.7
蚌 埠 市	Bengbu	45.8	-0.1	-5.8	-3.3	7.0	53.1
阜 阳 市	Fuyang	120.5	5.0	2.4	18.2	40.0	7.5
淮 南 市	Huainan	10.4	3.3	2.8	-5.8	20.1	-2.5
滁 州 市	Chuzhou	-16.0	17.9	17.3	3.7	15.2	17.0
六 安 市	Luan	18.2	16.2	18.0	28.2	44.6	-6.0
马鞍山市	Maanshan	55.3	10.2	22.0	-27.2	-21.4	72.0
芜 湖 市	Wuhu	91.6	2.8	6.4	-17.0	-8.7	27.0
宣 城 市	Xuancheng	2.4	10.2	13.6	-10.9	3.8	10.7
铜 陵 市	Tongling	-16.9	10.1	4.7	-21.9	25.1	17.4
池 州 市	Chizhou	0.3	16.4	0.3	43.0	7.9	109.4
安 庆 市	Anqing	78.1	10.2	12.0	8.2	20.1	8.9
黄 山 市	Huangshan	-24.5	0.9	-3.3	-6.2	12.9	30.2

地 区	Region	按控股情况分 According to the Holding Situation					
		国有控股 State Holding	集体控股 Collective Holding	私人控股 Private Holding	港澳台商控股 Hong Kong, Macao and Taiwan Holding Company	外商控股 Foreign Holding	其 他 Other
总 计	**Total**	**18.9**	**-23.7**	**1.9**	**-4.2**	**-18.1**	**14.3**
合 肥 市	Hefei	8.9	-42.0	2.6	-16.9	-1.1	58.4
淮 北 市	Huaibei	23.1	453.1	-20.8	55.4	10.0	36.1
亳 州 市	Bozhou	27.7	134.6	-2.6	2569.9		-3.3
宿 州 市	Suzhou	17.0	-13.6	7.3	-73.8	-86.5	-6.5
蚌 埠 市	Bengbu	30.9	-96.0	-8.3	62.6	-45.2	-20.1
阜 阳 市	Fuyang	16.6	24.3	1.3	-26.5	-65.9	4.7
淮 南 市	Huainan	9.1	-48.1	-8.6	331.5	4.5	119.8
滁 州 市	Chuzhou	23.6	-17.2	13.0	15.9	-26.9	22.7
六 安 市	Luan	17.7	-46.2	14.7	72.3	67.9	17.0
马鞍山市	Maanshan	43.5	112.6	1.8	-6.9	-48.8	-14.8
芜 湖 市	Wuhu	26.0	67.3	2.7	-41.2	1.1	-11.7
宣 城 市	Xuancheng	24.9	73.9	1.9	68.5	30.6	7.5
铜 陵 市	Tongling	33.7	-15.5	-8.3	-66.7	173.8	34.7
池 州 市	Chizhou	18.5	125.2	3.5	-57.0	51.2	90.8
安 庆 市	Anqing	19.4	57.7	6.1	21.7	-50.9	19.0
黄 山 市	Huangshan	22.1	31.6	-18.1	35.1	-59.1	3.9

5—9 各市按行业新增固定资产投资增长情况（2022年）
Growth of Investment in Newly Added Fixed Assets by Industry by Region (2022)

单位：%

地区	Region	本年新增固定资产 New Fixed Assets Added This Year	农林牧渔业 Agriculture, Forestry, Animal Husbandry and Fishery	采矿业 Mining	制造业 Manufacturing	电力、热力、燃气及水的生产和供应业 Production and Supply of Electricity, Heat, Gas and Water	建筑业 Construction	批发和零售业 Wholesale and Retail Trade	交通运输、仓储和邮政业 Transport, Storage, Post & Telecommunications	住宿和餐饮业 Accommodation and Catering Trade	信息传输、计算机服务和软件业 Information, Circulation Computer Services and Software
总计	**Total**	**-2.4**	**7.2**	**-11.3**	**3.5**	**-13.0**	**-63.1**	**-41.7**	**35.3**	**3.0**	**3.3**
合肥市	Hefei	10.0	34.1	1656.6	5.2	24.9	-93.6	-27.1	-51.4	-29.2	0.2
淮北市	Huaibei	22.5	-1.6	-10.3	9.0	-30.1		102.2	64.4		374.9
亳州市	Bozhou	8.6	-28.1	-83.2	-27.0	55.4		-85.2	120.5	-100.0	3445.2
宿州市	Suzhou	-35.0	146.7	528.2	-38.0	-44.5		442.2	6.2	-19.1	-77.0
蚌埠市	Bengbu	-29.9	-36.5		5.6	-53.1		-69.8	-15.4	433.0	
阜阳市	Fuyang	12.4	32.9		73.5	14.0		-94.1	5.8	-100.0	3025.3
淮南市	Huainan	-5.7	-38.0	-78.0	11.7	-40.8		-65.8	-4.4	-20.6	206.8
滁州市	Chuzhou	-44.0	-33.8		-37.9	-35.2		-100.0	15.4	-70.7	-100.0
六安市	Luan	-4.6	141.9	94.5	14.1	60.8		109.8	-1.2	-22.0	12.7
马鞍山市	Maanshan	-6.4	1.5	-79.3	7.0	62.0		-48.0	151.6	944.3	68.4
芜湖市	Wuhu	0.1	-10.1	954.7	-4.0	-59.6		-51.0	42.1	62.8	-26.6
宣城市	Xuancheng	-12.5	35.8	-5.0	-13.0	-53.0		-14.5	42.1	35.8	
铜陵市	Tongling	8.0	105.6	-75.2	19.6	73.3		1618.4	621.0	233.3	314.0
池州市	Chizhou	70.8	27.4	38.4	48.5	238.0	280.1	-63.1	841.8	78.4	-49.7
安庆市	Anqing	5.3	34.5	107.9	14.9	-42.0	216.1	26.7	-53.0	-9.6	-100.0
黄山市	Huangshan	0.4	70.4	-83.7	-14.0	-31.3	-65.3	-40.5	188.9	-35.8	20.4

地区	Region	金融业 Banking	房地产业 Real Estate	租赁和商务服务业 Leasing and Commercial Services	科学研究和技术服务业 Scientific Research and Technical Services	水利、环境和公共设施管理业 Water Conservancy, Environmental and Public Facilities Management	居民服务、修理和其他服务业 Residents Service, Repair and Other Services	教育 Education	卫生和社会工作 Health and Social Work	文化、体育和娱乐业 Culture, Sports and Entertainment	公共管理、社会保障和社会组织 Public Management, Social Security and Social Organization
总计	**Total**	**-36.1**	**-15.8**	**-7.1**	**120.5**	**25.1**	**6.1**	**-36.0**	**61.5**	**-9.0**	**-7.6**
合肥市	Hefei	-40.8	13.6	31.6	7.4	15.4	-21.5	-42.7	31.8	556.1	-41.5
淮北市	Huaibei		35.6	809.7	1881.9	77.4		39.5	-41.6	131.7	-46.9
亳州市	Bozhou		28.3	887.1	27015.0	-17.1		-49.2	80.7	-92.1	-67.8
宿州市	Suzhou		-48.6	-87.0	-93.9	-22.2	-83.3	-41.0	368.1	-60.3	-59.4
蚌埠市	Bengbu	-100.0	-72.0	8.3	-35.6	59.8	346.1	-36.5	193.9	419.6	-60.5
阜阳市	Fuyang	-100.0	-5.5	19.9	2378.5	204.8	-78.9	-62.2	11.0	-26.4	-39.9
淮南市	Huainan		-20.7	-66.3	284.2	5.7	25.1	-72.0	203.5	5.3	220.9
滁州市	Chuzhou		-61.7	223.9	-100.0	-18.2	68.4	-66.4	-71.8	75.2	-100.0
六安市	Luan		-58.5	-10.7	11.7	46.5	995.7	-33.1	55.4	-58.7	132.7
马鞍山市	Maanshan		-31.1	-78.7	815.3	-16.2	-47.3	-37.7	10.2	49.9	166.0
芜湖市	Wuhu	150.9	-8.1	-40.5	112.9	36.8	83.1	-32.9	206.5	-35.0	-61.6
宣城市	Xuancheng		-26.3	65.3	-43.7	66.0	56.9	-39.4	108.6	-8.3	-41.5
铜陵市	Tongling		-57.6	1079.1	309.8	98.6		301.7	103.0	113.3	-100.0
池州市	Chizhou		-47.9	-73.3		-16.0	-69.6	311.0	77.0	111.0	179.7
安庆市	Anqing		-7.3	-41.6	-28.8	54.8	-43.8	1.7	559.3	0.7	1.5
黄山市	Huangshan	344.8	-39.8	35.7	127.2	24.0	-11.5	-44.7	37.3	11.7	-2.9

5—10 各市按行业分固定资产投资增长情况（2022年）
Growth of Fixed Asset Investment by Industry by Region (2022)

单位：%

地 区 Region	固定资产投资 Investment in Fixed Assets	农林牧渔业 Agriculture, Forestry, Animal Husbandry and Fishery	采矿业 Mining	制造业 Manufacturing	电力、热力、燃气及水的生产和供应业 Production and Supply of Electricity, Heat, Gas and Water	建筑业 Construction	批发和零售业 Wholesale and Retail Trade	交通运输、仓储和邮政业 Transport, Storage, Post & Telecommunications	住宿和餐饮业 Accommodation and Catering Trade	信息传输、计算机服务和软件业 Information, Circulation Computer Services and Software
总　计 Total	**9.0**	**20.3**	**30.1**	**21.5**	**22.7**	**-31.6**	**-22.6**	**22.5**	**8.2**	**2.4**
合肥市 Hefei	9.1	52.2	-25.6	30.1	-6.7	-76.7	-4.3	16.0	36.0	2.2
淮北市 Huaibei	2.9	12.6	23.5	3.4	31.6		90.1	35.7		390.2
亳州市 Bozhou	8.8	15.6	-45.3	18.9	35.1		-87.4	84.3	-21.7	7424.4
宿州市 Suzhou	9.6	62.5	26.6	12.7	48.4		365.7	69.1	-18.4	42.4
蚌埠市 Bengbu	0.5	-32.4		-2.6	-11.8		-30.9	8.0	534.9	6221.2
阜阳市 Fuyang	6.5	0.7	23.2	40.4	84.9		28.5	11.1	-46.3	121.6
淮南市 Huainan	3.6	4.9	32.3	18.0	14.2		-46.7	25.6	-20.3	40.7
滁州市 Chuzhou	16.5	23.8	505.5	31.2	69.1		-69.7	18.6	-66.7	472.9
六安市 Luan	16.2	86.6	81.8	45.7	51.5	837.2	-8.4	58.2	77.7	113.9
马鞍山市 Maanshan	13.2	24.6	-11.4	26.7	-19.5		-52.2	70.4	120.4	11.2
芜湖市 Wuhu	5.4	-4.7	-22.9	6.8	23.5		-65.2	-18.9	15.9	-52.0
宣城市 Xuancheng	10.0	55.9	-23.2	25.0	-10.9		20.3	38.5	36.8	30.3
铜陵市 Tongling	8.8	44.6	101.5	23.5	-9.2		-57.1	80.2	-38.8	-72.6
池州市 Chizhou	15.0	32.2	380.9	23.5	21.3	112.0	-48.8	-35.6	42.9	-65.7
安庆市 Anqing	12.3	40.1	59.1	19.0	14.8	-49.0	33.7	33.9	85.4	12.3
黄山市 Huangshan	0.5	28.9	-77.6	3.2	13.7	-65.3	17.7	17.9	-27.9	42.0

地 区 Region	金融业 Banking	房地产业 Real Estate	租赁和商务服务业 Leasing and Commercial Services	科学研究和技术服务业 Scientific Research and Technical Services	水利、环境和公共设施管理业 Water Conservancy, Environmental and Public Facilities Management	居民服务、修理和其他服务业 Residents Service, Repair and Other Services	教育 Education	卫生和社会工作 Health and Social Work	文化、体育和娱乐业 Culture, Sports and Entertainment	公共管理、社会保障和社会组织 Public Management, Social Security and Social Organization
总　计 Total	**-21.4**	**-7.3**	**21.4**	**24.1**	**18.7**	**7.0**	**1.9**	**39.5**	**2.8**	**-5.1**
合肥市 Hefei	-47.8	-1.1	46.6	-25.0	13.9	56.9	2.9	8.5	2.4	-9.5
淮北市 Huaibei	62.3	-11.6	16.2	-13.0	23.0		-7.4	13.9	13.5	154.4
亳州市 Bozhou		-1.9	-30.3	252.1	4.6	249.1	11.8	41.0	-41.4	81.6
宿州市 Suzhou		-8.8	-4.2	11.1	37.3	209.0	6.0	100.1	22.2	-37.0
蚌埠市 Bengbu	-72.5	-3.9	73.3	-33.0	35.6	-23.8	-17.5	53.1	15.8	54.0
阜阳市 Fuyang	-73.6	-10.4	92.9	868.7	22.5	-47.4	-25.9	23.1	18.8	-56.3
淮南市 Huainan		-20.8	44.5	98.2	5.0	-37.8	15.3	129.9	-28.3	208.8
滁州市 Chuzhou		-2.5	5.7	61.7	24.0	99.9	15.9	3.8	51.5	-47.9
六安市 Luan	166.9	-12.1	32.1	-19.7	29.7	-37.4	10.4	52.4	-11.9	36.5
马鞍山市 Maanshan	-98.0	-6.8	-33.6	2.8	6.1	93.8	43.8	35.6	-18.6	20.5
芜湖市 Wuhu	256.8	-1.3	24.1	108.2	35.4	16.4	13.4	21.5	-19.2	-4.7
宣城市 Xuancheng		-24.2	43.4	106.4	22.4	102.2	34.2	92.1	12.4	-20.1
铜陵市 Tongling	-43.2	-28.1	58.2	0.7	12.2	-26.6	-27.5	72.6	26.3	-67.4
池州市 Chizhou	96.4	3.8	-18.9	4.4	25.8	-45.0	1.9	35.9	772.4	82.4
安庆市 Anqing		-1.9	31.4	11.7	-1.5	-39.0	74.1	85.7	-27.6	-26.9
黄山市 Huangshan	2040.6	-24.9	-31.5	-7.8	36.4	92.5	22.8	62.7	7.3	1.5

5—11 各市固定资产投资资金来源增长情况（2022年）
Growth of Capital Sources for Fixed Asset Investment by Region (2022)

单位：%

地 区	Region	本年资金来源合计 Total Sources of Funds for the Year	国家预算资金 State Budget Funds	国内贷款 Domestic Loans	债券 Bonds	利用外资 Foreign Investment	自筹资金 Self-raising Funds	其他资金来源 Other Sources of Funding
总 计	**Total**	**5.6**	**50.9**	**11.8**	**-66.7**	**-18.6**	**16.7**	**-20.5**
合肥市	Hefei	6.3	63.5	28.4		23.3	12.1	-12.5
淮北市	Huaibei	-5.4	44.3	9.3		-28.7	1.3	-36.2
亳州市	Bozhou	-2.8	0.8	23.2			9.6	-18.5
宿州市	Suzhou	4.8	45.8	-1.7		-86.6	25.7	-26.6
蚌埠市	Bengbu	-6.3	47.8	-2.3			-1.8	-30.2
阜阳市	Fuyang	8.2	151.9	12.9		628.9	18.6	-21.6
淮南市	Huainan	4.6	16.8	49.6		-46.3	22.0	-34.9
滁州市	Chuzhou	8.2	51.4	-7.6	-100.0	26.8	16.6	-13.7
六安市	Luan	18.8	43.1	-13.0		-73.5	50.4	-14.5
马鞍山市	Maanshan	13.7	140.3	-1.3		-76.1	30.4	-43.2
芜湖市	Wuhu	-5.4	27.2	-16.0		-63.5	4.2	-32.8
宣城市	Xuancheng	11.5	102.5	-35.4		-70.7	29.3	-31.9
铜陵市	Tongling	12.5	3.2	19.4		266.0	28.5	-31.4
池州市	Chizhou	12.6	2.5	34.3		-100.0	36.1	-24.9
安庆市	Anqing	10.6	51.4	-8.0		173.5	15.7	-8.9
黄山市	Huangshan	8.2	10.0	36.0		-3.5	19.9	-15.4

5—12　各市按建设性质项目分固定资产投资增长情况（2022年）
Growth of Investment in Fixed Assets by Construction Projects by Region (2022)

单位：%

地区	Region	新建 New Construction	扩建 Expansion Construction	改建和技术改造 Reconstruction and Technical Transformation
总计	**Total**	**16.0**	**30.4**	**20.6**
合肥市	Hefei	12.5	41.3	3.7
淮北市	Huaibei	13.9	14.3	17.3
亳州市	Bozhou	15.8	2.6	44.6
宿州市	Suzhou	28.2	9.7	34.3
蚌埠市	Bengbu	-1.4	88.7	24.0
阜阳市	Fuyang	15.9	22.0	27.0
淮南市	Huainan	25.4	-6.7	5.7
滁州市	Chuzhou	17.4	155.4	33.0
六安市	Luan	18.3	-5.0	125.4
马鞍山市	Maanshan	23.6	85.8	10.0
芜湖市	Wuhu	5.5	16.3	10.8
宣城市	Xuancheng	27.6	50.9	12.3
铜陵市	Tongling	34.1	88.4	-4.0
池州市	Chizhou	21.8	33.4	9.0
安庆市	Anqing	14.6	-21.5	26.9
黄山市	Huangshan	14.2	-33.1	39.4

5—13 各市民间投资和技改投资增长情况（2022年）
Growth of Private Investment and Technological Innovation Investment by Region (2022)

单位：%

地 区	Region	民间投资 Private Investment	技改投资 Investment in Technological Transformation
总 计	**Total**	**3.2**	**21.3**
合 肥 市	Hefei	9.8	22.8
淮 北 市	Huaibei	-13.0	22.3
亳 州 市	Bozhou	-3.8	27.7
宿 州 市	Suzhou	6.3	25.1
蚌 埠 市	Bengbu	-14.2	7.7
阜 阳 市	Fuyang	1.7	28.0
淮 南 市	Huainan	-3.9	9.5
滁 州 市	Chuzhou	13.8	34.1
六 安 市	Luan	14.5	61.6
马鞍山市	Maanshan	0.3	20.3
芜 湖 市	Wuhu	0.6	10.7
宣 城 市	Xuancheng	2.8	25.2
铜 陵 市	Tongling	-4.6	15.0
池 州 市	Chizhou	12.7	26.2
安 庆 市	Anqing	8.6	16.3
黄 山 市	Huangshan	-11.6	16.3

5—14 房地产开发主要指标
Main Indicators of Real Estate Development

指 标	Item	2010	2015	2020	2021	2022
企业个数 (个)	Number of Enterprises (unit)	3385	3620	4143	4240	3962
登记注册类型	Registration type					
内 资	Domestic Funded	3249	3534	4082	4176	3915
#国 有	State-owned Enterprises	136	60	53	22	50
集 体	Collective Enterprises	25	6	1	1	1
港、澳、台投资	Funded by Entrepreneurs from Hong Kong, Macao and Taiwan	78	57	44	43	31
外商投资	Foreign Funded	58	29	17	21	16
企业控股情况	Controlling Stake of Enterprises					
国有控股	Controlling Stake of State-owner	312	283	393	454	414
集体控股	Controlling Stake of Group	116	59	38	62	37
私人控股	Controlling Stake of Private	2620	2816	3265	3665	3110
港、澳、台商控股	Controlling Stake of Hong Kong, Macao and Taiwan Businessman	80	51	31	39	31
外商控股	Controlling Stake of Foreign Businessman	61	30	13	19	10
其 他	Other	196	381	403		360
本年完成投资额 (万元)	Investment Completed this Year (10000 yuan)	22518045	44248584	70422934	72632161	62034752
#住 宅	Residential Buildings	15952464	28491942	56367778	59768239	50828609
资金来源小计 (万元)	Source of Funds (10000 yuan)	28636982	49907807	89519935	95596395	71545853
#国内贷款	Domestically Loans	3237258	5642296	8930567	8453166	7053886
自筹资金	Fundraising	12110747	18601276	24200758	25262478	23003536
房屋建筑面积 (万平方米)	Floor Space of Buildings (10000 sq.m)					
施工面积	Floor Space Under Construction	17541.90	34244.67	44974.60	46812.59	40841.84
竣工面积	Floor Space Completed	3020.57	5537.74	5100.86	7012.89	5945.19
本年新开工面积	Floor Space Started this Year	7317.60	7759.35	11785.64	10434.89	6843.01
#住 宅	Residential Buildings	5770.46	5254.68	9243.72	8140.41	5237.57
商品房屋销售面积(万平方米)	Floor Space of Selling House (10000 sq.m)	4113.88	6174.09	9534.13	10460.90	6756.92
#住 宅	Residential Buildings	3604.87	5356.81	8695.35	9507.67	5872.99
实收资本合计 (万元)	Total Capital Hold (10000 yuan)	8603456	22029739	37079573	40139775	40686168
资产合计 (万元)	State Capital (10000 yuan)	54332428	168467240	347312551	369614732	375721639
负债合计 (万元)	Total Liabilities (10000 yuan)	40828272	132704740	279155283	291489704	292690504
资产负债率 (%)	Ratio of Liabilities to Assets (%)	75.15	78.77	80.38	78.86	77.90
主营业务收入 (万元)	Total Revenue (10000 yuan)	13150647	26455215	54741894	59562353	53425095
#土地转让收入	Land Transferred	81646	408642	69345	127121	277683

注：2022年房地产开发投资、商品房销售面积等指标数据与上年已公布的同期数据之间存在不可比因素，不能直接相比计算增速。

5—15　房地产开发投资（2022年）
Investment in Real Estate Development (2022)

指　标	Item	总　计 Total
计划总投资	Total Planned Investment	439764076
自开始建设累计完成投资	Accumulative Investment Actually Made Since Starting of Construction up to the End	306612125
本年完成投资	Investment Made this Year	62034752
#国有控股	State Controlling Share Hold Enterprises	11016522
按构成分：建筑工程	Grouped by Composition: Construction Project	39206589
安装工程	Installation Project	2132869
设备工器具购置	Purchase of Equipment and Instrument	388219
其他费用	Other Expenses	20307075
#旧建筑物购置费	Total Expenses of Purchasing Old Buildings	14057
土地购置费	Total Value of Land Purchased	18854148
按工程用途分：	Grouped by the Use of Project	
住　宅	Residential Buildings	50828609
#90平方米以下	Below $90m^2$	6045821
144平方米以上	Above of $144m^2$	3962627
办公楼	Office Buildings	1122855
商业营业用房	Houses for Business Use	5179260
其　他	Other	4904028
本年新增固定资产	Newly Increased Fixed Assets This Year	27283899
待开发土地面积　（平方米）	Land Space Prepared for Development　(sq.m)	29510787

单位：万元（10000 yuan）

内　资 Domestic Funded	国　有 State-owned Enterprises	集　体 Collective Enterprises	港、澳、台投　资 Funded by Entrepreneurs from Hong Kong, Macao and Taiwan	外商投资 Foreign Funded	中　央 Central Government	地　方 Local Government	其　他 Other
432071261	7041447		5431838	2260977	10763007	59992210	369008859
301657509	4629163		3517965	1436651	8996678	38782385	258833062
61521686	2141325		399298	113768	1412442	10115964	50506346
11016522	2141325				1400463	6372811	4689646
38864296	1331471		261075	81218	995626	5979956	32231007
2108572	32468		22138	2159	68335	216902	1847632
387153	2035		926	140	5931	40450	341838
20161665	775351		115159	30251	342550	3878656	16085869
14057	210					25	14032
18722574	714260		101866	29708	317231	3578552	14958365
50535510	1838429		216660	76439	1059884	8334681	41434044
6036359	275382		9431	31	52763	1357904	4635154
3941860	87864		7682	13085	75768	851294	3035565
1101162	49882		20645	1048	50478	103307	969070
5021271	73735		151554	6435	168084	656359	4354817
4863743	179279		10439	29846	133996	1021617	3748415
26897940	537241		278286	107673	648677	3265165	23370057
31082637	278156		560000	176031	369056	5573297	25876315

5—16 房地产开发企业财务状况（2022年）

Enterprise's Financial Situation in Real Estate Development (2022)

项目	Item	流动资产合计 Circulating Funds	#存货 Stock	固定资产原价 Original Value of Fixed Assets	累计折旧 Accumulated Depreciation	资产合计 Total Assets
总计	**Total**	**303376137**	**157224084**	**8235958**	**1739008**	**375721639**
国有及国有控股企业	State Controlling Share Hold Enterprises	90437180	43528032	4022934	553677	138051517
按注册类型分	**Grouped by Status of Registration**					
内资	Domestic Funded	299426179	155688492	7953688	1645384	370614981
#国有	State-owned Enterprises	9191795	3479760	279472	43938	16295026
集体	Collective Enterprises			438	438	4840
港、澳、台投资	Funded by Entrepreneurs from Hong Kong, Macao and Taiwan	3102594	1196024	194959	76546	3934385
外商投资	Foreign Funded	847364	339568	87311	17077	1172273
按隶属关系分	**Grouped by Administrative Relationship**					
中央	Central Government	6160632	2408738	110626	19071	8368353
地方	Local Government	66072302	32375698	3289596	407322	94420761
其他	Other	231143204	122439648	4835737	1312615	272932526
按资质等级分	**Grouped by qualification grade**					
一级	First Grade	17512984	6776201	438119	151335	23965148
二级	Second Grade	43902483	21608430	1045114	289424	53677335
三级	Third Grade	39904818	19343729	2248863	652438	50725673
四级	Forth Grade	5037143	3351627	157777	33204	6406206
暂定	Tentative	156987099	84588118	3477768	489157	186629507
其他	Other	40031611	21555979	868317	123450	54317770

5—17 各市房地产开发企业财务状况（2022年）

Enterprise's Financial Situation in Real Estate Development by Region (2022)

地区	Region	流动资产合计 Circulating Funds	#存货 Stock	固定资产原价 Original Value of Fixed Assets	累计折旧 Accumulated Depreciation	资产合计 Total Assets
总计	**Total**	**303376137**	**157224084**	**8235958**	**1739008**	**375721639**
合肥市	Hefei	96442740	45543136	2994158	717501	124610710
淮北市	Huaibei	7856619	4033055	308572	39322	9549556
亳州市	Bozhou	19404505	10543655	159375	24987	21113699
宿州市	Suzhou	16021321	8773833	726749	35700	21590201
蚌埠市	Bengbu	17886221	9196518	260838	63184	20447526
阜阳市	Fuyang	24675306	12984475	873952	139309	30530862
淮南市	Huainan	8969257	5034732	70439	31532	10649807
滁州市	Chuzhou	13649686	8177689	322125	51866	15323011
六安市	Luan	14664304	8341392	154573	35537	16164586
马鞍山市	Maanshan	8953127	4579343	277309	68432	10977548
芜湖市	Wuhu	29361420	15808718	861131	160825	34423619
宣城市	Xuancheng	15830883	7571223	456753	69919	25991055
铜陵市	Tongling	6862134	3294121	166121	66865	7672297
池州市	Chizhou	4162129	2342621	67854	25270	4750490
安庆市	Anqing	13621706	7745378	313391	138646	16438677
黄山市	Huangshan	5014781	3254194	222620	70113	5487995

单位：万元（10000 yuan）

负债合计 Total Liabilities	资产负债率(%) Ratio of Liabilities to Assets (%)	所有者权益合计 Owners Equity	实收资本 Capital Hold	主营业务收入 Main Business Income	土地转让收入 Revenue of Land Transfer	主营业务成本 Main Business Cost	营业利润 Operating profit	应付职工薪酬 The payable staff pay
292690504	**77.9**	**83031135**	**40686168**	**53425095**	**277683**	**45573620**	**3194917**	**1214015**
93367557	67.6	44683960	13779975	9307508	168874	7564494	1050954	203085
289427016	78.1	81187965	39594932	52916652	277683	45148009	3072418	1200320
10335635	63.4	5959391	1734678	966251		805284	12428	15772
4153	85.8	687	687	52		66	-138	42
2526558	64.2	1407827	877696	360214		296240	129806	9847
736930	62.9	435343	213540	148229		129371	-7306	3848
6064243	72.5	2304110	1176385	1606868		1317622	347776	40420
66863854	70.8	27556907	9565611	8443330	738	7009735	718334	163278
219762407	80.5	53170119	29944173	43374897	276945	37246262	2128808	1010317
17856379	74.5	6108769	4239510	2290735	350	1885838	355264	69793
39932150	74.4	13745185	4880560	5478715	130593	4452954	406865	120645
36547834	72.0	14177840	5601120	4594813	860	3846960	266214	122326
4414797	68.9	1991409	789248	745205	72494	620350	-25779	24750
152073910	81.5	34555597	20010221	35287010	73386	30460716	2041431	744358
41865435	77.1	12452336	5165509	5028617		4306803	150921	132144

单位：万元（10000 yuan）

负债合计 Total Liabilities	资产负债率(%) Ratio of Liabilities to Assets (%)	所有者权益合计 Owners Equity	实收资本 Capital Hold	主营业务收入 Main Business Income	土地转让收入 Revenue of Land Transfer	主营业务成本 Main Business Cost	营业利润 Operating profit	应付职工薪酬 The payable staff pay
292690504	**77.9**	**83031135**	**40686168**	**53425095**	**277683**	**45573620**	**3194917**	**1214015**
94404563	75.8	30206147	16357904	17265236	738	14712669	1699323	308625
7383078	77.3	2166478	670555	1210437		974017	70236	26633
16263919	77.0	4849780	1300887	2640294		2260908	73165	124764
15666322	72.6	5923879	2064389	3017642	7547	2671873	85639	66550
16749013	81.9	3698513	1424597	2535160		2191066	-10670	63954
24908949	81.6	5621913	3036540	5607041	11827	4896718	234424	117060
8784246	82.5	1865561	1880732	1230725	350	1032314	99317	43316
13103561	85.5	2219450	1557972	2762841	2	2360926	22325	80753
13427054	83.1	2737532	1649958	3574946		3222810	23800	73192
8341823	76.0	2635725	1261092	1395446	12267	1086707	120326	39448
29320015	85.2	5103604	2938288	4215626	130469	3260361	475071	65242
16568890	63.7	9422165	1980357	2857835	37669	2548441	196384	47219
6526172	85.1	1146125	985186	934195	123	851099	-13453	32807
3940993	83.0	809497	624770	662292	4076	522341	46268	17754
12571306	76.5	3867371	2204706	2688690	72616	2300041	53205	69419
4730598	86.2	757397	748236	826687		681331	19557	37280

5—18 房地产开发企业（单位）财务状况
Enterprise's Financial Situation in Real Estate Development

单位：万元（10000 yuan）

项目	Item	2010	2015	2020	2021	2022
年初存货	Opening Stock This Year	19892008	69197069	135091054	139697877	140507492
年末资产负债	**Assets and Liabilities at the Year-end**					
流动资产合计	Total of Current Assets	46759621	141925366	291886547	306692635	303376137
#应收账款	Receivable Accounts		4574491	10940390	10599901	15410632
存货	Stock	24613144	79781966	158898931	162973520	157224084
固定资产合计	Fixed Assets		4260390			
固定资产原价	Prime Cost of Fixed Assets	1537883	4300126	6423424	8756261	8235958
累计折旧	Progressive Depreciation	316551	857190	1475967	1643770	1739008
#本年折旧	Depreciation This Year	67026	183218	249724	285101	307545
在建工程	Projects In building		2318210	7696442	10106102	13796270
资产总计	Total of Assets	54332428	168467240	347312551	369614732	375721639
流动负债合计	Current Liabilities		111884489	219248516	227282898	224868390
#应付账款	Payables		11531651			
非流动负债合计	Non-Current Liabilities		20820251			
负债合计	Total of Liabilities	40828272	132704740	279155283	291489704	292690504
所有者权益合计	Total of Ownership Interest	13504156	35762501	68157268	78125028	83031135
#实收资本	Paid-in Capital	8603456	22029739	37079573	40139775	40686168
损益及分配	**Profit and Loss and Distribution**					
营业收入	Business Income		26973951	55850414	60443733	54351725
#主营业务收入	Main Business Earning	13150647	26455215	54741894	59562353	53425095
土地转让收入	Earning of Land Transfer	81646	408642	69345	127121	277683
商品房屋销售收入	Sales Revenue of Commercial Houses	12719888	24832862	53069473	57685174	51422548
房屋出租收入	Rental Income of Buildings	85698	169620	168766	193773	186472
其他收入	Other Income	263415	1044091	1300392	1402865	1387218
营业成本	Business Cost		20543191	45719615	51180462	46586818
#主营业务成本	Main Business Cost	9672150	20244368	44120002	49956305	45573620
营业税金及附加	Business Tax and Affixation		2188629	1602027	1479207	1291799
其他业务利润	Other Business Profit	36519	14218	69553	75443	54793
销售费用	Sales Expense	325905	934452	2235499	2437836	1793238
管理费用	Management Expense	539208	1184320	1586425	1640727	1349609
财务费用	Financial Expense	166459	610686	823498	959243	1015354
营业利润	Operating Profit	1547277	1657790	4436453	3728526	3194917
投资收益	Investment Yield	29217	135155	573312	826315	748158
利润总额	Total of Profit	1349105	1994345	4388932	3641738	3129930
应交所得税	Payable Income Tax	270053	567289	1277451	884504	765138
人工成本	**Labor cost**					
应付职工薪酬（贷方累计发生额）	Payable Employee Compensation Credit Cumulative Amount		727047	1226636	1370178	1214015

5—19 房地产开发企业（单位）投资、资金和土地情况
Investment, Funds and Land Condition of Real Estate Developer

单位：万元（10000 yuan）

指　标	Item	2015	2020	2021	2022
计划总投资	Total Planned Investment	251053015	436283521	465407730	439764076
自开始建设累计完成投资	Accumulative Investment Actually Made Since Starting of Construction up to the End	171677082	294679368	318904279	306612125
本年完成投资	Investment Made this Year	44248584	70422934	72632161	62034752
#国有控股	State-holding Stock	6134806	9455014	12841792	11016522
按构成分：建筑工程	Grouped by Composition: Construction Project	30569270	42206430	48566755	39206589
安装工程	Installation Project	5219369	3508706	2958334	2132869
设备工器具购置	Purchase of Equipment and Instrument	584514	735969	587715	388219
其他费用	Other Expenses	7875431	23971829	20519357	20307075
#旧建筑物购置费	Total Expenses of Purchasing Old Buildings	116710	61888	57230	14057
土地购置费	Total Value of Land Purchased	6419885	22162518	18727346	18854148
按工程用途分：	Grouped by the Use of Project				
住　宅	Residential Buildings	28491942	56367778	59768239	50828609
#90平方米以下	Below 90m^2	10547222	6129377	6740327	6045821
144平方米以上	Above of 144m^2	2353790	5336270	5480677	3962627
别墅、高档公寓	Villas and Good Apartments	668618			
办公楼	Office Buildings	2042490	1452056	1580550	1122855
商业营业用房	Houses for Business Use	10258620	7016767	6236674	5179260
其　他	Other	3455532	5586333	5046698	4904028
本年新增固定资产	Newly Increased Fixed Assets This Year	21065233	21783612	32395979	27283899
本年资金来源合计	Total by Source of Funds This Year	64989108	123510864	126745283	101883874
上年末结余资金	Surplus Funds at the End of Last Year	15081301	33990929	31148888	30338021
本年资金来源小计	Total Funds this Year	49907807	89519935	95596395	71545853
国内贷款	Domestic Loans	5642296	8930567	8453166	7053886
利用外资	Foreign Investment	10186	45900	5695	
自筹资金	Self-raising Fund	18601276	24200758	25262478	23003536
其他资金来源	Others	25654049	56342710	61875056	41488431
本年各项应付款合计	Total of All Payable Account This Year	14915267	25378952	26366751	26236288
#工程款	Project Account	7727866	15137073	15717790	14564990
待开发土地面积　（万平方米）	Land Space Prepared for Development　(10000 sq.m)	2472.35	3107.21	2522.57	2951.08

5—20 房地产开发企业（单位）施工、销售和待售情况（2022年）
Construction, Sale and for Sale in Real Estate Development Units (2022)

指 标	Item	合 计 Total	住 宅 Residential Buildings	#90平米以下 Below 90 sq.m	#144平米以上 Above of 144 sq.m	办公楼 Office Buildings	商业营业用房 Houses for Business Use	其 他 Others
			按用途分 Grouped by the Use of Project					
房屋施工面积 （万平方米）	Floor Space of Buildings Under Construction (10000 sq.m)	40841.84	30610.18			1046.85	3544.15	5640.67
#新开工面积	Newly Started	6843.01	5237.57			89.05	430.36	1086.04
房屋竣工面积 （万平方米）	Floor Space of Buildings Completed (10000 sq.m)	5945.19	4315.37			225.67	404.91	999.23
#不可销售面积	Not for Sale	224.61	47.79			22.30	24.39	130.13
住宅竣工套数 （套）	Sets of Commercial Residential Buildings Completed (set)		464655					
房屋竣工价值 （万元）	Value of Buildings Completed (10000 yuan)	20544608	15243724			819101	1756458	2725325
出租房屋面积 （万平方米）	Floor Space of Buildings for Renting (10000 sq.m)	15.50	0.10			0.40	11.58	3.42
商品房销售面积（万平方米）	Floor Space of Selling House (10000 sq.m)	6756.92	5872.99	329.06	405.55	89.00	328.26	466.68
#现房销售面积	Floor Space of Accomplished Buildings Sold	1008.63	694.72			30.19	138.13	145.60
期房销售面积	Floor Space of Futures Marketable Housings Sold	5748.29	5178.27			58.81	190.13	321.08
商品房销售额 （万元）	Total Sales of Commercial Houses (10000 yuan)	51603202	46911603	2417302	4793020	669841	2780150	1241608
#现房销售额	Sales Value of Accomplished Buildings	5643206	4023521			255712	986128	377845
期房销售额	Sales Value of Futures House	45959996	42888082			414129	1794022	863763
商品住宅销售套数 （套）	Sets of Commercial Residential Buildings Sold (set)		523163					
#现房销售套数	Sets of Accomplished Buildings Sold		61865					
期房销售套数	Sets of Futures House		461298					
待售面积 （万平方米）	Floor Space of Vacant Houses (10000 sq.m)	1881.95	898.45			109.77	538.62	335.12
待售1-3年	Vacant 1-3 Years	1070.72	567.30			48.17	259.66	195.58
待售3年以上	Vacant More than 3 Years	238.82	53.29			25.35	107.11	53.08

5—21 各市房地产开发企业（单位）个数（2022年）
Number of Enterprises for Real Estate Development by Region (2022)

单位：个（unit）

地 区	Region	企业个数 Number of Enterprises	内资企业 Domestic Funded Enterprises	#国有 State-owned	#集体 Collective-owned	#私营 Private Units	港澳台投资企业 Funded by Entrepreneurs from Hong Kong, Macao and Taiwan	外商投资企业 Foreign Funded Enterprises	国有控股 State-owned holdings
总 计	**Total**	**3962**	**3915**	**50**	**1**	**1765**	**31**	**16**	**414**
合肥市	Hefei	748	729	8		246	13	6	131
淮北市	Huaibei	115	112	2		55	1	2	23
亳州市	Bozhou	166	166	3		65			21
宿州市	Suzhou	254	252	4		179	1	1	30
蚌埠市	Bengbu	187	186	4		88	1		31
阜阳市	Fuyang	335	334	4		164	1		19
淮南市	Huainan	128	127	2		62	1		10
滁州市	Chuzhou	291	289	4		179		2	18
六安市	Luan	225	223	1		86	2		9
马鞍山市	Maanshan	161	157	6		73	2	2	24
芜湖市	Wuhu	251	249	3		90	2		15
宣城市	Xuancheng	209	208	4		95	1		25
铜陵市	Tongling	178	178	1		81			16
池州市	Chizhou	132	132			64			9
安庆市	Anqing	377	375	3	1	186	2		19
黄山市	Huangshan	205	198	1		97	4	3	14

5—22 各市按控股情况分的房地产企业（单位）个数（2022年）
Number of Real Estate Enterprises (units) by Controlled Holdings by Region (2022)

单位：个（unit）

地 区	Region	企业个数 Number of Enterprises	国有控股 State-owned Controlled Holdings	集体控股 Collective-owned Controlled Holdings	私人控股 Private Units Collective-owned Controlled Holdings	港澳台商控股 Funded by Entrepreneurs from Hong Kong, Macao and Taiwan Controlled Holdings	外商控股 Foreign Funded Enterprises Controlled Holdings	其他 Other
总 计	**Total**	**3962**	**414**	**37**	**3110**	**31**	**10**	**360**
合肥市	Hefei	748	131	9	513	13	3	79
淮北市	Huaibei	115	23	1	84	1	1	5
亳州市	Bozhou	166	21		118			27
宿州市	Suzhou	254	30	3	210		1	10
蚌埠市	Bengbu	187	31	3	138	1		14
阜阳市	Fuyang	335	19		288			28
淮南市	Huainan	128	10	5	108	1		4
滁州市	Chuzhou	291	18		248	1		24
六安市	Luan	225	9	2	176	3		35
马鞍山市	Maanshan	161	24		121	4	2	10
芜湖市	Wuhu	251	15		198			38
宣城市	Xuancheng	209	25	2	170			12
铜陵市	Tongling	178	16	4	144			14
池州市	Chizhou	132	9		114			9
安庆市	Anqing	377	19	6	315	1		36
黄山市	Huangshan	205	14	2	165	6	3	15

5—23 各市房地产开发建设投资总规模及完成投资（2022年）
General Scale and Actually Completed Investment in Real Estate Development by Region (2022)

单位：万元（10000 yuan）

地区	Region	计划总投资 Total Investment Actually Needed	自开始建设至本年底累计完成投资 Accumulative Investment Actually Made Since Starting of Construction up to the End	本年完成投资 Investment Made this Year	全部建成尚需投资 Further Investment Required for the Completion of Construction
总计	**Total**	**439764076**	**306612125**	**62034752**	**133151951**
合肥市	Hefei	136707920	91954923	14570872	44752997
淮北市	Huaibei	11408731	8051541	1839275	3357190
亳州市	Bozhou	23167680	15254032	3922275	7913648
宿州市	Suzhou	25475352	17517887	4445166	7957465
蚌埠市	Bengbu	24173943	19092499	3365669	5081444
阜阳市	Fuyang	40289258	28972527	7547582	11316731
淮南市	Huainan	15762875	10396630	1954894	5366245
滁州市	Chuzhou	25943089	15736191	5605906	10206898
六安市	Luan	24425899	16628994	3937154	7796905
马鞍山市	Maanshan	14216924	11664599	1990423	2552325
芜湖市	Wuhu	31264472	23121180	4998015	8143292
宣城市	Xuancheng	16316839	11538063	2129150	4778776
铜陵市	Tongling	13256777	10959792	1057872	2296985
池州市	Chizhou	8756461	6382901	887025	2373560
安庆市	Anqing	17398012	12169366	2608410	5228646
黄山市	Huangshan	11199844	7171000	1175064	4028844

5—24 各市按用途分的房地产开发企业（单位）完成投资额（2022年）

Actually Completed Investment of Enterprises for Real Estate Development by Region and by Use (2022)

单位：万元（10000 yuan）

地 区	Region	本年完成投资额 Investment Made this Year	住 宅 Residential Buildings	#90平米以下 Below 90 sq.m	144平米以上 Above of 144 sq.m	办公楼 Office Buildings	商业营业用房 Houses for Business Use	其 他 Other
总 计	**Total**	**62034752**	**50828609**	**6045821**	**3962627**	**1122855**	**5179260**	**4904028**
合肥市	Hefei	14570872	11487636	2353223	1137657	452438	1158875	1471923
淮北市	Huaibei	1839275	1676434	200590	107188	6007	41065	115769
亳州市	Bozhou	3922275	3272347	395218	192042	37771	379921	232236
宿州市	Suzhou	4445166	3786918	281054	92647	43056	336745	278447
蚌埠市	Bengbu	3365669	2822522	315301	297008	58875	198028	286244
阜阳市	Fuyang	7547582	6181783	394272	328373	195634	653011	517154
淮南市	Huainan	1954894	1577239	151348	74692	9211	221178	147266
滁州市	Chuzhou	5605906	4781304	621613	248225	38705	381492	404405
六安市	Luan	3937154	3120565	197912	208260	45542	532514	238533
马鞍山市	Maanshan	1990423	1655840	225390	176045	14629	183263	136691
芜湖市	Wuhu	4998015	4271053	376630	483412	40028	266604	420330
宣城市	Xuancheng	2129150	1764193	156821	309544	23643	212656	128658
铜陵市	Tongling	1057872	867886	55215	32115	4684	44532	140770
池州市	Chizhou	887025	781118	80971	52337	10747	49224	45936
安庆市	Anqing	2608410	2041643	83760	85124	41933	321172	203662
黄山市	Huangshan	1175064	740128	156503	137958	99952	198980	136004

5—25 各市房地产开发企业（单位）资金来源（2022年）

Sources of Funds of Enterprises for Real Estate Development by Region (2022)

单位：万元（10000 yuan）

地 区	Region	本年资金来源合计 Total Sources of Funds	上年末结余资金 Funds by the End of Last Year	本年资金来源小计 Total Funds This Year	国内贷款 Domestic Loans	#银行贷款 Bank Loan	自筹资金 Self-raising Funds
总 计	**Total**	**101883874**	**30338021**	**71545853**	**7053886**	**6359831**	**23003536**
合肥市	Hefei	35802742	11130010	24672732	3639697	3407229	6380756
淮北市	Huaibei	2337239	450859	1886380	219089	219089	751943
亳州市	Bozhou	5902884	1504792	4398092	405663	333306	1341180
宿州市	Suzhou	5630985	1163738	4467247	348692	244359	1684347
蚌埠市	Bengbu	5806505	1848709	3957796	268987	190257	1936614
阜阳市	Fuyang	10221375	3510607	6710768	424578	394924	2062380
淮南市	Huainan	2964058	1103156	1860902	276139	254001	410784
滁州市	Chuzhou	5806957	1305963	4500994	198207	159157	2062079
六安市	Luan	6012188	2053809	3958379	183691	151953	1248712
马鞍山市	Maanshan	2858095	754598	2103497	100537	97217	795715
芜湖市	Wuhu	6929480	1712185	5217295	364854	330230	1737310
宣城市	Xuancheng	3200124	1044816	2155308	179058	175163	684608
铜陵市	Tongling	1434453	484189	950264	96773	91273	376785
池州市	Chizhou	1167378	467190	700188	75450	61550	163544
安庆市	Anqing	3840795	1232847	2607948	124165	104817	639497
黄山市	Huangshan	1968616	570553	1398063	148306	145306	727282

5—26 各市房地产开发建设房屋建筑面积和造价（2022年）
Floor Space of Buildings and their Cost in Real Estate Development by Region (2022)

地　区	Region	施工房屋面积（平方米）Floor Space of Buildings Under Construction (sq.m)	新开工 Newly Started	竣工房屋面积（平方米）Floor Space of Buildings Completed (sq.m)	房屋建筑面积竣工率（%）Ratio of Floor Space of Buildings Completed (%)	竣工房屋价值（万元）Value of Buildings Completed (10000 yuan)	竣工房屋造价（元/平方米）Cost of Buildings Completed (yuan/sq.m)
总　计	**Total**	**408418419**	**68430140**	**59451912**	**14.6**	**20544608**	**3456**
合 肥 市	Hefei	81064366	15335992	23335924	28.8	9862230	4226
淮 北 市	Huaibei	14596209	2159052	1164164	8.0	177004	1520
亳 州 市	Bozhou	28437767	4485492	2831790	10.0	800082	2825
宿 州 市	Suzhou	30916857	5988090	1567483	5.1	444269	2834
蚌 埠 市	Bengbu	22273680	3235899	2069324	9.3	496096	2397
阜 阳 市	Fuyang	48033065	6274125	9144647	19.0	2814475	3078
淮 南 市	Huainan	14373806	2426364	1188828	8.3	326000	2742
滁 州 市	Chuzhou	31801966	6941304	2890772	9.1	777058	2688
六 安 市	Luan	31864034	4148676	1299840	4.1	332575	2559
马鞍山市	Maanshan	12708241	2747293	2089137	16.4	688025	3293
芜 湖 市	Wuhu	25894429	5314281	5198970	20.1	1697060	3264
宣 城 市	Xuancheng	17820936	2164478	2074695	11.6	641976	3094
铜 陵 市	Tongling	10642174	1808737	1056488	9.9	292270	2766
池 州 市	Chizhou	7391260	936013	656748	8.9	209529	3190
安 庆 市	Anqing	22827191	2886466	2248664	9.9	730727	3250
黄 山 市	Huangshan	7772438	1577878	634438	8.2	255232	4023

5—27 各市按用途分的房地产开发企业（单位）新开工房屋面积（2022年）
Floor Space Started in Real Estate Development by Region and by Use (2022)

单位：平方米（sq.m）

地区	Region	本年新开工房屋面积 Floor Space Started This Year	住宅 Residential Buildings	#90平米以下 Below 90 sq.m	144平米以上 Above of 144 sq.m	办公楼 Office Buildings	商业营业用房 Houses for Business Use	其他 Other
总计	**Total**	**68430140**	**306101848**			**10468453**	**35441455**	**56406663**
合肥市	Hefei	15335992	52014490			5721208	6991891	16336777
淮北市	Huaibei	2159052	12628938			47262	648172	1271837
亳州市	Bozhou	4485492	22062961			318496	2633407	3422903
宿州市	Suzhou	5988090	25523924			361422	2034767	2996744
蚌埠市	Bengbu	3235899	16289642			416625	2274994	3292419
阜阳市	Fuyang	6274125	37426794			1004877	3898867	5702527
淮南市	Huainan	2426364	11547741			179760	1204329	1441976
滁州市	Chuzhou	6941304	24999178			185762	1897088	4719938
六安市	Luan	4148676	24935253			325915	3478040	3124826
马鞍山市	Maanshan	2747293	10095568			121112	885955	1605606
芜湖市	Wuhu	5314281	19892105			298294	1741241	3962789
宣城市	Xuancheng	2164478	13868086			301260	1472636	2178954
铜陵市	Tongling	1808737	7229939			283449	1088966	2039820
池州市	Chizhou	936013	6102098			123145	539152	626865
安庆市	Anqing	2886466	16459035			531827	3120961	2715368
黄山市	Huangshan	1577878	5026096			248039	1530989	967314

5—28 各市商品房屋销售情况（2022年）
Selling of Commercial Houses by Region (2022)

地区	Region	房屋销售面积（平方米）Floor Space of Commercialized Buildings Sold (sq.m)	#住宅 Residential Buildings	现房 Completed Buildings	期房 Buildings Completed in Future	商品房销售额（万元）Total Sales of Commercialized Buildings (10000 yuan)	#住宅 Residential Buildings	现房 Completed Buildings	期房 Buildings Completed in Future
总计	**Total**	**67569224**	**58729931**	**10086347**	**57482877**	**51603202**	**46911603**	**5643206**	**45959996**
合肥市	Hefei	14591789	12378281	2363517	12228272	18115642	16681105	1518901	16596741
淮北市	Huaibei	1550503	1532034	274197	1276306	1070650	1056540	145117	925533
亳州市	Bozhou	4573999	4370150	485221	4088778	2672715	2519766	222848	2449867
宿州市	Suzhou	4786708	4626994	498305	4288403	2906447	2784637	257195	2649252
蚌埠市	Bengbu	3886856	3619942	793951	3092905	2350311	2183106	457186	1893125
阜阳市	Fuyang	7653430	7251664	384738	7268692	4789042	4488484	248642	4540400
淮南市	Huainan	1803240	1690181	139782	1663458	1168809	1095888	80589	1088220
滁州市	Chuzhou	8089650	6539642	852524	7237126	4612685	4012816	411122	4201563
六安市	Luan	4598360	4198128	646213	3952147	2666225	2430652	355301	2310924
马鞍山市	Maanshan	2150246	1617942	371238	1779008	1498225	1262248	181327	1316898
芜湖市	Wuhu	4924806	3888114	1133054	3791752	4161089	3684884	684699	3476390
宣城市	Xuancheng	2348885	2093713	426670	1922215	1616008	1466502	242805	1373203
铜陵市	Tongling	1537112	1101856	647435	889677	758817	570445	278020	480797
池州市	Chizhou	732889	583485	157011	575878	518030	428086	95768	422262
安庆市	Anqing	3269424	2442957	566063	2703361	1991510	1685220	267738	1723772
黄山市	Huangshan	1071327	794848	346428	724899	706997	561224	195948	511049

5—29 各市按用途分的商品房屋实际销售面积（2022年）

Floor Space of Commercial Houses Actually Sold by Use and by Region (2022)

单位：平方米（sq.m）

地区	Region	房屋销售面积 Floor Space of Selling House	商品住宅 Residential Buildings	#90平米以下 Below 90 sq.m	144平米以上 Above of 144 sq.m	办公楼 Office Buildings	商业营业用房 Houses for Business Use	其他 Other
总计	**Total**	**67569224**	**58729931**	**3290566**	**4055462**	**889986**	**3282552**	**4666755**
合肥市	Hefei	14591789	12378281	1656767	1871287	466353	498019	1249136
淮北市	Huaibei	1550503	1532034	53388	88022	1024	17445	
亳州市	Bozhou	4573999	4370150	151698	103163	16041	137708	50100
宿州市	Suzhou	4786708	4626994	144660	51967	37098	108129	14487
蚌埠市	Bengbu	3886856	3619942	174366	168195	32237	83245	151432
阜阳市	Fuyang	7653430	7251664	124984	119184	66666	260429	74671
淮南市	Huainan	1803240	1690181	22230	30886	47388	65419	252
滁州市	Chuzhou	8089650	6539642	333175	300008	15954	407215	1126839
六安市	Luan	4598360	4198128	144298	231081	53102	232684	114446
马鞍山市	Maanshan	2150246	1617942	82903	83284	9113	180299	342892
芜湖市	Wuhu	4924806	3888114	129411	465704	42633	259178	734881
宣城市	Xuancheng	2348885	2093713	65391	270279	9986	170428	74758
铜陵市	Tongling	1537112	1101856	117106	28305	9835	241125	184296
池州市	Chizhou	732889	583485	6694	50946	1715	107026	40663
安庆市	Anqing	3269424	2442957	7244	106398	64961	333866	427640
黄山市	Huangshan	1071327	794848	76251	86753	15880	180337	80262

5—30 各市按用途分的商品房待售情况（2022年）
Commercial House for Sale by Used by Region (2022)

单位：平方米（sq.m）

地区	Region	房屋待售面积 Square House for Sale	商品住宅 Residential Buildings	#90平米以下 Below 90 sq.m	144平米以上 Above of 144 sq.m	办公楼 Office Buildings	商业营业用房 Houses for Business Use	其他 Other
总计	**Total**	**18819543**	**8984480**			**1097671**	**5386198**	**3351194**
合肥市	Hefei	4059950	749332			572864	975027	1762727
淮北市	Huaibei	576424	448534				126670	1220
亳州市	Bozhou	805441	436981			29689	328206	10565
宿州市	Suzhou	979309	654644				294900	29765
蚌埠市	Bengbu	810496	518368			66107	183159	42862
阜阳市	Fuyang	430656	122365			28983	254798	24510
淮南市	Huainan	481964	271519			16240	161513	32692
滁州市	Chuzhou	529616	313171			12579	102320	101546
六安市	Luan	2205241	1684634			19366	446222	55019
马鞍山市	Maanshan	396702	207785			22874	151102	14941
芜湖市	Wuhu	744319	218481			102228	266446	157164
宣城市	Xuancheng	1163179	604143			14563	339192	205281
铜陵市	Tongling	1525802	468389			57187	526309	473917
池州市	Chizhou	1519442	977713			32718	459082	49929
安庆市	Anqing	1446022	696385			108913	450453	190271
黄山市	Huangshan	1144980	612036			13360	320799	198785

主要统计指标解释

固定资产投资

固定资产投资额是以货币表现的建造和购置固定资产活动的工作量，它是反映固定资产投资规模、速度、比例关系和使用方向的综合性指标。固定资产投资按经济类型可分为国有、集体、个体、联营、股份制、外商、港澳台商、其他等。按照管理渠道，全社会固定资产投资统计的范围包括：⑴城镇和农村500万元以上固定资产投资项目；⑵房地产开发投资；⑶农村非农户投资。

房地产开发投资

指房地产开发公司、商品房建设公司及其他房地产开发法人单位和附属于其他法人单位实际从事房地产开发或经营的活动单位统一开发的包括统代建、拆迁还建的住宅、厂房、仓库、饭店、宾馆、度假村、写字楼、办公楼等房屋建筑物和配套的服务设施，土地开发工程（如道路、给水、排水、供电、供热、通讯、平整场地等基础设施工程）的投资；不包括单纯的土地交易活动。

建设总规模

是指在报告期内所有施工项目的计划总投资。

在建总规模

是指在报告期末所有在建项目的计划总投资。

在建净规模

是指报告期末所有在建项目建成投产尚需的投资总量。

在建净规模＝在建总规模－未投产项目（期末在建）累计完成投资。

固定资产投资的资金来源

根据固定资产投资的资金来源不同，分为国家预算内资金、国内贷款、利用外资、自筹资金和其他资金来源。

⑴国家预算资金：包括一般预算、政府性基金预算、国有资本经营预算和社保基金预算。各类预算中用于固定资产投资的资金全部用为国家预算资金填报，其中一般预算中用于固定资产投资的部分包括基建投资、车购税、灾后恢复重建基金和其他投资。各级政府债券也归入国家预算资金。

⑵国内贷款：指报告期内企、事业单位向银行及非银行金融机构借入的用于固定资产投资的各种国内借款。包括银行利用自有资金及吸收的存款发放的贷款、上级主管部门拨入的国内贷款、国家专项贷款（包括煤代油贷款、劳改煤矿专项贷款等）、地方财政专项资金安排的贷款、国内储备贷款、周转贷款等。

⑶利用外资：指报告期内收到的用于固定资产投资的国外资金，包括统借统还、自借自还的国外贷款，中外合资项目中的外资，以及对外发行债券和股票等。国家统借统还的外资指由我国政府出面同外国政府、团体或金融组织签订贷款协议、并负责偿还本息的国外贷款。

⑷自筹资金：指建设单位报告期内收到的，用于进行固定资产投资的上级主管部门、地方和企、事业单位自筹资金。

⑸其他资金来源：指报告期内收到的除以上各种拨款。

固定资产投资按建设性质分

建设项目的性质一般分为新建、扩建、改建、迁建、恢复。基本建设按建设项目划分建设性质，更新改造、国有单位其他固定资产投资及城镇集体投资等按整个企业、事业单位的建设情况确定建设性质，房地产开发单位、农村投资等投资不划分建设性质。

⑴新建：一般是指从无到有、“平地起家”新开始建设的单位。有的单位原有的基础很小，经过建设后其新增加的固定资产价值超过原有固定资产价值（原值）三倍以上的也算新建。

⑵扩建：一般是指为扩大原有产品的生产能力，在厂内或其他地点增建主要生产车间（或主要工程）、独立的生产线或分厂的企业；事业单位和行政单位在原单位增建业务用房（如学校增建教学用房、医院增建门诊部或病床用房、行政机关增建办公楼等）也作为扩建。

⑶改建：一般是指现有企业、事业单位为了技术进步，提高产品质量，增加花色品种，促进产品升级换代，降低消耗和成本，加强资源综合利用和三废治理、劳保安全等，采用新技术、新工艺、新设备、新材料等对现有设施、工艺条件进行技术改造或更新（包括相应配套的辅助性生产、生活福利设施）。有的企业为充分发挥现有生产能力，进行填平补齐而增建不增加本单位主要产品生产能力的车间等，也属于改建。

固定资产投资按构成分

固定资产投资活动按其工作内容和实现方式分为建筑安装工程，设备、工具、器具购置，其他费用三个部分。

⑴建筑安装工程（建筑安装工作量）：指各种房屋、建筑物的建造工程和各种设备、装置的安装工程。包括各种房屋建造工程，各种用途设备基础和各种工业窑炉的砌筑工程；为施工而进行的各种准备工作和临时工程以及完工后的清理工作等；铁路、道路的铺设，矿井的开凿及石油管道的架设等；水利工程；防空地下建筑等特殊工程；以及各种机械设备的安装工程；为测定安装工程质量，对设备进行的试运工作。在安装工程中，不包括被安装设备本身的价值。

⑵设备、工具、器具购置：指购置或自制达到固定资产标准的设备、工具、器具的价值，固定资产的标准按财务部门规定。新建单位、扩建单位的新建车间按照设计和计划要求购置或自制的全部设备、工具、器具，不论是否达到固定资产标准均计入“设备、工具、器具购置”中。

⑶其他费用：指在固定资产建造和购置过程中发生的，除建筑安装工程和设备、工具、器具购置以外的各种应摊入固定资产的费用。

施工项目

指报告期内曾进行建筑或安装工程施工活动的建设项目，包括报告期内新开工项目、报告期以前开工跨入报告期继续施工的项目以及报告期施过工并在报告期内全部建成投产或停缓建的项目。

全部建成投产项目

工业项目是指设计文件规定形成生产能力的主体工程及其相应配套的辅助设施全部建成，经负荷试运转，证明具备生产设计规定合格产品的条件，并经过验收鉴定合格或达到竣工验收标准，与生产性工程配套的生活福利设施可以满足近期正常生产的需要，正式移交生产的建设项目。非工业项目是指设计文件规定的主体工程和相应的配套工程全部建成，能够发挥设计规定的全部效益，经验收鉴定合格或达到竣工验收标准，正式移交使用的建设项目。

商品住宅

指房地产开发企业（单位）建设并出售、出租给使用者，仅供居住用的房屋。

土地开发投资额

指房地产开发企业完成的前期工程投资，即路通、水通、电通、场地平整等（也称七通一平）所完成的投资。一般指生地开发成熟地的投资。在旧城区（老区拆迁）的开发中，如果有统一的规划，如政府有关部门批准的小区建设的前期工程中，有场地平整，原有建筑物、构筑物拆除，供水供电工程等工作量也可计算。未进行开发工程、只进行单纯的土地交易活动不作为土地开发投资统计。土地开发投资额在房屋用途分组中能分摊的部分就分摊，不能分摊的全部计入其他。

土地购置费

指房地产开发企业为取得土地使用权而支付的费用。土地购置费按当期发生数计入投资，如土地购置费为分期付款的，可分期计入投资；不计入新增固定资产。土地购置费支出包括：①通过草拟方式取得的土地使用权所支付的土地补偿费、附着物和青苗补偿费、安置补偿费及土地征收管理费等；②通过出让方式取得土地使用权所支付的出让金。

投资额按房屋工程用途分组

指投资额中用于各类房屋建设的投资。

住宅

指专供居住的房屋，包括别墅、公寓、职工家属宿舍和集体宿舍（包括职工单身宿舍和学生宿舍）等。但不包括住宅楼中作为人防用、不住人的地下室等。

本年完成开发土地面积

指报告期内对土地进行开发并已完成七通一平等前期开发工程，具备进行房屋建筑物施工或出让条件的土地面积。

本年购置土地面积

指在本年内通过各种方式获得土地使用权的土地面积。

本年土地成交价款

指进行土地使用权交易活动的最终金额。在土地一级市场，是指土地最后的划拨款和出让价；在土地二级市场是指土地转让、出租、抵押等最后确定的合同价格。土地成交价款与土地购置面积同口径，目的是正确计算平均土地购置价格。

房屋施工面积

指报告期内施工的全部房屋建筑面积。包括本期新开工的面积和上年开工跨入本期继续施工的房屋面积，以及上期已停建在本期恢复施工的房屋面积。本期竣工和本期施工后又停建缓建的房屋面积仍包括在施工面积中，多层建筑应填各层建筑面积之和。

房屋竣工面积

指报告期内房屋建筑按照设计要求已全部完工，达到住人和使用条件，经验收鉴定合格或达到竣工验收标准（实行房地产开发小区综合验收的城市，应经小区综合验收合格），可正式移交使用的各栋房屋建筑面积的总和。

实际销售面积

指报告期内已竣工的房屋面积中已正式交付给购房者或已签订（正式）销售合同的商品房屋面积。不包括已签订预售合同正在建设的商品房屋面积，但包括报告期或报告期以前签订了预售合同，在报告期又竣工的商品房屋面积。

Explanatory Notes for Major Statistical Indicators

Investment in fixed assets

amount of investment in fixed assets refers to the amount of money spent on the construction and purchase of fixed assets. It is a comprehensive indicator reflecting the scale, speed, proportional relationship and direction of use of fixed assets investment. According to the type of economy, investment in fixed assets can be divided into state-owned, collective, individual, joint venture, joint-stock system, foreign investors, Hong Kong, Macao and Taiwan businessmen, and others. According to the management channel, the scope of the statistics of the whole society's fixed assets investment includes: (1) Urban and rural fixed assets investment projects of more than 5 million yuan; (2) Investment in real estate development; (3) Rural non-household investment.

Investment in real estate development

refers to the real estate development companies, commercial housing construction and other real estate development company legal person units and is attached to other legal person units engaged in real estate development or business activity units unified development including the system construction, demolition also build houses, factories, warehouses, restaurants, hotels, resorts, office buildings, office buildings and other buildings and supporting facilities, Investment in land development projects (such as roads, water supply, drainage, power supply, heating, communications, site leveling and other infrastructure projects); Pure land transaction activities are not included.

Total construction scale

refers to the total planned investment of all construction projects during the reporting period.

Total size under construction

total planned investment in all projects under construction at the end of the reporting period.

Net size under construction

refers to the total amount of investment required by the end of the reporting period for all projects under construction to be completed and put into operation.

Net scale under construction = total scale under construction - projects not put into production (under construction at the end of the period) accumulated investment completed.

Sources of capital for investment in fixed assets

according to different sources of funds for fixed assets investment, it can be divided into funds within the state budget, domestic loans, foreign investment, self-raised funds and other sources of funds.

a) State budgetary funds include general budgets, budgets for government-managed funds, budgets for state capital operations and budgets for social security funds. All the funds used for fixed asset investment in various budgets are reported as state budget funds. The part used for fixed asset investment in general budgets includes infrastructure investment, car purchase tax, post-disaster recovery and reconstruction funds and other investments. Government bonds at all levels are also included in the national budget.

b) Domestic loans refer to all kinds of domestic loans borrowed by enterprises and institutions from banks and non-bank financial institutions for investment in fixed assets during the reporting period. These include loans issued by banks with their own funds and deposits, domestic loans allocated by higher competent departments, national special loans (including coal for oil loans, special loans for reforming coal mines through labor, etc.), loans arranged by special funds of local finance, domestic reserve loans, revolving loans, etc.

c) Utilization of foreign capital: refers to the foreign funds received during the reporting period for investment in fixed assets, including foreign loans borrowed and repaid by the government, foreign capital in sino-foreign joint venture projects, as well as the issuance of bonds and stocks. Foreign capital collectively borrowed and repaid by the state refers to foreign loans that the Chinese government signs loan agreements with foreign governments, organizations or financial organizations and is responsible for the repayment of principal and interest.

d) Self-raised funds refer to the self-raised funds received by the construction unit during the reporting period and used by the superior competent authorities, local authorities, enterprises and institutions for the investment in fixed assets.

f) Other sources of funding: refers to grants other than those received during the reporting period.

Investment in fixed assets is divided by the nature of construction

nature of construction projects is generally divided into new construction, expansion, reconstruction, relocation and restoration. The nature of capital construction is divided according to the construction project, the nature of renovation, other fixed assets investment of state-owned units and urban collective investment is determined according to the construction situation of the whole enterprise and public institution, and the nature of investment such as real estate development units and rural investment is not divided.

a) Build new: it is to point to to have from nothing commonly, "ground ground start up" the unit that starts building new. For some units whose original foundation is very small, the value of their newly added fixed assets after construction is more than three times the value of the original fixed assets (original value) is also counted as new construction.

b) Expansion: generally refers to the expansion of the original product production capacity, in the factory or other locations to build a major production workshop (or major engineering), independent production line or branch factory enterprises; Public institutions and administrative units in the original unit to build more business rooms (such as schools to build more teaching rooms, hospitals to build more outpatient department or bed rooms, administrative authorities to build office buildings, etc.) also as expansion.

c) Modification: It generally refers to existing enterprises and institutions to improve product quality, increase product varieties, promote product upgrading, reduce consumption and cost, strengthen comprehensive utilization of resources, treatment of three wastes, labor safety, etc., for the purpose of technological progress. Adopt new technology, new process, new equipment and new materials to carry out technical transformation or update of existing facilities and process conditions (including corresponding supporting auxiliary production and living welfare facilities). Some enterprises give full play to existing production capacity, undertake fill fill and add the workshop that does not increase this unit main product production capacity to wait, also belong to rebuild.

Investment in fixed assets is divided by composition

according to their work content and implementation mode, the investment activities of fixed assets can be divided into three parts: construction and installation works, purchase of equipment, tools and appliances, and other expenses.

a) Construction and installation work (construction and installation workload) : refers to the construction work of various houses and buildings and the installation work of various equipment and installations. Including a variety of housing construction projects, various uses of equipment foundation and a variety of industrial kiln masonry projects; Preparation and temporary works for the construction and clean-up work after completion; The laying of railways and roads, the digging of mines and the erection of oil pipelines; Water conservancy project; Air defense underground construction and other special projects; And the installation of various mechanical equipment; Test run of equipment to determine the quality of an installation project. In the installation project, the value of the installed equipment itself is not included.

b) Purchase of equipment, tools and appliances: refers to the value of purchased or self-made equipment, tools and appliances that meet the standards of fixed assets. The standards of fixed assets shall be stipulated by the financial department. All the equipment, tools and appliances purchased or self-made in accordance with the design and plan requirements of the new unit and the new workshop of the expanded unit, regardless of whether they meet the standards of fixed assets, shall be included in the "Purchase of Equipment, tools and appliances".

c) Other expenses refer to the expenses incurred during the construction and purchase of fixed assets, other than the construction and installation works and the purchase of equipment, tools and appliances, which should be allocated into fixed assets.

Construction project

refers to the construction projects in which construction or installation works have been carried out during the report period, including the new projects in the report period, the projects that started before the report period and continue to be constructed during the report period, and the projects that have been completed and put into operation or are suspended during the report period.

All completed and put into production

Industrial projects refers to the regulation form the production capacity of major projects and its corresponding auxiliary facilities completed, after the load test run, have in the production of qualified products designed condition, and identified qualified acceptance or meet completion inspection and acceptance standards, and production engineering supporting life welfare facilities can meet the needs of normal production of the recent, Formal handover of the construction project to production. Non-industrial project refers to the construction project that the main part of the project and the corresponding supporting projects specified in the design documents have been completed, can give full play to the benefits specified in the design, passed the appraisal or reached the completion acceptance standard, and is officially transferred to use.

Commodity residential house

refers to the housing built by real estate development enterprises (units) and sold or rented to users for residential use only.

Land development investment

refers to the real estate development enterprises completed the investment in the early stage of the project, namely road, water, electric, site leveling, etc. (also known as seven and one ping) completed investment. Generally refers to the development of raw land mature investment. In the old city (old area demolition) development, if there is a unified planning, such as the government departments approved by the district construction in the early stage of the project, there are site leveling, the original buildings, structures demolition, water supply and power supply engineering and other workload can also be calculated. Land transactions without development projects shall not be counted as land development investment. The land develops investment amount to be able to apportion part in building use group apportion, cannot apportion all calculate other.

Land purchase costs

refers to the fees paid by a real estate development enterprise for acquiring the right to the use of land. The land purchase cost shall be included in the investment according to the amount incurred in the current period. If the land purchase cost is paid by installments, it may be included in the investment by installments. It does not include new fixed assets. Land purchase expenses include: ① Land compensation fees, attachments and young seedlings compensation fees, resettlement compensation fees and land expropriation management fees paid by the land use right obtained through drafting; (2) Transfer fees paid by means of transferring land use rights.

Investment amount is grouped by housing project purpose

refers to the investment used in various types of housing construction.

Residential

refers to the housing exclusively for living, including villas, apartments, staff and workers' family dormitory and collective dormitory (including staff and workers' single dormitory and student dormitory). But does not include residential buildings as civil air defense, do not live in the basement, etc.

Land area to be developed this year

refers to the area of land that has been developed during the reporting period and has completed the preliminary development projects such as seven connections and one leveling, and is qualified for building construction or transfer.

Land area purchased this year

refers to the area of land acquired through various means during the year.

Land transaction price this year

refers to the final amount of land use right transactions. In the first-level land market, it refers to the final allocation and transfer price of land; In the secondary market of land, it refers to the final contract price of land transfer, lease and mortgage. Land transaction price and land purchase area with the same caliber, the purpose is to correctly calculate the average land purchase price.

Construction area

refers to the total building floor area under construction during the report period. It includes the area of newly started construction in the current period, the area of housing started in the previous year and continued construction in the current period, and the area of housing stopped in the previous period and resumed construction in the current period. The area of the building completed in the current period and the area of the building stopped or delayed after the construction in the current period shall still be included in the area under construction, and the total area of each floor shall be filled in for a multi-storey building.

Completed building area

refers to the total floor area of each building that can be formally transferred for use during the reporting period, which has been completed in accordance with the design requirements, meets the conditions for residents and use, and has passed the acceptance test or reached the completion acceptance standard (for cities that implement comprehensive acceptance test of real estate development communities, it shall pass the comprehensive acceptance test of the communities).

Actual sales area

refers to the area of the completed housing that has been formally delivered to the buyer or signed a (formal) sales contract during the reporting period. It does not include the area of the commodity housing under construction which has signed the pre-sale contract, but includes the area of the commodity housing which has signed the pre-sale contract during or before the report period and completed during the report period.

第六篇

Chapter 6

能源生产和消费

PRODUCTION AND CONSUMPTION OF ENERGY

简要说明

一、本篇主要内容有：能源生产、消费及品种构成，能源生产和消费弹性系数，近年来综合能源平衡表和电力平衡表，分行业分主要能源品种的消费量等。

二、2011 年及以前年份分行业主要能源品种消费量、分行业工业用水量为指全部国有及年销售收入 500 万元以上工业企业。2011 年起为全部国有及年销售收入 2000 万元以上工业企业，与历史年份不可比。

三、本篇资料取自省统计局能源处，按照国家统计局报表制度逐级汇总整理。

四、关于数据口径与计算的说明

1. 行业分类采用现行统一的国民经济行业分类国家标准。

2. 能源生产与消费弹性系数分别以能源生产、消费增长速度与国内生产总值增长速度相比求得。

Brief Introduction

I. Data in this chapter cover mainly the energy production, consumption and their composition, the elasticity ratio of energy production and consumption, the overall balance of energy and the balance of electricity, the consumption of energy by sector and by main variety.

II. The consumption of energy by sector and by main variety and industrial water consumption by sector include all state-owned industrial enterprises and the industrial enterprises with yearly sales revenue over five million yuan.

III. Data in this chapter are prepared and provided by the Division of Energy, Anhui Statistical Bureau, in accordance with the national reporting system.

IV. Coverage and calculation of data:

1. The state classification of national economic sectors is used in the classification of sectors.

2. The elasticity ratio of energy production is calculated as the quotient of the growth rate of energy production divided by the growth rate of GDP; and the elasticity ratio of energy consumption is calculated as the quotient of the growth rate of energy consumption divided by the growth of GDP.

6—1 能源生产和消费总量及电力生产和消费量
Total Production and Consumption of Energy and Electricity

年 份 Year	能源生产总量（万吨标准煤）Total Energy Production (10000 tons of SCE)	电力生产量（亿千瓦时）Electricity (100 million kWh)	能源消费总量（万吨标准煤）Total Energy Consumption (10000 tons of SCE)	电力消费量（亿千瓦时）Electricity (100 million kWh)
2005	6215.42	648.38	6505.98	581.65
2010	9673.79	1463.31	9414.00	1077.92
2014	9413.25	2033.92	12011.02	1585.18
2015	9972.64	2061.89	12301.23	1639.79
2016	9305.72	2252.69	12662.89	1794.98
2017	9145.34	2470.25	13018.71	1921.48
2018	9120.27	2741.22	13294.71	2135.07
2019	8943.62	2886.67	13869.73	2300.68
2020	8602.02	2808.97	14697.90	2427.50
2021	9317.48	3083.39	15342.63	2715.63
2022	9401.07	3298.77	15882.66	2993.22

注：电力生产量为全社会发电量。能源生产和消费量按等价热值计算。
a) Electricity production is the electricity generation of the whole society. Energy production and consumption are calculated at equivalent calorific value.

6—2 综合能源平衡表
Overall Energy Balance

单位：万吨标准煤（10000 tons of SCE）

指 标	Item	2010	2015	2020	2021	2022
可供消费的能源总量	**Total Energy Available for Consumption**	**9375.50**	**12298.66**	**14674.33**	**15346.51**	**15883.03**
一次能源生产量	Primary Energy Output	9673.79	9972.64	8602.02	9317.48	9401.07
能源消费总量	**Total Energy Consumption**	**9414.00**	**12301.23**	**14697.90**	**15342.63**	**15882.66**
在总量中:	Consumption by Sector:					
农、林、牧、渔业	Agriculture, Forestry, Animal Husbandry and Fishery	198.41	221.11	276.89	308.05	334.64
工 业	Industry	6977.07	8440.65	9535.76	9835.44	9923.85
建筑业	Construction	137.04	209.47	284.00	321.78	309.90
交通运输、仓储和邮政业	Transport, Storage and Postal Services	643.81	1052.17	1157.08	1156.05	1083.51
批发、零售业和住宿、餐饮业	Wholesale and Retail Trades, Hotels and Catering Services	170.98	317.69	462.95	562.58	661.24
其他行业	Other Sectors	289.56	515.98	871.23	1014.30	1124.44
生活消费	Household Consumption	997.11	1544.15	2109.99	2144.43	2445.07
在总量中:	Consumption by Usage:					
终端消费	Final Consumption	9269.33	12307.18	14859.25	15461.86	16151.78
#工 业	Industry	6832.40	8446.61	9697.12	9954.67	10192.97
加工转换损失量	Losses in Processing and Transformation	370.18	357.64	537.23	520.59	677.80
输配损失量	Losses in Transportation and Delivery	244.63	298.90	375.88	401.36	408.68
平衡差额	**Balance**	**-38.50**	**-2.57**	**-23.57**	**3.88**	**0.37**

6—3 能源生产弹性系数
Elasticity Ratio of Energy Production

年　份 Year	能源生产比上年增长（%） Growth Rate of Energy Production over preceding Year (%)	电力生产比上年增长（%） Growth Rate of Electricity Production over Preceding Year (%)	能源生产弹性系数 Elasticity Ratio of Energy Production	电力生产弹性系数 Elasticity Ratio of Electricity Production
2010	4.2	10.1	0.36	0.69
2015	5.9	1.4	0.68	0.16
2020	-3.8	-2.7		
2021	8.3	9.8	1.00	1.18
2022	0.9	7.0	0.26	2.00

注：能源生产增长速度按等价热值计算；电力生产增长速度按实物量计算。
a) The rate of rise of energy production is calculated on the basis of equal caloric value; The rate of rise of electricity production is calculated on the basis of real amount.

6—4 能源消费弹性系数
Elasticity Ratio of Energy Consumption

年　份 Year	能源消费比上年增长（%） Growth Rate of Energy Consumption over Preceding Year (%)	电力消费比上年增长（%） Growth Rate of Electricity Consumption over Preceding Year (%)	能源消费弹性系数 Elasticity Ratio of Energy Consumption	电力消费弹性系数 Elasticity Ratio of Electricity Consumption
2010	9.1	13.2	0.62	0.90
2015	2.7	3.4	0.31	0.40
2020	6.0	5.5	1.55	1.43
2021	4.4	11.9	0.53	1.43
2022	3.5	10.2	1.00	2.91

注：能源消费增长速度按等价热值计算；电力消费增长速度按实物量计算。
a) The rate of rise of energy consumption is calculated on the basis of equal caloric value; The rate of rise of electricity consumption is calculated on the basis of real amount.

6—5 能源加工转换效率
Efficiency of Energy Conversion

单位：%

年　份 Year	总效率 Total Efficiency	火力发电 Thermal Power Generation	炼　焦 Coking	炼　油 Petroleum Refining
2010	65.87	39.95	95.76	99.45
2015	68.14	41.46	95.20	99.50
2020	64.79	41.47	93.63	98.90
2021	64.60	41.78	93.54	99.70
2022	64.58	41.98	97.03	99.13

6—6 主要年份电力平衡表
Electricity Balance Sheet in Main Year

单位：亿千瓦时（100 million kWh）

指　标	Item	2010	2015	2020	2021	2022
可供量	**Total Energy Available for Consumption**	**1077.92**	**1639.79**	**2427.49**	**2715.63**	**2993.22**
生产量	Output	1463.31	2061.89	2808.97	3083.39	3298.77
水力发电及其它发电	Hydraulic Power Generation and Others	43.47	72.97	253.13	342.13	395.48
火　电	Thermal Power	1419.84	1988.92	2555.84	2741.26	2903.29
消费量	**Total Energy Consumption**	**1077.92**	**1639.79**	**2427.50**	**2715.63**	**2993.22**
在消费量中	Consumption by Sector					
农、林、牧、渔业	Agriculture, Forestry, Animal Husbandry and Fishery	11.91	16.85	37.48	44.34	56.68
工　业	Industry	777.18	1132.78	1550.80	1721.46	1830.72
#输配电损失量	Losses in Transmission	76.81	100.82	126.82	136.45	139.61
建筑业	Construction	14.75	25.21	39.53	47.38	46.67
交通运输、仓储和邮政业	Transport, Storage and Postal Services	14.58	26.74	50.90	61.81	61.33
批发、零售业和住宿、餐饮业	Wholesale and Retail Trades, Hotels and Catering Services	34.97	67.01	117.57	146.35	159.88
其他行业	Other Sectors	50.55	120.02	223.48	267.36	296.96
生活消费	Household Consumption	173.98	251.18	407.75	426.92	540.97

6—7 主要年份平均每天各种能源消费量
Average Daily Energy Consumption by Variety in Main Year

指　标		Item		2010	2015	2020	2021	2022
合　计	**（万吨标准煤）**	**Total**	**(10000 tons of SCE)**	**25.79**	**33.70**	**40.27**	**42.03**	**43.51**
原　煤	（万吨）	Coal	(10000 tons)	41.03	49.96	50.68	51.77	54.55
焦　炭	（万吨）	Coke	(10000 tons)	2.49	3.19	3.62	3.73	3.50
原　油	（万吨）	Crude Oil	(10000 tons)	1.31	1.89	1.95	2.06	1.59
燃料油	（万吨）	Fuel Oil	(10000 tons)	0.03	0.04	0.06	0.06	0.07
汽　油	（万吨）	Gasoline	(10000 tons)	0.54	1.25	1.89	1.91	1.64
柴　油	（万吨）	Diesel Oil	(10000 tons)	1.29	1.68	1.78	1.98	1.98
电　力	（亿千瓦小时）	Electricity	(100 million kWh)	2.95	4.49	6.65	7.44	8.20

6—8 主要年份生活能源消费量
Average Annual Energy Consumption for Households in Main Year

指 标	Item	2010	2015	2020	2021	2022
合 计 (万吨标准煤)	**Total (10000 tons of SCE)**	**997.11**	**1544.15**	**2109.99**	**2144.43**	**2445.07**
煤 炭 (万吨)	Coal (10000 tons)	312.00	256.08	23.68	22.66	11.58
液化石油气 (万吨)	Liquefied Petroleum Gas (10000 tons)	42.13	94.19	66.17	61.73	59.16
天然气 (亿立方米)	Natural Gas (100 million cu.m)	2.80	13.80	25.55	17.49	19.07
热 力 (万百万千焦)	Heat (10 billion kilo-joule)	1599.88	1157.41	2063.45	1715.57	1863.11
电 力 (亿千瓦小时)	Electricity (100 million kWh)	173.98	251.18	407.75	426.92	540.97

6—9 主要年份人均生活能源消费量
Annual per Capita Energy Consumption of Households in Main Year

指 标	Item	2010	2015	2020	2021	2022
平均每人生活消费能源(千克标准煤)	**Annual per Capita Consumption for Households (kg of SCE)**	**164.98**	**252.59**	**345.62**	**350.80**	**399.07**
煤 炭 (千克)	Coal (kg)	51.62	**41.89**	3.88	3.71	1.89
液化石油气 (千克)	Liquefied Petroleum Gas (kg)	6.97	15.41	10.84	10.10	9.66
天然气 (立方米)	Natural Gas (cu.m)	4.63	22.57	41.85	28.61	31.13
热 力 (万千焦)	Heat (10000 kilo-joule)	26.47	18.93	33.80	28.06	30.41
电 力 (千瓦小时)	Electricity (kWh)	287.86	410.87	667.90	698.39	882.93

注：按年平均常住人口数计算。

a) According to the annual average resident population is calculated.

6—10 主要年份能源消耗指标
Energy Consumption Indices in Main Year

年份 Year	单位地区生产总值能耗（等价值） Unit GDP Energy Consumption (Equal Values)	单位工业增加值能耗（规模以上，当量值） Energy Consumption per Unit of Industrial Added Value (Above Scale, Equivalent Value)	单位地区生产总值电耗 Unit GDP Electricity Consumption
	上升或下降（±%） Up or Down	上升或下降（±%） Up or Down	上升或下降（±%） Up or Down
2015	-5.6	-9.0	-4.9
2020	2.0	-0.9	1.6
2021	-3.6	-5.3	3.3
2022	0.0	-3.8	6.5

注：1、2010年，地区生产总值按照2005年可比价格计算；2015年，地区生产总值按照2010年可比价格计算；2020年，地区生产总值按照2015年可比价格计算；2021年，地区生产总值按照2020年可比价格计算。

2、计算单位地区生产总值能耗上升或下降时，相关发展速度保留1位小数。

a) In 2010, GDP was calculated at comparable prices in 2005; In 2015, GDP was calculated at comparable prices in 2010; In 2020, GDP is calculated at comparable prices in 2015. In 2021, GDP is calculated at 2020 comparable prices.

b) When calculating the increase or decrease of energy consumption per unit of GDP, the relevant development rate shall be kept at a decimal point.

6—11 各市能源消耗指标（2022年）
Energy Consumption Indices by Region (2022)

地区	Region	单位地区生产总值能耗（等价值） Unit GDP Energy Consumption (Equal Values)	单位工业增加值能耗（规模以上，当量值） Energy Consumption per Unit of Industrial Added Value (Above Scale, Equivalent Value)	单位地区生产总值电耗 Unit GDP Electricity Consumption
		上升或下降（±%） Up or Down	上升或下降（±%） Up or Down	上升或下降（±%） Up or Down
合肥市	Hefei	2.8	-1.9	9.0
淮北市	Huaibei	1.8	12.7	10.8
亳州市	Bozhou	-1.0	-10.2	8.6
宿州市	Suzhou	-0.3	-7.3	6.3
蚌埠市	Bengbu	11.0	11.8	10.4
阜阳市	Fuyang	1.4	-1.1	6.7
淮南市	Huainan	-3.6	-2.7	3.9
滁州市	Chuzhou	-2.4	-12.4	8.1
六安市	Luan	0.4	-7.3	10.7
马鞍山市	Maanshan	-4.8	-6.6	1.7
芜湖市	Wuhu	0.4	-2.2	3.5
宣城市	Xuancheng	0.3	-5.0	3.5
铜陵市	Tongling	-2.2	-2.4	5.4
池州市	Chizhou	-3.8	-13.5	3.5
安庆市	Anqing	-0.1	0.2	8.6
黄山市	Huangshan	-0.1	0.1	4.0

6—12 全社会用电情况
Electricity Used in Whole Society

单位：亿千瓦时（100 million kWh）

类　别	Types	2020	2021	2022
全社会用电量总计	**Total of Electricity Used in Whole Society**	**2427.50**	**2715.47**	**2993.22**
全行业用电量合计	Total of Electricity Used in Whole Trade	2019.76	2288.55	2452.25
第一产业	Primary Industry	28.59	37.73	47.12
第二产业	Secondary Industry	1589.40	1768.14	1876.70
第三产业	Tertiary Industry	401.77	482.67	528.43
城乡居民生活用电量合计	Electricity Used for Life	407.75	426.92	540.97
城镇居民	Urban	177.05	190.85	244.62
乡村居民	Rural	230.69	236.07	296.36
分行业用电	Grouped by Trade	2019.76	2288.55	2452.25
农、林、牧、渔业	Agriculture, Forestry, Animal Husbandry and Fishery	37.48	44.34	56.68
工　业	Industry	1550.22	1721.30	1830.72
#采矿业	Mining and Quarrying	83.95	87.86	88.95
制造业	Manufacturing	1120.20	1292.07	1368.76
电力、热力、燃气及水生产和供应业	Production and Supply of Electricity, Heat, Gas and Water	346.06	341.38	373.01
建筑业	Construction	39.53	47.38	46.67
交通运输、仓储和邮政业	Transport, Storage and Postal Services	50.90	61.81	61.33
信息传输、软件和信息技术服务业	Information Circulation, Computer Services and Software	27.57	32.23	37.00
批发和零售业	Wholesale and Retail Trades	93.36	116.58	127.78
住宿和餐饮业	Hotels and Catering Services	24.22	29.78	32.10
金融业	Financial Intermediation	6.47	7.73	8.76
房地产业	Real Estate	45.40	56.89	64.78
租赁和商务服务业	Leasing and Business Services	13.26	16.32	18.18
公共服务及管理组织	Public Service and Management Organization	131.35	154.18	168.24

注：2018年起，省电力公司电力报表的行业分类按照2017年新版《国民经济行业分类》（GB/T 4754—2017）标准实行。

a) Since 2018, the industry classification of the electricity report forms of provincial power companies was implemented in accordance with the 2017 new edition of the National Economic Industry Classification (GB/T 4754-2017).

6—13 电力建设情况
Electric Power Construction Situation

类　别		Types		2020	2021	2022
发电量	**（亿千瓦时）**	**Electric Power Generated**	**(100 million kWh)**	**2808.97**	**3083.39**	**3298.77**
线损率	**（%）**	**Electricity Loss Rate on Lines**	**(%)**	**6.20**	**5.80**	**5.35**
年末发电设备容量	**（万千瓦）**	**Power Generating Equipment Capacity (year-end)**	**(10000 kW)**	**7816.03**	**8465.74**	**9219.01**
架空线长度	**（公里）**	**Length of Overhead Lines**	**(km)**	**83036**	**87399**	**93398**
交流特高压		AC UHV		1232	1232	1232
直流特高压		DC UHV		1762	1762	4141
交流和直流500KV		500KV AC and DC		8467	8684	11023
220KV		220KV		18891	19698	19928
110KV		110KV		22244	24285	24979
35KV		35KV		30440	31738	32096
电缆长度	**（公里）**	**Length of Cable**	**(km)**	**1808.81**	**2101.00**	**2664.50**
220KV		220KV		35.43	39.00	397.10
110KV		110KV		800.08	885.00	1017.10
35KV		35KV		973.29	1177.00	1250.30
公用变电容量	**（万千伏安）**	**Public Transformer Capacity**	**(10000 kVA)**	**24223**	**26907**	**28195**
交流特高压		AC UHV		1200	1200	1200
直流特高压		DC UHV		1409	1409	1409
500KV		500KV		6161	6462	6662
220KV		220KV		8124	8562	9195
110KV		110KV		6435	6923	7320
35KV		35KV		2302	2351	2408
用电最高负荷	**（万千瓦）**	**Transport, Storage and Postal Services**	**(10000 kW)**	**4304.35**	**4442.30**	**5507.00**

注：1．2015年起，线损率按照省电力公司的合并口径（含所辖县公司）填报。
　　2．本表发电量取自全省能源平衡表。

a) Since 2015, the line loss rate has been reported in accordance with the combined caliber of the provincial power company (including the company in the county).
b) The power generation in this table is taken from the energy balance table of the whole province.

6—14 经销企业能源购进、销售与库存情况（2022年）
Energy Distribution Enterprise Purchase, Sales and Inventory (2022)

单位：万吨（10000 tons）

指　标	Item	年初商品库存量 Inventory At the Beginning of the Year	累计购进量 Total Purchase	#购自省外 Purchased from Outside the Province	累计销售量 Total Sales	#销往省外 Sold to the province	期末商品库存量 Inventories at the end of Period
原　煤	Coal	134.73	11945.27	8062.32	11957.29	4488.68	121.31
焦　炭	Coke	0.40	244.57	217.42	241.29	137.94	3.68
汽　油	Gasoline	28.59	598.15	410.85	587.75	23.13	39.46
柴　油	Diesel Oil	17.42	517.41	394.76	515.98	21.81	19.22
燃料油	Fuel Oil	0.20	16.54	15.98	16.62	5.14	0.12
液化石油气	Liquefied Petroleum Gas	0.57	34.39	6.13	34.17	1.82	0.78

6—15 主要年份全社会工业分行业用电量

Electricity Consumption of the Whole Society, Industry and Sub-industry in Major Years

单位：亿千瓦时（100 million kWh）

行业	Sector	2010	2015	2020	2021	2022
消费总量	**Total Consumption**	**777.18**	**1132.78**	**1550.22**	**1721.30**	**1830.72**
煤炭开采和洗选业	Mining and Washing of Coal	55.81	57.82	44.46	45.53	45.51
黑色金属矿采选业	Mining and Processing of Ferrous Metal Ores	13.63	20.63	21.32	22.58	24.08
有色金属矿采选业	Mining and Processing of Non-Ferrous Metal Ores	4.23	10.15	8.51	8.07	7.54
非金属矿采选业	Mining and Processing of Non-metal Ores	5.78	10.95	6.13	7.62	6.66
其他采矿业	Mining of Other Ores		3.70	3.28	3.80	4.82
农副食品加工业	Processing of Food from Agricultural Products	14.78	18.77	26.15	29.84	31.09
食品制造业	Manufacture of Foods	3.56	6.87	12.92	15.08	16.68
酒、饮料和精制茶制造业	Manufacture of Liquor, Beverages and Refined Tea	3.75	5.69	4.85	5.98	6.58
烟草制品业	Manufacture of Tobacco	1.01	1.25	1.57	1.72	1.72
纺织业	Manufacture of Textile	17.07	22.82	37.98	47.61	50.03
纺织服装、服饰业	Manufacture of Textile, Wearing Apparel and Accessories	2.97	4.23	8.28	9.83	10.83
皮革、毛皮、羽毛及其制品和制鞋业	Manufacture of Leather, Fur, Feather and Related Products and Footwear	1.15	1.19	3.13	3.71	3.71
木材加工和木、竹、藤、棕、草制品业	Processing of Timber, Manufacture of Wood, Bamboo, Rattan, Palm and Straw Products	9.61	12.20	15.26	19.11	18.49
家具制造业	Manufacture of Furniture	0.67	2.46	4.50	5.96	6.12
造纸和纸制品业	Manufacture of Paper and Paper Products	9.43	19.18	20.04	21.51	21.63
印刷和记录媒介复制业	Printing and Reproduction of Recording Media	2.75	2.30	3.48	4.19	4.30
文教、工美、体育和娱乐用品制造业	Manufacture of Articles for Culture, Education, Arts and Crafts, Sport and Entertainment Activities	1.40	0.79	2.60	3.05	3.25
石油、煤炭及其他燃料加工业	Petroleum, Coal and Other Fuel Processing Industries	3.38	8.36	21.12	23.96	23.60
化学原料和化学制品制造业	Manufacture of Raw Chemical Materials and Chemical Products	77.33	134.52	148.42	155.25	165.11
医药制造业	Manufacture of Medicines	5.33	6.93	14.52	16.87	18.30
化学纤维制造业	Manufacture of Chemical Fibres	7.01	11.45	8.08	10.56	10.69
橡胶和塑料制品业	Manufacture of Rubber and Plastics Products	15.39	27.50	51.48	63.63	65.28
非金属矿物制品业	Manufacture of Non-metallic Mineral Products	114.84	168.82	207.80	233.91	239.12
黑色金属冶炼和压延加工业	Smelting and Pressing of Ferrous Metals	126.24	148.02	183.99	199.48	192.22
有色金属冶炼和压延加工业	Smelting and Pressing of Non-ferrous Metals	16.61	35.23	42.19	46.75	55.99
金属制品业	Manufacture of Metal Products	22.05	38.96	72.27	85.64	87.35
通用设备制造业	Manufacture of General Purpose Machinery	12.42	13.69	22.42	28.36	30.00
专用设备制造业	Manufacture of Special Purpose Machinery	2.82	7.29	17.19	21.28	25.21
汽车制造业	Manufacture of Automobiles	12.49	19.77	20.54	26.87	34.03
铁路、船舶、航空航天和其他运输设备制造业	Manufacture of Railway, Ship, Aerospace and Other Transport Equipments		3.03	9.84	9.62	9.83
电气机械和器材制造业	Manufacture of Electrical Machinery and Apparatus	15.35	32.27	54.31	67.51	92.32
计算机、通信和其他电子设备制造业	Manufacture of Computers, Communication and Other Electronic Equipment	3.47	26.19	80.31	101.12	108.99
仪器仪表制造业	Manufacture of Measuring Instruments and Machinery		0.86	1.16	1.38	1.55
其他制造业	Other Manufacture	5.61	10.50	20.00	26.13	28.50
废弃资源综合利用业	Comprehensive Utilization of Waste Resources	0.90	1.56	3.43	5.64	5.58
金属制品、机械和设备修理业	Repair Service of Metal Products, Machinery and Equipment		0.17	0.35	0.53	0.69
电力、热力生产和供应业	Production and Supply of Electric Power and Heat Power	179.61	222.95	323.09	313.66	342.11
燃气生产和供应业	Production and Supply of Gas	1.20	2.26	1.23	1.36	1.35
水的生产和供应业	Production and Supply of Water	7.53	11.45	21.75	26.36	29.54

6—16 规模以上工业企业分行业取水情况（2022年）
Water Intake by Industries of Industrial Enterprises Above Designated Size (2022)

单位：万立方米（10000 M^3）

行 业	Sector	工业取水总量 Industrial Water Got Total Amount of Industrial Water Got	地表淡水 Earth's Surface Fresh Water	地下淡水 Undergr-ound Water	自来水 Tap Water	其他水 Other Water	重复用水数量 Repeat of Water Consump-tion
消费总量	**Total Consumption**	**478696.0**	**357383.1**	**39503.3**	**59295.5**	**7036.5**	**3140990.1**
煤炭开采和洗选业	Coal Mining and Dressing	8501.2	39.3	3264.8	45.1	170.8	14547.5
黑色金属矿采选业	Mining and Dressing of Ferrous Metals	2922.5	805.0	674.0	502.7	10.0	16381.7
有色金属矿采选业	Mining and Dressing of Nonferrous Metals	709.8	68.0	50.4	92.1		1193.6
非金属矿采选业	Mining and Dressing of Nonmetal Minerals	1507.5	1176.5	107.6	99.3	0.1	714.8
开采辅助活动	Mining Auxiliary Activities	6.9		5.6	1.3		
农副食品加工业	Agricultural and Non-staple Food Processing Industry	2287.7	131.0	635.5	1474.5	46.4	231.4
食品制造业	Food Production	2391.9	48.4	493.3	1779.4	47.7	675.5
酒、饮料和精制茶制造业	Wine, Drinks and Refined Tea Manufacturing	3128.4	707.7	801.0	1540.2	79.3	645.0
烟草加工业	Tobacco Processing	152.3		1.5	145.8	5.0	37.3
纺织业	Textiles	3356.9	1101.9	41.4	1961.5	43.9	1788.5
纺织服装、服饰业	Textile and Garment, Apparel Industry	689.1	33.8	41.5	609.6	4.2	2.3
皮革毛皮羽毛及其制品和制鞋业	Leather, Furs, Down and Related Products	913.0	247.5	62.2	486.5	13.0	653.3
木材加工及竹藤棕草制品业	Timber Processing, Bamboo, Cane, Palm Fiber and Straw Products	311.6	20.4	84.7	204.8	1.4	148.9
家具制造业	Furniture Manufacturing	136.9	5.2	10.4	121.3	0.0	2.9
造纸和纸制品业	Papermaking and Paper Products	3686.8	2928.5	223.3	467.1	68.0	1421.6
印刷和记录媒介复制业	Printing and Record Medium Reproduction	365.7	14.9	10.9	334.5	5.5	35.4
文教、工美、体育和娱乐用品制造业	Cultural and Educational Supplies Manufacturing, Industrial, Sporting and Entertainment	205.2	13.6	28.0	162.9	0.77	17.2
石油、煤炭及其他燃料加工业	Petroleum, Coal and Other Fuel Processing Industries	3940.5	775.3	0.2	2336.6	720.5	179790.0
化学原料和制品制造业	Raw Chemical Materials and Chemical Products	21936.9	10885.2	452.1	5612.1	3188.1	565655.7
医药制造业	Medical and Pharmaceutical Products	2359.8	341.7	246.8	1607.0	160.6	6819.3
化学纤维制造业	Chemical Fiber	591.4	99.2	181.3	252.7	58.2	1561.7
橡胶和塑料制品业	Rubber and Plastic Products	2460.7	35.6	112.6	1711.9	590.7	4725.0
非金属矿物制品业	Nonmetal Mineral Products	11795.1	5873.6	1678.5	4109.1	31.5	24573.9
黑色金属冶炼和压延加工业	Smelting and Pressing of Ferrous Metals	12492.5	11564.9	1.7	403.3	8.3	335255.1
有色金属冶炼和压延加工业	Smelting and Pressing of Nonferrous Metals	4324.6	191.4	107.1	3280.3	1.4	94245.8
金属制品业	Metal Products	1844.7	131.3	39.7	1660.9	12.6	233.5
通用设备制造业	Equipment in Current Use	1871.3	40.6	35.3	1794.6	0.9	115.1
专用设备制造业	Equipment in Special Use	1068.3	25.4	22.1	1018.8	2.0	37.4
汽车制造业	Automobile Manufacturing Industry	2311.0	57.5	32.2	2215.0	5.9	4833.2
铁路、船舶、航空航天和其他运输设备制造业	Railway, Shipbuilding, Aerospace, and Other Transportation Equipment Manufacturing Industry	783.0	59.3	6.4	657.4	0.1	112.4
电气机械和器材制造业	Electric Equipment and Machinery	5494.1	42.2	155.0	5273.7	15.8	750.0
计算机、通信和其他电子设备制造业	Computer, Communication and Other Electronic Equipment Manufacturing Industry	9034.2	33.8	33.7	8692.7	272.2	56765.8
仪器仪表制造业	Instrument Manufacturing	96.2	0.2	0.5	95.4	0.1	0.9
其他制造业	Other Manufacturing	112.5	12.1	19.6	80.8	0.0	5.4
废弃资源综合利用业	Comprehensive Utilization of Waste Resources	314.0	15.0	67.7	214.9	2.7	53.8
金属制品、机械和设备修理业	Metal Products, Machinery and Equipment Repair	108.3			108.3		0.5
电力、热力生产和供应业	Electricity, Heat Production and Supply Industry	51841.8	42254.6	1078.8	1806.1	1461.0	1826700.3
燃气生产和供应业	Production and Supply of Gas	67.3	0.5	2.1	64.6	0.1	78.7
水的生产和供应业	Production and Supply of Tap Water	312574.3	277602.0	28694.0	6270.5	7.8	179.8

6—17 规模以上工业企业分行业主要能源品种消费量（2022年）
Industrial Enterprises Above Designated Size Consume Major Energy Resources in Different Industries (2022)

行　业	Sector	原　煤（吨）Raw Coal (ton)	洗精煤（吨）Washed and Refined Coal (ton)
消费总量	**Total Consumption**	**199110502**	**17489278**
煤炭开采和洗选业	Coal Mining and Dressing	42566541	
黑色金属矿采选业	Mining and Dressing of Ferrous Metals	52428	
有色金属矿采选业	Mining and Dressing of Nonferrous Metals	980	
非金属矿采选业	Mining and Dressing of Nonmetal Minerals	190513	
开采专业及辅助性活动	Mining Profession and Auxiliary Activities		
农副食品加工业	Agricultural and Non-staple Food Processing Industry	1153	
食品制造业	Food Production	14	
酒、饮料和精制茶制造业	Wine, Drinks and Refined Tea Manufacturing	242604	
烟草制品业	Tobacco Processing		
纺织业	Textiles	22785	
纺织服装、服饰业	Textile and Garment, Apparel Industry	240	
皮革、毛皮、羽毛及其制品和制鞋业	Leather, Fur, Feather and Its Products and Footwear		
木材加工和木、竹、藤、棕、草制品业	Timber Processing, Bamboo, Cane, Palm Fiber and Straw Products	448	
家具制造业	Furniture Manufacturing		
造纸和纸制品业	Papermaking and Paper Products	1223770	
印刷和记录媒介复制业	Printing and Record Medium Reproduction	823	
文教、工美、体育和娱乐用品制造业	Cultural and Educational Supplies Manufacturing, Industrial, Sporting and Entertainment	2646	
石油、煤炭及其他燃料加工业	Petroleum, Coal and Other Fuel Processing Industries	1663778	8205478
化学原料和化学制品制造业	Raw Chemical Materials and Chemical Products	14883727	
医药制造业	Medical and Pharmaceutical Products	7683	
化学纤维制造业	Chemical Fiber	502	
橡胶和塑料制品业	Rubber and Plastic Products	232644	
非金属矿物制品业	Nonmetal Mineral Products	20085462	
黑色金属冶炼和压延加工业	Smelting and Pressing of Ferrous Metals	4119872	9283800
有色金属冶炼和压延加工业	Smelting and Pressing of Nonferrous Metals	405940	
金属制品业	Metal Products	43698	
通用设备制造业	Equipment in Current Use		
专用设备制造业	Equipment in Special Use		
汽车制造业	Automobile Manufacturing Industry		
铁路、船舶、航空航天和其他运输设备制造业	Railway, Shipbuilding, Aerospace, and Other Transportation Equipment Manufacturing Industry	14	
电气机械和器材制造业	Electric Equipment and Machinery	20375	
计算机、通信和其他电子设备制造业	Computers, Communications and Other Electronic Equipment Manufacturing Industry	11972	
仪器仪表制造业	Instrument Manufacturing		
其他制造业	Other Manufacturing		
废弃资源综合利用业	Comprehensive Utilization of Waste Resources	5966	
金属制品、机械和设备修理业	Metal Products, Machinery and Equipment Repair		
电力、热力生产和供应业	Production and Supply of Electric Power and Heating Power	113323923	
燃气生产和供应业	Production and Supply of Gas		
水的生产和供应业	Production and Supply of Tap Water		

其他洗煤（吨）Other Washed Coal (ton)	煤制品（吨）Coal Product (ton)	焦炭（吨）Coke (ton)	原油（吨）Crude Oil (ton)	汽油（吨）Gasoline (ton)	柴油（吨）Diesel Oil (ton)	天然气(气态)（万立方米）Natural Gas (Gaseous) (10000 cu.m)	热力（百万千焦）Heat (million kilo-joule)	电力（万千瓦时）Electric Power (10000 kWh)	生物燃料（吨标准煤）Biofuel (tons of SCE)
3207403	**31891**	**12760039**	**5795480**	**22343**	**258235**	**342774**	**142409234**	**15597306**	**3172464**
				960	17333	8422	1173785	395124	
				76	7433	119		219186	
				63	2419			33955	
				115	26175	90	2662151	85098	6044
				28	153			256	
				433	896	10233	1505080	228103	49949
		395		60	551	6666	1249227	90527	6871
		41		323	791	3096	4745004	74670	12208
				5	82	1111	155594	13309	
				35	133	7752	1284011	384913	6584
				387	77	762	147366	37040	4542
				172	162	1034	233775	29092	3462
				55	595	542	47266	83467	25120
			5	109	115	45	4	25194	
				201	2396	2674	16269379	243336	111733
				509	837	1891	175822	71340	930
				126	195	852	36783	33679	99
		85075	5794853		1524	70	13220822	222486	
428817				593	7514	28208	78137724	1701813	65524
				199	127	4205	6188327	139683	14390
						1910	2940933	52156	5488
				528	1452	14390	2901790	472660	62768
29295	225	48015	613	982	146427	127687	902665	1970432	44463
570480	31627	12374582		109	8282	12358	3968684	1911838	57
		11297		83	3238	25191	1197646	531700	2487
704	39	167559		980	2988	12978	173954	429877	3559
		71741		1652	2997	7029	53383	330784	616
		1333		1163	1827	2400	111830	155840	612
				1099	4366	12092	305256	389583	488
				150	297	1780		44833	266
			9	1559	1531	10334	472301	789967	4551
				506	364	15326	1391331	1113121	
				176	7	77		10903	
				18	63	39	72761	10961	
				78	1917	2697	55280	86611	21717
				71	253	336		7507	
2178108				7767	12427	3863	629301	3011029	2717581
				524	137	2052		8797	358
				413	145	445		153818	

6—18 规模以上工业企业能源购进、消费及库存（2022年）
Buys, Consumes and Stock of the Energy of Above Designated Size Industrial Enterprises (2022)

能源名称		Energy Item		购进量 Purchasing Amount	消费量 Consumption Amount 工业生产消费 Consumption of Industrial Production	#用于原材料 Used in the Raw Materials	年末库存量 Volume of Stock of the end of the Year
原　煤	（吨）	Raw Coal	(ton)	183611556	199110502	7509776	5035859
#无烟煤		Anthracite		4965938	4953121	822773	256133
炼焦烟煤		Byerlyte		47375	1134890		7124
一般烟煤		Generally Bituminous Coal		178598243	193022491	6687003	4772583
褐　煤		Lignite					18
洗精煤	（吨）	Washed and Refined Coal	(ton)	17539049	17489278		639191
其他洗煤	（吨）	Other Washed Coal	(ton)	3151856	3207403	362935	158872
煤制品	（吨）	Coal Product	(ton)	31893	31891		
焦　炭	（吨）	Coke	(ton)	6178153	12760039	1373	291695
其他焦化产品	（吨）	Other Coking Products	(ton)	154581	146122	60276	17840
焦炉煤气	（万立方米）	Coke Oven Coal Gas	(10000 cu.m)	68678	441452	59923	
高炉煤气	（万立方米）	Blast Furnace Gas	(10000 cu.m)	181509	4012623		
转炉煤气	（万立方米）	Converter Coal Gas	(10000 cu.m)	43484	319729		
发生炉煤气	（万立方米）	Producer Gas	(10000 cu.m)	271	271		
天然气(气态)	（万立方米）	Natural Gas(Gaseous)	(10000 cu.m)	332333	342774	38	34
液化天然气	（吨）	Liquefied Natural Gas	(ton)	52177	49469		90
煤层气	（万立方米）	Coalbed methane (CBM)	(10000 cu.m)	20113	44120	2148	1
原　油	（吨）	Crude Oil	(ton)	5786043	5795480		106529
汽　油	（吨）	Gasoline	(ton)	24280	22343	43	301
煤　油	（吨）	Kerosene	(ton)	2546	2415		375
柴　油	（吨）	Diesel Oil	(ton)	262775	258235	801	10894
燃料油	（吨）	Fuel Oil	(ton)	90216	85572		717
液化石油气	（吨）	Liquefied Petroleum Gas	(ton)	10827	4846	2	116
炼厂干气	（吨）	Refinery Gas	(ton)	900	300617		89
润滑油	（吨）	Lubricating Oil	(ton)	3197	2864	227	439
石　蜡	（吨）	Paraffin	(ton)	930	969	523	77
溶剂油	（吨）	Solvent Oil	(ton)	28624	28652	615	24
石油焦	（吨）	Refinery Coke	(ton)	80781	75152	6416	13094
石油沥青	（吨）	Petroleum asphalt	(ton)	51717	50143	44299	546
其他石油制品	（吨）	Other Petroleum Products	(ton)	798882	1845707	385613	4222
热　力	（百万千焦）	Heat	(million kilo-joule)	65001609	142409234		
电　力	（万千瓦时）	Electric Power	(10000 kWh)	37165910	15597306		
煤矸石(用于燃料)	（吨）	Coal Gangue (for fuel)	(ton)	2204779	2216264		17942
城市垃圾(用于燃料)	（吨）	Municipal Waste (for fuel)	(ton)	10510611	10368971		344218
生物燃料	（吨标准煤）	Biofuel	(tons of standard coal)	3323788	3172464		367763
余热余压	（百万千焦）	Afterheat Excess Pressure	(million kilo-joule)	4842877	103784936		
工业废料(用于燃料)	（吨）	Industrial waste (for fuel)	(ton)	1857	75650		871
其他燃料	（吨标准煤）	Other fuel	(tons of standard coal)	5478	5242		

6—19 地区能源消费
Regional Energy Consumption

单位：万吨标准煤（10000 tons of SCE）

指 标	Item	2020	2021	2022
能源消费总量（等价值）	Unit GDP Energy Consumption (Equal Values)	14697.90	15342.63	15882.66
农、林、牧、渔业能源消费	Energy Consumption in Agriculture, Forestry, Animal Husbandry and Fishery	276.89	308.05	334.64
工业和建筑业能源消费	Industrial and Construction Energy Consumption	9819.76	10157.21	10233.75
工业能源消费	Industry Energy Consumption	9535.76	9835.44	9923.85
建筑业能源消费	Construction Industrial Energy Consumption	284.00	321.78	309.90
服务业能源消费	Service Energy Consumption	2491.26	2732.93	2869.19
#交通运输、仓储和邮政业能源消费	Transportation, Storage and Postal Energy Consumption	1157.08	1156.05	1083.51
居民生活用能	Residences Life Energy Consumption	2109.99	2144.43	2445.07
城市居民	Urban	1231.34	1213.40	1357.58
农村居民	Rural	878.65	931.03	1087.49

6—20 各市全社会用电情况（2022年）
Electricity Used in Whole Society by Region (2022)

单位：亿千瓦时（100 million kWh）

地 区	Region	全社会用电量总计 Total of Electricity Used in Whole Society	全行业用电量合计 Total of Electricity Used in Whole Trade	第一产业 Primary Industry	第二产业 Secondary Industry	第三产业 Tertiary Industry	城乡居民生活用电量合计 Electricity Used for Life	城镇居民 Urban	乡村居民 Rural
总 计	**Total**	**2993.22**	**2452.25**	**47.12**	**1876.70**	**528.43**	**540.97**	**244.62**	**296.36**
合肥市	Hefei	500.92	406.95	3.75	251.42	151.78	93.98	69.03	24.95
淮北市	Huaibei	88.32	71.50	2.17	55.66	13.67	16.82	7.20	9.62
亳州市	Bozhou	105.39	67.08	3.59	35.80	27.69	38.32	12.56	25.76
宿州市	Suzhou	125.29	84.59	3.98	51.53	29.08	40.70	15.50	25.21
蚌埠市	Bengbu	117.01	89.54	3.97	57.15	28.42	27.47	12.82	14.66
阜阳市	Fuyang	206.66	139.24	6.07	84.24	48.93	67.42	16.81	50.61
淮南市	Huainan	108.80	82.45	2.48	58.58	21.39	26.35	12.02	14.34
滁州市	Chuzhou	283.12	247.15	5.01	209.20	32.94	35.97	15.45	20.52
六安市	Luan	158.35	120.71	3.03	86.32	31.36	37.64	11.62	26.01
马鞍山市	Maanshan	250.57	227.01	2.21	202.68	22.12	23.56	12.78	10.78
芜湖市	Wuhu	253.08	216.84	3.06	175.91	37.88	36.23	17.26	18.97
宣城市	Xuancheng	186.12	160.21	2.92	134.67	22.61	25.92	11.75	14.17
铜陵市	Tongling	114.00	102.96	0.51	89.77	12.68	11.03	6.06	4.97
池州市	Chizhou	103.82	91.95	0.97	80.97	10.01	11.87	4.90	6.97
安庆市	Anqing	151.95	116.63	2.40	88.61	25.63	35.32	12.61	22.71
黄山市	Huangshan	51.56	39.19	0.98	25.93	12.27	12.38	6.27	6.11

注：总计包括安徽电网主网架厂网损，各市不包括。
a) Total including Anhui power grid main grid plant network loss, excluding cities.

6—21 各市主要年份工业用电量
Industrial Electricity Used in Main Year by Region

单位：亿千瓦时（100 million kWh）

地 区	Region	2010	2015	2020	2021	2022
总 计	**Total**	**777.18**	**1132.79**	**1550.22**	**1721.30**	**1830.72**
合肥市	Hefei	64.10	130.93	189.98	223.28	239.87
淮北市	Huaibei	31.63	40.79	46.30	50.91	54.59
亳州市	Bozhou	13.42	21.47	24.79	28.51	32.97
宿州市	Suzhou	20.32	32.85	40.82	47.36	48.17
蚌埠市	Bengbu	34.32	37.43	46.65	49.40	55.33
阜阳市	Fuyang	36.89	58.21	72.32	79.91	80.02
淮南市	Huainan	47.49	55.68	55.79	59.02	57.42
滁州市	Chuzhou	30.39	90.73	155.73	182.26	205.72
六安市	Luan	24.42	31.99	63.89	75.30	83.53
马鞍山市	Maanshan	104.54	155.34	176.99	193.19	199.90
芜湖市	Wuhu	62.03	117.32	146.71	166.89	173.90
宣城市	Xuancheng	48.13	62.51	107.34	126.50	132.16
铜陵市	Tongling	47.08	68.51	78.24	83.34	89.12
池州市	Chizhou	18.82	39.13	64.76	74.46	80.07
安庆市	Anqing	44.41	53.42	71.11	80.04	85.74
黄山市	Huangshan	7.89	12.36	19.80	22.86	23.95

注：1. 2010年以后的工业用电量是区划调整后数据。

2. 总计包括安徽电网主网架厂网损，各市不包括。

a) Since 2010, the industrial electricity consumption is division after adjusting the data.

b) Total including Anhui power grid main grid plant network loss, excluding cities.

6—22 各市规模以上工业企业取水情况（2022年）
Water Intake by Industrial Enterprises Above Designated Size by Region (2022)

单位：万立方米（10000 M³）

地 区	Region	工业取水总量 Industrial Water Got Total Amount of Industrial Water Got	#地表淡水数量 The Earth's Surface Fresh Water	地下淡水数量 Undergr-ound Water	自来水数量 Tap Water	重复用水数量 Repeat of Water Consump-tion
总 计	**Total**	**478696.04**	**357383.11**	**39503.26**	**59295.47**	**3140990.05**
合肥市	Hefei	113552.42	95097.87	152.71	16202.51	366392.35
淮北市	Huaibei	20644.04	3059.39	7093.45	727.63	439042.32
亳州市	Bozhou	17021.48	8149.25	7918.54	499.27	91759.25
宿州市	Suzhou	14196.70	3337.13	9665.00	337.04	75215.79
蚌埠市	Bengbu	20741.49	17803.26	211.86	2471.16	166988.54
阜阳市	Fuyang	23104.69	12624.76	7073.90	1776.87	193133.15
淮南市	Huainan	41860.01	35665.96	4627.94	813.27	663515.34
滁州市	Chuzhou	39900.79	32952.82	891.44	5901.50	62381.29
六安市	Luan	17558.20	12216.47	473.35	3430.34	100130.72
马鞍山市	Maanshan	36383.03	32182.61	374.39	3130.83	274167.76
芜湖市	Wuhu	45919.37	38516.51	566.82	6055.78	146443.20
宣城市	Xuancheng	17753.19	12913.12	240.80	4489.74	37485.03
铜陵市	Tongling	24901.74	16852.08	96.11	5600.69	342045.36
池州市	Chizhou	11021.67	8966.68	13.32	1950.09	31939.40
安庆市	Anqing	28548.87	22653.59	81.82	4789.96	138714.94
黄山市	Huangshan	5588.37	4391.60	21.80	1118.78	11635.61

主要统计指标解释

能源生产总量

指一定时期内全省一次能源生产量的总和，是观察全省能源生产水平、规模、构成和发展速度的总量指标。一次能源生产量包括原煤，原油，天然气，水电、核电及其他动力能（如风能、地热能等）发电量，不包括低热值燃料生产量、太阳热能等的利用和由一次能源加工转换而成的二次能源产量。

能源消费总量

指全省国民经济各行业和居民家庭在一定时期消费的各种能源的总和。能源消费总量分为终端能源消费量、能源加工转换损失量和损失量三部分。

(1)终端能源消费量：指一定时期内全省各行业和居民生活消费的各种能源在扣除了用于加工转换二次能源消费量和损失量以后的数量。

(2)能源加工转换损失量：指一定时期内全省投入加工转换的各种能源数量之和与产出各种能源产品之和的差额，是观察能源在加工转换过程中损失量变化的指标。

(3)能源损失量：指一定时期内能源在输送、分配、储存过程中发生的损失和由客观原因造成的各种损失量，不包括各种气体能源放空、放散量。

能源生产弹性系数

是能源生产量的增长速度与国民经济增长速度之间的比值。计算公式为：

能源生产弹性系数＝能源生产总量年平均增长速度/国民经济年平均增长速度

本年鉴采用国内生产总值指标计算国民经济年平均增长速度。

电力生产弹性系数

是电力生产量的增长速度与国民经济增长速度之间的比值。计算公式为：

电力生产弹性系数＝电力生产量年平均增长速度/国民经济年平均增长速度

能源消费弹性系数

是能源消费增长速度与国民经济增长速度之间的比值。计算公式为：

能源消费弹性系数＝能源消费量年平均增长速度/国民经济年平均增长速度

电力消费弹性系数

是电力消费增长速度与国民经济增长速度之间的比值。计算公式为：

电力消费弹性系数＝电力消费量年平均增长速度/国民经济年平均增长速度

能源加工转换效率

指一定时期内能源经过加工、转换后，产出的各种能源产品的数量与同期内投入加工转换的各种能源数量的比率。它是观察能源加工转换装置和生产工艺先进与落后、管理水平高低等的重要指标。计算公式为：

能源加工转换效率＝能源加工、转换产出量/能源加工、转换投入量×100%

Explanatory Notes for Major Statistical Indicators

Total Energy Production

refers to a certain period of time the province's primary energy production is the sum of the province's energy production level, size, composition and development speed of the total indicators. The primary energy production includes the generation of raw coal, crude oil, natural gas, hydropower, nuclear power and other dynamic energy (such as wind energy, geothermal energy, etc.), excluding low calorific value fuel production, solar heat utilization and conversion from primary energy processing Of secondary energy production.

Total Domestic Energy Consumption

refers to the province's national economy and the families of various industries in a certain period of time the sum of the various energy consumption. The total energy consumption is divided into three parts: terminal energy consumption, energy processing conversion loss and loss.

a) terminal energy consumption: refers to a certain period of the province's various industries and residents living in a variety of energy consumption after deducting the conversion of secondary energy consumption and the amount of loss after the amount.

b) Loss During the Process of Energy Conversion: It refers to the total input of various kinds of energy for conversion, minus the total output of various kinds of energy in the province in a given period of time. It is an indicator to show the loss that occurs during the process of energy conversion.

c) Loss: It refers to the total of the loss of energy during the course of energy transport, distribution and storage and the loss caused by any objective reason in a given period of time. The loss of various kinds of gas due to gas discharges and stocktaking is excluded.

Elasticity Ratio of Energy Production

is the ratio of the growth rate of energy production and the growth rate of national economy. The formula is:

Elasticity Ratio of Energy Production=Average Annual Growth Rate of Energy Production / Average Annual Growth Rate of National Economy

This yearbook uses the Gross Domestic Product (GDP) indicator to calculate the average annual growth rate of the national economy.

Elasticity Ratio of Electricity Production

is the ratio of the growth rate of electricity production to the growth rate of the national economy. Its formula is:

Elasticity Ratio of Electricity Production=Average Annual Growth Rate of Electricity Production / Average Annual Growth Rate of National Economy

Elasticity Ratio of Energy Consumption

is the ratio of energy consumption growth rate and national economic growth rate. The formula is:

Elasticity Ratio of Energy Consumption=Average Annual Growth Rate of Energy Consumption / Average Annual Growth Rate of National Economy

Elasticity Ratio of Electricity Consumption

is the ratio of the growth rate of electricity consumption to the growth rate of the national economy. The formula is:

Elasticity Ratio of Electricity Consumption=Average Annual Growth Rate of Electricity / Average Annual Growth Rate of National Economy

Efficiency of Energy Processing and Conversion

refers to the ratio of the total output of energy products of various kinds after processing and conversion and the total input of energy of various kinds for processing and conversion in the same reference period. It is an important indicator to show the current conditions of energy processing and conversion equipment, production technique and management. The formula is:

Efficiency of Energy Processing & Conversion=Output of Energy After Processing & Conversion/Input of Energy for Processing & Conversion×100%

第七篇

Chapter 7

财政与金融

GOVERNMENT FINANCE AND FINANCE

简要说明

一、本篇反映全省财政收支、金融保险业发展状况。

二、财政收支资料来源于省财政厅财政决算。

三、金融保险业资料有以下三个部分：

1. 反映金融机构,包括中国人民银行、中资全国性大型银行、中资全国性中小型银行、中资区域性中小型银行、农村合作机构等信贷收支情况，资料由中国人民银行合肥中心支行提供；

2. 反映保险业务情况，资料由中国银行保险监督管理委员会安徽监管局提供；

3. 反映股票发行及筹资情况，资料由中国证券监督管理委员会安徽监管局提供。

Brief Introduction

I. Data in this chapter show the provincial government revenue and expenditure and the development of banking and insurance.

II. Data on the government revenue and expenditure come from the Department of Finance in the province. Data are based on the final financial accounts.

III. Data of banking and insurance include the following three parts:

1. Reflect the credit receipts and payments of financial institutions, including the People's Bank of China, large Chinese-funded national banks, small and medium-sized Chinese-funded national banks, small and medium-sized Chinese-funded regional banks, rural cooperative institutions, etc. Data are provided by Hefei Central Sub-branch of the People's Bank of China.

2. Reflect the insurance business, the information provided by the Anhui Supervision Bureau of the Bank of China Insurance Regulatory Commission.

3. Reflect the issuance and financing of shares, data provided by China Securities Regulatory Commission Anhui Supervision Bureau.

7—1 一般公共预算收支及增长速度
General Public Budget Revenue and Expenditure and Growth Rate

年 份 Year	一般公共预算收入 (万元) General Public Budget Revenue (10000 yuan)	一般公共预算支出 (万元) Expenditures in General Public Budgets (10000 yuan)	增长速度 (%) Increase Rate (%) 一般公共预算收入 General Public Budget Revenue	增长速度 (%) Increase Rate (%) 一般公共预算支出 Expenditures in General Public Budgets
2005	3340170	7130633	21.6	18.5
2010	11493952	25876135	33.0	20.8
2013	20750750	43496871	15.8	9.8
2014	22184418	46640973	6.9	7.2
2015	24543029	52390076	10.6	12.3
2016	26727920	55229501	8.9	5.4
2017	28124495	62038110	5.2	12.3
2018	30486705	65721484	8.4	5.9
2019	31827069	73922226	4.4	12.5
2020	32160079	74735925	1.0	1.1
2021	34981949	75910502	8.8	1.6
2022	35891411	83797840	9.9	10.4

注：2022年一般公共预算收入增长速度为同口径数据，是指将2022年和2021年同期新老政策留抵退税金额返加到收入中计算。

7—2 一般公共预算收入相当于生产总值的比例
General Public Budget Revenue As a Percentage of Gross Domestic Product

年 份 Year	一般公共预算收入 (万元) General Public Budget Revenue (10000 yuan)	生产总值 (亿元) Gross Domestic Product (100 million yuan)	一般公共预算收入相当于生产总值的比例 General Public Budget Revenue As a Percentage of Gross Domestic Product
2005	3340170	5675.9	5.9
2010	11493952	13249.8	8.7
2013	20750750	20584.0	10.1
2014	22184418	22519.7	9.9
2015	24543029	23831.2	10.3
2016	26727920	26307.7	10.2
2017	28124495	29676.2	9.5
2018	30486705	34010.9	9.0
2019	31827069	36845.5	8.6
2020	32160079	38061.5	8.4
2021	34981949	42565.2	8.2
2022	35891411	45045.0	8.0

7—3 税收收入和非税收入及比重
Total Revenue and Proportion of Tax and Non-tax

年 份 Year	绝 对 数 (万元) Total Revenue (10000 yuan)			比 重 (%) Proportion (%)	
	全 省 Total	税收收入 Tax Revenue	非税收入 Non-tax Revenue	税收收入 Tax Revenue	非税收入 Non-tax Revenue
2010	11493952	8665517	2828435	75.4	24.6
2015	24543029	17998922	6544107	73.3	26.7
2016	26727920	18575281	8152639	69.5	30.5
2017	28124495	19706808	8417687	70.1	29.9
2018	30486705	21807419	8679286	71.5	28.5
2019	31827069	22097280	9729789	69.4	30.6
2020	32160079	21995249	10164830	68.4	31.6
2021	34981949	23898951	11082998	68.3	31.7
2022	35891411	22467040	13424371	62.6	37.4

7—4 各项税收收入
Government Tax Revenue

单位：万元（10000 yuan）

年 份 Year	税收收入 Tax	增 值 税 Value-added Tax	营 业 税 Operation Tax	契 税 Contract Tax	企业所得税 Enterprises' Income Tax	个人所得税 Individual Income Tax
2010	8665517	1294839	2919300	959149	1065948	319746
2015	17998922	2731085	5868006	1725171	2355732	531350
2016	18575281	5303404	3099903	1854037	2332401	592815
2017	19706808	8033600		2442950	2747309	794104
2018	21807419	9059762		2376451	3346921	923496
2019	22097280	9423451		2319035	3709031	651118
2020	21995249	9432070		2262364	3625127	767409
2021	23898951	10075811		2620538	3924176	935293
2022	22467040	8450703		2315643	3925263	1051832

7—5 一般公共预算收支情况
General Public Budget Revenue and Expenditure

单位：万元（10000 yuan）

指　　标	Item	2021	2022
收入合计	**Total Revenue**	**34981949**	**35891411**
增值税	Value-added Tax	10075811	8450703
企业所得税	Enterprises' Income Tax	3924176	3925263
个人所得税	Individual Income Tax	935293	1051832
资源税	Resources Tax	334608	488541
城市维护建设税	Tax on Town maintenance and Construction	1633770	1634339
房产税	Tax on Real Estates	890701	1008438
印花税	Stamp Tax	372220	468038
城镇土地使用税	Tax on the Use of Urban Land	1129199	1133854
土地增值税	Land Value Added Tax	1429729	1292927
车船税	Vehicle and Ship Tax	283565	304896
耕地占用税	Tax on the Occupancy of Cultivated Land	227131	343533
契　税	Contract Tax	2620538	2315643
烟叶税	Leaf Tobacco Tax	6735	13792
环境保护税	Environmental Protection Tax	25708	27344
其他税收收入	Other Tax Revenue	9767	7897
专项收入	Expert Project Income	3137771	3223162
行政事业性收费	Administrative and Institutional Fees	1277208	1212719
罚没收入	Penalty and Confiscatory Income	1120042	976532
国有资本经营收入	Stated-owned Assets Profit	342999	304489
国有资源（资产）有偿使用	Income from the Paid Use of Stated-owned Resources (Assets)	4388100	6765029
其他收入	Other Income	816878	942440
支出合计	**Total Expenditure**	**75910502**	**83797840**
一般公共服务	General Public Service	5225729	5853117
外　交	Foreign Affairs		1630
国　防	National Defence	58084	64978
公共安全	Public Security	3089389	3452311
教　育	Education	13156630	14208664
科学技术	Science	4160874	5075556
文化旅游体育与传媒	Culture, Tourism, Sports and Media	860987	866360
社会保障和就业	Social Security and Employment	12295752	14271310
卫生健康	Health and Hygiene	7320016	8080816
节能环保	Energy Saving and Environmental Protection	1994541	2006851
城乡社区	Urban and Rural Communities	8580024	7690373
农林水	Agriculture and Forestry Water	9425474	9918819
交通运输	Transport	3039829	3612649
资源勘探工业信息等	Resource Exploration Industry Information, Etc	977562	1726713
商业服务业等	Business Services, etc	568048	708966
金　融	Financial	74036	986632
援助其他地区	Aid Spending Elsewhere	57362	62057
自然资源海洋气象等	Natural Resources, Marine Meteorology, etc.	649810	606186
住房保障	Housing Safeguard	2210902	2352799
粮油物资储备	Supplies of Grain and Oil Reserves	295219	270615
灾害防治及应急管理	Disaster Prevention and Emergency Management	369695	422352
债务付息	Debt Servicing	1459286	1475716
债务发行费用	Debt Issuance Costs	6646	4811
其他支出	Other Expenditure	34607	77559

7—6 各市一般公共预算收入（2022年）
General Public Budget Revenue by Region (2022)

单位：万元（10000 yuan）

地 区	Region	收入合计 Total Revenue	增值税 Value-added Tax	企业所得税 Enterprises' Income Tax	个人所得税 Individual Income Tax	资源税 Resources Tax
合肥市	Hefei	9092546	2997746	789884	276572	20999
淮北市	Huaibei	970317	381236	103193	11650	41657
亳州市	Bozhou	1481301	397785	90240	13458	14108
宿州市	Suzhou	1553455	462403	64812	12749	28313
蚌埠市	Bengbu	1740257	521956	75119	19623	2612
阜阳市	Fuyang	1848040	582014	101018	20224	27115
淮南市	Huainan	1203060	392394	54086	16697	67546
滁州市	Chuzhou	2778542	614226	123137	36797	35133
六安市	Luan	1612642	528695	104149	18477	39425
马鞍山市	Maanshan	2048752	834071	92967	34154	25736
芜湖市	Wuhu	3886020	1308086	280141	82459	31511
宣城市	Xuancheng	1885011	573721	94529	42097	40428
铜陵市	Tongling	1037838	407437	96495	8630	42746
池州市	Chizhou	831310	272218	51946	15168	52543
安庆市	Anqing	1748586	716696	70336	27482	16702
黄山市	Huangshan	907099	171778	26077	12084	1967

地 区	Region	城市维护建设税 Tax on Town Maintenance and Construction	房产税 Tax on Real Estates	印花税 Stamp Tax	城镇土地使用税 Tax on the Use of Urban Land	土地增值税 Land Value Added Tax
合肥市	Hefei	434694	361402	178191	131329	519435
淮北市	Huaibei	52713	23912	11120	31092	22838
亳州市	Bozhou	58225	34824	13682	57162	57987
宿州市	Suzhou	57266	30384	13735	38730	48349
蚌埠市	Bengbu	125237	39949	18757	51112	69681
阜阳市	Fuyang	95870	36000	17621	54334	101492
淮南市	Huainan	47013	30200	12916	35337	17388
滁州市	Chuzhou	92960	87702	28159	167694	67824
六安市	Luan	58852	39655	16172	64616	59987
马鞍山市	Maanshan	97252	62679	32771	56536	55617
芜湖市	Wuhu	226172	99091	52450	158622	76471
宣城市	Xuancheng	61913	52928	18028	121668	48923
铜陵市	Tongling	49499	25321	16430	48683	8925
池州市	Chizhou	31035	18517	9157	22708	12780
安庆市	Anqing	110092	40503	19718	62720	67217
黄山市	Huangshan	18234	22124	6627	28909	57189

7—6 续表 continued

地区	Region	车船税 Tax on Vehicles and Vessels	耕地占用税 Tax on the Occupancy of Cultivated Land	契税 Contract Tax	烟叶税 Leaf Tobacco Tax	环境保护税 Environmental Protection Tax	其他税收收入 Other Tax Revenue
合肥市	Hefei	75587	23904	893649		817	3131
淮北市	Huaibei	9815	2037	53255		795	107
亳州市	Bozhou	17170	19473	119817		284	-2
宿州市	Suzhou	19130	12471	116061		400	73
蚌埠市	Bengbu	18330	9303	84922		411	23
阜阳市	Fuyang	25844	48813	147526		430	541
淮南市	Huainan	11011	9186	60985		801	90
滁州市	Chuzhou	15739	72812	142220		605	332
六安市	Luan	16251	15930	114633		469	350
马鞍山市	Maanshan	11703	6075	76390		2943	96
芜湖市	Wuhu	26867	11677	173493	2219	2133	1811
宣城市	Xuancheng	17413	18304	99628	10330	958	550
铜陵市	Tongling	6361	3754	43195		847	5
池州市	Chizhou	6262	1890	32880	873	677	-3
安庆市	Anqing	19735	16756	96303		911	400
黄山市	Huangshan	7678	11732	60686	370	190	208

地区	Region	专项收入 Expert Project Income	行政事业性收费 Administrative and Institutional Fees	罚没收入 Penalty and Confiscatory Income	国有资本经营 State-owned Assets Profit	国有资源（资产）有偿使用 Income from the Paid Use of Stated-owned Resources (Assets)	其他收入 Other Income
合肥市	Hefei	1263682	195533	151910		481685	292396
淮北市	Huaibei	46587	26440	23388	92	93192	35198
亳州市	Bozhou	82216	48987	42942	338	380792	31813
宿州市	Suzhou	63894	85427	56754	15657	370928	55919
蚌埠市	Bengbu	113372	95751	55810	71985	324924	41380
阜阳市	Fuyang	108079	75114	106063	4071	250810	45061
淮南市	Huainan	71206	35088	41938	8200	258502	32476
滁州市	Chuzhou	149957	66267	116976	13371	873308	73323
六安市	Luan	91629	80705	58143		271520	32984
马鞍山市	Maanshan	103950	75654	52971		403079	24108
芜湖市	Wuhu	421382	118500	46807	178152	522425	65551
宣城市	Xuancheng	85462	40238	61083	416	475456	20938
铜陵市	Tongling	50742	45486	24317		139462	19503
池州市	Chizhou	42988	17510	23352	8870	195180	14759
安庆市	Anqing	120616	77126	62129	38	177134	45972
黄山市	Huangshan	29378	26986	28381	3299	364465	28737

7—7 各市一般公共预算支出（2022年）
Expenditures in General Public Budgets by Region (2022)

单位：万元（10000 yuan）

地区	Region	支出合计 Total Expenditure	一般公共服务 General Public Service	国防 National Defence	公共安全 Public Security	教育 Education	科学技术 Science
合肥市	Hefei	13801794	812285	9714	479103	2363239	2456708
淮北市	Huaibei	2140233	155447	1852	90854	396734	88766
亳州市	Bozhou	3971840	343665	4332	129592	815153	68306
宿州市	Suzhou	5021054	385894	3740	207089	979848	79216
蚌埠市	Bengbu	3595272	243341	2405	168429	664949	210502
阜阳市	Fuyang	6467379	480058	3531	253450	1308630	85741
淮南市	Huainan	2994527	238035	5459	156482	510961	44905
滁州市	Chuzhou	5134690	391538	3767	242805	841046	159453
六安市	Luan	5283131	408097	3784	186268	973745	61308
马鞍山市	Maanshan	3178088	227177	802	151769	423935	138429
芜湖市	Wuhu	5828795	360939	5599	224489	889423	730404
宣城市	Xuancheng	3485443	315241	1723	161012	456871	127557
铜陵市	Tongling	2008682	141518	926	90742	280788	138645
池州市	Chizhou	2018003	159723	1591	83823	275892	27505
安庆市	Anqing	5314193	407793	3246	191389	946874	134121
黄山市	Huangshan	2212819	197934	3748	120167	245631	54577

地区	Region	文化旅游体育与传媒 Culture, Tourism, Sports and Media	社会保障和就业 Social Security and Employment	卫生健康 Health and Hygiene	节能环保 Energy Saving and Environmental Protection	城乡社区 Urban and Rural Communities	农林水 Agriculture and Forestry Water
合肥市	Hefei	97195	1381453	1140501	531658	1991980	903136
淮北市	Huaibei	22070	281279	208842	33290	348305	228160
亳州市	Bozhou	25020	714510	634887	49533	110748	609632
宿州市	Suzhou	51772	776266	599471	109553	475837	781455
蚌埠市	Bengbu	29141	559045	371037	34780	416521	407047
阜阳市	Fuyang	42241	1128367	928638	113256	379810	995339
淮南市	Huainan	25572	509530	301466	59116	144707	564806
滁州市	Chuzhou	61214	776529	564930	69099	510175	797921
六安市	Luan	60572	845261	621256	95273	453361	985775
马鞍山市	Maanshan	45347	407771	267023	186436	619370	282119
芜湖市	Wuhu	74485	740152	532580	328372	610866	472576
宣城市	Xuancheng	41509	501655	374625	54541	420174	521385
铜陵市	Tongling	19952	296369	214151	31021	225724	211459
池州市	Chizhou	27458	303372	208989	67324	260907	295831
安庆市	Anqing	62683	747944	564575	107416	441812	941697
黄山市	Huangshan	54593	334172	215170	64699	269237	309559

7—7 续表 continued

单位：万元（10000 yuan）

地 区	Region	交通运输 Transport	资源勘探工业信息等 Resources Exploration Industry Information, Etc	商 业 服务业等 Commercial and Service Industry and So On	金 融 Financial	援助其他地 区 Aid Spending Elsewhere	自然资源海洋气象等 Natural Resources, Marine Meteorology, etc.
合 肥 市	Hefei	197378	429362	211882	208941		115611
淮 北 市	Huaibei	66952	20482	15502	540		11282
亳 州 市	Bozhou	127742	73077	17884	3643		15993
宿 州 市	Suzhou	258601	36560	17378	745		29878
蚌 埠 市	Bengbu	117908	37773	41088	3929		41274
阜 阳 市	Fuyang	202708	97071	37923	91714		37549
淮 南 市	Huainan	131354	29639	32025	3750		21154
滁 州 市	Chuzhou	196942	123780	12775	8133	80	65708
六 安 市	Luan	259240	33040	34794	3483		31403
马鞍山市	Maanshan	89146	41251	22949	3449	294	21579
芜 湖 市	Wuhu	165459	223205	58069	16408		35632
宣 城 市	Xuancheng	155781	102667	8596	1757		35510
铜 陵 市	Tongling	101618	37121	72118	627		19063
池 州 市	Chizhou	76798	21396	4644	1644		17335
安 庆 市	Anqing	266046	62485	94144	4318		31337
黄 山 市	Huangshan	121842	37928	14464	9773		16098

地 区	Region	住房保障 Housing Safeguard	粮油物资储 备 Supplies of Grain and Oil and Reserve Affairs	灾害防治及应急管理 Disaster Prevention and Emergency Management	债务付息 Debt Servicing	债务发行费 用 Debt Issuance Costs	其他支出 Other Expenditure
合 肥 市	Hefei	256025	14242	49645	146650	420	4666
淮 北 市	Huaibei	122421	3211	9897	33675	105	567
亳 州 市	Bozhou	137777	1635	15487	72912	255	57
宿 州 市	Suzhou	117657	13155	20871	74935	292	841
蚌 埠 市	Bengbu	165576	4140	17296	58905	186	
阜 阳 市	Fuyang	154379	12827	24377	88143	327	1300
淮 南 市	Huainan	138373	4878	22578	49520	172	45
滁 州 市	Chuzhou	166239	5278	35824	84665	280	16509
六 安 市	Luan	105960	6986	22690	87123	264	3448
马鞍山市	Maanshan	133816	3285	21618	87989	259	2275
芜 湖 市	Wuhu	178056	2751	21088	150992	456	6794
宣 城 市	Xuancheng	101314	2158	22465	71021	274	7607
铜 陵 市	Tongling	71195	2193	11482	38918	137	2915
池 州 市	Chizhou	113371	882	11415	57630	185	288
安 庆 市	Anqing	170402	11598	28485	87555	289	7984
黄 山 市	Huangshan	59309	2391	14703	44686	134	22004

7—8 各县（市）一般公共预算收入（2022年）
General Public Budget Revenue by County (City) (2022)

单位：万元（10000 yuan）

县（市） County (City)	收入合计 Total Revenue	增值税 Value-added Tax	企业所得税 Enterprises' Income Tax	个人所得税 Individual Income Tax	资源税 Resources Tax	城市维护建设税 Tax on Town Maintenance and Construction
合肥市本级 Hefei City at Its Own Level	5295727	1747040	495043	185446	12	291005
巢湖市 Chaohu	261875	78195	18848	5919	8118	9604
长丰县 Changfeng	549015	219564	24882	5824	3	18101
肥东县 Feidong	600543	240328	27923	5806		19335
肥西县 Feixi	638460	175634	30311	8225		17620
庐江县 Lujiang	262303	124269	19296	3024	12866	11025
淮北市本级 Huaibei City at Its Own Level	486366	213501	65460	6685	14366	32676
濉溪县 Suixi	283471	116201	27868	2000	19779	13113
亳州市本级 Bozhou City at Its Own Level	494230	155529	44416	5651	5	31662
涡阳县 Guoyang	209961	54728	12566	1677	6563	5538
蒙城县 Mengcheng	278201	52228	8729	1803	5654	5710
利辛县 Lixin	191768	45870	11555	1301	1886	4240
宿州市本级 Suzhou City at Its Own Level	557340	219797	26377	4542		27360
砀山县 Dangshan	145404	41785	1301	686		4509
萧县 Xiaoxian	205379	50068	10930	1080	7731	4516
灵璧县 Lingbi	142906	28359	4426	1418	452	3053
泗县 Sixian	150658	23687	3801	750		2335
蚌埠市本级 Bengbu City at Its Own Level	623045	165092	28232	6106	2577	86449
怀远县 Huaiyuan	264245	77825	5494	1293		6950
五河县 Wuhe	162023	43313	4365	1191	35	3878
固镇县 Guzhen	166577	41912	4241	1238		3739
阜阳市本级 Fuyang City at Its Own Level	352074	142064	23070	5028		43065
界首市 Jieshou	203222	100377	4894	2635		15104
临泉县 Linquan	185961	38816	9174	2071	41	4421
太和县 Taihe	215157	76806	9036	2392		9161
阜南县 Funan	155480	57879	7349	1428		4402
颍上县 Yingshang	311763	93674	26856	2740	23272	9008
淮南市本级 Huainan City at Its Own Level	443156	96074	23044	5512	14693	10030
凤台县 Fengtai	326592	154126	4606	3956	48174	14002
寿县 Shouxian	192337	38827	5091	1330	961	3592
滁州市本级 Chuzhou City at Its Own Level	604622	134533	38107	7865		41995
天长市 Tianchang	467416	127285	15801	3049	2145	13424
明光市 Mingguang	223923	36349	6135	2383	2229	4793
来安县 Laian	254334	59135	14475	2529	577	6132
全椒县 Quanjiao	245341	47355	10146	2034	3084	4518
定远县 Dingyuan	258047	37188	8182	1390	7004	3811
凤阳县 Fengyang	405000	83601	21004	13127	18212	8351

7—8 续表1 continued

单位：万元（10000 yuan）

县（市） County (City)	收入合计 Total Revenue	增值税 Value-added Tax	企业所得税 Enterprises' Income Tax	个人所得税 Individual Income Tax	资源税 Resources Tax	城市维护建设税 Tax on Town Maintenance and Construction
六安市本级 Luan City at Its Own Level	416189	95781	24073	5715		13147
霍邱县 Huoqiu	250186	87103	29134	1555	24099	7893
舒城县 Shucheng	218458	82012	8657	2126	3435	6987
金寨县 Jinzhai	200337	83742	8017	1835	3016	7003
霍山县 Huoshan	168601	60512	14342	1990	5407	8685
马鞍山市本级 Maanshan City at Its Own Level	726019	290732	32395	11298	5587	40729
当涂县 Dangtu	366020	158000	17287	7506	3338	14015
含山县 Hanshan	165323	69986	7188	1096	7549	5596
和县 Hexian	298824	132194	15628	7220	9262	12788
芜湖市本级 Wuhu City at Its Own Level	1480596	389274	122823	27991		123170
无为市 Wuwei	307749	108313	20316	1793	6647	11395
南陵县 Nanling	236708	95021	7004	2380	888	7439
宣城市本级 Xuancheng City at Its Own Level	276958	69180	13594	3108	1916	11223
宁国市 Ningguo	372265	120568	20865	15962	6113	13923
广德市 Guangde	359172	137342	25243	5343	10456	12141
郎溪县 Langxi	220504	67789	9151	2160	2139	6094
泾县 Jingxian	165847	59327	5733	1844	3641	4956
绩溪县 Jixi	88820	22790	3682	1450	259	2445
旌德县 Jingde	67977	15868	1579	2634	1885	1199
铜陵市本级 Tongling City at Its Own Level	472569	123340	61884	3469	20638	19323
枞阳县 Zongyang	122998	46729	7310	813	7483	4388
池州市本级 Chizhou City at Its Own Level	292470	82719	15293	3499	297	13596
东至县 Dongzhi	131913	29752	10645	2770	3741	2816
石台县 Shitai	28987	8524	958	4038	2544	528
青阳县 Qingyang	119093	41069	8142	2059	9928	3619
安庆市本级 Anqing City at Its Own Level	542112	213498	21380	10344	1186	51193
桐城市 Tongcheng	222780	71669	9388	4186	535	9970
潜山市 Qianshan	110808	38637	2248	825	867	3099
怀宁县 Huaining	165657	46857	12736	1774	10277	4197
太湖县 Taihu	86001	29372	2971	1341	547	2669
宿松县 Susong	105305	32789	3320	1323	2118	2669
望江县 Wangjiang	85906	34314	1938	2143		2666
岳西县 Yuexi	81232	30546	2537	1295	789	2364
黄山市本级 Huangshan City at Its Own Level	234983	33155	7389	2906		5301
歙县 Shexian	149180	36143	5555	2355	415	2977
休宁县 Xiuning	105178	18186	1904	941	608	1866
黟县 Yixian	43969	10340	1495	482	217	760
祁门县 Qimen	61959	15933	1338	504	364	1226

7—8 续表2 continued

单位：万元（10000 yuan）

县（市） County (City)	房产税 Tax on Real Estates	城镇土地使用税 Tax on the Use of Urban Land	土地增值税 Land Value Added Tax	耕地占用税 Tax on The Occupancy of Cultivated Land	契税 Contract Tax	其他各项税收 Other Income of Tax
合肥市本级 Hefei City at Its Own Level	123320	80627	62423	5069	657437	105263
巢湖市 Chaohu	8836	6857	9219	3136	16330	28255
长丰县 Changfeng	17609	12876	22588	1198	46826	8690
肥东县 Feidong	16980	11604	42545	3070	47110	33420
肥西县 Feixi	21734	12846	64763	1702	113291	12152
庐江县 Lujiang	6220	6519	4375	9729	12655	5577
淮北市本级 Huaibei City at Its Own Level	8950	9409	3608	927	41246	11427
濉溪县 Suixi	5843	9306	5699	1110	12009	5547
亳州市本级 Bozhou City at Its Own Level	15014	20578	23753		30135	12221
涡阳县 Guoyang	4703	7903	1225	6052	26924	5181
蒙城县 Mengcheng	5485	11387	7249	8334	24179	7121
利辛县 Lixin	2642	6534	17171	3684	16310	4076
宿州市本级 Suzhou City at Its Own Level	14319	20149	7929	1873	36550	13294
砀山县 Dangshan	1544	2103	6115	74	10563	4178
萧县 Xiaoxian	2022	3524	7834	3972	15075	3970
灵璧县 Lingbi	2375	2441	8126	86	12596	4124
泗县 Sixian	4378	2119	6293	2069	17194	4223
蚌埠市本级 Bengbu City at Its Own Level	12887	14416	12965	1169	53657	5837
怀远县 Huaiyuan	4520	8808	5686	5204	12634	4881
五河县 Wuhe	2238	3729	5031	2346	10808	2885
固镇县 Guzhen	2422	6911	4166	505	7823	5706
阜阳市本级 Fuyang City at Its Own Level	4251	7217	1428		6567	5292
界首市 Jieshou	3261	4294	5390	4791	12820	6965
临泉县 Linquan	2687	3814	12776	4576	24148	3367
太和县 Taihe	3752	6161	8498	1754	18787	5109
阜南县 Funan	1756	3572	14994	8585	12053	2855
颍上县 Yingshang	4319	6294	9473	17402	10527	5981
淮南市本级 Huainan City at Its Own Level	9506	16113	6352	581	40593	6447
凤台县 Fengtai	7695	5822	546	132	10706	8101
寿县 Shouxian	2415	2794	5289	8473	9686	2261
滁州市本级 Chuzhou City at Its Own Level	25717	38269	12831	81	50968	12850
天长市 Tianchang	14249	35517	10676	13802	24965	9103
明光市 Mingguang	2813	13819	8318	5631	6321	2107
来安县 Laian	8062	16982	13421	10508	12157	6622
全椒县 Quanjiao	14230	18748	4889	5854	14033	3489
定远县 Dingyuan	5093	9970	2238	7758	7850	2597
凤阳县 Fengyang	6620	19746	4983	11233	16216	4908

7—8 续表3 continued

单位：万元（10000 yuan）

县（市） County (City)	房产税 Tax on Real Estates	城镇土地使用税 Tax on the Use of Urban Land	土地增值税 Land Value Added Tax	耕地占用税 Tax on The Occupancy of Cultivated Land	契税 Contract Tax	其他各项税收 Other Income of Tax
六安市本级 Luan City at Its Own Level	8611	15240	16517	531	36575	3924
霍邱县 Huoqiu	4576	5412	2728	34	7375	4817
舒城县 Shucheng	5702	4602	6620	368	17530	3529
金寨县 Jinzhai	3360	5715	5774	7000	14300	7292
霍山县 Huoshan	4343	5069	2959	3622	11244	2923
马鞍山市本级 Maanshan City at Its Own Level	31114	22144	5324	368	39229	25644
当涂县 Dangtu	8661	8242	6986	798	12535	7549
含山县 Hanshan	3330	5058	3695	1346	6273	2445
和县 Hexian	5736	12936	2274	3441	13246	5541
芜湖市本级 Wuhu City at Its Own Level	40301	53424	5598	830	18058	41776
无为市 Wuwei	4206	10216	6001	2742	15636	4736
南陵县 Nanling	3343	10164	3742	1292	9810	4648
宣城市本级 Xuancheng City at Its Own Level	10774	48382	12221	1740	12344	8637
宁国市 Ningguo	8960	27838	5546	4269	18418	9129
广德市 Guangde	12815	15462	10080	3782	22349	7268
郎溪县 Langxi	8691	9430	5356	2970	12776	4760
泾县 Jingxian	1685	2668	2582	146	6139	2805
绩溪县 Jixi	1723	3302	5797	270	4082	1055
旌德县 Jingde	1707	1486	2147	1641	2706	1221
铜陵市本级 Tongling City at Its Own Level	11504	26112	1693	1938	23161	10362
枞阳县 Zongyang	2555	2548	2020	1340	6065	2172
池州市本级 Chizhou City at Its Own Level	9965	14147	8899	175	18421	5403
东至县 Dongzhi	2071	2164	228	190	4156	4894
石台县 Shitai	303	176	-921	179	745	393
青阳县 Qingyang	2582	4205	3722	1056	6500	2622
安庆市本级 Anqing City at Its Own Level	11084	20130	9543	4229	33822	12160
桐城市 Tongcheng	5957	11586	17436	1100	13567	4681
潜山市 Qianshan	1880	2215	3030	6819	7238	2802
怀宁县 Huaining	3975	5143	6555	3173	17013	4770
太湖县 Taihu	2103	3336	4854	118	5485	2577
宿松县 Susong	2071	2333	3024	472	7239	1892
望江县 Wangjiang	1610	1903	3621	624	7700	1861
岳西县 Yuexi	1699	2910	3318	221	4239	4582
黄山市本级 Huangshan City at Its Own Level	5283	5671	22095	60	23295	2362
歙县 Shexian	3321	3902	5116	1707	16305	2539
休宁县 Xiuning	1318	2407	5415	2261	3905	3244
黟县 Yixian	1356	1451	1213	1363	1869	422
祁门县 Qimen	1002	1108	906	4045	3407	699

7—8 续表4 continued

单位：万元（10000 yuan）

县（市） County (City)	专项收入 Expert Project Income	行政事业性收费 Administrative and Institutional Fees	罚没收入 Penalty and Confiscatory Income	国有资本经营 Stated-owned Assets Profit	国有资源(资产)有偿使用 Income from the Paid Use of Stated-owned Resources (Assets)	其他收入 Other Income
合肥市本级 Hefei City at Its Own Level	950757	73235	52639		276463	189948
巢湖市 Chaohu	19216	3686	19009		25926	721
长丰县 Changfeng	114269	12422	3931		22193	18039
肥东县 Feidong	83738	21555	15685		30875	569
肥西县 Feixi	62962	25293	11890		54984	25053
庐江县 Lujiang	18745	3421	8370		7582	8630
淮北市本级 Huaibei City at Its Own Level	28475	10413	9816	92	18280	11035
濉溪县 Suixi	14994	7698	6930		27344	8030
亳州市本级 Bozhou City at Its Own Level	35153	10514	15205		88663	5731
涡阳县 Guoyang	6462	4131	6254		58521	1533
蒙城县 Mengcheng	7882	4110	6031		112999	9300
利辛县 Lixin	5322	12646	5013	338	44039	9141
宿州市本级 Suzhou City at Its Own Level	26351	29209	18263	7000	95523	8804
砀山县 Dangshan	5890	27191	5980		32676	809
萧县 Xiaoxian	8818	3831	8802		68805	4401
灵璧县 Lingbi	4682	5342	9172		55040	1214
泗县 Sixian	3274	8210	5238	8657	54140	4290
蚌埠市本级 Bengbu City at Its Own Level	66190	36764	28132	29200	44009	29363
怀远县 Huaiyuan	15807	24874	6085		81610	2574
五河县 Wuhe	6119	15242	5926		50715	4202
固镇县 Guzhen	6555	8303	4785		65230	3041
阜阳市本级 Fuyang City at Its Own Level	34642	24055	24975	41	19251	11128
界首市 Jieshou	16322	2522	7372	2030	10473	3972
临泉县 Linquan	6931	6328	7361		54727	4723
太和县 Taihe	17205	18292	20886		14816	2502
阜南县 Funan	7874	6617	11119		12297	2700
颍上县 Yingshang	10964	10514	24726		40200	15813
淮南市本级 Huainan City at Its Own Level	36773	16215	20439	7000	108481	25303
凤台县 Fengtai	18093	5455	2561	400	41448	769
寿县 Shouxian	12796	5927	3479		86059	3357
滁州市本级 Chuzhou City at Its Own Level	38301	21393	29711	13371	117668	20962
天长市 Tianchang	23046	14094	28746		107637	23877
明光市 Mingguang	5947	3789	6086		114397	2806
来安县 Laian	15271	4168	7477		74342	2476
全椒县 Quanjiao	19604	6693	4471		79310	6883
定远县 Dingyuan	25694	4502	6887		115150	12733
凤阳县 Fengyang	10784	853	3850		179320	2192

7—8 续表5 continued

单位：万元（10000 yuan）

县（市） County (City)	专项收入 Expert Project Income	行政事业性收费 Administrative and Institutional Fees	罚没收入 Penalty and Confiscatory Income	国有资本经营 Stated-owned Assets Profit	国有资源(资产)有偿使用 Income from the Paid Use of Stated-owned Resources (Assets)	其他收入 Other Income
六安市本级 Luan City at Its Own Level	15717	25700	20826		111637	22195
霍邱县 Huoqiu	12708	19545	8644		33268	1295
舒城县 Shucheng	10141	7838	4595		49052	5264
金寨县 Jinzhai	16848	15038	255		18963	2179
霍山县 Huoshan	11912	3420	7371		23773	1029
马鞍山市本级 Maanshan City at Its Own Level	50437	16879	13867		127195	13077
当涂县 Dangtu	18299	31903	10029		55720	5152
含山县 Hanshan	7138	11401	3844		25557	3821
和县 Hexian	15312	7461	7184		47410	1191
芜湖市本级 Wuhu City at Its Own Level	315051	77794	21883	36689	159744	46190
无为市 Wuwei	19606	6988	3925	2052	77425	5752
南陵县 Nanling	16617	4503	5421	58411	3022	3003
宣城市本级 Xuancheng City at Its Own Level	11758	9134	22266	416	27130	13135
宁国市 Ningguo	17218	7415	8086		86361	1594
广德市 Guangde	19006	9801	11345		53576	3163
郎溪县 Langxi	9287	2100	3926		72957	918
泾县 Jingxian	7070	4987	4032		57378	854
绩溪县 Jixi	4006	2539	3611		30896	913
旌德县 Jingde	2135	2063	2820		26530	356
铜陵市本级 Tongling City at Its Own Level	32796	25400	12474		86965	11510
枞阳县 Zongyang	7363	6836	5124		13709	6543
池州市本级 Chizhou City at Its Own Level	13875	9272	9788	8870	64283	13968
东至县 Dongzhi	6030	2119	5661		54419	257
石台县 Shitai	2500	984	2475		5130	431
青阳县 Qingyang	5958	5033	5300		25605	103
安庆市本级 Anqing City at Its Own Level	51904	19439	18441		36656	27103
桐城市 Tongcheng	10700	11346	9768		38447	2444
潜山市 Qianshan	9234	4916	4155		21052	1791
怀宁县 Huaining	10282	21053	9914		3957	3981
太湖县 Taihu	4606	4044	5676		13637	2665
宿松县 Susong	4159	1282	629		39859	126
望江县 Wangjiang	4100	9766	5910		6081	1669
岳西县 Yuexi	3972	2197	6338		13157	1068
黄山市本级 Huangshan City at Its Own Level	6888	6820	8861	3275	90222	11400
歙县 Shexian	5401	4642	4913	2	51954	1933
休宁县 Xiuning	3000	1695	3559	22	52679	2168
黟县 Yixian	2040	963	1380		15879	2739
祁门县 Qimen	3113	1270	3019		20601	3424

7—9 各县（市）一般公共预算支出（2022年）
Expenditures in General Public Budgets by County (City) (2022)

单位：万元（10000 yuan）

县（市）	County (City)	支出合计 Total Revenue	一般公共服务 General Public Service	国防 National Defence	公共安全 Public Security	教育 Education	科学技术 Science	文化旅游体育与传媒 Culture, Tourism, Sports and Media	社会保障和就业 Social Security and Employment
合肥市本级	Hefei City at Its Own Level	6792521	271128	4623	278730	800371	1689719	60849	357342
巢湖市	Chaohu	680664	57387	1016	31406	149074	14799	3801	158682
长丰县	Changfeng	1269958	69988	546	34416	167505	347971	6459	160445
肥东县	Feidong	1104674	102765	1031	37473	160825	126699	6049	207164
肥西县	Feixi	1029343	79617	462	45447	168238	115753	8377	130366
庐江县	Lujiang	810659	66153	734	27020	154789	4980	4486	181660
淮北市本级	Huaibei City at Its Own Level	793843	46249	1557	52513	96490	43488	13046	97546
濉溪县	Suixi	788060	83447	295	25365	176335	27284	5357	100753
亳州市本级	Bozhou City at Its Own Level	1137397	78829	1871	49029	144308	31843	10464	61207
涡阳县	Guoyang	674653	54836	535	22445	159865	422	2816	177557
蒙城县	Mengcheng	704448	74055	355	20778	169107	7582	6646	156125
利辛县	Lixin	766786	65885	1501	26120	182785	395	2534	171367
宿州市本级	Suzhou City at Its Own Level	1421411	107391	1398	72965	78439	66154	23717	54558
砀山县	Dangshan	575548	42069	497	23164	141834	1217	3612	114076
萧县	Xiaoxian	803773	53364	511	30581	181369	5320	4495	177727
灵璧县	Lingbi	651097	54581		27267	174158	801	3001	135536
泗县	Sixian	620954	53846	884	29090	152335	855	13870	99898
蚌埠市本级	Bengbu City at Its Own Level	1139730	104725	1118	102898	101586	69754	19124	160492
怀远县	Huaiyuan	783784	45936	225	17733	186772	72390	2493	117226
五河县	Wuhe	503520	25984	341	16470	96397	26065	3122	101327
固镇县	Guzhen	470442	22953	155	17012	111493	11014	2403	73198
阜阳市本级	Fuyang City at Its Own Level	1592595	115645	1338	88382	111729	41212	15693	109368
界首市	Jieshou	475926	44014	245	18594	87643	24828	2590	93928
临泉县	Linquan	846077	58414		31933	240135	2021	6690	159777
太和县	Taihe	804912	54375	127	35412	169548	3097	4420	187153
阜南县	Funan	726366	44006	1052	23966	176666	2827	3149	171533
颍上县	Yingshang	909100	63809	290	28023	209355	7449	5706	196058
淮南市本级	Huainan City at Its Own Level	1128986	92767	4064	85237	120881	25298	10208	162377
凤台县	Fengtai	515594	34459	311	19543	97342	6643	3400	98013
寿县	Shouxian	780116	55896	546	27872	161352	10016	10133	120961
滁州市本级	Chuzhou City at Its Own Level	1153746	91295	1772	73987	94209	59863	26059	98639
天长市	Tianchang	736695	47456	393	39443	141736	27681	9146	107329
明光市	Mingguang	515603	40646	624	22432	83208	9467	3251	97205
来安县	Laian	427557	26905	237	17523	70176	6045	4974	83330
全椒县	Quanjiao	451162	32779	262	18598	68741	10205	3803	72884
定远县	Dingyuan	682848	47748	209	29479	105633	8540	2747	131715
凤阳县	Fengyang	647623	51216	230	28164	131388	22656	8202	111620

7—9 续表1 continued

单位：万元（10000 yuan）

县（市） County (City)	支出合计 Total Revenue	一般公共服务 General Public Service	国防 National Defence	公共安全 Public Security	教育 Education	科学技术 Science	文化旅游体育与传媒 Culture, Tourism, Sports and Media	社会保障和就业 Social Security and Employment
六安市本级 Luan City at Its Own Level	1196365	67710	1176	67663	110828	27580	22685	73328
霍邱县 Huoqiu	880820	69597	349	27303	200367	1671	5836	166054
舒城县 Shucheng	640181	47547	766	25523	140965	7375	8256	113589
金寨县 Jinzhai	793064	64458	43	22831	104689	3719	8968	186513
霍山县 Huoshan	395465	28335	200	17459	70737	5956	8252	60292
马鞍山市本级 Maanshan City at Its Own Level	1013894	90595	485	73188	87085	37097	28236	111723
当涂县 Dangtu	561715	33663		18727	84270	11947	5579	69979
含山县 Hanshan	425031	25419	112	16524	64653	10016	5550	67529
和县 Hexian	578078	30415		23109	81893	48142	4248	94447
芜湖市本级 Wuhu City at Its Own Level	2317469	116899	3094	109301	228295	384444	26874	236900
无为市 Wuwei	708428	37312	166	23548	166719	9754	18870	121077
南陵县 Nanling	430385	33202	65	19550	83700	26260	4549	90758
宣城市本级 Xuancheng City at Its Own Level	668822	69378	613	47094	24223	6556	9544	36890
宁国市 Ningguo	545436	48112	113	25295	74009	35320	7303	76784
广德市 Guangde	613281	57834	467	22095	84456	16851	5907	88548
郎溪县 Langxi	355264	38310		15180	70742	25650	4334	51354
泾县 Jingxian	329679	25077	196	17504	60868	3889	6757	67084
绩溪县 Jixi	179488	27509		10565	30000	9193	4167	29884
旌德县 Jingde	180270	17477		9989	18775	9736	1663	32300
铜陵市本级 Tongling City at Its Own Level	738827	54900	383	43941	60177	48278	12783	85647
枞阳县 Zongyang	483172	35801	151	19603	85243	36506	3038	89245
池州市本级 Chizhou City at Its Own Level	637095	43150	1079	36356	42978	15521	13447	56922
东至县 Dongzhi	425651	34338	8	18768	85682	3495	2721	70940
石台县 Shitai	155287	14339		6790	23289	447	3417	29328
青阳县 Qingyang	283375	19639	150	14624	37720	2656	4959	49779
安庆市本级 Anqing City at Its Own Level	1153915	74711	1118	55318	118081	29652	17210	134296
桐城市 Tongcheng	608989	38482	67	22668	137502	50344	7867	84078
潜山市 Qianshan	533628	46080	502	17112	102606	12355	5319	74937
怀宁县 Huaining	463614	38974	28	14428	90623	7773	6142	85526
太湖县 Taihu	506501	36738	49	17148	96776	608	6325	68205
宿松县 Susong	635076	48182	676	20252	159662	873	3771	86487
望江县 Wangjiang	466185	36749	172	17514	101276	13638	5582	78400
岳西县 Yuexi	478666	44807	634	18485	76119	17232	7343	68608
黄山市本级 Huangshan City at Its Own Level	529780	55422	1825	37637	40447	5836	21664	57985
歙县 Shexian	432521	20010	499	20037	63330	21485	5581	80669
休宁县 Xiuning	279842	27403		13980	34665	7280	4798	46715
黟县 Yixian	156234	15911	348	8641	12975	1980	9480	22187
祁门县 Qimen	224933	19328	306	9856	26340	4539	2523	38121

7—9 续表2 continued

单位：万元（10000 yuan）

县（市）	County (City)	卫生健康 Health and Hygiene	节能环保 Energy Saving and Environmental Protection	城乡社区 Expenses in Urban, Rural Areas and Communities	农林水 Agriculture and Forestry Water	交通运输 Transport	资源勘探工业信息等 Resources Exploration Industry Information, Etc	商业服务业等 Commercial and Service Industry and So On	金融 Financial
合肥市本级	Hefei City at Its Own Level	652101	340305	1226816	89601	108557	307174	117806	201743
巢湖市	Chaohu	54142	11852	33667	105428	9606	6028	1394	828
长丰县	Changfeng	76965	17351	51600	163530	20197	61050	46194	1710
肥东县	Feidong	66929	112944	29492	163917	19401	7905	4296	1056
肥西县	Feixi	88534	8918	110281	166553	26520	9782	6697	854
庐江县	Lujiang	66658	9163	37670	177661	12611	15197	2883	729
淮北市本级	Huaibei City at Its Own Level	115650	16818	143351	28899	56808	12715	8636	60
濉溪县	Suixi	49720	9752	87280	145468	6925	4680	1105	424
亳州市本级	Bozhou City at Its Own Level	363315	24139	63551	101855	59501	67431	13886	2480
涡阳县	Guoyang	61175	8799	9999	111147	16749	2471	1540	
蒙城县	Mengcheng	62903	6578	16446	134292	7042	207	134	
利辛县	Lixin	73889	4426	10426	143902	33754		369	
宿州市本级	Suzhou City at Its Own Level	330991	45712	330640	68737	131906	23308	2294	445
砀山县	Dangshan	38107	19669	41158	104204	12112	4791	7337	75
萧县	Xiaoxian	51262	25700	23776	174873	24676	1983	1755	
灵璧县	Lingbi	48289	5942	9386	123345	22012	4053	482	209
泗县	Sixian	41579	3553	48793	125021	23208	1501	388	
蚌埠市本级	Bengbu City at Its Own Level	219393	11631	125279	39983	65661	5222	5011	1497
怀远县	Huaiyuan	50379	6768	39877	153347	16066	1150	1707	655
五河县	Wuhe	32336	8471	30607	114595	12301	1138	1402	260
固镇县	Guzhen	27311	4599	53474	67321	20762	6237	22691	486
阜阳市本级	Fuyang City at Its Own Level	549979	18805	115472	110751	76031	50971	31622	89478
界首市	Jieshou	31195	52323	20778	66845	5350	3529	754	
临泉县	Linquan	63031	8760	40209	163986	28936	4935	975	
太和县	Taihe	55147	11597	57863	124510	30881	16730	2520	237
阜南县	Funan	60415	8637	12752	145957	19923	18019	403	11
颍上县	Yingshang	73807	10313	65130	167068	32554	1083	595	1700
淮南市本级	Huainan City at Its Own Level	195174	31408	65976	118400	89443	16835	14349	2445
凤台县	Fengtai	41161	15690	25813	99671	4993	3540	7353	1305
寿县	Shouxian	23713	2609	8260	284136	33538	5003	280	
滁州市本级	Chuzhou City at Its Own Level	245191	12532	115016	82867	46232	92915	4221	2017
天长市	Tianchang	65226	14694	67517	101196	33857	6323	2248	2444
明光市	Mingguang	41167	3435	65046	90988	12505	6012	284	282
来安县	Laian	34165	11234	43600	81083	14049	2230	1175	383
全椒县	Quanjiao	36589	5582	55731	101151	15434	5649	1203	182
定远县	Dingyuan	56107	7219	11828	184526	56799	1247	998	370
凤阳县	Fengyang	50318	9647	69874	105973	14684	4791	2017	1397

7—9 续表3 continued

单位：万元（10000 yuan）

县（市） County (City)	卫生健康 Health and Hygiene	节能环保 Energy Saving and Environmental Protection	城乡社区 Expenses in Urban, Rural Areas and Communities	农林水 Agriculture and Forestry Water	交通运输 Transport	资源勘探工业信息等 Resources Exploration Industry Information, Etc	商业服务业等 Commercial and Service Industry and So On	金融 Financial
六安市本级 Luan City at Its Own Level	313852	57598	155412	131175	97178	9903	6017	2443
霍邱县 Huoqiu	74979	4698	12285	232981	35558	6292	1342	
舒城县 Shucheng	50789	8080	33927	131132	38735	1484	541	72
金寨县 Jinzhai	48023	2025	116041	167006	24743	5	2010	30
霍山县 Huoshan	29436	4494	60364	67238	15480		1114	372
马鞍山市本级 Maanshan City at Its Own Level	137124	129797	169697	24325	38443	7153	7815	2682
当涂县 Dangtu	26037	7739	152674	80648	14620	14994	1478	356
含山县 Hanshan	35383	8928	86345	52888	20015	1148	726	20
和县 Hexian	30927	10587	98028	92034	11499	3466	4058	275
芜湖市本级 Wuhu City at Its Own Level	260689	276207	207317	108240	100841	66987	28433	11224
无为市 Wuwei	58629	9725	76919	118218	15954	933	698	179
南陵县 Nanling	39321	3482	28840	48453	14127	918	2262	1077
宣城市本级 Xuancheng City at Its Own Level	143676	19687	119563	56008	31550	51008	4113	1469
宁国市 Ningguo	37784	6530	83275	62391	18334	26767	835	
广德市 Guangde	65313	14724	79852	68952	45645	20652	1183	192
郎溪县 Langxi	25917	397	23169	49336	8261	3375	317	
泾县 Jingxian	24376	4451	29124	64333	9767	822	445	76
绩溪县 Jixi	15617	2914	8041	26015	5865	43	1407	20
旌德县 Jingde	13422	2574	21113	29702	11640		85	
铜陵市本级 Tongling City at Its Own Level	110404	24206	107854	16544	76263	26813	8654	227
枞阳县 Zongyang	36719	1368	17085	113260	13544	1027	417	123
池州市本级 Chizhou City at Its Own Level	92511	21182	136165	26895	38588	16572	3199	1289
东至县 Dongzhi	36671	9444	32660	86102	10974	786	232	285
石台县 Shitai	10265	4093	1438	40856	6977	295	121	70
青阳县 Qingyang	24990	2949	42132	51529	6735	101	529	
安庆市本级 Anqing City at Its Own Level	278267	38247	124939	163531	28690	15534	4073	956
桐城市 Tongcheng	34367	5998	51665	90634	26803	13398	1727	685
潜山市 Qianshan	37059	16646	37166	111856	29552	3000	2300	320
怀宁县 Huaining	43326	5595	20282	85494	19923	3191	1503	35
太湖县 Taihu	38534	15647	16846	125172	40291	8526	5963	1312
宿松县 Susong	36562	1945	60731	119831	50444	11632	7775	
望江县 Wangjiang	32938	6028	15489	98253	18400	1912	1254	985
岳西县 Yuexi	35605	6507	29363	99259	45482	2950	1895	10
黄山市本级 Huangshan City at Its Own Level	76174	32264	56573	25454	60201	13415	3688	3197
歙县 Shexian	39063	7874	38556	81392	16143	6131	1635	5546
休宁县 Xiuning	26797	4983	24884	57307	8165	3806	529	582
黟县 Yixian	11534	5082	25454	30401	2332	1259	1484	54
祁门县 Qimen	19428	4158	25241	37771	15287	3838	1035	216

7—9 续表4 continued

单位：万元（10000 yuan）

县（市） County (City)	援助其他地区 Aid Spending Elsewhere	自然资源海洋气象等 Natural Resources, Marine Meteorology, etc.	住房保障 Housing Safeguard	粮油物资储备 Supplies of Grain and Oil Reserves	灾害防治及应急管理 Disaster Prevention and Emergency Management	债务付息支出 Debt Payments	债务发行费用 Debt Issue Fee	其他支出 Other Expenditure
合肥市本级 Hefei City at Its Own Level		69755	92047	5512	25882	87604	208	4648
巢湖市 Chaohu		8251	17481	284	2515	12993	30	
长丰县 Changfeng		9020	23645	566	4462	6307	31	
肥东县 Feidong		12097	31933	731	4659	7277	31	
肥西县 Feixi		12361	32947	2405	4571	10609	33	18
庐江县 Lujiang		3965	24595	4221	3596	11832	56	
淮北市本级 Huaibei City at Its Own Level		5360	31253	963	4648	17491	65	237
濉溪县 Suixi		4642	44862	2232	3071	9027	36	
亳州市本级 Bozhou City at Its Own Level		6903	32093	730	6395	17527	40	
涡阳县 Guoyang		1391	26195	465	1929	14207	53	57
蒙城县 Mengcheng		4493	21857	211	1990	13600	47	
利辛县 Lixin		2814	29785	41	2530	14210	53	
宿州市本级 Suzhou City at Its Own Level		4680	37010	7827	8063	25068	97	11
砀山县 Dangshan		4002	6704	102	2668	8118	32	
萧县 Xiaoxian		6556	22853	70	3254	13593	55	
灵璧县 Lingbi		3739	22189	802	2068	13173	64	
泗县 Sixian		5852	7243	3538	2593	6889	18	
蚌埠市本级 Bengbu City at Its Own Level		17736	46223	1087	7655	33564	91	
怀远县 Huaiyuan		16997	40765	220	2133	10900	45	
五河县 Wuhe		2588	20522	1035	2302	6234	23	
固镇县 Guzhen		3695	18093	67	2092	5373	13	
阜阳市本级 Fuyang City at Its Own Level		10695	28146	3037	5554	17921	47	719
界首市 Jieshou		2267	13196	3090	1490	3251	16	
临泉县 Linquan		6290	13210	3026	3120	10593	36	
太和县 Taihe		9663	26399	1288	3255	10646	44	
阜南县 Funan		2132	18758	465	3846	11768	48	33
颍上县 Yingshang		5022	25119	196	2738	13037	48	
淮南市本级 Huainan City at Its Own Level		14198	43252	2827	10687	23083	77	
凤台县 Fengtai		4487	39268	618	3548	8406	30	
寿县 Shouxian		2118	14221	1433	3476	14505	48	
滁州市本级 Chuzhou City at Its Own Level	80	9872	60767	1569	12544	21852	69	178
天长市 Tianchang		26638	14153	766	2834	10586	29	15000
明光市 Mingguang		4332	23476	487	4203	6530	23	
来安县 Laian		6994	12504	607	2277	7097	27	942
全椒县 Quanjiao		4337	8007	5	3295	6697	25	3
定远县 Dingyuan		4990	15757	490	3571	12836	39	
凤阳县 Fengyang		7331	12525	844	4350	10252	37	107

7—9 续表5 continued

单位：万元（10000 yuan）

县（市） County (City)	援助其他地区 Aid Spending Elsewhere	自然资源海洋气象等 Natural Resources, Marine Meteorology, etc.	住房保障 Housing Safeguard	粮油物资储备 Supplies of Grain and Oil Reserves	灾害防治及应急管理 Disaster Prevention and Emergency Management	债务付息支出 Debt Payments	债务发行费用 Debt Issue Fee	其他支出 Other Expenditure
六安市本级 Luan City at Its Own Level		5417	18237	1351	4080	21856	46	830
霍邱县 Huoqiu		5194	20998	986	2482	11803	45	
舒城县 Shucheng		4070	10960	978	3476	9881	35	2000
金寨县 Jinzhai		2864	18042	324	3096	17594	40	
霍山县 Huoshan		4222	8232	521	3413	8695	35	618
马鞍山市本级 Maanshan City at Its Own Level	294	8153	25038	714	9121	23901	94	1134
当涂县 Dangtu		2833	15140	1129	2096	17445	47	314
含山县 Hanshan		2319	17414	714	2610	6683	35	
和县 Hexian		2899	22919	728	2648	15717	39	
芜湖市本级 Wuhu City at Its Own Level		12045	54686	1997	10443	72048	214	291
无为市 Wuwei		4224	28837	5	802	14183	50	1626
南陵县 Nanling		6636	13772	722	1930	10384	49	328
宣城市本级 Xuancheng City at Its Own Level		5432	18455	991	4682	17822	68	
宁国市 Ningguo		11937	16070	340	3354	10841	42	
广德市 Guangde		4835	17352	202	4017	11553	44	2607
郎溪县 Langxi		5911	16758		2231	8992	30	5000
泾县 Jingxian		2124	7329	91	2101	3256	9	
绩溪县 Jixi		1235	635	179	1501	4684	14	
旌德县 Jingde		709	6198	122	1090	3661	14	
铜陵市本级 Tongling City at Its Own Level		7705	22473	1261	5654	22008	82	2570
枞阳县 Zongyang		3490	16611	347	1824	7611	25	134
池州市本级 Chizhou City at Its Own Level		8405	52930	57	1414	28068	81	286
东至县 Dongzhi		1505	20186	186	2641	8000	25	2
石台县 Shitai		791	8519	15	1055	3169	13	
青阳县 Qingyang		4418	12667	237	1661	5878	22	
安庆市本级 Anqing City at Its Own Level		5740	26029	1933	4877	22790	76	7847
桐城市 Tongcheng		3289	25710	371	2227	11068	39	
潜山市 Qianshan		2427	17167	4328	4979	7892	25	
怀宁县 Huaining		4544	21579	3631	2120	8870	27	
太湖县 Taihu		4411	11509	249	3523	8629	40	
宿松县 Susong		4140	8916	133	4152	8816	30	66
望江县 Wangjiang		4163	23946	501	1165	7792	23	5
岳西县 Yuexi		2571	10892	452	2995	7410	24	23
黄山市本级 Huangshan City at Its Own Level		6693	12419	315	3187	13835	45	1504
歙县 Shexian		2412	10659	315	1158	9682	27	317
休宁县 Xiuning		2362	7776	361	2185	5246	18	
黟县 Yixian		691	2608	447	975	2376	5	10
祁门县 Qimen		1653	8414	454	1970	4443	12	

7—10 金融机构（含外资）人民币信贷资金平衡表（资金来源）
Financial Institutions (including foreign) RMB Credit Balance Sheet (funding)

（年末余额）(year-end)　　单位：万元（10000 yuan）

项　目	Item	2020	2021	2022
资金来源合计	**All Sources**	**648269406**	**713932214**	**806316377**
各项存款	Deposits	598978062	662718997	744926697
境内存款	Domestic Savings	598723549	662459387	744661345
住户存款	Household Savings	301172198	343298298	413505480
活期存款	Demand Deposits	97456824	104339148	118262494
定期及其他存款	And Other Deposits on a Regular Basis	203715374	238959150	295242987
非金融企业存款	Non-financial Corporate Deposits	160431473	173127104	178966612
活期存款	Demand Deposits	76771473	76423415	74523394
定期及其他存款	And Other Deposits on a Regular Basis	83660000	96703689	104443218
机关团体存款	Organizations Deposit	94006464	96370630	100313745
财政性存款	Fiscal Deposits	13431511	13469537	13016232
非银行业金融机构存款	Non-banking Financial Institutions Deposits	29681903	36193817	38859275
境外存款	Overseas Account	254513	259611	265352
金融债券	Financial Bonds	6346902	5640827	5749227
卖出回购资产	Sell Buy Assets	71023	97600	29000
借款及非银行业金融机构拆入	Borrowed Inter-bank Borrowing and Non-banking Financial Institutions	313691	732876	400276
应付及暂收款	Account Payable and Temporary Credit	16312148	17914767	19808790
各项准备	Every Capital Reserve	13880201	16381561	18110262
所有者权益	Owners' Equity	33030379	35294141	37986277
#实收资本	Paid-in Capital	12133828	11840753	12099900
其　他	Others	-20663000	-24848554	-20694152

注：1. 2019年人行对各项存款项目进行了调整，取消广义政府存款项目，将机关团体存款和财政性存款两个子项目单列，表7—11、7—12同。
2. 本表金融机构包括中国人民银行、政策性银行、国有商业银行、股份制商业银行、徽商银行、村镇银行、农村合作机构、邮储银行、财务公司、信托投资公司等。（下表同）

a) In 2019, the People's Bank of China adjusted various deposit items, cancelled the broad government deposit items, and separately listed two sub-items of institutional group deposit and financial deposit, with tables 7-11 and 7-12 being the same.

b) Financial institutions included in the people's bank of China, policy Banks, state-owned commercial Banks, joint-stock commercial Banks, the anhui merchants bank, village Banks, rural cooperative organizations, post office, Banks, financial companies, trust investment companies, etc. (the same as in the table below)

7—11 金融机构（含外资）人民币信贷资金平衡表（资金运用）
Financial Institutions (including foreign) RMB Credit Balance Sheet (fund use)

（年末余额）(year-end) 单位：万元（10000 yuan）

项目	Item	2020	2021	2022
资金运用合计	**Total of Capital Utilization**	**648269406**	**713932214**	**806316377**
各项贷款	Loans	515205192	581510003	670483850
境内贷款	Within the Boundaries Loan	514949796	581103152	669860734
住户贷款	Households Loans	214756881	245137611	266620832
短期贷款	Short-term Loan	41801179	51478644	64040148
消费贷款	Consumer Loans	13836447	16042080	18622552
经营贷款	Business Loans	27964732	35436564	45417595
中长期贷款	Medium and Long-term Loan	172955702	193658967	202580684
消费贷款	Consumer Loans	154614142	173291146	179501795
经营贷款	Business Loans	18341560	20367822	23078888
企（事）业单位贷款	Enterprise (business) Loan	300179915	335945540	403239902
短期贷款	Short-term Loan	89772297	89140821	99560326
中长期贷款	Medium and Long-term Loan	175241949	206191805	255481417
票据融资	Bill Financing	27908664	33164237	40549595
融资租赁	Financing Lease	6727256	7023109	7269766
各项垫款	The Advances	529748	425569	378798
非银行业金融机构贷款	Loans From Non-banking Financial Institutions	13000	20000	
境外贷款	Beyond Border Loan	255396	406852	623117
债券投资	Bond Investment	53661104	59345997	72325437
股权及其他投资	Equity and Other Investment	36303520	37636111	35491986
买入返售资产	Buy Back to Sell Assets	686603	1893663	2466986
存放非银行业金融机构款项	Storage of Non-banking Financial Institutions	156217	378276	439073
联行往来（净）	Jones Lang Lasalle Exchanges (net)	33237163	23891571	15299363
境内存放二级准备金	Stored in the Secondary Reserve	2353856	2349828	2276260
应收及预付款	Receivables and Prepayments	4669707	4835637	5350116
投资性房地产	Investment of Real Estate	9014	8259	7699
固定资产	Fixed Assets	4340886	4432698	4451867

7—12 金融机构（含外资）本外币合并信贷收支
Local and Foreign Financial Institutions (including foreign) Merging the Credit Balance of Payments

（年末余额）(year-end) 单位：万元（10000 yuan）

项　　目	Item	2020	2021	2022
各项存款	**Deposits**	**604683424**	**668685492**	**751960895**
境内存款	Domestic Savings	604234312	668088728	750763066
住户存款	Household Savings	302071141	344176097	414419429
活期存款	Demand Deposits	97970869	104864571	118772761
定期及其他存款	And Other Deposits on a Regular Basis	204100272	239311527	295646668
非金融企业存款	Non-financial Corporate Deposits	164977282	177825769	184104996
活期存款	Demand Deposits	79526635	79454441	77719332
定期及其他存款	And Other Deposits on a Regular Basis	85450647	98371329	106385664
机关团体存款	Organizations Deposit	94041621	96403253	100351770
财政性存款	Fiscal Deposits	13431511	13469537	13016232
非银行业金融机构存款	Non-banking Financial Institutions Deposits	29712758	36214071	38870638
境外存款	Overseas Account	449112	596764	1197829
各项贷款	**Loans**	**521249672**	**586698199**	**674662013**
境内贷款	Within the Boundaries Loan	519022978	584646594	672256433
住户贷款	Households Loans	214759560	245140831	266625611
短期贷款	Short-term Loan	41803742	51481798	64044851
中长期贷款	Medium and Long-term Loan	172955817	193659033	202580760
企（事）业单位贷款	Enterprise (business) Loan	304250419	339485763	405630823
短期贷款	Short-term Loan	91324794	90776387	100474209
中长期贷款	Medium and Long-term Loan	177759926	208096461	256958455
票据融资	Bill Financing	27908664	33164237	40549595
融资租赁	Financing Lease	6727256	7023109	7269766
各项垫款	The Advances	529778	425569	378798
非银行业金融机构贷款	Loans From Non-banking Financial Institutions	13000	20000	
境外贷款	Beyond Border Loan	2226693	2051605	2405579

7—13 各市金融机构（含外资）本外币合并信贷收支（2022年）

Local and Foreign Financial Institutions (including foreign) Merging the Credit Balance of Payments by Region (2022)

（年末余额）(year-end) 单位：万元（10000 yuan）

地 区	Region	各项存款 Deposits	住户存款 Household Savings	非金融企业存款 Non-financial Corporate Deposits	机关团体存款 Organizations Deposit	财政性存款 Fiscal Deposits	非银行业金融机构存款 Non-banking Financial Institutions Deposits	各项贷款 Loans
总 计	**Total**	**751960895**	**414419429**	**184104996**	**100351770**	**13016232**	**38870638**	**674662013**
合 肥 市	Hefei	230966379	80058769	78989412	47414560	7851376	15670131	235655494
淮 北 市	Huaibei	20518511	12941703	4445542	2974765	144952	4968	15951480
亳 州 市	Bozhou	32131296	23103676	5409027	3219616	380669	16830	31186694
宿 州 市	Suzhou	33947342	24436948	5551373	3567500	387013	1457	30344733
蚌 埠 市	Bengbu	30102622	19487828	6061269	4138174	346149	62483	29780024
阜 阳 市	Fuyang	53571557	41667161	6061926	5438293	232566	167687	47027317
淮 南 市	Huainan	29732597	20905760	4691647	3448447	195632	487886	21906695
滁 州 市	Chuzhou	40517977	25287619	9211399	4800785	719821	486787	40277640
六 安 市	Luan	38644415	26748180	6360011	4788730	651839	92082	33947408
马鞍山市	Maanshan	34158145	20115371	11067311	2161073	194908	585441	29110798
芜 湖 市	Wuhu	58484353	30456514	21941000	5031753	455794	484614	52852413
宣 城 市	Xuancheng	27795892	18043321	5745062	3302433	635355	63396	24111147
铜 陵 市	Tongling	21014732	13382982	5057553	1693297	66480	811502	16814197
池 州 市	Chizhou	15532937	11547329	2520913	1207686	246915	4975	12476292
安 庆 市	Anqing	46782143	33605846	7842766	4778059	313532	234947	34887648
黄 山 市	Huangshan	18317036	12560640	3144583	2386598	193181	26525	14466238
安徽省本部	Based in Anhui province	19742960	69782	4200		51	19668927	3865795

7—14 人民币信贷收支情况（2022年）
Credit Receipts and Payments (2022)

（年末余额）(year-end)　　　　单位：万元（10000 yuan）

项　目	Item	中资全国性大型银行 Chinese Large National Banks	中资全国性中小型银行 Chinese National Small and Medium-sized Banks	中资区域性中小型银行 Chinese Regional Small and Medium-sized Banks	村镇银行 Village Banks	农村合作机构 Rural Cooperative Organizations
各项存款	**Deposits**	**370775502**	**192045789**	**163289949**	**7859762**	**155430427**
境内存款	Domestic Savings	370615439	191941982	163289830	7859758	155430313
个人存款	Personal savings	223590048	59755241	129277388	5059797	124217591
#活期储蓄存款	Current Savings Account	77461555	16153926	24619448	754732	23864717
#定期储蓄存款	Time Deposit	78100232	29956022	98746992	4121165	94625828
#结构性存款	Structured Deposits	1208516	1558752	2539		2539
单位存款	Unit of Account	134404060	103247630	33967456	2799960	31167736
#活期存款	Demand Deposits	52935300	34443416	17190947	1527650	15663537
#定期存款	Time Deposits	24180045	18454966	8165308	636917	7528391
#保证金存款	Margin Deposits	3609594	9613831	2817531	136341	2681189
#结构性存款	Structured Deposits	2802200	3481719	800		800
国库定期存款	The Treasury Deposit	845606	1084900			
非存款类金融机构存款	The Deposit Financial Institutions Deposits	11775724	27854211	44986		44986
境外存款	Overseas Account	160063	103807	118	4	114
各项贷款	**Loans**	**326430058**	**206996847**	**123825430**	**6845607**	**116979822**
境内贷款	Within the Boundaries Loan	326011743	206804596	123825430	6845607	116979822
短期贷款	Short-term Loan	54320076	47082104	63829389	4242229	59587159
个人贷款	A Personal Loan	18103260	11642944	34188350	2918456	31269894
#个人消费贷款	Individual Consumption Loan	5613818	4828767	8149319	376691	7772628
单位贷款	Unit of The Loan	36216816	33084161	27838038	1323773	26514265
#经营贷款	Business Loans	27017824	26647824	27387190	1321993	26065197
#固定资产贷款	Fixed Asset Loan	546740	64184	215121	1780	213341
#并购贷款	Mergers and Acquisitions Loan	7500				
#贸易融资	Trade Financing	8644752	6372153	235727		235727
非存款类金融机构贷款	The Deposit Financial Institutions Loans		2355000	1803000		1803000
中长期贷款	Medium and Long-term Loan	256486821	149841483	44571168	2388200	42182968
个人贷款	Individual Loan	127276481	44928093	24896538	1875554	23020984
#个人消费贷款	Individual Consumption Loan	121562469	37438456	17830129	794010	17036120
单位贷款	Unit of the Loan	129095840	104693390	19674630	512645	19161984
#经营贷款	Management Loan	21488254	23002616	12301638	461946	11839693
#固定资产贷款	Fixed Asset Loan	105151929	79991014	7234881	50700	7184182
#并购贷款	M&A Loan	1977689	1212866	132870		132870
#贸易融资	Trade Financing	477967	486894	5240		5240
非存款类金融机构贷款	The Deposit Financial Institutions Loans	114500	220000			
票据融资	Overseas financing Loan	15202681	9528796	15400453	215162	15185291
各项垫款	Discount	2165	352212	24420	16	24404
境外贷款	Beyond Border Loan	418315	192251			

注：1．本表中资全国性大型银行包括国家开发银行、中国工商银行、中国农业银行、中国银行、中国建设银行、交通银行、中国邮政储蓄银行。

2．本表中资全国性中小型银行包括中国进出口银行、中国农业发展银行、中信银行、光大银行、招商银行、兴业银行、民生银行、华夏银行、徽商银行、九江银行、杭州银行、东莞银行、上海浦东发展银行、广发银行、渤海银行。

a) the Chinese national large Banks including China development bank, industrial and commercial bank of China, agricultural bank of China, bank of China, China construction bank, bank of communications, postal savings bank of China.

b) the Chinese national small and medium-sized Banks including the export-import bank of China, agricultural development bank of China, China everbright bank, China merchants bank, industrial bank, minsheng bank, huaxia bank, bank of anhui merchants bank, bank of jiujiang, hangzhou, dongguan bank, Shanghai pudong development bank, guangdong development bank, bank of the bohai sea.

7—15 上市公司数量
Number of Listed Companies

单位：家（unit）

年 份 Year	全省合计 Provincial Total	上交所 Shanghai Stock Exchange	深交所 Shenzhen Stock Exchange	北交所 Beijing Stock Exchange	仅发A股公司 A Share Only	发A、B股公司 A & B Share
2010	65	29	36		59	3
2012	78	29	49		72	3
2013	78	29	49		72	3
2014	80	31	49		74	3
2015	88	35	53		82	3
2016	93	37	56		87	3
2017	101	43	58		95	3
2018	103	47	56		97	3
2019	105	48	57		99	3
2020	126	57	69		120	3
2021	149	67	77	5	143	3
2022	161	72	82	7	155	3

注：仅发A股公司是指排除同时发行B股及H股的境内上市公司。

a) A-share only companies refer to domestic listed companies that exclude the simultaneous issuance of B shares and H shares.

7—16 股票发行及筹资情况
Issuing Summary for Stocks

年 份 Year	股票发行A股（万股） Amount Issued A Shares (10000 shares)	筹资额合计（万元） Raised Capital (10000 yuan)	A 股 A Shares	配股筹资 Shares Rights Issued	可转债筹资 Changeable Bonds	公司债 Corporate Bonds
2010	128849	1713126	1513126		200000	
2012	248280	1410770	415770			995000
2013	448722	2446186	1764186		32000	650000
2014	323193	1900684	1850684			50000
2015	209644	2718299	2183299			535000
2016	1140036	10357100	9970100			387000
2017	434290	4634079	3923779		119700	590600
2018	386365	5351411	3871411		230000	1250000
2019	650561	4412422	2836382		836040	740000
2020	135709	3516354	1753356	543092	919907	300000
2021	430093	12681100	4511110	396189	258200	7515600
2022	478703	13092501	1913320		1009131	10170050

注：1. 2016年以前股票发行包括首次公开发行、增发股票、认股权行权。

2. 2016年起股票发行包括首次公开发行、并购重组非公开发行、增发股票、认股权行权。

a) Prior to 2016, stock issuance includes initial public offering, additional shares and warrants.

b) Starting from 2016, stock issuance includes initial public offering, non-public offering of mergers and acquisitions, additional shares, and exercise of stock options.

7—17 各市股票发行及筹资情况（截至2022年）
Issuing Summary for Stocks by Region (As of 2022)

地 区	Region	上市公司（家）Number of Listed Companies (unit)	发行股票（只）Number of Listed Shares (unit)	股份总数（万股）Number of Shares (10000 share)	#无限售股份 Unlimited Shares	当年募集资金（万元）Raised Capital (10000 yuan)	#发行股票 Amount of Listed Shares
总 计	**Total**	**161**	**167**	**14858606**	**13346393**	**4182451**	**1913320**
合肥市	Hefei	75	77	5276369	4649978	2414698	940548
淮北市	Huaibei	4	4	538172	538172	300000	
亳州市	Bozhou	1	2	52860	52860		
宿州市	Suzhou						
蚌埠市	Bengbu	8	8	747370	719183	405099	245099
阜阳市	Fuyang	1	1	65780	65780		
淮南市	Huainan	2	2	282500	277697		
滁州市	Chuzhou	11	11	689261	422813	78000	78000
六安市	Luan	4	4	358659	350910	234000	
马鞍山市	Maanshan	7	8	1442297	1406854		
芜湖市	Wuhu	18	19	2754155	2457463	123020	22040
宣城市	Xuancheng	8	8	570897	479604	46032	
铜陵市	Tongling	11	11	1477503	1423007	179083	179083
池州市	Chizhou	4	4	135174	52011	357927	357927
安庆市	Anqing	5	5	200930	190580	44591	44591
黄山市	Huangshan	2	3	134187	133024		

注：1. 首次公开发行、并购重组非公开发行、增发股票、认股权行权募集资金包括在发行股票中。
2. 当年募集资金还包括可转债融资及公司债融资。

a) Initial public offering, merger and reorganization of non-public issues, rights to raise equity and stock rights to raise funds are included in the issuance of shares.

b) Funds raised in that year also include convertible bond financing and corporate bond financing.

7—18 保险公司业务经济技术指标（2022年）
Main Professional Technical Indicators of Insurance Companies (2022)

单位：万元（10000 yuan）

项　　目	Item	保费收入 Income From Premium	赔　付 Claim and Payment
合　计	**Total**	**14182419**	**5625464**
按公司类型分	**Divided By The Character of Company**		
财产保险公司	Property Insurance Companies	6048455	4037546
人身保险公司	Life Insurance Companies	8133964	1587918
按业务性质分	**Divided BY The Nature of The Business**		
财产保险业务	**Property Insurance Businesses**	**4869564**	**3191032**
企业财产险	Enterprise Property Insurance	110397	43648
家庭财产险	Family Property Insurance	60936	4568
机动车辆险	Motor Vehicle Insurance	3232949	2202812
工程保险	Engineering Insurance	37977	17981
责任保险	Liability Insurance	371490	149908
信用保险	Credit Insurance	40630	7197
保证保险	Guarantee Insurance	296054	198273
船舶保险	Ship Insurance	21281	9609
货物运输险	Freight Transport Insurance	35202	15040
特殊风险保险	Peculiar Risk Insurance	815	260
农业保险	Agriculture Insurance	613779	512366
其他保险	Other Insurance	48053	29371
人身保险业务	**Insurance Service of Life**	**9312855**	**2434432**
寿　险	Life Insurance	6460639	983099
健康险	Health Insurance	2504815	1349096
意外伤害险	Personal Accident Insurance	347402	102236

注：上述数据来源于各公司报送的保险数据，未经审计。因部分机构正在进行风险处置，行业汇总数据口径暂不包括这部分机构。

a) These data are from insurance data submitted by companies and are not audited. Because some institutions are in the process of risk disposal, the industry summary data caliber does not include these institutions.

主要统计指标解释

一般公共预算收入

指国家财政参与社会产品分配所取得的收入，是实现国家职能的财力保证。主要包括：

（1）税收收入：包括增值税、企业所得税、个人所得税、资源税、城市维护建设税、房产税、印花税、城镇土地使用税、土地增值税、车船税、耕地占用税、契税和烟叶税等。

（2）非税收入：包括专项收入、行政事业性收费收入、罚没收入、国有资本经营收入和国有资源（资产）有偿使用收入等。

一般公共预算支出

国家财政将筹集起来的资金进行分配使用，以满足社会各项事业发展和经济建设的需要，主要包括：

（1）一般公共服务：反映政府提供一般公共服务的支出。具体包括人大事务、政协事务、政府办公厅（室）及相关机构事务、发展与改革事务、统计信息事务、财政事务、税收事务、审计事务、海关事务、纪检监察事务、商贸事务、知识产权事务、民族事务、港澳台事务、档案事务、民主党派及工商联事务、群众团体事务、党委办公厅（室）及相关机构事务、组织事务、宣传事务、统战事务、对外联络事务、其他共产党事务支出、网信事务、市场监督管理事务、其他一般公共服务支出。

（2）公共安全：反映政府维护社会公共安全方面的支出。具体包括武装警察部队、公安、国家安全、检察、法院、司法、监狱、强制隔离戒毒、国家保密、缉私警察、其他公共安全支出等。

（3）教育：反映政府教育支出情况。具体包括教育管理事务、普通教育、职业教育、成人教育、广播电视教育、留学教育、特殊教育、进修及培训、教育费附加安排的支出、其他教育支出。

（4）科学技术：反映国家用于科学技术方面的支出。具体包括科学技术管理事务、基础研究、应用研究、技术研究与开发、科技条件与服务、社会科学、科学技术普及、科技交流与合作、科技重大项目、其他科学技术支出。

（5）文化旅游体育与传媒：反映政府在文化和旅游、文物、体育、新闻出版电影、广播影视、其他文化旅游体育与传媒支出。

（6）社会保障和就业：反映政府在社会保障与就业方面的支出。具体包括人力资源和社会保障管理事务、民政管理事务、补充全国社会保障基金、行政事业单位离退休、企业改革补助、就业补助、抚恤、退役安置、社会福利、残疾人事业、红十字事业、最低生活保障、临时救助、特困人员救助供养、补充道路交通事故社会救助基金、其他生活救助、财政对基本养老保险基金的补助、财政对其他社会保险基金的补助、退役军人管理事务、财政代缴社会保险费支出、其他社会保障和就业支出。

（7）卫生健康：反映政府用于卫生健康方面的支出。具体包括卫生健康管理事务、公立医院、基层医疗卫生机构、公共卫生、中医药、计划生育事务、行政事业单位医疗、财政对基本医疗保险基金的补助、医疗救助、优抚对象医疗、医疗保障管理事务、老龄卫生健康事务、其他卫生健康支出。

（8）节能环保：反映政府用于节能环保方面的支出。具体包括环境保护管理事务、环境监测与监察、污染防治、自然生态保护、天然林保护、退耕还林还草、风沙荒漠治理、退牧还草、已垦草原退耕还草、能源节约利用、污染减排、可再生能源、循环经济、能源管理事务、其他节能环保支出。

（9）城乡社区：反映政府用于城乡社区事务方面的支出。包括城乡社区管理事务、城乡社区规划与管理、城乡社区公共设施、城乡社区环境卫生、建设市场管理与监督、其他城乡社区支出。

（10）农林水：反映政府用于农林水事务方面的支出。具体包括农业农村、林业和草原、水利、扶贫、农村综合改革、普惠金融发展支出、目标价格补贴、其他农林水支出。

（11）交通运输：反映政府用于交通运输方面的支出。具体包括公路水路运输、铁路运输、民用航空运输、成品油价格改革对交通运输的补贴、邮政业支出、车辆购置税支出、其他交通运输支出。

信贷资金

指金融机构以信用方式积聚和分配的货币资金。金融机构信贷资金的来源有各项存款、金融债券、对国际金融机构负债、流通中现金、其他项目等；信贷资金的运用有各项贷款、有价证券及投资、黄金占款、外汇买卖、财政借款及在国际金融机构中的资产等。

存款

指企业、机关、团体或居民把货币资金存入银行或其他信贷机构保管，可随时或按约定时间支取款项，并取得一定利息的一种信用活动形式。根据存款对象或性质的不同可划分为住户存款、非金融企业存款、政府存款、非银行业金融机构存款等科目。它是银行信贷资金的主要来源。

贷款

指银行或其他信贷机构根据资金必须归还的原则，按一定利率，为企业、个人等提供资金的一种信用活动形式。我国银行贷款分为短期贷款、中长期贷款、融资租赁、票据融资、各项垫款、境外贷款等。

保费

指投保人为取得保险人在约定范围内所承担赔偿责任而支付给保险人的费用。

赔款

指保险人根据保险合同的规定，向被保险人支付的赔偿保险责任损失的金额。

给付

包括死伤医疗给付和满期给付。死伤医疗给付是指保险人根据人寿保险及长期健康保险合同的规定，因被保险人在保险期内发生保险责任范围内的保险事故支付给被保险人（或受益人）的金额。满期给付是指被保险人生存期满，保险人按人寿保险合同规定支付给被保险人的满期保险金额。

注：为反映机构改革和经济社会发展的最新变化，根据《2021 年政府收支分类科目》和《2018 中国统计年鉴》对部分财政、金融统计指标解释进行了修订。

Explanatory Notes for Major Statistical Indicators

General Public Budget Revenue

refers to the income obtained by the state finance participating in the distribution of social products, which is the financial guarantee for the realization of state functions. Mainly include:

1) Tax revenue: including value-added tax, enterprise income tax, individual income tax, resource tax, urban maintenance and construction tax, property tax, stamp tax, urban land use tax, land value-added tax, vehicle and vessel tax, farmland occupation tax, contract tax and tobacco tax, etc.

2) Non tax revenue: Include special revenue and administrative collect fees revenue, punish revenue, state-owned capital operation revenue and state-owned resource (asset) used revenue etc.

Expenditures in General Public Budgets

refers to the distribution and use of the funds the government finance has raised, so as to meet the needs of social various causes and economic construction and. It includes the following main items:

(1) General public Services: reflects government expenditure on the provision of general public services. Specific include National People's Congress, the Chinese people's political consultative conference affairs, government office (room) and the relevant agency business, the development and reform, statistics, financial affairs, tax, auditing affairs, customs affairs, discipline inspection affairs, commercial affairs, intellectual property affairs, ethnic affairs, Hong Kong, Macao and Taiwan affairs, archives, the democratic parties and federations of affairs, mass organizations, party committee Expenditures for the General Office (office) and related institutional affairs, organizational affairs, publicity affairs, United Front affairs, external liaison affairs, other Communist Party affairs, Internet and information services, market supervision and management affairs, and other general public services.

(2) Public security: reflects the government's expenditure on maintaining social public security. Specifically, it includes armed police forces, public security, national security, procuratorial work, courts, judiciary, prisons, compulsory isolation and drug rehabilitation, state secrecy, anti-smuggling police, and other public security expenditures.

(3) Education: reflects the government's expenditure on education. Specifically, it includes education management affairs, general education, vocational education, adult education, radio and television education, overseas education, special education, continuing education and training, expenses for additional arrangements for education expenses, and other education expenses.

(4) Science and technology: reflects the state's expenditure on science and technology. Specifically, it includes scientific and technological management affairs, basic research, applied research, technological research and development, scientific and technological conditions and services, social science, popularization of science and technology, scientific and technological exchanges and cooperation, major scientific and technological projects, and other scientific and technological expenditures.

(5) Culture, tourism, sports and media: reflects government expenditure on culture and tourism, cultural relics, sports, press, publication and film, radio, film and television, other culture, tourism, sports and media.

(6) Social security and employment: reflects government spending on social security and employment. Specific include human resources and social security management affairs, civil affairs, management affairs, supplement the national social security fund, retired administrative institution, enterprise reform subsidy, employment benefits, pension, retirement and resettlement, social welfare, undertakings for disabled persons, the cause of the Red Cross, the lowest life guarantee, temporary

assistance, strands personnel assistance support, supplement of road traffic accidents, the social assistance fund Financial subsidies to basic endowment insurance funds, financial subsidies to other social insurance funds, ex-servicemen's management affairs, social insurance premiums paid on behalf of the government, other social security and employment expenses.

(7) Health: Reflects government spending on health. Specifically, it includes health management affairs, public hospitals, primary medical and health institutions, public health, traditional Chinese medicine, family planning affairs, medical treatment of administrative institutions, financial subsidies to the basic medical insurance fund, medical assistance, special medical care, medical security management affairs, health care for the elderly, and other health expenditures.

(8) Energy conservation and environmental protection: reflects government expenditure on energy conservation and environmental protection. Including environmental management, environmental monitoring and supervision, pollution control, ecological protection, to protect natural forests, returning farmland to forest and grass, grazing ban, has reclamation sand desert governance, grassland conversion of grassland, energy conservation, pollution reduction, renewable energy and circular economy, energy management, energy conservation and environmental protection other spending.

(9) Urban and Rural Communities: reflect the Government's Expenditure on Urban and Rural Community Affairs. Including urban and rural community management affairs, urban and rural community planning and management, urban and rural community public facilities, urban and rural community environmental sanitation, construction market management and supervision, and other urban and rural community expenditures.

(10) Agriculture, forestry and water: reflects government expenditure on agriculture, forestry and water services. Specifically, they include agricultural and rural areas, forestry and grassland, water conservancy, poverty alleviation, comprehensive rural reform, inclusive financial development expenditure, target price subsidies, and other agricultural, forestry and water expenditure.

(11) Transportation: Reflects government spending on transportation. Specifically, it includes road and waterway transportation, railway transportation, civil aviation transportation, subsidies for transportation due to refined oil price reform, postal expenses, vehicle purchase tax expenses, and other transportation expenses.

Credit Funds

refers to the monetary funds accumulated and distributed by financial institutions through credit. Sources of credit funds of financial institutions include various deposits, financial bonds, liabilities to international financial institutions, cash in circulation, other items, etc.; The use of credit funds includes loans, securities and investments, gold deposits, foreign exchange trading, financial loans and assets in international financial institutions.

Deposit

it refers to a form of credit activity in which enterprises, government agencies, organizations or residents deposit monetary funds in banks or other credit institutions for safekeeping, can withdraw money at any time or at an agreed time, and obtain certain interest. According to the object or nature of deposit, it can be divided into household deposit, non-financial enterprise deposit, government deposit, non-banking financial institution deposit and other subjects. It is the main source of bank credit funds.

Loan

it refers to a form of credit activity in which banks or other credit institutions provide funds for enterprises and individuals at a certain interest rate according to the principle that funds must be returned. Bank loans in China are divided into short-term loans, medium-term and long-term loans, financial leasing, bill financing, various advances, overseas loans, etc.

Premium

is the fee paid by the insurant to the insurer to obtain the obligation of compensation from the insurance within the agreed terms.

Settled Claim

is the compensation paid by the insurer to the insurant in accordance with the insurance contract.

Payment

includes payment for death, injury or medical treatment and mature payment. Payment for death, injury or medical treatment refers to the money paid to the insurant (or the beneficiary) in accordance with the life or health insurance contract when the insurant encounters accidents within the insured period covered in the contract. Mature payment refers to the mature payment to the insurant in accordance with the life insurance contract at the end of the insured period.

Note: In order to reflect the latest changes in institutional reform and economic and social development, the interpretation of some fiscal and financial statistical indicators has been revised according to the Categories of Government Revenue and Expenditure in 2021 and China Statistical Yearbook in 2018.

第八篇

Chapter 8

物价指数

PRICE INDICES

简要说明

一、本篇价格指数资料，反映生产、流通与消费等环节的价格变动趋势和变动幅度。主要包括居民消费价格指数、商品零售价格指数、农产品生产者价格指数、工业生产者出厂价格指数、工业生产者购进价格指数。

二、价格指数统计由国家统计局安徽调查总队组织实施，各市、县调查队依据国家统计局统一制定的价格统计调查制度向基层采集原始数据汇总后上报。

三、消费、零售价格指数都是采用分层抽样调查方法编制的，以样本推断总体，被抽选的调查市县 19 个。

四、农产品生产者价格调查采用抽样调查和重点调查相结合的调查方法，调查采用月报和季报相结合的方式，目前我省抽选的调查县为 31 个。

五、工业生产者价格调查采用重点调查和典型调查相结合的方法，调查实行月报，调查对象包括全省 16 个市的 3100 余家工业企业。

Brief Introduction

I. Price index data reflects the trend and range of price changes in production, distribution and consumption. It mainly includes consumer price index (CPI), retail price index (RPI), producer price index (PPI) of agricultural products, producer price index (PPI) and producer purchase price index.

II. The statistics of price indices is organized by the NBS Survey Office in Anhui. The survey offices of the selected cities and counties collect statistical data from the grassroots units in accordance with the scheme of prices survey stipulated by the State Statistical Bureau, tabulate them and report them to higher agencies.

III.The consumption and retail price indices were compiled using stratified sampling survey methods. 19 cities and counties were selected for the survey.

IV. Survey on producer prices of agricultural products shall be conducted by combining sampling surveys with key surveys. The survey was conducted using a combination of monthly and quarterly reports, investigation county that my province selects at present is 31.

V. Data for the calculation of the price indices of industrial products are collected by Combination of key survey and typical survey method. The surveys are performed monthly including more than 3100 industrial enterprises in Anhui 16 cities.

8—1 各种价格总指数
Price Indices

上年=100（preceding year=100）

年 份 Year	居民消费价格指数 General Consumer Price Index	城市居民消费价格指数 Urban Areas	农村居民消费价格指数 Rural Areas	工业生产者出厂价格指数 Ex-factory Industrial Producer Price Index	工业生产者购进价格指数 Industrial Producer Purchasing Price Index
2005	101.4	101.0	101.9	103.3	107.2
2010	103.1	103.0	103.4	109.0	111.8
2014	101.6	101.7	101.5	97.4	97.2
2015	101.3	101.3	101.3	93.9	93.5
2016	101.8	101.8	101.6	98.5	98.4
2017	101.2	101.3	101.1	108.0	109.2
2018	102.0	102.0	102.0	103.0	105.3
2019	102.7	102.7	102.8	100.3	99.9
2020	102.7	102.5	102.9	99.1	98.5
2021	100.9	101.1	100.7	107.7	111.5
2022	102.0	102.1	101.8	103.2	104.0

8—2 各种价格定基指数
Fixed-base Price Indices

（1990=100）

年 份 Year	居民消费价格指数 General Consumer Price Index	城市居民消费价格指数 Urban Areas	农村居民消费价格指数 Rural Areas	工业生产者出厂价格指数 Ex-factory Industrial Producer Price Index	工业生产者购进价格指数 Industrial Producer Purchasing Price Index
2005	225.7	232.5	219.8	186.2	250.0
2010	260.9	268.1	255.1	218.2	326.6
2014	293.2	300.7	287.9	222.2	334.8
2015	297.0	304.6	291.6	208.6	313.0
2016	302.3	310.1	296.3	205.5	308.0
2017	305.9	314.1	299.6	221.9	336.3
2018	312.0	320.4	305.6	228.6	354.0
2019	320.4	329.1	314.2	229.4	353.7
2020	329.1	337.3	323.3	227.4	348.3
2021	332.1	341.0	325.6	244.9	388.4
2022	338.7	348.2	331.5	252.7	403.9

注：工业生产者出厂价格、工业生产者购进价格指数以1992年为100。
a) Index of producer price and purchase price for industrial producers was 100 in 1992.

8—3 居民消费价格分类指数（2022年）
Consumer Price Indices by Category (2022)

上年=100（preceding year=100）

类　　别	Item	全　省 Provincial Indices	城　市 Urban Indices	农　村 Rural Indices
居民消费价格总指数	**General Consumer Price Index**	**102.0**	**102.1**	**101.8**
食品烟酒	**Food Tobacco and Liquor**	**102.7**	**103.0**	**102.2**
食　品	Food	102.8	103.2	102.1
粮　食	Grain	102.0	101.8	102.3
薯　类	Potatoes	111.7	107.9	117.3
豆　类	Beans	104.0	104.5	103.1
食用油	Edible Oil	104.6	104.7	104.5
菜及食用菌	Vegetables and Edible Fungi	102.9	102.9	102.7
鲜　菜	Fresh Vegetables	102.3	102.3	102.1
畜肉类	Meat Class	97.3	97.7	96.6
禽肉类	Poultry Meat	105.4	105.4	105.5
水产品	Aquatic Products	96.6	97.0	95.7
蛋　类	Eggs	108.3	108.4	108.1
奶　类	Milk	101.7	102.3	100.5
干鲜瓜果类	Melons and Fruits	113.4	114.9	109.7
糖果糕点类	Candy Cakes Category	103.3	103.4	103.0
其他食品类	Other Food and Food Processing Services	103.5	103.5	103.6
茶及饮料	Tea and Beverages	105.9	105.2	107.0
烟　酒	Tobacco and Liquor	101.4	101.2	101.6
卷　烟	Cigarette	102.8	103.2	102.4
酒　类	Liquor	99.4	98.7	100.5
在外餐饮	Food for External Use	103.0	103.2	102.1
衣　着	**Clothing**	**101.3**	**101.0**	**101.9**
服　装	Garments	101.3	101.2	101.6
鞋　类	Footwear	101.2	100.3	103.0

8—3 续表 continued

上年=100（preceding year=100）

类　　别	Item	全　省 Provincial Indices	城　市 Urban Indices	农　村 Rural Indices
居　住	**Housing**	**99.8**	**99.8**	**99.6**
租赁房房租	Rental Housing Rentals	98.8	99.2	97.1
住房保养维修及管理	Housing Maintenance and Management	101.7	102.1	101.0
水电燃料	Water, Electricity and Fuel	102.3	101.4	103.9
自有住房	One's Own House	98.5	98.9	97.7
生活用品及服务	**Daily Necessities and Services**	**101.0**	**101.1**	**100.9**
家具及室内装饰品	Furniture and Interior Decorations	100.6	100.6	100.6
家用器具	Household Appliances	101.3	101.4	100.9
家用纺织品	Home Textiles	100.4	100.2	100.9
家庭日用杂品	Household Daily Groceries	99.6	99.5	99.8
个人护理用品	Personal Care Products	101.8	101.7	101.9
家庭服务	Family Service	104.0	104.2	103.4
交通通信	**Traffic Communication**	**105.3**	**105.4**	**105.2**
交　通	Traffic	107.6	107.6	107.7
通　信	Communication	99.0	99.0	99.0
教育文化娱乐	**Education Culture and Entertainment**	**102.8**	**103.1**	**102.1**
教　育	Education	103.7	104.3	102.5
文娱耐用消费品	Entertainment Durable Consumer Goods	98.7	98.3	99.7
旅　游	Traveling	101.5	101.5	101.3
医疗保健	**Medical Insurance**	**100.9**	**100.6**	**101.5**
药品及医疗器具	Medicine and Medical Equipment	100.2	99.7	101.1
医疗服务	Medical Service	101.2	101.0	101.6
其他用品及服务	**Other Supplies and Services**	**102.0**	**102.0**	**101.9**
其他用品	Other Supplies	102.6	102.5	102.9
其他服务	Other Services	101.2	101.5	100.4

8—4 调查市、县居民消费价格分类指数（2022年）

Consumer Price Indices by Category and by Surveyed City and County (2022)

上年=100（preceding year=100）

市 县 Surveyed City and County		总指数 General Index	食品烟酒 Food Tobacco and Liquor	食品 Food	#粮食 Grain	食用油 Edible Oil	菜及食用菌 Vegetables and Edible Fungi	鲜菜 Fresh Vegetables	畜肉类 Meat Class	禽肉类 Poultry Meat	水产品 Aquatic Products	蛋类 Eggs
合肥市	Hefei	102.4	103.6	103.7	100.1	102.8	101.6	100.6	98.3	109.7	97.5	108.0
淮北市	Huaibei	102.5	103.3	103.2	104.9	107.5	98.9	97.9	98.4	102.0	97.2	104.6
亳州市	Bozhou	101.9	103.6	104.3	103.8	108.1	102.1	101.7	97.3	106.0	97.2	104.3
宿州市	Suzhou	102.1	102.6	102.2	101.8	103.0	104.3	104.7	95.8	105.3	90.1	106.9
蚌埠市	Bengbu	101.9	102.2	102.1	100.0	105.0	101.6	100.9	97.6	100.8	96.9	108.5
阜阳市	Fuyang	101.9	102.2	102.0	101.4	103.3	99.6	98.3	95.0	105.3	97.0	115.9
淮南市	Huainan	101.9	103.0	103.5	104.0	104.8	102.7	102.4	99.6	105.7	96.8	111.0
滁州市	Chuzhou	102.1	102.1	102.4	98.8	106.5	99.4	98.4	101.6	104.9	99.5	103.4
马鞍山市	Maanshan	101.8	102.1	103.1	100.3	106.3	109.6	109.7	96.6	95.9	99.7	107.8
芜湖市	Wuhu	102.4	103.3	103.3	100.3	99.4	104.8	104.0	98.2	104.6	95.3	106.7
宣城市	Xuancheng	102.3	104.5	104.3	104.3	106.5	102.7	102.5	100.3	105.5	102.4	109.6
铜陵市	Tongling	102.0	102.5	103.8	102.0	100.3	105.4	105.4	97.3	109.3	92.7	111.9
安庆市	Anqing	102.2	102.2	102.1	100.1	107.1	104.3	104.1	96.8	107.7	91.0	106.8
六安市	Luan	102.0	102.7	103.2	103.8	109.3	105.3	104.6	96.1	104.7	99.2	105.5
庐江县	Lujiang	101.9	102.2	102.6	99.9	103.8	103.3	102.8	99.6	105.1	93.5	111.0
桐城市	Tongcheng	102.2	102.1	101.1	101.4	95.9	102.7	102.4	97.4	105.9	91.5	107.5
歙县	Shexian	102.2	102.8	103.1	101.9	106.6	106.2	106.0	93.8	103.6	98.6	113.8
阜南县	Funan	101.3	102.1	101.8	103.9	109.5	100.7	99.3	94.4	110.1	97.5	103.3
金寨县	Jinzhai	101.5	101.8	102.4	104.5	108.3	101.4	100.6	97.6	99.8	98.6	107.6

市 县 Surveyed City and County		干鲜瓜果类 Melons and Fruits	茶及饮料 Tea and Beverages	烟酒 Tobacco and Liquor	在外餐饮 Food for External Use	衣着 Clothing	居住 Housing	生活用品及服务 Daily Necessities and Services	交通通信 Traffic Communication	教育文化娱乐 Education Culture and Entertainment	医疗保健 Medical Insurance	其他用品及服务 Other Supplies and Services
合肥市	Hefei	115.9	107.9	100.9	104.8	101.2	100.3	101.4	104.8	103.2	100.3	102.1
淮北市	Huaibei	116.3	102.5	104.3	103.3	102.6	100.6	100.4	105.7	102.2	101.3	102.4
亳州市	Bozhou	122.9	106.3	104.0	101.0	101.2	98.6	101.5	104.3	103.4	100.2	101.8
宿州市	Suzhou	116.4	103.7	99.8	105.2	101.4	100.4	102.7	105.5	101.7	100.5	102.5
蚌埠市	Bengbu	113.4	100.4	104.0	101.7	100.4	100.3	100.9	105.4	101.8	101.5	102.4
阜阳市	Fuyang	113.0	105.8	101.0	102.8	101.8	98.3	100.9	106.0	107.4	98.9	101.8
淮南市	Huainan	115.3	102.9	100.7	102.8	100.1	99.7	100.2	105.0	103.1	100.0	100.6
滁州市	Chuzhou	110.1	102.2	100.7	101.8	100.8	100.2	101.1	105.1	104.1	101.8	101.8
马鞍山市	Maanshan	113.8	104.2	99.1	100.4	99.9	100.4	101.1	105.1	102.4	101.3	101.3
芜湖市	Wuhu	115.0	103.0	100.1	105.0	101.8	100.5	100.7	105.3	102.6	101.4	103.2
宣城市	Xuancheng	111.6	101.9	104.6	105.7	100.8	98.8	100.7	106.9	100.1	102.4	102.9
铜陵市	Tongling	115.8	98.1	99.4	101.0	101.0	99.2	102.1	106.6	102.7	100.4	102.1
安庆市	Anqing	115.3	104.4	102.1	102.0	101.8	100.2	101.4	106.1	103.0	101.3	102.3
六安市	Luan	111.8	111.3	100.4	101.9	99.9	99.9	100.5	106.1	103.2	99.9	101.9
庐江县	Lujiang	112.7	103.0	100.5	102.0	103.2	100.3	101.4	104.2	101.5	100.8	103.3
桐城市	Tongcheng	108.1	108.6	104.3	102.3	102.3	100.5	100.9	106.1	102.9	100.9	101.7
歙县	Shexian	111.5	108.5	100.9	102.6	100.4	101.8	101.4	105.6	100.6	100.4	101.1
阜南县	Funan	107.8	104.3	102.3	102.8	102.9	96.9	100.3	105.7	101.6	103.5	101.1
金寨县	Jinzhai	107.5	112.0	98.9	100.2	98.9	99.7	100.5	104.3	104.1	100.6	102.2

8—5 农产品生产者价格指数
Producer Price Indices of Agricultural Products

上年=100（preceding year=100）

类　别	Item	2015	2020	2021	2022
总指数	**General Index**	**99.76**	**115.62**	**101.26**	**102.78**
农业产品	**Agricultural Products**	**97.84**	**104.16**	**107.62**	**105.35**
谷　物	Cereal	98.25	104.23	106.38	106.97
小　麦	Wheat	97.93	101.80	107.23	117.35
稻　谷	Rice	99.27	103.41	103.62	98.39
玉　米	Corn	92.52	112.57	121.84	105.45
薯　类	Tubers	101.20	103.71	97.10	121.52
豆　类	Beans	95.64	120.42	115.87	106.96
油　料	Oil-bearing Crops	96.45	111.39	103.04	110.23
棉　花	Cotton	87.09	96.40	115.26	94.73
蔬　菜	Vegetables	99.96	100.97	109.49	100.55
茶	Tea	95.96	100.45	104.02	99.13
林业产品	**Forestry Products**	**95.26**	**102.90**	**102.17**	**100.42**
木　材	Timber	97.42	104.08	102.24	99.48
原　木	Logs	97.42	104.08	102.24	99.48
竹　材	Bamboo Material	93.01	98.75	100.49	100.82
牧　业(饲养动物及其产品)	**Animal Husbandry (Breeding Animals and Their Products)**	**105.05**	**129.32**	**83.73**	**97.83**
活牲畜	Livestock Breeding (Live Animals)	108.47	145.30	71.62	94.10
羊	Sheep and Goats	80.90	102.50	108.17	90.61
猪	Pig	112.38	153.26	63.98	93.90
家　禽	Poultry	101.43	94.89	102.05	103.93
鸡	Chicken	101.61	94.81	101.60	103.64
鸭	Duck	100.00	93.07	106.00	104.65
禽　蛋	Poultry Eggs	94.19	83.13	113.94	107.88
鸡　蛋	Chicken Eggs	94.21	83.23	113.77	106.91
渔　业	**Fishery**	**99.62**	**103.35**	**109.15**	**102.25**
淡水养殖产品	Aquatic products in Inland Water	99.62	103.35	109.15	102.25
养殖淡水鱼	Freshwater Fishes	100.47	103.69	108.65	99.79
养殖淡水虾	Freshwater Shrimps	103.53	98.02	112.00	111.90
养殖淡水蟹	Freshwater Crabs	90.15	92.28	113.28	115.61
其他淡水养殖产品	Other Freshwater Aquatic Products	94.79	102.91	103.20	96.97

8—6 工业生产者出厂价格主要分组指数（按生产生活资料分）
Producer Price Indices for Industrial Products by Category

上年=100（preceding year=100）

年份 Year	总指数 Total Industry Products	生产资料 Means of production	采掘 Mining & Quarrying	原材料 Raw Materials	加工 Manufa-cturing	生活资料 Consumer Goods	食品 Food	衣着 Clothing	一般日用品 Articles for Daily Use	耐用消费品 Durable Consumer Goods
2005	103.25	104.91	113.04	111.06	100.47	98.93	99.60	100.32	101.84	96.67
2010	108.98	110.86	111.45	116.89	108.12	103.03	104.96	101.97	102.67	100.45
2011	108.30	109.20	104.80	111.20	108.80	105.60	108.90	107.50	106.40	100.40
2012	98.30	97.00	96.90	99.20	96.00	101.70	102.60	103.10	100.30	101.10
2014	97.40	96.20	90.10	95.70	97.10	100.70	101.00	102.50	100.90	99.80
2015	93.94	91.65	81.10	91.02	93.12	100.17	99.91	101.37	100.02	100.33
2016	98.50	98.10	98.80	96.30	98.60	99.40	100.00	99.90	99.20	98.60
2017	107.98	110.80	126.41	114.71	108.17	101.06	101.37	101.45	100.51	100.95
2018	103.03	103.90	99.56	106.68	103.50	100.66	99.81	103.15	101.00	100.83
2019	100.34	100.12	108.83	99.19	99.60	100.90	101.58	102.33	100.56	99.83
2020	99.12	98.56	99.64	96.97	98.93	100.50	103.44	99.93	99.60	97.41
2021	107.72	110.13	127.30	114.14	107.73	101.37	101.63	102.04	102.50	99.95
2022	103.20	103.72	112.60	106.53	102.16	101.59	102.14	102.95	101.74	100.32

8—7 工业生产者出厂价格主要分组指数（按轻重工业分）
Sub-index of Light and Heavy industry of Ex-factory Industrial Producer Price Index

上年=100（preceding year=100）

年份 Year	轻工业 Light Industry	以农产品为原料 Using Farm Products as Raw Materials	以非农产品为原料 Using Non-farm Products Raw Materials	重工业 Heavy Industry	#采掘 Mining and	原料 Raw Materials	加工 Manufac-turing
2005	99.05	99.54	98.62	106.31	112.59	111.32	101.36
2010	104.77	106.38	103.19	111.36	110.97	116.63	108.11
2011	107.70	109.90	103.60	108.50	104.80	110.90	107.70
2012	101.40	101.30	101.50	97.10	96.90	99.30	96.10
2014	100.40	100.80	99.80	96.30	90.10	95.90	97.20
2015	99.64	99.47	99.96	91.82	81.10	91.17	93.33
2016	99.10	99.40	98.60	98.20	98.80	96.30	98.80
2017	101.81	102.18	101.28	110.74	126.41	114.37	108.02
2018	100.93	100.99	100.84	103.88	99.56	106.46	103.50
2019	99.99	100.66	99.02	100.50	108.83	99.57	100.01
2020	99.89	101.45	97.65	98.77	99.64	96.97	99.28
2022	103.53	102.16	105.17	102.99	112.60	106.93	100.79

8—8 工业生产者购进价格主要分组指数
Industrial Products Purchased from the Price Indices by Category

上年=100（preceding year=100）

年　份 Year	全部原材料 Total Raw and Other Materials	#燃料、动力类 Fuel and Power	黑色金属材料类 Ferrous Metals	有色金属材料和电线类 Nonferrous Metals	化工原料类 Industrial Chemicals	木材及纸浆类 Timber and Paper Pulp	建筑材料及非金属矿类 Building Materials and Nonmetal Mine Since	其他工业原材料及半成品类 Other Raw Materials and Semi-finished Products	农副产品类 Agricultural and Subsidiary Products	纺织原料类 Textile Raw Material
2005	107.13	114.95	108.07	116.42	106.87	103.47	106.55	104.35	98.16	95.41
2010	111.76	110.91	113.45	124.92	111.29	103.92	106.94	105.90	110.05	108.52
2011	110.80	112.90	110.10	116.10	109.50	108.70	117.40	103.90	116.30	112.10
2012	98.20	100.10	94.00	95.40	97.10	104.40	98.30	98.10	103.10	96.20
2014	97.20	93.30	95.90	95.60	98.30	100.40	99.80	98.40	100.80	99.10
2015	93.46	89.45	88.16	90.58	94.04	99.73	98.66	97.40	96.65	96.88
2016	98.40	95.70	97.10	101.60	96.80	99.50	96.10	99.70	98.50	100.80
2017	109.20	114.53	114.08	122.19	109.14	104.84	105.62	104.52	101.37	104.65
2018	105.27	110.10	106.79	107.81	104.43	103.08	106.91	104.09	107.13	104.09
2019	99.91	97.28	102.56	93.21	97.17	99.28	103.86	102.08	102.03	98.63
2021	111.52	117.81	119.76	121.21	114.55	102.89	109.97	105.55	103.78	104.38
2022	103.99	121.06	94.10	101.47	102.18	104.22	94.82	102.13	105.10	105.49

主要统计指标解释

居民消费价格指数

是度量消费商品及服务项目价格水平随着时间而变动的相对数，反映居民家庭购买的消费品及服务价格水平的变动情况。它是宏观经济分析和决策、价格总水平监测和调控以及国民经济经济核算的重要指标。其按年度计算的变动率通常被用来作为反映通货膨胀（或紧缩）程度的指标。

商品零售价格指数

商品的零售价格是商品在流通过程中最后一个环节的价格，是工业、商业、餐饮业和其他零售企业向城乡居民、机关团体出售生活消费品和办公用品的价格。商品零售价格指数，反映了市场商品零售价格的变动趋势和变动程度，为国家宏观调控和国民经济核算提供参考依据。同时，还可以在此基础上编制其他派生价格指数。

农产品生产者价格指数

是反映一定时期内，农产品生产者出售农产品价格水平变动趋势及幅度的相对数。该指数可以客观反映全省农产品生产者价格水平和结构变动情况，满足农业与国民经济核算需要。其中某代表品生产者价格指数是通过对全部有出售该产品行为的调查单位的个体指数进行几何平均求得的，类价格指数是通过对其所属的类（或代表品）的价格指数进行加权平均求得的。季度累计价格指数的计算方法与分季指数的计算方法相同。

工业生产者出厂价格指数

是反映各工业行业产品出厂价格总水平的变动趋势和程度的相对数。为国民经济核算、测算工业发展速度、宏观经济分析和调控、理顺价格体系提供依据。

工业生产者购进价格指数

是反映工业企业作为生产投入，而从物资交易市场和能源、原材料生产企业购买原材料、燃料和动力产品时，所支付的价格水平变动趋势和程度的统计指标，是扣除工业企业物质消耗成本中的价格变动影响的重要依据。

目前，我国编制的原材料、燃料和动力购进价格指数所调查的产品包括燃料动力、黑色金属、有色金属、化工、建材等九大类的900多种产品。

Explanatory Notes for Major Statistical Indicators

Resident's Consumer Price Index

As relative index which measures the change in price level of a group of representative consumer goods and services with the passage of time, reflecting the changes in prices of consumer goods and services purchased by residents. It is an important index of macroscopic economic analysis and decisions, general price level monitoring, adjustment and control, and national business accounting. Its changing rate by the year is usually regarded as reflecting the degree of inflation (or tightens).

Retail Price Index

Retail price of goods is the price of the last link in the circulating course. It is the price of consumer goods and official supplies sold to urban and rural residents or organs by industrial, commercial, catering trade and other retail enterprises. Retail price index reflects the trend and degree of changes in retail price of market commodities. It offers the consulting basis of national macroscopic adjustment and control and national business accounting. Besides, other deriving price indices could be worked out basing on it.

Producer Price Indices of Agricultural Production

reflect the trend and degree of changes in producers' prices received by farmers when they sell farm products during a given period. These indices depict the change in the level and structure of producer prices for farm products of the province and meet the needs of agricultural statistics and national accounts statistics. The producer price index for a given product is calculated as the geometrical mean of individual indices for all surveyed units which sell such product, and the indices for a product category is obtained as the weighted mean of price indices for all products in the category. Method for calculating accumulative quarterly indices is the same as for calculating the individual quarterly indices.

Ex-factory Price Index of Industrial Products

reflects the trend and degree of changes in general ex-factory prices of all industrial products. It offers basis of national business accounting, calculating industrial development speed, national macroscopic analysis, adjustment and control and rationalizing the price system.

Indices of Purchasing Prices of Raw Materials, Fuels and Power

reflect changes in the level and degree of prices paid by industrial enterprises when they purchase production input such as raw materials, fuels and power from the market or from other energy or raw materials producing enterprises. These indices provide important basis for measuring the material consumption of industrial enterprises after removing influence of price changes.

At present, over 900 products in 9 categories, including fuels and power, ferrous metals, non-ferrous metals, chemicals, building materials, are covered in China for the survey to produce indices of purchasing prices of raw materials, fuels and power.

第九篇

Chapter 9

城乡人民生活

LIVELIHOOD OF URBAN AND RURAL PEOPLE

简要说明

一、本篇资料内容主要反映城乡居民收支和生活状况，包括居民家庭基本情况、居民收支、消费水平、居住状况及主要消费品拥有量等。

二、本篇资料来源于城乡一体化住户调查。自 2013 年以来，城乡一体化住户调查整合城乡住户调查资源，统一调查指标、统一抽样方法、统一调查过程、统一数据处理和统一数据发布，由安徽调查总队根据国家统计局《住户收支与生活状况调查方案》组织实施，其调查目的是为全面了解全省和分市、县（区）城乡常住居民收入、生活现状及变化情况，全面准确地反映居民收入分配格局，满足各级政府制定政策计划和进行宏观管理的需要，以及社会各界的信息需求，为国民经济核算提供基础数据。

三、全体居民按收入五等份分组是指将所有调查户按人均可支配收入水平从低到高顺序排列，平均分为五个等份，处于最低 20%的收入群体为低收入组，依此类推依次为中间偏下收入组、中间收入组、中间偏上收入组、高收入组。

Brief Introduction

I. This chapter material content mainly reflects the urban and rural residents' income and living conditions, including residents family basic situation, income, consumption level, living condition and the main consumer ownership, etc.

II. This chapter material content is derived from the integrationization of urban and rural household survey. Since 2013, the integrationization of urban and rural household survey has been unifying urban and rural household survey resources unified index, sampling method and survey process, data processing and data releasing. According to the resident income and life condition investigation plan of the national bureau of statistics, the survey office in Anhui organized the implementation. Survey aim is for comprehensive understanding of the province and city and county (district) of urban and rural residents income, living status and changing situation, comprehensive accurately reflecting the residents income distribution pattern, providing for all levels of government policy planning and the need of macro management, and information demanding to the social, and basic data for the national economic accounting.

III. The quinquennial grouping of all households by income means that all surveyed households are arranged in order of per capita disposable income from the lowest to the highest, and divided into five equal groups on average. The income group at the bottom 20% is the low-income group, and so on, it is the lower middle income group, the middle income group, the upper middle income group, and the high income group.

9—1 人民物质文化生活情况
People's Material and Cultural Life

项　　目		Item		2021	2022
就　业		**Employment**			
城镇每一从业人口负担人数	（人）	Number of Persons Burdened by Each Employed Population in Cities and Towns	(person)	1.38	1.94
农村每一从业人口负担人数	（人）	Number of Persons Burdened by Each Employed Population in Rural Areas	(person)	1.50	1.91
城镇登记失业率	(%)	Urban Unemployment Rate	(%)	2.46	
收　入		**Income of Rural and urban Residents**			
城镇居民可支配收入	（元）	Annual per Capita Disposable Income of Urban	(yuan)	43009	45133
农村居民可支配收入	（元）	Annual per Capita Net Income of Rural Residents	(yuan)	18372	19575
城镇居民恩格尔系数	(%)	Engle Coefficient of Urban Households	(%)	32.0	33.3
农村居民恩格尔系数	(%)	Engle Coefficient of Rural Households	(%)	33.6	35.3
城镇非私营单位就业人员平均工资	（元）	Average Wage for the Employment of Urban Non Private Units	(yuan)	93861	
现住房面积	**（平方米）**	**Per Capita Floor Space of Residential Buildings**	**(sq.m)**		
城镇常住居民人均住房建筑面积		Urban Areas (Net)		42.3	42.4
农村常住居民人均住房建筑面积		Rural Areas (Net)		54.7	54.7
交　通		**Traffic**			
城镇每百户拥有家用汽车	（辆）	Number of Home Car per 100 Households in Urban Areas	(unit)	41.4	43.4
城镇每百户拥有摩托车	（辆）	Number of Motor Cycles per 100 Households in Urban Areas	(unit)	9.6	9.3
城市公用事业		**Public Utilities in Urban Areas**			
用水普及率	(%)	Water Penetration Rate	(%)	99.81	
燃气普及率	(%)	Gas Penetration Rate	(%)	99.48	
人均公园绿地面积	（平方米）	Per Capita Park Greenery Area	(sq.m)	14.49	
文　化		**Culture**			
城镇每百户有彩色电视机	（台）	Number of Color TV Sets per 100 Household in Urban Areas	(unit)	132.7	133.3
农村每百户有彩色电视机	（台）	Number of Color TV Sets per 100 Household in Rural Areas	(unit)	133.8	133.1
广播人口覆盖率	(%)	Broadcast Covering Ratio of Population	(%)	99.94	
电视人口覆盖率	(%)	TV Covering Ratio of Population	(%)	99.92	
教　育		**Education**			
每万人口中高等教育人数	（人）	Higher Education per 10,000 Population	(person)	309	
卫　生		**Public Health**			
每万人医院病床数	（张）	Number of Hospital Beds per 10000 Persons	(unit)	44.66	
每万人有执业（助理）医师数	（人）	Number of Licensed (Assistant) Physicians per 10000 Persons	(person)	24.22	

9—2 全体居民家庭基本情况
Basic Information About The Households of all The Residents

指　　标	Item	2021	2022
基本情况	**Basic Situation**		
户均常住人口 （人/户）	Permanent Residents per Household （person/home）	3.1	3.1
户均常住从业人口 （人/户）	Permanent Employees per Household （person/home）	2.1	1.6
平均每户家庭从业人口比重 （%）	Average Proportion of Working Population per Household （%）	69.6	51.9
平均每一从业人口负担人数（包括从业者本人） （人）	Number of Dependents per Employee Including Oneself （person）	1.4	1.9
恩格尔系数 （%）	Engel Coefficient （%）	32.6	34.1
户主文化程度 （%）	**Education Level of Householder （%）**		
未上过学	Not Been to School	2.4	2.3
小　学	Primary School	19.2	19.1
初　中	Junior Secondary School	47.3	47.2
高　中	Senior Secondary School	14.8	15.0
大学专科	Junior College	9.1	9.1
大学本科	Undergraduate college	6.4	6.6
研究生	Postgraduate	0.8	0.8
常住从业人员就业类型 （%）	**Job Situation （%）**		
雇　主	Employer	0.9	0.8
公职人员	Public Officer	1.8	1.8
事业单位人员	Institution Worker	5.1	5.2
国有企业雇员	State-owned Enterprise Employee	3.3	3.4
其他雇员	Other Employee	50.3	51.9
农业自营	Agricultural Self-employed	23.4	21.4
非农自营	Non-agricultural Self-employed	15.3	15.6
常住从业人员从事主要行业 （%）	**Industries Engaged （%）**		
第一产业	Primary Industry	25.2	23.0
第二产业	Secondary Industry	25.0	26.2
第三产业	Tertiary Industry	49.8	50.7
居民收入与支出情况	**Household Income and Expenditure**		
居民人均可支配收入 （元/人）	Per Capita Disposable Income of Residents （yuan/person）	30904.3	32745.2
居民人均现金可支配收入 （元/人）	Per Capita Disposable Cash Income （yuan/person）	28143.9	30261.7
现金可支配收入占可支配收入比重 （%）	Cash Disposable Income to Disposable Income （%）	91.1	92.4
居民人均消费支出 （元/人）	Per Capita consumer Expenditure （yuan/person）	21910.9	22541.9
居民人均现金消费支出 （元/人）	Per Capita Household Cash Consumption Expenditure （yuan/person）	17808.9	18379.0
现金消费支出占消费支出比重 （%）	Cash Consumption Expenditure Ratio of Consumption Expenditure （%）	81.3	81.5

9—3 全体居民可支配收入及构成
Household Disposable Income and Composition

指标	Item	2021	2022
可支配收入 （元/人）	**Disposable Income （yuan/person）**	**30904.3**	**32745.2**
工资性收入	Wages Income	16125.7	17122.0
经营净收入	Net Income From Business	6716.2	7103.5
第一产业经营净收入	Net Income From Primary Industry Operation	2336.5	2543.6
第二产业经营净收入	Net Income From Secondary Industry Operations	818.2	843.1
第三产业经营净收入	Net Income From Tertiary Industry Operations	3561.6	3716.7
财产净收入	Property Income	2167.6	2308.7
转移净收入	Transfer Income	5894.8	6211.1
转移性收入	Transfer Income	7246.2	7719.3
转移性支出	Transfer Expenditure	1351.4	1508.3
可支配收入构成 （%）	**Disposable Income （%）**	**100.0**	**100.0**
工资性收入	Wages Income	52.2	52.3
经营净收入	Net Income From Business	21.7	21.7
第一产业经营净收入	Net Income From Primary Industry Operation	7.6	7.8
第二产业经营净收入	Net Income From Secondary Industry Operations	2.6	2.6
第三产业经营净收入	Net Income From Tertiary Industry Operations	11.5	11.4
财产净收入	Property Income	7.0	7.1
转移净收入	Transfer Income	19.1	19.0
转移性收入	Transfer Income	23.4	23.6
转移性支出	Transfer Expenditure	4.4	4.6

9—4 全体居民按收入五等份分组的人均可支配收入
Per Capita Disposable Income of All Residents Divided Into Five Equal Groups

单位：元/人（yuan/person）

指标	Item	2021	2022
20%低收入组家庭人均可支配收入	20% of The Per Capita Disposable Income of Low-income Households	6194.7	6679.8
20%中间偏下收入组家庭人均可支配收入	Per Capita Disposable Income of Households in the Lower 20% of The Middle Income Group	15953.9	16486.2
20%中间收入组家庭人均可支配收入	Per Capita disposable Income of Households in The 20% Middle Income Group	24699.7	26226.3
20%中间偏上收入组家庭人均可支配收入	Per Capita disposable Income of Households in the Upper 20% of The Middle Income Group	37918.6	40325.2
20%高收入组家庭人均可支配收入	Per Capita Disposable Income of 20% of Households in The Top Income Group	78737.1	85519.1

9—5 全体居民消费支出
Consumption Expenditure of Total Residents

单位：元/人（yuan/person）

指　　标	Item	2021	2022
消费支出	**Consumption Expenditure**	**21911**	**22542**
食品烟酒	Food, Tobacco and Liquor	7143	7679
食　品	Food	4520	4791
烟　酒	Tobacco and Liquor	999	1149
饮　料	Drinks	189	223
饮食服务	Diet Service	1434	1516
衣　着	Clothing	1431	1413
衣　类	Clothing	1158	1141
鞋　类	Footwear	273	272
居　住	Residence	4665	4925
租赁房房租	Rent of Rentable Housing	103	104
住房维修及管理	Management and Maintenance of Housing	528	578
水、电、燃料及其他	Water, Electricity, Fuels and Others	738	831
自有住房折算租金	Converted Rent for Private Housing	3297	3412
生活用品及服务	Household Facilities, Articles and Service	1343	1354
家具及室内装饰品	Furniture and Interior Decorations	188	171
家用器具	Household Facilities	341	370
家用纺织品	Home Textiles	99	94
家庭日用杂品	Daily-Use Household Articles	324	331
个人护理用品	Personal Products	324	322
家庭服务	Household Service	67	67
交通通信	Traffic and Communications	2480	2484
交　通	Transportation	1789	1797
通　信	Communications	690	687
教育文化娱乐	Education, Cultural & Recreation Service	2585	2416
教　育	Education	2054	1912
文化和娱乐	Cultural and Recreation	531	505
医疗保健	Medicine and Medical Service	1784	1750
医疗器具及药品	Medical Instrument and Articles	381	357
医疗服务	Medical Service	1402	1393
其他用品和服务	Miscellaneous Commodities and Services	482	520
其他用品	Miscellaneous Commodities	253	290
其他服务	Miscellaneous Services	229	231

9—6 全体居民消费支出构成
Composition of Household Consumption Expenditure

单位：%

指　　标	Item	2021	2022
消费支出构成	**ConsumptionExpenditure**	**100.0**	**100.0**
食品烟酒	Food, Tobacco and Liquor	32.6	34.1
食　品	Food	20.6	21.3
烟　酒	Tobacco and Liquor	4.6	5.1
饮　料	Drinks	0.9	1.0
饮食服务	Diet Service	6.5	6.7
衣　着	Clothing	6.5	6.3
衣　类	Clothing	5.3	5.1
鞋　类	Footwear	1.2	1.2
居　住	Residence	21.3	21.8
租赁房房租	Rental House Rent	0.5	0.5
住房维修及管理	Management and Maintenance of Housing	2.4	2.6
水、电、燃料及其他	Water, Electricity, Fuels and Others	3.4	3.7
自有住房折算租金	Converted Rent for Private Housing	15.0	15.1
生活用品及服务	Household Facilities, Articles and Service	6.1	6.0
家具及室内装饰品	Furniture and Interior Decorations	0.9	0.8
家用器具	Household Facilities	1.6	1.6
家用纺织品	Home Textiles	0.5	0.4
家庭日用杂品	Daily-Use Household Articles	1.5	1.5
个人护理用品	Personal Products	1.5	1.4
家庭服务	Household Service	0.3	0.3
交通通信	Traffic and Communications	11.3	11.0
交　通	Transportation	8.2	8.0
通　信	Communications	3.2	3.0
教育文化娱乐	Education, Cultural & Recreation Service	11.8	10.7
教　育	Education	9.4	8.5
文化和娱乐	Cultural and Recreation	2.4	2.2
医疗保健	Medicine and Medical Service	8.1	7.8
医疗器具及药品	Medical Instrument and Articles	1.7	1.6
医疗服务	Medical Service	6.4	6.2
其他用品和服务	Miscellaneous Commodities and Services	2.2	2.3
其他用品	Miscellaneous Commodities	1.2	1.3
其他服务	Miscellaneous Services	1.0	1.0

9—7 全体居民年末主要耐用消费品拥有量
Ownership of Major Durable Consumer Goods by the End of The Year

单位：平均每百户（On average, every hundred households）

指　　标	Item	2021	2022
家用汽车	Household Automobile	35.6	38.0
摩托车	Motorcycle	16.8	16.4
助力车	Man-drawn Vehicle	115.1	114.5
洗衣机	Washing Machine	96.4	96.8
电冰箱（柜）	Refrigerator	104.3	104.0
微波炉	Microwave Oven	48.4	49.8
彩色电视机	Color TV	133.3	133.2
空调	Air Conditioner	169.3	172.4
热水器	Water Heater	97.4	96.7
排油烟机	Kitchen Ventilator	61.7	64.2
固定电话	Telephone	6.9	6.5
移动电话	Mobile Telephone	267.6	266.8
计算机	Computer	41.3	42.9
照相机	Camera	6.8	7.1

9—8 各市全体居民人均可支配收入
Per Capita Disposable Income of All Residents by Region

单位：元/人（yuan/person）

地　区	Region	2021	2022
安 徽 省	**Anhui**	**30904.3**	**32745.2**
合 肥 市	Hefei	46009.1	48820.5
淮 北 市	Huaibei	30737.5	32505.1
亳 州 市	Bozhou	24480.8	26070.1
宿 州 市	Suzhou	24289.7	25665.7
蚌 埠 市	Bengbu	31972.4	33733.0
阜 阳 市	Fuyang	24443.1	25925.4
淮 南 市	Huainan	31632.2	33390.1
滁 州 市	Chuzhou	28141.8	29910.0
六 安 市	Luan	24788.5	26510.9
马鞍山市	Maanshan	46557.3	49376.8
芜 湖 市	Wuhu	40500.9	43144.7
宣 城 市	Xuancheng	33720.2	35896.5
铜 陵 市	Tongling	32316.5	34136.4
池 州 市	Chizhou	28973.0	30963.7
安 庆 市	Anqing	27098.0	28802.5
黄 山 市	Huangshan	30573.9	32372.8

9—9 城镇居民家庭基本情况
Basic Conditions of Urban Households

项　　目		Item		2021	2022
平均每户常住人口	**(人)**	**Average Resident Population per Household**	**(person)**	**3.0**	**3.1**
平均每一就业者负担人数（包括就业者本人）	**(人)**	**Number of Persons Supported by Each Employee Including the Employee Himself or Herself**	**(persons)**	**1.38**	**1.94**
平均每人全部年总收入	**(元)**	**Average Total Annual Income Per Person**	**(yuan)**	**48026.7**	**51574.2**
#可支配收入		Disposable Income		43008.7	45133.2
工资性收入		Wages Income		25545.5	26773.3
经营净收入		Net Income From Business		6639.8	6986.6
财产净收入		Property Income		3882.7	4077.7
转移净收入		Transfer Income		6940.7	7295.5
平均每人消费性支出	**(元)**	**Per Capita Annual Living Expenditures for Consumption**	**(yuan)**	**26495.1**	**26832.4**
#食　品		Food		8468.6	8924.9
衣　着		Clothing		1794.9	1762.3
居　住		Residence		5822.9	6078.8
生活用品及服务		Supplies and Services		1671.2	1631.1
交通和通信		Transportation and Communications		3039.9	2910.0
教育文化娱乐服务		Education, Cultural & Recreation Service		3170.2	2877.8
医疗保健		Medicine and Medical Service		1891.2	1933.6
其他用品和服务		Other goods and Services		636.2	713.9
平均每人消费性支出构成（人均消费性支出=100）	(%)	**Composition of per Capita Annual Living Expenditures for Consumption**	**(%)**	**100.0**	**100.0**
#食　品		Food		32.0	33.3
衣　着		Clothing		6.8	6.6
居　住		Residence		22.0	22.7
生活用品及服务		Supplies and Services		6.3	6.1
交通和通信		Transportation and Communications		11.5	10.8
教育文化娱乐服务		Education, Cultural & Recreation Service		12.0	10.7
医疗保健		Medicine and Medical Service		7.1	7.2
其他用品和服务		Other goods and Services		2.4	2.7

9—10 城镇居民现金可支配收入及构成
Urban Residents Cash Disposable Income and Composition

指 标	Item	2021	2022
现金可支配收入 （元/人）	**Cash Disposable Income （yuan/person）**	**39884.1**	**45133.2**
现金工资性收入	Wages Income	25363.4	26773.3
现金经营净收入	Net Income From Business	6941.6	6986.6
第一产业经营净收入	Net Income From Primary Industry Operation	421.4	655.1
第二产业经营净收入	Net Income From Secondary Industry Operations	1190.2	1110.7
第三产业经营净收入	Net Income From Tertiary Industry Operations	5330.1	5220.8
现金财产净收入	Property Income	1203.7	4077.7
现金转移净收入	Transfer Income	6375.4	7295.5
现金转移性收入	Transfer Income	8448.6	9637.2
现金转移性支出	Transfer Expenditurc	2073.2	2341.7
现金可支配收入构成 （%）	**Composition of Cash Disposable Income （%）**	**100.0**	**100.0**
现金工资性收入	Wages Income	63.6	59.3
现金经营净收入	Net Income From Business	17.4	15.5
第一产业经营净收入	Net Income From Primary Industry Operation	1.1	1.5
第二产业经营净收入	Net Income From Secondary Industry Operations	3.0	2.5
第三产业经营净收入	Net Income From Tertiary Industry Operations	13.4	11.6
现金财产净收入	Property Income	3.0	9.0
现金转移净收入	Transfer Income	16.0	16.2
现金转移性收入	Transfer Income	21.2	21.4
现金转移性支出	Transfer Expenditure	5.2	5.2

9—11 城镇居民年末主要耐用消费品拥有量
Ownership of Major Durable Consumer Goods by Urban Residents at The Year-end

单位：平均每百户（On average, every hundred households）

指 标	Item	2021	2022
家用汽车	Household Automobile	41.4	43.4
摩托车	Motorcycle	9.6	9.3
助力车	Man-drawn Vehicle	107.0	107.1
洗衣机	Washing Machine	99.2	99.3
电冰箱（柜）	Refrigerator	102.6	102.7
微波炉	Microwave Oven	65.5	66.5
彩色电视机	Color TV	132.7	133.3
空调	Air Conditioner	199.3	201.4
热水器	Water Heater	101.2	100.6
排油烟机	Kitchen Ventilator	81.2	81.4
固定电话	Telephone	8.4	8.3
移动电话	Mobile Telephone	257.0	256.8
计算机	Computer	58.2	59.1
照相机	Camera	10.9	11.2

9—12 各市城镇居民人均可支配收入
Per Capita Disposable Income of Urban Residents by Region

单位：元/人（yuan/person）

地 区	Region	2021	2022
安徽省	**Anhui**	**43008.7**	**45133.2**
合肥市	Hefei	53207.6	56177.0
淮北市	Huaibei	39688.5	41700.7
亳州市	Bozhou	37318.9	39363.9
宿州市	Suzhou	37277.7	38910.5
蚌埠市	Bengbu	42656.0	44652.3
阜阳市	Fuyang	37379.0	39240.5
淮南市	Huainan	41375.0	43352.7
滁州市	Chuzhou	39025.3	41042.9
六安市	Luan	36793.5	38883.3
马鞍山市	Maanshan	56440.1	59420.1
芜湖市	Wuhu	48668.0	51481.1
宣城市	Xuancheng	46115.4	48596.4
铜陵市	Tongling	44453.7	46445.2
池州市	Chizhou	38756.0	41034.9
安庆市	Anqing	39416.1	41453.9
黄山市	Huangshan	41881.8	43799.9

9—13 农村居民家庭基本情况
Basic Conditions of Rural Households

指　　标	Item	2021	2022
平均每户常住人口　（人）	**Average Resident Population per Household　(person)**	**3.12**	**3.14**
平均每个从业者负担人口（含本人）　（人）	**On average, each practitioner bears the population (including himself)　(person)**	**1.50**	**1.91**
平均每人年收入　（元）	**Per Capita Annual Income　(yuan)**		
总收入	Total Revenue	25450	26987
#可支配收入	Disposable Income	18372	19575
工资性收入	Wages Income	6373	6861
经营性收入	Operating Income	6795	7228
财产性收入	Property Income	392	428
转移性收入	Transfer Income	4812	5058
平均每人年支出　（元）	**Per Capita Annual Expenditures　(yuan)**		
总支出	Total Expenditure	28585	26842
消费支出	Cash Consumption Expenditure	17163	17980
生产经营费用支出	Production and Operating Expenditure	5871	4201
财产性支出	Cash Property Expenditure	57	66
转移性支出	Cash Transfer Expenditure	604	622
部分商业保险支出	Part of Commercial Insurance Expenditure	56	41
购置资产及非经常性转移支出	Acquisition of Assets and Non-recurring Transfer Expenditure	3854	3125
借贷性支出	Lending Expenditure	980	806
总支出构成(总支出=100)　(%)	**Total Expenditure　(%)**	**100.0**	**100.0**
现金消费支出	Cash Consumption Expenditure	60.0	67.0
生产经营现金费用支出	Cash Production and Operating Expenditure	20.5	15.7
现金财产性支出	Cash Property Expenditure	0.2	0.2
现金转移性支出	Cash Transfer Expenditure	2.1	2.3
部分商业保险支出	Part of Commercial Insurance Expenditure	0.2	0.2
购置资产及非经常性转移支出	Acquisition of Assets and Non-recurring Transfer Expenditure	13.5	11.6
借贷性支出	Lending Expenditure	3.4	3.0

9—14 农村居民可支配收入及构成
Disposable Income and Composition of Rural Residents

指　　标	Item	2021	2022
可支配收入　（元/人）	**Disposable Income　(yuan/person)**	**18372**	**19575**
工资性收入	Wages Income	6373	6861
经营净收入	Net Income From Business	6795	7228
第一产业经营净收入	Net Income From Primary Industry Operation	4172	4551
第二产业经营净收入	Net Income From Secondary Industry Operations	519	559
第三产业经营净收入	Net Income From Tertiary Industry Operations	2105	2118
财产净收入	Property Income	392	428
转移净收入	Transfer Income	4812	5058
转移性收入	Transfer Income	5416	5680
转移性支出	Transfer Expenditure	604	622
可支配收入构成　（%）	**Disposable Income　(%)**	**100.0**	**100.0**
工资性收入	Wages Income	34.7	35.1
经营净收入	Net Income From Business	37.0	36.9
第一产业经营净收入	Net Income From Primary Industry Operation	22.7	23.3
第二产业经营净收入	Net Income From Secondary Industry Operations	2.8	2.9
第三产业经营净收入	Net Income From Tertiary Industry Operations	11.5	10.8
财产净收入	Property Income	2.1	2.2
转移净收入	Transfer Income	26.2	25.8

9—15 农村居民现金可支配收入及构成
Rural Residents Cash Disposable Income and Composition

指 标	Item	2021	2022
现金可支配收入 （元/人）	**Cash Disposable Income （yuan/person）**	**15988**	**18212**
现金工资性收入	Wages Income	6289	6764
现金经营净收入	Net Income From Business	4813	6286
第一产业经营净收入	Net Income From Primary Industry Operation	1908	3365
第二产业经营净收入	Net Income From Secondary Industry Operations	590	629
第三产业经营净收入	Net Income From Tertiary Industry Operations	2315	2293
现金财产净收入	Property Income	392	428
现金转移净收入	Transfer Income	4495	4734
现金转移性收入	Transfer Income	5099	5356
现金转移性支出	Transfer Expenditure	604	622
现金可支配收入构成 （%）	**Composition of Cash Disposable Income （%）**	**100.0**	**100.0**
现金工资性收入	Wages Income	39.3	37.1
现金经营净收入	Net Income From Business	30.1	34.5
第一产业经营净收入	Net Income From Primary Industry Operation	11.9	18.5
第二产业经营净收入	Net Income From Secondary Industry Operations	3.7	3.5
第三产业经营净收入	Net Income From Tertiary Industry Operations	14.5	12.6
现金财产净收入	Property Income	2.4	2.3
现金转移净收入	Transfer Income	28.1	26.0

9—16 农村居民消费支出
Consumption Expenditure of Rural Residents

单位：元/人（yuan/person）

指　　标	Item	2021	2022
消费支出	**Consumption Expenditure**	**17163**	**17980**
食品烟酒	Food, Tobacco and Liquor	5769	6354
食　品	Food	3766	4067
烟　酒	Tobacco and Liquor	925	1114
饮　料	Drinks	164	206
饮食服务	Diet Service	914	966
衣　着	Clothing	1054	1042
衣　类	Clothing	829	813
鞋　类	Footwear	225	229
居　住	Residence	3465	3699
租赁房房租	Rent of Rentable Housing	90	89
住房维修及管理	Management and Maintenance of Housing	404	491
水、电、燃料及其他	Water, Electricity, Fuels and Others	645	724
自有住房折算租金	Converted Rent for Private Housing	2327	2394
生活用品及服务	Household Facilities, Articles and Service	1003	1060
家具及室内装饰品	Furniture and Interior Decorations	132	140
家用器具	Household Facilities	253	302
家用纺织品	Home Textiles	77	72
家庭日用杂品	Daily-Use Household Articles	283	292
个人护理用品	Personal Products	231	230
家庭服务	Household Service	28	25
交通通信	Traffic and Communications	1899	2031
交　通	Transportation	1300	1423
通　信	Communications	599	607
教育文化娱乐	Education, Cultural & Recreation Service	1978	1926
教　育	Education	1668	1607
文化和娱乐	Cultural and Recreation	311	320
医疗保健	Medicine and Medical Service	1672	1554
医疗器具及药品	Medical Instrument and Articles	319	295
医疗服务	Medical Service	1353	1259
其他用品和服务	Miscellaneous Commodities and Services	322	315
其他用品	Miscellaneous Commodities	186	172
其他服务	Miscellaneous Services	136	142

9—17 农村居民消费支出构成
Composition of Rural Residents' Consumption Expenditure

单位：%

指标	Item	2021	2022
消费支出	**Consumption Expenditure**	**100.0**	**100.0**
食品烟酒	Food, Tobacco and Liquor	33.6	35.3
食　品	Food	21.9	22.6
烟　酒	Tobacco and Liquor	5.4	6.2
饮　料	Drinks	1.0	1.1
饮食服务	Diet Service	5.3	5.4
衣　着	Clothing	6.1	5.8
衣　类	Clothing	4.8	4.5
鞋　类	Footwear	1.3	1.3
居　住	Residence	20.2	20.6
租赁房房租	Rent of Rentable Housing	0.5	0.5
住房维修及管理	Management and Maintenance of Housing	2.4	2.7
水、电、燃料及其他	Water, Electricity, Fuels and Others	3.8	4.0
自有住房折算租金	Converted Rent for Private Housing	13.6	13.3
生活用品及服务	Household Facilities, Articles and Service	5.8	5.9
家具及室内装饰品	Furniture and Interior Decorations	0.8	0.8
家用器具	Household Facilities	1.5	1.7
家用纺织品	Home Textiles	0.4	0.4
家庭日用杂品	Daily-Use Household Articles	1.7	1.6
个人护理用品	Personal Products	1.3	1.3
家庭服务	Household Service	0.2	0.1
交通通信	Traffic and Communications	11.1	11.3
交　通	Transportation	7.6	7.9
通　信	Communications	3.5	3.4
教育文化娱乐	Education, Cultural & Recreation Service	11.5	10.7
教　育	Education	9.7	8.9
文化和娱乐	Cultural and Recreation	1.8	1.8
医疗保健	Medicine and Medical Service	9.7	8.6
医疗器具及药品	Medical Instrument and Articles	1.9	1.6
医疗服务	Medical Service	7.9	7.0
其他用品和服务	Miscellaneous Commodities and Services	1.9	1.7
其他用品	Miscellaneous Commodities	1.1	1.0
其他服务	Miscellaneous Services	0.8	0.8

9—18 农村居民主要食品消费量
Main Food Consumption of Rural Residents

单位：公斤/人（kg/person）

指　　标	Item	2021	2022
粮　食	Grain	172.5	163.1
谷　物	Cereals	156.2	148.3
薯　类	Tubers	2.9	2.3
豆　类	Beans	13.4	12.6
油　脂	Oil and Fats	10.9	9.3
#食用植物油	Edible Vegetable Oil	9.8	8.6
蔬菜及菜制品消费量	Vegetables and Processed Products	113.5	113.5
#鲜　菜	Fresh Vegetables	110.4	110.7
肉　类	Meat and Processed Products	27.6	32.1
#猪　肉	Pork	21.8	26.4
牛　肉	Beef	1.6	1.9
羊　肉	Mutton	0.9	0.9
禽　类	Poultry and Processed Products	15.8	15.1
水产品	Aquatic Products	13.9	12.9
蛋　类	Eggs and Processed Products	14.5	14.3
奶　类	Milk and Dairy Products	10.8	9.6
干鲜瓜果类	Dried and Fresh Melons and Fruits	53.6	51.8
#鲜瓜果	Fresh Melons and Fruits	49.3	51.6
坚果类	Nuts and Grain Products	3.4	
食　糖	Sugar	1.0	1.0

9—19 农村居民年末主要耐用消费品拥有量
Ownership of Major Durable Consumer Goods by Rural Residents at The End of The Year

单位：平均每百户（On average, every hundred households）

指　　标	Item	2021	2022
家用汽车	Household Automobile	29.5	32.2
摩托车	Motorcycle	24.3	24.2
助力车	Man-drawn Vehicle	123.8	122.6
洗衣机	Washing Machine	93.5	94.2
电冰箱（柜）	Refrigerator	106.1	105.5
微波炉	Microwave Oven	30.4	31.5
彩色电视机	Color TV	133.8	133.1
空调	Air Conditioner	137.5	140.6
热水器	Water Heater	93.4	92.5
排油烟机	Kitchen Ventilator	41.0	45.3
固定电话	Telephone	5.3	4.6
移动电话	Mobile Telephone	278.9	277.7
计算机	Computer	23.5	25.1
照相机	Camera	2.5	2.6

9—20 各市农村居民人均可支配收入
Per Capita Disposable Income of Rural Residents by Region

单位：元（yuan）

地 区	Region	2021	2022
安徽省	**Anhui**	18368	19575
合肥市	Hefei	26856	28727
淮北市	Huaibei	16504	17495
亳州市	Bozhou	16769	17872
宿州市	Suzhou	15913	16897
蚌埠市	Bengbu	19538	20687
阜阳市	Fuyang	15874	16871
淮南市	Huainan	16706	17722
滁州市	Chuzhou	17400	18630
六安市	Luan	16003	17216
马鞍山市	Maanshan	28331	30363
芜湖市	Wuhu	27202	29210
宣城市	Xuancheng	20565	22060
铜陵市	Tongling	18992	20264
池州市	Chizhou	19168	20602
安庆市	Anqing	16975	18130
黄山市	Huangshan	20298	21712

9—21 分市、县（市、区）居民人均可支配收入
Per Capita Disposable Income of Residents in Cities and Counties (cities and districts)

单位：元（yuan）

地区	Region	全体居民 Whole Population 2022	同比（±%） Compared With The Same	城镇居民 Urban Residents 2022	同比（±%） Compared With The Same	农村居民 Rural Residents 2022	同比（±%） Compared With The Same
安徽省	**Anhui**						
合肥市	**Hefei**	**48820**	**6.1**	**56177**	**5.6**	**28727**	**7.0**
瑶海区	Yaohai District	58044	5.6	58044	5.6		
庐阳区	Luyang District	64178	5.7	64178	5.7		
蜀山区	Shushan District	65319	5.7	65319	5.7		
包河区	Baohe District	66155	5.5	66155	5.5		
合肥高新区	Hefei New and High-tech Zone	52841	6.3	52841	6.3		
合肥经开区	Hefei Economic Zone	52816	6.0	52816	6.0		
合肥新站区	Hefei New Station District	49661	6.0	49661	6.0		
长丰县	Changfeng	35519	6.6	45432	5.6	27587	7.2
肥东县	Feidong	38088	6.6	47630	5.7	30197	7.1
肥西县	Feixi	39690	6.5	50189	5.5	30899	7.1
庐江县	Lujiang	34224	6.4	42573	5.6	26794	6.9
巢湖市	Chaohu	38605	6.4	45456	5.8	28228	7.0
淮北市	**Huaibei**	**32505**	**5.8**	**41701**	**5.1**	**17495**	**6.0**
杜集区	Duji District	37519	5.2	40238	5.0	18488	6.2
相山区	Xiangshan District	45562	5.2	47281	5.1	17981	5.9
烈山区	Lieshan District	32258	5.5	38912	4.9	17726	5.9
濉溪县	Suixi	24973	6.1	37883	5.3	17375	6.0
亳州市	**Bozhou**	**26070**	**6.5**	**39364**	**5.5**	**17872**	**6.6**
谯城区	Qiaocheng District	30058	6.4	42852	5.4	19800	6.5
涡阳县	Guoyang	23138	6.5	34959	5.5	16769	6.6
蒙城县	Mengcheng	25947	6.6	39689	5.7	18341	6.5
利辛县	Lixin	24454	6.5	38369	5.3	16598	6.7
宿州市	**Suzhou**	**25666**	**5.7**	**38910**	**4.4**	**16897**	**6.2**
埇桥区	Yongqiao District	30811	5.5	42753	4.3	17283	6.4
砀山县	Dangshan	26304	5.5	37470	4.4	17273	6.0
萧县	Xiaoxian	22978	5.8	36936	4.5	16769	6.0
灵璧县	Lingbi	22987	5.8	35127	4.4	16955	6.1
泗县	Sixian	21802	5.8	35286	4.2	16204	6.3
蚌埠市	**Bengbu**	**33733**	**0.1**	**44652**	**0.0**	**20687**	**0.1**
龙子湖区	Longzihu District	53560	0.0	55600	0.0	19614	0.1
蚌山区	Bengshan District	48008	0.1	49586	0.0	20360	0.1
禹会区	Yuhui District	39270	0.1	44497	0.1	19175	0.1
淮上区	Huaishang District	32146	0.1	45239	0.0	19519	0.1
蚌埠高新区	Bengbu New and High-tech Zone	38287	0.0	42828	0.0	19145	0.1
蚌埠经开区	Bengbu Economic Zone						
怀远县	Huaiyuan	28037	0.1	39529	0.0	20918	0.1
五河县	Wuhe	28668	0.1	39182	0.0	20830	0.1
固镇县	Guzhen	28517	0.1	39982	0.0	20964	0.1
阜阳市	**Fuyang**	**25925**	**6.1**	**39240**	**5.0**	**16871**	**6.3**
颍州区	Yingzhou District	36117	5.1	44208	4.4	19416	6.0
颍东区	Yingdong District	25681	6.4	37342	5.7	15884	6.3

9—21 续表1 continued

单位：元（yuan）

地 区	Region	全体居民 Whole Population 2022	同比（±%） Compared With The Same	城镇居民 Urban Residents 2022	同比（±%） Compared With The Same	农村居民 Rural Residents 2022	同比（±%） Compared With The Same
颍泉区	Yingquan District	29022	5.3	39616	4.1	17109	6.4
界首市	Jieshou	28713	5.9	41068	4.9	18414	6.4
临泉县	Linquan	21871	6.5	36105	5.3	16311	6.6
太和县	Taihe	26267	6.3	39286	5.5	17168	6.1
阜南县	Funan	22387	6.3	36022	5.4	16063	6.3
颍上县	Yingshang	25017	6.1	38884	5.0	17032	6.3
淮南市	**Huainan**	**33390**	**5.6**	**43353**	**4.8**	**17722**	**6.1**
大通区	Datong District	39874	4.9	45578	4.3	20864	6.5
田家庵区	Tianjiaan District	50929	4.9	51537	4.8	21840	5.3
谢家集区	Xiejiaji District	42324	4.3	44530	4.1	21011	6.2
八公山区	Bagongshan District	40900	5.4	41167	5.3	21265	6.6
潘集区	Panji District	32099	6.1	44441	5.4	19476	5.7
毛集实验区	Maoji Experimental District	26172	5.5	35266	4.7	19371	5.6
凤台县	Fengtai	27850	5.6	42097	4.5	19819	5.9
寿　县	Shouxian	22953	6.0	33221	5.0	15156	6.4
滁州市	**Chuzhou**	**29910**	**0.1**	**41043**	**0.1**	**18630**	**0.1**
琅琊区	Langya District	48673	0.0	50211	0.0	19769	0.1
南谯区	Nanqiao District	33198	0.1	46891	0.1	19194	0.1
滁州经开区	Chuzhou Economic Zone	40527	0.0	40527	0.0		
天长市	Tianchang	36775	0.1	43892	0.1	25960	0.1
明光市	Mingguang	27000	0.1	37466	0.1	17278	0.1
来安县	Laian	29676	0.1	43113	0.1	18612	0.1
全椒县	Quanjiao	29350	0.1	38677	0.1	19032	0.1
定远县	Dingyuan	24880	0.1	37039	0.1	17313	0.1
凤阳县	Fengyang	23259	0.1	33947	0.1	16434	0.1
六安市	**Luan**	**26511**	**6.9**	**38883**	**5.7**	**17216**	**7.6**
金安区	Jinan District	31670	6.9	43454	6.0	18342	7.3
裕安区	Yuan District	29924	6.9	44118	5.8	18458	7.4
叶集区	Yeji District	24238	7.1	35992	6.1	16837	7.4
霍邱县	Huoqiu	21416	7.2	34190	5.7	16124	7.6
舒城县	Shucheng	26363	6.8	36156	5.5	17320	7.9
金寨县	Jinzhai	22524	7.1	33353	5.3	16227	8.1
霍山县	Huoshan	31329	6.3	38240	5.5	19102	7.6
马鞍山市	**Maanshan**	**49377**	**6.1**	**59420**	**5.3**	**30363**	**7.2**
花山区	Huashan District	70731	5.3	70955	5.3	40909	7.1
雨山区	Yushan District	73202	5.2	73994	5.1	40157	7.1
博望区	Bowang District	44840	6.4	55153	5.4	33463	7.3
郑蒲港新区	Zhengpugang New District						
当涂县	Dangtu	43168	6.3	50144	5.6	34569	7.1
含山县	Hanshan	33749	6.6	42326	5.5	26891	7.4
和　县	Hexian	35909	6.3	43667	5.3	27081	7.3
芜湖市	**Wuhu**	**43145**	**6.5**	**51481**	**5.8**	**29210**	**7.4**
镜湖区	Jinghu District	57397	5.7	57794	5.7	35778	7.3
弋江区	Yijiang District	53881	5.8	53881	5.8		
鸠江区	Jiujiang District	45478	6.2	51746	5.6	31255	7.1

9—21 续表2 continued

单位：元（yuan）

地区	Region	全体居民 Whole Population 2022	同比（±%） Compared With The Same	城镇居民 Urban Residents 2022	同比（±%） Compared With The Same	农村居民 Rural Residents 2022	同比（±%） Compared With The Same
湾沚区	Wanzhi District	39440	7.1	48578	6.1	31763	7.7
繁昌区	Fanchang District	39855	6.9	48391	6.0	31583	7.6
三山经开区	Sanshan Economic Zone	37380	6.7	46772	5.7	31471	7.2
芜湖经开区	Wuhu Economic Zone	51574	6.0	51574	6.0		
无为市	Wuwei	35376	6.9	46968	5.9	25921	7.4
南陵县	Nanling	38178	6.8	46400	5.9	31683	7.4
宣城市	**Xuancheng**	**35897**	**6.5**	**48596**	**5.4**	**22060**	**7.3**
宣州区	Xuanzhou District	36605	6.3	48984	5.2	22383	7.4
宁国市	Ningguo	44461	6.2	53512	5.5	24806	7.1
广德市	Guangde	39569	6.4	52912	5.3	25049	7.5
郎溪县	Langxi	32052	6.7	47419	5.4	21295	7.3
泾县	Jingxian	28749	6.7	39862	5.6	19753	7.2
绩溪县	Jixi	30586	6.7	43373	5.8	18249	7.0
旌德县	Jingde	25397	6.6	34785	5.7	17630	6.9
铜陵市	**Tongling**	**34136**	**5.6**	**46445**	**4.5**	**20264**	**6.7**
铜官区	Tongguan District	56018	4.6	56049	4.6	37296	6.3
铜陵市郊区	Tongling Suburban District	31437	5.6	43522	4.4	18960	6.8
义安区	Yian District	37416	5.6	44527	4.5	31271	6.4
枞阳县	Zongyang	22638	6.1	33770	4.4	17346	6.9
池州市	**Chizhou**	**30964**	**0.1**	**41035**	**0.1**	**20602**	**0.1**
贵池区	Guichi District	33486	0.1	42603	0.1	21418	0.1
九华山风景区	Jiuhuashan Mountain Scenic Area	21039	0.1			21039	0.1
东至县	Dongzhi	29622	0.1	39062	0.1	20596	0.1
石台县	Shitai	22485	0.1	35654	0.1	14951	0.1
青阳县	Qingyang	31039	0.1	41980	0.1	21640	0.1
安庆市	**Anqing**	**28802**	**6.3**	**41454**	**5.2**	**18130**	**6.8**
迎江区	Yingjiang District	46335	6.1	52593	5.7	22584	6.7
大观区	Daguan District	45893	5.8	51482	5.5	21931	6.8
宜秀区	Yixiu District	29214	6.4	37179	5.8	22804	6.6
安庆开发区	Anqing Development Zone	50350	5.6	50350	5.6		
桐城市	Tongcheng	30252	6.1	40599	5.0	21392	6.9
潜山市	Qianshan	25809	6.3	40035	4.9	16843	6.9
怀宁县	Huaining	30217	6.3	41972	5.2	20642	7.0
太湖县	Taihu	23027	6.6	35394	5.4	16167	7.0
宿松县	Susong	22722	6.3	34428	5.3	16170	6.5
望江县	Wangjiang	23887	5.7	36128	4.2	16367	6.4
岳西县	Yuexi	22259	6.6	34376	5.1	16219	7.2
黄山市	**Huangshan**	**32373**	**5.9**	**43800**	**4.6**	**21712**	**7.0**
屯溪区	Tunxi District	46127	4.6	48010	4.5	23052	6.9
黄山区	Huangshan District	35256	5.6	46318	4.3	22443	7.2
徽州区	Huizhou District	35672	6.1	47719	5.0	22780	7.1
歙县	Shexian	28241	6.3	40090	4.8	21532	7.1
休宁县	Xiuning	27842	6.2	40076	4.7	21426	6.9
黟县	Yixian	28638	6.1	38862	4.4	21910	7.3
祁门县	Qimen	28335	6.1	40117	4.9	21365	6.7

主要统计指标解释

可支配收入

指调查户在调查期内获得的、可用于最终消费支出和储蓄的总和，即调查户可以用来自由支配的收入。可支配收入既包括现金，也包括实物收入。按照收入的来源，可支配收入包含四项，分别为：工资性收入、经营净收入、财产净收入、转移净收入。计算公式为：

可支配收入=工资性收入+经营净收入+财产净收入+转移净收入

其中：经营净收入=经营收入-经营费用-生产性固定资产折旧－生产税净额（生产税-生产补贴）

财产净收入=财产性收入-财产性支出

转移净收入=转移性收入-转移性支出

工资性收入

指就业人员通过各种途径得到的全部劳动报酬和各种福利，包括受雇于单位或个人、从事各种自由职业、兼职和零星劳动得到的全部劳动报酬和福利。

经营净收入

指住户或住户成员从事生产经营活动所获得的净收入，是全部经营收入中扣除经营费用、生产性固定资产折旧和生产税净额（生产税减去生产补贴）之后得到的净收入。

财产净收入

指住户或住户成员将其所拥有的金融资产和自然资源交由其他机构单位、住户或个人支配而获得的回报并扣除相关的费用之后得到的净收入。财产净收入包括利息净收入、红利收入、储蓄性保险净收益和转让承包土地经营权租金净收入等。

转移性收入

指国家、单位、社会团体对住户的各种经常性转移支付和住户之间的经常性收入转移。包括政府、非行政事业单位、社会团体对居民转移的养老金或退休金、社会救济和补助、政策性生活补贴、救灾款、经常性捐赠和赔偿以及报销医疗费等；住户之间的赡养收入、经常性捐赠和赔偿以及本住户非常住成员寄回带回的收入等。

消费支出

指住户用于满足家庭日常生活消费需要的全部支出，包括用于消费品的支出和用于服务性消费的支出。根据用途不同，消费支出可划分为食品烟酒、衣着、居住、生活用品及服务、交通通信、教育文化娱乐、医疗保健、其他用品及服务八大类。根据来源不同，消费支出可划分为现金消费支出、实物消费支出（含自产自用、来自单位、来自政府和其他社会组织）。

Explanatory Notes for Major Statistical Indicators

Disposable income

Refers to the sum of the final consumption expenditure and savings obtained by the survey households during the survey period, that is, the income that the survey households can use freely. Disposable income includes both cash and income in kind. According to the source of income, disposable income includes four items: wage income, net operating income, net property income and net transfer income. The calculation formula is:

Disposable income = wage income + net operating income + net property income + net transfer income

Among them: business net income = operating income - operating costs - productive fixed assets depreciation by net production tax (production tax - production subsidies)

Property income = property income - property spending

Transfer net income = metastatic income - transfer spending

Wage income

Refers to the employment through various means to get all the labor remuneration and benefits, including employed by units or individuals, is engaged in a variety of free lancing, part-time and sporadic labor to get all the labor remuneration and welfare.

Business net income

Refers to the resident or resident members engaged in the production and business operation activities of net income, is all operating income deducted operating expenses, productive fixed assets depreciation and net production tax (production tax less production subsidies) after the net income.

Property income

Refers to the resident or resident members should be owned by the financial assets, natural resources by other agencies and institutions and the resident or disposal and returns and net income after deducting costs associated. Property net income includes interest income, dividend income, net income and the transfer of contracted land management rights rental deposit sex insurance net income, etc.

Metastatic income

Refers to the various regular transfer payments made by the state, units and social organizations to households and the regular income transfer between households. Including pensions or retirement benefits transferred by the government, non-administrative institutions and social organizations to residents, social relief and subsidies, policy living subsidies, disaster relief funds, recurrent donations and compensation, and reimbursement of medical expenses; Maintenance income between households, recurrent donations and compensation, and income sent back by non-resident members of the household.

Consumer spending

Refers to the residents used to meet the needs of all family daily life consumption spending, including for consumer spending and for service consumer spending. According to different purposes, consumer spending can be divided into alcohol, tobacco, food, clothing, housing, household items and services, transportation, communication, education and cultural entertainment, health care and other products and services for the eight classes. According to different sources can be divided into consumer spending cash consumption expenditure, real consumer spending (including produce their own, from units, from government and other social organizations).

第十篇

Chapter 10

城市概况

GENERAL SURVEY OF CITIES

简要说明

一、本篇资料综合部分反映全省及16个地级城市市辖区社会、经济发展和城市建设的规模、效益及综合水平等基本情况。市政公用基础设施情况部分增加了9个县级市的资料。主要内容：

1. 人口及土地面积；

2. 综合经济指标；

3. 固定资产投资；

4. 教育、文化、卫生情况；

5. 财政、金融情况；

6. 人民生活情况；

7. 社会福利、劳动保险；

8. 市政公用基础设施情况。

二、本篇资料由安徽省统计局根据国家统计局《城市基本情况统计报表制度》搜集、汇总整理提供。市政公用基础设施情况资料由省住建厅提供。

Brief Introduction

I. The comprehensive part of this data reflects the scale, benefit and comprehensive level of social and economic development and urban construction in the whole province and 16 prefecture-level cities. The information of 9 county-level cities has been added to the situation of municipal public infrastructure. Main contents:

1. Population, area of land.

2. Comprehensive economic indicators.

3. Investment in fixed assets.

4. The conditions of education, culture and health care.

5. The conditions of finance and banking.

6. People’s livelihood.

7. Social welfare and labor insurance.

8. Municipal public infrastructure

II. Data are collected, summarized and provided by Anhui Provincial Bureau of Statistics according to the statistical report system of urban basic situation issued by the National Bureau of Statistics. Municipal public infrastructure information provided by the provincial Department of Housing and Construction.

10—1 地级城市基本情况（2022年）
Basic Statement of Cities at Prefectural Level (2022)

指　　标	Item	全　省 Province	#市区合计 City
人口及土地	**Population and Land**		
常住人口（万人）	Population of Permanent Residents (10000 persons)	6127.0	2452.9
建成区面积（平方公里）	Developed Area (sq.km)	3848	2225
综合经济	**General Economy**		
地区生产总值(当年价格)（亿元）	Gross Regional Product (at current price) (100 million yuan)	45045.0	23846.5
第一产业增加值	Added Value of Primary Industry	3513.7	771.6
第二产业增加值	Added Value of Secondary Industry	18588.0	9879.8
第三产业增加值	Added Value of Tertiary Industry	22943.3	13195.2
财政、金融	**Government Finance, Banking and Insurance**		
地方财政一般公共预算收入（亿元）	General Public Budget Revenue of Local Finance (100 million yuan)	3589.1	2146.3
地方财政一般公共预算支出（亿元）	General Public Budget Expenditure of Local Finance (100 million yuan)	8379.8	3779.2
一般公共服务支出	General Public Service	585.3	263.4
科学技术支出	Science	507.6	327.6
教育支出	Education	1420.9	561.9
文化旅游体育与传媒支出	Cultural Tourism, Sports and Media	86.6	40.9
卫生健康支出	Hygiene and Health	808.1	518.0
节能环保支出	Energy Saving and Environmental Protection	200.7	131.8
城乡社区支出	Urban and Rural Communities	769.0	508.7
交通运输支出	Transport	361.3	134.6
社会保障和就业支出	Social Security and Employment	1427.1	410.8
住房保障支出	Housing Security	235.3	113.1
人民币住户存款余额（亿元）	Deposits of Households (100 million yuan)	41350.5	19956.1
工　业	**Industry**		
规模以上工业企业数（个）	Number of Industrial Enterprises Above Designated Size (unit)	21484	9520
内资企业	Domestic Funded Enterprises	20567	8916
港澳台商投资企业	Funded by Entrepreneurs from Hong Kong, Macao and Taiwan	384	236
外商投资企业	Foreign Funded Enterprises	533	368

10—1 续表1 continued

指 标		Item		全 省 Province	#市区合计 City
流动资产合计	（亿元）	Total Circulating Funds	(100 million yuan)	29619.7	19289.5
营业收入	（亿元）	Operating Income	(100 million yuan)	46889.5	29697.2
利润总额	（亿元）	Total Profits	(100 million yuan)	2386.6	1393.8
邮 政		**Post**			
邮政行业业务收入	（亿元）	Revenue From Postal Business	(100 million yuan)	359.6	
快递业务收入	（亿元）	Income From Express Business	(100 million yuan)	237.5	153.1
国内贸易		**Domestic Trade**			
社会消费品零售总额	（亿元）	Total Retail Sales of Consumer Goods	(100 million yuan)	21518.4	11695.4
固定资产投资		**Investment in Fixed Assets**			
房地产开发投资	（亿元）	Total Investment in Real Estate Development	(100 million yuan)	6203.5	3568.9
#住 宅		Residential Buildings		5082.9	2868.8
商品房屋销售面积	（万平方米）	Floor Space of Selling House	(10000 sq.m)	6756.9	3476.6
#住 宅		Residential Buildings		5873.0	2940.9
商品房屋销售额	（亿元）	Total Sales of Commercial House	(100 million yuan)	5160.3	3037.6
#住 宅		Residential Buildings		4691.2	2745.0
商品房屋待售面积	（万平方米）	Square Commercial House for Sal	(10000 sq.m)	1882.0	1181.0
教育、文化、卫生		**Education, Culture and Public Health**			
学校数	（所）	Number of Schools	(unit)		
中等职业教育学校		Secondary Vocational Technical School		249	133
普通中学		Ordinary High School		3459	1160
普通小学		Ordinary Primary School		6509	1949

10—1 续表2 continued

指　　标	Item	全　省 Province	#市区合计 City
专任教师数（人）	Number of Full-time Teachers (person)		
中等职业教育学校	Secondary Vocational Technical School	32263	15373
普通中学	Ordinary High School	261293	97779
普通小学	Ordinary Primary School	269668	104279
在校学生数（万人）	Number of Student Enrollment (10000 persons)		
中等职业教育学校	Secondary Vocational Technical School	72.8	33.4
普通中学	Ordinary High School	348.9	128.5
普通小学	Ordinary Primary School	470.3	188.0
公共图书馆图书藏量（万册、件）	Quantity of Books in Public Libraries (10000 units)	4202.6	2132.5
医院数（个）	Number of Hospitals (unit)	1338	699
医院床位数（张）	Number of Hospital Beds (unit)	339157	178242
执业（助理）医师数（人）	Number of Practicing (assistant) Physicians (person)	185983	93927
注册护士数（人）	Registered Nurses (person)	221426	121060
人民生活	**People's Livelihood**		
城镇居民人均可支配收入（元）	Annual Per Capita Disposable Income of Urban Households (yuan)	45133	
城镇居民人均消费支出（元）	Per Capita Consumption Expenditure of Urban Residents (yuan)	26832	
每百户城镇居民家庭拥有	Per 100 Urban Households		
家用汽车（辆）	Automobile (unit)	43	
计算机（台）	Computer (unit)	59	
城镇居民人均住房建筑面积（平方米）	Per Capita Residential Floor Area of Urban Residents (sq.m)	42.4	
社会福利、劳动保险	**Social Welfare, Labor and Insurance**		
城乡居民基本养老保险参保人数（万人）	Number of Participants in Basic Old-age Insurance for Urban and Rural Residents (10000 persons)	3428.8	768.5
城市居民最低生活保障人数（万人）	Number of Urban Residents With Minimum Living Allowances (10000 persons)	27.6	14.9

10—2 地级城市市区基本情况（2022年）
Basic Statement of Cities at Prefectural Level by Region (2022)

指　　标	Item	合肥市 Hefei	淮北市 Huaibei	亳州市 Bozhou	宿州市 Suzhou
人口及土地	**Population and Land**				
常住人口 (万人)	Population of Permanent Residents (10000 persons)	532.3	103.2	152.7	177.5
建成区面积 (平方公里)	Developed Area (sq.km)	507	90	76	92
综合经济	**General Economy**				
地区生产总值(当年价格) (亿元)	Gross Regional Product (at current price) (100 million yuan)	8048.2	731.6	804.2	913.3
第一产业增加值	Added Value of Primary Industry	10.4	28.6	87.5	81.8
第二产业增加值	Added Value of Secondary Industry	2784.5	278.9	332.7	362.3
第三产业增加值	Added Value of Tertiary Industry	5253.3	424.2	384.1	469.1
财政、金融	**Government Finance, Banking and Insurance**				
地方财政一般公共预算收入 (亿元)	General Public Budget Revenue of Local Finance (100 million yuan)	671.8	68.7	80.1	90.9
地方财政一般公共预算支出 (亿元)	General Public Budget Expenditure of Local Finance (100 million yuan)	879.9	135.2	182.6	237.0
一般公共服务支出	General Public Service	42.2	7.2	14.9	18.2
科学技术支出	Science	182.8	6.1	6.0	7.1
教育支出	Education	155.9	22.0	30.3	33.0
文化旅游体育与传媒支出	Cultural Tourism, Sports and Media	6.8	1.7	1.3	2.7
卫生健康支出	Hygiene and Health	78.3	15.9	43.7	42.0
节能环保支出	Energy Saving and Environmental Protection	37.0	2.4	3.0	5.5
城乡社区支出	Urban and Rural Communities	167.9	26.1	7.4	35.3
交通运输支出	Transport	10.9	6.0	7.0	17.7
社会保障和就业支出	Social Security and Employment	54.1	18.1	20.9	24.9
住房保障支出	Housing Security	12.2	7.8	6.0	5.9
人民币住户存款余额 (亿元)	Deposits of Households (100 million yuan)	5219.1	750.6	808.3	977.7
工　业	**Industry**				
规模以上工业企业数 (个)	Number of Industrial Enterprises Above Designated Size (unit)	1128	355	359	589
内资企业	Domestic Funded Enterprises	982	341	355	574
港澳台商投资企业	Funded by Entrepreneurs from Hong Kong, Macao and Taiwan	55	5	3	8
外商投资企业	Foreign Funded Enterprises	91	9	1	7

蚌埠市 Bengbu	阜阳市 Fuyang	淮南市 Huainan	滁州市 Chuzhou	六安市 Luan	马鞍山市 Maanshan	芜湖市 Wuhu	宣城市 Xuancheng	铜陵市 Tongling	池州市 Chizhou	安庆市 Anqing	黄山市 Huangshan
134.1	212.6	156.7	80.8	197.3	101.6	246.4	77.3	83.8	61.2	81.1	54.3
155	156	128	120	82	104	265	75	91	49	163	72
1080.5	995.9	889.9	1031.3	904.4	1358.2	3556.0	519.2	1013.3	593.5	925.0	482.0
36.2	90.2	46.3	25.0	107.7	14.8	77.2	53.6	28.1	40.6	20.2	23.5
449.0	341.4	378.1	613.9	319.7	691.5	1698.1	210.8	547.6	303.3	403.6	164.5
595.3	564.3	465.5	392.4	476.9	651.9	1780.8	254.8	437.6	249.6	501.3	294.1
114.7	77.6	68.4	92.4	77.5	121.9	334.2	61.0	91.5	51.7	89.1	54.7
183.8	270.5	169.9	167.3	257.4	161.3	469.0	128.2	152.6	110.6	162.2	111.9
14.8	21.5	14.8	14.5	19.8	13.8	29.0	10.1	10.6	8.6	11.8	11.5
10.1	4.6	2.8	7.5	4.3	6.8	69.4	2.7	10.2	2.1	3.1	1.9
27.0	42.5	25.2	24.0	45.7	19.3	63.9	11.8	19.6	12.5	18.2	10.8
2.1	2.0	1.2	2.9	2.9	3.0	5.1	1.1	1.7	1.2	2.0	3.2
26.1	64.5	23.7	28.1	41.8	17.5	43.5	19.2	17.7	13.5	30.6	11.8
1.5	2.2	4.1	1.7	7.6	15.9	31.5	2.3	3.0	5.1	4.9	4.3
29.3	18.3	11.1	19.7	23.1	28.2	50.5	17.6	20.9	17.0	21.0	15.5
6.9	8.5	9.3	5.0	14.5	4.3	13.5	5.6	8.8	5.1	3.5	8.0
26.7	32.0	29.1	17.2	31.9	17.6	52.8	15.6	20.7	14.4	20.2	14.6
8.6	5.8	8.5	8.0	4.8	7.8	13.5	3.7	5.5	7.0	5.1	3.0
1027.1	1458.9	1329.1	619.2	1208.7	1043.3	2103.4	558.1	857.0	540.7	924.1	530.9
449	408	396	552	601	635	2032	554	484	386	327	265
427	396	386	482	586	579	1892	535	458	376	293	254
6	9	8	21	7	26	53	5	13	3	9	5
16	3	2	49	8	30	87	14	13	7	25	6

10—2 续表1 continued

指 标		Item		合肥市 Hefei	淮北市 Huaibei	亳州市 Bozhou	宿州市 Suzhou
流动资产合计	(亿元)	Total Circulating Funds	(100 million yuan)	5508.6	507.9	639.4	333.2
营业收入	(亿元)	Operating Income	(100 million yuan)	6915.8	769.5	778.3	735.7
利润总额	(亿元)	Total Profits	(100 million yuan)	263.3	97.1	66.6	45.1
邮 政		**Post**					
快递业务收入	(亿元)	Income From Express Business	(100 million yuan)	43.3	2.9	13.4	5.5
国内贸易		**Domestic Trade**					
社会消费品零售总额	(亿元)	Total Retail Sales of Consumer Goods	(100 million yuan)	3612.4	340.0	416.0	495.6
固定资产投资		**Investment in Fixed Assets**					
房地产开发投资	(亿元)	Total Investment in Real Estate Development	(100 million yuan)	1053.4	120.5	164.7	189.5
#住 宅		Residential Buildings		802.8	108.3	137.1	154.0
商品房屋销售面积	(万平方米)	Floor Space of Selling House	(10000 sq.m)	954.5	119.8	212.7	156.9
#住 宅		Residential Buildings		800.8	118.3	198.6	149.9
商品房屋销售额	(亿元)	Total Sales of Commercial House	(100 million yuan)	1297.0	84.0	124.4	108.9
#住 宅		Residential Buildings		1184.2	82.9	115.0	104.6
商品房屋待售面积	(万平方米)	Square Commercial House for Sal	(10000 sq.m)	317.4	54.0	33.4	41.6
教育、文化、卫生		**Education, Culture and Public Health**					
学校数	(所)	Number of Schools	(unit)				
中等职业教育学校		Secondary Vocational Technical School		29	3	5	6
普通中学		Ordinary High School		129	72	73	73
普通小学		Ordinary Primary School		177	103	236	238
专任教师数	(人)	Number of Full-time Teachers	(person)				
中等职业教育学校		Secondary Vocational Technical School		3010	515	1071	888
普通中学		Ordinary High School		17192	4641	6985	7884
普通小学		Ordinary Primary School		21244	4736	8884	10187

蚌埠市 Bengbu	阜阳市 Fuyang	淮南市 Huainan	滁州市 Chuzhou	六安市 Luan	马鞍山市 Maanshan	芜湖市 Wuhu	宣城市 Xuancheng	铜陵市 Tongling	池州市 Chizhou	安庆市 Anqing	黄山市 Huangshan
825.1	360.5	573.5	1078.6	461.7	1331.6	5254.7	354.4	989.0	415.1	468.6	187.6
1073.3	629.2	1278.6	1917.4	569.2	2823.7	6080.7	698.0	2815.8	1081.3	1237.5	293.2
70.8	21.3	43.5	65.5	28.4	83.8	398.9	26.4	96.2	35.2	38.2	13.5
9.9	10.4	3.9	8.9	8.6	5.0	19.4	5.1	2.8	2.7	7.5	3.7
760.3	866.4	570.9	358.3	585.1	502.3	1630.3	252.6	308.4	261.7	465.0	270.2
165.6	377.0	127.9	244.0	218.6	100.2	404.9	77.3	92.5	44.1	111.1	77.7
126.3	305.6	104.0	204.9	174.8	85.4	351.1	63.5	76.6	38.3	87.0	49.1
224.3	313.1	107.3	309.1	212.0	105.5	366.7	57.3	133.5	42.2	121.8	40.1
200.7	295.1	104.4	239.6	193.6	71.6	277.5	46.8	91.5	33.0	89.4	30.0
150.8	218.9	72.0	192.2	129.3	82.1	332.7	39.9	67.9	29.2	77.6	30.7
136.6	207.6	69.3	161.4	119.5	67.5	293.2	34.5	49.5	24.9	68.5	25.6
65.5	9.8	26.2	13.9	159.7	15.8	56.6	80.1	139.1	61.3	48.8	57.8
11	19	10	3	9	3	13	4	3	3	8	4
61	125	99	32	127	34	119	49	51	43	40	33
121	301	147	35	131	56	135	44	72	55	63	35
1083	2343	1065	478	914	428	1452	658	403	402	416	247
5364	10481	6561	2646	10447	3632	7784	3081	3667	2454	3199	1761
6664	10569	6421	2914	8617	3052	8317	3058	3134	2004	2513	1965

10—2 续表2 continued

指 标	Item	合肥市 Hefei	淮北市 Huaibei	亳州市 Bozhou	宿州市 Suzhou
在校学生数 （万人）	Number of Student Enrollment (10000 persons)				
中等职业教育学校	Secondary Vocational Technical School	6.9	1.1	1.9	2.5
普通中学	Ordinary High School	22.3	5.8	10.5	10.9
普通小学	Ordinary Primary School	38.7	8.3	15.9	17.8
公共图书馆图书藏量（万册、件）	Quantity of Books in Public Libraries (10000 units)	756.0	87.8	91.2	96.4
医院数 （个）	Number of Hospitals (unit)	146	58	32	40
医院床位数 （张）	Number of Hospital Beds (unit)	44876	7380	7339	9597
执业（助理）医师数 （人）	Number of Practicing (assistant) Physicians (person)	23407	3715	4765	5586
注册护士数 （人）	Registered Nurses (person)	31709	4663	6180	6443
人民生活	**People's Livelihood**				
城镇居民人均可支配收入 （元）	Annual Per Capita Disposable Income of Urban Households (yuan)	56177	41701	39364	38910
城镇居民人均消费支出 （元）	Per Capita Consumption Expenditure of Urban Residents (yuan)	32964	20542	20409	19047
每百户城镇居民家庭拥有	Per 100 Urban Households				
家用汽车 （辆）	Automobile (unit)	60	39	34	42
计算机 （台）	Computer (unit)	82	49	40	50
城镇居民人均住房建筑面积 （平方米）	Per Capita Residential Floor Area of Urban Residents (sq.m)	34	32	54	43
社会福利、劳动保险	**Social Welfare, Labor and Insurance**				
城乡居民基本养老保险参保人数 （万人）	Number of Participants in Basic Old-age Insurance for Urban and Rural Residents (10000 persons)	40.7	23.2	88.4	89.4
城市居民最低生活保障人数 （万人）	Number of Urban Residents With Minimum Living Allowances (10000 persons)	1.2	1.0	0.2	0.8

蚌埠市 Bengbu	阜阳市 Fuyang	淮南市 Huainan	滁州市 Chuzhou	六安市 Luan	马鞍山市 Maanshan	芜湖市 Wuhu	宣城市 Xuancheng	铜陵市 Tongling	池州市 Chizhou	安庆市 Anqing	黄山市 Huangshan
1.4	5.9	2.6	0.8	2.8	0.8	2.4	1.0	1.1	0.8	0.4	0.8
7.2	15.7	8.6	3.6	14.2	4.4	9.2	3.5	3.6	3.2	3.6	2.2
11.9	22.4	12.0	5.6	15.7	5.3	14.3	4.3	4.5	3.8	4.5	3.3
104.7	31.3	62.5	70.5	107.3	167.6	127.9	35.3	173.5	41.8	109.3	69.2
48	61	52	18	28	34	74	18	23	19	29	19
11576	17160	12210	4735	8988	6644	17724	5123	6413	3701	10040	4736
6006	9549	5680	2758	6948	3971	8796	2212	2989	1748	3695	2102
7702	11745	7369	3995	7935	5042	11002	3031	3775	2140	5367	2962
44652	39240	43353	41043	38883	59420	51481	48596	46445	41035	41454	43800
22118	20355	21625	21318	20369	32148	29518	29259	27403	20377	21191	25533
28	38	32	50	48	64	51	53	52	43	33	47
43	52	42	61	54	58	64	71	58	70	68	76
37	41	36	44	39	40	36	41	41	45	42	54
28.5	105.1	43.9	19.5	109.9	16.9	59.8	44.4	29.9	31.7	19.6	17.7
1.2	0.9	1.1	0.3	0.7	1.5	2.3	0.4	2.1	0.3	0.6	0.3

10—3 城市市政公用基础设施基本情况
Basic Statistics on Urban Public Utilities

指标	Item	2015	2020	2021	2022
城市面积	**Cities Areas**				
建成区面积 (平方公里)	Developed Areas (sq.km)	1926.36	2409.89	2460.17	2500.28
城市人口密度 (人/平方公里)	Population Density of Urban Districts (persons/sq.km)	2458	2655	2730	2744
供水、供气及供热	**Water Supply, Gas Supply and Heating**				
供水管道长度 (公里)	Length of the Pipeline for Supplying Water (km)	23842	36257	34120	35916
供水总量 (万立方米)	Annual Supply of Tap Water (10000 cu.m)	174263	238126	255083	261031
#居民家庭用水量	Water Consumption for Residential Use	68319	99121	101662	102099
人均日生活用水 (升)	Per Capita Water Consumption for Residential Use (liter)	168.90	197.37	190.23	194.31
用水普及率 (%)	Percentage of Population With Access to Tap Water (%)	98.79	99.60	99.81	99.76
天然气供气量 (万立方米)	Supply of Natural Gas (10000 cu.m)	234585	414417	451842	501514
#家庭用量	Consumption of Coal Gas for Residential Use	71773	128570	134921	151169
液化石油气供气量 (吨)	Liquefied Petroleum Gas (ton)	736312	157719	160115	159206
#家庭用量	Consumption of Liquefied Gas for Residential Use	104259	87248	82192	85158
供气管道长度 (公里)	Length of Gas Pipelines (km)	19949	32517	34774	35978
燃气普及率 (%)	Percentage of Population With Access to Gas (%)	97.55	99.24	99.48	99.42
集中供热面积 (万平方米)	Heated Area (10000 sq.m)	2683.76	2575.82	2555.35	2683.75
公共交通	**Public Traffic**				
公共汽（电）车总数 (辆)	Number of Public Transportation Vehicles (buses and trolley buses etc.) (unit)	18622	28331	28301	27785
出租汽车 (辆)	Taxi (unit)	55217	54136	55298	55205
市政工程	**Municipal Engineering**				
道路长度 (公里)	Length of Paved Roads (km)	13375	17750	19433	20372
道路面积 (万平方米)	Area of Paved Roads (10000 sq.m)	31010	43286	46184	48037
每人拥有 (平方米)	Area of Paved Roads per Population (sq.m)	20.82	24.29	23.74	24.57
排水管道长度 (公里)	Length of Sewer Pipelines (km)	24399	35393	36505	37867
建成区排水管道密度 (公里/平方公里)	Density of Sewer Pipelines (km/sq.km)	12.67	13.49	13.62	13.98
污水排放量 (万立方米)	Volume of Waste Water Discharged (10000 cu.m)	150642	208669	228288	227265
污水处理厂处理量 (万立方米)	Volume of Waste Water Treated (10000 cu.m)	138293	199819	219407	218797
城市绿化	**Forestation in Cities**				
绿化覆盖面积 (公顷)	Afforested Area (hectare)	112303	135493	144928	148248
#建成区	Developed District	79285	101232	108424	113324
园林绿地面积 (公顷)	Greenery Area of Gardens (hectare)	93786	119533	127602	132363
#建成区	Developed District	71582	92762	99276	102878
公园绿地面积 (公顷)	Park Greenery Area (hectare)	19913	26520	28190	33198
人均公园绿地面积 (平方米)	Per Capita Park Greenery Area (sq.m)	13.37	14.88	14.49	16.98
公园个数 (个)	Number of Parks (unit)	374	588	619	834
公园面积 (公顷)	Area of Parks (hectare)	12043	18795	20547	22931
市容环境卫生	**Environmental Sanitation**				
生活垃圾清运量 (万吨)	Volume of Disposal of Excrement (10000 tons)	491.94	660.70	714.90	745.42
生活垃圾无害化处理量 (万吨)	Environment-friendly Handling Capacity of the Domestic Rubbish (10000 tons)	489.74	660.70	714.90	745.42
生活垃圾无害化处理率 (%)	Living Refuse Treatment Rate (%)	99.55	100.00	100.00	100.00
公共厕所 (座)	Public Lavatory (unit)	3223	4769	6685	7092
#三类以上	Above Three Kinds	2813	4387	5787	6937

注：由于住建部制度修订，从2017年度起只统计用于城市生产和生活作燃料使用的气体能源。原先安庆市石化报送的约60万吨液化气系企业生产用原材料不再统计。

a) Due to the revision of the system of the Ministry of Housing and Urban-Rural Development, only the gas energy used for urban production and domestic fuel will be counted from 2017. Originally, about 600,000 tons of raw materials for production of liquefied gas enterprises submitted by Anqing Petrochemical Company are no longer counted.

10—4 各市城市建设情况（2022年）
Statistics on City Construction by Region (2022)

单位：平方公里（sq.km）

地 区	Region	城市现状建设用地面积 Urban Current Construction Land Area	#居住用地 For Residence	#公用设施用地 For Public Facilities	#道路与交通设施用地 Land for Roads and Traffic Facilities	#绿地与广场用地 Green Space and Square Land	征用土地面积 Land Put in Requisition for State Construction Projects	城市人口密度（人／平方公里）Population Density of Urban Area (persons/sq.km)
总 计	**Total**	**2426.81**	**704.78**	**179.33**	**459.56**	**297.13**	**177.05**	**2744**
合肥市	Hefei	453.86	135.52	53.89	106.55	23.98	51.55	5081
淮北市	Huaibei	99.01	35.60	7.44	11.62	9.75	12.70	3443
亳州市	Bozhou	76.00	20.94	3.75	17.01	16.45	0.53	4661
宿州市	Suzhou	91.56	28.24	4.08	19.48	13.42	1.95	3750
蚌埠市	Bengbu	154.97	50.41	11.07	26.54	12.20	32.90	2709
阜阳市	Fuyang	156.01	50.52	9.80	25.39	39.93	4.93	3177
淮南市	Huainan	128.14	46.40	1.17	22.51	34.64	2.65	2417
滁州市	Chuzhou	120.97	27.41	7.09	28.32	13.80	8.79	2453
六安市	Luan	82.38	27.61	8.28	17.03	5.87	2.46	3653
马鞍山市	Maanshan	93.23	25.87	7.05	9.85	3.67	0.65	4477
芜湖市	Wuhu	265.08	47.47	18.81	42.99	23.94	19.97	1758
宣城市	Xuancheng	74.30	18.10	5.51	15.88	8.09	3.47	2726
铜陵市	Tongling	87.24	24.31	7.34	13.99	5.71	5.68	1997
池州市	Chizhou	50.16	17.21	4.38	8.90	8.54	0.02	1230
安庆市	Anqing	164.72	45.42	10.33	29.57	23.88	5.30	2424
黄山市	Huangshan	60.62	20.85	3.84	11.93	9.04	1.07	767
桐城市	Tongcheng	26.03	10.35	1.78	3.64	0.49	0.51	1858
天长市	Tianchang	25.98	7.51	1.09	8.01	6.37	5.81	2421
明光市	Mingguang	29.00	8.35	1.85	7.46	3.18	2.24	4565
界首市	Jieshou	26.92	6.03	1.58	4.92	8.29	0.75	2445
宁国市	Ningguo	32.53	9.16	1.58	4.49	1.31	2.86	542
巢湖市	Chaohu	48.00	18.20	2.20	10.91	9.49	3.52	2051
潜山市	Qianshan	21.57	8.12	1.35	3.04	3.29	3.33	1139
无为市	Wuwei	25.11	7.02	2.05	3.23	7.40	2.21	1602
广德市	Guangde	33.42	8.16	2.02	6.30	4.40	1.20	4111

10—5 各市城市市政设施情况（2022年）
Basic Statistics on Municipal Infrastructure in Cities by Region (2022)

地 区	Region	年末实有道路长度（公里）Length of Paved Roads (year-end) (km)	年末实有道路面积（万平方米）Area of Paved Roads (year-end) (10000 sq.m)	城市桥梁数（座）Number of City Bridges (unit)	城市道路照明灯（盏）Number of Street Lights (unit)	城市排水管道（公里）Length of City Sewage Pipes (km)	污水管道 Sewage Pipeline
总 计	**Total**	**20372**	**48037**	**2414**	**1262908**	**37867**	**16922**
合肥市	Hefei	3332	9700	900	293814	9079	3792
淮北市	Huaibei	731	1655	50	32968	1145	494
亳州市	Bozhou	645	1798	17	49657	1384	599
宿州市	Suzhou	879	1933	119	58653	1205	584
蚌埠市	Bengbu	1338	2903	43	63090	1440	667
阜阳市	Fuyang	1261	2766	184	55174	1887	888
淮南市	Huainan	1096	2251	54	59151	1288	668
滁州市	Chuzhou	1018	2887	193	78539	2496	1183
六安市	Luan	691	2007	44	35357	1026	516
马鞍山市	Maanshan	983	2106	72	55919	1857	676
芜湖市	Wuhu	2103	4914	150	116299	3676	1278
宣城市	Xuancheng	603	1337	93	29433	1360	540
铜陵市	Tongling	780	1524	36	39933	1855	904
池州市	Chizhou	473	856	36	20785	819	344
安庆市	Anqing	1354	2616	118	82587	1487	1066
黄山市	Huangshan	659	1190	53	44052	921	427
桐城市	Tongcheng	244	499	13	13470	473	176
天长市	Tianchang	458	799	33	13970	512	239
明光市	Mingguang	328	747	19	21597	862	370
界首市	Jieshou	183	487	36	11349	399	169
宁国市	Ningguo	271	635	52	21229	520	227
巢湖市	Chaohu	442	1120	31	26400	1037	610
潜山市	Qianshan	105	289	16	11915	289	102
无为市	Wuwei	133	343	6	11050	262	82
广德市	Guangde	263	675	46	16517	587	323

10—6 各市城市设施水平（2022年）
Level of Public Facilities in Cities by Region (2022)

地 区	Region	城市用水普及率(%) Coverage Rate of Urban Population with Access to Tap Warer (%)	城市燃气普及率(%) Coverage Rate of Urban Population with Access to Gas (%)	人均城市道路面积(平方米) Per Capita Area of Paved Roads (sq.m)
总 计	**Total**	**99.76**	**99.42**	**24.57**
合肥市	Hefei	99.99	100.00	14.91
淮北市	Huaibei	100.00	100.00	22.89
亳州市	Bozhou	100.00	99.73	44.40
宿州市	Suzhou	100.00	100.00	31.33
蚌埠市	Bengbu	100.00	100.00	29.32
阜阳市	Fuyang	98.99	97.30	25.70
淮南市	Huainan	100.00	100.00	19.85
滁州市	Chuzhou	100.00	100.00	41.65
六安市	Luan	99.80	100.00	33.06
马鞍山市	Maanshan	100.00	100.00	26.74
芜湖市	Wuhu	100.00	98.89	25.91
宣城市	Xuancheng	97.94	99.19	37.24
铜陵市	Tongling	100.00	100.00	24.89
池州市	Chizhou	99.81	99.52	27.53
安庆市	Anqing	100.00	100.00	34.64
黄山市	Huangshan	100.00	95.00	33.61
桐城市	Tongcheng	97.59	97.88	29.31
天长市	Tianchang	100.00	100.00	41.33
明光市	Mingguang	93.10	95.67	40.91
界首市	Jieshou	96.48	96.48	25.56
宁国市	Ningguo	99.88	98.91	36.49
巢湖市	Chaohu	100.00	99.94	34.13
潜山市	Qianshan	97.72	83.31	23.54
无为市	Wuwei	100.00	100.00	17.29
广德市	Guangde	100.00	100.00	40.01

10—7 各市城市公共交通情况（2022年）

Basic Statistics on Public Transportation in Cities by Region (2022)

地区	Region	年末公共汽、电车交通运营数（辆）Number of Bus and Tram Traffic Operations at the end of the year (unit)	公共汽、电车运营线路总长度（公里）Total Length of Bus and Tram Lines (km)	公共汽、电车客运总量（万人次）Total Passenger Volume of Buses and Trams (10000 person-times)	出租汽车（辆）Number of Taxi (unit)
总　计	**Total**	**27785**	**81143**	**110951**	**55205**
合肥市	Hefei	6497	14951	34958	11552
淮北市	Huaibei	912	3083	3002	1638
亳州市	Bozhou	2017	4375	4494	3004
宿州市	Suzhou	1726	6185	3394	3033
蚌埠市	Bengbu	1607	3500	8073	3236
阜阳市	Fuyang	1918	3760	8038	3794
淮南市	Huainan	1469	1797	5077	3570
滁州市	Chuzhou	2004	5297	8696	3145
六安市	Luan	2219	9196	5793	3926
马鞍山市	Maanshan	1074	2641	3962	3234
芜湖市	Wuhu	1804	4244	8512	5380
宣城市	Xuancheng	1454	8930	4149	1909
铜陵市	Tongling	941	3366	4624	1945
池州市	Chizhou	471	3963	1688	1068
安庆市	Anqing	1304	3463	5393	3925
黄山市	Huangshan	368	2394	1098	846

10—8 各市城市绿地和园林（2022年）

Basic Statistics on Parks and Green Areas in Cities by Region (2022)

地区	Region	绿化覆盖面积（公顷）Green Areas (hectare)	建成区 Completed Area	绿地面积（公顷）Green Land Area (hectare)	公园绿地面积（公顷）Park Green Areas (hectare)	人均公园绿地面积（平方米）Park Green Areas (sq.m)	公园（个）Number of Parks (unit)	建成区绿地率(%) Per Capita Park Green Areas (%)	建成区绿化覆盖率(%) Green Covered Area as % of Completed Area (%)
总计	**Total**	**148248**	**113324**	**132363**	**33198**	**16.98**	**834**	**41.15**	**45.32**
合肥市	Hefei	26220	23283	22497	9705	14.92	295	40.30	45.96
淮北市	Huaibei	5120	4010	4713	1370	18.95	17	43.25	44.66
亳州市	Bozhou	4831	3342	4341	658	16.24	36	40.76	43.98
宿州市	Suzhou	6306	4051	5823	1162	18.84	39	41.20	44.20
蚌埠市	Bengbu	6961	6885	6332	1617	16.33	13	40.36	44.42
阜阳市	Fuyang	8395	7110	7596	1986	18.45	32	41.54	45.47
淮南市	Huainan	7719	5985	6261	2267	19.99	19	44.00	46.71
滁州市	Chuzhou	6071	5724	5466	1839	26.53	22	42.69	47.31
六安市	Luan	4608	3759	3657	1104	18.18	25	40.75	45.62
马鞍山市	Maanshan	6899	4665	6512	1169	14.85	24	42.77	44.73
芜湖市	Wuhu	13062	12151	12127	3121	16.45	48	40.98	45.84
宣城市	Xuancheng	5379	3401	4826	714	19.87	20	40.37	45.35
铜陵市	Tongling	8020	3999	7142	1007	16.45	19	40.89	43.95
池州市	Chizhou	2687	2350	2174	626	20.12	11	40.46	47.71
安庆市	Anqing	7256	7024	6974	1228	16.26	15	40.44	43.12
黄山市	Huangshan	14646	3432	13514	625	17.64	32	39.56	47.93
桐城市	Tongcheng	1268	1234	1154	266	15.61	10	40.10	43.01
天长市	Tianchang	1105	1098	1082	381	19.69	18	41.07	42.02
明光市	Mingguang	1388	1343	1243	344	18.83	28	40.12	44.76
界首市	Jieshou	1856	1152	1464	337	17.67	8	41.25	42.80
宁国市	Ningguo	1648	1577	1457	356	20.47	28	42.00	46.62
巢湖市	Chaohu	2290	2220	2232	530	16.15	28	44.41	46.25
潜山市	Qianshan	1060	921	899	223	18.14	9	36.10	41.86
无为市	Wuwei	1481	1149	1114	292	14.69	10	42.73	45.50
广德市	Guangde	1972	1457	1766	274	16.26	28	40.15	43.61

10—9 各市城市燃气情况（2022年）
Basic Statistics on Supply of Gas in Cities by Region (2022)

地区	Region	管道长度(公里) Length of Gas Pipelines (km)		全年供气总量 Volume of Gas Supply		用气人口(万人) Population with Access to Gas (10000 persons)	
		液化石油气 Liquefied Petroleum Gas	天然气 Natural Gas	液化石油气(吨) Liquefied Petroleum Gas (ton)	天然气(万立方米) Natural Gas (10000 cu.m)	液化石油气 Liquefied Petroleum Gas	天然气 Natural Gas
总计	**Total**	**189.60**	**35768.81**	**159205.82**	**501513.81**	**123.12**	**1820.88**
合肥市	Hefei		7578.55	39502.00	136263.61	10.30	640.10
淮北市	Huaibei		1537.84	9714.00	18499.00	10.08	62.23
亳州市	Bozhou		1838.10	12475.90	10067.17	5.86	34.53
宿州市	Suzhou		1324.51	2850.00	11398.52	1.84	59.85
蚌埠市	Bengbu	13.00	2588.41	1340.27	48281.00	3.26	95.76
阜阳市	Fuyang		1058.81	15863.00	14726.24	8.75	95.99
淮南市	Huainan		1731.96	8743.00	18672.57	8.62	104.75
滁州市	Chuzhou		1885.83	2792.00	24264.32	1.14	68.18
六安市	Luan		1345.53	153.00	16833.00	0.10	60.59
马鞍山市	Maanshan		1458.96	1989.00	34143.00	1.85	76.88
芜湖市	Wuhu	2.10	4335.58	21359.16	57965.28	13.02	174.56
宣城市	Xuancheng		848.19	2000.00	13904.24	3.00	32.63
铜陵市	Tongling		1226.73	6500.00	24612.85	6.50	54.73
池州市	Chizhou		957.74	2192.00	5794.59	2.60	28.35
安庆市	Anqing		1063.96	2950.00	14669.40	2.69	72.82
黄山市	Huangshan	153.50	826.80	5802.00	4609.51	16.08	17.57
桐城市	Tongcheng	21.00	457.70	6190.49	1935.00	5.85	10.80
天长市	Tianchang		674.61	960.00	7069.50	1.01	18.33
明光市	Mingguang		386.87	3500.00	5209.52	3.35	14.12
界首市	Jieshou		546.10	2070.00	1776.00	5.30	13.09
宁国市	Ningguo		390.00	5200.00	6803.49	4.90	12.30
巢湖市	Chaohu		1088.20	552.00	9600.50	0.48	32.31
潜山市	Qianshan		156.90	1280.00	1192.50	1.88	8.35
无为市	Wuwei		251.94	1128.00	3280.00	0.80	19.06
广德市	Guangde		208.99	2100.00	9943.00	3.86	13.00

10—10 城市供水用水情况
Water Supply and Water Use of Cities

年份 Year	综合生产能力(万立方米/日) Integrated Production Capacity (10000 cu.m/day)	地下水 Ground Water	供水总量(万立方米) Water Supply (10000 cu.m)	用水总量(万立方米) Water Use (10000 cu.m) #生产运营用水 Water Used for Business	公共服务用水 Water Used for Public Services	居民家庭用水 Water Used for Residents	其他用水 Other Water	人均日生活用水量(升) Per Capita Water Use (liter)
2006	1026.0	145.7	220174	102877	28373	57515	6778	237.84
2007	999.2	109.3	207574	116823	20918	48145	3780	180.40
2008	1728.7	109.4	195543	101119	19353	50323	3596	174.71
2009	2080.6	92.9	162243	67362	18656	49072	4248	160.96
2010	1992.8	99.2	160816	62871	19191	50889	5155	160.83
2011	820.2	103.2	158039	51387	18921	56014	5899	169.00
2012	1029.4	114.6	156888	47010	19443	59439	4406	165.45
2013	1074.0	98.8	161140	49071	20859	61328	5257	166.15
2014	1074.8	99.6	167781	49957	21627	64145	5217	166.72
2015	1094.8	98.5	174263	50110	22194	68319	4266	168.90
2016	1111.6	114.0	186543	51844	22167	76631	4677	180.19
2017	906.3	111.6	189892	52447	25090	79978	3642	188.11
2018	896.6	94.0	200824	54497	25438	86209	3561	190.68
2019	997.7	97.2	226762	66598	28072	91240	6830	194.49
2020	1079.0	95.0	238126	70811	28698	99121	7071	197.37
2021	1122.4	95.1	255083	78933	33084	101662	8890	190.23
2022	1143.6	90.5	261031	80573	36161	102099	9454	194.31

10—11 各市城市供水用水情况（2022年）

Water Supply and Water Use of Cities by Region (2022)

地 区 Region	综合生产能力（万立方米/日） Integrated Production Capacity (10000 cu.m/day)	地下水 Ground Water	供水总量（万立方米） Water Supply (10000 cu.m)	用水总量(万立方米) Water Use (10000 cu.m) #生产运营用水 Water Used for Business	公共服务用水 Water Used for Public Services	居民家庭用水 Water Used for Residents	其他用水 Other Water	人均日生活用水量（升） Per Capita Water Use (liter)
总 计 Total	**1143.6**	**90.5**	**261031**	**80573**	**36161**	**102099**	**9454**	**194.31**
合肥市 Hefei	241.4	0.1	68636	13629	12845	34776		200.61
淮北市 Huaibei	35.1	33.9	7424	2196	580	3562	58	156.94
亳州市 Bozhou	32.5	12.5	6034	1431	677	2592	11	221.11
宿州市 Suzhou	22.9	17.6	6963	2520	1189	2621	6	169.21
蚌埠市 Bengbu	78.0	0.4	19445	7548	5545	4636	38	281.67
阜阳市 Fuyang	38.2	9.5	11293	4105	440	5630	16	156.16
淮南市 Huainan	55.6	4.2	12482	2927	1609	5661	446	175.70
滁州市 Chuzhou	40.5		10268	4211	744	3481	541	166.97
六安市 Luan	48.5		7616	1055	992	3130	497	186.46
马鞍山市 Maanshan	130.5		16882	9279	1891	3436	753	185.38
芜湖市 Wuhu	117.7		29309	8200	2623	9413	3997	174.41
宣城市 Xuancheng	26.6	0.1	5803	1639	689	2548	75	252.28
铜陵市 Tongling	67.0		11362	3617	353	4628	1281	222.91
池州市 Chizhou	16.0		4396	821	1467	1650	10	276.61
安庆市 Anqing	52.4	0.1	13946	6988	2114	2851	433	180.13
黄山市 Huangshan	25.0		4846	1343	264	2286	154	199.38
桐城市 Tongcheng	10.5		2149	640	169	1131		214.56
天长市 Tianchang	15.0	5.0	3536	1215	360	808	767	165.60
明光市 Mingguang	9.1	0.6	1894	332	230	988	63	196.26
界首市 Jieshou	10.6	6.6	1485	266	87	883	2	144.63
宁国市 Ningguo	13.0		2713	882	21	1259	140	202.05
巢湖市 Chaohu	22.0		5409	3271	437	1190	48	135.84
潜山市 Qianshan	7.5		1476	491	67	778		192.81
无为市 Wuwei	17.0		3064	881	347	1441	18	246.58
广德市 Guangde	11.0		2601	1089	422	720	100	185.48

10—12 各市城市污水排放和处理情况（2022年）
City Sewage Emission and Processing by Region (2022)

单位：万立方米（10000 cu.m）

地区	Region	城市污水排放量 City Sewage discharge	城市污水处理总量 Total of Sewage Processing	污水处理厂处理量 Processing Amount of Sewage Processing Plant	其他污水处理量 Processing Amount of Others	城市污水处理率(%) Rate of City Sewage Treatment (%)	城市污水处理厂集中处理率(%) Central Processing Rate of Sewage Treatment Plant (%)
总　计	**Total**	**227265**	**222876**	**218797**	**4079**	**98.07**	**96.27**
合肥市	Hefei	61772	60552	59003	1549	98.02	95.52
淮北市	Huaibei	6051	5960	5960		98.49	98.49
亳州市	Bozhou	8980	8801	8801		98.01	98.01
宿州市	Suzhou	7124	7033	6518	515	98.73	91.50
蚌埠市	Bengbu	14518	14230	13798	432	98.02	95.04
阜阳市	Fuyang	10311	10188	10188		98.81	98.81
淮南市	Huainan	11601	11418	11129	290	98.42	95.93
滁州市	Chuzhou	9035	8828	8814	14	97.71	97.56
六安市	Luan	6473	6376	6247	129	98.50	96.50
马鞍山市	Maanshan	12295	12092	11742	350	98.35	95.50
芜湖市	Wuhu	25947	25447	24909	538	98.07	96.00
宣城市	Xuancheng	5228	5113	5113		97.80	97.80
铜陵市	Tongling	9090	8981	8981		98.80	98.80
池州市	Chizhou	3913	3834	3834		97.99	97.99
安庆市	Anqing	10061	9942	9701	241	98.82	96.43
黄山市	Huangshan	4315	4135	4135		95.83	95.83
桐城市	Tongcheng	1676	1616	1607	9	96.42	95.89
天长市	Tianchang	3070	3020	3020		98.36	98.36
明光市	Mingguang	1797	1756	1744	12	97.67	97.00
界首市	Jieshou	1645	1605	1605		97.58	97.58
宁国市	Ningguo	1922	1841	1841		95.80	95.80
巢湖市	Chaohu	4864	4718	4718		97.00	97.00
潜山市	Qianshan	1351	1320	1320		97.68	97.68
无为市	Wuwei	2146	2054	2054		95.70	95.70
广德市	Guangde	2080	2017	2017		96.99	96.99

10—13 各市城市市容环境卫生情况（2022年）

Basic Statistics on Urban Sanitation in Cities by Region (2022)

地区	Region	道路清扫保洁面积（万平方米）Road Cleaning Area (10000 sq.m)	生活垃圾清运量（万吨）Volume of Garbage Disposal (10000 tons)	生活垃圾无害化处理量（万吨）Volume of Garbage hazard-free Disposal (10000 tons)	生活垃圾无害化处理率（%）Living Refuse Treatment Rate (%)	市容环卫专用车辆设备总数（台）Number of Special Vehicles for Environmental Sanitation (unit)	公共厕所（座）Number of Public Lavatories (unit)
总　计	**Total**	**50253**	**745.42**	**745.42**	**100.00**	**12107**	**7092**
合肥市	Hefei	8844	237.14	237.14	100.00	1633	375
淮北市	Huaibei	1644	31.37	31.37	100.00	1336	158
亳州市	Bozhou	2693	19.58	19.58	100.00	315	446
宿州市	Suzhou	1927	23.29	23.29	100.00	434	573
蚌埠市	Bengbu	2903	37.64	37.64	100.00	879	630
阜阳市	Fuyang	3623	37.34	37.34	100.00	946	675
淮南市	Huainan	2990	38.09	38.09	100.00	468	466
滁州市	Chuzhou	2971	24.42	24.42	100.00	784	201
六安市	Luan	1829	28.75	28.75	100.00	389	408
马鞍山市	Maanshan	1740	34.85	34.85	100.00	216	141
芜湖市	Wuhu	4708	74.59	74.59	100.00	429	1066
宣城市	Xuancheng	1434	15.24	15.24	100.00	137	316
铜陵市	Tongling	1935	23.38	23.38	100.00	393	368
池州市	Chizhou	849	11.30	11.30	100.00	103	137
安庆市	Anqing	2586	25.55	25.55	100.00	851	359
黄山市	Huangshan	1175	12.21	12.21	100.00	428	85
桐城市	Tongcheng	456	6.34	6.34	100.00	419	32
天长市	Tianchang	886	8.32	8.32	100.00	92	136
明光市	Mingguang	1413	10.05	10.05	100.00	105	100
界首市	Jieshou	450	7.83	7.83	100.00	68	90
宁国市	Ningguo	930	5.37	5.37	100.00	308	106
巢湖市	Chaohu	832	11.09	11.09	100.00	710	78
潜山市	Qianshan	289	7.92	7.92	100.00	98	42
无为市	Wuwei	469	7.87	7.87	100.00	47	51
广德市	Guangde	677	5.90	5.90	100.00	519	53

主要统计指标解释

供水管道长度

指从送水泵至用户水表之间所有管道的长度。不包括新安装尚未使用、水厂内以及用户建筑物内的管道。

供水总量

指报告期供水企业（单位）供出的全部水量。包括有效供水量和漏损水量。

公共服务用水

指为城区社会公共生活服务的用水。包括行政事业单位、部队营区和公共设施服务、社会服务业、批发零售贸易业、旅馆饮食业以及社会服务业等单位的用水。

居民家庭用水

居民家庭用水指城市范围内所有居民家庭的日常生活用水。包括城市居民、农民家庭、公共供水站用水。

用水普及率

指报告期末城区内用水人口与总人口的比率。计算公式：

用水普及率=城区用水人口 /（城区人口+城区暂住人口）×100%

供气总量

指报告期燃气企业（单位）向用户供应的燃气数量。包括销售量和损失量。

燃气普及率

指报告期城区内使用燃气的人口与总人口的比率。计算公式：

燃气普及率=城区用气人口 /（城区人口+城区暂住人口）×100%

排水管道长度

指所有排水总管、干管、支管、检查井及连接井进出口等长度之和。

公园绿地

城市中向公众开放的、以游憩为主要功能，有一定的游憩设施和服务设施，同时兼有健全生态、美化景观、防灾减灾等综合作用的绿化用地。

公园面积

指报告期末综合公园、专类公园和带状公园的全部占地总面积。

Explanatory Notes for Major Statistical Indicators

Length of Water Supply Pipelines

refers to the total length of all the pipelines between the water pumps and the user water meters, excluding pipelines newly installed but not used yet, and in water plant, user building's pipeline as well as.

Volume of Water Supply

refers to the total volume of water supplied by water-works (units) during the reference period, including both the effective water supply and loss during the water supply.

Consumption of Water for Public Service

refers to the water consumption of urban society public service, including the consumption of government agencies and public institutions, military barracks, public facilities, wholesale and retail outlets, restaurants, hotels, and other units providing public services.

Consumption of Water for Residential Use

refers to the consumption of water for daily life of all households in the boundary of cities, including households of urban residents and farmers, and public water supply stations.

Percentage of Urban Population with Access to Tap Water

refers to the ratio of the urban population with access to tap water to the total urban population. The formula is:

Percentage of population with access to tap water=(Urban population with access to tap water) / (Urban population)×100%

Volume of Gas Supply

refers to the total volume of gas provided to users by gas-producing enterprises (units) in a year, including the volume sold and the volume lost.

Percentage of Urban Population with Access to Gas

population of urban areas using gas during the reference period and the ratio of the total population. Formula:

Percentage of population with access to gas = (Urban population with access to gas / Urban population) x 100%

Length of Urban Sewage Pipes

refers to the total length of general drainage, trunks. branch and inspection wells, connection wells, inlets and outlets, etc.

Park Green Area

refers to green areas open to the public for amusement and rest with the facilities of amusement, rest and services. Its function includes perfecting ecology, beautifying landscape, and preventing and reducing disaster.

Park Area

Total areas of including comprehensive park, community park, topic park, belt-shaped park.

第十一篇

Chapter 11

自然资源和环境保护

NATURAL RESOURCES AND ENVIRONMENT PROTECTION

简要说明

一、自然状况包括地域、气象状况。自然资源包括土地、气候、林木、水资源。

1. 林木资料来自省林业局；

2. 水资源资料由省水利厅和省水文局提供；

3. 气象资料由省气象中心整理提供。

二、环境保护统计资料由省生态环境厅提供，统计资料依据国家生态环境部制定的环境统计报表制度，由各市的环境统计年报汇总整理而成，主要包括“三废”排放与处理，反映各工业行业有关“三废”排放与处理的情况。

Brief Introduction

I. Natural conditions cover region and meteorological conditions. Natural resources cover land, climate, forest and water resources.

1. Forest data from the provincial Forestry Bureau;

2. Data on water conservancy are provided by the Water Conservancy Department and the Marine Products Bureau of Anhui Province.

3. The meteorological data are provided by the Provincial Meteorological Center.

II. Statistical data of environmental protection are provided by the Provincial Department of Ecology and Environment. According to the environmental statistical statement system formulated by the Ministry of Ecology and Environment of The People's Republic of China, the statistical data are summarized and sorted out from the environmental statistical annual reports of various cities, mainly including the discharge and treatment of "three wastes" and reflecting the discharge and treatment of "three wastes" in various industries.

11—1 自然状况
Natural Conditions

项　目		Item		2022
区　域		**Climate**		
土地总面积	(平方公里)	Total Land Area	(sq.km)	140140
山　区		Mountain		41162
平　原		Plain		34608
丘　陵		Hills		40448
圩　区		Low-lying Paddy Fields		12097
湖泊洼地		Lakes and Low-lying Lands		11122
山峰高程	**(米)**	**Height of Mountain Peak**	**(m)**	
大别山		DaBie Shan		1729.0
黄　山		Huang Shan		1864.8
九华山		JiuHua Shan		1344.4
天柱山		TianZhu Shan		1489.8
河流长度(安徽境内)	**(公里)**	**Length（Within the territory of Anhui Province）**	**(km)**	
淮　河		Huaihe River		430
长　江		Changjiang River		416
新安江		Xin An Jiang River		240
湖泊面积		**Area of Lakes**		
巢　湖	(平方公里)	ChaoHu Lake	(sq.km)	800
气　候		**Climate**		
年平均气温	(摄氏度)	Annual Average Temperature	(℃)	
淮北地区		HuaiBei Area		16.6
江淮地区		JiangHuai Area		17.3
沿江地区		Along Chang Jiang River		17.8
江南地区		Lying South of Chang Jiang		17.2
降水量	(毫米)	Precipitation	(mm)	
淮河流域		Huaihe River Basin		782.8
淮河上游区		The Upper Reaches of Huaihe River		791.9
淮河中游区		The Middle Reaches of Huaihe River		785.0
淮河下游区		The Lower Reaches of Huaihe River		719.6
沂沭泗河		Yishusi River		710.0
长江流域		Changjiang River Basin		1121.6
湖口以下干流		Main Rivers Below Hukou		1105.6
鄱阳湖水系		River System of Poyang Lake		1477.6
太湖水系		River System of Taihu Lake		1137.8
东南诸河		South-eastern Rivers		1554.7
钱塘江		Qiantang Jiang River		1554.7

11—2 自然资源
Natural Resources

项 目	Item	2021	2022
林木资源	**Forest Resources**		
人工造林面积 (千公顷)	Artificial Afforestation Area (1000 hectares)	35.77	22.64
水资源	**Water Resources**		
水资源总量 (亿立方米)	Total Resources (100 million cu.m)	883.26	545.19
淮河流域	Huaihe River Basin	303.45	174.79
淮河上游区	The Upper Reaches of Huaihe River	1.74	1.09
淮河中游区	The Middle Reaches of Huaihe River	292.96	170.02
淮河下游区	The Lower Reaches of Huaihe River	7.78	3.05
沂沭泗河	Yishusi River	0.97	0.63
长江流域	Changjiang River Basin	508.65	317.74
湖口以下干流	Main Rivers Below Hukou	479.13	296.37
鄱阳湖水系	River System of Poyang Lake	27.90	20.25
太湖水系	River System of Taihu Lake	1.62	1.12
东南诸河	South-eastern Rivers	71.16	52.66
钱塘江	Qiantang River	71.16	52.66
天然年径流量 (亿立方米)	Natural Annual Flow (100 million cu.m)	798.01	476.72
淮河流域	Huaihe River Basin	232.88	118.52
淮河上游区	The Upper Reaches of Huaihe River	1.07	0.55
淮河中游区	The Middle Reaches of Huaihe River	224.67	115.55
淮河下游区	The Lower Reaches of Huaihe River	6.75	2.23
沂沭泗河	Yishusi River	0.39	0.19
长江流域	Changjiang River Basin	493.98	305.55
湖口以下干流	Main Rivers Below Hukou	464.46	284.18
鄱阳湖水系	River System of Poyang Lake	27.90	20.25
太湖水系	River System of Taihu Lake	1.62	1.12
东南诸河	South-eastern Rivers	71.15	52.65
钱塘江	Qiantang River	71.15	52.65
地下水天然补给资源量 (亿立方米)	Natural Supply of Ground Water (100 million cu.m)	211.72	159.01
淮河流域	Huaihe River Basin	106.66	80.27
长江流域	Changjiang River Basin	94.52	69.74
新安江流域	Xinanjiang River Basin	10.54	9.00
淡水面积 (千公顷)	Freshwater Area (1000 hectares)		
#养殖面积	Cultivated Area	414.96	411.24
主要矿产保有总资源量	**Total Resources of Major Minerals**		
煤 炭 (亿吨)	Coal (100 million tons)	340.87	342.87
铁 矿 (矿石，亿吨)	Iron (Ore, 100 million tons)	51.94	52.96
铜 矿 (铜，万吨)	Copper (Metal, 10000 tons)	677.64	666.68
钼 矿 (钼，万吨)	Molybdenum (Metal, 10000 tons)	279.02	279.13
硫铁矿 (矿石，亿吨)	Pyrite Ore (Ore, 100 million tons)	7.80	7.76
水泥用灰岩 (矿石，亿吨)	Limestone for cement (Ore, 100 million tons)	131.70	138.61
玻璃用石英岩 (矿石，亿吨)	Limestone for glass (Ore, 100 million tons)	9.96	10.18
石 膏 (矿石，亿吨)	Gypsum (Ore, 100 million tons)	122.11	122.09
方解石 (矿石，亿吨)	Calcite (Ore, 100 million tons)	4.36	4.69

注：依据《固体矿产资源储量分类》（GB/T 17766—2020）的新分类要求，总资源量不再区分基础储量和资源量，按照探明资源量、控制资源量和推断资源量划分。因此，2020年及以后年度统计的数据为矿种的保有总资源量。

a) According to the new classification requirements of Solid Mineral Resources Reserves Classification (GB/T 17766-2020), the total resources are divided into proved resources, controlled resources and inferred resources instead of basic reserves. Therefore, the statistical data of 2020 and the year after are the total reserves of mineral species.

11—3 主要城市平均气温（2022年）
Monthly Average Temperature in Major Cities (2022)

单位：摄氏度（℃）

城 市	City	1月 Jan.	2月 Feb.	3月 Mar.	4月 Apr.	5月 May.	6月 June	7月 July	8月 Aug.	9月 Sept.	10月 Oct.	11月 Nov.	12月 Dec.	年平均 Annual Average
合 肥 市	Hefei	3.8	3.8	13.5	17.7	21.1	28	29.6	30	23.5	16.5	13.1	2.4	16.9
淮 北 市	Huaibei	2.4	3.3	11.5	17.2	21.8	29.2	28.3	28.8	23.1	16	12	1.6	16.3
亳 州 市	Bozhou	2.7	4	12.3	18.1	22	30	28.8	28.9	23.8	16.4	12.3	2.2	16.8
宿 州 市	Suzhou	2.2	3.1	11	16	20.9	28.9	28.3	28.4	22.3	15.7	11.9	1.2	15.8
蚌 埠 市	Bengbu	3.3	3.8	12.4	17.6	21.6	28.4	29	29.3	23.1	16.4	12.7	2.2	16.7
阜 阳 市	Fuyang	3.4	4.3	12.7	18.2	21.4	29.3	29.4	29.7	24.2	16.9	12.8	2.5	17.1
淮 南 市	Huainan	3.6	4	12.9	17.4	21.2	27.8	28.8	29.2	23.3	16.7	13.1	2.8	16.7
滁 州 市	Chuzhou	3.7	3.7	12.7	17.4	21	27.9	29.5	30.1	22.7	16.1	12.8	2.4	16.7
六 安 市	Luan	4.7	4.6	14.2	18.9	21.8	28.6	30.2	30.8	24.6	17.4	13.8	3.7	17.8
马鞍山市	Maanshan	5	4.6	14	18.3	21.5	27.6	30.8	31.6	24	17.8	14.5	4.6	17.9
芜 湖 市	Wuhu	5	4.5	14.2	18.1	21.6	27.9	31.1	31.5	24.3	17.7	14.6	4.2	17.9
宣 城 市	Xuancheng	5.3	4.4	14	17.9	21.1	27.3	30.7	31.4	23.8	17.7	14.9	4.2	17.7
铜 陵 市	Tongling	5.4	5	14.7	18.7	21.9	28.1	31.3	31.7	24.7	18	14.7	4.6	18.2
池 州 市	Chizhou	5.2	4.6	14.2	17.8	20.8	26.9	30.2	30.4	24.5	17.7	14.7	4.4	17.6
安 庆 市	Anqing	5.2	4.6	14.5	18	21	26.8	30.3	30.6	25	18	14.8	4.6	17.8
黄 山 市	Huangshan	6.5	5.1	14.6	17.6	20.7	25.9	30	31.3	25.5	18.6	16.4	4.9	18.1

11—4 主要城市降水量（2022年）
Monthly Precipitation in Major Cities (2022)

单位：毫米（millimeters）

城 市	City	1月 Jan.	2月 Feb.	3月 Mar.	4月 Apr.	5月 May.	6月 June	7月 July	8月 Aug.	9月 Sept.	10月 Oct.	11月 Nov.	12月 Dec.	全 年 Annual Total
合 肥 市	Hefei	79.3	32.5	174.2	65.1	5.7	99.2	135.7	6.6	0.2	107.2	89.5	10.4	805.6
淮 北 市	Huaibei	16.4	2.7	47.2	13.3	0.1	102.6	346.4	58.9		81.4	22	0.3	691.3
亳 州 市	Bozhou	17.7	1.9	42.8	9.8	5.3	112.9	464.4	135.1		94.4	20.3	2.9	907.5
宿 州 市	Suzhou	16.9	7.5	56.5	14.3	0.5	127.3	361.9	69	0.7	77.4	47.8	1.8	781.6
蚌 埠 市	Bengbu	32.3	17.7	113.6	58.3	3	214.7	213.1	40.3		94.3	44.9	2.2	834.4
阜 阳 市	Fuyang	31.7	8.7	173.8	79	15.3	108.1	161.5	98.7		127.3	58.4		862.5
淮 南 市	Huainan	48.5	27	163.8	25.4	8.7	204.2	177.7	72.9	1.7	85.5	49.9	1.2	866.5
滁 州 市	Chuzhou	82.9	23.2	152.9	76.3	23.4	85.9	114.5	36.4	25.8	108.6	87	3.3	820.2
六 安 市	Luan	88.7	33.6	214.5	58.9	22	166.5	92.8	18.9	0.2	83.1	81.9	11.4	872.5
马鞍山市	Maanshan	80.6	44.4	133.7	105.2	18.8	118.6	36.5	27	31.5	50.8	86.3	16.3	749.7
芜 湖 市	Wuhu	96.1	60	180.1	171.5	28.8	178.3	109.9	26.7	9.9	55.2	86.7	17.7	1020.9
宣 城 市	Xuancheng	122.5	67.8	225.5	197.2	51	212.2	43.7	24.4	65.4	52.2	103.7	33.5	1199.1
铜 陵 市	Tongling	117.7	57.3	217.6	135.9	28	224.5	80.8	110.3	0.6	46.1	77.3	25.8	1121.9
池 州 市	Chizhou	120.7	61.9	286.3	161.2	33.2	217.6	171.1	37.1	3	43.7	97.1	22.5	1255.4
安 庆 市	Anqing	109.4	51.1	264.3	194.3	36.7	282	89.7	3	0.1	35	89	15.6	1170.2
黄 山 市	Huangshan	124	107.3	255	203.4	202.2	299.9	47.3	49.4	1.4	26.2	93.5	44.3	1453.9

11—5 各市全年降水量（2022年）
Total Precipitation by Region (2022)

地 区	Region	年降水量 Precipitation 毫 米 (0.001m)	亿立方米 (100 million cu.m)	多年平均降水量（亿立方米）Average Precipitation in Many Years (100 million cu.m)	与上年比较 Compared With Last Year (±%)	与多年平均比较 Compared With The Average Precipitation of Many Years (±%)
总 计	**Total**	**979.8**	**1366.5**	**1643.3**	**-24.1**	**-16.8**
合肥市	Hefei	805.8	89.8	115.0	-28.0	-22.0
淮北市	Huaibei	674.6	18.5	23.0	-32.2	-19.6
亳州市	Bozhou	744.3	62.3	70.6	-23.0	-11.7
宿州市	Suzhou	688.2	68.4	84.5	-36.4	-19.0
蚌埠市	Bengbu	729.2	44.5	54.2	-18.7	-17.9
阜阳市	Fuyang	772.9	75.6	87.4	-17.6	-13.6
淮南市	Huainan	721.8	39.9	50.4	-28.7	-20.8
滁州市	Chuzhou	744.8	100.6	131.4	-23.0	-23.5
六安市	Luan	989.1	151.8	190.6	-29.8	-20.3
马鞍山市	Maanshan	818.9	32.3	43.1	-29.9	-25.0
芜湖市	Wuhu	1091.3	64.9	74.1	-20.5	-12.4
宣城市	Xuancheng	1315.1	162.3	179.2	-22.7	-9.5
铜陵市	Tongling	1056.5	30.9	39.9	-30.0	-22.6
池州市	Chizhou	1366.5	115.2	132.8	-23.1	-13.3
安庆市	Anqing	1158.4	157.6	191.2	-21.4	-17.6
黄山市	Huangshan	1546.9	152.0	175.7	-15.5	-13.5

11—6 流域分区全年降水量（2022年）
Total Precipitation by Area of Rivers (2022)

流域分区 River Area	年降水量 Precipitation 毫 米 0.001(m)	亿立方米 (100 million cu.m)	多年平均降水量（亿立方米）Average Precipitation in Many Years (100 million cu.m)	与上年比较 Compared With Last Year (±%)	与多年平均比较 Compared With The Average Precipitation of Many Years (±%)
总 计 Total	**979.8**	**1366.54**	**1643.34**	**-24.1**	**-16.8**
淮河流域 Huaihe River Basin	782.8	521.56	637.46	-26.6	-18.2
淮河上游区 The Upper Reaches of Huaihe River	791.9	2.93	3.46	-26.4	-15.3
淮河中游区 The Middle Reaches of Huaihe River	785.0	502.54	611.71	-26.5	-17.8
淮河下游区 The Lower Reaches of Huaihe River	719.6	13.96	20.03	-29.7	-30.3
沂沭泗河 Yishusi River	710.0	2.13	2.26	-30.4	-5.8
长江流域 Changjiang River Basin	1121.6	744.86	890.70	-23.4	-16.4
湖口以下干流 Main Rivers Below Hukou	1105.6	700.44	838.74	-23.8	-16.5
鄱阳湖水系 River System of Poyang Lake	1477.6	41.86	48.94	-16.1	-14.5
太湖水系 River System of Taihu Lake	1137.8	2.56	3.02	-22.9	-15.2
东南诸河 South-eastern Rivers	1554.7	100.12	115.18	-15.2	-13.1
钱塘江 Qiantang River	1554.7	100.12	115.18	-15.2	-13.1

11—7 各市水资源总量（2022年）
Water Resources by Region (2022)

单位：亿立方米（100 million cu.m）

地区	Region	天然年径流量 Natural Annual Flow by Region	山丘区地下水资源量 Ground Water Volume of Mountain and Hill Areas	山丘区河川基流量 River Flow of Mountain and Hill Areas	平原区降水入渗补给量 Permeated Precipitation Supply of Plain Areas	平原区降水入渗补给形成的河道排泄量 River Way Drainage Volume Caused by Permeated Precipitation Supply of Plain Areas	地下水资源与地表水资源不重复量 Amount of Non-repeat-calculated Water Between Ground Water and Surface Water	水资源总量 Total Amount of Water Resources by Region
总　计	**Total**	**476.72**	**76.63**	**73.89**	**76.35**	**10.62**	**68.47**	**545.19**
合肥市	Hefei	23.65	5.09	4.90	1.82	0.34	1.67	25.32
淮北市	Huaibei	2.18	0.30	0.07	3.30	0.06	3.47	5.65
亳州市	Bozhou	10.88			12.51	0.41	12.10	22.98
宿州市	Suzhou	10.47	1.01	0.36	13.05	0.38	13.32	23.79
蚌埠市	Bengbu	8.40	0.15	0.10	7.23	1.04	6.24	14.64
阜阳市	Fuyang	13.99			14.10	0.49	13.61	27.60
淮南市	Huainan	8.08	0.48	0.41	4.50	1.03	3.54	11.62
滁州市	Chuzhou	19.88	5.44	5.10	1.81	0.46	1.69	21.57
六安市	Luan	56.20	13.01	12.71	3.39	1.13	2.56	58.76
马鞍山市	Maanshan	9.91	0.75	0.70	2.51	0.83	1.73	11.64
芜湖市	Wuhu	24.31	2.21	2.02	4.56	1.90	2.85	27.16
宣城市	Xuancheng	74.67	11.99	11.84	1.88	0.47	1.56	76.23
铜陵市	Tongling	11.99	1.72	1.52	1.17	0.45	0.92	12.91
池州市	Chizhou	53.85	9.67	9.56	0.76	0.38	0.49	54.34
安庆市	Anqing	68.57	10.75	10.55	3.76	1.25	2.71	71.28
黄山市	Huangshan	79.69	14.06	14.05			0.01	79.70

11—8　流域分区水资源总量（2022年）
Water Resources by Area of Rivers (2022)

单位：亿立方米（100 million cu.m）

流域分区 River Area	天　然 年径流量 Natural Annual Flow by Region	山丘区地下 水资源量 Ground Water Volume of Mountain and Hill Areas	山丘区河 川基流量 River Flow of Mountain and Hill Areas	平原区降水 入渗补给量 Permeated Precipitation Supply of Plain Areas	平原区降水 入渗补给形成 的河道排泄量 River Way Drainage Volume Caused by Permeated Precipitation Supply of Plain Areas	地下水资源 与地表水资 源不重复量 Amount of Non-repeat-calculated Water Between Ground Water and Surface Water	水资源总量 Total Amount of Water Resources by Region
总　计 **Total**	**476.72**	**76.63**	**73.89**	**76.35**	**10.62**	**68.47**	**545.19**
淮河流域 Huaihe River Basin	118.52	16.65	15.08	59.55	4.85	56.27	174.79
淮河上游区 The Upper Reaches of Huaihe River	0.55			0.56	0.02	0.54	1.09
淮河中游区 The Middle Reaches of Huaihe River	115.55	16.23	14.83	57.57	4.50	54.47	170.02
淮河下游区 The Lower Reaches of Huaihe River	2.23	0.42	0.25	0.97	0.32	0.82	3.05
沂沭泗河 Yishusi River	0.19			0.45	0.01	0.44	0.63
长江流域 Changjiang River Basin	305.55	50.98	49.82	16.80	5.77	12.19	317.74
湖口以下干流 Main Rivers Below Hukou	284.18	47.10	45.94	16.80	5.77	12.19	296.37
鄱阳湖水系 River System of Poyang Lake	20.25	3.75	3.75				20.25
太湖水系 River System of Taihu Lake	1.12	0.13	0.13				1.12
东南诸河 South-eastern Rivers	52.65	9.00	8.99			0.01	52.66
钱塘江 Qiantang River	52.65	9.00	8.99			0.01	52.66

11—9 主要年份供水和用水情况
Water Supply and Water Use in Rural Area

年份 Year	供水总量(亿立方米) Water Supply (100 million cu.m)	地表水 Surface Water	地下水 Ground-water	其他 Others	用水总量(亿立方米) Water Use (100 million cu.m)	农业 Agricul-ture	工业 Industry	城镇公共 Urban Public	居民生活 Residents Live	生态环境补水 Ecological Protection	人均用水量(立方米/人) Per Capita Water Use (cu.m/person)
2010	292.50	258.54	33.08	0.89	292.50	167.54	94.32	4.91	23.40	2.30	491.60
2013	296.02	260.86	33.41	1.75	296.02	165.09	98.43	7.24	24.21	4.05	490.93
2014	272.09	239.93	30.31	1.85	272.09	142.83	92.71	7.40	24.50	4.65	447.30
2015	288.66	253.88	32.49	2.29	288.66	157.50	93.51	7.87	24.88	4.90	472.20
2016	290.65	256.10	32.02	2.53	290.65	158.60	93.09	8.29	25.08	5.59	471.10
2017	290.30	256.53	30.80	2.97	290.30	158.15	92.22	8.52	25.24	6.17	464.12
2018	285.81	251.47	29.82	4.51	285.81	153.99	91.05	8.74	25.36	6.67	452.00
2019	277.72	244.07	29.09	4.56	277.72	137.55	85.16	8.68	25.99	7.73	436.26
2020	268.30	233.83	28.68	5.79	268.30	144.51	80.37	8.23	26.89	8.30	430.40
2021	271.69	239.53	25.81	6.35	271.69	144.11	82.08	8.63	27.85	9.02	444.80
2022	300.46	268.96	24.12	7.38	300.46	175.72	78.87	8.30	27.82	9.75	491.0

11—10 各市供水和用水情况（2022年）
Water Supply and Water Use by Region (2022)

地区 Region	供水总量(亿立方米) Water Supply (100 million cu.m)	地表水 Surface Water	地下水 Ground-water	其他 Others	用水总量(亿立方米) Water Use (100 million cu.m)	农业 Agricul-ture	工业 Industry	城镇公共 Urban Public	居民生活 Residents Live	生态环境补水 Ecological Protection	人均用水量(立方米/人) Per Capita Water Use (cu.m/person)
合肥市 Hefei	32.98	31.08	0.02	1.87	32.98	19.63	4.37	2.36	4.55	2.07	345.3
淮北市 Huaibei	3.81	1.05	2.20	0.55	3.81	1.50	1.09	0.16	0.90	0.15	194.2
亳州市 Bozhou	11.08	5.54	5.12	0.42	11.08	6.84	1.70	0.25	1.88	0.40	222.9
宿州市 Suzhou	10.11	2.79	6.85	0.47	10.11	5.39	1.60	0.36	2.19	0.56	190.2
蚌埠市 Bengbu	14.77	12.80	1.66	0.31	14.77	11.22	1.05	0.41	1.48	0.61	445.9
阜阳市 Fuyang	18.82	10.92	7.30	0.60	18.82	11.75	2.70	0.44	3.23	0.70	230.7
淮南市 Huainan	20.92	19.88	0.39	0.65	20.92	11.96	6.12	0.50	1.48	0.87	689.7
滁州市 Chuzhou	25.10	24.16	0.34	0.60	25.10	19.37	2.57	0.44	1.95	0.77	624.4
六安市 Luan	33.22	32.66	0.08	0.49	33.22	28.62	1.51	0.49	1.71	0.88	756.3
马鞍山市 Maanshan	30.55	29.85	0.04	0.67	30.55	8.73	19.89	0.42	1.21	0.31	1406.9
芜湖市 Wuhu	30.95	30.83	0.00	0.12	30.95	11.19	16.74	0.71	1.74	0.58	836.2
宣城市 Xuancheng	15.54	15.40	0.05	0.09	15.54	11.62	1.59	0.43	1.30	0.60	623.7
铜陵市 Tongling	12.41	12.21	0.05	0.15	12.41	3.98	7.27	0.29	0.66	0.21	951.6
池州市 Chizhou	11.06	10.97	0.003	0.09	11.06	5.63	4.00	0.29	0.70	0.45	832.1
安庆市 Anqing	23.67	23.42	0.02	0.24	23.67	14.45	6.23	0.36	2.19	0.43	568.6
黄山市 Huangshan	5.48	5.39	0.01	0.07	5.48	3.84	0.42	0.40	0.64	0.16	412.4

11—11 环境综合整治
Environmental Improvement

指　　标	Item	2021	2022
环境质量	**Environment Quality**		
空气中颗粒物（粒径小于等于10μm）年均值（微克/立方米）	Annual Mean Value of Airborne Particulate Matter (particle size less than or equal to 10μm) (MCG/cu.m)	61	58
空气中颗粒物（粒径小于等于2.5μm）年均值（微克/立方米）	Annual Mean Value of Particulate Matter (particle size ≤ 2.5μm) in Air (MCG/cu.m)	35	35
空气中二氧化硫年均值（微克/立方米）	Annual Mean Value of Sulfur Dioxide in the Air (MCG/cu.m)	8	7
空气中二氧化氮年均值（微克/立方米）	Annual Mean Value of Nitrogen Dioxide in the Air (MCG/cu.m)	26	23
饮用水源水质达标率 (%)	Up-to-standard Rate of Drinking Water Quality (%)	98.7	99.1
区域环境噪声平均值(分贝(A))	The Average Indicator of Urban Noise (decibel)	55.1	55.1
交通干线噪声平均值(分贝(A))	The Average Indicator of Traffic Main Line Noise (decibel)	66.6	66.0
生态环境	**Eco-environment Protection**		
造林总面积 （万公顷）	Total Afforestation Area (10000 hectares)	17.99	14.75
自然保护区数 （个）	Number of Nature Reserves (above city-level) (unit)	44	41
#国家级	National Level	8	8
自然保护区面积 （万公顷）	Area of Nature Reserves (10000 hectares)	53.39	45.68
自然保护区面积占辖区面积比重 (%)	Area of Nature Reserves in Regions (%)	3.81	3.26
污染控制	**Pollution Control**		
一般工业固体废物综合利用率 (%)	General Industrial Solid Waste Comprehensive Utilization Rate (%)	91.05	
危险废物处置率 (%)	Rate of Treatment of Hazardous Waste (%)	94.61	
环境建设	**Environment Improvement**		
城市污水处理厂集中处理率 (%)	Rate of Concentrating Treatment of Sewage in the City (%)	96.11	96.27
城市燃气普及率 (%)	Rate of Gas Utilization in the City (%)	99.48	99.42
建成区绿化覆盖率 (%)	Green Coverage Rate in Constructed Areas (%)	44.07	45.32

注：1. 空气质量依据《环境空气质量标准》（GB3095—2012)及修改单（生态环境部公告2018年第29号）评价。
2. 省辖市空气质量达二级标准的城市数自2015年起采用新标准（《环境空气质量标准》（GB3095—2012））评价，与历史年份数据不可比。

a) Air quality was evaluated according to the Environmental Air Quality Standard (GB3095-2012) and the amendment (Announcement No. 29, 2018, of the Ministry of Ecology and Environment).

b) The air quality of the secondary standard of the provincial-level cities number since 2015, to adopt new standards (" ambient air quality standard "(GB3095-2012)), than with year of history data.

11—11 续表 continued

指　　标	Item	2021	2022
自然灾害	**Natural Disaster**		
发生地质灾害起数 (次)	Geological Disaster (unit)	80	54
#滑　坡	Landslide	30	13
崩　塌	Collapse	48	39
泥石流	Mudslide		1
地面塌陷	Surface collapse		1
人员伤亡 (人)	Casualties (person)		
#死亡人数	Deaths		
森林病虫害防治面积 (万公顷)	Forest Area Affected and Cured from Disease and Pests (10000 hectares)	36.2	33.5
环境污染	**Pollution**		
突发环境事件次数 (次)	Suddenly Environment Event Number (time)	2	3
#水污染	Water Pollution	1	3
大气污染	Air Pollution		
固体废物污染	Solid Waste Pollution	1	
人员伤亡 (人)	Personnel Casualty (person)		
污染直接经济损失 (万元)	Direct Economic Loss Due to Pollution (10000 yuan)	512.61	101.43
突发环境事件赔款总额 (万元)	Compensation Total Amount of Suddenly Environment Event (10000 yuan)		
污染损害罚款总额 (万元)	Fine Total Amount of Pollution Harm (10000 yuan)		
二氧化硫排放量 (万吨)	Sulphur Dioxide Discharge (10000 tons)	8.55	
#生活源二氧化硫排放量	Sulfur Dioxide Emissions From Domestic Sources	0.37	
氮氧化物排放量 (万吨)	Nitrogen Oxide Emissions (10000 tons)	44.58	
颗粒物排放量 (万吨)	Particulate Emissions (10000 tons)	11.73	
COD排放量 (万吨)	COD Discharge (10000 tons)	120.04	
氨氮排放总量 (万吨)	Ammonia Nitrogen Discharge (10000 tons)	4.33	
城镇生活污水排放量 (万吨)	Urban Consumption Waste Water Discharge (10000 tons)	226078	
#生活污水中化学需氧量排放量 (万吨)	COD Discharge from Urban Consumption Waste Water (10000 tons)	44.04	
#生活污水中氨氮排放量 (万吨)	Ammonia Nitrogen Discharge from Urban Consumption Waste Water (10000 tons)	2.67	
环境污染治理	**Investment in the Treatment of Environmental Pollution**		
省辖市空气质量达二级标准 (个)	Cities Directly under the Provincial Government Where the Air Quality Attains the Second Grade National Standards (unit)	10	6

注：2019年城镇生活污水排放量（万吨）和生活污水中化学需氧量排放量（万吨）均为生态环境统计业务系统内数值，生态环境部未对这两项数据基于二污普进行动态更新。

a) In 2019, urban domestic sewage discharge (ten thousand tons) and domestic sewage chemical oxygen demand discharge (ten thousand tons) are both values in the ecological and environmental statistics business system. The Ministry of Ecology and Environment has not dynamically updated these two the second pollution level.

11—12 环保系统机构、人员数
Environmental Protection Agencies and Persons Engaged

年份 Year	机构总数（个） Number of Agencies (unit)	人员总数（人） Total Number of Staff & Workers (person)	#科技人员 Scientific and Technical Personnel	#监测人员 Monitoring Personnel	#监察人员 Supervisory Personnel
2010	390	5722	2648	1767	2145
2013	419	5753		1624	2242
2014	425	5145		1594	1805
2015	408	5881		1596	1828
2016	458	5789		1666	2254
2017	483	5397		1636	1989
2018	297	6092		1568	2010
2019	419	5993		1517	1933
2020	400	5760	3999	1508	2491
2021	385	5775		1497	2579
2022	382	5753		1503	2495

注：自2014年起，数据为编制数,不含聘用人员。
a) Since 2014, the data for the preparation of the number, excluding the employment of personnel.

11—13 生活污染物排放
Discharge of Pollutants from Daily Life

年份 Year	城镇生活污水排放量（万吨） Volume of Urban Waste Water Discharged From Daily Life (10000 tons)	生活污水中化学需氧量排放量（吨） Absorption of Oxygen by Waste Water From Daily Life (ton)	生活及其他二氧化硫排放量（吨） Emission of Sulfur Dioxide From Daily Life and Others (ton)	生活及其他颗粒物排放量（吨） Domestic and Other Particulate Emissions (ton)
2010	113729	296274	48164	47958
2013	195091	436388	50928	44490
2014	202522	432220	52303	44368
2015	208928	427176	60002	44464
2016	190813	444042	49174	34267
2017	190594	459607	45796	35441
2018	196648	492465	38898	28082
2019	205797	493696	2743	8167
2020	223833	493554	3893	41607
2021	226078	440372	3711	37819

注：1. 生活及其他颗粒物排放量自2011年数据为生活源颗粒物排放量，不包括其他排放量。
2. 2019年城镇生活污水排放量（万吨）和生活污水中化学需氧量排放量（吨）均为生态环境统计业务系统内数值，生态环境部未对这两项数据基于二污普进行动态更新。

a) Domestic and other particulate emissions from 2011 data on particulate emissions from living sources, excluding other emissions.
b) In 2019, urban domestic sewage discharge (ten thousand tons) and domestic sewage chemical oxygen demand discharge (ten tons) are both values in the ecological and environmental statistics business system. The Ministry of Ecology and Environment has not dynamically updated these two data based on the second pollution level.

11—14 工业企业“三废”排放及治理
Discharge and Treatment of Waste Water, Waste Gas and Solid Wastes by Industry Enterprises

指 标	Item	2021
废 水	**Waste Water**	
工业废水排放总量 (万吨)	Total Volume of Waste Water Discharged (10000 tons)	42911.78
#工业废水COD排放量（万吨）	COD Discharge from Industrial Waste (10000 tons)	1.47
废 气	**Waste Gas**	
工业二氧化硫排放量 (万吨)	Volume of Sulphur Dioxide Emission (10000 tons)	8.17
工业颗粒物排放量 (万吨)	Industrial Particulate Emissions (10000 tons)	7.62
固体废物	**Solid Wastes**	
一般工业固体废物产生量 (万吨)	The Amount of General Industrial Solid Waste Generation (10000 tons)	14507.69
一般工业固体废物综合利用量 (万吨)	The Amount of General Industrial Solid Waste Comprehensive Utilization (10000 tons)	13593.92
一般工业固体废物综合利用率 (%)	General Industrial Solid Waste Comprehensive Utilization Rate (%)	91.05
一般工业固体废物贮存量 (万吨)	The Amount of General Industrial Solid Waste Storage (10000 tons)	729.40
一般工业固体废物处置量 (万吨)	The Amount of General Industrial Solid Waste Disposal (10000 tons)	813.00

注：2019年“一般工业固体废物贮存量（万吨）”均为生态环境统计业务系统内数值，生态环境部未对该项数据基于二污普进行动态更新。

a) The "general industrial solid waste storage volume (ten thousand tons)" in 2019 are all values in the ecological environment statistics business system, and the Ministry of Ecology and Environment has not dynamically updated the data based on the second pollution level.

11—15 各市工业废水排放及处理（2021年）

Discharge and Treatment of Industrial Waste Water by Region (2021)

地 区	Region	汇总工业企业个数（个）Number of Industrial Enterprises (unit)	工业废水排放总量（万吨）Total Volume of Waste Water Discharge (10000 tons)	#排入污水处理厂 Disperses into the Sewage Treatment Plants
总 计	**Total**	**7351**	**42911.78**	**23415.81**
合肥市	Hefei	700	6676.08	5916.79
淮北市	Huaibei	568	2009.31	769.21
亳州市	Bozhou	300	1028.16	551.40
宿州市	Suzhou	396	2328.16	1219.31
蚌埠市	Bengbu	369	1302.08	1278.60
阜阳市	Fuyang	584	1776.27	1129.81
淮南市	Huainan	232	3407.40	517.34
滁州市	Chuzhou	616	2782.35	2358.51
六安市	Luan	357	727.96	677.38
马鞍山市	Maanshan	434	7237.94	1141.24
芜湖市	Wuhu	644	3249.45	3121.38
宣城市	Xuancheng	794	2050.25	1777.93
铜陵市	Tongling	260	4723.40	927.51
池州市	Chizhou	492	687.53	406.88
安庆市	Anqing	354	2248.19	1137.68
黄山市	Huangshan	251	677.25	484.84

地 区	Region	工业废水中污染物排放量（吨）Total Volume Pollutant of Waste Water Discharge (ton)			废水治理设施数（套）Number of Facilities for Treatment of Waste Water (set)	废水治理设施处理能力（万吨／日）Handling Ability of Facilities for Treatment of Waste Water (10000 tons/day)
		#化学需氧量 COD	#石油类 Petroleum	#氨 氮 Ammonia & Nitrogen		
总 计	**Total**	**14657.16**	**101.25**	**771.55**	**3032**	**1000.93**
合肥市	Hefei	1643.83	4.44	39.81	439	46.38
淮北市	Huaibei	397.92	8.58	24.66	158	27.08
亳州市	Bozhou	194.95	0.74	6.58	102	9.14
宿州市	Suzhou	668.25	0.44	17.14	122	26.60
蚌埠市	Bengbu	544.24	0.36	14.43	137	19.10
阜阳市	Fuyang	864.25	8.50	176.13	226	22.98
淮南市	Huainan	930.39	1.64	92.05	72	79.45
滁州市	Chuzhou	1076.73	3.30	42.06	302	25.04
六安市	Luan	246.84	1.21	12.70	189	29.81
马鞍山市	Maanshan	2059.82	15.86	114.72	221	390.13
芜湖市	Wuhu	814.08	29.31	29.73	278	242.59
宣城市	Xuancheng	2321.48	12.36	84.80	271	13.94
铜陵市	Tongling	999.77	7.33	66.31	117	36.66
池州市	Chizhou	421.30	1.00	10.13	118	8.30
安庆市	Anqing	774.03	2.23	18.38	150	18.56
黄山市	Huangshan	699.28	3.95	21.94	130	5.17

11—16 各市工业废气排放及处理（2021年）
Emission and Treatment of Industrial Waste Gas by Region (2021)

地 区	Region	汇总工业企业个数（个）Number of Industrial Enterprises (unit)	工业废气治理设施数（套）Number of Facilities for treat-ment of Waste Gas (set)	工业二氧化硫排放量（吨）Volume of Sulphur Dioxide Emission by Industry (ton)	工业氮氧化物排放量（吨）Industrial Nitrogen Oxide Emissions (ton)	工业颗粒物排放量（吨）Industrial Particulate Emissions (ton)
总 计	**Total**	7351	17287	81701.19	139268.72	76226.63
合 肥 市	Hefei	700	2064	4552.89	9899.49	4593.90
淮 北 市	Huaibei	568	1311	5739.82	7719.19	4255.23
亳 州 市	Bozhou	300	518	2120.52	2197.53	1326.16
宿 州 市	Suzhou	396	910	3753.90	5427.85	2600.49
蚌 埠 市	Bengbu	369	609	1885.24	4085.83	716.87
阜 阳 市	Fuyang	584	1260	10402.75	7244.86	3853.83
淮 南 市	Huainan	232	414	11362.23	10469.57	2415.49
滁 州 市	Chuzhou	616	1273	4339.48	9432.40	4585.80
六 安 市	Luan	357	761	2878.83	5759.41	3452.82
马鞍山市	Maanshan	434	1504	11003.48	24538.58	10196.29
芜 湖 市	Wuhu	644	1443	8805.97	19881.99	12359.99
宣 城 市	Xuancheng	794	1750	2267.30	4651.22	5238.64
铜 陵 市	Tongling	260	597	2065.65	8769.06	8973.74
池 州 市	Chizhou	492	1847	6949.57	13259.10	7807.87
安 庆 市	Anqing	354	658	3083.81	5556.54	2577.70
黄 山 市	Huangshan	251	368	489.74	376.11	1271.81

11—17 各市工业固体废物产生及处理利用（2021年）
Discharge, Treatment and Utilization of Industrial Solid Wastes by Region (2021)

地　区	Region	汇总工业企业个数（个）Number of Industrial Enterprises (unit)	一般工业固体废物产生量（万吨）The Amount of General Industrial Solid Waste Generation (10000 tons)	危险废物产生量（万吨）The Amount of Hazardous Waste Generation (10000 ton)	一般工业固体废物综合利用量（万吨）The Amount of General Industrial Solid Waste Comprehensive Utilization (10000 ton)
总　　计	**Total**	**7351**	**14507.69**	**237.31**	**13593.92**
合 肥 市	Hefei	700	1308.73	18.51	1154.22
淮 北 市	Huaibei	568	1222.06	5.03	1181.49
亳 州 市	Bozhou	300	461.95	2.93	458.51
宿 州 市	Suzhou	396	629.20	4.96	622.48
蚌 埠 市	Bengbu	369	218.96	4.91	184.92
阜 阳 市	Fuyang	584	558.25	14.05	533.73
淮 南 市	Huainan	232	2639.49	5.27	2611.94
滁 州 市	Chuzhou	616	203.80	10.73	190.62
六 安 市	Luan	357	1273.24	5.82	1283.26
马鞍山市	Maanshan	434	2154.99	45.03	1986.15
芜 湖 市	Wuhu	644	613.16	47.68	458.66
宣 城 市	Xuancheng	794	504.58	9.88	513.63
铜 陵 市	Tongling	260	1464.82	41.66	1310.82
池 州 市	Chizhou	492	802.18	15.47	610.01
安 庆 市	Anqing	354	436.17	4.64	481.53
黄 山 市	Huangshan	251	16.11	0.73	11.96

地　区	Region	危险废物综合利用处置量（万吨）Quantity of Comprehensive Utilization and Disposal of Hazardous Waste (10000 tons)	一般工业固体废物贮存量（万吨）The Amount of General Industrial Solid Waste Storage (10000 tons)	一般工业固体废物处置量（万吨）The Amount of General Industrial Solid Waste Disposal (10000 tons)
总　　计	**Total**	**233.53**	**729.40**	**813.00**
合 肥 市	Hefei	18.36	232.20	25.76
淮 北 市	Huaibei	4.96	48.65	18.66
亳 州 市	Bozhou	2.75	3.75	2.73
宿 州 市	Suzhou	4.99	4.07	107.04
蚌 埠 市	Bengbu	4.56	4.76	29.66
阜 阳 市	Fuyang	13.61	0.59	24.45
淮 南 市	Huainan	5.27	21.01	16.89
滁 州 市	Chuzhou	10.33	0.24	13.27
六 安 市	Luan	5.66	5.39	18.58
马鞍山市	Maanshan	44.61	0.25	191.79
芜 湖 市	Wuhu	47.74	4.68	151.18
宣 城 市	Xuancheng	9.27	47.71	35.28
铜 陵 市	Tongling	39.98	167.09	138.64
池 州 市	Chizhou	16.05	188.51	31.83
安 庆 市	Anqing	4.64	0.44	3.15
黄 山 市	Huangshan	0.75	0.05	4.10

11—18 各市城市空气质量指标（2022年）
Ambient Air Quality in Main Cities by Region (2022)

单位：微克／立方米（MCG/cu.m）

地 区	Region	颗粒物（粒径小于等于10μm）(PM_{10}) Particulate Matter (particle size ≤ 10μm) (PM_{10})	颗粒物（粒径小于等于2.5μm）($PM_{2.5}$) Particulate Matter (particle size ≤ 2.5μm) ($PM_{2.5}$)	二氧化硫 (SO_2) Sulfur Dioxide	二氧化氮 (NO_2) Nitrogen Dioxide	空气质量达到及好于二级的天数比例 (%) As Good and Better air Quality in 2 Days (%)
全省平均	**Average**	**58**	**35**	**7**	**23**	**81.8**
合 肥 市	Hefei	63	32	8	31	86
淮 北 市	Huaibei	70	42	7	21	74
亳 州 市	Bozhou	68	41	7	15	74
宿 州 市	Suzhou	70	40	4	20	77
蚌 埠 市	Bengbu	66	37	10	25	79
阜 阳 市	Fuyang	67	41	7	22	75
淮 南 市	Huainan	66	41	8	19	80
滁 州 市	Chuzhou	56	32	8	25	80
六 安 市	Luan	56	33	7	19	85
马鞍山市	Maanshan	53	35	9	30	79
芜 湖 市	Wuhu	55	34	9	31	80
宣 城 市	Xuancheng	47	32	6	23	92
铜 陵 市	Tongling	60	34	9	29	84
池 州 市	Chizhou	51	33	7	22	82
安 庆 市	Anqing	52	34	7	23	84
黄 山 市	Huangshan	33	19	6	11	98

11—19 各市城市道路交通噪声监测情况（2022年）
Monitoring of Urban Road Traffic Noise in Key Cities by Region (2022)

地 区	Region	监测总长度（公里）Total Length of Roads (km)	路段平均宽度（米）Average Width of Roads (m)	平均车流量(辆/小时) Average Traffic Volume (car/hour)		噪声均值（分贝）Average Noise Value (dB)
				大型车 Large Car	小型车 Small Car	
总 计	**Total**	**2184.40**	**41.30**	**35**	**346**	**66.0**
合 肥 市	Hefei	591.70	34.90	77	468	68.8
淮 北 市	Huaibei	250.20	37.50	18	230	66.2
亳 州 市	Bozhou	53.20	51.80	16	572	63.9
宿 州 市	Suzhou	50.10	25.30	18	266	65.5
蚌 埠 市	Bengbu	122.20	33.90	36	490	67.0
阜 阳 市	Fuyang	29.40	45.90	20	341	65.7
淮 南 市	Huainan	56.00	18.60	42	451	67.1
滁 州 市	Chuzhou	295.30	44.90	22	171	63.9
六 安 市	Luan	68.30	49.90	21	306	65.6
马鞍山市	Maanshan	98.50	43.50	37	296	66.9
芜 湖 市	Wuhu	260.50	43.10	27	435	66.5
宣 城 市	Xuancheng	98.90	84.00	19	265	62.5
铜 陵 市	Tongling	31.30	34.00	40	547	66.6
池 州 市	Chizhou	28.90	36.00	124	461	68.8
安 庆 市	Anqing	73.40	44.90	24	262	65.5
黄 山 市	Huangshan	76.50	33.20	16	236	65.4

11—20 水资源情况
Water Resources

年份 Year	水资源总量（亿立方米）Total Water Resources (100 million cu.m)	地表水资源量 Surface Water	地下水资源量 Ground Water	地表水与地下水资源重复量 Duplicated Measurement Between Surface Water and Groundwater	人均水资源量（立方米／人）Per Capita Water Resources (cu.m/person)
2010	939.05	876.27	197.81	135.03	1578.20
2013	585.59	525.41	144.54	84.36	974.54
2014	778.48	712.86	178.91	113.29	1279.78
2015	914.12	850.19	193.71	129.78	1495.31
2016	1245.17	1179.23	219.26	153.32	2018.30
2017	784.90	717.82	200.95	133.87	1254.88
2018	835.78	766.67	203.67	134.56	1321.68
2019	539.87	482.10	144.85	87.08	848.07
2020	1280.41	1193.72	228.60	141.91	2053.82
2021	883.26	798.01	211.72	126.47	1446.12
2022	545.19	476.72	159.01	90.54	890.84

注：水资源总量=地表水资源量＋地下水资源量－地表水与地下水资源重复量。

a) Total Water Resources=Surface Water+Ground Water-Duplicated Measurement Between Surface Water and Groundwater.

11—21 各市水资源情况（2022年）
Water Resources by Region (2022)

地区	Region	水资源总量（亿立方米）Total Water Resources (100 million cu.m)	地表水资源量 Surface Water	地下水资源量 Ground Water	地表水与地下水资源重复量 Duplicated Measurement Between Surface Water and Groundwater	人均水资源量（立方米／人）Per Capita Water Resources (cu.m/person)
总计	**Total**	**545.19**	**476.72**	**159.01**	**90.54**	**890.84**
合肥市	Hefei	25.32	23.65	7.20	5.53	265.14
淮北市	Huaibei	5.65	2.18	3.70	0.23	287.97
亳州市	Bozhou	22.98	10.88	12.88	0.78	462.09
宿州市	Suzhou	23.79	10.47	14.29	0.97	447.81
蚌埠市	Bengbu	14.64	8.40	8.41	2.17	441.90
阜阳市	Fuyang	27.60	13.99	14.96	1.35	338.40
淮南市	Huainan	11.62	8.08	5.97	2.43	383.04
滁州市	Chuzhou	21.57	19.88	7.44	5.75	536.55
六安市	Luan	58.76	56.20	16.72	14.16	1337.86
马鞍山市	Maanshan	11.64	9.91	3.71	1.98	536.01
芜湖市	Wuhu	27.16	24.31	7.41	4.56	733.76
宣城市	Xuancheng	76.23	74.67	13.99	12.43	3060.09
铜陵市	Tongling	12.91	11.99	2.98	2.06	990.33
池州市	Chizhou	54.34	53.85	10.47	9.98	4087.25
安庆市	Anqing	71.28	68.57	14.82	12.11	1711.98
黄山市	Huangshan	79.70	79.69	14.06	14.05	6003.77

11—22　农村环境状况
The Environment of Rural Areas

年　份 Year	农村自来水普及率(%) Popularity Rate of Tape Water in Rural Areas (%)	农村户用沼气 Marsh Gas in Rural House		太阳能热水器面积（万平方米） Solar Water Heater Area (10000 sq.m)
		用户数（万户） Number of Users (10000 Households)	总产气量（万立方米） Total Volum Gas Production (10000 cu.m)	
2010	47.8	75.26	22334	422.12
2013	58.6	85.76	24693	520.07
2014	64.3	88.21	24516	539.60
2015	72.0	89.13	23992	568.58
2016	78.0	89.51	23125	586.29
2017	86.9	89.51	19447	595.39
2018	87.6	89.51	16787	604.52
2019	88.5	81.27	12857	586.23
2020	89.0	76.58	9788	601.56
2021	89.2	59.93	5824	599.69
2022	89.4	45.68	2137	587.93

11—23　各市农村环境状况（2022年）
The Environment of Rural Areas by Region (2022)

地　区	Region	农村自来水普及率(%) Popularity Rate of Tape Water in Rural Areas (%)	农村户用沼气 Marsh Gas in Rural House		太阳能热水器面积（万平方米） Solar Water Heater Area (10000 sq.m)
			用户数（万户） Number of Users (10000 Households)	总产气量（万立方米） Total Volum Gas Production (10000 cu.m)	
总　计	**Total**	**89.40**	**45.68**	**2137.00**	**587.93**
合肥市	Hefei	92.90	2.28	134.47	78.10
淮北市	Huaibei	81.20			28.51
亳州市	Bozhou	93.20	1.31	48.30	36.94
宿州市	Suzhou	93.90			27.87
蚌埠市	Bengbu	83.30	0.86	70.00	37.26
阜阳市	Fuyang	97.90	7.14	518.00	36.46
淮南市	Huainan	74.60	3.52	166.32	37.48
滁州市	Chuzhou	78.40	2.34	6.93	26.19
六安市	Luan	79.40	3.62	171.50	48.09
马鞍山市	Maanshan	98.60	1.51	2.87	42.37
芜湖市	Wuhu	96.80	0.01	1.33	59.43
宣城市	Xuancheng	91.10	3.13	24.01	30.33
铜陵市	Tongling	93.20	1.30	10.01	14.17
池州市	Chizhou	91.90	6.74	517.06	13.67
安庆市	Anqing	83.70	9.77	262.50	39.34
黄山市	Huangshan	92.50	2.15	203.32	31.73

11—24 突发环境事件情况
Environmental Accidents

年 份 Year	突发环境事件次数（次） Number of Environmental Accidents (time)	水污染 Water Pollution	大气污染 Air Pollution	固体废物污染 Solid Wastes Pollution	噪声与振动危害 Noise and Vibration Pollution	其 他 Other	直接经济损失（万元） Direct Economic Losses (10000 yuan)	突发环境事件赔款总额（万元） Total Compensation for Environmental Emergencies (10000 yuan)	污染损害罚款总额（万元） Total Fines for Pollution Damage (10000 yuan)
2010	30	10	8	5			231.60	23.00	133.00
2013	6	5	1				274.06	9.79	
2014	9	5	1	1			492.99	0.79	
2015	8	5	2			1	75.30	13.00	2.14
2016	3	1	1			1	16.00		
2017	4	1	2			1	6.20	10.00	
2018	4	4					3.70	5.00	
2019	5	2	3				109.40	20.00	20.00
2020	10	7	1			2	695.74	152.05	46.00
2021	2	1		1			512.61		
2022	3	3					101.43		

11—25 各市突发环境事件情况（2022年）
Environmental Accidents by Region (2022)

地 区	Region	突发环境事件次数（次） Number of Environmental Accidents (time)	水污染 Water Pollution	大气污染 Air Pollution	噪声与振动危害 Noise and Vibration Pollution	其 他 Other	直接经济损失（万元） Direct Economic Losses (10000 yuan)	突发环境事件赔款总额（万元） Total Compensation for Environmental Emergencies (10000 yuan)	污染损害罚款总额（万元） Total Fines for Pollution Damage (10000 yuan)
总 计	**Total**	**3**	**3**				**101.43**		
合肥市	Hefei	1	1				80.33		
淮北市	Huaibei								
亳州市	Bozhou	1	1				20.00		
宿州市	Suzhou								
蚌埠市	Bengbu								
阜阳市	Fuyang								
淮南市	Huainan								
滁州市	Chuzhou								
六安市	Luan								
马鞍山市	Maanshan								
芜湖市	Wuhu								
宣城市	Xuancheng								
铜陵市	Tongling	1	1				1.10		
池州市	Chizhou								
安庆市	Anqing								
黄山市	Huangshan								

11—26 地质灾害及防治情况
Geological Disasters and Prevention and Cure

年份 Year	发生地质灾害起数（次）Geological Disasters (time)	#滑坡 Land-slide	#崩塌 Collapse	人员伤亡（人）Casualties (person)	#死亡人数 Deaths	直接经济损失（万元）Direct Economic Losses (10000 yuan)	地质灾害防治项目（个）Number of Projects of Prevention of Geological Disasters (unit)	地质灾害防治投资（万元）Investment of Projects of Prevention of Geological Disasters (10000 yuan)
2010	338	143	164	12	6	2536.3	189	11352.0
2013	261	147	108	2	1	2247.8	624	29280.2
2014	126	49	70			590.4	537	21936.9
2015	616	312	272	2	1	13679.3	492	14205.5
2016	724	386	308			4616.4	982	25294.9
2017	58	23	33			175.2	920	30506.4
2018	113	40	69			484.4	460	23047.0
2019	178	98	68			1992.7	467	13413.6
2020	345	167	171			2132.9	1113	28656.4
2021	80	30	48			380.8	880	22215.5
2022	54	13	39			260.5	593	15099.2

11—27 各市地质灾害及防治情况（2022年）
Geological Disasters and Prevention and Cure by Region (2022)

地区	Region	发生地质灾害起数（次）Geological Disasters (time)	#滑坡 Land-slide	#崩塌 Collapse	人员伤亡（人）Casualties (person)	#死亡人数 Deaths	直接经济损失（万元）Direct Economic Losses (10000 yuan)	地质灾害防治项目（个）Number of Projects of Prevention of Geological Disasters (unit)	地质灾害防治投资（万元）Investment of Projects of Prevention of Geological Disasters (10000 yuan)
总　计	**Total**	54	13	39			260.5	593	15099.2
合肥市	Hefei							18	133.6
淮北市	Huaibei							2	10.0
亳州市	Bozhou							9	838.4
宿州市	Suzhou							4	18.0
蚌埠市	Bengbu							12	201.2
阜阳市	Fuyang							7	2165.1
淮南市	Huainan							17	225.0
滁州市	Chuzhou							24	1276.2
六安市	Luan							38	1878.2
马鞍山市	Maanshan							18	356.0
芜湖市	Wuhu							21	191.0
宣城市	Xuancheng	1		1			0.5	142	2490.6
铜陵市	Tongling							29	86.0
池州市	Chizhou	1		1			0.5	53	659.5
安庆市	Anqing	29	5	22			182.5	168	2292.2
黄山市	Huangshan	23	8	15			77.0	31	2278.2

11—28 自然保护基本情况
Basic Situation of Natural Protection

年份 Year	自然保护区 Nature Reserve 个数（个） Number of Nature Reserves (unit)	#国家级 Nation Level	面积（万公顷） Area of Nature Reserves (10000 hectares)	#国家级 Nation Level
2006	35		44.81	
2007	37		44.00	
2008	37		46.13	
2009	38		43.84	
2010	38	6	43.61	13.14
2011	38	7	43.20	13.92
2012	38	7	43.20	13.92
2013	39	7	41.28	13.92
2014	39	7	40.97	13.92
2015	40	7	41.35	13.92
2016	40	8	41.74	14.71
2017	40	8	41.74	14.71
2018	40	8	41.52	14.71
2019	43	8	52.54	14.71
2020	43	8	52.54	14.71
2021	44	8	53.39	14.71
2022	41	8	45.68	14.71

注：2022年自然保护地整合优化后，均为省级以上自然保护区，无市级自然保护区。

a) After the integration and optimization of nature protected areas in 2022, all of them will be nature reserves above the provincial level , and there will be no municipal nature reserves。

11—29 造林面积
Area of Afforestation

单位：公顷（hectares）

年 份 Year	造林总面积 Total Area of Afforestation	#人工造林 Manual Planting	按林种用途分 by Function of Forest 用材林 Timber Forests	经济林 By-product Forests	防护林 Protection Forests	薪炭林 Fuel Forests	特种用途林 Forests for Special Purpose
2010	65612	57012	17724	12380	33804	849	855
2013	208099	202766	72712	51817	73732	248	9590
2014	157745	150871	51701	44584	54826	426	6208
2015	128415	114350	47729	25173	39216	85	2144
2016	128042	91380	22717	30178	36595	131	1759
2017	144926	56667	11445	23615	20475	26	1106
2018	138493	55718	12682	29196	12985	145	710
2019	138746	51264	12923	23336	19300	450	160
2020	151465	59639	16009	23533	19514	362	1016
2021	179852	35774	12455	6665	16958	368	570
2022	147496	22639	10065	5791	6261	149	373

11—30 各市造林面积（2022年）
Area of Afforestation by Region (2022)

单位：公顷（hectares）

地 区	Region	造林总面积 Total Area of Afforestation	#人工造林 Manual Planting	按林种用途分 by Function of Forest 用材林 Timber Forests	经济林 By-product Forests	防护林 Protection Forests	特种用途林 Forests for Special Purpose
总 计	**Total**	**147496**	**22639**	**10065**	**5791**	**6261**	**373**
合肥市	Hefei	1772	1530	506	398	590	36
淮北市	Huaibei	876	342	31	36	244	31
亳州市	Bozhou	2769	661	156	2	503	
宿州市	Suzhou	6564	1714	426	194	1094	
蚌埠市	Bengbu	2115	1187	606	110	440	30
阜阳市	Fuyang	3078	626	185	20	323	99
淮南市	Huainan	2436	1490	693	56	712	30
滁州市	Chuzhou	8142	2885	1377	544	805	11
六安市	Luan	18719	1733	521	855	331	26
马鞍山市	Maanshan	2964	518	307	137	73	
芜湖市	Wuhu	4236	1285	866	306	112	
宣城市	Xuancheng	17152	899	692	181	22	3
铜陵市	Tongling	1956	422	195	191	18	18
池州市	Chizhou	15622	3007	2082	483	430	13
安庆市	Anqing	17608	3601	968	2185	378	70
黄山市	Huangshan	41487	739	454	93	186	6

主要统计指标解释

耕地

指种植农作物的土地，包括熟地，新开发、复垦、整理地，休闲地（含轮歇地、轮作地）；以种植农作物（含蔬菜）为主，间有零星果树、桑树或其他树木的土地；平均每年能保证收获一季的已垦滩地和海涂。耕地中包括南方宽度<1.0米，北方宽度<2.0米固定的沟、渠、路和地坎（埂）；临时种植药材、草皮、花卉、苗木等的耕地，以及其他临时改变用途的耕地。

园地

指种植以采集果、叶、根、茎、汁等为主的集约经营的多年生木本和草本作物，覆盖度大于50%和每亩株数大于合理株数70%的土地。包括用于育苗的土地。

林地

指生长乔木、竹类、灌木的土地，及沿海生长红树林的土地。包括迹地，不包括居民点内部的绿化林木用地，铁路、公路征地范围内的林木，以及河流、沟渠的护堤林。

草地

指生长草本植物为主的土地。

径流量

指在一定时段内通过河流某一过水断面的水量，用以反映一个国家或地区水资源的丰歉程度。计算公式为：

径流量=降水量-蒸发量

流域

每条河流都有自己的干流和支流，干支流共同组成这条河流的水系。每条河流都有自己的集水区域，这个集水区域就称为该河流的流域。

外流河

指直接或间接流入海洋的河流。供给外流河河水的区域称为外流区域。

内陆河

指在陆地内部干燥地区，河水沿途消失于沙漠或注入内陆湖泊的河流。供给内陆河河水的区域称为内陆区域。

矿产资源

矿产资源指由地质作用形成的，具有利用价值的，呈固态、液态、气态的自然资源，是社会生产发展的重要物质基础。目前我国已发现矿种有170多种，按其特点和用途，可分为能源矿产(如煤炭、石油、天然气、地热)、金属矿产(如铁矿、锰矿、铜矿、铅矿、铝土矿)、非金属矿产(如金刚石、石灰岩、粘土)和水气矿产(如地下水、矿泉水、二氧化碳气)四大类。其中：金属矿产按其物质成分和性质又可分为：黑色金属矿产、有色金属矿产、贵金属矿产、稀有金属矿产、稀土金属矿产、分散元素金属矿产六类。

平均气温

气温指空气的温度，我国一般以摄氏度为单位表示。气象观测的温度表是放在离地面约1.5米处通风良好的百叶箱里测量的，因此，通常说的气温指的是离地面1.5米处百叶箱中的温度。计算方法：月平均气温是将全月各日的平均气温相加，除以该月的天数而得。年平均气温是将12个月的月平均气温累加后除以12而得。

年平均相对湿度

指空气中实际水气压与当时气温下的饱和水气压之比。其统计方法与气温相同。

降水量

指从天空降落到地面的液态或固态(经融化后)水，未经蒸发、渗透、流失而在地面上积聚的深度。计算方法：月降水量是将全月各日的降水量累加而得。年降水量是将12个月的月降水量累加而得。

全年日照时数

指太阳实际照射地面的时数，通常以小时为单位表示。其统计方法与降水量相同。

水资源总量

指当地降水形成的地表和地下产水总量，即地表径流量与降水入渗补给量之和。

地表水资源量

指河流、湖泊以及冰川等地表水体中可以逐年更新的动态水量，即天然河川径流量。

地下水资源量

指地下饱和含水层逐年更新的动态水量，即降水和地表水入渗对地下水的补给量。

地表水与地下水重复计算量

指地表水和地下水相互转化的部分，即天然河川径流量中的地下水排泄量和地下水补给量中来源于地表水的入渗补给量。

供水总量

指各种水源为用水户提供的包括输水损失在内的毛水量。

地表水源供水量

指地表水体工程的取水量，按蓄、引、提、调四种形式统计。从水库、塘坝中引水或提水，均属蓄水工程供水量；从河道或湖泊中自流引水的，无论有闸或无闸，均属引水工程供水量；利用扬水站从河道或湖泊中直接取水的，属提水工程供水量；跨流域调水指水资源一级区或独立流域之间的跨流域调配水量，不包括在蓄、引、提水量中。

地下水源供水量

指水井工程的开采量，按浅层淡水、深层承压水和微咸水分别统计。城市地下水源供水量包括自来水厂的开采量和工矿企业自备井的开采量。

其他水源供水量

包括污水处理再利用、集雨工程、海水淡化等水源工程的供水量。

用水总量

指各类用水户取用的包括输水损失在内的毛水量。

农业用水

包括农田灌溉用水、林果地灌溉用水、草地灌溉用水、鱼塘补水和畜禽用水。

工业用水

指工矿企业在生产过程中用于制造、加工、冷却、空调、净化、洗涤等方面的用水，按新水取用量计，不包括企业内部的重复利用水量。

生活用水

包括城镇生活用水和农村生活用水。城镇生活用水由居民用水和公共用水（含第三产业及建筑业等用水）组成；农村生活用水指居民生活用水。

生态环境补水

仅包括人为措施供给的城镇环境用水和部分河湖、湿地补水，而不包括降水、径流自然满足的水量。

一般工业固体废物产生量

指未被列入《国家危险废物名录》或者根据国家规定的危险废物鉴别标准（GB5085）、固体废物浸出毒性浸出方法（GB5086）及固体废物浸出毒性测定方法（GB／T 15555）鉴别方法判定不具有危险特性的工业固体废物。计算公式是：

一般工业固体废物产生量=（一般工业固体废物综合利用量－其中：综合利用往年贮存量）+一般工业固体废物贮存量+（一般工业固体废物处置量－其中：处置往年贮存量）+一般工业固体废物倾倒丢弃量

一般工业固体废物综合利用量

指报告期内企业通过回收、加工、循环、交换等方式，从固体废物中提取或者使其转化为可以利用的资源、能源和其他原材料的固体废物量（包括当年利用的往年工业固体废物累计贮存量）。如用作农业肥料、生产建筑材料、筑路等。综合利用量由原产生固体废物的单位统计。

一般工业固体废物处置量

指报告期内企业将工业固体废物焚烧和用其他改变工业固体废物的物理、化学、生物特性的方法，达到减少或者消除其危险成分的活动，或者将工业固体废物最终置于符合环境保护规定要求的填埋场的活动中，所消纳固体废物的量。

一般工业固体废物贮存量　指报告期内企业以综合利用或处置为目的，将固体废物暂时贮存或堆存在专设的贮存设施或专设的集中堆存场所内的量。专设的固体废物贮存场所或贮存设施必须有防扩散、防流失、防渗漏、防止污染大气、水体的措施。

一般工业固体废物倾倒丢弃量

指报告期内企业将所产生的固体废物倾倒或者丢弃到固体废物污染防治设施、场所以外的量。

危险废物产生量

指当年全年调查对象实际产生的危险废物的量。危险废物指列入国家危险废物名录或者根据国家规定的危险废物鉴别标准和鉴别方法认定的，具有爆炸性、易燃性、易氧化性、毒性、腐蚀性、易传染性疾病等危险特性之一的废物。按《国家危险废物名录》（生态环境部、国家发展和改革委员会 2008 部令第 1 号）填报。

危险废物综合利用量

指当年全年调查对象从危险废物中提取物质作为原材料或者燃料的活动中消纳危险废物的量。包括本单位利用或委托、提供给外单位利用的量。

危险废物处置量

指报告期内企业将危险废物焚烧和用其他改变工业固体废物的物理、化学、生物特性的方法，达到减少或者消除其危险成分的活动，或者将危险废物最终置于符合环境保护规定要求的填埋场的活动中，所消纳危险废物的量。处置量包括处置本单位或委托给外单位处置的量。

危险废物贮存量

指将危险废物以一定包装方式暂时存放在专设的贮存设施内的量。专设的贮存设施指对危险废物的包装、选址、设计、安全防护、监测和关闭等符合《危险废物贮存污染控制标准》（GB18597-2001）等相关环保法律法规要求，具有防扩散、防流失、防渗漏、防止污染大气和水体措施的设施。

生活垃圾清运量

指报告期收集和运送到各生活垃圾处理厂(场)和生活垃圾最终消纳点的生活垃圾数量。生活垃圾指城市日常生活或为城市日常生活提供服务的活动中产生的固体废物以及法律行政规定的视为城市生活垃圾的固体废物。包括：居民生活垃圾、商业垃圾、集市贸易市场垃圾、街道清扫垃圾、公共场所垃圾和机关、学校、厂矿等单位的生活垃圾。

生活垃圾无害化处理率

指报告期生活垃圾无害化处理量与生活垃圾产生量的比率。在统计上，由于生活垃圾产生量不易取得，可用清运量代替。计算公式为：

生活垃圾无害化处理率＝生活垃圾无害化处理量/生活垃圾产生量×100%

森林面积

包括郁闭度0.2以上的乔木林地面积和竹林面积，国家特别规定的灌木林地面积，农田林网以及村旁、路旁、水旁、宅旁林木的覆盖面积。

人工林面积

指由人工播种、植苗或扦插造林形成的生长稳定，(一般造林3-5年后或飞机播种5-7年后)每公顷保存株数大于或等于造林设计植树株数80%或郁闭度0.20以上(含0.20)的林分面积。

森林覆盖率

以行政区域为单位的森林面积占区域土地总面积的百分比。计算公式为：

森林覆盖率＝森林面积/土地总面积×100%

活立木总蓄积量

指一定范围土地上全部树木蓄积的总量，包括森林蓄积、疏林蓄积、散生木蓄积和四旁树蓄积。

森林蓄积量

指一定森林面积上存在着的林木树干部分的总材积。

造林面积

指在宜林荒山荒地、宜林沙荒地、无立木林地、疏林地和退耕地等其他宜林地上通过人工措施形成或恢复森林、林木、灌木林的过程。

人工造林

指在宜林荒山荒地、宜林沙荒地、无立木林地、疏林地和退耕地等其他宜林地上通过播种、植苗和分植来提高森林植被覆被率的技术措施。

用材林

指以生产木材为主要目的的森林和林木，包括以生产竹材为主要目的的竹林。

经济林

指以生产果品，食用油料、饮料、调料，工业原料和药材为主要目的的林木。经济林是人们为了取得林木的果实、叶片、皮层、胶液等产品作为工业原料或者供食用所营造的林木，如油茶、油桐、核桃、樟树、花椒、茶、桑、果等。

防护林　指以防护为主要目的的森林、林木和灌木丛。包括水源涵养林，水土保持林，防风固沙林，农田、牧场防护林，护岸林，护路林等。

薪炭林

指以生产燃料为主要目的的林木。

特种用途林

指以国防、环境保护、科学实验等为主要目的的森林和林木。包括国防林、实验林、母树林、环境保护林、风景林，名胜古迹和革命纪念地的林木，自然保护区的森林。

滑坡

指斜坡上不稳定的岩土体在重力作用下沿一定软弱面(或滑动带)整体向下滑动的物理地质现象。

崩塌

指陡坡上大块的岩土体在重力作用下突然脱离母体崩落的物理地质现象。

Explanatory Notes for Major Statistical Indicators

Cultivated Land

refers to land mainly for the regular cultivation of farm crops (including vegetables), with some fruit trees, mulberry trees and others, covers cultivated land, newly-developed land, reclaimed land, consolidated land, fallow, beach land that can guarantee one harvest per year on average. It also covers fixed ditch, canal, road and sill (ridge) with width less than 1 meter in the South and 2 meters in the North, lands planted temporarily with herbs, grass, flowers and nursery stocks, and other cultivated land with temporary change of use.

Garden Land

refers to land for intensive cultivation of perennial woody plants and herbs to collect fruits, leaves, roots, stems and juice, with a covering rate over 50% and plant number per mu over 70% of rational plant number. Land for nursery is included.

Forestland

refers to land for planting arbor, bamboo, bush shrub and land in coastal zones for planting mangrove. It includes slash, but not the green belts in residential area, forests requested for railway and highway, and the dike protection forest around rivers and ditches.

Pastureland

refers to land mainly for the growth of herbs.

Volume of Runoff

refers to the total volume of water running through a certain cross section of a river during a certain period of time, reflecting the water resource condition in a country or a region. The formula for calculating volume of runoff is as follows:

Runoff =Precipitation-Evaporation

Drainage Area

Each river has its own main stream and branches to form the water system of the river. Each river has its own catchment's area, which is also called as the drainage area of the river.

Out-flowing Rivers

refer to rivers directly or indirectly flowing into the sea. The area providing water to the out-flowing rivers is called as out-flowing area.

Inland Rivers

refer to rivers in inland dry areas that die away in desert on the way or infuse into inland lakes. The area providing water to the inland rivers is called as inland area.

Mineral Resources

refer to useful minerals, with solid state, liquid state, gaseity, due to the geological process. Minerals are important natural resources, and important material base for social development. At present, there are more than 170 types of minerals discovered in China. They can be categorized into four groups: energy producing minerals (including coal, petroleum, natural gas and terrestrial heat), metallic minerals (including iron, manganese, copper, lead and bauxite), non metallic minerals (including diamond, limestone and clay), and water/gas related minerals (including ground water, mineral water and carbon dioxide). Metallic minerals can be further classified as ferrous, non-ferrous, noble metal, rare metal, rare earth metal and dispersed metals.

Average Temperature

refers to the air temperature. China uses centigrade as the unit. The thermometry used for weather observation is put in a breezy shutter, which is 1.5 meters high from the ground. Therefore, the commonly used temperature refers to the temperature in the breezy shutter 1.5 meters away from the ground. The calculation method is as follows:

Monthly average temperature is the summation of average daily temperature of one month divided by the actual days of that particular month.

Annual average temperature is the summation of monthly average of a year divided by 12 months.

Average Annual Relative Humidity

refers to the ratio of actual water vapour pressure to the saturation water vapour pressure under the current temperature. The calculation method is the same as that of temperature.

Volume of Precipitation

refers to the deepness of liquid state or solid state (thawed) water falling from the sky to the ground that has not been evaporated, infiltrated or run off. The calculation method is as follows:

Monthly precipitation is the summation of daily precipitation of a month.

Annual precipitation is the summation of 12 months precipitation of a year.

Annual Sunshine Hours

refer to the actual hours of sun irradiating the earth, usually expressed in hours. The calculation method is the same as that of the precipitation.

Total Water Resources

refers to total volume of surface water and groundwater and is measured as run-off for surface water and replenishment of groundwater with rainfall in local area.

Surface Water Resources

refers to total volume of year by year renewable dynamic resources which exist in rivers, lakes, glaciers and other surface water and are the natural run-off of rivers.

Groundwater Resources

refers to total volume of year by year renewable dynamic resources which exist in saturation aquifers of groundwater and are measured as replenishment of groundwater with rainfall and surface water.

Duplicated Measurement between Surface Water and Groundwater

refers to mutual exchange between surface water and groundwater, i.e. run-off of rivers includes some depletion into groundwater while groundwater includes some replenishment from surface water.

Water Supply

refers to gross water of various sources supplied to consumers, including losses during distribution.

Surface Water Supply

refers to withdrawals by surface water supply system, broken down with storage, flow, pumping and transfer. Supply from storage projects includes withdrawals from reservoirs; supply from flow includes withdrawals from rivers and lakes with natural flows no matter if there are locks or not; supply from pumping projects includes withdrawals from rivers or lakes with pumping stations; and supply from transfer refers to water supplies transferred from first-level regions of water resources or independent river drainage areas to others, and should not be covered under supplies of storage, flow and pumping.

Groundwater Supply

refers to withdrawals from supplying wells, broken down with shallow layer freshwater, deep layer freshwater and slightly brackish water. Groundwater supply for urban areas includes water mining by both waterworks and own wells of enterprises.

Other Water Supply Sources

include supplies by waste-water treatment, rain collection, seawater desalinization and other water projects.

Water Use

refers to gross water used by various water users, including losses during distribution.

Water Use by Agriculture

includes uses of water by irrigation of farming fields, forestry and orchards, irrigation of grassland, replenishment of fishing farms and water used by animal husbandry.

Water Use by Industry

refers to new withdrawals of water, excluding reuse of water within enterprises.

Water Use by Living Consumption

includes use of water for living consumption in both urban and rural areas. Urban water use by living consumption is composed of household use and public use (including tertiary industry and construction). Rural water use by living consumption includes water used by households.

Water Use by Ecological and Environmental Protection

includes replenishment of rivers and lakes and use for urban environment.

Common Industrial Solid Wastes Produced

refers to the industrial solid wastes that are not listed in the 《National Catalogue of Hazardous Wastes》, or not regarded as hazardous according to the national hazardous waste identification standards (GB5085), solid waste-Extraction procedure for leaching toxicity (GB5086) and solid waste-Extraction procedure for leaching toxicity (GB/T 15555). The calculation formula is as followed:

Common Industrial Solid Wastes Produced = (common industrial solid wastes utilized – the proportion of utilized stock of previous years) + common industrial solid waste stock + (common industrial solid wastes disposed – the proportion of disposed stock of previous years) + common industrial solid wastes discharged.

Common Industrial Solid Wastes Comprehensively Utilized

refers to volume of solid wastes from which useful materials can be extracted or which can be converted into usable resources, energy or other materials by means of reclamation, processing, recycling and exchange (including utilizing in the year the stocks of industrial solid wastes of the previous year) during the report period, e.g. being used as agricultural fertilizers, building materials or as material for paving road. Examples of such utilizations include fertilizers, building materials and road materials. The information shall be collected by the producing units of the wastes.

Common Industrial Solid Wastes Disposed

refers to the quantity of industrial solid wastes which are burnt or specially disposed using other methods to alter the physical, chemical and biological properties and thus to reduce or eliminate the hazard, or placed ultimately in the sites meeting the requirements for environmental protection during the report period.

Stock of Common Industrial Solid Wastes

refers to the volume of solid wastes placed in special facilities or special sites by enterprises for purposes of utilization or disposal during the report period. The sites or facilities should take measures against dispersion, loss, seepage, and air and water contamination.

Common Industrial Solid Wastes Discharged

refers to the volume of industrial solid wastes dumped or discharged by producing enterprises to disposal facilities or to other sites.

Hazardous Wastes Produced

refers to the volume of actual hazardous wastes produced by surveyed samples throughout the year of the survey. Hazardous waste refers to those included in the national hazardous wastes catalogue or specified as any one of the following properties in light of the national hazardous wastes identification standards and methods: explosive, ignitable, oxidizable, toxic, corrosive or liable to cause infectious diseases or lead to other dangers. The report of this indicator should follow the 《National Catalogue of Hazardous Wastes》 (the NO.1 Ministry Order in 2008 by the Ministry of Environment Protection and National Development and Reform Commission).

Hazardous Wastes Utilized

refers to the volume of hazardous wastes that are used to extract materials for raw materials or fuel throughout the year of the survey, including those utilized by the producing enterprise and those provided to other enterprises for utilization.

Hazardous Wastes Disposed

refers to the quantity of hazardous wastes which are burnt or specially disposed using other methods to alter the physical, chemical and biological properties and thus to reduce or eliminate the hazard, or placed ultimately in the sites meeting the requirements for environmental protection during the report period.

Stock of Hazardous Wastes

refers to the volume of hazardous wastes specially packaged and placed in special facilities or special sites by enterprises. The special stock facilities should meet the requirements set in relevant environment protection laws and regulations such as "Pollution Control Standards for Hazardous Waste Stock" (GB18597-2001) in regard to package of hazardous waste, location, design, safety, monitoring and shutdown, and take measures against dispersion, loss, seepage, and air and water contamination.

Consumption Wastes Transported

refers to volume of consumption wastes collected and transported to disposal factories or sites during the reference period. Consumption wastes are solid wastes produced from urban households or from service activities for urban households, and solid wastes regarded by laws and regulations as urban consumption wastes, including those from households, commercial activities, markets, cleaning of streets, public sites, offices, schools, factories, mining units and other sources.

Ratio of Consumption Wastes Treated

refers to consumption wastes treated over that produced. In practical statistics, as it is difficult to estimate, the volume of consumption wastes produced is replaced with that transported. It is calculated as:

Ratio of consumption wastes treated = consumption wastes treated / consumption wastes produced × 100%

Forest Area

refers to the area of trees and bamboo grow with a canopy density above 0.2 degree, the area of shrubby tree according to regulations of the government, the area of forest land inside farm land and the area of trees planted by the side of villages, farm houses and along roads and rivers.

Area of Man-made Forests

refer to the area of stable growing forests, planted manually or by airplanes, with a survival rate of 80% or higher of the designed number of trees per hectare, or with a canopy density of 0.20 degree or above after 3-5 years of manual planting or 5-7 years of airplane planting.

Forest Coverage Rate

Taking the administrative jurisdiction as the unit, the percentage of area of afforested land to the area of total land. The formula for calculating forest coverage rate is as follows:

Forestry coverage rate = Area of Afforested Land / Area of Total Land × 100%

Total Standing Stock Volume

refers to the total stock volume of trees growing in land, including trees in forest, trees in sparse forest, scattered trees and trees planted by the side of villages, farm houses and along roads and rivers.

Stock Volume of Forest

refers to total stock volume of wood growing in forest area, which shows the total size and level of forest resources of a country or a region.

Area of Afforestation

refers to the total area of land suitable for afforestation, including barren hills, idle land, sand dunes, non-timber forest land, woodland and "grain for green" land, on which acres of forests, trees and shrubs are planted through manual planting.

Manual Planting

refers to technical measures of sowing, planting seedlings and divided transplanting on land suitable for afforestation, including barren hills, idle land, sand dunes, non-timber forest land, woodland and "grain for green" land to increase vegetation coverage rate of forests.

Timber Forests

refer to forests which are mainly for the production of timber, including bamboo groves planted to harvest bamboos.

By-product Forests

refer to forests that mainly produce fruits, nuts, edible oil, beverages, indigents, raw materials and medicine materials. By-product forests are planted to harvest the fruits, leaves, bark or liquid of trees, and consume them as food or raw materials for the manufacturing industry, such as tea-oil trees, tung oil trees, walnut trees, camphor trees, tea bushes, mulberry trees, fruit trees, etc.

Protection Forests

refer to forests, trees and bushes planted mainly for protection or preservation purpose, including water resource conservation forests, water and soil conservation forests, windbreak and dune-fixing forests, farmland and pasture protection forests, riverside protection forests, roadside protection forests, etc.

Fuel Forests

refer to forests planted mainly for fuels.

Forests for Special Purpose

refer to forests planted mainly for national defence, environment protection or scientific experiments, including national defence forests, experimental forests, mother-tree forests, environment protection forests, scenery forests, trees in historical or scenic spots, forests in natural reserves.

Landslides

refer to the geological phenomenon of unstable rocks and earth on slopes sliding down along certain soft surface as a result of gravitational force.

Collapse

refers to the geological phenomenon of large mass of rocks or earth suddenly collapsing from the mountain or cliff as a result of gravitational force.

第十二篇

Chapter 12

农 业

AGRICULTURE

简要说明

一、本篇资料反映我省农业生产和农村经济的基本情况，内容主要包括乡镇（村）数、农业机械拥有量、农林牧渔业产值、主要产品产量等。

二、本篇资料来源：按照农村统计调查报表制度汇总、整理。

农村统计调查报表制度的统计范围包括各市、县（区）辖区的各种经济类型的全部农林牧渔业以及各非农行业附属的农林牧渔业生产单位，但不包括农业科学试验机构进行的农业生产。

农村统计调查报表制度按照国家统计局统一要求，由各市、县（区）调查队、统计局收集、汇总报送，采取抽样调查、典型调查、重点调查和其他调查所取得。部分指标及林业生产情况、渔业生产情况等指标均取自同级业务部门统计资料。

乡镇（村）数、农业机械拥有量、农垦系统农场基本情况等资料由省民政厅、省农业农村厅、省农垦总公司提供。

Brief Introduction

I. Data reflects the basic situation of agricultural production and rural economy in our province, including the number of towns (villages), agricultural machinery ownership, output value of agriculture, forestry, animal husbandry and fishery, output of main products, etc.

II. Data source: according to the rural statistical survey report form system summary, collation.

Statistical scope of the rural statistical survey report system includes all agriculture, forestry, animal husbandry and fishery of various economic types under the jurisdiction of cities, counties (districts) as well as agricultural, forestry, animal husbandry and fishery production units affiliated to non-agricultural industries, but does not include agricultural production conducted by agricultural scientific experimental institutions.

According to the unified requirements of the State Bureau of Statistics, the report forms of rural statistical investigations shall be collected, summarized and submitted by the investigation teams and the bureau of Statistics of the cities and counties (districts), and obtained through sampling surveys, typical surveys, key surveys and other investigations. Some indicators, forestry production, fishery production and other indicators are taken from the statistical data of business departments at the same level.

Number of towns (villages), ownership of agricultural machinery, basic information of agricultural reclamation system farms and other information shall be provided by the provincial Civil Affairs Department, the Provincial Department of Agriculture and Rural Affairs, and the Provincial Agricultural Reclamation Corporation.

12—1　乡（镇）、村数及主要农业机械年末拥有量
Number of Townships (towns), Villages and Year-end Ownership of Main Agricultural Machinery

指　　标		Item		2010	2015	2020	2021	2022
乡镇数	（个）	Number of Township and Town Governments	(unit)	1232	1249	1239	1236	1226
#镇个数		Number of Town Governments		869	946	968	997	1011
村民委员会	（个）	Number of Villagers' Committees	(unit)	15744	14688	14427	14252	14281
农业机械总动力	（万千瓦）	Total Agricultural Machinery Power	(10000 kW)	5409.78	6580.99	6799.50	6924.32	7070.11
农用大中型拖拉机	（台）	Number of Large and Medium Agricultural Tractors	(unit)	124660	220080	262506	276910	290952
小型拖拉机	（万台）	Number of Mini-tractors	(10000 units)	236.12	214.67	200.49	195.25	188.95
联合收获机	（台）	Combine Harvester	(unit)	102167	174156	227695	232655	238639
机耕面积	（千公顷）	Area Ploughed by Tractors	(1000 hectares)	4056.35	4287.86	7668.43	7646.18	7642.03
机播面积	（千公顷）	Seeded Area by Tractors	(1000 hectares)	3606.59	5003.90	6124.64	6281.76	6551.44
机收面积	（千公顷）	Harvest Area by Tractors	(1000 hectares)	5264.28	6440.64	7420.12	7314.10	7520.77

注：乡镇（包括城关镇）及村民委员会个数来源于省民政厅（下同）。
a) Number of township (including county towns) and villagers committee comes from the provincial Civil Affairs department (the same below).

12—2 主要年份农林牧渔业生产情况
Output of Farming, Forestry, Animal Husbandry and Fishery

指标	Item	2010	2015	2020	2021	2022
农产品产量（万吨）	Yield of Farm Crops (10000 tons)					
粮食	Grain	3207.71	4077.23	4019.22	4087.56	4100.13
谷物	Cereal	3055.91	3962.29	3901.88	3973.61	3979.98
#稻谷	Rice	1440.20	1616.80	1560.51	1590.43	1583.40
小麦	Wheat	1242.37	1661.05	1671.73	1699.73	1722.27
玉米	Corn	355.01	679.04	663.25	677.46	663.39
豆类	Beans	107.58	95.67	98.13	95.88	99.93
薯类	Tubers	44.22	19.27	19.22	18.07	20.21
油料	Oil-bearing Crops	176.13	171.45	162.47	167.14	173.42
#花生	Peanuts	68.06	70.02	72.33	71.82	72.38
油菜籽	Rapeseeds	101.05	96.57	85.30	91.06	96.40
芝麻	Sesame	0.87	1.03	1.99	2.27	2.25
棉花	Cotton	25.76	14.75	4.10	2.91	2.56
生黄红麻	Jute and Ambary Hemp	0.25	0.18	0.26	0.22	0.24
烟叶	Tobacco	1.77	2.63	2.04	2.01	2.18
#烤烟	Flue-cured Tobacco	1.71	2.52	2.02	1.99	2.15
蚕茧	Silkworm Cocoons	3.32	3.03	0.98	0.80	
茶叶	Tea	8.01	11.03	12.86	13.73	14.16
#绿茶	Green Tea	7.42	10.27	11.35	11.73	12.35
园林水果	Garden Fruits	235.88	301.81	367.82	383.54	396.25
农产品单位面积产量（公斤/公顷）	Yield of Farm Crops per Hectare (kg/hectare)					
谷物	Cereal	5194	6036	5926	6000	6034
棉花	Cotton	918	881	801	846	844
花生	Peanuts	4781	4987	4960	4913	4953
油菜籽	Rapeseeds	1966	2360	2434	2442	2452
芝麻	Sesames	1317	1501	1632	1678	1683
生黄红麻	Jute and Ambary Hemp	2658	2813	3752	3576	3482
烤烟	Flue-cured Tobacco	2712	2548	2355	2329	2326
茶园面积（千公顷）	Area of Tea Plantations at Year-end (1000 hectares)	127.24	156.98	194.71	205.01	209.27
果园面积（千公顷）	Area of Orchards at Year-end (1000 hectares)	109.06	130.82	166.29	168.49	167.62
大牲畜年末头数（万头）	Number of Large Animals (year-end) (10000 heads)	105.86	73.50	95.25	100.02	107.17
#牛	Cattle and Buffaloes	105.23	73.15	94.80	99.36	106.68
肉猪出栏头数（万头）	Number of Slaughtered Fattened Hogs (10000 heads)	2737.24	2872.20	2150.47	2797.76	2920.91
猪年末头数（万头）	Number of Hogs (year-end) (10000 heads)	1419.24	1484.09	1419.33	1582.50	1655.80
羊年末头数（万只）	Number of Sheep and Goats (year-end) (10000 heads)	473.08	417.99	597.87	612.82	635.66
肉类产量（万吨）	Output of Meat (10000 tons)	372.35	415.02	396.03	456.31	475.36
#禽肉	Poultry Output	110.80	145.02	181.05	183.41	191.80
奶类（吨）	Milk (ton)	191359	286170	376414	475559	507369
#牛奶	Cow Milk	191359	286170	376369	475506	507365
禽蛋（万吨）	Poultry Eggs (10000 tons)	126.70	155.01	184.22	177.10	186.66
淡水产品产量（万吨）	Total Output of Freshwater Aquatic Products (10000 tons)	193.31	209.30	232.41	236.50	245.50

注：2007—2017年数据根据第三次全国农业普查结果进行了修订和修正（下同）。
a) The 2007-2017 data were revised and revised according to the results of the third national agricultural census (the same below).

12—3 主要年份农作物播种面积
Sown Area of Crops in Major Years

单位：千公顷（1000 hectare）

指　标	Item	2010	2015	2020	2021	2022
粮 食	Grain Crops	6947.75	7280.73	7289.52	7309.61	7314.25
谷 物	Cereal	5883.75	6563.95	6584.00	6622.78	6595.82
#稻 谷	Rice	2338.63	2476.37	2512.08	2512.15	2496.48
小 麦	Wheat	2619.18	2857.97	2825.20	2846.00	2849.37
玉 米	Corn	864.08	1206.27	1234.76	1252.74	1228.94
豆 类	Beans	905.10	637.75	641.98	627.11	654.17
薯 类	Tubers	158.90	79.02	63.55	59.72	64.25
油 料	Oil-bearing Crops	691.87	574.91	521.44	542.20	561.90
棉 花	Cotton	280.75	167.46	51.20	34.43	30.29
生 麻	Raw Hemp	1.55	1.09	2.21	2.13	2.05
糖 料	Sugar Crops	3.59	3.05	2.70	2.48	2.32
烟 叶	Tobacco	7.54	10.25	8.64	8.62	9.33
蔬 菜	Vegetables	526.36	599.62	717.95	749.39	769.22

注：粮食（包括分类、品种）数据来源于国家统计局安徽调查总队（下同）。

a) The data of grain (including classification and variety) were obtained from Anhui Survey Team of National Bureau of Statistics (the same below).

12—4 农林牧渔业总产值及指数
Gross Output Value of Farming, Forestry, Animal Husbandry and Fishery and Related Indices

本表按当年价格计算。 (Data in value terms in this table are calculated at current prices.)

年份 Year	绝对数（万元） Gross Output Value (10000 yuan)					
	农林牧渔业总产值 Total of Farming, Forestry, Animal Husbandry and Fishery	农业 Farming	林业 Forestry	牧业 Animal Husbandry	渔业 Fishery	农林牧渔专业及辅助性活动 Professional and Auxiliary Activities
2010	28150185	14772975	1352804	8298046	2677885	1048475
2012	35522691	17864629	2094974	10741973	3491915	1329201
2013	38187303	19161918	2330736	11237306	3988152	1469191
2014	40242037	20270934	2830736	11340074	4175583	1624710
2015	41831434	20800862	2901057	12077885	4315202	1736428
2016	44323171	21370277	2910818	13197424	4661107	2183546
2017	45979418	22414199	3190831	13216891	4762099	2395398
2018	46727141	22536647	3329380	13158401	5056501	2646212
2019	51621338	23653942	3512838	16289006	5213091	2952462
2020	56809129	25254212	3874666	19001869	5425680	3252702
2021	60043101	28029266	4129049	18108607	6216648	3559532
2022	62779786	29370383	4733438	18125309	6602816	3947841

年份 Year	指数（%） Related Indices (%)					
	农林牧渔业总产值 Total of Farming, Forestry, Animal Husbandry and Fishery	农业 Farming	林业 Forestry	牧业 Animal Husbandry	渔业 Fishery	农林牧渔专业及辅助性活动 Professional and Auxiliary Activities
2010	104.46	103.24	107.64	104.93	105.47	110.54
2012	105.57	105.80	105.40	105.60	103.50	108.05
2013	103.41	103.24	106.93	102.01	104.63	107.94
2014	104.59	105.04	107.90	102.93	103.97	107.99
2015	104.20	104.92	105.69	102.66	103.35	105.71
2016	103.41	102.45	104.88	102.04	103.05	122.78
2017	104.08	104.44	109.61	101.86	103.24	108.40
2018	102.58	102.11	103.12	101.95	103.23	108.35
2019	102.26	103.42	104.30	98.17	103.30	108.20
2020	102.74	102.34	107.72	101.67	102.25	106.74
2021	109.35	103.35	98.45	121.25	104.15	108.05
2022	104.45	102.87	109.52	104.96	103.98	109.27

12—5　主要年份林业生产情况
Basic Data of Forest Production in Major Years

指　　标	Item	2010	2015	2020	2021	2022
营林情况　（公顷）	Management of Forest　(hectares)					
人工造林面积	Artificial Afforestation Area	57012	114350	59639	35774	22639
新封山育林面积	Area of Setting Apart Mountains for Forestation	20943	14066	42144	84577	75667
森林抚育面积	Area of Forest Tending	307795	560665	559572	515786	350601
油茶籽　（吨）	Tea-oil Seeds　(ton)	25864	78327	110180	129592	85807
板　栗　（吨）	Chestnuts　(ton)	137239	105870	99645	90965	94198
竹材采伐量　（万根）	Determination of Bamboo Cut　(10000 units)	9784	15724	20131	19797	18942
木材采伐量　（万立方米）	Determination of Timber Cut　(10000 cu.m)	458	567	536	612	551

12—6　主要年份茶叶、水果生产情况
Tea, Fruits Production in Major Years

单位：吨、公顷（ton，Hectares）

指　　标	Item	2010	2015	2020	2021	2022
茶叶产量	Tea	80149	110345	128603	137259	141632
#绿　茶	Green Tea	74192	102725	113547	117259	123525
园林水果产量	Garden Fruits	2358815	3018139	3678159	3835374	3962497
#苹　果	Apples	215407	198083	376245	372705	357441
梨	Pears	1006506	1154815	1275089	1283696	1350112
柑橘类	Citrus	11319	14915	32823	33151	32048
其他水果	Other Garden Fruits	1125583	1650326	1994002	2145778	2222716
#桃	Peaches	574309	758068	1051485	1160267	1225798
葡　萄	Grapes	211142	455286	534157	556987	572711
茶园面积	Tea Garden Area	127242	156982	194707	205012	209274
果园面积	Orchard Area	109061	130823	166286	168494	167617
#苹　果	Apples	12074	11348	11714	11435	11010
梨	Pears	39388	39742	41234	40720	40936
葡　萄	Grapes	7629	17152	26685	26423	26500

12—7 主要年份牲畜饲养情况
Number of Livestock in Major Years

单位：万头（万只） (10000 heads)

年 份 Year	大牲畜年末头数 Large Animals (year-end)	牛 Cattle and Buffaloes	肉猪出栏头数 Slaughtered Fattened Hogs	猪年末头数 Hogs (year-end)	羊年末只数 Sheep and Goats (year-end)	活家禽存栏只数 Poultry
2010	105.9	105.2	2737.2	1419.2	473.1	26216.2
2013	83.1	82.5	2888.2	1567.4	410.7	30315.1
2014	74.6	74.2	2990.4	1534.6	412.5	30712.8
2015	73.5	73.2	2872.2	1484.1	418.0	31020.8
2016	68.5	68.2	2760.4	1410.1	376.9	28904.6
2017	80.9	80.6	2828.9	1417.2	505.1	23018.5
2018	80.0	79.6	2837.4	1356.3	500.6	23524.9
2019	88.2	87.8	2292.6	1091.8	548.1	27406.5
2020	95.2	94.8	2150.5	1419.3	597.9	31024.1
2021	100.0	99.4	2797.8	1582.5	612.8	30285.4
2022	107.2	106.7	2920.9	1655.8	635.7	32284.2

注：全省猪、牛、羊、禽数据来源于国家统计局安徽调查总队（下同）。

a) Data of pigs, cattle, sheep and poultry in the whole province come from Anhui Investigation Team of National Bureau of Statistics (the same below).

12—8 主要年份畜产品产量
Output of Livestock Products in Major Years

单位：吨 (ton)

年 份 Year	肉类总产量 Output of Meat	禽肉产量 Poultry Output	生牛奶 Raw Milk	禽 蛋 Poultry Eggs	天然蜂蜜 Honey	蚕 茧 Silkworm Cocoons
2010	3723533	1108014	191359	1267030	16447	33177
2013	3980081	1293874	236741	1389427	20109	32247
2014	4073311	1299103	260392	1388606	19427	31080
2015	4150171	1450219	286170	1550134	16734	30328
2016	4079731	1539611	305344	1631743	17396	29497
2017	4151847	1464306	298412	1546998	17789	28940
2018	4217401	1506771	307961	1582579	21031	28904
2019	4028148	1745945	337551	1687029	17924	25978
2020	3960317	1810544	376369	1842236	16957	9755
2021	4563111	1834082	475506	1771000	18995	7968
2022	4753607	1918449	507365	1866634	18494	8454

12—9 农林牧渔业总产值（2022年）
Gross Output Value of Farming, Forestry, Animal Husbandry and Fishery (2022)

单位：万元（10000 yuan）

指　　标	Item	按可比价格计算 Calculated According to Constant Price	按当年价格计算 At Current Prices
农林牧渔业总产值	**Total Gross Output Value**	**62715194**	**62779786**
农业产值	**Gross Output Value of Farming**	**28832990**	**29370383**
谷物及其他作物	Cereal and Other Crops	14118691	14955500
谷　物	Cereal		11710751
薯　类	Tubers		156192
油　料	Oil-bearing Crops		1421253
豆　类	Beans		755678
棉　花	Cotton		55787
生　麻	Raw Hemp		11013
糖　类	Sugar Crops		24171
烟　叶	Tobacco		68700
其他农作物	Other Crops		751957
蔬菜、食用菌及花卉盆景园艺产品	Vegetables, Edible Fungus and Flowers and Plants Bonsai Horticultural Goods	10001557	9741994
水果、食用坚果、茶、饮料和香料	Fruits, Nut, Tea, Beverage and Spice	3839037	3806830
中草药材	Chinese Medicinal Herbs	873704	866058
林业产值	**Gross Output Value of Forestry**	**4522099**	**4733438**
林木的培育和种植	Cultivation and Planting of Woods	745828	758675
竹木采运	Lumbering and Transport of Bamboo and Timber	1421899	1417297
林产品	Forest Products	2354372	2557466
牧业产值	**Gross Output Value of Animal Husbandry**	**19006275**	**18125309**
牲畜饲养	Animals Breeding	3190753	2959066
#牛的饲养	Cattle and Buffaloes Breeding		848302
羊的饲养	Sheep and Goats Breeding		1695230
猪的饲养	Hogs Breeding	8823008	7989922
家禽的饲养	Poultry Breeding	6026516	6433043
狩猎和捕捉动物	Animals Hunting and Catching		
其他畜牧业	Other Animal Husbandry	965998	743278
渔业产值	**Gross Output Value of Fishery**	**6464303**	**6602816**
淡水产品	Freshwater Aquatic Products	6464303	6602816
#养　殖	Cultured		5394589
#鱼　类	Fishes		2968895
虾蟹类	Shrimps and Crabs		3440293
农林牧渔专业及辅助性活动产值	**Output Value of Professional and Auxiliary Activities**	**3889527**	**3947841**

12—10 农作物主要产品生产情况（2022年）
Production of Main Crops (2022)

指　　标	Item	播种面积（千公顷）Sown Area (1000 hectares)	产　　量（万吨）Yield (10000 tons)
粮食作物合计	Grain Crops	7314.25	4100.13
#夏收粮食	Summer-Harvest Crops	2849.93	1722.39
谷　物	Cereal	6595.82	3979.98
稻　谷	Rice	2496.48	1583.40
早　稻	Early Rice	171.40	101.10
中稻和一季晚稻	Middle-season Rice and Single-crop Late Rice	2143.94	1380.73
双季晚稻	Late Rice	181.13	101.57
小　麦	Wheat	2849.37	1722.27
冬小麦	Winter Wheat	2849.37	1722.27
玉　米	Corn	1228.94	663.39
其他谷物	Other Cereal	21.04	10.92
豆类合计	Beans	654.17	99.93
#大　豆	Soybean	610.71	94.22
薯　类	Tubers	64.25	20.21
#马铃薯	Potato	4.40	1.48
油料合计	Oil-bearing Crops	561.90	173.42
#花　生	Peanuts	146.15	72.38
油菜籽	Rapeseeds	393.16	96.40
芝　麻	Sesame	13.39	2.25
棉　花	Cotton	30.29	2.56
生麻合计	Fiber Crops	2.05	0.95
糖料合计	Sugar Crops	2.32	9.26
烟叶合计	Tobacco	9.33	2.18
中草药材	Crude Drugs	112.19	
蔬菜（含菜用瓜）	Vegetables (including gourd)	769.22	2537.70
瓜果类（果用瓜）	Melon and Fruit (Fruited Melon)	98.81	402.10
#西　瓜	Watermelon	74.04	318.34
草　莓	Strawberry	14.29	39.00
其他作物	Other Crops	33.24	

12—11　各市乡（镇）、村数（2022年）
Number of Townships (towns) and Villages by Region (2022)

地　区	Region	乡镇数（个）Number of Township and Town Governments (unit)	#镇数 Town Governments	村民委员会（个）Number of Villagers' Committees (unit)
总　计	**Total**	**1235**	**1011**	**14281**
合肥市	Hefei	81	70	1,137
淮北市	Huaibei	18	18	277
亳州市	Bozhou	79	72	1,227
宿州市	Suzhou	94	93	1,140
蚌埠市	Bengbu	55	47	878
阜阳市	Fuyang	149	125	1,487
淮南市	Huainan	71	59	825
滁州市	Chuzhou	94	85	950
六安市	Luan	130	95	1,744
马鞍山市	Maanshan	35	33	382
芜湖市	Wuhu	44	44	622
宣城市	Xuancheng	78	62	709
铜陵市	Tongling	31	27	363
池州市	Chizhou	45	37	574
安庆市	Anqing	130	85	1,286
黄山市	Huangshan	101	59	680

12—12 各市农、林、牧、渔业总产值及指数（2022年）

Gross Output Value of Farming, Forestry, Animal Husbandry and Fishery and Related Indices by Region (2022)

本表绝对数按当年价格计算，指数按可比价格计算。
Absolute figures in this table are calculated at current prices while indices are calculated at comparable prices.

地 区	Region	绝 对 数 （万元） Gross Output Value of Farming, Forestry, Animal Husbandry and Fishery (10000 yuan)					
		农林牧渔业总产值 Total of Farming, Forestry, Animal Husbandry and Fishery	农 业 Farming	林 业 Forestry	牧 业 Animal Husbandry	渔 业 Fishery	农林牧渔专业及辅助性活动 Professional and Auxiliary Activities
总 计	**Total**	**62779786**	**29370383**	**4733438**	**18125309**	**6602816**	**3947841**
合 肥 市	Hefei	5840878	3061534	285517	1307583	1022583	163661
淮 北 市	Huaibei	1508139	777403	51455	576834	59059	43389
亳 州 市	Bozhou	5294880	3316601	169105	1477266	126037	205871
宿 州 市	Suzhou	6716306	3163286	200164	2109433	120243	1123180
蚌 埠 市	Bengbu	4814917	2423773	135752	1618829	464475	172088
阜 阳 市	Fuyang	8737731	3841699	696731	2982578	276106	940617
淮 南 市	Huainan	2743268	1446056	70541	672037	488121	66513
滁 州 市	Chuzhou	5401991	2491547	190908	1396063	867083	456389
六 安 市	Luan	5110365	2406588	497321	1553558	528516	124382
马鞍山市	Maanshan	1913380	867447	33861	323840	545400	142832
芜 湖 市	Wuhu	3281493	1450662	238174	775503	713744	103410
宣 城 市	Xuancheng	3176904	1312161	392300	928853	398551	145039
铜 陵 市	Tongling	996538	468438	84262	176461	231362	36016
池 州 市	Chizhou	1728963	655970	261593	405217	304179	102004
安 庆 市	Anqing	4693242	1858976	454253	1442423	845547	92043
黄 山 市	Huangshan	1299550	654853	280586	302219	31150	30743

12—12 续表 continued

地区	Region	农林牧渔业总产值 Total of Farming, Forestry, Animal Husbandry and Fishery	农业 Farming	林业 Forestry	牧业 Animal Husbandry	渔业 Fishery	农林牧渔专业及辅助性活动 Professional and Auxiliary Activities
		指数（上年=100） Gross Output Value of Farming, Forestry, Animal Husbandry and Fishery (preceding year=100)					
总　计	**Total**	**104.45**	**102.87**	**109.52**	**104.96**	**103.98**	**109.27**
合肥市	Hefei	104.20	103.06	102.08	105.14	105.86	112.28
淮北市	Huaibei	103.97	103.19	100.93	104.84	105.04	112.20
亳州市	Bozhou	104.21	102.05	105.80	108.12	103.56	111.66
宿州市	Suzhou	105.13	103.53	97.11	106.33	113.39	108.04
蚌埠市	Bengbu	104.60	103.36	100.94	105.86	104.41	112.86
阜阳市	Fuyang	104.74	104.62	91.03	106.11	107.66	110.04
淮南市	Huainan	103.50	102.10	99.88	103.80	106.85	109.72
滁州市	Chuzhou	104.20	102.25	109.50	103.98	106.84	109.39
六安市	Luan	104.83	104.12	108.90	104.34	104.08	113.70
马鞍山市	Maanshan	104.33	103.00	102.88	106.22	104.98	107.65
芜湖市	Wuhu	104.51	102.92	104.02	107.22	105.21	106.97
宣城市	Xuancheng	104.92	102.47	109.55	105.64	104.78	112.61
铜陵市	Tongling	104.23	105.78	102.89	100.20	104.08	109.18
池州市	Chizhou	104.47	104.11	105.02	102.95	104.95	110.90
安庆市	Anqing	103.84	99.96	109.15	103.96	109.49	107.80
黄山市	Huangshan	105.03	103.05	110.43	105.22	103.98	104.17

注：全省农林牧渔业总产值指数按农产品生产者价格指数缩减计算。

a) The index of gross output value of agriculture, forestry, animal husbandry and fishery of the whole province reduces calculating according to producer's price index of agricultural products.

12—13 各市主要农业机械年末拥有量（2022年）
Agricultural Machinery at the Year-end by Region (2022)

地 区	Region	农业机械总动力（万千瓦）Total Power of Agricultural Machinery (10000 kW)	大中型拖拉机（台）Large and Medium Agricultural Tractors (unit)	小型拖拉机（台）Mini-tractors (unit)
总 计	**Total**	**7070.11**	**290952**	**1889534**
合肥市	Hefei	513.71	17789	172953
淮北市	Huaibei	286.23	17715	93770
亳州市	Bozhou	844.34	42894	122984
宿州市	Suzhou	856.22	44422	132052
蚌埠市	Bengbu	611.87	17697	279745
阜阳市	Fuyang	774.22	53451	110491
淮南市	Huainan	468.93	13892	201058
滁州市	Chuzhou	741.21	36384	362093
六安市	Luan	647.79	17267	153441
马鞍山市	Maanshan	162.39	4970	32708
芜湖市	Wuhu	234.40	6636	42592
宣城市	Xuancheng	256.03	4599	51997
铜陵市	Tongling	78.60	2150	9982
池州市	Chizhou	147.75	2015	24572
安庆市	Anqing	359.36	8841	86206
黄山市	Huangshan	87.06	230	12890

12—14　各市主要粮食作物播种面积（2022年）
Area Sown With Main Grain Crops in Each by Region (2022)

单位：公顷（hectare）

地　区	Region	粮食作物播种面积 Sown Area of Grain Crops	谷　物 Cereal	#稻　谷 Rice	小　麦 Wheat	玉　米 Corn	豆　类 Soybeans	薯　类 Potato
总　计	**Total**	**7314247**	**6595824**	**2496476**	**2849371**	**1228939**	**654174**	**64248**
合肥市	Hefei	525335	505334	355208	128887	19160	15452	4549
淮北市	Huaibei	276766	219200		135712	83488	57279	287
亳州市	Bozhou	875482	730683	4389	440543	279232	139361	5438
宿州市	Suzhou	939006	785835	1208	473424	308723	138600	14571
蚌埠市	Bengbu	518303	490422	104122	252390	126754	26551	1330
阜阳市	Fuyang	972939	830943	65069	502354	261886	134050	7947
淮南市	Huainan	531610	507572	280498	214688	12386	22650	1388
滁州市	Chuzhou	825142	781849	411337	329290	40532	38698	4595
六安市	Luan	611992	591932	406053	158934	26944	17526	2535
马鞍山市	Maanshan	176556	169015	116651	49542	2823	4521	3019
芜湖市	Wuhu	222679	212890	160436	42864	9591	7786	2003
宣城市	Xuancheng	219354	206701	154669	45243	6789	8675	3977
铜陵市	Tongling	101075	95536	78914	12890	3731	4762	777
池州市	Chizhou	120885	112677	89235	14665	8777	6637	1571
安庆市	Anqing	345835	313485	239741	47945	25319	25484	6866
黄山市	Huangshan	51288	41750	28945		12806	6141	3396

12—15 各市主要经济作物播种面积（2022年）
Area Sown to Main Cash Crops in Each by Region (2022)

单位：公顷 (hectare)

地 区	Region	经济作物 Cash Crop	油 料 Oil-bearing Crops	#花 生 Peanuts	油菜籽 Rapeseeds	芝 麻 Sesame	棉 花 Cotton	生 麻 Fiber Crops	糖 料 Sugar Crops
总 计	**Total**	**1619347**	**561900**	**146149**	**393159**	**13388**	**30291**	**2052**	**2315**
合肥市	Hefei	176658	61506	12600	47488	881	2709	36	166
淮北市	Huaibei	17198	2857	1171	1158	474	3		1
亳州市	Bozhou	166914	10167	7498	1670	935	688		24
宿州市	Suzhou	105821	29533	25228	4132	158	346		80
蚌埠市	Bengbu	122348	49517	46879	1927	651			42
阜阳市	Fuyang	177803	27497	7445	15533	4111	383	13	230
淮南市	Huainan	50390	12636	1683	10780	173	54		11
滁州市	Chuzhou	85945	39707	25351	13691	637	120		804
六安市	Luan	133860	54021	9150	43012	787	2189	1892	171
马鞍山市	Maanshan	58790	26497	740	25528	229	241	29	59
芜湖市	Wuhu	116869	35553	1375	33932	195	3247	80	179
宣城市	Xuancheng	68828	28712	1389	25786	129	85		70
铜陵市	Tongling	40137	23482	521	22819	142	1854		23
池州市	Chizhou	48495	33009	601	32063	346	971		36
安庆市	Anqing	204179	106728	4183	94517	3361	17327	2	61
黄山市	Huangshan	45111	20478	335	19127	179	73	0.2	359

12—15　续表　continued

单位：公顷（hectare）

地　区	Region	烟　叶 Tobacco	#烤　烟 Fluecured Tobacco	中草药材 Crude Drugs	蔬　菜 Vegeta-bles	瓜果类 Melon	#西　瓜 Water-melon	草　莓 Strawb-erry
总　计	**Total**	**9327**	**9254**	**112193**	**769223**	**98808**	**74043**	**14286**
合肥市	Hefei			1246	96615	10509	4357	5373
淮北市	Huaibei	0.3		565	10939	2833	2524	59
亳州市	Bozhou	41	41	60155	80034	13388	12224	252
宿州市	Suzhou			776	57253	16576	14926	1075
蚌埠市	Bengbu			1224	56762	9588	7496	700
阜阳市	Fuyang	39		9883	114309	21021	16225	1924
淮南市	Huainan	1		243	28200	7879	4611	2245
滁州市	Chuzhou			9500	31609	3196	2559	540
六安市	Luan			10223	62718	2230	1572	503
马鞍山市	Maanshan			75	29208	2366	1715	157
芜湖市	Wuhu	1912	1912	880	67107	3112	2066	425
宣城市	Xuancheng	6332	6300	4973	26245	1540	1033	233
铜陵市	Tongling			477	12761	849	550	224
池州市	Chizhou	590	590	2255	10622	916	538	48
安庆市	Anqing			4507	67701	1834	944	402
黄山市	Huangshan	411	411	5211	17139	970	703	127

12—16 各市主要农产品单位面积产量（2022年）
Yield of Major Farm Crops per Hectare by Region (2022)

单位：公斤/公顷（kg/hectare）

地区	Region	谷物 Cereals	棉花 Cotton	花生 Peanuts	油菜籽 Rapeseeds	芝麻 Sesame	烤烟 Fluecured Tobacco	蔬菜 Vegetables	瓜果类 Melon
总计	**Total**	**6034.09**	**844**	**4953**	**2452**	**1683**	**2326**	**32990**	**40695**
合肥市	Hefei	5752.77	707	3666	2698	1590		25943	26627
淮北市	Huaibei	6525.54	889	3815	2156	1132		39790	43939
亳州市	Bozhou	6787.48	814	6229	2599	1485	3629	40641	44312
宿州市	Suzhou	5501.73	741	5122	2220	1670		42576	48143
蚌埠市	Bengbu	5749.54		6710	1933	1265		48649	50007
阜阳市	Fuyang	6108.72	751	2790	2652	1810		41667	45981
淮南市	Huainan	6184.18	873	4909	2580	1578		32927	32776
滁州市	Chuzhou	5854.87	802	3598	2609	2259		34645	34154
六安市	Luan	5955.23	773	3723	2064	1128		21746	29918
马鞍山市	Maanshan	6223.81	823	2717	2735	1410		30600	30192
芜湖市	Wuhu	6465.72	914	3449	2785	2604	2868	26679	42969
宣城市	Xuancheng	6013.35	810	3425	2465	1805	2174	22632	27062
铜陵市	Tongling	5951.84	836	3534	2661	1915		26783	23470
池州市	Chizhou	5743.69	854	2784	2511	1778	2185	28698	18198
安庆市	Anqing	6014.57	869	2986	2350	1751		23639	22450
黄山市	Huangshan	6452.75	663	2488	1642	1366	2208	17964	21305

12—17　各市主要粮食作物产量（2022年）
Output of Major Food Crops in Each by Region (2022)

单位：吨（ton）

地区	Region	粮食 Grain	谷物 Cereal	#稻谷 Rice	小麦 Wheat	玉米 Corn	豆类 Beans	薯类（折粮） Potato (fold grain)
总　计	**Total**	41001255	39799803	15833990	17222740	6633874	999313	202139
合肥市	Hefei	2942285.1	2907071.6	2195120.6	600352.7	100140.5	21378.6	13834.9
淮北市	Huaibei	1513189.3	1430397.1		1021403.1	408994.0	81893.0	899.1
亳州市	Bozhou	5165899.1	4959494.9	20595.8	3226951.6	1678058.2	189934.1	16470.1
宿州市	Suzhou	4579504.8	4323453.7	7441.5	2785533.7	1520449.1	208762.9	47288.3
蚌埠市	Bengbu	2860206.2	2819705.0	612883.4	1537741.2	629178.6	36661.6	3839.7
阜阳市	Fuyang	5331323.9	5075999.5	336375.4	3298167.9	1433156.3	226872.1	28452.3
淮南市	Huainan	3176763.6	3138920.2	1869402.0	1202885.1	66633.1	33599.7	4243.7
滁州市	Chuzhou	4658667.4	4577622.8	2533222.6	1826768.2	214010.7	67258.5	13786.1
六安市	Luan	3560993.8	3525090.3	2640712.7	731523.7	152853.9	28113.7	7789.8
马鞍山市	Maanshan	1067966.0	1051919.1	784254.1	254518.4	13146.5	7215.6	8831.3
芜湖市	Wuhu	1396000.0	1376486.9	1106549.0	209776.0	60161.9	12821.4	6691.7
宣城市	Xuancheng	1267803.8	1242968.8	979457.1	222984.6	40527.1	12969.5	11865.4
铜陵市	Tongling	578346.8	568613.3	486231.4	56348.0	26033.9	7481.9	2251.6
池州市	Chizhou	665068.4	647180.3	545564.8	57168.2	44447.4	13175.5	4712.6
安庆市	Anqing	1945156.4	1885476.2	1522478.4	190617.1	170380.6	39212.9	20467.3
黄山市	Huangshan	292080.6	269403.7	193701.3		75702.4	11962.2	10714.7

12—18 各市主要经济作物产量（2022年）

Output of Main Cash Crops in Each by Region (2022)

单位：吨（ton）

地区	Region	油料 Oil-bearing Crops	#花生 Peanuts	油菜籽 Rapeseeds	芝麻 Sesame	棉花 Cotton	生麻 Fiber Crops	糖料 Sugar Crops
总计	**Total**	**1734163**	**723805**	**963969**	**22533**	**25579**	**9461**	**92562**
合肥市	Hefei	181932	46195	128114	1401	1914	34	6384
淮北市	Huaibei	7710	4469	2496	537	3		44
亳州市	Bozhou	52521	46708	4340	1388	560		669
宿州市	Suzhou	138692	129221	9175	264	257		2746
蚌埠市	Bengbu	319259	314549	3725	824			1460
阜阳市	Fuyang	70078	20770	41198	7441	288	80	13075
淮南市	Huainan	36341	8260	27808	273	47		312
滁州市	Chuzhou	128450	91224	35726	1439	97		29212
六安市	Luan	124445	34063	88766	888	1693	8933	4670
马鞍山市	Maanshan	72153	2010	69820	323	199	37	2277
芜湖市	Wuhu	99921	4742	94508	507	2966	362	6907
宣城市	Xuancheng	71286	4758	63565	232	69		1785
铜陵市	Tongling	62826	1843	60711	272	1550		745
池州市	Chizhou	82781	1672	80494	615	830		774
安庆市	Anqing	251862	12490	222124	5885	15059	16	1112
黄山市	Huangshan	33908	833	31401	245	49		20390

地区	Region	烟叶 Tobacco	#烤烟 Fluecured Tobacco	蔬菜 Vegetables	瓜果类 Melon	#西瓜 Watermelon	草莓 Strawberry
总计	**Total**	**21761**	**21527**	**25376958**	**4021000**	**3183420**	**389977**
合肥市	Hefei			2506502	279829	138787	122997
淮北市	Huaibei	1		435260	124465	115794	1493
亳州市	Bozhou	150	150	3252715	593251	555983	8301
宿州市	Suzhou			2437629	798007	746961	31166
蚌埠市	Bengbu			2761421	479455	379760	35605
阜阳市	Fuyang	132		4762960	966585	696919	73665
淮南市	Huainan	6		928522	258249	158802	64664
滁州市	Chuzhou			1095087	109152	95275	11252
六安市	Luan			1363851	66708	52317	10139
马鞍山市	Maanshan			893754	71442	57645	2326
芜湖市	Wuhu	5484	5484	1790378	133738	89488	8566
宣城市	Xuancheng	13792	13697	593973	41674	29570	5166
铜陵市	Tongling			341768	19929	13889	3918
池州市	Chizhou	1289	1289	304835	16674	14992	380
安庆市	Anqing			1600408	41181	21194	7846
黄山市	Huangshan	907	907	307895	20662	16046	2493

12—19 各市茶叶、水果生产情况（2022年）
Tea, Fruits Production by Region (2022)

单位：吨（ton）

地区 Region	茶叶 Tea	#绿茶 Green Tea	园林水果 Garden Fruits	#苹果 Apples	梨 Pears	葡萄 Grapes
总计 Total	**141632**	**123525**	**3962497**	**357441**	**1350112**	**572711**
合肥市 Hefei	2647	2623	242450	810	18293	83371
淮北市 Huaibei			160262	14324	8739	40059
亳州市 Bozhou			124026	1522	30006	21900
宿州市 Suzhou			2313019	331054	1124428	168478
蚌埠市 Bengbu			123944	1237	48884	28365
阜阳市 Fuyang			198008	7743	63525	48698
淮南市 Huainan			81959	43	17149	28690
滁州市 Chuzhou	548	548	164577	69	10313	46238
六安市 Luan	32330	27177	275538	209	8964	40745
马鞍山市 Maanshan	455	428	49325	277	5256	18546
芜湖市 Wuhu	2672	2246	67306	90	1704	24779
宣城市 Xuancheng	37541	34494	32602		5103	4604
铜陵市 Tongling	546	398	9353		872	2150
池州市 Chizhou	13957	9528	8564	10	420	1494
安庆市 Anqing	16055	15394	68399	53	4578	7663
黄山市 Huangshan	34881	30689	43166		1878	6930

12—20 各市牲畜饲养情况（2022年）
Number of Livestock by Region (2022)

单位：万头（万只）（10000 heads）

地区	Region	大牲畜年末头数 Large Animals (year-end)	牛 Cattle and Buffaloes	肉猪出栏头数 Slaughtered Fattened Hogs	猪年末头数 Hogs (year-end)	羊年末只数 Sheep and Goats (year-end)	活家禽只数 Poultry (year-end)
总　计	**Total**	**107.2**	**106.7**	**2920.9**	**1655.8**	**635.7**	**32284.2**
合肥市	Hefei	4.3	4.3	164.5	85.2	10.3	3770.3
淮北市	Huaibei	4.4	4.4	102.0	73.0	16.9	428.0
亳州市	Bozhou	9.5	9.4	359.0	193.8	100.8	1815.6
宿州市	Suzhou	14.3	14.2	430.5	275.1	194.2	3046.9
蚌埠市	Bengbu	14.6	14.6	191.7	108.4	55.5	2278.9
阜阳市	Fuyang	27.5	27.3	468.9	268.0	149.8	3010.6
淮南市	Huainan	5.2	5.2	123.1	66.5	19.6	1288.2
滁州市	Chuzhou	6.3	6.3	269.8	145.8	33.1	2890.1
六安市	Luan	5.4	5.4	253.5	141.6	22.8	2832.2
马鞍山市	Maanshan	1.1	1.1	44.0	22.2	6.9	763.5
芜湖市	Wuhu	1.1	1.1	60.6	38.2	3.6	2012.5
宣城市	Xuancheng	3.1	3.1	91.3	44.4	5.5	3180.3
铜陵市	Tongling	0.4	0.4	26.9	13.2	1.1	860.1
池州市	Chizhou	0.5	0.5	56.6	29.1	1.9	1065.7
安庆市	Anqing	7.7	7.7	203.4	109.2	11.1	2637.2
黄山市	Huangshan	1.8	1.7	75.2	42.2	2.5	404.0

12—21　各市畜产品产量（2022年）
Output of Livestock Products by Region (2022)

地　区	Region	主要肉类总产量（万吨）Output of Meat (10000 tons)	猪　肉 Pork	牛　肉 Beef	羊　肉 Mutton	禽　肉 Poultry
总　计	**Total**	**474.30**	**248.30**	**11.70**	**22.50**	**191.80**
合肥市	Hefei	35.52	13.70	0.37	0.30	21.15
淮北市	Huaibei	11.19	8.20	0.49	0.44	2.07
亳州市	Bozhou	42.47	29.73	1.17	3.00	8.56
宿州市	Suzhou	61.96	38.25	1.52	6.85	15.34
蚌埠市	Bengbu	43.23	16.24	2.04	2.81	22.14
阜阳市	Fuyang	67.33	41.54	2.81	5.46	17.52
淮南市	Huainan	19.82	11.30	0.62	0.89	7.02
滁州市	Chuzhou	40.84	22.06	0.75	1.02	17.02
六安市	Luan	37.31	20.98	0.44	0.91	14.98
马鞍山市	Maanshan	9.18	3.73	0.06	0.19	5.20
芜湖市	Wuhu	18.48	4.74	0.18	0.12	13.44
宣城市	Xuancheng	32.89	7.34	0.24	0.17	25.14
铜陵市	Tongling	4.56	2.49	0.03	0.03	2.01
池州市	Chizhou	9.10	5.01	0.07	0.04	3.98
安庆市	Anqing	32.99	16.63	0.78	0.24	15.34
黄山市	Huangshan	7.45	6.38	0.13	0.04	0.90

地　区	Region	生牛奶（万吨）Cow Milk (10000 tons)	禽　蛋（万吨）Poultry Eggs (10000 tons)	天然蜂蜜（吨）Honey (ton)	蚕　茧（吨）Silkworm Cocoons (ton)
总　计	**Total**	**50.70**	**186.66**	**18493.59**	**8453.71**
合肥市	Hefei	9.69	21.13	382.89	959.33
淮北市	Huaibei	2.01	4.43	57.66	
亳州市	Bozhou	1.21	8.86	237.25	6.40
宿州市	Suzhou	1.50	32.06	89.88	0.07
蚌埠市	Bengbu	24.25	9.71	14.68	
阜阳市	Fuyang	1.80	19.03	1022.52	1029.10
淮南市	Huainan	1.29	11.61	43.50	
滁州市	Chuzhou	0.85	13.65	135.10	
六安市	Luan	1.09	11.75	1006.99	1230.98
马鞍山市	Maanshan	5.76	3.54	2099.06	
芜湖市	Wuhu		9.00	698.30	
宣城市	Xuancheng		5.84	5429.52	1660.17
铜陵市	Tongling		3.35	23.53	
池州市	Chizhou	0.01	5.35	213.20	121.99
安庆市	Anqing		23.65	164.29	3086.27
黄山市	Huangshan	1.23	3.78	6875.22	359.40

12—22 各市水产品产量（2022年）
Output of Aquatic Products by Region (2022)

单位：吨（ton）

地 区	Region	水产品总产量 Total Aquatic Products	养殖产量 Cultured Products	捕捞产量 Fishing Products	鱼 类 Fish	虾蟹类 Crustacean	贝 类 Shell-fish	其它类 Others
总 计	**Total**	**2455031**	**2346395**	**108636**	**1558620**	**778215**	**54358**	**63838**
合肥市	Hefei	238621	232676	5945	107054	126488	1091	3988
淮北市	Huaibei	27256	26911	345	27151	93		12
亳州市	Bozhou	56485	52007	4478	49318	6726	389	52
宿州市	Suzhou	47976	45493	2483	41447	4463	95	1971
蚌埠市	Bengbu	132581	119616	12965	90984	24732	1777	15088
阜阳市	Fuyang	112495	102949	9546	74942	32676	1502	3375
淮南市	Huainan	186315	159336	26979	138552	40696	4224	2843
滁州市	Chuzhou	386939	374062	12877	224696	154847	5068	2328
六安市	Luan	247533	238120	9413	122047	118211	1757	5518
马鞍山市	Maanshan	123510	123434	76	58060	56191	8532	727
芜湖市	Wuhu	184113	179911	4202	120742	46364	3817	13190
宣城市	Xuancheng	117396	107039	10357	62505	48102	2933	3856
铜陵市	Tongling	110590	110580	10	79782	21442	7173	2193
池州市	Chizhou	147067	146361	706	115346	21333	7252	3136
安庆市	Anqing	322105	315382	6723	233025	75363	8507	5210
黄山市	Huangshan	14049	12518	1531	12969	488	241	351

12—23 国有农场基本情况
Basic Information on State Farms

指　　标		Item		2010	2015	2020	2021	2022
农场数	(个)	Number of Farms	(unit)	21	20	20	20	20
职工人数	(人)	Number of Staff and Workers	(person)	44759	38045	28835	15789	14410
耕地面积	(千公顷)	Cultivated Area	(1000 hectares)	34.75	29.56	29.21	30.08	32.93
农业机械总动力	(千瓦)	Total Power of Agricultural Machinery	(kW)	454679	454076	487978	483735	490352
农业机械拥有量	(台、辆)	Ownership of Agricultural Machinery	(unit)					
大中型农用拖拉机		Large and Medium Agricultural Tractors		2568	2886	2934	2716	2670
小型及手扶拖拉机		Mini and Walking Agricultural Tractors		6111	5244	4762	4732	4756
农用排灌动力机械		Machinery for Agricultural Drainage and Irrigation		5115	4173	6046	4999	4999
联合收获机		Combine Harvesters		1078	1372	1492	1422	1388
农用载重汽车		Trucks for Agricultural Use		181	175	829	186	53
农用化肥施用量	(吨)	Consumption of Chemical Fertilizers	(ton)	66814	70658	54787	54938	54157
农业总产值	(万元)	Gross Agricultural Output Value	(10000 yuan)	176197	204563	260937	255235	272963
农作物总播种面积	(千公顷)	Sown Area of Farm Crops	(1000 hectares)	68.53	59.31	50.17	49.98	50.93
粮食作物		Grain		61.04	55.13	47.32	46.96	47.49
棉　花		Cotton		3.77	0.32	0.04	0.03	0.03
油　料		Oil-bearing Crops		1.58	0.85	0.54	0.46	1.00
年末实有茶园面积		Area of Tea Plantations (year-end)		3.15	2.36	2.05	2.04	2.01
年末实有果园面积		Area of Orchards (year-end)		1.09	1.35	1.46	1.53	1.61
主要农产品产量		Yield of Major Farm Crops						
粮食作物	(吨)	Grain	(ton)	340720	341888	326282	343896	331387
棉　花	(吨)	Cotton	(ton)	5431	888	94	72	74
油　料	(吨)	Oil-bearing Crops	(ton)	3283	1977	1671	1238	2738
茶　叶	(吨)	Tea	(ton)	10894	12804	13789	14072	15432
水　果	(吨)	Fruits	(ton)	26589	13597	41555	43423	42626
畜牧业、渔业生产		Production of Animal Husbandry and Fishery						
大牲畜年末头数	(头)	Number of Large Animals (year-end)	(head)	7799	2462	2532	2312	1060
猪年末头数	(头)	Number of Hogs	(head)	38821	45099	27630	15158	26459
羊年末只数	(只)	Number of Sheep and Goats	(head)	5561	8692	9571	9676	4152
畜产品产量	(吨)	Output of Livestock Products	(ton)					
肉类总产量		Pork, Beef and Mutton		11037	15475	13833	12281	9281
#猪　肉		Pork		4553	6450	3757	5766	2581
生牛奶		Milk		19018	1510	1730	620	544
禽　蛋		Poultry Eggs		3346	1808	4365	4786	5001
水产品总产量	(吨)	Total Output of Aquatic Products	(ton)	4777	5741	14205	14267	13767

注：本表为农垦系统数据。
a) Data in this table cover those of the land reclamation department.

12—24 各县（市）乡（镇）、村数（2022年）
Number of Townships (towns) and Villages by County or City (2022)

县（市）	County (City)	乡镇数（个）Number of Township and Town Governments (unit)	#镇数 Town Governm-ents	村民委员会（个）Number of Villagers' Commit-tees (unit)
合肥市辖区	Hefei Region of City	8	7	98
巢湖市	Chaohu	12	12	125
长丰县	Changfeng	14	12	244
肥东县	Feidong	18	12	222
肥西县	Feixi	12	10	238
庐江县	Lujiang	17	17	210
淮北市辖区	Huaibei Region of City	7	7	64
濉溪县	Suixi	11	11	213
亳州市辖区	Bozhou Region of City	22	20	252
涡阳县	Guoyang	20	20	362
蒙城县	Mengcheng	14	12	268
利辛县	Lixin	23	20	345
宿州市辖区	Suzhou Region of City	24	24	310
砀山县	Dangshan	13	13	139
萧县	Xiaoxian	23	22	234
灵璧县	Lingbi	19	19	290
泗县	Sixian	15	15	167
蚌埠市辖区	Bengbu Region of City	12	8	175
怀远县	Huaiyuan	18	17	334
五河县	Wuhe	14	12	193
固镇县	Guzhen	11	10	176
阜阳市辖区	Fuyang Region of City	22	20	247
界首市	Jieshou	15	12	122
临泉县	Linquan	23	21	308
太和县	Taihe	31	30	282
阜南县	Funan	28	20	304
颍上县	Yingshang	30	22	224
淮南市辖区	Huainan Region of City	30	25	349
凤台县	Fengtai	16	12	213
寿县	Shouxian	25	22	263
滁州市辖区	Chuzhou Region of City	8	8	71
天长市	Tianchang	14	14	117
明光市	Mingguang	13	12	135
来安县	Laian	12	11	126
全椒县	Quanjiao	10	10	94
定远县	Dingyuan	22	16	196
凤阳县	Fengyang	15	14	211

12—24　续表　continued

县（市）	County (City)	乡镇数（个）Number of Township and Town Governments (unit)	#镇数 Town Governm-ents	村民委员会（个）Number of Villagers' Commit-tees (unit)
六安市辖区	Luan Region of City	40	29	606
霍邱县	Huoqiu	30	25	398
舒城县	Shucheng	21	15	394
金寨县	Jinzhai	23	13	213
霍山县	Huoshan	16	13	133
马鞍山市辖区	Maanshan Region of City	7	6	105
当涂县	Dangtu	11	10	115
含山县	Hanshan	8	8	94
和县	Hexian	9	9	68
芜湖市辖区	Wuhu Region of City	16	16	254
无为市	Wuwei	20	20	221
南陵县	Nanling	8	8	147
宣城市辖区	Xuancheng Region of City	15	12	159
宁国市	Ningguo	13	8	102
广德市	Guangde	9	6	103
郎溪县	Langxi	9	9	82
泾县	Jingxian	11	9	127
绩溪县	Jixi	11	8	75
旌德县	Jingde	10	10	61
铜陵市辖区	Tongling Region of City	15	12	173
枞阳县	Zongyang	16	15	190
池州市辖区	Chizhou Region of City	9	9	146
东至县	Dongzhi	15	12	234
石台县	Shitai	8	6	78
青阳县	Qingyang	13	10	116
安庆市辖区	Anqing Region of City	12	5	67
桐城市	Tongcheng	12	12	195
潜山市	Qianshan	16	11	164
怀宁县	Huaining	20	15	201
太湖县	Taihu	15	10	174
宿松县	Susong	21	9	185
望江县	Wangjiang	10	9	118
岳西县	Yuexi	24	14	182
黄山市辖区	Huangshan Region of City	26	18	168
歙县	Shexian	28	15	182
休宁县	Xiuning	21	11	153
黟县	Yixian	8	5	66
祁门县	Qimen	18	10	111

12—25 各县（市）农林牧渔业总产值（2022年）

Gross Output Value of Agriculture, Forestry, Animal Husbandry and Fishery by County or City （2022）

本表按当年价格计算　(Data in value terms in this table are calculated at current prices.)　　单位：万元（10000 yuan）

县（市）	County (City)	农林牧渔业总产值 Total of Farming, Forestry, Animal Husbandry and Fishery	农业 Farming	林业 Forestry	牧业 Animal Husbandry	渔业 Fishery	农林牧渔专业及辅助性活动 Professional and Auxiliary Activities
合肥市辖区	Hefei Region of City	164117	124752	30480	5366	561	2958
巢湖市	Chaohu	794024	432306	26547	153058	161887	20226
长丰县	Changfeng	1283409	688630	54446	295877	209358	35098
肥东县	Feidong	1328715	681067	62712	326731	224628	33577
肥西县	Feixi	1156514	517526	64460	389801	149708	35019
庐江县	Lujiang	1114099	621899	48440	132326	276219	35215
淮北市辖区	Huaibei Region of City	471730	236069	23320	170987	32483	8872
濉溪县	Suixi	1036409	541334	28135	405847	26576	34517
亳州市辖区	Bozhou Region of City	1596646	1142955	34884	350469	24550	43789
涡阳县	Guoyang	1261780	668639	27106	495570	23556	46909
蒙城县	Mengcheng	1315086	858427	58479	282071	47685	68424
利辛县	Lixin	1121367	646581	48636	349156	30246	46749
宿州市辖区	Suzhou Region of City	1568647	796238	37199	479918	31942	223350
砀山县	Dangshan	968315	498939	32968	194498	10200	231710
萧县	Xiaoxian	1507354	667340	76724	515912	20633	226745
灵璧县	Lingbi	1353913	613298	32877	456388	22902	228448
泗县	Sixian	1318076	587473	20395	462716	34566	212927
蚌埠市辖区	Bengbu Region of City	603233	367702	20520	138081	53302	23628
怀远县	Huaiyuan	1438926	750088	41907	416208	174142	56581
五河县	Wuhe	1266804	482981	38214	501802	198171	45636
固镇县	Guzhen	1505954	823002	35111	562738	38860	46243
阜阳市辖区	Fuyang Region of City	1786607	795023	218305	535733	37009	200537
界首市	Jieshou	697802	302484	59178	266824	9616	59700
临泉县	Linquan	2010866	906374	76765	789787	32116	205824
太和县	Taihe	1395180	503654	137859	526266	34507	192893
阜南县	Funan	1392049	728526	114032	354994	60200	134297
颍上县	Yingshang	1455228	605389	90589	509227	102657	147366
淮南市辖区	Huainan Region of City	886197	511986	19499	169590	160894	24228
凤台县	Fengtai	649591	353290	9955	191936	73414	20995
寿县	Shouxian	1207479	580780	41087	310510	253813	21290
滁州市辖区	Chuzhou Region of City	417932	190457	21087	130104	47537	28747
天长市	Tianchang	755146	348034	21089	130083	204082	51858
明光市	Mingguang	803122	311262	37597	162018	239040	53205
来安县	Laian	511790	234991	20226	160191	64528	31853
全椒县	Quanjiao	602936	225167	24351	160605	102762	90050
定远县	Dingyuan	1440148	773410	37498	393456	98048	137737
凤阳县	Fengyang	870916	408225	29061	259606	111085	62939

12—25 续表 continued

单位：万元（10000 yuan）

县（市）	County (City)	农林牧渔业总产值 Total of Farming, Forestry, Animal Husbandry and Fishery	农业 Farming	林业 Forestry	牧业 Animal Husbandry	渔业 Fishery	农林牧渔专业及辅助性活动 Professional and Auxiliary Activities
六安市辖区	Luan Region of City	1978813	985571	157868	654465	135474	45434
霍邱县	Huoqiu	1371785	517824	109507	505302	225162	13990
舒城县	Shucheng	758947	338533	76248	217145	94225	32796
金寨县	Jinzhai	557111	324939	79548	105196	23831	23597
霍山县	Huoshan	443710	239721	74150	71450	49824	8564
马鞍山市辖区	Maanshan Region of City	243707	84597	6120	48721	94322	9947
当涂县	Dangtu	613856	185100	6360	81427	311019	29950
含山县	Hanshan	486021	221067	13883	93597	79602	77873
和县	Hexian	569795	376683	7498	100095	60457	25062
芜湖市辖区	Wuhu Region of City	1394632	709159	87673	309521	250481	37798
无为市	Wuwei	1224531	512932	83446	284664	290258	53231
南陵县	Nanling	662330	228571	67055	181318	173005	12381
宣城市辖区	Xuancheng Region of City	955307	376207	46712	242828	242737	46823
宁国市	Ningguo	488204	228033	57429	167434	16647	18661
广德市	Guangde	525884	201362	100099	169440	29246	25737
郎溪县	Langxi	360440	150636	26836	80058	86812	16098
泾县	Jingxian	379199	144422	89699	120528	7592	16958
绩溪县	Jixi	304562	163495	17500	105008	5001	13558
旌德县	Jingde	163308	48005	54025	43558	10516	7204
铜陵市辖区	Tongling Region of City	454093	267719	33046	60968	70586	21775
枞阳县	Zongyang	542445	200719	51216	115493	160776	14241
池州市辖区	Chizhou Region of City	695164	266931	74297	175580	151423	26933
东至县	Dongzhi	676163	257639	86407	152449	118940	60728
石台县	Shitai	100779	53577	31488	13540	422	1753
青阳县	Qingyang	256857	77823	69401	63648	33395	12590
安庆市辖区	Anqing Region of City	366330	149981	21409	74378	111451	9112
桐城市	Tongcheng	699848	255373	68373	248673	118274	9154
潜山市	Qianshan	559031	269413	124085	143739	14147	7648
怀宁县	Huaining	492812	219760	29648	161442	63456	18506
太湖县	Taihu	611024	160011	78211	295616	70467	6720
宿松县	Susong	943320	354433	40174	236642	301245	10826
望江县	Wangjiang	668633	253092	18490	210854	159928	26270
岳西县	Yuexi	352243	196912	73864	71080	6579	3808
黄山市辖区	Huangshan Region of City	414371	184463	111699	91920	18108	8182
歙县	Shexian	352326	205243	39260	99186	3280	5357
休宁县	Xiuning	305543	138056	71111	78826	7120	10430
黟县	Yixian	90730	45174	23727	16625	1655	3549
祁门县	Qimen	136580	81916	34790	15662	987	3225

12—26 各县（市）主要粮食作物产量（2022年）

Area Sown With Main Grain Crops in Each by County or City (2022)

单位：吨 (ton)

县（市）	County (City)	粮食作物产量 Grain Crop Yield	谷物 Cereal	#稻谷 Rice	小麦 Wheat	玉米 Corn	豆类 Soybeans	薯类(折粮) Potato (fold grain)
巢湖市	Chaohu	396756.6	394424.2	285941.7	84478.7	24003.7	1356.3	976.1
长丰县	Changfeng	655463.7	645290.4	448140.3	168302.7	17689.7	5487.8	4685.5
肥东县	Feidong	637920.2	628024.4	492784.6	105900.6	29339.2	6656.0	3239.9
肥西县	Feixi	423242.1	418693.2	328923.1	86000.6	3469.5	3872.6	676.2
庐江县	Lujiang	758143.1	750264.8	587432.8	138886.5	23945.6	3649.4	4228.9
濉溪县	Suixi	1253259.8	1189229.1		849180.5	340048.7	63490.8	539.8
涡阳县	Guoyang	1288739.4	1184955.0		909884.0	270205.4	98002.4	5782.0
蒙城县	Mengcheng	1573821.4	1543965.5	14513.8	895208.4	610267.4	23586.1	6269.8
利辛县	Lixin	1388626.9	1358268.2	6082.0	812829.8	534332.9	27996.9	2361.8
砀山县	Dangshan	317326.7	306814.7		211197.9	95616.8	7709.7	2802.3
萧县	Xiaoxian	784938.8	765643.6		439831.0	322487.3	17060.4	2234.8
灵璧县	Lingbi	1098518.7	1052021.0		637819.0	411080.0	46002.4	495.3
泗县	Sixian	942664.7	832776.8	7441.5	574957.3	250273.7	68797.2	41090.7
怀远县	Huaiyuan	1260686.2	1252730.3	324583.0	690696.7	220734.0	7752.2	203.7
五河县	Wuhe	641863.9	625053.9	191694.8	330026.4	97554.2	15766.6	1043.5
固镇县	Guzhen	636763.5	631225.6	5648.7	358048.7	250721.5	3150.6	2387.4
界首市	Jieshou	400230.6	390698.8	1670.8	237417.1	151610.9	7262.3	2269.5
临泉县	Linquan	1064264.4	1045437.1		679298.5	364138.6	13190.9	5636.4
太和县	Taihe	1006882.1	895989.1		709324.1	186665.0	106033.4	4859.7
阜南县	Funan	892359.5	881114.8	134018.6	521630.4	222965.8	7271.1	3973.6
颍上县	Yingshang	1000811.2	958014.1	200685.9	587219.7	168508.5	34135.4	8661.7
凤台县	Fengtai	611682.1	604417.4	303420.8	288633.6	12362.9	6736.7	528.0
寿县	Shouxian	1769650.7	1750300.9	1111776.7	596256.4	42267.9	17131.1	2218.7
天长市	Tianchang	846112.9	845106.0	465666.3	369672.4	9767.3	738.0	268.9
明光市	Mingguang	673438.5	645057.7	269487.3	320578.6	54991.9	24717.7	3663.1
来安县	Laian	466231.9	461101.8	318767.2	130739.7	11594.9	1136.5	3993.5
全椒县	Quanjiao	423685.4	421494.7	292515.2	111603.9	17375.6	1530.3	660.4
定远县	Dingyuan	1169030.2	1150131.1	636494.8	451539.5	61200.1	16896.4	2002.8
凤阳县	Fengyang	833918.6	810777.5	392775.5	369509.1	45768.3	21778.6	1362.6

12—26 续表 continued

单位：吨（ton）

县（市）	County (City)	粮食作物产量 Grain Crop Yield	谷物 Cereal	#稻谷 Rice	小麦 Wheat	玉米 Corn	豆类 Soybeans	薯类(折粮) Potato (fold grain)
霍邱县	Huoqiu	1793998.6	1783427.3	1201988.5	542202.5	39236.4	8883.0	1688.3
舒城县	Shucheng	364930.8	360142.9	297067.2	34777.9	28297.8	3854.6	933.3
金寨县	Jinzhai	140835.7	137530.0	115833.4	11396.4	10300.2	2193.4	1112.3
霍山县	Huoshan	110811.4	108644.4	100723.9	111.3	7809.2	1389.6	777.4
当涂县	Dangtu	312358.5	306101.2	209917.6	87399.6	8784.1	3989.0	2268.2
含山县	Hanshan	258589.2	254123.9	204326.0	48412.6	1385.3	1416.4	3048.9
和县	Hexian	388651.2	384377.3	287998.0	93502.6	2876.6	864.2	3409.7
无为市	Wuwei	550376.4	543331.6	432458.8	82403.4	28469.5	3383.2	3661.6
南陵县	Nanling	358956.1	355962.1	325791.4	15657.6	14513.1	2014.2	979.8
宁国市	Ningguo	66341.0	65682.8	50158.1	5206.6	10318.1	504.0	154.2
广德市	Guangde	229931.1	225233.7	187650.2	33873.2	3710.4	3004.6	1692.8
郎溪县	Langxi	274485.5	267686.6	185493.2	79004.8	3188.6	3064.7	3734.2
泾县	Jingxian	115870.8	114029.9	105584.9	5334.1	3110.9	1031.7	809.3
绩溪县	Jixi	36859.8	32444.6	25328.4	738.4	6377.7	2570.5	1844.7
旌德县	Jingde	52056.4	51375.4	50102.6	46.7	1226.0	198.0	483.1
枞阳县	Zongyang	433582.9	427357.0	370123.9	43827.1	13406.0	4297.8	1928.1
东至县	Dongzhi	285475.4	277112.0	227516.5	29797.9	19797.6	5633.4	2730.0
石台县	Shitai	15323.8	13658.2	9347.3	417.6	3893.3	1352.0	313.7
青阳县	Qingyang	108868.2	104245.4	100597.5	2073.4	1574.4	3349.8	1273.0
桐城市	Tongcheng	317367.0	314837.4	259933.7	31822.0	23081.7	1574.0	955.6
潜山市	Qianshan	215320.7	213052.6	199771.3	8404.3	4876.9	1213.1	1054.9
怀宁县	Huaining	328312.3	322590.9	269524.7	10256.3	42809.9	3155.8	2565.6
太湖县	Taihu	216481.0	208669.6	157581.1	32392.8	18695.7	3245.7	4565.7
宿松县	Susong	406914.2	382223.7	301503.4	51114.1	27606.2	18210.9	6479.6
望江县	Wangjiang	303882.3	290299.3	213379.0	41596.9	35323.4	9675.6	3907.5
岳西县	Yuexi	82721.7	80699.7	63725.2	2702.8	14271.7	1497.1	525.0
歙县	Shexian	74000.3	66454.8	32207.8		34247.1	3668.3	3877.1
休宁县	Xiuning	74496.0	69699.4	53274.8		16424.6	3254.2	1542.4
黟县	Yixian	29619.1	28918.8	26688.1		2230.6	411.2	289.1
祁门县	Qimen	32135.7	29615.2	26635.2		2980.0	1262.2	1258.3

12—27 各县（市）主要经济作物产量（2022年）
Yield of Farm Crops and Area of Cultivated Land by County or City (2022)

单位：吨（ton）

县（市）	County (City)	油料 Oil-bearing Crops	油菜籽 Rapeseeds	棉花 Cotton	生麻 Raw Hemp	糖料 Sugar Crops
合肥市辖区	Hefei Region of City	1450	1299			
巢湖市	Chaohu	32361	24791	232	34	747
长丰县	Changfeng	24071	18330	75		366
肥东县	Feidong	74382	51552	663		1548
肥西县	Feixi	21302	13196	465		1059
庐江县	Lujiang	28366	18946	479		2664
淮北市辖区	Huaibei Region of City	2794	1590	1		44
濉溪县	Suixi	4916	907	2		
亳州市辖区	Bozhou Region of City	3842	595	437		
涡阳县	Guoyang	2704	322	12		632
蒙城县	Mengcheng	38865	1500	83		20
利辛县	Lixin	7110	1923	29		17
宿州市辖区	Suzhou Region of City	19975	657	68		2306
砀山县	Dangshan	9098	793	46		
萧县	Xiaoxian	10928	3316	31		415
灵璧县	Lingbi	14002	546	81		25
泗县	Sixian	84689	3863	31		
蚌埠市辖区	Bengbu Region of City	5286	1518			29
怀远县	Huaiyuan	30872	959			1316
五河县	Wuhe	40893	975			70
固镇县	Guzhen	242207	273			45
阜阳市辖区	Fuyang Region of City	15853	8259	85		3520
界首市	Jieshou	2770	1153	6	9	261
临泉县	Linquan	13460	6079	74	6	1995
太和县	Taihe	8173	4860	11	65	6160
阜南县	Funan	22130	15100	11		356
颍上县	Yingshang	7692	5747	102		783
淮南市辖区	Huainan Region of City	16205	13538	36		90
凤台县	Fengtai	5804	2952	4		222
寿县	Shouxian	14332	11318	7		
滁州市辖区	Chuzhou Region of City	3228	1994	15		
天长市	Tianchang	2323	1851			
明光市	Mingguang	44901	3192	8		25991
来安县	Laian	11588	5919	11		385
全椒县	Quanjiao	9591	7335	6		
定远县	Dingyuan	23903	5005	57		1547
凤阳县	Fengyang	32916	10430			1289

12—27 续表 continued

单位：吨（ton）

县（市）	County (City)	油料 Oil-bearing Crops	油菜籽 Rapeseeds	棉花 Cotton	生麻 Raw Hemp	糖料 Sugar Crops
六安市辖区	Luan Region of City	65736	44499	1012	8850	459
霍邱县	Huoqiu	20730	13210	1	71	3918
舒城县	Shucheng	24941	23785	669	12	293
金寨县	Jinzhai	8237	3051			
霍山县	Huoshan	4801	4221	10		
马鞍山市辖区	Maanshan Region of City	7397	7287			156
当涂县	Dangtu	23881	23837			8
含山县	Hanshan	21387	19953	134	37	1837
和县	Hexian	19488	18743	65		276
芜湖市辖区	Wuhu Region of City	52809	50305	1103		1654
无为市	Wuwei	35200	32843	1851	362	2208
南陵县	Nanling	11912	11360	12		3045
宣城市辖区	Xuancheng Region of City	14341	12954	25		667
宁国市	Ningguo	11256	10821	4		
广德市	Guangde	14321	13769	2		350
郎溪县	Langxi	8656	8298	36		78
泾县	Jingxian	8240	7652	3		271
绩溪县	Jixi	11844	8060			63
旌德县	Jingde	2627	2011			355
铜陵市辖区	Tongling Region of City	34300	33165	267		700
枞阳县	Zongyang	28526	27545	1283		45
池州市辖区	Chizhou Region of City	33018	32372	376		140
东至县	Dongzhi	35024	33632	429		587
石台县	Shitai	6423	6338	12		
青阳县	Qingyang	8316	8152	13		47
安庆市辖区	Anqing Region of City	13133	12085	1122		
桐城市	Tongcheng	25524	23671	532		
潜山市	Qianshan	17535	13583	917	16	12
怀宁县	Huaining	34556	32798	1811		475
太湖县	Taihu	20827	19857	1672		107
宿松县	Susong	52757	36835	3764		127
望江县	Wangjiang	83878	80015	5242		
岳西县	Yuexi	3651	3279			392
黄山市辖区	Huangshan Region of City	6212	5206			2552
歙县	Shexian	13782	13189	2		16523
休宁县	Xiuning	8033	7920	4		1089
黟县	Yixian	3681	3580	2		171
祁门县	Qimen	2200	1506	40		55

12—28 各县（市）茶叶、水果生产情况（2022年）

Tea, Fruits Production by County or City (2022)

单位：吨（ton）

县（市）	County (City)	茶叶 Tea	#绿茶 Green Tea	园林水果 Garden Fruits	#葡萄 Grapes
合肥市辖区	Hefei Region of City			33756	20507
巢湖市	Chaohu	676	652	12622	3617
长丰县	Changfeng			49978	6228
肥东县	Feidong	9	9	66168	3446
肥西县	Feixi	11	11	36957	13031
庐江县	Lujiang	1951	1951	42969	36542
淮北市辖区	Huaibei Region of City			139347	36016
濉溪县	Suixi			20915	4043
亳州市辖区	Bozhou Region of City			40070	5423
涡阳县	Guoyang			21986	3548
蒙城县	Mengcheng			27340	7334
利辛县	Lixin			34630	5595
宿州市辖区	Suzhou Region of City			114146	24382
砀山县	Dangshan			1707078	39091
萧县	Xiaoxian			402723	88963
灵璧县	Lingbi			65710	9092
泗县	Sixian			23362	6950
蚌埠市辖区	Bengbu Region of City			39554	8448
怀远县	Huaiyuan			32979	6931
五河县	Wuhe			26311	5685
固镇县	Guzhen			25100	7300
阜阳市辖区	Fuyang Region of City			48144	10662
界首市	Jieshou			16160	2830
临泉县	Linquan			67925	27669
太和县	Taihe			7546	1517
阜南县	Funan			45185	1545
颍上县	Yingshang			13048	4475
淮南市辖区	Huainan Region of City			38750	18315
凤台县	Fengtai			13689	2317
寿县	Shouxian			29520	8058
滁州市辖区	Chuzhou Region of City	441	441	13009	1882
天长市	Tianchang	15	15	6088	3546
明光市	Mingguang	27	27	24447	1718
来安县	Laian	10	10	22854	12669
全椒县	Quanjiao	52	52	27405	6107
定远县	Dingyuan	2	2	35980	10720
凤阳县	Fengyang	1	1	34794	9596

12—28 续表 continued

单位：吨（ton）

县（市）	County (City)	茶叶 Tea	#绿茶 Green Tea	园林水果 Garden Fruits	#葡萄 Grapes
六安市辖区	Luan Region of City	8476	8476	191796	8483
霍邱县	Huoqiu			65404	29388
舒城县	Shucheng	3464	3372	11847	1374
金寨县	Jinzhai	10805	10481	4350	1338
霍山县	Huoshan	9585	4848	2141	162
马鞍山市辖区	Maanshan Region of City	143	143	7328	4939
当涂县	Dangtu	2	2	20206	9160
含山县	Hanshan	258	230	16912	3291
和县	Hexian	52	52	4879	1156
芜湖市辖区	Wuhu Region of City	1906	1883	35826	15124
无为市	Wuwei	306	288	29450	9530
南陵县	Nanling	460	75	2030	125
宣城市辖区	Xuancheng Region of City	14103	12419	12483	2557
宁国市	Ningguo	3309	3309	5260	600
广德市	Guangde	7050	5749	3930	852
郎溪县	Langxi	7800	7800	4685	102
泾县	Jingxian	2904	2842	3041	200
绩溪县	Jixi	1680	1680	2246	94
旌德县	Jingde	695	695	957	200
铜陵市辖区	Tongling Region of City	288	264	7217	1345
枞阳县	Zongyang	258	134	2136	805
池州市辖区	Chizhou Region of City	2630	2059	3518	910
东至县	Dongzhi	4250	2660	1780	290
石台县	Shitai	6682	4435	1885	6
青阳县	Qingyang	395	374	1381	288
安庆市辖区	Anqing Region of City	31	31	10002	1190
桐城市	Tongcheng	554	554	1451	398
潜山市	Qianshan	3452	3398	3450	791
怀宁县	Huaining	98	98	9040	44
太湖县	Taihu	4407	3996	27600	1280
宿松县	Susong	520	402	8157	3262
望江县	Wangjiang	104	104	5139	485
岳西县	Yuexi	6890	6812	3559	213
黄山市辖区	Huangshan Region of City	3998	3924	4898	513
歙县	Shexian	10617	10617	33906	6208
休宁县	Xiuning	10306	9461	1315	60
黟县	Yixian	3045	2664	1737	87
祁门县	Qimen	6915	4024	1311	62

12—29 各县（市）畜牧业、渔业生产情况（2022年）
Production of Animal Husbandry, Fishery by County or City (2022)

县（市）	County (City)	出栏猪（万头）Slaughtered Fattened Hogs (10000 heads)	猪肉产量（万吨）Pork Production (10000 tons)	牛肉产量（万吨）Beef Production (10000 tons)	羊肉产量（万吨）Mutton Production (10000 tons)	禽肉产量（万吨）Poultry Production (10000 tons)	禽蛋产量（万吨）Egg Production (10000 tons)	水产品产量（吨）Aquatic Product Output (ton)
合肥市辖区	Hefei Region of City	0.47	0.04	0.03	0.003	0.27	0.19	576
巢湖市	Chaohu	13.10	0.95	0.02	0.08	1.92	2.32	44129
长丰县	Changfeng	50.33	4.38	0.08	0.11	4.93	4.90	46216
肥东县	Feidong	48.76	4.25	0.13	0.03	4.34	5.13	51213
肥西县	Feixi	37.31	3.05	0.05	0.03	7.36	6.07	42002
庐江县	Lujiang	14.54	1.04	0.05	0.05	2.33	2.52	54485
淮北市辖区	Huaibei Region of City	16.76	1.35	0.29	0.12	0.46	0.91	14304
濉溪县	Suixi	85.22	6.84	0.20	0.32	1.61	3.53	12952
亳州市辖区	Bozhou Region of City	93.19	7.35	0.35	0.61	1.14	3.16	13310
涡阳县	Guoyang	85.69	6.76	0.09	0.72	2.61	1.74	14832
蒙城县	Mengcheng	96.47	8.40	0.35	0.58	2.67	1.69	15210
利辛县	Lixin	83.63	7.22	0.39	1.09	2.14	2.28	13133
宿州市辖区	Suzhou Region of City	124.20	11.10	0.30	1.22	4.54	9.10	15007
砀山县	Dangshan	33.33	3.73	0.06	1.66	1.59	3.39	4898
萧县	Xiaoxian	72.98	6.24	0.29	1.97	2.72	8.76	8640
灵璧县	Lingbi	84.69	7.35	0.43	0.93	2.08	4.73	8110
泗县	Sixian	115.27	9.82	0.44	1.07	4.41	6.09	11321
蚌埠市辖区	Bengbu Region of City	18.79	1.50	0.14	0.08	2.68	1.15	17344
怀远县	Huaiyuan	57.87	5.05	0.50	1.25	4.00	1.99	49515
五河县	Wuhe	53.33	4.42	0.95	0.53	2.20	1.96	54192
固镇县	Guzhen	61.75	5.28	0.45	0.94	13.26	4.61	11530
阜阳市辖区	Fuyang Region of City	81.29	7.66	0.40	1.21	6.62	4.92	18293
界首市	Jieshou	31.28	2.94	0.16	0.63	1.13	1.75	6050
临泉县	Linquan	93.96	8.17	0.80	1.32	3.10	3.30	9600
太和县	Taihe	94.02	8.17	0.31	0.92	2.23	2.77	12262
阜南县	Funan	75.90	6.64	0.52	0.75	2.15	2.91	14457
颍上县	Yingshang	92.44	7.96	0.61	0.63	2.29	3.38	51833
淮南市辖区	Huainan Region of City	14.43	1.55	0.18	0.23	2.07	3.55	51738
凤台县	Fengtai	28.61	2.80	0.17	0.14	0.74	3.67	30317
寿县	Shouxian	80.06	6.95	0.27	0.53	4.22	4.38	104260
滁州市辖区	Chuzhou Region of City	15.60	1.19	0.02	0.15	1.08	0.53	25773
天长市	Tianchang	10.12	0.81	0.03	0.24	0.97	3.38	79350
明光市	Mingguang	34.50	2.65	0.18	0.11	2.60	2.43	78940
来安县	Laian	15.02	1.19	0.04	0.07	5.36	1.13	31006
全椒县	Quanjiao	33.32	2.38	0.06	0.10	3.03	1.10	71055
定远县	Dingyuan	126.62	11.00	0.15	0.17	2.02	2.36	42848
凤阳县	Fengyang	34.65	2.84	0.28	0.17	1.96	2.73	57967

12—29 续表 continued

县（市）	County (City)	出栏猪（万头）Slaughtered Fattened Hogs (10000 heads)	猪肉产量（万吨）Pork Production (10000 tons)	牛肉产量（万吨）Beef Production (10000 tons)	羊肉产量（万吨）Mutton Production (10000 tons)	禽肉产量（万吨）Poultry Production (10000 tons)	禽蛋产量（万吨）Egg Production (10000 tons)	水产品产量（吨）Aquatic Product Output (ton)
六安市辖区	Luan Region of City	91.40	7.37	0.09	0.29	6.74	2.08	62543
霍 邱 县	Huoqiu	116.02	9.95	0.11	0.44	3.28	6.22	118617
舒 城 县	Shucheng	19.56	1.47	0.05	0.02	3.70	2.76	39357
金 寨 县	Jinzhai	17.62	1.39	0.18	0.14	0.59	0.50	14062
霍 山 县	Huoshan	8.91	0.80	0.02	0.03	0.67	0.19	12954
马鞍山市辖区	Maanshan Region of City	2.50	0.20	0.03	0.04	0.78	0.36	14604
当 涂 县	Dangtu	9.47	0.81	0.004	0.07	1.14	1.34	64535
含 山 县	Hanshan	14.87	1.24	0.01	0.06	0.83	1.13	21053
和　县	Hexian	17.12	1.49	0.01	0.03	2.45	0.71	23318
芜湖市辖区	Wuhu Region of City	20.95	1.60	0.05	0.05	5.18	3.73	74936
无 为 市	Wuwei	18.59	1.49	0.10	0.05	2.24	1.95	71246
南 陵 县	Nanling	21.07	1.66	0.03	0.02	6.02	3.32	37931
宣城市辖区	Xuancheng Region of City	11.41	0.89	0.01	0.03	9.28	1.11	69031
宁 国 市	Ningguo	19.85	1.60	0.002	0.05	6.04	0.35	6429
广 德 市	Guangde	28.78	2.30	0.003	0.04	6.00	2.30	8120
郎 溪 县	Langxi	7.44	0.63	0.01	0.03	1.33	1.30	26850
泾　县	Jingxian	10.35	0.83	0.04	0.01	2.29	0.47	3180
绩 溪 县	Jixi	7.48	0.62	0.11	0.01	0.03	0.09	1795
旌 德 县	Jingde	5.98	0.47	0.07	0.01	0.17	0.21	1991
铜陵市辖区	Tongling Region of City	8.26	0.84	0.01	0.01	1.32	1.66	42920
枞 阳 县	Zongyang	18.64	1.65	0.02	0.02	0.69	1.68	67670
池州市辖区	Chizhou Region of City	27.26	2.39	0.04	0.02	1.41	1.73	67334
东 至 县	Dongzhi	18.94	1.70	0.01	0.02	1.23	1.48	58922
石 台 县	Shitai	1.60	0.14	0.003	0.002	0.06	0.14	270
青 阳 县	Qingyang	8.77	0.77	0.02	0.002	1.28	2.00	20541
安庆市辖区	Anqing Region of City	4.02	0.33	0.02	0.004	0.48	0.83	48028
桐 城 市	Tongcheng	26.70	2.23	0.05	0.02	0.75	7.80	40005
潜 山 市	Qianshan	24.15	1.95	0.03	0.04	1.04	1.76	5750
怀 宁 县	Huaining	28.62	2.33	0.01	0.02	2.21	3.75	29300
太 湖 县	Taihu	42.44	3.65	0.39	0.07	4.59	1.23	34432
宿 松 县	Susong	36.89	3.03	0.21	0.03	2.56	2.43	90426
望 江 县	Wangjiang	30.85	2.33	0.03	0.04	3.48	4.21	72793
岳 西 县	Yuexi	9.77	0.77	0.04	0.02	0.24	1.64	1371
黄山市辖区	Huangshan Region of City	13.29	1.12	0.06	0.01	0.33	0.58	7823
歙　县	Shexian	28.87	2.46	0.03	0.02	0.22	2.02	1424
休 宁 县	Xiuning	24.68	2.09	0.03	0.004	0.22	0.83	3302
黟　县	Yixian	4.63	0.40	0.01	0.001	0.07	0.13	789
祁 门 县	Qimen	3.68	0.31	0.001	0.003	0.06	0.22	711

主要统计指标解释

农林牧渔业总产值

农林牧渔业总产值是以货币表现的农林牧渔业全部产品总量和对农林牧渔业生产活动进行的各种支持性服务活动的价值。它反映一定时期内农林牧渔业生产总规模和总成果，是观察农林牧渔业生产水平和发展速度，研究农林牧渔业内部比例关系、农林牧渔业与工业、农林牧渔业与国家建设、人民生活比例关系的重要指标，同时也是计算农林牧渔业劳动生产率和农林牧渔业增加值的基础资料。1957 年以前的农业总产值中包括了厩肥和农民自给性手工业（如农民自制衣服、鞋、袜，自己从事粮食初步加工等）。1958 年及以后的农业总产值，林业中增加了村及村以下竹木采伐产值；牧业中取消了厩肥产值；副业中取消了农民自给性手工业产值，增加了村及村以下办的工业产值；渔业中增加了海洋捕捞水产品产值。1980 年及以后的农业总产值，在副业中增加了农民家庭兼营工业商品部分的产值。从 1984 年起村及村以下工业产值划归工业。从 1993 年起取消副业，将野生动物的捕猎划入牧业，野生植物采集和农民家庭兼营商品性工业划归农业。2003 年起，取消农业中的农民家庭兼营商品性工业，增加了农林牧渔服务业。

粮食产量

指全社会的产量。包括国有经济经营的、集体统一经营的和农民家庭经营的粮食产量，还包括工矿企业办的农场和其他生产单位的产量。粮食除包括稻谷、小麦、玉米、高粱、谷子及其他杂粮外，还包括薯类和豆类。其产量计算方法，豆类按去豆荚后的干豆计算；薯类（包括甘薯和马铃薯，不包括芋头和木薯）1963 年以前按每 4 公斤鲜薯折 1 公斤粮食计算，从 1964 年开始改为按 5 公斤鲜薯折 1 公斤粮食计算。城市郊区作为蔬菜的薯类（如马铃薯等）按鲜品计算，并且不作粮食统计。其他粮食一律按脱粒后的原粮计算。

油料产量

指全部油料作物的生产量。包括花生、油菜籽、芝麻、葵花籽、胡麻籽（亚麻籽）和其他油料。不包括大豆、木本油料和野生油料。花生以带壳干花生计算。

水产品产量

指人工养殖的水产品和天然生长的水产品的捕捞量。包括海水的鱼类、虾蟹类、贝类和藻类以及内陆水域的鱼类、虾蟹类和贝类，不包括淡水生植物。

猪、牛、羊肉产量

指当年出栏并已屠宰、除去头蹄下水后带骨肉（即胴体重）的重量。

期初（末）畜禽存栏头（只）数

指报告期初（末）养殖户（单位）饲养的大牲畜、猪、羊、家禽等畜禽的存栏数。

当年出栏头（只）数

指养殖户（单位）饲养的，供屠宰并已出栏的全部牲畜头（只）数。

农作物播种面积

指实际播种或移植有农作物的面积。凡是实际种植有农作物的面积，不论种植在耕地上还是种植在非耕地上，均包括在农作物播种面积中。在播种季节基本结束后，因遭灾而重新改种和补种的农作物面积，也包括在内。

农用化肥施用量

指本年内实际用于农业生产的化肥数量，包括氮肥、磷肥、钾肥和复合肥。化肥施用量要求按折纯量计算数量。折纯量是指把氮肥、磷肥、钾肥分别按含氮、含五氧化二磷、含氧化钾的百分之一百成份进行折算后的数量。复合肥按其所含主要成分折算。

农业机械总动力

指主要用于农、林、牧、渔业的各种动力机械的动力总和。包括耕作机械、排灌机械、收获机械、农用运输机械、植物保护机械、牧业机械、林业机械、渔业机械和其他农业机械（内燃机按引擎马力折成瓦（特）计算、电动机按功率折成瓦（特）计算）。不包括专门用于乡、镇、村、组办工业、基本建设、非农业运输、科学试验和教学等非农业生产方面用的动力机械与作业机械。

Explanatory Notes for Major Statistical Indicators

Gross Output Value of Farming, Forestry, Animal Husbandry and Fishery

gross output value of farming, forestry, animal husbandry and fishery is the total amount of all products of farming, forestry, animal husbandry and fishery and the value of various supporting services for farming, forestry, animal husbandry and fishery production. It reflects a certain period ecological-economic to produce total dimensions and total achievement, is to observe animal husbandry fishery production level and development speed, the ecological-economic internal proportion relations, animal husbandry, fisheries, animal husbandry, fishery and industry and national construction, an important index of proportional relationship between the people's life, but also calculate the ecological-economic labor productivity and the basis of the added value of ecological-economic data. Before 1957, the gross agricultural output value included barnyard manure and farmers' self-sustaining handicraft industries (such as self-made clothes, shoes and socks, and primary grain processing by themselves). The total output value of agriculture in 1958 and later, the output value of bamboo logging at and below the village level was added to forestry; The value of barnyard manure was abolished in animal husbandry; In the sideline, the output value of farmers' self-supporting handicraft industry was cancelled, and the output value of village and sub-village offices was increased. The output value of Marine fishery products increased in fishery. In 1980 and after the total agricultural output value, the sideline increased the output value of the part of industrial commodities that farmers' households concurrently owned. Since 1984, the industrial output value at and below the village level has been classified as industry. Since 1993, the sideline business has been abolished, and the hunting of wild animals has been classified into animal husbandry, while the gathering of wild plants and commercial industries run by farmers' families have been classified into agriculture. In 2003, farmers' households were not allowed to run commercial industries in agriculture, and services for agriculture, forestry, animal husbandry and fishery were increased.

Grain Yield

refers to the output of the whole society. It includes the grain output of state-owned enterprises, collectives and farmers' families, as well as the output of farms and other production units run by industrial and mining enterprises. Grain in addition to including rice, wheat, corn, sorghum, millet and other miscellaneous grains, also includes potatoes and beans. Its yield calculation method, beans according to the dry beans after pod calculation; Tubers (including sweet potatoes and potatoes, but not taro and cassava) were converted to 1 kilogram of grain per 4 kilograms of fresh potatoes before 1963, and changed to 1 kilogram of grain per 5 kilograms of fresh potatoes since 1964. Tubers as vegetables (such as potatoes, etc.) in the suburbs of the city are counted as fresh products and not counted as grain. Other grain shall be calculated according to the raw grain after threshing.

Yield of Oil-bearing Crops

refers to the total yield of oil bearing crops of various kinds, including peanuts, (dry, in shell) rapeseeds, sesame, sunflower seeds, flax seeds, and other oil bearing crops. Soybeans, oil-bearing woody plants, and wild oil-bearing crops are not included.

Output of Aquatic Products

refers to catches of both artificially cultured and naturally grown aquatic products, including fish, shrimps, crabs and shellfish in sea and inland water as well as seaweed. Freshwater plants are not included.

Output of Pork, Beef, and Mutton

refers to the meat of slaughtered hogs, cattle, sheep and goats with head, feet, and offal taken away.

Number of Livestock or Poultry in Stock at Beginning (or End)

refers to the number of large livestock, pigs, sheep, poultry and other livestock and poultry raised by farmers (units) at the beginning (end) of the report period.

Number of heads sold in the year

refers to the total number of animals raised by farmers (units) for slaughter and ready for sale.

Sown Area of Crops

refers to area of land sown or transplanted with crops regardless of being in cultivated area or non cultivated area. Area of land re-sown due to natural disasters is also included.

Consumption of Chemical Fertilizers in Agriculture

refers to the quantity of chemical fertilizers applied in agriculture in the year, including nitrogenous fertilizer, phosphate fertilizer, potash fertilizer, and compound fertilizer. The consumption of chemical fertilizers is required in calculation to convert the gross weight into weight containing 100% effective component (e.g. 100% nitrogen content in nitrogenous fertilizer, 100% phosphorous pent oxide contents in phosphate fertilizer, 100% potassium oxide contents in potash fertilizer). Compound fertilizer is converted with its major component.

Total Power of Farm Machinery

refers to total mechanical power of machinery used in farming, forestry, animal husbandry, and fishery, including plough , irrigation and drainage, harvesting, transport, plant protection, stock breeding, forestry and fishery. The power of internal combustion engines is required to convert horsepower into watts and the power of electric motors is required to be converted into watts. Machinery employed for non agricultural purposes, such as the machines used in township run and village-run industry, construction, non agricultural transport, scientific experiments and teaching, is excluded.

第十三篇

Chapter 13

工业

INDUSTRY

简要说明

一、本篇主要包括以下几部分汇总资料：

1. 全部工业企业按登记注册类型、行业分组的企业单位数和工业总产值(其中1995年后工业总产值均按新规定计算)。

2. 全部年主营业务收入在2000万元及以上的工业企业按地区和行业分组的主要经济指标和经济效益指标，主要包括工业总产值、工业增加值、资产、流动资产、固定资产、流动负债、所有者权益、营业收入、税金及附加、利润总额、应交增值税、总资产贡献率、资产负债率、成本费用利润率、流动资产周转次数等指标。

3. 大中型工业企业的主要经济指标和经济效益指标。

4. 主要工业产品产量和生产能力等。

二、1998年开始工业统计范围为全部国有企业及年主营业务收入在500万元及以上的非国有工业法人单位，2011年开始工业统计范围为年主营业务收入在2000万元及以上的工业法人单位。与历史年份不具可比性。

三、行业分类按《国民经济行业分类》(GB/T 4754-2017)标准划分。

四、资料来源：由省统计局工业处根据国家统计局工业统计报表制度收集、汇总、整理提供。

Brief Introduction

I. Data in this chapter cover the following parts:

1. The number of industrial enterprises, the gross industrial output value of all industrial enterprises classified by registration status and industrial division. (The gross industrial output value is calculated according to the new stipulation after 1995.)

2. Main economic indicators and efficiency indicators of all state-owned industrial enterprises, and of non-state enterprises each with an main business revenue of over five million yuan, classified by region and by industrial division, including gross industrial output value, industrial value-added, capital, circulating assets, fixed assets, liquid liabilities, owners' equity, Taxes and surcharges, sales profit, total profits, ratio of value-added to gross industrial output value, ratio of profits and taxes to funds and output value, turnover of working capital.

3. Main economic indicators and efficiency indicators of large and medium size industrial enterprises.

4. Output and production capacity of key industrial products.

II. Since 1998, the coverage of industrial statistics is all state-owned industrial enterprises and non-state enterprises each with main business revenue over five million yuan.

Data on gross industrial output value have been adjusted since 1995.

III. Data by branch of industry are based on <National Industrial Classification of all Economic Activities>((GB/T 4754-2017).

IV. Source of data: All data are prepared and provided by the Division of Industrial Statistics, Anhui Statistical Bureau, in accordance with the industrial statistical reporting system of SSB. Data are collected, tabulated and processed by the statistical bureau in the prefectures and cities.

13—1 工业分行业职工人数
Number of Staff and Workers in Industry by Industrial Branch

单位：人（person）

项 目	Item	2021	2022
总 计	**Total**	**2820498**	**2888522**
采矿业	**Mining**	**169155**	**155693**
煤炭开采和洗选业	Mining and Washing of Coal	133405	119464
石油和天然气开采业	Extraction of Petroleum and Natural Gas	344	321
黑色金属矿采选业	Mining and Processing of Ferrous Metal Ores	15933	15143
有色金属矿采选业	Mining and Processing of Non-Ferrous Metal Ores	4745	4494
非金属矿采选业	Mining and Processing of Non-metal Ores	14445	15742
开采专业及辅助性活动	Mining Profession and Auxiliary Activities	228	514
其他采矿业	Mining of Other Ores	55	15
制造业	**Manufacturing**	**2538252**	**2622045**
农副食品加工业	Processing of Food from Agriculture Products	109927	108564
食品制造业	Manufacture of Foods	56766	54314
酒、饮料和精制茶制造业	Manufacture of Wine, Beverages and Refined Tea	51645	51030
烟草制品业	Manufacture of Tobacco	6958	6743
纺织业	Manufacture of Textile	79674	83512
纺织服装、服饰业	Manufacture of Textile Wearing Apparel and Clothing	124129	116733
皮革毛皮羽毛及其制品和制鞋业	Manufacture of Leather, Furs, Feather and Related Products	38612	38137
木材加工及木竹藤棕草制品业	Processing of Timber, Manufacture of Wood, Bamboo, Rattan, Palm and Straw Products	37798	36198
家具制造业	Manufacture of Furniture	28037	28452
造纸及纸制品业	Manufacture of Paper and Paper Products	23206	23422
印刷和记录媒介复制业	Printing, Reproduction of Recording Media	37699	37205
文教工美体育和娱乐用品制造业	Manufacture of Culture, Education, Art, Sports and Entertainment Supplies	57901	57577
石油加工、炼焦和核燃料加工业	Processing of Petroleum, Coking and Processing of Nuclear Fuel	9605	9177
化学原料和化学制品制造业	Manufacture of Raw Chemical Materials and Chemical Products	121330	125909
医药制造业	Manufacture of Medicines	76296	79219
化学纤维制造业	Manufacture of Chemical Fibers	6357	6585
橡胶和塑料制品业	Manufacture of Rubber and Plastics	136672	141272
非金属矿物制品业	Manufacture of Non-metallic Mineral Products	197593	200225
黑色金属冶炼和压延加工业	Smelting and Pressing of Ferrous Metals	48944	47578
有色金属冶炼和压延加工业	Smelting and Pressing of Non-ferrous Metals	47658	45666
金属制品业	Manufacture of Metal Products	127959	134034
通用设备制造业	Manufacture of General Purpose Machinery	162801	172272
专用设备制造业	Manufacture of Special Purpose Machinery	112475	114880
汽车制造业	Manufacture of Automobile	210701	247610
铁路船舶航空航天和其他运输设备制造业	Manufacture of Railroads, Ships, Aerospace and Other Transportation Equipments	21682	23887
电气机械和器材制造业	Manufacture of Electrical Machinery and Equipment	279064	312502
计算机通信和其他电子设备制造业	Manufacture of Computers, Communication and Other Electronic Equipments	275562	266560
仪器仪表制造业	Manufacture of Measuring Instruments and Machinery	18605	19932
其他制造业	Manufacture of Others	9518	8837
废弃资源综合利用业	Industry of Comprehensive Utilization of Waste Resources	15869	16975
金属制品、机械和设备修理业	Industry of Metal Products, Machinery and Equipment Repair	7209	7036
电力、热力、燃气及水生产和供应业	**Electricity, Heat, Gas and Water Production and Supply Industry**	**113091**	**110783**
电力、热力生产和供应业	Production and Supply of Electric Power and Heat Power	78967	75817
燃气生产和供应业	Production and Supply of Gas	13025	13542
水的生产和供应业	Production and Supply of Water	21100	21424

注：不含规模以下私营单位。
a) Excluding scale under the private sector.

13—2 规模以上工业企业主要经济指标（2022年）

Main Indicators Above Designated Size Industrial Enterprises (2022)

项　目	Item	企业单位数（个）Number of Enterprises (unit)	资产合计 Total Assets
总　计	**Total**	**21484**	**56457.80**
总计中：	**Of the Total:**		
内资企业	Domestic Funded Enterprise	20567	50477.89
国有企业	State-owned Enterprise	126	1657.10
集体企业	Collective-owned Enterprise	16	10.90
股份合作企业	Share Holding Cooperative Enterprises	9	3.90
联营企业	Joint Owned Enterprises	4	8.99
有限责任公司	Limited Liability Corporations	3613	20154.50
股份有限公司	Share-holding Corporations Ltd.	408	13694.33
私营企业	Private Enterprises	16390	14947.69
其他企业	Other Enterprises	1	0.48
港澳台商投资企业	Enterprises Funded by Entrepreneurs from Hong Kong, Macao and Taiwan	384	2879.04
外商投资企业	Foreign Funded Enterprises	533	3100.87
总计中：	**Of the Total:**		
国有及国有控股企业	State Controlling Share Hold Enterprises	1110	20000.37
总计中：	**Of the Total:**		
轻工业	Light Industry	8140	11905.72
重工业	Heavy Industry	13344	44552.08
总计中：	**Of the Total:**		
大型企业	Large-sized Enterprises	279	25135.73
中型企业	Medium-sized Enterprises	1246	11409.25
小型企业	Small Enterprises	19959	19912.82

单位：亿元（100 million yuan）

流动资产合计 Circulating Funds	#存货 Stock	#产成品 Finished Product	固定资产原价 Original Value of Fixed Assets	固定资产累计折旧 Accumulated Depreciation of Fixed Assets	负债合计 Total Liabilities	流动负债 Liquid Liabilities
29619.67	**5594.82**	**2152.95**	**25786.30**	**10764.13**	**31899.84**	**25119.55**
26076.96	5005.70	1955.09	22956.58	9497.90	28515.18	22246.98
940.90	309.07	30.26	892.15	424.98	810.62	595.36
7.72	2.82	0.78	4.40	2.83	4.31	3.11
2.76	0.27	0.08	1.33	0.77	2.05	1.79
3.33	1.20	0.60	5.72	0.87	6.43	3.11
9497.52	1740.30	693.40	9659.17	3720.56	12337.01	9088.98
6426.37	793.28	256.21	6658.61	3309.13	6604.40	5195.40
9197.95	2158.72	973.74	5735.03	2038.67	8749.99	7358.87
0.42	0.04	0.04	0.16	0.10	0.37	0.37
1685.24	238.41	65.56	1250.49	532.75	1793.83	1507.20
1857.47	350.71	132.29	1579.23	733.49	1590.83	1365.36
7832.40	1255.08	351.14	13074.29	6038.64	10410.52	7145.51
7274.46	1891.66	740.25	4132.21	1624.17	6532.76	5809.10
22345.22	3703.17	1412.70	21654.09	9139.97	25367.07	19310.45
11970.23	1999.68	587.71	12766.74	5873.50	13995.97	10771.08
6130.25	1254.98	528.11	5156.03	2192.97	5897.43	4828.10
11519.19	2340.17	1037.12	7863.53	2697.66	12006.44	9520.36

13—2 续表1 continued

项　目	Item	所有者权益 Owners' Equity	#实收资本 Capital Hold
总　　计	**Total**	**24523.08**	**11423.31**
总计中:	**Of the Total:**		
内资企业	Domestic Funded Enterprise	21928.25	10049.10
国有企业	State-owned Enterprise	846.48	336.06
集体企业	Collective-owned Enterprise	6.58	1.25
股份合作企业	Share Holding Cooperative Enterprises	1.85	1.20
联营企业	Joint Owned Enterprises	2.56	2.56
有限责任公司	Limited Liability Corporations	7802.42	4620.13
股份有限公司	Share-holding Corporations Ltd.	7087.08	1777.09
私营企业	Private Enterprises	6181.16	3310.71
其他企业	Other Enterprises	0.12	0.10
港澳台商投资企业	Enterprises Funded by Entrepreneurs from Hong Kong, Macao and Taiwan	1084.78	596.93
外商投资企业	Foreign Funded Enterprises	1510.05	777.28
总计中:	**Of the Total:**		
国有及国有控股企业	State Controlling Share Hold Enterprises	9588.01	4323.30
总计中:	**Of the Total:**		
轻工业	Light Industry	5361.82	2273.15
重工业	Heavy Industry	19161.26	9150.16
总计中:	**Of the Total:**		
大型企业	Large-sized Enterprises	11139.76	4174.51
中型企业	Medium-sized Enterprises	5510.73	2530.47
小型企业	Small Enterprises	7872.58	4718.33

单位：亿元（100 million yuan）

营业收入 Business Revenue	营业成本 Business Cost	税金及附加 Taxes and Surcharges	利润总额 Total Profits	本年应付职工薪酬 Wages Payable in This Year	本年应交增值税 Value Added Tax Payable
46889.51	**40433.10**	**696.28**	**2386.60**	**3152.18**	**969.48**
40388.91	34656.28	669.12	2114.24	2778.60	886.76
1502.68	1053.44	294.45	48.95	124.43	64.55
10.51	8.42	0.10	0.44	1.47	0.24
3.30	2.74	0.02	0.14	0.43	0.13
1.58	1.14	0.03	-0.18	0.14	0.06
15588.52	13643.62	181.17	747.08	962.98	338.70
8166.28	6887.88	104.95	637.79	603.49	162.92
15115.65	13058.73	88.40	680.02	1085.64	320.13
0.39	0.31	0.00	0.01	0.02	0.02
3539.23	3273.77	12.08	88.37	150.67	32.28
2961.36	2503.04	15.08	183.99	222.91	50.44
13576.57	11599.50	488.65	656.62	1007.67	369.09
11123.23	9003.64	396.28	739.60	874.36	239.88
35766.28	31429.46	300.00	1647.00	2277.81	729.60
19859.89	17075.29	533.68	1026.53	1330.57	379.19
9197.79	7933.26	57.61	530.51	705.53	190.68
17831.83	15424.54	104.98	829.55	1116.08	399.61

13—2 续表2 continued

行 业	Sector	企业单位数（个）Number of Enterprises (unit)	资产合计 Total Assets
按行业分	**Grouped by Sector**		
煤炭开采和洗选业	Mining and Washing of Coal	19	2603.94
黑色金属矿采选业	Mining and Processing of Ferrous Metal Ores	57	397.64
有色金属矿采选业	Mining and Processing of Non-Ferrous Metal Ores	28	91.55
非金属矿采选业	Mining and Processing of Nonmetal Ores	239	911.72
开采专业及辅助性活动	Professional and Support Activities for Mining	3	7.22
农副食品加工业	Processing of Food from Agriculture Products	1412	1334.07
食品制造业	Manufacture of Foods	432	467.30
酒、饮料和精制茶制造业	Manufacture of Wine, Beverages and Refined Tea	268	924.46
烟草制品业	Manufacture of Tobacco	5	358.54
纺织业	Manufacture of Textile	769	717.63
纺织服装、服饰业	Manufacture of Textile Wearing Apparel and Clothing	661	260.13
皮革毛皮羽毛及其制品和制鞋业	Manufacture of Leather, Furs, Feather and Related Products	336	295.62
木材加工及木竹藤棕草制品业	Processing of Timber, Manufacture of Wood, Bamboo, Rattan, Palm and Straw Products	534	228.18
家具制造业	Manufacture of Furniture	249	224.49
造纸及纸制品业	Manufacture of Paper and Paper Products	245	617.11
印刷和记录媒介复制业	Printing, Reproduction of Recording Media	394	328.44
文教工美体育和娱乐用品制造业	Manufacture of Culture, Education, Art, Sports and Entertainment Supplies	571	232.14
石油、煤炭及其他燃料加工业	Processing of Petroleum, Coal and other Fuels	47	365.75
化学原料和化学制品制造业	Manufacture of Raw Chemical Materials and Chemical Products	1194	3318.99
医药制造业	Manufacture of Medicines	561	1244.62
化学纤维制造业	Manufacture of Chemical Fibers	68	175.26
橡胶和塑料制品业	Manufacture of Rubber and Plastics	1260	1525.66
非金属矿物制品业	Manufacture of Non-metallic Mineral Products	2522	5854.09
黑色金属冶炼和压延加工业	Smelting and Pressing of Ferrous Metals	136	1825.50
有色金属冶炼和压延加工业	Smelting and Pressing of Non-ferrous Metals	326	1477.72
金属制品业	Manufacture of Metal Products	1376	1635.80
通用设备制造业	Manufacture of General Purpose Machinery	1503	2286.13
专用设备制造业	Manufacture of Special Purpose Machinery	1114	1577.43
汽车制造业	Manufacture of Automobile	1156	4301.09
铁路船舶航空航天和其他运输设备制造业	Manufacture of Railroads, Ships, Aerospace and Other Transportation Equipments	208	397.79
电气机械和器材制造业	Manufacture of Electrical Machinery and Equipment	1504	6292.79
计算机通信和其他电子设备制造业	Manufacture of Computers, Communication and Other Electronic Equipments	1081	7290.39
仪器仪表制造业	Manufacture of Measuring Instruments and Machinery	185	325.38
其他制造业	Manufacture of Others	107	94.25
废弃资源综合利用业	Industry of Comprehensive Utilization of Waste Resources	251	386.77
金属制品、机械和设备修理业	Industry of Metal Products, Machinery and Equipment Repair	16	181.48
电力、热力生产和供应业	Production and Supply of Electric Power and Heat Power	373	4754.48
燃气生产和供应业	Production and Supply of Gas	139	492.57
水的生产和供应业	Production and Supply of Water	134	647.89

单位：亿元（100 million yuan）

流动资产合计 Circulating Funds	#存货 Stock	#产成品 Finished Product	固定资产原价 Original Value of Fixed Assets	固定资产累计折旧 Accumulated Depreciation of Fixed Assets	负债合计 Total Liabilities	流动负债 Liquid Liabilities
560.11	41.95	32.96	1449.48	622.52	1690.62	1060.41
120.99	11.65	7.25	284.06	118.19	185.32	153.80
41.58	4.73	3.44	47.01	19.71	66.29	54.69
387.85	51.06	8.04	151.76	64.07	529.52	234.58
3.50	0.47	0.31	2.37	0.56	4.73	3.03
794.18	273.44	107.38	515.10	163.70	702.11	604.00
250.47	78.66	26.76	246.21	97.05	268.16	230.50
597.10	219.59	45.93	310.50	121.30	383.11	341.42
258.64	179.46	10.52	157.05	92.09	109.36	108.06
366.71	107.60	63.15	311.20	120.56	377.33	321.63
172.05	41.98	20.61	110.45	49.42	156.92	144.23
191.81	47.94	23.76	83.67	28.38	168.30	150.60
141.47	38.13	18.49	85.31	33.85	119.77	105.26
133.01	30.56	9.55	73.52	21.72	130.95	122.91
245.43	48.07	22.67	216.08	89.45	379.11	284.33
198.80	42.57	17.26	152.44	67.32	156.82	141.59
153.50	51.79	22.13	74.87	27.31	133.31	120.50
106.22	39.95	12.04	352.29	190.97	217.88	190.50
1572.75	292.08	144.11	1665.16	652.37	1679.94	1248.10
749.24	199.13	97.46	409.61	156.87	612.42	552.38
100.71	17.73	9.00	63.14	27.47	98.96	87.70
834.60	180.30	84.92	693.38	306.20	719.59	635.47
3347.47	330.81	155.32	1931.71	754.52	2623.22	2186.25
806.24	218.39	63.71	1624.02	847.68	1115.17	931.07
961.86	270.63	74.78	502.39	216.16	938.74	771.99
1055.93	225.05	91.88	516.97	180.15	962.89	817.01
1446.29	317.24	112.10	719.47	296.43	1260.49	1070.98
1107.57	249.60	94.23	416.71	176.13	826.09	742.44
2540.37	395.41	183.21	1328.68	667.55	2956.90	2511.57
246.39	50.67	17.08	121.19	41.64	227.38	194.81
4351.10	761.56	343.86	1411.72	461.48	4157.58	3737.05
3703.86	589.96	181.82	3146.44	1125.44	3916.98	2784.86
234.47	33.69	12.12	86.18	39.19	129.90	121.47
59.12	13.04	6.75	24.08	9.35	50.11	45.71
254.45	36.25	14.87	93.87	26.69	196.16	161.70
144.25	30.02	2.27	41.61	21.02	61.61	41.84
998.30	51.65	3.03	5775.19	2624.38	2992.16	1764.91
186.42	10.67	5.40	239.61	76.41	254.54	187.67
193.85	11.34	2.79	346.81	128.07	337.72	151.81

13—2 续表3 continued

行 业	Sector	所有者权益 Owners' Equity	#实收资本 Capital Hold
按行业分	**Grouped by Sector**		
煤炭开采和洗选业	Mining and Washing of Coal	913.32	335.06
黑色金属矿采选业	Mining and Processing of Ferrous Metal Ores	212.32	116.56
有色金属矿采选业	Mining and Processing of Non-Ferrous Metal Ores	25.26	22.30
非金属矿采选业	Mining and Processing of Nonmetal Ores	381.74	118.32
开采专业及辅助性活动	Professional and Support Activities for Mining	2.49	1.26
农副食品加工业	Processing of Food from Agriculture Products	630.65	229.91
食品制造业	Manufacture of Foods	197.45	131.99
酒、饮料和精制茶制造业	Manufacture of Wine, Beverages and Refined Tea	541.35	131.86
烟草制品业	Manufacture of Tobacco	249.18	41.67
纺织业	Manufacture of Textile	340.01	136.12
纺织服装、服饰业	Manufacture of Textile Wearing Apparel and Clothing	102.37	52.62
皮革毛皮羽毛及其制品和制鞋业	Manufacture of Leather, Furs, Feather and Related Products	125.90	51.15
木材加工及木竹藤棕草制品业	Processing of Timber, Manufacture of Wood, Bamboo, Rattan, Palm and Straw Products	105.64	41.28
家具制造业	Manufacture of Furniture	93.50	234.94
造纸及纸制品业	Manufacture of Paper and Paper Products	237.74	99.15
印刷和记录媒介复制业	Printing, Reproduction of Recording Media	171.62	70.17
文教工美体育和娱乐用品制造业	Manufacture of Culture, Education, Art, Sports and Entertainment Supplies	98.28	45.58
石油、煤炭及其他燃料加工业	Processing of Petroleum, Coal and other Fuels	147.87	103.52
化学原料和化学制品制造业	Manufacture of Raw Chemical Materials and Chemical Products	1638.63	674.86
医药制造业	Manufacture of Medicines	632.05	258.89
化学纤维制造业	Manufacture of Chemical Fibers	76.30	43.21
橡胶和塑料制品业	Manufacture of Rubber and Plastics	804.00	355.83
非金属矿物制品业	Manufacture of Non-metallic Mineral Products	3226.73	857.46
黑色金属冶炼和压延加工业	Smelting and Pressing of Ferrous Metals	708.26	222.97
有色金属冶炼和压延加工业	Smelting and Pressing of Non-ferrous Metals	538.72	247.91
金属制品业	Manufacture of Metal Products	672.41	619.80
通用设备制造业	Manufacture of General Purpose Machinery	1024.02	453.44
专用设备制造业	Manufacture of Special Purpose Machinery	749.48	307.10
汽车制造业	Manufacture of Automobile	1337.18	695.85
铁路船舶航空航天和其他运输设备制造业	Manufacture of Railroads, Ships, Aerospace and Other Transportation Equipments	170.41	107.28
电气机械和器材制造业	Manufacture of Electrical Machinery and Equipment	2132.60	908.64
计算机通信和其他电子设备制造业	Manufacture of Computers, Communication and Other Electronic Equipments	3372.13	1919.21
仪器仪表制造业	Manufacture of Measuring Instruments and Machinery	195.48	65.57
其他制造业	Manufacture of Others	43.64	21.68
废弃资源综合利用业	Industry of Comprehensive Utilization of Waste Resources	190.62	96.05
金属制品、机械和设备修理业	Industry of Metal Products, Machinery and Equipment Repair	119.87	12.46
电力、热力生产和供应业	Production and Supply of Electric Power and Heat Power	1762.32	1370.51
燃气生产和供应业	Production and Supply of Gas	238.03	94.96
水的生产和供应业	Production and Supply of Water	309.38	121.84

单位：亿元（100 million yuan）

营业收入 Business Revenue	营业成本 Business Cost	税金及附加 Taxes and Surcharges	利润总额 Total Profits	本年应付职工薪酬 Wages Payable in This Year	本年应交增值税 Value Added Tax Payable
1144.16	816.63	24.94	177.83	242.85	76.82
241.10	157.33	5.69	47.87	23.21	12.58
34.40	27.26	0.85	0.64	4.74	1.15
259.90	152.39	11.16	53.36	17.20	13.60
5.53	5.15	0.03	0.10	0.16	0.01
1910.79	1731.78	4.54	83.70	85.11	12.38
516.43	440.59	2.48	17.15	38.31	8.86
579.65	318.01	53.16	111.25	69.44	31.61
508.71	138.74	289.40	25.56	47.92	46.55
594.32	529.70	3.23	20.28	57.74	10.18
324.53	280.30	2.07	9.20	66.70	10.99
312.87	274.82	1.47	19.06	22.86	6.80
277.94	245.14	1.60	12.45	19.01	4.51
197.52	161.49	1.16	10.80	21.10	5.41
358.24	317.48	2.09	35.04	30.10	8.99
307.91	254.11	1.84	21.38	28.60	6.29
222.73	190.39	1.31	10.65	31.46	6.84
763.98	658.08	77.65	11.13	17.46	12.39
2867.44	2406.42	16.13	234.72	143.02	45.67
839.22	613.85	5.76	72.53	66.35	22.18
97.13	86.45	0.59	4.64	5.69	0.62
1367.93	1149.02	8.10	87.16	129.53	25.78
3008.12	2476.89	23.86	272.19	175.24	78.17
2509.11	2397.17	9.95	-0.72	87.78	33.40
3035.05	2882.69	8.86	66.82	46.75	48.10
1955.08	1761.82	7.66	84.69	117.84	37.97
1800.56	1512.89	9.69	116.13	176.31	38.34
980.17	765.18	6.38	83.10	119.70	27.60
3780.65	3330.28	42.32	110.25	262.18	67.49
238.63	190.79	1.59	16.36	30.65	5.39
6333.12	5523.39	28.64	331.26	326.63	70.94
4649.91	4181.10	15.24	76.71	362.48	58.49
240.18	180.16	1.36	21.95	27.94	6.01
53.98	44.22	0.37	2.06	5.84	1.49
926.74	893.78	7.11	11.60	13.24	50.42
60.97	47.25	0.31	5.01	19.17	0.80
3045.62	2816.98	15.24	89.97	172.98	68.65
411.68	378.19	0.99	18.25	16.11	3.38
126.22	94.28	1.46	14.42	22.12	2.59

13—3 规模以上工业企业主要经济效益指标（2022年）

Main Indicators on Economic Benefit Above Designated Size Industrial Enterprises by Industrial Branch (2022)

项　目	Item
总　计	**Total**
总计中:	**Of the Total:**
内资企业	Domestic Funded Enterprise
国有企业	State-owned Enterprise
集体企业	Collective-owned Enterprise
股份合作企业	Share Holding Cooperative Enterprises
联营企业	Joint Owned Enterprises
有限责任公司	Limited Liability Corporations
股份有限公司	Share-holding Corporations Ltd.
私营企业	Private Enterprises
其他企业	Other Enterprises
港澳台商投资企业	Enterprises Funded by Entrepreneurs from Hong Kong, Macao and Taiwan
外商投资企业	Foreign Funded Enterprises
总计中:	**Of the Total:**
国有及国有控股企业	State Controlling Share Hold Enterprises
总计中:	**Of the Total:**
轻工业	Light Industry
重工业	Heavy Industry
总计中:	**Of the Total:**
大型企业	Large-sized Enterprises
中型企业	Medium-sized Enterprises
小型企业	Small Enterprises

总资产贡献率 (%) Ratio of Total Assets to Industrial Output Value (%)	资产负债率 (%) Assets-liability Ratio (%)	流动资产周转次数 (次/年) Number of Times of Annual of Turnover Circulating Funds (times/year)	工业成本费用利润率 (%) Ratio of Profits to Industrial Cost (%)
7.78	**56.50**	**1.58**	**5.40**
7.90	56.49	1.55	5.57
25.18	48.92	1.60	4.21
7.37	39.58	1.36	4.29
8.33	52.64	1.20	4.29
1.38	71.53	0.48	-10.41
7.02	61.21	1.64	5.06
7.20	48.23	1.27	8.45
7.84	58.54	1.64	4.69
6.25	75.62	0.95	2.26
4.88	62.31	2.10	2.57
8.49	51.30	1.59	6.62
8.40	52.05	1.73	5.25
11.99	54.87	1.53	7.32
6.66	56.94	1.60	4.83
8.32	55.68	1.66	5.57
7.28	51.69	1.50	6.09
7.39	60.30	1.55	4.87

13—3 续表 continued

行 业	Sector
按行业分	**Grouped by Sector**
煤炭开采和洗选业	Mining and Washing of Coal
黑色金属矿采选业	Mining and Processing of Ferrous Metal Ores
有色金属矿采选业	Mining and Processing of Non-Ferrous Metal Ores
非金属矿采选业	Mining and Processing of Nonmetal Ores
开采专业及辅助性活动	Professional and Support Activities for Mining
农副食品加工业	Processing of Food from Agriculture Products
食品制造业	Manufacture of Foods
酒、饮料和精制茶制造业	Manufacture of Wine, Beverages and Refined Tea
烟草制品业	Manufacture of Tobacco
纺织业	Manufacture of Textile
纺织服装、服饰业	Manufacture of Textile Wearing Apparel and Clothing
皮革毛皮羽毛及其制品和制鞋业	Manufacture of Leather, Furs, Feather and Related Products
木材加工及木竹藤棕草制品业	Processing of Timber, Manufacture of Wood, Bamboo, Rattan, Palm and Straw Products
家具制造业	Manufacture of Furniture
造纸及纸制品业	Manufacture of Paper and Paper Products
印刷和记录媒介复制业	Printing, Reproduction of Recording Media
文教工美体育和娱乐用品制造业	Manufacture of Culture, Education, Art, Sports and Entertainment Supplies
石油、煤炭及其他燃料加工业	Processing of Petroleum, Coal and other Fuels
化学原料和化学制品制造业	Manufacture of Raw Chemical Materials and Chemical Products
医药制造业	Manufacture of Medicines
化学纤维制造业	Manufacture of Chemical Fibers
橡胶和塑料制品业	Manufacture of Rubber and Plastics
非金属矿物制品业	Manufacture of Non-metallic Mineral Products
黑色金属冶炼和压延加工业	Smelting and Pressing of Ferrous Metals
有色金属冶炼和压延加工业	Smelting and Pressing of Non-ferrous Metals
金属制品业	Manufacture of Metal Products
通用设备制造业	Manufacture of General Purpose Machinery
专用设备制造业	Manufacture of Special Purpose Machinery
汽车制造业	Manufacture of Automobile
铁路船舶航空航天和其他运输设备制造业	Manufacture of Railroads, Ships, Aerospace and Other Transportation Equipments
电气机械和器材制造业	Manufacture of Electrical Machinery and Equipment
计算机通信和其他电子设备制造业	Manufacture of Computers, Communication and Other Electronic Equipments
仪器仪表制造业	Manufacture of Measuring Instruments and Machinery
其他制造业	Manufacture of Others
废弃资源综合利用业	Industry of Comprehensive Utilization of Waste Resources
金属制品、机械和设备修理业	Industry of Metal Products, Machinery and Equipment Repair
电力、热力生产和供应业	Production and Supply of Electric Power and Heat Power
燃气生产和供应业	Production and Supply of Gas
水的生产和供应业	Production and Supply of Water

总资产贡献率 (%) Ratio of Total Assets to Industrial Output Value (%)	资产负债率 (%) Assets-liability Ratio (%)	流动资产周转次数 (次/年) Number of Times of Annual of Turnover Circulating Funds (times/year)	工业成本费用利润率 (%) Ratio of Profits to Industrial Cost (%)
11.94	64.93	2.04	18.52
17.12	46.60	1.99	25.67
3.64	72.41	0.83	2.05
9.01	58.08	0.67	27.17
2.02	65.45	1.58	1.80
8.34	52.63	2.41	4.56
6.57	57.39	2.06	3.45
21.14	41.44	0.97	26.41
101.34	30.50	1.97	13.61
5.20	52.58	1.62	3.51
9.00	60.33	1.89	2.91
9.72	56.93	1.63	6.50
8.69	52.49	1.96	4.68
8.11	58.33	1.49	5.72
7.84	61.43	1.46	9.88
9.71	47.75	1.55	7.44
8.62	57.43	1.45	5.00
27.99	59.57	7.19	1.64
9.69	50.62	1.82	8.79
8.45	49.21	1.12	9.44
4.50	56.47	0.96	4.97
8.37	47.17	1.64	6.75
7.24	44.81	0.90	9.92
2.88	61.09	3.11	-0.03
9.20	63.53	3.16	2.26
8.56	58.86	1.85	4.50
7.60	55.14	1.24	6.80
7.78	52.37	0.88	9.16
5.49	68.75	1.49	3.03
5.92	57.16	0.97	7.32
7.22	66.07	1.46	5.53
2.46	53.73	1.26	1.67
9.07	39.92	1.02	9.85
5.06	53.17	0.91	3.92
18.70	50.72	3.64	1.26
2.68	33.95	0.42	8.78
4.97	62.93	3.05	3.06
4.75	51.68	2.21	4.59
3.44	52.13	0.65	12.48

13—4 国有控股工业企业主要经济指标（2022年）
Main Indicators of State-owned and State-holding Industrial Enterprises (2022)

项　目	Item	企业单位数（个）Number of Enterprises (unit)	资产合计 Total Assets
总　计	**Total**	**1110**	**20000.37**
总计中：	**Of the Total:**		
内资企业	Domestic Funded Enterprise	1062	19432.80
国有企业	State-owned Enterprise	126	1657.10
有限责任公司	Limited Liability Corporations	850	9423.34
股份有限公司	Share-holding Corporations Ltd.	80	8338.47
港澳台商投资企业	Enterprises Funded by Entrepreneurs from Hong Kong, Macao and Taiwan	21	312.66
外商投资企业	Foreign Funded Enterprises	27	254.90
总计中：	**Of the Total:**		
轻工业	Light Industry	153	1276.55
重工业	Heavy Industry	957	18723.82
总计中：	**Of the Total:**		
大型企业	Large-sized Enterprises	71	12876.20
中型企业	Medium-sized Enterprises	202	3128.53
小型企业	Small Enterprises	837	3995.64
按行业分	**Grouped by Sector**		
煤炭开采和洗选业	Mining and Washing of Coal	15	2582.53
黑色金属矿采选业	Mining and Processing of Ferrous Metal Ores	11	201.08
有色金属矿采选业	Mining and Processing of Non-Ferrous Metal Ores	6	35.38
非金属矿采选业	Mining and Processing of Nonmetal Ores	46	544.45
开采专业及辅助性活动	Professional and Support Activities for Mining	2	6.86
农副食品加工业	Processing of Food from Agriculture Products	30	52.75
食品制造业	Manufacture of Foods	6	3.11
酒、饮料和精制茶制造业	Manufacture of Wine, Beverages and Refined Tea	10	318.29
烟草制品业	Manufacture of Tobacco	5	358.54
纺织业	Manufacture of Textile	9	99.13
纺织服装、服饰业	Manufacture of Textile Wearing Apparel and Clothing	13	21.75
皮革毛皮羽毛及其制品和制鞋业	Manufacture of Leather, Furs, Feather and Related Products		
木材加工及木竹藤棕草制品业	Processing of Timber, Manufacture of Wood, Bamboo, Rattan, Palm and Straw Products	1	0.51
家具制造业	Manufacture of Furniture	1	6.03
造纸及纸制品业	Manufacture of Paper and Paper Products	4	13.34
印刷和记录媒介复制业	Printing, Reproduction of Recording Media	8	10.53
文教、工美、体育和娱乐用品制造业	Manufacture of Culture, Education, Art, Sports and Entertainment Supplies		
石油、煤炭及其他燃料加工业	Processing of Petroleum, Coal and other Fuels	4	268.56
化学原料和化学制品制造业	Manufacture of Raw Chemical Materials and Chemical Products	63	934.69
医药制造业	Manufacture of Medicines	25	115.81
化学纤维制造业	Manufacture of Chemical Fibers		
橡胶和塑料制品业	Manufacture of Rubber and Plastics	23	170.19
非金属矿物制品业	Manufacture of Non-metallic Mineral Products	150	2827.50
黑色金属冶炼和压延加工业	Smelting and Pressing of Ferrous Metals	10	1304.04
有色金属冶炼和压延加工业	Smelting and Pressing of Non-ferrous Metals	10	486.06
金属制品业	Manufacture of Metal Products	40	168.46
通用设备制造业	Manufacture of General Purpose Machinery	45	371.12
专用设备制造业	Manufacture of Special Purpose Machinery	53	279.27
汽车制造业	Manufacture of Automobile	60	1090.15
铁路船舶航空航天和其他运输设备制造业	Manufacture of Railroads, Ships, Aerospace and Other Transportation Equipments	16	185.30
电气机械和器材制造业	Manufacture of Electrical Machinery and Equipment	27	188.90
计算机通信和其他电子设备制造业	Manufacture of Computers, Communication and Other Electronic Equipments	54	2190.56
仪器仪表制造业	Manufacture of Measuring Instruments and Machinery	3	35.96
废弃资源综合利用业	Industry of Comprehensive Utilization of Waste Resources	6	47.48
其他制造业	Manufacture of Others	15	154.61
金属制品、机械和设备修理业	Industry of Metal Products, Machinery and Equipment Repair	3	151.82
电力、热力生产和供应业	Production and Supply of Electric Power and Heat Power	209	3941.85
燃气生产和供应业	Production and Supply of Gas	32	265.73
水的生产和供应业	Production and Supply of Water	94	562.20

单位：亿元（100 million yuan）

流动资产合计 Circulating Funds	#存货 Stock	#产成品 Finished Product	固定资产原价 Original Value of Fixed Assets	固定资产累计折旧 Accumulated Depreciation of Fixed Assets	负债合计 Total Liabilities	流动负债 Liquid Liabilities
7832.40	**1255.08**	**351.14**	**13074.29**	**6038.64**	**10410.52**	**7145.51**
7536.17	1171.00	336.24	12672.59	5814.94	10111.64	6942.97
940.90	309.07	30.26	892.15	424.98	810.62	595.36
3119.77	545.93	198.66	6197.00	2588.79	5358.45	3329.01
3470.23	314.48	106.55	5573.30	2798.37	3935.43	3014.89
134.70	26.97	3.40	239.19	118.41	176.90	99.33
161.52	57.11	11.50	162.51	105.29	121.99	103.21
784.51	319.24	61.27	455.88	225.48	480.22	424.60
7047.89	935.84	289.87	12618.41	5813.16	9930.31	6720.92
4981.57	800.10	180.20	8744.19	4324.87	6405.01	4673.41
1292.64	234.04	97.09	2145.39	1001.98	1491.46	1085.48
1558.19	220.93	73.85	2184.71	711.79	2514.05	1386.63
547.71	40.19	31.19	1436.14	614.24	1684.91	1054.83
56.88	2.84	1.85	164.25	69.67	71.58	63.97
3.18	0.97	0.55	34.82	11.99	23.97	17.89
229.63	40.75	2.03	38.59	17.62	314.24	110.24
3.16	0.43	0.31	2.32	0.53	4.52	2.83
34.98	18.47	8.70	22.47	9.01	35.35	31.46
1.95	0.87	0.51	1.84	0.75	1.01	0.99
231.11	66.58	14.11	48.79	21.01	102.62	99.86
258.64	179.46	10.52	157.05	92.09	109.36	108.06
43.33	5.63	3.87	40.92	21.19	35.79	28.69
13.36	0.59	0.29	11.96	5.67	9.28	8.67
0.17	0.06	0.05	0.30	0.01	0.40	0.37
5.43	0.08	0.01	0.90	0.76	5.21	4.91
8.54	4.94	3.77	6.56	2.92	5.59	3.61
6.66	1.38	0.70	6.38	3.52	3.28	2.74
52.52	21.75	4.79	295.91	170.55	148.21	131.87
286.13	45.96	20.68	633.08	219.63	517.30	281.46
64.04	18.15	8.02	52.58	21.41	56.65	51.97
77.48	17.12	9.85	91.20	42.33	72.19	64.49
1508.15	67.33	32.33	782.06	311.20	774.34	619.86
536.01	126.06	20.58	1254.03	660.17	785.15	680.48
286.95	121.92	15.70	243.79	123.82	231.27	173.29
117.02	26.79	14.32	54.45	24.38	87.66	69.62
225.44	36.84	14.12	103.26	54.78	175.87	124.92
181.83	40.14	15.54	57.09	23.70	177.65	145.17
676.48	81.93	45.93	360.96	190.26	783.70	659.00
128.95	21.78	9.42	55.42	22.89	96.76	85.21
95.96	18.87	9.72	47.81	12.05	127.61	98.82
929.24	150.67	38.47	1342.33	624.81	922.57	632.58
20.41	2.45	1.32	9.65	4.87	10.34	9.69
25.81	5.31	3.18	11.69	4.70	31.05	28.46
113.97	7.30	0.87	16.33	4.64	54.40	49.72
123.09	28.28	1.78	33.33	17.07	50.59	31.63
673.96	40.14	2.47	5244.59	2490.19	2489.57	1470.63
91.86	2.80	1.30	117.74	39.31	117.07	67.21
171.41	10.26	2.27	288.72	104.14	291.79	129.59

13—4 续表 continued

项　目	Item	所有者权益 Owners' Equity	#实收资本 Capital Hold
总　计	**Total**	**9588.01**	**4323.30**
总计中：	**Of the Total:**		
内资企业	Domestic Funded Enterprise	9319.33	4181.90
国有企业	State-owned Enterprise	846.48	336.06
有限责任公司	Limited Liability Corporations	4063.05	2700.47
股份有限公司	Share-holding Corporations Ltd.	4403.04	1141.31
港澳台商投资企业	Enterprises Funded by Entrepreneurs from Hong Kong, Macao and Taiwan	135.76	81.82
外商投资企业	Foreign Funded Enterprises	132.92	59.57
总计中：	**Of the Total:**		
轻工业	Light Industry	796.33	201.79
重工业	Heavy Industry	8791.68	4121.51
总计中：	**Of the Total:**		
大型企业	Large-sized Enterprises	6471.19	2361.08
中型企业	Medium-sized Enterprises	1637.07	1078.84
小型企业	Small Enterprises	1479.75	883.38
按行业分	**Grouped by Sector**		
煤炭开采和洗选业	Mining and Washing of Coal	897.62	332.32
黑色金属矿采选业	Mining and Processing of Ferrous Metal Ores	129.50	73.50
有色金属矿采选业	Mining and Processing of Non-Ferrous Metal Ores	11.41	9.83
非金属矿采选业	Mining and Processing of Nonmetal Ores	230.21	56.87
开采专业及辅助性活动	Professional and Support Activities for Mining	2.33	1.22
农副食品加工业	Processing of Food from Agriculture Products	17.39	10.90
食品制造业	Manufacture of Foods	2.10	0.60
酒、饮料和精制茶制造业	Manufacture of Wine, Beverages and Refined Tea	215.67	17.09
烟草制品业	Manufacture of Tobacco	249.18	41.67
纺织业	Manufacture of Textile	63.34	12.35
纺织服装、服饰业	Manufacture of Textile Wearing Apparel and Clothing	12.47	3.01
皮革毛皮羽毛及其制品和制鞋业	Manufacture of Leather, Furs, Feather and Related Products		
木材加工及木竹藤棕草制品业	Processing of Timber, Manufacture of Wood, Bamboo, Rattan, Palm and Straw Products	0.11	0.10
家具制造业	Manufacture of Furniture	0.82	0.55
造纸及纸制品业	Manufacture of Paper and Paper Products	7.75	1.16
印刷和记录媒介复制业	Printing, Reproduction of Recording Media	7.24	2.53
文教、工美、体育和娱乐用品制造业	Manufacture of Culture, Education, Art, Sports and Entertainment Supplies		
石油、煤炭及其他燃料加工业	Processing of Petroleum, Coal and other Fuels	120.35	82.77
化学原料和化学制品制造业	Manufacture of Raw Chemical Materials and Chemical Products	417.39	249.20
医药制造业	Manufacture of Medicines	59.16	32.78
化学纤维制造业	Manufacture of Chemical Fibers		
橡胶和塑料制品业	Manufacture of Rubber and Plastics	98.00	56.10
非金属矿物制品业	Manufacture of Non-metallic Mineral Products	2053.16	266.00
黑色金属冶炼和压延加工业	Smelting and Pressing of Ferrous Metals	518.89	129.48
有色金属冶炼和压延加工业	Smelting and Pressing of Non-ferrous Metals	254.79	118.03
金属制品业	Manufacture of Metal Products	80.80	36.77
通用设备制造业	Manufacture of General Purpose Machinery	195.25	100.15
专用设备制造业	Manufacture of Special Purpose Machinery	101.62	44.86
汽车制造业	Manufacture of Automobile	305.40	244.42
铁路船舶航空航天和其他运输设备制造业	Manufacture of Railroads, Ships, Aerospace and Other Transportation Equipments	88.54	56.68
电气机械和器材制造业	Manufacture of Electrical Machinery and Equipment	61.29	61.27
计算机通信和其他电子设备制造业	Manufacture of Computers, Communication and Other Electronic Equipments	1267.99	817.49
仪器仪表制造业	Manufacture of Measuring Instruments and Machinery	25.62	6.10
其他制造业	Manufacture of Others	16.44	10.77
废弃资源综合利用业	Industry of Comprehensive Utilization of Waste Resources	100.21	55.26
金属制品、机械和设备修理业	Industry of Metal Products, Machinery and Equipment Repair	101.24	6.61
电力、热力生产和供应业	Production and Supply of Electric Power and Heat Power	1452.28	1224.60
燃气生产和供应业	Production and Supply of Gas	148.66	59.56
水的生产和供应业	Production and Supply of Water	269.63	96.38

单位：亿元（100 million yuan）

营业收入 Business Revenue	营业成本 Business Cost	税金及附加 Taxes and Surcharges	利润总额 Total Profits	本年应付职工薪酬 Wages Payable in This Year	本年应交增值税 Value Added Tax Payable
13576.57	**11599.50**	**488.65**	**656.62**	**1007.67**	**369.09**
12855.07	10921.47	485.54	650.92	968.89	365.80
1502.68	1053.44	294.45	48.95	124.43	64.55
6170.47	5351.08	131.91	287.70	453.74	184.72
5174.48	4510.86	59.10	314.12	390.12	116.34
272.05	261.41	2.21	-5.55	27.05	2.21
449.46	416.62	0.90	11.25	11.73	1.08
1038.18	479.84	320.79	83.99	123.70	68.48
12538.39	11119.67	167.86	572.63	883.96	300.61
8829.87	7426.91	449.59	412.16	721.82	244.99
2263.81	2013.58	16.97	86.39	172.74	41.35
2482.90	2159.02	22.09	158.07	113.11	82.76
1115.77	791.07	24.44	177.56	239.81	75.18
116.73	61.11	3.64	33.02	15.32	8.19
16.97	12.23	0.65	0.00	3.40	0.87
83.84	48.99	3.85	19.04	5.72	4.16
5.26	4.94	0.03	0.07	0.15	0.00
74.97	67.38	0.17	1.92	2.48	0.56
2.85	2.25	0.02	0.22	0.42	0.03
165.28	44.23	28.66	42.46	37.97	13.95
508.71	138.74	289.40	25.56	47.92	46.55
45.57	41.12	0.32	-1.77	4.57	0.55
11.59	6.05	0.13	-0.07	4.75	0.99
0.34	0.32	0.00	0.02	0.02	-0.04
6.42	5.79	0.01	0.09	0.34	0.12
4.68	3.01	0.06	0.34	1.59	0.23
7.14	5.77	0.08	0.21	1.67	0.20
609.93	513.68	77.35	6.98	14.27	9.31
505.12	445.73	4.76	29.15	32.30	10.44
74.00	52.28	0.71	4.76	7.60	2.50
107.14	90.92	0.71	6.15	11.38	1.48
836.60	659.85	9.71	139.87	50.05	22.45
1507.23	1431.18	6.49	-1.20	61.95	11.46
1028.20	969.32	2.69	31.81	14.82	9.50
192.03	178.10	1.03	5.68	11.10	9.15
303.16	266.25	1.59	10.40	33.73	6.83
145.49	119.96	1.06	10.37	17.67	3.96
1045.88	971.27	5.45	-3.25	64.19	19.59
103.10	84.73	0.67	7.90	14.30	2.67
130.96	120.69	0.45	2.36	5.43	1.38
1055.22	936.09	4.52	31.53	92.02	13.09
9.86	6.79	0.03	0.99	1.36	0.09
11.06	7.46	0.12	0.22	1.83	0.06
560.39	547.62	4.14	3.35	2.75	30.85
40.69	31.06	0.15	3.39	14.57	0.10
2855.74	2679.30	13.93	51.26	163.18	59.03
183.35	171.16	0.44	6.48	7.54	1.39
103.96	82.14	1.16	9.73	18.85	2.16

13—5 国有控股工业企业主要经济效益指标（2022年）
Main Indicators on Economic Benefit of State-owned and State-holding Industrial Enterprises (2022)

项　目	Item
总　　计	**Total**
总计中:	**Of the Total:**
内资企业	Domestic Funded Enterprise
国有企业	State-owned Enterprise
有限责任公司	Limited Liability Corporations
股份有限公司	Share-holding Corporations Ltd.
港澳台商投资企业	Enterprises Funded by Entrepreneurs from Hong Kong, Macao and Taiwan
外商投资企业	Foreign Funded Enterprises
总计中:	**Of the Total:**
轻工业	Light Industry
重工业	Heavy Industry
总计中:	**Of the Total:**
大型企业	Large-sized Enterprises
中型企业	Medium-sized Enterprises
小型企业	Small Enterprises
按行业分	**Grouped by Sector**
煤炭开采和洗选业	Mining and Washing of Coal
黑色金属矿采选业	Mining and Processing of Ferrous Metal Ores
有色金属矿采选业	Mining and Processing of Non-Ferrous Metal Ores
非金属矿采选业	Mining and Processing of Nonmetal Ores
开采专业及辅助性活动	Professional and Support Activities for Mining
农副食品加工业	Processing of Food from Agriculture Products
食品制造业	Manufacture of Foods
酒、饮料和精制茶制造业	Manufacture of Wine, Beverages and Refined Tea
烟草制品业	Manufacture of Tobacco
纺织业	Manufacture of Textile
纺织服装、服饰业	Manufacture of Textile Wearing Apparel and Clothing
皮革毛皮羽毛及其制品和制鞋业	Manufacture of Leather, Furs, Feather and Related Products
木材加工及木竹藤棕草制品业	Processing of Timber, Manufacture of Wood, Bamboo, Rattan, Palm and Straw Products
家具制造业	Manufacture of Furniture
造纸及纸制品业	Manufacture of Paper and Paper Products
印刷和记录媒介复制业	Printing, Reproduction of Recording Media
文教、工美、体育和娱乐用品制造业	Manufacture of Culture, Education, Art, Sports and Entertainment Supplies
石油、煤炭及其他燃料加工业	Processing of Petroleum, Coal and other Fuels
化学原料和化学制品制造业	Manufacture of Raw Chemical Materials and Chemical Products
医药制造业	Manufacture of Medicines
化学纤维制造业	Manufacture of Chemical Fibers
橡胶和塑料制品业	Manufacture of Rubber and Plastics
非金属矿物制品业	Manufacture of Non-metallic Mineral Products
黑色金属冶炼和压延加工业	Smelting and Pressing of Ferrous Metals
有色金属冶炼和压延加工业	Smelting and Pressing of Non-ferrous Metals
金属制品业	Manufacture of Metal Products
通用设备制造业	Manufacture of General Purpose Machinery
专用设备制造业	Manufacture of Special Purpose Machinery
汽车制造业	Manufacture of Automobile
铁路船舶航空航天和其他运输设备制造业	Manufacture of Railroads, Ships, Aerospace and Other Transportation Equipments
电气机械和器材制造业	Manufacture of Electrical Machinery and Equipment
计算机通信和其他电子设备制造业	Manufacture of Computers, Communication and Other Electronic Equipments
仪器仪表制造业	Manufacture of Measuring Instruments and Machinery
废弃资源综合利用业	Industry of Comprehensive Utilization of Waste Resources
其他制造业	Manufacture of Others
金属制品、机械和设备修理业	Industry of Metal Products, Machinery and Equipment Repair
电力、热力生产和供应业	Production and Supply of Electric Power and Heat Power
燃气生产和供应业	Production and Supply of Gas
水的生产和供应业	Production and Supply of Water

总资产贡献率 (%) Ratio of Total Assets to Industrial Output Value (%)	资产负债率 (%) Assets-liability Ratio (%)	流动资产周转次数 (次/年) Number of Times of Annual of Turnover Circulating Funds (times/year)	工业成本费用利润率 (%) Ratio of Profits to Industrial Cost (%)
8.40	**52.05**	**1.73**	**5.25**
8.57	52.03	1.71	5.52
25.18	48.92	1.60	4.21
7.35	56.86	1.98	4.99
6.66	47.20	1.49	6.47
-0.01	56.58	2.02	-2.01
5.52	47.86	2.78	2.58
37.17	37.62	1.32	13.32
6.44	53.04	1.78	4.82
0.00			
9.43	49.74	1.77	5.15
5.14	47.67	1.75	3.96
7.63	62.92	1.59	6.81
11.93	65.24	2.04	19.04
22.67	35.60	2.05	42.08
5.82	67.75	5.34	-0.03
5.52	57.72	0.37	31.05
1.56	65.97	1.66	1.37
5.56	67.02	2.14	2.62
8.97	32.38	1.46	8.18
25.91	32.24	0.72	44.32
101.34	30.50	1.97	13.61
-0.19	36.11	1.05	-3.97
4.36	42.66	0.87	-0.63
-5.29	78.15	2.01	4.71
3.46	86.41	1.18	1.48
5.36	41.89	0.55	7.84
4.67	31.17	1.07	2.99
35.10	55.19	11.61	1.32
6.02	55.34	1.77	5.87
7.33	48.92	1.16	6.87
5.21	42.42	1.38	6.03
7.35	27.39	0.55	20.04
1.66	60.21	2.81	-0.08
9.62	47.58	3.58	3.23
9.65	52.03	1.64	3.01
5.22	47.39	1.34	3.53
6.14	63.61	0.80	7.49
2.32	71.89	1.55	-0.31
5.99	52.22	0.80	8.28
2.79	67.56	1.36	1.83
2.58	42.12	1.14	3.09
3.34	28.76	0.48	10.54
2.24	65.38	0.43	2.07
25.94	35.19	4.92	0.60
1.53	33.32	0.33	8.83
4.53	63.16	4.24	1.84
3.26	44.06	2.00	3.63
2.81	51.90	0.61	9.97

13—6 外商投资和港澳台商投资工业企业主要经济指标（2022年）

Main Indicators of Industrial Enterprises with Hong Kong, Macao, Taiwan and Foreign Funds (2022)

项　目	Item	企业单位数（个）Number of Enterprises (unit)	资产合计 Total Assets
总　　计	**Total**	**917**	**5979.91**
总计中:	**Of the Total:**		
港澳台商投资企业	Enterprises Funded by Entrepreneurs from Hong Kong, Macao and Taiwan	384	2879.04
外商投资企业	Foreign Funded Enterprises	533	3100.87
总计中:	**Of the Total:**		
轻工业	Light Industry	328	1592.50
重工业	Heavy Industry	589	4387.41
总计中:	**Of the Total:**		
大型企业	Large-sized Enterprises	56	2817.04
中型企业	Medium-sized Enterprises	156	1535.68
小型企业	Small Enterprises	705	1627.19
按行业分	**Grouped by Sector**		
黑色金属矿采选业	Mining and Processing of Ferrous Metal Ores	2	24.97
非金属矿采选业	Mining and Processing of Nonmetal Ores	2	5.22
农副食品加工业	Processing of Food from Agriculture Products	35	219.48
食品制造业	Manufacture of Foods	30	108.37
酒、饮料和精制茶制造业	Manufacture of Wine, Beverages and Refined Tea	21	141.80
纺织业	Manufacture of Textile	28	30.06
纺织服装、服饰业	Manufacture of Textile Wearing Apparel and Clothing	35	42.29
皮革毛皮羽毛及其制品和制鞋业	Manufacture of Leather, Furs, Feather and Related Products	16	52.71
木材加工及木竹藤棕草制品业	Processing of Timber, Manufacture of Wood, Bamboo, Rattan, Palm and Straw Products	2	2.00
家具制造业	Manufacture of Furniture	4	54.24
造纸及纸制品业	Manufacture of Paper and Paper Products	10	30.38
印刷和记录媒介复制业	Printing, Reproduction of Recording Media	13	30.65
文教工美体育和娱乐用品制造业	Manufacture of Culture, Education, Art, Sports and Entertainment Supplies	11	8.88
石油、煤炭及其他燃料加工业	Processing of Petroleum, Coal and other Fuels	2	53.49
化学原料和化学制品制造业	Manufacture of Raw Chemical Materials and Chemical Products	68	475.05
医药制造业	Manufacture of Medicines	24	71.44
化学纤维制造业	Manufacture of Chemical Fibers	3	22.70
橡胶和塑料制品业	Manufacture of Rubber and Plastics	50	217.07
非金属矿物制品业	Manufacture of Non-metallic Mineral Products	39	326.93
黑色金属冶炼和压延加工业	Smelting and Pressing of Ferrous Metals	5	30.96
有色金属冶炼和压延加工业	Smelting and Pressing of Non-ferrous Metals	7	241.45
金属制品业	Manufacture of Metal Products	33	132.78
通用设备制造业	Manufacture of General Purpose Machinery	69	294.48
专用设备制造业	Manufacture of Special Purpose Machinery	38	108.73
汽车制造业	Manufacture of Automobile	84	443.18
铁路船舶航空航天和其他运输设备制造业	Manufacture of Railroads, Ships, Aerospace and Other Transportation Equipments	9	45.29
电气机械和器材制造业	Manufacture of Electrical Machinery and Equipment	62	649.64
计算机通信和其他电子设备制造业	Manufacture of Computers, Communication and Other Electronic Equipments	80	1263.91
仪器仪表制造业	Manufacture of Measuring Instruments and Machinery	9	66.80
其他制造业	Manufacture of Others	1	3.85
废弃资源综合利用业	Industry of Comprehensive Utilization of Waste Resources	3	7.77
金属制品、机械和设备修理业	Industry of Metal Products, Machinery and Equipment Repair		
电力、热力生产和供应业	Production and Supply of Electric Power and Heat Power	53	454.56
燃气生产和供应业	Production and Supply of Gas	58	266.27
水的生产和供应业	Production and Supply of Water	11	52.54

单位：亿元（100 million yuan）

流动资产合计 Circulating Funds	#存货 Stock	#产成品 Finished Product	固定资产原价 Original Value of Fixed Assets	固定资产累计折旧 Accumulated Depreciation of Fixed Assets	负债合计 Total Liabilities	流动负债 Liquid Liabilities
3542.71	**589.12**	**197.85**	**2829.72**	**1266.24**	**3384.65**	**2872.56**
1685.24	238.41	65.56	1250.49	532.75	1793.83	1507.20
1857.47	350.71	132.29	1579.23	733.49	1590.83	1365.36
1055.93	177.01	72.11	633.80	311.44	868.18	793.94
2486.78	412.11	125.74	2195.92	954.80	2516.47	2078.63
1958.28	281.83	76.12	1082.93	495.18	1709.52	1581.97
740.10	160.94	61.51	906.87	442.86	775.61	610.80
844.33	146.35	60.23	839.92	328.20	899.52	679.80
4.31	0.58	0.29	20.38	11.36	12.59	9.12
3.90	0.01	0.01	1.04	0.61	2.37	2.37
142.44	35.73	14.86	68.96	27.71	120.51	99.71
51.46	9.85	4.48	76.30	37.79	65.87	63.47
78.73	24.67	4.45	72.28	34.65	69.35	52.95
17.02	6.71	2.40	16.50	6.35	16.93	14.71
30.31	4.37	0.96	20.67	10.90	27.54	24.11
28.75	5.00	2.17	20.21	9.54	26.98	26.11
1.69	0.43	0.36	0.20	0.11	2.11	1.71
30.28	2.80	0.68	7.09	2.88	35.67	35.38
12.05	2.47	1.08	26.54	11.14	8.94	4.89
21.16	2.73	1.23	18.51	10.62	10.72	9.90
7.51	2.72	1.22	2.64	1.40	4.05	3.53
19.18	5.46	1.52	40.43	13.86	35.71	26.11
215.08	24.37	12.83	190.60	93.88	200.43	146.80
39.70	13.87	5.26	36.55	16.24	28.29	22.59
11.12	4.33	2.96	18.01	10.83	10.60	7.86
127.35	31.59	14.56	180.01	112.50	89.66	78.72
176.36	26.82	14.04	173.85	63.94	148.61	138.01
20.83	5.53	3.06	27.72	19.67	15.33	14.32
175.63	48.92	9.22	68.48	41.13	171.33	128.82
76.83	18.65	5.96	51.79	19.44	58.72	47.55
180.68	43.48	7.10	101.63	45.00	145.70	140.03
70.94	27.50	8.57	62.93	35.85	34.61	29.72
284.40	50.32	20.34	186.46	98.17	221.45	193.75
36.15	8.89	0.47	6.38	2.30	35.48	28.39
494.97	53.00	28.99	176.77	92.42	389.96	372.49
841.21	106.32	23.01	482.32	147.97	937.61	851.13
44.96	4.07	1.55	36.67	20.10	26.65	23.37
2.73	0.27	0.07	1.39	0.67	0.47	0.45
4.42	0.21	0.08	3.82	2.20	2.99	2.25
149.84	8.12	0.26	446.70	200.25	257.93	145.35
128.62	7.84	3.61	140.21	45.77	141.45	111.01
12.10	1.52	0.21	45.67	18.99	28.03	15.89

13—6 续表 continued

项　目	Item	所有者权益 Owners' Equity	#实收资本 Capital Hold
总　计	**Total**	**2594.83**	**1374.21**
总计中:	**Of the Total:**		
港澳台商投资企业	Enterprises Funded by Entrepreneurs from Hong Kong, Macao and Taiwan	1084.78	596.93
外商投资企业	Foreign Funded Enterprises	1510.05	777.28
总计中:	**Of the Total:**		
轻工业	Light Industry	723.89	332.58
重工业	Heavy Industry	1870.94	1041.64
总计中:	**Of the Total:**		
大型企业	Large-sized Enterprises	1107.52	494.21
中型企业	Medium-sized Enterprises	760.07	388.64
小型企业	Small Enterprises	727.24	491.36
按行业分	**Grouped by Sector**		
黑色金属矿采选业	Mining and Processing of Ferrous Metal Ores	12.38	3.92
非金属矿采选业	Mining and Processing of Nonmetal Ores	2.85	0.67
农副食品加工业	Processing of Food from Agriculture Products	98.97	39.82
食品制造业	Manufacture of Foods	42.50	40.36
酒、饮料和精制茶制造业	Manufacture of Wine, Beverages and Refined Tea	72.45	35.09
纺织业	Manufacture of Textile	13.12	9.84
纺织服装、服饰业	Manufacture of Textile Wearing Apparel and Clothing	14.32	9.56
皮革毛皮羽毛及其制品和制鞋业	Manufacture of Leather, Furs, Feather and Related Products	25.73	10.15
木材加工及木竹藤棕草制品业	Processing of Timber, Manufacture of Wood, Bamboo, Rattan, Palm and Straw Products	-0.11	0.15
家具制造业	Manufacture of Furniture	18.56	4.21
造纸及纸制品业	Manufacture of Paper and Paper Products	21.44	18.70
印刷和记录媒介复制业	Printing, Reproduction of Recording Media	19.93	6.27
文教工美体育和娱乐用品制造业	Manufacture of Culture, Education, Art, Sports and Entertainment Supplies	4.82	2.71
石油、煤炭及其他燃料加工业	Processing of Petroleum, Coal and other Fuels	17.78	13.00
化学原料和化学制品制造业	Manufacture of Raw Chemical Materials and Chemical Products	274.61	98.75
医药制造业	Manufacture of Medicines	43.15	13.17
化学纤维制造业	Manufacture of Chemical Fibers	12.10	7.21
橡胶和塑料制品业	Manufacture of Rubber and Plastics	127.41	69.89
非金属矿物制品业	Manufacture of Non-metallic Mineral Products	178.33	159.28
黑色金属冶炼和压延加工业	Smelting and Pressing of Ferrous Metals	15.63	10.83
有色金属冶炼和压延加工业	Smelting and Pressing of Non-ferrous Metals	70.12	20.53
金属制品业	Manufacture of Metal Products	74.06	57.82
通用设备制造业	Manufacture of General Purpose Machinery	148.78	61.56
专用设备制造业	Manufacture of Special Purpose Machinery	74.12	51.54
汽车制造业	Manufacture of Automobile	221.73	84.67
铁路船舶航空航天和其他运输设备制造业	Manufacture of Railroads, Ships, Aerospace and Other Transportation Equipments	9.81	7.24
电气机械和器材制造业	Manufacture of Electrical Machinery and Equipment	259.67	82.63
计算机通信和其他电子设备制造业	Manufacture of Computers, Communication and Other Electronic Equipments	326.29	262.59
仪器仪表制造业	Manufacture of Measuring Instruments and Machinery	40.15	15.50
其他制造业	Manufacture of Others	3.38	2.33
废弃资源综合利用业	Industry of Comprehensive Utilization of Waste Resources	4.78	2.16
金属制品、机械和设备修理业	Industry of Metal Products, Machinery and Equipment Repair		
电力、热力生产和供应业	Production and Supply of Electric Power and Heat Power	196.63	121.62
燃气生产和供应业	Production and Supply of Gas	124.82	34.14
水的生产和供应业	Production and Supply of Water	24.50	16.28

单位：亿元（100 million yuan）

营业收入 Business Revenue	营业成本 Business Cost	税金及附加 Taxes and Surcharges	利润总额 Total Profits	本年应付职工薪酬 Wages Payable in This Year	本年应交增值税 Value Added Tax Payable
6500.59	**5776.82**	**27.16**	**272.36**	**373.58**	**82.72**
3539.23	3273.77	12.08	88.37	150.67	32.28
2961.36	2503.04	15.08	183.99	222.91	50.44
1655.56	1387.76	12.10	90.28	125.41	24.79
4845.04	4389.06	15.06	182.07	248.17	57.93
3730.04	3370.00	12.97	154.84	195.15	39.36
1182.56	991.50	7.14	69.43	103.19	22.04
1587.99	1415.32	7.05	48.09	75.24	21.33
10.84	5.99	0.38	2.69	1.11	0.75
2.68	1.21	0.10	0.82	0.16	0.13
322.48	293.62	0.97	16.34	14.89	2.46
154.16	128.70	0.86	-1.21	9.18	2.90
93.23	69.44	3.26	7.35	10.33	2.73
36.36	32.30	0.17	0.62	4.09	0.52
54.75	50.11	0.32	0.50	13.68	1.76
71.49	58.97	0.37	10.29	4.33	1.84
0.82	0.75	0.01	-0.01	0.09	0.00
46.94	35.67	0.25	0.19	4.51	1.15
34.11	32.29	0.15	-0.27	1.43	0.61
23.76	17.97	0.20	3.29	2.19	0.68
10.66	8.60	0.06	1.09	2.11	0.26
111.05	103.21	0.21	4.80	2.05	2.72
337.78	255.57	2.09	39.75	16.16	9.08
46.30	31.27	0.32	2.88	6.25	0.78
19.48	16.07	0.12	2.62	0.88	0.10
193.35	150.62	1.53	18.43	25.02	4.94
231.50	186.29	1.92	25.95	12.35	5.80
26.56	24.62	0.22	-0.62	1.56	0.30
911.67	877.82	0.63	11.23	4.61	-1.09
103.27	89.95	0.52	5.43	9.82	1.99
238.01	200.62	0.91	15.74	18.56	3.64
73.60	63.57	0.55	2.23	12.48	1.26
430.74	366.73	2.05	26.31	42.83	7.65
26.69	19.47	0.10	2.00	1.93	0.23
608.98	521.74	4.19	31.88	43.76	5.55
1779.58	1697.81	2.40	10.47	76.68	13.80
64.99	49.17	0.36	5.87	6.07	1.22
3.37	2.48	0.03	0.35	0.49	0.00
11.72	10.73	0.04	0.30	0.36	0.03
194.51	168.75	1.20	17.74	10.78	7.19
214.22	198.84	0.50	5.24	10.10	1.44
10.95	5.89	0.20	2.02	2.76	0.30

13—7 外商投资和港澳台商投资工业企业主要经济效益指标（2022年）

Main Indicators on Economic Benefit of Industrial Enterprises with Hong Kong, Macao, Taiwan and Foreign Funds (2022)

项　目	Item
总　　计	**Total**
总计中：	**Of the Total:**
港澳台商投资企业	Enterprises Funded by Entrepreneurs from Hong Kong, Macao and Taiwan
外商投资企业	Foreign Funded Enterprises
总计中：	**Of the Total:**
轻工业	Light Industry
重工业	Heavy Industry
总计中：	**Of the Total:**
大型企业	Large-sized Enterprises
中型企业	Medium-sized Enterprises
小型企业	Small Enterprises
按行业分	**Grouped by Sector**
黑色金属矿采选业	Mining and Processing of Ferrous Metal Ores
非金属矿采选业	Mining and Processing of Nonmetal Ores
农副食品加工业	Processing of Food from Agriculture Products
食品制造业	Manufacture of Foods
酒、饮料和精制茶制造业	Manufacture of Wine, Beverages and Refined Tea
纺织业	Manufacture of Textile
纺织服装、服饰业	Manufacture of Textile Wearing Apparel and Clothing
皮革毛皮羽毛及其制品和制鞋业	Manufacture of Leather, Furs, Feather and Related Products
木材加工及木竹藤棕草制品业	Processing of Timber, Manufacture of Wood, Bamboo, Rattan, Palm and Straw Products
家具制造业	Manufacture of Furniture
造纸及纸制品业	Manufacture of Paper and Paper Products
印刷和记录媒介复制业	Printing, Reproduction of Recording Media
文教工美体育和娱乐用品制造业	Manufacture of Culture, Education, Art, Sports and Entertainment Supplies
石油、煤炭及其他燃料加工业	Processing of Petroleum, Coal and other Fuels
化学原料和化学制品制造业	Manufacture of Raw Chemical Materials and Chemical Products
医药制造业	Manufacture of Medicines
化学纤维制造业	Manufacture of Chemical Fibers
橡胶和塑料制品业	Manufacture of Rubber and Plastics
非金属矿物制品业	Manufacture of Non-metallic Mineral Products
黑色金属冶炼和压延加工业	Smelting and Pressing of Ferrous Metals
有色金属冶炼和压延加工业	Smelting and Pressing of Non-ferrous Metals
金属制品业	Manufacture of Metal Products
通用设备制造业	Manufacture of General Purpose Machinery
专用设备制造业	Manufacture of Special Purpose Machinery
汽车制造业	Manufacture of Automobile
铁路船舶航空航天和其他运输设备制造业	Manufacture of Railroads, Ships, Aerospace and Other Transportation Equipments
电气机械和器材制造业	Manufacture of Electrical Machinery and Equipment
计算机通信和其他电子设备制造业	Manufacture of Computers, Communication and Other Electronic Equipments
仪器仪表制造业	Manufacture of Measuring Instruments and Machinery
其他制造业	Manufacture of Others
废弃资源综合利用业	Industry of Comprehensive Utilization of Waste Resources
金属制品、机械和设备修理业	Industry of Metal Products, Machinery and Equipment Repair
电力、热力生产和供应业	Production and Supply of Electric Power and Heat Power
燃气生产和供应业	Production and Supply of Gas
水的生产和供应业	Production and Supply of Water

总资产贡献率 (%) Ratio of Total Assets to Industrial Output Value (%)	资产负债率 (%) Assets-liability Ratio (%)	流动资产周转次数 (次/年) Number of Times of Annual of Turnover Circulating Funds (times/year)	工业成本费用利润率 (%) Ratio of Profits to Industrial Cost (%)
6.75	**56.60**	**1.83**	**4.38**
4.88	62.31	2.10	2.57
8.49	51.30	1.59	6.62
8.46	54.52	1.57	5.78
6.13	57.36	1.95	3.91
7.67	60.69	1.90	4.33
6.80	50.51	1.60	6.21
5.12	55.28	1.88	3.16
15.74	50.42	2.51	34.58
20.43	45.40	0.69	48.31
9.93	54.91	2.26	5.22
2.73	60.78	3.00	-0.82
9.71	48.91	1.18	8.81
4.45	56.34	2.14	1.72
6.32	65.13	1.81	0.93
23.61	51.18	2.49	16.57
0.24	105.45	0.49	-0.79
2.69	65.77	1.55	0.42
2.06	29.43	2.83	-0.77
13.96	34.99	1.12	16.15
15.88	45.67	1.42	11.31
15.18	66.76	5.79	4.52
11.00	42.19	1.57	13.29
6.04	39.60	1.17	6.52
12.84	46.68	1.75	15.08
12.03	41.31	1.52	10.61
10.41	45.45	1.31	12.56
-0.28	49.51	1.27	-2.29
4.83	70.96	5.19	1.27
6.57	44.22	1.34	5.48
7.05	49.48	1.32	7.04
3.92	31.83	1.04	3.13
8.36	49.97	1.51	6.50
4.07	78.34	0.74	8.02
7.00	60.03	1.23	5.54
2.36	74.18	2.12	0.59
10.83	39.89	1.45	9.90
9.73	12.29	1.23	11.79
4.50	38.46	2.65	2.67
6.76	56.74	1.30	9.98
2.73	53.12	1.67	2.49
5.20	53.36	0.91	20.21

13—8 私营工业企业主要经济指标（2022年）
Main Indicators of Private Enterprises (2022)

项 目	Item	企业单位数（个）Number of Enterprises (unit)	资产合计 Total Assets
总 计	Total	16390	14947.69
总计中:	Of the Total:		
私营独资	Private Sole-source Investment Enterprise	244	96.30
私营合伙	Private Partnership Enterprise	62	24.68
私营有限责任公司	Private Companies with Limited Liabilities	15407	12911.78
私营股份有限公司	Private Share-holding Companies with Limited Liabilities	677	1914.93
总计中:	Of the Total:		
轻工业	Light Industry	6720	4623.45
重工业	Heavy Industry	9670	10324.24
总计中:	Of the Total:		
大型企业	Large-sized Enterprises	55	2643.31
中型企业	Medium-sized Enterprises	524	2590.08
小型企业	Small Enterprises	15811	9714.30
按行业分	Grouped by Sector		
煤炭开采和洗选业	Mining and Washing of Coal	2	0.56
黑色金属矿采选业	Mining and Processing of Ferrous Metal Ores	37	143.70
有色金属矿采选业	Mining and Processing of Non-Ferrous Metal Ores	18	47.85
非金属矿采选业	Mining and Processing of Nonmetal Ores	149	157.51
开采专业及辅助性活动	Professional and Support Activities for Mining	1	0.36
农副食品加工业	Processing of Food from Agriculture Products	1200	701.49
食品制造业	Manufacture of Foods	350	226.85
酒、饮料和精制茶制造业	Manufacture of Wine, Beverages and Refined Tea	190	178.25
纺织业	Manufacture of Textile	666	378.03
纺织服装、服饰业	Manufacture of Textile Wearing Apparel and Clothing	557	169.34
皮革毛皮羽毛及其制品和制鞋业	Manufacture of Leather, Furs, Feather and Related Products	293	164.25
木材加工及木竹藤棕草制品业	Processing of Timber, Manufacture of Wood, Bamboo, Rattan, Palm and Straw Products	505	196.22
家具制造业	Manufacture of Furniture	220	122.90
造纸及纸制品业	Manufacture of Paper and Paper Products	206	114.00
印刷和记录媒介复制业	Printing, Reproduction of Recording Media	333	202.89
文教工美体育和娱乐用品制造业	Manufacture of Culture, Education, Art, Sports and Entertainment Supplies	536	198.75
石油、煤炭及其他燃料加工业	Processing of Petroleum, Coal and other Fuels	36	39.76
化学原料和化学制品制造业	Manufacture of Raw Chemical Materials and Chemical Products	853	805.40
医药制造业	Manufacture of Medicines	374	526.74
化学纤维制造业	Manufacture of Chemical Fibers	53	46.61
橡胶和塑料制品业	Manufacture of Rubber and Plastics	1045	677.91
非金属矿物制品业	Manufacture of Non-metallic Mineral Products	2060	1760.68
黑色金属冶炼和压延加工业	Smelting and Pressing of Ferrous Metals	108	253.13
有色金属冶炼和压延加工业	Smelting and Pressing of Non-ferrous Metals	241	252.33
金属制品业	Manufacture of Metal Products	1149	936.48
通用设备制造业	Manufacture of General Purpose Machinery	1157	878.82
专用设备制造业	Manufacture of Special Purpose Machinery	838	638.37
汽车制造业	Manufacture of Automobile	809	785.81
铁路船舶航空航天和其他运输设备制造业	Manufacture of Railroads, Ships, Aerospace and Other Transportation Equipments	151	82.69
电气机械和器材制造业	Manufacture of Electrical Machinery and Equipment	1131	2251.23
计算机通信和其他电子设备制造业	Manufacture of Computers, Communication and Other Electronic Equipments	629	1552.29
仪器仪表制造业	Manufacture of Measuring Instruments and Machinery	140	144.73
其他制造业	Manufacture of Others	88	26.76
废弃资源综合利用业	Industry of Comprehensive Utilization of Waste Resources	188	126.26
金属制品、机械和设备修理业	Industry of Metal Products, Machinery and Equipment Repair	8	7.44
电力、热力生产和供应业	Production and Supply of Electric Power and Heat Power	31	104.16
燃气生产和供应业	Production and Supply of Gas	22	26.64
水的生产和供应业	Production and Supply of Water	16	20.50

单位：亿元（100 million yuan）

流动资产合　计 Circulating Funds	#存　货 Stock	#产成品 Finished Product	固定资产原　价 Original Value of Fixed Assets	固定资产累计折旧 Accumulated Depreciation of Fixed Assets	负债合计 Total Liabilities	流动负债 Liquid Liabilities
9197.95	**2158.72**	**973.74**	**5735.03**	**2038.67**	**8749.99**	**7358.87**
65.69	16.47	9.27	33.13	11.82	58.58	49.97
14.93	3.94	1.82	9.94	3.53	15.71	13.71
7910.85	1841.53	857.66	5187.69	1816.88	7789.13	6529.84
1206.48	296.78	104.99	504.26	206.44	886.56	765.35
2850.87	860.86	410.27	1782.31	650.80	2636.65	2360.47
6347.08	1297.86	563.47	3952.72	1387.87	6113.34	4998.40
1293.40	323.30	127.34	1343.48	410.55	1599.61	984.69
1554.22	380.45	168.64	957.52	358.07	1396.06	1236.48
6350.33	1454.97	677.75	3434.03	1270.04	5754.31	5137.69
0.46	0.18	0.18	0.07	0.02	0.47	0.47
51.37	5.42	3.41	75.76	34.37	70.31	58.98
34.38	3.48	2.67	7.62	4.43	40.34	35.40
77.43	6.73	2.96	64.22	27.45	92.33	67.42
0.34	0.05	0.00	0.05	0.03	0.20	0.20
406.54	165.85	60.11	289.13	93.03	334.81	290.65
127.28	45.99	18.46	111.26	45.58	122.67	107.66
103.96	43.31	17.11	80.28	26.28	101.06	86.79
221.33	72.80	44.95	173.37	64.04	236.08	210.18
108.75	31.70	15.97	69.21	29.00	104.40	97.26
108.65	27.82	15.14	48.37	14.95	97.85	85.25
124.13	33.09	15.85	64.16	24.85	104.48	91.18
70.48	15.85	6.49	51.19	14.96	62.34	56.21
63.24	19.99	8.59	45.10	17.57	73.76	60.93
120.15	29.66	11.32	94.91	40.04	107.13	96.59
130.11	41.67	18.61	62.88	22.53	113.79	102.61
32.09	12.24	5.40	14.46	6.23	31.65	30.42
484.24	109.89	55.46	333.94	113.47	410.95	365.85
355.14	103.36	59.45	150.92	61.01	296.66	272.26
26.43	8.10	3.38	19.88	4.10	23.69	19.91
409.71	90.92	42.25	298.20	106.70	348.94	315.60
1198.16	166.06	75.97	624.89	252.21	1146.29	999.92
153.13	54.30	27.65	214.81	139.03	141.63	104.17
161.67	49.30	22.72	94.89	30.40	159.95	140.22
637.81	129.28	52.20	267.02	98.57	588.98	529.09
573.05	158.85	60.14	310.81	123.69	479.33	436.76
451.17	99.60	39.24	186.80	72.77	321.55	298.16
469.47	116.47	52.10	342.36	134.99	493.16	444.53
46.96	11.01	5.59	31.90	10.43	43.44	39.39
1511.49	300.70	155.83	622.80	198.58	1476.94	1270.18
651.27	167.71	56.79	823.16	178.69	863.93	426.70
111.09	14.98	4.91	26.66	10.70	68.14	65.44
19.59	5.20	2.79	8.35	3.05	12.44	11.19
81.55	15.32	9.51	43.15	13.82	71.54	61.10
5.27	0.88	0.24	2.36	0.94	3.14	2.86
52.69	0.34	0.06	54.57	12.71	77.38	54.87
9.82	0.49	0.16	16.87	4.06	18.66	17.89
7.53	0.13	0.10	8.64	3.37	9.60	4.55

13—8 续表 continued

项 目	Item	所有者权益 Owners' Equity	#实收资本 Capital Hold
总 计	**Total**	**6181.16**	**3310.71**
总计中:	**Of the Total:**		
私营独资	Private Sole-source Investment Enterprise	37.93	14.79
私营合伙	Private Partnership Enterprise	8.97	3.47
私营有限责任公司	Private Companies with Limited Liabilities	5105.14	2975.06
私营股份有限公司	Private Share-holding Companies with Limited Liabilities	1029.11	317.39
总计中:	**Of the Total:**		
轻工业	Light Industry	1980.82	1037.55
重工业	Heavy Industry	4200.34	2273.17
总计中:	**Of the Total:**		
大型企业	Large-sized Enterprises	1043.70	466.23
中型企业	Medium-sized Enterprises	1192.92	421.51
小型企业	Small Enterprises	3944.54	2422.98
按行业分	**Grouped by Sector**		
煤炭开采和洗选业	Mining and Washing of Coal	0.09	0.14
黑色金属矿采选业	Mining and Processing of Ferrous Metal Ores	73.39	34.38
有色金属矿采选业	Mining and Processing of Non-Ferrous Metal Ores	7.51	9.03
非金属矿采选业	Mining and Processing of Nonmetal Ores	64.73	28.77
开采专业及辅助性活动	Professional and Support Activities for Mining	0.16	0.04
农副食品加工业	Processing of Food from Agriculture Products	365.37	127.88
食品制造业	Manufacture of Foods	104.18	56.21
酒、饮料和精制茶制造业	Manufacture of Wine, Beverages and Refined Tea	77.20	37.60
纺织业	Manufacture of Textile	141.67	72.72
纺织服装、服饰业	Manufacture of Textile Wearing Apparel and Clothing	64.54	34.22
皮革毛皮羽毛及其制品和制鞋业	Manufacture of Leather, Furs, Feather and Related Products	65.83	27.96
木材加工及木竹藤棕草制品业	Processing of Timber, Manufacture of Wood, Bamboo, Rattan, Palm and Straw Products	90.50	34.77
家具制造业	Manufacture of Furniture	60.52	225.74
造纸及纸制品业	Manufacture of Paper and Paper Products	39.98	21.23
印刷和记录媒介复制业	Printing, Reproduction of Recording Media	95.75	42.99
文教工美体育和娱乐用品制造业	Manufacture of Culture, Education, Art, Sports and Entertainment Supplies	84.41	36.81
石油、煤炭及其他燃料加工业	Processing of Petroleum, Coal and other Fuels	8.12	6.64
化学原料和化学制品制造业	Manufacture of Raw Chemical Materials and Chemical Products	394.04	174.61
医药制造业	Manufacture of Medicines	229.96	92.46
化学纤维制造业	Manufacture of Chemical Fibers	22.93	7.93
橡胶和塑料制品业	Manufacture of Rubber and Plastics	326.90	139.90
非金属矿物制品业	Manufacture of Non-metallic Mineral Products	611.45	311.61
黑色金属冶炼和压延加工业	Smelting and Pressing of Ferrous Metals	109.58	43.63
有色金属冶炼和压延加工业	Smelting and Pressing of Non-ferrous Metals	92.12	54.43
金属制品业	Manufacture of Metal Products	347.00	443.07
通用设备制造业	Manufacture of General Purpose Machinery	397.87	146.06
专用设备制造业	Manufacture of Special Purpose Machinery	316.48	113.60
汽车制造业	Manufacture of Automobile	292.99	148.53
铁路船舶航空航天和其他运输设备制造业	Manufacture of Railroads, Ships, Aerospace and Other Transportation Equipments	39.24	18.09
电气机械和器材制造业	Manufacture of Electrical Machinery and Equipment	773.98	381.67
计算机通信和其他电子设备制造业	Manufacture of Computers, Communication and Other Electronic Equipments	687.08	354.29
仪器仪表制造业	Manufacture of Measuring Instruments and Machinery	76.58	31.85
其他制造业	Manufacture of Others	14.32	5.89
废弃资源综合利用业	Industry of Comprehensive Utilization of Waste Resources	54.72	20.56
金属制品、机械和设备修理业	Industry of Metal Products, Machinery and Equipment Repair	4.30	0.54
电力、热力生产和供应业	Production and Supply of Electric Power and Heat Power	26.77	15.59
燃气生产和供应业	Production and Supply of Gas	7.98	3.79
水的生产和供应业	Production and Supply of Water	10.90	5.47

单位：亿元（100 million yuan）

营业收入 Business Revenue	营业成本 Business Cost	税金及附加 Taxes and Surcharges	利润总额 Total Profits	本年应付职工薪酬 Wages Payable in This Year	本年应交增值税 Value Added Tax Payable
15115.65	**13058.73**	**88.40**	**680.02**	**1085.64**	**320.13**
123.05	106.19	0.61	6.56	8.24	2.29
23.86	19.66	0.35	1.05	2.50	0.75
13559.30	11812.38	76.56	544.22	961.60	286.63
1409.44	1120.50	10.88	128.18	113.30	30.47
5077.91	4403.12	27.60	240.85	398.83	89.87
10037.73	8655.61	60.80	439.17	686.81	230.26
2074.67	1861.57	16.79	41.71	139.24	22.56
2508.08	2114.88	15.84	177.13	223.81	67.25
10532.89	9082.28	55.77	461.18	722.59	230.33
2.48	2.33	0.00	-0.07	0.02	0.01
86.92	66.07	1.42	14.71	5.65	2.94
13.92	13.31	0.10	-0.59	0.80	0.09
95.49	58.19	3.66	13.75	5.44	5.00
0.27	0.21	0.00	0.03	0.01	0.01
1063.86	964.61	2.50	39.98	45.32	5.82
232.31	201.59	0.98	8.82	21.45	3.69
156.13	122.59	4.57	15.20	8.69	3.66
380.98	338.57	1.97	11.83	37.49	6.74
217.64	189.82	1.32	7.19	42.36	7.13
176.49	160.67	0.74	3.56	12.46	3.39
248.54	219.56	1.43	11.23	17.22	4.22
108.91	91.86	0.68	7.69	11.82	3.31
147.70	128.56	0.90	4.89	11.50	3.57
191.64	160.06	1.10	10.39	17.01	3.91
195.04	167.59	1.10	8.76	26.74	5.98
37.38	36.25	0.07	-0.95	1.00	0.31
934.61	786.85	4.26	62.32	48.94	14.81
423.18	342.49	2.54	22.78	24.57	9.86
43.98	38.57	0.31	2.07	2.80	0.87
762.45	648.71	4.09	41.21	65.04	14.95
1485.62	1252.86	8.95	65.83	89.40	40.15
625.93	610.76	2.35	-0.63	15.78	17.44
568.08	528.06	2.52	15.71	14.88	16.08
1190.39	1056.59	4.45	59.63	71.93	21.65
769.93	639.86	4.55	41.33	82.13	16.35
482.57	372.49	3.11	39.79	57.91	13.30
786.09	672.17	11.00	32.10	76.59	17.95
80.59	65.50	0.52	4.43	9.50	1.68
2393.83	2064.20	10.11	132.42	139.61	40.17
721.70	623.00	3.51	-18.08	97.22	12.67
119.80	93.18	0.70	10.43	11.82	3.36
31.58	27.52	0.17	1.68	2.36	1.30
282.16	269.37	2.41	3.97	6.86	16.20
6.65	5.30	0.04	0.90	0.64	0.11
17.00	11.85	0.10	3.17	0.85	0.91
26.62	23.48	0.10	0.92	1.16	0.36
7.16	4.08	0.07	1.64	0.68	0.21

13—9 私营工业企业主要经济效益指标（2022年）
Main Indicators on Economic Benefit of Private Industrial Enterprises (2022)

项　目	Item
总　　计	**Total**
总计中：	**Of the Total:**
私营独资	Private Sole-source Investment Enterprise
私营合伙	Private Partnership Enterprise
私营有限责任公司	Private Companies with Limited Liabilities
私营股份有限公司	Private Share-holding Companies with Limited Liabilities
总计中：	**Of the Total:**
轻工业	Light Industry
重工业	Heavy Industry
总计中：	**Of the Total:**
大型企业	Large-sized Enterprises
中型企业	Medium-sized Enterprises
小型企业	Small Enterprises
按行业分	**Grouped by Sector**
煤炭开采和洗选业	Mining and Washing of Coal
黑色金属矿采选业	Mining and Processing of Ferrous Metal Ores
有色金属矿采选业	Mining and Processing of Non-Ferrous Metal Ores
非金属矿采选业	Mining and Processing of Nonmetal Ores
开采专业及辅助性活动	Professional and Support Activities for Mining
农副食品加工业	Processing of Food from Agriculture Products
食品制造业	Manufacture of Foods
酒、饮料和精制茶制造业	Manufacture of Wine, Beverages and Refined Tea
纺织业	Manufacture of Textile
纺织服装、服饰业	Manufacture of Textile Wearing Apparel and Clothing
皮革毛皮羽毛及其制品和制鞋业	Manufacture of Leather, Furs, Feather and Related Products
木材加工及木竹藤棕草制品业	Processing of Timber, Manufacture of Wood, Bamboo, Rattan, Palm and Straw Products
家具制造业	Manufacture of Furniture
造纸及纸制品业	Manufacture of Paper and Paper Products
印刷和记录媒介复制业	Printing, Reproduction of Recording Media
文教工美体育和娱乐用品制造业	Manufacture of Culture, Education, Art, Sports and Entertainment Supplies
石油、煤炭及其他燃料加工业	Processing of Petroleum, Coal and other Fuels
化学原料和化学制品制造业	Manufacture of Raw Chemical Materials and Chemical Products
医药制造业	Manufacture of Medicines
化学纤维制造业	Manufacture of Chemical Fibers
橡胶和塑料制品业	Manufacture of Rubber and Plastics
非金属矿物制品业	Manufacture of Non-metallic Mineral Products
黑色金属冶炼和压延加工业	Smelting and Pressing of Ferrous Metals
有色金属冶炼和压延加工业	Smelting and Pressing of Non-ferrous Metals
金属制品业	Manufacture of Metal Products
通用设备制造业	Manufacture of General Purpose Machinery
专用设备制造业	Manufacture of Special Purpose Machinery
汽车制造业	Manufacture of Automobile
铁路船舶航空航天和其他运输设备制造业	Manufacture of Railroads, Ships, Aerospace and Other Transportation Equipments
电气机械和器材制造业	Manufacture of Electrical Machinery and Equipment
计算机通信和其他电子设备制造业	Manufacture of Computers, Communication and Other Electronic Equipments
仪器仪表制造业	Manufacture of Measuring Instruments and Machinery
其他制造业	Manufacture of Others
废弃资源综合利用业	Industry of Comprehensive Utilization of Waste Resources
金属制品、机械和设备修理业	Industry of Metal Products, Machinery and Equipment Repair
电力、热力生产和供应业	Production and Supply of Electric Power and Heat Power
燃气生产和供应业	Production and Supply of Gas
水的生产和供应业	Production and Supply of Water

总资产贡献率 (%) Ratio of Total Assets to Industrial Output Value (%)	资产负债率 (%) Assets-liability Ratio (%)	流动资产周转次数 (次/年) Number of Times of Annual of Turnover Circulating Funds (times/year)	工业成本费用利润率 (%) Ratio of Profits to Industrial Cost (%)
7.84	**58.54**	**1.64**	**4.69**
10.23	60.83	1.87	5.66
9.14	63.66	1.60	4.72
7.59	60.33	1.71	4.17
9.36	46.30	1.17	9.91
8.30	57.03	1.78	4.96
7.63	59.21	1.58	4.56
3.50	60.52	1.60	2.07
10.49	53.90	1.61	7.53
8.31	59.24	1.66	4.56
-8.25	83.42	5.37	-2.60
13.95	48.93	1.69	20.20
-0.55	84.30	0.40	-4.14
14.56	58.62	1.23	17.39
10.89	55.64	0.78	11.06
7.69	47.73	2.62	3.90
6.41	54.07	1.83	3.86
13.73	56.69	1.50	10.99
6.00	62.45	1.72	3.20
9.87	61.65	2.00	3.41
5.26	59.58	1.62	2.07
9.22	53.25	2.00	4.73
10.02	50.72	1.55	7.40
9.06	64.70	2.34	3.42
8.42	52.80	1.60	5.72
8.50	57.25	1.50	4.67
-1.00	79.59	1.16	-2.46
10.59	51.02	1.93	7.08
7.11	56.32	1.19	5.68
7.55	50.81	1.66	4.93
9.43	51.47	1.86	5.68
7.08	65.10	1.24	4.65
7.75	55.95	4.09	-0.10
14.35	63.39	3.51	2.82
9.86	62.89	1.87	5.24
7.70	54.54	1.34	5.60
9.22	50.37	1.07	8.91
8.29	62.76	1.67	4.27
8.61	52.54	1.72	5.77
8.51	65.61	1.58	5.85
0.57	55.66	1.11	-2.44
10.25	47.08	1.08	9.34
12.28	46.48	1.61	5.50
18.35	56.66	3.46	1.40
14.42	42.22	1.26	15.67
5.00	74.29	0.32	22.17
5.06	70.04	2.71	3.59
10.57	46.82	0.95	29.53

13—10 大中型工业企业主要经济指标（2022年）
Main Indicators of Large and Medium-sized Industrial Enterprises (2022)

项　目	Item	企业单位数（个）Number of Enterprises (unit)	资产合计 Total Assets
总　计	**Total**	**1525**	**36544.98**
总计中:	**Of the Total:**		
内资企业	Domestic Funded Enterprise	1313	32192.26
国有企业	State-owned Enterprise	37	1299.01
集体企业	Collective-owned Enterprise	1	1.80
股份合作企业	Share Holding Cooperative Enterprises		
有限责任公司	Limited Liability Corporations	524	12823.09
股份有限公司	Share-holding Corporations Ltd.	172	12834.97
私营企业	Private Enterprises	579	5233.39
港澳台商投资企业	Enterprises Funded by Entrepreneurs from Hong Kong, Macao and Taiwan	91	1997.44
外商投资企业	Foreign Funded Enterprises	121	2355.28
总计中:	**Of the Total:**		
轻工业	Light Industry	531	6966.58
重工业	Heavy Industry	994	29578.40
总计中:	**Of the Total:**		
大型企业	Large-sized Enterprises	279	25135.73
中型企业	Medium-sized Enterprises	1246	11409.25
按行业分	**Grouped by Sector**		
煤炭开采和洗选业	Mining and Washing of Coal	13	2578.33
黑色金属矿采选业	Mining and Processing of Ferrous Metal Ores	14	314.80
有色金属矿采选业	Mining and Processing of Non-Ferrous Metal Ores	4	31.78
非金属矿采选业	Mining and Processing of Nonmetal Ores	3	46.93
开采专业及辅助性活动	Professional and Support Activities for Mining		
农副食品加工业	Processing of Food from Agriculture Products	49	423.65
食品制造业	Manufacture of Foods	30	171.22
酒、饮料和精制茶制造业	Manufacture of Wine, Beverages and Refined Tea	26	680.44
烟草制品业	Manufacture of Tobacco	3	351.91
纺织业	Manufacture of Textile	55	359.91
纺织服装、服饰业	Manufacture of Textile Wearing Apparel and Clothing	54	94.91
皮革毛皮羽毛及其制品和制鞋业	Manufacture of Leather, Furs, Feather and Related Products	20	81.93
木材加工及木竹藤棕草制品业	Processing of Timber, Manufacture of Wood, Bamboo, Rattan, Palm and Straw Products	4	3.42
家具制造业	Manufacture of Furniture	14	126.52
造纸及纸制品业	Manufacture of Paper and Paper Products	11	454.37
印刷和记录媒介复制业	Printing, Reproduction of Recording Media	19	122.75
文教工美体育和娱乐用品制造业	Manufacture of Culture, Education, Art, Sports and Entertainment Supplies	19	23.86
石油、煤炭及其他燃料加工业	Processing of Petroleum, Coal and other Fuels	4	315.97
化学原料和化学制品制造业	Manufacture of Raw Chemical Materials and Chemical Products	64	2057.01
医药制造业	Manufacture of Medicines	58	551.61
化学纤维制造业	Manufacture of Chemical Fibers	5	101.30
橡胶和塑料制品业	Manufacture of Rubber and Plastics	59	785.26
非金属矿物制品业	Manufacture of Non-metallic Mineral Products	73	3260.78
黑色金属冶炼和压延加工业	Smelting and Pressing of Ferrous Metals	19	1695.52
有色金属冶炼和压延加工业	Smelting and Pressing of Non-ferrous Metals	34	928.57
金属制品业	Manufacture of Metal Products	74	786.17
通用设备制造业	Manufacture of General Purpose Machinery	110	1289.18
专用设备制造业	Manufacture of Special Purpose Machinery	69	762.61
汽车制造业	Manufacture of Automobile	159	3394.71
铁路船舶航空航天和其他运输设备制造业	Manufacture of Railroads, Ships, Aerospace and Other Transportation Equipments	15	241.41
电气机械和器材制造业	Manufacture of Electrical Machinery and Equipment	195	4968.43
计算机通信和其他电子设备制造业	Manufacture of Computers, Communication and Other Electronic Equipments	170	5930.61
仪器仪表制造业	Manufacture of Measuring Instruments and Machinery	15	201.27
其他制造业	Manufacture of Others	2	35.22
废弃资源综合利用业	Industry of Comprehensive Utilization of Waste Resources	7	123.08
金属制品、机械和设备修理业	Industry of Metal Products, Machinery and Equipment Repair	5	175.19
电力、热力生产和供应业	Production and Supply of Electric Power and Heat Power	28	2604.54
燃气生产和供应业	Production and Supply of Gas	9	234.65
水的生产和供应业	Production and Supply of Water	12	229.36

单位：亿元（100 million yuan）

流动资产合计 Circulating Funds	#存货 Stock	#产成品 Finished Product	固定资产原价 Original Value of Fixed Assets	固定资产累计折旧 Accumulated Depreciation of Fixed Assets	负债合计 Total Liabilities	流动负债 Liquid Liabilities
18100.48	**3254.65**	**1115.82**	**17922.77**	**8066.47**	**19893.40**	**15599.18**
15402.11	2811.89	978.20	15932.97	7128.43	17408.26	13406.41
814.66	295.83	24.64	701.11	387.78	568.84	485.65
1.52	1.13	0.02	1.03	0.85	0.45	0.45
5737.85	1091.73	427.50	6563.54	2777.93	7690.58	5813.84
6000.46	719.44	230.05	6366.30	3193.24	6152.71	4885.30
2847.62	703.75	295.99	2301.00	768.63	2995.68	2221.18
1238.18	177.43	41.93	805.95	369.14	1272.29	1132.24
1460.20	265.34	95.70	1183.85	568.90	1212.85	1060.53
4252.13	986.79	334.76	2224.57	941.85	3717.21	3323.94
13848.36	2267.86	781.07	15698.19	7124.62	16176.18	12275.24
11970.23	1999.68	587.71	12766.74	5873.50	13995.97	10771.08
6130.25	1254.98	528.11	5156.03	2192.97	5897.43	4828.10
554.24	40.93	31.96	1422.06	614.27	1651.90	1021.72
94.33	7.77	5.07	238.47	100.59	118.62	98.70
1.52	0.78	0.42	30.47	9.22	23.22	17.14
16.39	1.09	0.38	23.80	12.02	15.64	9.73
256.94	69.45	35.21	148.52	44.88	225.46	193.37
80.24	20.36	6.99	118.89	49.20	90.56	71.45
457.87	176.93	28.57	210.41	85.45	234.68	225.82
254.68	178.86	10.15	152.42	89.73	108.84	107.54
161.11	42.62	25.50	152.16	67.50	152.27	125.64
62.15	15.14	7.54	41.88	20.54	58.62	55.00
52.37	6.68	3.08	24.13	10.62	33.61	27.93
2.79	1.55	0.42	0.62	0.42	2.92	2.87
72.96	16.19	2.78	37.11	10.23	77.27	73.44
161.65	23.69	11.89	132.27	55.18	282.31	208.74
72.12	13.49	5.09	49.07	22.24	45.58	43.12
18.56	7.66	2.33	7.33	3.30	9.45	8.99
71.24	26.32	5.74	331.41	180.43	189.24	163.45
880.48	133.33	63.12	1101.40	459.68	1003.22	680.97
289.96	63.93	23.43	211.45	89.53	222.87	191.37
61.55	4.64	2.10	18.15	8.31	54.43	49.22
399.65	82.02	40.40	369.90	183.48	335.59	297.21
1735.68	117.43	59.62	940.23	392.87	937.58	779.10
715.26	187.95	45.88	1580.83	830.35	1032.40	859.41
555.60	209.48	44.86	398.51	184.40	510.34	399.81
475.39	108.29	34.66	243.27	80.84	442.38	351.47
822.00	180.77	53.33	389.67	175.96	631.98	528.57
523.75	117.50	44.58	179.30	82.32	367.00	319.40
1977.26	257.94	120.78	990.06	526.36	2389.89	2017.07
161.35	32.26	9.64	66.88	23.45	141.55	118.60
3403.08	579.47	257.00	1043.51	327.17	3363.12	3004.99
2780.11	438.50	117.72	2800.40	1028.83	3171.32	2132.62
144.33	16.52	5.00	55.20	27.40	73.86	69.40
21.72	3.87	2.94	2.08	1.01	19.66	17.58
84.81	6.64	1.14	15.58	4.47	27.96	23.43
140.13	28.89	2.03	38.55	19.17	58.21	38.77
362.77	25.30	1.00	4044.04	2117.47	1575.72	1122.13
103.02	5.57	2.39	117.65	46.47	119.52	77.94
70.42	4.82	1.06	190.07	80.38	92.95	64.74

13—10 续表 continued

项　目	Item	所有者权益 Owners' Equity	#实收资本 Capital Hold
总　计	**Total**	**16650.49**	**6704.99**
总计中:	**Of the Total:**		
内资企业	Domestic Funded Enterprise	14782.91	5822.13
国有企业	State-owned Enterprise	730.17	256.31
集体企业	Collective-owned Enterprise	1.35	0.51
股份合作企业	Share Holding Cooperative Enterprises		
有限责任公司	Limited Liability Corporations	5132.51	3060.07
股份有限公司	Share-holding Corporations Ltd.	6682.26	1617.50
私营企业	Private Enterprises	2236.62	887.73
港澳台商投资企业	Enterprises Funded by Entrepreneurs from Hong Kong, Macao and Taiwan	725.16	369.37
外商投资企业	Foreign Funded Enterprises	1142.43	513.49
总计中:	**Of the Total:**		
轻工业	Light Industry	3249.36	986.31
重工业	Heavy Industry	13401.13	5718.67
总计中:	**Of the Total:**		
大型企业	Large-sized Enterprises	11139.76	4174.51
中型企业	Medium-sized Enterprises	5510.73	2530.47
按行业分	**Grouped by Sector**		
煤炭开采和洗选业	Mining and Washing of Coal	926.43	331.53
黑色金属矿采选业	Mining and Processing of Ferrous Metal Ores	196.18	98.97
有色金属矿采选业	Mining and Processing of Non-Ferrous Metal Ores	8.55	8.96
非金属矿采选业	Mining and Processing of Nonmetal Ores	31.30	11.14
开采专业及辅助性活动	Professional and Support Activities for Mining		
农副食品加工业	Processing of Food from Agriculture Products	198.19	59.80
食品制造业	Manufacture of Foods	80.66	48.70
酒、饮料和精制茶制造业	Manufacture of Wine, Beverages and Refined Tea	445.76	78.10
烟草制品业	Manufacture of Tobacco	243.07	40.65
纺织业	Manufacture of Textile	207.65	55.51
纺织服装、服饰业	Manufacture of Textile Wearing Apparel and Clothing	36.29	16.54
皮革毛皮羽毛及其制品和制鞋业	Manufacture of Leather, Furs, Feather and Related Products	48.32	14.78
木材加工及木竹藤棕草制品业	Processing of Timber, Manufacture of Wood, Bamboo, Rattan, Palm and Straw Products	0.50	0.20
家具制造业	Manufacture of Furniture	49.25	13.39
造纸及纸制品业	Manufacture of Paper and Paper Products	172.06	54.86
印刷和记录媒介复制业	Printing, Reproduction of Recording Media	77.17	25.43
文教工美体育和娱乐用品制造业	Manufacture of Culture, Education, Art, Sports and Entertainment Supplies	14.41	5.52
石油、煤炭及其他燃料加工业	Processing of Petroleum, Coal and other Fuels	126.73	88.56
化学原料和化学制品制造业	Manufacture of Raw Chemical Materials and Chemical Products	1053.78	364.69
医药制造业	Manufacture of Medicines	328.75	118.48
化学纤维制造业	Manufacture of Chemical Fibers	46.87	22.04
橡胶和塑料制品业	Manufacture of Rubber and Plastics	449.67	167.05
非金属矿物制品业	Manufacture of Non-metallic Mineral Products	2323.20	380.78
黑色金属冶炼和压延加工业	Smelting and Pressing of Ferrous Metals	663.12	189.21
有色金属冶炼和压延加工业	Smelting and Pressing of Non-ferrous Metals	418.23	180.47
金属制品业	Manufacture of Metal Products	343.79	128.72
通用设备制造业	Manufacture of General Purpose Machinery	656.11	247.79
专用设备制造业	Manufacture of Special Purpose Machinery	395.61	141.52
汽车制造业	Manufacture of Automobile	1004.83	483.22
铁路船舶航空航天和其他运输设备制造业	Manufacture of Railroads, Ships, Aerospace and Other Transportation Equipments	99.86	62.94
电气机械和器材制造业	Manufacture of Electrical Machinery and Equipment	1605.30	562.87
计算机通信和其他电子设备制造业	Manufacture of Computers, Communication and Other Electronic Equipments	2759.29	1660.91
仪器仪表制造业	Manufacture of Measuring Instruments and Machinery	127.41	30.00
其他制造业	Manufacture of Others	15.56	7.27
废弃资源综合利用业	Industry of Comprehensive Utilization of Waste Resources	95.12	45.50
金属制品、机械和设备修理业	Industry of Metal Products, Machinery and Equipment Repair	116.98	10.51
电力、热力生产和供应业	Production and Supply of Electric Power and Heat Power	1028.82	886.68
燃气生产和供应业	Production and Supply of Gas	115.12	20.85
水的生产和供应业	Production and Supply of Water	136.40	36.55

单位：亿元（100 million yuan）

营业收入 Business Revenue	营业成本 Business Cost	税金及附加 Taxes and Surcharges	利润总额 Total Profits	本年应付职工薪酬 Wages Payable in This Year	本年应交增值税 Value Added Tax Payable
29057.68	**25008.55**	**591.29**	**1557.05**	**2036.09**	**569.87**
24145.08	20647.05	571.18	1332.78	1737.75	508.48
1354.96	930.52	293.39	39.16	113.45	61.30
1.88	1.02	0.05	0.05	0.30	0.00
10434.24	9164.48	144.68	471.88	688.67	203.11
7771.24	6574.58	100.44	602.85	572.28	154.27
4582.76	3976.45	32.63	218.84	363.05	89.80
2563.45	2373.40	8.92	72.73	121.98	22.43
2349.15	1988.10	11.20	151.54	176.36	38.96
6037.18	4586.98	369.85	535.90	498.26	155.32
23020.50	20421.57	221.44	1021.15	1537.83	414.55
19859.89	17075.29	533.68	1026.53	1330.57	379.19
9197.79	7933.26	57.61	530.51	705.53	190.68
1125.29	800.10	24.79	176.85	241.03	76.20
165.64	90.60	5.11	43.50	20.23	11.33
15.85	11.13	0.61	0.25	2.39	0.84
26.11	12.77	1.05	8.34	5.20	1.81
589.73	533.40	1.63	31.87	32.48	5.97
282.69	240.44	1.35	18.85	18.93	5.11
434.00	198.93	49.05	102.76	59.68	28.98
506.15	136.91	289.35	25.45	47.35	46.43
234.45	207.07	1.48	12.42	25.90	4.47
123.43	105.71	0.84	3.67	30.04	4.90
93.71	75.94	0.51	11.93	10.03	2.54
3.24	2.69	0.01	0.19	0.56	0.06
115.71	90.27	0.69	7.73	11.74	3.29
177.13	158.09	0.94	31.39	15.75	5.11
93.05	73.56	0.62	10.28	9.42	2.21
22.61	18.00	0.15	1.85	5.95	0.69
696.21	596.68	77.43	7.23	15.74	12.00
1402.94	1151.90	8.52	149.45	70.63	20.18
293.04	175.76	2.53	42.18	35.58	9.12
36.62	33.32	0.19	1.07	2.20	0.05
611.22	501.89	3.64	51.59	66.16	10.64
946.69	747.01	7.41	157.23	65.50	22.43
2197.97	2097.52	9.09	-1.50	81.61	29.30
1683.73	1575.71	5.75	54.90	31.68	29.85
809.73	745.79	2.92	31.76	48.86	9.90
1016.89	864.20	5.20	77.98	94.39	21.45
397.25	307.12	2.63	41.19	52.62	11.09
2893.54	2549.68	38.29	85.83	189.16	47.78
121.01	95.63	0.76	9.90	16.95	2.81
4992.92	4377.65	22.54	269.75	241.38	43.66
3850.78	3521.11	11.67	40.72	285.54	44.60
143.12	108.20	0.75	14.23	15.83	3.16
7.11	4.28	0.07	0.89	1.28	0.02
304.51	297.03	1.12	3.09	3.37	5.90
53.68	40.90	0.27	4.98	17.63	0.51
2426.89	2320.06	11.30	18.17	144.06	43.38
113.22	102.05	0.36	5.13	7.91	0.73
48.50	38.51	0.62	3.93	10.68	1.32

13—11 大中型工业企业主要经济效益指标（2022年）
Main Indicators on Economic Benefit of Large and Medium-sized Industrial Enterprises (2022)

项　目	Item
总　　计	**Total**
总计中:	**Of the Total:**
内资企业	Domestic Funded Enterprise
国有企业	State-owned Enterprise
集体企业	Collective-owned Enterprise
股份合作企业	Share Holding Cooperative Enterprises
有限责任公司	Limited Liability Corporations
股份有限公司	Share-holding Corporations Ltd.
私营企业	Private Enterprises
港澳台商投资企业	Enterprises Funded by Entrepreneurs from Hong Kong, Macao and Taiwan
外商投资企业	Foreign Funded Enterprises
总计中:	**Of the Total:**
轻工业	Light Industry
重工业	Heavy Industry
总计中:	**Of the Total:**
大型企业	Large-sized Enterprises
中型企业	Medium-sized Enterprises
按行业分	**Grouped by Sector**
煤炭开采和洗选业	Mining and Washing of Coal
黑色金属矿采选业	Mining and Processing of Ferrous Metal Ores
有色金属矿采选业	Mining and Processing of Non-Ferrous Metal Ores
非金属矿采选业	Mining and Processing of Nonmetal Ores
开采专业及辅助性活动	Professional and Support Activities for Mining
农副食品加工业	Processing of Food from Agriculture Products
食品制造业	Manufacture of Foods
酒、饮料和精制茶制造业	Manufacture of Wine, Beverages and Refined Tea
烟草制品业	Manufacture of Tobacco
纺织业	Manufacture of Textile
纺织服装、服饰业	Manufacture of Textile Wearing Apparel and Clothing
皮革毛皮羽毛及其制品和制鞋业	Manufacture of Leather, Furs, Feather and Related Products
木材加工及木竹藤棕草制品业	Processing of Timber, Manufacture of Wood, Bamboo, Rattan, Palm and Straw Products
家具制造业	Manufacture of Furniture
造纸及纸制品业	Manufacture of Paper and Paper Products
印刷和记录媒介复制业	Printing, Reproduction of Recording Media
文教工美体育和娱乐用品制造业	Manufacture of Culture, Education, Art, Sports and Entertainment Supplies
石油、煤炭及其他燃料加工业	Processing of Petroleum, Coal and other Fuels
化学原料和化学制品制造业	Manufacture of Raw Chemical Materials and Chemical Products
医药制造业	Manufacture of Medicines
化学纤维制造业	Manufacture of Chemical Fibers
橡胶和塑料制品业	Manufacture of Rubber and Plastics
非金属矿物制品业	Manufacture of Non-metallic Mineral Products
黑色金属冶炼和压延加工业	Smelting and Pressing of Ferrous Metals
有色金属冶炼和压延加工业	Smelting and Pressing of Non-ferrous Metals
金属制品业	Manufacture of Metal Products
通用设备制造业	Manufacture of General Purpose Machinery
专用设备制造业	Manufacture of Special Purpose Machinery
汽车制造业	Manufacture of Automobile
铁路船舶航空航天和其他运输设备制造业	Manufacture of Railroads, Ships, Aerospace and Other Transportation Equipments
电气机械和器材制造业	Manufacture of Electrical Machinery and Equipment
计算机通信和其他电子设备制造业	Manufacture of Computers, Communication and Other Electronic Equipments
仪器仪表制造业	Manufacture of Measuring Instruments and Machinery
其他制造业	Manufacture of Others
废弃资源综合利用业	Industry of Comprehensive Utilization of Waste Resources
金属制品、机械和设备修理业	Industry of Metal Products, Machinery and Equipment Repair
电力、热力生产和供应业	Production and Supply of Electric Power and Heat Power
燃气生产和供应业	Production and Supply of Gas
水的生产和供应业	Production and Supply of Water

总资产贡献率 (%) Ratio of Total Assets to Industrial Output Value (%)	资产负债率 (%) Assets-liability Ratio (%)	流动资产周转次数 (次/年) Number of Times of Annual of Turnover Circulating Funds (times/year)	工业成本费用利润率 (%) Ratio of Profits to Industrial Cost (%)
8.00	**54.44**	**1.61**	**5.74**
8.08	54.08	1.57	5.94
30.65	43.79	1.66	3.83
5.35	25.07	1.24	2.79
7.07	59.97	1.82	4.78
7.27	47.94	1.30	8.39
6.96	57.24	1.61	5.01
5.41	63.70	2.07	2.91
9.02	51.49	1.61	6.90
15.56	53.36	1.42	10.30
6.22	54.69	1.66	4.66
8.32	55.68	1.66	5.57
7.28	51.69	1.50	6.09
11.98	64.07	2.03	18.77
19.50	37.68	1.76	37.68
7.15	73.08	10.41	1.90
24.53	33.32	1.59	49.46
10.09	53.22	2.30	5.64
15.29	52.89	3.52	7.11
26.25	34.49	0.95	35.85
103.16	30.93	1.99	13.73
5.58	42.31	1.46	5.50
10.32	61.77	1.99	3.06
18.69	41.02	1.79	14.72
8.27	85.41	1.16	6.10
9.49	61.07	1.59	7.21
8.47	62.13	1.10	17.72
11.32	37.13	1.29	12.31
11.59	39.59	1.22	8.90
30.94	59.89	9.77	1.18
9.46	48.77	1.59	11.70
10.09	40.40	1.01	16.72
2.97	53.73	0.60	3.00
8.71	42.74	1.53	9.17
6.72	28.75	0.55	19.64
2.72	60.89	3.07	-0.07
10.32	54.96	3.03	3.38
6.08	56.27	1.70	4.04
8.43	49.02	1.24	8.16
7.50	48.12	0.76	11.39
5.40	70.40	1.46	3.10
5.37	58.63	0.75	8.84
7.07	67.69	1.47	5.73
2.05	53.47	1.39	1.06
8.83	36.70	0.99	10.82
3.53	55.81	0.33	13.00
8.84	22.72	3.59	1.02
2.55	33.23	0.38	9.97
4.03	60.50	6.69	0.76
2.69	50.94	1.10	4.65
2.65	40.53	0.69	8.41

13—12 各市全部规模以上工业企业主要经济指标（2022年）
Main Indicators Above Designated Size Industrial Enterprises by Region (2022)

单位：亿元（100 million yuan）

地　区	Region	企　业 单位数 （个） Number of Enterprises (unit)	资产合计 Total Assets	流动资产合计 Circulating Funds	固定资产原价 Original Value of Fixed Assets	负债合计 Total Liabilities	#流动负债 Liquid Liabilities
总　计	**Total**	**21484**	**56457.80**	**29619.67**	**25786.30**	**31899.84**	**25119.55**
合肥市	Hefei	2544	15064.24	8562.39	5974.16	8614.69	6810.04
淮北市	Huaibei	644	2320.97	940.71	1396.44	1347.91	1026.76
亳州市	Bozhou	735	1680.69	903.04	745.17	947.58	742.89
宿州市	Suzhou	1174	1207.68	568.74	682.36	697.77	508.79
蚌埠市	Bengbu	931	2169.27	1148.96	865.64	1197.71	958.39
阜阳市	Fuyang	1541	2038.23	978.75	1195.37	1209.63	898.48
淮南市	Huainan	848	2972.28	773.44	1850.91	1921.39	1082.50
滁州市	Chuzhou	2368	4962.92	2659.66	2263.71	2905.75	2355.19
六安市	Luan	1325	2358.45	1214.81	1141.75	1361.17	1021.60
马鞍山市	Maanshan	1401	3760.55	1851.37	2373.57	2164.50	1830.58
芜湖市	Wuhu	2264	8885.41	5345.63	2771.23	4543.37	3924.63
宣城市	Xuancheng	2097	2815.56	1502.39	1226.50	1557.64	1283.35
铜陵市	Tongling	624	1906.61	1046.84	1051.35	1062.31	849.92
池州市	Chizhou	703	1352.35	648.09	760.93	759.20	542.06
安庆市	Anqing	1730	2396.84	1136.20	1237.73	1275.74	1002.83
黄山市	Huangshan	555	565.75	338.67	249.48	333.47	281.56

地　区	Region	所有者权益 Owners' Equity	#实收资本 Total Capital Hold	营业收入 Business Revenue	营业成本 Business Cost	税金及附加 Taxes and Surcharges	利润总额 Total Profits	本年应交增值税 Value Added Tax Payable
总　计	**Total**	**24523.08**	**11423.31**	**46889.51**	**40433.10**	**696.28**	**2386.60**	**969.48**
合肥市	Hefei	6444.15	3034.07	11459.47	9922.20	121.55	447.79	157.73
淮北市	Huaibei	973.07	389.55	1553.92	1241.96	23.47	158.97	60.73
亳州市	Bozhou	732.48	262.88	1313.98	1054.62	32.90	95.08	33.12
宿州市	Suzhou	506.71	245.35	1252.81	1122.59	7.02	67.35	30.19
蚌埠市	Bengbu	971.56	415.06	1486.30	1205.38	84.34	81.81	33.94
阜阳市	Fuyang	828.41	386.03	1803.88	1559.91	47.14	79.13	54.70
淮南市	Huainan	1048.48	690.81	1672.13	1422.75	18.60	83.77	55.70
滁州市	Chuzhou	2056.68	1032.38	4708.98	4039.37	57.91	307.81	91.93
六安市	Luan	991.54	787.51	1773.95	1514.11	21.29	97.28	38.63
马鞍山市	Maanshan	1595.51	955.11	3909.48	3553.67	21.76	112.55	79.05
芜湖市	Wuhu	4332.30	1302.94	6212.03	5246.90	126.91	406.57	143.65
宣城市	Xuancheng	1256.34	534.33	2522.78	2172.88	17.73	135.21	56.96
铜陵市	Tongling	844.30	455.74	2936.41	2702.30	9.48	105.17	35.49
池州市	Chizhou	591.22	283.97	1466.16	1293.05	11.56	71.94	35.59
安庆市	Anqing	1119.19	541.88	2263.55	1911.26	91.75	114.82	51.21
黄山市	Huangshan	231.16	105.68	553.68	470.14	2.88	21.34	10.86

13—13 各市国有控股工业企业主要经济指标（2022年）
Main Indicators of State-owned and State Holding Majority Shares Industrial Enterprises by Region (2022)

单位：亿元（100 million yuan）

地区	Region	企业单位数（个）Number of Enterprises (unit)	资产合计 Total Assets	流动资产合计 Circulating Funds	固定资产原价 Original Value of Fixed Assets	负债合计 Total Liabilities	#流动负债 Liquid Liabilities
总计	**Total**	**1110**	**20000.37**	**7832.40**	**13074.29**	**10410.52**	**7145.51**
合肥市	Hefei	217	4794.33	1976.92	3190.43	2390.70	1720.62
淮北市	Huaibei	61	1449.62	486.40	1052.92	884.92	644.63
亳州市	Bozhou	45	751.29	299.43	439.77	384.61	256.13
宿州市	Suzhou	52	298.39	71.45	305.54	197.73	118.50
蚌埠市	Bengbu	64	735.88	357.83	441.19	388.51	295.85
阜阳市	Fuyang	38	617.29	140.60	538.91	348.04	206.45
淮南市	Huainan	74	2338.35	414.43	1505.66	1561.10	789.91
滁州市	Chuzhou	69	830.24	304.38	596.96	438.81	273.71
六安市	Luan	41	481.26	191.46	361.26	271.57	143.44
马鞍山市	Maanshan	84	1840.84	789.65	1616.83	1050.61	892.91
芜湖市	Wuhu	95	3195.90	1856.76	1002.11	1016.80	849.43
宣城市	Xuancheng	71	520.05	158.32	414.76	319.50	157.86
铜陵市	Tongling	58	828.97	394.75	648.98	423.70	320.48
池州市	Chizhou	45	439.93	118.05	309.63	236.39	116.79
安庆市	Anqing	82	819.60	252.53	606.54	456.73	341.36
黄山市	Huangshan	14	58.42	19.43	42.83	40.78	17.43

地区	Region	所有者权益 Owners' Equity	#实收资本 Total Capital Hold	营业收入 Business Revenue	营业成本 Business Cost	税金及附加 Taxes and Surcharges	利润总额 Total Profits	本年应交增值税 Value Added Tax Payable
总计	**Total**	**9588.01**	**4323.30**	**13576.57**	**11599.50**	**488.65**	**656.62**	**369.09**
合肥市	Hefei	2403.62	1334.88	2938.51	2561.02	85.48	86.11	55.13
淮北市	Huaibei	564.70	215.52	816.83	615.53	11.70	111.31	43.51
亳州市	Bozhou	366.68	117.52	375.97	225.74	28.05	59.18	19.14
宿州市	Suzhou	99.87	75.00	225.78	202.83	1.68	12.34	10.46
蚌埠市	Bengbu	347.37	163.80	543.06	400.83	79.86	26.20	18.07
阜阳市	Fuyang	269.25	125.51	356.51	270.38	35.36	30.95	15.25
淮南市	Huainan	777.24	564.48	1096.84	924.82	16.36	53.01	45.10
滁州市	Chuzhou	391.43	190.47	554.71	450.72	39.03	28.14	15.88
六安市	Luan	208.64	102.47	217.07	174.94	3.26	25.04	7.96
马鞍山市	Maanshan	790.23	367.38	2307.74	2165.35	13.72	24.34	51.61
芜湖市	Wuhu	2179.10	415.34	1272.45	1066.14	83.97	71.12	39.04
宣城市	Xuancheng	200.56	104.55	328.32	284.51	2.73	19.95	11.21
铜陵市	Tongling	405.27	222.83	1360.29	1256.73	4.60	53.88	16.65
池州市	Chizhou	203.54	106.18	218.00	178.60	3.54	22.76	4.82
安庆市	Anqing	362.87	207.35	928.01	789.10	79.10	30.14	14.72
黄山市	Huangshan	17.64	10.04	36.49	32.26	0.22	2.13	0.52

13—14 各市外商投资和港澳台商投资工业企业主要经济指标（2022年）

Main Indicators on Economic Benefit of Industrial Enterprises with Hong Kong, Macao, Taiwan and Foreign Funds by Region (2022)

单位：亿元（100 million yuan）

地区	Region	企业单位数(个) Number of Enterprises (unit)	资产合计 Total Assets	流动资产合计 Circulating Funds	固定资产原价 Original Value of Fixed Assets	负债合计 Total Liabilities	#流动负债 Liquid Liabilities
总计	**Total**	**917**	**5979.91**	**3542.71**	**2829.72**	**3384.65**	**2872.56**
合肥市	Hefei	186	2257.95	1639.17	827.07	1469.15	1347.40
淮北市	Huaibei	25	85.53	31.51	73.84	44.06	33.27
亳州市	Bozhou	8	29.19	14.49	17.15	15.97	13.91
宿州市	Suzhou	33	88.28	42.56	52.39	47.97	37.49
蚌埠市	Bengbu	43	344.38	120.36	111.50	130.98	75.70
阜阳市	Fuyang	20	133.06	47.41	87.06	88.27	47.14
淮南市	Huainan	24	158.81	54.29	158.49	85.20	60.87
滁州市	Chuzhou	118	655.68	271.22	451.29	321.59	264.18
六安市	Luan	31	84.53	38.61	56.38	42.83	35.27
马鞍山市	Maanshan	90	301.72	178.48	158.47	177.90	149.38
芜湖市	Wuhu	149	1105.57	681.26	459.38	562.24	495.55
宣城市	Xuancheng	61	119.42	69.67	60.29	54.40	44.73
铜陵市	Tongling	28	338.28	215.25	145.67	221.99	166.29
池州市	Chizhou	22	45.29	18.73	30.33	25.21	16.64
安庆市	Anqing	61	208.92	107.51	127.02	86.89	75.42
黄山市	Huangshan	18	23.29	12.18	13.40	10.01	9.31

地区	Region	所有者权益 Owners' Equity	#实收资本 Total Capital Hold	营业收入 Business Revenue	营业成本 Business Cost	税金及附加 Taxes and Surcharges	利润总额 Total Profits	本年应交增值税 Value Added Tax Payable
总计	**Total**	**2594.83**	**1374.21**	**6500.59**	**5776.82**	**27.16**	**272.36**	**82.72**
合肥市	Hefei	788.80	386.58	2616.41	2344.40	7.58	79.87	22.47
淮北市	Huaibei	41.47	24.29	73.94	62.50	0.58	4.50	1.25
亳州市	Bozhou	13.22	5.22	16.34	14.00	0.07	1.25	0.45
宿州市	Suzhou	40.31	19.07	95.99	81.87	0.40	10.35	1.80
蚌埠市	Bengbu	213.40	58.93	162.16	131.13	0.81	18.17	2.34
阜阳市	Fuyang	44.80	33.85	51.55	44.83	1.85	-8.97	0.88
淮南市	Huainan	73.61	41.26	101.54	85.20	0.59	11.49	3.43
滁州市	Chuzhou	334.10	239.22	652.21	590.55	2.74	20.64	14.97
六安市	Luan	41.70	25.15	76.01	62.48	1.61	6.07	2.52
马鞍山市	Maanshan	123.82	96.51	295.84	258.21	1.24	13.43	4.99
芜湖市	Wuhu	543.33	295.17	964.98	814.49	5.15	72.46	16.79
宣城市	Xuancheng	65.03	24.10	102.57	85.46	0.63	5.45	1.14
铜陵市	Tongling	116.29	51.82	1062.92	1014.01	1.29	19.79	3.28
池州市	Chizhou	20.09	14.83	45.91	39.01	1.25	2.96	1.01
安庆市	Anqing	121.60	54.92	161.28	130.72	1.25	14.08	4.99
黄山市	Huangshan	13.28	3.29	20.93	17.94	0.12	0.81	0.42

13—15 各市私营工业企业主要经济指标（2022年）
Main Indicators of Private Enterprises by Region (2022)

单位：亿元（100 million yuan）

地 区	Region	企业单位数（个） Number of Enterprises (unit)	资产合计 Total Assets	流动资产合计 Circulating Funds	固定资产原价 Original Value of Fixed Assets	负债合计 Total Liabilities	#流动负债 Liquid Liabilities
总 计	**Total**	**16390**	**14947.69**	**9197.95**	**5735.03**	**8749.99**	**7358.87**
合肥市	Hefei	1664	3650.83	2172.30	1359.95	2202.82	1612.29
淮北市	Huaibei	492	407.42	234.79	147.09	259.34	219.75
亳州市	Bozhou	543	544.18	368.23	166.39	333.78	304.42
宿州市	Suzhou	980	593.65	334.77	235.16	300.71	247.59
蚌埠市	Bengbu	686	571.76	367.46	176.76	359.81	321.97
阜阳市	Fuyang	1313	735.69	470.87	287.40	428.36	350.63
淮南市	Huainan	670	327.05	220.26	120.83	182.30	161.43
滁州市	Chuzhou	1898	1860.46	1148.49	662.13	1124.96	978.58
六安市	Luan	1072	842.90	475.00	364.92	507.52	448.01
马鞍山市	Maanshan	1041	744.53	494.45	283.09	433.49	382.89
芜湖市	Wuhu	1577	1331.66	862.05	541.00	772.53	701.23
宣城市	Xuancheng	1702	1294.03	796.32	523.48	753.45	692.59
铜陵市	Tongling	399	334.85	220.07	114.88	191.90	172.28
池州市	Chizhou	513	534.28	315.27	284.63	291.73	239.53
安庆市	Anqing	1419	856.74	513.37	340.65	415.00	348.34
黄山市	Huangshan	421	317.67	204.24	126.68	192.28	177.34

地 区	Region	所有者权益 Owners' Equity	#实收资本 Total Capital Hold	营业收入 Business Revenue	营业成本 Business Cost	税金及附加 Taxes and Surcharges	利润总额 Total Profits	本年应交增值税 Value Added Tax Payable
总 计	**Total**	**6181.16**	**3310.71**	**15115.65**	**13058.73**	**88.40**	**680.02**	**320.13**
合肥市	Hefei	1445.04	624.46	2913.03	2511.13	18.37	78.13	49.23
淮北市	Huaibei	148.08	89.09	390.44	353.96	1.77	5.54	7.98
亳州市	Bozhou	210.27	83.99	555.08	494.12	2.47	20.82	8.11
宿州市	Suzhou	290.68	107.94	735.42	666.42	3.84	33.40	11.39
蚌埠市	Bengbu	211.95	92.37	511.28	434.81	2.56	28.70	8.60
阜阳市	Fuyang	307.15	158.45	726.19	645.59	4.86	18.63	20.48
淮南市	Huainan	143.05	59.05	357.27	314.32	1.26	12.48	5.98
滁州市	Chuzhou	734.98	366.78	2036.75	1693.16	10.09	167.78	42.68
六安市	Luan	331.39	480.11	802.38	698.83	5.23	30.25	16.14
马鞍山市	Maanshan	310.66	340.69	812.16	701.98	4.04	29.75	14.94
芜湖市	Wuhu	557.28	237.81	1459.72	1232.49	8.32	87.89	39.06
宣城市	Xuancheng	539.62	249.38	1427.14	1234.76	11.13	64.33	36.76
铜陵市	Tongling	142.95	72.92	380.30	341.05	1.75	8.98	6.35
池州市	Chizhou	242.15	101.89	805.84	720.19	4.69	32.83	20.88
安庆市	Anqing	441.15	184.84	857.90	722.33	6.17	50.02	23.69
黄山市	Huangshan	124.76	60.94	344.75	293.61	1.84	10.50	7.87

13—16 各市大中型工业企业主要经济指标（2022年）

Main Indicators of Large and Medium-sized Industrial Enterprises by Region (2022)

单位：亿元（100 million yuan）

地区	Region	企业单位数（个） Number of Enterprises (unit)	资产合计 Total Assets	流动资产合计 Circulating Funds	固定资产原价 Original Value of Fixed Assets	负债合计 Total Liabilities	#流动负债 Liquid Liabilities
总计	**Total**	**1525**	**36544.98**	**18100.48**	**17922.77**	**19893.40**	**15599.18**
合肥市	Hefei	345	12185.78	6650.82	4994.50	6964.35	5400.32
淮北市	Huaibei	40	1546.95	594.87	950.31	851.73	680.60
亳州市	Bozhou	45	754.19	356.73	399.53	362.67	296.02
宿州市	Suzhou	48	344.13	161.50	277.32	198.36	155.77
蚌埠市	Bengbu	62	1137.61	586.18	431.69	551.78	457.80
阜阳市	Fuyang	76	916.79	357.25	773.44	510.82	369.19
淮南市	Huainan	40	2289.10	411.34	1504.56	1521.65	804.10
滁州市	Chuzhou	165	2655.30	1281.03	1451.11	1449.73	1139.42
六安市	Luan	82	1171.78	540.54	696.68	637.74	493.78
马鞍山市	Maanshan	84	2592.06	1113.26	1902.53	1501.74	1252.97
芜湖市	Wuhu	228	6825.43	3998.84	2056.84	3258.56	2814.42
宣城市	Xuancheng	136	1222.05	653.97	545.52	604.26	535.73
铜陵市	Tongling	40	1182.31	614.47	768.46	596.00	470.77
池州市	Chizhou	30	577.87	305.53	376.77	284.63	234.45
安庆市	Anqing	77	975.00	381.27	697.42	521.75	425.80
黄山市	Huangshan	27	168.65	92.89	96.08	77.63	68.04

地区	Region	所有者权益 Owners' Equity	#实收资本 Total Capital Hold	营业收入 Business Revenue	营业成本 Business Cost	税金及附加 Taxes and Surcharges	利润总额 Total Profits	本年应交增值税 Value Added Tax Payable
总计	**Total**	**16650.49**	**6704.99**	**29057.68**	**25008.55**	**591.29**	**1557.05**	**569.87**
合肥市	Hefei	5221.42	2432.43	9000.29	7858.66	110.78	330.05	108.31
淮北市	Huaibei	695.21	202.57	964.88	715.98	20.41	140.68	47.51
亳州市	Bozhou	391.52	86.80	581.30	415.59	28.70	61.35	20.86
宿州市	Suzhou	145.76	73.35	403.72	360.02	1.88	22.81	10.64
蚌埠市	Bengbu	585.83	179.90	748.64	567.56	80.57	50.86	22.52
阜阳市	Fuyang	405.98	166.89	972.00	832.06	41.77	58.09	32.59
淮南市	Huainan	767.45	531.76	1122.19	940.91	16.55	65.96	45.16
滁州市	Chuzhou	1205.57	565.16	2611.04	2261.71	45.80	157.39	47.28
六安市	Luan	534.04	271.59	908.22	765.76	15.41	62.10	22.79
马鞍山市	Maanshan	1090.32	455.90	2465.16	2267.33	12.28	65.28	33.98
芜湖市	Wuhu	3565.78	897.47	4480.77	3779.76	116.30	308.87	95.92
宣城市	Xuancheng	617.79	200.13	1018.01	874.03	7.91	68.84	21.21
铜陵市	Tongling	586.31	275.80	1706.84	1562.22	6.25	76.00	22.23
池州市	Chizhou	293.25	103.38	777.10	718.31	3.54	27.86	13.29
安庆市	Anqing	453.25	230.23	1128.57	948.65	82.28	49.89	22.48
黄山市	Huangshan	91.02	31.63	168.95	139.99	0.88	11.01	3.09

13—17　工业主要产品生产能力
Production Capacity of Major Industrial Products

项　目		Item		2021	2022
原　煤	(吨)	Raw Coal	(ton)	129502366	126312366
卷　烟	(万支)	Cigarettes	(10000 pieces)	11955500	12017500
棉纺锭／纺纱量	(锭／吨)	Cotton Spinning / Spinning Amount	(ingot/ton)	2026656	1787038
气流纺锭／纺纱量	(头／吨)	Air Spindle / Spinning Amount	(unit/ton)	180317	262773
棉布织机／布	(台／万米)	Cotton Looms / cloth	(unit/10000 meters)	31089	438487
原油加工能力／原油加工量	(吨/吨)	Processing Capacity of Crude Oil / Processing Amount of Crude Oil	(ton/ton)	9035714	9035985
焦　炭	(吨)	Coke	(ton)	15170000	13970000
烧碱(折100%)	(吨)	Caustic Soda (=100%)	(ton)	810000	878311
碳化钙(电石，折300升／千克)	(吨)	Calcium Carbide (calcium carbide, = 300 liters / kg)	(ton)	50000	50000
农用氮磷钾化学肥料总计(折纯)	(吨)	Total of Agricultural N, P and K Chemical fertilizers (=pure)	(ton)	4655830	5165440
初级形态塑料	(吨)	Primary form Plastic	(ton)	4303268	5073082
化学纤维	(吨)	Chemical Fiber	(ton)	1112413	1200980
硅酸盐水泥熟料	(吨)	Silicate Cement Grog	(ton)	156605700	160793372
水　泥	(吨)	Cement	(ton)	185689105	190229739
平板玻璃	(重量箱)	Plate Glass	(weight cases)	49077019	54079825
生　铁	(吨)	Pig Iron	(ton)	28199510	30241010
粗　钢	(吨)	Thick Steel	(ton)	37896000	38385500
钢　材	(吨)	Rolled Steel	(ton)	41523821	45483441
铁合金	(吨)	Ferroalloy	(ton)	106082	118609
金属切削机床	(台)	Metal-cutting Machine Tools	(unit)	23681	28701
挖掘机	(台)	Excavating Machine	(unit)	15120	15220
汽　车	(辆)	Motor Vehicles	(unit)	2061500	1725600
#基本型乘用车(轿车)		Basic Passenger Car (car)		1680000	1425000
民用钢质船舶	(载重吨)	Civil Steel Ship	(carrying capacity ton)	842819	1380280
太阳能电池	(千瓦)	Solar Battery	(kilowatt)	32077518	47707939
家用电冰箱	(台)	Household Refrigerators	(unit)	40677550	40011989
房间空气调节器	(台)	Air Conditioners	(unit)	46795659	42283110
微型计算机设备	(台)	Microcomputer Equipment	(unit)	51473932	54283527
移动通信手持机(手机)	(台)	Mobile Communication Handset (mobile phone)	(unit)	1885336	2005709
彩色电视机	(台)	Color TV	(unit)	28789547	19770000
发电设备容量总计／发电量	(万千瓦/万千瓦小时)	Capacity of Power Generation Equipment / Generating Capacity	(10000 kilowatt /10000 kilowatt hour)	6164.51	6808.60
#火电设备容量／发电量		Capacity of Thermal Power Equipment		5420.49	5534.50
水电设备容量／发电量		Capacity of Water Power Equipment		154.26	383.80
风电设备容量／发电量		Capacity of Wind Power Equipment		256.90	336.60

13—18 主要工业产品产量
Output of Major Industrial Products

项目		Item		2010	2015	2020	2021	2022
原煤	(万吨)	Raw Coal	(10000 tons)	13030	13404	11084	11274	11176.9
洗煤	(万吨)	Coal Washing	(10000 tons)	1603	4414	3629	3155	3317
铁矿石原矿量	(万吨)	Iron Ore Products	(10000 tons)	3237	4697	2616	3237	3242
铜金属含量	(吨)	Amount Contained of Copper	(ton)	129145	209072	81248	75720	99024
混合饲料	(万吨)	Blending Feed	(10000 tons)	121.9	100.1	60.6	77.4	91.7
原盐	(吨)	Raw Salt	(ton)	1461487	1496473	1553510	1415045	1281504
大米	(万吨)	Rice	(10000 tons)	1042.1	1713.3	1227.6	938.9	880.8
食用植物油	(万吨)	Edible Vegetable Oil	(10000 tons)	66.23	127.70	94.90	78.50	82.50
乳制品	(吨)	Dairy Products	(ton)	664812	943722	1245478	1182020	1033328
罐头	(吨)	Can (tin)	(ton)	308924	586059	453996	474557	525006.2
鲜、冻畜肉	(万吨)	Fresh and Frozen Meat	(10000 tons)	59.0	142.9	92.5	120.3	119.8
糖果	(吨)	Candy	(ton)	27682	87107	112571	161086	155767
酱油	(吨)	Soy Sauce	(ton)	41281	107292	50455	3070	2382
发酵酒精	(万千升)	Fermented Alcohol	(10000 kl)	68.0	37.4	29.7	29.5	30.2
白酒	(万千升)	Liquor	(10000 kl)	48.0	46.5	28.2	24.6	26.6
啤酒	(万千升)	Beer	(10000 kl)	154.1	119.2	76.0	79.5	84
精制茶	(吨)	Refined Tea	(ton)	178927	257143	216702	202312	176052
卷烟	(亿支)	Cigarettes	(100 million pieces)	1226	1269	1204	1218	1220
纱	(吨)	Yarn	(ton)	565419	1111904	786974	682639	640661
布	(万米)	Cloth	(10000 m)	108663	141398	79552	76550	49031
棉布	(万米)	Cotton Cloth	(10000 m)	82439	43565	33732	25232	16674
印染布	(万米)	Printing and Dyeing Cloth	(10000 m)	18392	18462	29305	17214	15137
绒线（毛线）	(吨)	Knitting Wool	(ton)	528	2227	567	559	
丝	(吨)	Silk	(ton)	6438	8057	3046	1904	2338
丝织品	(万米)	Silk Fabrics	(10000 m)	4005	7196	2037	1148	1085
服装	(万件)	Clothing	(10000 units)	53505	117020	80794	72017	70470
梭织服装		Shuttled Clothing		30888	79439	48929	42082	39331
针织服装		Knit Clothing		22617	37582	31865	29935	31139
人造板	(万立方米)	Man-made Board	(10000 cu.m)	573.0	1495.8	1157.9	1163.6	1050.4
机制纸及纸板	(万吨)	Machine-made Paper and Paperboard	(10000 tons)	221.1	306.3	406.6	422.4	401.3
纸制品	(万吨)	Paper Products	(10000 tons)	69.0	181.2	160.4	114.4	111.5
原油加工量	(万吨)	Volume of Processed Crude Oil	(10000 tons)	476.6	689.3	710.0	752.0	579
汽油	(万吨)	Gasoline	(10000 tons)	97.0	216.6	256.0	283.9	219.3
柴油	(万吨)	Diesel Oil	(10000 tons)	196.0	281.0	184.0	168.7	134.4
燃料油	(万吨)	Fuel Oil	(10000 tons)	12.4	1.8	14.0	23.7	24.5
液化石油气	(万吨)	Liquefied Petroleum	(10000 tons)	34.1	58.3	70.0	78.3	56.3
焦炭	(万吨)	Coke	(10000 tons)	839.6	958.5	1228.0	1252.6	1298
硫酸（折100%）	(万吨)	Sulfuric Acid (100%)	(10000 tons)	439.7	630.1	673.9	697.8	703.8
浓硝酸（折100%）	(万吨)	Enriched Nitric Acid (100%)	(10000 tons)	54.5	63.1	38.3	39.8	39.6
氢氧化钠（烧碱）（折100%）	(万吨)	Caustic Soda (100%)	(10000 tons)	29.0	72.0	85.5	75.1	81.0
碳酸钠（纯碱）	(万吨)	Soda Ash	(10000 tons)	35.4	76.9	88.8	83.3	91.4
合成氨	(万吨)	Synthetic Ammonia	(10000 tons)	266.4	344.8	326.2	303.8	319.9
农用氮肥磷钾化学肥料总计	(万吨)	Chemical Fertilizers	(10000 tons)	255.4	309.7	266.4	208.0	228.6
氮肥（折含N100%）	(万吨)	Nitrogen Fertilizers	(10000 tons)	201.5	228.3	170.4	164.0	176.7

13—18 续表 continued

项　　目		Item		2010	2015	2020	2021	2022
磷　肥	(万吨)	Phosphate Fertilizers	(10000 tons)	54.0	81.4	90.7	40.1	42.3
化学农药	(万吨)	Chemical Pesticide	(10000 tons)	15.1	19.8	16.1	22.4	19.3
塑料树脂及共聚物	(万吨)	Plastics	(10000 tons)	56.9	120.4	324.6	323.0	330.1
合成洗涤剂	(万吨)	Synthetic Detergents	(10000 tons)	74.6	79.4	101.6	102.8	105.8
化学原料药	(吨)	Chemical Medicine	(ton)	9208	40473	16717	16727	25179
中成药	(吨)	Traditional Chinese Medicine	(ton)	26190	49709	44885	42336	43798
化学纤维	(万吨)	Chemical Fiber	(10000 tons)	22.0	27.0	51.5	60.0	51.1
轮胎外胎	(万条)	Tires	(10000 units)	3744.3	2829.6	2777.0	3721.3	3986.6
塑料制品	(万吨)	Plastic Products	(10000 tons)	186.8	338.7	521.0	463.8	465.7
塑料薄膜	(吨)	Plastic Film	(ton)	166674	348278	584266	621093	614579
水　泥	(万吨)	Cement	(10000 tons)	7874	13085	14176	14992	14211
大理石板材	(万平方米)	Marble Plate	(10000 sq.m)	13.90	535.00	112.80	23.70	4.20
花岗石板材	(万平方米)	Granite Plate	(10000 sq.m)	109.82	497.60	307.40	80.10	29.90
平板玻璃	(万重量箱)	Plate Glass	(10000 weight cases)	1044.3	2302.5	4489.2	4637.0	4213.3
生　铁	(万吨)	Pig Iron	(10000 tons)	1844.9	2092.5	2537.3	2911.6	2956.5
钢　材	(万吨)	Rolled Steel	(10000 tons)	2446.4	3334.7	3607.5	3820.3	3963.0
铁道用钢材		Steel Use for Railway		11.9	12.5			
中小型钢材		Rolled-steel, Medium and Small		158.5	234.9	41.4	43.5	42.7
无缝钢管		Seamless Steel Pipe		20.0	72.6	33.7	38.2	47.0
线　材		Wire Rod		301.1	209.8	265.7	259.6	337.6
铜	(万吨)	Copper	(10000 tons)	83.1	131.1	105.8	110.0	111.4
工业锅炉	(蒸吨)	Industrial Boilers	(ton)	5196	31760	18886	5979	1668
发动机	(台)	engine	(10000 kW)		10418.8	9258.1	11910.9	11675.4
金属切削机床	(台)	Metal-cutting Machine Tools	(unit)	26283	81268	19728	18417	15111
起重设备	(吨)	Derrick Equipment	(ton)	334543	869451	91169	93282	94605
叉　车	(台)	Forklift	(unit)	40613	58094	112564	90687	84161
泵	(台)	Pump	(unit)	409494	2046093	10737814	7775627	6461802
轴　承	(万套)	Bearing	(10000 sets)	23665	76633	109653	114340	105704
矿山设备	(吨)	Mining Equipment	(ton)	74055	587194	310109	230775	329371
小型拖拉机	(台)	Mini-tractors	(unit)	17833	15316			
汽　车	(辆)	Motor Vehicles	(unit)	1244735	1257681	1160724	1452112	1746876
载货汽车		Trucks		273645	210804	230894	205458	92312
公路汽车		Coach		78426	37578	6450	4090	4167
交流电动机	(万千瓦)	Alternating Current Motor	(10000 kW)	1599.5	2200.0	2734.9	3235.3	2904
变压器	(万千伏安)	Transformer	(10000 KVA)	4136.9	4408.4	3729.1	3537.1	3557
蓄电池	(千伏安时)	Storage Battery	(KVA.h)	6610665	19170259	20208640	20828210	23094438
家用洗衣机	(万台)	Household Washing Machines	(10000 units)	1267.0	1725.2	2380.4	2627.4	2545.2
家用电冰箱	(万台)	Household Refrigerators	(10000 units)	2078.9	2888.2	2437.9	2381.4	2633.5
房间空气调节器	(万台)	Air Conditioners	(10000 units)	1666.1	3176.1	3009.7	3385.5	2691.1
电视机	(万部)	TV Sets	(10000 units)	395.3	1176.9	1611.8	1224.8	1026.3
#彩色电视机		Color TV		395.3	1176.9	1611.8	1224.8	1026.3
微型电子计算机	(万部)	Micro-computers	(10000 unit)	1.8	1801.5	3097.1	3694.8	2950.2
发电量	(亿千瓦时)	Electricity	(100 million kWh)	1443.9	2034.2	2682.0	2911.8	3135
火　电		Thermal Power		1420.2	1954.7	2527.0	2690.3	2882.9
水　电		Hydropower		18.9	30.9	41.0	55.7	52.8
煤　气	(亿立方米)	Gas	(100 million cu.m)	286.6	326.8	502.0	492.1	494.8

13—19 各市主要工业产品产量（2022年）
Output of Major Industrial Products by Region (2022)

项　　目		Item		合肥市 Hefei	淮北市 Huaibei	亳州市 Bozhou	宿州市 Suzhou
铁矿石原矿量	（万吨）	Iron Ore Products	(10000 tons)	634.5	47.1		
原　盐	（万吨）	Raw Salt	(10000 tons)				
大　米	（万吨）	Rice	(10000 tons)	70.3			
混合饲料	（万吨）	Blending Feed	(10000 tons)	1.2	4.7		24.8
食用植物油	（万吨）	Edible Vegetable Oil	(10000 tons)	48.6			
白　酒	（千升）	Liquor	(kl)		23866	135245	1535
精制茶	（吨）	Refined Tea	(ton)	18.4		2134.8	
纱	（吨）	Yarn	(ton)	15428	44183	7100	34739
布	（万米）	Cloth	(10000 m)	1701.6	520.2	1590.1	
机制纸及纸板	（万吨）	Machine-made Paper and Paperboard	(10000 tons)	12.7			90
原油加工量	（万吨）	Volume of Processed Crude Oil	(10000 tons)				
农用氮肥磷钾化学肥料总计	（万吨）	Chemical Fertilizers	(10000 tons)	26.3			
中成药	（吨）	Traditional Chinese Medicine	(ton)	2444.6		10329.3	55.8
化学纤维	（万吨）	Chemical Fiber	(10000 tons)	5.7			
轮胎外胎	（万条）	Tires	(10000 units)	3016.5			
水　泥	（万吨）	Cement	(10000 tons)	1446.1	602.4	246.9	684.4
平板玻璃	（万重量箱）	Plate Glass	(10000 weight cases)	420.6			
生　铁	（万吨）	Pig Iron	(10000 tons)				
钢	（万吨）	Steel	(10000 tons)				
成品钢材	（万吨）	Steel Products	(10000 tons)	137.8	2.3		
铜	（万吨）	Copper	(10000 tons)				
叉　车	（台）	Forklift	(unit)	79873			
汽　车	（辆）	Motor Vehicles	(unit)	571824			
载货汽车		Trucks		84527			
家用洗衣机	（万台）	Household Washing Machines	(10000 units)	2249.4			
家用电冰箱	（万台）	Household Refrigerators	(10000 units)	2079.4			
房间空气调节器	（万台）	Air Conditioners	(10000 units)	787.8	63.7		
彩色电视机	（万部）	Color TV	(10000 units)	634			
发电量	（亿千瓦时）	Electricity	(100 million kWh)	259.32	283.4	143.2	146

蚌埠市 Bengbu	阜阳市 Fuyang	淮南市 Huainan	滁州市 Chuzhou	六安市 Luan	马鞍山市 Maanshan	芜湖市 Wuhu	宣城市 Xuancheng	铜陵市 Tongling	池州市 Chizhou	安庆市 Anqing	黄山市 Huangshan
			3.4	2496.3	49.3	9.7				1.2	
			128.2								
40.3	55.7	262.4	136.3	131.4	23.4	40.6	22.7	7.6	6.9	78.9	4.5
10.6	1.4	25.3	15.5	1.2		1.5	5.5				
15.1	3.6	3.6		3.1	4.6	0.1	3.3		0.1	0.3	
6129.1	40290.3	185.2	7013.9	36070.9			8556	134.5	458.2	6058.2	
			117.5	4770.6			12446.5	6.1	10624.4	2400.7	143533.4
45095.5	201689	4573	17962.3	1111	3608	13899	44926.9		2298	203533.5	515
	2841.5	689.9			88.2	149.5	9751.7	3047.7		8651	19999.1
2	5.7	6.4	24.6	7	203.7	20.9	12.2			12.8	3.4
	88.2	17	16.6				13.3	55.6	3	8.5	
237.4	9055.8	2653.3	6463	1094.4	2338.3	4440.2	461			2671.6	1553.7
	2.7		19.9	9		0.1	3.7			10	
482.5			34.2			453.4					
345.5	461.5	789.5	1272.2	457	2059.7	2138.7	1068.4	1241.8	350.6	872.7	173.5
			840.4	720.5		2231.8					
				288.8	1790.8	449.2		249.7	178		
		38.4		417.5	2000.4	466.3	193.7	256.7	336.2		
	4.4	63.4	48.6	352.8	2023.1	513	301.3	276.1	238.1	2.1	
								111.4			
		1810		2478							
		1783			11792	1111015				50462	
		1783			6002						
			261.2	34.6							
			540.6	13.6							
			83.6			1690.7				65.3	
	8.4		370.6		13.3						
164.6	96.9	712.2	86.3	115.1	289.1	235.6655	113.1	230.5	52.9	192.1674	4.8

主要统计指标解释

工业

指从事自然资源的开采，对采掘品和农产品进行加工和再加工的物质生产部门。具体包括：(1)对自然资源的开采，如采矿、晒盐等（但不包括禽兽捕猎和水产捕捞）；(2)对农副产品的加工、再加工，如粮油加工、食品加工、缫丝、纺织、制革等；(3)对采掘品的加工、再加工，如炼铁、炼钢、化工生产、石油加工、机器制造、木材加工等，以及电力、燃气及水的生产和供应等；(4)对工业品的修理、翻新，如机器设备的修理等。

工业统计调查单位为工业法人单位。

工业法人单位指从事工业生产经营活动的法人单位。工业法人单位应同时具备以下条件：①依法成立，有自己的名称、组织机构和场所，能够独立承担民事责任；②独立拥有（或授权）使用资产，承担负债，有权与其他单位签订合同；③具有包括资产负债表在内的账户，或者能够根据需要编制账户。

国有控股企业

即原来的国有及国有控股企业，根据企业实收资本中国有经济成分的出资人的实际投资情况，或国有经济成分的出资人对企业资产的实际控制、支配程度进行分类。以下情况为国有控股：(1)在企业的全部实收资本中，国有经济成分的出资人拥有的实收资本（股本）所占企业全部实收资本（股本）的比例大于50%的国有绝对控股。(2)在企业的全部实收资本中，国有经济成分的出资人拥有的实收资本（股本）所占比例虽未大于50%，但相对大于其他任何一方经济成分的出资人所占比例的国有相对控股；或者虽不大于其他经济成分，但根据协议规定拥有企业实际控制权的国有协议控股。(3)投资双方各占50%，且未明确由谁绝对控股的企业，若其中一方为国有经济成分的，一律按国有控股处理。

本篇涉及的企业登记注册类型的解释详见综合篇。

轻工业

指主要提供生活消费品和制作手工工具的工业。按其所使用的原料不同，可分为两大类：(1)以农产品为原料的轻工业，是指直接或间接以农产品为基本原料的轻工业。主要包括食品制造、饮料制造、烟草加工、纺织、缝纫、皮革和毛皮制作、造纸以及印刷等工业；(2)以非农产品为原料的轻工业，是指以工业品为原料的轻工业。主要包括文教体育用品、化学药品制造、合成纤维制造、日用化学制品、日用玻璃制品、日用金属制品、手工工具制造、医疗器械制造、文化和办公用机械制造等工业。

重工业

指为国民经济各部门提供物质技术基础的主要生产资料的工业。按其生产性质和产品用途，可以分为下列三类：(1)采掘(伐)工业，是指对自然资源的开采，包括石油开采、煤炭开采、金属矿开采、非金属矿开采等工业；(2)原材料工业，指向国民经济各部门提供基本材料、动力和燃料的工业。包括金属冶炼及加工、炼焦及焦炭、化学、化工原料、水泥、人造板以及电力、石油和煤炭加工等工业；(3)加工工业，是指对工业原材料进行再加工制造的工业。包括装备国民经济各部门的机械设备制造工业、金属结构、水泥制品等工业，以及为农业提供的生产资料如化肥、农药等工业。

根据上述划分原则，修理业中以重工业产品为修理作业对象的划为重工业，反之划为轻工业。

资产总计

指企业过去的交易或者事项形成的、由企业拥有或者控制的、预期会给企业带来经济利益的资源。资产一般按流动性分为流动资产和非流动资产。其中流动资产可分为货币资金、交易性金融资产、应收票据、应收账款、预付款项、其他应收款、存货等；非流动资产可分为长期股权投资、固定资产、无形资产及其他非流动资产等。来源于会计“资产负债表”中“资产总计”项目的期末余额数。

流动资产合计

资产满足以下条件之一应归为流动资产：（1）预计在一个正常营业周期中变现、出售或耗用，主要包括存货、应收账款等；（2）主要为交易目的而持有；（3）预计在资产负债表日起一年内（含一年）变现；（4）自资产负债日起一年内，交换其他资产或清偿负债的能力不受限制的现金或现金等价物。包括货币资金、应收票据、应收账款、存货等项目。来源于会计“资产负债表”中“流动资产合计”项目的期末余额数。

固定资产原价

指企业在建造、购置、安装、改建、扩建、技术改造某项固定资产时所支出的全部货币总额。它一般包括买价、包装费、运杂费和安装费等。

负债合计

指企业过去的交易或者事项形成的，预期会导致经济利益流出企业的现时义务。负债一般按偿还期长短分为流动负债和非流动负债。来源于会计“资产负债表”中“负债合计”项目的期末余额数。

所有者权益合计

指企业投资人对企业净资产的所有权。企业净资产为企业全部资产与企业全部负债的差额，包括实收资本、资本公积、盈余公积、未分配利润等。根据会计“资产负债表”中“所有者权益”项的期末数填列。

营业收入

指企业经营主要业务和其他业务所确认的收入总额。营业收入包括“主营业务收入”和“其他业务收入”。来源于会计“利润表”中“营业收入”项目的本年累计数。

营业成本

指企业经营主要业务和其他业务所发生的成本总额。包括企业（单位）在报告期内从事销售商品、提供劳务等日常活动发生的各种耗费。包括“主营业务成本”和“其他业务成本”。来源于会计“利润表”中“营业成本”项目的本年累计数。

税金及附加

指企业因从事生产经营活动按税法规定应缴纳的消费税、城市维护建设税、资源税、环境保护税、教育费附加及房产税、土地使用税、车船使用税、印花税等相关税费。

利润总额

指企业在一定会计期间的经营成果，是生产经营过程中各种收入扣除各种耗费后的盈余，反映企业在报告期内实现的盈亏总额。来源于会计“利润表”中“利润总额”项目的本年累计数。

本年应交增值税

指企业按税法规定，从事货物销售或提供加工、修理修配劳务等增加货物价值的活动本期应交纳的税金。指企业在报告期应交增值税额。计算公式为：

本年应交增值税=销项税额-（进项税额-进项税额转出）

-出口抵减内销产品应纳税额-减免税款+出口退税

本年进项税额指工业企业在报告期内购入货物或接受应税劳务而支付的、准予从销项税额中抵扣的增值税额。

本年销项税额指工业企业在报告期内销售货物或提供应税劳务应收取的增值税额。

从业人员平均人数

是指报告期内每天拥有的从业人员人数。其计算公式为：

月平均人数=报告月内每天实有人数之和/报告月日历日数

季平均人数=季内各月平均人数之和/3

年平均人数=年内各月平均人数之和/12

总资产贡献率

反映企业全部资产的获利能力，是企业经营业绩和管理水平的集中体现，是评价和考核企业盈利能力的核心指标。计算公式为：

总资产贡献率（%）=（利润总额+税金总额+利息支出）/平均资产总额×100%

公式中：税金总额为产品销售税金及附加与应交增值税之和；平均资产总额为期初期末资产之和的算术平均值。

资产负债率

该指标既反映企业经营风险的大小，也反映企业利用债权人提供的资金从事经营活动的能力。计算公式为：

资产负债率（%）=负债总额/资产总额×100%

资产与负债均为报告期期末数。

流动资产周转次数

指一定时期内流动资产完成的周转次数，反映投入工业企业流动资金的周转速度。计算公式为：

流动资产周转次数=主营业务收入/全部流动资产平均余额

公式中：全部流动资产平均余额为期初和期末的流动资产之和的算术平均值。

成本费用利润率

反映企业投入的生产成本及费用的经济效益，同时也反映企业降低成本所取得的经济效益。计算公式为：

成本费用利润率（%）=利润总额/成本费用总额×100%

公式中：成本费用总额为主营业务成本、销售费用、管理费用、财务费用之和。

Explanatory Notes for Major Statistical Indicators

Industry

refers to the material production sector which is engaged in the extraction of natural resources and processing and reprocessing of minerals and agricultural products, including (1) extraction of natural resources, such as mining, salt production (but not including hunting and fishing); (2) processing and reprocessing of farm and sideline produces, such as grain and oil processing, food processing, silk reeling, spinning and weaving and leather making; (3) processing and reprocessing of mineral products, such as steel making, iron smelting, chemicals manufacturing, petroleum processing, machine building, timber processing, and production and supply of electricity, gas and water; (4) repairing and renovating of industrial products such as the machinery.

In industrial surveys, the units of enquiry are industrial corporate units.

Industrial corporate units refer to corporate units engaging in industrial production and operation activities, which meet the following requirements: (1) They are established legally, having their own names, organizations, location, and are able to take civil liability independently; (2) They possess (or are authorized to use) assets independently, assume liabilities and are entitled to sign contracts with other units; (3) They have accounts including the balance sheets or can compile the accounts according to the need.

State-holding Enterprises

cover the original state-owned enterprises and state-holding enterprises. They are classified according to the actual investment made by the contributors of state-owned part in the paid-in capital of the enterprises, or the degree of control or dominance of the contributors on the assets of the enterprises. The following cases are regarded as state-holding: (1) Absolute state-holding in which the contributors of state-owned parts possess more than 50% of all the paid-in capital (stocks) of the enterprises; (2) Relative state-holding in which the contributors of state-owned parts possess no more than 50% of the paid-in capital (stocks) of the enterprises, but more than that of any other contributors; or Agreed state-holding in which the contribors of state-owned parts possess no more than other contributors but have actual control over the enterprises according to agreements; (3) In the case both contributors possess 50% and it is not clear which one is in absolute holding position, the enterprise is regarded as state-holding enterprise if one of the contributor has state-owned elements.

For explanation of types of registration covered in this chapter, please refer to General Survey.

Light Industry

refers to the industry that produces consumer goods and hand tools. It consists of two categories, depending on the materials used:

(1) Industries using farm products as raw materials. These are the branches of light industry which directly or indirectly use farm products as basic raw materials, including the manufacture of food and beverages, tobacco processing, textile, clothing, fur and leather manufacturing, paper making, printing, etc.

(2) Industries using non-farm products as raw materials. These are the branches of light industry which use manufactured goods as raw materials, including the manufacture of cultural, educational articles and sports goods, chemicals, synthetic fibre, chemical products for daily use, glass products for daily use, metal products for daily use, hand tools, medical apparatus and instruments, and the manufacture of cultural and office machinery.

Heavy Industry

refers to the industry which produces capital goods, and provides various sectors of the national economy with necessary material and technical basis for production. It consists of the following three branches according to the purpose of production or the use of products:

(1) Mining, quarrying and logging industry, which refers to the industry that extracts natural resources, including extraction of petroleum, coal, metal and non-metal ores.

(2) Raw materials industry refers to the industry that provides various sectors of the national economy with raw materials, fuels and power. It includes smelting and processing of metals, coking and coke chemistry, chemical materials and building materials such as cement, plywood, and power, petroleum refining and coal dressing.

(3) Manufacturing industry which refers to the industry that processes raw materials. It includes machine-building industries which equip sectors of the national economy; industries producing metal structure and cement products; and industries producing means of agricultural production, such as chemical fertilizers and pesticides.

In accordance with the above principles of classification,

the repairing trades, which are engaged primarily in repairing products of heavy industry, are classified as heavy industry while those which are engaged in repairing products of light industry are classified as light industry.

Total Assets

refer to all resources that are owned or controlled by enterprises through previous trades or transactions with expectation of making economic profits. Classified by the degree of liquidity, total assets include current assets and non-current assets. Current assets can be classified into monetary capital, trading financial assets, notes receivable, accounts receivable, advanced payments, other receivables and inventories. Non-current assets can be divided into long-term equity investment, fixed assets, intangible assets and other non-current assets. Data on this indicator can be obtained from the year-end figures of total assets in the Balance Sheet of accounting records.

Total Current Assets

refer to the assets that meet one of the following requirements: (1) expected to be cashed, sold or used in a normal operation cycle, mainly including inventory and accounts receivable; (2) be owned for trading purpose mainly; (3) expected to be cashed in one year (including one year) from the day of the Balance Sheet; (4) unlimited cash or cash equivalents that can be exchanged with other assets or being capable of settling debts during one year since the day of the Balance Sheet. Included are monetary capital, notes receivable, accounts receivable and inventories. Data on this indicator can be obtained from the year-end figures of total current assets in the Balance Sheet of accounting records.

Fixed Assets Original Cost

refers to the total amount of money spent by an enterprise in the construction, purchase, installation, renovation, expansion and technological transformation of a fixed asset. It generally includes purchase price, packing fee, freight and miscellaneous expenses, installation fee, etc.

Total Liabilities

refer to payable liabilities of enterprises that accumulated from previous trades or transactions with expectation of economic profits leaking out. In terms of payment, it can be divided into liquid liabilities and long-term liabilities. Data on this indicator can be obtained from the year-end figures of total liabilities in the Balance Sheet of accounting records.

Total Owner's Equity

Refers to the ownership of the net assets of an enterprise by its investors. The net assets of an enterprise are the difference between its total assets and its total liabilities, including paid-in capital, capital reserves, surplus reserves, undistributed profits, etc. According to the final number of "owner's equity" in the accounting "balance sheet".

Business Revenue

refers to the total revenue recognized by an enterprise in its principal business and other business operations. Business revenue includes " revenue from principal Business" and " revenue from other business". It comes from this year's cumulative report of "business revenue" items from the "income statement".

Business Cost

refers to the total cost incurred by an enterprise in its principal business and other business operations. It includes various expenditures incurred by enterprises (units) in their daily activities of selling goods and providing labour services during the reporting period. It includes "Cost of principal business" and "Cost of other business". It comes from this year's cumulative report of "operating cost" items from the "income statement".

Taxes and Surcharges

To the consumption tax, urban maintenance and construction tax, resource tax, environmental protection tax, education surcharge, property tax, land use tax, vehicle and vessel use tax, stamp duty and other related taxes and fees that enterprises should pay according to the provisions of the tax law.

Total Profits

refers to the operation results in a certain accounting period, and it is the balance of various incomes minus various spendings in the course of operation, reflecting the total profits and losses of enterprises in reference period. Data are obtained from the this year's cumulative amount of total profits in the profit statement of the accounting record of enterprise.

VAT Payable This Year

according to the provisions of the tax law, enterprises should pay taxes in the current period for activities that increase the value of goods, such as selling goods or providing processing, repair and maintenance services. Refers to the value-added tax payable by the enterprise during the reporting period. The calculation formula is:

Value added tax payable this year = output tax amount - (input tax amount-transfer - out of input tax amount) - export deduction of tax payable on domestic products - tax relief + export tax refund

This year's input tax refers to the value-added tax paid by industrial enterprises for purchasing goods or receiving taxable services during the reporting period and allowed to be deducted from the output tax.

This year's output tax refers to the value-added tax payable by industrial enterprises for selling goods or providing taxable services during the reporting period.

Average number of employees

refers to the number of employees per day during the reporting period. The calculation formula is:

Average number of people per month = sum of actual number of people per day in the reporting month/number of calendar days in the reporting month

Quarterly Average Number = Sum of Monthly Average Number in Quarter /3

Annual Average Number = Sum of Average Number of Months in Year /12

Ratio of Profits, Taxes and Interests to Average Assets

reflects the profit-making capability of all assets of the enterprise and is a key indicator manifesting the performance and management and evaluating the profit-making potential of the enterprise. It is calculated as follows:

Ratio of Profits, Taxes and Interests to Average Assets (%) = (total profits + total taxes + interest payment) / average assets × 100%

In the above formula, total taxes is the sum of tax and extra charges on the sales of products and value-added tax payable; and average assets is the arithmetic mean of the sum of beginning assets and ending assets.

Ratio of Debts to Assets

reflects both the operation risk and the capability of the enterprise in making use of the capital from the creditors. It is calculated as follows:

Ratio of Debts to Assets (%) = total debts / total assets × 100%

Both assets and debts are figures at the end of the reference period.

Turnover of Working Capital

refers to the number of times of turnover of working capital in a given period of time, which reflects the speed of the turnover of working capital of industrial enterprises, and is calculated as follows:

Turnover of Working Capital = sales revenue of products / average balance of total working capital

In the above formula, average balance of total working capital refers to the arithmetic mean of the sum of working capital at the beginning and at the end of the reference period.

Ratio of Profits to Total Industrial Costs

refers to the ratio of profits realized in a given period to the total costs in the same period, which reflects the economic efficiency of input cost and is calculated as follows:

Ratio of Profits to Total Industrial Cost (%) = total profits / total costs × 100%

Total costs in the above formula are the sum of cost of products sold, marketing cost, management cost and financial cost.

第十四篇

Chapter 14

建筑业

CONSTRUCTION

简要说明

一、本篇资料反映我省建筑业概况和发展情况。主要包括建筑业企业生产经营情况，指标有企业个数、从业人员数、建筑业总产值、房屋建筑面积、机械设备、资产负债、利润税金、劳动生产率、技术装备率等。此外，2003 年及以前还包括农村建筑队主要指标。

二、建筑业企业资料由省统计局固定资产投资处提供。建筑业统计范围从 1996 年年报起由原城镇及城镇以上各种经济类型的建筑业企业扩大到具有建筑业资质等级的各种经济类型的建筑业企业，资料来源依据国家统计局制定的“建筑业统计报表制度”收集的有关年报资料。

Brief Introduction

I. Data in this chapter show the general situation and the development of the construction in the province. They cover mainly the situation of production and management of the enterprises of construction, including number of enterprises number of employed persons, gross output value, floor space of the building, machinery and equipment, assets and liabilities, profits and taxes, labor productivity, per capita machinery, etc. They also cover the main indicators of the rural construction teams at 2003 and before.

II. Data on the enterprises of construction in this chapter are provided by the Division of Statistics in Investment in Fixed Assets, Anhui Statistical Bureau. The coverage of construction statistics has been enlarged since 1996 when the annual statistical reports were submitted. The original coverage includes all the construction enterprises of various types of ownership at and above town level. The new coverage includes all the construction enterprises of various types of ownership with qualification. Data are collected in accordance with the “reporting scheme of construction statistics” stipulated by the National Bureau of Statistics.

14—1 建筑业企业概况
Main Indicators on Construction Enterprises

年 份 Year	总 计 Total	内 资 Domestic Funded	#国有企业 State-owned Enterprises	#集体企业 Collective Enterprise	港澳台商投资企业 Funded from Hong Kong, Macao and Taiwan	外 商投资企业 Foreign Funded	国 有控股企业 State Controlling Funded Hold Enterprises
企业单位数（个） Number of Enterprises (unit)							
2010	2469	2457	168	139	6	6	249
2013	2757	2745	122	85	5	7	234
2014	2807	2797	88	79	5	5	229
2015	2867	2857	72	70	4	6	223
2016	3037	3030	56	62	4	3	237
2017	3216	3208	53	58	4	4	231
2018	3980	3975	43	52	4	1	226
2019	4574	4568	36	47	5	1	229
2020	5878	5872	49	43	5	1	254
2021	7274	7268	60	40	5	1	306
2022	8362	8354	48	35	5	3	345
期末从业人员（万人） Number of Persons Engaged (10000 persons)							
2010	157.97	157.62	31.79	6.68	0.16	0.19	42.66
2013	176.88	176.62	21.48	4.17	0.13	0.13	38.52
2014	171.57	171.39	7.16	4.18	0.08	0.10	36.64
2015	168.82	168.65	6.16	3.75	0.08	0.09	32.13
2016	168.09	167.95	7.18	3.28	0.08	0.06	33.77
2017	171.56	171.43	3.45	2.99	0.07	0.05	33.74
2018	186.92	186.82	2.28	2.56	0.09		37.52
2019	198.40	198.35	1.90	2.18	0.04		40.59
2020	203.73	203.68	2.09	1.92	0.05		41.15
2021	196.15	196.11	2.16	1.86	0.05		40.04
2022	211.60	211.55	4.47	1.46	0.04	0.02	43.88
总 产 值（万元） Gross Output Value (10000 yuan)							
2010	28649619	28583665	8940053	743385	32530	33424	12034370
2013	49635516	49560201	9286296	605431	19409	55906	17750941
2014	54829260	54766827	4202697	634176	19529	42904	19626151
2015	56959353	56899036	3137078	634536	11800	48518	18858827
2016	60471125	60433001	3612219	569888	7026	26677	20500444
2017	68296702	68247114	1181390	576187	14160	35428	23956953
2018	78884540	78829984	672974	538159	54230	326	28105196
2019	85032583	84965307	631379	596117	67012	265	29729097
2020	93651164	93596064	1080189	610558	55099		33147899
2021	105840381	105795855	1393790	605693	44526		39355368
2022	117026336	116905700	2327533	491863	36739	83898	47560670

注：1．附营施工单位的生产活动在整个建筑生产活动中所占份额极小，加之资料不全，因而在总计中已略去。
　　2．2005年及以后年份为总承包和专业承包建筑业企业，城镇集体和农村建筑队不作统计。

a) The production activity of subsidiary construction units is omitted in the total because the portion is very small and the data are incomplete.

b) After 2005, Data are general contracting and professional contract of construction enterprises, Cities collective and construction crew of countryside doesn't count.

14—2 主要年份建筑业企业主要经济指标
Main Economic Indicators on Construction Enterprises

指　　标	Item	2010	2015	2020	2021	2022
企业单位数 (个)	Number of Construction Enterprises (unit)	2469	2867	5878	7274	8362
从业人数 (万人)	Staff and Workers (annual average) (10000 persons)	157.97	168.82	203.73	196.15	211.60
固定资产原价 (万元)	Original Cost of Fixed Assets (10000 yuan)	4034386	5676268	6850413	7127281	7209103
自有固定资产净值 (万元)	Fixed Assets Owned (net value) (10000 yuan)	2744333	4337451			
自有施工机械设备净值 (万元)	Net Value of Self-owned Construction Machinery and Equipment (10000 yuan)	1466999	1749198	1108484	1181337	909063
自有施工机械设备总台数 (台)	Total Number of Owned Construction Machinery and Equipment (unit)	415557	398670	207285	173832	176754
自有施工机械设备总功率 (万千瓦)	Total Power of Own Construction Machinery and Equipment (10000 kW)	663.58	904.82	472.76	512.00	404.49
建筑业总产值 (万元)	Gross Output Value of Construction (10000 yuan)	28649619	56959353	93651164	105840381	117026336
建筑工程	Construction Projects	25058430	48827159	79641512	89787579	100567355
安装工程	Installation Projects	2468351	4354850	6786347	7862917	8401565
其　他	Others	1122838	3777345	7223305	8189885	8057416
固定资产本年折旧 (万元)	Depreciation of Fixed Assets (10000 yuan)	260805	345217	425507	435117	532248
应付职工薪酬 (万元)	Payable Employee compensation (10000 yuan)		7791355	12581273	13839426	14197209
主营业务税金及附加 (万元)	Main Business Tax and Addition (10000 yuan)	1043879	1669272	470552	449506	433335
应交增值税 (万元)	Value Added Tax Payable (10000 yuan)			1703383	1770848	2121983
营业利润 (万元)	Business Profit (10000yuan)		1864170	2437436	2572879	2742762
利润总额 (万元)	Total Profits (10000 yuan)	983596	1872829	2487347	2608377	2776931
劳动生产率 (元/人)(按总产值计算)	Overall Labor Productivity (yuan/person) (In Terms of Gross Output Value)	177486	340696	457314	533025	507177
房屋建筑施工面积 (万平方米)	Floor Space of Buildings Under Construction (10000 sq.m)	23295.69	41479.74	49377.02	53887.36	49670.66
房屋建筑竣工面积 (万平方米)	Floor Space of Buildings Completed (10000 sq.m)	10512.36	15553.62	14516.04	14006.50	14856.90
房屋建筑面积竣工率 (%)	Ratio of Floor Space of Buildings Completed (%)	45.13	37.50	29.40	25.99	29.91
产值利润率 (%)	Ratio of Profit to Gross Output Value (%)	3.43	3.29	2.66	2.46	2.37

14—3 建筑业企业房屋建筑完成情况（2022年）
Floor Space of Buildings Completed by Construction Enterprises (2022)

指　标	Item	房屋建筑竣工面积（万平方米）Completed Area of Building Construction (10000 sq.m)	#国有控股企业 State Controlling Funded Hold Enterprises	房屋竣工价值（万元）Value of the Completed House (10000 yuan)	#国有控股企业 State Controlling Funded Hold Enterprises
总　计	**Total**	**14856.9**	**2991.4**	**24319740**	**6720253**
住　宅	Residential Buildings	8459.9	2125.6	14035398	4144242
商业及服务用房屋	Buildings Used for Business and Services	940.2	224.8	1677216	685397
办公用房	Office Buildings	458.3	57.7	719101	112062
科研、教育、医疗用房	Buildings Used for Scientific Research,Education, Medical Services	554.5	153.2	1097234	416771
文化、体育和娱乐用房	Buildings Used for Culture, Physical Training and Entertainment	153.7	41.0	307338	160106
厂房及建筑物	Workshops and Buildings	3633.5	305.3	5221660	633891
仓　库	Storehouses	113.7	0.6	143362	1376
其他用房	Others	543.0	83.1	1118432	566408

14—4 建筑业企业主要生产指标（2022年）
Main Indicators on Construction Enterprises (2022)

指标	Item	合计 Total Enterprises	总承包 General Contractor	专业承包 Professional Contractor
企业单位个数 (个)	Number of Enterprises in Charge of Construction (unit)	8362	6560	1802
签订的合同额 (万元)	Volume of Signed Contracts (10000 yuan)	241190897	221752553	19438343
直接从事建设单位承揽工程完成的产值 (万元)	Output Value of Projects Contracted by Construction Units Directly Engaged in Construction (10000 yuan)	103732117	92826953	10905164
自行完成施工产值	Output Value Completed by Self	102251961	91508513	10743447
分包出去工程产值	Engineering Subcontract Value	1480157	1318440	161717
从事建设单位以外承揽工程完成的产值 (万元)	Accomplished Output Value of the Project Not Taken from Construction Units (10000 yuan)	14774376	12058560	2715816
建筑业总产值 (万元)	Gross Output Value of Construction (10000 yuan)	117026336	103567073	13459263
#装饰装修产值	Decoration and Fixing UP	2958421	1513251	1445169
在外省完成产值	In Other Provinces	30410187	27538917	2871270
#建筑工程	Construction Projects	100567355	91792343	8775011
安装工程	Installation Projects	8401565	5624960	2776605
其　他	Others	8057416	6149770	1907647
竣工产值 (万元)	Output Value of Buildings Completed (10000 yuan)	43611070	39381776	4229295
房屋建筑施工面积 (万平方米)	Floor Space of Buildings Under Construction (10000 sq.m)	49670.66	47103.55	2567.11
#本年新开工	Newly Started Projects in this Year	16640.02	15322.89	1317.13
房屋建筑竣工面积 (万平方米)	Floor Space of Buildings Completed (10000 sq.m)	14856.90	13626.38	1230.52
房屋竣工价值 (万元)	Value of Buildings Completed (10000 yuan)	24319740	23093406	1226334
从事建筑业活动的平均人数 (万人)	Average Number of Persons Engaged in Construction Activities (10000 person)	230.74	198.18	32.57
从业人员 (万人)	Employed Persons at the Year-End (10000 person)	211.60	181.73	29.87
#工程技术人员	Engineering Technical Personnel	24.73	20.94	3.78
劳动生产率 (元/人)	Overall Labor Productivity (yuan/person)	507177	522604	413294
房屋建筑面积竣工率 (%)	Rate of Floor Space of Buildings Completed (%)	29.91	28.93	47.93

内资企业 Domestic Funded			港澳台商投资企业 Funded Enterprises from Hong Kong, Macao and Taiwan	外商投资企业 Foreign Funded	国有控股企业 State Controlling Funded Hold Enterprises	房屋建筑业 Building	土木工程建筑业 Civil Engineering	建筑安装业 Construction Installation Industry	建筑装饰和其他建筑业 Architectural Decoration and Other Construction Industry
	#集体 Collective-owned	#私营 Private							
8354	35	7505	5	3	345	4102	2841	511	908
240788739	653579	83746559	73068	329090	134872239	131858776	94819291	8131137	6381694
103672635	492214	50901639	36739	22743	41765310	55863055	38746821	5222304	3899937
102192479	490256	50573892	36739	22743	40731457	55081533	38112972	5193998	3863457
1480157	1958	327747			1033853	781522	633849	28305	36480
14713221	1607	6870550		61155	6829213	5616999	7833655	701022	622699
116905700	491863	57444442	36739	83898	47560670	60698533	45946627	5895021	4486156
2943755	1590	2219544	13933	732	408828	1292266	273930	200777	1191448
30395558	245183	8374883	14629		19784936	12785072	15162018	1632920	830177
100489651	236024	47811360	7812	69892	43011652	54966679	39456559	2777998	3366119
8371807	220541	4237298	25931	3827	2434291	3041551	2804286	2203768	351960
8044242	35298	5395784	2996	10179	2114727	2690302	3685782	913255	768078
43589706	388595	23221553	8800	12565	15394329	26065449	14061878	2106737	1377006
49582.15	222.95	24275.27	4.22	84	20005.18	42735.65	5708.81	607.91	618.28
16637.86	189.01	9839.76	2.16		4918.84	13659.62	2343.61	320.23	316.55
14851.32	187.38	9833.68	1.50	4.09	2991.41	12618.18	1622.23	410.91	205.58
24302071	183641	14147242	8800	8870	6720253	20548860	2834973	652381	283526
230.58	1.46	154.99	0.04	0.12	50.19	136.26	70.45	12.75	11.28
211.55	1.46	144.57	0.04	0.02	43.88	128.21	61.95	11.60	9.84
24.71	0.12	16.60	0.00	0.01	5.82	13.18	8.70	1.48	1.37
507005	336386	370639	902676	705022	947599	445462	652146	462333	397846
29.95	84.04	40.51	35.55	4.85	14.95	29.53	28.42	67.59	33.25

14—5 建筑业企业主要财务指标（2022年）
Main Financial Indicators on Construction Enterprises (2022)

指 标	Item	企业数（个）Number of Enterprises (unit)	流动资产合计 Circulating Funds	#存货 Stock
总 计	**Total**	**8362**	**87229783**	**8326201**
#国有控股企业	State Controlling Share Hold Enterprises	345	44240501	1942702
按登记注册类型分	**Grouped by registration Type**			
内资企业	Domestic Funded Enterprise	8354	87031998	8306965
国有企业	State-owned Enterprise	48	1465618	244915
集体企业	Collective-owned Enterprise	35	186701	64434
股份合作企业	Share Holding Cooperative Enterprises	13	53410	6321
联营企业	Joint Owned Enterprises			
国有独资公司	Wholly State-owned Company	95	12050775	687876
其他有限责任公司	Other Limited Liability Corporations	626	33869407	2069900
股份有限公司	Share-holding Corporations Ltd.	31	5669534	273249
私营企业	Private Enterprises	7505	33736517	4960265
其他企业	Other Enterprises	1	37	5
港澳台商投资企业	Enterprises Funded by Entrepreneurs from Hong Kong, Macao and Taiwan	5	75961	18444
外商投资企业	Foreign Funded Enterprises	3	121824	792
按国民经济行业分	**Grouped by Sector**			
房屋建筑业	Building	4102	41256367	5061786
土木工程建筑业	Civil Engineering	2841	38124511.9	2310749.7
#铁路道路隧道和桥梁工程建筑业	Railroad Road Tunnel &Bridge Engineering Enterprises	2076	23603386	1356465
建筑安装业	Construction Installation Industry	511	4626899	556655
建筑装饰和其他建筑业	Architectural Decoration and Other Construction Industry	908	3222005	397010
建筑装饰和装修业	Architectural Decoration and Decoration Industry	320	950956	147351
按资质等级分	**By Qualification Standard**			
施工总承包	Chief Construction Contract	6560	77272134	6850025
特 级	Top Grade	36	31505775	1010673
一 级	First Grade	457	21044931	2732453
二 级	Second Grade	1238	11565869	1489199
三级及以下	Third Grade and Below	4829	13155560	1617701
专业承包	Professional Contract	1802	9957648	1476176
一 级	First Grade	556	5103757	531484
二 级	Second Grade	828	3382128	678809
三级及以下	Third Grade and Below	418	1471763	265883

单位：万元（10000 yuan）

固定资产原价 Original Value of Fixed Assets	累计折旧 Progressive Depreciation	#本年折旧 Depreciation this Year	资产总计 Total of Assets	负债合计 Total of Liabilities	#流动负债 Current Liabilities	所有者权益 Owners' Equity	#实收资本 Capital Hold
7209103	**3263673**	**532248**	**109846962**	**81736684**	**72110798**	**28110854**	**13157894**
2671074	1311604	159531	57410178	46728151	42325110	**10682027**	4922009
7135803	3249260	530068	109561353	81538528	71996557	28023402	13111957
163982	82064	9990	1937020	1525913	1402905	411106	200793
69799	38878	2939	231538	127033	120491	104505	32603
8616	5020	1046	72830	42968	41877	29862	5269
793768	358074	47257	15239014	13000995	12086236	2238019	1181607
2168575	1063071	128749	44033275	34477356	30095835	9556422	4264927
340300	122831	17669	8385404	6503474	5219408	1881930	530386
3590664	1579271	322418	39662100	25860751	23029805	13801421	6896372
100	50		173	37		136	
29344	5485	839	102516	69992	67519	32524	10814
43956	8928	1342	183092	128164	46722	54928	35123
2752354	1116001	199368	50855296	38493359	32686974	12362010	5680482
3580627.7	1762911.9	258497.6	49688387.3	36940871.6	33645300.4	12747515.7	6126127.2
2223466	1112761	163167	30676427	23172062	21453509	7504366	3815423
553695	252515	50352	5561939	3841467	3573906	1720472	685424
322426	132245	24031	3741340	2460987	2204618	1280856	665862
62909	29251	5340	1065837	689718	610929	376119	211104
5970399	2713087	426971	98024624	73658039	64799326	24367161	11507684
1941391	948521	111640	44491316	35648583	30601446	8842733	3796926
1491102	714972	93698	23992283	17387411	16226014	6604873	2920267
1269632	552032	91552	13877234	9765279	8572846	4111955	2325434
1268274	497563	130081	15663791	10856766	9399020	4807601	2465057
1238704	550585	105277	11822338	8078645	7311472	3743693	1650211
453364	216547	39557	6010908	4212390	3881243	1798518	837862
467988	174130	39118	3972439	2748702	2433103	1223737	513540
317352	159908	26602	1838991	1117553	997127	721438	298809

14—5 续表 continued

指 标	Item	主营业务收入 Main Business Income	主营业务成本 Main Business Cost	主营业务税金及附加 Main Business Taxes and Additional
总 计	**Total**	**94785751**	**89445570**	**433335**
#国有及国有控股企业	State Controlling Share Hold Enterprises	41654563	39188509	105635
按登记注册类型分	**Grouped by registration Type**			
内资企业	Domestic Funded Enterprise	94690731	89365897	433126
国有企业	State-owned Enterprise	2144704	2011575	5354
集体企业	Collective-owned Enterprise	535190	454499	16648
股份合作企业	Share Holding Cooperative Enterprises	240966	228746	9854
联营企业	Joint Owned Enterprises			
国有独资公司	Wholly State-owned Company	12768286	12131108	32953
其他有限责任公司	Other Limited Liability Corporations	32277952	30583286	87675
股份有限公司	Share-holding Corporations Ltd.	3354609	3010777	10277
私营企业	Private Enterprises	43369024	40945907	270365
其他企业	Other Enterprises			
港澳台商投资企业	Enterprises Funded by Entrepreneurs from Hong Kong, Macao and Taiwan	37196	29904	110
外商投资企业	Foreign Funded Enterprises	57824	49769	100
按国民经济行业分	**Grouped by Sector**			
房屋建筑业	Building	46425848	44452312	234356
土木工程建筑业	Civil Engineering	38266626	35834047.9	134141.1
#铁路道路隧道和桥梁工程建筑业	Railroad Road Tunnel &Bridge Engineering Enterprises	24720468	23383273	88659
建筑安装业	Construction Installation Industry	6120277	5486253	45831
建筑装饰和其他建筑业	Architectural Decoration and Other Construction Industry	3973001	3672958	19008
建筑装饰和装修业	Architectural Decoration and Decoration Industry	1312778	1204840	5495
按资质等级分	**By Qualification Standard**			
施工总承包	Chief Construction Contract	82570734	78291076	363155
特 级	Top Grade	33966079	31901290	96703
一 级	First Grade	21392421	20420756	89224
二 级	Second Grade	11709594	11278470	82960
三级及以下	Third Grade and Below	15502640	14690561	94268
专业承包	Professional Contract	12215017	11154494	70180
一 级	First Grade	6421196	5822780	39592
二 级	Second Grade	3890942	3597707	21956
三级及以下	Third Grade and Below	1902880	1734007	8633

单位：万元（10000 yuan）

其他业务利润 Other Business Profit	销售费用 Operating Expense	管理费用 Management Expense	财务费用 Financial Expenses	营业利润 Operating Profit	利润总额 Total Profit	应交增值税 Value-added Tax Payable	本年应付工资薪酬 Total Payable Wages this Year
87380	**384244**	**2950390**	**578739**	**2742762**	**2776931**	**2121983**	**14197209**
66010	37052	740036	300575	1323570	1340941	629247	4020823
87380	384138	2945857	576963	2734553	2768580	2121077	14190910
1317	4039	54876	7387	61294	63342	34383	387070
120	635	56495	713	6191	6633	42991	103663
	570	3347	66	3779	4396	3252	31635
36490	12193	142397	77112	376342	387208	220691	1474403
37183	40997	814987	193949	987574	995949	507971	3342326
487	19686	92275	64196	185893	186645	41383	417868
11784	305817	1781461	233536	1113477	1124403	1270405	8433946
	200	20	6	4	4		
	105	3048	-60	3852	3936	817	4020
	1	1485	1836	4358	4415	89	2279
12656	136294	1175865	338265	1211897	1226036	1210208	7662862
68794.9	110251.2	1248050.7	206053.8	1254968.2	1267910.7	684853.1	4893711.7
39661	67186	665579	97477	759441	761209	417162	3120627
1122	105836	317658	15903	171809	171932	121877	892048
4807	31863	208816	18517	104088	111052	105044	748588
-4	6612	69910	6087	31487	32124	31614	191371
79199	230645	2267017	531664	2414865	2437170	1815908	12050607
57852	34284	558151	266133	937703	943157	410901	3368235
10345	50068	442584	100818	647019	653691	538026	3711238
2896	46112	473274	83617	338986	342299	372892	2259432
8106	100182	793009	81095	491157	498024	494089	2711702
8181	153599	683373	47075	327897	339761	306075	2146603
1678	105209	293092	21880	154233	156624	160819	1085321
5658	29495	259675	18299	114356	122486	100052	733004
845	18895	130606	6896	59308	60652	45204	328278

14—6 按登记注册类型分建筑业企业主要经济指标（2022）
According to the Construction Enterprise Registration Type Points Leading Economic Indicators (2022)

指标		Item		合计 Total Enterprises	内资企业 Domestic Funded
企业单位数	（个）	Number of Construction Enterprises	(unit)	8362	8354
从业人数	（万人）	Staff and Workers (annual average)	(10000 persons)	211.6	211.55
固定资产原价	（万元）	Original Cost of Fixed Assets	(10000 yuan)	7209103	7135803.4
建筑业总产值	（万元）	Gross Output Value of Construction	(10000 yuan)	117026336	116905699.6
建筑工程		Construction Projects		100567355	100489651.3
安装工程		Installation Projects		8401565	8371806.6
其　他		Others		8057416	8044241.7
固定资产本年折旧	（万元）	Depreciation of Fixed Assets	(10000 yuan)	532248	530067.5
应付职工薪酬	（万元）	Payable Employee compensation	(10000yuan)	14197209	14190910.4
主营业务税金及附加	（万元）	Main Business Tax and Addition	(10000yuan)	433335	433125.7
应交增值税	（万元）	Value-added Tax Payable	(10000yuan)	2121983	2121076.7
营业利润	（万元）	Business Profit	(10000yuan)	2742762	2734553.0
利润总额	（万元）	Total Profits	(10000 yuan)	2776931	2768579.7
房屋建筑施工面积	（万平方米）	Floor Space of Buildings Under Construction	(10000 sq.m)	49670.66	49582.15
房屋建筑竣工面积	（万平方米）	Floor Space of Buildings Completed	(10000 sq.m)	14856.90	14851.32
产值利润率	(%)	Ratio of Profit to Gross Output Value	(%)	2.37	2.37

#国 有 State-owned	#集 体 Collective-owned	港澳台商投资企业 Funded Enterprises from Hong Kong, Macao and Taiwan	#港澳台商独资企业 Hong Kong and Taiwan-funded Enterprises	外商投资企业 Foreign Funded
48	35	5	3	3
4.4695	1.4592	0.035	0.0189	0.0194
163981.6	69798.6	29343.5	1349.8	43955.8
2327533.3	491863.0	36738.9	23940.5	83897.6
1774766.9	236023.6	7811.5	7811.5	69891.7
469601.0	220541.4	25931.4	14233.4	3827.4
83165.4	35298.0	2996.0	1895.6	10178.5
9989.5	2938.6	838.7	61.3	1342.0
387069.8	103662.6	4020.2	2370.3	2278.6
5353.5	16648.1	109.9	75.4	99.5
34383.0	42991.4	816.7	538.3	89.2
61293.8	6190.5	3851.7	1952.8	4357.7
63342.1	6632.6	3936.1	1988.1	4415.1
709.23	222.95	4.22	4.22	84.29
251.81	187.38	1.50	1.50	4.09
2.72	1.35	10.71	8.30	5.26

14—7 各市建筑业企业房屋建筑完成情况（2022年）
Floor Space of Buildings Completed by Construction Enterprises by Region (2022)

地 区	Region	房屋建筑竣工面积（万平方米）Completed Area of Building Construction (10000 sq.m)	#住 宅 Residential Buildings	房屋竣工价 值（万元）Value of the Completed House (10000 yuan)	#住 宅 Residential Buildings
总 计	**Total**	**14856.90**	**8459.93**	**24319740**	**14035398**
合肥市	Hefei	5015.24	3523.71	9429043	6531772
淮北市	Huaibei	109.45	87.72	225284	175146
亳州市	Bozhou	397.74	130.13	425291	114970
宿州市	Suzhou	1008.73	394.99	1529711	667641
蚌埠市	Bengbu	991.46	679.96	2016281	1256817
阜阳市	Fuyang	586.30	309.53	754245	388036
淮南市	Huainan	114.37	60.46	163446	82637
滁州市	Chuzhou	1404.68	574.99	2340863	1021096
六安市	Luan	626.64	444.90	887051	615145
马鞍山市	Maanshan	485.87	251.46	784107	341399
芜湖市	Wuhu	1376.31	821.69	2039501	1234023
宣城市	Xuancheng	758.00	196.61	1038954	259413
铜陵市	Tongling	304.90	140.92	442176	199359
池州市	Chizhou	422.16	193.44	532574	278211
安庆市	Anqing	921.00	469.62	1211834	615619
黄山市	Huangshan	334.06	179.81	499380	254116

14—8 各市按登记注册类型和行业分的建筑业企业单位数（2022年）
Number of Construction Enterprises by Registration Status, Section and Region (2022)

单位：个（unit）

地 区 Region	合 计 Total Enterprises	内资企业 Domestic Funded	港澳台商投资企业 Funded by Entrepreneurs from Hong Kong, Macao and Taiwan	外商投资企业 Foreign Funded	国有控股企业 State-owned and State-controlled Enterprises	房屋工程建筑业 Building	土木工程建筑业 Civil Engineering	建筑安装业 Construction Installation Industry	建筑装饰和其他建筑业 Architectural Decoration and Other Construction Industry
总 计 Total	**8362**	**8354**	**5**	**3**	**345**	**4102**	**2841**	**511**	**908**
合肥市 Hefei	1909	1907	2		78	635	708	210	356
淮北市 Huaibei	37	36	1		8	20	15	1	1
亳州市 Bozhou	312	311	1		29	196	73	23	20
宿州市 Suzhou	380	380			18	232	105	24	19
蚌埠市 Bengbu	351	350		1	32	187	86	29	49
阜阳市 Fuyang	556	556			32	347	165	11	33
淮南市 Huainan	269	268		1	14	187	61	12	9
滁州市 Chuzhou	782	780	1	1	18	442	271	31	38
六安市 Luan	434	434			12	248	155	7	24
马鞍山市 Maanshan	273	273			8	166	69	18	20
芜湖市 Wuhu	980	980			23	481	341	51	107
宣城市 Xuancheng	391	391			19	203	135	22	31
铜陵市 Tongling	404	404			9	156	148	23	77
池州市 Chizhou	370	370			10	147	166	21	36
安庆市 Anqing	733	733			27	355	282	24	72
黄山市 Huangshan	181	181			8	100	61	4	16

14—9 各市按经济类型和行业分的建筑业总产值（2022年）
Overall Output Value of Enterprises in Charge of Construction by Ownership and Region (2022)

单位：万元（10000 yuan）

地区 Region	合计 Total Enterprises	内资企业 Domestic Funded	港澳台商投资企业 Funded by Entrepreneurs from Hong Kong, Macao and Taiwan	外商投资企业 Foreign Funded	国有控股企业 State-owned and State-controlled Enterprises	房屋工程建筑业 Building	土木工程建筑业 Civil Engineering	建筑安装业 Construction Installation Industry	建筑装饰和其他建筑业 Architectural Decoration and Other Construction Industry
总计 Total	**117026336**	**116905700**	**36739**	**83898**	**47560670**	**60698533**	**45946627**	**5895021**	**4486156**
合肥市 Hefei	56132673	56109425	23248		30961579	24068320	26533178	3141102	2390074
淮北市 Huaibei	966364	965671	692		748534	337884	627548	905	27
亳州市 Bozhou	1847394	1840624	6770		849102	1370917	329597	104183	42697
宿州市 Suzhou	6328747	6328747			1726277	2529821	2347810	1369667	81450
蚌埠市 Bengbu	6053152	6040587		12565	3778157	2026238	3766795	73978	186141
阜阳市 Fuyang	3741558	3741558			1194002	2203657	1445946	23450	68504
淮南市 Huainan	1135429	1074274		61155	309868	814068	246420	54783	20157
滁州市 Chuzhou	7873044	7856836	6029	10179	283699	6013074	1489776	226961	143232
六安市 Luan	3326449	3326449			219028	2283878	924392	60763	57417
马鞍山市 Maanshan	6924583	6924583			4066065	6035326	588892	128220	172145
芜湖市 Wuhu	9894915	9894915			1833716	5527500	3534909	285700	546807
宣城市 Xuancheng	3218434	3218434			575529	1706076	1238394	64281	209683
铜陵市 Tongling	2278917	2278917			284334	1253255	688042	90300	247321
池州市 Chizhou	1784390	1784390			193257	1025240	544853	147265	67031
安庆市 Anqing	4245554	4245554			459822	2625273	1390369	110953	118959
黄山市 Huangshan	1274735	1274735			77702	878007	249706	12511	134512

14—10 各市建筑业企业生产情况（2022年）

Production Indicators on Construction Enterprises by Region (2022)

地区	Region	企业单位个数（个）Number of Enterprises (unit)	总产值（万元）Total Output Value (10000 yuan)	建筑工程 Construction	安装工程 Installation	其他产值 Other Output Value	竣工产值（万元）Output Value of Buildings Completed (10000 yuan)
总计	**Total**	**8362**	**117026336**	**100567355**	**8401565**	**8057416**	**43611070**
合肥市	Hefei	1909	56132673	49407582	4631318	2093774	19039712
淮北市	Huaibei	37	966364	908198	24540	33625	281347
亳州市	Bozhou	312	1847394	1482365	250027	115002	773144
宿州市	Suzhou	380	6328747	4645978	866174	816596	3243008
蚌埠市	Bengbu	351	6053152	4237472	262075	1553605	3502410
阜阳市	Fuyang	556	3741558	3179836	266177	295545	1465221
淮南市	Huainan	269	1135429	947942	94071	93416	3222993
滁州市	Chuzhou	782	7873044	6901864	252492	718688	3290035
六安市	Luan	434	3326449	2787985	167706	370758	1414635
马鞍山市	Maanshan	273	6924583	6150853	383877	389853	1560797
芜湖市	Wuhu	980	9894915	8889377	430561	574977	2946467
宣城市	Xuancheng	391	3218434	2913452	120703	184278	1548554
铜陵市	Tongling	404	2278917	1915740	208868	154310	861301
池州市	Chizhou	370	1784390	1430586	154533	199270	831412
安庆市	Anqing	733	4245554	3588510	221477	435567	1822881
黄山市	Huangshan	181	1274735	1179615	66968	28152	707156

地区	Region	房屋建筑施工面积（万平方米）Floor Space of Building Under Construction (10000 sq.m)	房屋建筑竣工面积（万平方米）Floor Space of Building Completed (10000 sq.m)	自有施工机械设备 Machinery and Equipment Owned：净值（万元）Net Value (10000 yuan)	总台数（台）Number (unit)	总功率（万千瓦）Total Power (10000 kW)	期末从业人数（万人）Staff and Workers (10000 persons)
总计	**Total**	**49670.66**	**14856.90**	**909063**	**176754**	**404.49**	**211.60**
合肥市	Hefei	22201.79	5015.24	441150	91165	177.80	82.02
淮北市	Huaibei	636.40	109.45	9147	2721	3.24	1.22
亳州市	Bozhou	1593.22	397.74	7098	468	0.99	3.82
宿州市	Suzhou	2084.25	1008.73	142615	17001	86.13	13.61
蚌埠市	Bengbu	3107.52	991.46	32038	6146	9.23	9.51
阜阳市	Fuyang	1598.12	586.30	19314	17736	8.96	9.14
淮南市	Huainan	490.86	114.37	11132	1383	2.21	2.42
滁州市	Chuzhou	2963.39	1404.68	38732	3166	9.37	18.17
六安市	Luan	1593.71	626.64	37431	5238	10.74	11.52
马鞍山市	Maanshan	3460.20	485.87	33112	7907	23.57	8.12
芜湖市	Wuhu	3295.19	1376.31	39849	4270	14.02	20.50
宣城市	Xuancheng	2316.50	758.00	13040	1777	3.69	7.20
铜陵市	Tongling	1018.52	304.90	9122	4859	19.86	4.79
池州市	Chizhou	862.24	422.16	5861	1100	2.17	4.71
安庆市	Anqing	1748.90	921.00	59758	9180	26.72	11.30
黄山市	Huangshan	699.85	334.06	9664	2637	5.81	3.55

14—11 各市建筑业企业主要财务指标（2022年）
Main Financial Indicators on Construction Enterprises by Region (2022)

单位：万元（10000 yuan）

地区	Region	流动资产合计 Circulating Funds	固定资产原价 Original Value of Fixed Assets	累计折旧 Accumulated Depreciation	#本年 This Year	资产总计 Total Assets	负债合计 Total Liabilities	所有者权益 Owners' Equity	#实收资本 Capital Hold
总计	**Total**	**87229783**	**7209103**	**3263673**	**532248**	**109846962**	**81736684**	**28110854**	**13157894**
合肥市	Hefei	43433984	3110929	1509043	215144	54932891	43234364	11698527	5485979
淮北市	Huaibei	1409114	78398	37289	6689	1531661	1294932	236728	175303
亳州市	Bozhou	2519166	122188	38567	7939	3056544	2521031	535512	231013
宿州市	Suzhou	3920578	570915	259163	44976	4966104	3391433	1574670	628582
蚌埠市	Bengbu	6262480	164635	87587	17093	9581967	7276916	2305554	816845
阜阳市	Fuyang	3217367	216991	89892	19027	3726473	2685781	1040692	459525
淮南市	Huainan	1483466	94977	44238	5455	1622854	1336083	286771	192144
滁州市	Chuzhou	3926077	350034	140758	34603	5005200	3149633	1855640	913436
六安市	Luan	2752830	326812	140576	27193	3347038	1975582	1371456	691639
马鞍山市	Maanshan	4302208	265270	129533	14878	5177346	3665382	1511964	611214
芜湖市	Wuhu	4871839	670865	271604	58752	6042392	3992537	2049855	902111
宣城市	Xuancheng	1940195	218375	100282	22193	2247475	1557858	689617	409232
铜陵市	Tongling	1642876	204834	90244	15862	1922899	1353025	569873	319969
池州市	Chizhou	1714240	229266	66163	10978	2022652	1392667	629985	378237
安庆市	Anqing	2977098	461709	202374	25337	3608904	2196300	1412604	719471
黄山市	Huangshan	856268	122904	56361	6131	1054566	713161	341405	223195

地区	Region	主营业务收入 Main Business Income	主营业务成本 Main Business Cost	主营业务税金及附加 Main Business Taxes and Additional	销售费用 Operating Expense	管理费用 Management Expense	财务费用 Financial Expenses	营业利润 Operating Profit	利润总额 Total Profit	本年应付薪酬总额 Payable Salary This Year
总计	**Total**	**94785751**	**89445570**	**433335**	**384244**	**2950390**	**578739**	**2742762**	**2776931**	**14197209**
合肥市	Hefei	46449258	43278805	158567	179675	1207276	273828	1166645	1176492	6358930
淮北市	Huaibei	933466	1051791	6771	152	29450	8217	23740	25236	80242
亳州市	Bozhou	1683899	1639604	6325	8540	60280	19254	75034	76579	244078
宿州市	Suzhou	5529712	5120519	60946	40584	220460	60299	167171	166571	698471
蚌埠市	Bengbu	4458449	4237292	12840	3660	127332	39529	224883	226634	355781
阜阳市	Fuyang	2738270	2699401	19571	14691	104538	19306	85454	85273	449666
淮南市	Huainan	975166	973984	3562	1512	53970	5454	8417	9538	103247
滁州市	Chuzhou	4737516	4600681	21306	18317	155840	33630	143484	146359	1294249
六安市	Luan	3153206	3000001	16896	7874	121222	25100	103169	103906	590687
马鞍山市	Maanshan	6893683	6601414	19270	6406	148590	20932	200386	200844	545628
芜湖市	Wuhu	7806247	7301377	48367	54497	274418	20511	269873	280444	1805834
宣城市	Xuancheng	2608426	2459138	16228	10490	102578	11987	90553	89073	388341
铜陵市	Tongling	1625960	1635077	7009	10106	87713	3077	33904	34317	318481
池州市	Chizhou	1420526	1318948	7287	5917	61685	11514	49151	53544	213649
安庆市	Anqing	2792842	2616771	24163	20197	136430	20089	84092	84191	594108
黄山市	Huangshan	979127	910768	4228	1627	58609	6011	16808	17931	155819

主要统计指标解释

建筑业统计单位

指从事房屋、构筑物建造和设备安装活动的法人企业。建筑业法人企业应具有建筑业资质并能够独立核算，同时其应具备以下条件：①依法成立，有自己的名称、组织机构和场所，能够承担民事责任；②独立拥有和使用资产，承担负债，有权与其他单位签订合同；③独立核算盈亏，能够编制资产负债表。

建筑业总产值

是以货币形式表现的建筑业企业在一定时期内生产的建筑业产品和提供的服务的总和。建筑业总产值包括：

⑴建筑工程产值：指列入建筑工程预算内的各种工程价值。

⑵安装工程产值：指设备安装工程价值，不包括被安装设备本身的价值。

⑶其他产值：建筑业总产值中除建筑工程、安装工程以外的产值。包括房屋构筑物修理产值、非标准设备制造产值、总包企业向分包企业收取的管理费以及不能明确划分的施工活动所完成的产值。

a. 房屋构筑物修理产值：指房屋和构筑物修理所完成的产值，但不包括被修理房屋、构筑物本身价值和生产设备的修理价值。

b. 非标准设备制造产值：指加工制造没有定型的非标准生产设备的加工费和原材料价值(如化工厂、炼油厂用的各种罐、槽，矿井生产统一使用的各种漏斗、三角槽、阀门等)以及附属加工厂为本企业承建工程制作的非标准设备的价值。

房屋建筑施工面积

指在报告期内施过工的全部房屋建筑面积，包括本期新开工的房屋面积、上期施工跨入本期继续施工的房屋面积、上期停缓建在本期恢复施工的房屋面积、本期竣工的房屋面积及本期施工后又停缓建的房屋面积。

房屋建筑竣工面积

指在报告期内房屋建筑按照设计要求全部完工，达到了使用条件，经验收鉴定合格，正式移交使用单位的房屋建筑面积。

Explanatory Notes for Major Statistical Indicators

Statistical Unit in the Construction Industry

refers to a corporate enterprise engaged in the construction of buildings and structures and in the installation of equipment. A corporate construction enterprise should have qualification certificates with independent accounting system, and should meet the following 3 requirements: a) being set up in line with relevant legal basis, having its full name, organization and location, and capable of taking civil liabilities; b) independently possessing and using its assets and assuming its liabilities, and entitled to sign contracts with other institutions; and c) making independent accounts of its profits and losses, and capable of compiling its own balance sheet.

Gross Output Value of Construction

refers to total of construction products and services, expressed in money terms, produced or rendered by construction and installation enterprises during a given period of time. It includes:

(1) Output value of construction projects: the value of projects covered by the project budgets;

(2) Output value of installation projects: the value of the installation of equipment, (excluding the value of the equipment to be installed);

(3) Other output values: the output value of construction industry apart from that of construction projects and installation projects. It includes: output value of repair of buildings and structures; output value of non-standard equipment manufacturing; overhead expenses received by contracted enterprises from the sub-contracted enterprises and the completed output value of construction activities for which there is no clear definition.

a. Output value of repair of buildings and structures: the value created through the repairs of buildings or structures. It does not include the value of buildings or structures being repaired and the value of the repair of production equipment;

b. Output value of manufactured non-standard equipment: the value of non-standard production equipment, including raw materials and manufacturing cost, made for the construction project (i.e., chemical plant; kettles or tanks used by refineries; various fillers, triangle tanks, valves used by mines). It also includes the output value of equipment manufactured by subsidiary workshops.

Floor Space of Buildings Under Construction

refers to floor space of buildings under construction during the reference period, including the floor space of buildings for which construction has newly started; buildings for which construction has started earlier and is continuing during the reference period; and buildings for which construction has been suspended earlier but has restarted during the reference period; buildings completed during the reference period; and buildings under construction but construction has subsequently been during the reference period.

Floor Space of Buildings Completed

refers to the floor space of buildings that are completed in the reference period in accordance with the requirements of the design, up to the standard for being put into use, and having been checked and accepted by departments concerned as qualified ones.

第十五篇

Chapter 15

运输和邮电

TRANSPORT，POST AND TELECOMMUNICATION SERVICES

简要说明

一、交通运输业资料主要包括：铁路、公路、水路、民航四种运输方式的线路里程、运输设备拥有量，各种运输方式完成的货物运输量等。

邮电通信业资料主要包括：全省邮电局(所)及邮路情况，邮电通信主要电路及设备拥有量，主要邮电业务完成情况，邮电通信发展水平等资料。

二、有关交通运输资料分别来源于中国铁道上海局集团有限公司，省交通运输厅，民航安徽安全监督管理局，东航安徽分公司，省公安厅及本局有关年报资料。邮电通信业资料来源于省邮政管理局、通信管理局。

三、各部门资料调查范围及统计单位。

1. 铁路资料：来源于中国铁道上海局集团有限公司反馈数据。

2. 公路、水运、港口资料：公路和水运线路里程为年末通车和通航里程数(不含在建和未正式投入使用的公路和航道)由省交通运输厅提供。民用和公路营运车辆拥有量分别由省公安厅、省交通运输厅和农机局提供。

3. 民航运输资料：民航运输统计对象为我省境内从事民用航空运输飞行和通用飞行的东方航空公司安徽分公司。

4. 邮电通信资料：邮电通信包括邮政和电信业务。邮电业务量按业务范围分为国内业务量和国际及港澳业务量(对台业务量统计在港澳中)。

Brief Introduction

I. Data of transport cover mainly the length of the routes of railways, highways, waterways and civil aviation transport, the ownership of the transport equipment, the freight traffic and passenger traffic accomplished by various means of transportation.

Data of post and telecommunications cover mainly the situation of post and telecommunications offices and postal routes, the telephone lines, telegraph lines and the ownership of the telecommunication facilities, the principal postal and telecommunications services rendered, and the level of the development of the postal and telecommunications services, etc.

II. Relevant traffic and transportation data are from China Railway Shanghai Bureau Group Co., Ltd., Provincial Transportation Department, Anhui Safety Supervision and Administration Bureau of Civil Aviation, Anhui Branch of China Eastern Airlines, Provincial Public Security Department and the relevant annual reports of the Bureau. The data of the post and telecommunications industry shall come from the provincial postal administration and the communications administration.

III. The statistical coverage and statistical units of the various data:

1. Railway data: Feedback data from China Railway Shanghai Bureau Group Co., Ltd.

2. Data on highways, waterways and ports: The length of highways and waterways refer to the length open to traffic or navigation at the end of the year (not including the mileage of highways and waterways under construction but not officially put into use.) and Data are provided by the Department of Communication. Data on the stock of the highway civilian and transport business vehicles are provide by the Department of Public Security and Department of transportation and Agricultural Machinery Bureau .

3. Data on the civil aviation transport: The statistical units of the civil aviation transport include the enterprises registered in Anhui and engaged in the civil aviation transport flights and flights for general purpose, including the enterprises directly under the Civil Aviation Administration of Anhui Province or not under it.

4. Data on post and telecommunications: The post and telecommunications statistics cover postal and telecommunication services. The business volume of post and telecommunications is classified by business area into the domestic volume, the volume between China mainland and Hong Kong and Macao (including Taiwan) and the international volume.

15—1 交通运输业基本情况
Basic Conditions of Transportation

指标	Item	2010	2015	2020	2021	2022
运输线路长度（公里）	Length of Transportation Routes (km)					
铁路营业里程	Railways in Operation	2850	4169	5159	5263	5265
公路	Highways	149382	186940	236483	237411	237967
内河	Navigable Inland Waterways	5587	5729	5777	5775	5775
民航	Total Civil Aviation Routes	76303	103676	113559	31826	72079
#国际航线	International Routes	6575	15303	9157		2500
客运量总计（万人）	Total Passenger Traffic (10000 persons)	159597	87107	32570	27673	14695
铁路	Railways	5552	8553	9455	10996	7201
公路	Highways	153697	78072	22776	16284	7284
水运	Waterways	139	185	111	161	87
民航	Total Civil Aviation Routes	208	297	229	231	123
旅客周转量总计（万人公里）	Total Passenger-kilometers (10000 passenger-km)	15027550	12582090	7285606	7847152	5004008
铁路	Railways	4680584	6429489	5271179	6035436	4066717
公路	Highways	10101874	5748829	1681473	1478161	756104
水运	Waterways	2684	3843	1519	2130	1055
民航	Total Civil Aviation Routes	242408	399929	331435	331425	180132
货运量总计（万吨）	Total Freight Traffic (10000 tons)	228106	345756	374318	401242	393920
铁路	Railways	12091	10158	7549	7617	7769
公路	Highways	183658	230649	243529	259044	245982
水运	Waterways	32355	104947	123239	134580	140167
民航	Total Civil Aviation Routes	2.2	2.3	1.6	1.7	1.0
货物周转量总计（万吨公里）	Total Freight Ton-kilometers (10000 tons-km)	71536800	104025651	102091817	110239176	112364705
铁路	Railways	10165481	7393851	7009432	7825368	8035551
公路	Highways	50049069	47218724	34122365	37278807	36959840
水运	Waterways	11319581	49409946	60957621	65132585	67367860
民航	Total Civil Aviation Routes	2669	3130	2398	2416	1453
民用汽车拥有量（辆）	Number of Civil Vehicles Owned (unit)	2432339	5128318	9908541	10643900	11296878
载客汽车辆数	Number of Buses and Cars	1409937	4081562	8489544	9150111	9822229
载货汽车辆数	Number of Trucks	663361	875638	1326385	1400904	1381971
私人汽车拥有量	Number of Motor Vehicles Owned by Individuals	1661937	4231254	8724655	9397991	10049303
民用运输船舶拥有量（艘）	Number of Civil Transport Vessels (unit)	29186	28800	24539	24821	24519
#机动船	Motor Vessels	27041	27475	23757	24128	23890
驳船	Barges	2145	1325	782	693	629
私人运输船舶拥有量（艘）	Number of Private-owned Transport Vessels (unit)	4278	1882	1466	1576	1528
机动船	Motor Vessels	4262	1882	1466	1576	1528
驳船	Barges	16				

注：1. 2019年交通运输部组织的道路货物运输量专项调查，重新调整基数，客、货运量及周转量与2018年前数据不具可比性。

2. 运输线路长度中的内河长度为通航里程数。

a) In 2019, the Ministry of Transport organized a special survey on road freight transport volume, which readjusted the base. The passenger, freight volume and turnover volume were not comparable with the data before 2018.

b) Transportation line length of inland river navigation mileage in length.

15—2 运输路线长度
Length of Transportation Routes

单位：公里（km）

指　　标	Item	2010	2015	2020	2021	2022
铁　　路	**Railways**					
营业里程（省境内）	Length of Railways in Operation (within the boundaries of the province)	2850	4169	5159	5263	5265
公　　路	**Highways**					
公路里程	Total Length of Highways	149382	186940	236483	237411	237967
国道、省道	National and Provincial Routes	12412	13829	27947	28351	28860
县　道	County Routes	23970	24253	32571	32980	32452
乡　道	Village and town Routes	36226	36498	42769	42747	43458
专用公路	Special Highways	1004	1002	66	17	17
高速公路	Express-way	2929	4249	4904	5146	5477
一级公路	First Class	499	3166	5773	6171	6752
二级公路	Second Class	10504	10667	13188	13874	13837
三级公路	Third Class	15306	18920	20884	21606	21978
四级公路	Forth Class	113106	145875	191675	190590	189900
等外公路	Highway Below Class IV	7042	4063	59	23	23
在公路里程中：	Of the Total Length of Highways:					
晴雨通车里程	Length of Highways Opened to Traffic Despite Rain or Shine	145514	184290	236418	237388	237944
绿化里程	Length of Forestation Highways	60448	143833	206980	217263	220918
水　　运	**Waterways**					
内河航道通航里程	Length of Navigable Inland Waterways	5587	5729	5777	5775	5775
民　　航	**Total Civil Aviation Routes**					
国际航线	International Routes	6575	15303	9157		2500
国内航线	Domestic Routes	69728	88373	104402	92771	72079

15—3 运输线路质量
Quality of Transportation Routes

指　标	Item	2010	2015	2020	2021	2022
铁路营业里程　（公里）	**Length of Railways in Operation (km)**	**2850**	**4169**	**5159**	**5263**	**5265**
#复线里程　（公里）	Double-track Mileage (km)	1523	2753			
复线里程比重　(%)	Proportion of Double-track Mileage (%)	53.4	66.0			
公路线路里程　（公里）	**Length of Highways (km)**	**149382**	**186940**	**236483**	**237411**	**237967**
#等级公路里程　（公里）	Grade Highway Mileage (km)	142340	182877	236424	237388	237944
等级公路里程比重　(%)	Proportion of Mileage of Grade Highway (%)	95.3	97.8	100.0	100.0	100.0
内河航道里程　（公里）	**Length of Navigable Inland Waterways (km)**	**6507**	**6612**	**6628**	**6627**	**6627**
#等级航道里程　（公里）	Grade Channel Mileage (km)	5226	5345	5361	5359	5359
等级航道里程比重　(%)	Mileage Proportion of Grade Channel (%)	80.3	80.8	80.9	80.9	80.9

15—4 内河港口码头吞吐量
Volume of Passenger and Freight Handled in Ports of Inland Rivers

年　份 Year	旅客吞吐量（万人）Passenger Handled (10000 persons)	#旅客离港量 Out-port	货物吞吐量（万吨）Cargo Handled (10000 tons)	#集装箱（万标准箱）Container (10000 standard cases)
2010	69.18	57.00	32502.00	22.20
2013	78.52	41.35	39617.52	52.67
2014	76.38	39.52	43837.92	76.42
2015	62.14	31.79	48044.32	95.59
2016	64.31	32.59	51917.40	114.75
2017	54.71	27.56	51249.41	138.38
2018	57.71	29.15	51134.97	148.73
2019			55488.07	179.41
2020			54095.00	194.42
2021			58325.84	204.09
2022			60792.62	213.99

注：1. 2011年以后统计范围为通过能力在200万吨以上内河港口，以及从事外贸、集装箱的港口，与历年数据具有不可比性。
2. 港口吞吐量年报统计包含全省16个港口。
3. 2019年起旅客吞吐量及旅客离港量取消统计。

a) After 2011 statistic range are ports of capacity of 2000000 tons and over in inland river, and ports engaged in foreign trade, container port the data of the past years are not comparable.
b) The annual port throughput report includes 16 ports in the province.
c) Statistics on passenger throughput and passenger departure will be cancelled from 2019.

15—5 主要港口分货类吞吐量
Volume of Throughput in Major Ports by Type of Freight

单位：万吨（10000 tons）

货类	Type of Goods	2015	2020	2021	2022
吞吐量合计	**Total Throughput**	**1180.02**	**13536.65**	**13474.55**	**13504.01**
煤炭及制品	Coal and Products	777.91	2363.06	2503.69	2582.87
石油天然气及制品	Petroleum, Natural Gas and Products		120.56	148.43	185.43
金属矿石	Metal Ores	3.13	1168.76	1562.10	1666.71
钢铁	Steel and Iron	31.85	472.10	424.24	420.84
矿建材料	Mineral Building	8.80	4166.62	3325.61	2969.90
水泥	Cement	7.18	3485.67	3745.90	3754.84
木材	Timber		0.02	0.94	
非金属矿石	Nonmetal Ores	26.50	440.18	583.40	616.25
化肥及农药	Chemical Fertilizers and Pesticides	0.04	0.85	0.60	1.16
盐	Salt		21.60	26.13	16.57
粮食	Grain		56.44	52.55	41.85
机械、设备、电器	Machinery , Equipment, Electric Apparatus		0.85	2.23	0.28
化工原料及制品	Industrial Chemicals and Products	2.18	121.13	128.74	115.58
轻工、医药产品	Light industry, Medical Products		1.00	0.29	0.55
农林牧渔业产品	Agriculture, Forestry, Animal Husbandry and Fishery Products		11.51	8.21	2.76
其他	Other		322.43	1106.30	1128.42

注：2017年之前数据是安徽皖江物流（集团）股份公司涉水的吞吐量，以后是芜湖港的吞吐量数据。
a) The data before 2017 is the throughput of Anhui Wanjiang logistics (group) co., ltd. The throughput data of Wuhu Port will follow.

15—6 各市公路客货运输量（2022年）
Highway Passenger and Freight Traffic Volume By Region （2022）

地区	Region	客运量（万人）Passenger Traffic (10000 persons)	旅客周转量（万人公里）Passenger-kilometers (10000 passenger-km)	货运量（万吨）Freight Traffic (10000 tons)	货物周转量（万吨公里）Freight Ton-kilometers (10000 tons-km)
总计	**Total**	**7284**	**756104**	**245982**	**36959840**
合肥市	Hefei	1010	143537	28546	2568745
淮北市	Huaibei	110	30322	12379	2287491
亳州市	Bozhou	473	54184	30557	6515463
宿州市	Suzhou	200	25603	20555	3759169
蚌埠市	Bengbu	321	25137	31600	5965850
阜阳市	Fuyang	949	123463	33638	6022849
淮南市	Huainan	388	35047	9388	697978
滁州市	Chuzhou	283	38318	19192	3247240
六安市	Luan	498	80885	17595	2271270
马鞍山市	Maanshan	335	14362	4568	209921
芜湖市	Wuhu	575	41919	7192	766607
宣城市	Xuancheng	170	14007	11870	1015811
铜陵市	Tongling	100	15955	3356	180649
池州市	Chizhou	647	21442	5402	301113
安庆市	Anqing	650	61044	6285	681739
黄山市	Huangshan	574	30880	3857	467944

15—7 主要年份公路线路年底到达数（按技术等级分）
Length of Highway Routes at the Year-end (classified by technical level)

单位：公里（km）

年份 Year	公路里程总计 Total Length of Highways	等级路 Express-way and Class I to IV Highway	高速 Express-way	一级 First Class	二级 Second Class	三、四级公路 Third and Forth Class	等外公路 Highway Below Class IV
2010	149382	142340	2929	499	10504	128412	7042
2015	186940	182877	4249	3166	10667	164795	4063
2019	218295	217791	4877	5377	11676	195862	503
2020	236483	236424	4904	5773	13188	212559	59
2021	237411	237388	5146	6171	13874	212196	23
2022	237967	237944	5477	6752	13837	211878	23

15—8 公路线路年底到达数（按技术等级分）（2022年）
Length of Highway Routes at the Year-end (classified by technical level) (2022)

单位：公里（km）

项目	Item	公路里程总计 Total Length of Highways	等级公路 Expressway and Class I to IV Highway 合计 Total	高速 Express-way	一级 First Class	二级 Second Class	三级 Third Class	四级 Forth Class	等外公路 Highway Below Class IV
上年年底到达数	End of Last Year	237411	237388	5146	6171	13874	21606	190590	23
国道	National Routes	11172	11172	3711	3454	3465	533	9	
省道	Provincial Routes	17180	17156	1435	2342	5734	5462	2183	23
县道	County Routes	32980	32980		175	2919	11067	18819	
乡道	Village and town Routes	42747	42747		38	641	2326	39743	
专用公路	Highways for Special Use	17	17					17	
村道	Village Routes	133315	133315		163	1116	2218	129820	
本年新建数	Newly Built in This Year	1083	1083	331	409	81	31	232	
国道	National Routes	436	436	264	172	1			
省道	Provincial Routes	382	382	67	237	78			
县道	County Routes	3	3			2	1		
乡道	Village and town Routes	31	31			1	13	18	
专用公路	Highways for Special Use								
村道	Village Routes	231	231				17	214	
本年改建变更数	Changed in This Year	-527	-527		171	-117	341	-922	
国道	National Routes	-127	-127		63	-146	-42	-2	
省道	Provincial Routes	-183	-183		113	47	-374	32	
县道	County Routes	-530	-530		12	-39	317	-819	
乡道	Village and town Routes	679	679		3	19	331	327	
专用公路	Highways for Special Use								
村道	Village Routes	-366	-366		-19	3	110	-460	
本年年底到达数	End of This Year	237967	237944	5477	6752	13837	21978	189900	23
国道	National Routes	11481	11481	3974	3689	3319	491	7	
省道	Provincial Routes	17379	17356	1503	2692	5858	5088	2216	23
县道	County Routes	32452	32452		187	2882	11385	17999	
乡道	Village and town Routes	43458	43458		41	660	2670	40087	
专用公路	Highways for Special Use	17	17					17	
村道	Village Routes	133180	133180		143	1118	2345	129574	

15—9 各市公路线路年底到达数（按技术等级分）（2022年）
Length of Highway Routes at the Year-end by Region (classified by technical level) (2022)

单位：公里（km）

地区	Region	公路里程总计 Total Length of Highways	等级公路 Expressway and Class I to IV Highway 合计 Total	高速 Expressway	一级 First Class	二级 Second Class	三级 Third Class	四级 Forth Class	等外公路 Highway Below Class IV
总计	**Total**	**237967**	**237944**	**5477**	**6752**	**13837**	**21978**	**189900**	**23**
合肥市	Hefei	20154	20154	569	872	1658	2140	14914	
淮北市	Huaibei	5371	5371	95	190	587	665	3833	
亳州市	Bozhou	18254	18254	308	233	620	1905	15188	
宿州市	Suzhou	21251	21251	354	663	1215	1685	17334	
蚌埠市	Bengbu	11085	11085	272	304	586	1214	8709	
阜阳市	Fuyang	21309	21291	257	695	1017	2309	17013	18
淮南市	Huainan	9514	9514	209	199	542	941	7624	
滁州市	Chuzhou	20598	20593	647	563	1662	1695	16027	5
六安市	Luan	25307	25307	404	767	1343	2191	20603	
马鞍山市	Maanshan	7773	7773	194	349	403	823	6003	
芜湖市	Wuhu	11317	11317	328	427	662	832	9068	
宣城市	Xuancheng	13180	13180	433	393	718	1067	10569	
铜陵市	Tongling	5785	5785	163	189	357	305	4771	
池州市	Chizhou	9560	9560	327	272	699	744	7518	
安庆市	Anqing	22854	22854	393	333	934	1440	19754	
黄山市	Huangshan	7760	7760	419	117	527	1296	5401	
广德县	Guangde	3407	3407	74	119	147	440	2628	
宿松县	Susong	3487	3487	31	66	161	286	2942	

15—10 公路密度及通达情况
Density and Reaching Status of Highways

指标	Item	2010	2015	2020	2021	2022
公路密度	**Density of Highway**					
以国土面积计算（公里/百平方公里）	By Area of Territory (km/100 sq.km)	107.16	134.10	168.80	169.46	169.86
以人口数量计算（公里/万人）	By Population (km/10000 persons)	21.98	26.95	33.22	33.28	33.40
公路通达	**Reaching Status of Highways**					
乡镇数量（个）	Number of Townships (unit)	1382	1378	1233	1233	1233
#不通公路	Without Highway Communication					
不通公路乡镇所占比重（%）	Proportion of Townships Without Highway Communication (%)					
行政村数量（个）	Number of Villages (unit)	17274	17069	14393	14393	14248
#不通公路	Without Highway Communication	5	1			
不通公路行政村所占比重（%）	Proportion of Villages Without Highway Communication (%)	0.03	0.01			

15—11 主要年份民用车辆拥有量
Possession of Civil Vehicles

单位：万辆（10000 units）

指　　标	Item	2010	2015	2020	2021	2022
总　　计	**Total**	**909.66**	**1045.85**	**1482.44**	**1527.44**	**1574.09**
载客汽车	Passenger Vehicles	140.99	408.16	848.95	915.01	982.22
大　型	Large	3.82	4.41	5.54	5.47	5.21
中　型	Medium	4.94	2.69	2.26	2.09	1.85
小　型	Small	124.91	396.83	838.42	904.95	972.88
微　型	Minicar	7.31	4.22	2.73	2.51	2.28
载货汽车	Trucks	66.34	87.56	132.64	140.09	138.20
重　型	Heavy	20.24	30.37	45.49	48.63	45.89
中　型	Medium	12.41	3.68	3.47	3.12	2.61
轻　型	Light	33.12	53.28	83.66	88.32	89.68
微　型	Mini	0.56	0.23	0.02	0.02	0.02
其他汽车	Others	35.90	17.11	9.26	9.29	9.27
摩托车	Motorcycles	409.38	286.87	237.09	206.78	186.68
拖拉机	Tractors	248.58	236.68	234.10	234.10	234.10
挂　车	Trailers	8.45	9.46	20.39	22.16	21.62
其他类型车	Other Types of Vehicle	0.02	0.01		0.004	0.004
机动车驾驶员（万人）	Number of Motor Drivers (10000 persons)	692.42	1121.82	1700.34	1783.30	1852.38
#汽车驾驶	Automobile Drivers	475.65	977.45	1623.39	1711.70	1784.27

15—12 主要年份私人车辆拥有量
Possession of Private Vehicles

单位：辆（unit）

指　　标	Item	2010	2015	2020	2021	2022
总　　计	**Total**	**5726403**	**7086580**	**11092702**	**11463913**	**11912866**
载客汽车	Passenger Vehicles	1078206	3670696	7985547	8620936	9262632
大　型	Large	4293	837	493	425	346
中　型	Medium	22519	6980	4257	3961	3391
小　型	Small	988464	3622767	7954551	8592412	9236983
微　型	Minicar	62930	40112	26246	24138	21912
载货汽车	Trucks	285022	432142	684617	726004	738163
重　型	Heavy	28064	33303	37442	39892	37586
中　型	Medium	42674	15412	13591	12326	10726
轻　型	Light	209976	381491	633395	673639	689722
微　型	Mini	4308	1936	189	147	129
其他汽车	Others	298709	128416	54491	51051	48508
摩托车	Motorcycles	4058172	2850875	2361332	2058778	1856205
挂　车	Trailers	6249	4422	6706	7136	7350
其他类型车	Other Types of Vehicle	45	29	9	8	8

15—13 民用车辆拥有量营运情况（2022年）
Civilian Vehicles Capacity of Transportation Situation (2022)

单位：辆（unit）

指标	Item	总计 Total	营运 For Business	非营运 Not for Business	总计中 In the Total 进口 Import	个人 Individual	新注册 Registered Newly	报废 Write-off
总计	**Total**	**13379900**	**1101186**	**12268593**	**340103**	**11912866**	**1064143**	**151716**
#校车	The School Bus	10121				33	265	370
汽车	Number	11296878	865642	10421115	326499	10049303	922691	138175
载客汽车	Passenger Vehicles	9822229	165841	9646267	324065	9262632	814480	108553
#大型	Large	52089	39291	8910	133	346	2943	4194
中型	Medium	18519	3826	8460	245	3391	312	1667
小型	Small	9728774	122718	9606056	320265	9236983	811225	100827
微型	Minicar	22847	6	22841	3422	21912		1865
载货汽车	Trucks	1381971	678996	702975	2319	738163	100191	28405
#重型	Heavy	458907	447664	11243	1599	37586	20491	4479
中型	Medium	26054	19408	6646	3	10726	1543	949
轻型	Light	896844	211907	684937	717	689722	78130	22928
微型	Mini	166	17	149		129	27	48
其他汽车	Others	92678	20805	71873	115	48508	8020	1217
#三轮汽车	Tricar	23648	10729	12919		18829	2366	120
低速货车	Low-Speed Truck	10202	6868	3334		7163		184
摩托车	Motorcycles	1866759	21015	1845744	13587	1856205	124144	12617
普通	General	1731107	21013	1710094	13587	1721513	100611	12372
轻便	Portable	135652	2	135650		134692	23533	245
拖拉机	Tractors	2341001						
挂车	Trailers	216226	214528	1698	17	7350	17308	923
其他类型车	Other Types of Vehicle	37	1	36		8		1
机动车驾驶员（人）	Number of Motor Drivers (person)	18523793						
#汽车驾驶员	Automobile Drivers	17842657						

15—14 各市民用车辆拥有量（2022年）
Possession of Civil Vehicles by Region (2022)

单位：辆（unit）

地区	Region	汽车 Number	载客汽车 Buses and Cars	载货汽车 Ordinary Trucks	其他汽车 Other Motor Vehicles	摩托车 Motorcycle	拖拉机 Tractors	挂车 Trailers	其他类型车 Other Types of Vehicle	机动车驾驶员（人） Number of Motor Drivers (person)
总计	**Total**	**11296878**	**9822229**	**1381971**	**92678**	**1866759**	**2341001**	**216226**	**37**	**18523793**
合肥市	Hefei	2727532	2527260	186214	14058	131464		20076		3311847
淮北市	Huaibei	394221	345746	46152	2323	82324		12969		624848
亳州市	Bozhou	800143	607036	181047	12060	50171		26812		1299752
宿州市	Suzhou	772205	637886	126060	8259	117837		16923		1362784
蚌埠市	Bengbu	593394	474893	114723	3778	56451		33489	1	1060143
阜阳市	Fuyang	1169166	926140	228195	14831	212636		28444		1750551
淮南市	Huainan	441756	390869	47971	2916	96109		8447		952564
滁州市	Chuzhou	626636	541126	81038	4472	60744		18769		1142442
六安市	Luan	696625	582488	110065	4072	231596		13628		1597474
马鞍山市	Maanshan	384136	355087	26305	2744	101029		3888	35	695465
芜湖市	Wuhu	731809	676793	51984	3032	65193		5207		1173828
宣城市	Xuancheng	552677	486554	57229	8894	127041		10896		920840
铜陵市	Tongling	242874	219962	19976	2936	41873		3072	1	414215
池州市	Chizhou	232924	206846	24099	1979	103416		5329		434703
安庆市	Anqing	683363	616651	63886	2826	300230		4219		1328820
黄山市	Huangshan	247417	226892	17027	3498	88645		4058		453517
其他	Other									

15—15 各市私人车辆拥有量（2022年）
Possession of Private Vehicles by Region (2022)

单位：辆（unit）

地区	Region	汽车总计 Total	载客汽车 Passenger Vehicles	大型 Large	中型 Medium	小型 Small	载货汽车 Trucks	中型 Light-heavy	轻型 Light	其他汽车 Others
总计	**Total**	**10049303**	**9262632**	**346**	**3391**	**9236983**	**738163**	**10726**	**689722**	**48508**
合肥市	Hefei	2383531	2323395	33	1064	2318335	55705	251	54197	4431
淮北市	Huaibei	359411	332047	15	69	330639	26141	801	21839	1223
亳州市	Bozhou	708286	588757	38	198	585768	110071	1478	105166	9458
宿州市	Suzhou	704481	615576	29	210	612997	82958	1298	72171	5947
蚌埠市	Bengbu	500273	454232	76	272	452327	44457	647	42738	1584
阜阳市	Fuyang	1044816	891630	18	105	889070	145171	1072	141374	8015
淮南市	Huainan	394806	368769	15	227	367417	24852	259	24026	1185
滁州市	Chuzhou	544154	504268	12	113	502940	38260	593	34408	1626
六安市	Luan	619127	554271	17	247	552740	62983	1757	58796	1873
马鞍山市	Maanshan	340945	330039	15	39	329147	10054	136	9407	852
芜湖市	Wuhu	650221	629932	6	157	628788	19144	256	18431	1145
宣城市	Xuancheng	501705	462275	6	196	461300	33776	869	29645	5654
铜陵市	Tongling	220520	206968	25	139	206448	11497	109	10809	2055
池州市	Chizhou	211441	196285	4	24	196108	14112	262	11972	1044
安庆市	Anqing	640147	590565	34	306	589656	48489	781	44858	1093
黄山市	Huangshan	225439	213623	3	25	213303	10493	157	9885	1323

注：本表与15-13中私人汽车拥有量有差异，系取数时间节点不同造成，属合理波动。

a) The table 15-13 private car ownership has the difference and is reasonable, because of taking some time in different nodes.

15—16 公路营运汽车拥有量
Possession of Vehicles for Highway Business Transportation

年份 Year	汽车总计 (辆) Total Number (unit)	载客汽车 Passenger Car 辆数 (辆) Number (unit)	客位 (客位) Number of Seats (seat)	载货汽车 Trucks 辆数 (辆) Number (unit)	#普通载货汽车 Ordinary Trucks	吨位 (吨) Capacity (ton)	#普通载货汽车 Ordinary Trucks
2010	472861	36815	868682	436046	417858	2723868	2504762
2013	695637	34410	897033	661227	550291	4727364	4182303
2014	723137	33528	896263	689609	570989	5194403	4606239
2015	669790	29429	833188	640361	497353	5185429	4436908
2016	685228	29224	825011	656004	447396	5898712	2904883
2017	689867	28169	822520	661698	418424	6379438	2859672
2018	719683	25862	784811	693821	369831	7040325	2636022
2019	669591	22597	710023	646994	266830	8116936	2570478
2020	626225	19470	629395	606755	151710	9064562	2108963
2021	670875	17244	569812	653631	142781	9467985	2004399
2022	650977	14507	488579	636470	122239	9148146	1610882

注：不包含出租车、公交车（下同）。
a) Not including taxi, bus (the same below)。

15—17 各市公路营运汽车拥有量（2022年）
Possession of Vehicles for Highway Business Transportation by Region (2022)

地区	Region	汽车总计 (辆) Total Number (unit)	载客汽车 Passenger Car 辆数 (辆) Number (unit)	客位 (客位) Number of Seats (seat)	载货汽车 Trucks 辆数 (辆) Number (unit)	#普通载货汽车 Ordinary Trucks	吨位 (吨) Capacity (ton)	#普通载货汽车 Ordinary Trucks
总计	**Total**	**650977**	**14507**	**488579**	**636470**	**122239**	**9148146**	**1610882**
合肥市	Hefei	79453	2619	103660	76834	12830	1087617	179419
淮北市	Huaibei	30323	411	15962	29912	3913	445333	50896
亳州市	Bozhou	82729	561	23039	82168	13284	1043377	186859
宿州市	Suzhou	58919	499	19136	58420	11190	859253	145234
蚌埠市	Bengbu	87508	570	20274	86938	17574	1425845	245885
阜阳市	Fuyang	87447	1575	47741	85872	16252	1138118	226434
淮南市	Huainan	21614	1202	33688	20412	1937	314683	23936
滁州市	Chuzhou	51525	873	32625	50652	14550	743038	176589
六安市	Luan	47766	1092	38679	46674	12365	591907	146824
马鞍山市	Maanshan	13580	603	18389	12977	3667	179523	45124
芜湖市	Wuhu	17458	440	17907	17018	4439	218894	57341
宣城市	Xuancheng	29169	519	16232	28650	1869	449629	20595
铜陵市	Tongling	7488	327	12188	7161	1334	114152	18033
池州市	Chizhou	12665	351	11831	12314	1911	189643	24015
安庆市	Anqing	15566	1794	43883	13772	4170	214476	51347
黄山市	Huangshan	7767	1071	33345	6696	954	132660	12351

15—18 各市民用运输船舶拥有量（2022年）

Number of Civil Transport Vessels Owned by Region (2022)

地区	Region	总艘数（艘）Total Number (unit)	机动船 Motor Vessels 艘数（艘）Number (unit)	机动船 Motor Vessels 净载重量（吨）Dead Weight Tonnage (ton)	机动船 Motor Vessels 载客量（客位）Passenger Capacity (seat)	机动船 Motor Vessels 功率（千瓦）Drawing Power (kW)	驳船 Barges 艘数（艘）Number (unit)	驳船 Barges 净载重量（吨）Dead Weight Tonnage (ton)
总计	**Total**	**24519**	**23890**	**55490387**	**14924**	**11495989**	**629**	**351632**
合肥市	Hefei	1976	1969	3840745	1524	859500	7	4500
淮北市	Huaibei	82	82	44297		18001		
亳州市	Bozhou	1484	1460	2225742		568697	24	14346
宿州市	Suzhou	492	492	462600		133202		
蚌埠市	Bengbu	3147	3119	7140134		1762808	28	16439
阜阳市	Fuyang	2105	1802	4197862		839745	303	141621
淮南市	Huainan	1634	1392	3444305		688453	242	155728
滁州市	Chuzhou	883	883	715791		220342		
六安市	Luan	1530	1522	3718162	3098	612288	8	4128
马鞍山市	Maanshan	1118	1118	3372611	360	688604		
芜湖市	Wuhu	4073	4056	9915138	1784	2202300	17	14870
宣城市	Xuancheng	2801	2801	5778191	1285	882740		
铜陵市	Tongling	1347	1347	4146023		780862		
池州市	Chizhou	1130	1130	4890328		831162		
安庆市	Anqing	588	588	1578528	415	386148		
黄山市	Huangshan	129	129	19930	6458	21137		

15—19 各市私人运输船舶拥有量（2022年）

Number of Private-owned Transport Vessels Owned by Region (2022)

地区	Region	总艘数（艘）Total Number (unit)	机动船 Motor Vessels 艘数（艘）Number (unit)	机动船 Motor Vessels 净载重量（吨）Dead Weight Tonnage (ton)	机动船 Motor Vessels 载客量（客位）Passenger Capacity (seat)	机动船 Motor Vessels 功率（千瓦）Drawing Power (kW)
总计	**Total**	**1528**	**1528**	**1026923**		**370349**
合肥市	Hefei	215	215	172960		56584
淮北市	Huaibei					
亳州市	Bozhou					
宿州市	Suzhou					
蚌埠市	Bengbu					
阜阳市	Fuyang					
淮南市	Huainan					
滁州市	Chuzhou	3	3	1825		769
六安市	Luan					
马鞍山市	Maanshan	22	22	9159		6608
芜湖市	Wuhu					
宣城市	Xuancheng	1207	1207	792729		290080
铜陵市	Tongling	48	48	31469		9798
池州市	Chizhou	28	28	18136		6121
安庆市	Anqing					
黄山市	Huangshan	5	5	645		389

15—20 全省机场运输业务量（2022年）
Traffic Capacity of Airports (2022)

指　标	Item	运输起降架次（次）Number of Sorties of Taking-off and Landing	旅　客（人）Number of Passengers (person)	货邮合计（吨）Goods and Postal Parcels (ton)
总　计	**Total**	**76688**	**7070746**	**85013**
国内航线	Domestic Routes	75952	7070659	59937
港澳台航线	Hong Kong, Macao and Taiwan Routes	2	39	
国际航线	International Routes	734	48	25076
进　港	Arrival	38362	3105618	34030
国内航线	Domestic Routes	37996	3105603	30588
港澳台航线	Hong Kong, Macao and Taiwan Routes	1	15	
国际航线	International Routes	365		3442
出　港	Departure	38326	3965128	50983
国内航线	Domestic Routes	37956	3965056	29349
港澳台航线	Hong Kong, Macao and Taiwan Routes	1	24	
国际航线	International Routes	369	48	21634

注：货邮吞吐量不包括行李，2007以前年度包含行李。
a) Do not include baggage, goods or throughput of 2007 previous year includes luggage.

15—21 民航机场吞吐量（2022年）
Volume of Passenger and Freight Handled in Civil Airports (2022)

项　目	Item	旅客吞吐量（人）Passenger Handled (person)	#发运量 Delivered	货物吞吐量（吨）Cargo Handled (ton)	#发运量 Delivered
合　计	**Total**	**7070746**	**3965128**	**85013.0**	**50983.1**
合肥机场	Hefei Airport	5712698	3114866	76578.6	45614.7
黄山机场	Huangshan Airport	141352	86629	426.9	355.8
安庆机场	Anqing Airport	291105	212622	2138.7	2059.7
阜阳机场	Fuyang Airport	459524	258742	556.6	281.3
池州机场	Chizhou Airport	78861	45612	282.6	237.4
芜宣机场	Wuhu Xuanzhou Airport	387206	246657	5029.6	2434.2

15—22 东航安徽分公司基本情况
Basic Information of Anhui Branch of China Eastern Airlines

指　　标	Item	2015	2020	2021	2022
定期航班航线条数 （条）	Number of Civil Aviation Routes (unit)	65	87	61	45
#国内航线	Domestic Routes	59	84	61	45
定期航班线里程 （公里）	Length of Civil Aviation Routes (km)	103676	113559	92771	69579
#国内航线	Domestic Routes	88373	104402	92771	69579
民用航班飞行机场 （个）	Number of Civil Airports (unit)	51	48	40	36
民用飞机架数 （架）	Number of Civil Aircraft (unit)	15	19	19	19
客运量 （万人）	Passenger Traffic (10000 person)	297.13	229.13	231.35	123.10
旅客周转量 （万人公里）	Passenger-kilometers (10000 passenger-km)	399928.8	331435.5	331425.1	180136.19
货（邮）运量 （吨）	Freight Traffic (ton)	22896.5	16370.5	16736.9	9689.52
货（邮）周转量 （万吨公里）	Freight Ton-kilometers (10000 ton-km)	3130.38	2398.00	2416.08	1458.77
总周转量 （万吨公里）	Total Air Traffic Ton-kilometers (10000 ton-km)	38569.34	31733.15	31825.69	17379.89
#国际航线	International Routes	3320.70	763.06		0.78
国内航线	Domestic Routes	35248.64	30970.09	31825.69	17379.11

15—23 邮电业务基本情况
Basic Statistics of Postal and Telecommunications Services

指　　标	Item	2015	2020	2021	2022
邮电业务总量 （万元）	**Business Volume of Postal and Telecommunications Services (10000 yuan)**	**7400263**	**56632442**	**9876958**	**10446810**
函　件 （万件）	Number of Letters (10000 pcs)	8391	2434	4314	4687
国内普通包裹 （万件）	Domestic ordinary parcel (10000 pcs)	76	51	42	59
快　递 （万件）	Pieces of Express Mail Services (10000 pcs)	2991	220228	312665	353239
报刊期发数 （万份）	Issue of Newspapers and Magazines (10000 copies)	597	467	430	425
固定电话主叫通话时长 （亿分钟）	Landline Calling Number Call Duration (100 million minutes)	24.4	3.2	26.3	24.4
移动短信业务量 （万条）	Mobile Short Note Business Volume (10000 unit)	1774145	7128386	6151366	5742300
固定互联网宽带接入用户 （万户）	Internet Wide Band Turning on Users (10000 households)	887.94	2092.99	2335.82	2666.64
移动电话年末用户 （万户）	Year-end Mobile Phone Users (10000 subscribers)	4232.61	6025.55	6192.62	6379.39
#4G移动电话用户	4G Mobile Phone Subscribers	1253.74	4752.16	3978.48	3510.18
5G移动电话用户	5G Mobile Phone Subscribers			1263.89	2082.21
固定电话年末用户 （万户）	Number of Fixed Telephone Subscribers at Year-end (10000 subscribers)	739.43	559.54	541.02	521.43
邮路及农村投递路线总长度 （公里）	Length of Postal Routes and Rural Delivery Routes (km)	194231	323424	370139	389359
#汽车邮路	Highway Routes	44152	183779	229670	219414
铁路邮路	Railway Routes	1109	1109	4297	2407

注：邮电业务总量按上年不变单价计算（下同）。
a) Total amount of post and telecommunications services is calculated according to the constant unit price of the previous year (the same below).

15—24 各市邮电业务量（2022年）

Post and Telecommunication Services by Region (2022)

地区	Region	邮电业务总量（万元） Business Volume of Post and Telecommunications (10000 yuan)	邮政行业业务总量 Total Business Volume of Postal Industry	电信业务总量 Business Volume of Telecommunications	函件（万件） Number of Letters (10000 pcs)	快递（万件） Pieces of Express Mail Services (10000 pcs)	报刊期发数（万份） Newspapers and Magazines Circulation (10000 copies)
总计	**Total**	**10446810**	**4359966**	**6086844**	**4686.62**	**353238.78**	**424.64**
合肥市	Hefei	2748575	1389863	1358711	1061.27	132838.06	80.99
淮北市	Huaibei	272799	76702	196096	13.46	4613.87	10.13
亳州市	Bozhou	810113	385611	424503	18.46	39957.42	18.18
宿州市	Suzhou	640522	198318	442204	203.99	11568.57	26.15
蚌埠市	Bengbu	535037	228070	306967	23.40	19473.31	20.38
阜阳市	Fuyang	1010565	344855	665710	228.42	21932.16	39.67
淮南市	Huainan	394314	120912	273402	154.69	6086.71	18.02
滁州市	Chuzhou	593377	209215	384162	366.15	16111.12	26.91
六安市	Luan	616379	237388	378992	1755.86	12636.78	38.26
马鞍山市	Maanshan	342961	104233	238729	261.66	5514.80	18.83
芜湖市	Wuhu	782691	379257	403434	198.54	35917.83	24.08
宣城市	Xuancheng	389222	134681	254541	25.68	10451.30	22.09
铜陵市	Tongling	191779	68332	123447	13.39	3084.16	13.35
池州市	Chizhou	209103	63189	145915	7.13	2921.21	13.71
安庆市	Anqing	687283	348102	339182	214.00	25082.05	38.57
黄山市	Huangshan	221910	71239	150672	140.52	5049.42	15.32

地区	Region	国内普通包裹（万件） Domestic Ordinary Parcel (10000 pcs)	固定互联网宽带接入用户（万户） Internet Wide Band Turning on Users (10000 subscriber)	移动电话年末用户（万户） Number of Mobile Telephone Subscribers (10000 subscriber)	4G移动电话用户 4G Mobile Phone Subscribers	5G移动电话用户 5G Mobile Phone Subscribers	固定电话年末用户（万户） Year-end Installed Telephones (10000 subscriber)
总计	**Total**	**60.08**	**2666.64**	**6379.39**	**3510.18**	**2082.21**	**521.43**
合肥市	Hefei	11.34	487.99	1145.08	639.68	399.11	116.13
淮北市	Huaibei	2.02	90.75	217.95	120.15	71.47	16.06
亳州市	Bozhou	5.86	202.84	470.29	259.22	155.27	23.12
宿州市	Suzhou	1.83	212.82	521.83	294.26	162.23	25.78
蚌埠市	Bengbu	4.59	132.51	336.31	184.16	111.38	29.75
阜阳市	Fuyang	3.84	310.16	749.12	408.12	248.29	37.81
淮南市	Huainan	5.22	115.98	308.35	172.14	95.53	24.44
滁州市	Chuzhou	8.17	168.92	399.03	216.23	131.10	37.15
六安市	Luan	0.48	168.59	436.31	233.10	138.33	29.92
马鞍山市	Maanshan	1.59	103.21	251.80	139.80	78.13	22.38
芜湖市	Wuhu	4.32	180.14	414.01	224.21	137.00	42.17
宣城市	Xuancheng	3.40	122.18	282.64	152.52	89.29	26.51
铜陵市	Tongling	1.29	58.71	142.46	78.83	42.72	15.91
池州市	Chizhou	0.76	69.95	148.19	80.06	48.28	16.47
安庆市	Anqing	3.18	173.41	409.98	231.23	126.08	38.21
黄山市	Huangshan	2.19	68.48	146.06	76.47	48.00	19.63

注：由于统计口径变更，“邮政业务总量”指标变更为“邮政行业业务总量”，自2018年始，该指标口径变更。

a) Due to the change of statistical caliber, the index of "total postal business" was changed to "total postal industry business", and since 2018, the index caliber has changed.

15—25 邮电局所数及邮递线路（年底数）
Postal and Telecommunication Services Facilities (year-end)

单位：处（unit）

年份 Year	邮政信筒信箱 Postal Mailbox	邮路总长度（公里） Length of Postal Routes (km)	#汽车邮路 Highway Routes	铁路邮路 Railway Routes	农村投递线路（公里） Rural Delivery Routes (km)
2010	6693	45541	41321	2434	150902
2013	4641	48523	45995	2355	144838
2014	3704	46185	44960	1110	151640
2015	2401	45393	44152	1109	148838
2016	2511	61376	60144	1109	141849
2017	2533	185191	145859	1109	146126
2018	2273	146343	145227	1109	146884
2019	2219	159569	158460	1109	143644
2020	2177	184888	183779	1109	138536
2021	2152	233971	229670	4297	136168
2022	2156	253985	219414	2407	135374

注：由于邮政系统调整，2010年、2012年的邮路总长度与往年口径不同，不具可比性。

a) As the postal system adjustment, the caliber of Length of postal routes in 2010,2012 and previous years were different, did not have the comparability.

15—26 各市邮电局所数及邮递线路（2022年）
Postal and Telecommunication Services Facilities by Region (2022)

单位：处（unit）

地区	Region	邮政局所 Number of Post and Telecommunications Offices	邮政信筒信箱 Postal Mailbox	邮路总长度（公里） Length of Postal Routes (km)	#汽车邮路 Highway Routes	铁路邮路 Railway Routes	农村投递线路（公里） Rural Delivery Routes (km)
总计	**Total**	**1979**	**2156**		**218343**	**2407**	**135374**
合肥市	Hefei	187	249		59498	1109	13845
淮北市	Huaibei	49	58		865		4054
亳州市	Bozhou	102	114		11384		15000
宿州市	Suzhou	128	128		3695		15071
蚌埠市	Bengbu	90	96		60057		7742
阜阳市	Fuyang	196	198		10232	1298	10886
淮南市	Huainan	125	132		3748		4750
滁州市	Chuzhou	164	164		3004		10817
六安市	Luan	179	188		5404		15628
马鞍山市	Maanshan	72	85		1716		2940
芜湖市	Wuhu	97	126		22974		3566
宣城市	Xuancheng	135	147		5158		9478
铜陵市	Tongling	66	79		820		2664
池州市	Chizhou	78	86		2482		3548
安庆市	Anqing	189	203		24744		8781
黄山市	Huangshan	122	103		2562		6604

主要统计指标解释

铁路营业里程

又称营业长度（包括正式营业和临时营业里程），指办理客货运输业务的铁路正线总长度。凡是全线或部分建成双线及以上的线路，以第一线的实际长度计算；复线、站线、段管线、岔线和特殊用途线以及不计算运费的联络线都不计算营业里程。铁路营业里程是反映铁路运输业基础设施发展水平的重要指标，也是计算客货周转量、运输密度和机车车辆运用效率等指标的基础资料。

公路里程

是指凡达到交通运输部《公路工程技术标准》规定的技术等级公路，并经公路主管部门正式验收交付使用的里程。包括大中城市的郊区公路以及通过城镇街道的里程和桥梁、隧道、渡口的长度，不包括大中城市的街道、厂矿、林区生产用道和农业生产用道的里程。两条或多条公路共同经由同一路段，只计算一次，不得重复计算里程长度。按公路技术等级分：等级公路里程和等外公路里程，等级公路里程可分为高速公路、一级公路、二级公路、三级公路、四级公路里程。

内河航道里程

是指凡能通航机动船、木帆船以及运输排筏（指利用排筏经营运输），其枯水期水深在0.3米及以上的天然河流、人工河渠、湖泊、水库航道里程。不包括仅供放流木材的河道。湖泊、水库航道里程（库区航道）按固定航线计算。两省以河为界的航道里程，双方均按一半计算，以免重复。

民用航空航线里程

指民用运输班机飞行的航线长度。航线长度指机场之间的距离。航空航线里程以年末到达数为准，因气候关系不能全年通航的航线，按年末情况统计，如果年末能继续通航则计入总长度，否则应扣除不计。计算航线里程可按重复和不重复两种方法，前者是指各航线相加的总和，后者则要扣除各航线之间的重复区段计算。

货（客）运量

指在一定时期内，各种运输工具实际运送的货物（旅客）数量。它是反映运输业为国民经济和人民生活服务的数量指标，也是制定和检查运输生产计划、研究运输发展规模和速度的重要指标。货运按吨计算，客运按人计算。货物不论运输距离长短、货物类别，均按实际重量统计。旅客不论行程远近或票价多少，均按一人一次客运量统计；半价票、小孩票也按一人统计。

货物（旅客）周转量

指在一定时期内，由各种运输工具运送的货物（旅客）数量与其相应运输距离的乘积之总和。它是反映运输业生产总成果的重要指标，也是编制和检查运输生产计划，计算运输效率、劳动生产率以及核算运输单位成本的主要基础资料。计算货物周转量通常按发出站与到达站之间的最短距离，也就是计费距离计算。计算公式为：

货物（旅客）周转量＝Σ货物（旅客）运输量×运输距离。

民用汽车拥有量

指报告期末，在公安交通管理部门按照《机动车注册登记工作规范》，已注册登记领有民用车辆牌照的全部汽车数量。汽车拥有量统计的主要分类：根据汽车结构分为载客汽车、载货汽车及其他汽车；根据汽车所有者不同分为个人（私人）汽车、单位汽车；根据汽车的使用性质分为营运汽车、非营运汽车；根据汽车大小规格不同载客汽车分为大型、中型、小型和微型，载货汽车分为重型、中型、轻型和微型。

邮电业务总量（又称通信业务总量）

是以货币形式表现的通信企业为社会提供各类通信服务的总和。是用于观察通信业务发展变化总趋势的综合性总量指标。根据专业性质分为邮政行业业务总量和电信业务总量。电信业务总量又可细分为本地网通信业务总量、长途通信业务总量、移动通信业务总量、数据通信业务总量、电报业务总量等。按通信范围可分为：国内通信业务总量、国际及港澳台通信业务总量。计算公式为：

邮电业务总量＝Σ（各类通信业务量×不变单价）+出租代维及其他业务收入

＝邮政业务总量+电信业务总量

邮政业务总量＝Σ（各类邮政业务量×不变单价）+邮政出租代维及其他业务收入

电信业务总量＝Σ（各类电信业务量×不变单价）+电信出租代维及其他业务收入

移动电话用户

指通过移动电话交换机进入移动电话网、占用移动电话号码的电话用户。用户数量以报告期末在移动电话营业部门实际办理登记手续进入移动电话网的户数进行计算，一部移动电话统计为一户。计量单位：户。

电话用户

指接入国家公众固定电话网，并按固定电话业务进行经营管理的电话用户。1997 年以前，电话用户分为市内电话用户和农村电话用户。“市内电话用户”是指接入县城及县以上城市的电话网上的电话用户；“农村电话用户”是指接入县邮电局农话台及县以下农村电话交换点，以县城为中心（除市话用户外）联通县、乡（镇）、行政村、村民小组的用户。从 1997 年起，电话用户数分组调整为以用户所在区域划分为“城市电话用户”和“乡村电话用户”，与过去的按市内电话和农村电话划分方法不同。而电话用户总数、电话机总部数统计范围不变。

住宅电话用户

指安装在居民住宅或农民家里并按照住宅电话用户登记注册和收费的电话用户。包括私人付费、单位付费和按规定免费安装的住宅电话用户。

Explanatory Notes for Major Statistical Indicators

Length of Railways in Operation

refers to the total length of the trunk line under passenger and freight transportation (including both full operation and temporary operation). The calculation is based on the actual length of the first line even if this line has a full or partial double track or more tracks, excluding double tracks, station sidings, tracks under the charge of stations, branch lines, special-purpose lines and the non-payable connecting lines. The length of railways in operation is an important indicator to show the development of the infrastructure for the railway transport, and also the essential data to calculate volume of passenger freight transport, traffic density and utilization efficiency of the locomotives and carriages.

Length of Highways

refers to the length of highways which are built in conformity with the grades specified by the (Highway Engineering Standard) formulated by the Ministry of Transport, and have been formally checked and accepted by the departments of highways and put into use. The length of highways includes that of the suburb highways at large and medium-sized cities, highways passing through streets at small cities and towns, and also the length of bridges and ferries. It does not include the length of streets in big and medium-sized cities and highways built for the production purpose at factories, mines, forest areas and agricultural areas. If two or more highways go the same section of the way, the length of the section is only calculated for once and no duplication is allowed. They could be classified by technical level into class highway and substandard highways. Class highway includes express-way and first class, second class, third class and forth class highway.

Length of Navigable Inland Waterways

refers to the length of the natural rivers, artificial rivers and canals, lakes, and reservoirs open to navigation that deep in 0.3 meters and above in dry season, which enables the transport by motor vessel, wooden sailing boats and rafts (using rafts to transport), excluding river courses which are only used to float odd logs. If two provinces take river as circle, the length of section is only calculated half to both sides, so as not to repeat.

Length of Civil Aviation Routes

refers to the length of all routes for regular civil aviation flights and it is usually the distance between airports. The length is calculated at the end of the year as the standard. The lines that can't open all through the year because of the weather are calculated at the end of the year. If it could continue and open at the end of the year, it should be calculated, otherwise it should be deducted and disregarded. There are usually two ways to calculate the length: duplicated calculation and unduplicated calculation. The former is to put the length of all air routes together, and the later is not to allow the duplication in calculation.

Freight (Passenger) Traffic

refers to the volume of freight (passenger) transported with various means. Freight transport is calculated in tons and passenger traffic is calculated in the number of persons. Despite the type of freight and traveling distance, the freight transport is calculated in the actual weight of the goods: and despite the traveling distance and ticket price, the passenger traffic is calculated by the principle that one person can be counted only once in one travel. The passenger who travels with a half price ticket or a child ticket is also calculated as one person. The freight (passenger) traffic provides a quantitative measure to show how the transport industry serves the national economy and people, and is also an important indicator for planning the transport industry and for studying the development scale and speed of the transport industry.

Freight Ton-kilometers (Passenger-kilometers)

refer to the sum of the products of the volume of transported cargo (passengers) multiplying by the transport distance, usually using ton-kilometer and passenger-kilometer as units for measurement. Normally, the shortest distance between the departure station and the destination station (i.e., the payable distance) is the basis to calculate the freight ton-kilometers. This is an important indicator to show the total results of the transport industry, to prepare and examine the transport plan and to measure the efficiency, the labour productivity and the unit cost of transport. The formula is as follows:

Freight Ton-kilometers (Passenger-kilometers) =∑ {Freight (Passenger) Traffic × Distance of Transportation}

Measuring unit: ton-kilometer (person-kilometer)

Possession of Civil Motor Vehicles

refer to the total numbers of vehicles that are registered and received vehicles license tags according to the Work Standard for Motor Vehicles Registration formulated by the Transport Management Office under the department of public security at the end of the reference period. They are divided into categories. According to the structure of motor vehicles, they are divided into passenger vehicles, trucks and others; according to ownership into private vehicles and vehicles for the unit's use; according to kind of usage into working vehicles and non-working vehicles; and according to size of vehicles into large passenger vehicles, medium-sized passenger vehicles, small passenger vehicles and mini passenger vehicles, heavy trucks, light-heavy trucks, light trucks and mini-trucks.

Business Volume of Post and Telecommunications (Also called Business Volume of Communications)

refers to the total amount of communications services, expressed in currency terms, provided by communications enterprises for the society. It is a comprehensive indicator reflects the total trend of communication service. It could be divided into business volume of post and telecommunication by type and business volume of telecommunication includes business volume of local network, long-distance, mobile communication, digital communication and telegram. It could be divided into domestic, international and business volume of Hong Kong, Macao and Taiwan by the coverage. The formula is as follows:

Business Volume of Post and Telecommunications = Σ (Transaction of Communication Service × Constant Price) + Income from Leasing Maintenance and other Services

= Business Volume of Postal Services + Business Volume of Telecommunication Services

Business Volume of Postal Services =Σ (Transaction of Postal Service × Constant Price) + Income from Leasing, Maintenance and other Services

Business Volume of Telecommunication Services = Σ (Transaction of Telecommunication Service × Constant Price) + Income from Leasing, Maintenance and other Services

Mobile Telephone Subscribers

refer to the persons who own mobile telephone number connected with the mobile telephone communication network and have registered in mobile communication enterprises. The number of subscribers is calculated only when the subscribers who have gone through all the register formalities and entered into the mobile telephone network at the end of the report. One mobile telephone is treated as a subscriber.

Telephone Subscribers

refer to subscribers that are connected to the public line telephone network provided with telephone services. Before 1997, telephone subscribers were classified as city subscribers and village subscribers. City subscribers referred to those connected to city telephone networks in county towns and cities, while village subscribers referred to those connected to village telephone stations at and below counties. Since 1997, the classification of telephone subscribers was modified on the basis of physical location of the subscribers as "urban telephone subscribers" and "rural telephone subscribers", which is different from the previous classification of categorizing "local telephones" and "rural telephones", while the definition of total subscribers and total number of telephones remain unchanged.

Household Telephone Subscribers

refer to telephone sets installed in the dwelling units of residents or peasant families and registered and charged according to house telephone subscribers. They included three types of payment for the service: private payment, unit payment and free installing service.

第十六篇

Chapter 16

国内贸易

DOMESTIC TRADE

简要说明

一、本篇资料反映我省国内市场发展情况和批发零售业、餐饮业和住宿业商品经营情况。主要内容有批发零售业商品流通，限额以上批发零售企业、住宿餐饮企业财务状况，社会消费品零售总额、亿元商品交易市场成交情况等。

二、本篇资料是根据国家统计局的批发零售、住宿餐饮业统计报表制度进行搜集和加工整理。

本资料的调查范围：财务状况报表为各种经济类型的限额以上批发和零售业法人企业、住宿和餐饮业法人企业。社会消费品零售总额报表为有零售业务的各种经济类型的企业、行政事业单位。以上统计报表从基层起报，自下而上逐级综合上报，主要采取全面调查方法，局部资料有的以抽样调查推断，有的利用工商、税务等部门的有关资料推算。

三、限额以上批发和零售业、住宿和餐饮业统计限额标准：批发业：年主营业务收入在 2000 万元及以上；零售业：年主营业务收入在 500 万元及以上；住宿业：年主营业务收入在 200 万元及以上；餐饮业：年主营业务收入在 200 万元及以上。

Brief Introduction

I. This data reflect the situation of our province in the domestic market development and wholesale and retail, restaurant and hotel industry commodity business. Main contents are wholesale and retail commodity circulation, limitation above wholesale and retail enterprise, accommodation catering enterprises financial situation, total retail sales of social consumer goods, commodities trading market clinch a deal for $one hundred million.

II. Data in this chapter are collected and processed in accordance with the statistical reporting scheme on wholesale and retail sale trades as well as accommodation industry, catering trade, stipulated by the National Bureau of Statistics.

Statistical coverage: Statistics on financial conditions include all corporate enterprises of wholesale, retail, catering trade above the designated size and star size accommodation. Statistics on retail sales of consumer goods include all enterprises, institutional units and peasants engaged in retail sale business. The method used in data collection is a complete enumeration, under which all units are covered in the survey and data are reported from lower to higher level statistical offices. For local data, sample surveys are used, and in some cases, administrative registers from industrial and commercial administration and taxation administration are used in the estimation.

III. Statistical limit standard of wholesale and retail trade, accommodation and catering industry above designated size: wholesale industry: annual main business income is 20 million yuan and above; Retail industry: the annual main business income is 5 million yuan and above; Accommodation industry: the annual main business income is 2 million yuan and above; Catering industry: the annual main business income is 2 million yuan and above.

16—1 国内贸易基本情况
Basic Conditions of Domestic Trade

指　　标	Item	2010	2015	2020	2021	2022
法人机构　　（个）	**Number of Corporation Unit　(unit)**					
批发零售业	Engaged in Wholesale and Retail Trades	2449	6530	8471	9043	10203
住宿餐饮业	Accommodation and Catering Trade	1021	1780	2075	2198	2629
从业人员　　（万人）	**Persons Engaged　(10000 persons)**					
批发零售业	Engaged in Wholesale and Retail Trades	26.2	37.5	37.5	38.4	39.7
住宿餐饮业	Accommodation and Catering Trade	10.2	12.6	13.7	14.1	14.4
批发零售业　（亿元）	**Wholesale and Retail Trade　(100 million yuan)**					
商品购进总额	Total Purchases	4653.0	8389.5	13676.3	17665.1	19715.9
商品销售总额	Total Sale	5144.1	9454.9	15693.4	19727.8	21963.5
商品库存总额	Total Inventory	397.5	757.1	1054.0	973.7	1095.4
社会消费品零售总额（亿元）	**Total Retail Sales of Consumer Goods (100 million yuan)**	**5139.0**	**11184.9**	**18333.7**	**21471.2**	**21518.4**
按销售单位所在地分	By Location of Establishments					
城　镇	Urban			15102.1	17721.8	18094.4
#城　区	City			9940.2	11492.6	11633.6
乡　村	Rural			3231.6	3749.4	3424.0
按消费形态分	Grouped by consumption patterns					
餐饮收入	Catering income			1980.4	2920.9	2761.3
商品零售	Commodity retail			16353.3	18550.3	18757.1

注：1. 法人机构、从业人员、商品购进总额、销售总额、库存总额为限额以上口径。
　　2. 社会消费品零售总额城乡分组数据按行政区划调整进行调整。

a) Legal institutions, employees, total purchases of goods, total sales and total inventory are above the limit.

b) The total retail sales of social consumer goods and its grouping data were adjusted according to the change of Administrative Divisions .

16—2 限额以上批发零售、住宿餐饮业基本情况（2022年，按登记注册类型分）

Basic Conditions of Enterprises Above Designated Size in Wholesale and Retail Sale and Catering Trade by Registration (2022)

指　　标	Item	法人企业（个）Number of Corporation Enterprises (unit)	从业人数（人）Engaged Persons (person)
总　　计	**Total**	**12832**	**540642**
批发业合计	**Wholesale Trade**	**4731**	**150328**
国有控股	State-holding Enterprises	331	35374
内　资	Domestic-funded	4691	142360
国　有	State-owned	55	11730
集　体	Collective-owned	1	23
股份合作	Cooperative	3	45
有限责任公司	Limited Liability Corporations	731	42596
股份有限公司	Share-holding Corporations Ltd.	35	4447
私　营	Private	3858	83225
其　他	Other	8	294
港澳台商投资	With Investment from Hong Kong, Macao and Taiwan	20	4445
合资经营	Joint-venture	2	152
独资经营	With Sole Fund	16	3821
股份有限公司	Share-holding Corporations Ltd.		
其他投资企业	Other Investment Enterprises	2	472
外商投资	With Foreign Investment	20	3523
中外合资经营	Joint-venture	7	3157
外　资	Solely Foreign Funded	12	178
外商投资有限公司	Foreign Investment Corporations Ltd.	1	188
零售业合计	**Retail Trade**	**5472**	**246448**
国有控股	State-holding Enterprises	161	26085
内　资	Domestic-funded	5387	228142
国　有	State-owned	13	1747
集　体	Collective-owned	12	171
股份合作	Cooperative	8	210
联　营	Joint Ownership	2	48
有限责任公司	Limited Liability Corporations	730	66836
股份有限公司	Share-holding Corporations Ltd.	35	10645
私　营	Private	4582	148388
其　他	Other	5	97
港澳台商投资	With Investment from Hong Kong, Macao and Taiwan	55	12472
合资经营	Joint-venture	3	253
独资经营	With Sole Fund	48	10093
股份有限公司	Share-holding Corporations Ltd.	1	2032
其他投资企业	Other Investment Enterprises	3	94
外商投资	With Foreign Investment	30	5834
中外合资经营	Joint-venture	2	224
外　资	Solely Foreign Funded	25	4342
外商投资有限公司	Foreign Investment Corporations Ltd.	3	1268
其他外商投资企业	Other Foreign Funded Enterprises		

16—2 续表 continued

指　标	Item	法人企业(个) Number of Corporation Enterprises (unit)	从业人数(人) Engaged Persons (person)
住宿业合计	**Accommodation**	**849**	**40903**
国有控股	State-holding Enterprises	47	6374
内　资	Domestic-funded	839	39242
国　有	State-owned	7	553
有限责任公司	Limited Liability Corporations	158	15601
股份有限公司	Share-holding Corporations Ltd.	5	452
私　营	Private	668	22610
其　他	Other	1	26
港澳台商投资	With Investment from Hong Kong, Macao and Taiwan	6	1169
合资经营	Joint-venture	2	151
独资经营	With Sole Fund	4	1018
外商投资	With Foreign Investment	4	492
外　资	Solely Foreign Funded	4	492
餐饮业合计	**Catering Trade**	**1780**	**102963**
国有控股	State-holding Enterprises	28	3142
内　资	Domestic-funded	1773	100363
国　有	State-owned	5	543
集　体	Collective-owned	2	61
有限责任公司	Limited Liability Corporations	158	20791
股份有限公司	Share-holding Corporations Ltd.	5	365
私　营	Private	1601	78542
其　他	Other	2	61
港澳台商投资	With Investment from Hong Kong, Macao and Taiwan	4	583
合资经营	Joint-venture	1	34
合作经营	Cooperative operation	1	18
独资经营	With Sole Fund	2	531
外商投资	With Foreign Investment	3	2017
中外合资经营	Joint-venture	1	87
外　资	Solely Foreign Funded	2	1930

16—3 限额以上批发零售业商品购进、销售和库存情况（2022年，按注册类型分）

Total Purchases, Sales and Inventory of Enterprises Above Designated Size in Wholesale and Retail Trade by Registration (2022)

单位：万元（10000 yuan）

指 标	Item	购进总额 Total Purchases Value	#进口 Imports	销售总额 Total Sales Value	批发 Wholesale Value	零售 Retail Value	年末库存总额 Stock (year-end)
总 计	**Total**	**197158803**	**6713378**	**219635135**	**169075319**	**50314846**	**10953593**
批发业合计	**Wholesale Trade**	**156305903**	**6241624**	**172320303**	**165377175**	**6700663**	**6999736**
国有控股	State-holding Enterprises	64207302	4390180	68161469	66879874	1276954	2631474
内 资	Domestic-funded	137246140	6238063	147169710	141281567	5645677	6002246
国 有	State-owned	10839061	31913	13449655	13370708	78947	345054
集 体	Collective-owned	4864		5844	3705	2139	65
股份合作	Cooperative	17331		20839	20839		8560
有限责任公司	Limited Liability Corporations	71902951	4165190	76231771	74529054	1671252	3137330
股份有限公司	Share-holding Corporations Ltd.	6806719	1727231	5504138	5094026	408483	260289
私 营	Private	47451570	313729	51684980	48008097	3467511	2243376
其 他	Other	223645		272483	255137	17346	7573
港澳台商投资	With Investment from Hong Kong, Macao and Taiwan	9614648	1872	14726183	14725147	1037	503502
合资经营	Joint-venture	39473		40024	40024		
独资经营	With Sole Fund	9409663	1872	14498942	14497905	1037	497150
其他投资企业	Other Investment Enterprises	165512		187217	187217		6353
外商投资	With Foreign Investment	9445115	1690	10424410	9370462	1053949	493987
中外合资经营	Joint-venture	3063472	2	3996226	2964095	1032132	394604
外 资	Solely Foreign Funded	6245092	1688	6287040	6277444	9596	89241
外商投资有限公司	Foreign Investment Corporations Ltd.	136551		141144	128923	12221	10142
零售业合计	**Retail Trade**	**40852899**	**471753**	**47314832**	**3698144**	**43614184**	**3953858**
国有控股	State-holding Enterprises	8539325	15624	11167950	1869564	9298386	413130
内 资	Domestic-funded	37730216	380301	40830390	3144780	37683105	3733847
国 有	State-owned	1076586	2671	1107711	129296	978415	20913
集 体	Collective-owned	29794		32009	2	32007	282
股份合作	Cooperative	13890		15479	2579	12900	2871
联 营	Joint Ownership	7284		9229		9229	46
有限责任公司	Limited Liability Corporations	12449169	193987	13701162	729219	12971943	1092923
股份有限公司	Share-holding Corporations Ltd.	4041907		4518638	1050689	3467950	179607
私 营	Private	20097428	183642	21427139	1232995	20191639	2435167
其 他	Other	14159		19023		19023	2038
港澳台商投资	With Investment from Hong Kong, Macao and Taiwan	2303975	91453	2730395	16455	2713941	138484
合资经营	Joint-venture	68275		76747	210	76537	5272
独资经营	With Sole Fund	1703586	6514	1949407	15020	1934387	103680
股份有限公司	Share-holding Corporations Ltd.	520224	84938	685814		685814	27498
其他投资企业	Other Investment Enterprises	11891		18427	1225	17202	2034
外商投资	With Foreign Investment	818709		3754047	536909	3217138	81527
中外合资经营	Joint-venture	21963		26291		26291	3779
外 资	Solely Foreign Funded	793397		1844101	147575	1696526	68088
外商投资有限公司	Foreign Investment Corporations Ltd.	3349		1883656	389334	1494322	9660
其他外商投资企业	Other Foreign Funded Enterprises						

16—4 限额以上批发零售业商品购进、销售和库存情况（2022年，按行业分）

Total Purchases, Sales and Inventory of Enterprises Above Designated Size in Wholesale and Retail Trade by Sector (2022)

单位：万元（10000 yuan）

指 标	Item	购进总额 Total Purchases Value	销售总额 Total Sales Value	批 发 Wholesale Value	零 售 Retail Value	年末库存总 额 Stock (year-end)
总 计	**Total**	**197158803**	**219635135**	**169075319**	**50314846**	**10953593**
批发业合计	**Wholesale Trade**	**156305903**	**172320303**	**165377175**	**6700663**	**6999736**
农、林、牧、渔产品批发	Wholesale of Agriculture, Forest, Animal Husbandry and Fishery Products	3118348	3232666	3088550	140583	199055
谷物、豆及薯类批发	Wholesale of Corn, Bean and Potato	1597210	1658901	1587291	68427	141487
种子批发	Wholesale of Seed	210870	232799	230245	2554	31060
畜牧渔业饲料批发	Wholesale of Animal Husbandry and Fishery Feed	847132	860045	827071	32975	8478
棉、麻批发	Wholesale of Cotton, Linen	216550	221258	221258		7269
林业产品批发	Wholesale of Foresty Products	41639	42456	39932	2525	3279
牲畜批发	Wholesale of Livestock	22643	24262	17610	6653	99
渔业产品批发	Wholesale of Fishery Products	18953	19785	12638	7147	13
其他农牧产品批发	Wholesale of Other Agricultural Products	163352	173159	152508	20302	7369
食品、饮料及烟草制品批发	Wholesale of Food, Beverages and Tobaccos	16692635	21064801	19829093	1211205	1142880
米、面制品及食用油批发	Wholesale of Rice, Flour and Edible Oil	3805952	3951032	3839352	111680	524470
糕点、糖果及糖批发	Wholesale of Cakes, Candy and Sugar	441592	468585	433830	32678	4228
果品、蔬菜批发	Wholesale of Fruits, Vegetables	435081	484624	383803	100820	8267
肉、禽、蛋、奶及水产品批发	Wholesale of Meat, Poultry, Eggs, Milk and Aquatic Products	1562054	1677447	1552823	124410	73648
盐及调味品批发	Wholesale of Salt and Spices	173340	184037	170399	13638	10772
营养及保健品批发	Wholesale of Nutrition and Health Care Products	43444	52966	47892	5074	2048
酒、饮料及茶叶批发	Liquor, Beverage and Tea Wholesale	3770473	5065958	4399371	654682	262718
烟草制品批发	Wholesale of Tobaccos	5200020	7776993	7761718	13110	176899
其他食品批发	Wholesale of Other Food	1260678	1403158	1239905	155113	79830
纺织、服装及家庭用品批发	Wholesale of Textiles, Clothing and Household Goods	14344668	16533750	14542918	1979671	1077205
纺织品、针织品及原料批发	Wholesale of Textiles, Knitwear and Raw Materials	1167448	1226249	1216949	9300	41534
服装批发	Wholesale of Garments	849913	910300	884686	25613	51812
鞋帽批发	Wholesale of Shoes and Hats	108039	117193	103470	13723	2996
化妆品及卫生用品批发	Wholesale of Cosmetics and Health Supplies	1673067	2354079	2301178	52901	126904
厨具卫具及日用杂货批发	Wholesale of Kitchen Utensils and Daily Groceries	498227	592087	292237	299480	28668
灯具、装饰物品批发	Wholesale of Lamps and Decorative Items	789059	858595	825004	33592	68340
家用视听设备批发	Wholesale of Domestic Audio-visual Equipment	2185389	2282307	2160078	114492	89731
日用家电批发	Wholesale of Household Appliances	6959941	8049365	6628597	1417715	661736
其他家庭用品批发	Wholesale of Other Household Goods	113585	143575	130719	12856	5484

16—4 续表1 continued

单位：万元（10000 yuan）

指 标	Item	购进总额 Total Purchases Value	销售总额 Total Sales Value	批 发 Wholesale Value	零 售 Retail Value	年末库存总 额 Stock (year-end)
文化、体育用品及器材批发	Wholesale of Culture, Sports Appliances and Equipments	3987940	4244698	4010583	229654	255139
文具用品批发	Wholesale of Stationery	311172	338200	333469	3102	12244
体育用品及器材批发	Wholesale of Sporting goods and equipment	49356	51574	51574		4543
图书批发	Wholesale of Book	756601	876175	696144	180032	135522
音像制品、电子和数字出版物批发	Wholesale of Audio-visual Products, Electronic and Digital Publications	413130	414089	414089		51427
首饰、工艺品及收藏品批发	Wholesale of Jewelry, Crafts and Collectibles	650589	665088	631907	33181	24601
其他文化用品批发	Wholesale of Other Cultural Goods	1807093	1899572	1883399	13341	26802
医药及医疗器材批发	Wholesale of Medicines and Medical Appliances	10830972	13012091	12564886	422511	1029041
西药批发	Wholesale of Western Medicine	8134600	9311185	9041500	260877	778847
中药批发	Wholesale of Traditional Chinese Medicine	1307530	2007367	1865627	125855	90625
动物用药品批发	Wholesale of Animal Medicines	25390	32412	32412		87
医疗用品及器材批发	Wholesale of Medical Supplies and Equipment	1363452	1661128	1625348	35780	159482
矿产品、建材及化工产品批发	Wholesale of Mineral Products, Building Materials and Chemical Products	65518830	66116273	64572144	1515835	1475671
煤炭及制品批发	Wholesale of Coal and Related Products	20228320	20779619	20697114	79290	243802
石油及制品批发	Wholesale of Petroleum and Related Products	5786301	4395945	3701945	693999	190276
非金属矿及制品批发	Wholesale of Western Medicine	1175108	1239486	1236415	2270	32474
金属及金属矿批发	Wholesale of Metal Materials	19278670	19637635	19159953	463063	494420
建材批发	Wholesale of Building Materials	10664053	11438576	11264750	164167	230045
化肥批发	Wholesale of Chemical Fertilizer	2076196	2170124	2168371	1753	122939
农药批发	Wholesale of Pesticides	785956	805067	804370	698	40362
农用薄膜批发	Wholesale of Agricultural Film	30332	29720	29720		2054
其他化工产品批发	Wholesale of Other Chemical Products	5493894	5620101	5509506	110596	119300
机械设备、五金交电及电子产品批发	Wholesale of Machinery, Hardware and Electronic Equipment	31705377	37495393	36664477	824464	1605143
农业机械批发	Wholesale of Agricultural Machinery	306088	325019	299981	25038	16652
汽车及零配件批发	Wholesale of Motor Vehicles and Spare Parts	15315801	20234639	19885547	347499	978370
摩托车及零配件批发	Wholesale of Motorcycles and Their Parts	260216	294170	279847	14323	4669
五金产品批发	Wholesale of Hardware	495197	638069	601720	36350	18520
电气设备批发	Wholesale of Household Electrical Appliances	1271674	1381731	1359064	17809	76998
计算机、软件及辅助设备批发	Wholesale of Computer, Software and Assistant Appliances	10798734	11062174	10978271	83904	247351
通讯设备批发	Wholesale of Communication Equipment	849916	906404	823005	83399	91768
广播影视设备批发	Wholesale of Radio, Film and Television Equipment	167629	168862	119163	49699	5539
其他机械设备及电子产品批发	Wholesale of Other Mechanical Equipment and Electronic Products	2240122	2484325	2317881	166444	165277

16—4 续表2 continued

单位：万元（10000 yuan）

指标	Item	购进总额 Total Purchases Value	销售总额 Total Sales Value	批发 Wholesale Value	零售 Retail Value	年末库存总额 Stock (year-end)
贸易经纪与代理	Trade Broker and Agency	1221459	1301019	1300946	72	80637
贸易代理	Trade Agent	1215564	1294801	1294729	72	80637
其他贸易经纪与代理	Other Trade Broker and Agency	5896	6218	6218		
其他批发业	Other Wholesale Industry Art Agency	8885676	9319613	8803578	376667	134965
再生物资回收与批发	Recycling and Renewable Materials Wholesale	6306902	6679827	6471766	71704	115831
互联网批发	Wholesale of Internet	548449	492561	424750	67812	6679
其他未列明的批发	Wholesale of Other Unlisted	2030325	2147225	1907062	237151	12456
零售业合计	Total retail sales	**40852899**	**47314832**	**3698144**	**43614184**	**3953858**
综合零售	Integrated Retail	6918547	7720538	428253	7292285	630124
百货零售	Retail of General Merchandise	3338614	3694727	370312	3324415	304463
超级市场零售	Retail of Supermarkets	3416652	3838869	55958	3782911	310399
便利店零售	Retail of Convenience Store	77739	97457	1075	96382	7238
其他综合零售	Retail of Others	85542	89485	909	88577	8025
食品、饮料及烟草制品专门零售	Retail of Food, Beverages and Tobaccos	2258099	2516286	647499	1868604	549622
粮油零售	Retail of Grain and Oil	114972	126026	16546	109481	7422
糕点、面包零售	Retail of Cakes, Bread	64838	88236	2570	85666	2730
果品、蔬菜零售	Retail of Fruit, Vegetables	392363	474142	14248	459895	7738
肉、禽、蛋、奶及水产品零售	Retail of Meat, Poultry, Eggs, Milk and Aquatic Products	549453	558999	417320	141679	410584
营养和保健品零售	Retail of Nutrition and health care products	43980	48977	12379	36598	3621
酒、饮料及茶叶零售	Retail of Wine, tea and beverages	873075	972004	178706	793114	97047
烟草制品零售	Retail of Tobacco Products	24134	26390	125	26265	687
其他食品零售	Retail of Other Food	195286	221511	5604	215907	19792
纺织、服装及日用品专门零售	Special Retail of Textiles, Garments and Daily Consumer Articles	726679	914992	48034	866805	161397
纺织品及针织品零售	Retail of Textile and Knitwear	24021	29486	3209	26278	2129
服装零售	Retail of Garments	361321	494738	15785	478801	107109
鞋帽零售	Retail of Shoes and Hats	40418	51589	2684	48905	10890
化妆品及卫生用品零售	Retail of Cosmetics and Health Supplies	102597	116813	13720	103094	6656
厨具卫具及日用杂货零售	Retail of Kitchen Utensils and Daily Groceries	33112	37251	1933	35317	8493
钟表、眼镜零售	Retail of Watches, Glasses	66240	81664	292	81372	20452
自行车等代步设备零售	Retail of Bicycle and Other Transportation Equipment	50217	51985	1230	50755	4044
其他日用品零售	Retail of Other Daily Necessities	48754	51466	9181	42285	1625
文化、体育用品及器材专门零售	Retail of Culture, Sports Appliances and Equipments	1019839	1056824	18870	1037954	150732
文具用品零售	Retail of Stationery	63108	70568	3378	67189	5562
体育用品及器材零售	Retail of Sporting Goods and Equipment	13223	13771		13771	271
图书、报刊零售	Retail of Books, Newspapers	686237	683218	3471	679747	77547
音像制品、电子和数字出版物零售	Retail of Audio-visual Products, Electronic and Digital Publications	6083	6113	401	5712	299

16—4 续表3 continued

单位：万元（10000 yuan）

指　标	Item	购进总额 Total Purchases Value	销售总额 Total Sales Value	批　发 Wholesale Value	零　售 Retail Value	年末库存总　额 Stock (year-end)
珠宝首饰零售	Retail of Jewelry	116626	121769	6279	115491	42460
工艺美术品及收藏品零售	Retail of Arts and Crafts and Collectibles	43872	52665	262	52403	10352
乐器零售	Retail of Instruments	21524	22211	930	21281	9275
照相器材零售	Retail of Photographic equipment	5111	5550		5550	476
其他文化用品零售	Retail of Other Cultural Goods	64056	80959	4148	76811	4490
医药及医疗器材专门零售	Retail of Medicines and Medical Appliances	1405793	1627389	43577	1583812	222768
西药零售	Retail of Western Medicine	1372983	1588250	42138	1546112	216560
中药零售	Retail of Traditional Chinese Medicine	29924	35830	155	35675	6040
医疗用品及器材零售	Retail of Medical Supplies and Equipment	2886	3308	1284	2025	168
汽车、摩托车、零配件和燃料及其他动力销售	Sales of Automobiles, Motorcycles, Spare Parts and Fuel and Other Power	20777611	24533072	1977862	22555121	1695421
汽车新车零售	Retail of New Car	14411206	14552765	393148	14159617	1471061
汽车旧车零售	Retail of Used Car	206249	196862		196862	6832
汽车零配件零售	Retail of Auto Parts	53110	49176	406	48770	7266
摩托车及零配件零售	Retail of Motorcycles and Spare Parts	38929	42392	1244	41148	3024
机动车燃料零售	Retail of Motor Vehicle Fuel	6044694	9666458	1583064	8083305	207139
机动车燃气零售	Retail of Motor Vehicle Gas	23424	25419		25419	99
家用电器及电子产品专门零售	Special Retail of Household Electric Appliances and Electronic Products	2524645	2632743	170630	2460198	213385
家用视听设备零售	Retail of Home Audio-visual Equipment	1019415	1045736	27492	1018244	70344
日用家电零售	Retail of Household Appliances	692870	732974	51945	681029	62023
计算机、软件及辅助设备零售	Retail of Computer, Software and Assistant Appliances	246855	263510	29707	231889	16487
通讯设备零售	Retail of Communication Equipments	453681	469750	60332	409417	54795
其他电子产品零售	Retail of Other Electronic Products	111824	120774	1154	119620	9736
五金、家具及室内装修材料专门零售	Retail of Hardware, Furniture and Decoration Materials	454626	526276	38269	488007	28372
五金零售	Retail of Hardware	111349	129054	14224	114830	6336
灯具零售	Retail of Lamps	11201	11398	1958	9440	652
家具零售	Retail of Furniture	123369	139089	12750	126339	8846
涂料零售	Retail of Paint	9695	10637	190	10447	902
卫生洁具零售	Retail of Sanitary Ware	34970	37209	1330	35879	3889
木制装饰材料零售	Retail of Wooden Decorative Materials	52804	65820	3058	62763	1112
陶瓷、石材装饰材料零售	Retail of Ceramic, Stone Decoration Materials	40046	43743	2662	41082	2616
其他室内装修材料零售	Retail of Other Interior Decoration Materials	71192	89326	2098	87228	4019
货摊、无店铺及其他零售业	Retail of Stalls, No Shop and Other	4767060	5786713	325151	5461398	302037
互联网零售	Retail of Internet	4478993	5439746	318956	5120625	284334
邮购及电视、电话零售	Retail of Television, Telephone and Mail Order	67623	108406	1703	106703	4079
自动售货机零售	Retail of Vending Machine	2164	2375	43	2332	77
生活用燃料零售	Retail of Living Fuel	142333	161359	2098	159261	8570
其他未列明的零售	Retail of Other Unlisted	75946	74829	2351	72478	4979

16—5 限额以上批发零售业主要商品分类销售额（2022年）

Total Sales of Enterprises Above Designated Size in Wholesale and Retail Sale by Category of Main Commodities (2022)

单位：万元（10000 yuan）

指　标	Item	合　计 Total	批　发 Wholesale	零　售 Retail Sale
总　计	Total	**219158115**	**165880943**	**53277172**
粮油、食品、饮料、烟酒类	Grain and Edible Vegetable Oil, Food, Beverages, Tobacco and Liquor	35967023	23917998	12049025
粮油、食品类	Grain and Edible Vegetable Oil, Food	19382329	10652684	8729645
#粮油类	Grain and Edible Vegetable Oil	6810230	5289650	1520580
肉禽蛋类	Meat, Poultry and Eggs	3270537	2140384	1130153
水产品类	Aquatic Products	408377	89928	318449
蔬菜类	Vegetables	1332542	442834	889707
干鲜果品类	melons and Fruits	1378618	404841	973778
饮料类	Beverages	2282495	1156212	1126283
烟酒类	Tobacco and Liquor	14302199	12109101	2193098
服装鞋帽、针、纺织品类	Garments, Footwear, Hats, Knitwear and Textiles	4328280	1798039	2530241
服装类	Garments	2488284	695369	1792916
鞋帽类	Footwear and Hats	695751	265050	430701
针、纺织品类	Knitwear and Textiles	1144245	837621	306624
化妆品类	Cosmetics	1616145	764775	851371
金银珠宝类	Gold, Silver and Jewelry	1540310	645861	894448
日用品类	Articles for Daily Use	4471687	2425939	2045748
可穿戴智能设备	Wearable smart devices	42113	2021	40092
五金、电料类	Hardware and Electrical Materials	1186769	949147	237622
体育、娱乐用品类	Sports and Recreation Articles	371217	53098	318118
#照相器材类	Photographic Equipment Class	8795	65	8731
书报杂志类	Newspapers and Magazines	1433998	712531	721467
电子出版物及音像制品类	E-journal and Video Products	30743	2206	28536
家用电器和音像器材类	Household Appliances and Audio-visual Equipment	14153903	10625906	3527997
#能效等级为1级和2级的商品	Energy Efficiency Grade 1 and 2 Goods	7114429	6357375	757054
智能家用电器和音像器材	Smart Home Appliances and Audio and Video Equipment	3730474	3062878	667597
中西药品类	Traditional Chinese and Western Medicines	12973897	11244553	1729344
西　药	Western Medicines	8576155	7298689	1277466
中草药及中成药	Chinese Herbal Medicine and Proprietary Chinese Medicine	2213260	1957211	256050
文化、办公用品类	Cultural and Official Goods	10918494	10152481	766013
#计算机及其配套产品	Computer and Its Supporting Products	10178557	9908859	269698
家具类	Furniture	627122	142614	484508
通讯器材类	Communication Appliances	2332987	1380666	952321
#智能手机	A Smart Phone	1298662	701419	597243
煤炭及制品类	Coal and Related Product	20571910	20560991	10918
木材及制品类	Wood and Wooden Product	507787	507707	80
石油及制品类	Petroleum and Related Product	13982766	3944446	10038320
化工材料类	Raw Chemical Materials	8614372	8612305	2067
化肥类	Chemical Fertilizer	2526749	2525565	1184
金属材料类	Metal Materials	24718141	24708995	9146
建筑及装潢材料类	Building and Decoration Materials	7978611	7572964	405647
机电产品及设备类	Mechanical and Electrical Products	3587512	3485002	102510
农机类	Agricultural Machinery	284935	283745	1190
汽车类	Automobile	33271552	18321696	14949856
#新能源汽车	New Energy Vehicle	11909871	9979133	1930738
新车	New car	29022478	14759194	14263285
二手车	Used car	281713	7470	274243
种子饲料类	Seed and Feedstuff	1309758	1309698	60
棉麻类	Cotton, Hemp	139974	138964	1010
其他类	Other	12523160	11902362	620799

16—6 限额以上批发零售企业主要财务指标情况（2022年，按登记注册类型分）
Main Financial Indicators of Enterprises Above Designated Size in Wholesale and Retail Sale by Registration (2022)

指标	Item	流动资产合计 Circulating Funds	#存货 Stock
批发零售企业总计	**Total**	**84580222**	**11223748**
批发企业合计	**Wholesale Trade**	**70100310**	**7584060**
国有控股	State-holding Enterprises	26666403	2774665
内资	Domestic-funded	54599904	6535724
国有	State-owned	4153105	329552
集体	Collective-owned	1032	65
股份合作	Cooperative	13631	8377
有限责任公司	Limited Liability Corporations	27663814	3144109
股份有限公司	Share-holding Corporations Ltd.	4706528	434132
私营	Private	17956816	2612243
其他	Other	104978	7246
港澳台商投资	With Investment from Hong Kong, Macao and Taiwan	8670816	485000
合资经营	Joint-venture	13878	
独资经营	With Sole Fund	8624932	478681
其他投资企业	Other Investment Enterprises	32006	6319
外商投资	With Foreign Investment	6829590	563336
中外合资经营	Joint-venture	3013604	464865
外资	Solely Foreign Funded	3771995	88329
外商投资有限公司	Foreign Investment Corporations Ltd.	43992	10142
零售企业合计	**Retail Trade**	**14479911**	**3639688**
国有控股	State Controlling Share Hold Enterprises	2374016	458093
内资	Domestic-funded	12783658	3500738
国有	State-owned	110634	23972
集体	Collective-owned	1704	279
股份合作	Cooperative	8040	3324
联营	Joint Ownership	3595	41
有限责任公司	Limited Liability Corporations	4758788	1139253
股份有限公司	Share-holding Corporations Ltd.	958979	217195
私营	Private	6912751	2114931
其他	Other	29166	1743
港澳台商投资	With Investment from Hong Kong, Macao and Taiwan	845655	59594
合资经营	Joint-venture	13114	5691
独资经营	With Sole Fund	483596	51075
股份有限公司	Share-holding Corporations Ltd.	332618	821
其他投资企业	Other Investment Enterprises	16328	2008
外商投资	With Foreign Investment	850599	79356
中外合资经营	Joint-venture	7328	4056
外资	Solely Foreign Funded	845933	89174
外商投资有限公司	Foreign Investment Corporations Ltd.	-2663	-13874

单位：万元（10000 yuan）

固定资产合计 Total Fixed Assets	固定资产原价 Original Value of Fixed Assets	累计折旧 Progressive Depreciation	#本年折旧 Depreciation this Year	资产总计 Total of Assets	负债合计 Total of Liabilities	流动负债 Working Liabilities	所有者权益 Owners' Equity	#实收资本 Capital Hold	#个人资本 Individual Capital
4172535	**8416491**	**3435199**	**577526**	**103777036**	**77750029**	**68938214**	**25888005**	**13630755**	**1379947**
2101962	**3921705**	**1533071**	**309851**	**82440523**	**63589798**	**57557416**	**18795554**	**9393478**	**917574**
985109	1606168	566602	60156	33504275	22503366	19601859	10989841	4467612	21129
1808980	3332059	1251994	185891	65581115	47754524	42291611	17771419	8149087	900844
205732	475590	262713	25832	4583852	1944884	1802569	2634078	237311	2300
234	424	191	41	1246	152	152	1094	80	80
594	1132	537	104	18218	15343	15343	2875	4030	
834766	1256854	334044	46495	33370605	25620003	22642633	7739321	4770915	34798
148532	253626	103798	9858	7007151	4429298	3930258	2577853	708167	18130
608860	1326990	543584	102313	20461271	15644107	13800576	4778424	2383454	844805
10263	17444	7128	1248	138773	100738	100081	37775	45130	730
258355	503617	229863	119749	9820246	8865449	8302076	954796	1095814	
395	2461	2066	32	23486	18697	10737	4789	3865	
257788	500789	227621	119645	9763675	8818023	8262609	945652	1084049	
172	367	177	72	33085	28730	28730	4355	7900	
34627	86029	51214	4212	7039163	6969825	6963729	69338	148576	16730
32612	80748	47960	3940	3204200	3411148	3405127		124396	16680
2015	5263	3248	265	3790959	3514723	3514597	276236	24130	50
	19	6	6	44004	43954	44004	50	50	
2070572	**4494786**	**1902128**	**267675**	**21336513**	**14160231**	**11380798**	**7092451**	**4237278**	**462373**
647136	1342155	621150	64946	5030830	1778426	1045185	3209614	536045	4189
1790967	3844433	1557112	234187	18653917	12722124	10246109	5843762	3980232	461406
50492	142064	74269	8134	358272	94651	37452	221347	17703	
283	1551	470	109	3422	1401	494	2021	432	50
860	3590	1984	86	10047	4483	4046	5564	1380	635
0	20	19	4	3597	903	903	2693	120	
634017	1385776	538574	73488	7187826	5376754	4249157	1802755	1153378	32445
372959	724082	323358	32394	2218015	924946	714813	1293069	159302	6385
731879	1582723	617541	119849	8837602	6289454	5211661	2512021	2647217	421892
477	4627	898	124	35137	29532	27584	4293	700	
87367	297239	197842	16285	1153411	753365	649338	399749	162020	967
548	5702	3187	536	23914	9446	6734	14468	11110	40
79625	278443	188754	14612	728183	549608	450148	178278	107113	
5105	7949	2844	939	382898	185338	183483	197561	40100	
2088	5146	3057	197	18416	8973	8973	9443	3698	927
192239	353114	147174	17204	1529185	684742	485351	848940	95025	
299	4014	3688		13995	101462	97757	-87467	12582	
104774	194524	77895	9736	1205844	997398	882731	212942	82444	
87165	154575	65590	8022	309347	-414118	-495138	723464		

16—6 续表 continued

指 标	Item	主营收入 Project Settlement Income	营业成本 Operating Costs	税金及附加 Taxes and Surcharges
批发零售企业总计	**Total**	**195058691**	**181237116**	**1324619**
批发企业合计	**Wholesale Trade**	**154098201**	**144471279**	**1204835**
国有控股	State-holding Enterprises	60386758	56890849	1007941
内 资	Domestic-funded	131647790	123441384	1166825
国 有	State-owned	11793348	9720163	927530
集 体	Collective-owned	5171	4543	13
股份合作	Cooperative	18442	17197	57
有限责任公司	Limited Liability Corporations	67994194	64989211	125890
股份有限公司	Share-holding Corporations Ltd.	4950231	4807211	7213
私 营	Private	46635889	43687636	105572
其 他	Other	250514	215425	550
港澳台商投资	With Investment from Hong Kong, Macao and Taiwan	13222089	12798998	19419
合资经营	Joint-venture	26011	35337	59
独资经营	With Sole Fund	13027741	12619565	19043
其他投资企业	Other Investment Enterprises	168337	144097	316
外商投资	With Foreign Investment	9228322	8230896	18592
中外合资经营	Joint-venture	3534427	2765075	11282
外 资	Solely Foreign Funded	5568988	5346111	7185
外商投资有限公司	Foreign Investment Corporations Ltd.	124907	119711	125
零售企业合计	**Retail Trade**	**40960490**	**36765838**	**119784**
国有控股	State Controlling Share Hold Enterprises	9164541	8475116	26382
内 资	Domestic-funded	35151088	31559120	102657
国 有	State-owned	943360	903727	1472
集 体	Collective-owned	28208	27319	79
股份合作	Cooperative	12100	12146	89
联 营	Joint Ownership	8247	6620	20
有限责任公司	Limited Liability Corporations	11806165	10444724	41374
股份有限公司	Share-holding Corporations Ltd.	3505424	3317611	9117
私 营	Private	18832226	16831616	50483
其 他	Other	15359	15356	23
港澳台商投资	With Investment from Hong Kong, Macao and Taiwan	2536043	2168916	11816
合资经营	Joint-venture	70477	63895	588
独资经营	With Sole Fund	1842330	1634901	8859
股份有限公司	Share-holding Corporations Ltd.	606915	460375	2273
其他投资企业	Other Investment Enterprises	16321	9745	96
外商投资	With Foreign Investment	3273360	3037802	5312
中外合资经营	Joint-venture	23326	27549	69
外 资	Solely Foreign Funded	1625132	1464268	3305
外商投资有限公司	Foreign Investment Corporations Ltd.	1624902	1545985	1938

单位：万元（10000 yuan）

其他业务利润 Other Business Profit	销售费用 Operating Expense	管理费用 Management Expense	财务费用 Financial Expenses	营业利润 Operating Profit	利润总额 Total Profit	应交所得税 Payable Income Tax	本年应付工资薪酬 Total Payable Wages this Year
281819	**8320471**	**3269814**	**534222**	**2606725**	**2857575**	**859421**	**3608095**
131969	**5398103**	**2131694**	**344526**	**2054437**	**2254898**	**764709**	**2002815**
46073	1255783	636688	54499	1439272	1472935	364180	833287
124818	4331775	1664662	252885	2234040	2427471	726367	1722912
1490	148354	401308	-61687	753678	754543	216707	348467
	282	181	2	152	152	15	89
	191	356	798	-143	-139	7	218
52689	2238961	454927	160739	866051	943409	227900	656398
9404	105911	57539	20496	79160	80635	5421	109089
61235	1824514	718001	132231	542321	658764	276269	606171
	13563	32350	306	-7179	-9893	48	2480
199	209659	349626	100868	-237120	-234906	14966	175840
-30	529	587	-46	8058	7689		1170
230	186557	348212	100995	-245851	-243299	14653	168426
	22573	827	-81	674	704	313	6244
6952	856669	117406	-9227	57517	62332	23377	104064
6952	701425	88016	-16017	28039	28209	15611	99877
	146690	29153	6791	33199	37872	7766	2671
	8554	238	-1	-3720	-3749		1516
149849	**2922368**	**1138119**	**189696**	**552288**	**602678**	**94711**	**1605280**
44366	479270	181556	21707	249744	243456	22550	266532
136504	2435410	1048569	171226	441992	492649	81843	1434192
2867	43754	3584	1470	18917	18800	279	21936
	762	620	136	829	836	23	730
191	979	556	20	153	178	7	711
	443	415	52	697	698	118	529
66599	1017632	334674	68792	80416	96765	43864	531590
16427	179670	71637	8041	72219	67863	5546	105098
50421	1190947	636423	92676	268535	307223	32008	773098
	1225	660	38	226	287		499
9199	313819	55006	3870	35837	38382	9548	114867
297	6186	1248	-33	-914	-894	117	2698
5652	184835	30357	4148	25294	26107	6247	90904
1996	122443	21486	-162	5907	7484	1787	20439
1254	355	1915	-83	5550	5685	1397	826
4147	173139	34545	14599	74458	71647	3320	56222
1929	7196	1728	4005	-6241	-6437		800
2218	122244	22136	6738	26882	23697	3692	40136
	43700	10682	3856	53816	54386	-372	15285

16—7 限额以上批发零售企业主要财务指标情况（2022年，按行业分）

Main Financial Inventory of Enterprises Above Designated Size in Wholesale and Retail by Sector (2022)

(按2017年行业代码分组 Grouped by industry code for 2017)

指　标	Item	流动资产合计 Circulating Funds	#存货 Stock
总　计	**Total**	**84580222**	**11223748**
批发业合计	**Wholesale Trade**	**70100310**	**7584060**
农、林、牧、渔产品批发	Wholesale of Agricultural, Forestry, Animal Husbandry and Fishery Products	1331091	203685
食品、饮料及烟草制品批发	Wholesale of Food, Beverages and Tobaccos	9840713	1183585
#米、面制品及食用油批发	Wholesale of Rice, Flour and Edible Oil	1562029	532490
烟草制品批发	Wholesale of Tobaccos	2679533	165088
纺织、服装及家庭用品批发	Wholesale ofTextile, Clothing and Household Goods	6696744	1308200
#服装批发	Wholesale of Garments	470126	45958
文化、体育用品及器材批发	Wholesale of Culture, Sports Appliances and Equipments	3116334	372131
医药及医疗器材批发	Wholesale of Medicines and Medical Appliances	7530976	1063928
矿产品、建材及化工产品批发	Wholesale of Mineral Products, Building Materials and Chemical Products	18159674	1650605
#煤炭及制品批发	Wholesale of Coal and Related Products	3601777	257691
石油及制品批发	Wholesale of Petroleum and Related Products	959472	191533
金属及金属矿批发	Wholesale of Metal Materials	5911757	471168
建材批发	Wholesale of Building Materials	4984753	374962
化肥批发	Wholesale of Chemical Fertilizer	669396	135240
机械设备、五金交电及电子产品批发	Wholesale of Machinery, Hardware and Electronic Equipment	20358628	1614293
#汽车及零配件批发	Wholesale of Automobiles and Spare Parts	10174194	962345
电气设备批发	Wholesale of Electrical Equipments	580275	76777
计算机、软件及辅助设备批发	Wholesale of Computer, Software and Assistant Appliances	7366050	242029
贸易经纪与代理	Trade Broker and Agency	233678	82218
其他批发	Other Wholesale not Classified Elsewhere	2832473	105414
零售业合计	**Retail Trade**	**14479911**	**3639688**
综合零售	Integrated Retail	2732194	575839
#百货零售	Retail of General Merchandise	1409511	209379
超级市场零售	Retail of Supermarkets	1211789	351229
食品、饮料及烟草制品专门零售	Retail of Food, Beverages and Tobaccos	734372	190741
纺织、服装及日用品专门零售	Special Retail of Textiles, Garments and Daily Consumer Articles	377487	157244
#服装零售	Retail of Garments	208670	102430
文化、体育用品及器材专门零售	Retail of Culture, Sports Appliances and Equipments	736759	152538
#体育用品及器材零售	Sporting Goods and Equipment Retail	5839	687
图书、报刊零售	Books, Newspapers and Retail	521468	79017
医药及医疗器材专门零售	Retail of Medicines and Medical Appliances	798175	229757
#西药零售	Retail of Western Medicine	773338	221696
中药零售	Retail of Traditional Chinese Medicine	20407	6708
汽车、摩托车、燃料及零配件专门零售	Retail of Motor Vehicles, Motorcycles, Fuel and Parts	6130311	1749385
#汽车新车零售	Retail of New Cars	4404000	1495226
机动车燃油零售	Retail of Motor Vehicle Fuel	1643227	237335
家用电器及电子产品专门零售	Special Retail of Household Electric Appliances and Electronic Products	1072005	246621
#日用家电零售	Retail Sales of Household Appliances	323414	74820
计算机、软件及辅助设备零售	Retail of Computer, Software and Assistant Appliances	96419	19696
通信设备零售	Retail Sales of Communication Equipment	148607	56273
五金、家具及室内装饰材料专门零售	Special Retail of Hardware, Furniture and Decoration Materials	195891	35407
货摊、无店铺及其他零售	Stalls, No Shops and Other Retail Outlets	1702717	302158

单位：万元（10000 yuan）

固定资产合计 Total Fixed Assets	固定资产原价 Original Value of Fixed Assets	累计折旧 Progressive Deprecia-tion	#本年折旧 Deprecia-tion this Year	资产总计 Total of Assets	负债合计 Total of Liabilities	流动负债 Working Liabilities	所有者权益 Owners' Equity	#实收资本 Capital Hold	#个人资本 Individual Capital
4172535	**8416491**	**3435199**	**577526**	**103777036**	**77750029**	**68938214**	**25888005**	**13630755**	**1379947**
2101962	**3921705**	**1533071**	**309851**	**82440523**	**63589798**	**57557416**	**18795554**	**9393478**	**917574**
130722	201831	52356	10105	1944725	1201591	1066444	737011	320209	44224
366319	857059	407817	44463	11526062	6788668	6102210	4736004	1258997	249656
62725	117298	43796	3708	1822202	1531776	1383819	290426	142048	15638
178337	424004	245665	19722	2950452	473596	469648	2476512	28428	
92755	227189	108735	10906	7311719	6976438	6763982	332813	332171	58478
19682	43424	22840	1902	691598	527402	438959	164195	43410	10998
49554	76524	25255	3527	3727127	2454952	2343192	1271650	311635	19927
213094	504279	218321	35083	8434284	6535067	5350242	1883770	716582	87296
661058	1037276	331685	56185	23758344	16589500	14571986	7159365	4092637	324563
319516	385386	62147	9091	5130953	3059727	2955120	2069531	1534111	61600
115223	227525	106115	14726	1968639	1179294	654284	789263	161949	9868
77586	136293	51850	7694	6972687	5651872	5208961	1314254	1122657	101007
76154	152567	54862	14234	6224278	4244887	3471619	1978467	848341	94494
27810	44384	15177	1923	1181047	752672	730659	428375	160162	8679
375297	766024	353871	142917	22151251	19960350	18772707	2185864	2126345	106067
265241	539068	251117	120796	11643116	10343521	9538550	1295196	1745066	50008
5717	12295	5541	1162	606777	554600	544622	51539	28188	4500
14339	28371	13570	4266	7394218	7120114	7022047	274104	75050	3967
3870	5976	1708	536	239579	168258	163130	71320	34597	879
209293	245547	33324	6129	3347432	2914975	2423523	417757	200306	26483
2070572	**4494786**	**1902128**	**267675**	**21336513**	**14160231**	**11380798**	**7092451**	**4237278**	**462373**
660493	1582970	776314	81336	4854760	3874677	2936752	981602	638981	94500
399303	845241	381195	38180	2534224	1812643	1395169	724251	246114	52881
256493	726140	389935	41916	2193067	1955554	1476493	236285	380126	36445
54470	150236	61612	12165	917073	568679	460885	352886	134889	27520
66186	163166	24817	5594	566097	411626	305326	153684	89192	8835
61545	148087	19573	3926	373835	287952	204449	85786	71609	4050
35592	79430	37712	4597	892367	493266	348746	398527	84664	15588
152	1049	232	70	7748	5580	100	2168	300	
24439	53335	27807	2805	650436	341997	247618	308439	49599	2736
30101	74661	37466	6204	1074469	803920	696494	264082	116126	28421
29249	72370	36347	5958	1045016	782075	685598	256474	112106	28111
787	1933	842	215	24911	18837	9713	6074	3760	50
993656	2014567	837471	129744	9389410	5404822	4394838	3925292	1697450	185848
463446	934764	372098	73800	5511851	4375264	3780899	1122103	1295054	141387
528479	1069325	460704	55083	3775284	974314	569338	2758060	366781	41080
72532	122988	43352	7908	1294454	1017174	870188	268325	1228531	39214
13490	25700	10743	1965	382826	301091	255952	81350	137867	14156
3065	9838	5708	709	102936	63075	52995	37907	17307	5508
1925	4134	1710	425	153157	127338	115999	22387	1014489	4600
64005	100767	29055	5961	314256	200410	169523	104605	38551	14587
93538	206001	54329	14166	2033626	1385658	1198047	643449	208893	47861

16—7 续表 continued

指 标	Item	主营收入 Project Settlement Income	营业成本 Operating Costs
总 计	**Total**	**195058691**	**181237116**
批发业合计	**Wholesale Trade**	**154098201**	**144471279**
农、林、牧、渔产品批发	Wholesale of Agricultural, Forestry, Animal Husbandry and Fishery Products	3052150	2916716
食品、饮料及烟草制品批发	Wholesale of Food, Beverages and Tobaccos	18865568	15300266
#米、面制品及食用油批发	Wholesale of Rice, Flour and Edible Oil	3593525	3513333
烟草制品批发	Wholesale of Tobaccos	6875794	4892374
纺织、服装及家庭用品批发	Wholesale ofTextile, Clothing and Household Goods	14837691	12958204
#服装批发	Wholesale of Garments	858120	788639
文化、体育用品及器材批发	Wholesale of Culture, Sports Appliances and Equipments	3660881	3518327
医药及医疗器材批发	Wholesale of Medicines and Medical Appliances	11678099	9927690
矿产品、建材及化工产品批发	Wholesale of Mineral Products, Building Materials and Chemical Products	58766063	57554487
#煤炭及制品批发	Wholesale of Coal and Related Products	18263970	17917977
石油及制品批发	Wholesale of Petroleum and Related Products	3809951	3719582
金属及金属矿批发	Wholesale of Metal Materials	17880572	17644829
建材批发	Wholesale of Building Materials	10042277	9726526
化肥批发	Wholesale of Chemical Fertilizer	1857939	1944174
机械设备、五金交电及电子产品批发	Wholesale of Machinery, Hardware and Electronic Equipment	33797842	32587495
#汽车及零配件批发	Wholesale of Automobiles and Spare Parts	18357521	17971135
电气设备批发	Wholesale of Electrical Equipments	1237030	1195042
计算机、软件及辅助设备批发	Wholesale of Computer, Software and Assistant Appliances	9812881	9360768
贸易经纪与代理	Trade Broker and Agency	1195845	1139532
其他批发	Other Wholesale not Classified Elsewhere	8244062	8568564
零售业合计	**Retail Trade**	**40960490**	**36765838**
综合零售	Integrated Retail	6136242	5284201
#百货零售	Retail of General Merchandise	2655635	2256127
超级市场零售	Retail of Supermarkets	3331598	2899889
食品、饮料及烟草制品专门零售	Retail of Food, Beverages and Tobaccos	1936686	1653695
纺织、服装及日用品专门零售	Special Retail of Textiles, Garments and Daily Consumer Articles	803456	620855
#服装零售	Retail of Garments	425508	320318
文化、体育用品及器材专门零售	Retail of Culture, Sports Appliances and Equipments	985439	774913
#体育用品及器材零售	Sporting Goods and Equipment Retail	11341	9896
图书、报刊零售	Books, Newspapers and Retail	649303	495021
医药及医疗器材专门零售	Retail of Medicines and Medical Appliances	1465032	1148997
#西药零售	Retail of Western Medicine	1429251	1120264
中药零售	Retail of Traditional Chinese Medicine	32827	25971
汽车、摩托车、燃料及零配件专门零售	Retail of Motor Vehicles, Motorcycles, Fuel and Parts	21695091	20533650
#汽车新车零售	Retail of New Cars	13020271	12308918
机动车燃油零售	Retail of Motor Vehicle Fuel	8379746	7936130
家用电器及电子产品专门零售	Special Retail of Household Electric Appliances and Electronic Products	2253754	2057823
#日用家电零售	Retail Sales of Household Appliances	667535	604692
计算机、软件及辅助设备零售	Retail of Computer, Software and Assistant Appliances	236969	216744
通信设备零售	Retail Sales of Communication Equipment	419061	382659
五金、家具及室内装饰材料专门零售	Special Retail of Hardware, Furniture and Decoration Materials	470524	398822
货摊、无店铺及其他零售	Stalls, No Shops and Other Retail Outlets	5214267	4292884

单位：万元（10000 yuan）

税金及附加 Taxes and Surcharges	其他业务利润 Other Business Profit	销售费用 Operating Expense	管理费用 Management Expense	财务费用 Financial Expenses	营业利润 Operating Profit	利润总额 Total Profit	应交所得税 Payable Income Tax	本年应付工资薪酬 Total Payable Wages this Year
1324619	**281819**	**8320471**	**3269814**	**534222**	**2606725**	**2857575**	**859421**	**3608095**
1204835	**131969**	**5398103**	**2131694**	**344526**	**2054437**	**2254898**	**764709**	**2002815**
3198	8692	57870	39993	19122	44540	53204	2428	36173
954500	16620	1060359	598925	-56808	1271169	1286862	350905	687746
4764	4011	49220	27454	14409	20834	22117	3881	36882
921928	1630	115853	385212	-84242	754366	752336	216531	333762
29117	19184	1671995	177405	-16837	86719	94343	196861	233476
1121	1540	32373	16740	-2583	21510	22133	4407	16871
5739	1049	68483	37162	7533	60321	61812	-550	39636
41205	10218	1102293	360901	81417	288164	305186	68970	252187
79603	23581	590548	314440	128972	523301	575686	105239	301506
21605	1808	127455	56248	11683	211035	243586	48771	34032
4872	8643	84419	22839	10134	27115	27146	3797	70643
20362	3026	90774	74850	59919	26098	32865	6304	49740
23181	3217	118832	72108	34768	130455	140812	20116	77908
1472	2793	26499	18694	3668	31320	31321	5166	20454
49660	25898	782719	539328	142417	-266046	-229428	19300	411581
28821	23774	511847	368456	-64665	-401768	-394798	-9349	236063
1109	272	21534	13885	1056	7906	10292	1485	9830
10930	586	92712	45068	189820	102575	108329	15578	55048
1487	259	6043	4569	702	38903	39095	6630	5099
40326	26469	57793	58972	38007	7366	68137	14927	35412
119784	**149849**	**2922368**	**1138119**	**189696**	**552288**	**602678**	**94711**	**1605280**
35320	56726	715051	299773	64122	42037	50717	15678	451854
23430	23345	193855	176727	26110	66632	70137	10917	154121
11202	29792	506550	112883	37626	-24084	-19471	4561	284416
5283	1920	173346	77965	6851	54671	59168	9049	90863
3113	4373	106921	35395	7841	11904	14685	4580	64868
2234	307	81118	19642	6258	-341	1488	800	47603
4425	1835	88133	54826	3939	78874	75848	2502	71191
12		427	511	81	84	90	5	321
1664	1797	63878	41379	2804	62128	58626	25	55780
4278	1215	223457	72424	9132	30204	33101	6630	171509
4209	1195	218372	70776	8946	29598	32480	6592	166592
66	19	4855	1460	186	620	636	25	4467
44684	58608	765451	326458	79743	204955	218185	41327	455421
30110	45268	450471	258993	66932	5549	29376	26449	326635
14030	12516	303038	63295	12314	200202	189512	14495	121974
5192	4766	126048	75423	9391	11610	14453	2405	96557
1045	1667	36726	20585	3043	6013	6774	391	27364
375	177	7791	9975	607	4394	4757	225	8834
818	91	17616	19260	1142	4076	4829	782	20690
3069	243	51221	17462	2274	15118	15774	1224	28629
14419	20165	672741	178394	6403	102915	120746	11317	174389

16—8 限额以上住宿餐饮业经营情况（2022年）
Above Designated Accommodation Catering Business (2022)

指　　标	Item	营业额 Turnover
总　　计	**Total**	**3723786**
住宿业合计	**Total of Accommodation Enterprises**	**874389**
国有控股	State-holding Enterprises	164908
按登记注册类型分组	**Group by Registration Type**	
内　资	Domestic-funded	840239
国　有	State-owned	5126
集　体	Collective-owned	
联　营	Joint Ownership	
有限责任公司	Limited Liability Company	375431
股份有限公司	Share-holding Corporations Ltd.	10217
私　营	Private	449013
其　他	Other	453
港澳台商投资	With Investment from Hong Kong, Macao and Taiwan	26249
外商投资企业	Enterprises with Foreign Investment	7900
按国民经济行业分	**Divided by National Economy Industry**	
旅游饭店	Tourist Hotel	601602
一般旅馆	Common Hotel	245918
经济型连锁酒店	Economical Hotel Chain	122743
其他一般旅馆	Other General Hotels	123175
民宿服务	Homestay Service	6252
露营地服务	Campground Service	1659
其他住宿服务	Other Accommodation Service	18958
餐饮业合计	**Catering Trade**	**2849397**
国有控股	State-holding Enterprises	61336
按登记注册类型分组	**Group by Registration Type**	
内　资	Domestic-funded	2810600
国　有	State-owned	10063
集　体	Collective-owned	642
有限责任公司	Limited Liability Company	658086
股份有限公司	Share-holding Corporations Ltd.	7047
私　营	Private	2134009
其　他	Other	753
港澳台商投资企业	With Investment from Hong Kong, Macao and Taiwan	14873
外商投资企业	Enterprises with Foreign Investment	23925
按国民经济行业分	**Divided by National Economy Industry**	
正餐服务	Dinner	1813953
快餐服务	Fast Food	681117
饮料及冷饮服务	Drink and Cold Drink Service	48771
餐饮配送及外卖送餐服务	Catering and Delivery Services	297199
其他餐饮业	Other Catering Service	8358

单位：万元（10000 yuan）

客房收入 Room Revenue	餐费收入 Meals Income	商品销售收入 Commodity Sales	其他收入 Other Income	客 房 数 （间） Guestroom Number (unit)	床 位 数 （个） Bed Capacity (unit)	餐 位 数 （位） Number of Seating Arrangement (unit)
573565	**2819257**	**207056**	**123908**	**188253**	**291199**	**1543729**
442319	**298130**	**66533**	**67406**	**152667**	**232742**	**258664**
33956	51533	40954	38465	8842	14409	41135
426127	283976	65748	64389	149847	228397	252521
2036	2912	45	133	713	1312	4280
131531	137128	55676	51095	30380	47536	101439
6603	1345	547	1722	2061	3125	2583
285504	142591	9480	11439	116595	176290	144219
453				98	134	
12940	10130	573	2607	1825	2672	3809
3253	4024	213	410	995	1673	2334
245457	237358	60652	58134	67297	102210	196539
180957	52547	5027	7387	65872	94230	52641
99263	17033	2481	3967	26403	39157	11999
81694	35514	2546	3421	39469	55073	40642
4029	1838	352	34	6563	11853	2088
758	380	185	336	211	525	360
11118	6009	318	1513	12724	23924	7036
131246	**2521127**	**140523**	**56502**	**35586**	**58457**	**1285065**
7869	48256	3598	1612	1935	3315	27373
128928	2485394	140523	55755	35246	57844	1276750
2418	7155	127	362	376	589	3620
	615	28				550
35786	605874	7943	8483	8724	14168	222512
560	6405	20	62	326	454	4269
90164	1864593	132405	46847	25820	42633	1045078
	753					721
2318	12303		252	340	613	4310
	23430		495			4005
130905	1595132	59081	28835	35549	58387	1042716
	577068	77405	26644			192869
	46063	2052	656			1876
	294899	1937	363	8	12	46928
341	7965	48	4	29	58	676

16—9 限额以上住宿业和餐饮企业主要财务指标情况（2022年）

Main Financial Indicators of Enterprises Above Designated Size in Catering Trades by Status of Registration and by Sector (2022)

指　标	Item	流动资产合计 Circulating Funds	#存　货 Stock
总　计	**Total**	**2283729**	**146662**
住宿业合计	**Total of Accommodation Enterprises**	**1104485**	**59076**
国有控股	State-holding Enterprises	153445	7393
按登记注册类型分组	**Group by Registration Type**		
内　资	Domestic-funded	1062438	58336
国　有	State-owned	5602	396
集　体	Collective-owned		
联　营	Joint Ownership		
有限责任公司	Limited Liability Company	539825	24283
股份有限公司	Share-holding Corporations Ltd.	38221	233
私　营	Private	478238	33424
其　他	Other	553	
港澳台商投资	With Investment from Hong Kong, Macao and Taiwan	36131	452
外商投资企业	Enterprises with Foreign Investment	5916	288
按国民经济行业分	**Divided by National Economy Industry**		
旅游饭店	Tourist Hotel	794379	37891
一般旅馆	Common Hotel	251052	16355
经济型连锁酒店	Economical Hotel Chain	86802	5948
其他一般旅馆	Other General Hotels	164250	10408
民宿服务	Residential Service	10833	782
露营地服务	Campsite Service	25431	43
其他住宿服务	Other Accommodation Service	22790	4004
餐饮业合计	**Catering Trade**	**1179244**	**87585**
国有控股	State-holding Enterprises	38399	1234
按登记注册类型分组	**Group by Registration Type**		
内　资	Domestic-funded	1171506	86494
国　有	State-owned	2531	176
集　体	Collective-owned	149	14
有限责任公司	Limited Liability Company	288047	17186
股份有限公司	Share-holding Corporations Ltd.	2892	666
私　营	Private	877639	68397
其　他	Other	249	56
港澳台商投资企业	With Investment from Hong Kong, Macao and Taiwan	5415	572
外商投资企业	Enterprises with Foreign Investment	2323	520
按国民经济行业分	**Divided by National Economy Industry**		
正餐服务	Dinner	889983	71769
快餐服务	Fast Food	177370	12255
饮料及冷饮服务	Drink and Cold Drink Service	11016	815
餐饮配送及外卖送餐服务	Catering and Delivery Services	96748	2483
其他餐饮业	Other Catering Service	4127	263

单位：万元（10000 yuan）

固定资产合计 Total Fixed Assets	固定资产原价 Original Value of Fixed Assets	累计折旧 Progressive Depreciation	#本年折旧 Depreciation this Year	资产总计 Total of Assets	负债合计 Total of Liabilities	流动负债 Working Liabilities	所有者权益 Owners' Equity	#实收资本 Capital Hold	#个人资本 Individual Capital
1428796	**3040264**	**1272740**	**148663**	**5678985**	**4067648**	**2940801**	**1599770**	**1346114**	**200676**
919351	**1945135**	**842313**	**78703**	**3021614**	**2426834**	**1690682**	**585230**	**826964**	**79936**
171091	353747	176642	9622	505562	287827	247406	215168	191787	1688
793019	1690022	721441	70386	2697068	2066177	1497507	613656	681694	79936
4487	20520	11863	376	21913	9998	9739	11915	5013	
405370	951020	449159	31314	1336881	1083046	774058	251109	390365	4884
6964	11673	4709	492	92162	44671	28877	47492	21976	
375903	706507	255705	38198	1244666	927648	684018	302507	263924	75053
296	302	6	6	1446	814	814	632	416	
105785	214178	108449	7370	276134	308208	140926	-24388	137270	
20547	40935	12423	948	48412	52449	52249	-4037	8000	
742920	1598476	730666	58460	2240013	1861217	1268016	380633	685598	43743
137888	300141	104327	17262	637208	474605	337912	151217	112031	33614
51665	111137	32880	6118	242936	157776	98467	75495	40787	13368
86223	189004	71447	11144	394272	316829	239446	75722	71245	20246
4947	6666	1596	319	19944	17509	13908	2436	3286	1679
3002	5126	2124	256	55422	19017	19014	36405	15000	
30594	34725	3601	2406	69027	54487	51832	14540	11048	900
509446	**1095129**	**430427**	**69959**	**2657370**	**1640814**	**1250119**	**1014540**	**519151**	**120740**
34608	66314	30582	3419	96022	86262	43306	9759	54523	
502162	1083902	426856	69017	2627625	1618933	1232413	1006677	509360	120490
346	739	393	108	3868	5097	4168	-1228	1530	
1	300	298	2	151	952	952	-801	86	
125434	248941	101089	14740	600004	469273	385002	130392	123130	3290
197	33241	8902	1656	39343	24213	24036	15130	20550	
376184	800492	316112	52463	1984009	1119264	818121	863068	364065	117200
	189	61	48	250	135	134	115		
2839	5946	2751	307	9326	2675	2675	6651	6310	250
4445	5281	821	635	20420	19207	15031	1213	3480	
443308	960843	372586	58296	2121210	1332853	1019259	787469	435696	105608
57280	107078	45666	8022	393130	208555	140232	184487	66311	10114
716	3288	1357	340	17586	10355	7175	6191	2416	
5747	17814	7122	2857	117800	85692	80140	32109	13947	4297
2396	6107	3696	445	7644	3359	3312	4285	780	720

16—9 续表 continued

指 标	Item	主营收入 Project Settlement Income	营业成本 Operating Costs
总 计	**Total**	**3427432**	**2140459**
住宿业合计	**Total of Accommodation Enterprises**	**806524**	**420315**
国有控股	State-holding Enterprises	152360	75286
按登记注册类型分组	**Group by Registration Type**		
内 资	Domestic-funded	775174	409101
国 有	State-owned	4648	3028
集 体	Collective-owned		
联 营	Joint Ownership		
有限责任公司	Limited Liability Company	340765	159179
股份有限公司	Share-holding Corporations Ltd.	9020	3585
私 营	Private	420289	243140
其 他	Other	453	170
港澳台商投资	With Investment from Hong Kong, Macao and Taiwan	23642	7071
外商投资企业	Enterprises with Foreign Investment	7708	4143
按国民经济行业分	**Divided by National Economy Industry**		
旅游饭店	Tourist Hotel	550171	271718
一般旅馆	Common Hotel	230356	132278
经济型连锁酒店	Economical Hotel Chain	115144	66010
其他一般旅馆	Other General Hotels	115212	66268
民宿服务	Residential Service	6098	3880
露营地服务	Campsite Service	1659	1596
其他住宿服务	Other Accommodation Service	18241	10843
餐饮业合计	**Catering Trade**	**2620909**	**1720145**
国有控股	State-holding Enterprises	57203	44043
按登记注册类型分组	**Group by Registration Type**		
内 资	Domestic-funded	2584637	1701702
国 有	State-owned	9625	3817
集 体	Collective-owned	609	281
有限责任公司	Limited Liability Company	620139	341950
股份有限公司	Share-holding Corporations Ltd.	6373	3307
私 营	Private	1947159	1352122
其 他	Other	731	225
港澳台商投资企业	With Investment from Hong Kong, Macao and Taiwan	14434	5176
外商投资企业	Enterprises with Foreign Investment	21838	13267
按国民经济行业分	**Divided by National Economy Industry**		
正餐服务	Dinner	1725129	1071725
快餐服务	Fast Food	563080	422960
饮料及冷饮服务	Drink and Cold Drink Service	45934	22534
餐饮配送及外卖送餐服务	Catering and Delivery Services	279215	197558
其他餐饮业	Other Catering Service	7551	5368

单位：万元（10000 yuan）

税金及附加 Taxes and Surcharges	其他业务利润 Other Business Profit	销售费用 Operating Expense	管理费用 Management Expense	财务费用 Financial Expenses	营业利润 Operating Profit	利润总额 Total Profit	应交所得税 Payable Income Tax	本年应付工资薪酬 Total Payable Wages this Year
24298	**12949**	**822174**	**540639**	**50324**	**-14436**	**4977**	**14015**	**771809**
12966	**6350**	**221025**	**222411**	**27827**	**-67679**	**-61055**	**-171**	**238707**
2975	777	69850	34001	3977	-29464	-27233	-1273	64431
12543	6350	215748	199923	25268	-58396	-52563	-171	229310
23		1482	2239	56	-1804	-1330	1	2516
8020	3104	122284	90283	13095	-42223	-40459	-1209	116789
42		4997	2050	260	-1723	-1510		4080
4458	3246	86984	105159	11845	-12723	-9341	1037	105791
			192	12	77	77		134
66		4117	19053	2535	-7829	-7574		7562
357		1161	3435	24	-1454	-919		1834
10745	5130	174141	154177	21218	-61318	-55513	-831	173382
1848	1168	42805	60257	6194	-3823	-3153	639	59141
745	554	23168	29227	2462	-253	499	641	27319
1104	614	19638	31030	3731	-3571	-3651	-2	31823
17	2	800	2255	241	-952	-902	2	1666
12		317	417	-324	-273	-272		802
345	50	2963	5306	498	-1312	-1216	19	3716
11332	**6599**	**601148**	**318228**	**22497**	**53242**	**66032**	**14186**	**533103**
597	1760	10478	10572	605	-6743	-4702	240	19393
11301	6599	589579	309822	22317	54655	67248	14183	522418
11		4359	2048	34	-644	-538	2	3259
1		377	152	2	-204	-152		282
2418	3996	195783	83036	3740	5054	10150	5284	142871
208	-1	2332	2049	23	-1355	-1330	9	1569
8662	2603	386435	222431	18507	51710	59023	8888	374173
1		293	107	11	94	94	1	265
10		4900	5127	17	-795	-616	3	4115
21		6669	3278	163	-618	-600		6570
9733	5678	381813	244949	20585	26696	32197	7856	373719
1222	549	157791	38224	1308	15051	20672	4264	120724
45	378	17269	3149	133	3852	3909	499	9924
297	-6	41978	31454	445	7422	8937	1560	27352
36		2298	452	26	221	318	7	1384

16—10 限额以上批发和零售业连锁经营情况（2022年）
Basic Conditions of Chain-Enterprise Above Quota Wholesale and Retail (2022)

指　　标		Item		合　计 Total	直销店 Directly-run Shops	加盟店 Alliance Shops
门店总数	（个）	Gross Number of Shops	(unit)	9925	7589	2336
从业人数	（人）	Number of People Engaged	(person)	81400	75788	5612
零售营业面积	（平方米）	Area of Business	(sq.m)	7133942	6887867	246075
连锁门店商品购进额	（万元）	Total Purchases	(10000 yuan)	15058152	14654013	404139
#统一配送商品购进额		Centralized Purchase and Delivery		10286582	10017533	269049
#自有配送中心配送商品购进额		Total Revenue of Purchasing by Self Purchase and Delivery		3383964	3319617	64347
非自有配送中心配送商品购进额		Total Revenue of Purchasing by Non-self Purchase and Delivery		352071	319868	32204
连锁门店商品销售额	（万元）	Sales Value of Commodities	(10000 yuan)	17089960	16633604	456356
#零售额		Revenue of Retail Sales		12098649	11803137	295512

16—11 限额以上住宿和餐饮业连锁经营情况（2022年）
Basic Conditions of Chain-Enterprise Above Quota Lodging and food and Beverage Industry (2022)

指　　标		Item		合　计 Total	直销店 Directly-run Shops	加盟店 Alliance Shops
门店总数	（个）	Gross Number of Shops	(unit)	1290	1210	80
从业人数	（人）	Number of People Engaged	(person)	25829	25574	255
餐饮营业面积	（平方米）	Area of Business	(sq.m)	386444	384447	1997
客房数	（间）	Guestroom Number	(unit)	211	211	
床位数	（个）	Bed Capacity	(unit)	332	332	
餐位数	（位）	Number of Seating Arrangement	(unit)	172849	171859	990
连锁门店商品购进(采购)额	（万元）	Chain shops Commodity Purchasing Volume	(10000 yuan)	323487	311884	11603
#统一配送商品购进额		Centralized Purchase and Delivery		238032	237429	603
#自有配送中心配送商品购进(采购)额		Total Revenue of Purchasing by Self Purchase and Delivery		14489	13886	603
非自有配送中心配送商品购进(采购)额		Total Revenue of Purchasing by Non-self Purchase and Delivery		171695	171695	
连锁门店营业额	（万元）	Chain shops Turnover	(10000 yuan)	758037	752278	5759
#餐费收入		Catering Income		652731	647047	5684
商品销售额		Total Sales of Goods		72664	72664	

16—12 各市限额以上批发和零售业连锁经营情况（2022年）

Basic Conditions of Chain-Enterprise Above Quota Wholesale and Retail by Region (2022)

地 区 Region		门店总数 (个) Gross Number of Shops (unit)	从业人员 (人) Number of People Engaged (person)	零售营业面积 (平方米) Area of Business (sp.m)	商品购进总额 (万元) Total Purchases (10000 yuan)	#统一配送商品购进额 Centralized Purchase and Delivery	#自有配送中心配送 Total Revenue of Purchasing by Self	商品销售额 (万元) Sales Value of Commodities (10000 yuan)	零售额 Retail
总 计	**Total**	**9925**	**81400**	**7133942**	**15058152**	**10286582**	**3383964**	**17089960**	**12098649**
合 肥 市	Hefei	6195	61645	5869356	13009149	8549774	2848238	14906042	10083314
淮 北 市	Huaibei	92	440	4660	15966	15966	15966	21677	21677
亳 州 市	Bozhou	86	534	12686	14835	7596	7596	20511	20511
宿 州 市	Suzhou	767	895	28660	109431	109431		111922	111922
蚌 埠 市	Bengbu	519	3469	169188	192758	90985		248970	248970
阜 阳 市	Fuyang	542	3754	135664	222464	187161	70490	244449	199313
淮 南 市	Huainan	53	264	8761	6154	6154		10010	2691
滁 州 市	Chuzhou	611	2010	66533	49774	49774	49774	78578	78578
六 安 市	Luan								
马鞍山市	Maanshan	73	505	125402	287003	285753	285218	287393	267378
芜 湖 市	Wuhu	164	1888	82982	114463	114463	16917	140616	140616
宣 城 市	Xuancheng	353	2382	92297	88761	87399	82916	102696	102301
铜 陵 市	Tongling								
池 州 市	Chizhou	142	354	16887	10131	9995	3677	15064	15064
安 庆 市	Anqing	305	3077	515040	928173	766447	3173	890858	795140
黄 山 市	Huangshan	23	183	5826	9091	5683		11173	11173

16—13 各市限额以上住宿和餐饮业连锁经营情况（2022年）

Basic Conditions of Chain-Enterprise Above Quota Lodging and Food and Beverage Industry by Region (2022)

地 区 Region		门店总数 (个) Gross Number of Shops (unit)	从业人员 (人) Number of People Engaged (person)	餐饮营业面积 (平方米) Area of Business (sp.m)	客房数 (间) Guestroom Number (unit)	床位数 (个) Bed Capacity (unit)	餐位数 (位) Number of eating Arrangement (unit)	商品购进总额 (万元) Total Purchases (10000 yuan)	营业额 (万元) Turnover (10000 yuan)
总 计	**Total**	**1290**	**25829**	**386444**	**211**	**332**	**172849**	**323487**	**758037**
合 肥 市	Hefei	967	19151	256111			128871	251589	561513
淮 北 市	Huaibei								
亳 州 市	Bozhou								
宿 州 市	Suzhou								
蚌 埠 市	Bengbu								
阜 阳 市	Fuyang	56	174	3107			1035	947	2669
淮 南 市	Huainan								
滁 州 市	Chuzhou	2	13	1080			315	60	591
六 安 市	Luan								
马鞍山市	Maanshan	6	506	23000	211	332	5200	5644	8353
芜 湖 市	Wuhu								
宣 城 市	Xuancheng								
铜 陵 市	Tongling	255	5820	93146			36008	64153	181986
池 州 市	Chizhou								
安 庆 市	Anqing	4	165	10000			1420	1095	2926
黄 山 市	Huangshan								

16—14 各市限额以上批发零售企业主要财务指标情况（2022年）

Main Financial Indicators of Enterprises Above Designated Size in Wholesale and Retail by Region (2022)

地　区	Region	企业数（个）Number of Enterprises (unit)	流动资产合计 Circulating Funds	#存货 Stock	固定资产合计 Total Fixed Assets	固定资产原价 Original Value of Fixed Assets
总　计	**Total**	**10203**	**84580222**	**11223748**	**4172535**	**8416491**
合肥市	Hefei	2270	45142222	5489209	1414978	3066717
淮北市	Huaibei	260	1847662	252711	300823	383446
亳州市	Bozhou	466	2146523	313261	143000	263484
宿州市	Suzhou	618	2813165	308598	240860	441186
蚌埠市	Bengbu	589	2361948	346748	186865	378214
阜阳市	Fuyang	791	2808837	501399	185149	495812
淮南市	Huainan	417	1210555	215635	104248	232607
滁州市	Chuzhou	644	4415031	498855	274761	517995
六安市	Luan	614	1722601	278249	369771	563577
马鞍山市	Maanshan	250	1727989	330072	82797	200943
芜湖市	Wuhu	1320	10865226	1368623	318266	683500
宣城市	Xuancheng	345	1511507	186217	138644	290720
铜陵市	Tongling	256	2219923	318664	111625	210946
池州市	Chizhou	264	802110	123667	56233	130232
安庆市	Anqing	839	2374919	569463	192899	413618
黄山市	Huangshan	260	610006	122377	51615	143493

16—15 各市限额以上住宿和餐饮企业主要财务指标情况（2022年）

Main Financial Indicators of Enterprises Above Designated Size in Catering Trades by Status of Registration by Region (2022)

地　区	Region	企业数（个）Number of Enterprises (unit)	流动资产合计 Circulating Funds	#存货 Stock	固定资产合计 Total Fixed Assets	固定资产原价 Original Value of Fixed Assets
总　计	**Total**	**2629**	**2283729**	**146662**	**1428796**	**3040264**
合肥市	Hefei	518	797660	43203	436876	1022299
淮北市	Huaibei	58	35831	2498	8267	18099
亳州市	Bozhou	104	56596	2757	32210	73295
宿州市	Suzhou	137	79350	5639	71801	141585
蚌埠市	Bengbu	170	84925	7646	47693	99815
阜阳市	Fuyang	186	76458	6532	35068	79423
淮南市	Huainan	132	53790	4889	52557	93795
滁州市	Chuzhou	134	108277	15184	67192	148144
六安市	Luan	272	169149	15802	72941	171228
马鞍山市	Maanshan	56	55021	3876	25655	109095
芜湖市	Wuhu	235	180473	9069	140589	287367
宣城市	Xuancheng	118	95167	2749	98575	180762
铜陵市	Tongling	68	63220	8790	16437	33917
池州市	Chizhou	66	59868	2772	28327	81204
安庆市	Anqing	278	110335	11024	174716	292478
黄山市	Huangshan	97	257610	4233	119893	207759

单位：万元（10000 yuan）

累计折旧 Progressive Depreciation	#本年折旧 Depreciation this Year	资产总计 Total of Assets	负债合计 Total of Liabilities	#流动负债 Working Liabilities	所有者权益 Owners' Equity	#实收资本 Capital Hold	#个人资本 Individual Capital
3435199	**577526**	**103777036**	**77750029**	**68938214**	**25888005**	**13630755**	**1379947**
1360436	271959	55181665	43269182	38875249	11883451	7796949	483378
79672	9293	2330938	1706256	1530705	623531	202917	56963
95110	15878	2605250	1953826	1759251	648690	365283	62207
136479	18875	3468824	2586234	2355457	872179	289647	49958
154848	21352	2834487	2098111	1712102	733208	252045	48978
225049	36172	3407171	2165313	1684466	1240651	404828	100368
109055	11880	1480020	744686	642653	732333	241020	44076
192462	30726	5782915	4097391	3445866	1681072	558594	63025
156565	23594	2439448	1302661	1107398	1135443	274915	112922
95159	11543	2130589	1590247	1415696	536467	359850	22917
308222	51935	12753106	9991587	9207663	2738668	1815964	121122
127858	16474	1995745	1217176	973228	730880	205408	36592
88048	10326	2782664	2279076	1955673	500009	328735	24323
67051	9153	948773	522894	393698	425734	90538	23936
171921	27066	2839545	1735820	1451674	1101257	347310	86356
67264	11302	795898	489569	427436	304434	96754	42828

单位：万元（10000 yuan）

累计折旧 Progressive Depreciation	#本年折旧 Depreciation this Year	资产总计 Total of Assets	负债合计 Total of Liabilities	#流动负债 Working Liabilities	所有者权益 Owners' Equity	#实收资本 Capital Hold	#个人资本 Individual Capital
1272740	**148663**	**5678985**	**4067648**	**2940801**	**1599770**	**1346114**	**200676**
484413	43832	2054181	1503835	1067116	538830	469301	37506
9441	993	54217	40121	31715	14096	7979	1180
34576	6255	135754	96612	77059	39142	37811	5366
59992	7761	187502	136614	103050	47551	27335	6587
46389	6929	165785	97739	83034	67996	34248	10969
33056	5627	144660	85084	66943	57261	37447	19542
34388	2902	133256	86416	70691	46840	27411	15646
40685	8020	292681	194577	164768	97870	67146	9060
72288	11091	373010	279078	191217	93771	81149	21261
57108	5323	160457	134870	121749	25587	42400	3445
112865	16205	456687	297487	221392	158967	166237	10551
60563	8395	297875	197297	116649	99907	68799	8294
14352	2714	133427	89247	85790	43949	15112	6145
29201	3618	145524	109093	72185	36071	32801	7863
98084	10233	413166	229319	144610	183705	97266	31847
85340	8765	530803	490259	322836	48227	133672	5416

16—14 续表 continued

地 区	Region	主营收入 Project Settlement Income	营业成本 Operating Costs	税金及附加 Taxes and Surcharges	其他业务利润 Other Business Profit
总 计	**Total**	**195058691**	**181237116**	**1324619**	**281819**
合 肥 市	Hefei	86675150	80516942	345521	124492
淮 北 市	Huaibei	5598533	5351874	32329	8511
亳 州 市	Bozhou	5574604	4320386	77444	4338
宿 州 市	Suzhou	5680582	5274996	67560	5090
蚌 埠 市	Bengbu	5498384	5037600	58769	8710
阜 阳 市	Fuyang	6764810	6041517	112992	11566
淮 南 市	Huainan	4422670	4111792	54267	4162
滁 州 市	Chuzhou	8146290	7562509	76004	19071
六 安 市	Luan	4910769	4527462	78646	10147
马鞍山市	Maanshan	7181981	6816487	54998	4402
芜 湖 市	Wuhu	31227776	29348865	129771	61041
宣 城 市	Xuancheng	3073710	2755431	59423	4545
铜 陵 市	Tongling	8037948	8196622	36987	5405
池 州 市	Chizhou	2761073	2569848	31678	2090
安 庆 市	Anqing	7840521	7326431	79685	6156
黄 山 市	Huangshan	1663893	1478355	28548	2094

16—15 续表 continued

地 区	Region	主营收入 Project Settlement Income	营业成本 Operating Costs	税金及附加 Taxes and Surcharges	其他业务利润 Other Business Profit
总 计	**Total**	**3427432**	**2140459**	**24298**	**12949**
合 肥 市	Hefei	1520052	974695	8257	4323
淮 北 市	Huaibei	38559	24823	93	6
亳 州 市	Bozhou	83032	51380	698	435
宿 州 市	Suzhou	97078	62374	958	34
蚌 埠 市	Bengbu	133322	98538	785	858
阜 阳 市	Fuyang	126911	83480	951	735
淮 南 市	Huainan	85270	55895	359	103
滁 州 市	Chuzhou	122184	72083	1158	58
六 安 市	Luan	190630	121665	1282	607
马鞍山市	Maanshan	91535	61662	1146	436
芜 湖 市	Wuhu	232612	141805	2317	1153
宣 城 市	Xuancheng	81780	51432	1055	2364
铜 陵 市	Tongling	236771	96755	412	1076
池 州 市	Chizhou	46689	24378	454	195
安 庆 市	Anqing	263416	172561	2167	198
黄 山 市	Huangshan	77594	46935	2208	368

单位：万元（10000 yuan）

销售费用 Operating Expense	管理费用 Management Expense	财务费用 Financial Expenses	营业利润 Operating Profit	利润总额 Total Profit	应交所得税 Payable Income Tax	本年应付工资薪酬 Total Payable Wages this Year
8320471	**3269814**	**534222**	**2606725**	**2857575**	**859421**	**3608095**
4113862	1596683	356128	554255	633586	208151	1607952
123256	51961	16329	45050	48446	12482	62582
692202	136083	4779	258878	266226	74043	171863
128090	114103	11934	120002	117930	20520	89501
241585	124325	30119	78957	92542	21210	171055
276827	155446	22543	210570	216921	41186	184805
114204	75941	8434	91477	96079	19598	78629
318617	131609	12770	160486	162145	30789	199562
193567	104889	8630	295219	298918	66357	147372
216069	86222	10966	70894	88612	28992	113285
1322893	307761	13886	360700	434636	244722	368566
151558	83640	5134	103557	104964	24334	101981
75489	56855	11763	-21894	-804	11319	61553
62592	43910	2313	68697	67321	13429	45035
208568	144488	14832	173973	188609	30952	155866
81093	55901	3660	35903	41447	11335	48489

单位：万元（10000 yuan）

销售费用 Operating Expense	管理费用 Management Expense	财务费用 Financial Expenses	营业利润 Operating Profit	利润总额 Total Profit	应交所得税 Payable Income Tax	本年应付工资薪酬 Total Payable Wages this Year
822174	**540639**	**50324**	**-14436**	**4977**	**14015**	**771809**
432988	209417	17520	-15086	-2227	8157	327320
5623	8377	1191	-986	-704	35	9490
16045	16343	1027	-1840	-645	170	20093
17960	18924	1795	-4573	-3374	125	19626
18137	18436	1191	-198	-3338	108	20327
20654	17657	1110	4307	4515	266	29645
16282	12484	2082	-1933	-1522	171	14050
18916	23579	2196	5514	5381	339	30289
27043	37163	3323	1903	2237	373	43618
17420	15916	738	-6448	-5993	26	27912
38004	38179	2197	15101	16623	1394	52048
18159	20876	3329	-9428	-7571	122	25312
109505	25216	733	5858	6513	1577	76088
9591	12975	2195	-2725	-2444	-141	11678
39881	38788	6051	11873	12959	1341	41140
15968	26311	3646	-15776	-15432	-46	23175

16—16 各市限额以上批发零售业商品购进、销售和库存情况（2022年）

Total Purchases, Sales and Inventory of Enterprises Above Designated Size in Wholesale and Retail and Inventory by Region (2022)

单位：万元（10000 yuan）

地区	Region	从业人员（人）Persons Engaged (persons)	购进总额 Total Purchases Value	#进口 Imports	销售总额 Total Sales Value	批发 Wholesale Value	零售 Retail Value	年末库存总额 Stock (year-end)
总计	**Total**	**396776**	**197158803**	**6713378**	**219635135**	**169075319**	**50314846**	**10953593**
合肥市	Hefei	143258	87179568	4203197	98086127	77868558	20143061	5680041
淮北市	Huaibei	9113	6107573	8123	6447158	5556933	888124	230652
亳州市	Bozhou	17312	4549365	36527	6174722	4573926	1596498	275280
宿州市	Suzhou	16334	5557929	196	6333381	4215888	2115484	247975
蚌埠市	Bengbu	17387	5354985	186793	6193781	4400158	1791125	361752
阜阳市	Fuyang	28536	6926149	35024	7600573	4288664	3311909	474081
淮南市	Huainan	12493	4380721	3330	4960627	3698778	1261849	195112
滁州市	Chuzhou	22710	8369446	30486	8959921	6647188	2307250	432584
六安市	Luan	23629	4886200	26424	5555111	2971179	2583932	253129
马鞍山市	Maanshan	12775	7203604	27696	7717858	6053362	1661068	307468
芜湖市	Wuhu	38745	32278261	1303737	35110515	29470427	5592337	1199565
宣城市	Xuancheng	12191	3207509	9821	3635210	2272084	1341610	186328
铜陵市	Tongling	7055	8828144	82206	9308105	8328637	906382	341078
池州市	Chizhou	5763	2605220	144632	3074015	2136172	937842	117108
安庆市	Anqing	22956	8072524	585650	8578199	5563227	3006680	535016
黄山市	Huangshan	6519	1651607	29538	1899834	1030138	869696	116423

16—17 各市限额以上住宿餐饮业经营情况（2022年）

Above Designated Accommodation Catering Business by Region (2022)

单位：万元（10000 yuan）

地区	Region	从业人员（人）Persons Engaged (persons)	营业额 Turnover	客房收入 Room Revenue	餐费收入 Meals Income	商品销售收入 Commodity Sales	其他收入 Other Income	客房数（间）Guestroom Number (unit)	床位数（个）Bed Capacity (unit)	餐位数（位）Number of Seating Arrangement (unit)
总计	**Total**	**143866**	**3723786**	**573565**	**2819257**	**207056**	**123908**	**188253**	**291199**	**1543729**
合肥市	Hefei	56636	1714232	159921	1328568	140956	84787	32251	49675	551215
淮北市	Huaibei	2260	39773	11527	25836	135	2275	2976	4136	25299
亳州市	Bozhou	4678	85989	17856	65271	1805	1056	5276	8352	55347
宿州市	Suzhou	5247	101000	27308	68828	3967	897	7336	11468	44997
蚌埠市	Bengbu	4969	142100	19690	119612	1667	1131	15134	18806	107791
阜阳市	Fuyang	6913	139217	34938	98424	3503	2353	19066	24489	80662
淮南市	Huainan	4142	88723	14659	69265	3507	1292	4565	7059	51217
滁州市	Chuzhou	5480	125983	37527	81135	4757	2564	18267	32451	61812
六安市	Luan	9191	202852	51823	144056	5065	1909	11928	19538	100814
马鞍山市	Maanshan	4859	95206	12069	75524	1485	6127	3438	5383	38737
芜湖市	Wuhu	9019	245571	55469	168661	14680	6761	21301	31231	78212
宣城市	Xuancheng	5124	90123	29584	56239	2563	1737	9908	16151	71350
铜陵市	Tongling	8921	248546	11128	233053	3122	1244	8179	14294	67483
池州市	Chizhou	2434	48617	17737	30103	301	475	5554	9365	32763
安庆市	Anqing	9010	271708	53118	202730	13372	2489	14224	23576	114937
黄山市	Huangshan	4983	84148	19212	51953	6172	6811	8850	15225	61093

16—18 亿元以上商品交易市场情况（2022年）
Market Situation of Commodity Trading Above 100 million Yuan (2022)

指标	Item	市场个数（个）Number of Markets (unit)	总摊位数（个）Total Booth Number (unit)	总成交额（万元）Transaction Value (10000 yuan)
全省	**Total**	**93**	**123452**	**26683231**
综合市场	**Comprehensive Markets**	**42**	**76199**	**12079124**
生产资料综合市场	The Material of Production Comprehensive Markets	2	10481	1968885
工业品综合市场	Markets for Manufactured Goods	9	25074	1008362
农业品综合市场	Markets for Agricultural Goods	22	17472	6534261
其他综合市场	Other Comprehensive Markets	9	23172	2567616
专业市场	**Specialized markets**	**51**	**47253**	**14604107**
生产资料市场	The Material of Production Markets	9	4600	3495930
农产品市场	Agricultural Product Markets	16	11792	2636261
食品饮料烟酒市场	Food, Drink, Tobacco and Liquor	5	3406	548994
纺织品服装鞋帽市场	Textile, Clothing, Shoes and Hats	4	6433	553046
日用品及文化用品市场	Daily Necessities and Cultural Product Markets			
电器通讯器材电子设备市场	Electrical Communication Equipment Electronic Equipment Markets	1	3902	10511
医药医疗用品及器材市场	Medicine and Medical Supplies and Equipment Markets	1	6502	4500000
家具五金及装饰材料市场	Furniture, Hardware and Decorative Materials Markets	10	8146	784165
汽车摩托车及零配件市场	Automobile and Motorcycle Spare Parts Markets	3	888	1694043
花鸟鱼虫市场	Flower, Bird, Fish, Insect Markets	1	1320	215900
其他专业市场	Other Professional Markets	1	264	165257

16—19 各市亿元以上商品交易市场情况（2022年）
Market Situation of Commodity Trading Above 100 million Yuan by Region (2022)

地区	Region	市场个数（个）Number of Markets (unit)	总摊位数（个）Total Booth Number (unit)	营业面积（平方米）Business Area (sq.m)	总成交额（万元）Transaction Value (10000 yuan)
总计	**Total**	**93**	**123452**	**12270523**	**26683231**
合肥市	Hefei	25	33542	3357772	7927269
淮北市	Huaibei	5	5062	291396	517457
亳州市	Bozhou	3	9873	159207	4762694
宿州市	Suzhou	2	3600	811600	118710
蚌埠市	Bengbu	3	7374	856323	2128079
阜阳市	Fuyang	11	9229	1298849	3535035
淮南市	Huainan	4	2218	192400	206596
滁州市	Chuzhou	6	7928	1223131	650465
六安市	Luan				
马鞍山市	Maanshan	3	1087	46670	703904
芜湖市	Wuhu	11	23873	1575472	2285700
宣城市	Xuancheng	6	3601	44876	839609
铜陵市	Tongling	3	2059	255000	372535
池州市	Chizhou	4	3110	244505	204829
安庆市	Anqing	6	10476	1880922	2180157
黄山市	Huangshan	1	420	32400	250192

16—20 亿元以上商品交易市场摊位分类情况（2022年）
Classification of Commodity Exchange Markets of Transaction Value over 100 Million Yuan (2022)

指　　标	Item	年末出租摊位数（个）Number of Stalls Rented at the End of the Year (unit)	总成交额（万元）Transaction Value (10000 yuan)
合　　计	**Total**	**95924**	**26683231**
粮油、食品类	Grain and Oil, Food	24371	9736709
饮料类	Beverage Category	1888	374271
烟酒类	Smoke Wine	936	246711
服装鞋帽、针、纺织品类	Clothing, Shoes, Hats and Textiles	15978	1229994
化妆品类	Cosmetics	481	53895
金银珠宝类	Gold, Silver and Jeweler	36	946
日用品类	Articles for Daily Use	4867	306753
五金、电料类	Hardware & Electrical Materials	5305	430051
体育、娱乐用品类	Sports & Recreational Articles	365	25101
书报杂志类	Newspapers and Magazines	189	87491
电子出版物及音像制品类	E-journal and Video Products	27	623
家用电器和音像器材类	Household Appliances and Video Equipments	1511	224176
中西药品类	Traditional Chinese and Western Medicine	6521	4506666
文化办公用品类	Cultural and official Goods	908	197248
家具类	Furniture	2530	917943
通讯器材类	Communication Appliances	218	17230
煤炭及制品类	Coal and Related Products		
木材及制品类	Wood and Wooden Products	1053	256676
石油及制品类	Petroleum and Related Products	52	2000
化工材料及制品类	Raw Chemical Materials and Related Products	275	179547
金属材料类	Metal Materials	1935	3149893
建筑及装潢材料类	Building and Decoration Materials	11707	1712376
机电产品及设备类	Mechanical & Electrical Products	1331	372194
汽车类	Automobile	1070	1806587
种子饲料类	Seed and Feedstuff	314	56519
棉麻类	Cotton and Hemp	270	11295
其他类	Others	11786	780336

16—21 各市社会消费品零售总额（2022年）
Total Retail Sale of Consumer Goods in Major Years by Region (2022)

单位：万元（10000 yuan）

地 区	Region	社会消费品零售总额 Total Retail Sales of Consumer Goods	城 镇 Urban	城 区 City	乡 村 Rural	餐饮收入 Catering Income	商品零售 Commodity Retail
全 省	**Total**	215184119	180944479	116336211	34239640	27613421	187570698
合 肥 市	Hefei	50216208	47295608	38541191	2920600	5004600	45211608
淮 北 市	Huaibei	4948724	4011436	3222478	937288	277623	4671100
亳 州 市	Bozhou	11882193	9072174	4099119	2810020	1072059	10810134
宿 州 市	Suzhou	12240069	9180052	4085123	3060017	1493288	10746781
蚌 埠 市	Bengbu	12562408	10235881	7051114	2326527	1276822	11285586
阜 阳 市	Fuyang	22965023	17168796	11099687	5796227	2059954	20905069
淮 南 市	Huainan	8831269	6181888	4265503	2649381	1040560	7790709
滁 州 市	Chuzhou	15559696	12404189	6239307	3155506	1462611	14097084
六 安 市	Luan	11832476	8158753	4813010	3673723	1588250	10244225
马鞍山市	Maanshan	9582372	8702914	4581883	879458	1343871	8238501
芜 湖 市	Wuhu	19951164	17834861	14186252	2116303	2198560	17752604
宣 城 市	Xuancheng	7761512	6123833	3011467	1637679	736674	7024838
铜 陵 市	Tongling	4030229	3208126	2921783	822103	556172	3474057
池 州 市	Chizhou	4656395	3569425	2374114	1086970	622215	4034180
安 庆 市	Anqing	13069424	10008326	6686767	3061098	1236471	11832953
黄 山 市	Huangshan	5094957	3539217	2002967	1555740	585394	4509563

注：社会消费品零售总额城乡分组数据按行政区划调整进行调整。

a) The total retail sales of social consumer goods and its grouping data were adjusted according to the change of Administrative Divisions .

16—22 各县（市）社会消费品零售总额（2022年）
Total Retail Sale of Consumer Goods in Major Years by County or City (2022)

单位：万元（10000 yuan）

县（市）	County or City	社会消费品零售总额 Total Retail Sales of Consumer Goods	城镇 Urban	乡村 Rural	餐饮收入 Catering Income	商品零售 Commodity Retail
合肥市辖区	Hefei Region of City	36529029	36347208	181821	3616589	32912440
巢湖市	Chaohu	2276191	1968053	308138	162615	2113576
长丰县	Changfeng	3411340	2875587	535753	216478	3194862
肥东县	Feidong	3173360	2453209	720151	463036	2710324
肥西县	Feixi	2624279	2011858	612421	308276	2316003
庐江县	Lujiang	2202008	1639692	562316	237605	1964403
淮北市辖区	Huaibei Region of City	3400068	2553396	846672	198778	3201290
濉溪县	Suixi	1548656	1458040	90616	78846	1469810
亳州市辖区	Bozhou Region of City	4159676	3474781	684895	269271	3890405
涡阳县	Guoyang	2682046	2024708	657338	338576	2343470
蒙城县	Mengcheng	2543120	1941697	601423	229450	2313670
利辛县	Lixin	2497352	1630987	866365	234762	2262590
宿州市辖区	Suzhou Region of City	4956360	3288408	1667952	801245	4155115
砀山县	Dangshan	1952743	1845342	107401	103495	1849248
萧县	Xiaoxian	1972233	1566582	405651	143477	1828756
灵璧县	Lingbi	1833329	1421930	411399	313124	1520205
泗县	Sixian	1525404	1057789	467615	131947	1393457
蚌埠市辖区	Bengbu Region of City	7602507	6341114	1261393	644383	6958124
怀远县	Huaiyuan	2117321	1573722	543599	245602	1871719
五河县	Wuhe	1552405	1299705	252700	180409	1371996
固镇县	Guzhen	1290175	1021340	268835	206428	1083747
阜阳市辖区	Fuyang Region of City	8663796	6353453	2310343	818050	7845746
界首市	Jieshou	2130752	1615372	515380	179200	1951552
临泉县	Linquan	3157328	2278850	878478	272225	2885103
太和县	Taihe	4242759	3480997	761762	371834	3870925
阜南县	Funan	2313881	1948707	365174	201667	2112214
颍上县	Yingshang	2456507	1491417	965090	216978	2239529
淮南市辖区	Huainan Region of City	5709022	4118928	1590094	487236	5221786
凤台县	Fengtai	1478935	978375	500560	182992	1295943
寿县	Shouxian	1643312	1084586	558726	370332	1272980
滁州市辖区	Chuzhou Region of City	3583340	3416127	167212	175154	3408187
天长市	Tianchang	2430916	1984376	446540	255744	2175172
明光市	Mingguang	1782783	1369919	412864	260865	1521918
来安县	Laian	1534438	1194518	339921	147149	1387289
全椒县	Quanjiao	1818741	1383625	435117	176650	1642091
定远县	Dingyuan	1919620	1280146	639475	191666	1727954
凤阳县	Fengyang	2489857	1775479	714378	255383	2234474

16—22 续表 continued

单位：万元（10000 yuan）

县（市）	County or City	社会消费品零售总额 Total Retail Sales of Consumer Goods	城 镇 Urban	乡 村 Rural	餐饮收入 Catering Income	商品零售 Commodity Retail
六安市辖区	Luan Region of City	5851223	4517845	1333378	1052325	4798898
霍 邱 县	Huoqiu	1601416	1135411	466005	156879	1444537
舒 城 县	Shucheng	1744594	992674	751920	148465	1596129
金 寨 县	Jinzhai	1644360	878658	765702	149328	1495032
霍 山 县	Huoshan	990883	634165	356718	81252	909631
马鞍山市辖区	Maanshan Region of City	5022743	4843659	179084	691720	4331023
当 涂 县	Dangtu	1875177	1609029	266148	285737	1589440
含 山 县	Hanshan	1195706	975374	220332	180844	1014862
和 县	Hexian	1488745	1274853	213892	185569	1303176
芜湖市辖区	Wuhu Region of City	16302555	15417439	885116	1638687	14663868
无 为 市	Wuwei	2214296	1648700	565596	373138	1841158
南 陵 县	Nanling	1434313	768722	665591	186735	1247578
宣城市辖区	Xuancheng Region of City	2526112	1851872	674240	167969	2358143
宁 国 市	Ningguo	1334275	1238767	95508	149419	1184856
广 德 市	Guangde	1686297	1339634	346663	174386	1511911
郎 溪 县	Langxi	778038	572297	205741	77818	700220
泾 县	Jingxian	840435	613518	226917	101309	739126
绩 溪 县	Jixi	369299	333292	36007	36786	332513
旌 德 县	Jingde	227056	174453	52603	28987	198069
铜陵市辖区	Tongling Region of City	3083916	2772822	311094	452077	2631839
枞 阳 县	Zongyang	946312	435304	511008	104094	842218
池州市辖区	Chizhou Region of City	2616815	2377005	239810	259210	2357605
东 至 县	Dongzhi	1019024	563921	455103	147756	871268
石 台 县	Shitai	153672	88777	64895	25902	127770
青 阳 县	Qingyang	866884	539722	327162	189347	677537
安庆市辖区	Anqing Region of City	4649535	4366347	283188	455612	4193923
桐 城 市	Tongcheng	1606173	1336522	269651	198692	1407481
潜 山 市	Qianshan	1293171	969878	323293	131727	1161444
怀 宁 县	Huaining	1402600	994665	407935	133234	1269366
太 湖 县	Taihu	1145726	515577	630149	43792	1101934
宿 松 县	Susong	1151579	752145	399434	90799	1060780
望 江 县	Wangjiang	983592	653554	330038	89566	894026
岳 西 县	Yuexi	837048	419638	417410	93049	743999
黄山市辖区	Huangshan Region of City	2702159	2152674	549485	355634	2346525
歙 县	Shexian	1046528	628676	417852	76286	970242
休 宁 县	Xiuning	688160	347476	340684	60505	627655
黟 县	Yixian	238580	153847	84733	57920	180660
祁 门 县	Qimen	419530	256544	162986	35049	384481

主要统计指标解释

批发业

指批发商向批发、零售单位及其他企事业、机关单位批量销售生活用品和生产资料的活动，以及从事进出口贸易和贸易经纪与代理的活动。批发商可以对所批发的货物拥有所有权，并以本单位、公司的名义进行交易活动；也可以不拥有货物的所有权，而以中介身份做代理销售商。还包括各类商品批发市场中固定摊位的批发活动。

零售业

指百货商店、超级市场、专门零售商店、品牌专卖店、售货摊等主要面向最终消费者（如居民等）的销售活动。包括以互联网、邮政、电话、售货机等方式的销售活动，还包括在同一地点，后面加工生产，前面销售的店铺（如前店后厂的面包房）。不包括：谷物、种子、饲料、牲畜、矿产品、生产用原料、化工原料、农用化工产品、机械设备（乘用车、计算机及通信设备等除外）等生产资料的销售(列入批发业)；非零售单位附带的零售活动，如汽车修理单位销售汽车零件（列入单位主业所对应的行业类别中)；商业零售单位所在商厦的物业管理（列入物业管理）；商业零售单位所在的商品市场、商业大厦的市场管理活动（列入市场管理）。

批发和零售业商品购进、销售、库存额

指各种登记注册类型的批发和零售业企业(单位)以本企业(单位)为总体的，从国内、国外市场购进的商品总量，销售和出口的商品总量，库存的商品总量等情况。该指标可以反映商品流转过程中商品的购进、销售、库存之间的比例关系和存在的问题。

商品购进额

指从本企业以外的单位和个人购进（包括从国外直接进口）作为转卖或加工后转卖的商品金额（含增值税）。商品购进包括：（1）从工农业生产者、批发和零售业企业、住宿和餐饮业企业、出版社或报社的出版发行部门和其他服务业企业购进的商品；（2）从机关团体、事业单位购进的商品；（3）从海关、市场管理部门购进的缉私和没收的商品；（4）从居民收购的废旧商品等。不包括：（1）企业为本单位自身经营用，不是作为转卖而购进的商品，如材料物资、包装物、低值易耗品、办公用品等；（2）未通过买卖行为而收入的商品，如接受其他部门移交的商品、借入的商品、收入代其他单位保管的商品、其他单位赠送的样品、加工回收的成品等；（3）经本单位介绍，由买卖双方直接结算，本单位只收取手续费的业务；（4）销售退回和买方拒付货款的商品；（5）商品溢余。

商品销售额

指对本单位以外的单位和个人出售的商品金额（包括售给本单位消费用的商品，含增值税）。商品销售包括（1）售给城乡居民和社会集团消费用的商品；（2）售给农业、工业、建筑业、运输邮电业、服务业、公用事业等国民经济各行业用于生产、经营用的商品，包括售予批发和零售业作为转卖或加工后转卖的商品；（3）对国（境）外直接出口的商品。不包括：（1）未通过买卖行为付出的商品，如随机构变动移交给其他企业单位的商品、借出的商品、归还受其他单位委托代保管的商品、付出的加工原料和赠送给其他单位的样品等；（2）经本单位介绍，由买卖双方直接结算，本单位只收取手续费的业务；（3）购货退回的商品；（4）商品损耗和损失；（5）出售本单位自用的废旧物资。

商品库存额

指报告期末各种登记注册类型的批发和零售业企业(单位)已取得所有权的商品。它反映批发和零售业企业(单位)的商品库存情况和对市场商品供应的保证程度。商品库存包括：(1)存放在批发和零售业经营单位(如门市部、批发站、采购站、经营处)的仓库、货场、货柜和货架中的商品；(2)挑选、整理、包装中的商品；(3)已记入购进而尚未运到本单位的商品，即发货单或银行承兑凭证已到而货未到的商品；(4)寄放他处的商品，如因购货方拒绝付款而暂时存在购货方的商品；(5)委托其他单位代销(未作销售或调出)尚未售出的商品；(6)代其他单位购进尚未交付的商品。不包括：所有权不属于本单位的商品；委托外单位加工的商品；外贸企业代理其他单位从国外进口尚未付给订货单位的商品；代国家物资储备部门保管的商品等。

连锁总店（总部）

指负责连锁企业资源（商号、商誉、经营模式、服务标准、管理模式等等）的开发、配置、控制或使用等功能的企业核心管理机构。连锁经营是指经营同类商品或服务，使用统一商号的若干店铺，在同一总店（总部）的管理下，采取统一采购或特许经营等方式，实现规模效益的组织形式，包括直营连锁、特许连锁和自愿连锁三种形式。其中，直营连锁是指连锁店铺由连锁公司全资或控股开设，在总部的直接控制下，开展统一经营的连锁经营形式；特许连锁是指拥有注册商标、企业标志、专利、专有技术等经营资源的企业（特许人），以合同形式将其拥有的经营资源许可其他经营者（被特许人）使用，被特许人按合同约定在统一的经营模式下开展经营，并向特许人支付特许经营费用的连锁经营形式；自愿连锁是指若干个店铺或企业自愿组合起来，在不改变各自资产所有权关系的情况下，以同一个品牌形象面对消费者，以共同进货为纽带开展的连锁经营形式。

亿元以上商品交易市场

指年成交额在亿元及以上的商品交易市场。商品交易市场是指经有关部门和组织批准设立，有固定场所、设施，有经营管理部门和监管人员，若干市场经营者入内，常年或实际开业三个月以上，集中、公开、独立地进行生活消费品、生产资料等现货商品交易以及提供相关服务的交易场所，包括各类消费品市场、生产资料市场等。

社会消费品零售总额

指企业（单位、个体户）通过交易直接售给个人、社会集团非生产、非经营用的实物商品金额，以及提供餐饮服务所取得的收入金额。个人包括城乡居民和入境人员，社会集团包括机关、社会团体、部队、学校、企事业单位、居委会或村委会等。

Explanatory Notes for Major Statistical Indicators

Wholesale Trade

refers to the activities of wholesaler selling at wholesale commodities for daily use and capital goods to enterprises of wholesale and retail trades and other enterprises, institutions and government offices, including the activities of wholesaler engaged in import and export and acting as a trade agent. The wholesaler may have the right of ownership over the commodities of wholesale and trade in the name of its own's or a company, the wholesaler may not have the right of ownership, only acts an agent. The wholesale trade also include the activities of wholesaler at the fixed stalls of the wholesale market of different commodities.

Retail Trade

refers to the activities of department store, supermarket, franchised store, brand store, retail stall and on-the-spot-making-selling store selling commodities to the final consumers (citizens) by any means including internet, post, telephone, sales machine. Retail trade excludes the activities of sales of capital goods such a grain, seed, feed, livestock, mineral products, raw material for production, industrial chemicals, chemical products for farm, machine and equipment (vehicle, computer and communication equipment), and the activities of supplementary sales of non-retailer such as the sales of spare parts of car repair business (listed as branch in correspondence with principle business), property management of buildings of retail units (listed as property management); market management of commercial markets and buildings of retail units (listed as market management) .

Purchase, Sales and Stock of Commodities by Wholesale and Retail Trades

refer to the total volume of commodities purchased, total volume of sales and exports, and the stock of commodities by wholesale and retail enterprises (establishments) of different status of registration from domestic and overseas markets. This indicator reflects the relationship among purchase, sales and stock of commodities in the circulation of goods and reveals the existing problems.

Total Purchases of Commodities

refer to the total value of purchases of commodities by enterprises (establishments) from other establishments or individuals (including direct import from abroad) for the purpose of re-selling, either with or without further processing of the commodities purchased. The commodities include: (1) commodities purchased from agricultural and industrial producer, wholesaler, retailer, publishing house and other service business; (2) commodities purchased from institutions and government departments; (3) confiscated goods purchased from the customs authorities or market management agencies; (4) second-hand goods and wastes purchased from residents; The commodities exclude 1. commodities purchased by enterprises (establishments) for use in their own business operation, commodities obtained without buying or selling procedures such as materials, consumable goods of low value, office appliance, etc. 2. received goods without trading, such as goods handed over from others, borrowed goods, preserved goods for others, donated goods from others, processed and retrieved goods, etc. 3. goods of direct settlement between buyer and seller with handling fees introduced by others, 4. goods returned or refused to pay by the buyer, 5. excessive goods.

Total Sales of Commodities

refer to value of commodities sold by the establishments to other establishments and individuals (including goods sold for self consumption, including the value-added tax). The commodities include: (1) commodities sold to urban and rural residents and social groups for their consumption; (2) commodities sold to establishments in all industries for their production and operation, including agriculture, industry, construction, transportation, post and telecommunications, catering services, and public utility including commodities sold to wholesale and retail establishments for re-selling, with or without further processing; and (3) commodities for direct export to abroad. Excluded are (1) extended commodities without trading, such as goods handed over to other enterprises and institutions because of the change of organizations, lent goods, returned goods preserved for others, extended processing materials and samples donated to others, (2) goods of direct settlement between buyer and seller with handling fees introduced by others, 3. goods returned after purchase, (4) damaged and spoiled goods, (5) waste and used goods of self use,

Total Stock of Commodities

refers to total commodities possessed by wholesaler and retailer of various types of registration status at the end of the reference period, reflecting the commodity stock level of various wholesaler and retailer and the potential for market supply. It includes: (1) commodities located in storage, garages, counters, and shelves of operating places of wholesale and retail trades (such as sale stores, wholesale centres, procurement stations and operating offices); (2) commodities in the process of being selected, sorted, and packed; (3) commodities not arrived but recorded as purchase in the account, i.e. commodities not arrived but payment receipts for the commodities from the sellers or the banks arrived; (4) commodities deposited in other places rather than places mentioned above, for instance: commodities in the hold of purchasers temporarily due to the refusal of payment; (5) commodities entrusted to other units to sell but not sold yet; (6) commodities purchased for other units but not delivered yet. Commodities not included as stock are those not owned by the enterprises (units), commodities on commission for processing, imported commodities of agency of foreign trade enterprise but not yet delivered to ordering units and finally those put in stock on behalf of the state material reserves units.

Chain Head Stores (headquarter)

refer to the core leading stores responsible for development, allocation, administration and utilization of resources (name of stores, brand of stores, operation model, service standard, management way, etc.) of chain stores. Chain stores refers to the stores engaged in providing homogeneous commodities or services, with the central leadership of head store (headquarters) and guided by common policies, conduct centralized purchase and distributed selling of commodities, in order to gain better efficiency through standardized operation. The chain stores include regular chain stores, franchise chain stores and voluntary chain stores. Regular Chain store refers to chain stores that are invested or controlled by the headquarters. They operate under direct and unified management from the headquarters. Franchise chain store refers to the chain stores (franchisees) which are franchised with operation resources such as trade marks, names, patent and operation know-how by the franchisors in form of contract and pay the operation fees to the franchisors. Voluntary chain store refers to the stores operate jointly on the voluntary bases while maintaining their status of independent legal entities with full ownership of their assets. They sell goods of same brand from same channel of resource to the consumers.

Large Commodity Markets with Transaction Value over 100 Million Yuan

refers to the commodity markets with an annual transaction at and above 100 million. The commodity market refers to the markets approved and managed by related departments, where there are fixed sites, facilities, managers and administration offices, where there are a certain number of traders to operate for three month and above or all the year, where the commodities including the articles for daily consumption and capital goods and services are traded in a centralized, independent and open way. Such market includes markets of daily goods and market of capital goods, etc.

Total Retail Sales of Consumer Goods

refer to the amount obtained by enterprises (units, self-employed individuals) through direct sales of non-production and non-business physical commodity to individuals, social institutions, and revenue from providing catering services. Individuals include rural and urban households, population from abroad, social institutions include government agencies, social organizations, military units, schools, institutions, neighbourhood (village) committees.

第十七篇

Chapter 17

对外经济贸易

FOREIGN TRADE AND ECONOMIC COOPERATION

简要说明

一、我省进出口贸易的规模、进出口商品结构、贸易伙伴国的进出口总额以及三资企业的进出口变化情况，根据合肥海关资料加工整理。

二、利用外资资料来源于省商务厅，根据国家商务部和国家统计局共同制订的《利用外资统计制度》加工、整理而成。

三、外商投资企业注册登记情况。资料来源于省市场监管局，根据国家市场监管总局制订的《市场监督管理统计报表制度》进行统计、加工、整理而得。凡以市场监督管理机关核准注册，在我省的中外合资经营企业、中外合作经营企业、外商独资企业、中外股份公司、在华从事经营活动的外国及港澳台地区企业及外国公司在我省境内设立的分支机构均列入统计范围。

四、对外承包工程和劳务合作的发展状况。资料来源于省商务厅，根据国家商务部与国家统计局共同制订的《对外承包工程和劳务合作统计制度》通过全面调查方法进行加工、整理而得。

Brief Introduction

I. Data on scale of import and export, commodity structure, total volume of import and export to trade partner and change in import and export of joint, cooperative or exclusively foreign-funded ventures are collected in accordance with the data provided by the Hefei Customs.

II. Data on overall situation of the utilization of foreign capital in Anhui come from the Provincial Department of Commerce and are tabulated in accordance with the “Statistical Scheme on the Utilization of Foreign Capital” designed by the Ministry of Commerce and Economic Cooperation and the National Bureau of Statistics.

III. Registration of foreign-invested enterprises. Data from the provincial market supervision bureau, according to the State Administration for Market Regulation formulated "market supervision and management statistical statement system" for statistics, processing, sorting and obtained. All registered enterprises approved by the market supervision and administration authority in our province are included in the statistical scope, such as sino-foreign joint ventures, sino-foreign cooperative enterprises, wholly foreign-owned enterprises, sino-foreign joint stock companies, enterprises from Hong Kong, Macao and Taiwan engaged in business activities in China, and branches set up by foreign companies in our province.

IV. Data on development of the contracted projects, labor services cooperation and design and consultation service with foreign countries come from the Provincial Department of Commerce and are collected with the method of complete enumeration and are tabulated in accordance with the “Statistical Reporting Scheme on the Contracted Projects and Labor Services Cooperation with Foreign Countries” jointly stipulated by the Ministry of Commerce and Economic Cooperation and the National Bureau of Statistics.

17—1 对外经济贸易基本情况
Foreign Trade and Economic Cooperation

单位：万美元（USD 10000）

指标	Item	2010	2015	2020	2021	2022
进出口总额	**Total Imports and Exports**	**2427677**	**4880808**	**7859430**	**10700787**	**11315512**
出口总额	Total Exports	1241288	3311424	4557868	6337476	7141206
初级产品	Primary Products	78229	182463	144292	174786	190732
工业制成品	Industrial Manufactured Goods	1163059	3128960	4413576	6162690	6950474
进口总额	Total Imports	1186388	1569384	3301562	4363312	4174306
初级产品	Primary Products	629398	797477	1547241	2116756	1933525
工业制成品	Industrial Manufactured Goods	556991	771907	1753366	2246556	2240780
进出口差额	Import and Export Balance	+54900	+1742040	+1256306	+1974164	+2966900
利用外商直接投资	**Foreign Direct Investment Utilization**					
新批项目（个）	The New Projects (unit)	281	289	393	475	475
合同外资额	The Contract Amount of Foreign Investment	216462	393800	517192	688168	429034
实际利用外商直接投资额	The Actual Use of Foreign Direct Investment	501446	1361945	1830542	1929728	215507
外商投资企业基本情况	**The Basic Situation of Enterprises With Foreign Investment**					
年底登记户数（户）	At The End of The Registration Number (household)	2546	5063	8281	8490	8091
投资总额	The Total Amount of Investment	3032426	10648647	32270386	32476547	8285664
注册资本	Registered Capital	1734905	3091647	10222159	23629032	4905636
#外　方	Foreign	1293032	2234387	7538499	14853517	2924020
对外承包工程和劳务合作	**Foreign Contracted Projects and Labor Service Cooperation**					
对外承包工程新签合同额	Newly Signed Contract of Foreign Contracted Projects	151147	307024	280749	443690	545602
对外承包工程完成营业额	Foreign Contracted Projects Completed Turnover	192746	269258	250222	238506	239225
外派劳务人数（人）	Expatriate Population (person)	12631	10500	5233	581	1154
年末在外劳务人员（人）	At the end of the Year in Foreign Labor Service Personnel (person)	20236	23691	7716	3732	2206
对外投资	**Foreign Investment**					
新批境外企业（机构）数（家）	A new Batch of Overseas Enterprises (Institutions) Number (unit)	44	133	103	98	115
协议对外投资额	Agreement of Foreign Investment	112504	318197	120416	169127	172453
实际对外投资额	The Actual Amount of Foreign Investment	80966	96846	130729	135052	160912

注：2022年实际利用外商直接投资额统计口径是商务部口径，往年为省口径，数据不可比。

17—2 海关出口商品分类金额
Value of Exports by Category of Commodities (Customs Statistics)

单位：万美元（USD 10000）

指　　标	Item	2010	2015	2020	2021	2022
总　　额	**Total**	**1241288**	**3311424**	**4557868**	**6337476**	**7141206**
初级产品	Primary Goods	78229	182463	144292	174786	190732
食品及主要供食用的活动物	Food and Live Animals Used Chiefly for Food	47659	90668	84067	97259	101762
饮料及烟类	Beverages and Tobacco	129	217	672	1239	860
非食品原料	Non-edible Raw Materials	29947	36791	53194	66064	68447
矿物燃料、润滑油及有关原料	Mineral Fuels, Lubricants and Related Materials	65	403	3498	4637	8408
动、植物油脂及腊	Animal and Vegetable Oils, Fats and Wax	428	54384	2861	5587	11255
工业制成品	Manufactured Goods	1163059	3128960	4413576	6162690	6950474
化学品及有关产品	Chemicals and Related Products	148644	217230	352758	584747	664358
按原料分类的制成品	Finished Goods Classified by Raw Material	281446	906051	738331	933475	1062866
机械及运输设备	Machinery and Transport Equipment	421797	1210348	2283300	3240289	4071469
杂项制品	Miscellaneous Products	310905	644557	1015613	1385747	1131598
未分类的商品	Goods not Classified	267	150774	23574	18431	20183

17—3 海关进口商品分类金额
Value of Imports by Category of Commodities (Customs Statistics)

单位：万美元（USD 10000）

指　　标	Item	2010	2015	2020	2021	2022
总　　额	**Total**	**1186388**	**1569384**	**3301562**	**4363312**	**4174306**
初级产品	Primary Goods	629398	797477	1547241	2116756	1933525
食品及主要供食用的活动物	Food and Live Animals Used Chiefly for Food	27272	107868	284132	329820	297521
饮料及烟类	Beverages and Tobacco	110	596	4773	1917	2731
非食品原料	Non-edible Raw Materials	568818	643688	1149264	1628790	1465727
矿物燃料、润滑油及有关原料	Mineral Fuels, Lubricants and Related Materials	26226	28190	51265	79064	91150
动、植物油脂及腊	Animal and Vegetable Oils, Fats and Wax	6971	17136	57808	77165	76397
工业制成品	Manufactured Goods	556991	771907	1753366	2246556	2240780
化学品及有关产品	Chemicals and Related Products	60091	110446	182748	256190	253761
按原料分类的制成品	Finished Goods Classified by Raw Material	85325	174572	261255	338164	325758
机械及运输设备	Machinery and Transport Equipment	367495	224899	1094300	1351820	1489079
杂项制品	Miscellaneous Products	43856	100118	213920	299130	171572
未分类的商品	Goods not Classified	224	161872	1144	1254	611

17—4 海关进出口商品分类金额
Value of Imports and Exports by Category of Commodities (Customs Statistics)

单位：万美元（USD 10000）

品　　名	Item	2021		2022	
		出　口 Exports	进　口 Imports	出　口 Exports	进　口 Imports
总　　值	**Total**	**6337476**	**4363312**	**7141206**	**4174306**
初级产品	**Primary Goods**	**174786**	**2116756**	**190732**	**1933525**
食品及活动物	Food and Live Animals	97259	329820	101762	297521
活动物	Live Animals	587	631	634	
肉及肉制品	Meat and Related Products	306	176718	564	126115
乳品及蛋品	Dairy Products and Eggs	122	62687	151	47817
鱼、甲壳及软体类动物及其制品	Fish, Shellfish and Mollusks and Related Products	3619	1633	6079	2413
谷物及其制品	Cereals and Related Products	3673	18979	4685	24135
蔬菜及水果	Vegetables and Fruits	31480	33897	35962	52429
糖、糖制品及蜂蜜	Sugar, Sugar Products and Honey	11778	2048	13570	2114
咖啡、茶、可可、调味料及其制品	Coffee, Tea, Coco, Spices and Related Products	30377	5057	25748	2414
饲料（不包括未碾磨谷物）	Feed (excluding unbranded cereal)	9474	23267	7597	35193
杂项食品	Miscellaneous Food	5843	4903	6772	4891
饮料及烟类	Beverages and Tobacco	1239	1917	860	2731
饮　料	Beverages	586	1917	493	2731
烟草及其制品	Tobacco and Its Products	653		366	
非食用原料（燃料除外）	Inedible Material (excluding fuel)	66064	1628790	68447	1465727
生皮及生毛皮	Raw Hides and Raw Furs		398	18	222
含油子仁及果实	Oilseed Kernel and Fruit	5498	110216	4890	122426
生橡胶（包括合成橡胶及再生橡胶）	Raw Rubber (including synthetic rubber and reclaimed rubber)	3178	28395	1524	25934
软木及木材	Cork and Timber	3090	27439	2148	23377
纸浆及废纸	Paper Pulp and Waste Paper	3293	48904	5386	45582
纺织纤维（羊毛条除外）及其原料	Textile Fibers (excluding wool taps) and Related Waste Material	10357	16900	10484	13069
天然肥料及矿物（煤、石油及宝石除外）	Natural Fertilizer and Mineral (excluding coal, petroleum and precious stone)	5804	8676	4428	10752
金属矿砂及金属废料	Metal Ore and Metal Waste Material	855	1377696	958	1211397
其他动、植物原料	Other Animal and Plant Material	33987	10166	38610	12968
矿物燃料、润滑油及有关原料	Mineral Fuel, Lubrication Oil and Related Raw Material	4637	79064	8408	91150
煤、焦炭及煤砖	Coal, Coke and Briquette	252	64289	769	75735
石油、石油产品及有关原料	Petroleum, Petroleum Products and Related Material	4385	11066	7640	14737
天然气及人造气	Natural Gas and Person Gas-producing		3709		678
动植物油、脂及蜡	Animal Fat, Vegetable Oil and Wax	5587	77165	11255	76397
动物油、脂	Animal Fat	314	4038	521	2130
植物油、脂	Vegetable Oil	58	73043	101	73438
已加工的动植物油、脂及动植物蜡	Processed Animal Fat, Vegetable Oil and Wax	5215	85	10632	828
其他动植物油、脂及蜡	Other Animal Fat,Vegetable Oil and Wax				
工业制品	**Industrial Products**	**6162690**	**2246556**	**6950474**	**2240780**
化学成品及有关产品	Chemical Products and Related Products	584747	256190	664358	253761
有机化学品	Organic Chemical Products	197888	61902	244338	33769
无机化学品	Inorganic Chemical Products	20925	4842	36641	11005

17—4 续表 continued

单位：万美元（USD 10000）

品　　名	Item	2021 出口 Exports	2021 进口 Imports	2022 出口 Exports	2022 进口 Imports
染料、鞣料及着色料	Dyestuff, Tanning Material and Coloring Material	61957	15751	59471	15897
医药品	Medical and Pharmaceutical Products	59720	30313	64031	30581
精油、香料及盥洗、光洁制品	Essential Oil, Perfume, Sanitary and Surface Finishing Articles	22469	10768	19656	15404
肥　料	Fertilizer	44484		40981	
初级形状的塑料	Primary Shaped Plastics	55579	66554	67843	84198
非初级形状的塑料	Non-primary Shaped Plastics	35046	20241	45185	16783
其他化学原料及产品	Other Chemical Material and Products	72036	43828	86212	46124
按原料分类的制成品	Finished Goods Classified by Raw Material	933475	338164	1062866	325758
皮革、皮革制品及已鞣毛皮	Leather and Its Products and Tan Hide	2296	312	1601	225
橡胶制品	Rubber Products	58759	11353	67597	8652
软木及木制品（家具除外）	Cork and Wooden Products (excluding furniture)	57117	2963	60634	2674
纸及纸板、纸浆、纸及纸板制品	Paper, Paperboard, Paper Pulp and Paper Products	64252	10724	78770	8851
纺纱、织物、制成品及有关产品	Spinning, Fabric and Related Products	218311	59377	211455	33657
非金属矿物制品	Nonmetal Mineral Products	131282	39185	146607	33147
钢　铁	Iron and Steel	142965	18506	172948	21301
有色金属	Nonferrous Metal	91105	184307	122259	206845
金属制品	Metal Products	167388	11436	200995	10405
机械及运输设备	Machinery and Transportation Equipment	3240289	1351820	4071469	1489079
动力机械及设备	Dynamic Machinery and Equipment	103577	31272	97781	28692
特种工业专用机械	Special Industrial Machinery	116498	467477	150776	390805
金工机械	Metalworking	21954	20186	29140	23659
通用工业机械设备及零件	General Industrial Machinery Equipment and Accessories	464096	67709	500602	70948
办公用机械及自动数据处理设备	Office Machinery and Automatic Data Processing Equipment	713196	137191	804622	117460
电信和声音的录制及重放装置设备	Telecommunication, Sound Recording and Playing Equipment	172604	10826	115314	10922
电力机械、器具及其电气零件	Electric Machinery, Implements and Spare Parts	1196146	610493	1570878	834380
陆路车辆（包括气垫式）	Land Route Vehicles (including hover-motor)	401653	4145	726121	11317
其他运输设备	Other Transportation Equipment	50565	2518	76235	896
杂项制品	Miscellaneous Manufactured Articles	1385747	299130	1131598	171572
活动房屋、卫生水道、供热及照明装置	Prefabricated House, Sanitation, Water Pipe, Heating and Lighting Installation	77988	1323	68868	482
家具及其零件、褥垫及类似填充制品	Furniture and Accessories, Mattress, Bedding Articles	149700	653	158545	401
旅行用品、手提包及类似品	Box and Bag, Travel Goods	47675	122	67156	102
服装及衣着附件	Garments, Clothing Accessories	324958	2545	307911	891
鞋　靴	Footwear	55265	476	72426	210
专业、科学及控制用仪器装置	Professional, Scientific and Dominating Instrument	337061	226224	53268	100234
摄影器材、光学物品及钟表	Photographic Equipment, Optical Goods, Clocks and Watches	20872	38369	26110	43255
杂项制品	Miscellaneous Manufactured Articles	372229	29416	377313	25996
未分类的商品	Goods Not Classified	18431	1254	20183	611

17—5 安徽省同各国（地区）进出口总额
Anhui's Foreign Trade With Related Countries and Territories

单位：万美元（USD 10000）

国 别（地区）	Country (region)	2021 进出口总额 Total	2021 出口总额 Exports	2021 进口总额 Imports	2022 进出口总额 Total	2022 出口总额 Exports	2022 进口总额 Imports
合 计	**Total**	**10700787**	**6337476**	**4363312**	**11315512**	**7141206**	**4174306**
亚 洲	**Asia**	**4475652**	**2491214**	**1984438**	**4856912**	**2820059**	**2036853**
阿富汗	Afghanistan	521	515	6	552	552	
巴 林	Bahrain	3812	3743	69	4525	4481	45
孟加拉国	Bangladesh	35416	34709	708	38195	37391	804
不 丹	Bhutan	28	28		23	23	
文 莱	Brunei	885	885		807	782	25
缅 甸	Myanmar	26048	18232	7816	47285	32862	14423
柬埔寨	Cambodia	14909	14521	388	18543	17680	863
塞浦路斯	Cyprus	1066	1066		1091	1091	
朝 鲜	Korea DPR	230	230		843	843	
中国香港	Hong Kong	384842	378898	5944	372971	365953	7018
印 度	India	338422	281172	57250	302102	266511	35591
印度尼西亚	Indonesia	209703	107176	102527	251095	115808	135287
伊 朗	Iran	105250	62305	42945	190595	130707	59888
伊拉克	Iraq	21863	21845	18	34653	34653	
以色列	Israel	44956	25944	19012	56613	43164	13449
日 本	Japan	686279	255256	431023	640330	266176	374154
约 旦	Jordan	6297	5975	322	8988	8734	254
科威特	Kuwait	11304	10950	354	18572	18324	248
老 挝	Laos	7418	2918	4500	16430	9914	6516
黎巴嫩	Lebanon	3886	3829	57	12685	12684	
中国澳门	Macao	1160	1160		930	930	
马来西亚	Malaysia	208348	112814	95534	255549	115609	139940
马尔代夫	Maldives	636	636		685	685	
蒙 古	Mongolia	2708	2668	39.7	4846	3860	986
尼泊尔	Nepal	2626	2625	1	1844	1843	1
阿 曼	Oman	7345	6068	1277	10472	10158	314
巴基斯坦	Pakistan	76421	54991	21430	82274	62550	19724
巴勒斯坦	Palestine	323	323		264	264	
菲律宾	The Philippines	108235	75376	32859	135121	104961	30160
卡塔尔	Qatar	14500	8770	5730	19852	13845	6007
沙特阿拉伯	Saudi Arabia	78518	51969	26549	114717	94913	19805
新加坡	Singapore	166075	58590	107485	156295	81801	74493
韩 国	Republic of Korea	476983	180129	296854	550914	217980	332933
斯里兰卡	Sri Lanka	10190	9603	588	6620	6226	394
叙利亚	Syria	605	605		706	706	
泰 国	Thailand	196919	126791	70128	253071	166119	86952
土耳其	Turkey	81697	73515	8182	79395	72536	6859
阿联酋	United Arab Emirates	123814	90187	33627	127669	92719	34950
也门共和国	Arab Republic of Yemen	4909	4909		4350	4350	
越 南	Viet Nam	265345	228968	36377	287260	191725	95536
中国台湾	Taiwan	566184	113262	452922	530739	136511	394228
东帝汶	East Timor	409	409		903	903	
哈萨克斯坦	Kazakhstan	16053	16014	39	35927	35800	127
吉尔吉斯斯坦	Kirghiz Tanzania	2323	2323		3520	2639	881

17—5 续表1 continued

单位：万美元（USD 10000）

国 别（地区）	Country (region)	2021 进出口总额 Total	2021 出口总额 Exports	2021 进口总额 Imports	2022 进出口总额 Total	2022 出口总额 Exports	2022 进口总额 Imports
塔吉克斯坦	Tajikistan	704	578	126	1217	1110	106
土库曼斯坦	Turkmenistan	2235	2004	230	10117	10113	4
乌兹别克斯坦	Uzbekistan	37371	35727	1643	22309	20872	1437
非 洲	**Africa**	**506447**	**304303**	**202144**	**574589**	**360912**	**213677**
阿尔及利亚	Algeria	11711	11689	23	13223	13223	
安哥拉	Angola	4763	4763		12835	12770	65
贝 宁	Benin	2148	1358	790	5874	3278	2597
博茨瓦纳	Botswana	286	286		349	349	
布隆迪	Burundi	404	404		413	413	
喀麦隆	Cameroon	5875	5768	107	7563	7413	150
加那利群岛	Canary Is.	2	2				
佛得角	Cape Verde	409	409		463	463	
中 非	Central Africa	24	24		52	51	
塞卜泰(休达)	Sebtai (Ceuta)	0.4	0.4				
乍 得	Chad	427	427		733	283	451
科摩罗	Comoros	48	48		149	149	
刚 果	The Congo	1065	1065		1776	1277	499
吉布提	Djibouti	3272	3272		2373	2373	
埃 及	Egypt	63565	63296	269	51352	50657	695
赤道几内亚	Equatorial Guinea	375	375		177	177	
埃塞俄比亚	Ethiopia	12167	4799	7368	10142	3184	6957
加 蓬	Gabon	1108	338	771	2471	814	1657
冈比亚	Gambia	833	709	124	1044	949	95
加 纳	Ghana	23652	23092	560	24250	23280	970
几内亚	Guinea	4821	4821		6833	6833	
几内亚比绍	Guineabissau	15	15		9	9	
科特迪瓦	Cote D'ivoire	8368	7296	1072	8420	7995	426
肯尼亚	Kenya	7873	7604	269	13049	12555	494
利比里亚	Liberia	559	559		4884	4884	
利比亚	Libya	2416	2416		3891	3891	
马达加斯加	Madagascar	2123	2104	19	2091	2079	12
马拉维	Malawi	1016	914	102	687	426	261
马 里	Mali	2629	1228	1401	1142	651	491
毛里塔尼亚	Mauritania	7113	4256	2857	6621	4369	2252
毛里求斯	Mauritius	1459	1459		1680	1680	
摩洛哥	Morocco	9348	8353	995	12974	12587	387
莫桑比克	Mozambique	7813	6109	1704	9922	5588	4334
纳米比亚	Namibia	2059	1233	826	1668	1666	3
尼日尔	Niger	10001	470	9531	8898	502	8396
尼日利亚	Nigeria	42447	37277	5171	45755	41113	4641
留尼汪	Reunion	629	629		480	480	
卢旺达	Rwanda	281	281		410	410	
圣多和普林	St and More Spring	13	13		64	64	
塞内加尔	Senegal	10037	8210	1827	10729	9993	736
塞舌尔	Seychelles	143	143		136	136	
塞拉利昂	Sierra Leone	1541	1185	356	890	890	

17—5 续表2 continued

单位：万美元（USD 10000）

国 别（地区）	Country (region)	2021			2022		
		进出口总额 Total	出口总额 Exports	进口总额 Imports	进出口总额 Total	出口总额 Exports	进口总额 Imports
索马里	Somali	848	806	42	1167	1114	53
南 非	South Africa	73872	47571	26301	93655	70351	23304
西撒哈拉	Western Sahara	20	20				
苏 丹	Sudan	29494	2512	26983	30711	2975	27737
坦桑尼亚	Tanzania	11334	8504	2829	18586	13361	5224
多 哥	Togo	14166	7331	6835	14176	7496	6680
突尼斯	Tunisia	5147	5136	10	6939	6904	35
乌干达	Uganda	2490	1826	664	4216	3503	713
布基纳法索	Burkina Faso	1088	456	632	2519	492	2028
刚果(金)	Congo (DRC)	50656	6533	44123	71813	9065	62748
赞比亚	Zambia	54686	1801	52885	50362	1809	48553
津巴布韦	Zimbabwe	1901	1682	218	2283	2251	32
莱索托	Lesotho	348	348		47	47	
斯威士兰	Swaziland	408	408		998	998	
厄立特里亚	Eritrea	4555	74	4481	196	196	
马约特岛	Mayotte Island	57	57		149	149	
南苏丹共和国	Republic of South Sudan	538	538		286	286	
欧 洲	**Europe**	**1864331**	**1485638**	**378692**	**2030712**	**1686575**	**344137**
比利时	Belgium	56480	51848	4631	61885	58188	3698
丹 麦	Denmark	30570	27104	3465	28851	26454	2397
英 国	United Kingdom	183502	166671	16831	177096	163153	13943
德 国	Germany	346218	251526	94692	316472	228453	88019
法 国	France	108350	85545	22805	95070	79217	15854
爱尔兰	Ireland	13420	8471	4950	11892	9227	2665
意大利	Italy	106730	91048	15682	151431	134405	17026
卢森堡	Luxembourg	1669	857	812	2016	1793	222
荷 兰	Netherlands	246552	207481	39071	417869	353225	64644
希 腊	Greece	19127	17499	1628	21566	20174	1392
葡萄牙	Portugal	26033	24490	1543	23669	22527	1142
西班牙	Spain	125167	89709	35458	121991	94673	27318
塞浦路斯	Cyprus						
阿尔巴尼亚	Albania	1106	1066	40	1292	1209	83
安道尔	Andorra	8	8		43	43	
奥地利	Austria	36815	22395	14419	28627	19243	9385
保加利亚	Bulgaria	8471	7520	951	15815	15159	656
芬 兰	Finland	19525	14222	5302	19680	13469	6211
匈牙利	Hungary	37484	33337	4146	14953	14025	928
直布罗陀	Gibraltar	4	4				
冰 岛	Iceland	805	793	12	1060	1057	2
列支敦士登	Liechtenstein	78	53	25	236	89	147
马耳他	Malta	1234	1035	199	975	758	216
摩纳哥	Monaco	7	7		18	18	
挪 威	Norway	12895	11937	958	20709	19899	811
波 兰	Poland	91879	83630	8249	82489	76281	6208
罗马尼亚	Romania	14770	13794	976	14782	13609	1172
圣马力诺	SAN Marino	41	41		47	47	
瑞 典	Sweden	38613	29721	8892	32004	25569	6435
瑞 士	Switzerland	21550	17543	4007	23774	19581	4193

17—5 续表3 continued

单位：万美元（USD 10000）

国别（地区）	Country (region)	2021 进出口总额 Total	2021 出口总额 Exports	2021 进口总额 Imports	2022 进出口总额 Total	2022 出口总额 Exports	2022 进口总额 Imports
爱沙尼亚	Estonia	5300	4283	1017	5398	4778	620
拉脱维亚	Latvia	2930	2848	82	3443	2566	877
立陶宛	Lithuania	7093	6627	466	5405	5306	99
格鲁吉亚	Georgia	1803	1501	301	2333	2054	279
亚美尼亚	Armenia	14111	485	13625	6714	885	5829
阿塞拜疆	Azerbaijan	985	985		1706	1661	45
白俄罗斯	Byelorussia	7516	3643	3874	5172	3731	1441
摩尔多瓦	Moldora	710	595	115	644	616	28
俄罗斯	Russia	162332	129959	32373	219619	187825	31794
乌克兰	Ukraine	48514	20878	27636	17729	6484	11246
斯洛文尼亚	Slovenia	10012	9083	929	13290	12688	602
克罗地亚	Croatia	4699	4629	70	7577	7531	46
捷克共和国	Czech	38460	31400	7060	35265	28731	6534
斯洛伐克	Slovak	6345	5261	1084	6389	4913	1476
前南马其顿	Macedonia	373	336	37	438	423	15
波　黑	Bosnia & Herzegovina	920	665	255	651	573	77
梵蒂冈城国	Vatican City State	0.01	0.01				
法罗群岛	The Faroe Islands	2	2				
塞尔维亚	Serbia	2998	2985	13	12259	3903	8356
黑　山	Montenegro	126	118	9	353	348	5
拉丁美洲	**Latin America**	**1834126**	**770747**	**1063379**	**1742692**	**779778**	**962915**
安提瓜	Antigua	27	27		79	79	
阿根廷	Argentina	34358	24080	10278	42251	26271	15980
阿鲁巴岛	Aruba	162	162		213	213	
巴哈马	Bahamas	167	167		248	248	
巴巴多斯	Barbados	432	431	1	431	431	
伯利兹	Belize	94	94		248	214	34
玻利维亚	Bolivia	4805	3924	881	8246	4423	3823
博内尔	Bonaire	0.1	0.1				
巴　西	Brazil	397859	219591	178268	394386	246540	147846
智　利	Chile	551966	116720	435245	23	23	
开曼群岛	Cayman Islands	45	45		442360	102328	340032
哥伦比亚	Colombia	36776	34578	2198	38624	36589	2035
多米尼克	Dominica	54	54		282	282	
哥斯达黎加	Costa Rica	6420	5419	1001	8773	8036	737
古　巴	Cuba	1283	1283		718	579	139
库腊索岛	Curacao	143	143		269	269	
多米尼加	Dominican	6414	6252	162	10425	9966	459
厄瓜多尔	Ecuador	104621	28377	76244	134948	35903	99045
法属圭亚那	French Guiana	55	55		105	105	
格林纳达	Grenada	66	66		83	83	
瓜德罗普	Guaderopu	285	285		162	162	
危地马拉	Guatemala	8750	7232	1518	10447	10036	410
圭亚那	Guyana	640	640		1011	1011	
海　地	Haiti	1364	1364		960	959	1

17—5 续表4 continued

单位：万美元（USD 10000）

国 别（地区）	Country (territory)	2021 进出口总额 Total	2021 出口总额 Exports	2021 进口总额 Imports	2022 进出口总额 Total	2022 出口总额 Exports	2022 进口总额 Imports
洪都拉斯	Honduras	2201	2185	16	2630	2427	203
牙买加	Jamaica	2345	2345		2369	2369	
马提尼克	Matinik	48	48		99	99	
墨西哥	Mexico	283955	241425	42529	231361	198383	32978
蒙特塞拉特	Montserrat	0.01	0.01				
尼加拉瓜	Nicaragua	1183	1160	22	1144	1097	47
巴拿马	Panama	13584	11082	2502	38822	14905	23917
巴拉圭	Paraguay	3945	3836	109	3978	3837	141
秘 鲁	Peru	331831	38710	293121	318902	47740	271162
波多黎各	Puerto Rico	2696	2696	0.2	2775	2628	148
圣卢西亚	Saint Lucia	99	99		114	114	
圣马丁岛	Saint Martin Island	10	10		22	22	
圣文格林纳	Saint Article Greener	39	39		60	60	
萨尔瓦多	El Salvador	2101	2084	17	3221	3188	33
苏里南	Surinam	360	360		474	474	
特立—巴哥	Trinidad and Tobago	2562	834	1728	1111	1111	
特克—凯科	Turks &Caicos Is.	21	21		23	23	
乌拉圭	Uruguay	25590	8058	17532	31420	7698	23722
委内瑞拉	Venezuela	4709	4705	4	8598	8573	25
英属维尔京群岛	Virgin Is. (E)	3	3		6	6	
圣其茨尼维	St. Kitts-Nevis	25	25		20	20	
圣皮埃尔和密克隆	St. Pierre and Miquelon	0.003	0.003				
荷属安第列斯群岛	Antilles Is. (N)	11	11		45	45	
拉丁美洲其他	Other of Latin America	21	21		211	211	
北美洲	**North America**	**1583598**	**1160695**	**422903**	**1725660**	**1336816**	**388844**
加拿大	Canada	190935	116118	74817	198769	120295	78474
美 国	United States	1392650	1044565	348085	1526874	1216504	310370
格陵兰	Greenland	0.2	0.2		1	1	
百慕大	Bermuda Is.	12	12		16	16	
北美洲其他	Other of North America	0.01	0.01				
大洋洲	**Oceanic**	**435918**	**124878**	**311040**	**384436**	**157066**	**227370**
澳大利亚	Australia	371167.4	105459.8	265708	324193	134242	189951
库克群岛	Cook Islands	10	10		5	5	
斐 济	Fiji	860	858	1	1015	1015	
瑙 鲁	Nauru	0.01	0.01		1	1	
新喀里多尼	New Karidoni	386	386		514	514	
瓦努阿图	Vanuatu	138	136	2	169	164	5
新西兰	New Zealand	60678	15352	45326	54654	17240	37414
巴布亚新几内亚	Papua New Guinea	1328	1325	3	2185	2185	
所罗门群岛	Solomon Is.	203	202	1	199	199	
汤 加	Tonga	28	28		75	75	
萨摩亚	Samoa	189	189		231	231	
基里巴斯	Kiribati	50	50		77	77	
密克罗尼西	Micronesia	27	27		23	23	
马绍尔群岛	Marshall Island	80	80		114	114	
贝劳共和国	Palau	63	63		65	65	
法属波利尼西亚	French Polynesia	482	482		528	528	
瓦利斯和浮图纳	Wallis and Fortuna	48	48		13	13	

17—6 进出口商品贸易方式总值（2022年）
Total Value of Import and Export Trade Way (2022)

单位：万美元（USD 10000）

指 标	Item	进出口 Imports & Exports		出 口 Exports		进 口 Imports	
		金额 Value	增速(%) Growth (%)	金额 Value	增速(%) Growth (%)	金额 Value	增速(%) Growth (%)
总 计	**Total**	**11315512**	**5.74**	**7141206**	**12.68**	**4174306**	**-4.33**
一般贸易	General Trade	8252606	5.90	5521267	13.40	2731338	-6.58
国家间、国际组织间无偿援助和赠送的物资	Grants and Gifts of Materials Between Countries and International Organizations	70	-74.91	70	-74.91		
其他捐赠物资	Other Donated Materials	4	-86.67	4	-86.67		
加工贸易	Processing Trade	1834564	-6.33	1109691	-9.64	724873	-0.76
来料加工装配贸易	Assembly Processing Trade	153706	-1.14	70194	3.08	83512	-4.42
进料加工贸易	Processing With Imported Trade	1680858	-6.78	1039497	-10.39	641361	-0.26
加工贸易进口设备	Processing Trade Import Equipment	861	-63.09			861	-63.09
对外承包工程出口货物	Exports Contracted Projects	25929	-2.83	25929	-2.83		
租赁贸易	Leasing Trade	261	-93.47	261	-93.47		
外商投资企业作为投资进口的设备、物品	Foreign-invested Enterprises as the Import Investment of Equipment, Goods	1976	13.40			1976	13.40
出料加工	Material Processing	1534	-42.60	510	-37.01	1024	-45.03
易货贸易	Barter Trade	6	-99.92	2	-99.97	4	
保税物流	Bonded Logistics	1037671	57.84	428766	145.93	608906	26.04
海关特殊监管区域进口设备	Import Equipment from Special Areas Under Customs Supervision	84287	-58.71			84287	-58.71
其他贸易	Other Trade	75743	77.74	54706	106.19	21036	30.81

17—7 外国和港澳台地区直接投资（按行业）（2022年）
Foreign and Hong Kong, Macao and Taiwan Direct Investment (by Industry) (2022)

指　　标	Item	新签协议 Newly Signed Agreement 合同数（个） Number of Contracts (unit)	投资额（万美元） Investment (USD 10000)	实际投资合计（万美元） Total Actual Investment (USD 10000)	期末实有企业数（个） Number of Enterprises at the End of the Period (unit)	#本期新增企业 Newly Increased In this Period
总　　计	**Total**	**475**	**429034**	**215507**	**8255**	**628**
按国民经济行业分	**Grouped by Sector**					
农林牧渔业	Farming, Forestry, Animal Husbandry and Fishery	3	4689	9661	74	2
采矿业	Mining and Quarrying		316		23	
制造业	Manufacturing	121	135222	107520	1771	120
电力、热力、燃气及水的生产和供应业	Production and Supply of Electricity, Heat, Gas and Water	20	26658	4731	298	23
建筑业	Construction	3	9247		110	5
批发和零售业	Wholesale and Retail Trade	67	24387	3495	2361	120
交通运输、仓储及邮政业	Transportation, Storage and Postal Services	6	2546	3206	112	15
住宿和餐饮业	Accommodation and Catering Trade	5	126	30	693	82
信息传输、软件和信息技术服务业	Information Transmission, Software and Information Technology Services	21	12411	4941	557	32
金融业	Banking	3	-10	57	290	5
房地产业	Real Estate Trade	8	3835	8577	278	17
租赁和商务服务业	Leasing and Commercial Services	83	113622	7878	685	74
科学研究和技术服务业	Scientific Research and Technical Services	121	94704	64614	783	118
水利、环境和公共设施管理业	Water Conservancy, Environmental and Public Facilities Management	1	993	482	38	3
居民服务、修理和其他服务业	Residents Service, Repair and Other Services	2	67	315	82	1
教　育	Education				14	
卫生、社会工作	Health and Social Work	4	31		13	3
文化、体育和娱乐业	Culture, Sports and Entertainment	7	190		72	8
其他行业	Others				1	

17—8 外国和港澳台地区直接投资（按国别和地区）（2022年）

Direct Investment of Foreign Countries and Hong Kong, Macao and Taiwan by Countries and Regions (2022)

指标	Item	新签协议 Newly Signed Agreement 合同数（个） Number of Contracts (unit)	新签协议 投资额（万美元） Investment (USD 10000)	实际投资合计（万美元） Total Actual Investment (USD 10000)
合计	**Total**	**475**	**429034**	**215507**
中国香港	Hong Kong	181	274854	150158
印度	India			
印度尼西亚	Indonesia	1	266	
伊朗	Iran	3	86	
伊拉克	Iraq	1	500	
日本	Japan	14	3839	720
约旦	Jordan	1	75	
中国澳门	Macao	6	2713	
马来西亚	Malaysia	2	317	
尼泊尔	Nepal			
阿曼	Oman		44000	
巴基斯坦	Pakistan	7	632	
新加坡	Singapore	14	27906	37610
韩国	Republic of Korea	28	3918	556
叙利亚	Syria			
泰国	Thailand			
土耳其	Turkey	1	256	50
阿联酋	The United Arab Emirates			
也门共和国	Arab Republic of Yemen	4	583	
越南	VietNam	3	89	100
中国台湾	Taiwan	105	21144	3988
土库曼斯坦	Turkmenistan	2	107	
博茨瓦纳	Botswana		3	
喀麦隆	Cameroon			
刚果	The Congo	1	500	
埃及	Egypt	1	573	
赤道几内亚	Equatorial Guinea			
埃塞俄比亚	Ethiopia			
加纳	Ghana	3	122	
利比亚	Libya	1	500	
马达加斯加	Madagascar			
毛里求斯	Mauritius			
摩洛哥	Morocco			
尼日利亚	Nigeria	3	34	
卢旺达	Rwanda			
塞舌尔	Seychelles		600	35

17—8 续表 continued

指 标	Item	新签协议 Newly Signed Agreement 合同数（个）Number of Contracts (unit)	投资额（万美元）Investment (USD 10000)	实际投资合计（万美元）Total Actual Investment (USD 10000)
南 非	South Africa			
苏 丹	Sudan	3	50	
坦桑尼亚	Tanzania		8	
刚果(金)	The Democratic Republic of Congo	1	1000	
津巴布韦	Zimbabwe	1	9	
比利时	Belgium			
丹 麦	Denmark	2	1023	215
英 国	United Kingdom	5	2896	777
德 国	Germany	8	3755	2755
法 国	France	2	2951	386
爱尔兰	Ireland		377	9661
意大利	Italy		649	618
荷 兰	Netherlands	1	2004	674
西班牙	Spain	1	1	51
奥地利	Austria			
芬兰	Finland		69	
瑞 士	Switzerland		556	
亚美尼亚	Armenia			
阿塞拜疆	Azerbaijan	1	500	
白俄罗斯	Belarus	1	250	
俄罗斯	Russia	4	582	
乌克兰	Ukraine	2	29	
捷克共和国	Czech			27
阿根廷	Argentina		17	
伯利兹	Belize			50
巴 西	Brazil			400
开曼群岛	Cayman Islands	1	165	503
多米尼加共和国	Dominica.	1	40	9
英属维尔京群岛	Virgin	2	-4193	891
拉丁美洲其他	Other of Latin America			
加拿大	Canada	6	2539	43
美 国	United States	37	14891	2864
百慕大	Bermuda Is.			
澳大利亚	Australia	10	1887	92
斐济	Fiji	1	3796	
新西兰	New Zealand			
萨摩亚	Samoa	3	9566	2274
大洋洲其他	Other of Oceanic			

17—9 按国别（地区）对外投资
According to the Country (region) of Foreign Investment

国 别（地区）	Country (region)	新批境外企业(机构)数（个）A new Batch of Foreign Enterprises (institutions) (unit)		协议对外投资额（万美元）Foreign Investment Agreement（USD 10000）		实际对外投资额（万美元）Actual Foreign Investment（USD 10000）	
		2021	2022	2021	2022	2021	2022
合 计	**Total**	**98**	**115**	**169127**	**172453**	**135052**	**160912**
亚 洲	**Asia**	**55**	**77**	**126641**	**98903**	**100508**	**108339**
印度尼西亚	Indonesia	3	4	3400	2369	2835	17654
中国香港	Hong Kong	14	24	32610	11280	65772	46032
中国台湾	Taiwan		1		790		
泰 国	Thailand	2	4	1194	3737	1079	1109
缅 甸	Myanmar	11	1	31567	300	17	14
老 挝	Laos		1		1	1322	5336
马来西亚	Malaysia	1	2	100	550	138	346
日 本	Japan	3	4	260	467	86	154
韩 国	Republic of Korea	3	6	450	2264	173	615
印 度	India		2		4000	284	290
越 南	Viet Nam	2	3	2310	16589	746	1096
柬埔寨	Cambodia	1	1	25197	25800	621	329
巴基斯坦	Pakistan	1					109
菲律宾	The Philippines	2	2	999	299		
吉尔吉斯斯坦	Kirghiz Tanzania						
乌兹别克斯坦	Uzbekistan		2		12343	4500	6655
以色列	Israel						
新加坡	Singapore	7	10	12219	12585	22934	26808
沙特阿拉伯	Saudi Arabia						
哈萨克斯坦	Kazakhstan	4	3	16335	1625		
尼泊尔	Nepal	1					
土耳其	Turkey		1		3000		1414
阿联酋	The United Arab Emirates		2		560		255
蒙古	Mongolia		1		100		63
孟加拉国	Bangladesh		1		200		60
中国澳门	Macao		2		44		
非 洲	**Africa**	**2**	**5**	**579**	**6505**	**536**	**2630**
津巴布韦	Zimbabwe						
赞比亚	Zambia	1	1	102	200		
安哥拉	Angola						30
尼日利亚	Nigeria						
莫桑比克	Mozambique						
坦桑尼亚	Tanzania					1	
埃塞俄比亚	Ethiopia					37	33

17—9 续表 continued

国 别（地区）	Country (region)	新批境外企业(机构)数（个） A new Batch of Foreign Enterprises (institutions) (unit)		协议对外投资额（万美元） Foreign Investment Agreement (USD 10000)		实际对外投资额（万美元） Actual Foreign Investment (USD 10000)	
		2021	2022	2021	2022	2021	2022
多 哥	Togo					40	
喀麦隆	Cameroon						
南 非	South Africa	1		400	3000	402	819
刚果（金）	Fresh Fruit (gold)					5	
摩洛哥	Morocco			77	5	51	5
埃及	Egypt		1		100		
几内亚	Guinea		1		3000		1593
加纳	Ghana		2		200		
塞舌尔	Seychelles						150
欧 洲	**Europe**	**8**	**9**	**9769**	**17089**	**10251**	**24689**
英 国	United Kingdom				2235	960	801
德 国	Germany	1	2	4048	14323	4790	5530
法 国	France	2		3736	56	30	28
意大利	Italy					1942	1214
荷 兰	Netherlands		1				
俄罗斯	Russia		1	1493		1380	
匈牙利	Hungary						
爱尔兰	Ireland					7	16
卢森堡	Luxembourg	1		40		1130	17000
西班牙	Spain	2	3	341	350		
乌克兰	Ukraine	1		100		1	6
瑞 士	Switzerland	1		11		11	
比利时	Belgium		1		31		
塞尔维亚	Serbia		1		94		94
拉丁美洲	**Latin America**	**22**	**12**	**10202**	**18689**	**20523**	**9725**
巴 西	Brazil	6	1	2129	3000	3592	2494
格林纳达	Grenada						
墨西哥	Mexico		1	100	3000	1346	4487
秘 鲁	Peru					8	7
哥伦比亚	Colombia	4		2824			
玻利维亚	Bolivia	1	1				
多米尼加	Dominican Republic					1	
开曼群岛	Cayman Islands	1	3	1	8414	12271	2591
智 利	Chile	10	3	5148	1812	2906	
英属维尔京群岛	Virgin Is. (E)		1		15	400	
厄瓜多尔	Ecuador		2		2448		146
北美洲	**North America**	**5**	**9**	**1625**	**27904**	**3232**	**13483**
美 国	United States	4	8	1620	22404	3209	13462
加拿大	Canada	1	1	5	5500	23	21
大洋洲	**Oceanic**	**6**	**3**	**20311**	**3363**	**2**	**2046**
澳大利亚	Australia	6	3	20311	3363	2	2046

17—10 按国别（地区）对外承包工程和劳务合作
According to the Country (region) of Foreign Contracted Projects and Labor Service Cooperation

国 别（地区）	Country (region)	承包工程（万美元） Contracted Projects（USD 10000）				劳务合作（人） Labor Service Cooperation (person)			
		新签合同额 New Signing Stood		完成营业额 Complete Turnover		外派劳务人数 Field Services Number		年末在外人数 Out at the End of the Number	
		2021	2022	2021	2022	2021	2022	2021	2022
合 计	**Total**	**443690**	**545602**	**238506**	**239225**	**581**	**1154**	**3732**	**2206**
亚 洲	**Asia**	**171465**	**414645**	**157726**	**138324**	**45**	**282**	**2186**	**672**
阿 曼	Oman	237	954	1989	2475				
乌兹别克斯坦	Uzbekistan	16933	15810	7643	10046				
老 挝	Laos	884	3100	3192	3616		4		4
新加坡	Singapore	62	17774	10201	16341	14	0	49	36
巴基斯坦	Pakistan	25614	17398	23392	27496		19		19
科威特	Kuwait			3197				2	2
中国香港	Hong Kong		10820		2523		2		2
中国台湾	Taiwan			645					
尼泊尔	Nepal	6520	78	141	380				
蒙 古	Mongolia	25690	145884	6661	7488				
越 南	Viet Nam	22095	76569	36996	19276				
泰 国	Thailand		691	200	283				
印 度	India		0	517	299				
沙特阿拉伯	Saudi Arabia	32748	9835	4068	5273			626	
日 本	Japan					23	159	322	314
马来西亚	Malaysia			1546	495			657	
土耳其	Turkey	226		10315	4363			2	
孟加拉国	Bangladesh	5115	2242	15959	3624				
印度尼西亚	Indonesia	34384	66883	19432	14993		60	362	102
伊 朗	Iran								
中国澳门	Macao								
斯里兰卡	Sri Lanka			56	25				
柬埔寨	Cambodia	250	9850	5080	9090				
缅 甸	Myanmar					8	38	116	154
菲律宾	The Philippines		12797	4082	882				
文 莱	Brunei								
阿联酋	United Arab Emirates	705		42				6	
伊拉克	Iraq				447				
马尔代夫	Maldives						0	44	39
哈萨克斯坦	Kazakhstan		7200	2373	8396				
阿联酋	The United Arab Emirates		16761		514				
非 洲	**Africa**	**242187**	**77700**	**41120**	**58377**	**497**	**835**	**964**	**1464**
埃 及	Egypt					158	110	261	215
喀麦隆	Cameroon			264			52		52
埃塞俄比亚	Ethiopia	15966	18622	6232	6035				
赞比亚	Zambia	19146	5158	4523	4827		28		28
马拉维	Malawi	965	6	1456	293				
科特迪瓦	Cote D'ivoire		16610	88	222				
吉布提	Djibouti			39					
莫桑比克	Mozambique	1298	0	955	57				
阿尔及利亚	Algeria	29583		7533	12439	8	273	70	302
坦桑尼亚	Tanzania	628	564		699				
乌干达	Uganda				94				
突尼斯	Tunisia			74					
毛里塔尼亚	Mauritania								

17—10 续表 continued

国 别（地区）	Country (region)	承包工程（万美元） Contracted Projects（USD 10000）				劳务合作（人） Labor Service Cooperation (person)			
		新签合同额 New Signing Stood		完成营业额 Complete Turnover		外派劳务人数 Field Services Number		年末在外人数 Out at the End of the Number	
		2021	2022	2021	2022	2021	2022	2021	2022
几内亚	Guinea	99315		2989	17762	26	22	26	45
几内亚（比绍）	Guineabissau								
肯尼亚	Kenya								
加 纳	Ghana		810	105	547	11	8	11	12
安哥拉	Angola	74433	30165	7368	7811			1	1
赤道几内亚	Equatorial Guinea							7	
苏 丹	Sudan					2	14	2	16
马达加斯加	Madagascar			63				12	
刚果(布)	Fresh Fruit (cloth)			540	251				
刚果(金)	Fresh Fruit (gold)		5600	6564	5055	162	270	358	628
津巴布韦	Zimbabwe	74	166	856	401		3		3
塞拉利昂	Sierra Leone			27		3		3	3
尼日利亚	Nigeria	779		688	658	126	35	209	142
加 蓬	Gabon								
布基纳法索	Burkina Faso			92					
卢旺达	Rwanda								
毛里求斯	Mauritius			417	106			2	
利比里亚	Liberia				4				
贝 宁	Benin						15	1	14
博茨瓦纳	Botswana			77	44				
塞内加尔	Senegal					1	5	1	3
多 哥	Togo								
圣多美和普林西比	St and More Spring			169					
南苏丹	South Sudan				1072				
欧 洲	**Europe**	**16245**	**34048**	**22139**	**14039**				
俄罗斯联邦	Russia				286				
白俄罗斯	Byelorussia			2522					
英 国	United Kingdom								
黑 山	Montenegro								
塞尔维亚	Serbia		13288	600	1337				
匈牙利	Hungary			3939	573				
波 兰	Poland	16242	20760	15077	11843				
拉丁美洲	**Latin America**	**13796**	**16452**	**15334**	**19432**	**39**	**37**	**572**	**31**
委内瑞拉	Venezuela								
巴巴多斯	Barbados							1	
古 巴	Cuba								
玻利维亚	Bolivia		5800		531				
巴 西	Brazil								
巴拿马	Panama					8	2	540	1
格林纳达	Grenada								
厄瓜多尔	Ecuador			1811	2110	31	35	31	30
哥斯达黎加	Costa Rica		528	421	47				
智 利	Chile		4014		4014				
秘 鲁	Peru	13796	2713	13102	12591				
安提瓜和巴布达	Antigua and Barbuda				99				
墨西哥	Mexico		398		40				
北美洲	**North America**			**1200**	**5832**				
美 国	United States			1200	5832				
大洋洲	**Oceanic**		**2757**	**987**	**3221**				**39**
西萨摩亚	Western Samoa								
澳大利亚	Australia		2757	960	3221				
巴布亚新几内亚	Papua New Guinea								39
萨摩亚	Samoa			27					

17—11　外商投资企业年末企业数、投资总额及注册资本（2022年）
Number, Investment and Registered Capital of Foreign-funded Enterprises (2022)

项　目	Item	投资总额（万美元）Total Investment (USD 10000)	注册资本（万美元）Registered Capital (USD 10000)	#外　方 Capital Invested by Foreign Partner
按投资方式分	**Grouped by Type of Investment**			
#中外合资	Joint Ventures Enterprises	2660099	1514223	783444
中外合作	Cooperative Operation Enterprises	123965	42520	26531
外资企业	Foreign Investment Share Enterprises	459616	162956	157387
外商投资股份制	Foreign Invested Shareholding Enterprises	325609	273611	73250
按国民经济行业分	**Grouped by Sector**			
农林牧渔业	Farming, Forestry, Animal Husbandry and Fishery	235826	100316	82495
采矿业	Mining and Quarrying	20034	18172	10666
制造业	Manufacturing	4560603	2650432	1246055
热力、燃气及水的生产和供应业	Production and Supply of Electricity, Heat, Gas and Water	1046319	340127	230836
建筑业	Construction	73025	52491	37202
批发和零售业	Wholesale and Retail Trade	434010	365019	300131
交通运输、仓储及邮政业	Transportation, Storage and Postal Services	132231	77268	49862
住宿和餐饮业	Accommodation and Catering Trade	96236	91165	50165
信息传输、软件和信息技术服务业	Information Transmission, Software and Information Technology Services	160913	140538	126078
金融业	Banking	161084	193161	119829
房地产业	Real Estate Trade	388725	271473	178695
租赁和商务服务业	Leasing and Commercial Services	473933	499729	233753
科学研究和技术服务业	Scientific Research and Technical Services	2117379	1019024	825674
水利、环境和公共设施管理业	Water Conservancy, Environmental and Public Facilities Management	70147	27233	20032
居民服务、修理和其他服务业	Residents Service, Repair and Other Services	5366	16528	11466
教　育	Education	4223	1582	898
卫生、社会工作	Health and Social Work	20384	6522	4775
文化、体育和娱乐业	Culture, Sports and Entertainment	70878	54143	48116

17—12 各市外商投资企业年末企业数、投资总额及注册资本（2022年）

Number, Investment and Registered Capital of Foreign-funded Enterprises by Region (2022)

地 区	Region	企业数（个） Number of Registered Enterprises (unit)	投资总额（万美元） Total Investment (USD 10000)	注册资本（万美元） Registered Capital (USD 10000)	#外方 Capital Invested by Foreign Partner
总计	**Total**	**8091**	**8285664**	**4905636**	**2924020**
合肥市	Hefei	2804	4225898	2616028	1447545
淮北市	Huaibei	134	136092	64609	34958
亳州市	Bozhou	155	91928	51163	36210
宿州市	Suzhou	358	121402	50030	39702
蚌埠市	Bengbu	436	498967	273926	213855
阜阳市	Fuyang	254	178503	80620	53997
淮南市	Huainan	271	302397	132704	92541
滁州市	Chuzhou	565	383457	237454	188916
六安市	Luan	309	281264	118551	95384
马鞍山市	Maanshan	492	278475	140723	92232
芜湖市	Wuhu	814	871138	659297	330740
宣城市	Xuancheng	409	320781	171867	114136
铜陵市	Tongling	201	217159	102665	44789
池州市	Chizhou	224	128278	52643	39516
安庆市	Anqing	380	171096	104189	65157
黄山市	Huangshan	285	78829	49166	34343

17—13 各市商品进出口总额
Import and Export Commodities by Region

地区	Region	2021 进出口总额（万美元 USD10000） Total	出口总额 Exports	进口总额 Imports	2022 进出口总额（万美元 USD10000） Total	出口总额 Exports	进口总额 Imports
总计	**Total**	**10700787**	**6337476**	**4363312**	**11315512**	7141206	4174306
合肥市	Hefei	5145540	3140945	2004596	5427473	3452013	1975460
淮北市	Huaibei	179189	161872	17317	143949	129920	14030
亳州市	Bozhou	64701	48176	16525	65420	52903	12517
宿州市	Suzhou	166728	151814	14914	181105	168815	12290
蚌埠市	Bengbu	272360	130632	141727	300597	182134	118463
阜阳市	Fuyang	214028	172189	41839	203554	175378	28176
淮南市	Huainan	100933	94080	6853	119855	116368	3487
滁州市	Chuzhou	601461	497448	104013	626431	518934	107497
六安市	Luan	152207	139202	13005	152084	141626	10458
马鞍山市	Maanshan	726031	308866	417165	666222	315366	350856
芜湖市	Wuhu	1152008	757754	394254	1360779	946752	414027
宣城市	Xuancheng	282843	260578	22265	333831	306767	27063
铜陵市	Tongling	1082101	107742	974358	990893	112824	878069
池州市	Chizhou	143916	34366	109551	172667	49627	123039
安庆市	Anqing	250545	184819	65726	390594	308197	82397
黄山市	Huangshan	166196	146993	19203	180058	163581	16477

17—14 各市外商直接投资
Foreign Direct Investment by Region

地区	Region	项目（个） Number of Projects (unit) 2021	2022	合同外资额（万美元） Contract Value (USD 10000) 2021	2022	实际利用外资额（万美元） Used Value (USD 10000) 2021	2022
总计	**Total**	**475**	**475**	**688168**	**429034**	**1929728**	**215507**
合肥市	Hefei	175	140	394769	152222	374800	120517
淮北市	Huaibei	6	6	10187	12341	34825	4184
亳州市	Bozhou	7	15	7530	7044	51495	1610
宿州市	Suzhou	12	11	3259	10603	107710	2008
蚌埠市	Bengbu	26	12	44411	6239	124031	1972
阜阳市	Fuyang	10	18	7114	26042	46304	12937
淮南市	Huainan	10	10	4553	12013	40179	3222
滁州市	Chuzhou	27	28	41234	27047	170906	16266
六安市	Luan	24	20	18795	56750	67883	1596
马鞍山市	Maanshan	32	34	27291	19884	293661	14362
芜湖市	Wuhu	48	79	37329	39396	319657	23917
宣城市	Xuancheng	20	28	45913	19881	138615	6078
铜陵市	Tongling	9	8	2711	5792	45993	862
池州市	Chizhou	14	15	9708	8282	49341	1544
安庆市	Anqing	23	38	17288	16069	38021	4015
黄山市	Huangshan	32	13	16077	9429	26307	417

17—15 各市外国和港澳台地区直接投资（2022年）
Direct Investment of Foreign Countries, Hong Kong, Macao and Taiwan by Sector by Region (2022)

地 区	Region	新签协议 Newly Signed Agreement 合同数（个）Number of Contracts (unit)	投资额（万美元）Investment (USD 10000)	实际投资合计（万美元）Total Actual Investment (USD 10000)	期末实有企业数（个）Number of Enterprises at the End of the Period (unit)	#本期新增企业 Newly Increased In this Period
总 计	**Total**	**475**	**429034**	**215507**	**8091**	**626**
合肥市	Hefei	140	152222	120517	2804	230
淮北市	Huaibei	6	12341	4184	134	10
亳州市	Bozhou	15	7044	1610	155	13
宿州市	Suzhou	11	10603	2008	358	15
蚌埠市	Bengbu	12	6239	1972	436	21
阜阳市	Fuyang	18	26042	12937	254	23
淮南市	Huainan	10	12013	3222	271	18
滁州市	Chuzhou	28	27047	16266	565	38
六安市	Luan	20	56750	1596	309	24
马鞍山市	Maanshan	34	19884	14362	492	34
芜湖市	Wuhu	79	39396	23917	814	77
宣城市	Xuancheng	28	19881	6078	409	33
铜陵市	Tongling	8	5792	862	201	11
池州市	Chizhou	15	8282	1544	224	18
安庆市	Anqing	38	16069	4015	380	46
黄山市	Huangshan	13	9429	417	285	15

主要统计指标解释

进出口总额

指实际进出我国国境的货物总金额。包括对外贸易实际进出口货物，来料加工装配进出口货物，国家间、联合国及国际组织无偿援助物资和赠送品，华侨、港澳台同胞和外籍华人捐赠品，租赁期满归承租人所有的租赁货物，进料加工进出口货物，边境地方贸易及边境地区小额贸易进出口货物（边民互市贸易除外），中外合资企业、中外合作经营企业、外商独资经营企业进出口货物和公用物品，到、离岸价格在规定限额以上的进出口货样和广告品（无商业价值、无使用价值和免费提供出口的除外），从保税仓库提取在中国境内销售的进口货物，以及其他进出口货物。进出口总额用以观察一个国家在对外贸易方面的总规模。我国规定出口货物按离岸价格统计，进口货物按到岸价格统计。

商品经营单位所在地进、出口额

指所在地海关注册登记的有进出口经营权的企业实际进、出口额。

商品目的地进口额和商品货源地出口额

目的地进口额是指进口货物的消费、使用或最终抵运地的实际进口额；货源地出口额是指出口货物的产地或原始发货地的实际出口额。

利用外资

指我国各级政府、部门、企业和其他经济组织通过对外借款、吸收外商直接投资以及用其他方式筹措的境外现汇、设备、技术等。

对外借款

是我国利用外资的重要部分。指通过对外正式签订借款协议，从境外筹措的资金，包括外国政府贷款、国际金融组织贷款、外国银行商业贷款、出口信贷以及对外发行债券等。1996 年及以前还包括对外发行股票。

外商直接投资

指外国企业和经济组织或个人（包括华侨、港澳台胞以及我国在境外注册的企业）按我国有关政策、法规，用现汇、实物、技术等在我国境内开办外商独资企业、与我国境内的企业或经济组织共同举办中外合资经营企业、合作经营企业或合作开发资源的投资（包括外商投资收益的再投资），以及经政府有关部门批准的项目投资总额内企业从境外借入的资金。

对外承包工程

指各对外承包公司以招标议标承包方式承揽的下列业务：⑴承包国外工程建设项目，⑵承包我国对外经援项目，⑶承包我国驻外机构的工程建设项目，⑷承包我国境内利用外资进行建设的工程项目，⑸与外国承包公司合营或联合承包工程项目时我国公司分包部分，⑹对外承包兼营的房屋开发业务。对外承包工程的营业额是以货币表现的本期内完成的对外承包工程的工作量，包括以前年度签订的合同和本年度新签订的合同在报告期内完成的工作量。

对外劳务合作

指以收取工资的形式向业主或承包商提供技术和劳动服务的活动。我国对外承包公司在境外开办的合营企业，中国公司同时又提供劳务的，其劳务部分也纳入劳务合作统计。劳务合作营业额按报告期内向雇主提交的结算数(包括工资、加班费和奖金等）统计。

Explanatory Notes for Major Statistical Indicators

Total Imports and Exports at Customs

refer to the value of commodities imported into and exported from the boundary of China. They include the actual imports and exports through foreign trade, imported and exported goods under the processing and assembling trades and materials, supplies and gifts as aid given gratis between governments and by the United Nations and other international organizations, and contributions donated by overseas Chinese, compatriots in Hong Kong and Macao and Chinese with foreign citizenship, leasing commodities owned by tenant at the expiration of leasing period, the imported and exported commodities processed with imported materials, commodities trading in border areas (excluding mutual exchange goods), the imported and exported commodities and articles for public use of the Sino-foreign joint ventures, cooperative enterprises and ventures exclusively with foreign own investment. Also included are import or export of samples and advertising goods for whose CIF or FOB value are beyond the permitted ceiling (excluding goods of no trading or use value and free commodities for export), imported goods sold in China from bonded warehouses and other imported or exported goods. The indicator of the total imports and exports at customs can be used to observe the total size of external trade in a country. In accordance with the stipulation of the Chinese government, imports are calculated at CIF, while exports are calculated at FOB.

Import Export Value by Location of China's Foreign Trade Managing Units

refers to actual value of imports and exports carried out by corporations which have been registered by the local customhouse and are vested with right to run import export business.

Import Value of Commodities by the Places of their Destination and Export Value of Commodities by the Places of their Origin in China

The former indicator refers to the value of import commodities of the places of their consumption, utilization or the places of their final destination. The latter indicator refers to the value of export commodities of the places of their origin or the places of the commodities dispatched.

Utilization of Foreign Capital

refers to remittance, equipment and technology financed from abroad, by loans, foreign direct investment and other forms undertaken by the Chinese governments at all levels, by various departments, enterprises and other economic units.

Foreign Borrowings

an important part of China's utilization of foreign capital, it refer to funds borrowed from abroad through formal signing of borrowing agreements with foreign institutions, including loans of foreign governments, loans of international financial institutions, commercial loans of foreign banks, export credit, and funds raised by Chinese bonds (and shares before 1996) issued abroad.

Direct Investment by Foreign Entrepreneurs

refers to the investments inside China by foreign enterprises and economic organizations or individuals (including overseas Chinese, compatriots from Hong Kong and Macao, and Chinese enterprises registered abroad), following the relevant policies and laws of China, for the establishment of ventures exclusively with foreign own investment, Sino-foreign joint ventures and cooperative enterprises or for co-operative exploration of resources with enterprises or economic organizations in China. It includes the re investment of the foreign entrepreneurs with the profits gained from the investment and the funds that enterprises borrow from abroad in the total investment of projects which are approved by the relevant department of the government.

Contracted Projects with Foreign Countries

refer to projects undertaken by Chinese contractors (project contracting companies) through bidding process. They include: (1)overseas civil engineering construction projects financed by foreign investors; (2)overseas projects financed by the Chinese government through its foreign aid programs; (3)construction projects of Chinese diplomatic missions, trade offices and other institutions stationed abroad; (4)construction projects in China financed by foreign investment; (5)sub-contracted projects to be taken by Chinese contractors through a joint umbrella project with foreign contractor(s); (6)housing development projects. The business income from international contracted projects is the work volume of contracted projects completed during the reference period, expressed in monetary terms, including completed work on projects signed in previous years.

Service Cooperation with Foreign Countries

refers to the activities of providing technology and labour services to employers or contractors in the forms of receiving salaries and wages. Labour services providing by contractual joint ventures of Chine statistics of service co operation with foreign countries. The business income of labour service co operation is the income in the form of wages and salaries, overtime pay, bonuses and other remuneration received from the employers during the reference period.

第十八篇

Chapter 18

旅游

TOURISM

简要说明

一、旅游业发展情况。入境国际旅游(外国人、华侨、港澳同胞和台湾同胞)人数、不同经济类型的涉外饭店数量及规模情况的资料来源于省文化和旅游厅。

二、全省及各市国内旅游资料，是省文化和旅游厅根据文化和旅游部的抽样调查方案和工作要求，组织调查取得。

Brief Introduction

I. Development of tourism. The data on the number of inbound international tourists (foreigners, overseas Chinese, compatriots from Hong Kong, Macao and Taiwan) and the number and scale of foreign-related hotels of different economic types come from the provincial Department of Culture and Tourism.

II. Domestic tourism data of the province and municipalities are obtained by the provincial Department of Culture and Tourism according to the sampling survey plan and work requirements of the Ministry of Culture and Tourism.

18—1　旅游事业发展
Development of Tourism

指　　标	Item	2010	2015	2020	2021	2022
入境旅游人数　（人次）	Total Number of International Tourists Inbound (person-time)	1984174	4446289	692652	115134	48003
外 国 人	Foreigners	1173988	2591842	440040	60905	27001
港澳和台湾同胞	Compatriots from Hong Kong, Macao and Taiwan	810186	1854447	252612	54229	21002
国内旅游人数 （万人次）	Total Number of Domestic Tourists (10000 person-time)	15349	44404	47046	58066	49601
旅游收入	Income of Tourism					
国际旅游外汇收入(万美元)	Foreign Exchange Earnings (USD 10000)	82025.2	226287.5	27465.8	4531.7	2247.6
国内旅游收入 （亿元）	Earnings from Domestic Tourism (100 million yuan)	1094.8	3980.5	4221.5	5578.3	4640.2
旅游部门基本情况	**Basic Statement of Tourism Departments**					
旅游星级宾馆　（个）	Tourist Hotels With Star Class (unit)	453	441	262	242	217
#五星级	Five Star Class	14	26	30	27	23
四星级	Four Star Class	88	128	110	106	102
三星级	Three Star Class	182	214	110	101	87
二星级	Two Star Class	166	72	12	8	5
旅游涉外或星级宾馆	Tourist Hotels Concerning Foreign Affairs or With Star Class					
客　房　　（间）	Number of Rooms (unit)	44982	50546	39373	38740	34488
床　位　　（张）	Number of Beds (unit)	81867	87708	65660	64149	209752
客房出租率　（%）	Room Occupancy (%)	59.27	49.00	37.13	44.54	39.11
经营情况	Business Status					
营业收入　（亿元）	Business Income (100 million yuan)	50.38	50.89	32.04	35.64	35.27
利润总额　（万元）	Total Profits (10000 yuan)	21964.0	-24339.9	-41619.1	-30144.7	-29695.7

18—2 各市旅行社数
Number of Travel Agencies by Region

单位：个（unit）

地 区	Region	2018	2019	2020	2021	2022
总 计	**Total**	**1128**	**1193**	**1157**	**1185**	**1626**
合肥市	Hefei	239	255	252	254	435
淮北市	Huaibei	28	34	31	32	33
亳州市	Bozhou	25	25	26	27	36
宿州市	Suzhou	33	40	39	41	40
蚌埠市	Bengbu	45	47	46	45	68
阜阳市	Fuyang	42	42	41	49	66
淮南市	Huainan	61	65	62	62	64
滁州市	Chuzhou	52	55	55	66	75
六安市	Luan	52	45	47	46	72
马鞍山市	Maanshan	56	66	66	67	75
芜湖市	Wuhu	64	69	73	77	105
宣城市	Xuancheng	69	76	76	71	100
铜陵市	Tongling	28	31	30	29	40
池州市	Chizhou	71	69	62	63	81
安庆市	Anqing	99	96	70	70	107
黄山市	Huangshan	164	178	181	186	229

18—3 主要年份旅游景点基本情况
Basic Information of Tourist Attractions in Main Years

年　份 Year	A级旅游景点数(家) Number of A-class Tourist Attractions (home)	5A级景点 5 A Grade Scenic Spot	4A级景点 4 A Grade Scenic Spot	红色旅游基地数(个) Number of Red Tourist Bases (unit)
2018	600	11	194	
2019	605	11	194	
2020	625	12	203	181
2021	657	12	208	
2022	683	12	210	

18—4 各市旅游景点基本情况（2022年）
Basic Information of Tourist Attractions by Region (2022)

地　区	Region	A级旅游景点数(家) Number of A-class Tourist Attractions (home)	5A级景点 5 A Grade Scenic Spot	4A级景点 4 A Grade Scenic Spot	红色旅游基地数(个) Number of Red Tourist Bases (unit)
总　计	**Total**	**683**	**12**	**210**	
合 肥 市	Hefei	65	1	27	
淮 北 市	Huaibei	18		3	
亳 州 市	Bozhou	44		9	
宿 州 市	Suzhou	26		7	
蚌 埠 市	Bengbu	36		5	
阜 阳 市	Fuyang	39	1	6	
淮 南 市	Huainan	36		8	
滁 州 市	Chuzhou	45		8	
六 安 市	Luan	55	2	25	
马鞍山市	Maanshan	34	1	8	
芜 湖 市	Wuhu	36	1	11	
宣 城 市	Xuancheng	61	1	23	
铜 陵 市	Tongling	22		9	
池 州 市	Chizhou	40	1	17	
安 庆 市	Anqing	70	1	22	
黄 山 市	Huangshan	56	3	22	

18—5 各市旅游星级饭店（宾馆）住宿设施情况（2022年）
Accommodation Facilities of Hotels Concerning Foreign Affairs by Region (2022)

地 区	Region	饭 店（宾馆）（个）Number of Hotels (unit)	五星级 Five Star Class	四星级 Four Star Class	三星级 Three Star Class	二星级 Two Star Class	客 房（间）Number of Rooms (unit)	床 位（张）Number of Beds (unit)
总 计	**Total**	**217**	**23**	**102**	**87**	**5**	**34488**	**209752**
合肥市	Hefei	41	10	17	12	2	8870	13717
淮北市	Huaibei	3	1		2		460	712
亳州市	Bozhou	14	1	4	9		2095	3344
宿州市	Suzhou	5	1	2	2		743	1094
蚌埠市	Bengbu	7	1	3	3		1006	1707
阜阳市	Fuyang	4	1	1	2		805	1309
淮南市	Huainan	7		5	1	1	1130	1675
滁州市	Chuzhou	11		5	5	1	1669	155842
六安市	Luan	12	1	7	4		1883	3253
马鞍山市	Maanshan	6	2	4			1229	1960
芜湖市	Wuhu	20	1	8	11		2431	3826
宣城市	Xuancheng	13		9	4		1685	2902
铜陵市	Tongling	3		2	1		343	534
池州市	Chizhou	15		6	9		1673	2881
安庆市	Anqing	30		12	17	1	3882	6796
黄山市	Huangshan	26	4	17	5		4584	8200

注：本表星级宾馆（酒店）指2020年底止已得到国家旅游局或省旅游局批准的，不包括已报未批部分。

a) The star class of hotel in this table refer to be approved by the National Tourism Administration or Anhui Tourism Administration up to the Year-end of 2020 excluding those hed been reported but unapproved.

18—6　国际旅游外汇收入及构成
Foreign Exchange Earnings and It's Composition

指　标	Item	2010 数　额（万美元）Value (10000 USD)	2010 比　重（%）Percentage (%)	2015 数　额（万美元）Value (10000 USD)	2015 比　重（%）Percentage (%)	2021 数　额（万美元）Value (10000 USD)	2021 比　重（%）Percentage (%)	2022 数　额（万美元）Value (10000 USD)	2022 比　重（%）Percentage (%)
总　计	**Total**	**82025.2**	**100.0**	**226287.5**	**100.0**	**4531.7**		**2247.6**	
长途交通	Long Distance Transportation	26986.3	32.9	87392.2	38.6				
#民　航	Air	12385.8	15.1	46818.9	20.7				
铁　路	Railway	8202.5	10.0	12129.0	5.4				
汽　车	Highway	6398.0	7.8	8983.6	4.0				
游　览	Visiting	3691.1	4.5	7693.8	3.4				
住　宿	Accommodation	8776.7	10.7	19868.0	8.8				
餐　饮	Cater	7874.4	9.6	13192.6	5.8				
商品销售	Commodity Sale	19111.9	23.3	43990.3	19.4				
娱　乐	Entertainment	4839.5	5.9	10431.9	4.6				
邮电通讯	Postal and Communication	1886.6	2.3	4367.4	1.9				
市内交通	Local Transportation	1558.5	1.9	4548.4	2.0				
其他服务	Other Service	7300.2	8.9	34803.0	15.4				

注：2021、2022年受新冠肺炎疫情影响，入境旅游锐减，未进行入境旅游抽样调查，故年度数据暂缺。

a) In 2021 and 2022, due to the COVID-19 epidemic, inbound tourism decreased sharply, and no inbound tourism sampling survey was conducted, so the data of this year are temporarily missing.

18—7 接待外国人旅游人数（按国别分）
Number of Foreign Tourists by Country

单位：人次（person−time）

指 标	Item	2010	2015	2020	2021	2022
总 计	**Total**	**1173988**	**2591842**	**440040**	**60905**	**48003**
#日 本	Japan	135277	173519	39294	10259	4509
韩 国	Republic of Korea	405538	841117	31864	6612	3593
新加坡	Singapore	43507	143828	20817	1960	702
美 国	United States	101700	214812	66582	8410	4224
英 国	United Kingdom	49069	85577	20435	3194	979
法 国	France	63837	84823	29987	2591	1068
德 国	Federal Republic Of Germany	52934	95489	21016	2560	2029
俄罗斯	Russia	23990	53880	5627	783	304

18—8 国内旅游情况人数结构（按年龄、身份和职业分）（2022年）
Number of Domestic Tourists by Age, Identity and Occupation (2022)

单位：万人次（10000 person-time）

指 标	Item	按身份分组 By Identity			按职业分组 By Occupation								
		人数合计 Total	城镇居民 Urban Residents	非城镇居民 Unurban Residents	公务员 Public Servicers	事业单位工作人员 Institution Staff	企业工作人员 Enterprise Staff	社会团体工作人员 Social Organizations Staff	个体户 Self-employed	农民 Peasants	离退休人员 Retirees	学生 Students	其他 Other
合 计	**Total**	**49601.3**	**33757.9**	**15843.4**	**1680.9**	**8370.8**	**12484.2**	**5589.2**	**10395.0**	**1572.2**	**1623.7**	**7111.3**	**773.9**
55岁以上	55 and Over	3641.0	2375.9	1265.1	81.4	514.0	451.0	343.7	526.9	299.9	1357.1		67.0
45—54岁	45—54	6778.6	4470.4	2308.2	134.3	1211.8	1867.8	932.7	1749.5	450.7	266.6		165.2
35—44岁	35—44	13122.8	9217.9	3904.9	560.6	2514.1	4483.0	1676.5	3342.9	390.6			155.2
25—34岁	25—34	14362.9	10241.9	4121.0	735.0	3112.8	3870.5	1648.0	3743.9	294.3		730.2	228.2
24岁以下	24 and Under	11696.0	7451.8	4244.1	169.6	1018.1	1811.9	988.4	1031.7	136.7		6381.2	158.4

18—9　国内旅游主要经济指标
Main Economic Indicators of Domestic Tourism

年　份 Year	人　数 (万人次) Total Number (10000 persons)	总收入 (亿元) Total Income (100 million yuan)	一　日　游 One-day Tour 人　数 (万人次) Total Number (10000 persons)	一　日　游 One-day Tour 收　入 (亿元) Income (100 million yuan)	过夜旅游 Overnight Tour 人　数 (万人次) Total Number (10000 persons)	过夜旅游 Overnight Tour 收　入 (亿元) Income (100 million yuan)
2010	15349.0	1094.8	5332.0	212.7	10017.0	882.1
2013	33601.1	2903.2	11981.3	666.1	21619.8	2237.1
2014	37898.8	3309.7	14968.1	883.9	22930.7	2425.8
2015	44403.7	3980.5	19705.1	1244.9	24698.6	2735.6
2016	52241.2	4763.6	24472.0	1630.7	27769.2	3132.9
2017	62627.0	6002.4	31911.0	2306.3	30716.0	3696.1
2018	72147.2	7030.0	38727.2	2832.8	33420.0	4197.2
2019	81954.7	8291.5	45219.2	3401.2	36735.5	4890.3
2020	47046.5	4221.5	25136.8	1557.6	21909.7	2663.9
2021	58066.0	5578.3	32053.1	2174.9	26012.9	3403.4
2022	49601.3	4640.2	28606.1	1914.4	20995.2	2725.8

18—10　各市国内旅游主要经济指标（2022年）
Main Economic Indicators of Domestic Tourism by Region (2022)

地　区	Region	总收入 (亿元) Total Income (100 million yuan)	一　日　游 One-day Tour 人　数 (万人次) Total Number (10000 persons)	一　日　游 One-day Tour 收　入 (亿元) Income (100 million yuan)	过夜旅游 Overnight Tour 人　数 (万人次) Total Number (10000 persons)	过夜旅游 Overnight Tour 收　入 (亿元) Income (100 million yuan)
总　计	**Total**	**4640.2**	**28606.1**	**1914.4**	**20995.2**	**2725.8**
合肥市	Hefei	1006.0	4671.0	395.3	3505.5	610.6
淮北市	Huaibei	64.6	608.0	26.1	442.0	38.4
亳州市	Bozhou	160.4	1183.4	65.8	867.6	94.6
宿州市	Suzhou	130.1	1045.0	51.4	819.3	78.7
蚌埠市	Bengbu	220.5	1982.5	100.8	1268.1	119.7
阜阳市	Fuyang	152.4	1230.1	63.1	943.5	89.3
淮南市	Huainan	114.9	1045.9	50.9	734.0	63.9
滁州市	Chuzhou	179.9	1183.7	73.6	905.3	106.3
六安市	Luan	228.3	1589.9	94.2	1206.6	134.1
马鞍山市	Maanshan	211.2	1730.4	97.8	1094.3	113.4
芜湖市	Wuhu	505.9	2484.5	214.4	1743.4	291.5
宣城市	Xuancheng	223.6	1472.8	91.2	1148.6	132.4
铜陵市	Tongling	113.1	894.4	51.7	583.8	61.4
池州市	Chizhou	435.6	2349.2	173.6	1796.0	262.1
安庆市	Anqing	417.3	2549.7	182.7	1786.4	234.6
黄山市	Huangshan	476.6	2585.6	181.8	2150.9	294.7

18—11 国内旅游人均花费（2022年）
Per Capita Costs of Domestic Tourism (2022)

单位：元（yuan）

指　标	Item	平均每人花费 Per Capita Expenditure	交通费 Local Transportation	住宿费 Accommod-ation	餐饮费 Cater	购物费 Commodity Sale	游览费 Tour Admission Fee
总花费	Total Expenditure	935.5	188.0	130.1	165.5	224.0	83.7
一日游	One-day Tour	669.2	151.7		139.9	186.9	68.2
过夜花费	Overnight Tour	1298.3	237.4	307.3	200.4	274.6	104.9
#宾馆饭店	Living in Hotel	1418.5	243.3	438.4	204.4	277.6	109.1
#住亲友家	Living in Relative's or Friend's Home	1016.5	223.8		191.1	267.6	95.1

18—12 各市国内旅游人均花费（2022年）
Per Capita Costs of Domestic Tourism by Region (2022)

单位：元（yuan）

地　区	Region	平均每人花费 Per Capita Expenditure	交通费 Local Transportation	住宿费 Accommod-ation	餐饮费 Cater	购物费 Commodity Sale	平均逗留天数（天） Average Number of Days (day)
总　计	**Total**	**935.5**	**188.0**	**130.1**	**165.5**	**224.0**	**1.88**
合肥市	Hefei	1230.3	202.5	170.9	205.4	398.1	2.18
淮北市	Huaibei	614.8	130.9	86.7	117.3	156.9	1.76
亳州市	Bozhou	782.0	162.6	108.0	138.9	159.5	1.86
宿州市	Suzhou	698.0	178.7	105.7	123.1	105.3	1.86
蚌埠市	Bengbu	678.3	174.3	104.3	115.5	101.5	1.73
阜阳市	Fuyang	701.2	175.9	106.0	130.8	105.8	2.06
淮南市	Huainan	645.4	137.9	93.3	148.5	90.2	1.86
滁州市	Chuzhou	860.9	164.2	129.5	163.2	210.5	1.82
六安市	Luan	816.4	188.5	113.8	177.4	145.4	1.91
马鞍山市	Maanshan	747.8	163.5	102.1	156.4	135.5	1.71
芜湖市	Wuhu	1196.6	207.5	146.5	198.7	308.5	1.89
宣城市	Xuancheng	852.9	191.2	134.0	160.4	201.7	1.93
铜陵市	Tongling	764.9	166.1	108.0	160.0	163.2	1.66
安庆市	Anqing	1050.9	187.7	110.5	162.5	231.6	1.84
池州市	Chizhou	962.3	211.1	151.4	175.5	262.9	1.73
黄山市	Huangshan	1006.2	216.5	147.0	160.8	221.5	1.71

18—13 国家级黄山风景区旅游事业发展情况
Development of Tourism of Huang Shan Scenic at National Level

指　　标		Item		2010	2015	2020	2021	2022
接待人数	（人次）	Tourists Received	(person-time)	2518346	3182811	1511535	1674230	1396907
接待海外游客		Overseas Tourists		256753	160002	6854	7614	2551
国内游客		Domestic Tourists		2261593	3022809	1504681	1666616	1394356
营业收入	（万元）	Business Income	(10000 yuan)	168945	252527	228900	180249	207468
#游览设施		Touring Facilities		78812	104293	43601	53301	39647
住宿设施		Lodging Facilities		19832	31575	13648	14650	12257
娱乐设施		Entertainment Facilities		524	473	870	1106	670
餐饮设施		Catering Facilities		14580	22545	9373	10557	9057
商业设施		Commercial Facilities		785	709	1306	1658	1004
外汇收入	（万美元）	Foreign Exchange Earnings	(USD 10000)	5398	5354	234	263	99
涉外宾馆（酒店）住宿设施		Lodging Facilities of Tourist Hotels						
宾馆（酒店）	（个）	Number of Hotels	(unit)	14	10	10	10	9
#五星级		Five Star Class		2	3	3	3	3
四星级		Four Star Class		8	7	7	7	6
三星级		Three Star Class		1				
二星级		Two Star Class						
客　房	（间）	Number of Rooms	(unit)	2728	2474	1979	2109	1781
床　位	（张）	Number of Beds	(unit)	5690	5235	3650	3804	3370
客房出租率	（%）	Room Occupancy	(%)	51	51	32	29	27
旅游车辆	（辆）	Number of Touring Vehicles	(unit)	131	147	154	113	103
#大型车辆		Large-sized Vehicles		96	141	140	110	100
中型车辆		Middle-sized Vehicles		6	2	10	1	1
小型车辆		Small-sized Vehicles		29	4	4	2	2

18—14 国家级九华山风景区旅游事业发展情况
Development of Tourism of Jiu Hua Shan Scenic at National Level

指 标	Item	2010	2015	2020	2021	2022
接待人数 （人次）	Tourists Received (person-time)	4001139	9712500	7916841	8236027	7932914
接待海外游客	Overseas Tourists	150009	350011	5182		
国内游客	Domestic Tourists	3851130	9362489	7911659	8236027	7932914
营业收入 （万元）	Business Income (10000 yuan)	390008	1080332	996052	1030817	985847
#游览设施	Touring Facilities	156003	432131	358628	371094	335188
住宿设施	Lodging Facilities	97502	270083	249013	257704	276037
娱乐设施	Entertainment Facilities	7800	21509	9912	10205	11830
餐饮设施	Catering Facilities	58501	162049	258973	268012	266179
商业设施	Commercial Facilities	70201	194559	119526	123801	96613
外汇收入 （万美元）	Foreign Exchange Earnings (USD 10000)					
涉外宾馆（酒店）住宿设施	Lodging Facilities of Tourist Hotels					
宾馆（酒店） （个）	Number of Hotels (unit)	9	10			
#五星级	Five Star Class					
四星级	Four Star Class	2	3			
三星级	Three Star Class	7	7			
二星级	Two Star Class					
客 房 （间）	Number of Rooms (unit)	831	1064			
床 位 （张）	Number of Beds (unit)	1551	2014			
客房出租率 （%）	Room Occupancy (%)	65	62			
旅游车辆 （辆）	Number of Touring Vehicles (unit)	112	139	145	141	138
#大型车辆	Large-sized Vehicles	61	59	124	91	91
中型车辆	Middle-sized Vehicles	17	76	13	46	43
小型车辆	Small-sized Vehicles	34	4	8	4	4

主要统计指标解释

旅游人数

(1)入境旅游人数：指报告期内来我国观光、度假、探亲访友、就医疗养、购物、参加会议或从事经济、文化、体育、宗教活动的外国人、港澳台同胞等入境游客。统计时，外国人、港澳台同胞每入境一次统计1人次。

(2)出境人数：指中国（大陆）居民因公或因私出境前往其他国家、中国香港特别行政区、澳门特别行政区和台湾省观光、度假、探亲访友、就医疗养、购物、参加会议或从事经济、文化、体育、宗教活动的人数，即出境游客。统计时，按每出境一次统计1人次。

(3)国内旅游人数：指在报告期内在中国（大陆）观光游览、度假、探亲访友、就医疗养、购物、参加会议或从事经济、文化、体育、宗教活动的中国（大陆）居民人数，其出游的目的不是通过所从事的活动谋取报酬。统计时，国内游客按每出游一次统计1人次。

国际旅游(外汇)收入

指入境游客在中国（大陆）境内旅行、游览过程中用于交通、参观游览、住宿、餐饮、购物、娱乐等全部花费。

国内旅游收入

又称旅游总花费。指国内游客在国内旅行、游览过程中用于交通、参观游览、住宿、餐饮、购物、娱乐等全部花费。

国际旅行社

指经营业务范围包括入境旅游业务、出境旅游业务和国内旅游业务的旅行社。

国内旅行社

指经营范围仅限于国内旅游业务的旅行社。

星级饭店

指设备、设施、服务符合《旅游饭店星级的划分与评定》（GB/T14308-2010），通过相关旅游管理部门评定，并取得星级饭店称号的饭店（含预备星级饭店）。

Explanatory Notes for Major Statistical Indicators

Number of Tourists

(1) Visitor arrivals refer to the number of foreigners, Chinese compatriots from Hong Kong, Macao and Taiwan Chinese (mainland) who come to China (mainland) for sight-seeing, vacation, visiting relatives, medical treatment, shopping, attending conference, or to engage in economic, cultural, sports and religious activities. In compiling statistics, each time of entering China is counted as one person-time.

(2) Number of Chinese residents going abroad refer to the number of Chinese (mainland) residents going to other countries, Hong Kong Special Administrative region, Macao Special Administrative region and Taiwan for on official or private purposes, for sight-seeing, vacation, visiting relatives, medical treatment, shopping, attending conference, or to engage in economic, cultural, sports and religious activities. In compiling statistics, each time of leaving is counted as one person-time.

(3) Number of domestic tourists refers to the number of Chinese (mainland) residents who travel within China (mainland) for sight-seeing, vacation, visiting relatives, medical treatment, shopping, attending conference, or to engage in economic, cultural, sports and religious activities. In compiling statistics, each time of travelling is counted as one person-time.

Foreign Exchange Earnings from International Tourism

refer to the total expenditure of foreigners, overseas Chinese, Chinese compatriots from Hong Kong, Macao and Taiwan during their stay in the mainland of China on transportation, sighting, accommodation, food, shopping and entertainment.

Income from Domestic Tourism

refer to expenditure of domestic tourists on transportation, sighting, accommodation, food, shopping and entertainment while they travel.

International Travel Agencies

refer to travel agencies engaged in tourism entering China, Chinese residents going abroad and domestic tourism.

Domestic Travel Agencies

refer to travel agencies only engaged in domestic tourism.

Star-rated Hotels

refer to hotels rated with stars as assessed by the relevant tourism authorities according to GB/T14308-2010 standard with reference to their infrastructure, facilities and service levels.

第十九篇

Chapter 19

教育和科技

EDUCATION AND SCIENCE

简要说明

一、教育统计资料包括公办教育和民办教育、学历教育和非学历教育。具体有高等教育（研究生教育、普通高等教育和成人高等教育）中等教育（高中阶段教育和初中阶段教育）、初等教育（小学）、学前教育、特殊教育，以及教育经费等资料。主要指标包括学校数、在校学生数、招生数、毕业生数、教职工数和专任教师数、教育经费等。

教育事业统计资料由省教育厅提供；技工学校的资料由省人力资源和社会保障厅提供。

二、科技统计资料主要内容包括：全社会以及工业企业、政府部门属研究机构、高校的研究与试验发展（R&D）活动情况；国内外专利申请和授权情况；技术市场交易情况；开发区高新技术企业主要经济指标；科协系统科技活动情况；质量监督检验检疫等综合技术服务部门业务活动情况等。

资料来源：全省综合资料、企业及有关行业企事业单位的研究与试验发展（R&D）活动情况由省统计局文化产业处提供；政府部门属研究机构的研究与试验发展（R&D）活动情况、技术市场成交情况由省科技厅提供；科协系统科技活动资料由省科协提供；产品质量监督抽查、专利等资料，由省市场监管局提供。

Brief Introduction

I. Data on education cover the situations on education funded by government and non-government agencies, and the education with and without academic credentials including higher education (education of postgraduates, general higher education and adult education), secondary education (senior and junior high schools), elementary education (primary schools), preschool education, special education, and their expenditure. The main indicators include the number of schools, the number of students enrolled, the number of new students enrolled, the number of graduates, the number of staff and workers, the number of full-time teachers, sources and outlay of education funding, and education expenditure from the State budget.

The provincial Ministry of Education provides statistical data on education undertakings and education funding. Data on technical training schools are provided by provincial Ministry of Human Resources and Social Security.

II. The whole society as well as industrial enterprises, research institutions subordinated to government departments, colleges and universities of research and development (R&D) activities; Domestic and foreign patent application and authorization; Technology market; Development zone high-tech enterprises the main economic indicators; Association for science and technology system of science and technology activity; General administration of quality supervision, inspection and quarantine and other integrated technology services business activity, etc

Sources of data: Comprehensive data and research and development (R&D) activities of enterprises and institutions in related industries shall be provided by the Cultural Industry Division of the Provincial Bureau of Statistics. Research and experimental development (R&D) activities and technology market transactions of research institutions belonging to government departments shall be provided by the Provincial Science and Technology Department; S&t activity information of s&T system shall be provided by provincial s&T associations; Product quality supervision and spot check, patent and other materials, provided by the provincial market supervision bureau.

19—1 教育事业基本情况
Basic Statistics on Education

指 标	Item	2010	2015	2020	2021	2022
学校数 （所）	**Number of Schools (unit)**					
普通高等学校	Regular Institutions of Higher Education	100	108	115	121	121
中等职业学校	Secondary Vocational School	453	360	277	271	249
普通中等专业学校	General Secondary Vocational School	108	123	236		
中等技术学校	Secondary Technical School	95	109	225		
中等师范学校	Secondary Normal School	13	14	11		
职业中学	Vocational School	345	237	41		
普通中学	Ordinary High School	3738	3524	3507	3504	3459
高 中	High School	743	666	661	679	679
初 中	Junior High School	2995	2858	2846	2825	2780
小 学	Primary Schools	13997	9119	7464	6964	6509
幼儿园	Kindergartens	4018	6988	10876	11478	11577
特殊教育	Special Schools	62	68	77	77	77
专任教师 （万人）	**Number of Full-time Teachers (10000 persons)**					
普通高等学校	Regular Institutions of Higher Education	4.93	5.81	6.56	7.02	7.50
中等职业学校	Secondary Vocational School	2.17	2.72	2.76	3.12	3.23
普通中等专业学校	General Secondary Vocational School	0.77	1.11	2.59		
职业中学	Vocational School	1.40	1.61	0.17		
普通中学	Ordinary High School	23.01	22.72	24.76	25.65	26.13
高 中	High School	6.69	7.63	8.21	8.63	9.02
初 中	Junior High School	16.32	15.09	16.55	17.02	17.11
小 学	Primary Schools	24.57	23.83	26.04	26.90	26.97
幼儿园	Kindergartens	2.96	6.66	11.21	13.05	13.49
特殊教育	Special Schools	0.12	0.14	0.20	0.22	0.22
招生数 （万人）	**New Student Enrollment (10000 persons)**					
普通高等学校	Regular Institutions of Higher Education	29.69	35.00	46.29	47.31	46.16
中等职业学校	Secondary Vocational School	28.63	19.44	21.12	29.84	27.61
普通中等专业学校	General Secondary Vocational School	10.44	9.45	18.78		
职业中学	Vocational School	18.19	9.99	2.34		
普通中学	Ordinary High School	129.74	100.77	114.03	115.26	117.51
高 中	High School	42.41	36.33	39.08	39.10	42.09
初 中	Junior High School	87.33	64.44	74.95	76.16	75.42
小 学	Primary Schools	81.90	74.55	78.14	76.67	75.73
幼儿园	Kindergartens	66.60	97.48	85.41	68.81	62.00
特殊教育	Special Schools	0.22	0.51	0.60	0.65	0.66
在校学生 （万人）	**Student Enrollment (10000 persons)**					
普通高等学校	Regular Institutions of Higher Education	93.90	113.07	136.85	150.50	155.35
中等职业学校	Secondary Vocational School	77.61	58.43	56.36	75.21	72.80
普通中等专业学校	General Secondary Vocational School	28.93	27.53	50.04		
职业中学	Vocational School	48.68	30.90	6.32		
普通中学	Ordinary High School	406.58	303.63	337.31	346.21	348.86
高 中	High School	127.60	113.55	113.36	116.34	120.10
初 中	Junior High School	278.99	190.08	223.96	229.87	228.77
小 学	Primary Schools	460.44	422.50	468.24	468.73	470.25
幼儿园	Kindergartens	100.82	185.65	216.81	214.06	204.30
特殊教育	Special Schools	1.40	1.93	4.07	4.16	4.24
毕业生数 （万人）	**Graduates (10000 persons)**					
普通高等学校	Regular Institutions of Higher Education	23.22	29.25	32.68	32.70	41.89
中等职业学校	Secondary Vocational School	27.37	22.03	16.47	26.31	23.88
普通中等专业学校	General Secondary Vocational School	9.61	8.49	12.90		
职业中学	Vocational School	17.76	13.54	3.57		
普通中学	Ordinary High School	136.57	107.39	105.88	106.09	114.98
高 中	High School	44.38	43.30	35.13	35.99	38.07
初 中	Junior High School	92.19	64.09	70.75	70.10	76.92
小 学	Primary Schools	87.41	64.32	74.01	75.72	74.95
幼儿园	Kindergartens	38.89	70.40	80.34	77.83	77.53
特殊教育	Special Schools	0.16	0.13	0.37	0.56	0.61

注：2005—2020年，中等职业学校数据仅含普通中专和职业高中；自2021年起，中等职业学校数据包括普通中专、职业高中、成人中专学校以及其他中职机构（不计校数）和附设中职班（不计校数）；各类附设班专任教师数分别计入相应层次教师总数。

a) From 2005 to 2020, the data of secondary vocational schools only include ordinary technical secondary schools and vocational high schools; From 2021, data of secondary vocational schools include regular secondary vocational schools, vocational high schools, adult secondary vocational schools and other secondary vocational institutions (excluding the number of schools) and secondary vocational classes (excluding the number of schools); The number of full-time teachers of each supplementary class shall be counted into the total number of teachers at the corresponding level.

19—2 研究生数
Number of Postgraduates

单位：人（person）

年 份 Year	研究生数 Number of Postgraduates					
	在学人数 Student Enrollment	硕士 Master	招生数 New Student Enrollment	硕士 Master	毕业生数 Graduates	硕士 Master
2010	38991	34669	14047	12728	9302	8224
2015	50410	44517	17946	16158	15409	14115
2016	51738	45293	18523	16580	15994	14665
2017	57761	49842	22255	20013	16577	15209
2018	63464	54597	23870	21276	17705	16103
2019	70317	60348	25699	22737	18065	16456
2020	83896	72275	33955	30671	18348	16875
2021	98600	85114	36847	33154	20530	18521
2022	111060	95986	39012	35017	24105	21775

19—3 普通高等学校本科分科学生数
Number of Students of the Ordinary College Undergraduate Course Branch

单位：人（person）

项 目	Item	2021			2022		
		毕业生数 Graduates	招生数 New Student Enrollment	在校学生数 Student Enrollment	毕业生数 Graduates	招生数 New Student Enrollment	在校学生数 Student Enrollment
合 计	**Total**	**167216**	**206594**	**745625**	**190427**	**214806**	**767426**
哲 学	Philosophy	113	213	742	50	35	204
经济学	Economics	11617	11619	46835	12546	11274	45494
法 学	Law	3813	4734	17196	4378	4834	18717
教育学	Education	6264	8260	27200	7577	8682	27994
文 学	Literature	15335	20387	72548	19285	19604	73621
历史学	History	440	922	2779	599	775	2980
理 学	Science	12161	14933	55863	12965	15298	58882
工 学	Engineering	61078	75702	275633	67883	80029	286216
农 学	Agriculture	2883	3356	11594	3062	3370	11456
医 学	Medicine	12207	15394	61526	14065	17303	64772
管理学	Management	29852	37168	122070	35250	37877	122807
艺术学	Art	11453	13906	51639	12767	15725	54283

注：2013年起，根据教育部统一部署，使用新颁布的《高等学校本科专业目录》，新增了艺术学学科。

a) Since 2013, according to the unified deployment of the ministry of education, the use of new catalogue of the institutions of higher learning undergraduate, new art discipline.

19—4 普通高职高专（专科）分科学生数
Number of Students in Ordinary Vocational Colleges by Subject

单位：人（person）

项　目	Item	2021			2022		
		毕业生数 Graduates	招生数 New Student Enrollment	在校学生数 Student Enrollment	毕业生数 Graduates	招生数 New Student Enrollment	在校学生数 Student Enrollment
合　计	**Total**	**159788**	**266486**	**759366**	**228486**	**246795**	**786109**
农林牧渔大类	Farm, Forest, Animal and Fishery Category	1229	4026	13197	3461	2655	10808
资源环境与安全大类	Resource Environment and Security Category	572	2122	6543	1943	1460	5916
能源动力与材料大类	Energy Dynamics and Materials	1043	1696	4833	1286	1641	4940
土木建筑大类	Civil Architecture	10226	23942	66069	17382	15945	65993
水利大类	Water Conservancy Category	1013	1024	4036	1231	1159	3928
装备制造大类	Equipment Manufacturing Category	13833	24080	63325	18587	27839	72764
生物与化工大类	Biology and Chemical Industry	487	1169	3738	794	632	3629
轻工纺织大类	Light Industrial Textile Category	539	937	2968	992	956	2774
食品药品与粮食大类	Food and Medicine and Food	2525	3038	8505	2561	3399	8082
交通运输大类	Major Transportation Sectors	9793	15746	42880	13942	16460	47022
电子信息大类	Electronic Information Category	22177	36987	100882	29097	36485	110223
医药卫生大类	Medical and Health Category	25353	45968	132583	39631	42927	136562
财经商贸大类	Finance and Trade	34313	49778	155902	49873	39754	149514
旅游大类	Tourism Category	4904	6188	18848	6425	5966	17570
文化艺术大类	Cultural and Artistic Categories	5696	11698	29460	8022	11578	32651
新闻传播大类	News Communication	2074	2648	7674	2359	2618	7921
教育与体育大类	Education and Sports	19492	29057	76651	24022	30044	84468
公安与司法大类	Public Security and Judicial Categories	2714	2809	8318	2759	2357	8120
公共管理与服务大类	Public Administration and Services	1805	3573	12954	4119	2920	13224

19—5 普通本科高等学校分科专任教师数（2022年）
Number of Full-time Teachers in Regular Undergraduate Institutions of Higher Learning by Subject （2022）

单位：人（person）

项　目	Item	合　计 Total	正高级 With Chief Senior Title	副高级 With Deputy Senior Title	中　级 With Middle-rank Title	初　级 With Junior Title	未定职级 Undetermined rank
合　计	**Total**	**46316**	**6605**	**13889**	**17692**	**4926**	**3204**
哲　学	Philosophy	1522	148	403	607	223	141
经济学	Economics	2444	331	676	1019	286	132
法　学	Law	2198	237	552	784	413	212
教育学	Education	3679	286	1027	1521	487	358
文　学	Literature	5388	389	1360	2739	606	294
历史学	History	595	106	181	221	49	38
理　学	Science	6884	1680	2392	2030	438	344
工　学	Engineering	12610	1986	4011	4579	1144	890
农　学	Agriculture	944	219	281	305	86	53
医　学	Medicine	3661	668	1302	1252	233	206
管理学	Management	3803	411	1070	1505	493	324
艺术学	Art	2588	144	634	1130	468	212

19—6 普通高职高专（专科）专任教师数（2022年）
Number of Full-time Teachers in Ordinary Vocational Colleges (2022)

单位：人（person）

项目	Item	合计 Total	正高级 With Chief Senior Title	副高级 With Deputy Senior Title	中级 With Middle-rank Title	初级 With Junior Title	未定职级 Undetermined rank
总计	**Total**	**28643**	**1129**	**6490**	**10181**	**5723**	**5120**
#实习指导课	Practice Instruction Course	5997	195	1395	2464	1231	712
农林牧渔大类	Agriculture, Forestry, Husbandry and Fishery	342	27	111	102	52	50
资源环境与安全大类	Resource Environment and Security Categories	504	17	127	227	95	38
能源动力与材料大类	Energy, Power and Materials	402	12	115	103	53	119
土木建筑大类	Civil Construction Category	1169	48	234	471	235	181
水利大类	Water Conservancy Categories	157	11	51	46	37	12
装备制造大类	Equipment Manufacturing Category	2144	107	567	709	413	348
生物与化工大类	Biology and Chemical Industry	329	24	106	112	46	41
轻工纺织大类	Light Industry Textile Category	157	16	41	68	19	13
食品药品与粮食大类	Food, Medicine and Grain Categories	349	22	87	129	58	53
交通运输大类	Transportation Category	562	17	109	170	104	162
电子与信息大类	Electronics and Information Categories	3294	131	803	1174	605	581
医药卫生大类	Medical and Health Category	3095	176	851	1229	528	311
财经商贸大类	Financial and Commercial Categories	3399	138	723	1168	688	682
旅游大类	Tourism Categories	718	22	151	264	182	99
文化艺术大类	Culture and Art Category	2051	43	348	733	445	482
新闻传播大类	News Communication Category	276	11	63	96	59	47
教育与体育大类	Education and Physical Education	2397	66	511	842	539	439
公安与司法大类	Public Security and Judicial Categories	271	26	58	111	44	32
公共管理与服务大类	Public Administration and Service Categories	965	28	178	323	223	213
公共基础课	Public Basic Course	6062	187	1256	2104	1298	1217

注：从2021年起，教育部对职业学校学科进行了新的分类（下同）。

a) Starting from 2021, the Ministry of Education has made a new classification of vocational school subjects (The same below).

19—7 中等职业学校分科学生数（2022年）
Number of Students in Secondary Vocational Schools by Subject (2022)

单位：人（person）

项 目	Item	毕业生数 Graduates	招生数 New Student Enrollment	在校学生数 Student Enrollment
合 计	**Total**	**238826**	**276133**	**727997**
农林牧渔大类	Agriculture, Forestry, Husbandry and Fishery	21771	16649	46206
资源环境与安全大类	Resource Environment and Security Categories	4140	3779	4336
能源动力与材料大类	Energy, Power and Materials	155	379	831
土木建筑大类	Civil Construction Category	8562	9957	18667
水利大类	Water Conservancy Categories	622	77	320
装备制造大类	Equipment Manufacturing Category	22998	35683	87502
生物与化工大类	Biology and Chemical Industry	725	1018	1981
轻工纺织大类	Light Industry Textile Category	2768	2646	6195
食品药品与粮食大类	Food, Medicine and Grain Categories	867	910	2112
交通运输大类	Transportation Category	18934	17903	53904
电子与信息大类	Electronics and Information Categories	49201	58528	153815
医药卫生大类	Medical and Health Category	13538	21645	55251
财经商贸大类	Financial and Commercial Categories	22703	33072	84589
旅游大类	Tourism Categories	11575	14380	39875
文化艺术大类	Culture and Art Category	24928	24273	78662
新闻传播大类	News Communication Category	2949	2337	7883
教育与体育大类	Education and Physical Education	24992	24407	69835
公安与司法大类	Public Security and Judicial Categories	6	24	54
公共管理与服务大类	Public Administration and Service Categories	7392	8466	15979

注：中等职业学校包括原普通中专、成人中专和职业高中学校。从2021年起，教育部对职业学校学科进行了新的分类。

a) Secondary vocational schools include former ordinary technical secondary schools, adult technical secondary schools and vocational high schools. Starting from 2021, the Ministry of Education has made a new classification of vocational school subjects.

19—8 中等职业学校分科专任教师数（2022年）
Number of Full-time Teachers in Secondary Vocational Schools by Subject (2022)

单位：人（person）

项 目	Item	合 计 Total	正高级 With Chief Senior Title	副高级 With Deputy Senior Title	中 级 With Middle-rank Title	初 级 With Junior Title	未定职级 Undetermined rank
总 计	**Total**	**32263**	**160**	**8637**	**10020**	**7295**	**6151**
#实习指导课	Practice Instruction Course	2672	14	590	824	569	675
农林牧渔大类	Agriculture, Forestry, Husbandry and Fishery	1400	18	431	479	279	193
资源环境与安全大类	Resource Environment and Security Categories	210	1	46	81	61	21
能源动力与材料大类	Energy, Power and Materials	221	1	65	61	51	43
土木建筑大类	Civil Construction Category	593	5	189	200	118	81
水利大类	Water Conservancy Categories	41		10	18	12	1
装备制造大类	Equipment Manufacturing Category	2734	13	807	879	664	371
生物与化工大类	Biology and Chemical Industry	198	1	68	63	46	20
轻工纺织大类	Light Industry Textile Category	218	1	41	72	74	30
食品药品与粮食大类	Food, Medicine and Grain Categories	142		20	34	75	13
交通运输大类	Transportation Category	1333	10	271	372	354	326
电子与信息大类	Electronics and Information Categories	3781	27	912	1140	835	867
医药卫生大类	Medical and Health Category	1474	8	381	543	345	197
财经商贸大类	Financial and Commercial Categories	2199	8	528	692	529	442
旅游大类	Tourism Categories	1291	4	302	399	334	252
文化艺术大类	Culture and Art Category	3189	18	702	899	731	839
新闻传播大类	News Communication Category	146		27	47	39	33
教育与体育大类	Education and Physical Education	6450	23	1832	2172	1369	1054
公安与司法大类	Public Security and Judicial Categories	26		9	4	7	6
公共管理与服务大类	Public Administration and Service Categories	760	1	179	246	204	130
公共基础课	Public Basic Course	5857	21	1817	1619	1168	1232

19—9 技工学校数和学生数
Number of Technical Schools, Students, Staff and Teachers

年 份 Year	学校数（所） Schools (unit)	在校学生数（人） Student Enrollment (person)	毕业生数（人） Graduates (person)	招生数（人） New Student Enrollment (person)	教职工数（人） Staff and Teachers (person)
2010	93	93647	31393	31836	6716
2013	86	49126	17668	18570	6649
2014	83	44703	16922	16362	6537
2015	83	43809	18683	18979	6313
2016	86	56378	19328	24735	7676
2017	89	89513	16399	54595	7519
2018	81	127560	17979	61286	8996
2019	77	147807	22390	62465	9066
2020	93	184756	35929	84683	10615
2021	83	214135	44864	101229	11114
2022	86	241693	47595	89939	11954

注：1、学校数包括技师学院、高级技工学校和普通技工学校。
2、在校学生数包括初级、中级、高级及其以上学制教育和培训人数。
3、招生数包括招收的学制教育和培训人数。

a) the number of schools includes technician school, senior technical schools and ordinary technical schools.

b) the number of students Enrollment, includes students in primary, intermediate, advanced education ,over education system schools and the number of trained people.

c) the number of students enrolled in the school includes students enrolled in education system schools and the number of training people schools.

19—10 平均每万人口各级教育在校学生及构成情况
All Levels of Education Students per 10000 Population and Composition

年 份 Year	各级教育在校学生数占全省人口(%) All Levels of Education in the School Student Number Accounts for the Population (%)	平均每万人口中（人） On average every ten thousand people（person）					各级教育学生占学生总数（%） Education students at all levels of the total number (%)				
		高等教育 Higher Education	高中阶段 High School	初中阶段 Junior Middle School Stage	小 学 Primary Schools	学前教育 Preschool Education	高等教育 Higher Education	高中阶段 High School	初中阶段 Junior Middle School Stage	小 学 Primary Schools	学前教育 Preschool Education
2010	19.58	184	350	455	751	164	9.66	18.40	23.89	39.42	8.63
2015	19.11	231	324	312	695	305	12.36	17.37	16.73	37.19	16.34
2016	18.63	226	307	316	700	314	12.12	16.50	16.96	37.59	16.83
2017	18.83	225	298	326	711	324	11.88	15.82	17.33	37.76	17.22
2018	19.13	225	292	334	730	331	11.73	15.27	17.48	38.18	17.32
2019	19.78	245	291	346	731	334	12.54	14.94	17.78	37.55	17.18
2020	20.35	270	324	352	736	341	13.49	15.12	17.59	36.78	17.03
2021	21.44	309	314	377	768	351	14.59	14.82	17.78	36.26	16.56
2022	21.45	328	316	374	769	334	15.47	14.87	17.64	36.26	15.75

注：高等教育包括研究生、普通本专科、成人本专科；高中阶段包括普通高中、中等职业学校（普通中专、职业中学和成人中专）；初中阶段包括普通初中和职业初中。

a) Higher education includes graduate, general undergraduate and junior college, adult undergraduate and junior college; Senior high school includes ordinary senior high school, secondary vocational school (ordinary technical secondary school, vocational secondary school and adult secondary school); The middle school level includes regular middle school and vocational middle school.

19—11 各级各类学校生师比
At Various Levels and School Teacher Ratio

年 份 Year	普通高等学校 Regular Institutions of Higher Education	中等职业学校 Secondary Vocational School	普通高中 Ordinary High School	普通初中 Ordinary Junior High School	小 学 Primary Schools	幼儿园 Kindergartens
2010	18.0	35.4	19.1	17.1	18.7	34.1
2015	18.5	21.5	14.9	12.6	17.7	27.9
2016	18.3	20.8	14.3	12.8	17.9	25.4
2017	18.8	20.8	13.9	13.0	18.0	24.2
2018	18.2	21.4	13.7	13.2	18.3	23.0
2019	19.2	20.5	13.5	13.5	18.1	21.2
2020	20.0	20.4	13.8	13.5	18.0	19.3
2021		24.1	13.5	13.5	17.4	16.4
2022		22.6	13.3	13.4	17.4	15.1

注：本表2005年—2020年中等职业学校数据仅含普通中专和职业高中，2021年增加成人中专等，口径参照19—1表。

a) Data of secondary vocational schools in this table from 2005 to 2020 only include ordinary secondary vocational schools and vocational high schools, and adult secondary vocational schools will be added in 2021, with reference to Table 19-1.

19—12 各级学校女学生和女教师数
Number of Female Students and Teachers by Level of School

指　　标	Item	2010	2015	2020	2021	2022
女学生数（万人）	**Number of Female Students (10000 persons)**	**479.02**	**418.10**	**460.91**	**479.02**	**482.53**
普通高等学校	Regular Institutions of Higher Education	44.81	56.87	64.66	69.45	72.03
中等职业学校	Secondary Vocational School	38.19	29.05	26.29	35.02	33.41
普通中学	Regular Secondary Schools	186.49	139.43	154.95	159.03	159.83
小　学	Primary Schools	209.53	192.76	215.01	215.52	217.26
女学生占学生总数的百分比(%)	**Percentage of Female Students to Total Students (%)**	**45.97**	**46.58**	**46.15**	**46.03**	**46.08**
普通高等学校	Regular Institutions of Higher Education	47.72	50.30	47.20	46.15	46.37
中等职业学校	Secondary Vocational School	49.21	49.72	46.65	46.56	45.90
普通中学	Regular Secondary Schools	45.87	45.92	45.94	45.93	45.82
小　学	Primary Schools	45.51	45.62	45.92	45.98	46.20
女教师数（万人）	**Number of Female Teachers (10000 persons)**	**21.44**	**24.65**	**31.73**	**33.89**	**35.34**
普通高等学校	Regular Institutions of Higher Education	2.00	2.48	3.03	3.33	3.61
中等职业学校	Secondary Vocational School	0.82	1.05	1.25	1.47	1.58
普通中学	Regular Secondary Schools	7.91	8.77	10.93	11.63	12.15
小　学	Primary Schools	10.71	12.36	16.52	17.46	18.00
女教师占教师总数的百分比(%)	**Percentage of Female Teachers to Total Teachers(%)**	**39.07**	**44.76**	**52.79**	**54.05**	**55.35**
普通高等学校	Regular Institutions of Higher Education	40.56	42.62	46.23	47.38	48.12
中等职业学校	Secondary Vocational School	37.54	38.60	45.29	47.05	48.84
普通中学	Regular Secondary Schools	34.39	38.62	44.14	45.33	46.48
小　学	Primary Schools	43.58	51.86	63.44	64.91	66.73

注：从2021年起，各类附设班专任教师数分别计入相应层次教师总数。

a) Starting from 2021, the number of full-time teachers in each attached class will be counted into the total number of teachers at the corresponding level.

19—13 各级各类成人教育基本情况（2022年）
Basic Situation of Adult Education of All Types and at All Levels (2022)

单位：人（person）

指　标	Item	学校数（所）Schools (unit)	毕业生数 Graduates	招生数 New Student Enrollment	在校学生数 Student Enrollment	教职工人数 Teachers and Staff	专任教师 Full-time Teachers
成人高等教育	**Adult's Higher Education**	**6**	**111543**	**174650**	**342221**	**417**	**223**
#成人高等学校	Adult Education Schools	6	4687	9208	19587	417	223
广播电视大学	Radio and TV Universities	1	3692	5800	12975	297	175
职工、农民高等学院	Schools of Higher Education for Staff, Workers and Peasants	3	995	3408	6612	120	48
管理干部学院	Colleges for Management Cadres	1					
教育学院	Institute of Education	1					
成人技术培训学校	**Technical Training Schools for Adults**	**286**	**77896**		**103169**	**1918**	**1538**
职工技术培训学校	Technical Training Schools for Staff and Workers	30	32234		58349	931	867
农民技术培训学校	Technical Training Schools for Peasants	213	33341		36047	561	371
其他培训机构（含社会培训机构）	Other Training Organs (Including Social Training Organs)	43	12321		8773	426	300

19-14 民办教育基本情况（2022年）
Basic Information on Private Education （2022）

单位：人（person）

项　目	Item	校数（所）Number of Schools (unit)	毕业生数 Number of Students Graduated	招生数 New Enrollment	在校学生数 Enrolled Students	教职工数 Teachers and Staff	专任教师 Full-time Teachers
合　计	**Total**	**7154**	**826770**	**616825**	**2318233**	**236781**	**149085**
民办普通高等教育	Private Ordinary Higher Education	32	73087	94387	328194	16750	12906
民办中等职业教育	Private Secondary Vocational Education	91	56183	62270	181662	11223	8688
民办普通高中	Civilian-run Senior High Schools	232	80510	101517	267091	44340	20221
民办初中阶段教育	Private Junior High School Education	322	172525	84583	382593	34408	26029
民办小学	Civilian-run Primary Schools	223	86136	21541	273272	9470	17206
民办幼儿园	Civilian-run Kindergartens	6254	358329	252527	885421	120590	64035
#普惠性幼儿园	Universal Kindergarten	4615	278934	191589	699836	89904	47532

注：表中民办普通高中教职工数包括高级中学、完全中学和十二年一贯制学校的教职工及高中教师数；中等职业教育不含技工学校数字。
资料来源：安徽省教育厅。

a) In the table, the number of teaching staff in private ordinary high schools includes the number of teaching staff and high school teachers in senior high schools, complete high schools and 12-year system schools. Secondary vocational education does not include figures for technical schools.

Source: Anhui Municipal Commission of Education.

19—15 各市普通高等学校和中职学校情况（2022年）
General Institutions of Higher Learning and Secondary Vocational Schools by Region (2022)

单位：人（person）

地区	Region	学校数(所) Number of Schools (unit) 高等 Higher	中职 Secondary Vocational School	毕业生数 Number of Graduates 高等 Higher	中职 Secondary Vocational School	招生数 New Student Enrollment 高等 Higher	中职 Secondary Vocational School	在校学生数 Student Enrollment 高等 Higher	中职 Secondary Vocational School	中职学校专任教师数 Number of Full-time Teachers in Secondary Vocational Schools
总计	**Total**	**121**	**249**	**418913**	**238826**	**461601**	**276133**	**1553535**	**727997**	**32263**
合肥市	Hefei	54	49	179706	43723	191405	36885	667447	111176	5678
淮北市	Huaibei	4	5	15749	5931	14296	8075	46927	20874	918
亳州市	Bozhou	2	13	9590	17145	7563	18279	22517	45652	2419
宿州市	Suzhou	4	16	11070	22701	10678	35537	39645	74583	2920
蚌埠市	Bengbu	6	17	21286	15140	19560	19739	75645	52015	2088
阜阳市	Fuyang	6	32	15188	41038	18530	42952	61177	121266	4498
淮南市	Huainan	6	14	20428	9495	30902	14779	91581	43177	1518
滁州市	Chuzhou	4	10	18324	12988	19404	13859	62793	40351	1952
六安市	Luan	4	15	15776	21913	14990	20632	55574	52049	2004
马鞍山市	Maanshan	6	6	19577	7044	24950	9406	75993	22995	782
芜湖市	Wuhu	10	14	45414	12275	46494	8753	156010	33006	1729
宣城市	Xuancheng	1	11	2355	7921	4914	9273	15096	26645	1751
铜陵市	Tongling	3	5	11655	2987	14833	9604	46928	16378	624
池州市	Chizhou	3	6	10864	5221	13474	7816	41884	15533	666
安庆市	Anqing	5	26	15164	8211	20138	13076	60890	33787	2018
黄山市	Huangshan	3	10	6767	5093	9470	7468	33428	18510	698

19—16 各市特殊教育情况（2022年）
Basic Statistics on Special Education by Region (2022)

单位：人（person）

地区	Region	学校数(所) Number of Schools (unit)	毕业生数 Number of Graduates	招生数 New Student Enrollment	在校学生数 Student Enrollment	教职工数 Number of Staff and Teachers	专任教师数 Number of Full-time Teachers
总计	**Total**	**77**	**6102**	**6564**	**42421**	**2479**	**2225**
合肥市	Hefei	7	768	869	5031	305	332
淮北市	Huaibei	2	224	252	1361	47	41
亳州市	Bozhou	4	552	605	4681	219	200
宿州市	Suzhou	6	505	469	4233	230	202
蚌埠市	Bengbu	5	429	436	2916	120	115
阜阳市	Fuyang	7	952	1084	7410	323	304
淮南市	Huainan	3	386	381	2171	93	55
滁州市	Chuzhou	6	352	381	2192	161	138
六安市	Luan	7	506	625	3516	210	176
马鞍山市	Maanshan	4	112	115	982	82	79
芜湖市	Wuhu	6	247	243	1538	139	99
宣城市	Xuancheng	6	160	203	1343	140	122
铜陵市	Tongling	2	86	78	630	59	55
池州市	Chizhou	2	173	143	917	69	60
安庆市	Anqing	8	544	560	2881	240	214
黄山市	Huangshan	2	106	120	619	42	33

19—17 各市普通中学分城乡学校数和在校学生数（2022年）

Number of Regular Secondary Schools and Student Enrollment by Urban and Rural Areas and by Region (2022)

地 区	Region	学 校 数 （所） Number of Regular Secondary Schools (unit)							
		普通高中合 计 General Senior High School Total	城 区 Urban Areas	镇 区 Counties and Towns	乡 村 Rural Areas	初中合计 Junior High School Together	城 区 Urban Areas	镇 区 Counties and Towns	乡 村 Rural Areas
总 计	**Total**	**679**	**249**	**399**	**31**	**2780**	**475**	**1288**	**1017**
合肥市	Hefei	100	41	54	5	217	74	104	39
淮北市	Huaibei	21	14	7		104	44	34	26
亳州市	Bozhou	33	10	22	1	279	28	141	110
宿州市	Suzhou	48	8	40		205	11	117	77
蚌埠市	Bengbu	42	12	27	3	148	21	57	70
阜阳市	Fuyang	61	21	37	3	369	48	174	147
淮南市	Huainan	46	22	24		149	38	62	49
滁州市	Chuzhou	54	15	38	1	198	21	116	61
六安市	Luan	54	9	39	6	283	21	110	152
马鞍山市	Maanshan	19	9	9	1	85	20	34	31
芜湖市	Wuhu	46	28	16	2	164	54	76	34
宣城市	Xuancheng	21	9	11	1	121	25	64	32
铜陵市	Tongling	24	10	13	1	61	18	31	12
池州市	Chizhou	23	8	13	2	76	12	32	32
安庆市	Anqing	67	24	38	5	230	30	93	107
黄山市	Huangshan	20	9	11		91	10	43	38

地 区	Region	在校学生数 （人） Student Enrollment (person)							
		普通高中合 计 General Senior High School Total	城 区 Urban Areas	镇 区 Counties and Towns	乡 村 Rural Areas	初中合计 Junior High School Together	城 区 Urban Areas	镇 区 Counties and Towns	乡 村 Rural Areas
总 计	**Total**	**1200980**	**458856**	**713407**	**28717**	**2287654**	**661230**	**1278240**	**348184**
合肥市	Hefei	171998	82840	85278	3880	268762	137491	123119	8152
淮北市	Huaibei	39904	22252	17652		77562	32782	33380	11400
亳州市	Bozhou	111047	31670	76216	3161	262593	53231	168864	40498
宿州市	Suzhou	101806	15712	86094		241739	32543	172850	36346
蚌埠市	Bengbu	68101	20252	46376	1473	150059	22863	96881	30315
阜阳市	Fuyang	177854	50664	122658	4532	396980	75590	239991	81399
淮南市	Huainan	59835	26620	33215		124638	38586	62339	23713
滁州市	Chuzhou	67172	25719	41238	215	119326	40155	70693	8478
六安市	Luan	102358	34542	63518	4298	180680	47177	92701	40802
马鞍山市	Maanshan	36707	15560	20551	596	57774	24848	22343	10583
芜湖市	Wuhu	64785	42390	19179	3216	94724	52751	36160	5813
宣城市	Xuancheng	35241	21747	12410	1084	66673	28612	32726	5335
铜陵市	Tongling	24689	12072	12302	315	36230	16156	17903	2171
池州市	Chizhou	31700	13240	16678	1782	42044	14892	21257	5895
安庆市	Anqing	87268	35264	47839	4165	133011	31667	66552	34792
黄山市	Huangshan	20515	8312	12203		34859	11886	20481	2492

19—18 各市普通中学分城乡招生数和毕业生数（2022年）

Number of New Student Enrollment and Graduates of Regular Secondary Schools by Urban and Rural Areas and by Region (2022)

单位：人（person）

地区	Region	招生数 New Student Enrollment							
		普通高中合计 General Senior High School Total	城区 Urban Areas	镇区 Counties and Towns	乡村 Rural Areas	初中合计 Junior High School Total	城区 Urban Areas	镇区 Counties and Towns	乡村 Rural Areas
总计	**Total**	**420893**	**159308**	**250529**	**11056**	**754202**	**221887**	**418695**	**113620**
合肥市	Hefei	61601	30477	29690	1434	89523	47156	39915	2452
淮北市	Huaibei	14075	7870	6205		26501	11249	11471	3781
亳州市	Bozhou	39578	11618	26958	1002	86714	17050	56313	13351
宿州市	Suzhou	37220	5160	32060		81530	11486	56951	13093
蚌埠市	Bengbu	24658	7473	16495	690	51474	7524	33704	10246
阜阳市	Fuyang	62201	17148	43147	1906	134153	27074	80556	26523
淮南市	Huainan	21525	9158	12367		40823	13125	19544	8154
滁州市	Chuzhou	22668	8569	14026	73	38704	13781	22442	2481
六安市	Luan	35843	11726	22126	1991	56824	14782	28912	13130
马鞍山市	Maanshan	12855	5547	7100	208	18969	7896	7750	3323
芜湖市	Wuhu	21755	14362	6270	1123	30721	17747	11218	1756
宣城市	Xuancheng	12318	7630	4234	454	21329	9246	10731	1352
铜陵市	Tongling	8332	4054	4043	235	10763	5142	5010	611
池州市	Chizhou	10461	4371	5530	560	12925	4537	6535	1853
安庆市	Anqing	28598	11197	16021	1380	41785	10113	20940	10732
黄山市	Huangshan	7205	2948	4257		11464	3979	6703	782

地区	Region	毕业生数 Number of Graduates							
		普通高中合计 General Senior High School Total	城区 Urban Areas	镇区 Counties and Towns	乡村 Rural Areas	初中合计 Junior High School Total	城区 Urban Areas	镇区 Counties and Towns	乡村 Rural Areas
总计	**Total**	**380654**	**149211**	**222620**	**8823**	**769189**	**214293**	**432158**	**122738**
合肥市	Hefei	55016	25472	28214	1330	95362	48155	43578	3629
淮北市	Huaibei	13055	7254	5801		25698	10267	11900	3531
亳州市	Bozhou	33407	9813	22560	1034	88744	15810	58041	14893
宿州市	Suzhou	29306	5621	23685		74899	9825	54192	10882
蚌埠市	Bengbu	19417	6144	12972	301	45024	7501	28576	8947
阜阳市	Fuyang	55707	16862	37639	1206	131380	20468	81402	29510
淮南市	Huainan	17052	8005	9047		41008	12144	21402	7462
滁州市	Chuzhou	21965	8615	13247	103	41965	13141	25259	3565
六安市	Luan	33364	11448	20986	930	62133	15389	31466	15278
马鞍山市	Maanshan	12725	5687	6914	124	20049	8819	7650	3580
芜湖市	Wuhu	21446	13742	6776	928	32130	16240	13251	2639
宣城市	Xuancheng	11640	6661	4310	669	23898	10107	11590	2201
铜陵市	Tongling	8896	4128	4768		13765	5844	6948	973
池州市	Chizhou	11097	4534	5806	757	15099	5231	7736	2132
安庆市	Anqing	30114	12503	16170	1441	45934	11242	22132	12560
黄山市	Huangshan	6447	2722	3725		12101	4110	7035	956

19—19 各市普通高中、初中和小学分城乡专任老师数（2022年）
Regular Senior High School, Junior High School and Primary School by Urban and Rural Full-time Teachers by Region (2022)

单位：人（person）

地　区	Region	普通高中合计 General Senior High School Total	城　区 Urban Areas	镇　区 Counties and Towns	乡　村 Rural Areas	初中合计 Junior High School Total	城　区 Urban Areas
总　计	**Total**	**90183**	**35503**	**52459**	**2221**	**171110**	**47838**
合 肥 市	Hefei	13133	6063	6722	348	21796	10630
淮 北 市	Huaibei	3006	1736	1270		5779	2498
亳 州 市	Bozhou	7842	2327	5317	198	16165	3209
宿 州 市	Suzhou	7569	1205	6364		17162	2412
蚌 埠 市	Bengbu	4772	1502	3151	119	9902	1848
阜 阳 市	Fuyang	11194	3416	7524	254	24076	4344
淮 南 市	Huainan	4022	1987	2035		9135	2869
滁 州 市	Chuzhou	5455	1999	3417	39	10155	2777
六 安 市	Luan	7683	2685	4672	326	14293	2843
马鞍山市	Maanshan	3026	1416	1569	41	5096	1892
芜 湖 市	Wuhu	5257	3459	1543	255	8525	4065
宣 城 市	Xuancheng	2976	1690	1133	153	5791	2186
铜 陵 市	Tongling	2319	1005	1289	25	4127	1579
池 州 市	Chizhou	2378	949	1297	132	3499	1050
安 庆 市	Anqing	7877	3396	4150	331	12423	2766
黄 山 市	Huangshan	1674	668	1006		3186	870

地　区	Region	镇　区 Counties and Towns	乡　村 Rural Areas	小学合计 Primary School Total	城　区 Urban Areas	镇　区 Counties and Towns	乡　村 Rural Areas
总　计	**Total**	**93386**	**29886**	**269668**	**79163**	**118343**	**72162**
合 肥 市	Hefei	10178	988	36493	20672	13132	2689
淮 北 市	Huaibei	2337	944	9033	3708	2930	2395
亳 州 市	Bozhou	10171	2785	27784	5154	12377	10253
宿 州 市	Suzhou	12023	2727	29948	4410	15642	9896
蚌 埠 市	Bengbu	5962	2092	17274	3320	8304	5650
阜 阳 市	Fuyang	14329	5403	39197	6590	16975	15632
淮 南 市	Huainan	4418	1848	13500	3999	5526	3975
滁 州 市	Chuzhou	6303	1075	14732	4533	8439	1760
六 安 市	Luan	7353	4097	19787	4489	8823	6475
马鞍山市	Maanshan	2057	1147	7584	2765	3254	1565
芜 湖 市	Wuhu	3621	839	12853	6913	4513	1427
宣 城 市	Xuancheng	2921	684	8796	3478	4168	1150
铜 陵 市	Tongling	2148	400	5115	2064	2000	1051
池 州 市	Chizhou	1781	668	5166	1544	2420	1202
安 庆 市	Anqing	5888	3769	17192	3980	7265	5947
黄 山 市	Huangshan	1896	420	5214	1544	2575	1095

19—20 各市小学分城乡情况（2022年）

Primary Schools by Urban and Rural Conditions by Region (2022)

地 区	Region	学校数（所）Number of Primary Schools (unit)	城区 Urban Areas	镇区 Counties and Towns	乡村 Rural Areas	在校学生数（人）Student Enrollment (person)	城区 Urban Areas	镇区 Counties and Towns	乡村 Rural Areas
总 计	**Total**	**6509**	**873**	**1958**	**3678**	**4702546**	**1516553**	**2215959**	**970034**
合肥市	Hefei	470	166	183	121	638097	383626	232707	21764
淮北市	Huaibei	274	61	62	151	174005	73426	62198	38381
亳州市	Bozhou	908	54	193	661	500022	100054	252724	147244
宿州市	Suzhou	723	25	199	499	516178	72060	291559	152559
蚌埠市	Bengbu	544	45	111	388	321655	54252	177740	89663
阜阳市	Fuyang	1187	75	326	786	804378	162658	389515	252205
淮南市	Huainan	385	60	100	225	235899	83037	102261	50601
滁州市	Chuzhou	227	46	127	54	249113	88871	139309	20933
六安市	Luan	346	28	131	187	313626	92812	156507	64307
马鞍山市	Maanshan	179	45	57	77	121296	49331	53676	18289
芜湖市	Wuhu	236	80	98	58	212349	126560	72448	13341
宣城市	Xuancheng	132	30	68	34	132510	62130	60060	10320
铜陵市	Tongling	112	42	45	25	68897	35296	27002	6599
池州市	Chizhou	154	28	55	71	81327	31905	38445	10977
安庆市	Anqing	507	68	158	281	260336	72854	122450	65032
黄山市	Huangshan	125	20	45	60	72858	27681	37358	7819

地 区	Region	毕业生数（人）Number of Graduates (person)	城区 Urban Areas	镇区 Counties and Towns	乡村 Rural Areas	招生数（人）New Student Enrollment (person)	城区 Urban Areas	镇区 Counties and Towns	乡村 Rural Areas
总 计	**Total**	**749504**	**206031**	**361162**	**182311**	**757258**	**275103**	**352103**	**130052**
合肥市	Hefei	87208	48188	33973	5047	120285	74690	42761	2834
淮北市	Huaibei	26297	10776	10554	4967	29083	13002	10111	5970
亳州市	Bozhou	87934	14616	46161	27157	70923	16164	36391	18368
宿州市	Suzhou	84073	8893	48539	26641	78428	13050	44488	20890
蚌埠市	Bengbu	51338	8707	25042	17589	49770	8552	29478	11740
阜阳市	Fuyang	131451	21228	64413	45810	121204	29256	58580	33368
淮南市	Huainan	41785	12680	18106	10999	35857	14073	15485	6299
滁州市	Chuzhou	38578	12267	21958	4353	42529	16109	23664	2756
六安市	Luan	54371	13521	26779	14071	48900	16468	23915	8517
马鞍山市	Maanshan	18929	7403	8007	3519	20269	8666	9248	2355
芜湖市	Wuhu	30065	16110	11222	2733	36471	23626	11063	1782
宣城市	Xuancheng	21349	8892	10240	2217	21479	10459	9648	1372
铜陵市	Tongling	10529	4849	4320	1360	12202	6744	4471	987
池州市	Chizhou	12777	4315	6302	2160	14443	5818	6698	1927
安庆市	Anqing	41260	9798	19176	12286	43768	13593	20395	9780
黄山市	Huangshan	11560	3788	6370	1402	11647	4833	5707	1107

19—21 各市幼儿园基本情况（2022年）
Basic Statistics on Kindergartens by Region (2022)

单位：人（person）

地 区	Region	园 数（所）Number of Schools (unit)	离园人数 From the Number of Garden	招生数 New Student Enrollment	在园幼儿数 Number of children in the Kindergarten	教职工数 Number of Staff and Teachers	专任教师数 Number of Full-time Teachers
总 计	**Total**	**11577**	**775334**	**619956**	**2042987**	**237325**	**134909**
合肥市	Hefei	1563	117258	121404	361241	49870	24917
淮北市	Huaibei	370	30200	21942	76354	6640	4328
亳州市	Bozhou	1019	75603	53185	173965	17868	12527
宿州市	Suzhou	1551	86781	57334	211411	21690	14077
蚌埠市	Bengbu	748	54283	36805	117992	11403	6377
阜阳市	Fuyang	1833	119856	78828	288333	33666	19109
淮南市	Huainan	485	37992	28844	90262	9795	5858
滁州市	Chuzhou	662	41675	35406	126817	14016	8245
六安市	Luan	840	51151	38134	132546	16445	9121
马鞍山市	Maanshan	301	21275	21996	62085	7990	4168
芜湖市	Wuhu	580	33884	34636	100442	13602	7236
宣城市	Xuancheng	394	21261	19428	70696	9129	4958
铜陵市	Tongling	190	11370	9118	32786	4107	2256
池州市	Chizhou	175	14145	10369	36430	3969	2286
安庆市	Anqing	638	46498	40116	120777	12817	6845
黄山市	Huangshan	228	12102	12411	40850	4318	2601

19—22 各级各类学校教育经费收入情况（2022年）
Basic Statistics on Educational Funds in Various Schools (2022)

单位：万元（10000 yuan）

指标	Item	合计 Total	国家财政性教育经费 Government Appropriation for Education	一般公共预算教育经费 General Public Budget Funds for Education	民办学校中举办者投入 Conducting Investment of Voluntary School	捐赠收入 Donation Income	事业收入 Undertaking Revenue	其他收入 Other Income
总计	**Total**	**20532087**	**16580173**	**14200714**	**59545**	**5990**	**3368366**	**518013**
高等教育	Institutions of Higher Education	4264486	2551979	2218154	25120	2836	1397068	287485
普通高等学校	Regular Institutions of Higher Education	4223629	2538130	2206455	25120	2836	1370823	286721
本科学校	Undergraduate Courses Schools	2782637	1549680	1360519	23054	2759	959002	248143
专科学校	Junior College	175038	142151	104308			28759	4128
职业学校	Vocational Schools	1265954	846300	741629	2065	77	383062	34450
成人高等学校	Institutions of Higher Education for Adults	40857	13849	11699			26245	763
高中阶段教育	High School Education	3697525	2919347	2308469	8415	1738	720882	47144
中等职业学校	Vocational Secondary Schools	1226949	1052525	797725	5567	96	145985	22776
中等专业学校	Specialized Secondary Schools	1113660	950413	736005	4636	96	139498	19017
职业高中	Vocational Schools	24888	22196	16425	331		2361	
#农　村	Rural Areas	10485	8494	7916	331		1660	
技工学校	Technical Schools	80418	73361	39528			3298	3759
成人中等专业学校	Specialized Secondary Schools for Adults	7984	6555	5766	600		829	
普通高中	Senior Secondary Schools	2470576	1866822	1510744	2848	1642	574897	24368
#农　村	Rural Areas	1285023	937948	756801	1933	772	334271	10099
义务教育	Compulsory education	10195789	9450898	8242862	18281	799	581174	144638
普通初中	Regular Junior Secondary Schools	4175657	3724587	3272845	12489	470	385155	52956
#农　村	Rural Areas	2884120	2607918	2278053	7646	460	232231	35866
普通小学	Regular Primary Schools	6020132	5726311	4970017	5792	329	196019	91682
#农　村	Rural Areas	4120867	3938712	3377132	4867	281	121532	55475
特殊教育	Special Education	147245	146303	136524		147	69	726
学前教育	Preschool Education	1717991	1035195	897242	7730	466	644952	29648
#农　村	Rural Areas	983298	641866	539542	4000	116	333542	3774
其　他	Others	509051	476452	397463		5	24221	8373

19—23 全省科技活动基本情况
Basic Statistics on Scientific and Technological Activities

指　　标	Item	2010	2015	2020	2021	2022
科技活动	**Scientific and Technological Activities**					
研究与试验发展人员（万人）	Research and Experimental Developers (10000 persons)		20.48	27.88	35.02	37.50
研究与试验发展经费支出（亿元）	Expenditure on R&D (100 million yuan)	163.72	431.75	883.18	1006.12	1152.51
#基础研究	Basic Research	12.23	24.31	60.89	74.11	103.68
应用研究	Applied Research	15.66	33.48	78.46	84.22	96.77
试验发展	Experimental Development	135.83	373.96	743.83	847.80	952.06
#政府资金	Government Fund	36.07	86.42	134.83	146.48	186.56
企业资金	Self-raised Funds by Enterprise	118.86	331.07	720.22	834.25	934.54
#相当于GDP比例（%）	Proportion of Expenditure on R&D to GDP (%)	1.32	1.96	2.28	2.34	2.56
输出技术合同成交额（亿元）	**Export Technology Contract Turnover (100 million yuan)**	**46.15**	**190.53**	**742.44**	**1754.55**	**2216.72**
专　利	**Patent**					
专利申请授权量（件）	Total Patent Applications Authorized (unit)	16012	59039	119696	153475	156584
发　明	Creation and Inventions	1111	11180	21432	23624	26180
实用新型	Utility Models	8839	41094	84609	114415	115757
外观设计	Designs	6062	6765	13655	15436	14647

19—24 县级以上政府部门属研究与开发机构及科技信息与文献机构数、人员数

State-owned Research and Development Institutions and Information and Literature Institutions at and Above County Level and Persons Engaged

年 份 Year	合 计 Total		自然科学技术领域 Field of Natural Sciences and Humanities			社会、人文科学技术领域 Field of Social Sciences and Humanities			科技信息和文献机构 Scientific-technical Information and Literature Institutions		
	机 构（个）Institutions (unit)	从业人员（人）Employees (person)	机 构（个）Institutions (unit)	从业人员（人）Employees (person)	科技活动人员(人) S&T Personnel (person)	机 构（个）Institutions (unit)	从业人员（人）Employees (person)	科技活动人员(人) S&T Personnel (person)	机 构（个）Institutions (unit)	从业人员（人）Employees (person)	科技活动人员(人) S&T Personnel (person)
2010	104	6227	83	5405	4402	7	335	313	14	487	455
2014	97	7117	76	6468	5867	7	309	257	14	340	307
2015	95	7203	75	6514	5949	7	310	259	13	379	334
2016	93	6934	72	6169	5588	9	383	334	12	382	341
2017	93	7208	73	6465	6850	8	354	319	12	389	378
2018	90	7327	71	6588	7180	8	372	328	11	367	309
2019	84	7323	66	6580	7358	8	375	328	10	368	351
2020	80	7215	61	6452	8192	9	390	351	10	373	343
2021	82	7347	63	6590	9047	9	409	367	10	348	310
2022	75	7283	58	6575	9034	8	376	379	9	332	310

19—25 县级以上政府部门属研究与开发机构及科技信息与文献机构科技经费筹集和支出总额

Total Funds and Total Expenditures of State-owned Research and Development Institutions and Information and Literature Institutions at and Above County Level

单位：万元（10000 yuan）

年 份 Year	合 计 Total		自然科学技术领域 Field of Natural Sciences and Humanities			社会、人文科学技术领域 Field of Social Sciences and Humanities			科技信息和文献机构 Scientific-technical Information and Literature Institutions		
	科技活动收入 S&T Income	科技经费内部支出 Intramural Expenditure on S&T	科技活动收入 S&T Income	政府资金 Government Funds	科技经费内部支出 Intramural Expenditure on S&T	科技活动收入 S&T Income	政府资金 Government Funds	科技经费内部支出 Intramural Expenditure on S&T	科技活动收入 S&T Income	政府资金 Government Funds	科技经费内部支出 Intramural Expenditure on S&T
2010	191056	134839	172837	149390	118150	8210	5816	6851	10009	8608	9837
2014	272412	263631	255037	193514	250498	8512	6590	6338	8863	8059	6795
2015	302593	245986	284101	220104	230394	9923	6841	8160	8569	7954	7432
2016	278931	240220	257619	202083	221267	11947	8796	10180	9365	8094	8774
2017	361779	323452	334873	268752	302397	15791	11719	12257	11115	9647	8798
2018	400500	361335	368656	269594	337449	19168	9521	11572	12676	12300	12313
2019		354597			329012			16196			9390
2020		353984			331761			13998			8225
2021		383287			359820			14872			8594
2022		463328			433721			18656			10951

注：自2019年起，科技活动收入及政府资金数据不再统计。

a) Since 2019, data on revenue from science and technology activities and government funding will no longer be collected.

19—26 科协系统科技活动情况（2022年）

Basic Statistics on Scientific and Technological Activities of Associations for Science and Technology (2022)

项　　目		Item		科协合计 Total Number of Associations for Science & Technology	省科协 provincial Associations	省级学会 Provincial-level Learned Societies
机构数	**（个）**	**Number of Associations or Learned Societies**	**(unit)**	**161**	**1**	**160**
直属单位		Directly Under The Unit		4	4	
人员数	**（人）**	**Personnel**	**(person)**			
机　关		Associations		46	46	
直属单位		Enterprises and Non-profit Organizations Attached to Associations or Learned Societies		102	102	
学会理事		Members of Councils		12831		12831
学术活动		**Academic Activities**				
国内学术会议		Domestic Academic Meetings				
次　数	（次）	Number	(times)	212	2	210
参加人数	（人次）	Number of Participants	(person-time)	200000	1400	198600
交流论文数	（篇）	Number of Papers Presented	(unit)	11000		11000
国际学术会议		International Meetings Held in China				
次　数	（次）	Number	(times)	1		1
参加人数	（人次）	Number of Participants	(person-time)	1000		1000
交流论文数	（篇）	Number of Papers Presented	(unit)	41		41
国际民间科技交流		International Folk Exchange of S&T				
接待来访科技团组	（个）	International Group on S&T Received Home	(unit)			
接待总人数	（人次）	Person Received	(person-time)			
外派科技团组	（个）	Number of Study Tours Sent Aboard	(unit)			
外派总人数	（人次）	Total People Sent Aboard	(person-time)			
科技培训		**Training Program**				
参加培训人数	（人次）	Number of Training	(person-time)	304	304	
科普活动		**Activities for Popular Science**				
讲座次数	（次）	Number of Lectures	(times)	748	166	582
听讲座人数	（人次）	Number of Participants	(person-time)	92113	31000	61113
展览次数	（次）	Number of Exhibitions	(times)	53	8	45
参观展览人数	（万人次）	Number of Participants	(10000 person-time)	3.4	1	2
青少年科技竞赛次数	（次）	Number of Teenagers Participating in Science and Technology Competitions	(time)	62	8	54
未成年人参观科技场馆人次	（万人次）	Number of Visits by Minors to Science and Technology Venues	(10000 person-time)	16	16	
出　版		**Publications**				
科技期刊种数	（种）	Number of Academic Journals	(kind)	17		17
论文集种数	（种）	Number of Collections of Articles	(kind)			
论文集发行量	（册）	Number of Copies Distributed	(copies)			
科技报纸种数	（种）	Number of Scientific & Technological Newspapers	(kind)	3	1	2

注：自2020年始，省科协机构仅统计省级单位。

a) Since 2020, provincial associations for science and technology have counted only provincial units.

19—27 各市规上企业分行业创新情况（2022年）
Innovation of Enterprises by Industry by Region (2022)

地区	Region	企业数（个）companies (unit)	工业 Industry	建筑业 Construction Industry	服务业 Services	开展创新活动的企业所占比重(%) Proportion of Enterprises Carrying Out Innovative Activities (%)	工业 Industry
总计	**Total**	**39545**	**21392**	**3329**	**14824**	**51.5**	**67.8**
合肥市	Hefei	7634	2529	1231	3874	53.6	77.5
淮北市	Huaibei	1022	638	39	345	44.2	53.1
亳州市	Bozhou	1470	724	176	570	50.3	70.3
宿州市	Suzhou	2046	1174	113	759	45.4	56.8
蚌埠市	Bengbu	1865	925	109	831	50.5	75.8
阜阳市	Fuyang	2623	1534	152	937	55.1	69.2
淮南市	Huainan	1430	845	80	505	42.1	52.9
滁州市	Chuzhou	3413	2368	203	842	53.2	65.7
六安市	Luan	2261	1325	164	772	53.2	65.4
马鞍山市	Maanshan	1967	1378	148	441	58.2	71.1
芜湖市	Wuhu	4744	2256	298	2190	44.2	64.5
宣城市	Xuancheng	2710	2091	141	478	52.6	60.4
铜陵市	Tongling	1166	623	142	401	47.2	63.2
池州市	Chizhou	1203	703	81	419	54.6	73.4
安庆市	Anqing	3065	1724	203	1138	57.5	80.5
黄山市	Huangshan	926	555	49	322	55.3	71.7

地区	Region	建筑业 Construction Industry	服务业 Services	开展创新合作的企业所占比重(%) Proportion of Enterprises Engaged in Innovation Cooperation (%)	工业 Industry	建筑业 Construction Industry	服务业 Services
总计	**Total**	**35.5**	**31.6**	**33.3**	**45.3**	**22.3**	**18.5**
合肥市	Hefei	40.0	42.2	35.6	54.9	25.7	26.2
淮北市	Huaibei	48.7	27.3	30.9	37.9	41.0	16.8
亳州市	Bozhou	37.5	28.8	32.6	46.4	23.9	17.7
宿州市	Suzhou	33.6	29.4	27.7	35.6	25.7	15.7
蚌埠市	Bengbu	31.2	24.8	32.0	50.4	22.0	12.9
阜阳市	Fuyang	46.7	33.5	38.3	50.8	27.6	19.6
淮南市	Huainan	37.5	24.8	29.9	38.8	21.3	16.4
滁州市	Chuzhou	30.1	23.6	33.0	41.7	18.7	11.9
六安市	Luan	36.0	35.8	32.7	42.5	23.2	18.0
马鞍山市	Maanshan	25.7	28.6	39.4	48.5	16.2	18.6
芜湖市	Wuhu	35.6	24.5	29.3	43.8	20.5	15.6
宣城市	Xuancheng	30.5	24.9	31.3	36.8	15.6	11.7
铜陵市	Tongling	23.9	30.4	32.3	45.3	12.7	19.0
池州市	Chizhou	23.5	29.1	31.6	41.5	16.1	17.9
安庆市	Anqing	25.6	28.3	35.1	51.7	13.3	13.9
黄山市	Huangshan	38.8	29.5	37.8	50.6	28.6	17.1

19—28 规上企业创新情况（2022年）
Enterprise Innovation on Regulation (2022)

类别	Category	企业数（个）Number of Enterprises (unit)	开展创新活动 Carry out Innovation Activities	实现创新 Implement Innovation	占全部企业比重(%) Accounts for the Proportion of all Enterprises (%) 有创新活动 There are Innovation Activities	实现创新 Implement Innovation
总　　计	**Total**	**39545**	**20362**	**19442**	**51.5**	**49.2**
按行业分	**According to the Industry**					
采矿业	Mining	345	146	120	42.3	34.8
制造业	Manufacturing	20401	14103	13405	69.1	65.7
电力、热力、燃气及水的生产和供应业	Electricity, Heat, Gas and Water Production and Supply Industry	646	253	233	39.2	36.1
建筑业	Construction	3329	1181	1140	35.5	34.2
批发和零售业	Wholesale and Retail Trades	10138	2773	2750	27.4	27.1
交通运输、仓储和邮政业	Transport, Storage and Postal Services	1427	327	318	22.9	22.3
信息传输、计算机服务和软件业	Information Circulation, Computer Services and Software	770	551	510	71.6	66.2
租赁和商务服务业	Leasing and Commercial Services	1584	495	479	31.3	30.2
科学研究和技术服务业	Scientific Research and Technical Services	715	462	418	64.6	58.5
水利、环境和公共设施管理业	Water Conservancy, Environmental and Public Facilities Management	190	71	69	37.4	36.3
按地区分	**According to the Region**					
合 肥 市	Hefei	7634	4088	3912	53.5	51.2
淮 北 市	Huaibei	1022	452	446	44.2	43.6
亳 州 市	Bozhou	1470	739	704	50.3	47.9
宿 州 市	Suzhou	2046	928	877	45.4	42.9
蚌 埠 市	Bengbu	1865	941	917	50.5	49.2
阜 阳 市	Fuyang	2623	1446	1395	55.1	53.2
淮 南 市	Huainan	1430	602	595	42.1	41.6
滁 州 市	Chuzhou	3413	1816	1789	53.2	52.4
六 安 市	Luan	2261	1202	1152	53.2	51.0
马鞍山市	Maanshan	1967	1144	1113	58.2	56.6
芜 湖 市	Wuhu	4744	2098	1999	44.2	42.1
宣 城 市	Xuancheng	2710	1425	1366	52.6	50.4
铜 陵 市	Tongling	1166	550	534	47.2	45.8
池 州 市	Chizhou	1203	657	538	54.6	44.7
安 庆 市	Anqing	3065	1762	1608	57.5	52.5
黄 山 市	Huangshan	926	512	497	55.3	53.7

19—29 规上企业产品和工艺创新情况（2022年）
Product and Process Innovation of Enterprises on The Regulation (2022)

类　别	Category	企业数（个）Number of Enterprises (unit)	占全部企业比重(%) Accounts for the Proportion of all Enterprises (%)		
			开展产品或工艺创新活动企业 Enterprises Carrying out Product or Process Innovation Activities	实现产品创新企业 Realize Product Innovation Enterprises	实现工艺创新企业 Realize Process Innovation Enterprises
总　计	**Total**	**39545**	**40.9**	**24.4**	**30.7**
按行业分	**According to the Industry**				
采矿业	Mining	345	34.2	6.7	24.1
制造业	Manufacturing	20401	63.8	40.5	48.1
电力、热力、燃气及水的生产和供应业	Electricity, Heat, Gas and Water Production and Supply Industry	646	27.4	4.0	22.5
建筑业	Construction	3329	20.2	7.0	16.3
批发和零售业	Wholesale and Retail Trades	10138	8.6	4.1	6.6
交通运输、仓储和邮政业	Transport, Storage and Postal Services	1427	11.0	4.0	9.1
信息传输、计算机服务和软件业	Information Circulation, Computer Services and Software	770	63.5	40.0	39.9
租赁和商务服务业	Leasing and Commercial Services	1584	13.0	6.4	8.3
科学研究和技术服务业	Scientific Research and Technical Services	715	56.8	27.8	38.6
水利、环境和公共设施管理业	Water Conservancy, Environmental and Public Facilities Management	190	25.3	12.6	17.4
按地区分	**According to the Region**				
合肥市	Hefei	7634	41.6	23.4	31.2
淮北市	Huaibei	1022	33.4	16.1	27.7
亳州市	Bozhou	1470	36.6	21.0	28.4
宿州市	Suzhou	2046	33.2	19.1	24.3
蚌埠市	Bengbu	1865	40.3	25.7	29.3
阜阳市	Fuyang	2623	44.4	26.7	35.0
淮南市	Huainan	1430	28.9	13.9	23.4
滁州市	Chuzhou	3413	43.9	35.9	31.3
六安市	Luan	2261	41.1	24.1	32.4
马鞍山市	Maanshan	1967	51.5	29.7	40.4
芜湖市	Wuhu	4744	34.3	20.6	24.8
宣城市	Xuancheng	2710	44.2	28.4	33.3
铜陵市	Tongling	1166	37.1	23.6	29.0
池州市	Chizhou	1203	45.3	22.5	27.7
安庆市	Anqing	3065	47.1	22.7	35.5
黄山市	Huangshan	926	43.8	30.6	33.9

19—30　规上企业组织和营销创新情况（2022年）
Enterprise Organization and Marketing Innovation on Regulation (2022)

类　　别	Category	企业数（个）Number of Enterprises (unit)	占全部企业比重(%) Accounts for the Proportion of all Enterprises (%)		
			开展组织或营销创新活动企业 Enterprises Carrying out Organizational or Marketing Innovation Activities	实现组织创新企业 Realize the Organization of Innovative Enterprises	实现营销创新企业 Realize Marketing Innovation Enterprises
总　计	**Total**	**39545**	**36.8**	**29.4**	**26.7**
按行业分	**According to the Industry**				
采矿业	Mining	345	21.7	19.1	9.6
制造业	Manufacturing	20401	45.2	35.8	35.1
电力、热力、燃气及水的生产和供应业	Electricity, Heat, Gas and Water Production and Supply Industry	646	23.5	21.8	7.4
建筑业	Construction	3329	29.0	27.7	9.7
批发和零售业	Wholesale and Retail Trades	10138	26.2	18.6	20.9
交通运输、仓储和邮政业	Transport, Storage and Postal Services	1427	19.9	18.4	9.1
信息传输、计算机服务和软件业	Information Circulation, Computer Services and Software	770	52.3	46.5	34.8
租赁和商务服务业	Leasing and Commercial Services	1584	27.9	23.4	16.7
科学研究和技术服务业	Scientific Research and Technical Services	715	43.6	39.2	22.7
水利、环境和公共设施管理业	Water Conservancy, Environmental and Public Facilities Management	190	28.4	23.7	20.0
按地区分	**According to the Region**				
合 肥 市	Hefei	7634	40.5	33.3	26.6
淮 北 市	Huaibei	1022	33.6	25.7	25.9
亳 州 市	Bozhou	1470	38.5	31.6	27.6
宿 州 市	Suzhou	2046	32.6	25.2	24.3
蚌 埠 市	Bengbu	1865	36.0	28.7	26.0
阜 阳 市	Fuyang	2623	40.3	31.1	32.1
淮 南 市	Huainan	1430	33.1	27.0	23.4
滁 州 市	Chuzhou	3413	36.8	28.2	28.5
六 安 市	Luan	2261	39.7	31.5	30.2
马鞍山市	Maanshan	1967	36.9	29.6	26.3
芜 湖 市	Wuhu	4744	31.9	26.6	22.5
宣 城 市	Xuancheng	2710	33.9	27.0	24.2
铜 陵 市	Tongling	1166	34.2	27.4	23.5
池 州 市	Chizhou	1203	33.7	27.4	24.4
安 庆 市	Anqing	3065	39.0	30.9	30.2
黄 山 市	Huangshan	926	41.4	28.9	32.6

19—31 规上企业创新合作情况（2022年）
Innovation Cooperation of Enterprises in Accordance With Regulations (2022)

类别	Category	企业数（个）Number of Enterprises (unit)	占全部企业比重(%) Accounts for the Proportion of all Enterprises (%)			
			开展创新合作的企业 Enterprises Carrying out Innovation Cooperation	开展产学研合作的企业 Enterprises Carrying out Industry-university-research Cooperation	与高等学校开展创新合作的企业 Enterprises that Cooperate With Institutions of Higher Learning in Innovation	与研究机构开展创新合作的企业 Enterprises Engaged in Innovation Cooperation With Research Institutions
总计	**Total**	**39545**	**33.3**	**13.1**	**11.3**	**5.6**
按行业分	**According to the Industry**					
采矿业	Mining	345	21.2	11.0	9.6	7.5
制造业	Manufacturing	20401	46.3	20.9	17.9	8.9
电力、热力、燃气及水的生产和供应业	Electricity, Heat, Gas and Water Production and Supply Industry	646	25.2	7.4	5.6	3.9
建筑业	Construction	3329	22.3	5.9	4.9	2.4
批发和零售业	Wholesale and Retail Trades	10138	14.8	1.8	1.5	0.8
交通运输、仓储和邮政业	Transport, Storage and Postal Services	1427	12.2	1.7	1.3	0.7
信息传输、计算机服务和软件业	Information Circulation, Computer Services and Software	770	53.1	20.9	19.1	8.1
租赁和商务服务业	Leasing and Commercial Services	1584	18.9	4.6	4.2	1.3
科学研究和技术服务业	Scientific Research and Technical Services	715	44.5	26.4	24.3	12.0
水利、环境和公共设施管理业	Water Conservancy, Environmental and Public Facilities Management	190	24.7	6.8	6.3	5.8
按地区分	**According to the Region**					
合肥市	Hefei	7634	35.6	14.1	12.4	6.4
淮北市	Huaibei	1022	30.9	14.6	12.5	6.7
亳州市	Bozhou	1470	32.6	11.2	9.7	5.0
宿州市	Suzhou	2046	27.7	9.6	8.2	3.5
蚌埠市	Bengbu	1865	32.0	13.1	11.0	6.5
阜阳市	Fuyang	2623	38.3	14.4	13.0	6.1
淮南市	Huainan	1430	29.9	10.6	9.0	4.7
滁州市	Chuzhou	3413	33.0	12.1	9.5	6.1
六安市	Luan	2261	32.7	10.0	8.3	4.8
马鞍山市	Maanshan	1967	39.4	21.0	17.7	8.1
芜湖市	Wuhu	4744	29.3	12.5	11.3	4.7
宣城市	Xuancheng	2710	31.3	10.6	9.2	3.7
铜陵市	Tongling	1166	32.3	13.8	11.3	6.2
池州市	Chizhou	1203	31.6	14.1	11.2	5.9
安庆市	Anqing	3065	35.1	13.1	11.2	5.5
黄山市	Huangshan	926	37.8	16.5	15.0	5.8

19—32 规上工业企业创新情况（2022年）
Innovation of Industrial Enterprises on Regulation (2022)

类别	Category	企业数（个）Number of Enterprises (unit)	开展创新活动 Carry out Innovation Activities	实现创新 Implement Innovation	占全部企业比重(%) Accounts for the Proportion of all Enterprises (%) 有创新活动 There are Innovation Activities	实现创新 Implement Innovation
总计	**Total**	**21392**	**14502**	**13758**	**67.8**	**64.3**
按行业分	**According to the Industry**					
采矿业	Mining	345	146	120	42.3	34.8
制造业	Manufacturing	20401	14103	13405	69.1	65.7
电力、热力、燃气及水的生产和供应业	Electricity, Heat, Gas and Water Production and Supply Industry	646	253	233	39.2	36.1
按地区分	**According to the Region**					
合肥市	Hefei	2529	1960	1861	77.5	73.6
淮北市	Huaibei	638	339	334	53.1	52.4
亳州市	Bozhou	724	509	477	70.3	65.9
宿州市	Suzhou	1174	667	622	56.8	53.0
蚌埠市	Bengbu	925	701	688	75.8	74.4
阜阳市	Fuyang	1534	1061	1025	69.2	66.8
淮南市	Huainan	845	447	442	52.9	52.3
滁州市	Chuzhou	2368	1556	1535	65.7	64.8
六安市	Luan	1325	867	825	65.4	62.3
马鞍山市	Maanshan	1378	980	955	71.1	69.3
芜湖市	Wuhu	2256	1456	1377	64.5	61.0
宣城市	Xuancheng	2091	1263	1209	60.4	57.8
铜陵市	Tongling	623	394	379	63.2	60.8
池州市	Chizhou	703	516	401	73.4	57.0
安庆市	Anqing	1724	1388	1243	80.5	72.1
黄山市	Huangshan	555	398	385	71.7	69.4

19—33 规上工业企业产品和工艺创新情况（2022年）

Product and Process Innovation of Industrial Enterprises (2022)

类　别	Category	企业数（个）Number of Enterprises (unit)	占全部企业比重(%) Accounts for the Proportion of all Enterprises (%)		
			开展产品或工艺创新活动企业 Enterprises Carrying out Product or Process Innovation Activities	实现产品创新企业 Realize Product Innovation Enterprises	实现工艺创新企业 Realize Process Innovation Enterprises
总　计	**Total**	**21392**	**62.2**	**38.9**	**46.9**
按行业分	**According to the Industry**				
采矿业	Mining	345	34.2	6.7	24.1
制造业	Manufacturing	20401	63.8	40.5	48.1
电力、热力、燃气及水的生产和供应业	Electricity, Heat, Gas and Water Production and Supply Industry	646	27.4	4.0	22.4
按地区分	**According to the Region**				
合 肥 市	Hefei	2529	73.7	43.7	57.3
淮 北 市	Huaibei	638	47.0	23.2	40.0
亳 州 市	Bozhou	724	63.1	36.3	48.6
宿 州 市	Suzhou	1174	49.7	31.7	35.9
蚌 埠 市	Bengbu	925	70.2	46.7	51.1
阜 阳 市	Fuyang	1534	65.3	41.6	51.7
淮 南 市	Huainan	845	40.2	21.3	33.0
滁 州 市	Chuzhou	2368	59.2	50.1	42.1
六 安 市	Luan	1325	59.6	36.4	47.6
马鞍山市	Maanshan	1378	67.0	39.8	53.0
芜 湖 市	Wuhu	2256	59.3	36.1	42.6
宣 城 市	Xuancheng	2091	54.4	35.5	41.1
铜 陵 市	Tongling	623	58.4	39.0	45.6
池 州 市	Chizhou	703	69.1	35.1	41.3
安 庆 市	Anqing	1724	75.6	37.2	57.0
黄 山 市	Huangshan	555	66.1	48.1	51.0

19—34 规上工业企业组织和营销创新情况（2022年）
Organizational and Marketing Innovation of Industrial Enterprises on Regulation (2022)

类别	Category	企业数（个） Number of Enterprises (unit)	占全部企业比重(%) Accounts for the Proportion of all Enterprises (%)		
			开展组织或营销创新活动企业 Enterprises Carrying out Organizational or Marketing Innovation Activities	实现组织创新企业 Realize the Organization of Innovative Enterprises	实现营销创新企业 Realize Marketing Innovation Enterprises
总计	**Total**	**21392**	**44.2**	**35.1**	**33.9**
按行业分	**According to the Industry**				
采矿业	Mining	345	21.7	19.1	9.6
制造业	Manufacturing	20401	45.2	35.8	35.1
电力、热力、燃气及水的生产和供应业	Electricity, Heat, Gas and Water Production and Supply Industry	646	23.5	21.8	7.4
按地区分	**According to the Region**				
合肥市	Hefei	2529	53.6	43.2	39.0
淮北市	Huaibei	638	37.5	29.9	29.9
亳州市	Bozhou	724	47.9	38.8	37.3
宿州市	Suzhou	1174	36.9	28.2	29.1
蚌埠市	Bengbu	925	49.3	39.5	36.8
阜阳市	Fuyang	1534	47.1	36.2	40.0
淮南市	Huainan	845	38.7	31.0	27.8
滁州市	Chuzhou	2368	43.2	32.9	34.6
六安市	Luan	1325	45.4	36.9	35.2
马鞍山市	Maanshan	1378	42.5	34.0	31.4
芜湖市	Wuhu	2256	41.2	34.2	30.0
宣城市	Xuancheng	2091	37.0	30.1	26.9
铜陵市	Tongling	623	41.3	33.2	30.5
池州市	Chizhou	703	39.5	32.7	29.3
安庆市	Anqing	1724	48.8	38.6	39.9
黄山市	Huangshan	555	50.3	34.8	41.1

19—35 规上工业企业创新合作情况（2022年）
Innovation Cooperation Among Industrial Enterprises (2022)

类　　别	Category	企业数（个）Number of Enterprises (unit)	占全部企业比重(%) Accounts for the Proportion of all Enterprises (%) 开展创新合作的企业 Enterprises Carrying out Innovation Cooperation	开展产学研合作的企业 Enterprises Carrying out Industry-university-research Cooperation	与高等学校开展创新合作的企业 Enterprises that Cooperate With Institutions of Higher Learning in Innovation	与研究机构开展创新合作的企业 Enterprises Engaged in Innovation Cooperation With Research Institutions
总　　计	**Total**	**21392**	**45.3**	**20.3**	**17.4**	**8.7**
按行业分	**According to the Industry**					
采矿业	Mining	345	21.2	11.0	9.6	7.5
制造业	Manufacturing	20401	46.3	20.9	17.9	8.9
电力、热力、燃气及水的生产和供应业	Electricity, Heat, Gas and Water Production and Supply Industry	646	25.2	7.4	5.6	3.9
按地区分	**According to the Region**					
合 肥 市	Hefei	2529	54.9	25.4	22.1	12.2
淮 北 市	Huaibei	638	37.9	20.5	17.6	9.3
亳 州 市	Bozhou	724	46.4	20.9	18.0	9.5
宿 州 市	Suzhou	1174	35.6	14.7	12.4	5.1
蚌 埠 市	Bengbu	925	50.4	22.2	18.6	11.2
阜 阳 市	Fuyang	1534	50.8	22.8	20.6	9.9
淮 南 市	Huainan	845	38.8	15.5	12.9	7.0
滁 州 市	Chuzhou	2368	41.7	16.6	13.0	8.4
六 安 市	Luan	1325	42.5	15.2	12.5	7.3
马鞍山市	Maanshan	1378	48.5	27.6	23.2	10.5
芜 湖 市	Wuhu	2256	43.8	21.9	19.9	8.2
宣 城 市	Xuancheng	2091	36.8	13.3	11.7	4.6
铜 陵 市	Tongling	623	45.3	22.6	18.6	10.1
池 州 市	Chizhou	703	41.5	21.5	17.1	9.3
安 庆 市	Anqing	1724	51.7	21.7	18.8	8.8
黄 山 市	Huangshan	555	50.6	26.3	24.0	9.0

19—36 研究与试验发展人员（2022年）
Research and Experimental Development Personnel (2022)

指　标	Item	调　查单位数（个）Number of Investigation Units (unit)	有研究与试验发展活动单位 Activity for R&D	研究与试验发展人员（人）Staff of R&D (person)	#研究人员 Staff of Researcher	#全时人员 Staff of Full Time
总　计	**Total**	**28534**	**10230**	**375002**	**152307**	**233056**
按执行部门分组	**Grouped by Execution Department**					
科研机构	Scientific Research Institution	83	63	14912	12363	9881
高等学校	Institutions of Higher Learning	233	226	57896	49172	26147
企　业	Companies	27850	9635	288538	82707	188417
事业单位	Institution	368	306	13656	8065	8611
按隶属关系分	**Grouped by Subordination Relations**					
中　央	Central	397	174	42863	30164	30957
地　方	Local	28137	10056	332139	122143	202099

指　标	Item	研究与试验发展人员折合全时当量（人年）Full-time Equivalent of R&D Personnel (man-years)	#研究人员 Staff of Researcher	#基础研究 Basic Research	#应用研究 Apply Researcher	#试验发展 Experime-ntal and Develop-ment Researcher
总　计	**Total**	**252476**	**99839**	**19790**	**24983**	**207703**
按执行部门分组	**Grouped by Execution Department**					
科研机构	Scientific Research Institution	12823	8865	2835	4752	5236
高等学校	Institutions of Higher Learning	29174	25571	15509	11419	2246
企　业	Companies	199998	58361	298	5294	194407
事业单位	Institution	10481	7042	1148	3518	5814
按隶属关系分	**Grouped by Subordination Relations**					
中　央	Central	32511	22155	10066	6076	16369
地　方	Local	219965	77684	9724	18907	191334

19—37 研究与试验发展经费支出情况（2022年）
Research and Development Funds and Internal Expenditure (2022)

单位：万元（10000 yuan）

项目	Item	研究与试验发展经费支出 Expenditure for R&D	按活动类型分 By Activities 基础研究 Fundamental Research	应用研究 Applied Rescarch	试验发展 Experimental	#人员劳务费 Labor Expenses
总　计	**Total**	**11525148**	**1036810**	**967678**	**9520660**	**3561968**
按执行部门分组	**Grouped by Execution Department**					
科研机构	Scientific Research Institution	704893	202111	214654	288128	186775
高等学校	Institutions of Higher Learning	1198037	661427	418226	118384	437472
企　业	Companies	9219901	110086	186823	8922992	2786176
事业单位	Institution	402317	63186	147975	191156	151545
按隶属关系分组	**Grouped by Subordination Relations**					
中　央	Central	1661164	547206	265489	848469	521403
地　方	Local	9863984	489604	702189	8672191	3040565

19—38 高等学校科技活动情况
Basic Statistics on Higher Education for Scientific and Technological Activities

指　标	Item	2010	2015	2020	2021	2022
研究与试验发展（R&D）人员（人）	Research and experimental development (R&D) personnel (person)	19567	27710	45131	51910	57896
研究与发展人员全时当量（人年）	Full-time Equivalent of R&D Personnel (man.year)	7337	13541	23928	26620	29174
#基础研究	Fundamental Research	3273	6579	12306	14182	15509
应用研究	Applied Research	3471	6319	10593	10939	11419
试验发展	Experimental Development	595	644	1028	1499	2246
研究与发展经费支出（万元）	R&D Expenditure (10000 yuan)	141849	272859	800888	951248	1198037

19—39 各市研究与试验发展人员（2022年）
Research and Experimental Development Personnel by Region (2022)

地区	Region	调查单位数（个）Number of Investigation Units (unit)	有研究与试验发展活动单位 Activity for R&D	研究与试验发展人员（人）Staff of R&D (person)	#女性 Female	#研究人员 Staff of Researcher	全时人员 Staff of Full Time	博士毕业 Doctor
总计	**Total**	**28534**	**10230**	**375002**	**85947**	**152307**	**233056**	**28565**
合肥市	Hefei	5173	1586	131527	31692	72406	91867	19267
淮北市	Huaibei	767	155	13167	1468	2615	3670	493
亳州市	Bozhou	896	339	6503	2230	1839	3806	94
宿州市	Suzhou	1395	419	8198	2196	2988	4883	434
蚌埠市	Bengbu	1272	554	17574	4898	8159	11178	1219
阜阳市	Fuyang	1811	632	11629	3153	4324	7165	854
淮南市	Huainan	977	169	13064	2177	5956	4302	905
滁州市	Chuzhou	2699	1216	27770	6020	7781	18908	721
六安市	Luan	1586	588	14491	3919	3452	7814	413
马鞍山市	Maanshan	1668	898	22220	4069	7837	11679	772
芜湖市	Wuhu	3341	1066	47669	10324	18204	31904	2035
宣城市	Xuancheng	2328	877	21561	4576	4109	13427	124
铜陵市	Tongling	848	261	10613	2166	3243	5246	279
池州市	Chizhou	913	440	8321	1835	2235	4687	142
安庆市	Anqing	2183	726	13842	3317	4870	8278	598
黄山市	Huangshan	677	304	6853	1907	2289	4242	215

19—39 续表 continued

地 区	Region	硕士毕业 Master	研究与试验发展人员折合全时当量(人年) Full-time Equivalent of R&D Personnel (man-years)	#研究人员 Staff of Researcher	#基础研究 Basic Research	#应用研究 Apply Researcher	#试验发展 Experimental and Development Researcher
总 计	**Total**	**57641**	**252476**	**99839**	**19790**	**24982**	**207703**
合肥市	Hefei	30187	92528	49302	14185	14435	63907
淮北市	Huaibei	690	6651	1373	333	263	6055
亳州市	Bozhou	762	4113	1050	101	337	3675
宿州市	Suzhou	1318	5521	1858	179	413	4929
蚌埠市	Bengbu	3212	12225	5424	707	1027	10491
阜阳市	Fuyang	1726	7832	2749	385	628	6819
淮南市	Huainan	2037	6767	3232	845	1158	4764
滁州市	Chuzhou	2227	19684	5246	427	798	18459
六安市	Luan	1208	9941	2237	247	444	9250
马鞍山市	Maanshan	2728	13796	4820	378	648	12770
芜湖市	Wuhu	5929	33216	12018	1281	2460	29475
宣城市	Xuancheng	572	14505	2844	24	163	14318
铜陵市	Tongling	1323	5958	1709	140	619	5199
池州市	Chizhou	815	5480	1343	114	242	5124
安庆市	Anqing	1970	9410	3267	275	942	8193
黄山市	Huangshan	937	4849	1367	169	405	4275

19—40 各市研究与试验发展经费支出情况（2022年）
Research and Development Funds and Internal Expenditure by Region (2022)

单位：万元（10000 yuan）

地 区	Region	研究与试验发展经费 Expenditure for R&D	按活动类型分 By Activities			按支出用途分 By Expenditure	
			基础研究 Fundamental Research	应用研究 Applied Rescarch	试验发展 Experimental	日常性支出 Daily Expenditure	资产性支出 Assets Expenditure
总 计	**Total**	**11525148**	**1036810**	**967678**	**9520660**	**10176122**	**1349026**
合肥市	Hefei	4694764	787646	565281	3341836	4029439	665325
淮北市	Huaibei	272262	14174	10176	247911	263003	9259
亳州市	Bozhou	163139	3760	5201	154177	150258	12882
宿州市	Suzhou	190633	2564	11593	176477	172850	17784
蚌埠市	Bengbu	503194	44187	52883	406124	468548	34646
阜阳市	Fuyang	403507	18675	18385	366446	363471	40036
淮南市	Huainan	241150	33599	30327	177224	226120	15030
滁州市	Chuzhou	803765	19760	34592	749414	671138	132628
六安市	Luan	268788	4815	11408	252565	242429	26359
马鞍山市	Maanshan	780372	8165	17979	754227	734044	46327
芜湖市	Wuhu	1693995	80867	137760	1475368	1521770	172225
宣城市	Xuancheng	470085	2876	2923	464286	410050	60034
铜陵市	Tongling	350305	1846	20063	328396	315189	35116
池州市	Chizhou	204352	5181	11433	187738	165793	38559
安庆市	Anqing	352919	5924	31464	315531	322179	30741
黄山市	Huangshan	131919	2769	6210	122939	119843	12076

19—41 各市工业企业享受相关政策情况（2022年）
Industrial Enterprises Enjoy Relevant Policies by Region (2022)

地 区	Region	研究开发费用加计扣除减免税（万元）Total Research and Development Expense Counting Tax Reliefs (10000 yuan)	高新技术企业减免税（万元）Tax Reliefs of High and New Technology Enterprises (10000 yuan)
总 计	**Total**	**1390729**	**949140**
合肥市	Hefei	440630	233515
淮北市	Huaibei	48667	94420
亳州市	Bozhou	27284	5883
宿州市	Suzhou	26071	14080
蚌埠市	Bengbu	33618	21422
阜阳市	Fuyang	57471	22755
淮南市	Huainan	26005	6283
滁州市	Chuzhou	133891	120520
六安市	Luan	61799	38887
马鞍山市	Maanshan	87537	51650
芜湖市	Wuhu	173786	174937
宣城市	Xuancheng	79137	58793
铜陵市	Tongling	43367	23419
池州市	Chizhou	42905	21285
安庆市	Anqing	80530	43963
黄山市	Huangshan	28031	17328

19—42 工业企业科技活动基本情况
Basic Statistics on Science and Technology Activities of Industrial Enterprises

指　标	Item	2021	2022
有研究与试验发展活动的企业（个）	Number of Enterprises Having R&D Activities (unit)	7982	9135
有研究与试验发展活动的企业占全部企业的比重 (%)	Percentage of Enterprises Having R&D Activities to Total Number of Enterprises (%)	40.17	42.68
科技机构数（个）	Number of Scientific and Technological Institutions (unit)	6014	7286
R&D人员（万人）	R&D Personnel (10000 persons)	24.82	26.05
研究与试验发展折合全时人员（万人年）	Full-time Equivalent of R&D Personnel (10000 man-year)	17.04	18.08
科技机构科技活动人员数（万人）	Personnel Engaged in S&T Activities in S&T Institutions (10000 persons)	17.21	19.02
开发新产品经费支出（亿元）	Expenditure on New Product Development (100 million yuan)	908.83	1040.82
研究与试验发展经费支出（亿元）	Expenditure on R&D (100 million yuan)	739.12	820.65
#政府资金	Government Funds	17.97	23.74
#企业资金	Self-raised Funds by Enterprises	719.22	796.25
研究与试验发展经费支出占营业收入的比重 (%)	Proportion of Research and Experimental Development Expenditure to Operating Revenue (%)	1.65	1.68
引进境外技术经费支出（亿元）	Expenditure of Overseas Technology Introduction (100 million yuan)	2.25	1.53
消化吸收经费支出（亿元）	Expenditure for Assimilation of Technology (100 million yuan)	0.86	0.76
购买国内技术支出（亿元）	Expenditure for Purchase of Domestic Technology (100 million yuan)	16.54	7.01
专利申请数（件）	Patent Applications (piece)	75058	81620
#发明专利数	Invention Patents	30230	32625
拥有有效发明专利数（件）	Number of Effective Invention Patents (piece)	78480	91651

19—43　各市工业企业研究与试验发展基本情况（2022年）
Research and Development Basic Situation of Industrial Enterprise by Region (2022)

地区	Region	企业单位数（个）Number of Enterprises (unit)	#有研究与试验发展活动 Activity for R&D	#有研发机构 There are Research and Development Institutions	新产品销售收入（万元）Revenue of New Product Sales (10000 yuan)	研究与试验发展人员合计（人）Staff Of R&D (person)	#参加项目人员 Staff of Participating in Project	#女性 Female
总　计	**Total**	**21404**	**9135**	**7286**	**175804744**	**260535**	**244348**	**51805**
合肥市	Hefei	2540	1137	772	49692884	64280	59936	13333
淮北市	Huaibei	638	135	96	3472922	11773	11425	1014
亳州市	Bozhou	724	326	171	2752855	5493	5100	1732
宿州市	Suzhou	1174	392	338	5407878	5652	5316	1365
蚌埠市	Bengbu	925	489	380	4804681	10498	9748	2381
阜阳市	Fuyang	1534	578	588	7228091	9215	8657	2255
淮南市	Huainan	845	142	114	1530357	9156	8798	958
滁州市	Chuzhou	2368	1162	1049	27767122	24642	23367	4888
六安市	Luan	1325	547	293	6218176	12288	11576	3142
马鞍山市	Maanshan	1378	835	755	13757689	18097	16575	3079
芜湖市	Wuhu	2257	958	611	24084452	37395	35236	7234
宣城市	Xuancheng	2091	824	713	8426766	20232	18646	4158
铜陵市	Tongling	623	241	145	6330378	8464	7960	1259
池州市	Chizhou	703	411	313	5944508	6979	6571	1305
安庆市	Anqing	1724	679	697	5929554	11148	10476	2456
黄山市	Huangshan	555	279	251	2456431	5223	4961	1246

地区	Region	#研究人员 Staff of Researcher	#全时人员 Staff of Full Time	研究与试验发展人员折合全时当量合计（人年）Total Work Volume of Conversion Staff of Full Time (person year)	#研究人员 Staff of Researcher	应用研究人员 Staff of Apply Researcher	试验发展人员 Staff of Experimental and Development Researcher
总　计	**Total**	**69448**	**168393**	**180814**	**49188**	**4569**	**175970**
合肥市	Hefei	23441	49486	47093	17245	2427	44579
淮北市	Huaibei	1536	3093	5957	860	41	5793
亳州市	Bozhou	1181	3581	3727	802	119	3608
宿州市	Suzhou	1307	3890	4124	965	18	4106
蚌埠市	Bengbu	2686	7187	7838	1960	206	7631
阜阳市	Fuyang	2620	6215	6526	1881	197	6329
淮南市	Huainan	3006	2427	4549	1482	246	4256
滁州市	Chuzhou	5538	17461	17941	4068	123	17819
六安市	Luan	2012	6945	8787	1469	31	8756
马鞍山市	Maanshan	5114	9538	11505	3328	143	11355
芜湖市	Wuhu	11201	26826	27592	8349	448	27139
宣城市	Xuancheng	3272	12395	13428	2139	91	13338
铜陵市	Tongling	1504	4558	5042	949	180	4861
池州市	Chizhou	1322	4212	4879	957	33	4846
安庆市	Anqing	2733	6928	7774	1962	232	7536
黄山市	Huangshan	975	3651	4052	772	35	4017

19—44 各市工业企业研究与试验发展经费情况（2022年）
Research and Development Funds Basic Situation of Industrial Enterprise by Region (2022)

单位：万元（10000 yuan）

地区	Region	研究与试验发展经费内部支出合计 Expenditure for R&D	按活动类型分组 Grouped by Active Type		按支出用途分组 Grouped by Using of Funds			
			应用研究支出 Applied Research Expenditure	试验发展支出 Experiment Development Expenditure	经常费支出 Normal Funds Expenditure	#人员劳务费 Salary	资产性支出 Capital Expenditure	#土建工程 Construction Project
总计	**Total**	**8206500**	**169023**	**7928228**	**7489090**	**2261330**	**717410**	**15587**
合肥市	Hefei	2549784	63890	2386862	2311578	758493	238206	2684
淮北市	Huaibei	243169	1473	234982	239672	79424	3497	656
亳州市	Bozhou	139103	1203	137900	131729	17101	7374	1103
宿州市	Suzhou	159636	233	159394	145441	37423	14195	353
蚌埠市	Bengbu	294620	6563	288057	278777	83443	15843	408
阜阳市	Fuyang	322202	5905	316297	301585	63252	20617	811
淮南市	Huainan	169160	7250	159521	166245	84199	2915	87
滁州市	Chuzhou	714704	2723	711982	608147	145745	106557	1588
六安市	Luan	223813	1513	222298	207733	59089	16080	502
马鞍山市	Maanshan	667275	2273	664818	628650	158560	38625	1172
芜湖市	Wuhu	1412209	61296	1350482	1296000	448868	116209	3000
宣城市	Xuancheng	437462	1599	435532	380547	97855	56915	1452
铜陵市	Tongling	309685	6053	303632	281359	79790	28326	493
池州市	Chizhou	166939	1031	165908	136511	35721	30429	561
安庆市	Anqing	284520	5895	278496	270196	83539	14324	596
黄山市	Huangshan	112220	125	112070	104920	28828	7299	122

地区	Region	按资金来源分组 Grouped by Source of Funds			研究与试验发展经费外部支出 Outside Expenditure	#对境内研究机构支出 Foreign Research Institutions	#对境内高等学校支出 Domestic University
		政府资金 Government	企业资金 Enterprise	境外资金 Overseas Funds			
总计	**Total**	**237363**	**7962483**	**4102**	**500703**	**63094**	**49301**
合肥市	Hefei	66125	2482699	822	278680	15295	20676
淮北市	Huaibei	2976	240193		11108	2161	5476
亳州市	Bozhou	1611	137444		10039	7688	498
宿州市	Suzhou	1984	157652		3892	1305	947
蚌埠市	Bengbu	5133	286931	1395	8035	2237	1665
阜阳市	Fuyang	13889	308235		17584	7239	4362
淮南市	Huainan	2985	166173		19874	8134	1200
滁州市	Chuzhou	15171	699343	186	13290	2075	1707
六安市	Luan	3104	220666		3006	561	198
马鞍山市	Maanshan	7254	659438	16	17840	2311	2452
芜湖市	Wuhu	84821	1326118	781	86748	9985	5649
宣城市	Xuancheng	12163	424420	876	10474	531	789
铜陵市	Tongling	3170	306507		4255	1866	463
池州市	Chizhou	7941	158972	26	2693	418	701
安庆市	Anqing	8118	276390		10400	1160	2149
黄山市	Huangshan	916	111303		2786	129	370

19—45 各市工业企业自主知识产权和技术情况（2022年）
Self-owned Intellectual Property Rights and Technology Situation Industrial Enterprise by Region (2022)

地 区	Region	专利申请数（件）Number of Patent Application (unit)	发明专利 Patent of Invention	有效发明专利数（件）Invention Number of Patents Effectively (unit)	发表科技论文（篇）Publish Technical Papers (unit)	拥有注册商标数（件）Registered Trademark Number (unit)
总　计	**Total**	**81620**	**32625**	**91651**	**3455**	**41526**
合肥市	Hefei	28599	14181	31957	1542	15037
淮北市	Huaibei	1744	787	1357	305	1075
亳州市	Bozhou	1326	510	1852	75	2666
宿州市	Suzhou	2128	635	1975	17	827
蚌埠市	Bengbu	2301	845	3055	93	1630
阜阳市	Fuyang	3504	1492	4494	93	2691
淮南市	Huainan	1610	410	1613	200	602
滁州市	Chuzhou	6970	2232	6903	125	2243
六安市	Luan	3737	1109	3636	102	1588
马鞍山市	Maanshan	5004	1890	6979	252	1601
芜湖市	Wuhu	11044	3976	14611	356	6316
宣城市	Xuancheng	4903	1629	4309	56	1628
铜陵市	Tongling	1750	570	2412	91	741
池州市	Chizhou	1665	581	1429	23	607
安庆市	Anqing	3881	1359	3780	116	1203
黄山市	Huangshan	1454	419	1289	9	1071

地 区	Region	形成国家行业标准数（项）National and Industry Standard Number (item)	引进境外技术经费支出（万元）Expenditure on the Introduction of Overseas Technology (10000 yuan)	消化吸收经费支出（万元）Digestion Absorption Funds Expenditure (10000 yuan)	购买境内技术经费支出（万元）Expenditure on Purchasing Domestic Technology (10000 yuan)	技术改造经费支出（万元）Technological Transformation Funds Expenditure (10000 yuan)
总　计	**Total**	**1896**	**15259**	**7550**	**70056**	**3001962**
合肥市	Hefei	803	7924	1098	28923	601595
淮北市	Huaibei	45			257	82818
亳州市	Bozhou	38			163	9399
宿州市	Suzhou	21			3890	131653
蚌埠市	Bengbu	67			583	43997
阜阳市	Fuyang	70			1800	83559
淮南市	Huainan	43			4844	272109
滁州市	Chuzhou	77	1		3498	178982
六安市	Luan	51	92	19	4753	75199
马鞍山市	Maanshan	132	2487	2356	2292	770625
芜湖市	Wuhu	175	4617	3367	15132	329102
宣城市	Xuancheng	130	126	710	8	40976
铜陵市	Tongling	91			132	91096
池州市	Chizhou	30	5		154	24263
安庆市	Anqing	102	6		3219	237076
黄山市	Huangshan	21			409	29512

19—46 省级以上开发区主要经济指标
Main Economic Indicators of Development Areas above the Provincial Level

项 目	Item	2020	2021	2022
全区经营（销售）收入 （万元）	Business (Sales) Income (10000 yuan)	529513697	663560337	797509957
规模以上工业营业收入	Industrial Operating Income Above Scale	284323335	351929509	403514556
资质以内建筑业营业收入	Business Income of Construction Industry Within Qualification	39349194	44313077	45932448
限额以上批发零售业销售收入	Sales Revenue of Wholesale and Retail Trade Above Quota	88456989	109007104	123470442
限额以上住宿餐饮业营业收入	Operating Income of Catering Industry With Accommodation Above Limit	1228492	1740124	2126331
房地产业销售收入	Real Estate Sales Revenue	21168530	24528980	20897387
规模以上服务业企业营业收入	Business Income of Service Enterprises Above Scale	20663484	28648312	30369853
进出口总额 （万美元）	Total Import and Export (USD 10000)	6173590	8641927	9304870
出口额	Export	3708401	5273854	6006861
进口额	Import	2465190	3368073	3298009
税收总额 （万元）	Total Tax (10000 yuan)	20287199	26579286	30180691
财政收入 （万元）	Financial Revenue (10000 yuan)	26878021	30777462	38438172
利用外商直接投资情况	Foreign Direct Investments			
当年新批进区外商投资企业 （个）	Foreign Investment Enterprises Entered this Year(unit)	301	315	337
利用内资情况（在建亿元以上项目）	Domestic Investment (Construction project of one hundred million yuan of above)			
项目个数 （个）	Project Number (unit)	3701	4749	4740
到位省外境内资金额 （万元）	In Place of Domestic Funds Outside the Province (10000 yuan)	91851655	123908399	143894709

19—47 部分国家级开发区主要经济指标（2022年）
Main Economic Indicators of Some National Development Zones (2022)

指标		Item		合肥高新技术产业开发区 Hefei New High Technology Industry Development District
全区经营（销售）收入	（万元）	Business (Sales) Income	(10000 yuan)	44087375
规模以上工业营业收入		Industrial Operating Income Above Scale		22506122
资质以内建筑业营业收入		Business Income of Construction Industry Within Qualification		6534068
限额以上批发零售业销售收入		Sales Revenue of Wholesale and Retail Trade Above Quota		7857982
限额以上住宿餐饮业营业收入		Operating Income of Catering Industry With Accommodation Above Limit		286203
房地产业销售收入		Real Estate Sales Revenue		1944376
规模以上服务业企业营业收入		Business Income of Service Enterprises Above Scale		4954008
进出口总额	（万美元）	Total Import and Export	(USD 10000)	800725
出口总额		Total Export		660119
进口总额		Total Import		140606
税收总额	（万元）	Total Tax	(10000 yuan)	2740460
财政收入	（万元）	Financial Revenue	(10000 yuan)	4138072
新批进区外商投资企业	（个）	Number of Foreign Funded Enterprises Approved Into Development Areas	(unit)	41
实际利用外商直接投资额	（万美元）	Foreign Direct Investment Amount Actually Used this Year	(USD 10000)	6864
亿元以上省外境内投资项目	（个）	Investment Projects (outside the province, Above 100 million yuan)	(unit)	44
亿元以上项目到位省外境内资金额	（万元）	Investment Projects of Gaining Fund (outside the province, Above 100 million yuan)	(10000 yuan)	1799000

合肥经济技术开发区 Hefei Economy and Technology Development District	芜湖经济技术开发区 Wuhu Economy and Technology Development District	芜湖高新技术产业开发区 Wuhu New High Technology Industry Development District	蚌埠高新技术产业开发区 Bengbu New High Technology Industry Development District	马鞍山经济技术开发区 Maanshan Economy and Technology Development District	马鞍山慈湖高新技术开发区 Maanshan New High Technology Industry Development District	铜陵经济技术开发区 Tongling Economy and Technology Development District	安庆经济技术开发区 Anqing Economy and Technology Development District	滁州经济技术开发区 Chuzhou Economy and Technology Development District	池州经济技术开发区 Chizhou Economy and Technology Development District
68907585	36921031	18315246	8214516	9495478	7930119	23276082	12684539	17497975	5594228
33408131	24552221	8223914	4083132	5062560	4610965	16899459	7958039	13038069	2597147
5726710	93316	735539	2213389	168431	225649	394318	144554	1293512	606924
26016761	10008619	4989930	972598	1931409	1047498	1654159	2033746	2552002	1376394
62598	23623	59355	6973		6192	12023	17935	8834	33985
759831	322800	817885	203085	138436		132832	265650	298963	168035
2933554	1920452	1290794	17553	941767	135298	133254	150525	306595	252320
2048686	833095	52881	39543	53644	53529	554723	199044	212814	60611
1177189	612230	43069	24921	45498	50512	69687	143788	152862	20192
871497	220865	9812	14622	8146	3017	485036	55256	59952	40419
1601500	1128791	1327600	558081	188857	271931	266229	1481342	562750	334342
2915383	1180604	399276	161506	340235	282787	390707	287592	619568	535956
30	12	10	3	3	5	1	4	5	6
67070	12090	7517	235	9662	138	862		2836	508
86	110	97	25	52	49	97	40	15	56
1137402	3342188	2308307	1241024	1865150	1402770	2770166	1920002	2432000	910815

19—48 各市省级以上开发区主要经济指标（2022年）

Main Economic Indicators of Development Areas above the Provincial Level by Region (2022)

地 区	Region	全区经营（销售）收入（万元） Business (Sales) Income (10000 yuan)	规上工业营业收入 Industrial Operating Income Above Scale	资质以内建筑业营业收入 Business Income of Construction Industry Within Qualification	限额以上批发零售业销售收入 Sales Revenue of Wholesale and Retail Trade Above Quota	限额以上住宿餐饮业营业收入 Operating Income of Catering Industry With Accommodation Above Limit	房地产业销售收入 Real Estate Sales Revenue	规模以上服务业营业收入 Business Income of Service Enterprises Above Scale	进出口总额（万美元） Total Import and Export (USD 10000)
总 计	**Total**	**797509957**	**403514556**	**45932448**	**123470442**	**2126331**	**20897387**	**30369853**	**9304870**
合肥市	Hefei	226910944	108409686	20611203	51097952	866776	6967449	13687860	4126163
淮北市	Huaibei	14761023	8904963	702371	2474449	20007	154248	656386	137095
亳州市	Bozhou	21029933	11206185	1474970	4896157	68906	1867528	909051	62828
宿州市	Suzhou	31933494	8582466	1700153	2450472	31731	763259	921599	136811
蚌埠市	Bengbu	20995323	11087573	2794672	1871978	32337	532771	235786	132631
阜阳市	Fuyang	45039795	26301674	2296299	4882755	106478	2040293	1218143	196750
淮南市	Huainan	13988469	7721952	545510	3481963	12654	536475	418020	91560
滁州市	Chuzhou	52715496	40352169	3515454	5777825	91457	1651936	884958	614324
六安市	Luan	23454985	14512651	2463006	3038511	277057	1359804	745815	149501
马鞍山市	Maanshan	42300839	24205312	977779	5230240	44929	595419	1755917	389175
芜湖市	Wuhu	167358485	55793308	4254592	22558601	179881	1287529	5046066	1285013
宣城市	Xuancheng	32766574	21551641	1665865	2391071	38950	1373708	545683	322303
铜陵市	Tongling	36917387	25109605	792132	5211317	195241	164397	947600	982914
池州市	Chizhou	20507350	12740516	1096037	2434739	53800	309477	734923	170398
安庆市	Anqing	35922558	21947983	765770	4841252	89643	977235	1505872	353102
黄山市	Huangshan	10907302	5086872	276638	831160	16485	315859	156172	154303

地 区	Region	出口额 Export	进口额 Import	税收总额（万元） Total Tax (10000 yuan)	财政收入（万元） Financial Revenue (10000 yuan)	新批进区外商投资企业（个） Foreign Investment Enterprises Entered this Year (unit)	实际利用外商直接投资（万美元） Foreign Direct Investment Amount Actually Used this Year (USD 10000)	亿元以上省外境内投资项目个数（个） Investment Projects (outside the province, Above 100 million yuan) (unit)	亿元以上项目到位省外境内资金额（万元） Investment Projects of Gaining Fund (outside the province, Above 100 million yuan) (10000 yuan)
总 计	**Total**	**6006861**	**3298009**	**30180691**	**38438172**	**337**	**244142**	**4740**	**136534155**
合肥市	Hefei	2687363	1438801	7926781	12538642	99	112859	362	9737228
淮北市	Huaibei	126448	10647	573977	605964	7	4748	104	4551514
亳州市	Bozhou	50353	12475	2482095	2211775	5	1609	268	8566864
宿州市	Suzhou	129389	7422	695841	792441	10	1726	258	6210110
蚌埠市	Bengbu	104036	28595	908518	534687	6	519	174	7851864
阜阳市	Fuyang	169441	27309	2188739	6397444	13	9822	365	9243884
淮南市	Huainan	89570	1991	563862	644781	4	2597	131	3041224
滁州市	Chuzhou	509379	104945	2049304	2360170	16	16470	376	14767355
六安市	Luan	139907	9594	1504201	1697398	14	10677	223	6013377
马鞍山市	Maanshan	258666	130509	1455408	1893043	36	33528	499	11995224
芜湖市	Wuhu	872444	412569	3917011	3181136	47	35100	640	24498659
宣城市	Xuancheng	296232	26071	1445860	1666048	25	5855	403	8989032
铜陵市	Tongling	111153	871761	680165	815024	8	2221	233	4507306
池州市	Chizhou	46455	123943	917484	1155635	13	1593	302	6115510
安庆市	Anqing	278590	74512	2483641	1504757	29	4402	259	9000821
黄山市	Huangshan	137437	16866	387804	439227	5	417	143	1444183

19—49 合肥国家高新技术产业开发区企业经营状况（2022年）

Enterprises Business of Hefei National Development Zone for New and High-level Technology Industries (2022)

经济类型 Ownership	企业数（家） Enterprises (unit)	总产值（万元） Gross Output Value (10000 yuan)	总收入（万元） Total Revenue (10000 yuan)	技术性收入 Technical Revenue	利税总额（万元） Total Pre-tax Profit (10000 yuan)	利润 Profit	出口创汇（万美元） Foreign Exchange Earned Through Export (USD 10000)	年末职工人数（人） Number of Staff and Workers at Year-end (person)	全员劳动生产率（万元/人） Overall Labor Productivity (10000 yuan /person)
总计 Total	**3308**	**59347633**	**88035344**	**21086984**	**10030090**	**4943485**	**2302755**	**371811**	**236.8**
国有经济 State-owned	59	7345279	13328445	4492285	2540527	2726236	108363	56034	237.9
私营企业 Private	1760	6333214	12713590	924019	223513	302169	229939	84522	150.4
股份制经济 Share Holding	1349	25967830	42070974	6674883	5274672	1536269	1129693	187510	224.4
中外合资 Sino-foreign Joint Venture	21	2168827	2318910	1860	125578	51624	100837	11294	205.3
港澳台侨与大陆合资 China-Hong Kong/macao/ Taiwan Joint Venture	9	1140661	1200120	26616	281355	30301	38343	5397	222.4
港澳台侨独资企业 H.K/Macao/Taiwan Funded	10	12659381	12963587	8899031	1343295	157316	642969	13335	972.1
其他经济 Others	100	3732442	3439718	68289	241150	139569	52610	13719	250.7
总计中：三资企业 Joint, Cooperative or Exclusively Foreign-funded Ventures	44	3452849	5338494	4695	388123	168532	145559	20352	262.3

19—50 合肥国家高新技术产业开发区产品概况（2022年）

Products of Hefei National Development Zone for New and High-level Technology Industries (2022)

单位：万元（10000 yuan）

技术领域	Field of Technology	产值 Output Value	年销售收入 Annual Sales Revenue	出口额 Volume of Export
总计	**Total**	**59345620**	**88016158**	**15488559**
电子与信息	Electronics and Information Industry	22200729	31512597	8225278
生物医药技术	Biology and Medicine	6806946	7157713	330863
新材料	New Materials	1827252	2554678	147839
光机电一体化	Photoelectric, Mechanical and Electrical products	7212954	8505937	1875780
新能源高效节能	New Energy Sources and Energy Saving Devices	11123891	16169775	3439573
环境保护	Environmental Protection	229072	540383	5482
航空航天技术	Aviation Technology	5833	23353	478
核应用技术	Nuclear Application Technology	11307	11307	
其他高技术	Other High-level Technology	9489364	14323676	853819
非高技术	Unhigh-level Technology	438271	7216738	609447

注：根据国家外汇交易中心公开的信息可知，在2022年我国人民币与美元的“平均汇率为6.7261。

a) According to the Information released by the State Foreign Exchange Trade System, the average exchange rate between China's RMB and the US dollar in 2022 will be 6.7261.

19—51 全省监督抽查产品质量情况
Results of Sampling Check on Product Quality Under Provincial Supervision

年份 Year	抽查企业（个） Number of Enterprises Selected (unit)	无不合格品企业数（个） Number of Enterprises Without Products Unqualified	抽查产品 Products Selected in Sampling（类） Number of Types	（种） Number of Kinds	合格产品（批次） Number of Products Qualified (kind)	样品合格率（%） Rate of Sample Products Qualified (%)
2010	11459	10154	12	110	12954	90.77
2013	13851	13086	12	134	16397	93.93
2014	2728	2585	8	88	2953	95.26
2015	2291	2181	8	79	2558	96.00
2016	3440	3193	8	86	3476	93.32
2017	3814	3568	7	81	3762	93.72
2018	2699	2608	8	90	2979	96.94
2019	4036	3597	10	109	4064	89.09
2020	3253	3016	10	109	3566	93.57
2021	3188	2954	10	116	3376	93.59
2022	3901	3638	10	140	5162	94.43

注：根据省政府减轻企业负担的要求，2014年我省对企业产品定检明显减少。

a) According to the requirements of the provincial government to reduce the burden of enterprises, in 2014, the province of enterprise products regular checks were significantly reduced.

19-52 技术市场成交情况（2022年）
Situation of Technological Markets （2022）

项目	Item	成交项目（项） Transaction Projects (item)	成交金额（万元） Transaction Value (10000 yuan)
按卖方分合计	**Seller Total**	**29492**	**22168504**
企业法人	Enterprise Artificial Person	20881	21417753
事业法人	Institution Artificial Person	8287	434876
社团法人	Social Organization Artificial Person	85	20131
自然人	Natural Person	133	22521
机关法人	Agencies & Organization Artificial Person	37	229998
其他	Others	69	43225
按买方分合计	**Buyer Total**	**30190**	**30729883**
企业法人	Enterprise Artificial Person	25879	27638840
事业法人	Institution Artificial Person	1798	1423942
社团法人	Social Organization Artificial Person	43	4670
自然人	Natural Person	136	30059
机关法人	Agencies & Organization Artificial Person	2270	1593768
其他	Others	64	38604

19—53 三种专利申请授权量
Three Kinds of Patent Applications Granted

单位：项（item）

指 标	Item	2010	2015	2020	2021	2022
申请授权量合计	**Total Applications Authorized**	**16012**	**59039**	**119696**	**153475**	**156584**
发 明	Creations and Inventions	1111	11180	21432	23624	26180
实用新型	Utility Models	8839	41094	84609	114415	115757
外观设计	Designs	6062	6765	13655	15436	14647
申请受权人情况	**Authorized Person of the Application**					
个 人	Individual	4852	9457	16866	19083	13246
大专院校	Universities and Colleges	503	5374	10044	11536	11513
科研单位	Research Institutions	364	781	1405	1679	1866
企 业	Enterprises	10254	43200	89940	119226	128313
机关团体	Government Agencies and Organizations	39	227	1441	1951	1646

19—54 各市三种专利申请授权量（2022年）
Three Kinds of Patent Applications Granted by Region (2022)

单位：项（item）

地 区	Region	申请授权量合计 Total Applications Authorized	发 明 Creations and Inventions	实用新型 Utility Models	外观设计 Designs	申请受权人情况 Authorized Person of the Application: 个 人 Individual	大专院校 Universities and Colleges	科研单位 Research Institutions	企 业 Enterprises	机关团体 Government Agencies and Organizations
总 计	**Total**	**156584**	**26180**	**115757**	**14647**	**13246**	**11513**	**1866**	**128313**	**1646**
合肥市	Hefei	59340	12734	42076	4530	2531	6035	1696	48441	637
淮北市	Huaibei	3822	519	3142	161	406	131	3	3256	26
亳州市	Bozhou	3692	437	2471	784	955	78	1	2603	55
宿州市	Suzhou	4972	670	3735	567	899	115	3	3882	73
蚌埠市	Bengbu	6202	751	4682	769	787	592	36	4734	53
阜阳市	Fuyang	7089	1074	4907	1108	1533	138	12	5287	119
淮南市	Huainan	4512	696	3399	417	607	1081	8	2785	31
滁州市	Chuzhou	11219	1427	8669	1123	818	544		9811	46
六安市	Luan	6820	672	5118	1030	1238	168	7	5288	119
马鞍山市	Maanshan	9669	1797	7438	434	289	630	8	8718	24
芜湖市	Wuhu	16836	2879	12339	1618	771	1589	55	14177	244
宣城市	Xuancheng	6251	634	5227	390	400	59	3	5755	34
铜陵市	Tongling	3263	332	2711	220	253	38	1	2952	19
池州市	Chizhou	3015	403	2304	308	282	68	15	2625	25
安庆市	Anqing	7437	882	5553	1002	1234	121	12	5958	112
黄山市	Huangshan	2445	273	1986	186	243	126	6	2041	29

主要统计指标解释

普通高等学校

指按国家规定的设置标准和审批程序批准举办的，通过国家普通高等教育招生考试，招收高中毕业生为主要培养对象，实施高等学历教育的全日制大学、独立设置的学院和高等专科学校、高等职业学校及其他普通高教机构。

成人高等学校

指按照国家规定的设置标准和审批程序批准举办的，指通过全国成人高等教育招生考试，招收具有高中毕业或同等学历的人员为主要培养对象，利用函授、业余、脱产等多种形式对其实施高等学历教育的学校。包括职工高等学校、农民高等学校、管理干部学院、教育学院、独立函授学院、广播电视大学、其他成人高教机构等。其他成人高教机构是承担国家成人招生计划任务不计校数的机构。

小学学龄儿童入学率即小学学龄儿童净入学率

指小学教育在校学龄人口数占小学教育国家规定年龄组人口总数的百分比。计算公式为：

小学净入学率＝小学在校学龄人口数/小学校内外学龄人口数×100%

财政性教育经费

包括财政预算内教育经费，各级政府征收用于教育的税费，企业办学校教育经费，校办产业、勤工俭学和社会服务收入用于教育的经费。

研究与试验发展（R&D）

指在科学技术领域，为增加知识总量，以及运用这些知识去创造新的应用进行的系统的创造性的活动，包括基础研究、应用研究、试验发展三类活动。国际上通常采用 R&D 活动的规模和强度指标反映一国的科技实力和核心竞争力。

基础研究

指为了获得关于现象和可观察事实的基本原理的新知识(揭示客观事物的本质、运动规律，获得新发现、新学说)而进行的实验性或理论性研究，它不以任何专门或特定的应用或使用为目的。其成果以科学论文和科学著作为主要形式。用来反映知识的原始创新能力。

应用研究

指为获得新知识而进行的创造性研究，主要针对某一特定的目的或目标。应用研究是为了确定基础研究成果可能的用途，或是为达到预定的目标探索应采取的新方法(原理性)或新途径。其成果形式以科学论文、专著、原理性模型或发明专利为主。用来反映对基础研究成果应用途径的探索。

试验发展

指利用从基础研究、应用研究和实际经验所获得的现有知识，为产生新的产品、材料和装置，建立新的工艺、系统和服务，以及对已产生和建立的上述各项作实质性的改进而进行的系统性工作。

R&D 人员

指参与研究与试验发展项目研究、管理和辅助工作的人员，包括项目（课题）组人员，企业科技行政管理人员和直接为项目（课题）活动提供服务的辅助人员。反映投入从事拥有自主知识产权的研究开发活动的人力规模。

R&D 人员全时当量

指全时人员数加非全时人员按工作量折算为全时人员数的总和。例如：有两个全时人员和三个非全时人员（工作时间分别为 20%、30%和 70%)，则全时当量为 2+0.2+0.3+0.7=3.2 人年。为国际上比较科技人力投入而制定的可比指标。

R&D 经费内部支出合计

指调查单位用于内部开展 R&D 活动（基础研究、应用研究和试验发展）的实际支出。包括用于 R&D 项目（课题）活动的直接支出，以及间接用于 R&D 活动的管理费、服务费、与 R&D 有关的基本建设支出以及外协加工费等。不包括生产性活动支出、归还贷款支出以及与外单位合作或委托外单位进行 R&D 活动而转拨给对方的经费支出。

R&D 经费内部支出中政府资金

指 R&D 经费内部支出中来自各级政府部门的各类资金，包括财政科学技术拨款、科学基金、教育等部门事业费以及政府部门预算外资金的实际支出。

R&D 经费内部支出中企业资金

指 R&D 经费内部支出中来自本企业的自有资金和接受其他企业委托而获得的经费，以及科研院所、高校等事业单位从企业获得的资金的实际支出。

新产品销售收入

指报告期企业销售新产品实现的销售收入。

发明（专利）

指对产品、方法或者其改进所提出的新的技术方案。是国际通行的反映拥有自主知识产权技术的核心指标。

实用新型（专利）

指对产品的形状、构造或者其结合所提出的适于实用的新的技术方案。反映具有一定技术含量的技术成果情况。

外观设计（专利）

指对产品的形状、图案、色彩或者其结合所作出的富有美感并适于工业上应用的新设计。反映拥有自主知识产权的外观设计成果情况。

Explanatory Notes for Major Statistical Indicators

Regular Institutions of Higher Education

refers to the national standards set by the provisions of the approval and approval procedures, through the national general higher education entrance examination, recruiting high school graduates as the main training object, the implementation of higher education full-time university, independent set of colleges and colleges, higher Vocational schools and other general institutions of higher education.

Institutions of Higher Education for Adults

refers to the provisions of the country in accordance with the provisions of the standards and approval procedures approved by the National Adult Higher Education Admissions Examination, to recruit high school graduates or equivalent qualifications as the main training object, the use of correspondence, amateur, full-time and other forms of its implementation Higher education of the school. Including the institutions of higher education for workers, peasant higher schools, management cadres colleges, educational colleges, independent correspondence schools, radio and television universities, other adult higher education institutions. Other adult institutions of higher education are institutions that are responsible for the national adult enrollment program.

The enrollment rate of primary schoolchildren is the net enrollment rate of primary school age children

refers to the percentage of the total number of school-age population in primary school education in primary school age group. The formula is:

Primary school enrollment rate = primary school population of school age population / primary school school age population ×100%

Government Appropriation for Education

refers to State budgetary fund for education, taxes and fees collected by governments at all levels that are used for education purpose, education fund for enterprise-run schools, income from school-run enterprises, work-study programme and social services that are used for education purpose.

Research and Development (R&D)

refers to systematic and creative activities in the field of science and technology aiming at increasing the knowledge and using the knowledge for new application. R&D includes 3 categories of activities: basic research, applied research and experimentation for development. The scale and intensity of R&D are widely used internationally to reflect the strength of S&T and the core competitiveness of a country in the world.

Basic Research

refers to empirical or theoretical research aiming at obtaining new knowledge on the fundamental principles regarding phenomena or observable facts to reveal the intrinsic nature and underlying laws and to acquire new discoveries or new theories. Basic research takes no specific or designated application as the aim of the research. Results of basic research are mainly released or disseminated in the form of scientific papers or monographs. This indicator reflects the innovation capacity for original knowledge.

Applied Research

refers to creative research aiming at obtaining new knowledge on a specific objective or target. Purpose of the applied research is to identify the possible uses of results from basic research, or to explore new (fundamental) methods or new approaches. Results of applied research are expressed in the form of scientific papers, monographs, fundamental models or invention patents. This indicator reflects the exploration of ways to apply the results of basic research.

Experiments and Development

refer to systematic activities aiming at using the knowledge from basic and applied researches or from practical experience to develop new products, materials and equipment, to establish new production process, systems and services, or to make substantial improvement on the existing products, process or services. Results of experiment and development activities are embodied in patents, exclusive technology, and monotype of new products or equipment. In social sciences, experiment and development activities refer to the process of converting the knowledge from basic or applied researches into feasible programmes (including conduct of demonstration projects for assessment and evaluation). There are no experiment and development activities in the science of humanities. This indicator reflects the capability of transferring the results of S&T into technique and products, and measures the realization of S&T in spearheading the economic and social development.

Scientists and Engineers

refer to persons who have completed university or higher education or obtained titles of senior and middle level professional positions.

R&D Personnel

refer to persons engaged in research, management and supporting activities of R&D, including persons in the project teams, persons engaged in the management of S&T activities of enterprises and supporting staff providing direct service to the research projects.

This indicator reflects the size of personnel engaged in R&D activities with independent intellectual property.

Full-time Equivalent of R&D Personnel

refers to the sum of the full-time persons and the full-time equivalent of part-time persons converted by workload. For instance, if there are 2 full-time persons and 3 part-time workers (20%, 30% and 70% of working hours respectively on R&D activities), the full-time equivalent are 2+0.2+0.3+0.7=3.2 person-years. This is an internationally comparable indicator of S&T manpower input.

Total Internal Expenditure of Funds on R&D

refers to the real expenditure of surveyed units on their own R&D activities (basic research, application study, test and development) including direct expenditure on R&D activities, indirect expenditure of management and services on R&D activities, expenditure on capital construction and material processing by others. Excluding the expenditure on production activities, return of loan, and fees transferred to cooperated and entrusted agencies on R&D activities.

Internal Expenditure of Government Funds

refers to the expenditure of funds on R&D activities from government agencies at different levels, including appropriate funds on science and technology from financial departments, scientific funds, operating expenses from education departments and the real expenditure of extra budgetary funds from government agencies.

Internal Expenditure of Funds of Enterprises

refers to the expenditure of funds on R&D activities from self-raised funds of enterprises and funds from other enterprises through entrustment, and the expenditure of funds of institutions, such as institution of scientific research and universities, from enterprises.

Sales Income of New Products

refers to the real sales income of new products of the enterprises at the reporting period.

Patented Inventions

refer to new technical proposals to the products or methods or their modifications. This is universal core indicator reflecting the technologies with independent intellectual property.

Patented Utility Models

refer to the practical and new technical proposals on the shape and structure of the product or the combination of both. This indicator reflects the condition of technological results with certain technical content.

Designs

refer to the aesthetics and industrially applicable new designs for the shape, pattern and colour of the product, or their combinations. This indicator reflects the appearance design achievements with independent intellectual property.

第 二 十 篇

Chapter 20

卫生和社会服务

PUBLIC HEALTH AND SOCIAL SERVICES

简要说明

一、本篇主要反映卫生、民政、劳动保障事业的发展情况。

卫生部分主要包括卫生机构、卫生人员、卫生设施，医疗服务，农村和社区卫生、妇幼保健、医疗保障制度等情况。

民政事业和劳动保障统计资料主要包括社会服务企事业机构、人员、床位情况，社会救济情况，社区服务设施和农村社会保障网络情况，婚姻服务情况等情况。

二、卫生部分的资料来自省卫生健康委员会。民政事业和劳动保障统计资料分别由省民政厅、省人力资源和社会保障厅依据统计报表制度整理提供。省人力资源和社会保障厅提供的分市数据，均为老区划口径数据。

Brief Introduction

I. Data in this chapter mainly reflect the development of public health, civil affairs, labor and social security.

The health part mainly includes health institutions, health personnel, health facilities, medical services, rural and community health, maternal and child health care, medical security system and so on.

Civil affairs and labor security statistics mainly include social service enterprises and institutions, personnel, beds, social relief, community service facilities and rural social security network, marriage services and so on.

II. Information for the Ministry of Health comes from the provincial Health Boards. The statistics of civil affairs and labor security are arranged and provided respectively by the provincial civil affairs department and the provincial Human resources and social security Department according to the statistical statement system. Municipal data provided by the provincial Department of human resources and social security are old district data.

20—1 医疗卫生机构数
Number of Health Institutions

单位：个（unit）

年　份 Year	总　计 Total	#医　院 Hospitals	社区卫生服务中心(站) Community Health Service Center (station)	乡　镇卫生院 Township Hospitals	村卫生室 Village Health Room	疾病预防控制中心(防疫站) Disease Prevention and Controlling Center (Epidemic Prevention Station)	专科疾病防治院(所.站) Specialized Disease Prevention and Treatment Canters (stations)	妇　幼保健机构 Maternity and Child Care Centers	急救中心(站) First-aid Center (station)	卫　生监督所 Health Supervision Centers
2010	23019	730	1730	1437	15636	124	50	119	11	110
2013	24645	938	1942	1387	15310	120	50	121	13	113
2014	24824	968	1941	1398	15288	121	48	121	14	113
2015	24853	1018	1930	1382	15295	121	47	121	14	113
2016	24388	1042	1908	1371	15276	121	47	120	14	112
2017	24484	1095	1882	1367	15331	121	48	118	15	113
2018	24926	1140	1891	1365	15317	120	45	120	16	112
2019	26436	1241	1858	1380	15549	119	42	121	15	113
2020	29391	1388	1869	1356	15710	121	43	123	19	105
2021	29554	1338	1814	1347	15630	122	41	126	19	113
2022	30176	1338	1827	1339	15601	124	41	127	22	112

20—2 医疗卫生机构人员数
Number of Engaged Persons in Health Institutions

单位：人（person）

年　份 Year	人员合计 Total	卫生技术人员 Medical Technical Personnel	#执业(助理)医师 Licensed (Assistant) Doctors	注册护士 Registered Nurse	每万人口卫生技术人员数 Number of Health Technicians per 10,000 Population
2010	247493	205403	81097	76550	34.48
2013	353835	253549	98630	103404	42.05
2014	365650	267964	103738	111544	44.05
2015	377387	280768	107792	119303	45.70
2016	390346	296668	113810	128434	47.88
2017	407530	313546	120857	138166	50.13
2018	426851	333492	126782	149703	52.74
2019	454616	361240	138407	163390	56.75
2020	503226	412247	164325	188253	67.56
2021	519677	435334	172670	200980	71.21
2022	553360	471176	185983	221426	76.90

注：因《2021国家卫生健康统计调查制度》指标口径调整，卫生技术人员包括从事临床或监督工作并同时从事管理工作的人员（如院长、书记等），口径略大于往年数（下同）。

a) Due to the adjustment of the indicator caliber of 2021 National Health Statistical Survey System, the caliber of health technical personnel includes those engaged in clinical or supervisory work and management work at the same time (such as deans and secretaries), which is slightly larger than the number of previous years (the same below).

20—3 医疗卫生机构、床位、人员数（2022年）
Number of Health Units, Beds and Staff (2022)

指　　标	Item	机构数（个）Health Institutions (unit)	床位数（张）Beds (unit)	人员数（人）Persons Engaged (person)	卫生技术人员 Medical technical Personnel
总　计	**Total**	**30176**	**443917**	**553360**	**471176**
医　院	Hospitals	1338	339157	330332	290569
综合医院	Comprehensive Hospitals	741	219571	229293	202965
中医医院	Hospitals of Traditional Chinese Medicine	148	51151	46610	41635
中西医结合医院	Hospitals Combined by Medium Doctors	48	5509	5658	5014
专科医院	Specialized Hospitals	357	58014	47158	39715
口腔医院	Stomatological Hospitals	38	616	2698	2219
眼科医院	Ophthalmology Hospitals	61	3637	4242	3329
耳鼻喉科医院	Ear, Nose and Throat Hospitals	5	385	258	242
肿瘤医院	Malignant Tumour Hospitals	8	3405	4120	3701
心血管病医院	Cardiovascular Disease Hospitals	2	451	401	337
妇产(科)医院	Gynecology Hospitals	31	3351	5404	4327
儿童医院	Children's Hospitals	5	1779	2423	2047
精神病医院	Mental Hospitals	73	25007	10013	8409
传染病医院	Infection Hospitals	8	3802	2760	2416
皮肤病医院	Dermatological Hospitals	6	304	415	344
结核病医院	Tubercle Hospitals	1	1100	1168	1065
麻风病医院	Leprosy Hospitals	2	30	13	6
骨科医院	Orthopedic Hospitals	18	2726	2491	2191
康复医院	Rehabilitation Hospitals	28	4855	3980	3379
整形外科医院	Plastic Surgery Hospital	6	281	518	394
美容医院	Cosmetology Hospitals	9	506	889	623
其他专科医院	Other Specialized Hospitals	56	5779	5365	4686
护理院（中心）	Nursing Hospitals	44	4912	1613	1240
基层医疗卫生机构	The Basic Medical Institutions	28205	92363	187008	151844
社区卫生服务中心(站)	Community Health Service Center (station)	1827	11312	26147	24013
社区卫生服务中心	Community Health Center	369	11312	15858	14343
社区卫生服务站	Community Health Service Station	1458		10289	9670
卫生院	Commune Hospitals	1347	80355	70691	65329
街道卫生院	Hospitals in the Streets	8	370	496	442
乡镇卫生院	Township Hospitals	1339	79985	70195	64887
中心卫生院	Center Hospitals	447	39282	33028	30630
乡卫生院	Rural Hospitals	892	40703	37167	34257
村卫生室	Village Health Room	15601		42860	18394
门诊部	Outpatient Departments	1611	696	22637	20313
诊所、卫生所、医务室	Clinics、Health Institute、Medical Office	7819		24673	23795
专业公共卫生机构	Professional Public Health Institutions	475	11287	30743	25146
疾病预防控制中心	Disease Prevention and Controlling Center	124		7921	6232
专科疾病防治院（所、站）	Specialized Disease Prevention and Treatment Canters (stations)	41	1514	2084	1726
健康教育所（站、中心）	Health Education Offices (stations or centers)	6		41	17
妇幼保健院	Maternity and Child Care Centers	127	9767	15042	12785
急救中心（站）	First-aid Center (station)	22	6	1236	702
采供血机构	Blood Collecting and Supply Organizations	28		1555	1271
卫生监督所(中心)	Health Supervision Centers	112		2818	2385
计划生育技术服务机构	Birth Control Technical Services	15		46	28
其他卫生机构	Other Health Institutions	158	1110	5277	3617
康复医疗机构	Medical Institutions for Rehabilitation	12	1110	382	303
医学科学研究机构	Research Institutes of Medical Science	10		214	98
医学在职培训机构	Medical On-the-job Training Organizations	15		229	120
临床检验中心（所、站）	Clinical Testing Center (station)	5		281	201
健康体检中心	Physical Examination Centers	20		960	801
医疗辅助性机构	Medical Auxiliary Institutions	86		3112	2070
统计信息中心	Statistical Information Center	5		43	2
其　他	Other	5		56	22

20—4 医疗卫生机构各类人员数（2022年）
Persons Engaged in Health Care Institutions by Type of Occupation (2022)

单位：人（person）

指标	Item	合计 Total	卫生技术人员 Medical Technical Personnel	执业(助理)医师 Licensed (Assistant) Doctors	注册护士 Registered Nurse	药师(士) Pharmacist	技师(士) Technology Division
总计	**Total**	**553360**	**471176**	**185983**	**221426**	**17136**	**27634**
按经济类型分	**By the type**						
公立	The Public	387468	328023	131949	147463	13344	19801
国有	State Owned	286775	253424	91893	122680	10407	16315
集体	Collective Owned	100693	74599	40056	24783	2937	3486
非公立	Non-Public	165892	143153	54034	73963	3792	7833
#联营	Joint Ownership	2102	1725	679	848	63	91
私营	Private	107796	95171	37372	48918	2293	4597
按主办单位分	**According To The Organizer**						
政府办	Set Up by Government	336071	299220	113344	139299	12679	19017
#卫生部门	The Health Sector	333075	296794	112397	138114	12588	18885
社会办	Set Up by Society	113263	79132	35612	34640	2218	4510
个人办	Set Up by Individual	104026	92824	37027	47487	2239	4107

指标	Item	其他 Other	乡村医生和卫生员 Village Doctors and Assistants	其他技术人员 Other Technical Personnel	管理人员 Administrative Personnel	仅从事管理的人员 full-time personnel	工勤技能人员 Logistics Technical Workers
总计	**Total**	**18997**	**24607**	**20095**	**27381**	**13388**	**24094**
按经济类型分	**By the type**						
公立	The Public	15466	21523	15137	17367	8371	14414
国有	State Owned	12129	548	12946	15278	7627	12230
集体	Collective Owned	3337	20975	2191	2089	744	2184
非公立	Non-Public	3531	3084	4958	10014	5017	9680
#联营	Joint Ownership	44	151	67	102	62	97
私营	Private	1991	1142	2948	5909	3023	5512
按主办单位分	**According To The Organizer**						
政府办	Set Up by Government	14881	213	14694	16693	8114	13830
#卫生部门	The Health Sector	14810	213	14448	16343	7939	13681
社会办	Set Up by Society	2152	23597	2743	5305	2634	5157
个人办	Set Up by Individual	1964	797	2658	5383	2640	5107

20—5 各市医疗卫生机构人员数（2022年）
Number of Persons Engaged in Health Institutions by Region (2022)

单位：人（person）

地　区	Region	合　计 Total	卫　生 技术人员 Medical Technical Personnel	执业(助理)医师 Licensed (Assistant) Doctors	注　册 护　士 Registered Nurse	药　师 (士) Pharmacist	技　师 (士) Technology Division
总　计	**Total**	**553360**	**471176**	**185983**	**221426**	**17136**	**27634**
合肥市	Hefei	100689	86966	32743	42920	2840	5975
淮北市	Huaibei	17307	14511	5885	6616	569	791
亳州市	Bozhou	40782	33387	12768	16284	1123	1829
宿州市	Suzhou	42796	36549	15228	16670	1278	1921
蚌埠市	Bengbu	32717	27691	10649	13351	1001	1627
阜阳市	Fuyang	71062	59923	23869	28008	2047	3685
淮南市	Huainan	26226	21952	8410	10258	868	1316
滁州市	Chuzhou	36356	31835	12402	15506	959	1446
六安市	Luan	35936	30112	13156	12795	1146	1673
马鞍山市	Maanshan	19505	16827	6601	7812	594	1045
芜湖市	Wuhu	33495	29050	11642	13622	1150	1601
宣城市	Xuancheng	22317	19215	7288	9237	824	1083
铜陵市	Tongling	12442	10607	4189	4836	490	657
池州市	Chizhou	11777	10338	4223	4585	413	542
安庆市	Anqing	36928	31014	12719	13778	1294	1717
黄山市	Huangshan	13025	11199	4211	5148	540	726

地　区	Region	其　他 Other	乡村医生和卫生员 Village Doctors and Assistants	其　他 技术人员 Other Technical Personnel	管理人员 Administrative Personnel	仅从事管理的人人员 full-time personnel	工勤技能人　员 Logistics Technical Workers
总　计	**Total**	**18997**	**24607**	**20095**	**27381**	**13388**	**24094**
合肥市	Hefei	2488	1541	4291	6265	3413	4478
淮北市	Huaibei	650	499	881	642	378	1038
亳州市	Bozhou	1383	3751	1261	1226	724	1659
宿州市	Suzhou	1452	2355	1373	1605	806	1713
蚌埠市	Bengbu	1063	1156	1412	1272	777	1681
阜阳市	Fuyang	2314	4444	2339	3321	1335	3021
淮南市	Huainan	1100	1139	1148	1749	633	1354
滁州市	Chuzhou	1522	1762	1007	1546	445	1307
六安市	Luan	1342	2473	1243	1670	899	1209
马鞍山市	Maanshan	775	529	599	994	593	957
芜湖市	Wuhu	1035	812	1112	2032	1106	1415
宣城市	Xuancheng	783	710	894	952	382	1116
铜陵市	Tongling	435	529	407	714	378	521
池州市	Chizhou	575	472	331	722	301	335
安庆市	Anqing	1506	2014	1443	2095	952	1505
黄山市	Huangshan	574	421	354	576	266	785

20—6 各市医疗卫生机构数（2022年）
Number of Medical Health Institutions by Region (2022)

单位：个（unit）

地区	Region	总计 Total	#医院 Hospitals	社区卫生服务中心（站） Community Health Service Center (station)	乡镇卫生院 Township Hospitals	村卫生室 Village Health Room
总计	**Total**	**30176**	**1338**	**1827**	**1339**	**15601**
合肥市	Hefei	3703	221	182	95	1130
淮北市	Huaibei	884	69	144	28	351
亳州市	Bozhou	2568	86	134	92	1338
宿州市	Suzhou	2158	99	76	108	1227
蚌埠市	Bengbu	1664	112	163	56	937
阜阳市	Fuyang	3273	135	134	159	1808
淮南市	Huainan	1678	82	168	80	849
滁州市	Chuzhou	1983	69	120	94	1059
六安市	Luan	2752	50	158	133	1916
马鞍山市	Maanshan	1089	65	98	38	429
芜湖市	Wuhu	1791	98	142	52	732
宣城市	Xuancheng	1485	59	60	79	827
铜陵市	Tongling	636	30	58	26	359
池州市	Chizhou	1089	40	20	59	615
安庆市	Anqing	2325	89	132	135	1400
黄山市	Huangshan	1098	34	38	105	624

地区	Region	疾病预防控制中心(防疫站) Disease Prevention and Controlling Center (Epidemic Prevention Station)	专科疾病防治院(所.站) Specialized Disease Prevention and Treatment Canters (stations)	妇幼保健机构 Maternity and Child Care Centers	急救中心(站) First-aid Center (station)	卫生监督所 Health Supervision Centers
总计	**Total**	**124**	**41**	**127**	**22**	**112**
合肥市	Hefei	13	10	12	6	11
淮北市	Huaibei	5	1	5	1	2
亳州市	Bozhou	5		5		5
宿州市	Suzhou	6	4	6	1	6
蚌埠市	Bengbu	8	1	9	1	4
阜阳市	Fuyang	9	3	10	2	9
淮南市	Huainan	8	2	10	1	7
滁州市	Chuzhou	9	1	9	1	9
六安市	Luan	8		9	1	7
马鞍山市	Maanshan	7	2	7	1	7
芜湖市	Wuhu	10	3	9	1	9
宣城市	Xuancheng	9	1	8	1	8
铜陵市	Tongling	3	1	4	1	5
池州市	Chizhou	6	3	4	1	6
安庆市	Anqing	10	9	12	2	9
黄山市	Huangshan	8		8	1	8

20—7 各市医疗卫生机构床位数（2022年）
Number of Beds of Medical Health Institutions by Region (2022)

单位：张（unit）

地　区	Region	总　计 Total	#医　院 Hospitals	#综合医院 Comprehensive Hospitals	中医医院 Hospitals of Traditional Chinese Medicine	中西医结合医院 Hospitals Combined by Medium Doctors
总　计	**Total**	**443917**	**339157**	**219571**	**51151**	**5509**
合 肥 市	Hefei	70891	61791	36602	5838	1618
淮 北 市	Huaibei	12847	9866	6891	1381	
亳 州 市	Bozhou	34152	23477	13976	6308	811
宿 州 市	Suzhou	36918	24094	17479	4107	302
蚌 埠 市	Bengbu	26021	22223	17128	2487	555
阜 阳 市	Fuyang	59867	43126	25944	7151	30
淮 南 市	Huainan	21017	16848	11968	1095	
滁 州 市	Chuzhou	28515	20269	14026	3032	756
六 安 市	Luan	34282	21929	14119	4737	209
马鞍山市	Maanshan	15544	11614	8014	2075	
芜 湖 市	Wuhu	27634	23820	15380	3525	160
宣 城 市	Xuancheng	17545	13507	7792	2452	102
铜 陵 市	Tongling	9705	7995	4966	725	419
池 州 市	Chizhou	9537	7909	5057	1431	241
安 庆 市	Anqing	29495	22810	14671	3942	80
黄 山 市	Huangshan	9947	7879	5558	865	226

地　区	Region	专科医院 Specialized Hospitals	社区卫生服务中心（站） Community Health Service Center (station)	乡镇卫生院 Township Hospitals	专科疾病防治院(所.站) Specialized Disease Prevention and Treatment Canters (stations)	妇幼保健机构 Maternity and Child Care Centers
总　计	**Total**	**58014**	**11312**	**79985**	**1514**	**9767**
合 肥 市	Hefei	14736	1612	5180	16	1503
淮 北 市	Huaibei	1594	595	1685	256	426
亳 州 市	Bozhou	2282	1030	9079		554
宿 州 市	Suzhou	2206	1064	11263	55	419
蚌 埠 市	Bengbu	2053	499	3083	20	196
阜 阳 市	Fuyang	9291	1558	13183		1770
淮 南 市	Huainan	3729	476	2591	393	695
滁 州 市	Chuzhou	2455	737	6846	200	449
六 安 市	Luan	2344	463	10198		1684
马鞍山市	Maanshan	1225	906	1809	24	624
芜 湖 市	Wuhu	4695	547	2887	110	259
宣 城 市	Xuancheng	3161	593	3154	20	99
铜 陵 市	Tongling	1885	303	884	20	460
池 州 市	Chizhou	1110	40	1371	148	60
安 庆 市	Anqing	4117	725	5200	252	494
黄 山 市	Huangshan	1131	164	1572		75

20—8 医疗机构门诊、住院服务情况（2022年）
The Situation of Outpatient Service and Hospitalization Service in Medical Institution(2022)

机构类别	Institution Category	总诊疗人次数（万人次）Total Number of Patients Treated (10000 person-times)	门、急诊 Out-patients and Emergency Patients	入院人数（人）Hospital Admissions (person)	出院人数（人）Being Out of Hospital (person)	每百门、急诊入院人数（人）Hospital Admissions per 100 Out-patient Times and Emergency Patient-times (person)
总　计	**Total**	**37000.33**	**34313.00**	**9747905**	**9633481**	**4.03**
#医　院	Hospitals	14359.86	13846.03	8446586	8334525	6.10
社区卫生服务中心(站)	Community Health Service Centers	3319.75	2889.75	110602	109794	0.38
卫生院	Commune Hospitals	7446.94	6708.26	959074	958944	1.43
村卫生室	Village Clinics	6455.39	5974.80			
门诊部	Clinics	1380.89	1033.83	10848	10848	0.10
诊所、卫生所、医务室	Clinics、Health Institute、Medical Office	3288.41	3132.94			
专科疾病防治院	Specialized Disease Prevention and Treatment Centers (stations)	13.89	11.63	8963	8985	6.45
妇幼保健机构	Maternity and Child Care Centers	671.09	652.79	210656	209209	3.14
康复医疗机构	Medical Institutions for Rehabilitation	2.38	1.22	1176	1176	4.93

20—9 重大传染病救治及救助情况
Significant Infectious Diseases Treatment and Rescue Situation

指　　标	Item	2020	2021	2022
重大传染病救治财政投入（万元）	Significant Financial Investment for Treatment of Infectious Diseases (10000 yuan)			
艾滋病	AIDS	4066	2400	2400
结核病	Tuberculosis	1150	810	810
晚期血吸虫病	Advanced Schistosomiasis	2100	2050	2025
重大传染病免费救治（人）	Free Treatment of Major Infectious Diseases (person)			
艾滋病	AIDS	9725	10188	9703
结核病	Tuberculosis	9043	9057	8820
晚期血吸虫病	Advanced Schistosomiasis	4234	4115	4028

20—10 医疗机构病床使用情况（2022年）
Utilization of Hospital Beds(2022)

机构类别	Type of Hospital	病床周转次数（次）Turnover of Beds (times)	病床工作日（日）Number of Days per Bed in Use in a Year (days)	病床使用率（%）Utilization Rate of Beds（%）	出院者平均住院日（日）Average Hospitalization Period (days)
总　计	**Total**	**24.5**	**219.1**	**60.02**	**8.5**
医　院	Hospitals	27.3	249.7	68.42	8.8
社区卫生服务中心（站）	Community Health Service Centers	12.5	101.1	27.69	6.2
卫生院	Commune Hospitals	13.8	108.5	29.71	6.9
专科疾病防治院（所、站）	Specialized Disease Prevention and Treatment Centers (stations)	6.6	169.3	46.4	22.7
妇幼保健机构	Maternity and Child Care Centers	27.0	151.2	41.43	5.5
康复医疗机构	Medical Institutions for Rehabilitation	2.8	74.5	20.41	23.7

20—11 主要年份医院病床使用情况
Utilization of Hospital Beds in Main Years

年 份 Year	实有床位(张) Hospital Beds (number)	出院人数(人) Patients Discharged from Hospitals (person)	病床周转次数(次) Turnover of Beds (time)	病床工作日(日) Number of Days per Bed in Use in a Year (days)	病床使用率(%) Utilization Rate (%)	出院者平均住院日(日) Average Stay Days in Hospital (day)
2010	122171	3718022	31	313	85.9	10
2013	171508	5544366	33	317	86.8	9
2014	187730	8181303	34	320	87.7	9
2015	202713	6502924	34	310	85.0	9
2016	216448	7037582	35	309	84.6	9
2017	233142	7841303	36	315	86.3	9
2018	253264	8227956	34	304	83.3	9
2019	271517	8765828	34	303	83.1	9
2020	317229	8094679	28	264	72.2	9
2021	318142	8300162	28	260	71.2	9
2022	338266	8334525	27	250	68.4	8.8

注：自2016年起，部分没有医疗运营的医院病床未参与汇总。

a) Since 2016, some hospital beds without medical operation have not participated in the summary.

20—12 各市医院病床使用情况（2022年）
Utilization of Hospital Beds by Region (2022)

地 区	Region	实有床位(张) Hospital Beds (number)	出院人数(人) Patients Discharged from Hospitals (person)	病床周转次数(次) Turnover of Beds (time)	病床工作日(日) Number of Days per Bed in Use in a Year (days)	病床使用率(%) Utilization Rate (%)	出院者平均住院日(日) Average Stay Days in Hospital (day)
总 计	**Total**	**338266**	**8334525**	**27**	**250**	**68.4**	**8.8**
合肥市	Hefei	61139	1626099	29	273	74.9	8.9
淮北市	Huaibei	9866	263328	27	266	73.0	9.4
亳州市	Bozhou	23477	560577	29	247	67.6	7.7
宿州市	Suzhou	24094	591431	28	233	63.8	7.9
蚌埠市	Bengbu	22203	567128	28	248	68.0	8.3
阜阳市	Fuyang	43126	1083669	27	226	61.9	8.9
淮南市	Huainan	16749	361266	24	232	63.5	9.0
滁州市	Chuzhou	20269	480703	27	224	61.4	8.2
六安市	Luan	21929	483029	27	253	69.4	8.9
马鞍山市	Maanshan	11614	267200	26	237	65.0	8.8
芜湖市	Wuhu	23820	526592	25	248	68.1	9.7
宣城市	Xuancheng	13387	358614	29	269	73.6	8.2
铜陵市	Tongling	7995	179531	23	263	72.0	11.5
池州市	Chizhou	7909	185385	27	239	65.5	8.4
安庆市	Anqing	22810	608752	30	281	77.0	9.3
黄山市	Huangshan	7879	191221	25	229	62.7	9.7

20—13 主要年份乡镇卫生院病床使用情况
Utilization of Hospital Beds of Township Hospitals in Main Years

年 份 Year	实有床位(张) Hospital Beds (number)	出院人数(人) Patients Discharged from Hospital (person)	病床周转次数(次) Turnover of Beds (time)	病床工作日(日) Number of Days per Bed in Use in a Year (days)	病床使用率(%) Utilization Rate (%)	出院者平均住院日(日) Average Stay Days in Hospital (day)
2010	48944	1495925	32	194	53.1	5
2013	49781	1709374	36	228	62.4	6
2014	50871	1706132	35	226	62.0	6
2015	50973	1596190	33	221	60.6	7
2016	51316	1563326	32	221	60.6	7
2017	56560	1718011	33	224	61.2	6
2018	58458	1540988	29	204	55.9	7
2019	60278	1230615	23	175	47.9	7
2020	69165	1065565	17	132	36.3	7
2021	70681	848061	14	107	29.4	7
2022	79985	957133	14	109	29.8	6.9

20—14 各市乡镇卫生院病床使用情况（2022年）
Utilization of Hospital Beds of Township Hospitals by Region (2022)

地 区	Region	实有床位(张) Hospital Beds (number)	出院人数(人) Patients Discharged from Hospital (person)	病床周转次数(次) Turnover of Beds (time)	病床工作日(日) Number of Days per Bed in Use in a Year (days)	病床使用率(%) Utilization Rate (%)	出院者平均住院日(日) Average Stay Days in Hospital (day)
总 计	**Total**	**79985**	**957133**	**14**	**109**	**29.8**	**6.9**
合肥市	Hefei	5180	54912	13	107	29.4	6.6
淮北市	Huaibei	1685	18624	12	113	31.0	7.0
亳州市	Bozhou	9079	190045	23	167	45.7	6.5
宿州市	Suzhou	11263	197675	20	150	41.0	7.5
蚌埠市	Bengbu	3083	24563	10	89	24.4	7.2
阜阳市	Fuyang	13183	182777	15	99	27.1	6.2
淮南市	Huainan	2591	14468	8	61	16.7	5.9
滁州市	Chuzhou	6846	36805	7	65	17.8	7.8
六安市	Luan	10198	147595	19	145	39.7	6.5
马鞍山市	Maanshan	1809	4299	3	59	16.3	16.0
芜湖市	Wuhu	2887	5676	3	21	5.8	7.0
宣城市	Xuancheng	3154	17107	6	78	21.4	11.9
铜陵市	Tongling	884	1553	2	30	8.1	7.4
池州市	Chizhou	1371	11441	11	95	26.0	7.6
安庆市	Anqing	5200	42822	10	71	19.4	6.2
黄山市	Huangshan	1572	6771	5	51	14.1	7.8

20—15 主要年份村卫生室基本情况
The Basic Situation of Health Room in Main Years

年 份 Year	机构数（个） Health Institutions (unit)	按设置、主办单位分 Grouped by Managing Organization					乡村医生和卫生员（人） Rural Doctors and Health Workers (person)		
		村 办 Set Up by Village	乡卫生院设点 Spot of Township Commune Hospital	联合办 Joint Set Up	私人办 Private Set Up	其 他 Others		乡村医生 Rural Doctors	卫生员 Health Workers
2010	15636	7912	3501	1020	1748	1455	55784	53638	2146
2013	15310	7823	3507	1454	945	1581	51640	48365	3275
2014	15288	7215	3152	1481	947	2493	48261	45217	3044
2015	15295	7192	3182	1484	947	2490	45914	42955	2959
2016	15276	7155	2771	1936	928	2486	43365	40470	2895
2017	15331	7083	2850	1880	900	2618	40869	38000	2869
2018	15317	7106	2965	1849	872	2525	37606	34969	2637
2019	15549	7080	3135	1839	894	2601	35006	32601	2405
2020	15710	7360	2812	2174	829	2535	30776	28791	1985
2021	15630	9169	280	2408	762	3011	26769	25292	1477
2022	15601	9169	105	2520	766	3041	24466	23281	1185

20—16 各市村卫生室基本情况（2022年）
The Basic Situation of Health Room by Region (2022)

地 区	Region	机构数（个） Health Institutions (unit)	按设置、主办单位分 Grouped by Setting Up and Managing Organizations					乡村医生和卫生员（人） Rural Doctors and Health Workers (person)		
			村 办 Set Up by Village	乡卫生院设点 Spot of Township Commune Hospital	联合办 Joint Set Up	私人办 Private Set Up	其 他 Others		乡村医生 Rural Doctors	卫生员 Health Workers
总 计	**Total**	**15601**	**9169**	**105**	**2520**	**766**	**3041**	**24466**	**23281**	**1185**
合肥市	Hefei	1130	243	2	479	42	364	1530	1480	50
淮北市	Huaibei	351	327		16	3	5	499	498	1
亳州市	Bozhou	1338	912		255	24	147	3726	3523	203
宿州市	Suzhou	1227	860		144	42	181	2355	2281	74
蚌埠市	Bengbu	937	820	2	20	7	88	1156	1118	38
阜阳市	Fuyang	1808	1268		111	3	426	4439	3845	594
淮南市	Huainan	849	189	1	311	45	303	1138	1103	35
滁州市	Chuzhou	1059	976	1	41		41	1757	1676	81
六安市	Luan	1916	783		772		361	2468	2447	21
马鞍山市	Maanshan	429	282		3	38	106	529	521	8
芜湖市	Wuhu	732	313	43	61	51	264	803	768	35
宣城市	Xuancheng	827	509	7	22	193	96	704	699	5
铜陵市	Tongling	359	176	21	20	7	135	495	483	12
池州市	Chizhou	615	353	10	20	106	126	456	454	2
安庆市	Anqing	1400	886	11	145	55	303	1993	1971	22
黄山市	Huangshan	624	272	7	100	150	95	418	414	4

20—17 民政行业单位基本情况（2022年）
Basic Conditions of Civil Affairs Agencies (2022)

项　　目	Item	单位数 （个） Number of Enterprises (unit)	职工人数 （人） Number of Staff and Workers (person)
民政行政机关	Civil Affairs Administrative Departments	121	2270
提供住宿的社会工作机构	A Social Work Agency That Provides Accommodation	2713	27787
养老机构	Pension Agency	2619	26315
精神疾病服务机构	Mental Illness Services	3	200
儿童福利和救助机构	Child Welfare and Assistance Agency	33	689
其他提供住宿机构	Other Accommodations	58	583
不提供住宿的社会工作机构	A Social Work Agency That Does Not Provide Accommodation	29926	110755
#社区服务机构和设施	Community Service Agencies and Facilities	19320	88230
民政部门直属康复辅具机构	Rehabilitation AIDS Institutions Directly Under the Civil Affairs Department	1	27
低保服务机构	Subsistence Allowance Service Institutions	22	116
彩票发行机构	Lottery Agency	44	520
社会组织	Social Organization	36900	452268
社会团体	Social Groups	16917	182153
基金会	Foundation	195	1375
民办非企业单位	Private Non-enterprise Units	19788	268740
基层群众自治组织	Community-level Self-governing Organizations	18009	91465
居委会	Residents' Committees	3728	21956
村委会	Village Committee	14281	69509
其他社会服务机构	Other Social Service Agencies	175	3112
婚姻登记服务机构	Marriage Registration Service	31	214
殡葬服务机构	Funeral Services	144	2898
其他事业单位	Other Institutions	23	167

20—18 全省民政服务事业费支出情况
Expenditure on Civil Affairs Service in the Province

单位：万元（10000 yuan）

指　　标	Item	2010	2015	2020	2021	2022
总　　计	**Total**	**971558**	**1812234**	**2151615**	**2170805**	**2446945**
社会福利	Social Welfare	48429	183619	459355	500783	636174
社会救助	Social Assistance	543753	987512	1536107	1494942	1622250
民政管理事务	Civil Administration	35842	79831	117803	126289	137378
行政事业单位离退休	Retired Administrative Institutions	11670	16394	7917	8971	11922
其　他	Other	47592	44852	30480	39820	39222

20—19 社会福利事业单位基本情况（2022年）
Basic Statistics on Social Welfare Institutions (2022)

项　目	Item	单位数（个）Number of Homes (unit)	工作人员（人）Number of Staff and Workers (person)	床　位（张）Number of Beds (unit)	年末收养人数（人）Number of Persons Housed (person)
提供住宿的法定社会工作机构	A Statutory Social Work Agency That Provides Accommodation	2713	27787	377134	135751
养老机构	Pension Agency	2619	26315	366453	132267
#社会福利院	Social Welfare Home	55	1329	10502	4141
精神疾病服务机构	Mental Illness Services	3	200	315	80
#社会福利医院	Social Welfare Hospital	3	200	315	80
儿童福利和救助保护机构	Child Welfare and Rescue Protection Agency	33	689	5789	2490
#儿童福利机构数	Number of Child Welfare Institutions	27	639	5239	2457
未成年人救助保护中心数	Number of Juvenile Rescue and Protection Centers	6	50	550	33
其他提供住宿机构	Other Accommodation Agencies	58	583	4577	914

20—20 享受补助、救济人员情况
Persons Receiving Subsidies or Relief Funds

单位：人、元/人月（person、Yuan/man-month）

指　标	Item	2021	2022
最低生活保障	**Minimum Living Guarantee**	**2085965**	**1974970**
城镇居民最低生活保障人数	Number of Persons Receiving Lowest Cost-of-living in Urban Area	316695	276271
农村居民最低生活保障人数	Number of Persons Receiving Lowest Cost-of-living in Rural Area	1769270	1698699
城市最低生活保障平均标准	Average Standard of Urban Minimum Living Standards	686.3	738.0
农村最低生活保障平均标准	Average Standard of Subsistence Allowances for Rural Residents	684.9	727.5
特困人员救助供养	**Relief and Support for the Poor**	**345520**	**336339**
农村特困人员救助供养	Assistance and Support for Rural Poor People	334386	324404
城市特困人员救助供养	Assistance and Support for Urban Poor People	11134	11935
临时救助	**Temporary Relief**	**102061**	**95766**
其他生活救助（传统救助等）	**Other Living Assistance (traditional assistance, etc.)**	**14605**	**13464**

20—21 婚姻服务情况
Number of Marriage and Divorces

指 标		Item		2010	2015	2019	2020	2021	2022
内地居民登记结婚	(对)	Registered Marriages	(couple)	650861	737989	539233	471309	420214	338852
初 婚	(人)	First Marriages	(person)	1038265	1240023	833006	709881	625206	509349
再 婚	(人)	Remarriages	(person)	263457	238179	250100	233739	215860	168355
离 婚	(对)	Divorces	(couple)	109634	181207	250107	237650	150041	143175
离婚率	(‰)	Divorce Rate	(‰)	3.22	5.22	7.04	6.67	4.21	4.02

注：本表数据由民政厅、法院提供。

a) The data in this table were provided by Provincial Civil Affairs Department and court.

20—22 各市婚姻服务情况（2022年）
Number of Marriage and Divorces by Region (2022)

地 区	Region	内地居民登记结婚 (对) Registered Marriages (couple)	初 婚 (人) First Marriages (person)	再 婚 (人) Remarriages (person)	登记离婚数 (对) Quantity of Registered Divorcing (couple)	离婚率 (‰) Divorce Rate (‰)
总 计	**Total**	**338852**	**509349**	**168355**	**107378**	**3.01**
省本级	Provincial Level	410	820		75	
合肥市	Hefei	50401	71643	29159	16809	4.22
淮北市	Huaibei	11038	16714	5362	3803	3.48
亳州市	Bozhou	31813	50218	13408	8605	2.57
宿州市	Suzhou	31661	48505	14817	8809	2.67
蚌埠市	Bengbu	18593	26602	10584	7285	3.77
阜阳市	Fuyang	50984	80471	21497	14467	2.69
淮南市	Huainan	16079	23006	9152	5376	2.77
滁州市	Chuzhou	22998	34549	11447	7570	3.34
六安市	Luan	23176	35652	10700	7307	2.51
马鞍山市	Maanshan	10579	14858	6300	3824	3.37
芜湖市	Wuhu	18396	27079	9713	6130	3.16
宣城市	Xuancheng	12339	16936	7742	5073	3.67
铜陵市	Tongling	6501	9651	3351	2045	2.43
池州市	Chizhou	6278	9451	3105	2089	2.60
安庆市	Anqing	21695	34411	8979	5887	2.25
黄山市	Huangshan	5911	8783	3039	2224	3.01

注：本表数据由民政厅提供，离婚人数不包括法院的调解和判决离婚数。

a) Data in this table are provided by provincial department of civil affairs. The number of divorces excludes those mediated and judged by courts.

20—23 城乡居民最低生活保障情况
Basic Living Allowances for Urban and Rural Residents

年 份 Year	城乡居民最低生活保障 People Receiving Lowest Cost-of-living in Urban and Rural Area			
	城镇低保人数（万人） Number of Persons Receiving Lowest Cost-of-living in Urban Area (10000 person)	保障金额（万元） Amount of Money (10000 yuan)	农村低保人数（万人） Number of Persons Receiving Lowest Cost-of-living in Rural Area (10000 person)	保障金额（万元） Amount of Money (10000 yuan)
2010	88.40	197149.3	214.62	195417.7
2015	64.67	281671.7	196.33	387606.0
2020	34.43	232200.2	183.68	943603.4
2021	31.67	210046.0	176.93	920214.9
2022	27.63	216091.2	169.87	1007464.4

20—24 各市城乡居民最低生活保障情况（2022年）
Basic Living Allowances for Urban and Rural Residents by Region (2022)

地 区	Region	城乡居民最低生活保障 People Receiving Lowest Cost-of-living in Urban and Rural Area			
		城镇低保人数（人） Number of Persons Receiving Lowest Cost-of-living in Urban Area (person)	保障金额（万元） Amount of Money (10000 yuan)	农村低保人数（人） Number of Persons Receiving Lowest Cost-of-living in Rural Area (person)	保障金额（万元） Amount of Money (10000 yuan)
总 计	**Total**	**276271**	**216091**	**1698699**	**1007464**
合肥市	Hefei	19731	19372	125278	110652
淮北市	Huaibei	14129	10739	34640	22592
亳州市	Bozhou	7583	5454	220674	117073
宿州市	Suzhou	24049	15295	232386	125308
蚌埠市	Bengbu	18381	15130	70934	43692
阜阳市	Fuyang	23515	17456	276174	149278
淮南市	Huainan	17001	14515	85538	50479
滁州市	Chuzhou	19885	15473	105751	63854
六安市	Luan	25691	17776	174278	101061
马鞍山市	Maanshan	20802	16467	37121	26350
芜湖市	Wuhu	27966	26374	61172	39587
宣城市	Xuancheng	8025	6236	58519	37407
铜陵市	Tongling	22954	16854	20947	12218
池州市	Chizhou	6411	4452	44735	25035
安庆市	Anqing	14299	10283	121037	66108
黄山市	Huangshan	5849	4217	29515	16770

20—25 工伤保险情况
Situation of Employment Injury Insurance

单位：人、万元（person, 10000 yuan）

项　目	Item	2015	2020	2021	2022
参保人数	Insurance Population	5288777	6838599	7180480	8180729
农民工人数	Number of Rural Workers	1464977	1293927	1755964	2400024
享受伤残待遇人数	Number of Enjoy Wounded and Disabled Treatment Population	71780	53455	74419	55507
享受工伤保险待遇的职业病人数	Number of Enjoy Industrial Injury Insurance Treatment Population	2606	1662	1931	1345
因工死亡人数	Number of On-duty Deaths	610	877	967	850
供养亲属人数	Number of Support Relatives	11105	13237	13271	13097
基金收入	Fund Revenue	216014	150822	246699	331347
基金支出	Fund Expense	162053	245673	294174	335967
累计结余	Accumulative Surplus	374900	374942	327466	322846
省级调剂金	Provincial Adjustment Funds	40935	41562	39026	36445

20—26 各市职工基本医疗保险情况（2022年）
Basic Medical Insurance for Employees by Region (2022)

地　区	Region	参保人数(人) Insurance Population (person)			基金(万元) Fund (10000 yuan)			
		合计 Total	职工小计 Total of Staffs & Workers	退休人员小计 Total of Retirees	收入 Income	支出 Expenditure	累计结余 Accumulative Surplus	个人账户 Personal Account
总　计	**Total**	**10633068**	**7724289**	**2908779**	**4639457**	**3151104**	**7811853**	**2943410**
合 肥 市	Hefei	3147211	2566060	581151	1592095	1097570	2992297	668649
淮 北 市	Huaibei	465821	278006	187815	224773	161244	365513	215009
亳 州 市	Bozhou	331634	263541	68093	161610	109521	343793	100360
宿 州 市	Suzhou	367503	269718	97785	136128	91927	342759	104847
蚌 埠 市	Bengbu	576370	368881	207489	221046	169150	299339	156038
阜 阳 市	Fuyang	584388	446165	138223	235037	159304	386608	173121
淮 南 市	Huainan	622366	329157	293209	210759	198694	232084	159864
滁 州 市	Chuzhou	632894	481191	151703	264546	187352	459205	227881
六 安 市	Luan	460696	339830	120866	191939	126252	365501	132013
马鞍山市	Maanshan	633839	395604	238235	273077	207245	302742	153869
芜 湖 市	Wuhu	977944	721162	256782	368492	104516	645844	333498
宣 城 市	Xuancheng	500830	376613	124217	213329	123742	322548	124216
铜 陵 市	Tongling	337140	211937	125203	125340	102774	185554	104083
池 州 市	Chizhou	203632	151449	52183	90034	59510	148758	70040
安 庆 市	Anqing	530839	346233	184606	218489	171143	248154	119315
黄 山 市	Huangshan	259961	178742	81219	112762	81159	171155	100606

注：合肥市医疗保险基金收入、支出、累计结余项目中包含省本级相应项目基金。

a) The medical insurance fund income,expenditure and accumulative surplus of Hefei city including provincial corresponding item fund.

20—27 城镇职工基本养老保险情况
Basic Endowment Insurance for Urban Employees

年 份 Year	参保职工 （人） Active Contributors (person)		离休、退休退职人员年末人数（人） Retirees at the Year-end (person)	基金收支情况 （万元） Revenue and Expenses (10000 yuan)		
	年末数 Number at the year-end	#企业 Enterprises		基金收入 Fund Revenue	基金支出 Fund Expense	累计可用结余基金 Total Usable Balance
2010	4920498	4824616	1774880	3432478	2708340	3529725
2013	5922049	5812695	2191238	6249422	4688128	7454218
2014	5969045	5860399	2323449	6807025	5441083	8820160
2015	6108539	6001183	2466593	7917525	6313752	10423933
2016	6343078	6237503	2579290	8394118	6965752	11852299
2017	7541145	6491344	3228587	10202349	8115654	13938994
2018	7988093	6874864	3429090	21051657	18176103	16814548
2019	8602847	7437652	3566938	16594395	14311418	19045435
2020	9143979	7944079	3691471	15014999	15472778	18587656
2021	10031546	8795815	3810220	19698676	17039419	21246913
2022	11830490	10583528	3978736	18828806	16618642	23457077

注：因试点改革单位口径部分调整，历年数据有部分调整。
a) Due to the partial adjustment of the caliber of the pilot reform unit, the data over the years have been partially adjusted.

20—28 各市城镇职工基本养老保险情况（2022年）
Basic Endowment Insurance for Urban Employees by Region (2022)

地 区	Region	参保职工 （人） Active Contributors (person)		离休、退休退职人员年末人数（人） Retirees at the Year-end (person)	基金收支情况 （万元） Revenue and Expenses (10000 yuan)		
		年末数 Number at the year-end	#企业 Enterprises		基金收入 Fund Revenue	基金支出 Fund Expense	累计可用结余基金 Total Usable Balance
总 计	**Total**	**11830490**	**10583528**	**3978736**	**18828806**	**16618642**	**23457077**
合肥市	Hefei	3838690	3706739	512421	3931501	2000411	116021
淮北市	Huaibei	410761	372109	146283	466814	513768	568939
亳州市	Bozhou	441051	361454	115970	515354	472978	59443
宿州市	Suzhou	445614	348541	166556	649861	686870	66596
蚌埠市	Bengbu	569926	501985	236802	650434	935744	39521
阜阳市	Fuyang	592772	453978	216268	968278	889915	36041
淮南市	Huainan	458086	398011	250860	713455	909244	67132
滁州市	Chuzhou	648903	567232	236260	885476	854755	43097
六安市	Luan	467031	374906	190101	702278	741346	101182
马鞍山市	Maanshan	487785	440522	282824	675737	1084444	19036
芜湖市	Wuhu	925490	855235	392347	1194931	1313520	47225
宣城市	Xuancheng	635815	577560	216939	628907	681730	107541
铜陵市	Tongling	255600	222145	142958	385471	497905	11115
池州市	Chizhou	231916	197289	73469	271649	277240	10525
安庆市	Anqing	650029	551832	274357	857463	1049341	63653
黄山市	Huangshan	257889	216805	103401	369213	421547	36629

注：总计数中含省直数据。
a) Provincial data is contained in the total number.

20—29 主要年份城乡居民参加基本医疗保险情况
Participation of Urban and Rural Residents in Basic Medical Insurance in Major Years

年　份 Year	参保人数（万人）People Participated in Medical Insurance (10000 person)			基金收支情况（万元）Revenue and Expenses (10000 yuan) 基金收入 Revenue		
	城乡居民 Urban and Rural Residents	原城镇居民 Former Urban Residents	原新农合 Former New Rural Cooperative Medical System	城乡居民 Urban and Rural Residents	原城镇居民 Former Urban Residents	原新农合 Former New Rural Cooperative Medical System
2012		975	5044		321603	1487170
2013		945	5150		417549	1895768
2014		1017	5191		372422	2129677
2015		974	5191		451113	2551820
2016		840	5121		473304	2854539
2017		1299	4654		802481	2907727
2018		1615	4687		1070620	3178810
2019	5843			4367939		
2020	5753			4763005		
2021	5651			4889463		
2022	5443			5052455		

年　份 Year	基金收支情况（万元）Revenue and Expenses (10000 yuan) 基金支出 Expenses			累计结余 Balance at Year-end		
	城乡居民 Urban and Rural Residents	原城镇居民 Former Urban Residents	原新农合 Former New Rural Cooperative Medical System	城乡居民 Urban and Rural Residents	原城镇居民 Former Urban Residents	原新农合 Former New Rural Cooperative Medical System
2012		236587	1428581		356475	441263
2013		344626	1775728		402958	550375
2014		326502	2064647		448820	595287
2015		370514	2232031		520002	884885
2016		370684	2549181		592066	1127740
2017		664496	2746777		794527	1078125
2018		1005906	3203518		936516	1178239
2019	4440048			2084462		
2020	4487822			2359645		
2021	4897447			2351661		
2022	4782689			2621426		

注：1．2014年基金收支数据不包含市级统筹单位上解下拨基金收支。

2．2019年原城镇居民和原新农合医保整合为城乡居民基本医疗保险，不再单独区分。

a) 2014 fund balance of payments data does not include the city as a whole unit over financing the fund balance of payments.

b) In 2019, the original urban residents and the original new rural cooperative medical insurance will be integrated into the basic medical insurance for urban and rural residents, and no separate distinction will be made.

20—30 各市城乡居民参加基本医疗保险情况（2022年）

Participation of Urban and Rural Residents in Basic Medical Insurance by Region (2022)

地　区	Region	参保人数（人）People Participated in Medical Insurance (person)	基金收支情况（万元）Revenue and Expenses (10000 yuan) 基金收入 Revenue	新冠疫苗财政补助 Financial Subsidies for COVID-19 Vaccines	基金支出 Expenses	疫苗清算费用 Vaccine Clearing Costs	累计结余 Balance at Year-end
总　计	**Total**	**54433683**	**5052455**	**7249**	**4782689**	**40409**	**2621426**
合肥市	Hefei	5533814	511611		555036		158323
淮北市	Huaibei	1529248	144029		155045	1439	84010
亳州市	Bozhou	5449680	522478	837	499620	3081	225293
宿州市	Suzhou	5316185	490459	884	426102	5806	331633
蚌埠市	Bengbu	2922681	274324		239433	1900	209953
阜阳市	Fuyang	8706071	800733	2661	764345	6552	373804
淮南市	Huainan	2687277	248640	2498	220769	3948	232031
滁州市	Chuzhou	3466244	325357		304080	2798	183491
六安市	Luan	4746049	439771		419243	939	209291
马鞍山市	Maanshan	1556093	137984		157947	4659	48444
芜湖市	Wuhu	2720111	252707		144379	1426	258064
宣城市	Xuancheng	2103306	197402		179045	2285	78616
铜陵市	Tongling	1152642	107666		113513	1313	25651
池州市	Chizhou	1267461	122752	369	124383	1916	33131
安庆市	Anqing	4164352	372497		368798	1087	119792
黄山市	Huangshan	1112469	104044		110952	1261	49899

注：1. 合肥市参保人数、基金收入、支出、累计结余项目中包含省本级相应项目基金。
2. 淮南市清算新冠病毒及接种费用各级财政补助2021年未入账，该市当期收入中新冠病毒疫苗及接种费用财政补助金额为0。
3. 合肥市新冠病毒疫苗及接种费用均从职工基本医疗保险基金中支出，该市当期收入中新冠病毒疫苗及接种费用财政补助金额和当期支出中新冠疫苗及接种费用清算金额为0。

a) In Hefei City, number of insurance, fund income and expenditure, the accumulative surplus items include in the provincial level corresponding project fund.

b) Huainan City's liquidation of novel coronavirus vaccine and inoculation costs all levels of financial subsidies have not been recorded in 2021, and the amount of financial subsidies for novel coronavirus vaccine and inoculation costs in the current income of the city is 0.

c) Novel coronavirus vaccine and vaccination costs in Hefei are all incurred from the basic medical insurance fund of employees. The financial subsidy amount for novel coronavirus vaccine and vaccination costs and the liquidation amount for new coronavirus vaccine and vaccination costs in the current period of the city's income are 0.

20—31 各市失业保险基本情况（2022年）
Basic Information About Unemployment Insurance by Region （2022）

单位：万人（10000 persons）

地区	Region	本年参保人数 Contributors This Year				
		合计 Total	企业 Enterprises	国有企业 State-owned Enterprises	集体企业 Collected-owned Enterprises	事业单位 Institutions
总计	**Total**	**663.58**	**527.46**	**129.45**	**11.93**	**101.81**
合肥市	Hefei	231.51	201.41	78.04	3.61	12.20
淮北市	Huaibei	28.54	25.68	7.38	0.24	2.86
亳州市	Bozhou	22.41	15.72	2.31	0.39	6.02
宿州市	Suzhou	16.02	11.16	1.35	0.18	4.43
蚌埠市	Bengbu	30.02	22.18	4.41	0.63	7.08
阜阳市	Fuyang	38.10	21.88	3.75	1.04	15.18
淮南市	Huainan	31.31	26.54	12.80	1.17	3.68
滁州市	Chuzhou	33.82	24.17	3.75	1.25	8.41
六安市	Luan	29.13	19.50	3.45	0.74	8.12
马鞍山市	Maanshan	31.91	25.74	3.85	0.77	4.47
芜湖市	Wuhu	59.87	50.76	1.25	0.21	7.12
宣城市	Xuancheng	31.78	25.77	1.35	0.74	5.32
铜陵市	Tongling	18.25	14.50	1.71	0.21	3.37
池州市	Chizhou	11.92	8.53	1.01	0.30	2.99
安庆市	Anqing	34.38	24.01	1.87	0.33	7.71
黄山市	Huangshan	14.60	9.92	1.15	0.12	2.86

地区	Region	领取失业保险金人数 Beneficiaries of Unemployment Insurance this year	基金（万元） Fund (10000 yuan)		
			收入 Income	支出 Expenditure	累计结余 Accumulative Surplus
总计	**Total**	**8.04**	**463226.00**	**521502.00**	**817596.00**
合肥市	Hefei	3.60	161625.00	208928.00	1530.00
淮北市	Huaibei	0.28	21187.00	19374.00	12599.00
亳州市	Bozhou	0.17	14296.00	10141.00	14701.00
宿州市	Suzhou	0.13	10304.00	10112.00	407.00
蚌埠市	Bengbu	0.43	19320.00	22789.00	
阜阳市	Fuyang	0.33	23921.00	20599.00	438.00
淮南市	Huainan	0.25	27530.00	20178.00	10738.00
滁州市	Chuzhou	0.49	24306.00	22537.00	19271.00
六安市	Luan	0.17	18616.00	13813.00	
马鞍山市	Maanshan	0.55	23792.00	25704.00	1016.00
芜湖市	Wuhu	0.55	38158.00	33455.00	
宣城市	Xuancheng	0.21	18728.00	14553.00	11299.00
铜陵市	Tongling	0.24	13928.00	18059.00	
池州市	Chizhou	0.12	7445.00	5829.00	13.00
安庆市	Anqing	0.34	22077.00	18976.00	6895.00
黄山市	Huangshan	0.19	9460.00	8977.00	10004.00

20—32 城乡居民基本养老保险情况
Situation of Rural and Rural Residents Endowment Insurance

单位：万人、万元（10000 persons, 10000 yuan）

项　目	Item	2020	2021	2022
参保人数	People Participated in	3490	3458	3429
年末领取养老金人数	At the end of the Number of Pensioners	915	914	963
本年基金收入	This Fund Income	2539796	2947535	3894849
个人缴费	Individual Paying	770561	1118448	1986958
集体补助	Collective Subsidy	122	95	61
政府补贴	Government Subsidy	1542018	1584058	1683564
利息收入	Interest Income	143974	153071	202065
其他收入	Other Earning	4158	8495	8719
转移收入	Income Transfer	16486	5489	4325
本年基金支出	This Fund Spending	1470826	1571862	1836246
养老金支出	Old-age Pension Expenditure	1431601	1532431	1797258
其他支出	Other Spending	754	5	8
转移支出	Transfer Spending	12425	1885	2572
年末基金滚存结余	Fund Blance Year-end	5886482	7262155	9320758

注：自2014年起，对城乡居民基本养老保险情况相关指标进行微调。

a) Since 2014, the basic old-age insurance for urban and rural residents is related indicators for fine-tuning.

20—33 各市生育保险情况（2022年）
Birth Insurance Situation by Region (2022)

地　区	Region	参保人数（人） Insurance Population (person)	#女　性 Female	基金收支情况（万元） Revenue and Expenses (10000 yuan)：待遇支出 Treatment Expenditure
总　计	**Total**	**7571174**	**3234237**	**240494**
合肥市	Hefei	2566060	1127221	138926
淮北市	Huaibei	265168	87794	4962
亳州市	Bozhou	263541	115464	7380
宿州市	Suzhou	269718	124719	5283
蚌埠市	Bengbu	368881	171899	7628
阜阳市	Fuyang	462197	208591	7920
淮南市	Huainan	329170	117555	5580
滁州市	Chuzhou	481191	205137	7386
六安市	Luan	321654	132282	6519
马鞍山市	Maanshan	395603	165024	7345
芜湖市	Wuhu	631474	255566	15963
宣城市	Xuancheng	376375	169662	6533
铜陵市	Tongling	210251	83728	2900
池州市	Chizhou	151449	63257	2921
安庆市	Anqing	316787	131673	8682
黄山市	Huangshan	161655	74665	4567

注：合肥市含省直数据。基金收支不包含市级统筹单位上解下拨基金收支。

a) Hefei data was made. Fund more than balance does not include the city as a whole unit over financing the fund balance of payments.

20—34 人力资源服务机构综合情况（2022年）
Human Resources Service Organization Comprehensive Situation (2022)

项　目		Item		公共就业服务机构 Public Employment Service Organization	公共人才服务机构 Public Talented Person Service Organization	国有性质服务企业 State-owned Service Enterprise	私营性质服务企业 Private Service Enterprise
服务机构数	(个)	Service Organization	(unit)	16	9	79	3079
从业人员人数	(人)	Population of Jobholder	(person)	183	86	3953	63298
#大专及以下		Junior College and Below					
本　科		Undergraduate Course					
硕士及以上		Master and Above		23	3	61	916
#取得职业资格人数		Obtaining Professional Qualification Population		42	11	290	7761
设立固定招聘场所	(个)	Fixed Employment Advertise Place	(unit)	39	8	64	2722
总资产	(万元)	Total Assets	(10000 yuan)	12098	2342	92719	2669861
建立人力资源服务网站	(个)	Human Resources Service Network	(unit)	245	5	44	1015
全年营业总收入	(万元)	Annual Business Gross Income	(10000 yuan)			2715023	4584775

注：仅统计县以上机构。
a) Only institutions above the county level are counted.

20—35 人力资源服务业务基本情况（2022年）
Human Resources Service Basic Situation (2022)

项　目	Item	公共就业服务机构 Public Employment Service Organization	公共人才服务机构 Public Talented Person Service Organization	国有性质服务企业 State-owned Service Enterprise	私营性质服务企业 Private Service Enterprise
服务人员总数（人）	Total of Service Personnel Registration (person)	183	86	3953	63298
登记要求流动人员（人）	Number of Registration Requesting Flowing Personnel (person)				
#大专及以下	Junior College and Below				
本　科	Undergraduate Course				
硕士及以上	Master and Above	23	3	61	916
实现就业和流动人数（人）	Realizing Employment and Flowing Population (person)	196573	163256	662848	7295371
服务用人单位数（个）	Number of Service Personnel Units (unit)	24964	27029	25085	884001
#国有企、事业单位	State-owned Enterprise and Institution	3346	1064	1263	68833
私营企业	Private Enterprise Foreign-funded Enterprise	22727	22456	20699	539081
外资企业	Foreign-funded Enterprise	3452	1314	280	26566
建立人力资源数据库（个）	Establishment Human Resources Database (unit)				
现存数据库求职信息总量（人次）	Total of Extant Database Seeking Employment Information (person time)				
#全年入库求职信息	Whole Year Warehousing Seeking Employment Information				
现场招聘服务	Scene Employment Advertise Service				
举办招聘会次数（次）	Number of Times of Conducting Job Fair (time)	2271	1613	2015	12892
#毕业生专场	Graduate Specially	490	275	378	2979
农民工专场	Peasant Laborer Specially	187	60	499	3136
参会用人单位（家）	Attending the Meeting Employer (unit)	49836	22521	11087	132532
提供招聘岗位（个）	Providing Employment Post (unit)	431312	654739	314720	2744200
参会求职人数（人）	Attending the Meeting Seeking Employment Population (person)	170236	144029	498484	3018611
网络招聘服务（条）	Network Employment Advertise Service (unit)				
发布岗位信息	Issue Post Information	59834	356934	575775	4636751
发布求职信息	Issue Seeking Employment Information	55327	4380	976653	9995227
劳务(人才)派遣服务	The Service (talented person) to Dispatch to Serve				
派遣单位（个）	Detached Organization (unit)	23	24	4929	22714
派遣人员总量（人）	Total of Detached Personnel (person)	143	134	142994	618311
登记要求派遣人数（人）	Registration Requesting Detached Population (person)				
人力资源管理咨询	Human Resources Management Consulting				
服务用人单位（个）	Service Employer Unit (unit)	970	224	2873	30143
人力资源外包服务	Human Resources Outsourcing Service				
服务用人单位（个）	Service Employer Unit (unit)			2756	79341
流动人员档案管理	Flowing Personnel Record Management				
现存档案数量（人）	Number of Extant File (person)	190199	317692	207695	256100
依托档案提供服务（次）	Depending on the File to Provide Service (time)	79068	61428	72054	205504
培训服务	Training Service				
举办培训班（个）	Conducting Training Class (unit)	1511	129	687	5341
参加人数（人）	Participating Population (person)	6329	4439	40868	308425
测评服务	Evaluation Service				
测评人数（人）	Evaluation Population (person)	1845		52464	640704
猎头服务	Headhunting Service				
成功推荐人才（人）	Successful to Recommend Talented Person (person)	124		1485	21195

20—36 各市职业技能评价鉴定综合情况（2022年）

Comprehensive Situation of Vocational Skill Evaluation and Appraisal by Region (2022)

单位：人（person）

地 区	Region	评价机构数（个）Number of Appraisal Institution (unit) 小计 Total	#职业技能等级认定机构 Vocational Skill Rating Agency	#职业技能鉴定机构 Vocational Skill Appraisal Agency	考评人员人数 Number of Evaluation Staff	鉴定考核人数 Appraisal Number of Assessment 小计 Total	初级 Primary	中级 Middle-level	高级 High level
总 计	**Total**	**838**	**785**	**53**	**21139**	**610664**	**175334**	**284680**	**141316**
合肥市	Hefei	207	200	7	6839	184259	12369	99926	69649
淮北市	Huaibei	23	19	4	1178	32063	9018	16841	5684
亳州市	Bozhou	26	21	5	906	31077	11965	13293	5623
宿州市	Suzhou	11	9	2	434	19612	8764	9232	1231
蚌埠市	Bengbu	58	54	4	993	26496	2967	17969	5015
阜阳市	Fuyang	55	49	6	903	27474	11807	10147	5281
淮南市	Huainan	35	31	4	1402	49537	27571	15693	4722
滁州市	Chuzhou	65	56	9	1258	25849	14085	6460	4857
六安市	Luan	21	21		498	37987	19034	13244	5370
马鞍山市	Maanshan	44	44		930	34235	9763	18407	5263
芜湖市	Wuhu	30	29	1	969	37313	2558	27208	6998
宣城市	Xuancheng	58	52	6	1106	31533	12564	11308	7332
铜陵市	Tongling	15	15		754	14983	4504	6735	3450
池州市	Chizhou	41	38	3	575	11214	6809	1938	2316
安庆市	Anqing	77	75	2	1345	28131	12396	10418	5021
黄山市	Huangshan	72	72		1049	18901	9160	5861	3504

地 区	Region	技师 Technician	高级技师 Senior Technician	获取证书人数 Number of Obtaining a Certificate 小计 Total	初级 Primary	中级 Middle-level	高级 High level	技师 Technician	高级技师 Senior Technician
总 计	**Total**	**7765**	**1569**	**536243**	**157136**	**251178**	**120985**	**5650**	**1294**
合肥市	Hefei	1814	501	151010	9949	83849	55702	1132	378
淮北市	Huaibei	478	42	26492	7412	13938	4795	319	28
亳州市	Bozhou	191	5	27397	10334	11941	4939	178	5
宿州市	Suzhou	296	89	17740	7864	8565	1012	221	78
蚌埠市	Bengbu	475	70	24504	2451	16919	4625	439	70
阜阳市	Fuyang	175	64	25024	10123	9551	5119	169	62
淮南市	Huainan	1377	174	43485	25267	13561	3863	679	115
滁州市	Chuzhou	444	3	23938	12822	6036	4637	440	3
六安市	Luan	285	54	34765	17804	11873	4763	271	54
马鞍山市	Maanshan	666	136	28755	7963	15590	4733	366	103
芜湖市	Wuhu	418	131	34375	2285	25279	6314	379	118
宣城市	Xuancheng	278	51	30000	11960	10594	7136	263	47
铜陵市	Tongling	243	51	12414	3545	5714	2928	190	37
池州市	Chizhou	119	32	11077	6702	1928	2303	112	32
安庆市	Anqing	232	64	26907	11903	10044	4677	220	63
黄山市	Huangshan	274	102	18360	8752	5796	3439	272	101

注：本年合肥市数据中包含省直。

a) This year in hefei data contains was made.

主要统计指标解释

医疗卫生机构

指从卫生（卫生计生）行政部门取得《医疗机构执业许可证》《计划生育技术服务许可证》，或从民政、工商、机构编制管理部门取得法人单位登记证书，为社会提供医疗服务、公共卫生服务或从事医学科研和医学在职培训等工作的单位。医疗卫生机构包括医院、基层医疗卫生机构、专业公共卫生机构、其他医疗卫生机构。

医院

包括综合医院、中医医院、中西医结合医院、民族医院、各类专科医院和护理院，不包括专科疾病防治院、妇幼保健院和疗养院，包括医学院校附属医院。

基层医疗卫生机构

包括社区卫生服务中心、社区卫生服务站、街道卫生院、乡镇卫生院、村卫生室、门诊部、诊所(医务室)。

专业公共卫生机构

包括疾病预防控制中心、专科疾病防治机构、妇幼保健机构（含妇幼保健计划生育服务中心）、健康教育机构、急救中心（站）、采供血机构、卫生监督机构、取得《医疗机构执业许可证》或《计划生育技术服务许可证》的计划生育技术服务机构。

其他医疗卫生机构

包括疗养院、临床检验中心、医学科研机构、医学在职教育机构、卫生监督（监测、检测）机构、医学考试中心、农村改水中心、人才交流中心、统计信息中心等卫生事业单位。

卫生人员

指在医疗卫生机构工作并由单位支付工资的人员。包括在编及合同制人员、返聘和临聘本单位半年以上人员（如护士、医师等），不包括离退休人员、退职人员、离开本单位仍保留劳动关系人员、返聘和临聘本单位不足半年人员。多点执业医师一律计入第 1 执业单位在岗职工数，不再计入第 2、3 执业单位在岗职工数。

卫生技术人员

包括执业医师、执业助理医师、注册护士、药师（士）、检验技师（士）、影像技师、卫生监督员和见习医（药、护、技）师（士）等卫生专业人员。不包括从事管理工作的卫生技术人员(如院长、副院长、党委书记等)。

其他卫生技术人员

包括见习医(药、护、技)师(士)等卫生专业人员，不包括药剂员、检验员、护理员等。见习医师(士)指毕业于高中等院校医学专业但尚未取得医师执业证书的医师和医士。

其他技术人员

指从事医疗器械修配、卫生宣传、科研、教学等技术工作的非卫生专业人员。

管理人员

指担负领导职责或管理任务的工作人员。包括从事医疗服务、公共卫生、医学科研与教学等业务管理工作的人员；主要从事党政、人事、财务、信息、安全保卫等行政管理工作的人员。

工勤技能人员

指承担技能操作和维护、后勤保障、服务等职责的工作人员。工勤技能人员分为技术工和普通工。技术工包括护理员(工)、药剂员(工)、检验员、收费员、挂号员等，但不包括实验员、技术员、研究实习员(计入其他技术人员),经济员、会计员和统计员等(计入管理人员)。

乡村医生和卫生员

指从当地卫生和计生行政部门获得“乡村医生”证书的人员；卫生员是指村卫生室中未获得“乡村医生”证书的人员。

实有床位数

指年底固定实有床位数，包括正规床、简易床、监护床、超过半年加床、正在消毒和修理床位、因扩建或大修而停用床位。不包括产科新生儿床、接产室待产床、库存床、观察床、临时加床和病人家属陪侍床。

城镇居民最低生活保障人数

指在报告期末家庭平均收入在当地规定的最低生活保障线以下的城镇居民数。包括“三无”对象，失业人员和在职、下岗、退休人员等。

农村居民最低生活保障人数

指报告期末在建立农村最低生活保障制度的地区，得到当地政府或集体给予最低生活保障的农业人口家庭人数。

离婚率

指当年离婚人数占户籍人口的比重，计算公式为：

离婚率＝当年离婚人数/户籍人数×1000‰。

社区服务设施数

指报告期末设立的以非营利为目的，为本社区居民服务，特别是为老年人、残疾人、儿童服务的社区服务中心、活动站、服务站、养老院、老年公寓（托老所），残疾人工疗站、残疾儿童日托所、家务服务站、婚姻介绍所等福利性设施以及职工社会保险管理服务的机构数。几种不同类型的社区服务单位，共用一个场所的，只能统计为一个社区服务设施。成为社区服务设施的条件：（1）是独立核算单位；（2）有固定的从业人员；（3）有一定的服务项目；（4）有一定的场所。

城镇职工基本养老保险

1.（参保）职工人数

指报告期末按照国家法律、法规和有关政策规定参加基本养老保险并在社保经办机构已建立缴费记录档案的职工人数，包括中断缴费但未终止养老保险关系的职工人数，不包括只登记未建立缴费记录档案的人数。

2.（参保）离退休人员人数

指报告期末参加基本养老保险的离休、退休和退职人员的人数。

3.基金收入

指根据国家有关规定，由纳入基本养老保险范围的缴费单位和个人按国家规定的缴费基数和缴费比例缴纳的养老保险基金，以及通过其他方式取得的形成基金来源的收入。包括单位和职工个人缴纳的基本养老保险费、基本养老保险基金利息收入、上级补助收入、下级上解收入、转移收入、财政补贴和其他收入。

4.基金支出

指按照国家政策规定的开支范围和开支标准从养老保险基金中支付给参加基本养老保险的个人的养老金、丧葬抚恤补助，以及由于保险关系转移、上下级之间调剂资金等原因而发生的支出。包括离休金、退休金、退职金、各种补贴、医疗费、死亡丧葬补助费、抚恤救济费、社会保险经办机构管理费、补助下级支出、上解上级支出、转移支出、其他支出等。

5.基金累计结余

指报告期末基本养老保险基金收支相抵后的累计余额。

城镇职工基本医疗保险

1.参保人数

指报告期末按国家有关规定参加相应基本医疗保险的人数。

2.基金收入

指由用人单位和个人按照国家规定的缴费基数、缴费比例或缴费标准缴纳的基本医疗保险基金，财政补助资金以及通过其他方式取得的形成基金来源的款项，包括：单位缴纳收入、个人缴纳收入、财政补助收入（含医疗救助补助个人收入）、财政补贴收入、利息收入、其他收入和转移收入等。

3.基金支出

指按照国家政策规定的开支范围和开支标准，从基本医疗保险基金中支付给参保人员的医疗保险待遇支出，包括住院医疗费用支出、门急诊医疗费用支出、个人账户基金支出、其他支出、转移支出等。

4.基金累计结余

指报告期末基本医疗保险基金累计结余金额。

失业保险

1.参保人数

指报告期末按照国家法律、法规和有关政策规定参加了失业保险的城镇企业、事业单位的职工及地方政府规定参加失业保险的其他人员的人数。

2.基金收入

指报告期内筹集的失业保险基金的总额，包括失业保险费收入、利息收入、财政补贴收入、其他收入、转移收入、上级补助收入、下级上解收入。

3.基金支出

指报告期内为保障失业人员基本生活、促进其再就业等支出的基金总额，包括失业保险金支出、医疗补助金支出、丧葬补助金和抚恤金支出、职业培训和职业介绍补贴支出、其他费用支出、其他支出、转移支出、补助下级支出、上解上级支出等。

4.基金累计结余

指报告期末失业保险基金收支相抵后的累计余额。

工伤保险

1.参加保险人数

指报告期末依据国家有关规定参加工伤保险的职工人数和有雇工的个体工商户的雇工数。

2.享受保险待遇人数

指年初至报告期末因工伤或职业病而享受工伤保险待遇的人数。为享受工伤医疗待遇中未评定等级的人数、享受伤残待遇人数以及享受因工死亡待遇人数之和。

3.基金收入

指根据国家有关规定，由参加工伤保险的单位按国家规定的缴费基数和缴费比例缴纳的工伤保险基金，以及通过其他形式取得的形成基金来源的款项。包括：单位缴纳的社会统筹基金收入、财政补贴收入、利息收入、其他收入、转移收入等。

4.基金支出

指按照国家政策规定的开支范围和开支标准从工伤保险基金中支付给参加工伤保险的人员及供养直系亲属工伤保险待遇支出及其他支出。包括工伤医疗费、伤残补助金、工亡补助金、护理费、丧葬补助费、工伤预防费用、职业康复费用和其他支出。

5.基金累计结余

指报告期末工伤保险基金累计结余金额。

Explanatory Notes for Major Statistical Indicators

Medical and Health Care Institutions

refers to the health (health care) administrative departments to obtain "medical institutions permit", "family planning technical service permit", or from the civil affairs, industry and commerce, institutional management and management departments to obtain legal person registration certificate for the community to provide medical services, public Health services or engaged in medical research and medical on-the-job training and other work units. Medical and health institutions include hospitals, primary health care institutions, professional public health institutions, other medical and health institutions.

Hospitals

Including general hospitals, Chinese medicine hospitals, Chinese and Western medicine hospitals, ethnic hospitals, all kinds of specialist hospitals and nursing homes, excluding specialist disease prevention and treatment hospital, maternal and child health centers and nursing homes, including medical college affiliated hospitals.

Health Care Institutions at Grass-root Level

include community health service centers, community health service stations, urban health centers, township health centers, village clinics, outpatient departments and clinics (health centers).

Specialized Public Health Institutions

include centers for disease control and prevention, specialized disease prevention and treatment institutions, women and children care agencies(including women and children health care family planning service center), health education institutions, first aid centers, blood gathering and supplying institutions, health supervision and inspection agencies, and family planning technical service centers that obtained the Certification of Health Care Institution or certification of family planning technical service centers.

Other Medical and Health Care Institutions

including medical centers, clinical testing centers, medical research institutions, medical in-service education institutions, health supervision (monitoring, testing) institutions, medical examination centers, rural water centers, talent exchange centers, statistical information centers and other health institutions.

Health Care Employees

means a person who works in a medical and health institution and is paid by a unit. (Including nurses, physicians, etc.), excluding retirees, retirees, leaving the unit still retain labor relations personnel, re-employment and employment of the unit is not enough Half a year staff. Multi-point practitioners are included in the number of workers in the first practice in the number of workers, no longer included in the first 2,3 units in the number of workers on duty.

Medical Technical Personnel

refer to the professional staff engaged in health care, including licensed doctors, licensed assistant doctors, registered nurses, pharmacists, laboratory technicians, imaging staff, health care supervisors and intern doctors, pharmacists, nurses, and technical personnel, excluding the medical technical personnel engaged in managerial job (e.g. president, vice president and secretary of the party committee etc).

Other health technical personnel

including trainee medical (medicine, nursing, skills) (and), and other health professionals, not including the apothecary, inspector, nurse, etc. Trainee doctors graduated from high school (and) such as college medical professional but not yet get physicians practicing certificate of doctors and healers.

Other technical staff

refers to is engaged in medical equipment and replacement, health education, scientific research, teaching and other technical work of health professionals.

Management personnel

refers to the leadership or management shoulder the task of staff. Including medical services, public health, medicine, scientific research and teaching personnel for the management of the business such as; Mainly engaged in the party and government, personnel, finance, information, security and other administrative work.

Those logistics skills personnel

means for skills operation and maintenance, logistics, services and other staff duties. Those logistics skills staff divided into technical and direct labor. Technology including caregivers (engineering), apothecary (work), the analyst, cashier, registered member, etc., but does not include laboratory technician, technician, research assistant (included in the other technicians), economy, accountant and statistician (included in the management personnel).

Rural doctors and medical corpsman

from the local health and family planning administrative department of personnel to obtain "country doctor" certificate; Medics refers to not get "country doctor" certificate in village clinics.

Actual data

refers to the fixed end of actual data, including regular bed, simple bed, guardianship, more than half a year, an additional disinfection and repair, because of the expansion or overhaul and stop using bed. Not including obstetrics bed of newborn babies, delivery room to look obstetric table, inventory bed, bed, temporary extra bed and escort, the bed of the patient's family.

Minimum living allowances for urban residents

refers to the number of those whose average family income is below a minimum local standard by the end of the reporting period, including both the employed and unemployed, laid off and retired, and those jobless people without stable residence or valid IDs.

Number of Rural Residents Entitled to Minimum Living Allowances

refers to the number of those receiving the minimum living allowances from the local government or community in the rural areas where this allowances system is in place as of the end of the reporting period.

The divorce rate

Refers to the number of divorce proportion of the population, the calculation formula is:

Divorce rate = the number of divorce, the household registration number * 1000 ‰.

Number of Service Facilities in Communities

refers to the number non-profit welfare facilities set up community residents' in particular the community-based centers that serve senior citizens, the handicapped or children, recreational centers, service centers, nursing homes, apartments for the elderly (nursery for the aged), work and treatment stations for the handicapped, day-care centers for handicapped children, domestic help agencies and dating services, as well as social insurance management agencies for the employees. Different types of community service providers that share the same premise are regarded as one community service facility. The requirements for a social service facility of communities include: (1) independent accounting; (2) fixed employees; (3) provision of certain services; and (4) with certain places.

Basic old-age insurance for urban workers

1. Number of staff and workers covered

refer to staff and workers participating in the basic pension insurance programme according to national laws, regulations and related policies at the end of the reference period, who have already had payment records in social security management agencies, including those who have interrupt payment without terminating the insurance programme. Those who have registered in the programme but with no payment records are not included.

2. Number of retirees participating in the basic pension insurance programme

refer to the number of retirees participating in basic pension insurance programmes by the end of the reference period.

3. Revenue of the basic pension insurance programme

refers to payments made by employers and individuals participating in the pension insurance programme in accordance with the basis and proportion stipulated in State regulations, and income from other sources that become source of pension insurance fund, including the premium paid by employers and staff and workers, interest income, subsidies from higher level agencies, income as transfer from subordinate agencies, transferred income, government financial subsidies and other income.

4. Expenditure of basic pension insurance programme

refer to payment made on pensions and funeral subsidies to those retired and resigned people covered in pension insurance programmes according to related national policies on scope and standard of expenditure. Also included are expenditure which arises due to shift of the insurance relationship or adjustment of funds among agencies. More specifically, included are pensions for resigned people, pensions for retired people, pension for people quitting jobs, various subsidies, medical fees, funeral subsidies, compensation payments, management fees for social security agencies, expenses on subsidies to lower subordinates, expenses as transfer to agencies at higher level, transferred expenditure and other expenditure.

5. Balance of basic pension insurance programme

refers to the balance of basic pension insurance funds at the end of the reference period after deducting expenses from revenue.

Basic medical insurance for urban workers

1. Number of people participating in the insurance programme

refers to people participating in the basic medical care insurance programme according to related regulations as at the end of reference period.

2. Revenue of the insurance programme

refers to payments made by employers and individuals participating in the medical care insurance programme in accordance with the basis and proportion stipulated in State regulations, and income from other sources that become source of medical insurance fund, including income paid by units, individual paid income, financial assistance's income (including individual income from medicaid), financial subsidies' income, interest income, transfer income and other income.

3. Expenditure of the insurance programme

point to the expenditure scope that sets according to national policy and expenditure standard, the treatment of medical treatment insurance that pays in fund of insurance of primary medical treatment to ginseng protect personnel defray, include defray of medical treatment charge of charge of medical treatment of be in hospital, door emergency treatment, individual account fund defray, other defray, transfer defray.

4. Balance of the basic medical care insurance programme

refers to the balance of medical care insurance funds at the end of the reference period.

Unemployment Insurance

1. Number of people covered

refers to staff and workers in urban enterprises or institutions who have participated in the unemployment insurance programme according to relevant policies and regulations, and other people who have participated according to local government regulations, as at the end of reference period.

2. Revenue of the unemployment insurance programme

refers to the total unemployment insurance funds raised in the reference period, including unemployment insurance premium, interest income, financial subsidies, other income, transferred income, subsidies from higher level agencies and income as transfer from subordinate agencies..

3. Expenditure of the unemployment insurance programme

refers to total expenses during the reference period to guarantee the basic livelihood of unemployed people, and to encourage their re-employment. Included are unemployment relief, medical fees, funeral subsidies, compensation payments, training expenses, management fees for unemployment insurance agencies, subsidies to lower level agencies, expenses as transfer to higher level agencies, transferred expenditure and other expenditure.

4. Balance of the unemployment insurance programme

refers to the balance of revenue of the programme after deducting expenses at the end of the reference period.

Work Injury Insurance

1. Number of people covered

refers to staff and workers who have participated in the work injury insurance programme and number of employees in private business according to relevant national regulations at the end of the reference period.

2. Number of beneficiaries

point to the total amount of the unemployed insurance fund that raises money inside report period, include income of unemployment insurance premium income, accrual income, fiscal allowance income, other income, transfer income, income of upper allowance, lower solution income.

3. Revenue of the work injury insurance programme

refers to payments made by employers participating in the work injury insurance programme in accordance with the basis and proportion stipulated in State regulations, and income from other sources that become source of work injury insurance fund, including income of social comprehensive funds paid by employers, government financial subsidies, interest income and other income.

4. Expenditure of the work injury insurance programme

refers to payments made from work injury insurance funds to those who participated in the work injury insurance programme and their direct dependents within the scope and standards of expenditure according to related national policies, and other expenditure, including medical fees for work injury, injury and disability subsidies, death subsidies, nursing fees, funeral subsidies, injury prevention fees, occupational rehabilitation fees and other expenditure.

5. Balance of the work injury insurance programme

refers to the balance of the work injury funds at the end of the reference period.

Maternity Insurance

1. Number of people covered

refers to people who have participated in the maternity insurance programme according to relevant regulation at the end of the reporting period.

2. Number of enjoying insurance

refers to people of sum who enjoy treatment of industrial injury insurance, medical treatment for not rating work-related injuries , the disability beneficiaries and the worker death and treatment at the beginning of the year to the end of the reporting period.

3. Revenue of maternity insurance

refers to payments made by employers participating in the maternity insurance programme in accordance with the basis and proportion stipulated in State regulations, and income from other sources that become source of maternity insurance fund, including income of funds paid by employers, interest income ,transfer income and other income.

4. Expenditure of the maternity insurance programme

refers to payments made from maternity insurance funds to staff and workers who participate in the maternity insurance programme within the scope and standards of expenditure in accordance with related national policies, expenses paid for pregnancy, child delivery or surgeries related to family planning, and other expenditure, including allowance for child bearing, medical fees and other expenditure.

5. Balance of the maternity programme

refers to the balance of the maternity insurance funds at the end of reference period.

第二十一篇

Chapter 21

文化和体育

CULTURE AND SPORTS

简要说明

一、本篇主要反映文化、体育、新闻出版、广播电影电视事业的发展情况。

文化部分主要包括艺术表演团体、艺术表演场所、公共图书馆、文化馆、文化站、广播、电视、新闻出版以及文物等文化事业的机构、人员、经费和业务活动情况。体育部分主要包括群众体育和竞技体育，主要内容有体育系统职工情况，竞技体育成绩，群众体育活动等情况。

二、根据各部门制定的统计报表制度汇总加工整理而成。艺术业、图书馆业、群众文化服务业的资料主要来自省文化旅游厅；文物资料来自省文物局；广播、电视、新闻出版资料来自省新闻出版局；体育部分的资料来自省体育局。

Brief Introduction

I. Data in this chapter mainly reflect the development of culture; sports; news and publication; and radio broadcasting, films and television.

Data on culture cover mainly the situations on institutions, personnel and business activities of cultural undertakings including arts performing groups and performance venues; public libraries; museums; cultural centres; archives; cultural stations; broadcasting; films; television; news and publication; and cultural relics. Data on sports cover mass sports (sports for all) and athletic sports, including mainly the number of staff and workers in sports departments, number of stadiums and gymnasiums, achievements in athletic sports events, mass sports activities and the international exchanges of sports delegations.

II. According to the statistical statement system formulated by various departments, it is summarized and processed. The materials of art industry, library industry and mass cultural service industry mainly come from the provincial department of culture and Tourism; Cultural relics data from the provincial bureau of Cultural Heritage; Radio, television, press and publication materials from the provincial Press and Publication Bureau; The information of sports comes from provincial sports bureau.

21—1 文化艺术和文物事业机构、人员情况（2022年）
Number of Institutions and Personnel in Culture, Art and Cultural Relies (2022)

机构类别	Category of Institution	机构数（个）Number of Institutions (unit)	从业人员（人）Number of Persons Engaged (person)
文化及相关产业	**Culture and Relative Industry**	**16108**	**76121**
艺术业	Art Industry	3956	42398
艺术表演团体	Art Performance Troupes	3806	40665
话剧、儿童剧、滑稽剧团	Drama, Children's Play and Comedy Troupes	17	356
歌舞、音乐类	Song and Dance, Musicals	209	3922
京剧、昆曲类	Peking Opera and Kunqu Opera	8	496
#京　剧	Beijing Opera Troupes	8	496
地方戏曲类	Local Opera	2144	12609
杂技、魔术、马戏类	Acrobatics, Magic and Circus	418	5198
曲艺类	Folk Arts	94	1802
综合性艺术表演团体	Comprehensive Art Performing	916	16282
其　他	Other		
艺术表演场所	Art Centers	150	1733
#剧场、影剧院	Theaters and Music Halls	58	1067
图书馆事业	Library Business	133	1736
群众文化事业	Mass cultural undertakings	1635	6246
省级文化馆、群众艺术馆	Provincial Cultural Center, Mass Art Museum	1	37
市级文化馆、群众文化馆	Municipal Cultural Centers, Mass Cultural Centers	17	304
县、市文化馆	County and City Cultural Centers	105	1157
文化站	Cultural Stations	1512	4748
#乡镇文化站	Township Cultural Stations	1275	4061
文化部门教育机构	Cultural sector Educational Institutions	4	83
文艺科研	Literary and Scientific Research	10	142
文化科技研究	Cultural Science and Technology Research	3	37
综合性艺术研究	Comprehensive Artistic Research	3	21
地方戏艺术研究	Local Opera art Research	3	77
其他科研机构	Other Scientific Research Institution	1	7
文化市场经营单位	Cultural Market Management Unit	11691	29529
文物业	Total of Cultural Relic Organization	314	3969
文物机构合计	Total Heritage Institutions	89	611
#文物保护管理机构	Cultural Relic Protection Management Organization	80	483
文物科研机构	Scientific and Research Historical Relics Agency	1	54
博物馆合计	Museums	225	3358
艺术类博物馆	Art Museum	21	168
综合性博物馆	Comprehensive Museum	96	1592
历史类博物馆	History Class Museum	67	1044
自然科技类博物馆	Natural Science and Technology Museum	8	107
其它博物馆	Other Museum	33	447

注：艺术事业机构数，包括非公有制艺术表演团体及场所。
a) Number of art institutions, including the non-public sectors of the performing arts groups and places.

21—2 艺术表演团体演出情况（2022年）
Basic Statistics on Performance of Art Troupes (2022)

种 类	Item	演出场数（场）Number of Performances (shows)	到农村演出 Shows in Rural Areas	国内演出观众人数（千人次）Number of Audience While Perfoming at Home (1000 person-times)
总 计	**Total**	**337200**	**162800**	**52285**
国有剧团	Troupes Sponsored by State-owned Units	7500	4400	4062
集体经营剧团	Troupes Sponsored by Collective Units	200	100	95
其 他	Other	329600	158200	48128
按剧种分	**Art Troupes**			
话剧、儿童剧、滑稽剧团	Drama, Children,s Play and Comedy Troupes	4900	200	315
歌舞、音乐类	Song and Dance, Musicals	13700	7400	4568
京剧、昆曲类	Peking Opera and Kunqu Opera	300	100	263
#京 剧	Beijing Opera Troupes	300	100	263
地方戏曲类	Local Opera	65200	41800	16374
杂技、魔术、马戏类	Acrobatics, Magic and Circus	133800	54600	12773
曲艺类	Folk Arts	7100	4200	1267
综合性艺术表演团体	Comprehensive Art Performing	112200	54500	16726
其 他	Other			

注：演出场数包括非公有制企业数据。
a) Doing a including non-public enterprise data.

21—3 群众艺术馆、文化馆站业务活动及经费情况（2022年）
Basic Statistics on Activities and Expenditures of Mass Art Centers and Cultural Centers (2022)

项 目	Item	总 计 Total	群众艺术馆、文化馆 Mass Art Centers Cultural Centers	文化站 Cultural Stations
单位数 （个）	Number of Units (unit)	1635	123	1512
举办展览 （个）	Exhibition (unit)	6777	1220	5557
组织文艺活动 （次）	Art Performances and Story-telling Sessions (times)	49716	9080	40636
举办训练班	Training Courses			
班 次 （次）	Number of Classes (times)	34966	15989	18977
培训人次 （万人次）	Training People (10000 person-times)	215	68	147
群众艺术馆、文化馆负责指导单位	Units Responsible for Guiding Mass Art Centers and Cultural Centers			
馆办文艺团体 （个）	Literature Groups Hold by Art and Cultural Buildings	429		
群众业余演出团、队 （个）	Part-time Art Groups (unit)	14923		
总支出 （万元）	Total Expenditures (10000 yuan)	66995	36577	30417

21—4 公共图书馆业务活动及经费情况（2022年）
Facilities, Services and Expenditures of Public Libraries (2022)

项目	Item	总计 Total	省级公共图书馆 Public Libraries at Provincial Level	地市级公共图书馆 Public Libraries at Prefectural Level	县级公共图书馆 Public Libraries at County Level
公共图书馆（个）	Number of Public Libraries (unit)	133	1	23	109
总藏量（万册）	Total Collections (10000 volumes)	4203	404	1266	2532
#本年新增藏量	New Reserves This Year	373	15	119	239
图书	Books	3735	329	1150	2256
古籍	Ancient Works	63	35	16	12
报刊	Newspapers and Periodicals	200	38	66	96
开架书刊	Open Books and Periodicals	2504	119	857	1527
实际持证读者数（千个）	Actual Number of Cardholder Readers (1000 unit)	3555	282	1764	1509
图书流通情况	Circulation of Books				
总流通人次（万人次）	Total Number of Circulation (10000 person-times)	5197	164	2299	2733
书刊文献外借册次（万册次）	volume-times of borrowing books (10000 volume-times)	2501	105	813	1582
为读者服务举办各种活动	Service Activities Provided for Readers				
次数（万次）	Number of Activities (10000 times)	1.17	0.07	0.33	0.77
参加人数（万人次）	Number of Readers Involved (10000 person-times)	829.55	19.71	438.53	371.31
总支出（万元）	Total Expenditures (10000 yuan)	56135	9080	19642	27413
#基本支出	Basic Expenditures	27582	5779	9805	11998
#新增藏量购置费	The New Inventory Purchase Expense	7179	710	3017	3452
公用房屋建筑面积（万平方米）	Floor Space of Public Buildings (10000 sq.m)	71.35	3.69	26.36	41.30
#书库	Stack Rooms	11.13	0.87	4.48	5.78
阅览室	Reading Rooms	25.87	0.97	10.49	14.41
阅览室座席数（个）	Seating Capacity of Reading Rooms (unit)	63069	1545	25027	36497

注：总藏量不包括电子图书。

a) A total does not include electronic books.

21—5 博物馆、文物机构业务活动及经费情况（2022年）
Facilities, Services and Expenditures of Museums and Cultural Relic Agencies (2022)

项目	Item	文物保护管理机构 protection and Management Agencies	文物科研机构 Scientific and Research Historical Relics Preservation	其他文物机构 Other Agencies	博物馆 Museums
藏品（件）	Number of Units (unit)	34936	19763		916154
#一级品	Number of Exhibitions (unit)	202	27		6627
业务活动	Art Performances and Story-telling Sessions				
陈列展览（个）	Training Courses (unit)	20			1299
参观人次（万人次）	Number of Classes (10000 person-times)	120			1405
#未成年人	Minors	18			348
总支出（万元）	Total Expenditures (10000 yuan)	19096	7450		73760
#基本支出	Basic Expenditures	8387	1859		32323

21—6　全省档案事业基本情况（2022年）
Provincial Archives Cause Basic Situation (2022)

项　　目	Item	合　计 Total	国家综合档案馆 National Comprehensive Archives	国家专门档案馆 National Special Archives	部门档案馆 Departmental Archives	企业档案馆 Enterprise Archives	事业单位档案馆 Archives of Institutions
档案馆个数（个）	**Number of National Archives (unit)**	**164**	**125**	**16**	**4**	**4**	**15**
建筑面积（万平方米）	**Floor Space of Building (10000 sq.m)**	**72.45**	**64.41**	**4.56**	**0.66**	**0.56**	**2.26**
馆藏档案情况	**Files Collected in Archives**						
纸质档案	Paper Files						
全　宗（个）	Full Archives (unit)	16290	16054	155	5	37	39
案　卷（千卷）	Records (1000 rolls)	33013.72	27583.09	2212.97	2163.77	345.98	707.91
新中国成立前档案	Archives Before the Founding of New China	95.16	94.42	0.02	0.04	0.33	0.35
新中国成立后档案	Archives After the Founding of New China	32918.56	27488.66	2212.95	2163.73	345.66	707.56
以件为保管单位档案（千件）	Documents Shall Be the Archives of The Storage Unit (1000 piece)	34779.87	32556.70	31.83	120.13	230.78	1840.43
新中国成立前档案	Archives Before the Founding of New China	83.99	83.92	0.01			0.06
新中国成立后档案	Archives After the Founding of New China	34695.88	32472.78	31.82	120.13	230.78	1840.37
录音磁带、录像磁带、影片档案（千盘）	Audio Tape, Video Tape, Film Archive (1000 disc)	32.97	27.78	2.00	0.49	1.43	1.26
照片档案（千张）	Photo Archives (1000 rolls)	1476.44	438.89	505.41	2.04	157.85	372.26
实物档案（千件）	Physical File (1000 piece)	166.47	89.83	0.24	0.37	7.27	68.77
档案利用情况	**File Utilization**						
本年利用档案人次（人次）	Persons Using Files in the Year (person-times)	320570	244133	12818	26610	8092	28917
本年利用资料人次（人次）	Persons Using Datas in the Year (person-times)	4129	3776	10	172	45	126
本年利用档案数量（万卷件次）	Files Used in the Year (10000 roll.times)	134.65	115.79	4.46	3.48	3.62	7.30
本年利用资料数量（册次）	Datum Used in the Year (volume-times)	21734	20700	10	521	143	360
本年编研档案、资料（万字）	Files and Data Prepared and Studied in the Year (10000 Chinese characters)	5528.30	4225.20		100.00	12.00	1191.10

资料来源：安徽省档案局。
Source: Anhui Municipal Bureau of Archives.

21—7 广播、电视事业发展情况
Basic Statistics on Broadcasting and Television Stations

指标		Item		2021	2022
职工人数	(人)	Number of Staff and Workers	(person)	27329	27914
广播电视台	(座)	Broadcasting and TV Station	(set)	78	78
省级广播电视台		Provincial Broadcasting and TV Station		1	1
市级广播电视台		City Broadcasting and TV Station		16	16
县级广播电视台		County Broadcasting and TV Station		61	61
中波发射台及转播台	(座)	Number of Broadcast Transmission Stations and Relaying Stations	(set)	23	23
中波发射机功率	(千瓦)	Broadcast Power of Transmitters	(kW)	1382.6	1406.6
广播人口覆盖率	(%)	Listener Rating	(%)	99.94	99.95
调频电视发射台及转播台	(座)	FM TV Station and Broadcast Station	(set)	105	105
调频发射机功率	(千瓦)	Frequency Modulation Transmitter Power	(kW)	699.4	708.2
电视发射机功率	(千瓦)	Power of Transmitters	(kW)	520.0	455.65
电视人口覆盖率	(%)	Viewer Rating	(%)	99.92	99.94

21—8 广播、电视覆盖率
Listeners and Viewers Rate

指标	Item	覆盖人口（万人） Covered Population (10000 persons)		覆盖率（%） Covering Ratio (%)	
		2021	2022	2021	2022
广　播	**Broadcasting**	**7112.37**	**7121.83**	**99.94**	**99.95**
中央台节目	Program I of China National Broadcasting	7095.31	7106.13	99.70	99.73
省级台节目	Program I of Provincial Broadcasting	7099.95	7111.04	99.76	99.80
地市级台节目	Program I of Prefectural (city) Broadcasting	6990.30	7012.06	98.22	98.41
县级台节目	Programs of County Broadcasting	4967.21	5010.80	69.79	70.32
电　视	**Television**	**7110.91**	**7121.11**	**99.92**	**99.94**
中央台节目	Relaying Program I of CCTV	7110.54	7121.07	99.91	99.94
省级台节目	Program I of Provincial Television	7107.72	7118.97	99.87	99.91
地市级台节目	Programs of Prefectural (city) Television	6991.35	7014.54	98.24	98.44
县级台节目	Programs of County Television	5033.67	4999.19	70.73	70.16

21—9 广播、电视节目制作时间
Produces Length of Broadcasting and Television

单位：小时（hour）

指标	Item	2021	2022
广播节目制作	**Production of Broadcasting**	**286798**	**305526**
新　闻	News Programs	49211	51002
专　题	Special Subject Programs	82549	83138
综　艺	Variety Entertainment	41439	44631
广播剧	Broadcasting Play	4759	5029
广　告	Advertisement	29432	30691
其　他	Others	79408	91035
电视节目制作	**Production of TV Programs**	**78637**	**77187**
新　闻	News Programs	29002	29803
专　题	Special Subject Programs	19033	17991
综　艺	Variety Entertainment	5568	4310
影视剧	TV Play	267	309
广　告	Advertisement	12146	11215
其　他	Others	12621	13559

21—10 广播、电视宣传基本情况（2022年）
Basic Statistics on Broadcasting and Television (2022)

项目	Item	节目套数（套）Number of Programs (set)	全年公共节目播出时间（小时）Time of Program Transmission All the Year (hour)	制作节目时间（小时）Time of Making Program (hour)	#新闻节目 News Programs	专题节目 Special Subject Programs	综艺节目 Variety Emtertainment
无线广播合计	**All Radio Broadcasting Stations**	**111**	**656160**	**305526**	**51002**	**83138**	**44631**
省 级	Provincial	9	75729	54835	7016	18321	4824
市县级	City and County	102	580431	250691	43986	64817	39807
电视播映合计	**All Television Stations**	**133**	**742314**	**77187**	**29803**	**17991**	**4310**
省 级	Provincial	7	49576	13136	5230	1402	669
市县级	City and County	126	692738	64051	24573	16589	3641

注：全省广播电视节目制作时间包括各级广播电视台和社会影视节目制作机构制作的时间。

a) The provincial radio and television programme production time including broadcast television and film and television programme production social organizations at all levels to make the time.

21—11 图书、杂志和报纸出版数量
Number of Books, Magazines and Newspaper Published

年份 Year	图书 Books Published 种类（种）Number of Publications (kind)	新出版 New Publications	总印数（万册）Printed Copies (10000 copies)	总印张数（万印张）Printed Sheets (10000 sheets)	杂志 Magazines Published 种类（种）Number of Publications (kind)	每期平均印数（万册）Average Printed Copies Per Issue (10000 copies)	总印数（万册）Printed Copies (10000 copies)	总印张数（万印张）Printed Sheets (10000 sheets)	报纸 Newspapers Published 种类（种）Number of Publications (kind)	每期平均印数（万册）Average Printed Copies Per Issue (10000 copies)	总印数（万份）Printed Copies (10000 copies)	总印张数（万印张）Printed Sheets (10000 sheets)
2010	5646	2669	23891	163954	178	404	5842	23115	98	519	116988	470953
2013	9440	5469	25800	200400	180	397	6227	26000	98	517	124700	509100
2014	9934	5227	25579	192396	180	355	5627	24474	98	500	121176	464623
2015	8902	4832	27329	207650	180	313	5251	24574	98	480	104830	375622
2016	9441	5212	24892	182768	180	291	5017	23305	98	363	79488	201261
2017	9745	4864	30704	235287	180	259	4399	20008	98	325	71577	155571
2018	10040	4248	32077	236527	180	233	4321	19742	98	299	67725	139280
2019	10066	3767	28760	226531	180	202	3742	16996	98	265	61730	119914
2020	10015	3210	31793	248971	180	185	3485	15820	94	241	56092	109568
2021	10121	3558	32294	266689	180	176	3443	16301	88	234	54808	103041
2022	10181	3285	32772	276178	181	173	3429	15516	85	215	50871	95116

21—12 主要年份少年儿童读物和课本出版情况
Number of Books Published for Children and Textbooks in Major Years

年份 Year	种数（种） Number of Publications (kind)		总印数（万册） Printed Copies (10000 copies)		总印张（千印张） Printed Sheets (1000 sheets)	
	儿童读物 Books for Children	课本 Textbooks	儿童读物 Books for Children	课本 Textbooks	儿童读物 Books for Children	课本 Textbooks
2010	1094	449	1489	10563	90700	789666
2015	1244	1091	1927	11827	153008	853487
2019	1532	800	3272	10916	191386	791319
2020	1456	751	3158	14689	190915	1077107
2021	1868	727	2810	13615	184936	1005899
2022	1249	739	2298	14591	158447	1049611

21—13 主要年份出版印刷生产情况
Conditions of Printing in Main Year

年份 Year	企业数（个） Number of Enterprises (unit)	工业销售产值（万元） Industrial Sales Value (10000 yuan)	印刷产量 Output of Printing 黑白（万令） Black and White (10000 ream)	印刷产量 Output of Printing 彩色（万对开色令） Color (10000 bisect color ream)	装订产量（万令） Output of Bookbinding (10000 ream)	用纸量（万令） Amout of Paper Used (10000 ream)
2010	258	302870	1094.23	2715.25	809.97	1040.70
2015	258	488208	858.99	3876.95	999.02	1737.36
2019	322	575133	796.68	3961.56	1311.85	1840.68
2020	338	511912	586.70	4103.56	984.66	1395.37
2021	359	567442	501.69	4777.96	1007.82	1189.42
2022	354	540016	441.10	4312.29	875.82	1047.30

21—14 主要年份出版物发行机构数和网点数
Issuing Institutions and Spots of Publication in Main Year

年份 Year	发行机构合计（处） Total	国有书店及国有发行点 State-owned Bookstore and Issuing Spots	出版社 Press	网上书店 Online Bookstore	文化教育广电邮政系统 Cultural, Educational Broad-casting and Postal Systems	新华书店系统外批发网点 Wholesale Spots Outside Xinhua Bookstore	集体个体零售 Collective and Personal Retail	新华书店系统出版社自办发行从业人数(人) Persons Engaged in Own Issuance of Presses of Xinhua Book-Store System (persons) 全部职工 All Staff	#国有书店及发行点 State-owned Bookstores and Issuing Spots
2010	7723	579	11	1	3576	330	3226	5029	4878
2015	8275	630	11	77	3657	302	3598	5073	5008
2019	8796	642	8	1140	1831	381	4794	6019	5851
2020	9129	780	9	1364	1936	470	4570	6088	5914
2021	9480	776	9	1565	1936	441	4753	6191	5990
2022	9635	802	9	1592	1936	445	4851	6152	5951

21—15 规模以上文化及相关产业法人单位基本情况（2022年）
Basic Information of Cultural and Related Industry Legal Entities above Designated Size(2022)

单位：万元 (10000 yuan)

项目	ProJect	企业单位数（个）Number of Enterprises (unit)	年末从业人数（人）Engaged Persons at Year-end (person)	资产总计 Total assets	营业收入 Total Revenue	利润总额 Total profit	应交增值税 Value-added Tax Payable
总　计	**Total count**	**2568**	**239877**	**43007011.3**	**27426003.1**	**1337690.4**	**442063.5**
按行业类别分	**Divided by industry category**						
新闻信息服务	News information service	95	14740	845095.8	945320.5	88591.2	18434.4
内容创作生产	Content creation and production	571	51413	5752977.5	4453915.1	419403.7	77767.7
创意设计服务	Creative design service	285	23129	4795826.6	3173201.8	233644.3	49766.4
文化传播渠道	Cultural communication channel	227	14037	4579945.9	2675758.8	111718.9	30000.2
文化投资运营	Cultural investment operation	13	2210	6696805.6	130994.6	-368424.5	1776.2
文化娱乐休闲服务	Culture, entertainment and leisure	155	9592	3350007.4	244222.4	-36819.9	5918.3
文化辅助生产和中介服务	Culture assists production and intermediary services	552	49698	8224968.2	5871673.3	554301.5	141981.4
文化装备生产	Production of cultural equipment	132	16199	1292517.4	1272125.4	49222.8	19257.9
文化消费终端生产	Cultural consumption terminal	538	58859	7468866.9	8658791.2	286052.4	97161
按产业类型分	**Divided by industry type**						
文化制造业	Cultural manufacturing industry	1147	140203	16769539.6	13466904.9	910849.5	269302.6
文化批发和零售业	Cultural wholesale and retail	444	14414	5203869.8	5908888.4	141501.2	46325.8
文化服务业	Cultural service industry	977	85260	21033601.9	8050209.8	285339.7	126435.1
按领域分	**By domain**						
文化核心领域	Core area of culture	1346	115121	26020658.8	11623413.2	448113.7	183663.2
文化相关领域	Culture-related field	1222	124756	16986352.5	15802589.9	889576.7	258400.3

注：表中部分数据因四舍五入，存在总计与分项合计不等的情况。

a)Note: Some data in the table are not equal to the total and sub-item total due to rounding.

21—16 分地区规模以上文化及相关产业法人单位基本情况（2022年）
Basic Information of Cultural and Related Industry Legal Entities above Designated Size by Region(2022)

单位：万元（10000 yuan）

地区	Region	法人单位数（个）Number of legal entity (unit)	年末从业人员（个）Engaged Persons at Year-end (person)	资产总计 Total assets	营业收入 Total Revenue	利润总额 Total profit	应交增值税 Value-added Tax Payable
全省	**Total**	**2568**	**239877**	**43007011.3**	**27426003.1**	**1337690.4**	**442063.5**
合肥市	Hefei	492	75594	19320104.8	12604925.3	381996.9	156104.2
淮北市	Huaibei	39	2589	178882.9	153100.8	10607.9	2089.1
亳州市	Bozhou	78	9102	5039655.8	410307.2	-30074.2	15105.9
宿州市	Suzhou	181	9976	1331204.2	1548556.1	61518.2	36510.3
蚌埠市	Bengbu	124	10867	920104	721483.7	14123.6	10763.1
阜阳市	Fuyang	252	18142	1152363.8	1006422.5	35733.4	24602
淮南市	Huainan	80	3989	337011.1	314726	883.2	3546.5
滁州市	Chuzhou	257	31191	1479372	2446270.4	69993.7	40267.7
六安市	Luan	109	10244	1199480.1	693563.6	23897.9	6998.9
马鞍山市	Maanshan	127	10826	5034216.4	1875340.3	320159.5	40020.8
芜湖市	Wuhu	227	14102	2092862.2	2423182.3	300272.1	32797.6
宣城市	Xuancheng	169	12258	844562.2	838891.4	45767.6	17539.4
铜陵市	Tongling	82	4388	332222.4	281930.4	13787.8	5887.4
池州市	Chizhou	78	6523	1103981.9	419485.8	4217.6	9709.2
安庆市	Anqing	193	12111	1416547.4	1084935.2	56083.7	28558.8
黄山市	Huangshan	80	7975	1224440.1	602882.1	28721.5	11562.6

21—17 全省体育场地数（2022年）
Number of Stadiums and Gymnasiums (2022)

指 标		Item		总 计 Total
综合指标		**Composite Indicator**		
人均体育场地面积	（平方米）	Sports Area per Capita	（sq.m）	2.62
体育场地数量	（万个）	Number of Sports Venues	（10000 unit）	21.41
基础运动场地		**Basic Sports Field**		
田径场地	（万个）	Athletic Field	（10000 unit）	1.04
游泳场地	（个）	Swimming Venue	（unit）	1044
球类运动场地		**Ball Court**		
足球场地	（个）	A Football Field	（unit）	7184
篮球场地	（万个）	Basketball Court	（10000 unit）	4.65
排球场地	（个）	Volleyball Venue	（unit）	3428
乒乓球场地	（万个）	Table Tennis Court	（10000 unit）	5.80
羽毛球场地	（万个）	Badminton Court	（10000 unit）	1.85
冰雪运动场地		**Ice and Snow Sports Field**		
滑冰场地	（个）	Skating Ground	（unit）	13
滑雪场地	（个）	Skiing	（unit）	5
体育健身场地		**Sports and Fitness Area**		
全民健身路径	（万个）	National Fitness Path	（10000 unit）	4.22
健身房	（个）	Gym	（unit）	7114
健身步道	（万公里）	Fitness Trails	（10000km）	1.45

21—18 体育系统职工人数（2022年）
Number of Staff and Workers in Sports System (2022)

单位：人（person）

人员分类	Category of Personnel	合 计 Total	#优秀运动队 Excellent Sports Teams	体育运动学校 Physical Education and Sports Schools	业余学校 Sparetime Sports Schools	公共体育场馆 Public Stadiums and Cymnasiums	机关 Officers
总 计	**Total**	**3008**	**970**	**200**	**370**	**259**	**1209**
公务员	Public Servants	653					653
运动员	Athletes	572	572				
专职教练员	Full-time Coaches	421	114	86	218	3	
专职文化教师	Full-time Teachers	165	53	78	34		
科技人员	Scientific and Technical Personnel	2	1	1			
医务人员	Medical Personnel	6	4	1	1		
管理人员	Administrative Personnel	296	113	14	49	120	
其 他	Others	893	113	20	68	136	556

21—19 等级运动员、等级裁判员发展人数（2022年）

Number of Athletes and Referees in Grades by Type of Sports (2022)

单位：人（person）

运动项目	Item	等级运动员 Number of Athletes in Grades	运动健将 International Master of Sports	一级 First Grade Sportsman	二级 Second Grade Sportsman	等级裁判员 Number of Referees in Grades	国际、国家级 International National Referees	一级 First Grade Referees	二级 Second Grade Referees
总　计	**Total**	**2540**		**513**	**2027**	**1614**		**627**	**987**
田　径	Track and Field	642		32	610				57
游　泳	Swimming	334		59	275			1	5
体　操	Gymnastics	71		65	6				
举　重	Weightlifting	22		6	16			1	
拳　击	Boxing	54		18	36				
中国式摔跤	Chinese style wrestling	7		2	5				8
国际式摔跤	Wrestling	87		31	56			1	
柔　道	Judo	28		7	21				
跆拳道	Kickboxing	39		14	25			40	
击　剑	Fencing	53		12	41				
赛　艇	Racing Shell	50		9	41			45	
皮划艇	Canoeing	24		8	16			46	
射　击	Shooting	24		19	5			9	
足　球	Football	26			26			17	19
篮　球	Basketball	190		17	173			44	12
排　球	Volleyball	213		64	149			48	8
乒乓球	Table Tennis	73		17	56			1	2
羽毛球	Badminton	51		14	37			75	442
网　球	Tennis	61		28	33				
手　球	Handball	171		37	134				198
技　巧	Skill								
武　术	Wu Shu	194		2	192			84	
其　他	Others	126		52	74			215	236

注：等级运动员与等级裁判员为当年市以上体育行政部门审批数。一级裁判员审批已下放协会，此项数据目前缺失。

a) Number of Grade athletes and referees is approval number in the year above the city level of the sports administrative departments. The first-class referee's approval has been delegated to the association, and this data is currently missing.

21—20 体育活动基本情况
Basic Statement of Sports

指　　标	Item	2010	2015	2020	2021	2022
举办全民健身活动次数　　（次）	Times of Activities That the Whole Nation in Health Conducted (times)		2176	5191	3723	
参加全民健身活动人数　　（万人）	People Participating the Activities That the Whole Nation in Health (10000 person)	324.76	337.88	396.00	345.00	523.00
优秀运动员　　（人）	Number of Athletes in Grades (person)	852	657	1754	2377	
运动健将	International Master of Sports	159	185	57	40	
一级运动员	First Grade Sportsman	280	207	349	811	513
二级运动员	Second Grade Sportsman	160	125	1348	1526	2027
等级教练员人数　　（人）	Number of Coaches in Grades (person)	652	633	594	647	638
等级裁判员发展人数（人）	Number of Referees in Grades (person)	864	489	641	1038	1614
在国内外比赛中获奖牌数　　（枚）	Number of Medals Won in the Matches Both Inside and Outside the Country (unit)	160.0	116	124	126	117
金　牌	Gold Medals	57.0	35	28	38	34
银　牌	Silver Medals	42	31	38	43	37
铜　牌	Bronze Medals	61	50	58	45	46
体育社会组织总数　　（个）	Total Number of Sports Social Organizations (unit)				2835	3042
#体育社会团体	Sports Community				2291	2422
体育基金会	Sports Foundation				2	66
体育类民办非企业单位	Sports Private Non-enterprise Units				542	554

注：1．优秀运动员2008年以前为等级运动员。
2．由于裁判员审批制度改革，2015年我省未审批一级裁判员，以致裁判员发展人数比上年大幅度减少。

a) Before 2008, Top athletes were athlete in Grades .

b) Due to the referee for examination and approval system reform, in 2015 our province level for examination and approval of the referee, so that the number of referees development greatly reduced over the previous year.

主要统计指标解释

文化及相关产业

指为社会公众提供文化、娱乐产品和服务的活动以及与这些活动有关联的活动的集合。根据提供文化、娱乐产品和服务活动的属性特点，划分为公益性文化活动和经营性文化活动两大类。

文化及相关产业是第三产业的重要组成部分。是在我国《国民经济行业分类》基础上的派生分类，有文化服务和相关文化服务两大类：

艺术表演团体

指由文化部门主办或实行行业管理（经文化市场行政部门审批或已申报登记并领取相关许可证），专门从事表演艺术等活动的各类专业艺术表演团体，含民间职业剧团。如话剧团、方言话剧团、滑稽剧团、儿童剧团、歌剧团、木偶团、皮影团等以及由若干剧种组成的综合性专业艺术表演团体。不包括群众业余文艺表演团体。

艺术表演场所

指由文化部门主办或实行行业管理（经文化市场行政部门审批或已申报登记并领取相关许可证），有观众席、舞台、灯光设备，公开售票、专供文艺团体演出的文化活动场所。附属于文化部门机构内非独立核算的剧场、排演场，公开营业的也应单独统计。

广播节目综合人口覆盖率

指根据国家广电总局制定的《广播电视人口覆盖率统计技术标准和方法》进行统计调查的，在对象区内采用无线、有线、卫星等技术手段能够收听到包括中央、省、地市、县广播节目其中任意一套的人口数占全省总人口数的百分比。

电视节目综合人口覆盖率

指根据国家广电总局制定的《广播电视人口覆盖率统计技术标准和方法》进行统计调查的，在对象区内采用无线、有线、卫星等技术手段能够收看到包括中央、省、地市、县级电视节目中任意一套的人口数占全省总人口数的百分比。

等级运动员人数

指经考核正式批准授予等级运动员称号的人数。运动员等级分为国际级运动健将、运动健将、一级运动员、二级运动员、三级运动员、少年级运动员。

等级裁判员人数

指经考核正式批准授予等级裁判员称号的人数。裁判员等级分为国际裁判、国家级裁判、一级裁判、二级裁判、三级裁判。

体育场

指设有标准田径跑道（400 米环形跑道至少 8 条，直跑道 8-10 条）、标准足球场（场地为 105×68 米）等的室外体育场地。

体育馆

指设有比赛和练习场地、看台和辅助用房等设施，可开展球类、体操等单项或多项体育比赛，固定座席大于 500 个的室内体育建筑。

Explanatory Notes for Major Statistical Indicators

Culture and Related Industries

refer to the aggregate of activities, providing the mass with culture goods, amusement goods and services. According to the characteristics of culture goods, amusement goods and services, they can be classified into two categories, or nonprofit cultural activities and profit cultural activities.

Culture and related industries is the important component of the tertiary industry. These are the derivative sector from the Industrial Classification of the National Economy and are composed of two categories of culture services and related cultural services.

Arts Performance Troupes

refer to the various professional performing arts groups, which sponsored by the cultural sectors or guided by the cultural society (approved by the cultural market administration, or registered and permitted with the relative certificate), including non-governmental troupes, such as drama troupes, dialect troupes, comedy troupes, children troupes, Opera troupes, puppetry troupes, Shadowgraph troupes, etc., comprehensive professional arts performance troupes. The mass amateur arts performance troupes are not included.

Arts Performance Places

refer to the various sites for cultural activities, which sponsored by the cultural sectors or guided by the cultural society (approved by the cultural market administration, or registered and permitted with the relative certificate), with the facility of auditorium, stage, and lighting, and selling tickets in public. The theaters and rehearse sites which are affiliated to the cultural sectors without independent financial accounts which are open to the public should be covered independently.

Radio Coverage of Population

refers to the percentage of population, which can listen to one of central, provincial, city, prefecture, and county radio programs by wireless, cable, satellite and other technical means, in the surveying area, to national total population, according to Statistical Standard and Method on Television and Radio Coverage of Population established by the State Administration of Broadcasting, Film and Television.

Television Coverage of Population

refers to the percentage of population, which can watch one of central, provincial, city, prefecture, and county television programs by wireless, cable, satellite and other technical means, in the surveying area, to national total population, according to Statistical Standard and Method on Television and Radio Coverage of Population established by the State Administration of Broadcasting, Film and Television.

Number of Athletes in Grades

refers to the number of athletes who have been given titles through examination. The titles of athletes include international masters of sports, masters of sports, first-grade, second-grade and third-grade sportsmen and young athletes.

Number of Referees in Grades

refers to the number of referees who have been given titles after examination. They are classified as international referees, national referees and referees of the first, second and third grades.

Stadiums

refers to outdoor sports venues with standard track and field runways (at least 8 circular runways and 8-10 straight runways in 400 meters) and standard football fields (with a site of 105×68 meters).

Gymnasiums

refers to an indoor sports building with facilities such as competition and practice venues, stands and auxiliary rooms, which can carry out single or multiple sports competitions such as ball games and gymnastics, and has more than 500 fixed seats.

第二十二篇

Chapter 22

公共管理及其他

PUBLIC MANAGEMENT AND OTHERS

简要说明

本篇主要包括社会活动参与、公检法司、残疾人事业和妇联干部情况等内容。

一、社会活动参与的内容主要包括历届安徽省人大代表和政协委员情况以及工会组织和妇联组织情况。

二、公检法司的资料主要包括公安机关的刑事案件立案情况和治安案件查处情况，交通、火灾事故情况，人民检察院的办案情况，人民法院审理案件和收结案情况，以及律师、公证、调解工作等情况。

Brief Introduction

Data in this chapter show statistics on participation in social activities, public security, procuratorial, legal and judicial affairs, disabled persons, women's Federation cadres and so on.

I. Data on participation in social activities cover mainly information on representatives to the National People's Congress (NPC), members of the Chinese People's Political Consultative Conference (CPPCC) and National trade unions. Data on number of NPC and CPPCC representatives are provided by NPC and CPPCC respectively.

II. Data on public security, procuratorial, legal and judicial affairs cover information such as criminal cases registered and offense cases handled by the public security agencies, traffic or fire accidents, cases handled by procuratorate's offices, cases accepted and settled by the people's courts, and statistics on lawyers, notarization and mediation.

22—1 历届安徽省人民代表大会代表人数
Number of Anhui Province the National People's Congress Represents

单位：人（person）

			代表总数 Total Number of Deputies	#女 代 表 Female Deputies	占代表总数（%） As Percentage to Total	少数民族代表 Ethnic Minority Deputies	占代表总数（%） As Percentage to Total
一 届	First Congress	(1954)	448	69	15.40	8	1.79
二 届	Second Congress	(1958)	496	68	13.71	9	1.81
三 届	Third Congress	(1964)	497	96	19.32	9	1.81
五 届	Fifth Congress	(1978)	998	196	19.64	28	2.81
六 届	Sixth Congress	(1983)	813	167	20.54	34	4.18
七 届	Seventh Congress	(1988)	729	157	21.54	28	3.84
八 届	Eighth Congress	(1993)	729	164	22.50	27	3.70
九 届	Ninth Congress	(1998)	728	195	26.79	35	4.81
十 届	Tenth Congress	(2003)	732	204	27.87	33	4.64
十一届	Eleventh Congress	(2008)	730	212	29.04	34	4.66
十二届	Twelfth Congress	(2013)	730	210	28.77	34	4.66
十三届	Thirteenth Congress	(2018)	723	225	31.12	37	5.12

22—2 历届政协安徽省委员会委员人数
Number of Anhui Province Political Consultative Conference Committee Member

单位：人（person）

			委员总数 Total Number of Deputies	#中国共产党委员 Deputies from the Communist Party of China	占委员总数（%） As Percentage to Total	少数民族委员 Ethnic Minority Deputies	占委员总数（%） As Percentage to Total
一 届	First Congress	(1954)	171	53	30.99	6	3.51
二 届	Second Congress	(1958)	308	88	28.57	8	2.60
三 届	Third Congress	(1964)	372	108	29.03	18	4.84
四 届	Fourth Congress	(1978)	506	297	58.70	21	4.15
五 届	Fifth Congress	(1983)	724	231	31.91	30	4.14
六 届	Sixth Congress	(1988)	694	234	33.72	40	5.76
七 届	Seventh Congress	(1993)	705	245	34.75	40	5.67
八 届	Eighth Congress	(1998)	730	273	37.40	37	5.07
九 届	Ninth Congress	(2003)	740	278	37.57	37	5.00
十 届	Tenth Congress	(2008)	745	286	38.39	38	5.10
十一届	Eleventh Congress	(2013)	745	297	39.87	39	5.23
十二届	Twelfth Congress	(2018)	738	291	39.43	39	5.28

22—3 妇联组织及工作情况
Basic Statistics of Women's Associations

项　目	Item	2020	2021	2022
妇联组织数　（个、所）	Number of Women's Associations (unit)	19226	19609	19619
表彰情况	Basic Statistics on Commendation			
评选巾帼建功标兵数　（人）	Women Pacesetters in Performing Meritorious Services (person)	1064	1558	1477
巾帼文明示范岗数（个、所）	Number of Woman's Civilization Demonstration Posts (unit)	178	344	1070
三八红旗手　（人）	March 8th Red Banner Winners (person)	4405	3955	4393
三八红旗集体　（个）	March 8th Red Banner Groups (unit)	1041	1174	1424
五好文明家庭　（户）	"Five Good" Civilized Families (household)	2293	1698	1633

22—4 工会组织情况
Basic Statistics on Trade Unions

年　份 Year	工会基层组织数（个） Number of Grassroots Unions (unit)	全省已建工会组织的基层单位职工与会员人数（万人） Membership and Number of Staff and Workers in Grassroots Unions (10000 person)					工会专职工作人员人数（万人） Number of Full-time Personnel of Unions (10000 person)
		职工人数 Number of Staff and Workers	#女职工 Female	#农民工 Rural Workers	会员人数 Membership	#女会员 Female	
2010	61256	710.23	243.77	228.28	666.37	231.71	2.98
2015	123883	957.04	339.71	399.88	904.72	330.53	2.78
2019	91269	880.64	329.99	363.03	819.72	312.48	2.89
2020	100236	953.00	358.52	418.22	892.44	340.41	3.18
2021	109571	1011.31	377.52	456.10	961.29	362.17	3.27
2022	115357	1061.36	395.13	491.35	1013.13	379.37	3.83

22—5 妇女参政议政状况
Basic Conditions on Women's Participating in the Administration and Discussion of State Affairs

项　　目	Item	2015	2020	2021	2022
省(区、市)人大代表数　(人)	Provincial (area, city) National People's Congress number　(persons)	740	707	730	728
#女　性	Female	208	224	228	228
省(区、市)政协委员数　(人)	Provincial (area, city) CPPCC Member Number　(persons)	740	738	737	739
#女　性	Female	166	173	183	180
中共党员人数　(万人)	The number of members of the Communist Party of China　(10000 persons)	350.99	365.62	378.21	383.30
#女　性	Female	75.13	90.86	97.81	100.03
省级政府领导班子中女干部配备率　(%)	Female Cadres Portion of Provincial Rank Government Leading Group　(%)	100.00	100.00	100.00	100.00
地级政府领导班子中女干部配备率　(%)	Female Cadres Portion of Region Rank Government Leading Group　(%)	75.00	100.00	81.25	81.30
县级政府领导班子中女干部配备率　(%)	Female Cadres Portion of County Rank Government Leading Group　(%)	90.10	91.30	100.00	95.19

22—6 妇女卫生保健状况
Basic Conditions on Women Hygiene

项目	Item	2015	2020	2021	2022
妇幼保健机构病床数 （张）	Number of Sickbeds in Maternity and Child Care Organs (unit)	3454	7498	8044	9767
妇幼保健机构医生数 （人）	Number of Doctors in Maternity and Child Care Organs (person)	2305	4026	4352	4971
孕产妇系统管理率 (%)	Percentage of Pregnant and Lying-in Women Under System Management (%)	85.30	89.86	91.37	92.39
住院分娩率 (%)	Percentage of Childbirths in Hospital (%)	99.95	99.99	99.99	99.99
孕产妇死亡率 （1/10万）	Death Rate of Pregnant and Lying-in Women (1/100 thousand)	17.26	8.00	5.83	10.77
已婚育龄妇女避孕率 (%)	Contraception Rate of Married Women in Their Childbearing Age (%)	87.05			
婚前医学检查率 (%)	Percentage of Medical Examinations Before Marriage (%)	94.00	96.15	94.29	93.78

注：2018年数据现按照卫生资源与医疗服务法定报表调整。

a) The data for 2018 is now adjusted according to the statutory report of health resources and medical services.

22—7 儿童卫生保健状况
Basic Conditions on Children Hygiene

项目	Item	2015	2020	2021	2022
婴儿死亡率 (‰)	Death Rate of Infants (‰)	4.54	3.47	2.80	2.70
5岁以下儿童死亡率 (‰)	Death Rate of Children Below Five (‰)	6.85	4.85	4.05	4.08
住院分娩出生缺陷发生率 (‰)	Rate of Childbirth Defects in Hospital (‰)	11.52	27.80	30.76	32.57
卡介苗接种率 (%)	Rate of Inoculating With BCG Vaccine (%)	99.80	99.95	99.96	99.64
脊髓灰质炎疫苗接种率 (%)	Rate of Inoculating With Polio Vaccine (%)	99.75	99.83	99.87	99.72
百白破疫苗接种率 (%)	Rate of Inoculating With Joint Vaccine of Pertussis, Diphtheria and Tetanus (%)	99.56	99.85	99.87	99.70
麻疹疫苗接种率 (%)	Rate of Inoculating With Measles Vaccine (%)	99.75	99.84	99.89	99.76
乙肝疫苗接种率 (%)	Rate of Inoculating With Hepatitis B Vaccine (%)	99.92	99.91	99.92	99.73
7岁以下儿童保健管理率 (%)	Percentage of Children Below Seven Under Health Management (%)	90.91	92.65	93.34	93.45
0—6个月婴儿纯母乳喂养率(%)	0-6 Month Baby Breastfeeding rate (%)	65.77	72.52	74.65	74.16
5岁以下儿童中重度贫血患病率 (%)	Prevalence of Severe Anemia Rate of Children Under 5 Years of Age (%)	0.85	0.39	0.38	0.31
5岁以下儿童低体重患病率(%)	Low Weight Rate of Children Under 5 Years of Age (%)	0.66	0.52	0.52	0.51

22—8 残疾人事业基本情况
Basic Information of People with Disabilities

指　　标	Item		2020	2021	2022
康　复	**Rehabilitation**				
社区康复	Community Rehabilitation				
开展社区康复服务工作的市辖区（个）	Municipal Districts Carrying Out Community Rehabilitatioı Services	(unit)	51	51	51
开展社区康复服务工作的县（市）（个）	Counties (cities) Carrying Out Community Rehabilitation Services	(unit)	60	62	62
社区康复协调员（人）	Community Rehabilitation Coordinator	(person)	17402	17405	17651
康复机构	Rehabilitation Organization				
残疾人康复机构（个）	Rehabilitation Institution for Disabled Persons	(unit)	295	304	309
#残联系统康复机构	Rehabilitation Mechanism for Disabled Persons' Federation System		63	67	57
康复机构在岗人员（人）	On-the-job Personnel in Rehabilitation Institutions	(person)	8570	9979	10877
康复人才	Rehabilitation Talents				
培训康复管理人员（人次）	Training of Rehabilitation Management Personnel	(person-time)	1267	1656	1999
培训康复业务人员（人次）	Training of Rehabilitation Personnel	(person-time)	6423	7584	13389
培训社区康复协调员（人）	Training of Community Rehabilitation Coordinators	(person)	16327	16447	16925
教　育	**Education**				
普通高等院校录取残疾考生（人）	Colleges and Universities Admit Disabled Candidates	(person)	616	570	674
社会保障和托养	**Social Security and Support**				
托养服务	Care Service				
托养机构（个）	Support Mechanism	(unit)	410	464	332
本年度机构托养残疾人（人）	This Year, The Organization Supports The Disabled	(person)	3501	3870	2536
本年度享受居家服务残疾人（人）	Disabled People Who Enjoy Home Service This Year	(person)	16333	18351	19133
本年度接受“阳光家园计划”资助的人数（人）	Number of Recipients of "Sunshine Home Project" This Year	(person)	13305	13649	22899

22—8 续表 continued

指标		Item		2020	2021	2022
就业		**Employment**				
城乡持证残疾人就业人数	（人）	Number of Persons With Certified Disabilities Employed in Urban and Rural Areas	(person)		521685	513280
盲人按摩机构	（个）	Massage Institution for The Blind	(unit)		347	372
残疾人就业资金支出	（万元）	Expenditure on Employment Funds for Disabled Persons	(10000 yuan)	21063	21010	22365
农村实用技术培训	（人次）	Rural Practical Technology Training	(person-time)		15112	13166
残疾人就业帮扶基地	（个）	Employment Support Base for The Disabled	(unit)		112	110
维权		**Activist**				
省级残疾人信访		Petition for Disabled People at Provincial Level				
来信	（件）	Letters	(unit)	359	556	519
来访	（人次）	Visit	(person-time)	3662	2554	2239
#集体访批次	（批次）	Group Visit Batch	(batch)	5	7	1
集体访人次	（人次）	Group Visits	(person-time)	71	89	10
来电	（通）	Call	(unit)	4463	4927	712
残联组织建设		**Organization Building of Disabled Persons' Federation**				
省市县乡残联实有人员	（人）	Provinces, Cities, Counties and Townships Disabled Persons' Federation Has Actual Personnel	(person)	3604	3571	3674
乡镇（街道）、村（社区）残疾人专职委员实有人数	（人）	Actual Number of Full-time Members of Disabled People in Villages and Towns (streets) and Villages (communities)	(person)	17298	15665	15810

22—9 律师、公证、调解、司法鉴定、法律援助工作基本情况
Basic Statistics on Lawyers, Notarization and Mediation

指标		Item		2010	2015	2020	2021	2022
律师工作		**Lawyers**						
律师事务所	(个)	Number of Law Offices	(unit)	500	668	919	967	1019
律　师	(人)	Lawyers	(person)	5019	7687	15988	18418	21088
专职律师		Full-time Lawyers		4411	6913	11813	13118	14635
兼职律师		Part-time Lawyers		281	381	455	484	499
公职律师		Government Lawyers		97	205	2971	3851	4740
公司律师		Corporation Counsel		11	11	571	796	1044
法援律师		Legal Aid Lawyers		246	185	178	169	170
聘请担任常年法律顾问的单位	(处)	Number of Units With Permanent Legal Advisors	(unit)	10945	16941	26582	32661	29127
民事、经济诉讼代理	(件)	Civil, Economic Litigation Agents	(case)	69615	121621	246149	315117	328565
刑事诉讼辩护及代理	(件)	Defense and Agent of Criminal Cases	(case)	15164	25107	57033	70557	58765
行政诉讼代理	(件)	Agent of Administrative Action	(case)	1428	3621	7332	10310	9812
非诉讼法律事务	(件)	Number of Non-litigious Legal Affairs	(case)	5188	8783	9973	14548	12684
法律援助机构数	(个)	Number of Legal Aid Institutions	(unit)	126	125	123	123	123
妇女儿童法律援助工作站数	(个)	Number of Legal Aid Stations for Women and Children	(unit)	114	143	131	227	228
法律援助工作人员数	(人)	Number of Legal Aid Workers	(person)	450	507	455	439	489
办理法律援助案件数	(件)	Number of Legal Aid Cases Handled	(case)	24715	73558	90465	90765	88804
法律援助受援人数	(人)	Number of Recipients of Legal Aid	(person)			105638	94178	129712
#得到法律援助机构援助的妇女人数		Number of Women Assisted by Legal Aid Agencies		7064	18394	19762	19132	19216
得到法律援助机构援助的儿童人数		Number of Children Assisted by Legal Aid Agencies		2365	4956	4978	6183	6926
司法鉴定工作		**Judicial Appraisal Work**						
司法鉴定机构	(个)	Forensic Institution	(unit)	104	118	96	100	101
司法鉴定人	(人)	Judicial Expert	(person)	1493	1698	1522	1584	1799
办理司法鉴定案件数	(件)	Number of Cases of Judicial Expertise Handled	(case)	37927	86958	140275	165172	154749
公证工作		**Notarization**						
公证机构	(个)	Notary Organ	(unit)	84	83	86	86	86
公证人员	(人)	Notaries personnel	(person)	769	893	1043	1071	1065
#公证员		Notaries		350	394	378	406	406
公证员助理		Assistant Notaries		201	256	339	319	289
办理公证事项	(件)	Notarized Matters	(unit)	375828	320383	305291	323057	280221
#涉外及港澳台公证事项		And Hong Kong, Macao and Taiwan Notarization Matters Involving Foreign Elements	(case)	53614	56578	30499	35117	32399
人民调解工作		**Number of People's Mediation**						
司法所工作人员	(人)	Judicial Office Staff	(person)	4307	4911	5754	5967	7263
人民调解委员会	(个)	Number of people's Mediation Committees	(unit)	23094	20866	20603	20854	21108
人民调解员	(人)	People's mediators	(person)	139366	103912	102981	103005	101916
调解民间纠纷	(件)	Number of Civil Disputes Mediated	(case)	329660	630117	541957	554694	573830

22—10 劳动人事争议仲裁委员会受理及处理案件情况（2022年）
Accepted and Settled Cases by Labor Dispute Arbitration Committee (2022)

单位：件（case）

案件类别	Category of Cases	合计 Total	国有企业 State-owned Enterprises	城镇集体企业 Urban Collective-owned Enterprises
上期未结案件数	**Number of Cases Left Over from Last Period**	**755**	**11**	**3**
案件受理情况	**Cases Accepted**			
案件数	Number of Cases	43496	1552	22
#集体争议案件数	Number of Collective Disputes	87	2	2
涉及劳动者人数（人）	Number of Related to Laborers (person)	47405	1581	556
#集体争议涉及劳动者人数	Number of Collective Dispute Related Laborers	2280	23	506
案件处理情况	**Case Settled**			
结案件数	Number of Cases Settled	43559	1548	25
处理方式	**Manners of Settlement**			
仲裁调解	By Mediation	30745	986	5
仲裁裁决	By Arbitration Lawsuit	12152	468	20
其他方式	Others	662	94	
处理结果	**Result of Settlement**			
用人单位胜诉	Won by Units	3437	375	
劳动者胜诉	Lawsuit Won by Laborers	17139	541	15
双方部分胜诉	Lawsuit Partly Won by Both Parties	19589	453	7
本期未结案数	**Number of Cases Unsettled**	**692**	**15**	
案外调解争议数	**Number of Cases Settled by Other Forms**	**6964**	**249**	

案件类别	Category of Cases	外商投资及港澳台投资企业 Foreign Funded and Hong Kong, Macao & Taiwan Chinese Funded Enterprises	私营企业 Private Enter-prises	其他 Others
上期未结案件数	**Number of Cases Left Over from Last Period**	**1**	**724**	**16**
案件受理情况	**Cases Accepted**			
案件数	Number of Cases	231	40450	1241
#集体争议案件数	Number of Collective Disputes	1	62	20
涉及劳动者人数（人）	Number of Related to Laborers (person)	242	43178	1848
#集体争议涉及劳动者人数	Number of Collective Dispute Related Laborers	12	1275	464
案件处理情况	**Case Settled**			
结案件数	Number of Cases Settled	228	40532	1226
处理方式	**Manners of Settlement**			
仲裁调解	By Mediation	147	28835	772
仲裁裁决	By Arbitration Lawsuit	81	11183	400
其他方式	Others		514	54
处理结果	**Result of Settlement**			
用人单位胜诉	Won by Units	50	2876	136
劳动者胜诉	Lawsuit Won by Laborers	63	16143	377
双方部分胜诉	Lawsuit Partly Won by Both Parties	106	18517	506
本期未结案数	**Number of Cases Unsettled**	**4**	**642**	**31**
案外调解争议数	**Number of Cases Settled by Other Forms**	**7**	**6650**	**58**

22—11 公安机关立案的刑事案件情况
Criminal Cases Registered in Public Security Organs

案件类别	Category of Cases	立案（起）Number of cases Registered (case)		构成（%）Composition (%)	
		2021	2022	2021	2022
总　计	**Total**	**202846**	**190434**	**100.00**	**100.00**
杀　人	Homicide	225	187	0.11	0.10
伤　害	Appeals Against Criminal Detention	2331	2474	1.15	1.30
抢　劫	Robbery	141	141	0.07	0.07
强　奸	Rape	1243	1305	0.61	0.69
拐卖妇女儿童	Abducting Women and Children	112	53	0.06	0.03
盗　窃	Larceny	59493	47879	29.33	25.14
诈　骗	Fraud	87644	64761	43.21	34.01
伪造、变造货币，持有使用伪造货币	Forging and Fabricating Bills or Using Forged Bills	33	51	0.02	0.03
其　他	Others	51624	73583	25.45	38.64

22—12 公安机关受理、查处治安案件情况
Offense Cases Against Public Order Handled by Public Security Organs

单位：起（case）

案件类别	Category of Cases	2021		2022	
		受理 Number of Cases Accepted to be Treated	查处 Number of Cases Investigated and Treated	受理 Number of Cases Accepted to be Treated	查处 Number of Cases Investigated and Treated
总　计	**Total**	**430909**	**414716**	**376976**	**361096**
扰乱单位、公共场所秩序	Disturbing Unit & Public Order	2467	2418	2228	2139
寻衅滋事	Making Trouble	3279	3261	2936	2842
阻碍执行职务	Handling Public Affairs	1298	1284	1189	1151
非法携带枪支、弹药、管制刀具	Illegal Holding of Gun、Ammo & Tube Cutting Tool	320	310	331	319
违反危险物质管理规定	Violation of Management Rule of Dangerous Material	2048	1984	1621	1556
殴打他人	Hitting other People	112381	110116	94217	91976
盗　窃	Stealing	103267	95643	101410	94277
诈骗、抢夺、敲诈勒索财物	Swindle Snatch & Blackmail Blackmailing Money & Goods	27113	25110	22578	21078
哄　抢	Making Scramble	48	48	73	73
卖淫、嫖娼	Prostitution & Go Whoring	5897	5747	4831	4752
赌博或为赌博提供条件	To Gamble or Provide for Gambling	13631	13395	13680	13346
其　他	Other	159160	155400	131882	127587

22—13 各市公安机关立案的刑事案件情况（2022年）
Criminal Cases Registered in Public Security Organs By Region (2022)

单位：起（case）

地 区	Region	总 计 Total	杀 人 Homicide	伤 害 Injury	抢 劫 Robbery	强 奸 Rape	拐卖妇女儿童 Abducting Women and Children
总 计	**Total**	**190434**	**187**	**2474**	**141**	**1305**	**53**
合肥市	Hefei	42840	18	223	38	151	4
淮北市	Huaibei	7000	5	78	3	50	2
亳州市	Bozhou	11269	22	298	10	156	1
宿州市	Suzhou	14417	25	253	16	162	6
蚌埠市	Bengbu	9609	18	205	5	113	7
阜阳市	Fuyang	19263	29	389	17	201	13
淮南市	Huainan	6446	7	95	3	65	2
滁州市	Chuzhou	13667	3	191	11	71	6
六安市	Luan	12625	9	163	13	83	1
马鞍山市	Maanshan	7084	3	88	5	37	1
芜湖市	Wuhu	14375	8	124	9	58	2
宣城市	Xuancheng	7034	9	89	3	47	
铜陵市	Tongling	4668	4	54	1	18	
池州市	Chizhou	4226	4	53	1	27	
安庆市	Anqing	11829	20	114	6	56	6
黄山市	Huangshan	4082	3	57		10	2

地 区	Region	盗 窃 Larceny	诈 骗 Fraud	伪造、变造货币，持有使用伪造货币 Forging and Fabricating Bills or Using Forged Bills	其 他 Others	青少年刑事案件作案成员占全部作案成员比重(%) Proportion of Young People In Criminal Cases
总 计	**Total**	**47879**	**64761**	**51**	**73583**	**16.4**
合肥市	Hefei	9525	13804	18	19059	14.1
淮北市	Huaibei	1377	2575		2910	22.1
亳州市	Bozhou	3329	2304	3	5146	22.7
宿州市	Suzhou	3458	3870	5	6622	11.2
蚌埠市	Bengbu	2322	3652	1	3286	20.8
阜阳市	Fuyang	5015	6287	9	7303	13.8
淮南市	Huainan	1383	1765	1	3125	22.3
滁州市	Chuzhou	4230	4992	2	4161	14.9
六安市	Luan	3524	3748		5084	18.7
马鞍山市	Maanshan	1793	2069	1	3087	19.8
芜湖市	Wuhu	3855	6872	4	3443	11.3
宣城市	Xuancheng	1994	3015		1877	15.2
铜陵市	Tongling	1436	1930	1	1224	14.8
池州市	Chizhou	1090	1578	4	1469	19.4
安庆市	Anqing	2730	4516	2	4379	16.7
黄山市	Huangshan	818	1784		1408	12.7

22—14 各市公安机关查处治安案件情况（2022年）

Investigation of Public Security Cases by Public Security Organs By Region （2022）

单位：起（case）

地 区	Region	总 计 Total	扰乱单位、公共场所秩序 Disturbing Unit & Public Order	寻衅滋事 Making Trouble	阻碍执行职务 Handling Public Affairs	非法携带枪支、弹药、管制刀具 Illegal Holding of Gun、Ammo & Tube Cutting Tool	违反危险物质管理规定 Violation of Management Rule of Dangerous Material
总 计	**Total**	**361096**	**2139**	**2842**	**1151**	**319**	**1556**
合肥市	Hefei	93504	452	363	182	31	338
淮北市	Huaibei	16892	122	104	35	9	41
亳州市	Bozhou	22017	90	96	41	11	41
宿州市	Suzhou	22039	53	207	40	8	50
蚌埠市	Bengbu	11520	66	157	45	8	145
阜阳市	Fuyang	33648	311	852	221	38	280
淮南市	Huainan	12332	80	149	60	6	106
滁州市	Chuzhou	26738	144	126	68	24	27
六安市	Luan	28727	180	152	100	40	160
马鞍山市	Maanshan	10098	98	65	62	10	42
芜湖市	Wuhu	26013	115	86	68	24	64
宣城市	Xuancheng	12022	69	141	66	47	91
铜陵市	Tongling	10641	134	73	42	13	20
池州市	Chizhou	4888	35	53	19	11	5
安庆市	Anqing	20702	117	117	63	23	126
黄山市	Huangshan	9315	73	101	39	16	20

地 区	Region	殴打他人 Hitting Other People	盗 窃 Stealing	诈骗、抢夺、敲诈勒索财物 Swindle Snatch & Blackmail Blackmailing Money & Goods	哄 抢 Making Scramble	卖淫、嫖娼 Prostitution & Go Whoring	赌博或为赌博提供条件 To Gamble or Provide for Gambling	其 他 Other
总 计	**Total**	**91976**	**94277**	**21078**	**73**	**4752**	**13346**	**127587**
合肥市	Hefei	22020	16197	5774	42	1123	1651	45331
淮北市	Huaibei	4282	2243	507		24	63	9462
亳州市	Bozhou	4454	7426	523		44	194	9097
宿州市	Suzhou	5425	5969	1071		193	364	8659
蚌埠市	Bengbu	3912	2742	353		129	498	3465
阜阳市	Fuyang	8424	13432	1622	5	394	1398	6671
淮南市	Huainan	3427	3801	948		74	395	3286
滁州市	Chuzhou	6148	10646	1460	4	328	2381	5382
六安市	Luan	9239	6675	1963	10	169	801	9238
马鞍山市	Maanshan	2594	3761	1115		124	479	1748
芜湖市	Wuhu	7798	6371	1612	2	797	1790	7286
宣城市	Xuancheng	2263	4510	1226	10	90	534	2975
铜陵市	Tongling	2947	2137	586		110	452	4127
池州市	Chizhou	1342	1225	319		119	273	1487
安庆市	Anqing	5684	5903	1755		225	881	5808
黄山市	Huangshan	2017	1239	244		809	1192	3565

22—15　检察机关处理申诉案件情况（2022年）
Appeals Handled by Procurator's Offices (2022)

单位：件（case）

案件类别	Category of Cases	受理 Cases Accepted	立案复查 Cases Registered of Reinvestigation	结案 Cases Settled	改变原决定 Original Decision Changed
总计	**Total**	**7262**	**148**	**163**	**11**
不服刑事拘留	Appeals Against Criminal Detention	1			
不服不立案	Appeals Against Rejection of The Case	242			
不服逮捕	Appeals Against Arrest	3			
不服不批捕	Appeals Against Rejection of Arrest	9	1	1	
不服不起诉	Appeals Against Rejection of Prosecute	167	83	86	7
不服撤案	Appeals Against Withdrawal of the Case	21	1	1	
不服原免于起诉	Appeals Against Original Exemption of Lawsuit	1			
不服刑事判决	Appeals Against Judgment of Criminal Case				
不服劳教	Appeals Against Judgment of Reeducation Through Labor	1236	49	61	2
其他	Others	5582	14	14	2

22—16　人民法院行政一审案件受理结案情况（2022年）
People's Courts Have Accepted and Concluded Cases of First Instance (2022)

单位：件（case）

项目	Item	受理 Cases Accepted	结案 Cases Settled	判决 Judgment	不予立案 Not to File a Case	驳回起诉 Reject	撤诉 Withdraw	调解 Mediation	其他 Other
总计	**Total**	**11340**	**10689**	**5581**	**352**	**1880**	**2299**	**90**	**487**
公安	Public Security	1145	1056	618	37	80	265		56
资源	Resources	1507	1444	709	34	293	293	7	108
城建	City Construction	2501	2342	1254	67	507	389	28	97
工商	Industry and Commerce	217	198	71	7	47	67	2	4
卫生	Health	32	31	18	1	3	8	1	
环保	Environmental Protection	75	65	27	3	4	22	1	8
交通	Traffic	56	52	22	2	7	21		
税务	Tax	28	27	12		6	8		1
其他	Others	5779	5474	2850	201	933	1226	51	213

22—17　人民法院刑事一审案件受理结案情况（2022年）
People's Courts Have Accepted and Concluded Criminal Cases of First Instance (2022)

单位：件（case）

案件类别	Category of Cases	受理 Cases Accepted	结案 Cases Settled
总计	**Total**	**47992**	**45223**
危害公共安全罪	Offences Against Public Security	19302	19114
破坏社会主义市场经济秩序罪	Offences Against Socialist Economic Order	2437	2048
侵犯公民人身权利、民主权利罪	Offences Against Citizens' Personal and Democratic Rights	5534	5014
侵犯财产罪	Offences Against Properties	9077	8427
妨碍社会管理秩序罪	Offences Against Social Management of order	11031	10129
危害国防利益罪	Offences Against National Defense	7	7
贪污贿赂罪	Offences on Corruption and Bribery	550	443
渎职罪	Offences on Dereliction of Duty	49	39
其他	Others	5	2

22—18 人民法院合同纠纷一审案件受理结案情况（2022年）
Settlement of Cases of First Instance Concerning Contract Disputes in People's Courts (2022)

单位：件（case）

项目	Item	受理 Cases Accepted	结案 Cases Settled	判决 Judgement	不予受理 Off the Docket
总计	**Total**	**539001**	**527885**	**231170**	**4530**
确认合同效力	Confirm the Validity of the Contract	1419	1351	687	4
买卖合同	Sales Contract	66143	64672	27376	141
建设用地使用权合同	Construction Land Use Right Contract	81	78	41	
房地产开发经营合同	Real Estate Development and Operation Contract	81	69	38	1
房屋买卖合同	Housing Sales Contract	24955	24334	12025	16
赠与合同	Contract of Gift	754	726	349	
借款合同	Loan Contract	177105	174160	86165	908
银行卡	Bank Card	33997	33880	19946	504
租赁合同	Lease Contract	23202	22524	10594	39
承揽合同	Contract of Hired Work	8032	7803	3431	38
建设工程合同	Construction Contract	27910	25573	12388	74
运输合同	Contract of Carriage	2898	2844	1298	3
委托合同	Commissioning Contract	2093	2023	974	28
土地承包经营权合同纠纷	Disputes Over Contracted Land Management Rights	1284	1273	236	
服务合同	Service Contract	7958	7833	2718	8
其他	Others	161089	158742	52904	2766

项目	Item	驳回起诉 Reject	撤诉 Withdraw	调解 Mediation	其他 Other
总计	**Total**	**15794**	**165865**	**104769**	**5757**
确认合同效力	Confirm the Validity of the Contract	147	377	88	48
买卖合同	Sales Contract	1784	17540	17027	804
建设用地使用权合同	Construction Land Use Right Contract	6	22	8	1
房地产开发经营合同	Real Estate Development and Operation Contract	7	16	5	2
房屋买卖合同	Housing Sales Contract	454	5842	5803	194
赠与合同	Contract of Gift	17	220	111	29
借款合同	Loan Contract	4774	42432	38699	1182
银行卡	Bank Card	1328	8201	3470	431
租赁合同	Lease Contract	594	6131	4839	327
承揽合同	Contract of Hired Work	174	1957	2079	124
建设工程合同	Construction Contract	874	6642	5207	388
运输合同	Contract of Carriage	81	671	744	47
委托合同	Commissioning Contract	82	470	392	77
土地承包经营权合同纠纷	Disputes Over Contracted Land Management Rights	61	285	691	
服务合同	Service Contract	390	3217	1374	126
其他	Others	5021	71842	24232	1977

22—19 人民法院婚姻家庭、继承、权属、侵权纠纷及其他民事一审案件受理结案情况（2022年）

Settlement of Marriage and Family, Inheritance, Ownership, Infringement Disputes and Other Civil Cases of First Instance in People's Courts (2022)

单位：件（case）

项目	Item	受理 Cases Accepted	结案 Cases Settled	判决 Judgement	不予受理 Off the Docket
总计	**Total**	**222214**	**217955**	**99803**	**460**
婚姻家庭	Marriage and Family	88725	87929	34650	81
继承	Inheritance	2650	2559	1103	7
物权	Real Right	12238	11724	5317	115
知识产权与竞争	Intellectual Property and Competition	10948	10851	3468	3
劳动争议、人事争议	Labor Disputes and Personnel Disputes	19320	18879	9505	98
与公司、证券、保险、票据等有关的民事	Civil Affairs Related to Companies, Securities, Insurance, Bills, Etc.	25011	24466	12208	37
侵权责任	Tort Liability	51899	50684	27528	22
特殊诉讼程序案件	Special Procedure Cases	3212	2885	1819	9
其他	Others	8211	7978	4205	88

项目	Item	驳回起诉 Reject	撤诉 Withdraw	调解 Mediation	其他 Other
总计	**Total**	**4236**	**46010**	**64799**	**2647**
婚姻家庭	Marriage and Family	920	14945	36699	634
继承	Inheritance	79	609	731	30
物权	Real Right	929	3481	1724	158
知识产权与竞争	Intellectual Property and Competition	103	6080	1040	157
劳动争议、人事争议	Labor Disputes and Personnel Disputes	622	2943	5046	665
与公司、证券、保险、票据等有关的民事	Civil Affairs Related to Companies, Securities, Insurance, Bills, Etc.	723	6757	3980	761
侵权责任	Tort Liability	562	8938	13501	133
特殊诉讼程序案件	Special Procedure Cases	145	483	360	69
其他	Others	153	1774	1718	40

22—20 主要年份交通事故发生情况
Traffic Accidents in Main Years

指　标	Item	2010	2015	2020	2021	2022
交通事故发生数　（起）	Number of Traffic Accidents (case)	7714	13736	10706	10284	8668
一次性死亡三人以上事故	Accidents With More Than Three Deaths One Time	54	26	19	17	13
交通事故损失　（万元）	Losses of Traffic Accidents (10000 yuan)	2349.6	6122.5	5526.8	5168.8	4259
一次性死亡三人以上事故	Accidents With More Than Three Deaths One Time	116.6	181.2	102.0	66.4	54

22—21 交通事故情况（2022年）
Basic Statistics on Traffic Accidents (2022)

指　标	Region	发生数（起）Number of Traffic Accidents (case)	死亡人数（人）Number of Deaths (person)	受伤人数（人）Number of Injuries (person)	损失折款（万元）Losses Covnerted Into Cash (10000 yuan)
总　计	**Total**	**8668**	**2215**	**9198**	**4259.1**
#一次性死亡三人以上事故	Accidents With More Than Three Deaths One Time	13	46	20	53.7
一般事故	General Accident	8655	2169	9178	4205
机动车	Motor-driven Vehicles	5551	1733	5496	3315.0
汽　车	Automobiles	4603	1531	4306	3232.0
摩托车	Motorcycles	1483	315	1753	536.0
拖拉机	Tractors	90	31	77	100.0
农业运输车	Transport Vehicles for Agricultural Use	74	17	85	16.0
非机动车	Non-motor-driven Vehicles	2345	328	2942	379.0
#自行车	Bicycles	117	42	109	35.0
#其它非机动车	Other Non-motor-driven Vehicles	2228	286	2833	344.0
行人、乘车人	Pedestrians	116	42	94	90.0

注：机动车相关指标有重复计算。

a) Motor vehicle related indicators have repeated calculation.

22—22 各市交通事故情况（2022年）
Basic Statistics on Traffic Accidents by Region (2022)

地区	Region	合计 Total 发生数（起）Number of Traffic Accidents (case)	死亡人数（人）Number of Deaths (person)	受伤人数（人）Number of Injuries (person)	损失折款（万元）Losses Converted Into Cash (10000 yuan)	城区 Urban Areas 发生数（起）Number of Traffic Accidents (case)	死亡人数（人）Number of Deaths (person)	受伤人数（人）Number of Injuries (person)
总计	**Total**	**8668**	**2215**	**9198**	**4259**	**4381**	**770**	**4596**
合肥市	Hefei	1342	412	1237	1316	840	174	773
淮北市	Huaibei	266	53	287	25	188	20	203
亳州市	Bozhou	619	176	648	122	141	39	127
宿州市	Suzhou	209	80	224	91	57	12	59
蚌埠市	Bengbu	1081	217	1199	444	879	131	982
阜阳市	Fuyang	321	133	292	163	54	21	36
淮南市	Huainan	714	115	834	154	301	44	340
滁州市	Chuzhou	210	159	118	271	93	62	51
六安市	Luan	689	184	796	527	250	44	285
马鞍山市	Maanshan	238	69	227	59	162	34	170
芜湖市	Wuhu	624	65	702	133	312	39	315
宣城市	Xuancheng	360	138	331	216	158	30	156
铜陵市	Tongling	114	60	105	55	35	20	32
池州市	Chizhou	304	86	322	91	163	17	193
安庆市	Anqing	1216	205	1488	513	520	58	631
黄山市	Huangshan	361	63	388	78	228	25	243

22—23 灾害情况（2022年）
Statistics on Disasters (2022)

项　目	Item	自然灾害直接经济损失（亿元）Direct Losses of Natural Disasters (100 million yuan)	农业经济损　失 Agricultural Losses	农作物灾害（万公顷）Area of Crop Disaster (10000 hectare) 受灾面积 Areas Covered	绝收面积 Areas of Total Crop Failure	受灾人口（万人）Population Covered (10000 persons)
总　计	**Total**	**20.21**	**19.47**	**39.04**	**1.60**	**263.34**
#旱　灾	Drought	16.67	16.67	36.48	1.45	229.98
洪 涝 灾	Floods	1.09	0.86	1.91	0.13	18.19

注：旱灾、洪涝灾中每个地块受灾一次即统计一次，但总计中全年每个地块只统计受灾最重的一次。
a) Each plot of land affected by drought and flood is counted once, but in total, each plot of land affected by the disaster is counted only once in the whole year.

22—24 救灾情况
Statistics on Disaster Relief

单位：万元 (10000 yuan)

项　目	Item	财政资金投入 Investment of Financial Fund 2021	2022	救灾物资投入（折款）Input of Relief Materials (discount) 2021	2022
总　计	**Total**	**23269.7**	**25363.6**	**1322.0**	**1371.6**
中　央	Central Government	19340.0	19030.0	16.6	0.0
省　级	Provincial-level	2959.0	3000.0	380.1	514.5
地　市	Prefecture-level	76.4	273.0	373.3	284.1
县　级	County-level	894.3	3060.6	552.0	573.0

22–25 福利彩票
Welfare Lottery

项　目	Item	2021	2022
福利彩票发行额　（亿元）	Circulation of Welfare Lottery (100 million yuan)	44.39	48.11
福利彩票公益金提取额　（亿元）	Public Welfare Funds Drawn from Welfare Lottery (100 million yuan)	14.53	15.67

22–26 体育彩票
Sport Lottery

项　目	Item	2021	2022
体育彩票销售额　（亿元）	Circulation of Sport Lottery (100 million yuan)	75.19	101.86
体育彩票公益金提取额　（亿元）	Public Welfare Funds Drawn from Sport Lottery (100 million yuan)	19.58	25.06

主要统计指标解释

律师

指依法取得律师执业证书，接受委托或者指定，为当事人提供法律服务的执业人员。

公证人员

指在公证处工作的人员总称，包括公证处主任、副主任、公证员、公证员助理和其他从事辅助性工作的人员。

公证文书

指公证处根据当事人申请，依照事实和法律，按照法定程序制作的，具有法律效力的司法证明文书。

调解人员

指在人民调解委员会担负调解民间一般民事纠纷和轻微违法行为引起纠纷的工作人员，包括调解委员会的委员和调解小组的调解员。

调解民间纠纷

指调解委员会依照法律规定，根据自愿原则，用说服教育的方法调解民间发生的有关民事权利和义务的争执，促成当事双方达到协议和谅解，解决纠纷。包括婚姻家庭纠纷，财产权益纠纷等，不包括法院受理调解的民事案件数。

人民检察院直接立案侦查案件

指按照管辖的规定，由人民检察院直接立案侦查的贪污贿赂犯罪、渎职犯罪、国家机关工作人员利用职权实施的侵犯公民人身权利和民主权利的犯罪以及经省级人民检察院决定立案侦查的国家机关工作人员利用职权实施的其他重大犯罪案件。

立案

指检察机关对犯罪线索进行初步调查后，认为存在职务犯罪事实并需要追究刑事责任时，依法决定作为刑事案件进行侦查的诉讼活动，是追究犯罪的开始。

大案

贪污贿赂犯罪案件指贪污、贿赂数额在5万元以上，挪用公款案在10万元以上，其他案件在50万元以上。渎职犯罪大案一般为直接经济损失5万元以上，死亡1人以上或者重伤3人以上的案件；或虽然没有造成经济损失和伤亡，但犯罪情节恶劣或造成严重后果的案件。

要案

指县、处级以上干部的犯罪案件。该指标主要反映职务犯罪案件中县、处级以上干部被人民检察院依法立案侦查的情况。

青少年罪犯

指人民法院在报告期内判决发生法律效力的有罪判决中14周岁以上不满25周岁的罪犯。其中14周岁以上不满18周岁的罪犯为未成年罪犯。

行政案件

指公民、法人和其他组织不服行政机关作出的具体行政行为，向人民法院提起行政诉讼，人民法院依法审理的案件。

单独赔偿

指单独提起行政赔偿的案件。当事人对行政行为的合法性没有争议，就行政侵权造成的损害赔偿单独提起赔偿诉讼。

受理劳动争议案件数

指劳动争议仲裁委员会根据国家有关规定，对劳动争议当事人的申请予以审查，符合受理条件而正式立案、准备处理的劳动争议案件数。

结案

是指人民法院在统计报告期内，审理完毕或认为不需要再审理，决定结束审理或者做出实体或程序方面处理的案件数。

Explanatory Notes for Major Statistical Indicators

Lawyers

refers to the legally obtained a lawyer's practice certificate, accept entrust or specify, for the parties to provide legal services practitioners.

Notary Personnel

refers to the floorboard of notarization work personnel, including the notary office director and deputy director, notaries, assistant notaries, and other personnel engaged in the work of supporting.

Notary Documents

refer to the judicial notary documents drawn up at the request of the interested party and are in accordance with facts and the law and following certain legal proceedings.

Mediators

refer to workers on people's mediation committees responsible for mediating in civil disputes and cases of slight infraction of the law. They include members of the mediation committees and mediators of mediation groups.

Mediation of Civil Disputes

refers to mediation committees' work in mediating in civil disputes concerning civil rights and duties through persuasion and education in accordance with the provisions of law on a voluntary basis, so as to solve disputes by helping the parties involved come to an agreement and understanding. These disputes include divorce cases and disputes over property ownership, but exclude the civil cases to be handled by the court.

Cases Registered and Handled Directly by People's Procuratorate Offices

refer to those serious criminal cases that, according to the functional jurisdiction, are registered and handled by the People's Procuratorate Offices, including the ones on bribery and corruption, the ones on abuse and dereliction of duty, offences against citizens' personal and democratic rights by government officials abusing their powers; and that are registered and handled by the provincial Procuratorate offices in relation to other major crimes committed by government officials by abusing their powers.

Acceptance of Case

refers to the decision made by the procurators office to confirm the act of crime after initial investigation and to start legal proceedings of the case as criminal case.

Large Case

In case of corruption and bribery, it refers to the case involves a bribery of over 50000 yuan, or a misappropriation of over 100000, or other cases involving 500000 yuan. In case of offence on dereliction of duty, it refers to the case that causes an economic loss of over 50000, loss of one life, or severe injury of 3 persons; or a case that displays extremely disgusting behavior of the offender or results in grave aftermath.

Key Cases

refer to crimes committed by county and director-level officials. This indicator reflects the situation of those county and director-level officials involved in criminal cases registered and handled by People's Procuratorate offices.

Juvenile Criminals

refers to the offenders within the age range of 14 to 25 convicted guilty by the court during the reporting period while those between 14 and 18 are defined as minor offenders.

Administrative Cases

refers to the cases filed by citizens, corporations and other organizations against the specific administrative conducts of administrative authorities and handled by the court.

Separate Compensation

refers to cases that are separately filed for administrative compensation by the party who has no dispute on the legality of administrative conducts but brings proceedings separately to claim for damages caused by administrative tort.

Number of Labour Disputes Cases Accepted

refers to the number of cases of labour disputes submitted that, after being reviewed by the labour dispute arbitration committees in line with the relevant national regulations, are accepted and registered for treatment.

Cases Settled

refers to the number of cases During the report period that are finished or need not checked, are determined in finishing and are Made a substantive or procedural aspects of processing.

第二十三篇

Chapter 23

省级和县级主要经济指标及位次

MAIN ECONOMIC INDICATORS AND THEIR ORDERS OF PRECEDENCE OF PROVINCE AND COUNTY

简要说明

一、本篇包括全国分省（市）主要年份经济指标及位次和本省县级主要经济指标及位次。

二、各县资料均来自本年鉴各篇。

三、人均指标依据年平均人数计算。

Brief Introduction

I. This chapter includes main economic indicators and their orders of precedence of provinces and counties of Anhui in major years.

II. Data of counties are extracted from the concerned data in other chapters in this yearbook.

III. Per capita indicators are calculated in accordance with annual average population.

23—1 全国分省（市）主要年份生产总值及位次（2022年）

Gross Domestic Product and Their Orders of Precedence in Major Years by Province or City（2022）

本表按当年价格计算 (Data in value terms in this table are calculated at current prices.) 单位：亿元（100 million yuan）

省（市） Province or City	生产总值 Gross Domestic Product	位次 Order of Precedence	第一产业 Primary Industry	位次 Order of Precedence	第二产业 Secondary Industry	位次 Order of Precedence	第三产业 Tertiary Industry	位次 Order of Precedence
全国 National Total	**1210207**		**88345**		**483165**		**638698**	
北京 Beijing	41610.9	13	111.5	30	6605.1	23	34894.3	5
天津 Tianjin	16311.3	24	273.1	28	6038.9	24	9999.3	22
河北 Hebei	42370.4	12	4410.3	8	17050.1	11	20910.0	13
山西 Shanxi	25642.6	20	1340.4	25	13840.8	14	10461.3	20
内蒙古 Inner Mongolia	23158.6	21	2653.7	15	11241.8	18	9263.1	23
辽宁 Liaoning	28975.1	17	2597.6	16	11755.8	15	14621.7	16
吉林 Jilin	13070.2	26	1689.1	22	4628.3	26	6752.8	26
黑龙江 Heilongjiang	15901.0	25	3609.8	11	4648.9	25	7642.2	25
上海 Shanghai	44652.8	11	97.0	31	11458.4	17	33097.4	6
江苏 Jiangsu	122875.6	2	4959.4	6	55888.7	1	62027.5	2
浙江 Zhejiang	77715.4	4	2324.8	20	33205.2	4	42185.4	4
安徽 Anhui	**45045.0**	**10**	**3513.7**	**12**	**18588.0**	**10**	**22943.3**	**12**
福建 Fujian	53109.9	8	3076.2	13	25078.2	6	24955.5	10
江西 Jiangxi	32074.7	15	2451.5	19	14359.6	13	15263.7	15
山东 Shandong	87435.1	3	6298.6	1	35014.2	3	46122.3	3
河南 Henan	61345.1	5	5817.8	3	25465.0	5	30062.2	7
湖北 Hubei	53734.9	7	4986.7	5	21240.6	7	27507.6	9
湖南 Hunan	48670.4	9	4602.7	7	19182.6	9	24885.1	11
广东 Guangdong	129118.6	1	5340.4	4	52843.5	2	70934.7	1
广西 Guangxi	26300.9	19	4269.8	9	8938.6	20	13092.5	19
海南 Hainan	6818.2	28	1417.8	24	1310.9	30	4089.5	28
重庆 Chongqing	29129.0	16	2012.1	21	11693.9	16	15423.1	14
四川 Sichuan	56749.8	6	5964.3	2	21157.1	8	29628.4	8
贵州 Guizhou	20164.6	22	2861.2	14	7113.0	22	10190.4	21
云南 Yunnan	28954.2	18	4012.2	10	10471.2	19	14470.8	17
西藏 Tibet	2132.6	31	180.2	29	804.7	31	1147.8	31
陕西 Shaanxi	32772.7	14	2575.3	17	15933.1	12	14264.2	18
甘肃 Gansu	11201.6	27	1515.3	23	3945.0	27	5741.2	27
青海 Qinghai	3610.1	30	380.2	27	1585.7	29	1644.2	30
宁夏 Ningxia	5069.6	29	407.5	26	2449.1	28	2213.0	29
新疆 Xinjiang	17741.3	23	2509.3	18	7271.1	21	7961.0	24

注：本表数据为初步核算数。

a) Data in this table are preliminary accounting data.

23—2 全国分省（市）主要年份固定资产投资及位次
Urban Investment in Fixed Assets and Their Orders of Precedence in Main Years by Province or City

单位：亿元（100 million yuan）

省（市） Province or City	2010	位次 Order of Precedence	2015	位次 Order of Precedence	2020年 增速(%)及位次 Growth Rate and Rank in 2020		2021年 增速(%)及位次 Growth Rate and Rank in 2021		2022年 增速(%)及位次 Growth Rate and Rank in 2022	
全国 National Total	**270251.99**		**551590.04**		**2.9**		**4.9**		**5.1**	
北京 Beijing	5350.84	22	7446.02	26	2.2	26	4.9	21	3.6	19
天津 Tianjin	6252.22	20	11814.57	21	3.0	23	4.8	22	-9.9	30
河北 Hebei	14621.72	6	28905.74	5	3.2	21	3.0	25	7.9	9
山西 Shanxi	5845.23	21	13744.59	17	10.6	2	8.7	10	5.9	17
内蒙古 Inner Mongolia	8838.67	12	13529.15	18	-1.5	29	9.8	8	17.6	1
辽宁 Liaoning	15793.64	4	17640.37	13	2.6	25	2.6	26	3.6	19
吉林 Jilin	7695.62	16	12508.59	20	8.3	4	11.0	4	-2.4	25
黑龙江 Heilongjiang	6495.85	19	9884.28	24	3.6	19	6.4	14	0.6	22
上海 Shanghai	5106.86	24	6349.39	27	10.3	3	8.0	11	-1.0	24
江苏 Jiangsu	22809.04	1	45905.17	2	0.3	27	5.8	20	3.8	18
浙江 Zhejiang	11980.32	8	26664.72	6	5.4	11	10.8	5	9.1	5
安徽 Anhui	**11104.35**	**9**	**23803.93**	**10**	**5.1**	**13**	**9.4**	**9**	**9.0**	**6**
福建 Fujian	7992.46	14	20973.98	11	-0.4	28	6.0	17	7.5	11
江西 Jiangxi	8470.19	13	16993.90	14	8.2	5	10.8	5	8.6	7
山东 Shandong	22585.11	2	47381.46	1	3.6	19	6.0	17	6.1	15
河南 Henan	15799.22	3	34951.28	3	4.3	14	4.5	23	6.7	13
湖北 Hubei	9959.91	10	26086.42	7	-18.8	31	20.4	1	15.0	2
湖南 Hunan	9301.29	11	24324.17	9	7.6	9	8.0	11	6.6	14
广东 Guangdong	15270.71	5	29950.48	4	7.2	10	6.3	15	-2.6	26
广西 Guangxi	6719.29	17	15654.95	15	4.2	15	7.6	13	0.1	23
海南 Hainan	1278.62	29	3355.40	29	8.0	6	10.2	7	-4.2	27
重庆 Chongqing	6597.78	18	14208.15	16	3.9	18	6.1	16	0.7	21
四川 Sichuan	12552.58	7	24965.56	8	2.8	24	5.9	19	6.0	16
贵州 Guizhou	2945.78	27	10676.70	22	3.2	21	-3.1	30	-5.1	28
云南 Yunnan	5308.93	23	13069.39	19	7.7	8	4.0	24	7.5	11
西藏 Tibet	463.26	31	1295.68	31	5.4	11	-14.2	31	-18.0	31
陕西 Shaanxi	7744.17	15	18231.03	12	4.1	16	-3.0	29	8.1	8
甘肃 Gansu	3054.73	26	8626.60	25	7.8	7	11.1	3	10.1	4
青海 Qinghai	967.44	30	3144.17	30	-12.2	30	-2.9	28	-7.6	29
宁夏 Ningxia	1397.52	28	3426.42	28	4.0	17	2.2	27	10.2	3
新疆 Xinjiang	3274.20	25	10525.42	23	16.2	1	15.0	2	7.6	10

注：各省数据不包括跨地区项目投资。

a) Every provincial data does not include inter-regional project investment.

23—3 全国分省（市）主要年份房地产开发企业本年完成投资及位次

Major Years Real Estate Development Enterprises Completed Investment in Current Year and Ranking and Ranking by Province or City

本表按当年价格计算 (Data in value terms in this table are calculated at current prices.) 单位：亿元（100 million yuan）

省（市） Province or City		2021	位次 Order of Prece-dence	增长 Growth (%)	2022	位次 Order of Prece-dence	增长 Growth (%)
全 国	**National Total**	**147602.08**		**4.4**	**132895.41**		**-10.0**
北 京	Beijing	4139.03	14	5.1	4178.46	2	1.0
天 津	Tianjin	2769.98	12	6.2	2127.94	24	-23.2
河 北	Hebei	5023.87	5	9.2	4982.97	4	-0.8
山 西	Shanxi	1945.23	10	6.3	1764.20	13	-9.3
内蒙古	Inner Mongolia	1234.13	16	4.9	978.28	22	-20.7
辽 宁	Liaoning	2900.72	27	-2.6	2362.00	20	-18.6
吉 林	Jilin	1540.92	13	5.5	1014.84	29	-34.1
黑龙江	Heilongjiang	935.97	30	-4.8	628.64	27	-32.8
上 海	Shanghai	5035.18	8	7.2	4979.54	5	-1.1
江 苏	Jiangsu	13477.45	21	2.3	12406.88	12	-7.9
浙 江	Zhejiang	12389.11	6	8.5	12939.52	1	4.4
安 徽	**Anhui**	**7263.22**	**18**	**3.1**	**6811.72**	**11**	**-6.2**
福 建	Fujian	6195.61	19	2.8	5515.45	15	-11.0
江 西	Jiangxi	2528.83	10	6.3	2209.27	16	-12.6
山 东	Shandong	9819.75	17	3.9	9225.91	10	-6.0
河 南	Henan	7874.35	22	1.2	6793.36	17	-13.7
湖 北	Hubei	6121.93	1	25.2	6172.01	3	0.8
湖 南	Hunan	5427.83	4	11.2	5180.30	9	-4.6
广 东	Guangdong	17465.85	23	0.9	14962.97	18	-14.3
广 西	Guangxi	3733.93	28	-2.9	2307.38	30	-38.2
海 南	Hainan	1379.62	19	2.8	1158.37	19	-16.0
重 庆	Chongqing	4354.96	25	0.1	3467.60	21	-20.4
四 川	Sichuan	7831.88	9	7.1	7500.01	7	-4.2
贵 州	Guizhou	3383.06	26	-1.0	2403.69	26	-28.9
云 南	Yunnan	4309.93	29	-4.3	3152.02	25	-26.9
西 藏	Tibet	141.97	31	-14.2	60.68	31	-57.3
陕 西	Shaanxi	4441.00	24	0.8	4254.79	7	-4.2
甘 肃	Gansu	1525.88	3	12.6	1481.66	6	-2.9
青 海	Qinghai	442.51	15	5.0	296.15	28	-33.1
宁 夏	Ningxia	466.95	7	7.8	419.95	14	-10.1
新 疆	Xinjiang	1501.43	2	19.1	1158.86	23	-22.8

23—4 全国分省（市）主要年份农林牧渔业总产值及位次

Gross Output Value of Farming, Forestry, Animal Husbandry, and Fishery and Their Orders of Precedence in Main Years by Province or City

本表按当年价格计算 (Data in value terms in this table are calculated at current prices.) 单位：亿元（100 million yuan)

省（市）	Province or City	2010	位次 Order of Precedence	2015	位次 Order of Precedence	2020	位次 Order of Precedence	2021	位次 Order of Precedence	2022	位次 Order of Precedence
全国	**National Total**	**69319.76**		**107056.36**		**137782.17**		**147013.4**		**156065.94**	
北京	Beijing	328.02	26	368.24	28	263.43	30	269.51	29	268.18	31
天津	Tianjin	317.33	27	467.44	27	476.44	28	509.26	28	521.44	28
河北	Hebei	4309.42	3	5978.88	5	6742.49	8	7018.67	8	7667.41	8
山西	Shanxi	1047.85	22	1522.64	24	1935.84	24	2134.02	24	2211.59	25
内蒙古	Inner Mongolia	1843.57	18	2751.55	20	3472.36	20	3815.12	19	4316.76	18
辽宁	Liaoning	3106.53	9	4686.71	10	4582.56	14	4927.73	15	5180.03	15
吉林	Jilin	1850.28	16	2880.62	16	2976.00	21	2972.32	21	3217.91	21
黑龙江	Heilongjiang	2536.30	12	5044.93	9	6438.11	9	6459.97	10	6718.24	10
上海	Shanghai	287.03	29	302.62	30	279.82	29	268.93	30	273.53	30
江苏	Jiangsu	4297.14	4	7030.76	3	7952.59	4	8279.72	6	8733.8	6
浙江	Zhejiang	2172.86	14	2933.44	15	3496.94	19	3579.21	20	3752.31	20
安徽	**Anhui**	**2955.45**	**10**	**4390.80**	**11**	**5680.91**	**12**	**6004.31**	**12**	**6277.98**	**12**
福建	Fujian	2307.06	13	3717.87	13	4901.07	13	5200.97	13	5502.56	13
江西	Jiangxi	1900.58	15	2859.10	17	3820.74	18	3998.09	18	4223.81	19
山东	Shandong	6650.94	1	9549.63	1	10190.58	1	11468.01	1	12130.71	1
河南	Henan	5734.20	2	7641.27	2	9956.35	2	10501.2	2	10952.24	2
湖北	Hubei	3501.99	8	5728.56	6	7303.64	7	8296.44	5	8939.33	4
湖南	Hunan	3787.47	6	5630.75	7	7511.96	6	7662.36	7	8160.13	7
广东	Guangdong	3754.86	7	5520.03	8	7901.92	5	8305.84	4	8892.29	5
广西	Guangxi	2720.99	11	4197.12	12	5913.28	11	6524.39	9	6938.53	9
海南	Hainan	821.31	25	1323.91	25	1821.02	25	2014.79	25	2272.04	24
重庆	Chongqing	1021.13	23	1738.15	22	2749.05	22	2935.65	22	3068.45	22
四川	Sichuan	4081.81	5	6377.84	4	9216.40	3	9383.32	3	9859.75	3
贵州	Guizhou	997.82	24	2738.67	21	4358.62	15	4691.97	16	4908.67	16
云南	Yunnan	1810.53	19	3383.09	14	5920.52	10	6351.82	11	6635.8	11
西藏	Tibet	100.77	31	149.46	31	233.53	31	255.34	31	278.62	29
陕西	Shaanxi	1666.06	20	2813.50	18	4056.61	17	4313.44	17	4601.93	17
甘肃	Gansu	1057.02	21	1722.09	23	2103.61	23	2439.54	23	2680.74	23
青海	Qinghai	201.32	30	319.27	29	507.10	27	528.53	27	566.21	27
宁夏	Ningxia	305.94	28	483.02	26	703.07	26	759.81	26	845.92	26
新疆	Xinjiang	1846.18	17	2804.42	19	4315.61	16	5143.12	14	5169.04	14

23—5 全国分省（市）主要年份工业增速位次
Growth Rank of Industry in Main Years by Province or City

本表按当年价格计算 (Data in value terms in this table are calculated at current prices.)

省（市） Province or City	2010年 增速位次 Growth Rank in 2010	2015年 增速位次 Growth Rank in 2015	2020年 增速位次 Growth Rank in 2020	2021年 增速位次 Growth Rank in 2021	2022年 增速位次 Growth Rank in 2022
全 国 National Total					
北 京 Beijing	27	27	19	1	31
天 津 Tianjin	1	4	23	23	28
河 北 Hebei	22	25	13	29	15
山 西 Shanxi	8	30	8	7	4
内蒙古 Inner Mongolia	14	7	27	28	3
辽 宁 Liaoning	18	31	21	30	29
吉 林 Jilin	12	22	2	30	30
黑龙江 Heilongjiang	26	28	17	26	24
上 海 Shanghai	17	29	22	9	27
江 苏 Jiangsu	24	11	5	6	16
浙 江 Zhejiang	23	25	9	3	19
安 徽 Anhui	**4**	**7**	**6**	**17**	**12**
福 建 Fujian	11	6	20	12	14
江 西 Jiangxi	9	5	14	8	7
山 东 Shandong	27	17	10	14	16
河 南 Henan	14	7	28	27	16
湖 北 Hubei	4	7	31	2	10
湖 南 Hunan	7	14	12	22	6
广 东 Guangdong	19	18	24	16	23
广 西 Guangxi	1	12	25	21	19
海 南 Hainan	16	24	30	11	25
重 庆 Chongqing	1	2	7	10	22
四 川 Sichuan	6	12	15	13	21
贵 州 Guizhou	25	3	10	3	26
云 南 Yunnan	27	21	18	19	5
西 藏 Tibet	30	1	1	3	2
陕 西 Shaanxi	13	19	26	25	7
甘 肃 Gansu	21	20	4	17	13
青 海 Qinghai	10	16	29	15	1
宁 夏 Ningxia	19	14	16	24	10
新 疆 Xinjiang	31	23	2	19	7

注：工业为月度快报口径。
a) Data in the table are preliminary statistics.

23—6 全国分省（市）主要年份社会消费品零售总额及位次
Total Retail Sales of Consumer Goods and Their Orders of Precedence in Main Years by Province or City

本表按当年价格计算 (Data in value terms in this table are calculated at current prices.)　　单位：亿元（100 million yuan）

省（市） Province or City		2021	位次 Order of Precedence	增长 Growth (%)	2022	位次 Order of Precedence	增长 Growth (%)
全　国	**National Total**	**440823.2**		**12.5**	**439732.5**		**-0.2**
北　京	Beijing	14867.7	12	8.4	13794.2	13	-7.2
天　津	Tianjin	3769.8	26	5.2	3572.0	26	-5.2
河　北	Hebei	13509.9	14	6.3	13720.1	14	1.6
山　西	Shanxi	7747.3	21	14.8	7562.7	21	-2.4
内蒙古	Inner Mongolia	5060.3	23	6.3	4971.4	23	-1.8
辽　宁	Liaoning	9783.9	18	9.2	9526.2	18	-2.6
吉　林	Jilin	4216.6	24	10.3	3807.7	25	-9.7
黑龙江	Heilongjiang	5542.9	22	8.8	5210.0	22	-6.0
上　海	Shanghai	18079.3	11	13.5	16442.1	11	-9.1
江　苏	Jiangsu	42702.6	2	15.1	42752.1	2	0.1
浙　江	Zhejiang	29210.5	4	9.7	30467.2	4	4.3
安　徽	**Anhui**	**21471.2**	**8**	**17.1**	21518.4	8	**0.2**
福　建	Fujian	20373.1	9	9.4	21050.1	9	3.3
江　西	Jiangxi	12206.7	15	17.7	12853.5	15	5.3
山　东	Shandong	33714.5	3	15.3	33236.2	3	-1.4
河　南	Henan	24381.7	5	8.3	24407.4	5	0.1
湖　北	Hubei	21561.4	7	19.9	22164.8	7	2.8
湖　南	Hunan	18596.9	10	14.4	19050.7	10	2.4
广　东	Guangdong	44187.7	1	9.9	44882.9	1	1.6
广　西	Guangxi	8538.5	20	9.0	8539.1	19	0.0
海　南	Hainan	2497.6	28	26.5	2268.4	28	-9.2
重　庆	Chongqing	13967.7	13	18.5	13926.1	12	-0.3
四　川	Sichuan	24133.2	6	15.9	24104.6	6	-0.1
贵　州	Guizhou	8904.3	19	13.7	8507.1	20	-4.5
云　南	Yunnan	10731.8	16	9.6	10838.8	16	1.0
西　藏	Tibet	810.3	31	8.7	726.5	31	-10.3
陕　西	Shaanxi	10250.5	17	6.7	10401.6	17	1.5
甘　肃	Gansu	4037.1	25	11.1	3922.2	24	-2.8
青　海	Qinghai	947.8	30	8.0	842.1	30	-11.2
宁　夏	Ningxia	1335.1	29	2.6	1338.4	29	0.2
新　疆	Xinjiang	3584.6	27	17.0	3240.5	27	-9.6

注：根据第四次全国经济普查结果对2018年社会消费品零售总额进行了修订，2019年相应进行调整。

a) According to the results of the fourth national economic census, the total retail sales of social consumer goods in 2018 was revised and adjusted accordingly in 2019.

23—7 全省分县（市）主要经济指标及位次（2022年）
Main Economic Indicators and Their Orders of Precedence of All Counties (2022)

县（市）	County (City)	生产总值（亿元）Gross Domestic Product (100 million yuan) 指标 Amount	位次 Order of Precedence	人均生产总值（元）Per Capita Gross Domestic Product (yuan) 指标 Amount	位次 Order of Precedence	一般公共预算收入（万元）General Public Budget Revenue (10000 yuan) 指标 Amount	位次 Order of Precedence	一般公共预算支出（万元）Expenditures in General Public Budgets (10000 yuan) 指标 Amount	位次 Order of Precedence
巢湖市	Chaohu	608.01	6	83402	10	261875	17	680664	20
长丰县	Changfeng	823.83	3	103496	5	549015	3	1269958	1
肥东县	Feidong	859.39	2	95754	6	600543	2	1104674	2
肥西县	Feixi	1068.36	1	108684	4	638460	1	1029343	3
庐江县	Lujiang	601.45	7	67579	23	262303	16	810659	7
濉溪县	Suixi	571.18	8	61783	30	283471	13	788060	11
涡阳县	Guoyang	451.69	17	38689	51	209961	28	674653	21
蒙城县	Mengcheng	458.83	14	41730	46	278201	14	704448	18
利辛县	Lixin	386.77	22	32791	55	191768	33	766786	14
砀山县	Dangshan	262.03	39	34252	53	145404	44	575548	30
萧县	Xiaoxian	431.61	18	41421	47	205379	29	803773	9
灵璧县	Lingbi	324.43	32	33292	54	142906	45	651097	22
泗县	Sixian	293.24	34	38865	50	150658	42	620954	26
怀远县	Huaiyuan	357.25	25	38046	52	264245	15	783784	12
五河县	Wuhe	272.87	37	51534	38	162023	40	503520	37
固镇县	Guzhen	301.73	33	60166	31	166577	36	470442	41
界首市	Jieshou	411.49	19	63896	28	203222	30	475926	40
临泉县	Linquan	460.27	13	27963	58	185961	34	846077	6
太和县	Taihe	533.63	10	38937	49	215157	27	804912	8
阜南县	Funan	327.05	31	27905	59	155480	41	726366	16
颍上县	Yingshang	505.03	11	42227	45	311763	10	909100	4
凤台县	Fengtai	348.50	27	64892	27	326592	9	515594	35
寿县	Shouxian	259.90	40	31143	56	192337	32	780116	13
天长市	Tianchang	686.11	4	112847	3	467416	4	736695	15
明光市	Mingguang	288.33	35	59145	33	223923	23	515603	34
来安县	Laian	392.21	21	93383	7	254334	19	427557	47
全椒县	Quanjiao	336.61	30	84363	9	245341	21	451162	44
定远县	Dingyuan	380.09	23	56393	35	258047	18	682848	19
凤阳县	Fengyang	495.38	12	77951	14	405000	5	647623	23
霍邱县	Huoqiu	282.38	36	29945	57	250186	20	880820	5

23—7 续表1 continued

县（市）	County (City)	生产总值（亿元）Gross Domestic Product (100 million yuan)		人均生产总值（元）Per Capita Gross Domestic Product (yuan)		一般公共预算收入（万元）General Public Budget Revenue (10000 yuan)		一般公共预算支出（万元）Expenditures in General Public Budgets (10000 yuan)	
		指标 Amount	位次 Order of Precedence	指标 Amount	位次 Order of Precedence	指标 Amount	位次 Order of Precedence	指标 Amount	位次 Order of Precedence
舒城县	Shucheng	375.73	24	54101	36	218458	26	640181	24
金寨县	Jinzhai	236.44	45	47814	40	200337	31	793064	10
霍山县	Huoshan	205.72	48	72182	19	168601	35	395465	50
当涂县	Dangtu	558.65	9	134777	1	366020	7	561715	31
含山县	Hanshan	250.69	42	74279	16	165323	39	425031	49
和县	Hexian	353.47	26	85898	8	298824	12	578078	29
无为市	Wuwei	609.91	5	73750	18	307749	11	708428	17
南陵县	Nanling	341.78	29	78480	12	236708	22	430385	46
宁国市	Ningguo	454.28	15	116932	2	372265	6	545436	32
广德市	Guangde	404.29	20	80616	11	359172	8	613281	27
郎溪县	Langxi	214.77	46	69058	22	220504	25	355264	51
泾县	Jingxian	155.16	52	57149	34	165847	37	329679	52
绩溪县	Jixi	101.57	55	74139	17	88820	52	179488	57
旌德县	Jingde	65.17	57	59245	32	67977	56	180270	56
枞阳县	Zongyang	196.66	50	42338	44	122998	47	483172	38
东至县	Dongzhi	259.46	41	65936	26	131913	46	425651	48
石台县	Shitai	34.21	59	43580	42	28987	59	155287	59
青阳县	Qingyang	191.38	51	77955	13	119093	48	283375	53
桐城市	Tongcheng	452.04	16	76294	15	222780	24	608989	28
潜山市	Qianshan	237.19	44	53846	37	110808	49	533628	33
怀宁县	Huaining	344.93	28	69542	21	165657	38	463614	43
太湖县	Taihu	210.85	47	48978	39	86001	53	506501	36
宿松县	Susong	262.52	38	42966	43	105305	50	635076	25
望江县	Wangjiang	202.49	49	43972	41	85906	54	466185	42
岳西县	Yuexi	132.35	54	40975	48	81232	55	478666	39
歙县	Shexian	237.38	43	66493	24	149180	43	432521	45
休宁县	Xiuning	137.69	53	66038	25	105178	51	279842	54
黟县	Yixian	54.37	58	72013	20	43969	58	156234	58
祁门县	Qimen	90.89	56	63118	29	61959	57	224933	55

23—7 续表2 continued

县（市）	County (City)	农林牧渔业总产值（万元）Gross Output Value of Farming, Forestry, Animal Husbandry and Fishery (10000 yuan)		城镇居民人均可支配收入（元）Per Capita Disposable Income of Urban Residents (yuan)		农村居民人均可支配收入（元）Per Capita Disposable Income of Rural Residents (yuan)		社会消费品零售总额（万元）Total Retail Sale of Consumer Goods (10000 yuan)	
		指标 Amount	位次 Order of Precedence	指标 Amount	位次 Order of Precedence	指标 Amount	位次 Order of Precedence	指标 Amount	位次 Order of Precedence
巢湖市	Chaohu	794024	27	45456	9	28228	5	2276191	13
长丰县	Changfeng	1283409	14	45432	10	27587	6	3411340	2
肥东县	Feidong	1328715	11	47630	5	30197	4	3173360	3
肥西县	Feixi	1156514	19	50189	3	30899	3	2624279	6
庐江县	Lujiang	1114099	21	42573	15	26794	9	2202008	15
濉溪县	Suixi	1036409	22	37883	38	17375	35	1548656	32
涡阳县	Guoyang	1261780	16	34959	51	16769	46	2682046	5
蒙城县	Mengcheng	1315086	13	39689	28	18341	32	2543120	7
利辛县	Lixin	1121367	20	38369	36	16598	47	2497352	8
砀山县	Dangshan	968315	23	37470	39	17273	40	1952743	19
萧县	Xiaoxian	1507354	2	36936	42	16769	45	1972233	18
灵璧县	Lingbi	1353913	10	35127	50	16955	43	1833329	22
泗县	Sixian	1318076	12	35286	49	16204	53	1525404	34
怀远县	Huaiyuan	1438926	6	39529	29	20918	22	2117321	17
五河县	Wuhe	1266804	15	39182	31	20830	23	1552405	31
固镇县	Guzhen	1505954	3	39982	26	20964	21	1290175	41
界首市	Jieshou	697802	31	41068	20	18414	31	2130752	16
临泉县	Linquan	2010866	1	36105	45	16311	50	3157328	4
太和县	Taihe	1395180	7	39286	30	17168	41	4242759	1
阜南县	Funan	1392049	8	36022	46	16063	57	2313881	12
颍上县	Yingshang	1455228	4	38884	33	17032	42	2456507	10
凤台县	Fengtai	649591	35	42097	17	19819	26	1478935	36
寿县	Shouxian	1207479	18	33221	59	15156	58	1643312	28
天长市	Tianchang	755146	29	43892	11	25960	10	2430916	11
明光市	Mingguang	803122	26	37466	40	17278	39	1782783	24
来安县	Laian	511790	44	43113	14	18612	30	1534438	33
全椒县	Quanjiao	602936	38	38677	35	19032	29	1818741	23
定远县	Dingyuan	1440148	5	37039	41	17313	38	1919620	20
凤阳县	Fengyang	870916	25	33947	56	16434	48	2489857	9
霍邱县	Huoqiu	1371785	9	34190	55	16124	56	1601416	30

23—7 续表3 continued

县（市）	County (City)	农林牧渔业总产值（万元）Gross Output Value of Farming, Forestry, Animal Husbandry and Fishery (10000 yuan)		城镇居民人均可支配收入（元）Per Capita Disposable Income of Urban Residents (yuan)		农村居民人均可支配收入（元）Per Capita Disposable Income of Rural Residents (yuan)		社会消费品零售总额（万元）Total Retail Sale of Consumer Goods (10000 yuan)	
		指标 Amount	位次 Order of Precedence	指标 Amount	位次 Order of Precedence	指标 Amount	位次 Order of Precedence	指标 Amount	位次 Order of Precedence
舒城县	Shucheng	758947	28	36156	43	17320	37	1744594	25
金寨县	Jinzhai	557111	41	33353	58	16227	51	1644360	27
霍山县	Huoshan	443710	48	38240	37	19102	28	990883	47
当涂县	Dangtu	613856	36	50144	4	34569	1	1875177	21
含山县	Hanshan	486021	47	42326	16	26891	8	1195706	42
和县	Hexian	569795	39	43667	12	27081	7	1488745	35
无为市	Wuwei	1224531	17	46968	7	25921	11	2214296	14
南陵县	Nanling	662330	34	46400	8	31683	2	1434313	37
宁国市	Ningguo	488204	46	53512	1	24806	13	1334275	39
广德市	Guangde	525884	43	52912	2	25049	12	1686297	26
郎溪县	Langxi	360440	50	47419	6	21295	20	778038	53
泾县	Jingxian	379199	49	39862	27	19753	27	840435	51
绩溪县	Jixi	304562	54	43373	13	18249	33	369299	56
旌德县	Jingde	163308	56	34785	52	17630	34	227056	58
枞阳县	Zongyang	542445	42	33770	57	17346	36	946312	49
东至县	Dongzhi	676163	32	39062	32	20596	25	1019024	46
石台县	Shitai	100779	58	35654	47	14951	59	153672	59
青阳县	Qingyang	256857	55	41980	18	21640	15	866884	50
桐城市	Tongcheng	699848	30	40599	21	21392	18	1606173	29
潜山市	Qianshan	559031	40	40035	25	16843	44	1293171	40
怀宁县	Huaining	492812	45	41972	19	20642	24	1402600	38
太湖县	Taihu	611024	37	35394	48	16167	55	1145726	44
宿松县	Susong	943320	24	34428	53	16170	54	1151579	43
望江县	Wangjiang	668633	33	36128	44	16367	49	983592	48
岳西县	Yuexi	352243	52	34376	54	16219	52	837048	52
歙县	Shexian	352326	51	40090	23	21532	16	1046528	45
休宁县	Xiuning	305543	53	40076	24	21426	17	688160	54
黟县	Yixian	90730	59	38862	34	21910	14	238580	57
祁门县	Qimen	136580	57	40117	22	21365	19	419530	55

附　录

APPENDIX

简要说明

一、附表 1：安徽农民工非农就业基本情况，由国家统计局安徽调查总队提供。

Brief Introduction

Ⅰ. The attached schedule 1 : Basic Situation of Non-agricultural Employment of Migrant Workers in Anhui Province, data is from Anhui Province survey organization of National bureau of statistics.

附录　安徽农民工非农就业基本情况

Basic Situation of Non-agricultural Employment of Migrant Workers in Anhui Province

指　　标	Item	2020	2021	2022
农民工总量　　(万人)	**Total Number of Migrant Workers　　(10000 person)**	**1967.4**	**1981.3**	**1996.6**
外出农民工	Outgoing Migrant Workers	1342.1	1311.1	1264.0
住户中外出农民工	Migrant Workers Migrant Workers	858.3	885.6	838.5
举家外出农民工	Family Migrant Workers	483.9	425.5	425.5
本地农民工	Local Migrant Workers	625.2	670.2	732.6
外出农民工不同地区就业比例（%）	**Employment Proportion of Migrant Workers in Different Regions (%)**			
去往本省	Go to the Province	38.9	38.1	43.2
#去往乡外县内	Go to the County Outside the County	18.5	17.5	19.5
去往县外省内	Go to the County Outside the Province	20.3	20.6	23.7
去往省外	Go Outside the Province	61.1	61.9	56.8
#去往东部地区	Go to the Eastern Region	56.8	57.8	52.5
去往京津冀地区	Go to Beijing-Tianjin-Hebei Region	1.8	2.6	2.4
去往江浙沪地区	Go to Jiangsu, Zhejiang and Shanghai Region	49.2	49.5	45.5
去往中部地区（安徽除外）	Go to the Central Area (Except Anhui)	2.1	2.4	2.4
去往港澳台及国外	Go to Hong Kong, Macao, Taiwan and Abroad	0.1	0.3	0.0
不同行业农民工就业比例　　（%）	**Proportion of Migrant Workers Employed in Different Industries (%)**			
第一产业	Primary Industry	0.4	0.4	0.4
第二产业	Secondary Industry	47.4	47.8	48.2
#制造业	Manufacturing	23.3	22.4	24.4
建筑业	Construction	21.8	23.4	21.6
第三产业	Tertiary Industry	52.2	51.7	51.4
#批发和零售业	Wholesale and Retail Trades	12.6	12.9	13.0
交通运输、仓储和邮政业	Transport, Storage and Post	7.1	7.2	7.3
住宿和餐饮业	Hotels and Catering Services	7.6	7.0	6.7
居民服务、修理和其他服务业	Services to Households, Repair and Other Services	12.2	12.5	12.5
不同劳动合同农民工所占比例（%）	**Proportion of Migrant Workers With Different Labor Contracts (%)**			
无固定期限劳动合同工	Non-fixed Term Labor Contract Workers	13.0	11.3	9.0
一年及以上劳动合同工	One Year and Above Labor Contract Workers	23.5	21.4	26.6
一年以下劳动合同工	A Year of Labor Contract Workers	3.7	5.7	6.6
没有劳动合同	There is No Labor Contract	55.9	58.2	54.2
其　他	Other	3.8	3.4	3.6
外出务工月收入　　（元）	**Monthly Income for Migrant Workers　　(yuan)**	**5455.4**	**6041.4**	**6309.0**